# Twentieth-Century Literary Criticism

Volume 9

# Twentieth-Century Literary Criticism

**Excerpts from Criticism of the
Works of Novelists, Poets, Playwrights,
Short Story Writers, and Other Creative Writers
Who Lived between 1900 and 1960,
from the First Published Critical Appraisals
to Current Evaluations**

**Dennis Poupard
Editor**

**Thomas Ligotti
James E. Person, Jr.
Associate Editors**

**Gale Research Company
Book Tower
Detroit, Michigan 48226**

## STAFF

Dennis Poupard, *Editor*

Thomas Ligotti, James E. Person, Jr., *Associate Editors*

Mark W. Scott, *Senior Assistant Editor*

Earlene M. Alber, Jane Dobija, Kathleen Gensley, Sandra Giraud, Denise B. Grove, Marie Lazzari,
Serita Lanette Lockard, Denise Wiloch, *Assistant Editors*

Sharon K. Hall, Phyllis Carmel Mendelson, *Contributing Editors*

Robert J. Elster, Jr., *Production Supervisor*
Lizbeth A. Purdy, *Production Coordinator*
Eric Berger, Michael S. Corey, Paula J. DiSante, Brenda Marshall, Janet S. Mullane,
Gloria Anne Williams, *Editorial Assistants*

Robert J. Elster, Jr., *Research Coordinator*
Ann Marie Dadah, Jeannine Schiffman Davidson, Karen Rae Forsyth, Barbara Hammond,
Robert J. Hill, James A. MacEachern, Mary Spirito, Margaret Stewart, Carol Angela Thomas,
*Research Assistants*

Linda M. Pugliese, *Manuscript Coordinator*
Donna D. Craft, *Assistant Manuscript Coordinator*
Colleen M. Crane, Maureen A. Puhl, Rosetta Irene Simms, *Manuscript Assistants*

L. Elizabeth Hardin, *Permissions Supervisor*
Filomena Sgambati, *Permissions Coordinator*
Janice M. Mach, *Assistant Permissions Coordinator*
Patricia A. Seefelt, *Photo Permissions*
Mary P. McGrane, Susan D. Nobles, Anna Pertner, *Permissions Assistants*
Elizabeth Babini, Margaret Chamberlain, Virgie T. Leavens, Joan B. Weber, *Permissions Clerks*

Copyright © 1983 by Gale Research Company

Library of Congress Catalog Card Number 76-46132

ISBN 0-8103-0220-9
ISSN 0276-8178

# CONTENTS

# PREFACE

It is impossible to overvalue the importance of literature in the intellectual, emotional, and spiritual evolution of humanity. Literature is that which both lifts us out of everyday life and helps us to better understand it. Through the fictive lives of such characters as Anna Karenin, Lambert Strether, or Leopold Bloom, our perceptions of the human condition are enlarged, and we are enriched.

Literary criticism can also give us insight into the human condition, as well as into the specific moral and intellectual atmosphere of an era, for the criteria by which a work of art is judged reflects contemporary philosophical and social attitudes. Literary criticism takes many forms: the traditional essay, the book or play review, even the parodic poem. Criticism can also be of several kinds: normative, descriptive, interpretive, textual, appreciative, generic. Collectively, the range of critical response helps us to understand a work of art, an author, an era.

## The Scope of the Book

The usefulness of Gale's *Contemporary Literary Criticism (CLC)*, which excerpts criticism on current writing, suggested an equivalent need among literature students and teachers interested in authors of the period 1900 to 1960. The great poets, novelists, short story writers, and playwrights of this period are by far the most popular writers for study in high school and college literature courses. Moreover, since contemporary critics continue to analyze the work of this period—both in its own right and in relation to today's tastes and standards—a vast amount of relevant critical material confronts the student.

Thus, *Twentieth-Century Literary Criticism (TCLC)* presents significant passages from published criticism on authors who died between 1900 and 1960. Because of the difference in time span under consideration *(CLC* considers authors who were still living after 1960), there is no duplication between *CLC* and *TCLC.*

Each volume of *TCLC* is carefully designed to present a list of authors who represent a variety of genres and nationalities. The length of an author's section is intended to be representative of the amount of critical attention he or she has received from critics writing in English, or foreign criticism in translation. Critical articles and books that have not been translated into English are excluded. Every attempt has been made to identify and include excerpts from the seminal essays on each author's work. Additionally, as space permits, especially insightful essays of a more limited scope are included. Thus *TCLC* is designed to serve as an introduction for the student of twentieth-century literature to the authors of that period and to the most significant commentators on these authors.

Each *TCLC* author section represents the scope of critical response to that author's work: some early criticism is presented to indicate initial reactions, later criticism is selected to represent any rise or fall in an author's reputation, and current retrospective analyses provide students with a modern view. Since a *TCLC* author section is intended to be a definitive overview, the editors include between 30 and 35 authors in each 600-page volume (compared to approximately 75 authors in a *CLC* volume of similar size) in order to devote more attention to each author. An author may appear more than once because of the great quantity of critical material available, or because of a resurgence of criticism generated by events such as an author's centennial or anniversary celebration, the republication of an author's works, or publication of a newly translated work or volume of letters.

## The Organization of the Book

An author section consists of the following elements: author heading, biocritical introduction, principal works, excerpts of criticism (each followed by a citation), and an annotated bibliography of additional reading.

- The *author heading* consists of the author's full name, followed by birth and death dates. The unbracketed portion of the name denotes the form under which the author most commonly wrote. If an author wrote consistently under a pseudonym, the pseudonym will be listed in the author heading and the real name given in parentheses on the first line of the biocritical introduction. Also located at the beginning of the biocritical introduction are any name variations under which an author wrote, including transliterated forms for authors whose languages use nonroman alphabets. Uncertainty as to a birth or death date is indicated by a question mark.

- The *biocritical introduction* contains biographical and other background information about an author that will elucidate his or her creative output. Parenthetical material following several of the biocritical introductions includes references to biographical and critical reference series published by the Gale Research Company. These include *Dictionary of Literary Biography* and past volumes of *TCLC*.

- The *list of principal works* is chronological by date of first book publication and identifies genres. In the case of foreign authors where there are both foreign language publications and English translations, the title and date of the first English-language edition are given in brackets. Unless otherwise indicated, dramas are dated by first performance, not first publication.

- *Criticism* is arranged chronologically in each author section to provide a perspective on any changes in critical evaluation over the years. In the text of each author entry, titles by the author are printed in boldface type. This allows the reader to ascertain without difficulty the works discussed. For purposes of easier identification, the critic's name and the publication date of the essay are given at the beginning of each piece of criticism. Unsigned criticism is preceded by the title of the journal in which it appeared. For an anonymous essay later attributed to a critic, the critic's name appears in brackets in the heading and in the citation.

  Beginning with Volume 9, important critical essays will be prefaced by *explanatory notes* as an additional aid to students using *TCLC*. The explanatory notes will provide several types of useful information, including: the reputation of a critic; the reputation of a work of criticism; the specific type of criticism (biographical, psychoanalytic, structuralist, etc.); and the growth of critical controversy or changes in critical trends regarding an author's work. In many cases, these notes will cross-reference the work of critics who agree or disagree with each other.

- A complete *bibliographical citation* designed to facilitate location of the original essay or book by the interested reader accompanies each piece of criticism. An asterisk (*) at the end of a citation indicates the essay is on more than one author.

- The *annotated bibliography* appearing at the end of each author section suggests further reading on the author. In some cases it includes essays for which the editors could not obtain reprint rights. An asterisk (*) at the end of a citation indicates the essay is on more than one author.

Each volume of *TCLC* includes a cumulative index to critics. Under each critic's name is listed the author(s) on which the critic has written and the volume and page where the criticism may be found. *TCLC* also includes a cumulative index to authors with the volume numbers in which the author appears in boldface after his or her name. A cumulative nationality index is another useful feature in *TCLC*. Author names are arranged alphabetically under their respective nationalities and followed by the volume number(s) in which they appear.

## Acknowledgments

No work of this scope can be accomplished without the cooperation of many people. The editors especially wish to thank the copyright holders of the excerpts included in this volume, the permission managers of many book and magazine publishing companies for assisting us in locating copyright holders, and the staffs of the Detroit Public Library, University of Detroit Library, University of Michigan Library, and Wayne State University Library for making their resources available to us. We are also grateful to Michael F. Wiedl III for his assistance with copyright research and to Norma J. Merry for her editorial assistance.

## Suggestions Are Welcome

Several features have been added to *TCLC* since its original publication in response to various suggestions:

- Since Volume 2—An *Appendix* which lists the sources from which material in the volume is reprinted.

- Since Volume 3—An *Annotated Bibliography* for additional reading.

- Since Volume 4—*Portraits* of the authors.

- Since Volume 6—A *Nationality Index* for easy access to authors by nationality.

- Since Volume 9—*Explanatory notes* to excerpted criticism which provide important information regarding critics and their work.

If readers wish to suggest authors they would like to have covered in future volumes, or if they have other suggestions, they are cordially invited to write the editor.

# AUTHORS TO APPEAR
# IN FUTURE VOLUMES

Ady, Endre 1877-1919
Agate, James 1877-1947
Agustini, Delmira 1886-1914
Aldanov, Mark 1886-1957
Aldrich, Thomas Bailey 1836-1907
Annensy, Innokenty Fyodorovich 1856-1909
Arlen, Michael 1895-1956
Bal'mont, Konstantin 1867-1943
Barea, Arturo 1897-1957
Barry, Philip 1896-1946
Bass, Eduard 1888-1946
Benet, William Rose 1886-1950
Benjamin, Walter 1892-1940
Benson, E(dward) F(rederic) 1867-1940
Benson, Stella 1892-1933
Bentley, E(dmund) C(lerihew) 1875-1956
Berdyaev, Nikolai Aleksandrovich 1874-1948
Beresford, J(ohn) D(avys) 1873-1947
Bergson, Henri 1859-1941
Bethell, Mary Ursula 1874-1945
Binyon, Laurence 1869-1943
Bishop, John Peale 1892-1944
Blackmore, R(ichard) D(oddridge) 1825-1900
Blasco-Ibáñez, Vicente 1867-1928
Bojer, Johan 1872-1959
Bosman, Herman Charles 1905-1951
Bottomley, Gordon 1874-1948
Bourget, Paul 1852-1935
Bourne, George 1863-1927
Brancati, Vitaliano 1907-1954
Brandes, Georg (Morris Cohen) 1842-1927
Broch, Herman 1886-1951
Bromfield, Louis 1896-1956
Bryusov, Valery (Yakovlevich) 1873-1924
Byrne, Donn (Brian Oswald Donn-Byre) 1889-1928
Caine, Hall 1853-1931
Campana, Dina 1885-1932
Cannan, Gilbert 1884-1955
Chatterji, Sarat Chandra 1876-1938
Churchill, Winston 1871-1947
Corelli, Marie 1855-1924
Corvo, Baron (Frederick William Rolfe) 1860-1913
Crane, Stephen 1871-1900
Crawford, F. Marion 1854-1909
Croce, Benedetto 1866-1952
Davidson, John 1857-1909
Day, Clarence 1874-1935
Dazai, Osamu 1909-1948

De Gourmont, Remy 1858-1915
Delafield, E.M. (Edme Elizabeth Monica de la Pasture) 1890-1943
Delisser, Herbert George 1878-1944
DeMille, Cecil B(lount) 1881-1959
DeMorgan, William 1839-1917
DeVoto, Bernard 1897-1955
Döblin, Alfred 1878-1957
Douglas, (George) Norman 1868-1952
Douglas, Lloyd C(assel) 1877-1951
Dreiser, Theodore 1871-1945
Drinkwater, John 1882-1937
Dujardin, Edouard 1861-1949
Durkheim, Emile 1858-1917
Duun, Olav 1876-1939
Eisenstein, Sergei 1898-1948
Ellis, Havelock 1859-1939
Ewers, Hans Heinz 1871-1943
Fadeyev, Alexandr 1901-1956
Fargue, Leon-Paul 1876-1947
Feydeau, Georges 1862-1921
Field, Michael (Katherine Harris Bradley 1846-1914 and Edith Emma Cooper 1862-1913)
Field, Rachel 1894-1924
Fisher, Rudolph 1897-1934
Flecker, James Elroy 1884-1915
Fletcher, John Gould 1886-1950
Freeman, Douglas Southall 1886-1953
Freeman, John 1880-1929
Freud, Sigmund 1853-1939
Gladkov, Fydor Vasilyevich 1883-1958
Glyn, Elinor 1864-1943
Gogarty, Oliver St. John 1878-1957
Golding, Louis 1895-1958
Gosse, Edmund 1849-1928
Gould, Gerald 1885-1936
Grahame, Kenneth 1859-1932
Gray, John 1866-1934
Grieg, Nordahl 1902-1943
Griffith, D(avid) W(ark) 1875-1948
Guiraldes, Ricardo 1886-1927
Gumilyov, Nikolay 1886-1921
Gwynne, Stephen Lucius 1864-1950
Haggard, H(enry) Rider 1856-1925
Hale, Edward Everett 1822-1909
Hall, (Marguerite) Radclyffe 1886-1943
Harris, Frank 1856-1931
Hergesheimer, Joseph 1880-1954
Hernandez, Miguel 1910-1942
Herrick, Robert 1868-1938
Hewlett, Maurice 1861-1923
Heyward, DuBose 1885-1940
Hichens, Robert 1864-1950
Hilton, James 1900-1954
Hofmannsthal, Hugo Von 1874-1929

Holtby, Winifred 1898-1935
Hope, Anthony 1863-1933
Hudson, Stephen 1868-1944
Hudson, W(illiam) H(enry) 1841-1922
Hulme, Thomas Ernest 1883-1917
Ivanov, Vyacheslav Ivanovich 1866-1949
Jacobs, W(illiam) W(ymark) 1863-1943
James, Will 1892-1942
James, William 1842-1910
Jerome, Jerome K(lapka) 1859-1927
Jones, Henry Arthur 1851-1929
Khodasevich, Vladislav 1886-1939
Kuttner, Henry 1915-1958
Kuzmin, Mikhail Alexseyevich 1875-1936
Lang, Andrew 1844-1912
Lawson, Henry 1867-1922
Leverson, Ada 1862-1933
Lewisohn, Ludwig 1883-1955
Lindsay, (Nicholas) Vachel 1879-1931
Lonsdale, Frederick 1881-1954
Loti, Pierre 1850-1923
Louys, Pierre 1870-1925
Lowndes, Marie Belloc 1868-1947
Lubitsch, Ernst 1892-1947
Lucas, E(dward) V(errall) 1868-1938
Lynd, Robert 1879-1949
MacArthur, Charles 1895-1956
Machado de Assis, Joaquim Maria 1839-1908
Manning, Frederic 1887-1935
Marinetti, Filippo Tommaso 1876-1944
Marriott, Charles 1869-1957
Martin du Gard, Roger 1881-1958
McCrae, John 1872-1918
Mencken, H(enry) L(ouis) 1880-1956
Meredith, George 1828-1909
Mistral, Frederic 1830-1914
Mitchell, Margaret 1900-1949
Monro, Harold 1879-1932
Monroe, Harriet 1860-1936
Moore, Thomas Sturge 1870-1944
Morgan, Charles 1894-1958
Morley, Christopher 1890-1957
Murnau, F(riedrich) W(ilhelm) 1888-1931
Murray, (George) Gilbert 1866-1957
Musil, Robert 1880-1939
Nervo, Amado 1870-1919
Nietzsche, Friedrich 1844-1900
Norris, Frank 1870-1902
Ogai, Mori 1862-1922
Olbracht, Ivan (Kemil Zeman) 1882-1952
Ophuls, Max 1902-1957

9

## Authors to Appear in Future Volumes

Péguy, Charles 1873-1914
Pickthall, Marjorie 1883-1922
Pinero, Arthur Wing 1855-1934
Platonov, Audrey 1899-1951
Pontoppidan, Henrik 1857-1943
Porter, Eleanor H(odgman) 1868-1920
Porter, Gene(va) Stratton 1886-1924
Prevost, Marcel 1862-1941
Quiller-Couch, Arthur 1863-1944
Rappoport, Solomon 1863-1944
Reid, Forrest 1876-1947
Riley, James Whitcomb 1849-1916
Rinehart, Mary Roberts 1876-1958
Roberts, Elizabeth Madox 1886-1941
Röhmer, Sax 1883-1959
Rolland, Romain 1866-1944
Rolvaag, O(le) E(dvart) 1876-1931
Rosenberg, Isaac 1870-1918
Rourke, Constance 1885-1941
Roussel, Raymond 1877-1933
Runyon, Damon 1884-1946
Ruskin, John 1819-1900

Sabatini, Rafael 1875-1950
Santayana, George 1863-1952
Seeger, Alan 1888-1916
Service, Robert 1874-1958
Seton, Ernest Thompson 1860-1946
Slater, Francis Carey 1875-1958
Slesinger, Tess 1905-1945
Solovyov, Vladimir 1853-1900
Spitteler, Carl 1845-1924
Squire, J(ohn) C(ollings) 1884-1958
Steiner, Rudolph 1861-1925
Stockton, Frank R. 1834-1902
Stroheim, Erich von 1885-1957
Sturges, Preston 1898-1959
Sudermann, Hermann 1857-1938
Symons, Arthur 1865-1945
Tabb, John Bannister 1845-1909
Tey, Josephine (Elizabeth Mackintosh) 1897-1952
Thomas, (Philip) Edward 1878-1917
Toller, Ernst 1893-1939
Tolstoy, Alexei 1882-1945

Turner, W(alter) J(ames) R(edfern) 1889-1946
Vachell, Horace Annesley 1861-1955
Valera y Alcala Galiano, Juan 1824-1905
Van Dine, S.S. (William H. Wright) 1888-1939
Van Doren, Carl 1885-1950
Vazov, Ivan 1850-1921
Verhaeren, Émile 1855-1916
Wallace, Edgar 1874-1932
Wallace, Lewis 1827-1905
Washington, Booker T(aliaferro) 1856-1915
Webb, Mary 1881-1927
Webster, Jean 1876-1916
Welch, Denton 1917-1948
Wells, Carolyn 1869-1942
Wister, Owen 1860-1938
Wren, P(ercival) C(hristopher) 1885-1941
Wylie, Francis Brett 1844-1954

Readers are cordially invited to suggest additional authors to the editors.

# Annie (Wood) Besant

## 1847-1933

English essayist, lecturer, historian, and editor.

Though she wrote over four hundred books and pamphlets, Besant is best remembered not as an author but as one of the preeminent social critics, activists, and religious zealots of her age. Her commitment to such controversial causes as birth control and home rule for India earned her wide recognition during her lifetime. At various times in her long career Besant embraced, among other beliefs, theism, atheism, the free thought movement, Fabian socialism, and eventually Theosophy. To each cause she devoted her considerable talents and energies, both as an orator and as a writer.

Besant grew up in impecunious circumstances following her father's death, but was able to receive a liberal, progressive education when Ellen Marryat, a sister of novelist Frederick Marryat, offered to tutor her. From her childhood Besant was devoutly religious. She spent hours in prayer, fasting, and meditation. Her religious feelings were at their height when, at twenty, she met and married orthodox clergyman Frank Besant. Much later her friend and fellow Theosophist William T. Stead would write: "She could not be the bride of heaven, and therefore became the bride of Mr. Frank Besant. He was hardly an adequate substitute." The two were unsuited to each other, and after six years they separated. Having rejected both her marriage and her childhood faith, Besant began her life-long search for a formal system of belief she could accept. She first became involved with the free thought movement after attending a lecture by the movement's leader, Charles Brad-laugh. It was as a free thinker that Besant began her own career as a public speaker. In 1876 Besant and Bradlaugh were involved in a celebrated obscenity trial for publishing and distributing birth control information. Later, after embracing socialism, Besant led a strike of exploited match-factory workers in London which resulted in major labor reforms. Bernard Shaw was unwittingly responsible for her conversion from socialism to Theosophy by giving her a review copy of Helena P. Blavatsky's *The Secret Doctrine*. After she adopted Theosophy, Besant forsook her earlier causes, even repudiating her stand on birth control. However, it was as a Theosophist that she achieved some of her most noteworthy reforms. In India, where she eventually settled, she helped to improve and desegregate educational facilities and was instrumental in establishing the Central Hindu College, the first institute of higher education in India to teach Indian subjects and admit Indian students. Though Besant did not live to see India achieve home rule, her efforts toward this goal were a major factor in its final realization.

Critical commentary on Besant's writing has naturally centered on her controversial topics, and not on her technique as a writer. Her biographer, Theodore Besterman, wrote that her early pamphlets on religion and atheism "were straightforward and methodical but uninspired presentations." Critics of her later works concur with this view. "Her writing was apt to be dull and unremarkable, except when she was really indignant," Margaret Cole has noted. It was as an orator— "the greatest woman orator of England," according to Shaw— that Besant excelled. Those who attended her lectures praised

*Courtesy of Prints and Photographs Division, Library of Congress*

her ringing voice, intense self-confidence, and masterful control of her subject. Her writing is best when her hastily composed essays capture the power of her spoken words.

Despite her relative obscurity today, Besant remains a significant personality in modern British history. In her private quest for a spiritual truth, she contributed much to the struggles of the poor and the working classes in England and abroad. She has left her mark on British labor laws, on the face of modern education in India, and on the shape of modern Theosophical thought.

## PRINCIPAL WORKS

*On the Deity of Jesus of Nazareth*  (essay)  1873
*Essays by Mrs. Besant*  (essays and speeches)  1875
*On the Nature and Existence of God*  (essay)  1875
*The Gospel of Atheism*  (essay)  1877
*The Law of Population: Its Consequences and Its Bearing upon Human Conduct and Morals*  (essay)  1877
*My Path to Atheism*  (essays)  1877
*Marriage: As It Was, As It Is, and As It Should Be*  (essay) 1879
*History of the Great French Revolution*  (history)  1883
*Why I Am a Socialist*  (essay)  1886
*Why I Do Not Believe in God*  (essay)  1887

---

**ANNIE BESANT   (essay date 1893)**

In a century that boasts so much of what is new, amid nations that ever seek some fresh discovery, it may seem as though a view of life dating from the hoariest antiquity would have but little chance of welcome, would find but scant approval. Theosophy is the oldest of all archaic teachings; its name counts but some fifteen centuries, but the thing covered by the name antedates the most ancient of the nations known to Western man. . . . It was old when, five thousand years ago, Shri Krishna taught it as his kingliest mystery to his beloved disciple Arjuna, on the plain of the Kurus. . . . To-day it is freshly promulgated in order that it may reinvigorate the attenuated belief in the spiritual life that Christendom has preserved, and make that belief once more a living force that may triumph over materialistic luxury and materialistic science. It not only affirms but it demonstrates the reality of the spiritual life, transferring the soul from the realm of faith to the realm of knowledge, and enabling the patient and devoted student to enter on a path the goal of which is, in very truth, the vision of the Divine.

The Esoteric Philosophy—to give it its commonest name—postulates an eternal essence of being, limitless, incognizable, from which arises manifestation, the breathing forth of a universe, thought taking form; in it the root of spirit and of matter, the dual aspect of the one eternal substance, a duality inseparable from manifested existence. This manifested existence is found in the present universe to be evolved through seven distinct stages of being—states of consciousness regarded as spiritual, planes of differentiated forms regarded as material. Each of these seven gradations has its own spiritual forces, its own material forms, entities of which one pole is spirit, the other matter; these poles being present in each, as the positive and negative poles of a magnet. There is no entity that is pure spirit; there is no entity that is pure matter; one or other aspect may predominate, but both must be present. On the highest plane matter has its subtlest, its most sublimated form; on the lowest plane spirit has its most restricted and confined energy: but they are indivisible, their union indissoluble throughout the

whole of the present cycle of evolution. These seven planes can be investigated, lived in, by perfected men, so that their existence becomes a matter of knowledge, and is subject to continual reverification as new students advance to proficiency in the spiritual life; for to the eye of spirit "Nature has no veil in all her kingdoms," and human consciousness is capable of working on each of these planes of being, and of transferring itself without breach of continuity from one plane to another. Those perfected men who have achieved this power are called Adepts, Mahâtmâs, Masters, and so on. They are men who have quickened the slow processes of natural evolution by strenuous efforts, resolute will, long-continued and loving self-abnegation; they have done swiftly what the race is doing slowly, and, as the Elder Brothers of Humanity, they labor ever still for human progress, holding in trust for the race all they have attained, teaching those who have already progressed sufficiently far to profit by their instructions, ever watching to take advantage of every opportunity by which a human soul may be helped forward to the light. . . .

The possibility of consciousness transcending physical conditions is now so thoroughly established that it is scarcely worth while to offer arguments in proof thereof to educated and thoughtful persons. In the mesmeric trance and in many allied conditions consciousness escapes from the bondage of physical matter and manifests powers and capacities loftier and more piercing than those of normal life. Clairvoyance, clairaudience, are among its most familiar demonstrations, and the evidence is here so abundant as to be within the easy reach of every student. These phenomena belong, for the most part, to the astral world, in its various sub-stages and higher and lower regions. Manifestations of great genius, on the other hand, are the successful attempts of consciousness on the higher mental plane to impress itself on the lower, and some analyses of their own experiences from the pens of such men as Mozart and Tennyson suggest lines of corroborative testimony to the truth of Theosophic teachings on this head. Serious students of Occultism learn methods of training which gradually evolve the power of thus passing from plane to plane at will, and thus accumulate experience which adds to the wealth and variety of the ever-increasing store of evidence to the reality of these superphysical states.

What is done by the student deliberately after he has reached a certain stage of development is done for him in the earlier stages, and normally for all humanity, by the process of reincarnation. Reincarnation is the successive inhabiting of body after body by the spiritual Ego, the higher nature of man. This Ego, the true "I," is eternal, alike ingenerable and indestructible, springing from the divine source, a spark individualized from the flame of the divine life. Dwelling in the man of flesh, its true consciousness masked and unable to manifest itself through the gross covering that envelops it, it gathers the teachings of experience, the lessons of earthly life. Then, passing through the gateway of death to the higher states of consciousness, it gradually shakes off its garments worn in earthly life, and, as pure soul clad in form of ethereal texture, it dwells awhile apart from the turmoil of earth, assimilating the experience it has gathered, and thus formulating the capacities which, on its return to earth, will appear as innate characteristics. Thus each succeeding life is molded by the lives that went before it, and the experienced, often-incarnated Ego brings with him to his new life-lesson all that he has been able to build into his own spiritual nature from the experiences of his past. (p. 665)

The conception of man as a spiritual being, sprung from one divine source, passing through a common evolution, trained by the one method of reincarnation, traveling towards the single goal of spiritual perfection—all this tends to lay deep and sure the basis for the Universal Brotherhood of man. We cannot despise, for mere outward differences of rank and wealth and culture, the brother souls that started with us on the long pilgrimage, that have lived with us, worked with us, suffered with us, through countless æons. We have all been poor and rich so many times, so often lofty and so often low in social rank, so often learned and ignorant, so often wise and foolish—how should we despise each other in any one brief stage of our long pilgrimage? Brotherhood becomes so patent as a fact in nature that it inevitably works itself into our lives as a living truth, and further study of minuter truths only makes more definite and more complete our recognition of this sublime and potent verity.

In a brief article such as this nothing more can be done than give barest outlines of great teachings—poor presentment of richest store. But those who study shall find satisfaction; those who patiently seek the light shall behold it; and that great Science of the Soul, which is the trunk whence the religions of the elder world have sprung, shall serve once more as stem wherefrom shall branch out the more glorious religions of the centuries that lie before humanity. (pp. 665-66)

> *Annie Besant, "What Theosophy Is," in* The Outlook, *October 14, 1893, pp. 665-66.*

## REV. ANSON P. ATTERBURY (essay date 1893)

[Under the heading **"What Theosophy Is,"** Mrs. Annie Besant has presented] a short but comprehensive statement concerning "the Esoteric Philosophy." As ordinarily described, this so-called system of religion is the dreariest waste imaginable; under Mrs. Besant's light yet potent touch, fountains gush forth from the desert, flowers bloom, a beautiful transformation is effected—in about two thousand words. It takes genius to accomplish such results.

Certain statements made in the article referred to are somewhat startling to one who attempts to verify them. Thus, Mrs. Besant says, concerning Theosophy, that "the thing covered by the name antedates the most ancient of the nations known to Western man." Undoubtedly some idea of "religion"—undefined and perhaps undefinable—is as old as the human race. But to claim that the doctrines which Theosophy includes are thus hoary with antiquity is indeed interesting to a student of modern and Western science. . . . To have information direct from astral spheres that materialistic evolution has been taught from the year 4000 B.C.—or further back—down to our own time, is indeed an item of news "interesting if true."

"The thing covered by the name" includes other doctrines, concerning which it is certainly surprising to hear such claims for antiquity. If only some records could be brought from the mountain fastnesses of Thibet, and published from the Mahatmas and for the enlightenment of the lower Western races, giving definite proof that somebody, at least a thousand years ago, believed anything at all approaching to the conglomeration of ideas "covered by the name" Theosophy, the claim as to the antiquity of this system would be worth investigation. Undoubtedly, some thoughts concerning religion, imbedded in the Vedic writings of the far past, are included in the Theosophic presentations of the present. But to say that "the thing covered by the name antedates" other religious beliefs, and so may

rightly claim the reverence due to antiquity, is mere childishness of assertion, without either proof or expectation of acceptance.

Mrs. Besant confidently affirms concerning Theosophy that it "demonstrates the reality of the spiritual life." We should be glad to have it demonstrated—even by a Theosophist. But the kind of spiritual life that it "demonstrates" is something hardly satisfactory. The chilly astral life that it asserts, the final absorption into Nirvana—a vague something, which is nothing, assumed without proof . . . is hardly a satisfactory answer to the innate longings of the human soul. And the authority of an elusive Mahatma, whom "eye hath not seen and ear hath not heard," is insufficient evidence of such "things unseen."

A system of philosophy like Theosophy, which makes spirit and matter but the "dual aspect of the one eternal substance," and then makes that "one eternal substance" the only approach to any idea of God that the religion contains, is both foolish and Godless. It is philosophic nonsense thus to identify matter and spirit; in spite of modern materialist assertion, mankind instinctively rejects the idea. To claim that a stone is only a soul in an early stage of development is indeed an astral sublimation of thought.

The so-called proof of the whole system of Theosophy rests upon the existence and testimony of Mahatmas, men "who have quickened the slow processes of natural evolution by strenuous efforts, resolute will, long-continued and loving self-abnegation." But cold criticism must refuse to accept the existence of such creatures, or at least to believe in their taking such part on earth, until better evidence is adduced than has thus far been presented. . . . The exposure of [Mme. Blavatsky's] fraudulent spiritualistic phenomena, made by the agents of the London Society for Psychical Research, vainly denied by the Theosophical Society, is sufficient to answer all claims of Theosophy which are based upon occult phenomena. If these Mahatmas exist, as is claimed by Theosophists, they must do something better than thus far they have done before they will be cordially received by an incredulous Western world. If they exist, and "labor still for human progress," why have they been so long in telling us, and so very shadowy in their appearance, and so charlatan-like in their manifestations? We cannot help remarking to them that it would be well to seek some introduction other than through Mme. Blavatsky, if they desire successfully to "labor still for human progress"—at least so far as concerns communication with the Western world.

In the short space of her article Mrs. Besant has compressed assertion sufficient to require a volume should even partial response be attempted for all. It is, however, most interesting to see how fair a presentation may be made of matters inconceivably foolish—if only there be sufficient assumption, assertion, and assurance. But the superficial credulity of many may be trusted.

> *Rev. Anson P. Atterbury, "Correspondence: 'What Theosophy Is'," in* The Outlook, *October 28, 1893, p. 778.*

## *THE SPECTATOR* (essay date 1894)

Like many other people who feel that they have suffered from the misconceptions and misrepresentations of the world, Mrs. Besant has written an *apologia pro vitâ suâ* in the form of an autobiography [*Annie Besant: An Autobiography*]. Not that she professes any intention of offering an explanation or defence for the opinions which brought about her hostile attitude towards society—or, perhaps, we should rather say which attracted the hostility of society towards herself—for the only reason that she gives for telling the story of her life is the hope that the tale may prove profitable to others whose lives are darkened by the same troubles and doubts which she has experienced in her own. Whether or not her book is likely to have this effect, is a question which need not be considered. But there is one result which may attend her labours, and not an undesirable one. Her history may induce society to be less hasty and more charitable in passing judgment upon those who rebel against the opinion of the majority. That Mrs. Besant has herself chiefly to thank for the unenviable notoriety which she achieved is true enough; but that does not acquit the world of having treated her with scant justice, or of lending a credulous ear to charges which could not be fairly made against her. The autobiography before us has every appearance of being a truthful and perfectly honest production. . . . [This] self-drawn portrait is by no means without interest. It is that of a woman of considerable ability and but little knowledge, of an independent mind and very dependent affections, an alternate prey to religious fervour and religious doubt, unselfish in the matter of material advantage and painfully self-centred, possessed of most of the Christian virtues, but absolutely devoid of Christian humility. There are many forms of egoism; few more insidious than that which besets Mrs. Besant. She herself seems only to have half-recognised its existence. "Looking back to-day over my life," she writes, "I see that its keynote—through all the blunders, and blind mistakes, and clumsy follies—has been a longing to sacrifice to something felt as greater than the self." And, she adds, the sacrifice was to her the "supremely attractive thing;" to make it required no painful surrender of her own wishes, rather it was a "joyous springing forward along the easiest path." For which reason she is ready to disclaim all credit for self-denial and self-sacrifice. But there her reasoning stops short. She does not pursue it to the logical conclusion that there was self-indulgence in yielding to the longing for sacrifice, and, apparently, she fails to realise how extremely selfish some of her sacrifices were. It is possible to be self-seeking in the matter of spiritual as well as material advantage, and to do injury to other people's spiritual interests by attaching an altogether inordinate importance to one's own. Mrs. Besant's sense of the importance of her own convictions was deplorably exaggerated.

It might very well be that this longing for sacrifice was the keynote of her earlier life. But, to be brutally candid, it was a longing to sacrifice what other people cared for, in order to obtain what Mrs. Besant cared for. The supreme luxury, in her eyes, was a conspicuous martyrdom. . . . To do her justice, she seems to have felt no doubts on the subject herself, entertaining a perfectly genuine enthusiasm for her own heroism. There is something rather piteous, as well as ludicrous, in the blindness that shut her eyes to the real state of affairs. Endowed with a fatal facility of speech, she set herself to teach long before she had learnt, with the result that her own ignorance grew the more confirmed. Even in the light of such knowledge as she has now attained, she views her past labours with perfect self-complacency, and quotes long passages from her essays on atheism—the name which she gives to the crude form of utilitarianism which served her for the time as a religious creed—with unconcealed satisfaction. . . .

Orthodox society had probably never heard of her or her teaching, had she not wilfully provoked prosecution, by publishing a certain pamphlet, with whose ideas, by the way, she did not

agree. One thing at least stands to the credit of her honesty; while she exaggerates the importance of her crusade, she does not exaggerate the scanty equipment with which she undertook it. She did not care for politics, she says, because the necessary compromises of political life were intolerable to her. In other words, the recognition of two sides to every question, the task of collecting information on both sides, and the anxious consideration of all available evidence before passing judgment, were things which she abhorred. How youthfully ignorant was her enthusiasm may be seen on almost every page of her book. Her religious convictions were formed and abandoned with equal haste; and it was with the utmost fervour and the least possible understanding that she professed herself successively a Christian, a Theist, an Atheist, a Socialist, and a Theosophist. (p. 309)

And this is the woman to whom the world wanted to affix the label of "Dangerous,"—one who has never outgrown the romantic ideals and unreasoning enthusiasm of a clever schoolgirl. Clever, she undoubtedly was, and one cannot help thinking that she might have made an honourable name for herself in more than one walk in life had she brought herself to undergo the necessary training and discipline. Even the book before us shows signs of a very considerable literary capacity. The portrait that she draws of Mr. Bradlaugh is full of interest, though presenting rather a one-sided view of that remarkable man; and there are occasional passages which rise to a high point of eloquence. (p. 310)

> *"Mrs. Besant's Autobiography," in* The Spectator *(©1894 by* The Spectator*), Vol. 72, No. 3427, March 3, 1894, pp. 309-10.*

**W. E. GLADSTONE**  (essay date 1894)

[*Annie Besant: An Autobiography*] presents to us an object of considerable interest. It inspires sympathy with the writer, not only as a person highly gifted, but as a seeker after truth, although it is to be regretted that at a particular point of the narrative the discussion borders on the loathsome. Indeed, it becomes hard to conceive by what mental process Mrs. Besant can have convinced herself, that it was part of her mission as a woman to open such a subject as that of the Ninth Chapter, in the face of the world, and in a book meant for popular perusal. Instruction will be derived from the work at large; but probably not exactly the instruction intended by the authoress. Her readers will find that they are expected to feel a lively interest in her personality: and, in order that this interest may not be disappointed, they will find her presented to their view in no less than three portraitures, at different portions of the volume. They will also find, that the book is a spiritual itinerary, and that it shows with how much at least of intellectual ease, and what unquestioning assumptions of being right, vast spaces of mental travelling may be performed. The stages are, indeed, glaringly in contrast with one another; yet their violent contrarieties do not seem at any period to suggest to the writer so much as a doubt whether the mind, which so continually changes in attitude and colour, can after all be very trustworthy in each and all its movements. This uncomfortable suggestion is never permitted to intrude; and the absolute self-complacency of the authoress bears her on through tracts of air buoyant and copious enough to carry the Dircæan swan. Mrs. Besant passes from her earliest to her latest stage of thought as lightly, as the swallow skims the surface of the lawn, and with just as little effort to ascertain what lies beneath it. An ordinary mind would suppose that modesty was the one lesson which she could not have failed to learn from her extraordinary permutations; but the chemist, who shall analyse by percentages the contents of these pages, will not, I apprehend, be in a condition to report that of such an element he can find even the infinitesimal quantity usually and conveniently denominated a 'trace.' Her several schemes of belief, or non-belief, appear to have been entertained one after another, with the same undoubting confidence, until the junctures successively arrives for their not regretful, but rather contemptuous, rejection. They are nowhere based upon reasoning, but they rest upon one and the same authority—the authority of Mrs. Besant. In the general absence of argument to explain the causes of her movements, she apparently thinks it sufficient to supply us with her three portraits, as carrying with them sufficient attestation. If we ask upon which of her religions, or substitutes for religion, we are to place reliance, the reply would undoubtedly be, upon the last. Yes; but who is to assure us that it will be the last? It remains open to us to hope, for her own sake, that she may yet describe the complete circle, and end somewhere near the point where she began. (pp. 317-18)

*W. E. Gladstone, "True and False Conceptions of the Atonement," in* The Nineteenth Century, *Vol. XXXVI, No. 211, September, 1894, pp. 317-31.\**

**BEPIN CHANDRA PAL**   (essay date 1913)

Mrs. Besant has been, for more than a quarter of a century, one of the most prominent figures in our public life. And today, there is, perhaps, not another person, in any Indian province, to whom the heart of awakened India goes with greater reverence and deeper affection than it does to this strange woman from beyond the seas.

A magnetic personality, a finished orator, a capable organiser, endowed with large powers of imagination and sympathy, and with a very rare combination of the subtle wisdom of the diplomat with the fervour of the prophet, Mrs. Besant's influence over a very large section of our English-educated countrymen has been hardly less than that of any other leader of thought in India of the present generation.

In the earlier years of her consecrated service to India, she very materially helped to wean away the sympathies of [a] good many English-educated Indians, especially in the South, from the so-called free-thought and secularism of the middle-nineteenth-century European culture, and very largely rehabilitated for them the faith and philosophy of their fathers. In her latest activities she has been a most powerful influence to wean away [a] good many people from separatist ideals of isolated sovereign national independence, and draw them to the higher ideal of federated and co-operative inter-nationalism. . . . (pp. 1-4)

[No] one else could have stemmed the tide of this so-called free-thought and secularism, so far as this large class of people were concerned, so successfully as Mrs. Besant has undoubtedly done. Hide-bound Hindu orthodoxy may not have been seriously affected by her apologetics and exegetics, which did not always follow the lines of the ancient exegetical literature of our race. Her readings of Hindu philosophy and her interpretations of Hindu rituals, may have seemed to some as a medley of modern scepticism and ancient supernaturalism. But notwithstanding all this, one cannot reasonably refuse to acknowledge the immense debt that the present generation of English-educated Hindus owe to her. One may question the validity of her spiritual claims. One may not accept her science

as true or her philosophy as sound. There may be,—indeed, there are—the widest possible difference of opinion in the country about these matters. But no one, I think, can refuse to admit the very patent fact that large numbers of our educated countrymen, especially in Madras, would not have been what they are to-day . . . without her teachings and the inspiration of her magnetic personality.

To many people, who have carefully observed Mrs. Besant's career, as it is gradually evolved through successive stages or phases of traditional faith and rational doubt, of gross materialism and subtle theosophy,—her character and personality seem to be a puzzling mystery. And this mystery has been, very largely, I think, the one supreme secret of her success in life. (pp. 5-9)

*Bepin Chandra Pal, "Mrs. Annie Besant: A Character Sketch" (originally published in* The Hindu Review, *1913), in his* Mrs. Annie Besant: A Psychological Study, *Ganesh & Co., Publishers, 1917, pp. 1-12.*

**BEPIN CHANDRA PAL**   (essay date 1917)

[It may not] be very easy to discover Mrs. Besant's real philosophy of life. She has professed and preached so many different and even contradictory doctrines, that it is no easy thing to find out either the least common multiple or the greatest common measure of her strange and rich intellectual repertory. Yet there must be some sort of a secret unity or affinity even in these strange collections or they could never have found a place in an individual intellectual life and evolution. Mrs. Besant's changes have been somewhat violent, and one cannot indeed feel sure even now that she has reached the last of these. Nor do they prove any serious mental or moral disqualification. The men or women who change not from youth to age, except in the body, may be considered very steady and respectable, but whether they actually live or simply vegetate may also be very pertinently questioned. And whatever else Mrs. Besant has or has not done, there can, I think, be absolutely no question about the fact that she has lived her life and not simply vegetated. She has changed many a time. But changes have no meaning unless they are worked upon something that persists, unchanged, through all these changes. . . . That something is at once the least common multiple and the greatest common measure of our changing lives. It is that something which constitutes the most vital element in our real philosophy of life. To understand the value of Mrs. Besant's spiritual life one must seek and discover this permanent and persistent factor of her inner life and character.

Born a Christian, married to a priest of the established Church in England her first intellectual allegiance was naturally given to the creeds and dogmas of popular Protestant Christianity. Nor was she a half-hearted Christian, either. Mrs. Besant's forceful nature never can engage itself half-heartedly in any pursuit, whether intellectual or moral, social or religious. She believed in every Christian doctrine, faithfully followed the religious exercises of the Church, and threw herself with unstinted enthusiasm into the parochial works of her husband's congregation. But all of a sudden, a domestic calamity, the death of her only child, a daughter to whom she was much devoted, scattered her house of sands. . . . [John Stuart] Mill's problem faced her. Why is there death, disease, sorrow, degradation, vice, sin,—all these multitudinous evils in this world? How are these reconciled with the beneficence of the responsible Ruler of the Universe? The only answer that Mill found for this question was that God is either not-good, or He is not-powerful enough to keep down evil. . . . Mrs. Besant thus found out by bitter personal experience,—or more correctly speaking, she thought that she had discovered,—that there was no God like the God whom she had all her life believed in and prayed to. (pp. 33-9)

[Mrs. Besant's unbelief was] more than mere agnosticism, it developed into positive atheism. This intellectual assertiveness has been a prominent feature of her character. It was equally present in her early Christianity, as in her subsequent atheism and secularism. It was a prominent feature in her subsequent Theosophy also. What did not exist to her, could not exist in the universe. What was true to her, must be true universally and for all. In theory, Theosophy has little room, really, for any kind of absolutism. A system or doctrine that proclaims the truth of *all* religions, which believes, like Hinduism, in evolution and adhikariveda—in the religious and the spiritual life, cannot be absolutist in any sense of the term. In practice, however, like many other universalist doctrines, Theosophy is clearly, absolutist. It is, therefore, that we so frequently found at one time, an irritating impatience of other ideas and ideals, other doctrines and disciplines, in Mrs. Besant. In India her condemnation of almost all our modern religious movements . . . had at one time been both exceedingly narrow and exceedingly bitter. This narrowness was inconsistent with the true spirit of Theosophy. This bitterness is unknown in those who have attained high spiritual life, at least in India, and among the Hindus. But I do not blame Mrs. Besant for it. These things are constitutional in her. All extraordinarily ardent natures are narrow: and absolute devotion to a particular school or system or sect naturally, breeds bitter antagonism against opposite or rival schools, systems or sects. It is only when these ardent and devoted souls attain superior spiritual elevation, or are called to some large practical work, needing combined and organised efforts of many minds of diverse castes and culture that these limitations drop off their mind and character like the dry leaves of autumn. (pp. 41-5)

> *Bepin Chandra Pal, in his* Mrs. Annie Besant: A Psychological Study, *Ganesh & Co., Publishers, 1917, 725 p.*

**GEOFFREY WEST** (essay date 1928)

In 1891 W. T. Stead declared Mrs. Annie Besant to be one of the three most remarkable women of his time. The other two were Mrs. Booth and Mrs. Butler, both, like Mrs. Besant, of the "apostolic type," "propagandists militant." They, to a very great extent, belong to a now faded past, and their prominence has dwindled in memory; Mrs. Besant, however, is with us still, and if her star has in some degree sunk lower in the West, that has been by her own choice and that it might rise the more splendidly shining in the East. All that she was then seems to-day but the preface to what she was to become, and to agree that she was remarkable then is necessarily to agree that she is to-day doubly remarkable.

She is, though, far more than a mere phenomenon. Her work, even her work of forty and fifty years ago, is significant for us to-day where that of Mrs. Booth and Mrs. Butler is forgotten. Her sufferings, her labours, and her victories were the birth-pangs wherein an attitude essentially familiar was shaped and produced, an attitude at least more tolerant and understanding, expressed in a wider sympathy and a concern with the spirit rather than the letter of belief, more human if some-

times less humane, taking a broader and possibly profounder if more bewildered view. It is no longer the fashion to denigrate things Victorian, but to study the life of Mrs. Besant is to realize how many of the swaddling cruelties which public opinion in the sixties and seventies lent all its weight to enforce, would be possible no longer—or only under the most unusual circumstances. In the change thus marked she has played her part, and a great part, and whatever our final attitude to her, this debt must be acknowledged. She battled for free thought in days when hell was an ever-threatening reality, and even intelligent clergymen—leaders of religious thought—declared it the Church's duty, not hers, to ascertain the truth; she strove against the subjection of women, for their education and equality. . . . She gave in the seventies the first popular impulse to the modern birth-control movement by her public defence of its principles in the face of every insult and ascription of obscene motive; she upheld upon platform and in print the rights of smaller nationalities at a time when the intoxication of empire still rose unrestrained. She was a socialist before Socialism became respectable, an advocate and organizer of Trade Unions when even the workers accepted them unwillingly, a propagandist against royalty, capital punishment, the existing land system, and for woman suffrage and equal justice. Upon all these issues she was, if never alone, a pioneer, and time has justified her; there is not one which is not to-day either so fully accepted that it is taken for granted or would not be discussed with a vastly wider tolerance than even she, probably, dreamed of. She fought, it is clear to us to-day, on the side of the angels, and it might seem ironic—were it not that we instinctively take it for granted—that like all agents of heaven she was attacked most bitterly by the godly.

There was indeed, it appears, scarcely a public controversy from the seventies to the nineties, touching intellectual, social, or political freedoms, with which she did not identify herself upon the unpopular side; typify her era she certainly does not, but she may be said to have summed it up in very large degree simply by the extent to which she ran counter to its most cherished beliefs and prejudices, fought against the storm of its reactionary forces. (pp. 9-13)

But her significance is more than this, and it is rather in this additional respect that her later progress into Theosophy becomes relevant. For though throughout her life she has been deeply involved in politics, the essential fact concerning her is that she has been from first to last a religious adventurer, a spiritual pilgrim. (p. 13)

Mrs. Besant appears to many to have shared with Booth and Stead—to mention two contemporary figures—an overwhelming instinct and desire for religion together with inadequate equipment for its apprehension, lacking those sensitive refinements of the spiritual nature which alone give hope of victory. The religious heart is, unfortunately, no warrant of the religious soul. Mrs. Besant, no doubt, regards Theosophy as her final triumph; by that alone, Theosophists will say, her name must be carried to posterity. . . . (pp. 162-63)

[Mrs. Besant] has been since Madame Blavatsky's death the living centre of the [Theosophical] Society, which has under her Presidency gone forward from strength to strength, to prosperity and influence; but only time can show whether without her it can preserve its position. For herself, whatever its fate, it appears undeniable that in Theosophy Mrs. Besant has increasingly rejected her earlier ideals, denied what, at her most masculine, her most modern, her most significant, she stood for. (p. 167)

[Mrs. Besant is] a woman of overwhelming personality, yet even as such, though her fellow-workers seem unable to express adequately their admiration, she appears to have made little impression upon her contemporaries in general, to have appealed scarcely at all to their imaginations. Of her greatness as an orator there can be no doubt—though here it might be truer to call her a public speaker, for she has always been primarily a propagandist. It is difficult to imagine that many of her speeches will be read in future years, for their own sake, as literature. Their matter is everything, their manner nothing, they are contributions to controversy rather than to knowledge, and when the dust of their particular conflict drifts to earth, they will lie—as many of them already do—forgotten beneath it. Something the same may be said of her voluminous writings; he must needs be a hardy soul who, save as a student, essays to read them. Style she has never had, and though haste may account for the more formless sentences and paragraphs to be found occasionally in her work, it is difficult to reconcile them with the smallest degree of literary intention or feeling. At her best she can express herself straightforwardly, with admirable directness, yet even her *Autobiography,* which of all her writings possesses the greatest general interest, must be read for its tale rather than its telling. Its significance, that is to say, is all upon the surface, in its plain facts; it is useless to seek below for deeper meaning. There is in its pages no hidden harmony, no voice of the soul, no secret beauty.

Is not this the lack which runs throughout, which helps to account for one's ultimate feeling that gifted as undoubtedly she is, she is possibly less gifted than a superficial study of her achievements might suggest? Is it not that what talents she has possessed she has always controlled with a skill and completeness amounting to genius, and always directly and forcefully to a single end? She has been at all times utterly sincere, utterly certain of her cause, of its righteousness, its nobility, its triumph; at all times she has looked steadfastly forward, made at every change the cleanest of cuts with the entanglements of the past. All these things make for the utmost efficiency, but they no more indicate richness of personality than they do spiritual power. It might be suggested that Mrs. Besant probably has more in common with, say, Mr. Henry Ford than with such teachers as Buddha and Jesus. She herself is to be found, to an unusual degree, in her work, and she must be estimated, again to an unusual degree, by the tangible results of her labours. (pp. 167-70)

[Her work], her life-long battle for freedom of thought and of speech, for truth and for enlightenment, in politics and in religion, and in England and in India, certainly will stand; it has already become part of history. Yet even here it is arguable that she originated nothing, gave nothing to the world which otherwise it must have lacked, but which now is its imperishable heritage; that what she did was simply—*it is a great service*—to hasten processes already existing. The modern spirit would have come to birth without her, even had it been born with more difficulty, after delay. Even of her work in India this may be held to be wholly true. She has been in this respect rather an assistant than a creator; she has added to the sum-total of progress only relatively, and though her immortality in her work can be considered assured, it is not unlikely to be an anonymous immortality.

For herself, she leaves no distinctive body of writings, no vitally original thought, to carry on her name. As a phenomenon of sheer energy of unfailing courage, of noble sincerity, she will live always in the memories of all who have known

her; her fame beyond that point, considering her present position, seems curiously problematical.

Mrs. Besant is, it may again at this point be asserted, one of the most remarkable of living women, and to suggest that she is for our time rather than for all time in no way detracts from her uniqueness, or from the gratitude which we to-day, as the direct beneficiaries of her herculean labours and sacrifices, owe to her. It is the exaggerated claims of her enthusiastic admirers which make some attempt to restore proportion occasionally essential. Only when they are moderated does it seem possible that she will be given the wider admiration which, for her services, is her due. (pp. 170-72)

> *Geoffrey West, in his* Annie Besant *(copyright © 1928 by The Viking Press, Inc.; reprinted by permission of the publishers), Viking Penguin, 1928, 174 p.*

**THEODORE BESTERMAN** (essay date 1934)

In 1877 Mrs Besant published her *The Gospel of Atheism,* in which she attempted to define her attitude. She begins by making it clear that the Atheist does not assert that there is no God, but that he merely declares that he has no conception of the meaning of God. . . . In fact, the Atheist refuses to believe anything about that of which he knows nothing; he neither denies nor affirms. But he does deny that which he knows to be untrue. Thus, in Mrs Besant's example, he will affirm that three times one are three, and he will deny that three times one are one. So far, so good. The point just made is perhaps not quite so sound philosophically as Mrs Besant thought; still, if we accept it, what then?

It must be owned that no further definite ideas can be derived from Mrs Besant's *Gospel.* It contains such outbursts of eloquence as: "Atheist is one of the grandest titles a man can wear; it is the Order of Merit of the world's heroes." . . . But beyond that there is nothing.

Elsewhere, however, Mrs Besant made a more reasoned attempt to justify Atheism as a positive creed. She set out from a species of monism, regarding it as manifest to all "who will take the trouble to think steadily," that matter and spirit are only varying manifestations of one eternal and underived substance. From this rather dangerous position Mrs Besant argued that the Deity must necessarily be that eternal and underived substance. "Thus," she continues, "we identify substance with the all-comprehending and vivifying force of nature." This is a little difficult to follow. If we are prepared, as was Mrs Besant, to take up an extreme monistic attitude by a mere assertion, without argument, this procedure could conceivably be allowed for the sake of the argument. Having taken up this position it by no means follows as a necessity that the basic substance must be the Deity. Granting even this, however, how can we maintain that we have "thus" identified substance both with God and with nature? The argument obviously has not even the semblance of reason. We can see, however, that the triple assumption was essential to Mrs Besant's case, for she proceeds to point out, having made it, that "we simply reduce to a physical impossibility the existence of the Being described by the orthodox as a God possessing the attributes of personality."

Having thus dismissed the notion of a personal God, justly enough, perhaps, however little one may agree with the course of the argument, Mrs Besant inquired whether *any* idea of God could be attained. She concluded, or rather, asserted, that evidence was lacking, that we could grasp only phenomena, implying presumably (quite unjustifiably) that phenomena are incapable of yielding any evidence of God. (pp. 62-5)

[In *The Gospel of Atheism*] we find what we shall find again and again in Mrs Besant's intellectual life. Possessing to a high degree the faculty of vivid and lucid exposition, she often mistook the *exposition* of a problem for its *explanation*. . . . Mrs Besant undoubtedly gives us, in telling phrases and in a really brilliant simile, a picture of the difference between life and death, but it is merely a picture that tells a story, without in the least elucidating it. (p. 67)

It is when she turned to the practical implications of Atheism that we see the Mrs Besant of the 'seventies and 'eighties at her best. In ethics, after all, the practical side vastly overbalances the philosophical; indeed, it is probably true to say that ethics is not at all a normative science. In other words, in a public person, we need not worry about the roads by which he has reached his convictions, so long as the latter are good. Thus, though one may feel convinced that Mrs Besant's utilitarianism was philosophically false, it cannot be denied that in going up and down the country delivering lectures . . . she was doing much good. . . . (pp. 69-71)

[That Mrs Besant's atheism] was the product of a schooled and penetrating intellect cannot justly be maintained. It clearly springs from a restless and insufficiently instructed mind, from warm and benevolent feelings, and from a wholly sincere urge for well-doing. (p. 71)

Mrs Besant's style is largely undistinguished by felicity of language or structure. . . . Almost every phrase [from an 1899 quotation] is commonplace: "wonders of science," "grandeur of philosophy," "lines of beauteous colour," "gracious living curves," and so on. There is practically no use of the subtler rhetorical tricks of the classical orators. What has to be said is said in a simple, quiet manner, with the first words that come to the lips, and with an almost total lack of artful devices. (p. 79)

What then is the secret? It is I think this: Mrs Besant had the greatest of all oratorical gifts, the ability to project herself into her audience, mentally to incorporate herself with it, so that the audience almost feel that *it* is speaking rather than some outside entity. . . . Her use of similes and metaphors was severely restricted but always effective, her vocabulary simple and homely. All in all, it is small wonder that Mr Shaw, writing in 1924, said that at this time "Annie Besant was the greatest orator in England, perhaps the greatest in Europe. Whether it is possible for her to be still that at seventy-seven I do not know; but I have never heard her excelled; and she was then unapproached." (pp. 79-80)

> *Theodore Besterman, in his* Mrs. Annie Besant: A Modern Prophet *(reprinted by permission of the Estate of T.D.N. Besterman), Kegan Paul, Trench, Trubner & Co., Ltd., 1934, 273 p.*

## ADDITIONAL BIBLIOGRAPHY

Braden, Charles Samuel. "Theosophy." In his *These Also Believe: A Study of Modern American Cults and Minority Religious Movements*, pp. 221-56. New York: The Macmillan Co., 1950.*
> History of the Theosophical Society, including discussion of Besant's role. Braden focuses mainly on the American branch of the Theosophical Society led by Katherine A. Tingley.

Bright, Esther. *Old Memories and Letters of Annie Besant*. London: The Theosophical Publishing House, 1936, 172 p.
> Reminiscence interspersed with letters from Besant.

Cole, Margaret. "Annie Besant." In her *Women of To-day*, pp. 191-232. 1938. Reprint. Freeport, N.Y.: Books for Libraries Press, 1968.
> Biographical sketch.

Fremantle, Anne. *This Little Band of Prophets: The Story of the Gentle Fabians*. London: George Allen & Unwin, 1960, 256 p.*
> History of the London Fabians, who included Besant, George Bernard Shaw, Sidney Webb, Hubert Bland, and Henry Hyde Champion among their number.

Manvell, Roger. *The Trial of Annie Besant and Charles Bradlaugh*. New York: Horizon Press, 1976, 182 p.
> Account of the events leading up to the obscenity trial of Besant and Bradlaugh. Manvell provides a study of the relationship between Besant and Bradlaugh, as well as a transcript of the four-day trial.

Nethercot, Arthur H. *The First Five Lives of Annie Besant*. Chicago: The University of Chicago Press, 1960, 418 p.
> Detailed, noncritical biography of Besant from her birth until her first trip to India in 1893.

Nethercot, Arthur H. *The Last Four Lives of Annie Besant*. Chicago: The University of Chicago Press, 1963, 483 p.
> Second volume of Nethercot's biography of Besant, concentrating on her activities in India and with the Theosophical Society.

Smith, Warren Sylvester. "The Non-Christians." In his *The London Heretics: 1870-1914*, pp. 27-194. New York: Dodd, Mead & Co., 1968.*
> Brief approbatory study of Besant's public careers as a Socialist and a Theosophist. Smith theorizes that Besant was emotionally unstable because of the celibacy she adopted after converting to Theosophism.

[Stead, William T.] "Mrs. Besant: Theosophy's New Leader." *The Review of Reviews* IV, No. 4 (December 1891): 540-47.
> Brief sketch of Besant's life. Stead traces Besant's changing philosophies up to her involvement with Helena Blavatsky and the Theosophical Society.

Venkatachalam, G. "Annie Besant." In his *Profiles*, pp. 161-67. Bombay: Nalanda Publications, 1949.
> Praises Besant's great skill as an orator, but finds her greatest gift to be her ability to get "things done properly and promptly," citing particularly her work toward Indian home rule.

Williams, Gertrude Marvin. *The Passionate Pilgrim: A Life of Annie Besant*. New York: Coward-McCann, 1931, 382 p.
> Lengthy noncritical biography which attempts to analyze the reasons for Besant's devotion to so many varied movements.

# Tadeusz Borowski

## 1922-1951

(Also translated as Theodore) Polish short story writer, poet, essayist, historian, and journalist.

As a survivor of the concentration camps in Auschwitz and Dachau, Borowski belongs to a group of Eastern European writers who drew upon their experiences under the Nazi occupation to create a distinctive body of literature which has since been called the "literature of atrocity." His best-known contribution to this literature is a collection of short stories entitled *Kamienny świat (This Way for the Gas, Ladies and Gentlemen, and Other Short Stories)*. A fierce portrayal of human brutality, the harshness of this work is intensified by Borowski's refusal to depict his characters as exclusively good or evil. Indeed, it is the author's unwillingness to romanticize the plight of the death-camp victims which has made him inaccessible for most readers, and has led critics to label him a nihilist. But Borowski's detached cynicism also conceals a highly moralistic attitude towards humanity—one which stresses responsibility and guilt even among the victims of Auschwitz and Dachau.

Born of Polish parents in the Soviet Ukraine, Borowski experienced from an early age the hardships of poverty and political oppression. In 1926 his father was transported to an Arctic labor camp as punishment for dissident activities; four years later his mother was sent to a settlement in Siberia. The young Borowski was forced upon the care of an aunt until his family was reunited in Poland before the Second World War. During the war, the Nazis occupied Poland and banned education for Poles. Borowski was forced to complete his secondary education in the Warsaw underground. After graduating, he took several different jobs and continued his studies by attending secret lectures at Warsaw University. While there, Borowski became acquainted with a promising group of poet-conspirators and published his first volume of poetry, *Gdziekolwiek ziemia*. Shortly thereafter, he was arrested by the Gestapo when he fell into a trap set for his activist friends. Borowski passed through several prisons and concentration camps in Poland and Germany before ending in Auschwitz. While there, he repeatedly witnessed the betrayal of one prisoner by another in the struggle for survival. Borowski himself took this course when he accepted an assignment from the camp adminstration to work as a hospital orderly, a job that possibly saved his life, but also made him an instrument of the Nazi system. He was eventually freed by American forces in 1945. The following year he returned to Warsaw, where he published his most significant works on the Holocaust: *This Way for the Gas, Ladies and Gentlemen* and *Pozegnanie z Maria*. In 1949 Borowski became a fierce Stalinist in the Communist party and engaged in intelligence work during the early years of the cold war. His literary activity as a communist consisted mainly of polemical articles written for a Warsaw newspaper which, although considered by critics his weakest work, won a prize from the government. The ultimate irony in Borowski's life lies in the circumstances of his death: after surviving the gas chambers of Auschwitz, he chose to take his own life by asphyxiation when he was twenty-nine years old.

From the outset, Borowski's literary efforts were shaped by his wartime experiences. *Gdziekolwiek ziemia*, which was written during the Nazi occupation, took as its theme the total destruction of humanity in the extermination camps. In his collections published after the war—*Pozegnanie z Maria* and *This Way for the Gas, Ladies and Gentlemen*—Borowski became the first writer in Poland to truthfully depict the harsh realities of life in the camps. Unlike his contemporaries, Borowski refused to divide his characters into such rigid categories as "victims" and "criminals." Instead, he presents the camp-system itself as the anonymous antagonist in his stories. According to Andrzej Wirth, the key to understanding Borowski's fiction lies in his unique conception of tragedy. Wirth contends that Borowski's model "has nothing to do with the classical conception based on the necessity of choice between two systems of value"; rather, his tragedy is based on the inability of his characters to choose because every choice is evil.

Borowski's Auschwitz stories and poetry have consistently elicited a wide array of critical reactions. While he achieved notoriety during his brief lifetime as one of Poland's outstanding literary figures, he was, nonetheless, bitterly attacked for his cynicism and amorality. The anti-heroes of his short stories, who lacked courage and compassion, came into direct conflict with the more romantic heroes who populated the fiction of his contemporaries. Catholic critics especially denounced him as a nihilist, and the Communist party criticized his work as decadent, amoral, and Americanized. Recent critics, however, have offered a more objective evaluation of Borowski's work. They consider his detachment from his subject matter not as a moral stance, but as a literary device consciously used by the author to capture the bleak reality of prison camp existence.

Borowski's works are among the most brutal to come out of the Nazi concentration camps. According to Czech critic Jan Kott, Borowski's Auschwitz stories constitute "one of the cruelest testimonies to what men did to men, and a pitiless verdict that anything can be done to a human being."

## PRINCIPAL WORKS

*Gdziekolwiek ziemia* (poetry) 1942
*Imiona nurtu* (poetry) 1945
*Poszukiwania* [with K. Olszewski] (poetry) 1945
*Byliśmy w Oświęcimiu* [with K. Olszewski and J. Nel Siedlecki] (history) 1946
*Kamienny świat* (short stories) 1948
  [*This Way for the Gas, Ladies and Gentlemen, and Other Short Stories*, 1967]
*Pożegnanie z Marią* (short stories) 1948
*Utwory zebrane*. 5 vols. (short stories, poetry, essays, and journalism) 1954

---

**SIMON GRAY** (essay date 1967)

Tadeusz Borowski's collection of short stories and reports is, at least in translation, an achievement of direct and courageous observation. The vocabulary of moral outrage has helped us to live with the concentration camp without helping us to live imaginatively in it. Eichmann in the dock, discussions on the meaning of evil, the images of those skeletal and freakish survivors that evoke a disgust we hurriedly convert into pity—and that special and English fluency provoked by the unspeakable. Belsen, Auschwitz, Dachau have become our symbols for the European nightmare, accommodated into our modern mythology. But Borowski looks at the concentration camp as if it were first of all a community of men and women, governed by unalterable instincts and formed by necessary habits. The constant need for human contact—in the persecutors as well as in the condemned—the clinging to ridiculous hopes and useless possessions; and at the same time the grotesque corruptions that become accepted as the consequence of the gift for survival. These terse descriptions, almost anecdotal in form, become an oblique commentary on the negotiations we conduct daily in our own, civilised ways. But in the last forlorn pages we suddenly discover how much that sympathetic watchfulness cost Borowski. The eye that focused so unflinchingly on the human details—the man who knew what, above all, must be preserved in himself—can now see, in the safety of his rediscovered city, 'only a world of stone.' (pp. 622-23)

*Simon Gray, "A Man of Style," in* New Statesman *(©1967 The Statesman & Nation Publishing Co. Ltd.), Vol. 73, No. 1886, May 5, 1967, pp. 622-23.\**

**ANDRZEJ WIRTH** (essay date 1967)

[*Wirth demonstrates that the traditional design of tragedy does not apply to Borowski's fiction because the relationship between criminal and victim in the Nazi system is an anonymous one. This is one of the most thorough critical treatments of Borowski's short stories.*]

[A] historical point of view enters our speculation at the moment when we begin to treat Borowski's work as a document of the so-called "martyrological literature," a term we use to describe literature whose themes are the contemporary crimes against humanity. Historians assure us that in scope and refinement these have surpassed everything previously recorded. If this is so, and it surely is, we have to assume that new crimes call for a new literature. The design of tragedy based on a Creon-Antigone situation in relation to the tragedy of mass annihilation in Auschwitz is as useless as the Shakespearean tragedy of the "great steps" by which History ascends amid dynastic murders.

The specific, always detectable tone of Borowski's stories, is the outcome of the conception of tragedy which he adopted. It has nothing to do with the classical conception based on the necessity of choice between two systems of value. The hero of Borowski's stories is a hero *deprived of all choice*. He finds himself in a situation without choice because every choice is base. The tragedy lies not in the necessity of choosing but in the impossibility of making a choice. The emergence of such situations, whose inhumanity lies in their lack of any alternative, Borowski describes as characteristic of the new times. **"Boy with a Bible"** is about a random collection of people awaiting death in one cell. Even the solidarity of people about to die together is absent. Each faces death alone and isolated from his chance colleagues. Even the cause for which they are dying cannot be revealed either to the enemy or the other victims. (pp. 45-6)

Attempts to apply the traditional design of tragedy to describe the critical experience of our century, which the planned extermination of people has become, have not only proved fruitless but somehow, because of their inadequacy, have discredited the subject, which could not be shown as the struggle with fate of an outstanding individual. The wholesale character of the tragedy made the individualistic, exemplary presentation impossible. . . .

The relationship between the criminal and his victim had become blurred. It could no longer be presented as the classical relationship between Creon and Antigone. And not only because there is no longer an "outstanding" criminal or an "outstanding" victim as understood by classical tragedy, but also because the relation between the murderer and the victim is now an anonymous one. (p. 46)

Mass murder then—the critical experience of our times—demands from the writer a revision of artistic means. Tragedy in life does not automatically become tragedy in art. The question which Tadeusz Borowski must have asked himself was how to make the death of millions a tragedy in terms of *literature*. The answer, contained in his Auschwitz stories, calls for an analysis. It seems that it was there that a solution was found which is valid as a formula for contemporary literature.

Right from the beginning Borowski is conscious of the inadequacy of the classical design of tragedy to express the tragedy of the twentieth century, particularly its climax, the mass murder. The awareness of this leads him to a momentous artistic discovery. Borowski does not make either the victim or the murderer the hero of his stories. The first eventuality demands that the individual be given exceptional positive qualities, which because they are crushed by a superior force, excite the feeling of tragedy. Borowski is aware that this solution is inadequate in relation to the contemporary situation. Attempts in this direction result in a pale and *pretentious sentimentality.* The other possibility which has been tried, always with the same result, leads to a *demonization of the criminal.* This too is, in the circumstances, an inadequate solution.

A feature of crime in the concentration-camp system is not the sharp delineation of the murderer but rather his withdrawal outside the *situation* established by the system. Borowski discovers the optimum vantage point for his themes, Goethe's "der prägnante Punkt" ["the meaningful point"], when he presents them through the eyes of a third party which is not unequivocally either the murderer or the victim. He combines the features of both in the figure of a "Kapo" or some other character professing the ethic of such a go-between between the torturer and the victim. In adopting this position from which to shape his narrative Borowski overcomes the traditional tragic design and demonstrates the problem inherent in the *ambivalence* of the criminal and the victim. At the same time he shifts the weight of accusation from an elusive criminal on to the Nazi *system* which forces its victims on to a narrow path leading to crime. Yet this criminal system is not *"fate,"* something irrevocable. It can and is questioned by another system intent on wiping out social sources of crime. What is irrevocable is the *situation* which the criminal system creates. This situation develops according to certain fixed norms which are not "fate" in general but *"fate created by the system."* From this Borowski draws his conception of tragedy, based not on an opposition between the criminal and his victim, but on the value destroying the *automatic* character of the situation. (pp. 47-8)

The new conception of tragedy, unfolding in a world of *destroyed values,* was in a way the principle underlying the best stories of the Auschwitz cycle. From a systematic application of this principle springs the specific tone which makes Borowski distinguishable in the mass of Polish martyrological literature. This tone is one of apparent cynicism, moral indifference and an uncontrollable "moral insanity." It serves as the prism through which the narrator of Borowski's stories sees the camp reality.

In the Auschwitz cycle the narrators have certain features in common. In each case he is a victim collaborating in crime. Within the system of extermination he has found a comparatively comfortable position of a mediator between victims and their tormentors and plays this role with relish. In both **"A Day in Harmenze"** and **"Ladies and Gentlemen: into the Gas Please"** the narrator is a *vorarbeiter* [foreman] who says of himself in a camp decimated by hunger: "Work is easy after breakfasting on a quarter of bacon with bread and garlick and a tin of condensed milk." In **"People Marching"** the narrator constantly stresses his special position within the system of extermination: "At the time I would normally sit down to my lunch, which was better than I ever had at home, people would be marching this way and that." This is the vantage point from which the narrator observes the crowd moving to the crematorium. In the **"Death of a Freedom Fighter"** the narrator has reached his position thanks to shrewdness and experience acquired while struggling to remain alive. This enables him to view the camp victims from a distance without compassion and with indifferent scorn.

In stories where the narrator is invested with positive humane qualities and his place in the system of mass extermination

lacks the ambiguities I have described, the artistic effect is weakened. This happens in **"At Home in Auschwitz"**: here the author identifies himself with the narrator and offers *direct* comments. He either metes out justice to the cruel world in highminded declarations or demands it rhetorically: "For maybe we shall have to report to the living about this camp and about this time of deceit and take a stand in defense of the dead." The incommensurability between fact and the moralist's commentary, once a certain bound of inhumanity is passed, becomes evident and thus underlines the artistic significance of the method Borowski used in his best camp stories.

From the special position of the narrator poised between the victim and the murderer emerges that unexpected *"alienation effect,"* in the flash of which Borowski portrays the truth about the camps. This alienation effect is brought about by the description of unimaginable crimes as if they were something almost natural. "One day was very much like another. People emerged from trains and marched—this way and that . . . Nights followed days, rains came after draughts." Within this poetic framework we come across this tremendous sentence: "I returned with the ball and passed it to the wing. Between two corner shots 3,000 people were gassed behind my back." (**"People Marching"**). Crime comes as a shock to the reader because it goes unnoticed by the indifferent narrator who is playing football, and also because that which is most unnatural is shown as an almost natural biological process. One is shocked into an awareness of the unnaturalness of mass extermination because it is presented as natural.

In **"Farewell to Mary"** the alienation effect is brought about through a demonstration of how the occupation alters the natural function of men and events. A warehouse in the suburbs serves for a wedding reception, a school becomes a prison, people are turned into goods, the manager of a building firm trades in gold, a poet is a storekeeper, compassion becomes scorn at the expense of tragedy: "In the night policemen would help the *goods* through a window of the school, and these would either immediately vanish in the nooks of the street, or, injuring themselves terribly would climb over the barbed wire into the yard of our firm where they would wander aimlessly till dawn, because the office was of course shut. They were mostly young women." (My italics). Treating people as objects, the transformation of man into an object as a result of an inhuman situation, is Borowski's constant theme. The description of man in a situation in which he has become an *object* is the crux of the camp stories.

The reduction of human beings to objects is accompanied either by the destruction of values I have described or the transformation of values into their opposites. (pp. 49-51)

Borowski reached the poetry of his best camp stories gradually. In **"Farewell to Mary"** nature descriptions still have the traditional expressive functions: "To the right of the house, against the background of a stormy sky, the leafless tree, motionless in the wind and wreathed in milky puffs from passing steam engines, stands dramatically."

This portrayal of nature mirrors the dramatic character of events which are to follow, but in later stories natural descriptions serve as *contrast.* Murder takes place in an arcadian setting of splendidly opulent nature. (p. 51)

The use of nature description for contrast is in effect one of the deliberate methods of creating the alienation effect. Another method is that of a *situational and emotional inversion.* A labor camp without real work: "They work not with their hands but with their eyes.'' (**"A Day in Harmenzach"**); forced labor which gives satisfaction to the laborer: "I am digging a ditch. The light handy shovel seems to move on its own. The clods of moist earth give easily and fly into the air." In **"The Battle of Grünwald"** a girl from Poland dies, *after the war,* while escaping *into* a camp. In **"A Day in Harmenze"** a *guard* asks a *prisoner* for a pair of shoes. In **"Ladies and Gentlemen: into the Gas Please"** a Red Cross ambulance is going back and forth carrying gas for killing people.

Borowski's work, in its artistically climactic moments, has become an expression of a will to give witness to the *unbelievable* truth about the fate which man has prepared for man in the twentieth century. In cherishing this noble desire Borowski is not unique in world literature. The uniqueness of his position lies in that his writing *does* in fact give witness to this truth. Artistic as well as ordinary human courage was needed to achieve this; and artistic resourcefulness as well. Borowski possessed all these qualities. He was able to depict tragedy outside the classical laws of tragedy. He created tragedy according to a new law: a tragedy without alternative, without choice, without competing values. He demonstrated prototypes of situations which are tragic in themselves. Situations created by a system which had treated man as an object, as a thing, and taken away from him the possibility of being human. Borowski had the courage to say this. He also had the courage to formulate a principle that once a certain limit of inhumanity is passed, the differentiation between tormentor and victim becomes fluid. (pp. 51-2)

The truth about death in the twentieth century neither makes a villain out of the murderer nor does it attempt an apotheosis of the victim. The emphasis in the accusation shifts on to the *Nazi system* which has created the inhuman situation. "I wished to describe what I have experienced, but who in the world will believe a writer using an unknown language? It's like trying to persuade trees or stones" (**"Nazis"**). Borowski's fear has proved unfounded. His truth is a discovery, doubtless terrifying, which was made in the name of world literature and forms a part of it. (p. 52)

> *Andrzej Wirth, "A Discovery of Tragedy," translated by Adam Czerniawski, in* The Polish Review *(© copyright 1967 by the Polish Institute of Arts and Sciences in America, Inc.), Vol. XII, No. 3, Summer, 1967, pp. 43-52.*

**GEORGE ECKSTEIN** (essay date 1968)

[The short pieces in *This Way to the Gas, Ladies and Gentlemen*] are remarkable in the unsentimental, unflinching frankness with which they face the universal brutality, including that of the inmates [of Auschwitz] themselves and especially of the various camp functionaries among them.

The author describes these functionaries, who virtually ran the camp administration for the SS, from the *Kapo* down to the privileged "Special *Kommandos*," such as those who received the new arrivals from the cattle trains and had access to some of their possessions. To be able to participate in the camp apparatus, to wiggle an "easy" job, a place in the infirmary on a certain day, a pair of shoes, an extra bowl of soup—matters of life and death! . . . All this—so indispensable for survival—had a price, a heavy price including one's own brutalization.

Borowski does not evade these unpleasant facts; he stresses them, because they were the bitter essence of life in the Nazi concentration camp. There is a class society in camp, and he himself belongs to one of the privileged groups: he is young and healthy, Polish (packages from home!), at times a hospital orderly, at times the foreman of a small labor gang; he has contact with the political group that is struggling for positions of influence in the camp administration. **"A Day at Harmenz"** illustrates the constant infighting, the briberies and thefts, aggressive group action, and sly deceptions on which survival depends—and also the unspeakable brutality with which the weaker prisoners are eliminated. (p. 185)

Borowski has an unerring eye and ear for the grotesqueness, the absurdity of life in this condition. In a way, the whole book is a collection of examples. To mention one more: in the **"Death of Schillinger"** the author tells the story of one of the most brutal Nazi Lagerführer who is eventually shot by a naked Jewish girl whom he tries to pull out of a mass being driven to the gas chambers. As he lies dying in pain, he groans, "O God, what have I done to deserve such suffering!" The man who tells of this "irony of fate" is himself a member of the *Sonderkommando* who (a second irony) drove this girl and her group into the gas chambers after this incident and (triple irony) is liquidated with all his colleagues in the end, after the *Sonderkommando's* last-minute attempt at saving themselves through a revolt.

In the midst of this all-perverting brutality, there are flashes of humaneness—unsentimental and offhanded. You can't afford to go soft: such as the passage in **"The Man with the Package"** where the Prussian-Jewish doctor from Berlin teaches his assistant understanding for the camp *"Schreiber"* who has fallen from grace and who—doomed, and knowing he is doomed—yet clings to a small package with a few belongings on his last walk, naked, to the gas.

In **"Auschwitz, our Home,"** Borowski blames hope itself—"hope that makes people go without a murmur to the gas chambers, keeps them from risking revolt . . . compels man to hold on to one more day of life . . ." (pp. 185-86)

> *George Eckstein, "The Festering Sore," in* Dissent *(© 1968, by Dissent Publishing Corporation), Vol. XV, No. 2, March-April, 1968, pp. 184-86.\**

**CZESŁAW MIŁOSZ** (essay date 1969)

Critical toward all the Polish complexes of "martyrdom" and toward the resistance movement, [Borowski] preferred to write poetry, and his mimeographed volume, *Wherever the Earth (Gdziekolwiek Ziemia* . . .), differed radically from the work of his contemporaries and colleagues such as Baczyński or the group of *Art and the Nation*. Like them, however, he took much from the Second Vanguard, but while they dissolved images into a sort of emotional mist, he strove for sharpness, even harshness. Yet, though the strong metrical patterns give the impression of manly vigor, his poems are the most desperate of those produced during the Nazi occupation. In them, the torture and death of "us slaves" (Poles) is stripped of all meaning, even of an anticipated meaning for posterity, and the catastrophe acquires all the earmarks of a macabre prank played by blind and indifferent forces of history, similar to a cataclysm of nature. . . . [Many of Borowski's Auschwitz stories were collected] under the title *Farewell to Mary (Pożegnanie z Marią* . . .), The treatment of the subject puzzled and even caused indignation among the critics. No such presentation of life in a concentration camp yet existed in literature, where there is no clear division into victims and criminals. The camp is shown as an infernal machine, forcing prisoners, its victims, into a struggle for survival at any price, be it at the expense of the weaker among them. All notions of good and bad behavior tumble down; ''good'' equals toughness and resourcefulness; ''evil'' equals lack of cunning or of physical strength. The narrator, who bears the author's first name (Tadeusz), is one of those tough fellows who organize their life in the camp quite well, steal, barter, know how to avoid overexertion while laboring, and look on with detachment, if not with a sarcastic grimace, at the daily processions of thousands destined for the gas chambers. The moral ambiguity is emphasized by the tone of the narrative, which is a bragging one; connivance of prisoners with their overseers is evoked in a matter-of-fact way. No overt moral judgment is passed. Borowski thus achieves an effect of cruelty which remains unsurpassed by any testimony on Nazi camps.

In his craft, he learned much from Hemingway, especially how to outline a situation through idiomatic dialogue without author's commentary. Actually, Borowski was a desperate moralist. His stories place on trial our entire Western civilization, which made such crimes possible. The stories set in Germany after the entrance of American troops betray a deep sense of outrage at the ''normalcy'' that will soon relegate Nazi genocide to the sphere of vague recollections or, more probably, of silence. We refer here to another book of short stories: *The World of Stone (Kamienny świat . . .).* (pp. 488-89)

[Later, he] put his talent at the disposal of the [Communist] Party, writing mostly journalism. His style was forceful and often brilliant, in spite of an unceremonious twisting of facts. . . . After *Farewell to Mary,* which Marxist critics denounced as the work of a nihilist, tainted with the American literature of violence, Borowski plunged into an aggressive campaign for Socialist Realism. (p. 489)

In spite of its apparent contradictions, Borowski's work stands as a whole, unified by his chase after some unshakable moral values. The bitterness of his early poems grew out of his disagreement with the belief in the redeeming virtue of Polish heroism. His Auschwitz stories, seemingly written in cold blood, are actually a most hot-blooded protest. He embraced a dogmatic Marxism because of the same stubborn search, as he found in it a promise of rescue for mankind. And since he was a man of scrupulous integrity, he was doomed to fail in his new duty as a ''politically reliable'' writer. (p. 490)

> *Czesław Miłosz, ''World War II and the First Twenty Years of People's Poland,'' in his* The History of Polish Literature *(copyright © 1969 by Czesław Miłosz; reprinted by permission of the University of California Press), Macmillan, 1969, pp. 441-532 (and to be reprinted by the University of California Press, 1983).**

**JAN KOTT**   (essay date 1976)

Borowski was the greatest hope of Polish literature among the generation of his contemporaries decimated by the war. . . . [His] Auschwitz stories, however, are not only a masterpiece of Polish—and of world—literature. Among the tens of thousands of pages written about the holocaust and the death camps, Borowski's slender book continues to occupy, for more than a quarter century now, a place apart. The book is one of the cruelest of testimonies to what men did to men, and a pitiless verdict that anything can be done to a human being. (pp. 11-12)

[Borowski's first volume of poetry], **Wherever the Earth,** predicted in classical cadences the extermination of mankind. Its dominant image was that of a gigantic labor camp. Already, in that first volume of poetry, there was no hope, no comfort, no pity. The last poem, **''A Song,''** concluded with a prophecy delivered like a sentence: ''We'll leave behind us iron scrap / and the hollow, mocking laugh of generations.'' (pp. 14-15)

Borowski's Auschwitz stories are written in the first person. The narrator of three of the stories is a deputy Kapo, Vorarbeiter Tadeusz. The identification of the author with the narrator was the moral decision of a prisoner who had lived through Auschwitz—an acceptance of mutual responsibility, mutual participation, and mutual guilt for the concentration camp. ''It is impossible to write about Auschwitz impersonally,'' Borowski wrote in a review of one of the hagiographic books about the camp. ''The first duty of Auschwitzers is to make clear just what a camp is. . . . But let them not forget that the reader will unfailingly ask: But how did it happen that *you* survived? . . . Tell, then, how you bought places in the hospital, easy posts, how you shoved the 'Moslems' [prisoners who had lost the will to live] into the oven, how you bought women, men, what you did in the barracks, unloading the transports, at the gypsy camp; tell about the daily life of the camp, about the hierarchy of fear, about the loneliness of every man. But write that you, you were the ones who did this. That a portion of the sad fame of Auschwitz belongs to you as well.'' (pp. 21-2)

In Borowski's Auschwitz stories the difference between executioner and victim is stripped of all greatness and pathos; it is brutally reduced to a second bowl of soup, an extra blanket, or the luxury of a silk shirt and shoes with thick soles, about which Vorarbeiter Tadeusz is so proud. (p. 23)

Borowski describes Auschwitz like an entomologist. The image of ants recurs many times, with their incessant march, day and night, night and day, from the ramp to the crematorium and from the barracks to the baths. The most terrifying thing in Borowski's stories is the icy detachment of the author. ''You can get accustomed to the camp,'' says Vorarbeiter Tadeusz. Auschwitz is presented from a natural perspective—a day like any other. Everything is commonplace, routine, *normal.* ''. . . first just one ordinary barn, brightly whitewashed—and here they proceed to asphyxiate people. Later, four large buildings, accommodating twenty thousand at a time without any trouble. No hocus-pocus, no poison, no hypnosis. Only several men directing traffic to keep operations running smoothly, and the thousands flow along like water from an open tap.'' (pp. 24-5)

Borowski called his book about Auschwitz ''a voyage to the limit of a particular experience.'' At the limit of that experience Auschwitz is no exception but the rule. History is a sequence of Auschwitzes, one following the other. (p. 25)

> *Jan Kott, ''Introduction,'' translated by Michael Kandel (copyright © Jan Kott, 1976; copyright © 1959 by Maria Borowski; translation copyright © 1967 by Penguin Books Ltd; reprinted by permission of Viking Penguin Inc.), in* This Way to the Gas Ladies and Gentlemen, and Other Short Stories *by Tadeusz Borowski, translated by Barbara Vedder, Penguin Books, 1976, pp. 11-26.*

**HAMIDA BOSMAJIAN**   (essay date 1979)

> [*This is part of a larger work in which Bosmajian considers the effect of the Nazi reign of terror upon the creative activity of several authors, Borowski among them.*]

[Borowski's] stories, while they can be arranged to give the illusion of beginning, middle, and end, are really memory shards in which he retraces his guilt, reacts aggressively against it, and mocks himself profoundly as an artist in a world of stone. (p. 45)

[In **"This Way for the Gas, Ladies and Gentlemen,"** we see] how a young man, the narrator Tadek, incorporated Auschwitz. . . . Tadek, who works at the ramp, actively participates in sending thousands to their deaths. Yet the nonmetaphysically inclined Tadek also arrives at metaphysical intimations; for the magnitude of decreation around him evokes such resonances in **"This Way for the Gas,"** internalizes them in **"A Visit,"** and disgorges them in aggressive apocalyptic visions in **"The World of Stone."**

The uncreating world of the concentrationary universe is a world of lies and deceit, as is already evident in the title of **"This Way for the Gas, Ladies and Gentlemen,"** and is confirmed as the reader becomes conscious of the fact that within the twenty pages of this short story 15,000 people have been gassed. Speed intensifies throughout the narrative as Tadek races through the account of his participation in preparing the victims of three transports for their deaths. In the beginning he and his composers seem to eagerly await the first transport, for also at the ramp is "Canada," the land of plenty, where the inmates get supplies for survival. The narrator's tone is objective, casual, and cynical. . . . Typical of Borowski's style is the climactic but ironic use of parallelisms. [A distant] church steeple obviously points to something that transcends this world. But whatever that might be, it has no contact with the two groups of men who conspire within this confined, narrow ground of evil. (pp. 49-50)

After the wagons have been emptied, the inmates must clean up the "Schweinerei" (pig's mess); the physical and moral stain must appear to have been removed. Among the human refuse in the wagon, Tadek finds "squashed, trampled infants, naked little monsters, with enormous heads and bloated bellies. We carry them out like chickens, holding several in each hand." . . . Pity is consistently undercut as the narrator moves from infants to monsters, to chickens, and to the seemingly unaffected diversionary attitude of the SS man who sees but does not choose to see. Shocked, the women refuse to take the little bodies; but a tall, grey-haired woman accepts them and addresses Tadek as "my poor boy," a personalized phrase that overwhelms him, not with tears, but with intense, physical fatigue and with the refusal to look at people individually. (pp. 50-1)

With the arrival of the second transport brutality increases and deception diminishes. A woman, aware that she would go to the gas chamber if defined as a mother, denies her child but is killed by a Russian inmate. As Tadek once again struggles with nausea, there emerges from the train a girl that belongs to another time and world. She "descends lightly from the train, hops to the gravel, looks around inquiringly as if somewhat surprised. Her soft, blond hair has fallen on her shoulders in a torrent." Her wise and mature look defines her as in the know as she insists on going to the gas chamber. She is a totally absurd but true appearance of personhood and dignity in this world of deceit; her knowledge, however, leads her to seek death. . . . [Only] the human being can contain such knowledge, for there is no god who contains or refuses to contain so much suffering.

This is particularly evident after Tadek has cleaned up the wagons of the second transport and rests against the rails: "The

sun has leaned low over the horizon and illuminates the ramp with a reddish glow: the shadows of the trees have become elongated, ghostlike. In the silence that settles over nature at this time of day, the human cries seem to rise all the way to the sky." . . . No ear will receive the cries that rise from this constricted and seemingly eternal narrow ground. Tadek, who sees all this, describes it in a language resonant with religious connotations, a language similar to the images of Nelly Sachs in "Landscape of Screams"; for the precision of Borowski's attempt to imitate reality and Sachs's precise use of the literalness of the word approximate each other. (p. 51)

Nausea is a momentary and illusory relief for a man who has made such a world part of his being that his sense of ego has been lost. In the sketches **"A Visit"** and **"The World of Stone,"** Tadek describes the state of such a man after liberation. He admits in **"A Visit"** that "I have never been able to look at myself". . . . Self-knowledge is a myth for the former concentration camp inmate, for his self is constituted of what he saw. **"A Visit"** is a visit of the people who claimed his kinship, as is evident in the twice-repeated whisper of a dying man: "Brother, brother." Tadek had to fail as his brother's keeper, for he had thousands of brothers and sisters who claimed his kinship. As the repetition of "I saw, I saw, I saw" reveals, Tadek has only been able to fulfill the final request of the victims, namely, that he remember what happened. He is now housed in his memory but is unhoused in his present world as he sits "in someone else's room," where in a moment he will feel "homesick for the people I saw then." He can visit them all, and they will be his visitation. Because he is defined through them alone, because there is no room for self-knowledge, his consciousness is nothing but a house for the memory of the victims. The world that once swallowed him is now contained within him.

In **"The World of Stone"** the alienated narrator reacts aggressively against the "intimate immensity" (Bachelard) of himself as the anagogic container of the world of Auschwitz. Growing within him "like a foetus inside a womb" is the terrible knowledge and foreboding that "the Infinite Universe is inflating at incredible speed." He wants to retain it like "a miser," afraid that solid matter will dissolve into emptiness like a "fleeting sound." Demonic knowledge crowds and pressures the confines of his being, a knowledge that cannot be transformed into the logos of speech because it would not generate an individualized creation; rather, it would generate a chaos of emptiness, reminiscent of smoke and air or the cries that rose all the way to the sky from the ground of Auschwitz. (pp. 52-3)

[In **"The World of Stone"**] Tadek is left with the choice of chaos as void or a world of stone, the latter symbolized by the "massive cool building made of granite" where he works. But granite does not protect him; he knows it "cannot keep the world from swelling and bursting like an over-ripe pomegranate, leaving behind but a handful of contracted, grey, dry ashes," an image which is a grotesque inversion of Mallarmé's "Afternoon of a Faun." In Borowski's world of stone there may be a volcanic eruption of aggression, there may be ashes, but no queen of love visits the daydreamer.

Tadek concludes that, because the world has not yet blown away, he intends to write and "grasp the true significance of the events and people I have seen." His matter is great and worthy of "an immortal epic," but the act of writing would mean a concession to the illusion of normality in which he does not want to participate. Tadek and the other victim-survivors of the concentrationary universe have not left us, who are still caught in the illusion of reprieve, the conclusive comfort of a great epic. They have left us partial visions, short stories, sketches, and fragments and retained ''with a miser's piercing anxiety'' . . . the world which swallowed them and which they swallowed with open eyes. (pp. 53-4)

> *Hamida Bosmajian, ''The Rage for Order: Autobiographical Accounts of the Self in the Nightmare of History,'' in her* Metaphors of Evil: Contemporary German Literature and the Shadow of Nazism *(© 1979 by The University of Iowa Press), University of Iowa Press, 1979, pp. 27-54.**

## LAWRENCE L. LANGER   (essay date 1982)

[In *This Way for the Gas, Ladies and Gentlemen*] Borowski's strategy is to fuse techniques of fiction with details of fact in a way that obliterates usual sources of tension in literature and introduces us dramatically to the atmosphere of what I have abstractly called the world of choiceless choice. He draws us not into an imaginative (and imagined) world, but into the daily routines of Auschwitz itself, then takes us beyond history by manipulating tone and point of view and enfolding the narrated events with an insulating irony to try to salvage some of the reader's disintegrating admiration for human nature. Slowly it becomes clear that his own disintegrating admiration is at stake too, as he struggles, in his own words, ''to tell the truth about mankind to those who do not know it.''

For Borowski, the concepts of heroism and villainy died with the first deportations to the deathcamps. In a searching exposition of the theoretical basis of Borowski's literary achievement, Andrzej Wirth examines the original idea of tragedy that evolved in his work following his dismissal of those two concepts [see excerpt above]. New crimes, Wirth assumes, call for a new literature. . . . Borowski, perhaps more powerfully than any other writer on the subject, discredits the argument that an exemplary individual attitude or act could be pitted against a system of mass extermination. . . . Hence the victim could not transform himself, like Melville's Ahab, into a unique hero or, again like Ahab, create a unique antagonist from machinery of destruction that was deliberately designed to reduce all its victims to interchangeable ash. . . . As a consequence, both the nature of good and the source of evil were blurred, as was the traditional relationship between hero and antagonist, a Hamlet and a Claudius, Antigone and Creon, Othello and Iago. (pp. 103-04)

The title of Borowski's volume, *This Way for the Gas, Ladies and Gentlemen* (which is also the title of the initial story), is itself an ironic farewell to politeness, to human consideration, and an introduction to a pitiless world of stone (as Borowski called one of his Polish Auschwitz volumes) from which a new human identity, a deathcamp identity, is to be chiseled. The old identities, as Wirth observes, which attributed exceptional positive qualities to the hero and extraordinary cruelty to the villain, were simply insufficient to portray the actual conditions of Auschwitz. Such efforts, Borowski felt, would sentimentalize the hero and demonize the villain, reflecting not the authenticity of the deathcamp experience but the commentator's habit of viewing that experience (often instinctively) through the comforting lenses of traditional literature. (p. 105)

Although Borowski transforms the ordeal of Auschwitz into literature, he refuses to treat his subject as material to be artistically manipulated. If anything, his *reader* becomes his ma-

terial, a sensibility whose premises about character and conduct will be disorganized by the experience of reading and reformulated after absorbing the substance of the artist's unorthodox vision. Both the behavior and the attitude of Borowski's characters violate our expectations of decency (and often of monstrosity too), leaving us with the problem of reconciling old values with a new reality. Since Borowski need not pretend to have invented this reality—Auschwitz has already ''happened''—his challenge is to ensure that we do not confuse it with familiar assumptions about the pre-Holocaust world. . . . By using narrative points of view from *within* the system of extermination, by presenting as normal, actions that we intuitively regard as perverse, Borowski moves a step beyond . . . the dual universe of free or meaningless choice. His vision of system-created fate reflects a version of survival that is inaccessible in straightforward accounts of life in the deathcamps. He simply eliminates the destroyed half of that dual universe. (pp. 105-06)

The apparent cynicism of Borowski's narrators is not merely a literary device; it represents an honest attempt to suggest how Auschwitz ''denatured'' human character. ''It is impossible to write about Auschwitz impersonally,'' Borowski once said in a review of a book about the camp that praised the behavior of survivors and victims. . . . Fear and loneliness do not breed heroes or villains in this atmosphere. Life here breeds lice, and because of this the opening line of the story **''This Way for the Gas''**—''All of us walked around naked''—introduces us to an unrecognizable Eden, where men and women exist not by naming the beasts but by being confused with them, breathing (while their garments are being deloused) not the glorious air of paradise restored but the odor of Cyclone B, ''an efficient killer of lice in clothing and of men in gas chambers.'' . . . It is as if the world of organized creation were disintegrating back into chaos through a natural process, devoid of the signs of apocalypse, still under the control of men, while the unprepared reader—like the confused original arrivals at Auschwitz—must find his way around an alien terrain.

Delousing is a vital controlling image for the deathcamp experience, not as metaphor but as literal reflection of a place where men and women did not choose heroic death and were not even killed like human beings, but were *exterminated*. . . . For Borowski, Auschwitz was a place where people were exterminated, or survived in order to avoid extermination. In normal times, we may admire the spiritual strength of those who can draw on a quiet faith to confront impending disaster; Borowski allows no such luxury, not because he is an enemy of faith, but because he knows how such an emphasis can distort what he calls ''the daily life of the camp.'' (pp. 106-08)

In the culture of coping that was Auschwitz, the living did not control the dead—the dead controlled the living. The survivor depended for his life—for the time being, anyway—on the death of someone else. If the tragic figure is a man who through action or moral attitude rebels against his destiny, what are we to make of Borowski's narrator, who helps to drive victims from the cattle cars, unloads their belongings, watches them being led off to the gas chambers, feels rage at his involvement in their fate rather than pride at his triumph over his own, and finds in an attack of nausea little escape from an environment that dehumanizes everyone—murderer, victim, and survivor? . . . [The narrator] is victim himself of the only permissible form of charity, the camp law that dictates that ''people going to their death must be deceived to the very end.'' . . . (pp. 109-10)

Their death pollutes his life while it ensures his survival: he will get from the transport the new shoes that he needs. He is left only a choice between evils, between extermination and continued existence in Auschwitz. . . . In the context of all those corpses, we are surprised by his question from another world—"Listen Henri, are we good people?" . . .—a question both irrelevant and intolerable. It is irrelevant because the idea of the "good" echoes a system of values that the Nazis have perverted, leaving a vacuum that makes such a question unanswerable; and intolerable because the narrator, powerless to denounce or attack the original agents of evil, who are unidentifiable in any case, finds himself hating their victims, a situation that he himself calls pathological. And the reader, who shares with Borowski a vantage point wider than any of his characters, who still inhabits the other world that the narrator has been wrenched from, suffers most of all from what he is forced to witness: the invitation to the gas in the story's title includes us all.

Its fatal odor lingers in our memory as Borowski mercilessly confronts us with moments of dehumanization so overwhelming that they temporarily obliterate instances of compassion that might have balanced them. Compassion we expect, even in adversity; but the terror of extermination generated consequences that leave us morally speechless. . . . (p. 110)

Borowski is determined to follow the images of men as they evolve under the tutelage of Auschwitz, even though his pursuit may shatter all cherished humanisms of the past. The risk is great, since it raises the challenge of rebuilding new humanisms from fragments of discord that pierce the heart with potentially incurable wounds. He complicates his vision, and our task of interpreting it, by acknowledging the multiple realities of the deathcamp universe, where human reactions shift with the state of one's hunger, the relative security of one's future (depending on which Kommando one was assigned to), and the simple fact of whether or not one was Jewish. Borowski's non-Jewish narrator in **"A Day at Harmenz"** (Harmenz was one of the many subcamps surrounding Auschwitz) is openly contemptuous of the Jew Becker, who when he was camp senior at a Jewish camp elsewhere in Poland had had his own son hanged for stealing bread from the other prisoners. Borowski's secure narrator habitually denounces those who violate his sense of human decency with imprecations like "pig" and "swine" (favorite SS imprecations too), and Becker does not escape his scorn. But the confrontation that follows shifts our sympathies rapidly as we are drawn into a world where human decencies like the loyalty of father to son are poisoned by unprecedented conditions of being. . . . But just as we begin to understand the justification for Becker's version of survival, Borowski's narrator undermines our insight with a further exchange: "'And you, you never ate anything but your own ration?' 'That was different. I was a camp senior'." . . . A morality determined by diet seems a bizarre juxtaposition to readers accustomed to one founded on values less nutritive; Borowski's story records the genesis of this unfamiliar system for gauging human conduct. (pp. 111-12)

Two essential rituals of the deathcamp dominate the action of ["**A Day at Harmenz**"], framing the perimeters of the prisoners' existence: the noontime "meal," and a selection for the gas chambers. In Borowski's universe, men cannot afford the luxury of inviolate spirits or uncontaminated attitudes: the pressure of events allows no leisure for such self-indulgence. The practical law of survival motivates the narrator, who is foreman of his work detail, to snatch a large caldron of soup from the next Kommando and substitute one of his own that is half the size. A similar rule induces the Kapo to distribute second helpings of soup to the stronger and healthier workers: "The sick, the weaklings, the emaciated, have no right to an extra bowl of water with nettles. Food must not be wasted on people who are about to go to the gas chamber." . . . Borowski's ironic tone cannot disguise the fact that within the inhuman limitations of Auschwitz there is a grain of reason in this sensible cruelty, similar to the principle followed by prisoner-doctors of designating hopeless cases for selection in order to save convalescing ones. The idea that men suffer in body to endure in spirit is meaningless here, as is the more traditional view of sacrifice: we suffer, that others may live. The deathcamp corrupts this to read, "Let others suffer, so that we may live," and in the wake of this perverse but inescapable system of morality given the minimal inclination toward sainthood of ordinary men, charity becomes an exclusive prerogative of the fortunate few, not a source of spiritual grace, while the reader gropes in vain to share with the victims a terror he cannot identify with. (p. 113)

Borowski's refusal to spiritualize the experience of suffering in the deathcamp creates distance rather than recognition, and the reader is left with a sense of humanity so violated (and violating) that there is nothing and no one to identify with. . . . Even Borowski's Polish biographer was driven to conclude after reading the Auschwitz stories that in the world of stone, the living are always right, the dead are always wrong. But Jan Kott, who introduces Borowski's stories in English, corrects this misleading conclusion: "If the dead are wrong and the living are always right, everything is finally justified: but the story of Borowski's life and that which he wrote about Auschwitz show that the dead are right, and not the living." (pp. 113-14)

[Borowski] refuses to gratify the reader's need to find justification in the survivor. If mutual support occasionally helped friends or relatives to hold out for a time (as Mrs. Haneczka gave food to the narrator before he began to receive packages from home), *ultimately* private support ensures one life at the expense of another, since there is not enough food to go around (as the narrator tells the Greeks who plead with him to intervene with Mrs. Haneczka, "If you're hungry, ask her for food yourself. Let her give it to you" . . .). The narrator is forced, not by his own nature—and this is vital if we are to understand Wirth's theory of a tragedy beyond choice—but by the situation in Auschwitz which controls him even though he did not help to create it, to participate in a kind of deathcamp "justice" that is always allied with the death of someone else. In this sense the living are always "wrong," since they so rarely are able to perform their deeds in behalf of everyone's life. And the dead are "right" maybe only because they have not been saved by a "justice" that is not just. They do not bear the burden of lingering doubts, of unspecified guilt, of unjustified blame. (p. 114)

All the first-person narrators of Borowski's Auschwitz stories recognize that their identities have been permanently scarred by their encounter with extermination. Even the narrative impulse is an inadequate defense against the disintegrating coherence of their lives; the profusion of images intrudes on their inner world and transforms it into a reflection of the Holocaust universe itself. One narrator, after surviving and returning home, finds—in one of Borowski's most vivid tropes—that routine living "cannot keep the world from swelling and bursting like an over-ripe pomegranate, leaving behind but a handful of grey, dry ashes.'' . . . One senses from Borowski's vision that a thin film of ash will soil any bright hopes that may have survived from the pre-Holocaust world.

Borowski is one of the few commentators to pursue in detail the ambiguity of hope in the deathcamp universe. In a singular passage from his longest story, **"Auschwitz, Our Home (A Letter),"** the narrator reflects in a letter to his fiancée in the women's camp on the value of hope, and before our eyes the celebration of this traditional virtue dissolves into a bitter lament at its deceptive power. . . . Indeed, a burning residue of psychological truth smolders in these lines, for only when they surrendered hope and embraced despair did the remnant of Jews in the Warsaw ghetto, in Sobibor and Treblinka, in the last Sonderkommando of Birkenau acknowledge that destruction was upon them and mobilize the will to action. (pp. 117-18)

The author of the abortive love letters in **"Auschwitz, Our Home"** wrestles with one of the crucial bequests of the Holocaust: how to reconcile his memories of love *before* the camp with anticipations of a future infected by experiences *of* the camp. Those experiences transform survival for him into a *negative* principle: "Our only strength is our great number—the gas chambers cannot accommodate all of us." . . . His dialogue with his beloved is really a monologue with himself, a struggle to explain how the abnormal, through habit and familiarity, grows to seem normal—a process he records even as he disputes its logic. (p. 119)

[If Auschwitz] has not canceled beauty, truth, and moral virtue forever (and Borowski does not suggest that it has), it has challenged and perhaps corrupted their meaning for the narrator and other survivors like him. The reader participates in two realities: one where love, beauty, truth, and moral virtue continue to flourish (at least in inspiration) despite the Holocaust; and another where in a perpetual present of the imagination, men reenact the ordeal of extermination. For Borowski they are separate but intersecting realms, although he reverses the connection promoted by commentators like [Viktor] Frankl and [Bruno] Bettelheim. Whereas they argue that reliance on prior values can ease the severity of the deathcamp ordeal, Borowski insists that the severity of the ordeal undermines the unity and potency of all prior values. (p. 120)

The originality of Borowski's vision is that it portrays a world where consequences are not connected to choice. Since the deathcamp universe eliminated conditions that support worth, the victim could not ''choose'' life and remain human. He could strive for life and, if lucky, remain *alive;* but this was a struggle between states of being, not competing values. Borowski concentrates unerringly on situations that confirm this view. (p. 123)

Borowski challenges us to identify with [his characters] . . . even though the world of competing values that we inhabit comfortably as readers urges us toward revulsion at their acts. Wirth's principle of a new tragedy outside the familiar classical laws operates here; he argues that Borowski "demonstrated prototypes of situations which are tragic in themselves." If we can accept the idea of human behavior resulting from situations into which men are thrust *despite* their ethical convictions, then we cannot evaluate their conduct with familiar moral imperatives, by praising survivors for clinging to inner values in adversity, or blaming victims for cooperating in their own extermination. Such attitudes, Borowski would assert, derive from a misconception of the deathcamp *situation*. Several survivors in one of his stories become spokesmen for a point of view that we might call the disenchanting truth of Auschwitz: "in this war morality, national solidarity, patriotism and the ideals of freedom, justice and human dignity had all slid off man like a rotten rag . . . there is no crime that a man will not commit in order to save himself." . . . Such cynicism is part of our heritage from the Holocaust, to be measured alongside those more optimistic versions that still celebrate the individual and minimize the transfiguring—or disfiguring—power of the situation. (p. 124)

*Lawrence L. Langer, "Auschwitz: The Death of Choice," in his* Versions of Survival: The Holocaust and the Human Spirit *(reprinted by permission of the State University of New York Press; © 1982 State University of New York),* State University of New York Press, 1982, pp. 67-129.*

---

## ADDITIONAL BIBLIOGRAPHY

Pochoda, Elizabeth. "Books Considered: 'This Way for the Gas, Ladies and Gentlemen' by Tadeusz Borowski." *The New Republic* CLXXIV, No. 15 (10 April 1976): 31.
> Brief discussion of Borowski's major work.

Shechner, Mark. "Survival Declined." *The Nation* 222, No. 24 (19 June 1976): 760-62.*
> Review of *This Way for the Gas* in which Shechner praises Borowski for his "detachment" and ability to control the content of his stories.

# (William) Wilfred Campbell

## 1861-1918

Canadian poet, dramatist, essayist, novelist, and editor.

Along with Bliss Carman, Archibald Lampman, Duncan Campbell Scott and Charles G. D. Roberts, Campbell belongs among the "Confederation" poets, a group that reflected the nationalistic optimism of Canadians after the formation of the Dominion of Canada. His volume entitled *Lake Lyrics,* containing poems that praise the beauty of Canada's lake district, earned him the sobriquet "The Lake Poet." He also had the reputation of being a free thinker, and authored scathing criticism of Victorian utilitarianism. In spite of the resentment his opinions frequently provoked, Campbell enjoyed a good deal of popular success with his poetry.

Campbell was born in Berlin, Ontario. When he was ten years old, his family moved to the lake district of Ontario between Georgian Bay and Lake Huron. Here he developed the sensitivity toward nature that later characterized all of his work. As a young man he decided to study for the ministry, as his father and grandfather had done. He was ordained in 1885, but left the ministry in 1891 because he felt that church dogma and his official position were too much of a restriction on his freedom of speech. It was during his ministerial studies in the unsettlingly liberal atmosphere of the Episcopal Divinity School in Cambridge, Massachusetts, that Campbell first experienced the intellectual discontent that remained with him for the rest of his life.

Campbell's unorthodox ideas frequently led to controversy. He caused a scandal when, in 1892, he referred to the Christian symbol of the cross as a "myth." This observation appeared in "At the Mermaid Inn," a literary column Campbell wrote in conjunction with Scott and Lampman for the *Toronto Globe.* Campbell was forced to publish a disclaimer of his remarks when the editor of the *Globe* denounced him in print. The poet's controversial position is a reflection of his study of mythological systems in order to arrive at a personally acceptable body of truths. Late in his life, Campbell's spiritual restlessness and discontent led him to abandon his earlier ideas on mythology in literature and life, and to adopt an elaborate personal system founded on more conventional religious beliefs. Such changes in outlook typify the undercurrent of dissatisfaction that runs through Campbell's poetry, which V. B. Rhodenizer attributes to the frustration of an artist who would like to be satisfied with transcendental, intuitive revelations of truth, but whose sense of logic craved reassurances of a more tangible nature.

As an author, Campbell experimented in several genres, with mixed results. Most critics agree that while his novels are competent efforts, his narrative style is not exciting. Critics are divided over the merits of his dramas, the most important of which are *Hildebrand* and *Mordred.* These were written in verse in imitation of Shakespeare, though their medieval subjects are received from Tennyson, revealing the strength of the Victorian poet's influence on Campbell. Campbell acknowledged Tennyson as his poetic model and often, as in the poem "Lancelot," this influence is apparent. However, Campbell's verse is far less polished than Tennyson's, and his meters

and rhymes are often considered jarring. But Campbell deliberately left his verses in this state, believing that "the spirit and not the form makes earth's literature."

While Campbell's descriptive *Lake Lyrics* made his reputation, the best of his later poems are either narratives or patriotic hymns in praise of imperial Britain. With *The Dread Voyage, and Other Poems* and *Beyond the Hills of Dream,* Campbell began to introduce an element of the fantastic into his poetry. Unearthly subjects figure prominently in many of the better known works from this later period. "A Mother," which was probably Campbell's most popular poem, deals with the return of a woman from the grave to claim her young child. Today, however, Campbell is remembered primarily for his nature lyrics, poems that indicate, to many critics, the extent to which the Canadian imagination has been shaped by the Canadian landscape.

## PRINCIPAL WORKS

*Snowflakes and Sunbeams*  (poetry)  1888
*Lake Lyrics*  (poetry)  1889
*The Dread Voyage, and Other Poems*  (poetry)  1893
*Mordred and Hildebrand*  (dramas)  1895
*Beyond the Hills of Dream*  (poetry)  1899
*The Collected Poems of Wilfred Campbell*  (poetry)  1905

*Ian of the Orcades* (novel) 1906
*A Beautiful Rebel* (novel) 1909
*The Beauty, History, Romance and Mystery of the Canadian Lake Region* (essays) 1910
*The Scotsman in Canada* (essays) 1911
*Sagas of Vaster Britain* (poetry) 1914
*Poetical Works of Wilfred Campbell* (poetry) 1922
*\*At the Mermaid Inn* [with Archibald Lampman and Duncan Campbell Scott] (essays) 1979

*This work is a collection of essays that originally appeared in the newspaper *Toronto Globe* in 1892-93.

------

**WILLIAM MORTON PAYNE** (essay date 1890)

[In his **"Lake Lyrics"**] Mr. Campbell sings fluently, and with feeling, of the lake region and of the aspects of nature in the northern wilds. His verse is somewhat lacking in finish, but evinces a deep and true poetical sympathy with nature, and occasionally produces a pure and sustained lyric note. (p. 282)

> William Morton Payne, "Recent Books of Poetry," in The Dial *(copyright, 1890, by The Dial Publishing Company, Inc.), Vol. X, No. 118, February, 1890, pp. 279-83.\**

**WILLIAM MORTON PAYNE** (essay date 1893)

Mr. Campbell's verses [in **"The Dread Voyage"**] are characterized by an imaginative grasp of nature, and especially of nature in her sadder or sterner moods, that is often singularly impressive. The approach of winter, the sweep of the storm, and the majesty of the icebound northern wastes, are themes to which the author frequently recurs, and which he continues to associate with the corresponding phases of human emotion. This interpenetration of the soul of man and the soul of the physical world may be taken as the predominant thought of Mr. Campbell's work. When in quiet vein, he gives us tender verses like [those in] **"An August Reverie"**. . . . A deeper melancholy breathes from the stanzas to **"Autumn,"** which cannot fail to suggest the great ode of Keats. . . . A tribute to Robert Browning is one of the noteworthy poems of the collection. Mr. Campbell's chief defects are an occasional diffuseness, a use of awkward inversions, and a certain waywardness in his attitude toward the laws of rhythmical structure.

> William Morton Payne, "Recent Books of Poetry: 'The Dread Voyage'," in The Dial *(copyright, 1893, by The Dial Publishing Company, Inc.), Vol. XX, No. 177, November 1, 1893, p. 269.*

**THE CRITIC** (essay date 1894)

**"The Dread Voyage"** is Mr. Campbell's second book. As was to be expected, it is an improvement over **"Lake Lyrics,"** which was his first. In it he deals with more serious subjects, gives wider play to his imaginative faculty, and keeps his lyric powers more in restraint than heretofore. Occasional faults of rhyme and lapses from the rules governing the poet's art are still to be observed in his work, but at the same time one has to acknowledge that his touch has become surer and firmer, and that in a poem wholly imaginative in its conception, as is **"The Last Ride,"** he is capable of doing a fine thing. This

poem, with its marginal gloss, is the most conspicuous one in the volume, although it finds commendable company in **"The Dread Voyage," "Sir Lancelot," "The Children of the Foam"** and **"The Mother,"** any one of which is sufficiently good to add considerably to Mr. Campbell's reputation. The least successful features of the collection are the sonnets, none of which but seems to show that it came with more or less cramping of thought and expression. The lyrics, however, are nearly always free in their music, winning in their fancy and charming in their picturesqueness. Mr. Campbell's title as Laureate of the Lakes is not to be questioned. He is their interpreter and knows their every secret. (p. 235)

> "Canadian Poetry and Verse," in The Critic *(© The Critic 1894; reprinted with the permission of the Thomas More Association, Chicago, Illinois), Vol. XXI, No. 633, April 7, 1894, pp. 235-36.\**

**THE ATHENAEUM** (essay date 1895)

Mr. W. Campbell, in all the contents of his volume named, from a short mysterious lyric scarcely worth the especial honour for which it is chosen, **'The Dread Voyage,'** shows much literary control of diction and a good amount of poetic fancy. But a perusal of the whole volume leaves an impression of his lacking material for his poems: his themes do not seem inevitable, like those of a poet's inspiration, or a thinker's deep impressions, or a songster's impulse, but as if they were the result of searchings for something on which to employ the poetic faculty, and as if any other would have served the purpose equally well. Fuller thought, deeper feeling, are needed to give his expression that tone of reality without which verse, no matter how able, fails to gain a hold on the required sympathies of the reader. There is no reason to assume that he has not these to give his work, if he will. An excessive use of alliteration in the crude consecutive form vexes the ear in Mr. Campbell's verse: he gives us, to take an instance, in the compass of three lines "brawling brooklets," "murmurous mirth," "life's leash," "young year"; and this duplication of consonants goes on incessantly. The alliteration which can be so great an oral charm is the returning to dominant initial consonants before their sounds have quite died out in the ear, not the hammering at them in consecutive words; it uses some interval, according to its rhythm, if it be but of one short word. Of course there are cases of this more musical alliteration also in Mr. Campbell's poems—and indeed some *must* occur, if but accidentally, in any harmonized writing, sound suggesting responsive sound, whether the writer be conscious of it or not—but it is the hammering alliteration which he especially adopts, and it fills his verse with uncomfortable *staccato* passages. Objection must be taken to sundry dialect solecisms—such as "back of" for *behind*—and to occasional strainings after grandiose expression—as "some golden majesty of stairs." The study after Tennyson, **'Sir Lancelot,'** is so entirely imitative that it is strange that the exercise should have been given a place among Mr. Campbell's published poems; but the other contents of the volume are written with the due self-reliance of one who has no longer to look to imitation, but to self-development, for the strengthening of his powers. (p. 257)

> "Colonial Verse," in The Athenaeum, *No. 3539, August 24, 1895, pp. 256-57.\**

**LAWRENCE J. BURPEE** (essay date 1900)

While Mr. Campbell's reputation rests mainly on his work in verse, he has also produced some very creditable prose, chiefly in the nature of short stories. (p. 425)

Before proceeding to consider Mr. Campbell as a lyrist, it may be convenient here to refer somewhat briefly to his dramatic work. In this he is less well-known than as a lyrical poet, only two of his dramas having as yet been published in book form. These are **"Mordred"** and **"Hildebrand."** . . . **"Mordred"** is a tragedy, founded on Malory's Arthurian legend. Mr. Campbell, while following the general narrative of Malory, which he condenses into five acts, draws therefrom very different conclusions. To the elder writer Mordred was the personification of evil, deformed in soul as well as in body. In the present drama Mordred at first reveals deep affection for his father, King Arthur; but, on being rudely rebuffed by the king and treated with contempt by his knights, his love is turned to hate; and, encouraged by his evil genius, Vivien, he in the end compasses the destruction of the Round Table. The action of the drama is well developed, as is also the play of mind upon mind. Mordred's intellectual power is cleverly contrasted with the physical strength of the knights, and the ultimate ruin of the latter shown to have been largely due to their too great reverence for mere animal strength, and their contempt for the power of the mind. **"Hildebrand"** is a much shorter performance. It is a historical tragedy, dealing with the life and character of the famous Pope, his struggle for supremacy with Henry IV. of Germany, and his enforcement of the celibacy of the clergy.

Of these two dramas, the former is more ambitious in every way, and, on the whole, contains the better workmanship. While not perfect in construction, and lacking, perhaps, some of the qualities that go to make up the highest form of drama, it is, unquestionably, a powerful piece of work, and establishes the fact that Mr. Campbell possesses no mean ability in this direction. (pp. 425-26)

[In 1889 Mr. Campbell] collected the best of [his] verses in a book, under the title: **"Lake Lyrics."** This was favorably received in England and the United States, as well as throughout Canada. It at once placed him among the best of the minor poets of America, and earned for him the title of "The Lake Poet." The deep earnestness of his love for the "mighty, restless lakes" marked him as above the rank of a mere poetaster, and insured serious consideration from those best qualified to judge. His early years had been spent beside Huron's shore, and he naturally became deeply imbued with its ever-varying moods. . . . His lines are full of color and music, and, rail though we may at the poverty and inherent worthlessness of descriptive poetry in general, one cannot fail, possessing a modicum of imagination, to enjoy thoroughly his delightfully vivid pictures of the great inland seas. . . . (p. 427)

In 1893 Mr. Campbell published his second book of verse: **"The Dread Voyage."** In this volume, although descriptive poetry is given a place, it is much less prominent than in **"Lake Lyrics."** The poet is gradually cutting himself free from the Druidic or Nature school of verse. The human note is now the predominating one. At the same time, it may be said that the fascination of the weird and mystical side of humanity has laid perhaps too great hold on him, and gives a certain obscurity to some of his poems—such as the **"Dread Voyage"** and the **"Were-Wolves."** Though perfectly legitimate, and possessing many technical fine qualities, these hardly constitute the highest type of verse, and certainly do not represent Mr. Campbell at his best.

The poet also possesses an amiable weakness, shared by many of his fellow-lyrists, of giving favorite words a prominence rather unfair to their synonyms. For instance, the two words

"yea" and "ken" crop up persistently throughout his several books of verse. This is certainly not the result of a weak vocabulary; on the contrary, Mr. Campbell's work reveals a very catholic taste in the choice of words. It is, rather, a case of lexicological favoritism.

In **"Sir Lancelot"** our poet gives a somewhat Tennysonian picture of the great knight—Tennysonian not in a plagiaristic sense, but in the interpretation of the old legend. In **"Mordred,"** on the other hand, it will be remembered that he substituted for Tennyson's idealistic conception one even more realistic and rationalistic than Malory's. (p. 429)

**"Unabsolved"** is a remarkable dramatic monologue, instinct with intense, restrained feeling. It is based on the confession of a man who went with one of the expeditions to save Sir John Franklin's party, and who, being sent ahead, saw signs of them, but through cowardice was afraid to tell. He makes confession on his deathbed, and, filled with a terrible remorse, refuses to accept absolution. . . . The one poem of Mr. Campbell's which is probably most widely known is **"The Mother."** This appeared for the first time in *Harper's Magazine*, in April, 1891, and was immediately copied by a great many papers throughout Canada and the United States, receiving very flattering notices. The *Chicago Inter-Ocean* devoted a leading article to it, saying, among other things, that it was "the nearest approach to a great poem which had cropped out in current literature for many a long day." As a matter of curiosity, this may be compared with what a Canadian writer, Mr. Waldron, said of the same poem:

> The wanton repetition of coarse suggestions of the charnel house is not compensated by the mawkish sentiment of the poem, or by the questionable beauty of its scenery.

It is unnecessary to point out, especially to any one who has read the poem, that the above cannot be dignified with the name of criticism; it is simply vulgar abuse. (pp. 430-31)

The **"Harvest Slumber Song"** may be placed beside **"Little Blue Eyes and Golden Hair,"** as representing the under current of gentleness running through [Mr. Campbell's] verse—that which appeals to the heart rather than to the mind. The preëminent lyrical quality and high ethical teaching of Mr. Campbell's poetry is well shown by a little poem called **"Love."** . . .

I think it will be seen that the poet has reached a much higher level in the **"The Dread Voyage"** than in his first book, **"Lake Lyrics."** He has thrown off the veil of pessimism which brooded over some of his earlier work, and there is now found in it a more hopeful, optimistic ring. (p. 431)

**"Beyond the Hills of Dream,"** it is hardly too much to say, is one of the most important books of verse appearing in recent years on either side of the Atlantic. As **"The Dread Voyage"** marked an improvement on **"Lake Lyrics,"** even more does the present volume show an advance beyond all Mr. Campbell's previous work. There is in it a seriousness and sincerity of purpose, and the expression of a definite doctrine of life, which, combined with its high technical workmanship, place its author in the forefront of living poets. Especially significant are the selections which are made from his previous books for embodiment in the new one. These are poems dealing definitely with the human side of life, exposing such qualities as love, remorse, devotion, self-sacrifice, pathos. They represent the highest range of the poet's previous achievement, and reveal, above all, that sincerity which is the most important of all qualities in a man-of-letters, and without which his work, though it contain the very fruit of genuis, is worth nothing, and can never hope to appeal successfully to the great heart of humanity.

The title poem is an imaginative piece of work, sensuous, and rich in delicate color and haunting music. It is of a quite fairy lightness. . . . (p. 432)

In addition to the serious ethical purpose of this book, there runs through it a new and significant vein—a stirring note of imperialism. The poet sings the unity of the British race. This patriotic strain first finds expression in the jubilee ode, **"Victoria,"** and is continued through the succeeding poems, **"England,"** **"Sebastian Cabot,"** and **"The World-Mother,"** reaching its most significant note in **"The Lazarus of Empire."** (p. 434)

It is giving Mr. Campbell nothing more than his due to say that, especially in his latest book, he has produced verses of very high merit, both as to substance and construction. His work contains the qualities that go to make up genuine poetry—that is to say, sincerity, originality, strength, and refinement. (p. 436)

> Lawrence J. Burpee, "A Canadian Poet," in The Sewanee Review *(reprinted by permission of the editor; published 1900 by The University of the South), Vol. VIII, No. 4, October, 1900, pp. 425-36.*

## A. ST. JOHN ADCOCK  (essay date 1906)

Mr. Campbell says in a prefatory note [to **The Collected Poems of Wilfred Campbell** that] "there is no doubt that poetry is first and last a high emotion"; and no one will dispute that, if we add that it is never great poetry except there be a high intellect behind the emotion. But if we agree that "simplicity and directness are essential to the highest class of verse," we shall have to send Swinburne and Shelley and a few more out into the cold with the minor poets. Poetry cannot be cramped and limited in this fashion; there are great things that are best said simply and directly, and there are things as great that the spirit cannot look on without dazzled eyes, or speak of but with hints and shadowed words; surely there is a beauty of mystery as well as of clearness, of starlight as well as of sunlight.

Personally, my preference is for that same simplicity and directness, and for those large and human themes that are best handled simply and directly, and these themes and such handling of them will delight you everywhere as you turn the pages of Mr. Campbell's volume. He voices clearly and with strength and sweetness "the eternal appeal from life and nature," letting "the thought and imagination dwell upon the human, and nature as affecting the human, rather than upon the mere objective nature, as solely an aesthetic aspect." He has points of kinship with Wordsworth and Arnold; he thinks and feels as they might have thought and felt, but thought and feeling and utterance are none the less sharply and finely individual. There is tenderness and dignity, splendour and sonority in the **"Elegiac Verses,"** in the Sonnets, the Patriotic Poems, the Dramatic Verse, the Poems on the Affections; but, on the whole, for a certain haunting music, a certain sheer getting to the heart of life, perhaps you will go back to some of the lyrics in the two sections of Elemental and Human Verse, and the Nature Verse. Nothing could well be more exquisite in its kind than **"The Spring Spirit,"** with its rapturously wistful opening:

> I, poor Satyr in the glade,
> Saw a wonder, half afraid.

It is impossible to represent the book adequately by quotation, and it is not necessary to try. Mr. Campbell has a deservedly high reputation in Canada; rumours of it reached us long since; and his name on the cover will assure him of a welcome here which none who give will regret giving. (p. 177)

> A. St. John Adcock, "A Canadian Poet," in The Bookman, *London, Vol. XXX, No. 179, August, 1906, pp. 176-77.*

## THE TIMES LITERARY SUPPLEMENT  (essay date 1923)

The poetry of Wilfred Campbell, though often ineffectual, is often beautiful. He is not original enough in content and in method—particularly, in phrase—to impress deeply in our memories his name in association with a special art. Eloquent in general terms, he does not strike out as a rule his own watchwords; his verse is of a formal charm. We hear through him the voice of culture and patient reflection. Such names as Mozart, Paganini, Turner, Bacon, Coleridge occur in his poetry; and their influences appear also. As an elegiac poet, Campbell is well endowed and noteworthy in the trial. Perhaps his best sustained poem is that which laments his friend Lampman. . . . Campbell himself, in love of nature and in sweetness of rhyme, was worthy of Lampman's friendship. Returning at times through his work is the sad glory of autumn, ushering in the mood of requiem. Of season and scene he knew how to hint the character, and most of all, of the time when woods are calm and bright.

> "Annotated List of New Books and Reprints: 'The Poetical Works of Wilfred Campbell'," in The Times Literary Supplement (© *Times Newspapers Ltd. (London) 1923; reproduced from* The Times Literary Supplement *by permission), No. 1111, May 3, 1923, p. 306.*

## CARL F. KLINCK  (essay date 1942)

> [*Klinck's* Wilfred Campbell: A Study in Provincial Victorianism *is the most complete study available on Campbell's life, times, and the influences that shaped his work.*]

Through poems which were sometimes amazingly guiltless of conscious artistry, Campbell preached Supernaturalism, the infinite and eternal possibilities of the human soul. In the days of **The Dread Voyage** he had studied the possibilities for evil, dwelling upon sin and the "red wolves" of passion which make man their prey. He portrayed the destructive powers of hate and lust in **"The Were-Wolves,"** **"The Vengeance of Saki,"** **"The Last Ride,"** **Mordred,** and **The Brockenfiend;** and the spiritual desolation of those who have fled responsibilities in **"The Dreamers,"** **"Unabsolved"** and **"Sir Launcelot."** Among such depressing pieces he brought to completion only a few contrasting studies of man's love.

But dramatic sketches of a happier kind grew more numerous through the years, as Campbell gradually neglected his theory which set too high a value upon "the gloomy, despairing and tragic." By the time he published his **Collected Poems** he was positively a messenger of faith and hope. He studied now man's heroic possibilities for good. His complete picture of man was nobly inspiring. He had dramatized man as infinitely capable of love in **"Lazarus,"** **"The Mother,"** **"The Hebrew Father's**

Prayer'' and "Out of Pompeii"; now he also dramatized man as infinitely capable of courage in "Peniel," "Henry A. Harper" and "The Blind Caravan," as infntely capable of loyalty in "Ahmet" and the play *Morning,* and as infinitely capable of noble aspiration in "Phaethon" and "The Discoverers." In "Harper" especially, he insisted that the godlike in man appears not only in "rare hours" when the world looks on, but also "in the common round of life's slow action."

Campbell is at his best in "The Discoverers," a poem which rose above its "occasion," the three hundredth anniversary of the discovery of the Maritime Canadas, to become a hymn to the glory of man in the highest, man in the service of his brothers and his God. . . . (pp. 252-53)

All of these poems were in circulation before 1908. But even at that date Darwinism had not stopped writhing under Campbell's sturdy feet. Since the theme of natural beauty was as constant as the theme of Man, he could not escape the science of Nature. Naturalism and Supernaturalism were still at war. . . . [In his unpublished notes] he said that "both [the natural idea and the supernatural idea] are vast and important influences and, like all great influences founded on truth, cannot be denied." "It is in them and between them," he added, "[that] the old basic truth we are seeking is to be found." (p. 254)

An entry in the Diary of March 2, 1910 suggests that the poet had a vision of things unattempted yet in prose or rhyme. He contemplated a major effort . . .—an epic poem to justify the ways of Earth to man!

It was to treat the evolutionary-divine origin of the human race.

> "The subject of greatest interest to man," said Campbell, "is that of the immortality of the soul. Do men live after death? is the greatest question of life. And after studying the question from all sides, I have come to the conclusion that the true solution of the matter is closely connected with the mystery surrounding the origin of man. Solve the one and you solve the other."

His evidence tended to prove the descent, rather than the ascent, of man; divine, not natural, selection; a "dual" origin; and the race as the treasury of man's ideal nature. By establishing such principles he hoped to effect a synthesis of all his teachings in the spirit of "My Creed." (pp. 254-55)

"There is as much evidence to prove that man descended in the scale as that he ascended," he said. Through many pages he submitted his "evidence extant from ethnology, mythology, history, literature, archaeology and development of civilization" to prove the descent. "All great peoples," he declared in a summary of his main argument, "have the belief that they were descended from the gods, and all great peoples go back to a still greater civilization or past." (p. 255)

His theory of the dual origin of man was essential to a system which denied the evolution of man's higher nature while it admitted that the "Darwinian idea" was "a partial truth" perhaps explaining man's animal nature. Recognizing his own lack of scientific training, Campbell made no attempt to debate against the biologists. He conceded that the lower man had evolved through natural selection, and he gave an ambiguous, though possibly mystic, interpretation of "natural" as "by intervention of the divine." He went only so far with the materialists, and then fought them off the ground which he called his own, that of the soul.

It is easy to recognize the prehistoric man of popular scientific books in Campbell's "lower man," who lived in a crude primal world closely associated with the beasts and reptiles; he was "a brownie or Caliban or pixie—an earth creature with no conscience and no soul but something that provided room for a soul." Distinct from this animalman at first, was a "higher man," possessed of vast powers over matter, space and time; a good picture of him is available, for "Christ was a reincarnation of what man was in the beginning." This "god-man" lived in Atlantis (to which "all traditions point as the Garden of Eden") described as a "great mountain continent in the centre of the Atlantic, shut off from the other centres of primal life by a vast expanse of ocean—the Gulf Stream is the rim of the vast warm ocean which surrounded the land—an eternal beautiful summer where no extremes were felt and where no evil, sin, pain or grief could enter."

Man today is the descendant of the two stocks, "one half of earth, one half of God." The divine man, in "one dire hour," was grafted on the natural one. This was the Fall, this fusion with the lower order of being. The reasons for the Fall, hidden in mystery too deep for our comprehension, concern us less than the tragic results. (pp. 255-56)

Such a system has only one sure defence against the cold logic of the scientist. It must be regarded as resting, not upon logic, but upon intuition. It is not pseudo-science; it is mythology. In this way, in the autumn of his life, when the drums of Europe were beginning to beat in his ears, Campbell was preparing his exit speech, a defiant gesture of his final reckoning with Darwinism, of his triumph over doubt, of his trust in imperishable things. Compounded of all the best the poet had tasted and known—Calvinism without creeds, delight in nature for its earthly sake, the transcendental "dream," faith rather than reason, the will to believe in immortality, and a pleasant interpretation of anthropological and historical facts—compounded of these, Campbell's private mythology was admirably suited to the purposes of epic poetry. (p. 257)

In the light of the normal progress of poetic thought about nature during the nineteenth century, one might also remark glibly that Campbell had gone backwards. The mythological stage being a thing of the distant past, such thought has ranged normally through the metaphysical concept of Wordsworth and the transcendentalism of Emerson to the naturalism of Thomas Hardy; Campbell's [*The Dread Voyage, The Collected Poems,* and *Sagas of Vaster Britain*] . . . seem to show a curious reversal of the process. (pp. 257-58)

Campbell, paradoxically, takes his place among the "moderns" when his case is reviewed beside Professor Tindall's revelations concerning D. H. Lawrence [in *D. H. Lawrence & Susan His Cow*]. The latter, after groping through Methodism, transcendentalism, Platonism and confusion, developed a "private religion"—"as a substitute for an orthodox belief"—since "after Darwin and Huxley, acceptance of the Christian miracles and forms became impossible for many men of religious temper and training." (p. 258)

The result may be a religion strictly "private" or influenced by theosophy (as was that of W. B. Yeats, A. E. and D. H. Lawrence), by spiritualism, or by other organized movements. Such religions do not require a theology, a logical basis; they are, indeed, by definition and by nature "unconscious," "organic," non-logical. And such religions are not, therefore, slaves to science; they bend anthropology and all other branches of science to their will, shaping for their own purposes what they cannot ignore.

Campbell's mythology was a part of this religious movement. Having revealed the dual origin of man, "one half of earth, one half of God," he used it as a basis for his ethics. What man, he said in effect, will choose to be Caliban when he can be Ariel? It is a sufficient argument for idealism without the promise of eternal advantages. And thus the strands of Campbell's thought weave themselves into a recognizable pattern. His extraordinary respect for the past seems necessary to his system. The God-like in man is not all lost; what remains of him must be defended with life itself. The various great races, whose memories grope back to Atlantis, are the storehouses of mankind, each with its special remembrance of the endowments of man as he was in his perfect state. Institutions and traditions of all kinds, principles of honour and morality, written and unwritten laws, heroic deeds and utterances of great men, habits of self-discipline and self-improvement, works of art—all these the treasury of a race contains as priceless elements of the first divine order. Each individual is entrusted with a share of responsibility in preserving his people's vision of the perfect man.

From the dim past comes not only civilization, but also the counterpart and corrective which we call Nature. Not all the glittering objects in a race's storehouse are worth keeping. Not everything out of the past is sacred; much of it is better scrapped. The gold must be tested and only the purest retained. But by whom and by what standards shall it be tested? The answer is simple and direct: by our sovereign selves under the guidance of Nature. Nature is our Mother from the beginning of life and our loving teacher of eternal truth. She nursed our ancestors of the "lower sort" but also those of the "higher sort." Even the God-man rejoiced in the dawns and sunsets, the waters and shores, the woods and fields of perpetual summer on Atlantis. We are still "brothers to the birds and grasses," heirs of the sublime urge, and sharers of beauty before which the soul bows in reverence. "Man and Nature are one where the soul is concerned." Man may love Nature; for he cannot truly love her without also loving God. Indeed, he loses Life and Love if he neglects what she reveals through the mysterious avenues of dream.

The past and the present are interrelated. What they mean to us depends upon ourselves, upon our obedience to our "inward, mystic flame of life," which draws power from some "fountain-head where sense hath never been." (pp. 258-60)

Final criticism of Campbell the poet will not be pronounced for several generations. He was in many ways a very choice provincial representative of that era which passed away with the Great War of 1914-1918. He will share with his age and province the praises and condemnations of posterity. The lowest estimate of him will indicate that he was not so much germinative as typical—one of the Imperialists, one of the anti-dilettantes, one of the literary pioneers of Ontario—a teacher rather than a creator, a spokesman rather than a philosopher. The highest estimate will indicate that he captured much beauty in the midst of the commonplace and that he wedded artistry to manly thought—that, in short, a number of his best poems deserve an equal place with those of more famous contemporaries.

And any estimate which is based upon knowledge of him will assert with gratitude that he was a man of lofty spirit who trusted in poetry as the noblest vehicle to convey the idealism which made his life significant and his work not wholly perishable. (pp. 261-62)

*Carl F. Klinck, in his* Wilfred Campbell: A Study in Provincial Victorianism *(copyright © McGraw-Hill Ryerson Limited, 1942; reprinted by permission of the author), Ryerson Press, 1942, 289 p.*

## D.M.R. BENTLEY   (essay date 1979)

[Campbell] saw Pan as an apt image of the poet. Campbell was by all accounts, of a . . . melancholy, pessimistic complexion . . . and, hence, he tended to see both the myth of the goat-god and the fate of the poet through dark-tinted spectacles. Campbell's incidental references to Pan, in ["**The Lyre Degenerate**" and in "**The Tragedy of Man**"] . . . , tend to bear out Carl Klinck's observation that, characteristically, he "dwells . . . less upon the joys of Pan's songs than upon the tragedy of his life and death." This observation is directed specifically at Campbell's only extended treatment of Pan—the poem entitled "**Pan the Fallen**" which was included in his third volume, *The Dread Voyage and Other Poems*. . . . (p. 64)

Campbell's Pan, a less attractive figure even than the one in Lampman's "The Poets," is a "grotesque shape," "Part man, but mostly beast, / Who drank and lied, and snatched what bones / Men threw him from their feast." In "**Pan the Fallen**," the god with "pipes and goatish hoof" is a moribund figure of fun, a clown and an entertainer, whom "man despised / . . . And still would have it so." Beneath Pan's "sardonic" mask, "Elfin music," and "clownish play," however, the speaker of the poem discerns a gaze which is directed towards "some far heaven / Whence a soul had fallen down." Eventually the "careless" people who had rewarded Pan for his entertainment with "earthflung pence" become "tired for a time of his antics" and leave him to starve and, ultimately, to die in the "dust" of the "empty" marketplace. But in death the god's "tired face" is "turned towards heaven" and suffused by a "softer light" and a "peace ineffable." "**Pan the Fallen**" concludes with a description of the reaction of the "careless" people when, in the moonlight, they discover the dead god. . . . Although, as Klinck says, Campbell does not "labour the obvious moral" of the poem, it is abundantly clear that in "**Pan the Fallen**" he is dealing with the fate of the poet in a callous and unthinking society. While Campbell's sombre—and slightly sentimental—use of Pan as a type of the poet is reminiscent of Lampman's "The Poets," "**Pan the Fallen**" also echoes forward to such poems as Layton's "Cold Green Element" and Klein's "Portrait of the Poet as Landscape." Like the later Canadian poets, Campbell offers a dark, albeit not unrelievedly negative view of the poet as an outsider to whom recognition comes, if at all, too late. (pp. 64-5)

*D.M.R. Bentley, "Pan and the Confederation Poets" (reprinted by permission of the author), in* Canadian Literature, *No. 81, Summer, 1979, pp. 59-71.**

## BARRIE DAVIES   (essay date 1979)

[*In his introduction to* At the Mermaid Inn, *the collection of columns written by Archibald Lampman, Wilfred Campbell and Duncan Campbell Scott for the* Toronto Globe, *Davies comments on the interests and contributions of each of the writers.*]

'**At the Mermaid Inn**' is a work of great importance and fascination because it is a complex record of three writers' involvement in the special problems not only of their time and place, but perhaps ours; for tendencies and reactions initiated in the nineteenth century have persisted with an increasing sense of anxiety and crisis into our own time. The column, which ran for almost eighteen months in the Toronto *Globe,* from 6 February 1892 until 1 July 1893, is one of the best guides we have to prevailing intellectual tastes and currents at the same time as it rivets our attention to peculiarly Canadian complexities. . . .

Campbell and Lampman provided the more outspoken and controversial pieces. Scott tended to hold aloof from contemporary issues and his voice is more arcane and monotone. He left it largely to Lampman and Campbell to discuss contemporary concerns, the tone of their writing modulating from anger, indignation, and urgency to sadness and rueful bewilderment. (p. vii)

A reading of the bewildering number of eclectic topics in the 'Mermaid Inn' columns, which range from pets, open fireplaces, and a new kind of gold separator, to sea serpents, Wilhelm II's sense of humour, and Trappist monks, could induce an antiquarian or a whimsical interest. . . . On 25 September 1976, *The Globe and Mail* revived 'the famous literary column, The Mermaid Inn,' and chose Hugh MacLennan to begin it. MacLennan in a nostalgic mood wrote:. . .

> Happy men they seem to have been of the old
> Mermaid column, at least to the extent that they
> did not have to worry about politics.

He completely misses the troubled and abrasive nature of a column whose authors were well aware that the political chicaneries of Parliament Hill had contributed to a state of national crisis, and where Lampman expressed his dismay about the vanishing forests and 'the awful destructiveness' of his contemporaries. . . . Anyone who reads the nineties column with the attention it commands can only note Keats's poem ["At the Mermaid Inn"] as fraught with sinister, unintentional ironies. We must avoid the Elysium or Arcadian fallacy, and the equally fallacious 'modernist' one, which perversely attributes modernism to earlier writers engrossed by problems which continue to perplex our era. Because Lampman, Campbell, and Scott wrote of urbanization, socialism, or the changing position of women does not make them more modern than Carlyle, Ruskin, Morris, or Mill.

The disposal of two more fallacies will clear the ground for a more accurate scrutiny of **'At the Mermaid Inn.'** The notion that a considerable time-lag in news of literary and political developments existed between Canada and the rest of the English-speaking world is made untenable by even a cursory reading of the material. If such a lag existed it was a matter of weeks or months and not decades. Tennyson's or Whitman's death, the Shelley centenary, the election of a poet laureate, the morality of Hardy's *Tess,* the barbarity of Kipling's *Barrack-Room Ballads,* Symon's definition of the poet—all are debated with a freshness and intensity which we would hope for in the literary section of the best modern newspapers. Finally, the preoccupation with the affairs of the English-speaking world could only be interpreted as colonial voyeurism by the most myopic of present-day nationalists. Lampman, Campbell, and Scott did not ignore the complexity of the Canadian experience in favour of the sentimental confusions of nationalism, and that in itself is evidence of maturity. But greater evidence lies in the discriminating handling of English and American writers, methods, and institutions, and the judicious selection of what was appropriate to Canadian writers, methods, and institutions.

'**At the Mermaid Inn**' constitutes a defence of the imaginative life and the values of art in a time which had come to dismiss them as impractical. (pp. viii-x)

Wilfred Campbell, formerly the Reverend W. W. Campbell and then a layman by choice, plunged into the persistent nineteenth-century debate concerning the authority of the Bible. . . . Campbell the international debater received a national reproof from the editor of *The Globe,* speaking no doubt for the majority of his 40,000 readers. He emphatically repudiated Mr Campbell's religious ideas. . . . Campbell's rejection of institutional religion, though in conflict with orthodox rigidity, did of course duplicate the attitudes of many intellectuals in North America and England. The grounds for the rejection of, and the possible alternatives to, orthodoxy are clearly reiterated by Campbell in the column. Institutional religion, we are told on three occasions, is conservative, reactionary, or inert. The church has ceased to be an active force in society, is ceremony without ethics, a tool of capitalism, indifferent to the 'destitution, degradation and misery' within the shadow of its spire and the sound of its bell. Its adherents are depicted as narrow, hypocritical, and devoted to a 'sect-prejudice' and 'pharisaism' which perpetuate many moral and aesthetic crimes, actively increasing human distress while simultaneously condemning those who seek to expose them through literature and art as 'abominations of the evil one.' Sectarian theology, moreover, could not survive the findings of Darwin, 'Higher Criticism,' anthropology, geology, and archaeology, and in Campbell's opinion a religion 'bolstered up by ignorance' was but 'poor and tottering' anyway. For, in *The Globe* columns at least, the -isms and -ologies and dreadful clinking hammers did not bring to Campbell the doubts and perplexities of Arnold and Ruskin. What emerged instead was something close to the exaltation of man as in Swinburne, or the transcendentalism of Emerson. . . . (pp. x-xi)

Throughout the nineteenth century the effects of materialization and vulgarization were observable. Like sceptical and honest men elsewhere in England and America, Lampman, Campbell, and Scott in what we now see as an age of crisis protested against trends exacerbated in a country which had not had time to develop. . . . Utilitarian political theories and laissez-faire economics, evangelical religion and the equation of prosperity and industrial expansion with happiness provided the recognizable temper of the age. In Canada especially, where these movements were felt by many to be the prerequisites for nationhood, reservations and alternative ideals were not encouraged. Nevertheless, one of the dominant notes here is satirical, if that term includes an antipathy to the attitudes and tendencies of the age, a refusal to compromise because of the pressures of society, an exercise of intelligence and sensibility devoted to closing the breach between the actual and the ideal. Irony and satire are not modes of indifference, but modes of concern.

Had the nineteenth century produced a juster, more equitable, more democratic society? Neither Campbell nor Lampman thought so. Instead they focus attention on a new feudalism based on money, a brutal division between the plutocratic few and the impoverished mob caused by the man who, as Campbell puts it, is 'but a two-legged animal, who preys on his species and believes in the creed that might is right.' The improper distribution of wealth and the motives of an acquisitive society are exposed. Money is sought for the sake of splendour, for 'the power with which it arms,' or from the 'purely brute instinct' of 'watching the pile grow.'. . . The 'ideal plan' would include massive infusions of socialism, which all these writers endorsed, resulting in a 'paradise of the philosopher and the poor man,' where there are 'no rich men and no poor and the labouring man is King.' Not in England, however, or North America, which is 'too full of practical politicians and railway magnates to be a fit place for any simple and honest man to live in.'

The varied symptoms of corruption lead to the same diagnosis that the age is preoccupied by materialism and utilitarianism. Campbell, like Arnold, pointed to 'hurry and change,' to an inflexible demand for practical knowledge and studies to the detriment of the imaginative, creative, and humane. The age is obsessed with a joyless and 'monstrous puritanical notion' that ensures that 'the mass of mankind were only made to be worked.' Recreation therefore is construed as shocking idleness, and 'to grant a holiday is almost to overturn the world.' The Christmas Eve column for 1892 ends with a poem dedicated to 'The Galley Slaves.' Whether the future will bring an improvement is dubious, for parents moulded by social pressures continue to force their children into 'such paths as appear to be desirable or honourable to them' and are therefore partly responsible for 'a fair proportion of the mental and moral ruin we see about us.'

Progress then is change, but is divorced by Lampman, Campbell, and Scott from moral improvement as they continue their dissection of society by looking at another downtrodden segment, women. The extra legal, moral, and social inequities from which women suffer are unequivocally condemned, and equal rights and opportunities are advocated in the sure knowledge that not only women, but men and society as a whole will benefit. . . . (pp. xi-xiii)

It ought to be clear by now that **'At the Mermaid Inn'** is important because it reflects many of the issues, conflicts, and general temper of the age. (p. xiii)

Roy Daniells once made explicit the connection between the land and self-awareness, and stated that it was no accident that Canadian poets of the late nineteenth century were concerned with landscape. Just as the concern with landscape was no accident, so, it seems to me, it was inevitable that the characteristic qualities of the 'landscape' should be conflict coupled with an intense need for resolution. There is no better commentary on post-Confederation poetry, on 'landscape,' than **'At the Mermaid Inn.'**

Confederation did not create a nation, declared Campbell, for a quarter of a century later Canada was but 'the scattered and intractable materials of which a nation may be made.' If it were a complex fate to be an American, then the complexity of trying to be a Canadian seemed overwhelming. 'I speak here,' writes Campbell, 'as a Canadian and one who loves his country, but who loves her too well to bury the dangers to her progress, that all true Canadians only see too well, in cowardly evasions for the sake of creating a false hope.'. . . Campbell's article follows immediately after Scott's, which is written from the point of view of 'an enthusiastic Canadian, one who believes that his country is the brightest and best on earth' and will therefore 'indulge in a little flaunting of the maple leaf.' The poverty of the language here is equal to the poverty of the thought as Scott tritely imagines a future in which present obstacles have been miraculously overcome and when 'we will serve as the example to the world of a people welded by a national spirit and a national love.'. . . Perhaps Scott's overblown rhetoric was responsible for the vehemence which Campbell expresses: 'If there is one thing I detest, it is a

tendency to self-deception and to avoid grim realities.' There is an intricate and tough-minded optimism in Campbell's realization that the conflicts and antagonisms need to be fully expressed. What he most fears as 'the greatest danger to the country lies in trying to smother as inimical what is but the natural expression of this stage of our development.' A national sentiment will be formed by, and will include, what are paradoxically either impediments or characteristics, such as sheer size, regionalism, sectionalism, 'old country feuds of racial, religious, or other origin,' and the subtleties of a relationship to Britain and the United States.

Lampman wrote buoyantly about the conflicting extremes of the Canadian climate, 'of the restless and violent alternatives of heat, and tempest, and rain, of foliage and frost' and its effect upon national character. It was a very different matter when he and his fellow writers pondered the moral, intellectual, and aesthetic climate. In a country hardly out of a 'money-getting and home building stage' the utilitarianism of the nineteenth century was focussed and intensified. The lack of audacity, the puritanism, the prudery and 'frostbite at the roots of the Canadian imagination' of Frye, Bush, E. K. Brown, and Smith receive early expression in Lampman's complaint that 'in a country like this, where people talk so much about progress and prosperity and so forth, the number of those who count artistic and aesthetic development as one of the things to be sought after is so few.'. . . What could be more unpropitious than an ethos made up of a 'binder-twine' mentality, to adopt Lampman's phrase, in conjunction with Campbell's sense of 'pharasaism' and colonial self-contempt. . . . That Canada was not a nation is reflected in the absence of truly national institutions. In two separate columns on a single Saturday, Campbell condemns Canadian universities for failing to be centres 'of the best culture and aspirations of the growing national life.' Part of the reason for that failure lies in the fact that so few of the professors of literature and history 'are truly Canadians in birth, hope, sympathy, and education.'. . . Likewise, Lampman on two occasions comments upon the 'poor and average-looking room' of the 'so-called national gallery' as symbolic of a contempt for anything not immediately perceived as useful. He censures both the government and the wealthy for their complete lack of interest in 'the beauty, the honour, the real well-being of this country.'

It is hardly surprising, then, that talented Canadians felt obliged to leave, and the evaluation of the meaning of this exodus is one of the persistent concerns of the column. (pp. xiv-xv)

Lampman and Campbell, then, would have agreed with Scott that Canada did not furnish writers with opportunities to live by their writing. Where they disagreed was in the strength of their conviction that this was a fault which could and must be remedied. Hence the most persistent and crucial concern of **'At the Mermaid Inn'** lies in the series of attempts to create an atmosphere in which art and artists could flourish. (p. xvii)

The recently formed Association of American Authors prompted Campbell to write that a similar organization in Canada might change unfavourable circumstances. . . . But literary fellow feeling was more often desired than perceived by Campbell, for he felt that 'the grave weakness in our literary conditions is the same as that at the bottom of our national existence.'

This weakness he defines as disunity caused by 'a bundle of cliques, each determined to get what it calls its right and caring little for matters outside of its own interests.' (p. xviii)

The issue was critical, for Lampman, Campbell, and Scott equated a mature national consciousness with a reliable market for books and a just appreciation of indigenous talent. (p. xix)

**'At the Mermaid Inn'** makes it clear that there is a continuum of sensibility and a history of ideas which ought to enable us, in future, to be more specific and confident about the implications of the word Canadian when we speak of Canadian literature. (p. xxi)

> *Barrie Davies, in his introduction to his* At the Mermaid Inn: Wilfred Campbell, Archibald Lampman, Duncan Campbell Scott in "The Globe" 1892-93 *(© University of Toronto Press 1979), University of Toronto Press, 1979, pp. vii-xxi.*\*

## ADDITIONAL BIBLIOGRAPHY

Brown, E. K. "Canada and Its Poetry." In his *On Canadian Poetry,* pp. 129-44. Ottawa: The Tecumseh Press, 1973.*
  Briefly discusses the reasons for Campbell's popularity in his own day.

Frye, Northrop. "The Masters". In his *The Bush Garden: Essays on the Canadian Imagination,* pp. 118-42. Toronto: Anansi, 1971.*
  Includes a brief reference to Campbell in an essay discussing how Canadian landscape has shaped Canadian literature.

Sykes, W. J. "Wilfred Campbell." In *Leading Canadian Poets,* edited by W. P. Percival, pp. 37-44. Toronto: Ryerson Press, 1948.
  Biocritical sketch. Sykes was a longtime friend of Campbell's and his remarks are appreciative.

# Anatole France

## 1844-1924

(Pseudonym of Jacques Anatole François Thibault) French novelist, short story and novella writer, essayist, critic, biographer, dramatist, and poet.

During his lifetime, France was widely recognized as his country's greatest author, distinguishing himself in two widely diverse areas of literature: wistful storytelling and trenchant satire. He gained immense popularity with such works as *Le livre de mon ami (My Friend's Book)* and *Le crime de Sylvestre Bonnard (The Crime of Sylvestre Bonnard)*, the first written perceptively from a child's point of view, the second from that of an old man. Toward the end of the nineteenth century France's involvement with the Dreyfus Affair marked a change not only in his life but in his works, which subsequently reflected a new social and political awareness. These later works, including *L'île des pingouins (Penguin Island)* and *Le dieux ont soif (The Gods Are Athirst)*, were never as popular with readers or critics. After his death, France's reputation suffered a marked decline and it is presently undergoing reevaluation.

The only son of a Paris bookseller and his wife, France adopted his father's nickname as his own pseudonym. He was educated at the Jesuit Collège Stanislas, an experience which left him with a profound distrust of religious institutions and a hatred for clergymen. France credited a lifetime of indiscriminate reading, rather than his formal education, with providing most of his considerable erudition. France's family was very close, and he lived with his parents until his marriage at thirty-five. Critics believe the unhappy marriage of the Bergerets in *Le mannequin d'osier (The Wicker-Work Woman)* is at least partly based on France's first marriage, which ended in divorce. In the early 1880s France became a member of the literary salon of Léontine de Caillavet. She became the guiding force in his life, insuring that he wrote regularly and that he appeared in the most socially advantageous settings. She edited his work and even wrote articles and book introductions in his name. Mme. de Caillavet's tireless campaigning on his behalf was an important factor in France's 1896 election to the French Academy. After her death, France began living with her personal secretary, whom he eventually married. France was awarded the Nobel Prize in literature in 1921. In 1922 his complete works were placed on the Index of Forbidden Books, in response to prolonged and vehement Catholic criticism of his work.

France began his career with novels and stories of a highly conservative, conventional nature. His first critical and popular success came with *The Crime of Sylvestre Bonnard*. The eponymous hero, a retiring bibliophile unsuited to worldly dealings, was the first of many similar characters, who were to some extent based on France himself: Jérôme Coignard from *La rôtisserie de la reine pédauque (The Queen Pédauque)*, Jean Servien from *Les désirs de Jean Servien (The Aspirations of Jean Servien)*, and Monsieur Bergeret from "L'histoire contemporaine." As his fame grew, France began to treat more controversial themes with an increased tendency toward exoticism, as evidenced in *Thaïs, Le lys rouge (The Red Lily)*, and the stories in *Balthasar*, works which illustrate France's hedonistic and nihilistic philosophy.

The writing of the four-novel series "L'histoire contemporaine" spanned a period of great change for France. Until this time, France had never aligned himself with any political cause. In this he resembled M. Bergeret from the first novel in the series, *L'orme du mail (The Elm-Tree on the Mall)*, who would withdraw from daily affairs to ruminate on the follies of humankind. However, during the composition of the third novel in the series, *L'anneau d'améthyste (The Amethyst Ring)*, France became for the first time in his life actively involved with a social cause—the Dreyfus Affair. Though he had previously repudiated Zola and his school of literary Naturalism, France was aware of the miscarriage of justice in the sentencing of Dreyfus, and he was the first major literary figure to sign Zola's famous "J'accuse." His new involvement was reflected by the covert political activities of some of the characters in *The Amethyst Ring*. Unjust political and legal systems became a recurring theme in France's writing. The short story "Crainquebille" is probably France's most well-known indictment of judicial injustice. As he grew in social awareness, satire became one of France's chief literary tools, of which he made increasing use in such later novels as *Penguin Island, The Gods Are Athirst*, and *The Revolt of the Angels*. These are considered by some critics to be excessive in their flippancy and ridicule of religion and patriotism, while others praise their iconoclasm along with their artistry.

While France received lavish praise from critics during his lifetime, he was ignored or disparaged after his death. The nostalgic sentiment of his early work appealed to fewer critical readers than it once had, and the social and political issues that inspired his satires are now primarily of historical interest. It is only in the last decade that a significant number of critics have offered favorable rereadings of his works. Critics reevaluating France have found a new and more complex appreciation for the artistic qualities of his fiction and his sophisticated handling of literary forms. Murray Sachs, in particular, has noted France's role as one of the seminal French short story writers, whose efforts in that genre contributed to the "prestigious place enjoyed by the short story today in the French literary world." Though only recently reappraised by critics, France has always remained popular with readers, primarily for his insightful stories of childhood and for his masterful portrayal of such characters as Bonnard and Bergeret, gentle book-loving men much like France himself.

## PRINCIPAL WORKS

*Alfred de Vigny* (essay) 1868
*Le noces corinthiennes* (drama) 1876
  [*The Bride of Corinth*, 1920]
*Jocaste. Le chat maigre* (novellas) 1879
  [*Jocasta. The Famished Cat*, 1912]
*Le crime de Sylvestre Bonnard* (novel) 1881
  [*The Crime of Sylvestre Bonnard*, 1890]
*Les désirs de Jean Servien* (novel) 1882
  [*The Aspirations of Jean Servien*, 1912]
*Le livre de mon ami* (novel) 1885
  [*My Friend's Book*, 1913]
*Balthasar* (novellas and short stories) 1889
  [*Balthasar*, 1909]
*La vie littéraire*. 4 vols. (criticism) 1889-92
  [*On Life and Letters*. 4 vols., 1910-24]
*Thaïs* (novel) 1890
  [*Thaïs*, 1891]
*L'étui de nacre* (short stories) 1892
  [*The Mother-of-Pearl Box*, 1892]
*La rôtisserie de la reine Pédauque* (novel) 1893
  [*The Queen Pédauque*, 1910]
*Le jardin d'epicure* (essays) 1894
  [*The Garden of Epicurus*, 1908]
*Le lys rouge* (novel) 1894
  [*The Red Lily*, 1905]
*\*Le mannequin d'osier* (novel) 1897
  [*The Wicker-Work Woman*, 1910]
*\*L'orme du mail* (novel) 1897
  [*The Elm-Tree on the Mall*, 1910]
*\*L'anneau d'améthyste* (novel) 1899
  [*The Amethyst Ring*, 1919]
*\*Monsieur Bergeret à Paris* (novel) 1900
  [*Monsieur Bergeret in Paris*, 1921]
*L'affaire Crainquebille* (short stories) 1901
  [*Crainquebille, and Other Profitable Tales*, 1915]
*Histoire comique* (novel) 1903
*L'île des pingouins* (novel) 1908
  [*Penguin Island*, 1909]
*Vie de Jeanne d'Arc*. 2 vols. (biography) 1908
  [*The Life of Joan of Arc*, 1909]
*Les contes de Jacques Tournebroche* (short stories) 1909
  [*The Merrie Tales of Jacques Tournebroche*, 1910]
*Les dieux ont soif* (novel) 1912
  [*The Gods Are Athirst*, 1913]

*La revolte des anges* (novel) 1914
  [*The Revolt of the Angels*, 1914]
*Le petit Pierre* (novel) 1918
  [*Little Pierre*, 1920]
*Les sept femmes de la Barbe-Bleue et autres contes merveilleux* (short stories) 1919
  [*The Seven Wives of Bluebeard and Other Marvellous Tales*, 1920]
*La vie en fleur* (novel) 1922
  [*The Bloom of Life*, 1923]
*Oeuvres complètes*. 25 vols. (novels, short stories, novellas, poetry, essays, criticism, biography, and dramas) 1925-37

*These works are collectively referred to as *L'histoire contemporaine*.

---

**G. MONOD** (essay date 1883)

[It is a] mixture of reality, sensibility, and poetry which forms the merit of the children's stories M. France has given us under the title of **"Le Petit Bonhomme."** M. France is a writer who will make his mark; he has not yet achieved the reputation which his talents will command. He has the gift which is of all gifts the rarest amongst French authors—freshness. (p. 375)

> *G. Monod, "Contemporary Life and Thought in France," in* The Living Age *(copyright 1883, by the Living Age Co.), n.s. Vol. XLIII, No. 2042, August 11, 1883, pp. 361-76.*

---

*THE NATION* (essay date 1885)

[M. Anatole France, in **'Le Livre de mon ami'**], has written something charming and exquisite. It is not a story, though it is full of attractive and interesting people. It recalls sometimes, but does not resemble, the most delicate and ethereal of [Charles Lamb's] *Essays of Elia*. It is a book for summer holidays or long winter evening hours of rest; a book to be read slowly and reread like a poem. It is made up of the scattered recollections of the earliest childhood and boyhood of a dreamer not yet old. This is the first and larger half of the book, and is called 'Le livre de Pierre.' The remainder is 'Le livre de Suzanne,' "tiré tout entier des papiers de mon ami," and composed of all that was found there that was connected in any way with the childhood of his little daughter. Among the most delightful chapters of this delightful book is the one in which Pierre relates how Suzanne, "qui ne s'était pas encore mise à la recherche du beau," applied herself to it with extreme ardor at the age of three months and twenty days. The exquisite grace and charm of these few pages, the subtile and delicate observation, the fine and tender mockery, are characteristic of the author of **'Le Crime de Sylvestre Bonnard,'** which revealed to the world five or six years ago that M. Anatole France, besides being a savant, was a poet with a fine and rare fancy, and above all a tender and sympathetic heart. After all, it is not Pierre, nor Suzanne, nor any of the other personages in **'Le Livre de mon ami,'** who gives to the book its peculiar charm; it is M. Anatole France himself. The work is probably in no sense an autobiography, any more than the earlier one was; but, like that, it leaves the reader with the feeling that he has penetrated to what is finest and best in the character of a very charming writer, as no memoirs would ever have enabled him to do. (pp. 75-6)

*"Recent French Literature," in* The Nation *(copyright 1885* The Nation *magazine, The Nation Associates, Inc.), Vol. XLI, No. 1047, July 23, 1885, pp. 75-7.*

## LAFCADIO HEARN  (essay date 1890)

The author of **"Le Crime de Sylvestre Bonnard"** is not classifiable,—though it would be difficult to name any other modern French writer by whom the finer emotions have been touched with equal delicacy and sympathetic exquisiteness.

If by Realism we mean Truth, which alone gives value to any study of human nature, we have in Anatole France a very dainty realist;—if by Romanticism we understand that unconscious tendency of the artist to elevate truth itself beyond the range of the familiar, and into the emotional realm of aspiration, then Anatole France is betimes a romantic. And, nevertheless, as a literary figure he stands alone: neither by his distinctly Parisian refinement of method, nor yet by any definite characteristic of style, can he be successfully attached to any special group of writers. He is essentially of Paris, indeed;—his literary training could have been acquired in no other atmosphere; his light grace of emotional analysis, his artistic epicureanism, the vividness and quickness of his sensations, are French as his name. But he has followed no school-traditions; and the charm of his art, at once so impersonal and sympathetic, is wholly his own. How marvellously well the author has succeeded in disguising himself! It is extremely difficult to believe that the diary of Sylvestre Bonnard could have been written by a younger man; yet the delightful sexagenarian is certainly a young man's dream.

M. Anatole France belongs to a period of change,—a period in which a new science and a new philosophy have transfigured the world of ideas with unprecedented suddenness. All the arts have been more or less influenced by new modes of thought,—reflecting the exaggerated materialism of an era of transition. The reaction is now setting in;—the creative work of fine minds already reveals that the Art of the Future must be that which appeals to the higher emotions alone. Material Nature has already begun to lure less, and human nature to gladden more;—the knowledge of Spiritual Evolution follows luminously upon our recognition of Physical Evolution;—and the horizon of human fellowship expands for us with each fresh acquisition of knowledge,—as the sky-circle expands to those who climb a height. The works of fiction that will live are not the creations of men who have blasphemed the human heart, but of men who, like Anatole France, have risen above the literary tendencies of their generation,—never doubting humanity, and keeping their pages irreproachably pure. In the art of Anatole France there is no sensuousness: his study is altogether of the nobler emotions. What the pessimistic coarseness of self-called "Naturalism" has proven itself totally unable to feel, he paints for us truthfully, simply, and touchingly,—the charm of age, in all its gentleness, lovableness, and indulgent wisdom. The dear old man who talks about his books to his cat, who has remained for fifty years true to the memory of the girl he could not win, and who, in spite of his world-wide reputation for scholarship, finds himself so totally helpless in all business matters, and so completely at the mercy of his own generous impulses,—may be, indeed, as the most detestable Mademoiselle Préfère observes, "a child"; but his childishness is only

the delightful freshness of a pure and simple heart which could never become aged. His artless surprise at the malevolence of evil minds, his tolerations of juvenile impertinence, his beautiful comprehension of the value of life and the sweetness of youth, his self-disparagements and delightful compunctions of conscience, his absolute unselfishness and incapacity to nourish a resentment, his fine gentle irony which never wounds and always amuses: these, and many other traits, combine to make him one of the most intensely living figures created in modern French literature. (pp. v-viii)

But it is not because M. Anatole France has rare power to create original characters, or to reflect for us something of the more recondite literary life of Paris, that his charming story will live. It is because of his far rarer power to deal with what is older than any art, and withal more young, and incomparably more precious: the beauty of what is beautiful in human emotion. And that writer who touches the spring of generous tears by some simple story of gratitude, of natural kindness, of gentle self-sacrifice, is surely more entitled to our love than the sculptor who shapes for us a dream of merely animal grace, or the painter who images for us, however richly, the young bloom of that form which is only the husk of Being! (pp. viii-ix)

*Lafcadio Hearn, in his introduction to* The Crime of Sylvestre Bonnard (Member of the Institute) *by Anatole France, Harper & Brothers, 1890, pp. v-ix.*

## *THE ATLANTIC MONTHLY*  (essay date 1891)

[It is] in the early Christian centuries, that M. Anatole France has laid the scene of his latest novel, *Thaïs*. To readers of English speech *Thaïs* will be very likely to suggest a comparison with [Walter Pater's] *Marius the Epicurean*. Neither book is an historical novel, in the ordinary sense of the word; each is the result of intellectual curiosity and of literary fastidiousness. M. Anatole France is a *délicat;* one might go a step further, and say a *raffiné*. . . . *Marius the Epicurean* was a careful and elaborate performance, but it somehow lacked salt. It appealed to the intellect, but failed to stimulate it. We confess that, for our own part, we prefer *Thaïs,* with its beauty, not of artistic research, but of art, and its indication of an intelligence perpetually alive, and abounding in little surprises of idea and unlooked-for delicacies of phrase.

M. Anatole France takes us, not to Italy, but to Egypt; to a desert peopled with anchorites, and an Alexandria inhabited by philosophers of all schools and dilettanti of every shade. (p. 414)

[No] outline can convey an idea of the manner in which it is told, the suavity of touch, the fine, delicate irony. Primarily, it is neither a novel, nor a study of the epoch, nor a philosophic treatise. It is a piece of Parisian platonism, a sort of poem in prose, in which truths are tied up in paradox, and the poetry is infused with a mockery which would be fatal to the poetic spirit, if the two contradictions were not brought into harmony by that individuality which marks all M. France's writing. (p. 415)

The philosophy of *Thaïs* is just now being actively discussed in Paris, where protests against its skepticism are made not only by the adherents of established faiths, but by a large party of "young France" in healthy reaction against the long-preached gospel of negation. What is it, on the whole, this philosophy? Is it a defense of the Hellenic spirit, a protest against Hebraism, such as Matthew Arnold uttered in far different, graver, more authoritative tones? We cannot undertake to say. A number of creeds appear to crumble under the persiflage of M. France's pen; we find insinuations of malicious irony delicately turned against Hebraism, Christianity, asceticism, systems of philosophy, and theories of creation. If any reader of skeptical yearnings can discover in the book a consistent doctrine of negation, he is welcome to set down his footstool and worship; if any find a windmill to attack, he will do well to sharpen his lance: the only danger in either case will be that of having overweighed M. France's gravity as a writer, and undervalued his intelligence. For a reader willing to take a turn round the spheres merely for enjoyment and intellectual exercise, a reader enamored of literary grace, glad of an occasional side-light upon life and of the companionship of a mind of much fineness and individuality, *Thaïs* may prove a draught of pleasure with a delicate aroma of philosophy. (pp. 415-16)

> *"Two French Novels," in* The Atlantic Monthly, *(copyright © 1891, by The Atlantic Monthly Company, Boston, Mass.), Vol. LXVII, No. CCCCI, March, 1891, pp. 414-17.\**

**MAURICE BARING** (essay date 1895)

M. France has chosen a few charming themes, and played them in different keys with many variations. *Le Crime de Sylvestre Bonnard* is the contemplation of an old philosophical bachelor; *Le livre de mon ami* is a child's garden of prose. He has written stories about contemporaries of Solomon, of pre-Evites even (*La fille de Lilith*), and stories about Anglo-Florentines. He has charmed us with philosophy and with fairy-tales, and diverted us with the adventures of poets, politicians, and madmen of every description. His criticism he has defined in a famous phrase as "the adventures of his soul among masterpieces." And his creative works are not so much the observations of a mind among men as the subdued and delicate dreams of a soul that has fallen asleep, tired out by its enchanting adventures. He has himself confessed that he is not a keen observer. (p. 264)

[The] phrase "adventures of the soul" is singularly suited to him. In his whole work we trace the phases and the development of a gentle admiration. In the *Livre de mon ami* M. France tells the story of his childhood. . . .

It is very rare that a man of letters can look back through the prison-bars of middle-age with eyes undimmed by the mists of his culture and philosophy, and see the ingenuous phases, the gradual progress from thrill to thrill of awakening, that take place in the soul of a child.

M. France has evoked these early "frissons" with a magic wand. And the penetrating psychology with which childish "états-d'âme" are revealed is no less striking than the charm and poetry which animate them.

The very pulse of the machine is laid bare; at the same time, the book is as loveable and lovely as a child's poem by Victor Hugo or Robert Louis Stevenson. (p. 265)

Before altogether leaving M. France's writings about children, I must mention another supreme achievement in this province: his fairy tale *Abeille*, which is to be found in a collection of short stories called *Balthasar*. Mr. Lang hit the right nail on the head when he said that people do not write good fairy stories now, partly because they do not believe in their own stories, partly because they try to be wittier than it has pleased heaven to make them. M. France believes in *Abeille;* one has only to read the story to be convinced of the fact. As for being

wittier than God has pleased to make him, M. France is far too sensible to attempt an almost impossible task.

There is no striving after modernity in *Abeille;* it is neither paradoxical nor elaborate, but a real fairy tale, where there are stately *grandes dames,* trusty squires, perfidious water-nymphs, industrious dwarfs, and disobedient children. It is a genuine fairy tale, told with the sorcery that baffles analysis, which only the elect who believe in fairies can feel and appreciate. . . . (p. 268)

M. France, in the first fine rapture of a Hellenic revival, wrote **"Les Noces Corinthiennes,"** a fine and interesting poem, dealing with the melancholy sunset of Paganism and the troubled moonrise of Christianity. It is a period of which he is very fond; and he has made it the subject of one of his most important books—*Thais.* (p. 269)

[*Thais*] is the story of a conversion in the early Christian times. (p. 270)

The contrast between the end of Paganism and the beginning of Christianity, between the sceptical and brilliant world of Alexandria and the savage life of the Anchorites, is drawn with consummate art. It is a thoughtful story, exquisitely told, containing some of M. France's most brilliant pages and some of his finest touches of irony.

Books of this kind, *Thais, Balthasar, L'Etui de Nacre,* a collection of little masterpieces in a *genre* which M. France has made his own, and *Le Puits de Sainte Claire* . . . is what M. France has done by the way, so to speak. In these we do not trace the growth of his mind so much as in his other books. But as far as perfection of form and delicacy of touch go, they are perhaps the most finished things he has done. (pp. 270-71)

After the dreamy childhood of little Pierre [in *Livre de mon ami*] comes the feverish period of youth; there is an agitated violence about M. France's work of that time which completely disappears later on.

*Les Désirs de Jean Servian,* a study of youthful, ineffectual passion, is rather crude and unsatisfactory; M. France has not yet found his medium. *Jocaste* is a violent piece of melodrama, set in an atmosphere of hard pessimism. *Le Chat Maigre* is merely an interlude, a caprice of fancy. Yet here M. France has a subject after his own heart, and he is completely successful. It is the story of a youth who comes from Haiti to pass his *baccalauréat;* he lives in a *cénacle* of madmen, and so vague and irresponsible is he himself, that it never occurs to him that they are mad. M. France's love of madmen, of the *fantoches* of humanity, is one of his most decided characteristics. He draws a distinction between madness and insanity. Madness, he says, is only a kind of intellectual originality. Insanity is the loss of the intellectual faculties. M. France leavens all his books with mad characters, introducing us like this to the most quaint and amusing types.

In these early books M. France was giving vent to the various phases of his youth. The restless preludes played on the tremulous reeds were soon to be merged into the broad music of the mellow diapasons. (pp. 271-72)

In M. France's case the shifting restlessness of youth has only helped to make middle-age more tolerant, as we note in *Le Crime de Sylvestre Bonnard.* (p. 272)

*Le Crime de Sylvestre Bonnard* is M. France's masterpiece. . . . M. Bonnard is a child at heart, and his tenderness is exquisite.

Delightful, too, is his pedantry, which leads him to handle romantic subjects and ideas with the most elegant precision and unfaltering exactitude. As for his language, it is the purest and most distinguished French; it is needless to say more. (pp. 272-73)

The complement of Sylvestre Bonnard is the Abbé Jérome Coignard, the hero of *La Rôtisserie de la reine Pédauque.* M. Coignard, who lived and died in the last century, was a priest. . . . (p. 273)

The laws of men, he says, are founded on utility, a fallacious utility, since no one knows what in reality befits men and is useful to them. For this reason he breaks them, and is ready to do it again and again. (p. 274)

[It is] by the primrose path that M. l'Abbé seeks his salvation, relying on the cleansing dews of repentance. He is the most subtle and entertaining arguer conceivable, but his voyage to salvation by a ''voie detournée'' is nevertheless brought to an abrupt end. In abetting the elopement of a lovely Jewess with a young marquis, he is pursued by the Jewess's angry father, who takes him to be his daughter's seducer, and murders him on the Lyons road. He died at the age of fifty-eight, after receiving the last sacraments, in an odour of repentance and sanctity, and earnestly urging his young pupil to disregard his old advice and forget his philosophy. . . . (pp. 274-75)

Fortunately we are still able to be led astray by the subtlety of his discourses. They almost make us doubt whether the Kingdom of Heaven does not sometimes consist in words. We may add that ''**Les opinions de Jérome Coignard**'' is perhaps a more edifying book than ''**La Rôtisserie de la Reine Pédauque**,'' where his discourses are blent with a record of his deeds.

We have now considered almost all M. France's works, with the exception of *Le Lys Rouge,* which stands apart as his sole effort in the province of the modern analytic novel. The book is not very characteristic of M. France, although it contains some brilliant writing, notably a dialogue, near the beginning, on Napoleon, and a fine study of an artist's jealousy; the Florentine atmosphere also is successfully rendered; but we would willingly give up the romantic part of the book for one of the Abbé Coignard's discourses or Sylvestre Bonnard's reveries. (p. 275)

[The] shadows of irony which temper the colour of [M. France's] dream let us more than suspect that ''even while singing the song of the Sirens, he still hearkens to the barking of the Sphinx.'' Like Mr. Stevenson, he has struck sombre and eloquent chords on the theme of *pulvis et umbra.* He loves to remind us that a time will come when our descendants, diminishing fast on any icy and barren earth, will be as brutal and brainless as our cave-dwelling ancestors. (p. 276)

M. France is neither a pessimist nor an optimist, but both; since he feels that the world is neither good nor bad, but good *and* bad. (p. 277)

The burden and keynote of M. France's works may be found in the most blessed words of the blessed saint: ''Everywhere I have sought for happiness and found it nowhere, save in a corner with a book.'' (pp. 277-78)

> Maurice Baring, ''M. Anatole France'' (reprinted by permission of the Trustees of the Maurice Baring Will Trust), in Yellow Book, Vol. V, No. 3, April, 1895, pp. 263-79.

## FREDERIC TABER COOPER (essay date 1898)

Anatole France's right to a place among contemporary critics rests mainly upon a series of articles which originally appeared in the Paris *Temps,* and which were subsequently reprinted in four volumes under the general title of *La Vie Littéraire.* In the preface to the first of these volumes, he sets forth in his usual entertaining and candid fashion his theories regarding literary criticism. His creed, so far as he can be said to have any, is of the simplest: he reduces the whole art to a matter of individual taste. A critic's judgment of a book is, in his eyes, at best only the expression of a personal opinion; the possibility of reducing criticism to an exact science, or of adopting a purely objective attitude in estimating literary work, he absolutely denies. (p. 129)

And of objective criticism . . . he has this to say:

> There is no such thing as objective criticism, any more than there is an objective art; and all those who flatter themselves that they put anything else than themselves into their works are dupes of the most fallacious illusion. . . .

And accordingly, M. France does talk about himself abundantly, confidently and always entertainingly, not only in his critical essays but in everything which comes from his facile pen. . . .

[In] a system which avowedly rejects accepted standards for the comparative anarchy of individual preference, the personality of the critic becomes of paramount interest. . . . [An] estimate of Anatole France the Critic resolves itself very largely into an estimate of Anatole France the Man. It must be admitted, however, that his is a complicated nature. Sceptic, erudite and moralist, poet, novelist and Epicurean, he does not lend himself readily to analysis. (p. 130)

Much emphasis has been laid upon M. France's scepticism, and with good reason, for it has not only tinged all his writings, but is becoming more accentuated in each succeeding volume. . . .

For the most part, M. France's scepticism is of the insouciant, laughing sort which makes him, as he has often been called, a ''most dangerous antagonist to the spirit of faith and chastity''; yet he too sometimes has his dark moments of discouragement, moments when he questions whether it is not ''wiser to plant cabbages than to write a book,'' and when he enviously watches the threshers of grain, ''simple artisans of what is the work par excellence.'' (p. 131)

A fundamental article of his literary creed is that ''all books, even the most admirable, seem infinitely less precious for what they contain than for what the reader puts into them.'' And in reading the various essays and reviews which go to make up his *Vie Littéraire,* we cannot help feeling that they owe their value, not to the merits of the books which he discusses, but to the thoughts which they have suggested to him, and which he in turn reveals to us. Taken as a whole his opinions on the great works in literature are what may be called normal; thus Shakespeare is ''the poet of humanity; his place is everywhere, where there are men capable of feeling the beautiful and the true. He is like Homer, above the level of the people.'' But while he admits the claims of Homer and Shakespeare, Racine and Corneille, M. France is sufficiently catholic in his tastes to find something to praise in Bourget and Maupassant, Baudelaire and Verlaine. Although not in sympathy with the naturalistic school, he recognises that ''Flaubert and the Goncourts inaugurated in a masterly fashion a form of methodical literature, and that Zola, with *L'Assommoir* and *Germinal,* has powerfully carried on the work begun."' . . .

For the most part Anatole France is a kindly critic, praising when he can, and touching upon what he regards as faults with an indulgent irony. (p. 132)

Frederic Taber Cooper, "Living Continental Critics: Anatole France," in The Bookman, *New York (copyright, 1898, by George H. Doran Company), Vol. VIII, No. 2, October, 1898, pp. 129-34.*

## EDMUND GOSSE (essay date 1903)

M. Anatole France is what they used to call a Pyrrhonist in the seventeenth century—a sceptic, one who doubts whether it is worth while to struggle insanely against the trend of things. (pp. 187-88)

After many efforts, more or less imperfectly successful, M. France seems at last to have discovered a medium absolutely favourable to his genius. He has pursued his ideal of graceful scepticism from period to period. He has sought to discover it in the life of late antiquity (*Thaïs*), in the ironic *naïveté* of the Middle Ages (*Balthasar* and *Le Puits de Sainte Claire*), in the humours of eighteenth-century deism (*La Rôtisserie de la Reine Pédauque* and *M. Jérôme Coignard*), in the criticism of contemporary books (*La Vie Littéraire*), in pure philosophical paradox (*Le Jardin d'Épicure*). Only once, in my opinion, has he ceased to be loyal to that *sagesse et élégance* which are his instinctive aim; only once—in that crude *Le Lys Rouge,* which is so unworthy of his genius in everything but style. With this exception, through fifteen delightful volumes he has been conscientiously searching for his appropriate medium, and, surely, he has found it at last. (pp. 188-89)

The two books which M. Anatole France published in 1897 belong to the new category. Perhaps it was not every reader of *L'Orme du Mail* who noticed the words "*Histoire Contemporaine*" at the top of the title-page. But they are repeated on that of *Le Mannequin d'Osier,* and they evidently have a significance. Is this M. Anatole France's mode of indicating to us that he is starting on some such colossal enterprise as a [Balzac's] *Comédie Humaine,* or a series like [Zola's] *Les Rougon Macquart?* Nothing quite so alarming as this, probably, but doubtless a series of some sort is intended; and, already, it is well to warn the impetuous reader not to open *Le Mannequin d'Osier* till he has mastered *L'Orme du Mail,* at the risk of failing to comprehend the situation. The one of these books is a direct continuation of the other.

There was no plot in *L'Oreme du Mail.* We were introduced, or rather invisibly suspended within, a provincial city of France of to-day, where, under all species of decorous exteriors, intrigues were being pushed forward, domestic dramas conducted, the hollowness of intellectual pretensions concealed and even—for M. Anatole France knows the value of the savage note in his exquisite concert—brutal crimes committed. With a skill all his own, he interested us in the typical individualities in this anthill of a town, and he knows how to produce his effects with so light and yet so firm a hand, that he never for a moment wearied us, or allowed us to forget his purpose. (pp. 189-90)

Readers of *L'Orme du Mail* were prepared for the entertainment which was bound to follow. (p. 190)

[But] we are not quite happy. *Le Mannequin d'Osier* is not so gay a book as its predecessor, and the Pyrrhonism of M. Anatole France seems to have deepened upon him. The air of insouciance which hung over the sun-lighted Mall has faded away. . . . In the new book, M. Bergeret, who took a secondary place in *L'Orme du Mail,* comes into predominance. His sorrows and squalor, the misfortunes of his domestic life, his consciousness of his own triviality of character and mediocrity of brain—those are subjected to cruel analysis. The difference between *L'Orme du Mail* and *Le Mannequin d'Osier* is that between the tone of Sterne and of Swift. . . . It is curious to find [a] Swift-like tone proceeding out of the Shandean spirit which has of late marked the humour of M. Anatole France. (pp. 191-92)

The intelligent part of the English public has been successfully dragooned into the idea that M. Anatole France is the most ingenious of the younger writers of Europe. . . . Yet, one can but wonder how many of his dutiful English admirers really enjoy his books—how many, that is to say, go deeper down than the epigrams and the picturesqueness; how many perceive, in colloquial phrase, what it is he is "driving at," and, having perceived, still admire and enjoy. It is not so difficult to understand that there are English people who appreciate the writings of Ibsen and of Tolstoi, and even, to sink fathoms below these, of D'Annunzio, because although all these are exotic in their relation to our national habits of mind, they are direct. But Anatole France—do his English admirers realise what a heinous crime he commits?—for all his lucidity and gentleness and charm, Anatole France is primarily, he is almost exclusively, an ironist.

In the literary decalogue of the English reader the severest prohibition is "Thou shalt not commit irony!" This is the unpardonable offence. . . . No one who has endeavoured for the last hundred years to use irony in England as an imaginative medium has escaped failure. . . . Is it because the great example of irony in our language is the cruel dissimulation of Swift? Is it that our nation was wounded so deeply by that sarcastic pen that it has suspected ever since, in every ironic humorist, "the smiler with the knife"?

But the irony of M. Anatole France, like that of Renan, and to a much higher degree, is, on the contrary, beneficent. It is a tender and consolatory raillery, based upon compassion. His greatest delight is found in observing the inconsistencies, the illusions of human life, but never for the purpose of wounding us in them, or with them. His genius is essentially benevolent and pitiful. This must not, however, blind us to the fact that he is an ironist, and perhaps the most original in his own sphere who has ever existed. (pp. 193-94)

The design of the author, as always—as most of all in that most exquisite of his books, *Le Jardin d'Épicure*—is to warn mankind against being too knowing and too elaborate. Be simple, he says, and be content to be deceived, or you cannot be happy. . . . Over and over again he has preached that intelligence is vanity, that the more we know about life the less we can endure the anguish of its impact. He says somewhere—is it not in *Le Lys Rouge?*—that the soul of man feeds on chimeras. Take this fabulous nourishment from us, and you spread the banquet of science before us in vain. We starve on the insufficiency of a diet which has been deprived of all our absurd traditional errors, "nos idées bêtes, augustes et salutaires." It is strange that all the subtlety of this marvellous brain should have found its way back to the axiom, Unless ye become as little children, ye cannot enter into the kingdom of heaven.

These reflections may bewilder those who take up the *Histoire Comique* as a work of mere entertainment. They may even be scandalised by the story; and indeed to find it edifying at all, it is needful to be prepared for edification. (pp. 195-96)

It would perhaps be difficult to point to a single book which M. Anatole France has published in which his theory that only two things, beauty and goodness, are of any importance in life, seems at first sight to be less prominent than in his *Histoire Comique*. But it prevails here, too, we shall find, if we are not hasty in judgment. And if we do not care to examine the philosophy of the story, and to reconcile its paradoxes with ethical truth, we can at least enjoy the sobriety, the precision, the elasticity of its faultless style. If the reader prefers to do so, he may take *Histoire Comique* simply as a melancholy and somewhat sensuous illustration of the unreasonable madness of love, and of the insufficiency of art, with all its discipline, to regulate the turbulent spirit of youth. (p. 197)

*Edmund Gosse, "The Irony of M. Anatole France" (1903), in his* French Profiles, *revised edition, William Heinemann, 1913 (and reprinted by Books for Libraries Press, 1970), pp. 185-97.*

### JOSEPH CONRAD (essay date 1904)

["*Crainquebille*"] purports, by the declaration of its title-page, to contain several profitable narratives. The story of Crainquebille's encounter with human justice stands at the head of them; a tale of a well-bestowed charity closes the book with the touch of playful irony characteristic of the writer on whom the most distinguished amongst his literary countrymen have conferred the rank of Prince of Prose.

Never has a dignity been better borne. M. Anatole France is a good prince. He knows nothing of tyranny but much of compassion. The detachment of his mind from common errors and current superstitions befits the exalted rank he holds in the Commonwealth of Literature. (p. 43)

The dignity will suffer no diminution in M. Anatole France's hands. He is worthy of a great tradition, learned in the lessons of the past, concerned with the present, and as earnest as to the future as a good prince should be in his public action. It is a Republican dignity. And M. Anatole France, with his sceptical insight into all forms of government, is a good Republican. He is indulgent to the weaknesses of the people, and perceives that political institutions, whether contrived by the wisdom of the few or the ignorance of the many, are incapable of securing the happiness of mankind. He perceives this truth in the serenity of his soul and in the elevation of his mind. He expresses his convictions with measure, restraint and harmony, which are indeed princely qualities. He is a great analyst of illusions. He searches and probes their innermost recesses as if they were realities made of an eternal substance. And therein consists his humanity; this is the expression of his profound and unalterable compassion. He will flatter no tribe, no section in the forum or in the market-place. (p. 44)

[The] reasoning of M. Anatole France is never confused. His reasoning is clear and informed by a profound erudition. Such is not the case of Crainquebille, a street hawker, charged with insulting the constituted power of society in the person of a policeman. The charge is not true, nothing was further from his thoughts; but, amazed by the novelty of his position, he does not reflect that the Cross on the wall perpetuates the memory of a sentence which for nineteen hundred years all the Christian peoples have looked upon as a grave miscarriage of justice. (p. 46)

Crainquebille, who has lived pushing every day for half a century his hand-barrow loaded with vegetables through the streets of Paris, has not a philosophic mind. Truth to say he has nothing. He is one of the disinherited. Properly speaking, he has no existence at all, or, to be strictly truthful, he had no existence till M. Anatole France's philosophic mind and human sympathy have called him up from his nothingness for our pleasure, and, as the title-page of the book has it, no doubt for our profit also.

Therefore we behold him in the dock, a stranger to all historical, political or social considerations which can be brought to bear upon his case. He remains lost in astonishment. Penetrated with respect, overwhelmed with awe, he is ready to trust the judge upon the question of his transgression. In his conscience he does not think himself culpable; but M. Anatole France's philosophical mind discovers for us that he feels all the insignificance of such a thing as the conscience of a mere street-hawker in the face of the symbols of the law and before the ministers of social repression. Crainquebille is innocent; but already the young advocate, his defender, has half persuaded him of his guilt.

On this phrase practically ends the introductory chapter of the story. . . . And this opening chapter without a name—consisting of two and a half pages, some four hundred words at most—is a masterpiece of insight and simplicity, resumed in M. Anatole France's distinction of thought and in his princely command of words.

It is followed by six more short chapters, concise and full, delicate and complete like the petals of a flower, presenting to us the Adventure of Crainquebille. . . . We see, created for us in his outward form and innermost perplexity, the old man degraded from his high estate of a law-abiding street-hawker and driven to insult, really this time, the majesty of the social order in the person of another police-constable. It is not an act of revolt, and still less of revenge. Crainquebille is too old, too resigned, too weary, too guileless to raise the black standard of insurrection. He is cold and homeless and starving. He remembers the warmth and the food of the prison. He perceives the means to get back there. Since he has been locked up, he argues with himself, for uttering words which, as a matter of fact he did not say, he will go forth now, and to the first policeman he meets will say those very words in order to be imprisoned again. (pp. 46-8)

But this policeman is full of philosophic superiority, disdain, and indulgence. He refuses to take in charge the old and miserable vagabond who stands before him shivering and ragged in the drizzle. And the ruined Crainquebille, victim of a ridiculous miscarriage of justice, appalled at this magnanimity, passes on hopelessly down the street full of shadows where the lamps gleam each in a ruddy halo of falling mist. (p. 49)

Besides "**Crainquebille**" this volume contains sixteen other stories and sketches. To define them it is enough to say that they are written in M. Anatole France's prose. . . . [It] is difficult to read M. Anatole France without admiring him. He has the princely gift of arousing a spontaneous loyalty, but with this difference, that the consent of our reason has its place by the side of our enthusiasm. He is an artist. As an artist he awakens emotion. The quality of his art remains, as an inspiration, fascinating and inscrutable; but the proceedings of his thought compel our intellectual admiration. (pp. 51-3)

[There] are other sketches in this book, more or less slight, but all worthy of regard—the childhood's recollections of Professor Bergeret and his sister Zoé; the dialogue of the two upright judges and the conversation of their horses; the dream of M. Jean Marteau, aimless, extravagant, apocalyptic, and of all the dreams one ever dreamt, the most essentially dreamlike. The vision of M. Anatole France, the Prince of Prose, ranges over all the extent of his realm, indulgent and penetrating, disillusioned and curious, finding treasures of truth and beauty concealed from less gifted magicians. Contemplating the exactness of his images and the justice of his judgment, the freedom of his fancy and the fidelity of his purpose, one becomes aware of the futility of literary watch-words and the vanity of all the schools of fiction. Not that M. Anatole France is a wild and untrammelled genius. He is not that. Issued legitimately from the past, he is mindful of his high descent. He has a critical temperament joined to creative power. He surveys his vast domain in a spirit of princely moderation that knows nothing of excesses but much of restraint. (p. 54)

> *Joseph Conrad, "Anatole France: 'Crainquebille'" (originally published as "Anatole France," in* The Living Age, *Vol. XXIV, No. 3140, September 10, 1904), in his* Notes on Life and Letters, *J. M. Dent & Sons Ltd., 1921, pp. 43-54.*

## ANDREW LANG   (essay date 1908)

> [*This is the earliest and best-known critical disagreement with France's interpretation of the life of Joan of Arc. Lang attacks France's interpretation from an historical and not a literary point of view.*]

In Balzac's tale, *Le Chef d'Oeuvre Inconnu,* a painter devotes too many years to the achievement of a masterpiece. When he shows the long-hidden treasure at last, the spectators find nothing but a blur, a meaningless blotch of colours, in which no form is visible save the beautifully designed foot of a woman.

The *Vie de Jeanne d'Arc,* by M. Anatole France, reminds me of the *Chef d'Oeuvre Inconnu.* The distinguished author is known to have worked at his topic for some twenty years, and he has a large, perhaps an exhaustive, knowledge of the literature of his theme. Yet the figure of the Maid, as represented by him, seems to myself a blur, in which nothing is clearly seen but the beauty of the heart of the heroine. The artist, from the first pages of his Preface, appears to be perplexed; to hold no consistent view, to hold two contradictory views at once.

In the forefront of the evidence about a heroine who is, he says, "from the first, and perhaps for ever, enclosed in the flowery thicket of legends," M. France places the testimony of her own replies to her French judges, at Rouen, in 1431. "We all know the value of the answers of the Maid; they are heroically candid, and usually (*le plus souvent*) are transparently clear." Yet "her unceasing hallucinations usually (*le plus souvent*) made her incapable of distinguishing the true from the false." (p. 982)

[The] Maid, as interpreted for us by M. France, is a girl whose replies to her judges are "heroically sincere, and, usually, pellucid," and also is a girl "who cannot, usually, discern what is true from what is false." M. France "does not raise a doubt against her honesty," and he accuses her of a deliberately fraudulent exhibition of herself in a sham trance!

For the statement of M. France that the poor girl was "perpetually hallucinated," and so could not tell truth from falsehood, I am not aware that there is a single line of evidence in any record. . . .

The point is that no sign or trace of "dissociation," or loss of normal consciousness, of trance, or of ecstasy, of anything but the keenest sense of her actual surroundings, is ever reported (as far as I can discover) in the case of Jeanne d'Arc. If she occasionally heard her Voices through the hubbub of her clerical tormentors at Rouen, her replies prove that she, at the same time, retained all her acuteness of intellect. The portrait is hopelessly blurred, is rendered unrecognisable, by M. France when he says that the Maid was "perpetually hallucinated." He gives no evidence for his assertion, and I have found none. (p. 983)

[M. France] has really produced no living and recognisable portrait of the Maid. But the portrait is not clouded so much by these unreconciled contradictions in the handling, as by the pervading tone and atmosphere of the whole book. The tone of M. France, except in some generous passages of praise, is *narquois,* is grudging, one may even say is *grunching.* . . . M. France's ruling tendency is the desire, conscious or subconscious, to prove that Jeanne was not so very wonderful after all; that she was but one of a class of visionaries—usually futile, usually given up to the mortification of the flesh, and usually credited with such marvels as St. Colette exhibited when she floated about in the air. . . . (pp. 986-87)

The renown of Jeanne d'Arc owes nothing to legend, to mythical accretions, but it is the desire of M. France to regard her as perhaps for ever lost in the fairy "forest of legend." (p. 987)

> *Andrew Lang, "The Chef D'oeuvre of M. Anatole France," in* The Fortnightly Review *(reprinted by permission of Contemporary Review Company Limited), n.s. Vol. LXXXIII, No. CCCXCVIII, June, 1908, pp. 982-93.*

## ARNOLD BENNETT   (essay date 1908)

> [*In a rare negative evaluation of France during his lifetime, Bennett is motivated not by outraged religiosity, but by literary considerations. Though admitting France's genius, Bennett finds fault with the structure of his novels.*]

There is less enthusiasm—that is to say, less genuine enthusiasm—for Anatole France than there used to be. The majority, of course, could never appreciate him, and would only buy him under the threat of being disdained by the minority, whose sole weapon is scorn. And the minority has been seriously thinking about Anatole France, and coming to the conclusion that, though a genius, he is not the only genius that ever existed. . . . Anatole France's last two works of imagination did not brilliantly impose themselves on the intellect of his country. **"L'Histoire Comique"** showed once again his complete inability to construct a novel, and it appeared to be irresponsibly extravagant in its sensuality. And **"Sur La Pierre Blanche"** was inferior Wells. The minority has waited a long time for something large, original, and arresting; and it has not had it. The author was under no compulsion to write his history of Joan of Arc, which bears little relation to his epoch, and which one is justified in dismissing as the elegant pastime of a savant. If in Anatole France the savant has not lately flourished to the detriment of the fighting philosopher, why should he have spent years on the **"Joan of Arc"** at a period when Jaurès urgently needed intellectual aid against the doctrinairism of the International Congress? Jaurès was beaten, and he yielded, with the result that Clemenceau, a man far too intelligent not to be a practical Socialist at heart, has become semi-reactionary for want of support. This has not much to do with literature. Neither has the history of Joan of Arc. To return to literature, it . . . is indubitable that Anatole France is slightly acquiring the reputation of a dilettante. (pp. 60-1)

In **"L'Ile des Pingouins"** he returns, in a parable, to his epoch. For this book is the history of France "from the earliest time to the present day," seen in the mirror of the writer's ironical temperament. It is very good. It is inimitable. It is sheer genius. One cannot reasonably find fault with its amazing finesse. But then one is so damnably *un*reasonable! One had expected—one does not know what one had expected—but anyhow something with a more soaring flight, something more passionate, something a little less gently "tired" in its attitude towards the criminal frailties of mankind! . . . [When] an Anatole France grows wearily indulgent before the spectacle of life, one is inclined to wake him by throwing "Leaves of Grass" or "Ecce Homo" (Nietzsche's) at his head. For my part, I am ready to hazard that what is wrong with Anatole France is just spiritual anaemia. (pp. 61-2)

> *Arnold Bennett, "Anatole France" (originally published under the pseudonym, Jacob Tonson, in* The New Age, *n.s. Vol. IV, No. 1, October 29, 1908), in his* Books and Persons: Being Comments on a Past Epoch, 1908-1911 *(copyright, 1917, by George H. Doran Company; copyright renewed © 1945 by Marie Marguerite Bennett; reprinted by permission of the Estate of the late Arnold Bennett), Doran, 1917, pp. 59-62.*

### G. K. CHESTERTON    (essay date 1908)

A considerable time ago (at far too early an age, in fact) I read Voltaire's "La Pucelle," a savage sarcasm on the traditional purity of Joan of Arc, very dirty, and very funny. I had not thought of it again for years, but it came back into my mind this morning because I began to turn over the leaves of the new **"Jeanne d'Arc,"** by that great and graceful writer, Anatole France. It is written in a tone of tender sympathy, and a sort of sad reverence; it never loses touch with a noble tact and courtesy, like that of a gentleman escorting a peasant girl through the modern crowd. It is invariably respectful to Joan, and even respectful to her religion. And being myself a furious admirer of Joan the Maid, I have reflectively compared the two methods, and I come to the conclusion that I prefer Voltaire's.

When a man of Voltaire's school has to explode a saint or a great religious hero, he says that such a person is a common human fool, or a common human fraud. But when a man like Anatole France has to explode a saint, he explains a saint as somebody belonging to his particular fussy little literary set. Voltaire read human nature into Joan of Arc, though it was only the brutal part of human nature. At least it was not specially Voltaire's nature. But M. France read M. France's nature into Joan of Arc—all the cold kindness, all the homeless sentimentalism of the modern literary man. There is one book that it recalled to me with startling vividness, though I have not seen the matter mentioned anywhere; Renan's "Vie de Jésus." It has just the same general intention: that if you do not attack Christianity, you can at least patronise it. My own instinct, apart from my opinions, would be quite the other way. If I disbelieved in Christianity, I should be the loudest blasphemer

in Hyde Park. Nothing ought to be too big for a brave man to attack; but there are some things too big for a man to patronise. (pp. 267-68)

> *G. K. Chesterton, "The Maid of Orleans," in his* All Things Considered *(reprinted by permission of Miss D. E. Collins), John Lane Company, 1908, pp. 267-73.*

### H. L. MENCKEN    (essay date 1915)

Consider now, beloved, Monsieur Jacques-Anatole Thibault France *de l'Académie Française,* an ancient of three score and ten, a veritable patriarch of letters, the *doyen* of French authors, but still full of the joy of life, the Old Adam, the unquenchable gayety of the Gaul: as Nietzsche would say, still fit for dancing with arms and legs. Old Anatole, indeed, goes back to the dark ages, almost to the crusades. (p. 260)

And yet, as I say, the fires of youth are still in the veteran. His Indian Summer is pert, sunshiney, Spring-like. He leaps and cavorts. . . . [No] denials, you may be sure, will ever cure him of the *cacoëthes scribendi;* he will keep on writing until that dark (and, let us hope, distant) day when the inexorable embalmer casts upon him a sinister and appraising eye. In proof whereof here is the last fruit of his fancy: **The Revolt of the Angels,** the liveliest and most delightful piece of fooling that I have seen in many a long day, a book of waggery and gusto all compact, a literary *scherzo* that warms the cockles of the heart. (pp. 260-61)

It is written with unfailing address, ingenuity and charm. The characters are well imagined; the incidents, for all their grotesquerie, still show an ingratiating reasonableness; there is a constant play of tart, Rabelaisian humor. Old Anatole, indeed, is the natural heir of François in our time. He has something of the same hand for elaborate, elephantine satire; he is full of the same amazing erudition, the same overwhelming allusiveness; he has the same keen eye for all that is empty and ridiculous in theological and ecclesiastical rumble-bumble. With it all, he is a far more delicate artist than Rabelais, though, of course, by no means so colossal a humorist. He never stoops to grossness, even in the midst of his most daring fooling. His urbanity never gives way to the staggering savagery of Pantagruel's creator. In its essence, to be sure, **The Revolt of the Angels** is one of the most impious books ever written, but you will search it in vain for any obvious violation of the decencies. It is, in brief, the clowning of an artist and a gentleman. (p. 262)

> *H. L. Mencken, "Anatole France: A Gamey Old Gaul" (originally published in* The Smart Set, *Vol. XLV, No. 1, January, 1915), in his* H. L. Mencken's "Smart Set" Criticism, *edited by William H. Nolte (copyright © 1968 by Cornell University; used by permission of the publisher, Cornell University Press), Cornell University Press, 1968, pp. 260-62.*

### J. MIDDLETON MURRY    (essay date 1919)

Whether the present generation will produce great poetry, we do not know. We are tolerably certain that it will not produce wise men. It is too conscious of defeat and too embittered to be wise. . . . But precisely because they are not wise, they will seek the company of wise men. Their own attitude will not wear. The ecstasy will fail, the will to renunciation falter; the gray reality which permits no one to escape it altogether will filter like a mist into the vision and the cell. Then they will turn to the wise men. They will find comfort in the smile to which they could not frame their own lips, and discover in it more sympathy than they could hope for.

Among the wise men whom they will surely most frequent will be Anatole France. His company is constant; his attitude durable. There is no undertone of anguish in his work like that which gives such poignant and haunting beauty to Tchehov. He has never suffered himself to be so involved in life as to be maimed by it. But the price he has paid for his safety has been a renunciation of experience. Only by being involved in life, perhaps only by being maimed by it, could he have gained that bitterness of knowledge which is the enemy of wisdom. . . . [Anatole France] has seen men as it were in profile against the sky, but never face to face. Their runnings, their stumblings and their gesticulations are a tumultuous portion of the landscape rather than symbols of an intimate and personal possibility. They lend a baroque enchantment to the scene.

So it is that in all the characters of Anatole France's work which are not closely modelled upon his own idiosyncrasy there is something of the marionette. They are not the less charming for that; nor do they lack a certain logic, but it is not the logic of personality. They are embodied comments upon life, but they do not live. (pp. 47-8)

The chasm between living and being wise (which is to be *raisonnable*) is manifest. The condition of living is to be perpetually surprised, incessantly indignant or exultant, at what happens. To bridge the chasm there is for the wise man only one way. He must cast back in his memory to the time when he, too, was surprised and indignant. No man is, after all, born wise, though he may be born with an instinct for wisdom. Thus Anatole France touches us most nearly when he describes his childhood. The innocent, wayward, positive, romantic little Pierre Nozière [in *Le Petit Pierre*] is a human being to a degree to which no other figures in the master's comedy of unreason are. And it is evident that Anatole France himself finds him by far the most attractive of them all. He can almost persuade himself, at moments, that he still is the child he was. . . . (pp. 49-50)

To know a thing too well is by worlds removed from not to know it at all, and Anatole France does not elsewhere similarly attempt to indulge the illusion of unbroken innocence. He who refused to put a mark of interrogation after 'What is God,' in defiance of his mother, because he knew, now has to restrain himself from putting one after everything he writes or thinks. . . . Yes, Anatole France is wise, and far removed from childish follies. And, perhaps, it is precisely because of his wisdom that he can so exactly discern the enchantment of his childhood. So few men grow up. The majority remain hobbledehoys throughout life; all the disabilities and none of the unique capacities of childhood remain. There are a few who, in spite of all experience, retain both; they are the poets and the *grands esprits*. There are fewer still who learn utterly to renounce childish things; and they are the wise men. (pp. 50-1)

Not otherwise is it with us and Anatole France. We may have little in common with his thought—the community we often imagine comes of self-deception—but it is sweet for us to inhabit his mind for a while. (p. 51)

*J. Middleton Murry, "The Wisdom of Anatole France (originally published in* The Athenaeum, *No. 4640, April 4, 1919), in his* Aspects of Literature *(reprinted by permission of The Society of Authors as the literary representative of the Estate of John Middleton*

*Murry),* W. Collins Sons & Co. Ltd., *1920, pp. 46-51.*

**JULES LEMAÎTRE**    (essay date 1921)

Sylvestre Bonnard is the glory of M. Anatole France. He is the most original figure that he has portrayed. He is M. Anatole France himself as he would like to be, as he will be, perhaps as he already is. Grown old? Not at all, for, in the first place, if M. Bonnard's intellect is seventy years of age, his heart has remained young, he is able to love. And then he belongs to an age in which people become old very early. Sylvestre Bonnard sums up in himself all that is best in the soul of that age. Other ages have incarnated the best of themselves in the citizen, in the artist, in the knight, in the priest, in the man of the world: the nineteenth century in its decline, if we wish to retain only the most eminent of its qualities, is an elderly scholar, a bachelor, very intelligent, very meditative, very ironical, and very gentle. (pp. 16-17)

Now, what sort of novels would M. Sylvestre Bonnard write? Precisely those of M. Anatole France. The habit of meditation and of retiring within oneself scarcely develops the gift of inventing stories and extraordinary combinations of events. This gift seems of even small value to aged meditative persons (at least unless it reaches as exceptional a degree as in the elder Dumas, for example). M. Sylvestre Bonnard therefore could not write romances of adventure or even romantic novels. Add to this a fear of what is rhetorical, of the emphasis of expression which tragic stories almost always require. And, finally, what interests M. Bonnard most are not the surprises of fortune nor dramatically violent situations, but the habitual conduct of the world and of men. To the man who reflects much, everything seems singular enough, and to him who knows how to look at it the most ordinary reality is a spectacle of continual surprise.

Thus M. France-Bonnard will tell us very simple stories. (pp. 18-19)

If, as a rule, the subject is trifling, the characters are alive. What characters? What human masks will an old scholar like Sylvestre Bonnard prefer to represent? Those from which he differs most must for that very reason make most impression upon him. He is as much of a thinking being as it is possible to be; he will therefore especially depict unthinking beings, those who abandon themselves without distrust to excesses of speech and gesture, who are least in the secret of the human comedy, eternal dupes of themselves and of the external world. (pp. 20-1)

'There is nothing in the world for me except words, so much of a philologist am I,' says Sylvestre Bonnard. 'Each of us dreams the dream of life in his own way. I dream that dream in my library.' But the dream one dreams in a library so as to enrich it with the dream of many other men, does not cease to be personal. M. Anatole France's stories are, above all, the stories of a great scholar, of an excessively learned and subtle mandarin; but out of all the proffered booty he has made a choice which was determined by his own temperament, by his own originality; and perhaps it would not be a bad definition of him to say that he is a learned and tender humorist in love with antique beauty. It is remarkable, at any rate, that this rich intelligence owes almost nothing (unlike M. Paul Bourget) to the literatures of the North; it seems to me to be the extreme and very pure product of the Greek and Latin tradition alone.

I perceive, as I end, that I have not said at all what I intended to say. M. Anatole France's books are those which I should most like to have written. I believe I understand and feel them completely; but I love them so much that I have not been able to analyse them without a little agitation. (pp. 41-2)

> *Jules Lemaître, "Anatole France," in his* Literary Impressions, *translated by A. W. Evans, Daniel O'Connor, 1921, pp. 1-42.*

## JOHN GALSWORTHY (essay date 1923)

In his long writing career—he began in 1868 and was still writing at his death in 1924—[Anatole France] only thrice, if I am not mistaken, assumed the rôle of novelist pure. *Le Crime de Sylvestre Bonnard, Le Lys Rouge* and *L'Histoire Comique* stand out in method from his other work. In them alone is he chiefly student of human character and teller of a tale. In his other books he is first the philosopher and satirist. Even a work of art so remarkable as *Thais,* a perfect piece of recreation, is in essence critical, and was forged out of a satiric heart. The Bergeret series, though they contain many admirable portraits, was the work of one preoccupied with riddling the prejudices rather than painting the features of human beings. The short masterpiece *Le Procurateur de Judée* presents an unforgettable effigy of Pontius Pilate, but it was written to clothe in perfection a satiric thought. Poor **"Crainquebille"** is a very human figure, yet it is rather as a walking indictment of human justice that we cherish and remember him. Even little dog Riquet conveys his tail-fluttering criticism of human habits. Anatole France was a subtle and deadly fencer, rather than a trenchant swordsman like Voltaire; his victims still don't know that they are dead. They read him yet, and call him *maître.* Unsurpassed for lucidity and supple elegance, his style was the poetry of pure reason. He was very French. We shall never perhaps see again so perfect an incarnation of the witty French spirit. Not without justification did he take the *nom de plume* of France. . . . [He was] a humanist, the most convinced and proselytising of them all. Born fortunately too late for the glory of being burned or beheaded, he succeeded in being excommunicated by the Vatican. . . . He excelled in the ironic mingling of values. *Le Jongleur de Notre Dame*—how tender his irony could be! Loving the pagan, he yet seems to have reverenced the heart of the Sermon on the Mount, for *Heureux les Simples* is the moral of many of his tales. . . . He revelled in shredding away from the core of Christianity with his thin chased knife all pretences, shams, and superstitions. One reads *Crainquebille* and knows that injustice was anathema to his spirit. *L'Affaire Dreyfus* brought Anatole France out of the groves of his philosophic fancy, and *L'Anneau d'Amethyste* was a contribution to Justice almost as potent as Zola's *J'Accuse.* Though a declared Socialist, latterly of an extreme type, he failed, as is usual with men of letters, to influence politics. His direct indulgence in political propaganda stirred no waters. But his diffused and temperamental criticism has cleared away much superstition and deeply affected modern thought. (pp. 148-50)

> *John Galsworthy, "Six Novelists in Profile: An Address" (1923), in his* Candelabra: Selected Essays and Addresses *(copyright © 1932 John Galsworthy; copyright renewed © 1960 by A.J.P. Sellar and R. H. Sauter; reprinted with permission of Charles Scribner's Sons), Charles Scribner's Sons, 1933, pp. 133-54.\**

## YEVGENY ZAMYATIN (essay date 1924)

If someone were to watch the progress of our earthly culture from a neighboring planet, he would—across a distance of hundreds of millions of miles—see only the highest peaks. And if he were to draw an atlas of our culture for the past quarter of a century, the highest summit on the map of Russia would, of course, be Lev Tolstoy, and the highest summit on the map of France would be Anatole France. These two names represent not only the spiritual poles of two nations, but also the poles of two cultures: one which casts off into the unknown from the shore called European civilization, and another which remains, to destroy and to build, on this shore. And these two lofty names throw their shadow on everything below. Tolstoy is the absolute, emotion, faith (even if it refracts in the form of faith in reason); France is all relativism, irony, skepticism.

In spite of their polarity, the same energy flows through both positive and negative electrons. And the same energy of revolution animates these two poles, Tolstoy and France. Both are great heretics. Many of their works have won the highest honor a writer can expect, a listing in the catalog of proscribed books.

Nevertheless, the polarity remains. Our efforts to assimilate France are merely testimony to the natural, lusty appetite of youth, which is sometimes tempted by the indigestible. The touchstone which demonstrated to me with particular force the polarity of France in relation to us was Blok's response to him. Blok said that he could not accept France: "He is somehow unreal, he is all irony." France was "unreal" to Blok because France was a real European, through and through; because, of the two possible solutions of the problem of life, Blok, Russia, chose the tragic, with hatred and with love that stopped at nothing, while France chose the ironic, with its relativism and skepticism—also stopping at nothing.

"It takes extraordinary spiritual strength to be an atheist," says Monsieur Larive-du-Mont in France's story, **"The Shirt,"** when the conversation turns to how difficult it is to die. Monsieur du-Mont is right. But we must add that it takes even greater strength of spirit to be an atheist, a skeptic, a relativist—and yet live fully and love life. Anatole France passed this ordeal by fire—indeed, not even by fire, but by something still more terrible, by cold. Remaining a skeptic to the very end, he loved life with a young and tender love to the very end. "The irony that I invoke," said France, "is not cruel. It does not mock either love or beauty. It teaches us to laugh at evil men and fools, whom, without it, we might be weak enough to hate."

France died in deep old age. But he died very young. Just recently, when he was over seventy, he gave world literature a gift of the most characteristically Francian, the most French, the gayest, the most merciless, and the wisest of his works— **The Revolt of the Angels.** And therefore we experience his death not as the natural end of an artist who had completed his earthly journey, but as a violation, as something unnatural—as we experience the death of the young. (pp. 296-97)

> *Yevgeny Zamyatin, "Eight Writers and One Painter: Anatole France, an Obituary" (1924), in his* A Soviet Heretic: Essays by Yevgeny Zamyatin, *edited and translated by Mirra Ginsburg (reprinted by permission of The University of Chicago Press; © 1970 by The University of Chicago), University of Chicago Press, 1970, pp. 296-97.*

**E. M. FORSTER** (essay date 1927)

*Thais,* by Anatole France, is the shape of an hour-glass.

There are two chief characters, Paphnuce the ascetic, Thais the courtesan. Paphnuce lives in the desert, he is saved and happy when the book starts. Thais leads a life of sin in Alexandria, and it is his duty to save her. In the central scene of the book they approach, he succeeds; she goes into a monastery and gains salvation, because she has met him, but he, because he has met her, is damned. The two characters converge, cross, and recede with mathematical precision, and part of the pleasure we get from the book is due to this. Such is the pattern of *Thais.* . . . It is the same as the story of *Thais,* when events unroll in their time-sequence, and the same as the plot of *Thais,* when we see the two characters bound by their previous actions and taking fatal steps whose consequence they do not see. But whereas the story appeals to our curiosity and the plot to our intelligence, the pattern appeals to our æsthetic sense, it causes us to see the book as a whole. We do not see it as an hour-glass—that is the hard jargon of the lecture room which must never be taken literally. . . . We just have a pleasure without knowing why, and when the pleasure is past, as it is now, and our minds are left free to explain it, a geometrical simile such as an hour-glass will be found helpful. If it was not for this hour-glass the story, the plot, and the characters of Thais and Paphnuce would none of them exert their full force, they would none of them breathe as they do. (pp. 214-15)

> *E. M. Forster, "Pattern and Rhythm," in his As-*
> *pects of the Novel (copyright, 1927, by Harcourt*
> *Brace Jovanovich, Inc.; renewed, 1955, by E. M.*
> *Forster; reprinted by permission of the publisher; in*
> *Canada by Edward Arnold Ltd. in connection with*
> *Kings College, Cambridge and The Society of Au-*
> *thors as the literary representatives of E. M. For-*
> *ster's Estate), Harcourt, 1927, pp. 213-42.\**

**EDMUND WILSON** (essay date 1940)

[France's] immensely amusing *Contemporary History,* with its smiling but deadly analysis of the upper strata of French society, is the product of the Dreyfus period. At the beginning of *The Elm Tree on the Mall,* as if as a keystone and justification of the work, France, evidently remembering his father, plants an intelligent cobbler's son. Piédagnel, the brilliant child of humble parents, has aroused the sympathetic interest of the Abbé at the head of the seminary where Piédagnel is studying for the priesthood. But the boy is weak in doctrine; he is found to have been copying down erotic poems by Verlaine and Leconte de Lisle. The Abbé begins to be afraid that he may be rearing another Renan, and, though reluctantly, he dismisses the boy just at the moment when the ritual of the Church is beginning esthetically to move him. Piédagnel, with no aptitude for a manual trade, is sent back to the cobbler's shop; the Church has abruptly closed to him the hopes which it had been encouraging, it is suppressing the same gifts which it has stimulated. But Piédagnel goes out with a passion in his heart which, France tells us, is to fill his whole life: the "hatred of the priest."

This incident told with the French brevity and coolness of which Anatole France was a master, with the art which does not allow us to feel the full force of what we have been reading till we have finished the last line, is one of the most effective things of the kind that Anatole France ever wrote. Yet we are somewhat surprised as we go on to discover that it is to have no

sequel. From these first chapters we might have supposed that Piédagnel was to figure as a hero; but the cobbler's son never reappears. The character who turns into the hero is M. Bergeret, another Sylvestre Bonnard, less sentimentalized and more ironic. M. Bergeret is a humble professor of Latin, who has been compelled by the science department to hold his classes in a depressing basement (belles lettres by Anatole France's time are losing their faith in science and are no longer so eager for an alliance with it). Later, Bergeret takes a stand on Dreyfus, attracts a certain amount of public attention, goes to Paris and gets a better chair. What France has done is to telescope in Piédagnel his own situation with his father's—the shoemaker's grandson with the shoemaker's son; and then allow M. Bergeret, who corresponds to the mature France with the Collège Stanislas well behind him, to substitute himself for Piédagnel. A whole set of steps in the social ladder has been jumped between Bergeret in Paris and Piédagnel in his provincial town. And thereafter Anatole France himself is to be Bergeret successful. (pp. 58-9)

France was much preoccupied with history; he wrote a whole series of novels and short stories—they make, indeed, the bulk of his writing—which attempt to catch the essence of various periods from Homer's Greece to Napoleon III's Paris. Even his studies of contemporary France he labels *Contemporary History.* But how far away now, in a few decades, Michelet's vision of history seems when we look back from Anatole France! It is characteristic of France that he should, as I have said, aim merely at catching the essence of a period. He has already become one of the great practitioners of a cult which is later to be carried further: the cultivation of intelligence for its own sake. Let us understand phenomena and appreciate them: it gives pleasure and it is a mark of superiority to be able to see how things work and how an infinite variety of things are good in an infinite variety of kinds. But there we may leave them; we need not attempt to systematize them or to draw conclusions on which we may act. France has not yet come quite so far as this. He does, as we shall see, sometimes try to build systems and he occasionally makes gestures of public action. But he no longer has anything like Michelet's exalted and unfading vision of the combat of liberty with fatality, man with nature, spirit with matter, which had been so plain in the dawn of the century. It becomes a favorite game of France's irony to show, with something not unlike complacency, how freedom, spirit and man are defeated. Homer's song of the evils that flowed from the wrath of Achilles is broken up by the quarreling of cowherds; Jeanne d'Arc, preaching war, finds a following and becomes a national heroine where a similarly hallucinated young woman who has been inspired to preach peace and Christian love, walking the walls at the siege of Paris, is promptly picked off by an arrow. Yet there is no general coherence to the picture. In *The Procurator of Judea,* France takes a cue from Renan. Renan, in telling about Paul before Gallio, had pointed out the irony of the incident: to Gallio, the man in authority, the cultivated Roman, Paul had been an unprepossessing nobody. Yet the civilization of Gallio was doomed; it was Paul who represented the future. In *The Procurator of Judea,* Pilate has forgotten Christ. But later France is to try it the other way: in *On the White Stone,* he demonstrates that in the long run the future was really to belong to Gallio, since it was to be the kind of civilization imagined by enlightened Romans that was ultimately to hold the field when Christianity had come and gone. Yet France wrote pretty travesties of saints' legends whose shades of ironic tenderness Voltaire would never have understood. And the affair of Thaïs and Paphnuce is a drama where we sympathize equally with the courtesan and with the saint. Sometimes he amused himself with pure exercises of the historic imagination, such as the story of Caesar's conquests from the point of view of one of the Gallic chieftains whom the Romans are reducing to subjection. It is the miscellaneous learning of the bookstore, unorganized by any large purpose, the undisciplined undirected curiosity of the indolent lover of reading. (pp. 59-61)

It has become the fashion to disparage France as a writer; but that is partly because people expect to find in him things that he cannot supply, even though he may sometimes attempt to do so—and not for the things that are actually there. For Anatole France does not represent merely a dimming of the eighteenth-century Enlightenment as Taine and Renan do; he shows that tradition in full disintegration; and what he is telling, with all his art and wit, is the story of an intellectual world where principles are going to pieces. The moralist in Anatole France, the Paphnuce, the Gamelin, is always in conflict with the sensualist, the great preacher of *volupté* as the sole solace for human futility; and the moralist becomes more and more odious as the sensualist becomes more and more sterile.

In his political role, France is a socialist; yet the whole purpose of two of his later books, **The Gods Are Thirsty** and **The Revolt of the Angels,** is to show that revolutions must eventually result in tyrannies at least as oppressive as those they were designed to displace. And when he undertakes, in **Penguin Island,** to write a sort of outline of history, he has modern industrial civilization blasted off the face of the earth by embittered proletarian anarchists. But no freer and more reasonable order succeeds: the rebels are wiped out with their masters, and such men as are left on earth return to their original condition as tillers of the soil. We are back with the cycles of Vico again and might as well not have got rid of God. . . . Anatole France is a professed reformer and optimist, who is always relapsing into cynicism or gloom, and giving way to the worst suspicions of the mechanistic character of life and the total insignificance of humanity. He reads the astronomical articles in Larousse and makes great play with the vision of mankind alone in the awful empty universe, a mere disease on the face of the earth—a vision that has seemed terrible with Pascal, still tragic in Leopardi, still productive of nobly-ringing verses in the poetry of Alfred de Vigny, a little overdone and ridiculous in the novels of Thomas Hardy, and which has come down, in Anatole France, with his dressing-gown, his slippers and his Larousse, to the level of entertaining conversation. (pp. 61-3)

> *Edmund Wilson, "Decline of the Revolutionary Tradition: Anatole France," in his* To the Finland Station *(reprinted by permission of Farrar, Straus and Giroux, Inc; copyright © 1940, 1972, by Edmund Wilson; renewed © 1968, by Edmund Wilson), Harcourt, Brace and Company, 1940 (and reprinted by Farrar, Straus and Giroux, 1953, pp. 65-79).*

**ANDRÉ MAUROIS** (essay date 1942)

During the years that followed the death of Anatole France it was the "right thing" amongst the younger men no longer to admit that he had been a great writer. That post-war period was violent and crude. Minds that had lost their bearings demanded sweeping assertions, fearing error less than doubt. Culture went against the grain, compassion bored, and irony exasperated. For that generation the art of Anatole France could have no appeal. But we foresee another generation of young men who will "discover" with delight the **Histoire Contemporaine** and **Les Dieux ont Soif**. Formal perfection is the surest

guarantee of permanence. What is written in a style combining ingenuity with purity of diction and depicts emotions that are eternal is proof against time's ravages. Better still if the emotions thus depicted are those by which the author himself has been moved. The encounter between a writer of genius and a theme bound up with the tastes and spiritual conflicts of his adolescent years rarely fails to bring forth a work of the first rank. By such a predisposed affinity Anatole France was destined to write the best of his novels on the theme of the French Revolution. (p. vii)

[In his father's bookshop] Anatole France had come to be on intimate terms with Robespierre, Marat and their clan down to its humblest members. (pp. vii-viii)

Did he share their sentiments? That question has given rise to endless controversy. According to his political tendencies and personal bias each reader tries to bring the book into line with his own views. Let us try to analyze it as a chemist analyzes a solution, without prejudice. Évariste Gamelin is a monster. If, to safeguard the Revolution, he has to guillotine his friends, he will cause the wisest and most charming heads to fall, without compunction. But this monster is a patriot. He is brave and risks his own neck as he sacrifices those of others. He is disinterested and genuinely believes that the sole object of his cruel acts is to promote the welfare of mankind. A sentimentalist, he melts into tears of loving-kindness at the prospect of the joys in store for poor humanity, once the Revolution has purged the State of scoundrels. Unfortunately these scoundrels persist in their evil practices, stern measures still are called for, and torrents of "tainted blood" must still be shed. What is wrong with Évariste Gamelin? Why should his very real virtues bring forth only bloodshed and betrayal? Because he is convinced of being in possession of the Truth. To make men equal and contented, this fanatic is quite prepared to kill them all.

There is no shadow of doubt as to the horror the bloodthirstiness of such a man as Gamelin inspires in Anatole France. No one has depicted with more severity the Revolutionary Tribunal, its scorn for the rights of those arraigned before it, the infamy of the accusers, the baseness and subservience of the judges. France does not believe that the Terror was a necessity or that it led to happy results. Gamelin's old mother takes a much saner view of it than does her son. "I am no aristocrat. I have seen the great in the full tide of their power, and I can bear witness that they abused their privileges. . . . But never tell me the Revolution is going to establish equality, because men will never be equal; it is an impossibility, and, let them turn the country upside down to their heart's content, there will still be great and small, fat and lean in it." In the days of Thermidor the people of Paris were weary of Revolution; they considered it had lasted too long. Anatole France brings out this weariness. "Believe me, friend, the Revolution is a bore. . . ." (pp. viii-ix)

Of the various characters in the novel the one that seems most nearly to express the author's view is Brotteaux, the ex-aristocrat. His philosophy is that of the "Garden of Epicurus" and regards pleasure as the goal of life. Brotteaux is devoted to Reason, but not fanatically so. He might well have said in the words of his creator: "The more I ponder over human life, the more I am convinced that Irony and Pity should be called to witness and to judgment on it. The former smiles and makes life amiable; the latter weeps and gives it sanctity. The irony I have in mind is not a cruel one. It does not scoff at love or beauty. It is gentle and good-natured. It tempers anger with a smile and teaches us to laugh at fools and rascals whom otherwise we might be weak enough to hate.'' Brotteaux does not hate even Évariste who has him put to death so stupidly. At the scaffold's foot, in a scene that recalls *Les Misérables,* a friar asks the old Epicurean for his prayers. In short, Anatole France regards Brotteaux as a sort of saint. But a voluptuary saint, who even in the tumbrel taking him to the guillotine lets his eyes linger with admiration and regret on a girl's white bosom.

Does the fact that France depicts so tellingly the blood-lust of the terrorists and the philosophic resignation of their victims oblige us to infer he is against the Revolution? Are there good grounds for such a view, or would not such an attitude on his part be wholly incompatible with what we know of his political career? Was he not to be seen, towards the close of his life, on the platforms of revolutionary parties? To these questions there is only one answer possible, Walt Whitman's remark: "Do I contradict myself? Very well, then, I contradict myself." In the course of his long life Anatole France was a conservative and a revolutionary turn by turn—and simultaneously at whiles. (pp. ix-x)

In any case why, in a novel, should he be expected to take sides? A great artist does not sit in judgment. "When I write about horse-thieves," Chekov said, "some people expect me to declare that stealing horses is a crime; but that's none of my business, I leave that to the courts." If *Les Dieux ont Soif* achieves a great and permanent beauty it is because Anatole France is not trying in it to press home a "lesson", but to depict men's lives as they were in those stormy times. He puts into the mouths of Brotteaux the Epicurean, Longuemare the priest, Blaise the merchant, and the grim fanatic Gamelin, the remarks that they would actually have made. Each man, searching his conscience, honestly believes his conduct justified. Wherein all alike are self-deceived—except, possibly, Brotteaux, whose sanity of outlook is preserved by scepticism. (p. xi)

The novel closes with Robespierre's execution and that of Gamelin. The wheel has come full circle; those who heap insults on them as they pass by in the tumbrel are the same people who had heaped insults on their victims. The vendors of revolutionary prints re-set their shop-windows with displays of "Robespierre's Foul Conspiracy". All great social upheavals are followed by such revulsions of opinion. Some months after Cromwell's death the populace of London gave a triumphal welcome to Charles Stuart, whose father the same populace had hooted to the scaffold. The revolution brought off by Lenin and Trotzky found fruition, after Lenin's death, with Trotzky's exile. The truth is that mankind comprises a relatively stable aggregate of virtues and shortcomings. Those who try to uplift it above itself, or to abase it below its natural level, may be sure of seeing it one day swing back abruptly and with terrifying violence to the norm. "There are elements," France said, "in human nature that revolutions cannot change." (p. xii)

*André Maurois, "Introduction" (copyright, 1942, by The Nonesuch Press; reprinted by permission of the author and the author's agents, Scott Meredith Literary Agency, Inc., 845 Third Avenue, New York, New York, 10022), in* The Gods Are A-Thirst *by Anatole France, translated by Alfred Allinson, The Nonesuch Press, 1942, pp. vii-xii.*

**V. S. PRITCHETT** (essay date 1944)

Despite his artifice, his epicureanism, his air of ripeness and skepticism, [Anatole France] is at heart an adolescent writer.

His world—as he says toward the end of his last autobiographical book, *The Bloom of Life*—is the world of desire and illusion. His way is the primrose path of nostalgia, sensual pessimism and self-love. The famous irony is the artful weapon of the bookish man who never grows up, who tastes life and history. They are a gourmet's dish, sweetened by the senses, salted by horror. He observes, but does not experience; and, beginning as a dreamer, a writer of historical pastiche, a faunlike comedian of the museums and the libraries, he ends in moral nihilism. One is reminded of his own phrase about Van Dongen's portrait in his old age: "It makes me look like a Camembert that is running."

The notes of tenderness and the naïve which appear in both the sentimental and the savage writings of Anatole France led many critics to feel that, if he was appalled by human nature, he also pitied it. But now one begins to doubt. One does not pity men until one understands their dignity. As one reads his life and rereads his books one builds a picture of Anatole France shut up in a daydream world, protected by all the authority of a superb culture, tortured by self-pity and not by pity for mankind. His reminiscences of childhood and youth, his essays in the archaic improprieties of history, and his two or three realistic novels reveal a man who chooses to exploit the pleasure, the terrors and the final anarchy of a personal solitude. He became a kind of Gibbon who has lost the love of liberty in the love and hatred of himself and who, tactfully withdrawing from the battle of history, contents himself with the footnotes. It is the course of the bookish man, the man who has tippled the illusions of the library and whose irony scarcely conceals the complacency of the noncombatant. One might suppose, after reading his novel about the Terror, *The Gods are Athirst,* that the French Revolution was an idle piece of human sadism caused by boredom or some northern incursion of the sirocco, and that the forces of history are really nothing but the agglomerated aberrations of human character. The complacency of this view is as shocking as the Terror. It is not a cold complacency; it is the complacency of the daydream and self-love.

To this passive and cunning view of life, Anatole France brought the genial resources of his unorganized reading, the power to crystallize it in anecdote and to link the anecdotes together, with the subtlety and wit of the French tradition. One is rummaging in a second-hand bookshop—and, of course, he was the son of a famous bookseller—and each volume has its human habit and voice. As a novelist Anatole France was less a creator of characters than a compressor of them. He squeezed them out of books, as wine drips out of the press. His naïve priests and his fanatics, his trenchermen and his sluts, his always bedable girls, his politicians gulled by their own corruption are the fantasies of the library, jocosely or morbidly removed from the treadmill of life. There is scathing diagnosis—see his handling of the Dreyfus case in *Penguin Island*—there is art. But a heavy price is paid for this intellectual high-coloring of France's characters: we cannot take them seriously. They have wine instead of blood; sex but not vitality. The Terror in *The Gods are Athirst* does not terrorize except as a theory about the Terror. We are engaged by the sensational notion that hundreds offered themselves voluntarily to the guillotine, that the Moscow confessions were anticipated, that a woman would cling to her lover with a wilder ardor and attain an even more powerful satisfaction, when she knew he had that morning condemned innocent men peremptorily to death. For we know that some women do offer themselves to murderers with special zeal. And yet, in the end, we put down this novel which was to blast the puritan out of us and to replace him by the mellow and stoical reader of Lucretius—we put it down with the feeling that we have been tricked. Surely, we say, huge scenes have been left out. Surely it is perverse to personify the Revolution in a narrow prig like Gamelin and to treat the Terror as an outburst of self-righteousness or to isolate it as a clinical instance of insanity. Is it enough to regard the Terror merely as one of the frenzies of human nature? Was it not inevitable and therefore tragic? Is it not an insult to those cartloads of human beings jolting toward the guillotine, to give them the pathos of marionettes, to treat them as a cat treats a mouse, to use them as a psychiatrist's anecdote? The sadism and pity of Anatole France are certainly powerful and unrelenting in this book; but, in the end, one comes to regard it as a piece of erotica, while its judgment—that after revolutions have done their worst, life eventually goes on exactly as before—relies on an obvious confusion of ideas. (pp. 359-62)

> *V. S. Pritchett, "The Centenary of Anatole France" (originally published as "Books in General," in* The New Statesman and Nation, *Vol. XXVII, No. 689, May 6, 1944), in his* The Living Novel & Later Appreciations *(copyright 1947, © 1964, renewed 1975 by V. S. Pritchett; reprinted by permission of Literistic Ltd.), revised edition, Random House, 1964, pp. 359-64.*

### BEATRICE YOUNG and LISELOTTE MARKUS   (essay date 1952)

Anatole France states that: "In questions of literature there is not a single opinion that cannot easily be opposed by a contradictory opinion." Thus by his own words he supports the verdict of those who have tried to discuss his literary activity, for it is impossible to classify Anatole France. He does not fit into any category. (p. 22)

The philosophy of Anatole France has long been the despair of critics. Whenever they fitted him into a niche, he removed himself from it in his succeeding book or article. Although a self-confessed skeptic, he admires the highest values and believes in them, as can be seen in his **Le Livre de Mon Ami.** In **L'Orme du Mail,** after violent denunciations of the political activity of the Third Republic with all its pettiness, and in spite of his anti-Semitic bias, which [Jacques] Roujon claims to perceive, he takes both his hero and himself into the thick of the conflict raging around the Dreyfuss Case. While he attacks without scruple all that arouses his ire, his concern with the subtleties of religious belief is such that, like Voltaire, he cannot be regarded as one without religious faith, even though his faith may take on unconventional form. (pp. 23-4)

[His] individualism, so pronounced that it transcends the indefinable barriers surrounding literary periods, links Anatole France most completely to our present era. In **The Queen Pedauque,** he is a man of the Renaissance; in **Thaïs,** with its classical simplicity and psychological conflict, he is a contemporary of Racine, even though some of his ideas hint toward Voltaire; in **The Red Lily** he suggests the *fin de siècle;* in **L'Orme du Mail** he merges himself into the problems of his own time; in **Le Génie Latin** he feels himself in every age; and it is above all in the timeless **Sylvestre Bonnard** that he has won his greatest fame and keeps his highest place in literature. It is from his eternal viewpoint, free from the shackles of time, that he is able to survey the history of mankind and write with mellow irony his **Penguin Island.**

Our times today are burdened with tremendous masses and varieties of information, opinion and invention. Much that is welcomed one year is outmoded the next, to be reinstated the year after that. The constancy of change is the only permanent factor within the endless whirl. This is bewildering. In order to withstand the cataclysm of our times, we need Anatole France's sensitive understanding and his wise and smiling serenity. (p. 24)

> *Beatrice Young and Liselotte Markus, "Anatole France," in* The Modern Language Journal, *Vol. XXXVI, No. 1, January, 1952, pp. 22-4.*

### J. B. PRIESTLEY   (essay date 1960)

By 1924 Anatole France, with his immense reputation both at home and abroad, had enjoyed a very long reign. Moreover, as we know, the literary world of the Twenties had its own new values and standards. So it is not surprising that his death should have been followed by attacks on his work, reputation, personality; though we may feel that the savagery of these attacks did not exhibit French criticism—or criticism elsewhere that followed Paris fashion—in a favourable light. After the knives had done their work, he was ignored. And all these hoots and howls, and, even more, the silence that followed them, have largely succeeded in keeping two new generations of readers away from him, have reduced his fame to a shred of what it was throughout the Western world during the last thirty years of his life. There is no more dramatic example, in this whole age, of the sudden collapse of a great reputation. But if the noise of it reached him beyond the grave, Anatole France would not have been shocked, for he had no more illusions about enduring fame than he had about most other things. . . . And sooner or later, if the pleasures of reading are to continue, Anatole France will reappear, not quite the giant he seemed to be once, but still dwarfing the writers who made haste to attack him.

The case against him is easily made: he lacks the creative energy and depth of a master novelist; his thought is not original; his famous style has not a contemporary tone and ring, and too often suggests an eighteenth-century pastiche; his elaborate scepticism and irony, at a time when, unlike Voltaire, he ran no risks, can be irritating or wearisome; and his novels of contemporary life, if we except **Crainquebille,** seem thin and unreal. Much of him—his sly sensuality, his mocking rationalism, his antique-shop tastes, his scholarly dilettante airs, his general view of man and society—suggests a nineteenth-century background, fading rapidly in the years before the First War, and gone for ever after it. But all this does not dispose of him, except in the limited terms of literary fashion; it leaves the best of him, in its own unique mixture of qualities, quite untouched. For there is nobody like him. It is not an accident that this essentially French writer—and no writer of his time or since is more completely French or owes so little to any outside influences—should have had so great a reputation throughout the Western world. He had something of his own to offer it. (pp. 338-39)

His was an odd development: his earliest writing suggests an elderly smiling sceptic; with increasing fame, fortune, and years, his work reverses the usual trend, displays a more youthful inventiveness, adds a suggestion of generous anger and breadth of compassion to its mockery and irony, makes use of its wit as a weapon against injustice in every form. His fundamental pessimism is still there, but, unlike so much of the pessimism that was growing and deepening with the age, it is not savage and wounding, a kind of revenge, but has pity in it. *Crainquebille,* as early as 1902, sounds a note that later writers echo over and over again. Perhaps his sardonic fable about the penguins who acquired souls, and with them a history, is over-long (an unusual fault with him), building too much on its basic idea; but his *Les Dieux ont soif,* superbly narrated, is not only the story of the French Revolution but of all major violent revolutions, in which Death, taking charge, is hungry and refuses to be satisfied; and there is more than Voltairean irony in the final twists and turns, the metaphysical paradoxes, of *La Révolte des anges.* These later works will one day recapture readers in many countries, who will then perhaps go back to *Thaïs,* to a short story like *The Procurator of Judea,* or to some of the old literary *causerie* pieces, glinting with irony and wise mischief, all so pleasant and easy to read, and all—except of course for those critics who have dismissed this author as a mere fake—so hard to write. When the literary world is tired of alternating doses of syrup and vinegar, perhaps it will return with pleasure to the light dry wine of Anatole France. (pp. 339-40)

> *J. B. Priestley, "Mostly before 1914," in his* Literature and Western Man *(copyright © 1960 by J. B. Priestley; reprinted by permission of A D Peters & Co Ltd), Harper & Brothers, 1960, pp. 336-69.* *

## DUSHAN BRESKY (essay date 1969)

[*In his book-length critical study, Bresky examines such aspects of France's work as his vocabulary, diction, and use of humor and ambiguity. He devotes chapters to France's poetic technique, his eroticism, and the supernatural and utopian elements of his fiction.*]

France's thought is dynamic. His work reflects many shades of *pessimisme jouisseur,* yet his lifelong wisdom, for all its evolution and range is homogeneous. Like Epicure, he thinks that the goal of life is pleasure, and his art reflects this hedonistic belief. Pleasure is not merely sensual; it is the many-sided experience of all human faculties. Francean pleasure implies agreeable sensual stimulation, intellectual inspiration, and the spiritual enjoyment provoked by human love, pity, and irony, which he says is the joy of wisdom; Francean pleasure implies heroic pathos which springs from man's awareness of his own tragic destiny. Art offers to man's imagination the same range of sensual and spiritual enjoyment. Its practical goal is to give pleasure; its ideal goal is the creation of beauty, which to France is the purest form of joy. He believes that the aesthetic enjoyment a writer offers should not require any excessive effort, intellectual or spiritual, from the reader. (p. 223)

There are various ways of surprising the reader and of stimulating his imagination. The main thing is to offer him something he does not know or which he does not expect, thus satisfying his inborn hunger for novelty and change. . . . In France's work is an abundance of "autre chose". This *autre chose* surprises the reader's imagination and, through it, stimulates his intellectual and sensual and intuitive faculties. Such an aesthetic value has many significant topical and formal aspects. For this reason, any general critical evaluation which tries to prove that one or two "dominant" qualities of France's art or of his temperament are particular "keys" to his art is open to the charge of over-simplification. . . . France exploits all the traditional figures of speech to dramatize his subject matter, oxymorons, antitheses, numerous periphrases, understatements, euphemisms, hyperbole, metaphors, similes, and

other less common rhetorical effects. These are welcome "deviations" from gray lexical or syntactic normalcy. The same can be said of the aphorism and the florid sentence. The musicality of France's prose is another rich source of aesthetic enjoyment. Extensive illustrations show France's use of rhythm, rhyme, harmony, assonances, and sonorous euphonies. In some instances, his prose is so pervaded with rhythm that it is possible to arrange it into one or more versions of free verse.

To express a mythical atmosphere in rhythmical terms, France creates an illusion of ancient metric prosody, in particular, dactylic hexameters. France also imitates the primitive rhymes and assonances of hagiographic literature in his parodies of the medieval legends. Often, to emphasize the pagan-Christian conflicts he is so fond of dramatizing, France parallels his topical contrasts with metrical contrasts: the pagan elements are expressed in harmonious *vers libres* which vaguely echo the dactyls; the Christian and medieval topics are stylized by primitive rhymes and assonances. Of course, France did not limit his use of rhythm and rhyme to the legends; he applied them in most of his works.

Veiling the subject in poetry is one of France's subtle skills. The harsh realities of life disappear; everything is suffused with a timeless charm or mysterious gloom. The lyrical effects in France's prose depend on a refined combination of poetic subject and exceptional stylistic skill. Radiant visions of mythical life as in "**Amycus Célestin**", "**Le Saint Satyre**", "**Le Chanteur de Kymé**", or in *La Révolte des anges,* are typical examples of this alliance of lyrical style and matter. The Greco-Roman past is not the only source of France's rich lyrical inspiration. He finds poetry everywhere: in the arid sands of Africa, along the snowy road which leads to the ominous gate of M. d'Astarac's lonely mansion, in Brotteaux's attic, facing the night skies over revolutionary France, or under the elm tree where M. Bergeret meditates about the futility of life. France is able to grasp and make permanent the poetry of each situation. (pp. 223-25)

Most critics of France's style emphasize his extraordinary stylistic ease, but France himself points out that such ease is usually an illusion. He compares a good style to a sun ray: its complex nature is revealed only if it is resolved into a spectrum. His own style ideally exemplifies his thesis. It is clear, precise, concise, and it projects the subject matter in elegant contours and shades. His rhymes, assonances, alliterations, and numerous euphonies give his prose a pleasing melody and his rhythms give it graceful cadence. France's art of expression was inspired by the finest influences in the French tradition: La Fontaine's charming free verse, the disciplined lyricism of Racine, Voltaire's elegant art of satirical understatement and the musicality of Verlainean diction. . . . An analysis of his diction and rhythmical, euphonious prose leaves little doubt that his extraordinary stylistic brilliance alone makes him a classic. The discipline of his diction, syntax and poetic technique is not always so evident in his composition. Yet the frequent charge of critics that France's works are poorly composed is not fully justified. The critics tend to forget that his short stories and essays, which represent a substantial part of his work, are generally well constructed. His novels are digressive and composed in the tradition of great *prosateurs* such as Rabelais, Cervantes, Lesage, Voltaire, Fielding, Dickens or Gogol. Yet, like them, France turns this weakness to a relative advantage. His art of suave digression, comparable to that of Horace or La Fontaine, can stimulate like any other aesthetic feature. It is characteristic of him to use a short digressive subordinate clause for comical or unusual effects. France also weaves into his text countless digressive anecdotes, citations, and major interpolations. Some of them are detrimental to his art, others add aesthetic charm. Unity and economy of form is not an infallible dogma; it can occasionally be violated to advantage. The aesthetic glow of digression may stimulate the *connoisseur* and divert the average reader. (pp. 225-26)

In spite of the vicissitudes of critical fashion, France will always rate with Shaw as the greatest satirist of his era, and with Rabelais, Molière and Voltaire as one of the greatest French wits. Much of this reputation depends on the excellence of his style, which is a faithful servant of his humor. Humor, irony in particular, is paramount in France's art. Some critics would hesitate to consider humor an aesthetic value. (p. 226)

This analysis considers humor as one of many aspects of art. It seems inaccurate to reduce the aesthetics of masterpieces such as *Thaïs*, "Balthasar", **"Le Jongleur de Notre Dame"**, **"Le Procurateur de Judée"**, **"Le Saint Satyre"**, **"Le Chanteur de Kymé"**, *Les Dieux ont soif*, and *La Révolte des anges* to irony alone. Besides, France's irony itself has diverse facets and effects. It can express many different attitudes: sympathy and gratitude, sardonic contempt and hatred, gentle blame, mischievous or melancholy joy. It may playfully draw a benign caricature or etch an acid satire. Grave and sublime irony, vehicles of France's significant themes, usually contain a latent paradox and do not always provoke laughter.

Although less significant in France's art than his irony, the second aspect of humor, farce, is by no means rare. His early novel, *Le Chat maigre,* is mainly farcical, and so is his collection of licentious short stories, *Les Sept Femmes de la Barbe-Bleue*. One finds highly farcical short stories in all his collections and long farcical passages are blended with irony and *gauloiseries* in all his major novels. Farce is not necessarily a low form of art, it is often sublime, especially when it is elevated to the metaphysical level.

Closely related to irony, are the many ambiguities, paradoxes, contradictions, and contrasts. These features, just as deservedly as irony, could be regarded as the "key" to France's art. Although less pervasive than pure irony, they are a constant ingredient in France's prose and create a variety of effects— many are comical and licentious, others are symbolic and, like irony, often express a higher universal meaning.

France's contradictions and paradoxes provide perhaps the sharpest spice of aesthetic surprise; they give an unmistakable tang to his prose. They often outgrow their aphoristic form and, like symbolism or grave irony, may suggest a universal meaning or reveal an unknown spiritual perspective. Thus the extended paradox is raised to a paradoxical controversy, or to major conflict. France, the skeptic and polemist, likes to dwell on the hidden discords in social and ethical conventions, general beliefs or philosophical and religious doctrines. These controversial ideas are disseminated through the typical Francean heroes, learned scholars, and wise men such as Bonnard, Nicias, Coignard, M. d'Astarac, Choulette, Bergeret, Doctor Trublet, and Brotteaux. The sagacious satyrs, fallen angels, and Satan are frequent challengers of Christian moral and social standards. *La Révolte des anges* dramatizes the most significant of France's paradoxical controversies. It formulates his pagan creed and expresses his profound sympathy for the underdog, Satan. Satan is not the supreme evil in France's view but a Promethean Lucifer, a friendly titan, who worships the two mythical charioteers, Apollo and Dionysos. France also depicts

the clash between Christianity and paganism in several short stories, never failing to present paganism as a more charming and more natural cult. (pp. 227-28)

France stimulates the reader by eroticism and *gauloiserie* in almost all his works. He has a sensual and hedonistic conception of love. In this respect his erotic subjects are in the tradition of Ovid, Boccaccio, La Fontaine, and the *galant* literature of the eighteenth century. Without considering his early poetic work, it may be said that **Jocaste, Thais, Le Lys rouge, Histoire comique,** and **Les Dieux ont soif** contain France's serious love themes. (pp. 228-29)

France frequently stimulates less definite urges than the undeniable animal instincts of sex, fear and pugnacity. One of these is man's attraction towards the unknown. This curiosity is stimulated most intensely by the supernatural element: miracles and supernatural beings have always aroused human curiosity. A skeptic such as France would hardly take miracles, ghosts, angels and devils seriously, but they are one of his favorite topical ingredients. [Loring B.] Walton, referring to France's skepticism, talks about his distaste for the miraculous. France certainly satirizes the miraculous, but the term "distaste" does not seem to characterize France's attitude. France does not believe in the miracle, but the idea of it constantly amuses and attracts him. One might say that France has a taste for the supernatural, in spite of his irreverence toward it. This interest of the skeptic in the supernatural is one of the paradoxes in France's wisdom and in his art. . . . It is irrelevant whether France believes in supernatural phenomena or whether he satirizes them. The fact that he treats supernatural and utopian topics so often, in an era of naturalistic and psychological novels, indicates that in his choice of subject matter France relies on the classical tradition, in which supernatural topics are a desirable source of aesthetic pleasure.

France's parodies of the old legends dealing with the supernatural keep the original exotic or historical setting. Both the exotic and the historical are typical aspects of what is designated in this study as *bizarrerie*. This term includes subjects striking for their oddness or strangeness. In general, *bizarrerie* contributes to the topical richness so characteristic of France's style, in the wider sense of the word. It illustrates, most unexpectedly, France's general ideas. In some instances, the *bizarrerie* borders on the controversial; in other cases it has a purely decorative function. France's controversial or comical heroes such as Tudesco, Bonnard, Coignard, Pigeonneau, or Bergeret, have a bizarre streak which usually originates in their humanism and in their unconventional social code. The minor *bizarreries* are decorative. Most of France's works include either a bizarre theme or at least a bizarre hero. Bizarre scenes and topics are especially evident in **Le Chat maigre, Le Crime de Sylvestre Bonnard, Thaïs, La Rôtisserie de la Reine Pédauque, Les Dieux ont soif, L'Ile des Pingouins, La Révolte des anges**, and in most of the short stories. France's bizarre heroes include Paphnuce, Marquis Tudesco, Choulette, and many characters from **L'Ile des Pingouins** and, from the short stories, heroes ranging from M. Pigeonneau to the Grand Saint Nicolas.

Aesthetic incongruities gain part of their effect from being "unexpected", but they excite chiefly by some rare or unusual quality, such as a sudden contrast or conflict, a supernatural element, humor, or eroticism. Occasionally, however, one finds in France's prose instances where unexpectedness is the main source of surprise. . . . Like his Epicurean *Weltanschauung* and like his style and wit, France's life-long contact with classical literature strengthens both the formal and the spiritual cohesion of the whole work. His style and wit account for a great deal of structural unity; they assimilate and reconcile many discrepancies, but alone they could never account for an entirely harmonious synthesis of all aesthetic factors. To achieve this, the author has to express a coherent wisdom which can interpret, or at least face, any aspect of life. (pp. 229-32)

> *Dushan Bresky, in his* The Art of Anatole France *(a revision of a thesis presented at the University of Washington in 1962; reprinted by permission of the author),* Mouton Publishers, 1969, 268 p.

### MURRAY SACHS   (essay date 1974)

Perhaps the single most significant contribution Anatole France made to the short story genre was simply that he practised it—assiduously, regularly and with distinction. The writing of short stories was, for Anatole France, neither a convenient journalistic 'gagne-pain' nor a form of relaxation between longer works (as was patently the case for many nineteenth-century authors), but rather a serious art form which he strove earnestly to master, and then to develop as far as his gifts would take him. The regularity with which his carefully-revised tales were collected into book form, over a thirty-year period, testifies eloquently to the importance he attached to the short story form as a means of artistic expression, and a genre for which he felt he had a special aptitude. . . . It was probably Maupassant who first won a really large audience for the short story, but it was Anatole France who assured the continuity of that ready audience's attention into the twentieth century, by the originality and high quality of his work in that genre. It is not too much to suggest that Anatole France's role, as the most celebrated man of letters at the turn of the century, was decisive in making the genre of the short story artistically and economically attractive for all French authors of the twentieth century. From Proust and Gide to Sartre and Camus and on to the New Novelists and beyond, there is scarcely a prose writer of any consequence in the twentieth century who has not done serious work in this genre. The prestigious place enjoyed by the short story today in the French literary world is the direct consequence of the painstaking skill of nineteenth-century authors like Mérimée, Maupassant and Anatole France, who gradually built a durable aesthetic tradition for this genre.

Beyond this general contribution, there was a particular domain which Anatole France made distinctively his own in the short story. He had never shown any major interest in depicting the quality of everyday life in his fiction, nor was he primarily intent on spinning a good yarn for its own sake, nor on portraying an especially fascinating personality, nor on creating a dramatically tense atmosphere, though all of those elements do occur, on occasion, as secondary characteristics of his stories. Neither reality, nor plot, nor character, nor mood is the animating objective of his fictional creations, but idea. It is always some thought or concept which is the starting-point for his stories, and the source of both their shape and their ultimate meaning. Whether they take the form of legend or historical recreation, pure fantasy or contemporary satire, playful pastiche or private drama, ancient document or modern case-history, the one constant and distinctive feature of every story is that an idea is at its vital centre. There are few, if any, other imaginative artists of whom it can be said quite so absolutely that ideas are his prime source of inspiration and the trigger of his creative faculties. His is not a pictorial, or analytical, or affective art, but predominantly an art of abstraction and cerebration. (pp. 56-7)

The statement of the central theme in any Anatole France novel or short story always has the form of a paradox, an incongruity, or an absurdity. For this was the irreducible essence of his view of man, which his subject, his style and his tone all helped him express.

As for form and technique, Anatole France's key contribution to the short story genre was the invention of what might be called the multi-resonant tale. He disdained surprise endings, vignettes, and mood pieces, and strove instead to concentrate the focus of each story on a single concept which would expand and echo ambivalently and on several levels in the reader's mind at the story's conclusion. The perfect model of this kind of multi-resonant tale is **'Le Procurateur de Judée'**, which is constructed totally around the last sentence, and which leaves the reader with multiple unresolved ironies to ponder regarding history, religion, politics and the role of individuals in history. Nor does the effect depend upon the last sentence as a surprise, since the reader has been led to await this sentence with growing anticipation throughout the story. What the last sentence does is to put the last brick in place in a careful structure which the reader can only then grasp in its entirety, and in which he can suddenly recognize many layers of conflicting meanings. Anatole France employed many variations on this formula, once he had worked it out, but the essential elements in it, however variously arranged, can always be found in every successful story he ever wrote: namely, the steadfast concentration on a single theme, the patient building of a significant structure, and the expanding, multivalent insights of the conclusion. These elements define the *conte francien*, that distinctive short story type which is Anatole France's own special addition to the development of the genre, the invention of which may yet turn out to be the literary achievement which will best assure his enduring fame.

For in the perspective of literary history, it is now quite clear that Anatole France played an essential role in helping to establish a literary tradition of the artistic short story in France, and that he was able to do so not merely because he happened to write many good short stories, but because the storytelling talent was the very essence of his creative ability. Even his novels and his autobiographical writings, which bulk so large in his *oeuvre,* can be shown to be constructed from original conceptions and on the basis of techniques which are by nature those of the short story. It seems increasingly likely that the primary place Anatole France will come to occupy in the literary history of France is that of a great teller of exemplary tales—exemplary by reason both of the ideas they propose and the standard of excellence they set. (pp. 57-9)

> *Murray Sachs, in his* Anatole France: The Stories *(© Murray Sachs 1974), Edward Arnold, 1974, 62 p.*

### WAYNE C. BOOTH   (essay date 1976)

[*In his introduction to a 1976 translation of* Thaïs, *excerpted below, Booth discusses modern criticism's neglect of France's fiction and offers a sophisticated analysis of the author's much admired strongpoint—the style and structure of his books. Booth considers the "hourglass pattern" which E. M. Forster perceived in* Thaïs *(see excerpt above) a misrepresentation of the novel's design.*]

[The shape of an hourglass] was intended by E. M. Forster as a summary of "the pattern" of ***Thaïs*** [see excerpt above]. (p. 2)

The neat formula for a neat story is indeed in itself pleasing—so pleasing conceptually that it has been borrowed by other critics when they needed an illustration of neat fictional form. There are only two things wrong with it: it bears hardly any relation at all to what we find in France's version, and, if taken seriously, it will surely discourage anyone from wanting to read the book. All of the pleasure is in the summary. Why bother to read more than a hundred pages, when the form can be experienced in three sentences?

What is worse, by using the hourglass figure, Forster makes his summary sound more interesting, "aesthetically," than it is. What he *describes* is really no more interesting than an X. One can only assume that he chose the hourglass because it suggests a more beautiful symmetry than one finds in two crossed straight lines. (p. 3)

[The story of *Thaïs*] has about as much similarity to an hourglass as *King Lear* has to a Christmas tree. Such a priest encountering such a courtesan and moving to such a doom does not produce symmetrical images. There is no clear crossing from salvation to doom, by Paphnutius; he is damned from the beginning. And there is no crossing from damnation to salvation, by Thaïs; she is blessed throughout. There is, in fact, very little movement at all. (pp. 6-7)

Perhaps no one can now read *Thaïs* without wondering at first how it ever could have been *widely* popular. And aside from that historical question, what is one to *do* with all this freight of ideas that seem so thoroughly dated: this bland cosmopolitanism, this easy skepticism about all moral commitment (the sort of thing that made Edmund Wilson in the thirties reverse the high praise he had given in the twenties), the heavy anticlericalism, the precious celebrations of Eros (resembling the "carnal mysticism" that Malcolm Cowley was later to describe as one of the four main "tendencies" in the literary culture of the twenties), the dilettantish taking up of this or that commitment, always softened with expressions of worldly-wise detachment—such seeming ideas, really only slogans that serve to confirm one generation of readers and to turn off the next, merely get in our way. When one reads, for example, the young James Branch Cabell's adulatory words about France in his introduction to the translation of *The Queen Pedauque* . . . , one can see that Cabell's praise for what he takes to be a literary quality, France's peculiar kind of irony, is really a celebration of the one right attitude toward life: the stance of the ironic man. When everyone who was anyone took up with "irony and pity," the catchphrase originally applied to France, the phrase summarized a complex of "ideas" and "feelings" about life that was exciting while it lasted but that inevitably passed with the coming of the thirties and then of World War II. By 1939, none of Anatole France's classics could any longer be found on *The Modern Library* list. With the passing of the fashion in his ideas, Anatole France—so one might argue—rightly sank from view.

A second lost appeal has followed from the first: the excitement of encountering a living figure as representative intellectual. It is easy to find contemporary evidence that readers identified with France in ways that went beyond the effects of any one work. He stood for them in the battle of life, as it were, representing one possible way of coping with the terrors of a universe recently unmasked as cold and impersonal. Everybody who was anybody had learned that if you scratch beneath the surface of things, as all great thinkers for more than two centuries had been doing, you find a heart of darkness, a terrifying emptiness where once men had seen God. And here was a man

who had probed as far into that abyss as anyone, and yet he could *do* things with it—he could *write* about how to live with it; and what was perhaps even more important, he could live intensely, celebrating life and its sensual pleasures even while scoffing at those who took those pleasures too seriously. Thus such a figure comes to *represent* me, in my time.

But of course later generations must seek other representatives: France will be replaced by Gide and Proust, Gide and Proust by Camus and Sartre, Camus and Sartre by—whoever happens to be your present intellectual hero or heroine. And once the *person* has lost all magical powers, the *works* must make their way on their own.

The question now becomes: did the initial decline of *Thaïs*, as the ideas lost their flash and "the master" faded from view, leave us with a work of art worth preserving?

The great public figure, more famous for being a writer than for his actual writings, was also famous for his sayings, among them one that went like this: "I have only two enemies: Christ and chastity." But what of readers who have decided not to hate but to be indifferent to Christ, who no longer have before them any models of chastity that might be hated or feared? Must not such readers inevitably find *Thaïs* boring, because it seems to depend on outmoded battles with Christ and chastity? Only, I would suggest, if they insist on reading it as "a novel."

Many readers recognized from France's earliest publication that he was "not a novelist" but rather a "man of ideas." Some few found him merely a "mental dilettante," as Paul West later put it, with "nothing coherent to say," a man who tried "to reconcile high intellectual ambitions with an impossibly cluttered mind," but one who redeemed the clutter by creating "a prose of immaculate concision which only Camus and Colette have equalled." Far more, as I have suggested, found his appeal, particularly in the earliest years, in the ideas themselves, though it was always difficult to make a case for any great originality or profundity. What was not generally recognized, and what has now been forgotten, is how much the "delicate style" and the "exquisite form" that were most often the explicit points of praise, are inseparable, in France, from the "ideas"—how the form is made out of the ideas, in ways that make both freshness and profundity fairly unimportant. (pp. 10-12)

To read the work at all, we must engage in a kind of philosophical conversation with its author, a conversation in which we never receive his words direct. . . . [In *Thaïs* we] read, "The ancients of the desert extended their power to include sinners and godless men. Their benevolence was sometimes terrible." The delight here, for the reader who sees himself and France together as among the godless (even if the identification is only for the duration of the book), comes from the seemingly slight but powerful difference between the word *terrible* as spoken by the pious and naive narrator, and the word *terrible* as spoken by the insinuating author.

"Paphnutius had a profound knowledge of the ways of faith. He knew hearts well enough to recognize that Timocles was not in God's grace, and the day of salvation had not yet come to this hell-bent soul." "Profound" may be again a bit heavy and a bit easy, but coming as a response to the long account by Timocles (the skeptic), Paphnutius' judgment is wonderfully silly.

"Crobyle [the slave girl] called him [Paphnutius] her sweet satrap and held up the mirror for him to see himself, and

Myrtale tweaked his beard. Paphnutius, however, was praying and did not notice them.'' At such moments, we hear the overt account in a voice that could be Paphnutius' own conscience-bound rationalizations. We are, in fact, so often inside his mind that we come to think of the whole story as if told by him, though of course there is much told that he could never tell. But the covert voice of the author is even stronger. Thus the effect here is almost as absurd as if it read: ''Myrtale tweaked my beard, but I was praying and did not notice her.''

''Since God, whose ways are inscrutable, did not deem it appropriate to enlighten his servant, Paphnutius, plunged into doubt, decided to think about Thaïs no longer.'' Such a sentence might, in some works, be taken at face value. Except perhaps for the word ''appropriate,'' which seems odd, it could all be written with total piety. But when we encounter the sentence as we move into the last part of *Thaïs,* we have long since known that every word carries both the meaning it might have for the ignorant, self-deluded Paphnutius and the meaning it has for the enlightened, skeptical reader: God's ways *are* inscrutable for the would-be saint, and they are even more inscrutable for the reader who is fairly certain that no God exists. God did not deem it appropriate to enlighten poor Paphnutius, as *he* sees it; as *we* see it, there could be no light in the direction Paphnutius is pursuing. Paphnutius ''decided to think about Thaïs no longer''—and we of course know that, driven as he is by secret lusts, he has no power to make that decision. He is lost, has been lost from the beginning, because his prayers are empty gestures toward an empty sky.

All the delight of such writing thus comes in the precise texture from line to line. We need not be among those who think that all of the implied author's claims to sophistication are indeed sophistication. Though we shall no doubt lose some of the titillation that certain ''ideal readers'' of his own time must have known, we can easily make ourselves, with his help, into the kind of (temporary) sophisticate who can distinguish what is sound from what is blind in the narrator's point of view. We are not even disturbed greatly when we find many passages in which the ironies are too complex for deciphering: we know that we are in good hands, and that no doubt we could, with just a bit more effort, make it all out clearly. Indeed it increases our pleasure if we can feel that France is always just a bit ahead of us: there is more here than meets even *our* discerning eyes.

Besides, our assumed position entails the belief that the world cannot, after all, be ''made out.'' Paphnutius and the narrator think it is all simple, even when God is inscrutable; but *we* know that it is ultimately baffling to the core. Pursued by a vision of Thaïs with her bare breast ''filmed over with the blood oozing from her open heart,'' Paphnutius becomes more anxious. ''His suffering was a cruel affliction. But, as his body and soul remained pure in the midst of these temptations, he trusted in God and gently reproached him.'' On the one hand, we have no doubts about the gross impurity of his body and soul; and we know that the phrase ''trusted in God'' and the word ''gently'' must be retranslated. But was it a cruel affliction or not? Yes and no. Perhaps. The words are what Paphnutius thinks, but are they not also, in another sense, what we can believe? Often, very often, we cannot tell. And not being able to tell becomes part of our pleasure. Indeed, the mixtures become more and more complex as the work proceeds. The narrative voice itself occasionally takes on some of France's sophistication—yet we have little trouble with this ''inconsistency of point of view.'' The implied author as ironic man never changes.

I use the word ''philosophical'' for this kind of conversation with misgivings. It is certainly not coherent philosophizing, yet no one who lacks an interest in philosophical ideas can ever enjoy it very much. I feel equal diffidence in calling the whole of *Thaïs* a ''novel of ideas,'' though that's the only term we have for works (actually of many different sorts) in which our attention is more on thoughts than on the fate of the characters. The trouble is that though the author pretends that the ideas matter very much, they matter to him and to us very little *as ideas,* since they are (even, I suspect, for most of the more alert original readers) subordinated to the intellectual pleasure of hearing at least two voices talking at once, one of them betraying itself to the other.

We have no name, I think, for the kind of work in which the central interest is a philosophical conversation with the implied author, conducted ''behind the main character's back,'' with the author presenting himself as ''the ironic man.'' It might be described as a subvariety of that large class of works that Sheldon Sacks has named the apologue—works in which the invention and disposition of characters and episodes are determined more by a pattern of ideas than by the development of characters and their fate. But the trouble is that here we have no real *pattern* of ideas. E. M. Forster's hourglass betrays the work no worse than would a schematic statement of how the author's various truths interrelate. France was never a systematic philosopher. He changed his mind often. Though he was always ''a skeptic,'' he embraced throughout his life a succession of dogmas. If it was true that Henry James's mind was never violated by an idea, it was true of France that his mind was raped almost daily. There *were* times in his later life, particularly after he committed himself in the Dreyfus affair, when he stood for a relatively clear position as a pro-socialist critic; Georg Lukacs was later to make of him almost a proto-Marxist hero, far more penetrating in his criticism of bourgeois culture than a Hugo and the equal of a Zola. But no reader can emerge from *Thaïs* with a clear sense of what the novelist is *for.* It is essential to the special mocking tone of *Thaïs* that no firm assertions can be attributed to the author; our only clear picture at the end is of what he is against: all passionate ideological commitments are absurd, even though some are more absurd than others. After skepticism has done its work, what abides—and that on very shaky ground—is simply Venus and all that she stands for: beauty, tenderness, a tolerant generosity (with limits: Thaïs is proud that she has not sold herself to those who do not love her) and a simplicity shared by Thaïs and by some—strangely not all—of the beasts and birds. (pp. 13-18)

[Among] the works that drive us into thought, using the whips of irony, with just enough pain and threat to arouse our pity for the victims and yet not so much as to risk our souls, I can think of none better than *Thaïs.* The twentieth century has subjected us all to a literature that risks much more. Most of France's important successors could no longer ''amorously toy'' with the abyss, and some of them, like Samuel Beckett, have even tried to find ways of saying that in all honesty nothing can be said. Such differences of what we might almost call ''surface depth'' and ''apparent daring'' will always affect to some degree our judgment on our contemporaries and on writers of our recent past. But with a finely wrought piece of fiction now nearly a century old, the dating has done most of the damage it can ever do. We should now be ready to recognize that the ''elitist'' ideas were, after all, not *that* bad, were not in fact all that different from those that became downright popular fifty or seventy-five years later. It is surely time now to look again at this masterful stylist who, even when he was most skeptical about whether assertion was possible or writing worthwhile, could still carve out from the accumulation of doubts a work of art as splendid as *Thaïs*. (pp. 23-4)

> *Wayne C. Booth, in his introduction to* Thaïs *by Anatole France, translated by Basia Gulati (reprinted by permission of The University of Chicago Press; translation © 1976 by The University of Chicago), University of Chicago Press, 1976, pp. 1-24.*

## DIANE WOLFE LEVY (essay date 1978)

Anatole France was a master story-teller, and his short stories rank among his best-known and most interesting works. If the short story form imposes certain restrictions, it can also result in a refinement and condensation of both thought and technique. France's ironic and detached manner and his careful craftsmanship appear at their best in this showcase genre. (p. 9)

[In *Les Sept Femmes de la Barbe-Bleue et autres contes merveilleux*], the last of his eight collections of short stories, France uses a complex system of parody to provide the reader with constant and often paradoxical surprises throughout the text. . . .

*Les Sept Femmes de la Barbe-Bleue* reiterates France's life-long concern with history and epistemology, and returns to the legendary, supernatural, and religious themes he so often used throughout his career. (p. 10)

France did not value history for any absolute, factual contribution to the sum of human knowledge. He considered it an art rather than a science, whose sole value lay in its beauty. . . . (p. 13)

This skepticism with regard to history's accuracy combined with an appreciation of its symbolic grandeur can be seen in *Clio*, a small volume of five short stories published in 1900. As the title indicates, all are inspired by the Muse of History. In them, France elaborates his oblique view of history, focusing on an incidental anecdote (as in **"La Muiron"**) or an historical fact seen from an unusual viewpoint (the "bas bout de la table" in **"Le Roi Boit"**) in order to illuminate one of the many facets of the human side of the past. The two most prominent stories in the collection emphasize spiritual values rather than facts. The historical background of **"Le Chanteur de Kymé"** is of interest because of the light it sheds on the creative spirit and the role of the artist, unappreciated by his contemporaries as well as the reader who is unaware, until the last sentence, that the aged bard of the story is Homer. And in **"Komm l'Atrébate,"** history remains an overwhelming and incomprehensible force, crushing individual action or resistance. (pp. 13-14)

The mainspring of France's stories is the relationship between reality and illusion and the paradoxical values which he assigns them. Even in *La Vie de Jeanne d'Arc*, France had toyed with notions of veracity. . . . But in *Les Sept Femmes* paradox and parody, the most characteristic traits of France's thought, together form the essential mechanism of the work. This paradox is not merely the tension between the real and the supernatural which is present in all fantastic tales: such non-ironic tension can be found in France's straightforward tales of mystery and suspense such as **"L'Ombre"** or **"La Fille de Lilith."** In the tale of the fantastic, the supernatural intrudes into the real world, provoking undeniable and yet inexplicable events. In *Les Sept Femmes*, however, France pretends to impose the same rational evaluations on both kinds of phenomena: real and fantastic.

The longest of the stories in *Les Sept Femmes*, **"La Chemise,"** provides a key to the others. The protagonist, Christophe V, represents the modern mentality—withering for lack of illusion. Real life is "false": we need the mysterious, the "merveilleux" which gives life its true meaning. But paradoxically, the "merveilleux" cannot exist, for if it did it would by definition annul itself. . . . Christophe V's search for the magic talisman, the shirt of a happy man, is thus doomed to failure.

This paradox is incorporated into the very structure of the first three stories in the collection through France's manipulation of the traditional forms of the fairy tale and saint's legend. Each of the stories is based on a "type populaire"—a tale "legitimized" by a well-known text. Two, Bluebeard and the Sleeping Beauty, are taken from Perrault; the third, the legend of St. Nicolas, is based on the popular legend and children's song. These models arouse certain expectations concerning plot and character on the part of the reader, as well as fundamental concepts of reality and illusion. A simple variant or retelling of a tale may alter certain details but never changes what France has called the "fonds pueril et sacré" of the story. In these irreverant versions, however, France deliberately alters these fundamental elements. The ironic tone already present in Perrault's tales is magnified in France's stories. France also exaggerates the tendency for realism which is characteristic of the French folktale (and is also emphasized in Perrault's stories). France knowingly confuses this realism with historical veracity, a notion completely alien to fiction. Thus, by altering the reader's concept of fiction, he necessarily alters the perception of reality.

The satire in *Les Sept Femmes* is double. France's parodies or "reprises transformistes" of traditional tales are not directed simply against his protagonists. France uses these parodies to mock scholarly and scientific methods and attitudes, much as Voltaire, in his article on Gargantua, uses the parody of a fictional character to ridicule religious beliefs. This kind of indirect attack creates an atmosphere of mock seriousness at the same time that it debases the target (by association with the fictional character). Voltaire's brief satire ends with the same paradox which France develops more extensively in his stories; what is fictional is "real," thus accepted reality must be fictional. . . . But while Voltaire's narrator is clearly his own persona, France's satire is directed against the narrator as well as the protagonist in two of the stories, **"Les Sept Femmes de la Barbe-Bleue"** and **"Le Grand Saint Nicolas."** The events related in the stories and often the very language of the narration undermine the professed objectives of the narrator, whose unreliability is clearly revealed. In much the same way, reason founders in the face of reality in **"La Chemise."**

There is yet another level to France's irony in these stories. All irony (and all parody, which is inherently ironic) depends on the collaboration of *destinateur* and *destinataire*. . . . The reader and author form an elite which mocks the foolishness or perversity of the many. This collaboration is particularly important for France, whose style leans so heavily toward pastiche, parody and allusion. Nevertheless, France does not allow his reader to enjoy an entirely privileged position since the stories are based on the manipulation of the reader's attitudes and preconceptions. Indeed, France's technique depends on the frustration of the reader's expectations; a process which parallels the dramatic irony developed in the plot.

The humor of France's stories is Bergsonian in its contrast of the vital and the mechanical. They center on a rigid character whose expectations are constantly frustrated because he persistently fails to adapt to circumstances. France's characters are victims of illusion as well as prisoners of reality. Their rigidity is shared by narrator and reader alike, and all, to a greater or lesser degree, are implicated in France's irony. The criticism of all rational endeavor in **"La Chemise"** extends this irony to existential proportions. . . . (pp. 16-19)

The pervasiveness of France's irony has been considered a form of artistic "paralysis" by some of his critics. But irony is far from crippling in **Les Sept Femmes de la Barbe-Bleue.** These short stories offer a unique example of the integration of manner and form. Ironic contrast, opposition and paradox are not only used as narrative techniques but are incorporated into the basic structure of the text. (p. 19)

> *Diane Wolfe Levy, in her* Techniques of Irony in Anatole France: Essay on "Les sept femmes de la Barbe-Bleue," *U.N.C. Department of Romance Languages, 1978, 165 p.*

---

## ADDITIONAL BIBLIOGRAPHY

Axelrad, Jacob. *Anatole France: A Life without Illusions, 1844-1924.* New York: Harper & Brothers, 1944, 480 p.
    Noncritical biography.

Brousson, Jean Jacques. *Anatole France Himself: A Boswellian Record.* Translated by John Pollock. Philadelphia: J. B. Lippincott Co., 1925, 356 p.
    Transcription of France's casual remarks, conversations, and reminiscences, taken down by his secretary.

Cerf, Barry. *Anatole France: The Degeneration of a Great Artist.* New York: The Dial Press, 1926, 303 p.
    Critical study designed to undermine France's reputation. Cerf writes that "France's books constitute a valuable reflection of the successive currents of thought in which he lived," but that his books date quickly and his novels gradually degenerate to accommodate a growing taste for decadence, scorn, and irony.

Chevalier, Haakon. *The Ironic Temper: Anatole France and His Time.* New York: Oxford University Press, 1932, 288 p.
    Early biography with little critical evaluation of France's writing. Chevalier concludes that various "insufficiencies"—primary among them a lack of coherence—kept France from greatness.

Durant, Will. "Anatole France." In his *Adventures in Genius,* pp. 252-300. New York: Simon and Schuster, 1931.
    Favorable discussion of France's life and works. Durant discusses France's epicureanism, skepticism, socialism, and his attitude toward women.

Guérard, Albert Léon. "Anatole France." In his *Five Masters of the French Romance,* pp. 39-96. New York: Charles Scribner's Sons, 1917.
    Divides France's career into four major periods: an idyllic phase, a satiric phase, a Voltairian phase, and a socialist phase. Guérard concludes that "the primacy of Anatole France in French literature is unchallenged."

Jefferson, Carter. *Anatole France: The Politics of Skepticism.* New Brunswick, N.J.: Rutgers University Press, 1965, 294 p.
    Biographical study of France's political attitudes and how they changed throughout his life.

Kémeri, Sándor [pseudonym of Mme. Bölöni]. *Rambles with Anatole France.* Translated by Emil Lengyel. Philadelphia: J. B. Lippincott, 1926, 335 p.
    Personal reminiscence by France's secretary and traveling companion of a recuperative trip to Italy taken during France's sixty-sixth year.

Kennett, W.T.E. "The Themes of *Penguin Island*." *Romantic Review* XXXIII, No. 3 (October 1942): 275-89.*
    Explores the idea of an imaginary penguin island in the voyage literature of the sixteenth through twentieth centuries, concluding with France's *Penguin Island.*

May, James Lewis. *Anatole France: The Man and His Work; An Essay in Critical Biography.* 1924. Reprint. Port Washington, N.Y.: Kennikat Press, 1970, 261 p.
    Biographical account, focusing on France's formative years. In the second half of his book, May discusses France's works.

Rascoe, Burton. "Anatole France the Skeptic." In his *Titans of Literature: From Homer to the Present,* pp. 430-52. New York: G. P. Putnam's Sons, 1932.
    Compares France and Remy de Gourmont, and considers them both "among the most emancipated intelligences the world has produced."

Sachs, Murray. "The Present As Past: Anatole France's *Histoire Contemporaine.*" *Nineteenth-Century French Studies* V, Nos. 1-2 (Fall-Winter 1976-77): 117-28.
    Examination of the literary and artistic purpose of the *Histoire Contemporaine.* Sachs feels critics often overlook this aspect of the series to focus on its political and satirical purpose.

Schaffer, Aaron. "Anatole France and Poetry." *PMLA* XLVII, No. 1 (March 1932): pp. 262-82.
    Study of France's attitude toward poets and poetry as expressed in his novels and stories.

Searle, William. "Anatole France and the Maid: A Naturalistic View." In his *The Saint and the Skeptics: Joan of Arc in the Work of Mark Twain, Anatole France, and Bernard Shaw,* pp. 57-96. Detroit: Wayne State University Press, 1976.
    Examination of France's interpretation of Joan of Arc as a victim of a nervous disorder, who was manipulated by an unscrupulous clergy.

Shanks, Lewis Piaget. *Anatole France: The Mind and the Man.* New York: Harper & Brothers Publishers, 1932, 236 p.
    Psychological biography of France, meant "to reconcile the works and the author." Shanks concludes that France was essentially conservative.

Smith, Helen B. *The Skepticism of Anatole France.* Paris: Les Presses Universitaires de France, 1927, 131 p.
    Early study of the skeptical trend in France's works, including a primarily French-language source bibliography.

Stewart, Herbert L. *Anatole France the Parisian.* New York: Dodd, Mead & Co., 1927, 394 p.
    Early noncritical biography, focusing primarily on France's social activism.

Walton, Loring Baker. *Anatole France and the Greek World.* Durham, N.C.: Duke University Press, 1950, 334 p.
    Analysis of France's preoccupation with "*les anciennes formes de la vie.*" This well-documented study of France's Hellenic influences is less accessible to English-language readers because frequently quoted material and virtually all of the footnoted references are in French.

# Mary (Eleanor) Wilkins Freeman

## 1852-1930

(Also wrote under pseudonym of Constant Reader) American short story writer, novelist, poet, and dramatist.

Freeman was the most prolific writer of the New England local colorists and the first of that school to portray this rural environment in a realistic and unsentimental manner. At their best, her stories and novels powerfully depict the fate of individuals bound by tradition or habit to a decaying social system. The most accomplished treatment of this theme can be seen in her first two volumes of short stories, *A Humble Romance* and *A New England Nun*. Noted for their scathing portraits of New England life, the stories in these collections launched Freeman's career as a significant commentator on post-Civil War rural America.

Freeman was born in Randolph, Massachusetts. When she was fifteen her family moved to Brattleboro, Vermont, where she lived until her middle thirties. As a young woman she lived with her family, publishing children's stories and verse in various magazines. Within a seven-year period, both Freeman's sister and parents died, leaving her with only a part interest in a small business. She returned to Randolph to live with friends and continue her writing. Her short stories began appearing in such magazines as *Harper's Bazaar* and *The Boston Sunday Budget*, which published her first non-juvenile story, "A Shadow Family," in 1882. Several collections of short stories, and the novels *Jane Field*, *Pembroke*, and *Jerome, a Poor Man*, eventually established Freeman's reputation in the United States and Europe as a prominent writer of realistic local-color fiction. In the early 1890s she met Charles M. Freeman, a doctor seven years her junior, and in 1902, after a number of broken engagements, they were married. Though she continued writing, Freeman abandoned many of the concerns voiced in her early fiction and ventured into new genres, such as the ghost story, romance, and historical novel. These were never as critically or popularly successful as her New England fiction. Freeman's marriage was also unsuccessful. Charles Freeman was an alcoholic who was periodically confined to a mental institution, and Freeman herself developed an addiction to tranquilizers and sleeping medications. She obtained a legal separation from her husband prior to his death and spent her last years alone. In 1927 she became one of the first women elected to the National Institute of Arts and Letters.

"A young writer should follow the safe course of writing only about those subjects she knows thoroughly," Freeman wrote, and her best works are those that deal with life in the post-Civil War New England of her own experience. *A Humble Romance* and *A New England Nun* are considered her most typical works. The title stories of these collections, as well as "The Revolt of Mother," "A Village Singer," and "A Conflict Ended," earned Freeman critical notice as a "student of the will." In these stories, the principal characters, repressed victims of a decaying social system, assert themselves against friends, family, or society. These early stories can be classified as realistic, but Freeman's realism is not that of other local colorists, such as Sarah Orne Jewett and Harriet Beecher Stowe, who faithfully reproduced social and physical details of their

*The Bettmann Archive*

particular settings. Rather, Freeman's New England, as Larzer Ziff noted, "could be anywhere rural and neglected." Her concern was to present personality types common to New England rather than the particulars of its cultural milieu.

Freeman's first novels, *Jane Field*, *Pembroke*, and *Jerome, a Poor Man*, though generally well-received by most critics, were attacked by others for their lack of depth and substance. Many argued that while Freeman was skillful at crafting a short story around the idiosyncrasies of a leading character, this method was insufficient to sustain a novel. As Charles Miner Thompson remarked, *Jane Field* "is simply a short story of unusual length," and all of her novels are similarly episodic and disjointed. Her later forays into subjects outside her New England landscape—such as the historical novel *The Heart's Highway*, the social-problem novel *The Portion of Labor*, and the detective novel *An Alabaster Box*, coauthored with Florence Morse Kingsley—display the same weaknesses, and are further flawed by her unfamiliarity with these new genres. Thompson has called her novels "experiments" which were for the most part failures—"obviously outside the range of her abilities."

In recent years some of Freeman's short fiction, especially "The Revolt of Mother," has received renewed critical attention because of its relevance to early American feminism. Freeman's primary concern, however, was to depict individuals of either sex striving toward liberation from the repressive social conditions of the rural village in the late 1800s. Her insight into the strong and sometimes twisted personalities that could develop under these circumstances was extensive, and she portrayed these people and their times with vividness and sympathy.

(See also *Dictionary of Literary Biography, Vol. 12: American Realists and Naturalists.*)

## PRINCIPAL WORKS

*Decorative Plaques* [with George F. Barnes]   (poetry and
    verse)   1883
*A Humble Romance, and Other Stories*   (short stories)
    1887
*A New England Nun, and Other Stories*   (short stories)
    1891
*Young Lucretia, and Other Stories*   (short stories)   1892
*Giles Corey, Yeoman*   (drama)   1893
*Jane Field*   (novel)   1893
*Pembroke*   (novel)   1894
*Madelon*   (novel)   1896
*Jerome, a Poor Man*   (novel)   1897
*Silence, and Other Stories*   (short stories)   1898
*The Jamesons*   (novel)   1899
*The Heart's Highway*   (novel)   1900
*The Love of Parson Lord, and Other Stories*   (short stories)
    1900
*The Portion of Labor*   (novel)   1901
*Understudies*   (short stories)   1901
*Six Trees*   (short stories)   1903
*The Wind in the Rosebush, and Other Stories of the*
    *Supernatural*   (short stories)   1903
*The Givers*   (short stories)   1904
*The Debtor*   (novel)   1905
*By the Light of the Soul*   (novel)   1906
*The Fair Lavinia, and Others*   (short stories)   1907
*The Shoulders of Atlas*   (novel)   1908
*The Winning Lady, and Others*   (short stories)   1909
*The Butterfly House*   (novel)   1912
*The Copy-Cat, and Other Stories*   (short stories)   1914
*An Alabaster Box* [with Florence Morse Kingsley]   (novel)
    1917
*Edgewater People*   (short stories)   1918

---

### [W. D. HOWELLS]   (essay date 1887)

[Take] a number of studies like *A Humble Romance, and Other Stories,* by Miss Mary E. Wilkins, and you have the air of simple village life as liberally imparted as if all the separate little dramas were set in a single frame and related to one another. The old maids and widows aging and ailing and dying in their minute wooden houses; the forlorn elderly lovers; the simple girls and youths making and marring love; the husbands and wives growing apart and coming together; the quarrels and reconciliations; the eccentricities and the heroisms; the tender passions and true friendships; the funerals and weddings; the hates and spites; the injuries; the sacrifices; the crazy consciences; the sound common-sense—are all suggested and expressed in a measure which, we insist, does not lack breadth, though each sketch is like the sentences of Emerson, "an in-

finitely repellent particle," and will have nothing to do with any other, so far as community of action is concerned. Community of character abounds: the people are of one New England blood, and speak one racy tongue. It might all have been done otherwise; the lives and fortunes of these villagers might have been interwoven in one texture of narrative; but the work would not necessarily have gained breadth in gaining bulk. Breadth is in the treatment of material, not in the amount of it. The great picture is from the great painter, not from the extensive canvas. Miss Wilkins's work could hardly have given a wider sense of life in a Yankee village and the outlying farms if it had greater structural unity. It has unity of spirit, of point of view, of sympathy; and being what the author intended, we ask no other unity of it; many "broader" views lack this unity which is so valuable. Besides, it has humor of a quaint, flavorous sort, it has genuine pathos, and a just and true respect for the virtues of the life with which it deals. . . . What is notable in all the descriptions is the absence of literosity; they are as unrhetorical as so many pictures of Torguénief's, or Björnson's, or Verga's, and are interesting proofs of the fact that the present way of working is instinctive; one writer does not learn it from another; it is in the time, in the air, and no critic can change it. When you come to the motives of these little tales, the simplicity and originality are not always kept; sometimes they ring false, sentimental, romantic; but even then they are true in the working out of character, though this does not redeem them from the original error. For the most part, however, they are good through and through, and whoever loves the face of common humanity will find pleasure in them. They are peculiarly American, and they are peculiarly "narrow" in a certain way, and yet they are like the best modern work everywhere in their directness and simplicity. They are somewhat in the direction of Miss [Sarah Orne] Jewett's more delicate work, but the fun is opener and less demure, the literature is less refined, the poetry is a little cruder; but there is the same affectionate feeling for the material, a great apparent intimacy with the facts, and a like skill in rendering the Yankee parlance. (p. 640)

[*W. D. Howells,*] *"Editor's Study,"* in Harper's New Monthly Magazine (*copyright © 1887 by* Harper's New Monthly Magazine), *Vol. LXXV, No. CCCCXLVIII, September, 1887, pp. 638-42.**

### THE ATLANTIC MONTHLY   (essay date 1891)

[It is] the disposition of Miss Wilkins to single out for her subjects highly accented phases of New England life. In her latest collection [*A New England Nun*] Miss Wilkins has included twenty-four stories. The book is charged with tender sentiment, yet once only, so far as we remember, at the close of the moving story of Christmas Jenny, does the author introduce anything which may be likened to an artistic use of sentiment. In this story the figures of the girl and her lover make the kind of foil which we are used to in German sentimental literature. The touch here, however, is so slight as almost to escape notice. It serves chiefly to remind one how entirely Miss Wilkins depends for her effects upon the simple pathos or humor which resides in the persons and situations that are made known through a few strong, direct disclosures. The style is here the writer. The short, economical sentences, with no waste and no niggardliness, make up stories which are singularly pointed, because the writer spends her entire strength upon the production of a single impression. The compression of these stories is remarkable, and almost unique in our literature, and it is gained without any sacrifice of essentials and by no mere narrowness of aim, but by holding steadily before the mind the central, vital idea, to the exclusion of all by-thoughts, however interesting they may be. Hence it happens frequently that the reader, though left satisfied on the main issue, is piqued by the refusal of the storyteller to meet his natural curiosity on other points. (p. 847)

Miss Wilkins, with her passion for brevity, her power of packing a whole story in a phrase, a word, although she gives her characters full rein sometimes, naturally relies chiefly upon her own condensed report of persons, incidents, and things. Sententious talk, though not unknown in New England, runs the risk of being unnaturally expressive, and Miss Wilkins shows her fine artistic sense by not trusting to it for the expression of her characters. As a rule, the speech of the New England men and women in her stories is very simple and natural; her art lies in the selection she makes of what they shall say, the choice of a passage which helps on the story. Thus the brevity of speech which is in itself a characteristic of New England people is not made to carry subtleties or to have a very full intrinsic value, nor is it a mere colloquialism, designed to give color and naturalness, but it is the fit expression which conveys a great deal to the reader, because, like the entire story, it is a condensation, an epitome.

Of the genuine originality of these stories it is hard to speak too strongly. There is, indeed, a common character to the whole series, an undertone of hardship, of loss, of repressed life, of sacrifice, of the idolatry of duty, but we suspect this is due more to the prevailing spirit of New England life than to any determining force of Miss Wilkins's genius. For the most part, she brings to light some pathetic passage in a strongly marked individuality, and the variety of her characterizations is noticeable. Now and then she touches a very deep nature, and opens to view a secret of the human heart which makes us cry out that here is a poet, a seer. Such an effect is produced by the most powerful story in the book, **"Life Everlastin'."** More frequently she makes us exclaim with admiration over the novelty, yet truthfulness, of her portraitures, as in **"The Revolt of Mother"** and the story which gives the title to her book. Always there is a freedom from commonplace, and a power to hold the interest to the close which is owing, not to a trivial ingenuity, but to the spell which her personages cast over the reader's mind as soon as they come within his ken. He wonders what they will do; and if he is surprised at any conclusion, the surprise is due, not to any trick in the author, but to the unexpected issue of an original conception, which reflection always shows to be logical and reasonable.

The humor which is a marked feature of Miss Wilkins's stories is of a pungent sort. Every story has it, and it is a savor which prevents some, that otherwise would be rather painful, from oppressing the reader unduly. (pp. 847-48)

> *"New England in the Short Story," in* The Atlantic Monthly, *(copyright © 1891, by The Atlantic Monthly Company, Boston, Mass.), Vol. LXVII, No. CCCIV, June, 1891, pp. 845-50.*

## WILLIAM MORTON PAYNE (essay date 1898)

[In the photographic realism of Miss Wilkins] nature counts for little, and life for nearly everything, a life, moreover, that is pictured with touches whose delicacy suggests Jane Austen or Meissonnier. **"Jerome, a Poor Man"** is the most ambitious of Miss Wilkins's books, and its realism is not so uncompro-

mising as to refuse absolutely admission of the elements of romance. Although the hero is "a poor man," and although we are spared no detail of his grim struggle with poverty, he is allowed the good fortune of a windfall in the shape of a legacy, and his toil leads in the end to prosperity and happiness. The story of this legacy involves the one questionable point in the whole scheme of the book. As a boy, impelled by a great desire to help those who are, like himself, struggling for the means of subsistence, Jerome makes a vow that if he ever becomes possessed of any large sum of money he will distribute it indiscriminately among the poor of his township. The legacy permits fulfilment of this rash vow, and we are not sure that the author does not believe such indiscriminate charity to be desirable and really helpful to its beneficiaries. Her main object is, of course, to illustrate the effect of this conduct upon two other men, who are shamed into something like emulation of it, and to close the book in a sort of Christmas atmosphere of good will toward men. But the moral is still questionable from the standpoint of a sound sociology, and we wish that the main result might have been achieved by some other means. The heroine, appropriately named Lucina, is not a success, and we can hardly wish Jerome joy in the possession of so insipid and doll-like a creature. But men in love do not always know what is best for them, and a familiar moral is thus pointed once more. (pp. 79-80)

> *William Morton Payne, "Recent Fiction: 'Jerome, a Poor Man'," in* The Dial *(copyright, 1898 by The Dial Publishing Company, Inc.), Vol. XXIV, No. 279, February 1, 1898, pp. 79-80.*

## CHARLES MINER THOMPSON (essay date 1899)

Nearly every character in [*Pembroke*] is a monstrous example of stubbornness,—of that will which enforces its ends, however trivial, even to self-destruction. The people are not normal; they are hardly sane. Such is Miss Wilkins's village, and it is a true picture; but it wholly represents New England life no more than [a] dying apple orchard wholly represents New England scenery. (pp. 665-66)

The realist makes it his boast that he tells the truth, but he exercises as rigid a selection in incidents and characters as the most arrant romancer, and, as this novel of *Pembroke* aptly illustrates, tells a story often as far away from average truth. . . . If *Pembroke* gives a picture of New England life which is more fairly to be called incomplete than inaccurate, the reason lies in the personality of the writer and the nature of her environment, the two factors of her limitations. And so the real task is, not to find fault with her for not going outside the circle of her talent, but to measure the length of its radius, and to guess, if possible, what determined it. (p. 666)

What influence the accident of [her] environment had upon Miss Wilkins becomes plain when we consider that the best part of any story-teller's equipment lies in his store of vivid childhood memories. There is evidence that Miss Wilkins remembers the time when the electric cars did not slide, with griding trolley, through the streets of modern, prosperous Randolph. In no book of hers are there mountains such as those which stand behind and in front of Brattleboro, nor is there any broad and beautiful river perpetuating her memories of the Connecticut. The scenery—never in any case much dwelt upon—is that of a flat country, of eastern Massachusetts, of Randolph. And from Randolph, too, she got her knowledge of the trade of shoemaking as it was before the days of the factory. But the circumstance that her formative period was spent in Brattleboro, and the internal evidence of her work, otherwise than in the exceptions named, suggest, if they do not command, the conclusion that the larger part of her material was obtained there. The narrow field for the observation of life thus afforded her was still further restricted, of course, by the fact of her sex. Had she been a boy, she would have roamed the fields, gone fishing and hunting, had the privilege of sitting in the country store and listening to the talk of the men of evenings; she would have taken an interest in the local politics, and have learned to look at life as the men look at it, with the larger and more catholic view which is theirs not by virtue of greater insight, but by virtue of the undeniably larger, freer lives they are permitted to live. As she was a girl, her outlook was confined to the household; her sources of information were the tales of gossiping women, which would naturally relate mostly to the family quarrels and dissensions that are the great tragedies of their lives.

To the restriction of environment and of sex must also be added the restriction of temperament. Miss Wilkins has a keen and deep sense of humor, but it is never so keen and deep as her sense of the pathetic, and when a scene or a situation is in quarrel between them, her sense of humor is sure to come lamely off. The most distinctly humorous of her stories, and also one of her best and best known, is **"The Revolt of Mother."** In this, a situation which in the hands of a writer more exclusively humorous would be laughable becomes in hers one over which it seems heartless to smile, so clearly is its underlying pathos revealed. Without burdening too much the weary back of heredity we may recall her witch-persecuting Puritan ancestors in Salem, and, remembering Hawthorne's similar ancestry, say to ourselves that she was probably a serious, imaginative child, with a faculty for brooding over questions of conduct, who could be expected to feel the pathos in the humorous stories, and deeply to relish the grim and tragic ones. (p. 668)

Is it any wonder that such a mind, working on such material, should have produced as its first work such stories as compose the volume entitled *A Humble Romance*? (p. 669)

[This book] came with the force of a new revelation of New England to itself. The literary merit of the stories was remarkable. The short, terse sentences, written in the simplest, homeliest words, had a biting force. Its skillfully lavish use of homely detail, always accurate, always significant, gave it an astonishing reality. The paragraphs were as simple and direct as the sentences, and each advanced the story swiftly and easily upon its predestined course. There was no wavering from the direct line, there were no stumbling-blocks of impertinent description or incident, no superfluities even. There was no annoying striving after elegance of diction, no self-conscious attempt at cleverness of phrase or an artistic manner. Everywhere was the sharp definiteness of the writer who sees clearly. Everywhere was the unconsciousness of an absorbed artist, not preoccupied with theories of art, with personal vanities, with fear of the critics or anxiety to please the public, but dominated by the one idea of setting down accurately the definite vision which her imagination had conceived and matured, and which now of necessity must be born. The stories had, furthermore, a certain rare quality which always gives strength to fiction. It is the air on the part of the author of being exterior to his story and irresponsible for it, of seeming to say, "I do not explain, I do not justify, I find no fault, I neither laugh over them nor grieve; these events are not of my invention,—they happened. I report them, and allege nothing about them except

that they are true." It is this quality, as much as any, which gives a peculiar impressiveness to the tales of Guy de Maupassant. So far as method is concerned, his story called in its English version *A Bit of String* might have been written by Miss Wilkins.

A good literary style is always more or less of a miracle. It cannot be acquired by industry, it cannot be taught in the schools. Like any other aptitude of the mind it may be trained and perfected, but it is essentially a gift of nature. A gift of nature, then, we must call Miss Wilkins's style. . . . But excellent as in many respects the style of this first book was, it yet had numerous and serious blemishes. Although direct references to bygone writers and now and then the use of a word in an obsolete sense showed Miss Wilkins to be acquainted with literature of a good sort, her style was deficient in grace, in music, as if written by one whose ear is untrained by any attentive listening to the rich harmonies of old prose. And it was deficient also in correctness and in elegance: it was to some degree an uneducated and uncultured style. . . . Miss Wilkins, as a writer, belongs to the noble army of the self-made. These defects of form show how much, in the beginning, she was hampered by the lack of a liberal education in literature, just as the limitations of substance show how much she is hampered by the lack of a liberal education in life. . . . The romancer, the poet, the philosopher, may live and die in his own library and yet write well, but the novelist who reports men in their habit as they lived must write of the life he knows. And as Miss Wilkins is such a writer, the limitations of her environment determine the scope of her work, and they are unfortunately great. If we keep them in mind, the fact is not surprising that of the twenty-eight stories in *A Humble Romance* every one is told from the point of view of some woman,— and that there are very few which do not deal with one of those family or neighborhood quarrels which have been referred to as the staple of the women's gossip in small country towns. The book is, in fact, a collection of twenty-eight special cases of unhappiness among a peculiarly isolated and small-minded class of countrywomen. Their mental attitude is caught with astonishing precision, but by this very success the stories gain an atmosphere at once narrow and mean. They are saved from being unpleasant by their undeniable pathos, and by being so thoroughly human, if petty, as readily to excite sympathy. As the author may not be asked to spoil her effect by labeling her incidents special cases, it becomes easy to see how distorted and untruthful an impression of New England life—an impression all the more untruthful in the general because so accurate in the particular—she would succeed unconsciously in conveying. (pp. 669-70)

I confess that in considering Miss Wilkins's work I ask myself again and again, with a never failing and perhaps impertinent curiosity, what circumstances in her life could so have revealed to her and impressed upon her imagination the awful power for evil of a perverted will. But her favorable environment and Puritan ancestry make it easy to understand how the problem of the will, once it had attracted her attention, should appeal with extraordinary force to one of her analytic, brooding, somewhat sombre temperament, and how it should seem to be laid upon her, as with a heavy hand, to embody her impressions in dramatic form. The dramatic value of unreasonable stubbornness is her own personal discovery, the particular thing which gives her work psychological interest and distinction. I know of no writer who has treated it so persistently, so variously, who has seemed so infatuated with it. In no study of New England character—in the form either of history or of fiction—has the native strength of will been made so prominent. Consciously or unconsciously, she has seized upon it and set it forth as the keystone of New England character. It is not the exclusive possession of New England people, of course; but that it is in a marked degree characteristic no one can doubt. The stubborn Puritan came to no relaxing land, but to one from which only dogged perseverance could wring a living, and so it is not strange if his descendants have acquired a character which may be described as granitic. . . . It is easy to understand the success of a book which reproduces with a great wealth of accurate and homely detail a life which is still close to the richest and most cultivated of us, and which is of the very fibre of our thought and character,—a book which, in a land where women are the larger portion of the reading public, is written exclusively from the feminine point of view; but I choose to think that it was mainly the insistence upon a fine basic quality of New England character which made *A Humble Romance* come with all the force of a new revelation of New England to itself.

This long examination of *A Humble Romance* would be disproportionate were not this first book, and its succeeding sister volume, *A New England Nun,* in a way a brief memorandum of Miss Wilkins's entire message to the world, which her later work, for the most part, only serves to amplify and make clear. When one begins to read the novels, the short stories assume almost the aspect of preliminary sketches of their scenes and episodes, for they are similar not only in substance, but in method. Those cogent reasons which publishers urge, reinforced by the ambition which every writer of fiction feels to try his hand in the most important form of his art, made it inevitable that, sooner or later, Miss Wilkins should write novels. But, natural as it was, it is none the less regrettable. For years she studied the shorter form and wrote in it,—years which necessarily left their indelible impress upon her talent. . . . Miss Wilkins, whose earliest and longest training has been in the short story, thinks in the length of the short story. Her novels, with the apparent exception of *Jane Field,* which is simply a short story of unusual extent, have the air of a chronological series of short stories about the same people. She has never been able to see the larger proportions of the novel in their proper perspective. Moreover, in writing short stories she taught herself, with a thoroughness the results of which she will never be able wholly to overcome, a genuine mastery of the short, terse sentence. (pp. 671-72)

Mastery in the methods of the short story, and a fixed habit of writing in short sentences, are not the most useful qualifications to bring to the task of writing novels. Many lessons of technique have to be laboriously unlearned by the writer thus trained when he attempts the new and ampler form. That Miss Wilkins has succeeded in overcoming the results of her earliest training in any measure is due, no doubt, to the artistic restlessness which is one of her most marked characteristics. She has written for children; she has written society verses; she wrote little prose poems in the day, fortunately brief, when they were popular under the absurd name of "etchings" or "pastels in prose"; she has tried her hand more than once at the drama, as *Giles Corey, Yeoman,* remains to witness; she has written a detective story; she has tried historical fiction; and she has composed romances not only of the kind in which passionate love is the theme, but also of the kind in which, as in Hawthorne, idealistic beauty is the end. Some of these experiments have been so obviously outside the range of her abilities that those who have watched her progress with a loving solicitude—and these are not a few—have trembled for her

future. But whether partial failures or full successes, they showed artistic health, a talent curious about itself and ambitious to miss no possible development, a commendable desire to find out for itself its own strength and its own limitations. And these experiments have served their useful purpose in developing both her talent and her style.

As a result of her practice in so many varieties of composition, she has advanced much in her understanding of the form of the novel; but it has had its chief effect, naturally enough, upon her style. In the art of constructing sentences she has made really remarkable gain. Those who are interested in style simply as style will find much to reward their curiosity in tracing her progress from the direct bald statements of her earliest manner through the florid sentences of *Madelon* and the long loose ones of *Jerome* to the really excellent prose style which she at last attains in "**Evelina's Garden,**" a story in her latest work, *Silence.* But the point here is that the practice which gave her talent its direction was not of the kind to fit her for the writing of novels. She made herself a specialist in the beginning, and, like all specialists, made her irretrievable sacrifice of possibilities of development.

In the novels, as in the short stories, the will is still the theme. Willfulness, of a good or bad kind, is still the predominating characteristic of the people, from stern Jane Field, whose sense of justice and whose self-confident determination to judge moral questions for herself lead her stubbornly to pursue the path of crime, to haughty Jerome, ready to sacrifice everything good and sweet in life upon the altar of his own inordinate, willful pride. But *Pembroke*—her first real novel, and to my mind unquestionably the best—contains the most complete summary of her observations upon the stubbornness of the New England character. Its plot . . . shows clearly enough why it should be, in an artistic sense, her most successful novel. The scene and the characters are those which she knows in every detail of their interior and exterior life; its psychological problems are those which have most interested her, and upon which she has thought most deeply and persistently. The novel is great by its fidelity to life, by its dignity of theme, and by its social significance. On the other hand, it has the expected and unavoidable defects. The first impulse of the reader is to dispute the assumption that such a community as Pembroke ever existed; but on reflection he will admit that although it may not actually exist, it could be easily assembled, and that the exaggeration of which it is indubitably guilty is due to a legitimate selection, for the purpose of artistic emphasis, of circumstances unusual in combination, but in themselves and separately usual enough. Then, being the study of an entire community, it lacks any broad central current of interest. The reader is lost in a multitude of details, episodes, and characters, out of which he emerges rather with a sense of the undesirableness of an uncontrollable will than with any definite idea of one or two supremely interesting characters or of a connected chain of events. The sense of confusion inevitable in a study of a community is increased by the writer's inability, already noted, not to deal with separate episodes as if they were short stories. It is owing to this lack of homogeneity, partly necessary, partly due to want of skill, that what one remembers about the novel are particular pages and passages of great beauty and strength. Many people would refer to *Pembroke,* I think, as the novel which contained—let us say for example—that capital description of the boy Ephraim's solitary, joyous coasting, pages remarkable for their rich blending of humor and pathos.

In two important technical respects *Jerome* is a better novel than *Pembroke;* for it has a strong central interest in the personality of its hero which binds its many short-story-like episodes together, and its style, in Miss Wilkins's later acquired manner of flowing sentences pleasantly varied in cadence and in length, makes it much more easily readable. Jerome himself, however, is a most unsympathetic person. The reader cannot help feeling a growing impatience with this wrong-headed young man, who, in a way repugnant to all common sense, insists upon taking the very roughest and hardest road to the success for which his strength of character plainly destines him. Besides, the plot, slight and weak at best, shocks one's sense of average probabilities. But worse than all, Miss Wilkins departs from that fine impartiality of the disinterested observer, which gives such force to her short stories and to *Pembroke,* and becomes a preacher and a sentimentalist. The book is written to insinuate an accusation against the present social system. . . . [It] is redeemed, however, by many excellent pages of narrative, description, and character drawing, in which Miss Wilkins reaches as high levels of artistic achievement as she has ever attained. Although not the strongest of her novels, it is easily the most readable. (pp. 672-74)

A plausible argument could indeed be made to show that the best realists are idealists at heart, whose very sensitiveness has made them more ready than the average person to perceive ugly realities, and who have consciously or unconsciously tried to rouse sluggish humanity to endeavor by unsparing pictures of the petty and the mean and the ignoble in human life. Were such an argument to be made Miss Wilkins would furnish a telling example; for back of all her work is the idea, the sense of the mystery of human life, the question, "Why is this?" and she gently pushes selected incidents and characters before you, as if filled with the desire to learn, from any one who knows, the meaning of these problems,—clues doubtless, each one in its degree, to the answer to the Great Problem. Her preoccupation with the mystery of life shows itself in little ways,—in the sense which some persons have of the unreality of her people; in her indifference to scenery, which she may well consider as of small moment in comparison with human beings; in her indifference to accuracy in antiquarian detail as compared with artistic truth. Behind all her work one feels that he encounters the questioning eyes of an idealist. Although she is ranked in the popular judgment as a realist, there is in her work the purest vein of romance and ideality, and even a certain touch of mysticism and allegory, which allies her, however distantly, to the literary family of Hawthorne. These qualities may be noticed even in her early short stories, and in *Pembroke* their presence, in spite of their bungling and mechanical expression here, is to be perceived in the physical deformity which seems to accompany Barney Thayer's deformity of character. They show themselves most conspicuously, if not most agreeably, however, in *Madelon.* Like her other volumes in describing the fortunes of people of various kinds and degrees of stubbornness, it is unlike them in having romantic love for its theme, and in presenting as one of its principal characters, Lot Gordon, a man in whom mysticism and ideality are unexpectedly the most notable qualities. They show themselves most charmingly in "**Evelina's Garden,**" a little tale which is a gem of its kind, and which shows that Miss Wilkins can command at least a hesitating comparison to the author of the most beautiful American romances. It is to be hoped that she will cast aside in favor of this kind of work the tales of antiquarian interest, such as "**Silence**" itself, which ought to be moving but is not, and "**The Little Maid at the Door.**" She does not breathe freely in the musty atmosphere of colonial history. Her Puritans, with their stilted speech, are uncommonly tiresome.

How is such a writer to be classified? I think she cannot be classified at all. A modest and conscientious artist, unfortunately limited by an imperfect education in books, and by an equally imperfect experience of life; who has cultivated her great natural gift for expression to the best of her opportunities and ability, and used it to set forth as vividly as possible such few of the multitudinous aspects of life as her temperament and environment have permitted her to see,—that is Miss Wilkins. Only writers of mediocre ability—natural imitators—can be put in a class and accurately labeled. A really original writer, like Miss Wilkins, no matter how limited, is *sui generis.* She can be described, she cannot be classified. But if she must have her tag, the most nearly satisfactory will be that which declares her an idealist masquerading in the soiled and ragged cloak of realism. (pp. 674-75)

> *Charles Miner Thompson, "Miss Wilkins: An Idealist in Masquerade," in* The Atlantic Monthly *(copyright © 1899, by The Atlantic Monthly Company, Boston, Mass.; reprinted with permission), Vol. LXXXIII, No. CCCCXCIX, May, 1899, pp. 665-75.*

**MARY E. WILKINS FREEMAN**   (essay date 1917)

It occurs to me that I have never read a severe criticism of an author's own work by the author, and that it may be an innovation. I am therefore proceeding to criticize the story by which I consider myself lamentably best known, and that is "**The Revolt of Mother.**" It was in an evil day I wrote that tale. It exposed me to much of which I could not dream. This very morning I have a letter concerning that story. Somebody wishes to use it in a book. I fear I am mostly known by "**The Revolt of Mother.**" My revolt against the case is perfectly useless. People go right on with almost Prussian dogmatism, insisting that "**The Revolt of Mother**" is my one and only work. It is most emphatically not. Were I not so truthful, having been born so near Plymouth Rock, I would deny I ever wrote that story. I would foist it upon somebody else. It would leave me with a sense of freedom I have not known since that woman moved into her husband's barn in print.

In the first place all fiction ought to be true, and "**The Revolt of Mother**" is not in the least true. When I wrote that little tale I threw my New England traditions to the winds and trampled on my New England conscience. Well, I have had and still have retribution. It is not a good thing to produce fiction which is not true, although that sounds paradoxical. The back bone of the best fiction is essential truth, and "**The Revolt of Mother**" is perfectly spineless. I know it, because I am of New England and have lived there. I had written many true things about that cluster of stainless states and for a change I lied.

Sometimes incessant truth gets on one's nerves. It did on mine. There never was in New England a woman like Mother. If there had been she most certainly would not have moved into the palatial barn which her husband had erected next the mean little cottage she had occupied during her married life. She simply would have lacked the nerve. She would also have lacked the imagination. . . . If Mother had lived all those years in that little cottage she would have continued to live there. Moving into the new barn would have been a cataclysm. New England women seldom bring cataclysms about their shoulders. (pp. 25, 75)

It is a dreadful confession, but that woman called "Mother" in "**The Revolt of Mother**" is impossible. I sacrificed truth when I wrote the story, and at this day I do not know exactly what my price was. I am inclined to think gold of the realm. It could not have been fame of the sort I have gained by it. If so I have had my punishment. Not a story since but somebody asks ''Why not another **'Revolt of Mother'?''** My literary career has been halted by the success of the big fib in that story. Too late I admit it. The harm is done. But I can at least warn other writers. When you write a short story stick to the truth. If there is not a story in the truth knit until truth happens which does contain a story. Knit, if you can do no better at that than I, who drop more stitches than any airplane in Europe can drop bombs. You can at least pull out the knitting, but a story printed and rampant is a dreadful thing, never to be undone. (p. 75)

> *Mary E. Wilkins Freeman, ''Who's Who—and Why: Mary E. Wilkins Freeman, an Autobiography,'' in* The Saturday Evening Post *(reprinted from The Saturday Evening Post © 1917, copyright renewed © 1945, The Curtis Publishing Company), Vol. 190, No. 23, December 8, 1917, pp. 25, 75.*

## FRED LEWIS PATTEE (essay date 1920)

[It is] the short stories of her earlier collections, *A Humble Romance* and *A New England Nun,* with *Pembroke* which followed, that will give [Miss Wilkins] her final place among American writers. In these we have her first spontaneous work, work that is hers alone and that has furnished a short story type which no one may imitate without detection any more than one may imitate the work of Irving or of Poe. This element of originality is the first that must be considered by the critic. We of a later day, to whom the manner has become familiar, do not realize how startlingly novel these tales appeared to their first readers. . . . The first surprise at the work of Miss Wilkins came from her method, her peculiar perspective, her style, her startling originality. She appeared suddenly, almost without forebears; seemingly she had been influenced by no one. (p. xix)

This independence accounts for many crudities in her earlier work, and it accounts also for most of those elements in her short stories that have given her the place that is hers. She was herself and no one else. Her short-sentence structure is a part of her personal equation; it is her literary length of stride. When she attempts more elaborate structure she becomes self-conscious and unconvincing. All her efforts in her novels to gain a more flowing style have been unable to give her the long-sentence habit. . . . [Miss Wilkins] presents her material intensely with no more thought of ornamentation than had her Puritan ancestors when they poured out their burning convictions of sin and salvation. Everywhere repression. The dialogue moves swiftly without explanation; every coloring adjective is primly removed.

The center of her art, the beginning and the end of it, is humanity, the individual soul. She plunges at once *in medias res,* usually with the name of her leading character. Her backgrounds are incidental. There is as little description in her best stories as there is in an old ballad. Swiftly she introduces her two or three or four characters, they reveal themselves by means of dialogue, they become often fearfully alive, they grip at the heart or the throat, and then suddenly with a throb the story is done, like a ballad. Unlike Bret Harte or Miss Murfree or Hardy, with whom the physical landscape is often one of the characters in the tale, she so strips her narratives of background that they become universal in their atmosphere and setting. The grim story **''Louisa''** might be a translation from the Russian; **''A Village Lear''** might be passed as a story of Egdon Heath. The most of her stories are localized only by the fact that her characters are such as are found solely within the confines of the old New England Puritanism. Her chief use of landscape, as has been suggested, is Hawthornesque—the use of it symbolically, poetically, as an interpreting or contrasting touch in her human tragedy or comedy. (pp. xx-xxi)

This intensity, repressed with New England severity, is the only style that could fitly treat the material that her conscience and her stern sense of truth furnished her—the only material that she knew. Her characters are like plants that have sprung up from a sterile soil. As subjects for fiction in the older interpretation of fiction they seem impossible. . . . In the stories of Miss Wilkins even the children are victims: little Anna Eliza finally confesses to her grandmother that she lost her patchwork on purpose; little Patience, after a heroic struggle with herself, braves the terrors of the old Squire's presence and gives him back the sixpence prize he had awarded the best scholar in the school, because at the critical moment some one had whispered to her the answer to his question. In these tales we see not the New England of Mrs. Stowe, the New England of the high tide period, nor that of Miss Jewett, the New England of the transition: it is the picture of the swift decline and the final wreckage, the distorted fragments of what once had been glorious. It is the fifth act of the Puritan drama. A half-century before the minister would have been the central figure of a New England village picture; in *A New England Nun* there are only four ministers mentioned, all of them minor figures, spineless and effeminate. (pp. xxi-xxii)

[Miss Wilkins] stands external to her material and seemingly she is irresponsible for it. She makes no comment; her characters seemingly are alone responsible for the story—they develop themselves. It is the art of the old ballad which was anonymous; the subjective is absent. (p. xxiii)

Only in parts and passages is her work of *Spoon River Anthology* texture. In soul she is a romanticist and a poet. Even in her most depressing material there is little of realism in the Zola sense of the term. Her New England critics declare that her vision, so far as at least New England character is concerned, is astigmatic; that she has given caricatures rather than realistic studies from the life. They are wrong and they are right. In reality, her characters are of the Dickens type, not photographs but paintings, idealizations of the truth, individuals intensely alive, yet drawn not from the life, but from the heightened images projected by their creator's imagination. They are therefore, in reality, like the characters of Dickens, mythological creations. Their author, a nunlike soul who has lived her whole life like an Emily Brontë in the seclusion of a little village, frail of body and delicate of health, over-imaginative, poetic, intense, creates in the quiet of her study her own world. . . . How far unconsciously she has written autobiography we may never know, and yet we know this, that the writer of fiction which is at all worth our study can have no secrets, and that inevitably he spins his web from his own heart. One need say no more. Her characters mostly are unmarried women. Of the central figures in the twenty-four stories of *A New England Nun* nineteen are unmarried females and all but five of them are past middle age. Or, to go still wider, there are in the book, leaving out merely incidental personages, sixty-seven characters, all but sixteen of whom are women, just half of them unmarried.

With such material there are infinite possibilities for depressed realism, and yet seldom are we sent away depressed. Almost all her stories, and some of them against the very protest of nature, end happily. The lover returns, the hapless maiden, pathetically patient through years of waiting, is married at last; justice is done and all is well. . . .

Her favorite theme is revolt. Her tale opens with a study of repression. The central figure is bound by inherited forces which hold him as with steel. Sometimes the force is external, as in the case of Mrs. Penn in **"The Revolt of 'Mother,'"** but more often is it internal. On the surface of the life there is apparent serenity and reserve, but beneath there is an increasing fire. Then suddenly the barriers break and the strength of the recoil is in proportion to the strength of the repression. (pp. xxiii–xxiv)

She does not present her material merely to entertain. In all her stories there is far more than the story. **"The Revolt of 'Mother,'"** for instance, might furnish a thesis on the homes of farmers, and yet no one may call it a purpose story. There are times when the preacher that is within every descendant of New-Englanders gets the better of the artist, but it is not often. . . . Never does she present unlovely pictures simply to display them. Kipling's robust cynicism is in a world apart from hers. She thinks well of life; she hates oppression with her whole New England soul, and she sends her reader away always more kindly of heart, more tolerant, more neighborly, in the deeper sense of the word.

Her kinship is with Hawthorne rather than with the realists. Both worked in the darker materials of New England Puritanism; both were romancers and poets, both were seekers after truth, and both were able to throw over their work a subtle atmosphere that was all their own. Hawthorne, writing as he did in the mid-nineteenth century, in the mild noon of later German romance, suffused his work with the rich glow that the later writer, bound by her more prosaic times, was unable to find; she, however, equal to him in her command of pathos and of emotional intensity, was able to surpass him in her command of gripping situation and her powers of compelling characterization. Of the generation born since the war she alone may be compared with this earliest depicter of the New England soul. (pp. xxv–xxvi)

> *Fred Lewis Pattee, "Introduction" (copyright 1920 by Harper & Row, Publishers, Inc.; renewed 1947 by Fred Lewis Pattee; reprinted by permission of Harper & Row, Publishers, Inc.), in* A New England Nun, and Other Stories *by Mary E. Wilkins Freeman, Harper & Brothers, 1920, pp. vii–xxvi.*

## ARTHUR MACHEN   (essay date 1923)

[*Machen presents the whole of* Hieroglyphics, *from which this excerpt is taken, as an attempt to reproduce the critical discourses of an anonymous "literary hermit."*]

[Miss Wilkins's tales] are all pervaded and filled with an emotion which I can hardly think that the writer has realised. Well, I find it difficult to express exactly what I mean, but I think that the whole impression which one receives from these tales is one of loneliness, of isolation. Compare Miss Wilkins with Jane Austen, the New England stories with *Pride and Prejudice.* You might imagine, at first, that in one case as in the other there is a sense of retirement, of separation from the world, that Miss Austen's heroines are as remote from the great streams and whirlpools of life as any Jane Field or Charlotte of Massachusetts. But in reality this is not so. The people in the English novels are in no sense remote; they are merely

dull. . . . "Remoteness" is an affection of the soul, and wicker-figures, dressed up in the clothes of a period, cannot have any such affections predicated of them; and consequently though Emma or Elizabeth may appear very quaint to us from the contrast between the manners of this century and the last, they cannot be remote. But that does seem to me the quality of those books of Miss Wilkins's; the people appear to be very far off from the world, to live in an isolated sphere, and each one lives his own life, and dwells apart with his own soul, and in spite of all the trivial chatter and circumstance of the village one feels that each is a human being moved by eminently human affections. (pp. 153–54)

I claimed, I think, literary merit for Miss Wilkins because her books give out an impression of loneliness. (pp. 157–58)

So this is my plea for Miss Wilkins. I think that . . . she has painted a society, indeed, but a society in which each man stands apart, responsible only for himself and to himself, conscious only of himself and his God. You will note this, if you read her carefully, you will see how this doctrine of awful, individual loneliness prevails so far that it is carried into the necessary and ordinary transactions of social life, often with results that are very absurd. Many of the people in her stories are so absolutely convinced of their "loneliness," so certain that there are only two persons in the whole universe—each man and his God—that they do not shrink from transgressing and flouting all the social orders and regulations, in spite of their very strong and social instinct drawing them in the opposite direction. You remember the man who vowed that under certain circumstances he would sit on the meeting-house steps every Sunday? He kept his vow—for ten years, I think—and he kept it in spite of his profound horror of ridicule, of doing what other people didn't do, in spite of his own happiness; but he kept it because he realised his "loneliness," because he saw quite clearly that he must stand or fall by his own word and his own promise, and that the opinions of others could be of no possible importance to him. The instance is ludicrous, even to the verge of farce, and yet I call it a witness to the everlasting truth that, at last, each man must stand or fall alone, and that if he would stand, he must, to a certain extent, live alone with his own soul. It is from this mood of lonely reverie and ecstasy that literature proceeds, and I think that the sense of all this is diffused throughout Miss Wilkins's New England stories. (pp. 159–60)

> *Arthur Machen, in his* Hieroglyphics: A Note upon Ecstasy in Literature, *Alfred A. Knopf, 1923, 166 p.*\*

## F. O. MATTHIESSEN   (essay date 1931)

Miss Wilkins was not shaped by any previous writer. In fact she would not read anything which she thought might influence her. She had not even read Miss Jewett. But whether she was conscious of it or not, her view of the New England temperament was very like Mrs. Stowe's. Yet there is this significant difference. Mrs. Stowe saw that the tragedy of New England lay in the relentless wrestling of the mind against the forces of evil. The abnormal struggle of the conscience cast a shadow across the lives of nearly every one who grew up here, the shadow in which Hawthorne dwelt and which formed the very substance of his romances. Miss Wilkins does not portray this struggle, but the result of generations of such a struggle. Her characters do not brood much upon the mysteries of sin and death, but the pattern of existence into which they are born has been warped and twisted by all the intense introspection of their ancestors. Mrs. Stowe thought of New England as the region which had cradled the destinies of America; Miss Wilkins simply sees the implications of life in a country town from which the high tide of achievement has long since fallen away.

Her vision is uncompromising; her extraordinary power comes from the unflinching directness with which she sets down even the harshest facts. Unlike Miss Jewett she is never the detached spectator watching what is going on about her; she and her characters are one. She can present all the essential elements of a situation in a few blinding sentences the very blunt and awkward shortness of which intimates the kind of life she is creating. Her power of catching the actual cadences of speech is equally great; she conveys the baffled groping for words that resorts to well-worn idioms, the stupid reiteration of phrases which reveal a man's efforts to hide a sudden emotion or the cumbersome processes of his slow mind in reaching an unexpected meaning. The parts of her stories one remembers are these flashes of illumination: Deborah Thayer's discovery of her daughter's pregnancy while she is making her try on a new dress; the pathetic spectacle of old Polly Moss trying to play ball with the children . . . ; the sinister impression of the almshouse in the glimpse of a door flying open and a little figure running down the corridor. . . . (pp. 405-06)

Mary Wilkins is unsurpassed among all American writers in her ability to give the breathless intensity of a moment. She does not build up to it laboriously. She rarely even uses the word which the situation carries to the reader. (p. 406)

The readers of the eighties and nineties often found Miss Wilkins morbid and depressing. They asserted that her view of the New England nature was one-sided and distorted, that the people she drew were not typical but mere exaggerations. In one limited sense they were right. The sharply unexpected sentences with which she often ends her stories, as when she makes Candace Whitcomb, the village singer, ask her rival to sing for her as she lies on her death bed, and then gasp with almost her final breath: ''You flatted a little on—soul''; the angularities and eccentricities of her characters sometimes remind us that she was working in the prevailing mode of the local colorists, which was the mode of Dickens and caricature. But such defects are on the surface. Mary Wilkins possessed what few of her contemporaries seem to have been able to understand, a deeply rooted feeling that life was a tragedy. She herself never fully explored the implications of this feeling; she never achieved a complete expression of it in any of her stories. (pp. 407-08)

Actually the effect of Miss Wilkins's work is rarely depressing. The qualities that she emphasizes are to be seen in Delia Caldwell, the very characteristic heroine of *A Conquest of Humility.* Her tall, full figure stood like a young pine tree as if she contained all the necessary elements of support within herself. She would have been handsome except for her thick and dull complexion; there was a kind of stiff majesty in her attitude; she had the air of being one who could accomplish great things but might grind little ones to pieces. . . . She faces the world so unquiveringly that her mother finds her unnatural, but Delia Caldwell contains within herself a strange poise unknown to weaker natures. She is sustained by her self-respect.

Similar courage supports a great many of Miss Wilkins's characters, the courage that is born of loneliness. The struggle of the heart to live by its own strength alone is her constant theme, and the sudden revolt of a spirit that will endure no more from circumstance provides her most stirring dramas. Sometimes

the revolt is violent, as when old woman Magoun feeds her granddaughter deadly nightshade rather than let her fall into the hands of her debauched father. More frequently it is gently pathetic. In a great many instances it gains a happy end, for beneath the surface of her realistic detail Miss Wilkins is burningly romantic: the girl manages by sheer force of will to support herself and avoid a man she does not love, or the lover returns from the West after many years to marry the old maid. Mary Wilkins knows that the solitary spirit ends in defeat. . . . (pp. 408-09)

It is staggering to realize that after her first two collections of stories, [*A Humble Romance* and *A New England Nun*] . . . , Mary Wilkins printed more than thirty-five volumes. She wrote novels, a detective story about the Borden murder, serials, a play, and sketches of New Jersey where she lived after her marriage in 1902. None of her later work has anything like the strength that I have been describing. It is commonplace, frequently sentimental, and lacking in any positive virtues of style. It makes her remark that she did not want to be a writer at all ring in one's ears. In retrospect it now appears that she told all she knew about life in those first stories. As stories they were frequently clumsy and stiff, fitted to a fairly ordinary pattern, owing their effect to single passages rather than to the shaping of the whole. She was not naturally an artist. She had the one great gift of poignant intensity, and a determination to face the truth. (p. 409)

> *F. O. Matthiessen, ''New England Stories,'' in* American Writers on American Literature, *edited by John Macy (reprinted by permission of Liveright Publishing Corporation; copyright 1931 by Liveright Publishing Corporation; copyright renewed © 1959 by Liveright Publishing Corporation), Liveright, 1931, pp. 399-413.*\*

**BABETTE MAY LEVY** (essay date 1946)

Harriet Beecher Stowe, Rose Terry Cooke, Sarah Orne Jewett, Mary E. Wilkins Freeman—their rhythmic names bring to mind a picture of New England and a type of gentle story. These women wrote hundreds of studies of New England life. Mrs. Freeman alone produced over two hundred shorter tales as well as twelve novels and, although her predecessors and fellow-authors did not approach this fertility, their contributions are not meager. (p. 338)

[During the 1880s and 1890s, Mrs. Freeman] wrote what are usually considered her most sensitive studies of New England life. The world she portrayed consists of a number of extremely unpleasant older people, some in poorhouses, some still making life miserable for their relatives; a great many middle-aged women, a few of them married to somewhat nebulous husbands, more of them widowed or single; some—but not too many—attractive young women in their twenties, most of them on the verge of ''a decline'' because of a misunderstanding with their wooers; and a few exceptionally beautiful yellow-haired girl-children, always being sent alone on long errands or trips so that they can be temporarily lost. No one in a Freeman story reads or has any intellectual interests; no one goes to church for any other reason than that to do so is a respectable Sunday habit. With one notable exception, these people live in small towns or even more rural neighborhoods. *The Portion of Labor* . . . has its setting in a factory town, and the population boasts its normal masculine complement. Mrs. Freeman always shows a slightly class-conscious New England, although this usually is not a dominant theme in her tales. In this one novel the newer aspects of the class-struggle, labor versus capital, unions versus paternalistic owners, stand out clearly; especially sad is the fate of the over-aged worker. For Mrs. Freeman, however, the difference between the upper and lower classes is mostly a matter of the freedom they allow themselves in expressing their emotions: better-bred men and women conceal their feelings and desires, the untutored are not ashamed to show theirs; in particular, the women are not embarrassed at being caught in an obvious struggle to get married.

Mrs. Freeman, fearful of losing her characteristic touch, refused to read the work of other local colorists, and it should be noted that, in contrast to other delineations, her version of New England is curiously lacking in restraint. Conservative, much-enduring women suffer endless trials with a patience that would amaze Job; suddenly they rebel and take matters into their own hands. Only once does an abrupt insurrection of this sort fail. Poor Jane Field, maddened by the thought of her young daughter's dying of consumption for lack of a little money, thinks she can administer justice better than her God apparently was doing. Her agony of mind after she has cheated in getting what is rightfully hers, is most convincing evidence of the survival of this Puritan conscience. But most of Mrs. Freeman's heroines, with lesser goals at stake than the pathetic Mrs. Field's, are saved by good old New England ''faculty''— and by this time ''faculty'' included not a little determination and stubbornness. . . . Gifts, incidentally, play a large part in many of Mrs. Freeman's stories. Her Yankees are thrifty to penuriousness, but never have such gifts been dispensed so freely. This generosity ranges from the presentation of splendid rag-dolls to the quiet handing over of less attractive lovers; one man, in a really moving tale, has so strongly the desire to give that he finally gives as his last gift his honesty. Diligent and poverty-stricken women who sew and crochet half the year to make their Christmas gifts, bestow the results of this labor on everyone with whom they have the slightest acquaintance. One well-to-do city man celebrates the Yule season by giving eight hundred and forty chess sets to his friends. Similar extremes may be seen in the diets of Mrs. Freeman's characters. Never did women require less for their polite, frugal repasts—a dish of rhubarb, a cup of custard, a bit of quince preserve are the heartiest additions to the lean fare. [In **"The Love of Parson Lord,"**] Parson Lord and his daughter dine regularly on a brown loaf, a pitcher of milk, and tea made of sage leaves. On the other hand, when the good man realizes that a growing girl might like a different menu, he provides oranges and pineapples, plump partridges and quail. And what feasts there are at Thanksgiving family gatherings, quilting parties and picnics! Then everyone has his fill of ''pinky'' hams and roasted chickens, of rich pound and chocolate cakes, of whipped-cream, mince, and cranberry pies, and of dozens of other delectables.

There is a naïve, not too convincing air about all this rebellion of the weak, this prodigal exchange of gifts among the habitually parsimonious, this lavish feasting of the hungry. Nevertheless, many of Mrs. Freeman's woman characters possess an innate dignity of soul that compels admiration. . . . Nor are these New England women stupid; largely unschooled they may be, but they possess the type of homely wit that enables one of them to say, quite casually:

> I dun' no' of anything that gets cold any quicker
> than lamb broth, unless it's love.

When there is nothing else to admire in Mrs. Freeman's characters, their very resoluteness of purpose may compel sympathy. Typical is the fiercely proud Mrs. Edwards, a painfully convincing character in an otherwise fantastic tale called *Jerome;* confined to her rocking-chair, she becomes more and more twisted in mind as poverty conquers her. But if no one can like Mrs. Edwards, no one, meeting her in life or in fiction, can forget her or blame her for her unpleasant failings. (pp. 353-56)

Both Mrs. Stowe and Miss Jewett saw isolation as intensifying much that was typical of New England; but for Mary E. Wilkins Freeman it was New England's besetting sin of pride that led to isolation, both physical and spiritual. In this theory, Mrs. Freeman turned back to the oldest explanation of all: New England's ministers since the first settlement in the New World had been telling their congregations that their sin lay in their pride—an accusation, indeed, that all preachers in all ages and all places have been inclined to stress. Except for the moving story *Jane Field,* Mrs. Freeman largely, and somewhat strangely, ignored the religious implications of self-pride as the source of all evil inasmuch as it turns man from dependence on God. She considered the evil of pride as it daily manifested itself in the community: the woman who cannot bring herself to ask help of the most willing friends and neighbors, the man who cannot make himself speak at the right moment to save his own or someone else's happiness. The tragedy is twofold and cumulative, for not only do people need to humble themselves to the point of admitting that no one is self-sufficient, but they also have no right to deprive their fellow men of the exercise of charitable instincts. Mrs. Freeman, then, in contrast to Mrs. Stowe and Miss Jewett, held that isolation was as much the result of the Yankee character as the cause of the latter's distinctive quality; like Mrs. Cooke, but thinking in far more definite terms, she held New Englanders fully responsible for themselves and their individuality. (pp. 357-58)

*Babette May Levy, "Mutations in New England Local Color," in* The New England Quarterly *(copyright 1946 by* The New England Quarterly*), Vol. XIX, No. 3, September, 1946, pp. 338-58.\**

**EDWARD FOSTER**  (essay date 1956)

The germ of [Miss Wilkins' first novel,] *Jane Field,* might have been some slight contact with one of the patients of the Vermont Insane Asylum who came to the door of the Wilkins house at 3 Chase Street in the late '60's. For at the close of the novel, Mrs. Field is obsessed in a way which will mark her as ''queer'' through all the rest of her life.

The setting permits the novelist to use more of her observation than had entered any earlier work. It is first Green River, almost any of the villages in the West River Valley near Brattleboro, then Elliott which strongly suggests Randolph. For purposes of humorous contrast, Miss Wilkins can play off the countrified awkwardness of her Green River ladies against the relative sophistication of Elliott manners. Customs and especially travel by railroad suggest a time in the '70's; the feeling is always retrospective. These are the quaint and twisted doings of ancient aunts and grandmothers. And here are poverty, pride, and the New England conscience doing their awesome work. (p. 115)

Despite the amateurishness of the complications, the struggle at the center of *Jane Field* is meaningful and potentially dramatic. The deepest demands of a New England woman are pitted against each other: Mrs. Field must cherish her daughter; she must also maintain her selfhood by living within the village code, and especially the commandment, "Thou shalt not steal." Nor was Jane Field the only village mother who was caught within this dilemma; it must have occurred frequently in these unusually hard times. Equally significant is the denouement— the break, the confession, the mind which will never fully recover from a conflict too long sustained.

The most telling moments are those which take us into Mrs. Field's consciousness to suggest the terror of her lonely struggle. (pp. 116-17)

The effect of such probings of the spirit is heightened by the moral and religious norms implied steadily within the novel. Whatever Miss Wilkins' personal convictions may have been, she writes here in the spirit of a latter-day Calvinism. The majesty of God and the heroic temper of the "saints" are gone; but there is no questioning of His justice or of the finality of His commandments. It is precisely in her hours of guilty torment that Mrs. Field must cling most closely to the tenets of her faith. (p. 117)

One can notice these elements of power in *Jane Field* without being convinced that M. E. Wilkins could write a novel in 1892. The illusion is overwhelming when we are within the mind of her heroine; but the representation of the struggle in action and dramatic scene is commonplace, implausible, uneven in tone. Since the conception of the character precluded cleverness and quick thinking as attributes, Mrs. Field must move through endless scenes, in which Elliott people are always about to discover the deception, using no artifices beyond silence or mumbled words. Frequently the effect of her clumsiness is comic—moments of calculated humor for which the reader is grateful. More often one is simply impatient with the minor characters who are too easily deceived; they seem to be stooges cut carelessly out of the whole cloth. (pp. 117-18)

One puts down this work with questions rarely raised by the short stories. Is *Jane Field* to be taken as a comic novel of village manners, touched with a little grimness? Is it "homespun tragedy"? Or was Miss Wilkins seeking again the note of tragicomedy maintained so firmly in some of the stories? The last is the most plausible answer. She seems to have attempted a maneuver which she had virtually mastered in the short form without fully understanding its difficulties in the novel. (p. 118)

[Despite] its nominally "happy" ending and its deference to a modish objectivity of treatment, [*Pembroke*] is a deeply felt plea for the natural expression of normal feeling. By the same token, it is also M. E. Wilkins' fullest exploration of the "diseased will" which blocks the expression of feeling, a theme touched frequently in earlier stories. By the nature of its subject, it is intensely dramatic, and the dramatic conflicts are boldly realized. (p. 126)

Lest there be any doubt of the moral import of her novel, Miss Wilkins expressed it bluntly in her 1899 "Introductory Sketch" for the "Biographical Edition" of *Pembroke*. It was, she wrote, "originally intended as a study of the human will in different phases of disease and abnormal development, and . . . to prove the truth of a theory that its cure depended upon the capacity of the individual for a love which could rise above all consideration of self." (p. 128)

Conan Doyle called *Pembroke* "the greatest piece of fiction since *The Scarlet Letter*." Though his praise was excessive, the comparison with Hawthorne is interesting. Miss Wilkins at her best rivals her predecessor in understanding the dark side of human nature, nor is her method as far from his as might be supposed. She is of course more "realistic," yet the note of poetic suggestiveness is frequently heard. The unfinished house of *Pembroke* is a symbol of great power, a power fully and imaginatively developed. (p. 131)

[*Madelon*] is Miss Wilkins' gesture toward violence and passion. Though the setting, Ware Center, Vermont, was familiar enough to her readers, the plot and its chief actors were cut from new cloth. Madelon Hautville is a half-breed, Indian and French Canadian; she is also wildly beautiful and intensely amorous. The tale is scarcely under way before she is stabbing Burr Mason because he prefers another girl. His cousin Lot Gordon takes the crime on his own head, substituting his weapon for hers, and goes to prison. As Madelon announces her guilt to everyone, she meets only blank incredulity, an irony reminiscent of Raskolnikov's confessions in *Crime and Punishment*. At length Burr Mason, who is still living, states that he committed the deed himself, an attempt at suicide. Then follows the whole second half of the novel—a confusion of cross purposes and twisted but uninteresting motives. Lot Gordon gradually emerges as an infinitely fine and poetic hero.

Clearly Miss Wilkins was attempting "strong" incidents and a frankly romantic tone even as she sought to preserve some of the sobriety in observation and character delineation of her earlier stories. Such a blending of styles is not impossible, but it is not achieved in *Madelon*. It is obviously and disturbingly uneven. (pp. 138-39)

Warned presumably by the failure of *Madelon*, Miss Wilkins returned [in *Jerome, a Poor Man*] to the subject she knew— New England middle class character, represented with minimal sensationalism. She allowed herself room for turning around, for developing her protagonist from boyhood to a point of stability in his late twenties. Whereas *Jane Field* was little more than novella and *Pembroke* a short novel, *Jerome* contains nearly two hundred thousand words. Perhaps it should be viewed as her fairest and most generally acceptable treatment of a Yankee village; but frequently the reader is disturbed by new notes, new mannerisms which do not come off. Considering the long succession of weak novels which will follow, one concludes that *Jerome* is the watershed between Miss Wilkins' firm writing in the novel and her later unrewarded experimentation.

Despite its surface realism, *Jerome* is virtually an allegory of unhealthy pride expressed in compulsive rejection of gifts and in sacrificial generosity. (p. 144)

Since *Jerome,* despite its diatribes against the rich and avaricious, is in no sense a proletarian novel, the outcome is clearly in sight. . . . [For the turns of plot], it is only necessary to say that they are occasionally well-conceived but more frequently thin and awkward. One notes again that Miss Wilkins cannot maintain an even texture of incident through a sustained action.

But, as in *Jane Field* and in *Pembroke,* there is continued cogency in the psychological analysis. (pp. 145-46)

For significance of theme, *Jerome* must be ranked with the best short stories and with *Jane Field* and *Pembroke*. It resembles *Jane Field* in setting in that Miss Wilkins was drawing upon observation of both Randolph and Brattleboro. Jerome's "Upham" seems to be a rather successful fusing of the two towns. Steady references to shoe manufacturing in the domestic stage and a crucial episode concerning the building of a shoe factory suggest Randolph in the '40's and '50's. The landscape is hilly Brattleboro; important scenes mention the Hayes Tavern of West Brattleboro and the flooding of the "Graystone brook," rather obviously a reminiscence of the flooding of the Whetstone of Brattleboro, which was one of the town's memorable disasters. *Jerome* is like *Pembroke* in bringing to its readers a group of well-conceived minor characters—the broken father, the proud and domineering mother, the miser Simon Bassett, the spinster Camilla.

Yet it prefigures the later and inferior novels. Though closely kin in spirit to Barney of *Pembroke,* young Jerome differs from him significantly. He is a perfectionist, deadly set in his determination to grapple with his own spirit and a hostile world, and he is without humor. Granting that the type is worthy of study, one cannot escape an impression of sheer boredom. He will reappear in feminine guise as Ellen in *The Portion of Labor* and as Maria in *By the Light of the Soul.* Moreover this character will increasingly seem to be a projection—not of the whole Mary E. Wilkins, who is not dull but—of the writer in an attitude of tense spiritual striving.

Almost equally alarming are the village gentry who here appear for the first time in a Wilkins novel. The fact that they are, with the exception of avaricious Dr. Prescott, mannerly, charming, dignified, generous is not to be held against them as fictional creations. Such qualities were needed in Miss Wilkins' pages; such human beings certainly lived in the villages. It is rather that the writer, who is completely at ease with her middle class characters, seems uncomfortable when she introduces us to the Squire and his lady, a little too much on her own best behavior. There will be more of this uncertainty as later stories and novels bring more of the gentry to us.

One of the quiet sources of richness in the earlier stories and novels was the restrained employment of symbolism. Though treated only in connection with two or three stories and *Pembroke,* it is felt lightly in virtually all of Miss Wilkins' writing. The symbols work their way precisely because they seem to emerge from ordinary observation and casual reflection; they blend easily with surface realism because, for the most part, they do not suggest a conscious striving for symbolic effect. In *Jerome,* the symbolism is conscious, overt, sustained. (pp. 146-47)

The social criticism of *Jerome,* expressed partly in the vaguely socialistic diatribes of the cobbler Ozias Lamb and in the previously unmentioned hocus-pocus about a will and gifts to the community, is . . . decorative and sentimental. Miss Wilkins sympathized with the poor and was at least lightly aware of the 'nineties trend toward radical social and economic thought, but she was unready for close and honest fictional exploration of the issues.

*Jerome* is today a readable novel—less dramatic than *Pembroke,* equally mordant as an analysis of neurotic pride, better balanced as an interpretation of a New England village. (pp. 148-49)

*The Portion of Labor* is Miss Wilkins' most ambitious and least successful novel. In some two hundred thousand words, the author attempted to build a companion piece for *Jerome,* to trace the development of a lower-middle class girl of a "shoe town" from childhood through adolescence and young womanhood into the safe port of a good marriage. The town is perhaps Brockton; the time, the troubled '80's and '90's; the chief incident, an unsuccessful strike of shoe workers.

Ellen Brewster, the heroine, is asking Jerome's question, "Where is my happiness?" The minor middle class characters are as usual limned with fine insight, but the mill owner and his family are seen through eyes too much dazzled by wealth and position. For close thinking and sound knowledge of the economic system of the '90's, Miss Wilkins substituted the moralism and sentiment which marred Elizabeth Stuart Phelps, *The Silent Partner.* After harrowing us with sharply observed details of worker degradation and poverty, she concluded that such was the will of God and a fine schooling in "character." Calvinistic determinism is linked with economic conservatism and decorated with a touch of self-righteousness. This, in general, is the "portion of labor"; but sentiment enters to arrange the marriage of the worker heroine with the owner's son.

Ellen is the "Wilkins character" mentioned in comment on *Jerome,* hardly as neurotic as the boy but sufficiently tedious in her ecstasies of self-sacrifice, her commitment to perfection, her tense demand for happiness. After this pattern is once grasped, it will bear repetition only if the writer is amplifying her analysis of its limitations. The amplification does not occur in *The Portion of Labor.* (pp. 154-55)

[The serialized novel, *By the Light of the Soul,*] is Mrs. Freeman's boldest attempt to realize the possibilities of the subjective and religious elements of *Jerome* [and] *The Portion of Labor.* . . . For precision and fullness of detail in the treatment of minor characters and of the New Jersey and New England setting, it is a realistic and regional novel—another *Pembroke;* in the development of the inner life of its heroine, Maria Edgham, it appears to be lightly disguised spiritual autobiography. (pp. 169-70)

*By the Light of the Soul* is also a feebly plotted novel. The major complication, which shapes Maria's life more than any other external factor, is her unconsummated marriage at sixteen, under preposterous circumstances, to the boy Wollaston Lee. Contriving with little plausibility objections against annulment or divorce, Mrs. Freeman spun out the frustrations latent in this marriage through nearly three hundred pages; other complications are almost as thin. And one may also dismiss Maria Edgham, like Ellen Brewster of *The Portion of Labor,* as a tedious bore.

So much for *By the Light of the Soul* as another unsuccessful novel. It is rewarding however as a comment on Mrs. Freeman's emotional and spiritual growth, especially on her conception of the "old maid." For she would never forget that her own marriage had come very late. (p. 170)

[The setting of *The Shoulders of Atlas*] is "East Westland," a small shoe town much like her own Randolph. The people of the novel might have walked directly out of **"A New England Nun"** or *Pembroke.* Structurally, the new novel also resembles *Pembroke,* for it is a series of variations on a single theme developed in the lives of closely connected characters.

It is the theme, principal or subordinate, of much realistic tragedy. "Everyone bore, seen or unseen, the burden of his or her world upon straining shoulders. The grand pathetic tragedy, inseparable from life, moved multiple at the marriage feast." (p. 176)

*The Shoulders of Atlas* is a valuable complement to Mrs. Freeman's earlier comment on New England ways and character. Moving away from the theme of neurotic pride, it touches other abnormalities fostered by material poverty and an overly rigid cultural ideal. In thought and observation, it is a distinguished novel. The prose is always adequate and frequently pungent and suggestive in the manner of the early stories. Structurally, however, *The Shoulders of Atlas* is a poor thing; for Mrs. Freeman could not bring herself to attempt the hard thinking about incident and complication which her theme of "burdens" seems to require. She had undertaken a realistic subject, realistic in the sense that it seems to demand a matching of broadly typical traits with broadly typical incidents. Her plot draws much too heavily upon a hocus-pocus of concealed and altered wills and melodramatic poisoning. And the commonplace conclusion—a general pairing off of all unattached males and females—is merely a reiteration of the Victorian assurance that love is best. (p. 177)

In selecting characters and situations and traits, [Mrs. Freeman] was guided naturally by her own sensibility. She exaggerated the numerical importance of the women and of the elderly people; she made little attempt to represent fairly the variety of "adjustments" to village life which must have existed. It is hard to believe that no New England villagers of the last half century were able to come to fruitful terms with themselves and their culture, but no fully rounded figure appears in a Freeman story or novel. Though the great majority must have lived as easy, if mediocre, conformists, such people appear only rarely in the writings and then in minor roles. The reader gains no sense of their numerical weight in the towns.

Her truth is of a narrower and more precious kind—a superb understanding of the undefeated neurotics, occasionally men, more often women. Always they are dowered with the primary virtues of a traditional society—courage and loyalty and a strong sense of duty. If they are intensely individualistic, they must also bear the individual's burden of alienation from family and group and ultimately from self. Neither code nor church can bring them peace, yet their gestures of revolt are never quite conclusive, never fully satisfying. Necessarily, they are frustrated and neurotic to a degree. Yet the thrust toward love and achievement and a sense of belonging cannot be killed. They are all—these striving neurotics—seeking a wholeness of spirit and a fullness of life almost impossible of attainment in the village as Mrs. Freeman knew it.

That much is the fruit of sympathetic understanding, but there is something more. For in the loose and popular sense of the term, Mrs. Freeman was a philosophic writer; for herself and her major characters, she sought meaning in life and believed that fulfillment and happiness were not unattainable. (pp. 190-91)

> *Edward Foster, in his* Mary E. Wilkins Freeman *(copyright 1956 by Hendricks House, Inc., reprinted by permission of the publisher), Hendricks House, 1956, 229 p.*

## ABIGAIL ANN HAMBLEN  (essay date 1966)

Women writers of Mary Wilkins' day—even of her later day—did not often come to terms with raw sex. They wrote "love stories" if they wished to be popular, but these were of a decided "moonlight and roses" type. The more serious novelists, while not ignoring the subject, certainly were not inclined to frankness. And so it is interesting to see how clear-eyed and forthright Mary Wilkins could be. Though she never deliberately exploited it, she never side-stepped the question of simple physical appeal—or of downright lust.

In *Jerome* a rather charming incident shows the dawning of desire on the part of an immature girl. Lucinda finds Jerome, the boy she loves, asleep in the woods. As she stands looking down at him she has the "sense of a great mystery." She understands suddenly how love can make a man and woman literally one. . . . The whole scene with the waking boy, the caress, the long kiss, the gasping words, is beautiful, but it is distinctly physical, and not in the tradition of "romantic" stories.

It has a reality similar to that of the Rose Berry story in *Pembroke.* Rose is very young and intense; the reader knows immediately that something underlies her vehement commiseration with Charlotte over the quarrel with Barney. (p. 55)

Though she is defiant with denial when Charlotte confronts her with the accusation that she is running after Barney—"'and you don't even care anything for him; you haven't even that for an excuse. . . . You've lowered yourself'"—she recognizes the truth in Charlotte's words. She feels some sense of guilt, but she feels something else, too. She is conscious of "an injured and bewildered feeling, as if somewhere in this terrible nature, at whose mercy she was, there was some excuse for her."

A much more detailed account of girlish lust with "some excuse" is found in *The Shoulders of Atlas.* . . . Though the novel as a whole is inferior to *Pembroke,* in the presentation of Lucy Ayres it builds upon the lightly-sketched-in figure of Rose Berry. Lucy is psychopathic in the intensity of her desire for Horace Allen. When she comes upon him making love to Rose Fletcher in the orchard, she hides herself to stand watching and listening, her face "terrible"; she is "full of an enormous, greedy delight," yet in the grip of "the most horrible agony and a more horrible joy." She is "like a fanatic who dances in fire." A friend feels that her love for the young man is "in a way an insult to him," but her mother is more understanding: "'Sometimes, quite often, it may happen that too heavy a burden, a burden which has been gathering weight since the first of creation, is heaped upon too slender shoulders. This burden may bend innocence into guilt and modesty into shamelessness, but there is no more reason for condemnation than in a case of typhoid fever. Any man of good sense and common Christianity should take that view of it.'" No one needs to be reminded that even by 1908 such an attitude towards the excesses of sexual passion was far from common. (p. 56)

[*Madelon*] exhibits a love as intense, but less sordid than Lucy's, and on a much grander scale. The heroine is unlike most of Mary Wilkins' women. Usually they have great self-control and great strength, but Madelon goes beyond them in these things—she is primitive in her love and in her self-denial. Fiery and unforgettable, she reminds the reader of Cathy Heathcliffe. (Incidentally, Mary Wilkins greatly admired *Wuthering Heights.*) The novel would have been an artistic achievement if it had stopped after the first two-thirds, with Madelon's marriage to the repulsive yet pitiable Lot Gordon in payment for his refusing to testify against the man she loved. That love can be a terrible thing, demanding an excruciating sacrifice, would then have been the thesis. It is regrettable that Mary Wilkins, heedless of the compelling theme that had come alive under her hand, saw fit to drag her story out in a mush of sentimentality and improbabilities. But even as it stands it is notable for its vivid Brontë-like heroine with her unyielding passion. (pp. 56-7)

That Mary Wilkins was conscious of the past is evident, for many of her stories have a seventeenth- or eighteenth-century setting. For example, in the collection *Silence and Other Stories* . . . the title story concerns the Deerfield Massacre (1703) and

"**The Little Maid at the Door**" is about the Salem witchcraft fright. There is a vivid picture of eighteenth-century Massachusetts in the mild little children's tale, "**The Adventures of Ann, the Bound Girl of Samuel Wales, of Braintree, in the Province of Massachusetts Bay**" in *In Colonial Times*. . . . In *The Love of Parson Lord and Other Stories* . . . , "**Catherine Carr**" describes the way in which a girl and her grandmother save the girl's lover from the British during the War of 1812. (p. 57)

[There] is a certain charm about these stories set in long-ago times. And there is real power in "**Silence**," which tells of the horrors of an Indian massacre. It contains one of the most effective pieces of description Mary Wilkins ever wrote. The reader stands beside the young girl as she peers from her dormer window at the holocaust below: "Deerfield village was roaring with flames, the sky and snow were red, and leaping through the glare came the painted savages, a savage white face and the waving sword of a French officer in their midst." There are "awful war whoops" and "death-cries," and "close under her window, the dark sweep of the tomahawk, the quick glance of the scalping-knife, and the red starting of caps of blood. . . ." This is a true re-creation of history, and not only of facts— the mood, the emotion, are all deftly and subtly woven into a graphic, unforgettable word-scene. The Deerfield Massacre comes alive.

It is to be regretted that Mary Wilkins felt that, in the interests of her popularity, she must write a costume novel. "Historical romances" were much in vogue in 1900, when *The Heart's Highway* was published. The time of the novel is 1682, the place Virginia, the dramatis personae cavaliers and adventurers. The language is impossibly high-flown, as are the actions of the hero, Harry Maria Wingfield. (pp. 57-8)

The story as a whole is florid, garnished with a rhapsodic style, ending with a triumphantly flourishing sentence to the effect that the "blazon of love" is the only one which holds good forever "through all the wilderness of history." . . .

During the period following the Civil War, the wave of feeling against "social injustice" gained momentum. Rich versus poor, labor versus capital, became big questions in American life, and author after author took up the cudgels for the poor, and for labor. Mary Wilkins was not indifferent to suffering and injustice, and the agonized revolt of the poverty-stricken. In *Jerome* . . . she shows an awareness of unrest. Ozias Lamb, the philosophical cobbler, is given to impassioned speeches: "'What right has one man with the whole purse, while another has not a penny in his pocket!'" The boy Jerome meditates on this, and, deciding that it is wrong for the rich to have everything, the poor nothing, resolves that if he ever becomes wealthy he will give to the poor. (p. 58)

This is really as far as Mary Wilkins' opinions go on the question of inequality. . . . [In *The Portion of Labor*] she takes up the problem of the labor-capital struggle. In addition to being overlong, with some very trashy patches of writing, it is distinctly unsatisfying as a tract. The author is seen to waver; she can hardly make up her mind which side she is on, and so she helplessly tries to reconcile them, with the result that she cannot possibly be taken seriously.

Her factory owners, the Lloyds, have many good qualities, and are shown to have their problems, too (a rather remarkable touch in a labor novel). In addition some of her workers are shown to be free of envy and resentment, wishing only for the privilege of honest work. . . . (p. 59)

Mary Wilkins understood the ravages of poverty, but she did not understand the economic struggle of her time. She was manifestly unfit to write about the problem of abolishing poverty and she would have been well advised not to do so. *The Portion of Labor* is almost embarrassingly inadequate.

One little-known—and very small—part of Mary Wilkins' writing is that devoted to crimes, ghosts, or mysterious doings. *The Wind in the Rose-Bush and Other Stories of the Supernatural* . . . is overwhelming in its concentrated eeriness. The reader almost unconsciously feels that the author is enjoying herself in these strange tales: there is a shiver on each page, because the ghosts are "real" ghosts, with no nonsense about scientific explanations. It is imagination—an imagination used to the contemplation of practicalities—gone riot.

For a great deal of the effect of horror comes from the matter-of-fact, humdrum settings in which the stories are laid, and the calculating, worldly-minded men and women who people them. For instance, the title story begins calmly, "Ford Village has no railroad station, being on the other side of the river from Porter's Falls . . .", and the first person introduced is the ex-schoolteacher, Miss Rebecca Flint, "tall and spare and pale." In the end the denouement is presented in the curt, semiliterate lines of a village postmaster's letter.

The very events in these stories concern ordinary things. In "**The Southwest Chamber**" a water pitcher, just filled, is found dry and dusty; a night cap is tried on the person sleeping in the bed; the pattern of the chintz changes, etc. In "**The Shadow on the Wall**," a dead man's shadow is seen each evening when the lamps are lit. In "**The Wind in the Rose-Bush**" a young girl's nightgown is found laid out as in a coffin. "**The Lost Ghost**" describes a small girl, dead of neglect, who keeps appearing in her shroud saying wistfully, "'I can't find my mother.'" As a variation, "**Luella Miller**" tells about a woman whose very existence is death to those near her. Any reader with a taste for this sort of thing will find Mary Wilkins' spectres and victims convincing and entertaining.

Those who prefer a practical mystery will appreciate more such a story as "**The Gold**," a story of hidden treasure during Revolutionary War times. This has a well-worked-out solution which cannot possibly be guessed. (p. 60)

Tales of this type were, of course, aside from the main stream of Mary Wilkins' work, but they are interesting to consider, for they show the way in which her agile fancy could amuse itself. And above all, it is significant that they are not Gothic; they are about *New England* ghosts and murderers. (p. 61)

*Abigail Ann Hamblen, "Certain Minor Aspects of Mary Wilkins' Work" (© 1966; reprinted by permission of the author), in her* The New England Art of Mary E. Wilkins Freeman, *The Green Knight Press, 1966, pp. 55-61.*

**PERRY D. WESTBROOK** (essay date 1967)

*The Debtor,* laid entirely in Jersey, is essentially a silly story. Some of the intentional humor, to be sure, comes off reasonably well. One can smile at the wiles of the four-flusher Carroll, not an uncommon suburban type, as he dupes the tradespeople of Banbridge. These townsfolk are, of course, the "natives," the residents from long before the commuters moved in; and, as such, Mrs. Freeman, the specialist in village character, makes them come to life. Most likable is Anderson, a lawyer turned grocer, a bachelor approaching middle age, who marries Carroll's daughter Charlotte. Charlotte herself, however, is enough to spoil a whole book. A simpering nincompoop, she is the product of a degree of sentimentality that Mrs. Freeman had hitherto not displayed. More realistically conceived is Carroll's hatred for the business rival who has ruined him—a hatred so consuming that it becomes directed against himself and, in accord with the Freudian theory of suicide, almost leads him to take his own life. But an occasional psychological insight and several amusing and lifelike characters are not enough to salvage over five hundred pages of fiction blemished by pervasive mawkishness and a preposterous plot. By any standards, *The Debtor* is a failure. By the standards of Mrs. Freeman's best fiction, it is an abysmal failure.

More can be said for *By the Light of the Soul,* an undertaking of some two hundred thousand words. The title indicates the novel's theme—the Emersonian notion that the soul in itself is a source of insight adequate to guide us through the moral labyrinths of life. Friends of Mrs. Freeman considered the book to be a spiritual autobiography. The heroine, Maria Edgham, in her childhood is a replica of the child Mary Wilkins—a pretty, bright, somewhat spoiled, intensely sensitive girl. (pp. 162-63)

Some readers have termed Maria Edgham a bore. Truly her dreary, unwavering seriousness, her will that can ruthlessly smother her most turbulent emotions, if these in any way threaten to lead her from the straitest path of duty, her morbidly acute conscience, her fiercely determined charitableness towards the poor, and above all her readiness to condemn all others who fall short of her own superhuman standards—all these traits are tiresome. . . . Yet in her moments of mystical transport as well as in her loyalty to her family, Maria is not totally obnoxious. Certainly Mrs. Freeman did not mean her to be.

One reason Maria becomes a bit ludicrous to the reader is that the plot of the novel provides only the feeblest motivation for her powers of will and endurance. The central device is a marriage, never consummated, that a dull-witted parson forced on her and a high-school classmate while the two were wandering in New York City in search of Maria's little sister who had run away from home. . . . Inevitably, of course, Maria's younger sister Evelyn falls in love with Maria's "husband"; and equally inevitably this occurs at the moment, deferred for fifteen years, when Maria and her spouse are beginning to be attracted to each other and are on the verge of entering into actual union. Maria's will power and sense of duty surge. She flees, changes her name, gets a report printed that she is dead. The sister is free to marry her "brother-in-law," and she does so. In the context of such tomfoolery, Maria's otherwise impressive and valid, if repelling, strength of character becomes unconvincing and irrelevant.

Yet even this novel is not totally without strength. It catches the atmosphere of the New Jersey commuting town in which the first half is laid. Shifting to a Massachusetts mill city, as if Mrs. Freeman were seeking more familiar ground, the action becomes more credible; and the setting continues to be interesting, especially the glimpses of the decay and demoralization in which people on the undesirable side of the river live. Prostitution, drunkenness, and criminal neglect of children are presented with a "naturalism" that either Crane or Dreiser would find to his taste.

In *By the Light of the Soul,* Mrs. Freeman voices more outspokenly than ever before her awareness of the folly of mankind. As in many of her works, there is a character [Henry Stillman] who takes petty reprisals against destiny for assigning him to a distasteful life, in this case life in a run-down industrial town. . . . (pp. 163-65)

Despite his folly, Henry through the years has acquired a bitter realization of the weakness of humanity. Was Mrs. Freeman's marriage with an alcoholic bringing her to a similarly grim knowledge? Was she perhaps regretting her plunge into matrimony in her late middle age? At any rate she mercilessly lampoons the elderly spinster, Maria Stillman, otherwise a sensible woman, for her clumsy machinations to ensnare the husband of her dead sister. (p. 165)

[In] Mrs. Freeman's own childhood home, as well as in most of her books, merciless female domination of spineless males was the rule. Yet in this novel the married men seem more discontented, more disillusioned than ever before. One scorns them rather than sympathizes with them—which was becoming more and more Mrs. Freeman's feeling about her fellow mortals. She was approaching Mark Twain's indignation against "the damned human race." In addition to folly, she reveals in *By the Light of the Soul* behavior describable only as gratuitous malice. When a girl runs away, the neighbors secretly gloat while they pretend to comfort the mother; and when a school-girl is jilted by her lover, her classmates covertly exult.

Mrs. Freeman had always done her best writing in short fiction. . . . Of [her later stories] an occasional one ranked with the best she had written, but the days of whole volumes of distinguished tales were past. Only a brief glance at these later collections is worthwhile. (pp. 165-66)

[*The Givers*] is composed largely of Christmas stories, competent in their evocation of New England settings, especially of the blizzards and gales of December, and in their characterization. But they are sentimental in plot, as is not unusual for their genre. Yet few even of these are downright mawkish. The male and female solitaries who people them do, of course, have joy brought into their dreary existences in accord with the season—but the joy is always a lasting one, involving basic transformations of their lives. (p. 166)

*The Fair Lavinia and Others* [is] a volume of tales with titles like "Amarina's Roses," "Eglantina," and "The Willow-Ware," and dealing for the most part with small-town gentlefolk. . . . [These] tales are pretty much without substance. The only exception is "The Gold," laid in Revolutionary days, and telling the story of a farmer who has a goldsmith convert his inherited precious metal into andirons, doorknobs, drawer handles, and the like, which he puts to their normal use about his house just as if they were made of brass. . . . As a tale of greed that destroys a human soul, this story is powerful. The final scene, when neighbors break into the farmhouse one icy winter day and find the old miser dead before his fireplace hearth with the andirons and doorknobs glittering in the cold sunlight, is comparable to the scene of Judge Pyncheon's death in *The House of the Seven Gables.*

The next collection, *The Winning Lady and Others* . . . , was considered by some to be the best that Mrs. Freeman had published—an estimate that is unfounded. . . . [In] all her later stories and novels, Mrs. Freeman's style was gaining fluency and complexity at the expense of the unadorned simplicity and directness that had contributed so much to the effectiveness of her earlier work. Glibness was supplanting feeling and was hanging like a veil between the author and her material. (pp. 166-67)

*The Butterfly House* [is] an attempt to satirize the pettinesses of life in a New Jersey suburb. Understandably, the reviewers found the novel to be evidence of a serious decline in its author's powers. The satire, which centers upon the doings of clubwomen, is dull; and the plot, which hinges upon one woman's posing as the author of another woman's anonymously published best-selling novel, is preposterous without being humorous. But the depiction of the utter selfishness of the impostor, who psychologically is "obliged to commit an ignoble deed in order to render her soul capable of tasting to the full . . ." . . . , is effective. (p. 168)

[*The Copy-Cat and Other Stories*] contains the last stories of merit that Mrs. Freeman wrote. The first six are about children in an unnamed village, apparently suburban but with many rural characteristics. The children are real, "as chokeful of mischief as a pod of peas." . . . Several of them appear in more than one story, as do some of the adults. The series provides a view of village life as lived by youngsters, and this life, as Mrs. Freeman depicts it, is much less fraught with the clash of wills and eruption of passions than that of the adult villagers in her usual story. Avoiding sentimentality, these tales underscore the wholesomeness of small-town childhood, but the children are for the most part of prosperous families in a prosperous community that sends its progeny to a private school. In earlier collections or novels, for example *Jerome,* Mrs. Freeman presented the spectacle of childhood blighted by extreme poverty, both of spirit and of things.

In addition to truly delightful stories of childhood, *The Copy-Cat* contains several other pieces of a quality that marks a real, if brief, resurgence of Mrs. Freeman's talents. Among these are two stories of revolt. "**Dear Annie**" tells of a young woman's rebellion against exploitation by her sister and by her weak-willed father, the village minister. . . . Less sensational than "**The Revolt of Mother,**" the story is more effective because it records a plausible spiritual growth, over an extended period, both in Annie and in her relatives.

The other story of revolt, "**The Balking of Christopher,**" is one of the loveliest things Mrs. Freeman ever wrote. In it the revolt is not against another person or a family but against God and the duty orthodox religion enjoins. All his life Christopher had attempted to do his duty, and Providence had always thrown obstacles in his way—fire, drought, flood, sickness, death. One spring morning Christopher decides he will not do his duty, which that day is to plough the South Field. . . . In many instances Mrs. Freeman had questioned the wisdom of devoting a life solely to duty, and she does so again in this story. (pp. 169-70)

*An Alabaster Box,* the final novel to bear Mrs. Freeman's name on its title page, was written in collaboration with Florence Morse Kingsley. It elicited from one reviewer the remark that Mrs. Freeman stood in need of re-establishing her reputation and from another the comment that she would do better to avoid collaboration in the future. While a sorry excuse indeed for a novel, *An Alabaster Box* is interesting as a final statement of some of Mrs. Freeman's attitudes. The plot, though improbable, is simple: Mr. Andrew Bolton, a banker in the village of Brookville, embezzles money entrusted to him, goes to jail for his crime, but does not make good the grievous losses suffered by the townspeople. . . . As an indictment of the corporate meanness of a small town, *An Alabaster Box* is as bitter as Mark Twain's *The Man That Corrupted Hadleyburg* though decidedly weaker in ironic effect, characterization, and style.

Mrs. Freeman's last collection of short fiction, *Edgewater People* . . . , is also her poorest. Purporting to be a study of the process of growth of four villages that are the offshoot of one ancient settlement, the book is actually a loosely connected series of stories that happen to have their setting in the same area. Certain characters reappear several times, but their presence in no way demonstrates Mrs. Freeman's contention that communities, like individuals, inherit identical qualities from a common forebear. . . . The most notable character in the volume, Sarah Edgewater, is a mere distorted echo of the strong-willed New England women who had populated Mrs. Freeman's earlier work. The subject of one of the stories, Sarah's conquering a pathological fear of loneliness by transforming her hate and resentment towards her sister into love, is psychologically convincing as an idea but not as it is developed in this instance. The idea was infinitely better handled in *Pembroke.* Equally pathetic as an echo is "**Value Received,**" based on the theme that one who gives has a sacred duty to receive from the giver in turn. As presented in "**Old Lady Pingree**" in *A Humble Romance* the theme had cogency, as it also did in "**The Selfishness of Amelia Lamkin.**" As developed in "**Value Received,**" by methods not worth mentioning, it is ludicrous. But most distressing of all in the volume is the blind chauvinism evident in several of the stories, notably "**Both Cheeks,**" in which the conversion of a pacifist into a bloodthirsty militarist is presented as the ultimate in spiritual growth.

As with many a person of less than first-rate intellect, World War I brought out all the second-rate in Mrs. Freeman. The first line of a poem she contributed to a volume called *America in the War* (1918), edited by Louis Raemakers, is sufficient evidence: "America wakes! The White Christ has called her. . . ." The war was, of course, only a secondary influence in Mrs. Freeman's artistic collapse. Her age (almost seventy), the exhausting drainage of her energies during forty years of fantastically prolix writing, and her husband's alcoholism merging into psychosis—these are reasons enough for artistic bankruptcy. No more volumes and only a handful of fugitive pieces appeared during the last twelve years of her life. (pp. 170-72)

With *A Humble Romance* and *A New England Nun* Mrs. Freeman established a reputation that endured throughout her life and only in the past decades has shown signs of serious decline. Reviews of her work over a period of forty years were overwhelmingly favorable. (pp. 172-73)

[A writer] with universal overtones but with microscopic focus upon one area of the nation, Mrs. Freeman represents regionalism at its very best. Nor is the region that engages her talents a negligible backwater in American culture. It is one that was seminal and transcontinentally influential in forming the American character and in establishing the national values. No major Northern author of the nineteenth century failed to realize this function of New England. (p. 177)

> *Perry D. Westbrook, in his* Mary Wilkins Freeman *(copyright © 1967 by Twayne Publishers, Inc.; reprinted with permission of Twayne Publishers, a Division of G. K. Hall & Co., Boston), Twayne, 1967, 191 p.*

**SUSAN ALLEN TOTH** (essay date 1973)

[*Toth discusses several of Freeman's stories in which characters strive to retain their individuality and independence in the face of constant pressure from the community to conform. Toth's inter-*

*pretation of this often complex and positive outlook differs from the usual critical interpretation of Freeman's characters as inflexible and bound by tradition.*]

[For years, literary historians have viewed] Freeman as a pessimistic recorder of New England's decline. Larzer Ziff sees in her tales "the piercing northern night which had descended on a land now barren," Jay Martin sweepingly enfolds her characters into one general type, "the humorless, vacant, mindless, narrow New Englander," and Austin Warren has clinically classified her morbid cases of New England conscience. After concluding that most critics since 1900 have treated Freeman as "a historian of New England rural life and as an anatomist of the Puritan will in its final stages of disintegration," Perry Westbrook himself stresses Freeman's sociological value as "our most truthful recorder in fiction of New England village life," a life drawing to an isolated and impoverished conclusion by the 1880's and 1890's.

Although these judgments have sound basis, their cultural and historical focus on gloom, misery, decay, and extinction has obscured the real dramatic conflict at the heart of Freeman's best short stories. It is a conflict whose positive aspects need to be recognized. Many of her characters suffer, but they also fight their way to significant victories. Living in drab poverty, they still struggle with courageous spirit towards self-expression and independence. This vital struggle is far from being dated as a past or purely local condition that existed only in New England in the decades following the Civil War.

Freeman has a surprisingly modern and complex sense of the constant mutual adjustment necessary between individual and community, between need for independence and social insistence on conformity, between private fulfillment and social duties. Her men and women must assert themselves in ingenious ways to maintain their integrity in the face of community pressures, and Freeman records their varying successes with a wry but sympathetic spirit.

Despite their strikingly modern themes, many of these stories have never received adequate critical attention. Some, like "**A Village Singer**," have been often anthologized but seldom discussed. Some, like "**A Church Mouse**," have been praised only in passing, and then mainly for their bitter irony or pathos. Others, like "**Arethusa**" and "**A Slip of the Leash**," have long been hidden from notice and out of print. It is time to release Freeman's best fiction from its restrictive label as morbid cultural documentation and to read these powerful and relevant short stories on their own carefully developed and detailed terms.

Individual and community clash intensely in Freeman's world because organized society is inherently hostile to the needs and demands of its constituents. Life is a constant battleground for all. The sense of this underlying hostility sets Freeman's New England stories far apart in tone from those of her contemporaries. . . . Freeman's isolated villages are far from harmonious social groups. No long-established, mutual reservoir of good will provides sustenance for the business of day-to-day living. In Freeman's villages, each individual must battle the community in order to define his rights and responsibilities.

This problem of definition is often raised by the very old. While in Jewett's fiction the aged are valued as guardians of tradition and as wise advisers to the younger generation, in Freeman's stories the old must fight for their survival with all their strength, a strength fortunately dependent on character rather than on physical heartiness. The old, rather than the younger generation, institute rebellion and demand social justice. (pp. 82-4)

"**A Village Singer**" is one of Freeman's best dramatizations of this problem. A deceptively quiet opening places the story in the beginning of spring, when new life is whispering in the village. . . . When the new leading soprano rises to sing her solo in the church, we learn that Candace Whitcomb, "the old one, who had sung in the choir for forty years," has been dismissed because the congregation feels her voice has become cracked and uncertain. The subtle relationship between the inevitable arrival of spring and the abrupt dismissal of the aged woman gives the congregation's action an unfeeling harshness, like an indifferent act of nature.

Suddenly, in the midst of the new singer's solo, Candace's strong, angry voice rises into the church; she is sitting at her nearby window and playing her small organ to drown out her rival. Everyone is shocked, and later that evening, after Candace has interrupted the second service, the rather timorous minister calls on her to remonstrate. Candace's reply, full of indignant justice, asserts the demands of her humanity and indicts the callous congregation. . . . [An] outpouring of direct, forceful prose shows Freeman's vernacular dialogue at its best, running freely and clearly but with individual speech rhythms and idiomatic speech forms. . . . (pp. 84-5)

Candace's anger against the congregation who have turned her off after a lifetime of service has transformed her into what Freeman explicitly calls a Napoleonic figure. Freeman's respect for the old woman's refusal to give in to dismissal and despair is evident. . . . Candace is not merely a "humorless, vacant, mindless, narrow New Englander" as she sits at her organ and pours all her strength into a defiant song. She is a genuine heroine.

The story ends with a quiet return to the opening picture of approaching spring. Worn out by her defiant vigils and by her self-assertion, Candace becomes rapidly ill and dies. As the fever begins to affect her, she stands at her doorway and sees a forest fire raging in the distance: "She watched with a dull interest the flames roll up, withering and destroying the tender green foliage." This image of her own destruction is carried subtly to the final paragraph of the story, when Candace as a gesture of forgiveness has asked the new soprano to sing for her. After the song, Candace looks up at the young girl and delivers a final thrust, revealing "the old shape of a forest tree through the smoke and flame of the transfiguring fire the instant before it falls: 'You flatted a little on—soul,' said Candace."

Taking a petty incident, the replacement of an old singer with a younger one, Freeman has turned it into a challenge to selfish community spirit, an individual's refusal to be denied humanity and justice, and a sometimes humorous, occasionally pathetic but never maudlin character study of a remarkable old woman. Without wasting space on superfluous description . . . , Freeman uses setting and detail for their maximum effect. Dialogue is sharply to the point, and Candace's monologues provide most of the necessary exposition in terse, clear, idiomatic prose. Even the hint of symbolism is subtle and unobtrusive. "**A Village Singer**" is typical of Mary Wilkins Freeman at her best.

"**A Village Singer**" is only one of several fine stories that pit old and no longer fully productive members of a community against its attempt to dispose of them. One such story, low-keyed and little-known, is "**A Church Mouse**," a parable of the feminine will to survive even in the harshest of male worlds.

Hetty, the heroine, is a woman who has grown old in household service and now has no place to go, not even a poorhouse, since her village has not built one. Deciding to apply for the job of tending the local church, she moves without permission, stove, bedstead and all, into the chimney-corner of the church gallery. Hetty survives there for a while, since she keeps the church spotless, but one Sunday morning the congregation can smell the faint odor of yesterday's turnips, Hetty's meager meal. They are outraged, not because the old woman has had no assistance or charity, but because she has defiled the meetinghouse. . . . As all the men in the community assemble to evict her forcibly, Hetty's fate looks bleak. . . . But Hetty's courage and resourcefulness have aroused the support of other women in the community. Realizing Hetty's plight, the deacon's wife arrives with the voice of chiding conscience to silence the men and to assure Hetty she can remain in the church. The men are routed, and Hetty wakes next morning joyously to ring the Christmas bell.

Hetty has won her right to home and independence, by asserting her rights and accepting responsibility in return, as she also expects the community to do. Like Candace in **"A Village Singer,"** she refuses to accept the status of an unprofitable figure in village accounts. . . . [She] demands recognition of her humanity from those who do not want to be reminded of it. For her as well as for Candace, Freeman has admiration and respect.

The old are not the only members of Freeman's communities who must struggle to maintain their independence, their rights or their plain individuality. Young as well as old must protect themselves against the constant intrusion of village demands. These demands may take the form of an insatiable curiosity that threatens individual privacy at every turn. In the background of Freeman's stories the village gossips are always scurrying, waiting to carry news—preferably disastrous—to their neighbors. These stories are filled with the sounds of eager footsteps entering rooms unannounced; doors flung open into dining rooms, parlors, and even bedrooms; low voices exchanging confidences about someone who has just crossed the threshold.

Against this background of whispers and opened doors, the characters of Freeman's world try to live according to their own consciences. Their determination to be true to themselves in face of community demands provides dramatic conflict in several of Freeman's best stories. Some, like Esther Gay in **"An Independent Thinker,"** wish to be free to follow their own conclusions about religion. (pp. 86-9)

Some of Freeman's independent thinkers have been singled out for praise by critics. Ziff, for example, selects the story of a village agnostic, **"Life Everlastin',"** as one of her best; and Foster finds **"A Tardy Thanksgiving,"** the story of a woman who refuses to celebrate Thanksgiving when she has nothing for which to rejoice, as the "freshest and most satisfying" of the whole collection in *A Humble Romance*. Praise for these stories, however, sometimes obscures their real meaning. Freeman's characters are often cited for "going against the grain of the community," as though their defiant gestures are merely attempts at rebellion against the village code. But Freeman puts much more emphasis on the positive drive towards fulfillment that motivates her strong characters, a fulfillment of what they believe to be their own true selves. They do not fight simply for their ideas but for their independence; they demand, quite simply, a measure of individual freedom. This is not a petty goal, nor is their struggle a futile one.

Among the least noticed of Freeman's stories are those that explore this urge towards self-fulfillment and that insist upon an individual's inviolable right to his own personality. **"Arethusa,"** a story never thoroughly discussed by any critic of Freeman, is one expression of this theme. Although it lacks the finished terseness and dramatic finality of some of her earlier stories, it has a charm of its own. . . . **"Arethusa"** describes a girl who is wild, secret, and blooming only to herself. Lucy is a strange girl, who takes little interest in ordinary domestic life, and who prefers to roam the fields, particularly the green marshes where the arethusa and other flowers grow. . . . Uninterested in men, Lucy alarms her stolid mother. . . . Worried about Lucy's future, her mother finally manages to persuade her to accept Edson Abbott, a young man who is strong, firm, but diplomatic in his wooing. Her acceptance is hardly a joyful assent. . . . (pp. 90-1)

Freeman ends **"Arethusa"** with an ironic thrust at Lucy's self-satisfied husband. . . . Even though Lucy's strange character may seem peculiarly unbalanced to modern readers, Freeman's vision of an inviolable personality is strongly presented. Freeman has sympathy for any character who wants to be "forever her own," whether one's integrity requires holding fast to a particular opinion or to one's whole emotional nature.

Men as well as women need to "be one's own," as Freeman makes plain in one of her interesting failures, **"The Slip of the Leash."** . . . [This] story is one of her few never collected in a hard-cover volume and it remains almost unknown today. Set "in one of the far Western states," it lacks the sharp-edged specificity and clear focus of her New England stories, but it does have a haunting premise. Perhaps modeled on Hawthorne's "Wakefield," it tells of Adam Anderson, over forty years old with a wife and four children, who leaves his small world because he fears he is losing a sense of his own soul. He loves his family, but he still feels "exultation that he had broken away from that love and its terrible monotony of demand." Freeman is not very sure at describing unleashed wildness, volcanic forces, and deep passions as they manifest themselves outside the tight restraints of a New England village; still she manages to imbue Adam with a kind of weird reality. After some random adventures, he returns as a sort of wild man to live like a hermit in the wood near his old home and to watch his family struggle with their farm. Eventually, as his family becomes poorer and more desperate, Adam returns to them and to his old life. He has found he cannot ignore his ties and responsibilities, but at least he has gained "an infinite preciousness of renewed individuality."

Through Freeman's stories march a procession of characters like Adam, Lucy of **"Arethusa,"** Candace Whitcomb of **"A Village Singer,"** and others like them. They assert their right to individuality, even if they must affront village society to do so. Although their circumstances may be small and confining, their characters are strong and courageous. (pp. 92-3)

[These characters'] integrity, strength, and initiative go far to redeem the barren settings in which they are placed. . . . Far from being only the gloomiest of realists or the sternest of social historians, Mary Wilkins Freeman is also a writer of vital and complex short stories whose positive force is vastly underestimated. The struggles she depicts of individual and community glow with an intense and modern light. (p. 93)

*Susan Allen Toth, "Defiant Light: A Positive View of Mary Wilkins Freeman," in* The New England Quarterly *(copyright 1973 by The New England*

Quarterly), *Vol. XLVI, No. 1, March, 1973, pp. 82-93.*

**ALICE GLARDEN BRAND**   (essay date 1977)

[*In a standard interpretation of Freeman's character types, Brand generalizes about Freeman's male characters, describing them as ignorant and bestial; she sees Freeman's female characters as apathetic creatures, vulnerable to the pressures of the social order and for the most part mindlessly consenting to the rural parochialism which structures their lives.*]

Freeman's characters are the New England peasantry. They are the leftovers of society—the spinsters, widows and widowers, bachelors, and elderly—living civilized but neglected lives. Women dominate the action in her stories. But her men, as antiheros, cannot be extricated from the action. Each human silhouette implicates the other. They, as archetypes, bear a frightening timelessness because, in the evolution of human behavior, they are prevalent and ubiquitous.

Freeman's men are the nadir of humanity. Their ignorance is exceeded only by their bestiality. If they choose to assert, they are aggressive. If they choose to withdraw, they are foolish. In either case, the men are unable to cope with conflict in ways other than those established by the rural society. Socially prescribed behaviors for men (as for women) were inflexible and unsatisfying.

Freeman is also as harsh with her women; but she is more discriminating when she defines their characteristics. In early stories, women, particularly the young, sense the inevitability of their existences as vulnerable to the social order. Society placed a premium on marriage, self-control, and impassiveness. Women's apathy was a mindless consent to rural parochialism. As Freeman becomes angrier and bolder, her women become angrier and bolder. When Freeman's men exemplify ignominy, female aggression is conspicious and justifiable. Nevertheless, self-destructive tendencies permeate that aggression. This response is never far from Freeman's thematic center. (pp. 83-4)

In her fiction, spanning the years 1887 to 1928, relationships between men and women were seen in an unchanging framework. Women were charged with the responsibility for preserving men's egos. Men were charged with the responsibility for potency, a facade for incompetence and ignorance. Women faithfully lived out frustrations. Thus, men and women reinforced each other's roles. (pp. 83-4)

Freeman's people are in the eye of a storm. A rare few manage to reach the fringe of the storm but they are never free to move through it. Few seem at the edge of great profundities, but self-analysis is avoided by a fictional cloture which was culturally defined. Freeman's central characters do not have life-affirming experiences. They are inexorably drawn to stasis within predatory or parasitic relationships. The fictional noise is trivia: housekeeping, animals, religious imperatives, gossip—the legitimate blur on more primal frustrations. Men and women are endowed with immunity from the impulses of the other. They respond with composite deceptions. Because the characters act outside themselves, the spiritual center of this writing is Freeman's contempt for their emotional bondage.

Freeman's rifle fire barely misses a relational abnormality by ego diminution. The common denominators of men are plain; they are gullible, vain, intellectually feeble, and emotionally illiterate. Men are most noxious when they live out their pas-

sions and vices. Unhealthy passivity traditionally associated with women is seen in Jim Bennett [in **"Coronation"**] and Marcus Woodman [in **"A Conflict Ended"**]. . . . Clearly, in Freeman's stories, behavioral anomalies are not sexually stereotyped.

Freeman's rifle-fire barely misses a relational abnormality in which men and women are equal targets. However, she endows her women with responses which are more differentiated than those assigned her men. Young women bear ambiguous and silent resentments, refusing to recognize them as aberrations. The young women are more likely to abdicate their identities; in effect, young women relinquish roles they never had, because they have learned to externalize authenticity. Freeman also attacks sacrificing and self-indulgent women as the breed of traditional martyrs. Most, she condemns women who exhibit open hostility. The status of spinster, or of those elderly married, made women eligible for self-expression; but self-expression was commonly refracted through a prism of hate. Aging intractably, these women possessed unremitting guile played out in manipulative schemes. If they chose to fight for autonomy, they fought wrong. That they were incapable of self-exploration is taken for granted. But the anger embedded in their actions is complex and its genesis inaccessible to them.

Women's anger distorted their perception because it could not be confronted and examined. Beneath their anger were such complex fears as fear of their sexuality and fear of social and religious penalty. Yet more basic than these fears was a sense of helplessness. Dependence further obscured their consciousness. When Freeman's characters reached out from helplessness they reached out in fury—they attacked. While their violence was controlled it was nevertheless maladaptive; their aggressive acts devoured their integrity and the integrity of their partners. In short, their anger betrayed them.

Anger was one condoned method for coming to terms with a world which limited personal responses. Freeman's characters did not question their rage even when it dominated their responses. Without this confrontation they could never hope to understand and cope with it, just as they could never hope to understand and deal with their helplessness or their passivity.

Freeman's fiction describes a near-perfect social indoctrination regarding admissible emotions. Puritan society did not allow the peasantry the mental tools needed to define their feelings. Rural existence meant maintaining a socially defined equilibrium with a prescribed set of unexamined emotions. In sum, the religious and social dogma did not merely slow the evolution of self-experience; it fragmented, inverted, obscured, or obliterated it.

Throughout her stories, Freeman's cynical view of rural parochialism remains constant and clear. The social order perpetuated itself by controlling every aspect of rural life. Sex roles were inflexible and inviolate. Men and women shared an understandable yet a pathological need to cling to these roles. They orbited around their partners, working, in effect, to ensnare themselves in unhealthy relationships. The relational aberrations in these stories are indiscriminate and pervasive. Freeman is unsparing in her misanthropy.

Freeman's creative work was didactic. She taught the balance of inner and outer worlds by weighting her fiction with the outer world.

Are cultural scars the required prelude to contemporary self-definition? Does reading Freeman make a difference? In tracing femaleness from passivity to rage or extinction, Freeman focuses on the struggles for woman's identity. In tracing maleness from impotence to aggression and bestiality, she extrapolates his inhumanities. Finally, in delineating the peasant culture, she offers human experience sufficiently basic to give breadth to its contemporary interpretations.

She reminds the reader that tradition distorts identity. She implicates emotional disguises which undermine self-exploration. With almost slavish repetition, she records archaic behaviors which perpetuate anger and defend it mindlessly. She forces the reader to confront rage and search for its genesis.

She was more than didactic. She was a palatable propagandist because her messages were ulterior and multiple. Her narratives were subversive; heavy with unspoken possibilities. She was a civilized critic of destructive human behaviors and by documenting these behaviors she pressed for their eradication. (pp. 98-100)

> *Alice Garden Brand, "Mary Wilkins Freeman: Misanthropy As Propaganda," in* The New England Quarterly *(copyright 1977 by* The New England Quarterly*), Vol. L, No. 1, March, 1977, pp. 83-100.*

**JOSEPH R. McELRATH, JR.**    (essay date 1980)

Mary E. Wilkins Freeman's **"The Revolt of Mother"** is a short story which is now receiving a good deal of attention because of its relevance to the history of American feminism. The mother in revolt is one of those tough-minded, self-aware, and determined females that began to appear at the close of the nineteenth century when the so-called "New Woman" was assuming clear definition. And there's no need to quibble over feminists' characteristic distortions and general hobby-horse riding: Sarah Penn *is* the real thing, a female who successfully revolts against and liberates herself from a familial situation of pernicious male dominance. There is, however, a more important reason for modern readers to focus upon this particular Freeman tale. It is one of her best. Artistically, it transcends the many, many similar pieces that Freeman produced for the American magazine and book reading public of the 1880s and '90s.

It should be stressed here that **"The Revolt of Mother"** is magazine fiction. . . . The reason for this emphasis is that in a collection of Freeman's stories—and this applies to all of them—the quality of individual stories is frequently overlooked or blurred as one finishes a tale and then quickly moves on to the next. In the collections there is a quality of sameness which cannot be denied. Freeman worked with regional types, and by the time one finishes a collection of ten tales he usually knows all he wants to, thank you, about the New England spinster, the New England widow, the New England old folks, and the New England schoolmistress. Freeman's contemporaneous popularity and claim to attention in literary history cannot be fully understood until one forces himself to read her works as they first appeared. Freeman initially drew attention to herself as the author of individual tales which were published in individual issues of magazines. They were originally designed to be read in this manner, and they appear at their best when considered thus. (p. 255)

[Freeman, in **"The Revolt of Mother",**] abruptly seduces the reader into her fictional world and deliberately arranges her tensely emotional material in a series of crises, each of which seems to momentarily function as a climactic conclusion. With a rapid pace she seems to resolve the central conflict of the story, only to renew the same conflict. Then she quickly moves to another apparent resolution, whereupon that "resolution" complicates matters further. When the actual conclusion finally does occur—providing the most surprising and unexpectedly emotional resolution of all—the sympathetic reader who delights in complication piled upon complication receives a rich reward: a happy ending totally unanticipated by the crisis-ridden and foreboding events that led up to it. If masterful artistry involves the writer's ability to manipulate the reader's mind and emotions to the point of self-forgetfulness and total immersion in the workings of a tale, **"The Revolt of Mother"** is a masterwork. At the least, it is a classic example of the artful use of anticlimax as a deliberate narrative device.

Forewarned of a revolt because of the title, the reader begins the story with the expectation of a crisis which will soon develop. . . . Without even the "exposition of background data" one expects to find attending the introduction of the principal characters, Freeman immediately proceeds to dramatize the story's emotional conflict and to build toward the first (apparent) resolution.

**"The Revolt"** begins *in media res,* with the two main characters assuming definition through their actions and the imagery assigned by Freeman to them. . . . (pp. 256-57)

Father—Adoniram Penn—is . . . introduced as the unsavory villain of the piece, a defiant man who will have his way and who will brook no opposition to his plans. . . .

The sensationality of the opening is enhanced when the reader is allowed a view of the personality questioning Adoniram. (p. 257)

It is Adoniram who then retreats, although he does not change his mind about the barn. He temporarily defuses the situation by his withdrawal; and Freeman then turns to the Mother, explaining through dialogue that Adoniram has conspired to build the barn without her consent and against her known desires. By the time son Sammy reveals to Mother that Father also intends to buy four more cows, the first "act" of the story with its crisis/climax is complete. A stiff-necked Adoniram and equally willful Mother have completed their initial confrontation, and Adoniram has won the contest. Mother does silently return to her kitchen, where we soon discover that she is in no way as sinister as her husband seems and that, while she is strong-willed, she is clearly a sympathetically conceived victim of her husband's obstinate nature.

This constitutes the first resolution of conflict in **"The Revolt of Mother,"** and hence the usefulness of a dramatic term such as "act" in explaining the short story. The first section of the story functions as a one-act play: a conflict was introduced; it moved toward a muted but real climax; and the conflict was resolved by the withdrawal of Adoniram and the capitulation of Mother.

But, the story, and the conflict, as it turns out, have only begun. The second act opens with Mother, saying "nothing more," entering her pantry. As Adoniram expressed his emotionality by roughly handling the mare, Mother likewise employs the means at hand: "a clatter of dishes" is heard. She attempts to resign herself to the situation in dutiful, housewifely fashion. But as she begins washing dishes with her daughter Nanny, the attempt seems to be failing. Her behavior bristles with suppressed rage. Mother "plunged her hands vigorously into the water" as Nanny identifies the cause of the conflict initiated in act one: "'don't you think it's too bad father's going to build that barn, much as we need a decent house to live in?'" That this is the root of resentment is confirmed by Mother who then "scrubbed a dish fiercely." Her anger is finally articulated: "'You ain't found out yet we're women-folks, Nanny Penn'." . . . (pp. 257-58)

Nanny goes on to lament the fact that her impending wedding will take place in their ill-decorated "box of a house." She is not exaggerating about the house. . . . Nanny is upset; Mother is upset. But then Mother goes on to display the nobility of character which makes her such a positively fashioned heroine in the eyes of the reader and which, by way of contrast, makes Adoniram seem an even blacker villain. For forty years Adoniram has promised a decent house but has built only the structures he felt he needed for his business. Mother has just passed through the most recent and greatest betrayal of that promise. Yet she has strength of character enough not to exact revenge by turning Nanny against her father. She attempts to appreciate the finer points of her situation, reminding Nanny that "a good many girls don't have as good a place as this." . . . Then she notes what a blessing it is that Adoniram built a cooking shed for them so that they would not have to bake in the house during hot weather.

A few hours later, with both of the children out of the way, a second crisis is initiated by Mother. She calls Adoniram from his work, sits him down, reminds him that she has never complained before, and begins to complain at length about his placing barns and cows above familial obligations. She delivers a brilliantly passionate monologue, clearly vindicating her claim that she and her children have been wronged. "Mrs. Penn's face was burning; her mild eyes gleamed. She had pleaded her little cause like a Webster," hearing in response only Adoniram's blunt reply, "'I ain't got nothin' to say.'" . . . That resolves the crisis. Adoniram shuffles out; Mother goes to the bedroom, and later comes back to the kitchen with reddened eyes. Renewed conflict—crisis—resolution.

A third act begins with Nanny returning to the kitchen miffed, sarcastically suggesting that her wedding might better be held in the new barn which will undoubtedly be nicer than the house. Nanny notes her mother's peculiar expression when she completes this pettish suggestion. It will become clear to the reader several hundred words later that this constitutes actual "crisis" moment of the narrative structure (determining the outcome of the tale): it is here that Mother decides to make the barn their new home should the opportunity afford itself. At present, though, Freeman withholds this information and runs the risk of maintaining reader interest with a peculiar kind of suspense. The question that comes to mind at this point is, where can the story possibly be going? In view of the many paragraphs remaining, *something* is certainly about to happen. But it is simply unthinkable, given the information Freeman has fed the reader, that Adoniram will change his mind.

The story leaps ahead through the spring months during which the barn is being constructed, and Freeman relates that Mother no longer speaks of the matter. We are duped into thinking that Mother has, indeed, resigned herself to the egotism of her husband—that the conflict of acts one and two has been truly resolved. Freeman now elaborates upon Adoniram's villainy, once again confirming the belief that Mother's situation is a hopeless one. (pp. 258-59)

A maxim occurs to Mother after Adoniram's departure [on a buying-trip]: "'Unsolicited opportunities are the guide-posts

of the Lord to the new roads of life.'" . . . She forthwith gives directions to the help: move all of the household belongings to the barn. The event is a grandly liberating and heroic one, even if it does seem destined to produce an unhappy outcome. (pp. 259-60)

Most of the fourth act is given to the rising action leading to the true "climax" of the narrative structure and its rapidly executed denouement and conclusion. What *will* Adoniram do when he returns? We know only the most negative things about his character: he has seemed violent; he has acted in the most egotistical and pig-headed ways; he has been curt with Mother beyond the point of simple rudeness; and he expects no one to cross him, least of all Mother. We are free to imagine only dire consequences.

Reader interest is heightened through more suspense. The local characters begin ruminating over the probable outcome of this revolt; they loiter about the neighborhood on the day of Adoniram's return to see what will happen. We know that Mother is not going to back down. When the local minister comes to reason with her, she is shelling peas "as if they were bullets," and when she looks at him there is in her eyes "the spirit that her meek front had covered for a lifetime." . . . (p. 260)

What the reader does not expect after all that has occurred is a comic reversal. But Freeman does end this tale of impending tragedy with a startling turn to a tragicomic resolution. And the truly amazing thing is that she turns the tables on the reader as convincingly as she does. Adoniram shows none of the anger that seemed to be so great a part of his nature at the story's beginning. Adoniram shows no anger at all. Rather, he is totally bewildered, able only to say "'Why, mother!'" again and again as he tries to grasp the change that has taken place. . . . He totally capitulates, promising to finish the new barn as a house. There is no resentment. Instead there is the first show of his love for Mother in the whole tale: "'Why, mother,' he said, hoarsely, 'I hadn't no idee you was so set on't as all this comes to'." . . . He is telling the truth, oddly enough. Freeman had withheld the fact that Adoniram's could be, and was, a sensitive and loving nature—albeit an extraordinarily dense one. It is one of the most complicated trick-endings in all of nineteenth-century American short fiction. Freeman did all that she could to suppress suspicion that such an ending could be even remotely possible. Her mastery is especially made manifest when we think back over the story and note how she developed the scenes to obscure positive personality traits in Adoniram which were actually there all the time. (pp. 260-61)

The reassuring testimony to the admixture of good and evil in human nature with which Freeman startles the reader at the conclusion of **"The Revolt"** is vintage Howellsian realism at its enduring best. **"The Revolt"** is also, to speak more plainly, literary gimmickry at its best. It is so well executed that, while some readers may resent the withholding of *the* fact about Adoniram that changes everything, the rest of us can enjoy the notion that love can sometimes conquer all, in 1890 and even in the 1980s. (p. 261)

*Joseph R. McElrath, Jr., "The Artistry of Mary E. Wilkins Freeman's 'The Revolt'," in* Studies in Short Fiction *(copyright 1980 by Newberry College), Vol. 17, No. 3, Summer, 1980, pp. 255-61.*

ADDITIONAL BIBLIOGRAPHY

Brooks, Van Wyck. "Country Pictures." In his *New England: Indian Summer,* pp. 455-73. E. P. Dutton & Co., 1940.\*
    Discusses the contrast between "dearth, decay, and dessication" and the "vigour of life" in New England, and considers Freeman, together with Robert Frost, Rudyard Kipling, Edwin Arlington Robinson, Edith Wharton, and Eugene O'Neill, as the authors who best portrayed both of these aspects of New England life.

"Novels of American Life." *The Edinburgh Review,* No. CCCLXXXIV (April 1898): 386-414.\*
    Early favorable review of *Pembroke.* The critic praises Freeman's portrayal of New England character types, but mentions that her range is limited.

Hirsch, David H. "Subdued Meaning in 'A New England Nun'." *Studies in Short Fiction* II, No. 1 (Fall 1964): 124-36.
    Interprets in psychoanalytic and mythic terms one of Freeman's best-known stories.

Quina, James H. "Character Types in the Fiction of Mary Wilkins Freeman." *Colby Library Quarterly* IX, No. 8 (December 1971): 432-39.
    Divides Freeman's character types into four groups: the control groups who maintain the status quo; the ascetics who have withdrawn from life; those who rebel against the status quo; and those who moderate between the second and third character types.

Sherman, Sarah W. "The Great Goddess in New England: Mary Wilkins Freeman's 'Christmas Jenny'." *Studies in Short Fiction* 17, No. 2 (Spring 1980): 157-64.

Mythic interpretation of "Christmas Jenny." Sherman interprets the eponymous character as an archetypal earth mother or fertility symbol.

Toth, Susan Allen. "Mary Wilkins Freeman's Parable of Wasted Life." *American Literature* XLII, No. 4 (January 1971): 564-67.
    Comparison of Freeman's "The Three Old Sisters and the Old Beau" with Hawthorne's "The Wedding Knell," stressing the differences in the authors' approaches to similar story lines.

Williams, Blanche Colton. "Mary Wilkins Freeman." In her *Our Short Story Writers,* pp. 160-181. 1922. Reprint. Freeport, N.Y.: Books for Libraries Press, 1969.
    Discussion of Freeman's short fiction, analyzing some of her main characters.

Wood, Ann Douglas. "The Literature of Impoverishment: The Women Local Colorists in America, 1865-1914." *Women's Studies* 1, No. 1 (1972): 3-45.\*
    Places Freeman in relation to other women local colorists from the late 1800s and early 1900s, including Sarah Orne Jewett, Rose Terry Cooke, and Kate Chopin. The differences between the local colorists and the pre-Civil War women romantic novelists are discussed.

Ziff, Larzer. "An Abyss of Inequality: Sarah Orne Jewett, Mary Wilkins Freeman, Kate Chopin." In his *The American 1890s: Life and Times of a Lost Generation,* pp. 275-305. New York: The Viking Press, 1966.\*
    Argues against Freeman's classification as a major author of regional fiction, saying that the New England of her stories "could be anywhere rural and neglected," and that "she seems not to have had a sense of her craft and not to have grown with it."

# (Gibran) Kahlil Gibran

## 1883-1931

(Also transliterated as Khalil; also Jibrān and Jabrān) Lebanese poet, aphorist, short story writer, novelist, and dramatist.

Author of the immensely popular *The Prophet*, Gibran is one of the most commercially successful poets of this century. His small books, biblical in style and often illustrated with his own allegorical drawings, have been translated into twenty languages, making him the most widely known writer to emerge from the Arab-speaking world. Gibran's poetry and prose are recognized for their metrical beauty and emotionally evocative language. They also demonstrate an ecstatic spiritualism and a serene love of humanity. Gibran's mysticism led Auguste Rodin to call him "the William Blake of the twentieth century."

Born of Maronite Christian parents in the village of Bsherri, Gibran was a talented child who exhibited advanced abilities in drawing, building, modeling, and writing. As a teenager he went to Paris and studied art under Rodin at the École des Beaux Arts. There he began his first serious experiments in literature, writing prose poems and short plays in Arabic. In 1904 Gibran moved to the United States, where he met Mary Haskell, a Bostonian headmistress who became both his inspiration and adviser. His best works—*The Prophet, Sand and Foam*, and *Jesus the Son of Man*—were written during his years in the United States. By the time of his death, Gibran's work was known throughout the English- and Arabic-speaking world, and the term "Gibranism" had, in many circles, become a common literary term, describing any mystical, poetic expression of one's philosophy.

Gibran's early works—*'Arā'is al-muruj (Nymphs of the Valley), Al-arwāh al-mutamarridah (Spirits Rebellious), Al-ajniha al-mutakassira (The Broken Wings)*, and *Dam 'ah wabtisāmah (A Tear and a Smile)*—are interesting for the light they shed on his development as an artist. All of these, in some way, depict Gibran's typical hero who, with his eloquent tongue, conquers both the feudal lords of the Lebanese aristocracy and a clerical system which is fundamentally anti-Christian. *The Prophet* is considered Gibran's most satisfying work. It was the first book in which he was able to poetically convey his belief in love as a unifying force in nature. In *The Prophet*, Gibran expressed what N. Naimy has called his "triple longing": a longing for the country of his birth, for a utopian society in which he can feel at home, and for a higher world of metaphysical truth. Perhaps Gibran's most important work after *The Prophet* is *Jesus the Son of Man*. In this book, Gibran attempted to portray Christ through the impressions of a number of his contemporaries. Though certain critics have commented on the Nietzschean influence apparent in Gibran's portrait, others argue that Gibran's concept of Christ was shaped more by Blake, especially since his Jesus is not God incarnate, but an ordinary man who has elevated himself from the human to the divine.

Gibran has received little serious treatment from American and European critics. Most maintain that his work, though concerned with important themes, is too poised and didactic.

Some, such as Khalil S. Hawi, believe that Gibran's prophecy and oracular wisdom was simply a literary disguise for a philosophy based on primitivism and escapism. Generally, most critics agree that Gibran had the refined sensibility of a true poet and a gift for language, but that he often marred his work by relying on shallow epigrams and trite parables.

Despite his critics' reservations, Gibran remains the most popular Arab writer of the twentieth century, both inside and outside the Arab-speaking world. In his quest for spiritual truth he exerted a significant influence over the younger generations of the Middle East and the United States. Decades after his death, his work still attracts a wide audience.

(See also *TCLC*, Vol. 1.)

## PRINCIPAL WORKS

*'Arā'is al-muruj*   (short stories)   1910
  [*Nymphs of the Valley*, 1948]
*Dam 'ah wabtisāmah*   (poetry and prose)   1914
  [*Tears and Laughter*, 1946; also published as *A Tear and a Smile*, 1950]
*The Madman*   (poetry and prose)   1918
*The Forerunner*   (poetry and prose)   1920

*Al-arwāh al-mutamarridah* (short stories) 1922
  [*Spirits Rebellious,* 1946]
*The Prophet* (poetry) 1923
*Sand and Foam* (aphorisms) 1926
*Jesus the Son of Man* (prose) 1928
*The Earth Gods* (poetry and prose) 1931
*The Wanderer* (aphorisms and prose) 1932
*Manzūmāt* (poetry) 1934
  [*Prose Poems,* 1934]
*\*The Secrets of the Heart* (poetry and prose) 1947
*\*The Broken Wings* (poetry) 1957
*Beloved Prophet* [with Mary Haskell] (letters) 1972

*These works were previously published in Arabic.

---

### THE NATION   (essay date 1918)

Disciples of the modern cult of things Eastern will possibly
welcome the specimen of the work of the Arab sage, Kahlil
Gibran, which [has recently been] . . . published in the shape
of **"The Madman"**. . . . Of Gibran, Rodin said: "The world
should expect much from this poet painter of Lebanon. He is
the William Blake of the twentieth century." We think, however, that most Westerners will find the work repellent in its
exotic perversity, and will lay it aside with an uncomprehend-
ing shake of the head, for East is East and West is still West,
and Tagore has not really succeeded in bridging the chasm
between them, nor do we think that Gibran will do so. The
most appealing of these parables is **"The Wise Dog"**—though
we frankly prefer La Fontaine. . . .

> *"Notes: 'The Madman',"* in The Nation *(copyright
> 1918 The Nation magazine, The Nation Associates,
> Inc.), Vol. 107, No. 2791, December 28, 1918, p.
> 812.*

### JOHN HAYNES HOLMES   (essay date 1928)

Readers of Mr. Gibran's earlier work, **"The Prophet,"** published in many editions in this country and translated into more
than twenty languages, will know what to expect in [*Jesus the
Son of Man*]. Here is the same poet, with the same austere
purity of thought, the same amplitude and beauty of phrase,
the same wisdom, serenity and lofty vision. Only in this case
his mind is centered upon a single theme, the immortal Galilean, instead of being scattered, as in the earlier volume, over
the far-flung problems of life and death.

Kahlil Gibran has attempted a unique and daring experiment.
He has told the story of Jesus, not as the single biographer or
historian would tell it, but as it would be told, section by
section, episode after episode, by those who had contact with
the Master either for a moment or over a more extended period.
Somewhat after the fashion of Browning in "The Ring and the
Book," he lets character after character speak, each telling
what he has seen, or felt, or known. Most of the characters
are the familiar figures in the Gospels—the disciples, Mary
Magdalen, the other Mary, John the Baptist, Caiaphas, Pilate
and his wife, Zacchaeus, Nicodemus, Joseph of Arimathea.
Others are frankly imaginative, such as Rafca, the bride of
Cana, a Persian philosopher in Damascus, Elmadan the Logician, Rumanous, a Greek Poet, Barca, a merchant of Tyre,
and a cobbler in Jerusalem. Some of the characters speak twice,

as John on Patmos, and Mary Magdalen "thirty years later."
The last witness is a man from Lebanon, "nineteen centuries
afterward." There are seventy-seven personages in all, and
each comes with his offering of interpretation and devotion to
lay it upon the single altar of the Galilean. Friends and enemies,
Jews and Gentiles, Pharisees and sinners, men and women—
all speak. It is like the many variations of some master musician
upon a single theme. Different keys, different harmonies, but
always the same great melody.

If any man were fitted to attempt this adventurous task it is
Mr. Gibran. First of all he is a countryman of Jesus, himself
the man of Lebanon who speaks in the last pages of the book.
He therefore knows Palestine, its people, the cadences of their
speech and the insights of their spirit. It is as though a contemporary sat down, at a belated hour, to write another and
different gospel.

Nor is this as imprudent as it sounds, for Gibran is, secondly,
a poet. It is difficult to describe the mystery of his verse. It
has a simplicity which is disarming and yet a majesty which
at times is overwhelming. It murmurs through long stretches
like a quiet brook and then suddenly crashes like a thunder
storm. Its supreme qualities are, perhaps, the ample phrase
which paints a picture in a few words and the rhythmic stress
and cadence which give perfect balance to lovely words. How
unforgettable the description of the virgin, Mary. . . .

Now and again the poet dares a direct comparison with the
New Testament, as in the parable of the shepherd in South
Lebanon. I heard Mr. Gibran read this parable once and I
thought then, as I think now, that it matches the Scripture
standard.

This book even invites the supreme test by giving speech to
the Nazarene himself. . . .

His writing is not unworthy of the theme which the poet has
chosen for his work.

> *John Haynes Holmes, "A Poet Interprets a Prophet,"
> in* New York Herald Tribune Books *(© I.H.T. Cor-
> poration; reprinted by permission), December 2, 1928,
> p. 6.*

### MIKHAIL NAIMY   (essay date 1934)

> [*Naimy draws parallels between Nietzsche's Zarathustra and Gi-
> bran's Almustafa, in the following excerpt from his* Kahlil Gibran:
> A Biography.]

[*The Prophet*] was not all of Gibran's making. Much of it is
fashioned after Nietzsche's Zarathustra. It seems that Gibran
who had been able to set his mind and imagination free of the
influence of Nietzsche's mind and imagination had not been
able to free himself from the great German's style and form.
Perhaps he was quite unconscious of the fact.

Nietzsche takes for a mouthpiece a prophet called Zarathustra.
Gibran, a prophet called Almustafa.

Nietzsche's Zarathustra walks a stranger among men giving
them now and then of his wisdom; when tired of his exile
among them, he retires to his "Happy Isles." Gibran's Almustafa is also a stranger among men; when weary of his exile
he returns to the "isle of his birth."

Nietzsche's Zarathustra on bidding his disciples farewell towards the end of the First Part of the book says to them in
part, "Now do I bid you lose me and find yourselves; and only

when you have all denied me, will I return unto you.'' Gibran's Almustafa bids his friends farewell and says to them among other things: ''But should my voice fade in your ears, and my love vanish in your memory, then I will come again.''

Zarathustra at the beginning of the Third Part, while preparing to leave his Happy Isles for the world, ascends a high mountain, and in ascending reveals the burdens of his heart. Looking at the sea in the distance, he addresses it thus: ''Ah, this somber, sad sea, below me! Ah, this somber nocturnal vexation! Ah, fate and Sea! To you must I now *go down*!'' Almustafa ascends a hill outside Orphalese, and after speaking long to his heart, looks at the sea and says, ''And you, vast sea, sleeping mother, who alone are peace and freedom to the river and the stream. Only another winding will this stream make; only another murmur in this glade, and then shall I come to you, a boundless drop to a boundless ocean.''

As Zarathustra is Nietzsche in another form, so is Almustafa Gibran under a borrowed name. Both are subjective creations, veiled with symbol and metaphor sufficiently to hide their authors' identities from the ordinary reader. To one, however, who knew Gibran as I knew him the veil appears quite thin and transparent. The twelve years Almustafa spent in waiting for his ship are the twelve years Gibran had lived in New York up to the writing of the prelude to the *Prophet*. The city of Orphalese is no other than New York. Almitra ''who had first sought and believed in him'' is Mary Haskell. ''The isle of his birth'' is Lebanon. His promise to return to the people of Orphalese is but a re-affirmation of his old belief in re-incarnation which holds that those who leave the earth with their accounts unsettled, whether with men or things, must be reborn again and again until they break their last bond with the earth. Viewed from another angle and in a broader light Orphalese may be taken to symbolize the earth, and Almustafa's exile in it to refer to the detachment of the individual spirit from the All-Spirit during its earthly pilgrimage. The ''isle of birth'', then, would be the bosom of the All-Spirit, or the centre of Life Universal. The author leaves the margin wide for the reader's imagination; and therein lies one of the secrets of his art.

Though close and striking is the kinship in form and style between *The Prophet* and ''Thus Spake Zarathustra'', the two books are far apart in substance. For that substance Gibran is indebted mainly to his imagination which was able to tap the ever bubbling springs of the Spirit Universal where all thirsty spirits must slake their thirst. If you, therefore, are struck by the great similarity between Almustafa's sermons and the out-givings of many prophets and *sufis* of the East, be slow to accuse Gibran of giving you borrowed ideas. Say rather that he culled those ideas, bravely and independently, from the same garden where men with an imagination unshackled of weights and measures have always culled theirs. The ideas may not be new, to be sure. Is there anything new under the sun? But they are put forward in words which look and sound almost new; so rhythmic are they, so palpitating with life, so bright of color and so graceful of line, and yet so few in number, that only a pedant, or one color-blind, or one deaf to music, can really find any major fault with them. In this book, more than in any other of his books, Gibran's style reaches its very zenith. Many metaphors are so deftly formed that they stand out like statues chiselled in the rock. To some they may look like riddles—enigmatic and incomprehensible. Such readers must blame their own eye and ear, their poverty of spirit, before they blame the author.

In *The Prophet* Gibran's imagination, looking at life, found it to be one and the same essence—Love. It also found all men to be equal partners in that essence, the only difference being in the realization and application of that truth. (pp. 187-90)

Almustafa lift his hearers [to spiritual heights], his speech sparkling with poetic similes drawn from nature in her various moods, and closely modeled after the Bible even to the extent of borrowing bodily certain expressions such as ''You have been told . . . but I say unto you''; or ''Verily I say unto you,'' and others. But the language flows so smoothly, so naturally, and carries the reader so readily to its goal, that he overlooks all borrowed forms and turns. Hardly can he lay the book down without feeling that his heart has been enriched by the experiences and contemplations of Almustafa's heart, and that his soul's eye has been opened up unto the truth and beauty of the Universal Soul. (p. 191)

*Mikhail Naimy, in his* Kahlil Gibran: A Biography *(copyright 1950 by Mikhail Naimy; originally published in 1934), Philosophical Library, 1950, 267 p.*

## TALMAGE C. JOHNSON   (essay date 1948)

*[Johnson finds Gibran to be a prophet of despair, whose thought seems to mirror the growing disillusionment of the post-World War II Western world.]*

[Gibran is] the modern Oriental prophet, poet and philosopher. The Western world, baffled and confused by the discovery that ''the heart has gone out of Progress'' and that secular materialism has been unable to protect its own gains, listens hopefully. Not understanding exactly what he says, it is the more convinced that he is saying something of vast import. The notes of pessimism and fatalism which a few years ago would have been summarily rejected now strike a responsive chord. Tired of conflict, many are ready to agree with him who declares: ''I am a stranger, and I shall remain a stranger until the white and friendly wings of Death carry me home into my beautiful country. There, where light and peace and understanding abide, I will await the other strangers who will be rescued by the friendly trap of time from this narrow dark world.'' . . . Gibran puts it more delicately than do the Jehovah's Witnesses!

We shall not find in this man from the East the salvation which our hearts tell us we must have or perish. He is too gloomy a prophet, too inconsistent and too far separated from the workaday world. But he may well bring us to a re-examination of a Savior in whom East and West did meet, and we may meet again and again the universal Christ. . . .

Perhaps Gibran, the Oriental mystic, understands better certain aspects of Christianity than do we more practically minded Occidental Christians. We can profit from his fresh presentation of these aspects. . . .

[*The Secrets of the Heart*] is a translation of earlier writings than those which first brought Gibran to the attention of the Western world. It does not add greatly to his stature, for its editor claims too much when he says that ''his earliest—like his latest—writings project timeless universal truths.'' To some extent they do, but not nearly so effectively as his later works. In these earlier writings, he is definitely more Oriental and less universal than in some of the later ones.

*Talmage C. Johnson, ''Never the Twain—,'' in* The Christian Century *(copyright 1948 Christian Century Foundation; reprinted by permission from the Feb-*

ruary 4, 1948 issue of The Christian Century), Vol. LXV, No. 5, February 4, 1948, p. 144.

**ROBERT HILLYER** (essay date 1950)

[*A noted poet and professor of English, Hillyer discusses common themes in Gibran's canon, and traces the development of Gibran's philosophy in* A Tear and a Smile. *Hillyer finds the work a crucial one in Gibran's life and artistic development.*]

*A Tear and a Smile* includes much of Kahlil Gibran's earliest work, and, with the interesting prose poem written in Paris on his twenty-fifth birthday, marks the beginning of a more mature and affirmative response to life. Like those of many romantic poets, of the East or the West, his youthful flights were toward the white radiance of eternity, away from a world that seemed largely in the hands of injustice and violence. The recoil of a sensitive mind from reality frequently takes revolutionary forms of which political revolution is merely the most obvious. With Gibran the revolt was not directed toward institutions so much as toward the individuals who became the accomplices of abstract evil, of greed, injustice, and bloodshed. Most of the human figures in his early works are therefore personifications, with the result that parable and allegory are the usual method. His later works, more frankly homiletic, gain from the abandonment of the indirect narrative style and present a bolder acceptance of hope for felicity in the here and now. (p. vii)

Gibran's figure of the Poet stands at the top of his hierarchy, far and away the highest of mankind. As contemplation of the stars may lift the spirit of some, or the sea the spirit of others, so in Gibran's case the background of his time-scarred country provided a vision of the great and the small, the many and the one, the things that perish and the things that endure, which is the measuring-rod of the poets. (pp. x-xi)

In his youthful revolt against priestcraft he showed a spiritual affinity to the English poet William Blake. As time went on, other aspects of the Occidental mystic's philosophy combined to influence Gibran's writings and his drawings as well. The kinship was clearly discernible and acknowledged. Many convictions were common to both: a hatred of sham and binding orthodoxy, personified by evil priests; the manumission of physical love from the bonds of convention in order to attain spiritual completeness; the perception of beauty in the moment that seems to be fleeting but is, in truth, everlasting; and the discovery of miracles in seasonal nature and the commonplace things of daily living. Both warred against reason in the name of imagination. Both defied the snares of logic to cut a straight wingpath directly to God. (p. xi)

In Gibran's *Prophet* a separate character is assigned to the Poet, yet they are two aspects of the same entity, the highest emanation of Man. The poet can sin only in denying his own nature—and in all Gibran's pages no poet commits such a sin. (p. xii)

"The Poet's Death Is His Life" is a dialogue between the poet and Death, showing Death as the poet's friend and consummate love, who alone can set his spirit free and, as men are gradually enlightened, endow with his prophecies a fairer world. We approach here a conception of the poet as one who gives his life for the redemption of mankind. The logical assumption that Jesus was the ultimate Poet was to Gibran a not unnatural conclusion.

More orthodox conceptions of Christ, as formulated by the churches, were repulsive to him. If the Poet was incapable of

wrong, the Priest, at least in these early works, could do no right. . . . In *Nymphs of the Valley* we read the story of the poor boy tormented by the wicked monks; in *Spirits Rebellious* it is the Priest who pronounces the curse over the bodies of the bride and her lover who died faithful to their love.

We of the West cannot weigh the factual truth of Gibran's portrayal of the priesthood in his youthful works. It may be that the Syrian Church of his boyhood was indeed the purveyor of corruption, the jeweled bauble empty of significance, the oppressor of the poor, as he describes it. Remnants of Byzantine splendor along with Byzantine decay may cling to the Eastern churches; the poet's indignation cannot be wholly without reference to observed conditions. (pp. xiii-xiv)

Yet it must be remembered that the Oriental method of personifying institutions and summoning an entire situation into one symbol was characteristic of Gibran's work, especially in his novitiate as poet. Truth to a large design, as in Byzantine art, sometimes demanded the distortion of details. His realism consisted in the massing of general effects to emphasize concepts that he believed to be the ultimate reality. Thus he was at the opposite pole from contemporary realists who overwhelm large themes in an avalanche of careful detail. In this fact lies much of Gibran's appeal for the reader who wearies of the modern Occidental technique, which so often leads to the gutter and away from the stars. The photographic reproduction of actuality with no reference to the more expansive designs of Truth and Justice, Beauty and Peace, would have held no interest for Gibran.

In this symbolic usage, parallel to the good Poet and the bad Priest, we find the Poor Man, who is always oppressed, and the Rich Man, who is always the oppressor. In infancy the Prince's son is hailed with songs of praise as one who "will be to you a pride and delight and the heir to the inheritance of my great forefathers. Rejoice then . . . for your future now belongs to this scion of our house." At the same time a poverty-stricken woman gives birth to her son, and "when the noise of the multitudes in the streets had died the wretched woman placed the infant in her lap and looked into its shining eyes, and she wept as though she would baptize the child with her tears. 'Have compassion on us, O Lord!'" And thus the separate destinies of the rich and the poor are spun out until even in death the division persists, as in "**The City of the Dead.**" . . . [Here, despite] the impressiveness of the conclusion, we are aware that the symbolic method in such a story is far too generalized to support the scrutiny of truth. It becomes little more than sentimentalism, gilded by the rays of uncertain artistry. Sentimentalism of this kind is the prevailing weakness of young romantics, including, at times, the young Blake.

With the Poor Man and the Priest, the Lover completes the trinity of noble personages. In the early parables physical union, but delicately hinted at, is the consummation, the release of the soul. There is no sustained emphasis on the sensualism we associate with the love poetry of the Orient, and even the discernible echoes from the *Song of Songs* are chastened and become rather remote. (pp. xiv-xvi)

Death is the ultimate lover. It may come as a king whose hand is laid upon the lost shepherd; it may come as a woman of unearthly beauty clothed in a garment white as snow. It is life itself in perfected form. (p. xvii)

The life after death, however, is a separate theme that undergoes a change through Gibran's writings. The early stories indicate a belief in the doctrine of reincarnation that seems more than a literary device. In *Nymphs of the Valley* there is the story of the lovers who meet again after two thousand years in the ruins of the temple of Astarte, and there complete the noble passion that was frustrated so long before, by the priests of a faith whose altars now lie open to the wind and rain. But later Gibran seems to have joined the neo-Platonists in their belief in the return of the individual soul to God.

Evidently Gibran left behind him very early his childhood conception of individual redemption and survival as taught in Christianity. In the theory of reincarnation of the soul the identity half persists through a succession of new experiences with no recollection of what has gone before except in occasional flashes of revelation. At last he surrendered his last vestige of belief in the survival of the individual and spoke of the reunion of that particle of deity, that small kingdom of God within each man, with the all-embracing Godhead. The rest is the dross of this world, gratefully to be relinquished as the soul takes its lonely flight back to its Source.

*A Tear and a Smile* exhibits this somewhat emotional philosophy at its most untamed. If the parables and observations lack the serenity of *The Prophet* or *The Madman*, they have some compensating vigor, almost a rashness, of approach, natural to a young writer who, had he been born in the West, would have been a late recruit to the romantic school. The book is more Eastern, however, than his later writings. It is probable that in these Arabic compositions he was writing for his countrymen at home and in exile. (pp. xvii-xviii)

In the beginning of [*A Tear and a Smile*] we are told that the tear of sorrow purifies the heart and that the smile of joy warms it with understanding. Spiritual hunger is the goal of life; the quest is its own fulfillment. To realize a dream is to lose it, and the satisfied of this world are the most wretched of people. Divested of personification, these ideas may be presented without sentimentalism. They are best left undramatized, and that fact was borne in upon the maturing poet. (p. xviii)

Gibran's strength developed not from a change of technique but from a change in emphasis. It would be unnatural for a mature poet to continue to express nothing but loathing for the world in which he lives, and always to point "yonder." Such grimly maintained irony in English and American poetry of the past generation has resulted in a wasteland of lamentations which, on analysis, prove to be but the vulgar exposure of personal woes and inadequacies. The phrasing is tough, but the core is effeminate. Poetry cannot proceed along a series of negations. Gibran's best work, embellished though it is with Asian metaphor, develops manlier qualities. Hope, cheerfulness, and anger displace the perhaps overworked tears and smiles, and they increase as the poet grows older.

The second half of [*A Tear and a Smile*] is in the main given over to these more positive moods. "**The Widow and Her Son**" is a dignified little *genre* piece wherein the treasure of the humble is adequately realized. Patriotism is the inspiration of "**A People and Destiny**," wherein Syria, personified as a shepherdess, consults with Destiny, in the guise of an old man, with something keener than mere wistfulness for a vanished past. "Behold the sun rising from out of darkness"—the conclusion of "**Peace**"—becomes gradually the prevailing theme. The Sun, moreover, is not only that eventual and spiritual orb to be reached through the gates of suffering and death, but the good daily sun, warming the earth to a genial response, a felicity in the here and now, an assurance of terrestrial bliss.

Thus in his first flights the poet sped toward eternity and saw the world as a place where misfortune must purify the soul for its reunion with God. Then the increasing warmth of life led him to be less dualistic: the material world became informed with the heavenly light. Gibran's ripened philosophy was anticipated in several of the selections [in *A Tear and a Smile*], prominently in "**My Birthday**," written in Paris when he became twenty-five. In this piece he explicitly turns away from his past writings and drawings in the sudden arrival of a joy he had not imagined: a meaning in the faces of people, their voices rising upward in the streets of the city, children at play, young men and old, and so beyond that city, not in escape but in understanding, to "the wild parts in their awful beauty and voiced silence," then on to the sea, the stars, and "all the contending . . . forces of attraction and repulsion . . . created and borne by that Will, timeless and without limit." We are reminded of the climax of Victor Hugo's famous "Extase." . . . (pp. xix-xxi)

At the end Gibran discovers and acknowledges that "humanity is the spirit of divineness on earth," and "what I now say with one tongue, tomorrow will say with many."

The poet grows up. The detestable Priests and Rich Men disappear; the impeccable Poets and Lovers take on more lively attributes than mere flawlessness. Eternity becomes more than a distant star wherein we shall quench the small, wandering fire of our being. It begins to shine through the earth, not away from it. (p. xxi)

> *Robert Hillyer, in his introduction to* A Tear and A Smile *by Kahlil Gibran (copyright 1950, copyright renewed 1977, by Alfred A. Knopf, Inc.; reprinted by permission of the publisher), Knopf, 1950 (and reprinted by Knopf, 1972), pp. vii-xxi.*

### SUHAIL IBN-SALIM HANNA (essay date 1968)

[*Hanna draws parallels between the life and work of Gibran and that of Walt Whitman, examining similarities in tone, style, and philosophy in* The Prophet *and* "Song of Myself."]

[Hamilton A.R. Gibb] once suggested that "the brilliant writers of the young Syro-American school were engaged in the creation of a new literary art, the 'prose poem' (*shir manthur*), which owed its inspiration to Walt Whitman and English free verse." This insight, though mentioned in passing by Professor Gibb, is penetrating indeed. A close, even a cursory, analysis of Gibran's work reveals a marked similarity to that of Whitman. Specifically, Gibran's spiritual yearnings, his broad vision, his mystical strength, his celebration of the self, his blend of Oriental and Occidental ideas—these and other qualities can be found in Whitman's poetry. In style, Gibran, like Whitman, broke away from conventional verse forms and made use of a loose, irregular, at times chanting, rhythm. These two rather broad parallels characterize, in a general way, the writings of the two poets. Whitman in "Song of Myself" and Gibran in *The Prophet* wrote what might be considered their finest and most fully realized works. Devoted primarily to these two works, the present analysis delineates the motifs and style used by Gibran and earlier by Whitman; moreover, it maintains that Gibran's work reflects a conscious, not a mere coincidental, return to the poetry of Walt Whitman.

Mysticism is one of the main, pervasive elements in *The Prophet* and in "Song of Myself." (pp. 175-76)

[*The Prophet*], like "Song of Myself," is concerned with the life of the author. Both works, however, are not autobiographical studies in the strict sense of the term. They do not treat

Gibran or Whitman as central characters, each with his own distinctive mind, attitudes, and personality. For underlying both works is the profound realization that man's soul partakes, in a Platonic manner, of a Higher Soul. The poet's soul, Gibran and Whitman believe, tends to be fused with other selves; his life, with all its love, joy, pain, hope, becomes a vital part of the lives of his fellowmen. *The Prophet* and ''Song of Myself,'' then, are less the single ''journal of a soul'' than they are ''the way of all souls.''

There are many stages in a man's life. Some are sinuous and turbulent; others meander but are relatively calm. Yet they are all a part of the same stream and the same life. From the varied stages in Gibran's life, one can graph a clear pattern. In his early years, for example, Gibran seemed to cling to a bold, rebellious, heretical mode, one that was Nietzschian in character. It took Gibran, as Naimy demonstrated, a good while before he finally shook off the shackles of Nietzschian pessimism and unrest. In the later stages of his life (which ended at the age of forty-eight), Gibran began to reject the spirit of the nineteenth century rebel and to assert a stronger belief in the ideas of the Enlightment of the eighteenth century. Like Whitman, Gibran came to see, even accept, the reality of a benevolent and harmonious universe. (pp. 176-77)

In a mystical experience, the nature and reality of God are vital features. To Gibran and Whitman, God is not the Christian God of the New Testament or the Jehovah of the Old. In *Jesus the Son of Man,* Gibran strips Christ of his traditional divinity and assigns to him the virtues of the most noble, lofty, inspiring human ideal. In a not dissimilar mode, Whitman suggests in ''Chanting the Square Deific'' an idea that is radical to the mind of a Christian. In this poem, God is not a trinity but a quaternity. The Old Testament God is generally thought to control nature; but the God underlying both *The Prophet* and ''Song of Myself'' is immanent in character; his divinity is within nature. Historically, he is the Lord of the Upanishads in which the Brahman ''is all in all''—the One (absolute, eternal, all-encompassing Consciousness). In a crucial sense, this God is not really a person, but a principle; not a figure, but a force. ''Perhaps,'' Gibran once speculated, ''we are nearer to Him each time we try to divide Him and find Him indivisible.'' With the ancient Indian mystics, both poets believe that from God all living creatures emanate and to Him they all return. (pp. 177-78)

Fundamentally, Gibran thought, if a union with the Omnipresent is to be meaningful, the mystic ''must renounce his individual self to find it in the infinite All-Self. He must not hate any man, for he becomes all men.'' In this belief, Gibran seemed to be attuned to the chant that Whitman sang in the fifth section of ''Song of Myself.'' . . . In his mysticism, then, Gibran, like Whitman, identified his human self (*atman* or *jivatman,* to use the terms of Upanishadic literature) with other selves. In the process, his real self would merge with the stuff of the infinite All-Self, with the Brahman, with Emerson's Over-Soul, indeed with God.

Besides the telling blend of mysticism that pervades *The Prophet* and ''Song of Myself,'' the two works share a common structure. Both are not primarily logical but psychological in form. They are not geometrical figures but musical progressions. As music, *The Prophet,* like ''Song of Myself,'' is not really a symphony with contrasting movements. It, moreover, does not follow an operatic pattern in the strict sense with an overture, arias, recitatives, and a finale. In connection with its true structure, what has been noted of Whitman's masterpiece clearly

applies to *The Prophet:* ''It comes closer to being a rhapsody of tone poem, one that modulates from theme to theme, often changing in key and tempo, falling into reveries and rising toward moments of climax, but always preserving its unity of feeling as it moves onward in a wave-like flow.'' It can further be added that Gibran, like Whitman, ''preferred to let one image suggest another image, which in turn suggests a new statement of mood or doctrine. His themes modulate into one another by pure association, as in a waking dream, with the result that all his transitions seem instinctively right.''

It also might be useful to conceive of *The Prophet* and ''Song of Myself'' as dramas with the poet himself assuming the central role. Both works portray the poet's entry into a mystical state, his journey through its various stages, and finally his emergence from that state. Almustafa—Gibran's ''Prophet of God, in quest of the uttermost''—is very much like Whitman's bard who loafs, invites his soul, and chants, ''A call in the midst of the crowd'' with a ''voice, orotund sweeping and final.'' In both cases, the body of the work, or its firm narrative structure, rests in the poet's view of the vast and colorful spectrum of man's destiny. What the poet says has been revealed to him directly in his mystical experience. Thus, in a real sense, the poet dons the mantel of prophecy. He feels the urge to grapple with the larger questions of life, such as religion, time, evil, faith, death, God, pain, immortality. What has been referred to as Whitman's ''sermon'' in ''Song of Myself'' parallels the account that Almustafa, the chosen and the beloved, gave to his first believer who begged him: ''Now therefore disclose us to ourselves, and tell us all that has been shown you of that which is between birth and death.'' (pp. 178-80)

Just before Gibran bids his last farewell to the people of Orphalese, he reasserts a feeling towards God that is universal and pantheistic. The same sentiment is echoed by Whitman at the end of the ''sermon'' in ''Song of Myself.'' Both, as suggested earlier, feel the presence of a God clothed—in a metaphorical, not real, sense—with personal attributes. Whitman, for instance, refers to ''the hand of God'' as ''the promise of my own''; similarly, ''the spirit of God is the brother of my own.'' Gibran is also mindful of a God with human traits when he asserts:

> God listens not to your words save when
> He Himself utters them through your lips.

Their most clear and marked parallel, however, is in their intense belief in God's presence in all places, in all things, and at all times. (pp. 183-84)

These, then, are just a few of the parallels that can be found in Whitman's ''Son of Myself'' and *The Prophet* of Khalil Gibran. From these works and others, one can draw still more themes, approaches, and attitudes that the two poets share. But a crucial question remains: of what value are such parallels to the student of Gibran? In general, these parallels not only add another possible source of Gibran's doctrine but also suggest a new avenue to his style. (p. 185)

With the Bible, Blake, and Nietzsche, the impact of Whitman on Gibran's style should be considered. There are, as it has been illustrated, sufficient parallels in their thinking to suggest a possible dialogue between the two poets. Gibran seems to be quite sympathetic with Whitman's mystical longings. He appears—at least when he wrote *The Prophet* and later—to appreciate the ''barbaric yawp'' of the American poet, his general message with all its optimism, its faith in man, religion, knowledge, progress, and God. Not only did Gibran accept Whitman's message, but he also seemed to imitate his medium.

The major stylistic features that appear in *The Prophet* can also be found in "Song of Myself." The most common ones are: the abandonment of metrical and rhymed verse; the use of a rhythmical, irregular chant that resembles in its cadences, repetitions, and parallelisms, the harmonies of the biblical psalms. There are others, and very striking ones at that. In his prose poems, for instance, Gibran often makes use of the rhetorical question, a technique frequently found in Whitman's work, including "Song of Myself." (pp. 186-87)

Besides the rhetorical question as an integral part of a prose poem, the two poets also catalogued their emotions, attitudes, visions, and the like. . . . Gibran, perhaps with Whitman as his guide, made use of the catalogue. "Love," he urged in *The Prophet*, "has no desire but to fulfill itself." Then he cautioned:

> But if you love and must needs have desires,
> let these be your desires:
> To melt and be like a running brook that sings
> its melody to the night.
> To know the pain of too much tenderness.
> To be wounded by your own understanding of
> love;
> And to bleed willingly and joyfully.

Another feature, closely related to the "cataloging device," deals with the repetition of an initial word such as "but," "and," "for," "nor," to sustain the flow, thought, even logic of a theme. (pp. 188-89)

In *The Prophet* and "Song of Myself," the underlying concern, being essentially a dramatization of a mystical experience with the poet assuming the central role of prophet or teacher, is clear enough. That there is an entrance, a progression, and an emergence from a mystical state is also apparent. In both cases the poet, who echoes man's ideals and sentiments, is the one who is celebrated. All attention is focused on his thoughts, moods, and visions. Certainly, neither Almustafa of *The Prophet* nor the "Manhattan Kosmos" of "Song of Myself" is blessed with a polymathic mind. Both, nevertheless, have fresh, bright insights which penetrate the depth of human existence. Through their visions both poets illuminate the shadows which give form, shape, and meaning to the life of man.

Gibran and Whitman, to generalize further, are members of the poet-prophet cult. Many bards belong to that group, with few more eloquent than Shelley. His *Defence of Poetry*, although incomplete, remains as one of the most stirring manifestos of the poet's role. Here Shelley assigns to the poet the dual task of legislator and prophet. The poet "not only beholds intensely the present as it is, and discovers those laws according to which present things ought to be ordered, but he beholds the future in the present, and his thoughts are the germs of the flower and the fruit of latest time." As their works indicate, Gibran and Whitman saw in Shelley's plea a mature insight. (p. 190)

Their farewell, or emergence from the mystical state, embodies, in a sense, the major elements the two poets share. Whitman and Gibran, having finished their "sermons," get ready to leave their people. The farewell comes as a fitting climax to their mission. Both have preached on religion, God, knowledge, death, and other so-called larger issues of life; now they have finished. But they can not leave their fellowmen, whose

spirit they have merged with their own, without a final assurance. . . . From their farewells (which suggest a similarity in structure), one can draw clear parallels in theme and style.

In *The Prophet*, it becomes rather obvious, Gibran utilized many of the motifs and stylistic devices used earlier by Whitman. From nearly all the examples—even the ones picked at random to illustrate the parallels in their style—one can detect a close relationship in attitude, a kinship in outlook and experience.

In works beside *The Prophet* and "Song of Myself," one can find many other parallels between Gibran and Whitman. The notion, for example, of the transmigration of the soul is clearly outlined in **"The Poet from Baalbeck."** In this work Gibran eulogizes the Lebanese poet Khalil Effandi Mutran and praises the great soul that was incarnate in the poet's body. In "Song of Myself," in "Song of Prudence," and in other poems, Whitman expresses a similar belief.

It has been shown thus far that many of the ideas and forms of *The Prophet* can be found in Whitman's poetry and in "Song of Myself" in particular. The phrase "can be found" is used advisedly here, for the really critical issue that remains to be discussed is whether Gibran's poetry "can be traced" to the writings of the American poet. Studies might try to show—at the risk of belaboring the obvious—that Gibran's work reflects the impact of Indian mysticism, Platonism in all its forms, and, of course, the Bible. More specifically, the influence of Nietzsche and Blake has been suggested, and quite cogently. But even in light of these varied sources, one can still trace the major traits of Gibran's work to the poetry of Walt Whitman. There was between Gibran and Whitman, as it has been pointed out, a close kinship in experience, mode, and outlook—too close to be dismissed as one of the interesting coincidences of literary history. To maintain, then, that Gibran's writings reflect a conscious, and not a mere coincidental, return to Whitman is a sound and tenable hypothesis. (pp. 191-93)

> *Suhail ibn–Salim Hanna, "Gibran and Whitman: Their Literary Dialogue," in* Literature East and West *(© Literature East and West Inc.), Vol. XII, Nos. 2, 3 & 4, 1968, pp. 174-98\* [the excerpt of Gibran's poetry used here was originally published in his* The Prophet *(copyright 1923 by Kahlil Gibran; renewed copyright 1951 by Administrators C.T.A. of Kahlil Gibran Estate and Mary G. Gibran; reprinted by permission of Alfred A. Knopf, Inc.), Knopf, 1931]*

### KHALIL S. HAWI (essay date 1972)

[*In one of the few detailed examinations of Gibran's style and the major influences on his work, Hawi presents what has become the standard contemporary assessment of Gibran's art.*]

Gibran's language was not entirely new, but merely took a step further the trend developed by his predecessors, the Christian writers from the sixteenth century down to al-Bustāni and Marrāsh in the nineteenth. Of the last two, al-Bustāni differed from Gibran in his use of language, which was purely utilitarian, while Gibran's was chiefly artistic. Marrāsh, again, although he put the language to artistic use, had philosophical and scientific interests which Gibran lacked, and made great use of terms drawn from these disciplines, but never learnt to use them artistically. (pp. 251-52)

[Gibran] belongs without any doubt to the Christian literary tradition, and owes a great deal to the language of the Protestant version of the Bible and the artistic part of Marrāsh's language. A proof of Gibran's debt to the language of the Bible is provided by his lavish quotations from it, which do not stand out in any way from the texture of his style. Gibran's improvement on the language of the Bible and Marrāsh was in the direction of refinement and in a new way of using words such as we see in the European Romantics, making possible the expression of some delicate emotions and tones. We must agree with Gibran when he says that "the only means for the revival of the language is in the heart of the poet, on his lips and between his fingers". It is amazing how he himself, as we shall see, was able to extend the scope of Arabic, simply by means of familiar words, to regions unknown to it before. One of his virtues, which he may have cultivated consciously, was to avoid departing from the familiar language even when expressing such elevated themes as mysticism and pantheism, which he could do very successfully without recourse to the highly specialized, if not positively eccentric, language of the ancient Arab mystics and pantheists. (pp. 252-53)

All this shows that he gave deliberate thought to the problems of language, and therefore his choice of familiar speech was based on principle and was not, as many critics have thought, due to carelessness and lack of proficiency in the traditions of the language. (p. 253)

Taking the rhythm of his style first from the point of view of formal pattern, we observe that parallelism in various forms is one of its chief characteristics. The most common of these is antithetical parallelism, sometimes complete and sometimes incomplete. It is used more profusely in his Arabic than in his English writings, especially in his early and middle phases, the reason being that during this period his mind was entangled in various aspects of dualism, which were bound to have their effect upon the rhythm of his style and on other aspects of it as well. Thus, in his early writings we find a large number of statements which are antithetically balanced, such as "I would rather die of longing than live in boredom". His love of antitheses at that time even extended to the general title of the collection of prose poems on which he was engaged, which is *A Tear and a Smile.* Later in his middle phase he could not for instance address the night without evoking the day, and sometimes he could not praise the first without disparaging the second. (p. 254)

Although antithetical parallelism was never quite abandoned in his later writings, after he had come to believe in the unity of existence, in pantheism, it took on a different significance, since he now saw the dualism of things as apparent rather than real. Sentences such as "For what is evil but good tortured by its own hunger and thirst?" and "Who knows but a crystal is mist in decay" and the like are not sharply antithetical because the opposition between good and evil, crystal and mist is resolved by the assertion that these opposites are in reality one. (p. 257)

The spirit which informs the rhythm of [Gibran's early] writings is pure emotionalism, which may account for their other qualities such as grace, sweep, alternation of tone and the use of similar or synonymous words for their emotive value in the expression of excitement, irritation or anger. It must be this emotional persuasiveness which renders the pervading prolixity of his style inoffensive. Yet we meet in the same writings short and pregnant sentences dropped brusquely on to the page, and meant to evoke a wider significance than the words used would normally convey. (pp. 259-60)

It is evident that a style whose rhythm is informed by emotionalism will appeal by its rhythm to the emotions. It may appeal to the imagination as well, through its imagery. (p. 260)

Since Gibran's works teem with particular images, we may first pick a few at random from his early writings, such as the following picture of Lebanon in the moonlight:

> The whole of Lebanon appeared beneath these
> silvery rays like a youth reclining on his arm
> beneath a delicate veil which does and does not
> hide his limbs.

It is evident that Gibran sees his country with a discerning eye. He tries in other passages to exploit the evocative power of the word 'Lebanon' itself, with all its geographical and historical associations, and frequently uses the names of other places or of men and gods, for the same purpose. Another pair of images full of subtle suggestion is the following, by which he tries to convey the impression of a song within him which he cannot or rather does not want to utter:

> It is more redolent than the fragrance of jas-
> mine; what throat shall enslave it? It is more
> protected than the virgin's secret; what (mu-
> sical) strings can violate it?

(pp. 260-61)

It may be said that this kind of imagery could have been introduced into Arabic by any poet who had saturated himself in the European Romantic school but to us it does not seem so simple, for we believe that he must have been not only well acquainted with the Romantics but actually transformed by them, and must in addition have had an unusual gift for language and a painter's eye for the secrets of light and shade. It is true that a good many of his images are, like some of his parallelisms, simply constructed out of sharp oppositions and painted in black and white . . . , but whenever he managed to shake this tendency off he was capable, as we have seen, of subtle, suggestive and evocative writing. What is more, he could endow the art of word-painting with a sense of mystery, due as much to his ethereal, spiritual flights as to his idealization of the real. (pp. 261-62)

Gibran's structural images are either allegories or visions of life or some aspect of it. The allegories, in which concepts, general trends and qualities are personified, are more abundant than the visions in his early and middle phases. Yet he may have drawn no distinction between them, as he seems to look at both in the same way and give them the same name and form. In a prose poem of the middle phase, entitled **'Ru'ya'** **"Vision"**, he tells of three ghosts the poet meets on the sea shore; they assert the ultimate reality and unity of love, rebellion and liberty. We have a strong impression that the ghosts are really these three ideas personified. Yet Gibran has some structural images which really do contain visions of life, such as the image of life as processions in a poem which bears the same title, **al-Mawakib** which was written at the end of his middle phase. An earlier poem, also entitled **'Ru'ya'**, which is a vision of the human heart as a dead bird in a cage, convinces us, despite the presence in it of an element of personification, that it really is a vision, that the poet is describing something he really saw in his mind's eye, and not merely using a device.

As most of these poems end with a moral, most often expressed epigrammatically, there is a strong element of the parable in them. In the prose poem **'Amām 'Arsh al-Jamāl'**, **"the Daughter of the Forest"** teaches the poet the truth about beauty. . . .

In another prose poem **'Bayn al-Kharā'ib'**, Solomon and his beloved conclude their discourse with this epigram: "Eternity keeps naught save love, for it is in its own likeness".

We would have called these poems parables pure and simple, especially as they are written in prose, had it not been for the emotional elevation of their rhythm and the work of imagination in the creation of their particular images, but we can still see in their parabolical and epigrammatic qualities the seeds of the parables and epigrams Gibran was later to write. It is also owing to rhythm and imagery that these poems can tolerate a great number of abstract words and still remain at a high level of poetical intensity, without appearing abstract in content and structure. (pp. 262-63)

When we pass from *al-'Awāsif* to *The Madman* new tendencies are clearly manifested. These are intensity of thought, brevity of expression, a growing use of symbolism, the emergence of a new type of symbol and the insistent use of parable. However, the intensity of thought does not cause any loss in emotional vehemence, both being present in equal proportions in most of the pieces in the book. Gibran did not preserve this balance in all his later writings, either in Arabic or in English. *The Forerunner, The Wanderer* and almost all the Arabic works after *The Madman* are overwhelmingly conceptual and abstract, and are hence much inferior to *The Madman* as literature.

It seems to us that in this book he let his mind participate in the process of creation as an instrument of control, and thus was able for the first time to achieve brevity, control and pregnancy of expression unmixed with the prolixity which had been his greatest fault. It must also have been at this time that he began to cultivate these qualities with determination. Mrs. Young [his friend and biographer] tells us that his motto as a writer was "the inevitable word in the inevitable place". This was certainly not his aim before *The Madman*, when he habitually mixed brief sentences with long meandering paragraphs.

After *al-'Awāsif*, Gibran's belief in pantheism led him to search for symbols which could represent adequately the basic idea behind it, the unity of all existence. In *The Madman* he used various different symbols for this, in one place the sea, with the brook to represent man, in another the greater sea, and in a third the tree whose root is man and whose blossoms are God. In *al-Mawākib* the symbol used for the same idea was the forest, the pipe or flute being the guide to and within it. In a poem called **'al-Bahr'** which we cannot date precisely, but which may belong to the same year as *al-Mawākib* or a little later, he returns to the symbol of the sea.

This kind of symbolism may be called analogical, for it can only be used by one who believes that there is a correspondence between the visible and the invisible, and that visible phenomena reveal the reality of those unseen, or as Goethe, himself a pantheist, says, "the particular represents the universal, not as a dream or a shadow, but as the living and instantaneous revelation of the unfathomable". In this way, we believe, the symbol of the sea is meant to reveal the unfathomable reality of the unity of all existence, especially when in *The Prophet*, Gibran significantly calls it "mother". Crystal and mist, representing two states of one and the same thing, definite, particular existence and its dissolution into universal life, are analogical symbols of the same kind, and so is the idea of death as a "rest upon the wind", which means that it is only temporary, and that eventually one must return to life. (pp. 265-67)

Despite his wide use of symbols, Gibran was not and did not intend to be a symbolist poet in the modern sense. The element of symbolism which entered his art did not prevent him from continuing his old custom of asserting morals and general precepts directly; he did not abandon his old didacticism, for this strain is conspicuous in his later parables and epigrams. The pantheistic mystic who needed symbols to express his meaning was also a poet-prophet who wanted to preach the truth. All the same, in the parables of *The Madman*, Gibran is more discreet and indirect in offering his general precepts than in his earlier poems or in the later parable of *The Forerunner* and *The Wanderer*.

To turn to Gibran's epigrams; as we have already said, they had their prototype in the conclusions of some of his poems. This is not all; they also have roots in another aspect of his earlier poetry, the frequent occurrence of sentences which, like the traditional Arabic line of verse, can stand independent of their context and can easily be isolated from it. Gibran's use of the epigram, *per se*, was wide enough; he wrote one entire book, *Sand and Foam*, in this form, and all his later works which are not parabolical are extremely epigrammatical in style. If we take *The Prophet* as an example, it will be seen that not only the sermons, but even the nostalgic, lyrically meditative prologue and epilogue obey this rule. The same thing is to a great extent true of *The Earth Gods*, which is supposed to be a poem. Again, of his Arabic works, *al-Mawākib* is highly epigrammatical, especially the part spoken by the Old Man, where almost every line is deliberately designed as an epigram and meant to be quoted as a proverb. The other later works in Arabic, of which **'Iram Dhāt al-'Imād'** is the most important, are at least partly epigrammatical. Because of this, Gibran's Arabic epigrams are far more numerous than one would suppose from counting those he explicitly designed as such, and journalists who like to adorn their pages with the sayings of great men find in his works a fertile field for exploitation, as do many preachers and other speakers in Lebanon and the United States.

But if this tendency to pithy expression in his style generally, let alone the aphorisms of *Sand and Foam*, has won Gibran such a great host of admirers, and, we might say, popularizers, this was at the expense of unity in his writings as a whole. How can unity be achieved in a work whose smallest subsection is self-contained? Even his later theory of the art of writing, "the inevitable word in the inevitable place", betrays an undue attention to components, to the parts at the expense of the whole. Let us take *The Prophet* which is generally considered his masterpiece, and look at it as a complete structure. Behind the attempts to perfect the sermons and each epigrammatical sentence in them lies an artistic carelessness which allowed him to leave the Prophet standing on his feet from morning to evening delivering sermon after sermon, without pausing to consider that the old man might get tired, or that his audience might not be able to concentrate on his sermons for so long. To prevent the book from turning into a mere collection of sermons, Gibran should have thought of a more complex plot, in which real characters came together and interacted and more action took place. (pp. 267-69)

*Khalil S. Hawi, in his* Kahlil Gibran: His Background, Character and Works *(copyright © 1972 by the Arab Institute for Research and Publishing; reprinted by permission of the Literary Estate of Khalil S. Hawi),* The Arab Institute for Research and Publishing, 1972, 311 p.

## N. NAIMY (essay date 1974)

[*Naimy divides Gibran's literary career into three distinct periods: his early works which deal with the social problems in Lebanon; his middle works which focus on humanity's disrespect for God's creation; and his final works which stress the unity of life on earth. Elsewhere in his essay Naimy points to the influence Nietzsche had on Gibran's work.*]

In speaking about work to the people of Orphalese, Gibran's Prophet, Almustafa, says, "Work is love made visible." It is only fair to Gibran, therefore, that we should treat his literary works, eight in Arabic and an equal number in English, as various manifestations of this love. Had Gibran been primarily a thinker, a student addressing himself to the study of his philosophy would probably have been able to establish a Gibranian system of thought and a well-defined theory of love. But Gibran was primarily a poet and a mystic in whom thought, as in every good poet and good mystic, is a state of being rather than a state of mind. A student of Gibran's philosophy, therefore, finds himself more concerned not with his ideas but with his disposition; not with his theory of love but with Gibran the lover. That Gibran had started his literary career as a Lebanese emigrant in twentieth-century America, passionately yearning for his homeland, may, perhaps give a basic clue to his disposition and intellectual framework.

To be an emigrant is to be an alien. But to be an emigrant mystical poet is to be thrice alienated. To geographical alienation is added estrangement from both conventional human society at large, and also the whole world of spatio-temporal existence. Therefore such a poet is gripped by a triple longing: a longing for the country of his birth, for a utopian human society of the imagination in which he can feel at home, and for a higher world of metaphysical truth. This triple longing provided Gibran with the basis for his artistic creativity. Its development from one stage of his work to another is only a variation in emphasis and not in kind; three strings of his harp are always to be detected and towards the end of his life they achieve almost perfect harmony in his master-piece, *The Prophet,* where the home country of the prophet Almustafa, the utopian state of human existence and the metaphysical world of higher truth become one and the same. (pp. 55-6)

[Between his essay *Music* and *The Prophet*], Gibran's writings as well as his thought seem to have passed through two stages: the youthful period of his early Arabic works, *Nymphs of the Valley, Spirits Rebellious, Broken Wings* and *A Tear and a Smile,* published between 1907 and 1914, and the relatively more mature stage of *Processions, The Tempests, The Madman,* his first work in English, and *The Forerunner,* his second, all leading up to *The Prophet.*

It is only natural that in his youthful stage Gibran's longing in Chinatown, Boston, where he first settled, for Lebanon, the country of the first impressionable years of his life, should dominate the two other strings in his harp. *Nymphs of the Valley* is a collection of three short stories; *Spirits Rebellious* consists of another four, while *Broken Wings* can easily pass for a long short story. Overlooking names and dates, the three books can safely be considered as one volume of eight collected short stories that are similar in both style and conception, even to the point of redundancy; in all of them Lebanon, as the unique land of mystic natural beauty, provides the setting. The different heroes, though their names and situations vary from story to story, are in essence one and the same. They are unmistakably Khalil Gibran the youth himself, who at times does not even bother to conceal his identity, speaking in the first person

singular in *Broken Wings* and as Khalil in "Khalil the Heretic" of *Spirits Rebellious.* This first-person hero is typically to be found challenging pretenders to the possession of the body and soul of his beloved Lebanon. These pretenders in the nineteenth and early twentieth century are, in Gibran's reckoning, the feudal lords of Lebanese aristocracy and the church order. The stories are therefore almost invariably woven in such a way as to bring Gibran the hero, or a Gibran-modelled hero, into direct conflict with representatives of one or another of those groups. (pp. 56-7)

It is easy to label Gibran in this early stage of his career as a social reformer and a rebel, as he was indeed labelled by many students of his works in the Arab world. His heroes, whose main weapons are their eloquent tongues, are always engaged in struggles that are of a social nature. There are almost invariably three factors here: innocent romantic love, frustrated by a society that subjugates love to worldly selfish interests, a church order that claims wealth, power and absolute authority in the name of Christ but is in fact utterly antichrist, and a ruthlessly inhuman feudal system. However, in spite of the apparent climate of social revolt in his stories Gibran remains far from deserving the title of social reformer.

To be a reformer in revolt against something is to be in possession of a positive alternative. But nowhere do Gibran's heroes strike us as having any real alternative. The alternatives, if any, are nothing but the negation of what the heroes revolt against. Thus their alternative for a corrupt love is no corrupt love, the sort of utopian love that we are made to see in *Broken Wings;* the alternative for a feudal system is no feudal system, or the kind of systemless society we end up with in *Spirits Rebellious;* and the alternative for a Christless church is a Christ without any kind of church, a madman in the kind of role in which John [in *Nymphs of the Valley*] has found himself. Not being in possession of an alternative, a social reformer in revolt is instantly transformed from a hero into a social misfit. Thus Gibran's heroes have invariably been heretics, madmen, wanderers, and even prophets and Gods. As such they all represent Gibran the emigrant misfit in Chinatown, Boston, drawn in his imagination and longing to Lebanon, his childhood's fairyland, who is not so much concerned with the ills that corrupt its society as with the corrupt society that defiles its beauty. What kind of Lebanon Gibran has in mind becomes clearer in a relatively late essay in Arabic, in which his ideal of Lebanon and that of the antagonists whom he portrays in his stories are set against one another.

The best that Gibran the rebel could tell those corrupters of Lebanese society in this essay entitled "**You Have Your Lebanon and I have Mine**" is not how to make Lebanon a better society, but how beautiful is Lebanon without any society at all. (pp. 58-9)

It is no wonder that this kind of rebel should wind up his so-called social revolt at this stage of his career with the publication of a book of collected prose poems entitled *A Tear and a Smile*. The tears, which are much more abundant here than the smiles, are those of Gibran the misfit rather than the rebel in Boston, singing in an exceedingly touching way of his frustrated love and estrangement, his loneliness, homesickness and melancholy. The smiles, on the other hand, are the expression of those hitherto intermittent but now more numerous moments in the life of Gibran the emigrant when Lebanon, the land of mystic beauty, ceases to be a geographical expression, and is gradually metamorphosed in his imagination into a metaphysical homeland. After such rudimentary attempts as his short story **"The Ash of Generations and the Eternal Fire"** in *Nymphs of the Valley,* expressive of his belief in reincarnation, Gibran has managed in his prose poems of *A Tear and a Smile* to give his homesickness a clear platonic twist. His alienation has become that of the human soul entrapped in the foreign world of physical existence, and his homesickness has become the yearning of the soul so estranged for rehabilitation in the higher world of metaphysical truth whence it has originally descended. It is for this reason that human life is expressed by a tear and a smile: a tear for the departure and alienation and a smile for the prospect of a home-coming. The historic analogy of the sea in this respect becomes common from now on in Gibran's writings; rain is the weeping of water that falls over hills and dales estranged from the mother sea, while running brooks sound the happy song of home-coming. (pp. 59-60)

When Gibran's homeland, the object of his longing, was Lebanon, his anger was directed against those who in his view had defiled its beauty. But now that his homeland had gradually assumed a metaphysical Platonic meaning, his attack was no longer centred on local clergy, church dogma, feudalism and the other corrupting influences in Lebanon, but rather on the shamefully defiled image that man, the emigrant in the world of physical existence, has made of the world of God, his original homeland. Not only Lebanese society, but rather human society at large has become the main target of Gibran's disgust and bitterness throughout the second stage of his career. This kind of disgust constitutes the central theme in Gibran's long Arabic poem *Processions* . . . and his book of collected Arabic essays *The Tempests* . . . , his last work in Arabic, as well as in his first two works in English, [*The Madman* and *The Forerunner*] . . . , both of which are collected parables and prose poems.

The hero in Gibran's poetico-fictional title-piece in *The Tempests,* Youssof al-Fakhry in his cottage among the forbidding mountains, becomes a mystery to the awe-stricken neighbourhood. (p. 60)

Looking at the rest of men from the tower of life, from his giant God-self which he has so recognized at a rare moment of awakening, Youssof al-Fakhry sees them in their forgetful day-to-day earthly existence, at the bottom of the tower. In their placid unwillingness to lift their eyes to what is divine in their natures, they appear to him as disgusting pigmies, hypocrites and cowards. (pp. 60-1)

In **"The Grave-Digger"**, another poetico-fictional piece in *The Tempests,* these men who have sold their souls, and who constitute in Gibran's reckoning the rest of human society, are dismissed as dead, though in the words of the hero, modelled in the lines of Youssof al-Fakhry, "finding none to bury them, they remain on the face of the earth in stinking disintegration." . . .

To be the only sane man among fools is to appear as the only fool among sane men. If life, as Youssof al-Fakhry says, is a tower whose bottom is the earth and whose top is the world of the infinite, then to clamour for the infinite in one's life is to be considered an outcast and a fool by the rest of men clinging to the bottom of the tower. This is precisely how the Madman in Gibran's first English work, *The Madman,* gained his title. (p. 61)

*Processions,* Gibran's long poem in Arabic, is a dialogue between two voices. Upon close analysis, the two voices seem to belong to one and the same man: another of those Gibranian madmen, or men who have become Gods unto themselves.

This man would at one time cast his eyes downwards at people living at the bottom of the tower, and consequently raise his voice in derision and sarcasm, poking fun at their unreality, satirizing their Gods, creeds and practices, and ridiculing their values, ever doomed, blind as they are, to be at loggerheads. At another instant he would turn his eyes to his own sublime world beyond good and evil, where dualities interpenetrate giving way to unity, and then he would raise his voice in praise of life absolute and universal.

To achieve self-fulfilment is to achieve serenity and peace. That Gibran and his heroes are still mad Gods, grave-diggers and enemies of mankind, filled with bitterness despite their claim of having arrived at the summit of life's tower, reveals that Gibran's self-fulfilment throughout this second stage of his work is still a matter of wishful thinking and make-believe rather than an accomplished fact. Too preoccupied with his own painful loneliness in his transcendental quest, Gibran the madman or superman, it seems, has failed hitherto not only to feel the joy of self-realization at the summit, but also to recognize the tragedy of his fellow-men supposedly lost in the mire down below. Consequently instead of love and compassion, people could only inspire in him bitterness and disgust.

The stage of anger and disgust was succeeded in Gibran's development by a third stage, that of *The Prophet,* his *chef d'oeuvre, Jesus the Son of Man* and *The Earth Gods.* The link is to be found in *The Forerunner* . . . , his book of collected poems and parables. To believe, as Gibran did, that life is a tower whose base is earth and whose summit is the infinite is also to believe that life is one and indivisible. For the man on top of life's tower to reject those who are beneath, as Gibran had been doing up to this point, is to undermine his own height and become lower than the lowest he rejects. (pp. 61-2)

Gibran's belief in the unity of life, which has hitherto made only intermittent and at times confused appearances in his writings, has now become, with all its implications with regard to human life and conduct, the prevailing theme of the rest of his works. If life is one and infinite, then man is the infinite in embryo, just as a seed is in itself the whole tree in embryo. . . .

Seeing man in this light, Gibran can no longer afford to be a grave-digger. A new stage has opened in his career. Men are divine and, therefore, deathless. If they remain in the mire of their earthly existence, it is not because they are mean and disgusting, but because the divine in them, like the fire in a piece of wood, is dormant though it needs only a slight spark to be released into a blaze of light.

Consequently, it is not a grave-digger that men need, but an igniter; a Socratic mid-wife, who would help man release the God in himself into the self that is one with God. Therefore in this new stage Gibran the grave-digger and the madman gives way to Gibran the prophet and the igniter. (p. 63)

It is not hard to see that Almustafa the Prophet is Gibran himself, who in 1923 had already spent almost twelve years in New York city, the city of Orphalese, having moved there from Boston in 1912, and that the isle of his birth is Lebanon to which he had longed to return. But looking deeper still Almustafa can further symbolize the man who, in Gibran's reckoning, has become his freer self; who has realized the passage in himself from the human to the divine, and is therefore ripe for emancipation and reunion with life absolute. His ship is death that has come to bear him to the isle of his birth, the Platonic world of metaphysical reality. As to the people of Orphalese, they stand for human society at large in which men, exiled in their spatio-temporal existence from their true selves, that is, from God, are in need in their God-ward journey of the guiding prophetic hand that would lead them from what is human in them to the divine. Having made that journey himself, Almustafa presents himself in his sermons throughout the book as that guide.

Stripped of its poetical trappings, Gibran's teaching in *The Prophet* is found to rest on the single idea that life is one and infinite. As a living being, man in his temporal existence is only a shadow of his real self. To be one's real self is to be one with the infinite to which man is inseparably related. Self-realization, therefore, lies in going out of one's spatio-temporal dimensions, so that the self is broadened to the extent of including everyone and all things. Consequently man's only path in self-realization, to his greater self, lies in love. Hence love is the theme of the opening sermon of Almustafa to the people of Orphalese. No man can say "I" truly without meaning the totality of things apart from which he cannot be or be conceived. Still less can one love oneself truly without loving everyone and all things. So love is at once an emancipation and a crucifixion: an emancipation because it releases man from his narrow confinement and brings him to that stage of broader self-consciousness whereby he feels one with the infinite, with God; a crucifixion because to grow into the broader self is to shatter the smaller self which was the seed and confinement. (p. 64)

To the student of Gibran's literary art, *Jesus the Son of Man* may offer some novelty, but not so to the student of his thought. Gibran in this book tries to portray Christ as he understands him by inviting a number of Christ's contemporaries to speak of him each from his own point of view. Their views combined in the mind of the reader are intended to bring out the desired portrait. But names, places and situations apart, the Jesus so portrayed in the book is not so much a new development of the Biblical Christ, as he is the old Biblical Nazarene transformed into another Gibranian Almustafa. Like Almustafa he is described as "The chosen and the beloved", who after several previous rebirths is come and will come again to help lead men to their larger selves. He is not a God who has taken human form, but an ordinary man of ordinary birth who has been able through spiritual sublimation to elevate himself from the human to the divine. His several returns to earth are the several returns of the eagle who would not taste the full freedom of space before all his fledgelings are taught to fly. . . .

Therefore Gibran's Jesus was neither meek nor humble nor characterized by pity. His return to earth is the return of a winged spirit, intent on appealing not to human frailties, but to the power in man which is capable of lifting him from the finite to the infinite. (p. 67)

In *The Prophet*, Gibran the thinker reaches his climax. His post-*Prophet* works, with the possible exception of *The Earth Gods* . . . , the last book published in his lifetime, have almost nothing new to offer. (p. 68)

[*The Wanderer*] published posthumously, is a collection of parables and sayings much in the style and spirit of *The Forerunner* . . . , published three years before *The Prophet*. As to *The Garden of the Prophet,* also published posthumously . . . , it should be dismissed outright as a fake and a forgery. Gibran, who had planned *The Garden of the Prophet* to be an expression of Almustafa's state of being and teachings after he had arrived in the isle of his birth from the city of Orphalese, had only time left to write two or three short passages for that book.

Other passages were added, some of which are translations from Gibran's early Arabic works, and some possibly written by another pen in imitation of Gibran's style. The result was a book attributed to Gibran, in which Gibran's poetry and thought are brought to a most unhappy state of chaos and confusion.

This leaves us with *The Earth Gods* as the complete work with which Gibran's career comes to its conclusion. And a fitting conclusion it is indeed.

The book is a long prose poem where, in the words of Gibran, "The three earth-born Gods, the Master Titans of Life" hold a discourse on the destiny of man.

Gibran, who throughout his career was a poet of alienation and longing, strikes us in *The Prophet* and in *Jesus the Son of Man,* Almustafa's duplicate, as having arrived at his long-cherished state of intellectual rest and spiritual fulfilment. Almustafa and Christ, who in Gibran's reckoning are earth-born Gods, reveal human destiny as being man's gradual ascent through love and spiritual sublimation towards ultimate reunion with God, the absolute and the infinite. It is possible that Gibran began to have second thoughts about the philosophy of his prophet towards the end of his life. Otherwise why is it that instead of one earth God, one human destiny, he now presents us with three who apparently are in disagreement?

Shortly after *Jesus the Son of Man,* Gibran, who had for some time been fighting a chronic illness, came to realize that the fates were not on his side. Like Almustafa, he must have seen his ship coming in the mist to take him to the isle of his birth and in the lonely journey towards death, armed as he was with the mystic convictions of Almustafa, he must have often stopped to examine the implications of his philosophy.

In his farewell address to the people of Orphalese, Almustafa saw his departure as "A little while, a moment of rest upon the wind". But what of this endless cycle of births and rebirths? If man's ultimate destiny as a finite being is to unite with the infinite, then that destiny is a virtual impossibility. For the road to the infinite is infinite, and man's quest as a traveller through reincarnation is bound to be endless and fruitless.

Therefore comes the voice of Gibran's first God. . . . (pp. 68-9)

If man in his ascent to the infinite is likened to a mountain-climber, [as the first God suggests, then] moments of gloom and helplessness only occur when he casts his eyes towards the infinitely removed summit beyond. It is not so when he casts his eyes downwards and sees the heights he has already scaled. The loneliness and gloom then give way to optimism and reassurance. For a journey that can be started is a journey that can be concluded. Gibran on his lonely voyage must have turned to see this other implication in Almustafa's philosophy. There we hear the voice of the second God, whose eyes are turned optimistically downwards. His philosophy is that the height of the summit is a part of the lowliness of the valley beneath. That the valley is now transcended is a reassurance that the summit can be considered as already conquered. For to reach the summit is to reach the highest point to which a valley could raise its depth. Man's journey to God is therefore a journey inwards and not an external quest. . . .

Yet in Gibran's lonely journey towards death, a voice not so pessimistic as that of his first God nor so optimistic as that of the second is heard. This voice, coming perhaps from the youthful past of *Broken Wings* and *A Tear and a Smile,* though not part of Almustafa's voice, is yet not out of harmony with it. It is the voice of someone who has come to realize that man has so busied himself philosophizing about life that he has forgotten to live it. Rather than the climber terrified by the towering height of the summit or reassured by the lowliness of the valley, here is a love-intoxicated youth in the spring meadows on the mountainside. (p. 70)

Thus Gibran, [through the words of the third God], concludes his life-long alienation. His thought in the twilight of his days seems to have swung back to his youth where it first started. (p. 71)

> N. Naimy, "The Mind and Thought of Kahlil Gi-bran," in Journal of Arabic Literature *(copyright 1974 by E. J. Brill), Vol. V, 1974, pp. 55-71.*

## EUGENE PAUL NASSAR  (essay date 1980)

[*Nassar examines the effect of cultural alienation on Gibran's work.*]

Many of [the] merits and defects [of Gibran's works] are intimately bound to [the author's] struggle to live within two cultures, the Lebanese-Arab and the American. In Gibran's case, the struggle led him to adopt a pseudo-wisdom posture which can be called "exultant dualism." Gibran's personal psychic suffering in maintaining the posture before his audience is variously demonstrated in some of his best, certainly most poignant, lyrical moments. These lyric passages, which constitute the most authentic Gibran, dramatize the pangs of cultural discontinuity. (p. 21)

The early New York years were overcast for Gibran by the terrible fate of Lebanon during the Great War (fully one-third of the population of the Mountain starved). His chronic melancholia pervades the prose-poems in Arabic of this period. But he was finding success in America, where he most wanted it; here, both his symbolic drawings and his life drawings of famous artists and other notables, were popular. . . . Though his reputation in the Arabic world grew in the Twenties as a result of further collections of his earlier prose-poems in Arabic, Gibran now turned all of his literary energies and aspirations to the slim books of poems, parables, and aphorisms in English, and he turned his draftsman abilities to the illustration of these books.

The continuity of tone that runs throughout the works of Gibran is that of lonely alienation, of a yearning for connections. Beneath all his prophetic masks, Gibran's lyric cry for connection reveals his most authentic voice. Hungering for real unity, Gibran is ever attempting to lift himself up by his own bootstraps to deliver truths or at least prolegomena to the multitudes in old societies or new on social and cosmic questions. But ever behind these pronunciamentos is the Gibran of unsureness, of profound melancholy, of tragic vision. Gibran is at home neither in the old culture nor in the new, and an unresolved dualism vitiates much of the work when, as so often occurs, it pretends to resolution.

The reader of the translations from the Arabic and of the English works of Gibran will find in each a confusing series of self-projections and investitures. Gibran was of the mold of William Blake: both angry social reformer of old cultural contexts and the prophet of an expanding cosmic consciousness beyond any need of a given cultural context. Most often and fundamentally, however, he emerges as a lonely poet finding solace only in the poetic consciousness or imagination. He wants desperately

to trumpet a Humanism with absolutist foundations, but at the center of his vision (a center he keeps trying to shroud in mist), he is a tragic dualist whose exultation is fixed only in the idea of an ever-upwards-striving human spirit. . . . The humanism [expressed in such poems as **"We and You,"** **"A Visit from Wisdom,"** and *The Broken Wings*] is much like both the humanism of Gibran's mentor, William Blake, and the early humanism of Percy Shelley. The young poet aspires to the energy of Blake, the social ardency of the early Shelley, and the cosmic euphoria of the Whitman of the *Song of Myself;* what Gibran really achieves, however, are dramatizations of the inextricable dualisms in Blake's *Songs of Innocence and Experience,* the tragic tone of Shelley's *The Triumph of Life,* the solitary laments of Whitman's "Out of the Cradle" or "When Lilacs Last in the Dooryard Bloom'd."

Gibran always struggles to extricate himself from a melancholic position; at times he attempts this with a shell of toughness and bitterness which he, according to Naimy, fashioned after Nietzsche; often he attempts it through a brand of transcendentalism that seems a fusion of his own intuitions with his knowledge of Emerson, Naimy, and others. Neither role convinces as much as does the lyric voice of the poet who is often ashamed of both roles.

The bitter Yusif El Fakhri, in the philosophic dialogue, **"The Tempest,"** has withdrawn from civilization. . . . But though Fakhri sought solitude only to avoid civilization, he has had "religious" experiences. . . . Such momentary psychic experience [as he describes] is not to be denied; Gibran's poetry is often of such moments. The question is whether in Gibran's mind such moments of "mysticism" or "cosmic consciousness" are in fact intuitive glimpses into a higher reality for an immortal soul, or only esthetic apprehensions of the evolutionary potential in man's creative imagination. And the truth of the matter, demonstrably so, is that Gibran was tortured by the question, wanting to assert the one to his audience, while believing the other. (pp. 23-6)

There is a very moving and revealing Arabic poem of nightmare, confession, and self-analysis called **"Between Night and Morning"** in *The Tempests.* . . . This poem consists of two related nightmares. The first is of the poet's harvesting fruit trees of his own planting. After the harvest is given away to the people (his Arabic readers, specifically the Christian-Lebanese), the poet discovers his fruit is as bitter as gall. . . . Another tree is planted "in a field afar from the path of Time," watered with "blood and tears," but not one of the people will now taste of this sweet fruit of sadness, and the poet withdraws to his solitude. The second nightmare is of a boat of the poet's own building, "empty . . . except of rainbow colors." . . . [The poet] sails the seas to fill his boat with worthy cargo, but his people will not welcome him back, though the boat is full. And he withdraws, unable to speak or sing, even as dawn approaches. Both nightmares are obvious allegories of Gibran's guilt feeling with regard to his art and his audience. (pp. 27-8)

It is within this melancholy context that the record of Gibran's euphoric moments, and the quasi-theology around which he fashions those moments, must be read.

*The Prophet* is an extended flight on the wings of a dubious idea that Gibran derived from Blake, Whitman, and Nietzsche, that the evolving godliness in man is god enough for exultant worship. . . . The "Greater Self," "Larger Self," "Vast Man" (cf. Blake's "Eternal Great Humanity Divine,") within us is the God of *The Prophet* (and, to be sure, of *Jesus, Son of Man*). . . . [This] may seem acceptable doctrine in some theological (Emersonian) circles. However, to other (particularly Lebanese-Christian) circles, it is heretical because the speaker, Gibran, wants 1) to do without a Godhead existing independently of man while pretending to the absolute authority of such, and 2) to do without any promise of ego-immortality while pretending sufficient compensation in the immortality of the Life Force, that is, in the succeeding generations of man evolving an ever wider and wider consciousness.

Whitman's "Myself" is much the same as Gibran's "Larger Self." In fact, *The Prophet* is deeply influenced by the *Song of Myself*. Both works are devious enough to obscure the problem of evil in the euphoric, cosmic moment. . . . In both the *Song of Myself* and *The Prophet* we have, in fact, dualism pretending to unity. . . . [Gibran's vision, as revealed in *The Prophet,* is] of a dualistic spiral; the wider the consciousness is expanded, the greater the awareness of *both* joy and pain, good and evil. Gibran's Arabic prose poem, "The Ambitious Violet," is of a violet that would be a rose for a day so as to have a moment in the sun, a rose that is willing to then be dashed by the tempest. Or, as Gibran's "Jesus" says it, "The lilies and the brier live but a day, yet that day is eternity spent in freedom." . . . One need not de-emphasize the importance of ecstatic psychic or mystic moments. A moment in eternity is a different blessing than to be eternally in eternity. Thus, the bluff one often senses in both Gibran and Whitman. What is moving in both poets is their otherwise tortured consciousness of this bravado. It is not, however, a bravado likely to bluff the Christian-Lebanese peasant in general, or the Christian-Lebanese peasant in Gibran.

Gibran's later work, *The Earth Gods,* is in many ways a more satisfying work than *The Prophet.* In this book, the "second god" strikes the true tonality of the artist-as-only-savior central to Gibran. . . . The first god speaks only of weariness, bitterness, and a death-wish; the third god speaks of merely human dancers and mere human love, everfresh. All three gods represent attitudes of the poet in a complex inner debate with no possible resolution save that all three are capable of being caught momentarily by the beauty of the young lovers and by their dance in the ancient "sacred grove." . . . The third god would build some transcendental truths upon this love, but the second god protests. . . . [The] gods are "earth-bound." The poem ends with the third god finally agreeing with his brother:

> Better it is for us, and wiser,
> To seek a shadowed nook and sleep in our
> earth divinity,
> And let love, human and frail, command
> the coming day. . . .

The voice of the lyric Gibran here persuades the prophetic Gibran; the poet persuades the transcendental philosopher. (pp. 29-32)

Gibran was born into an ancient and rich hill-culture in the Lebanese Mountain. He was separated from this culture, but he also separated himself from it. That culture as I know it from my immigrant parents and their peers is one that humanizes nature, the universe, and God in terms of the Lebanese family, its garden, and its mountain village. . . .

This idyllic vision, attained, of course, only fitfully, had sufficient power to cause the ambiguous love-hate, accusatory-guilty relationship of Gibran with the Old Country and its—(his)—people. . . . (p. 33)

The fundamental tone of Gibran then is lyric, tragic, alienated, punctuated by a series of struggles for transcendence and/or involvement. (It is worth noting that Gibran's art work too, his drawings, oils, washes, whatever merit they have standing alone before the artist's eye, are deeply illustrative of his fundamental tonality—pain and alienation and longing pervading them almost to the exclusion of any sense of joy.) Gibran is hardly a Blake or Whitman, not having their linguistic and imagistic vitality (though his style—obviously dependent on the King James Bible—is of considerable emotive and evocative power). But their "transcendental" thinking is much alike, often embracing the "exultant dualism" which is a pretense of an achieved unity covering a morass of conflicts. All three poets labor under the burden of their transcendent self-projections of unitary truths and are wholly convincing only when wholly absorbed in dramatizations of their dualistic experiences. To put Gibran in this company, at least in terms of similarity of theme and substance, is both to save him from his cultists and to place him, rightly, far more within the Western than an Eastern poetic tradition. (p. 34)

*Eugene Paul Nassar, "Cultural Discontinuity in the Works of Kahlil Gibran," in* MELUS *(copyright, MELUS, The Society for the Study of Multi-Ethnic Literature of the United States, 1980), Vol. 7, No. 2, Summer, 1980, pp. 21-36 [the excerpt of Gibran's poetry used here was originally published in his* The Earth Gods *(copyright 1931 by Kahlil Gibran; renewed copyright 1959 by Administrators C.T.A. of Kahlil Gibran Estate, and Mary K. Gibran; reprinted by permission of Alfred A. Knopf, Inc.), Knopf, 1931]*

---

## ADDITIONAL BIBLIOGRAPHY

Naema, Michael. "The Gift of Genius." *Lotus Afro Asian Writings* 18, No. 4 (October 1973): 169-76.
   Tribute and analysis. Naema examines a number of Gibran's early works with the intention of demonstrating the poet's genius.

Young, Barbara. *This Man from Lebanon: A Study of Kahlil Gibran.* New York: Alfred A. Knopf, 1972, 188 p.
   Biography. Young does not attempt a detailed account of Gibran's life, but develops a portrait of the poet based on personal reminiscences.

# Charlotte (Anna) Perkins (Stetson) Gilman

## 1860-1935

American short story writer, essayist, novelist, and autobiographer.

Gilman was one of the most prominent feminists and social thinkers at the turn of the century. Her *Women and Economics,* an examination of women's place within the economic sphere, earned her wide recognition, and for several decades she was considered the leading intellectual of the women's movement. Both her fiction and her nonfiction, after years of neglect, have been rediscovered by modern feminists. These works show not only the iconoclastic nature of Gilman's thought, but also reveal that she was one of the first women writers to introduce humor and satire into feminist literature. Gilman is best known today for her least characteristic work, ''The Yellow Wall Paper,'' in which she portrayed with dramatic intensity and authenticity a young woman's mental breakdown.

Quite early in her life Gilman displayed the independence she later advocated for women in her lectures and her writing. In her youth she insisted on remuneration for her household chores, and as a young woman she paid her mother room and board, supporting herself as a teacher and as a commercial artist. At twenty-four, after a long courtship, she married a young artist, Charles Walter Stetson. Following the birth of their daughter, Katharine Beecher, Gilman grew increasingly despondent. She consulted noted Philadelphia neurologist S. Weir Mitchell, who prescribed his renowned ''rest cure'': complete bed rest and limited intellectual activity. Gilman credited this experience with driving her ''so near the borderline of utter mental ruin that I could see over.'' She removed herself from Mitchell's care, and eventually left her husband, traveling with her daughter to California where she supported herself by lecturing and writing. ''The Yellow Wall Paper,'' written almost fifteen years later, is her angry indictment of Mitchell's ''cure'' and her protest against the dependent position of women in society. While in California, Gilman helped to edit feminist publications, assisted in the planning of the California Women's Congresses of 1894 and 1895, and was instrumental in founding the Women's Peace Party. She spent the next several years lecturing in the United States and England on women's rights and on labor reform. In 1900 she remarried, and continued her dedication to various causes. One of her most important works was her monthly journal *The Forerunner,* published from 1909 through 1916. Gilman wrote nearly all of the copy for this journal, which served as a vehicle for advancing social awareness and has been called her ''single greatest achievement.'' In 1935, having learned that she suffered from inoperable cancer, Gilman took her life, saying in a final note that ''when one is assured of unavoidable and imminent death, it is the simplest of human rights to choose a quick and easy death in place of a slow and horrible one.''

*Women and Economics* had its origin in Gilman's studies of Darwinism and the sociology of Lester Ward. She argued that women's secondary status in society, and especially women's economic dependence on men, is not a fact of nature, but the result of culturally enforced behavior. In questioning whether there were fundamental differences in potential between the sexes, Gilman was not expressing new ideas. However, as Carl

*Courtesy of Prints and Photographs Division, Library of Congress*

Degler noted, ''no one in her time focussed the arguments so sharply and stated them so cogently and lucidly as she did.'' Gilman had a sure instinct for logical fallacies, and she demonstrated great skill in pointing out faulty reasoning in opposing arguments. In other nonfiction works, such as *Concerning Children, Human Work,* and *The Man-Made World,* Gilman suggested that women should work outside of the home to fully develop their potential. She proposed ''baby gardens'' where working mothers could leave their children with childcare professionals.

In her fiction, Gilman portrayed women adapting themselves to exciting new lives. She had little talent for imaginative writing; in fact, her fiction was for the most part didactic. She ''gave little attention to her writing as literature,'' writes critic Ann J. Lane. ''She wrote quickly, carelessly, to make a point.'' Her last three fictional works, *Moving the Mountain, Herland,* and *With Her in Ourland,* are Utopian novels that develop her ideas of equality for women. Unlike most Utopian fiction, in Gilman's works it is people's attitudes, rather than existing technology, that have changed radically.

Gilman's best work of fiction, ''The Yellow Wall Paper,'' is also her least typical. In the story, a young wife and mother's inexorable mental deterioration is recounted in the first person. This terse narrative gains in chilling effect when it is read with knowledge of Gilman's own breakdown. Originally interpreted solely as a horror story, most modern critics agree with Ann D. Wood that "The Yellow Wall Paper" reflects Gilman's "nightmare vision of sick women dependent on male doctors who use their professional superiority as a method to prolong their patients' sickness and, consequently, the supremacy of their own sex."

Since the end of World War I, Gilman's economic theories have been increasingly disregarded. However, as more and more women enter the job market, her sociological studies gain in significance. Many modern feminist nonfiction works reflect the influence of Gilman's ideas, and readers are rediscovering, in Gilman's fiction and nonfiction alike, much that is relevant to contemporary problems.

## PRINCIPAL WORKS

*In This Our World*   (poetry)   1893
*Women and Economics*   (essay)   1898
*The Yellow Wall Paper*   (short story)   1899
*Concerning Children*   (essay)   1900
*The Home: Its Work and Influence*   (essay)   1903
*Human Work*   (essay)   1904
*What Diantha Did*   (novel)   1910
*The Crux*   (novel)   1911
*The Man-Made World*   (essay)   1911
*Moving the Mountain*   (novel)   1911
*Benigna Machiavelli*   (novel)   1914; published in journal
   *The Forerunner*
*With Her in Ourland*   (novel)   1916; published in journal
   *The Forerunner*
*His Religion and Hers*   (essay)   1923
*The Living of Charlotte Perkins Gilman*   (autobiography)
   1935
*\*Herland*   (novel)   1978
*The Charlotte Perkins Gilman Reader*   (short stories and
   novel fragments)   1980

*This work was written in 1915.

---

**HENRY AUSTIN**   (essay date 1895)

Charlotte Perkins Stetson, of California, several years ago gave promise of making a unique little niche for herself in literature, when she published in the *Nationalist Magazine* a subtly satirical poem, called **"Similar Cases."** Her first book of verse, entitled *In This Our World* . . . , raises her promise into the rank of performance. It is truly one of the most quaint and startling verse-books of the year. The cover with its hint of cloudy, Ethiopian sky, two overburdened camels and two stunted palms, upspringing from one root, recalls at once Olive Schreiner's *Three Dreams in a Desert* and gives the key to the purpose of the author.

The contents of this little volume fully justify the first opinions formed by various critics of Mrs. Stetson's capacity. Here is a woman with a sense of humour and at the same time, in spots, peculiarly without that saving sense; for some things in the book, if read by themselves, would tempt a critic to class it simply as another curiosity of literature.

One is repelled every now and then by the "ultra-barbaric yawp" of this Californian Apostle of the New Woman, but one is brought to bay, after all, and compelled to admit considerable reason for the dissatisfaction, the militant pessimism that pervades her utterances. (pp. 335-36)

But the trouble with most pessimistic philosophers is that they overstate their case. To listen too seriously to Mrs. Stetson's raging dithyrambs about the washtub and her denunciations of the **"Holy Stove"** might make one believe that she had often been obliged to rise betimes and light the fire, while her liege lord was smoking that *ne plus ultra* of Bohemianism, a cigar before breakfast; whereas this book itself is proof enough that Mrs. Stetson has had leisure to "loaf and invite her soul," and to express her Womanhood in one of the highest channels possible—namely, the "building of the lofty rhyme."

For, *malgré* her infelicitous eccentricities of thought and technique, much of her work is lofty in tone and in tones. There is a fine, throbbing, human quality about it. There are passages of grave and potent eloquence. . . .

Mrs. Stetson has very little Nature-worship in her verse, very little word-painting of the scenic sort. Her concern, chiefly, is Human Nature—Man and Woman—and especially the New Woman of whose arrival we have heard so much lately that some of us are weary in advance. But occasionally Mrs. Stetson can throw words together, as Turner threw colours, and produce an intense sense of picture. (p. 336)

Mrs. Stetson is generally happy in her closing line. She has a sense of climax quite unusual. For example, in a poem where she fights the idea of Vanity as a peculiarly feminine attribute, she clinches a clever *tu quoque argumentum ad hominem* thus: . . .

> Feminine Vanity! Hark to these men!
> Vanity's wide as the world is wide—
> Look at the peacock in his pride—
> Is it a hen?

But the Stove with its crackling fire seems determined to sound the dominant note in her poetry and in an earnest appeal to the **"Young Wife"** it appears, as by right divine, in the second stanza

> Are you content with work? To toil alone,
> To clean things dirty and to soil things clean,
> To be a kitchen maid—be called a Queen—
> Queen of a cook-stove throne?

It would, however, be unjust to convey an impression that the Stove succeeds in its demoniac purpose of dominating Mrs. Stetson. She escapes into larger and nobler fields of thought than those coloured by her probable failure to become a good cook, and she says many fine and valuable things, and some things, of course, which a friendly editor would have prevented her from printing, as if he could, because they are flat—as flat, for instance, as her fall of fancy, called **"Mr. Rockefeller's Prayer."** In most of that class of her verses, like **"Similar Cases"** and **"The Survival of the Fittest,"** where she assails with the cold logic of science and the charming warmth of ridicule the present industrial system, whose inherent injustice affords historic assurance of its overthrow and change into something better, Mrs. Stetson's humorous and vigorous muse is at her best, because at her largest. The *Weltschmerz* blots out the Ego; the *lacrymae rerum* put out the fires of the Cook-stove. . . .

And who can deny the poetic intensity of her poem **"Mothers,"** in which with a kind of sublime audacity she compares the whole race to a baby and claims for woman the mission of being the saviour of the future? There is a veiled hint of this, one remembers, on the last page of Hawthorne's immortal *Scarlet Letter* to Posterity. . . .

In fine, this little book, *In This Our World*, is exceedingly well worth reading for what it says and for what it signifies. (p. 337)

> *Henry Austin, "'In This Our World',"* in The Book-
> *man, New York (copyright, 1895, by George H. Doran*
> *Company), Vol. I, No. 5, June, 1895, pp. 335-37.*

### THE AMERICAN FABIAN  (essay date 1897)

["**Similar Cases**"] is a curious biological satire and has been quoted from one end of the land to the other, appearing now in the lectures of learned professors of natural science, and again furnishing trenchant arguments for the political agitators. In its few verses it shows a panorama of instantaneous photographs of the world-old contention between the spirit of Progress and the sluggish mass of skeptical conservatism. It tells us that among our humble progenitors in the animal world there appeared now and then a radical who experienced the same pages of progressiveness and sweet pains of discontent that we advanced reformers know. The little eohippus, forefather of the horse, declares his intention to rise in the scale of being; the anthropoidal ape announces "I'm going to be a man"; the neolithic man expresses in turn his confidence of rising to civilization. All these progressives meet the fate of their kind; jeered at for his temerity, each in turn is summarily crushed by the good old argument—*"You would have to change your nature."* The writer draws a caustic brush over this dictum. What satire could be keener than her demure explanation? . . .

An instance of the way this poem has touched the mark is the fact that many "last verses" have been added by reformers of all shades and creeds everywhere—each feeling that a further illustration of his own particular conviction was necessary to bring this picture of the march of evolution up to date.

A volume of Mrs. Stetson's poems entitled **"In This Our World"** . . . has been widely commented upon. It is a collection of singularly fresh and vigorous pieces—not poetry in the lofty meaning of the word, and, indeed, the author lays no claim to the title of poet, but in the trenchant parables she deftly cuts into her page is teaching of the highest order. If it is not poetry it certainly is not prose. . . .

Curiously enough—and yet from another aspect not surprising at all—this strange, passionate, mocking woman comes of long lines of Puritan stock, with a stern ancestry of orthodox deacons and Unitarian "come-outers" behind her. Her grandmother was Mary Beecher, daughter of the redoubtable Rev. Lyman Beecher and sister of the famous Henry Ward and Harriet Beecher. . . .

Mrs. Stetson has shown evidences of possessing both strains of the Beecher talent, humor, pathos and graphic descriptive ability as a writer, combined with the power of the preacher. She has repeatedly filled pulpits in the West and in the East with credit to her cause and to them. . . . Her speeches [in England] were everywhere received with favor; her view of **"Women in Evolution"** being by competent critics hailed as a distinct contribution to this somewhat threadbare subject. (p. 2)

We have spoken of Mrs. Stetson's work as not taking rank in the annals of true poetry, but there are signs that a further development may place her in that list before long. If the power to concentrate into close, highly-charged rhythmic diction whole areas of human experience and give in a verse the entire atmosphere of some region of human life be real poetry, then Mrs. Stetson's lines called **"The Wolf at the Door"** . . . are certainly entitled to this rank. We think it far and away the best thing she has yet produced. There is the very still, creeping horror of poverty in the lines:

> The slow, relentless padding step
> That never goes astray.

And what but genius could sum up the inherited misery of overworked generations in the solemn words:

> We are born to hoarded weariness,
> As some to hoarded gold.

The analogy of the figure carries a double reflex meaning in the dependence of one of the statements upon the other. The writer is too much of an artist to say it, but the reader hears the undertone of stern reminder that the "hoarded weariness" is *because* of the "hoarded gold." (pp. 2-3)

Hood's "Song of the Shirt" and Mrs. Browning's "The Cry of the Children" struck pangs of self-reproach into the public conscience. This poem of Charlotte Perkins Stetson's portrays perhaps no less forcibly the ghastly persecutions of the unceasing poverty which hangs over thousands of human beings in our day.

A different but equally pointed arraignment is contained in her little verses on **"Charity."** In these lines of child-story Mrs. Stetson touches with light satire the whole indictment against the despotism of private property. . . . (p. 3)

> *"Charlotte Perkins Stetson: A Daring Humorist of*
> *Reform,"* in The American Fabian, *Vol. III, No. 1,*
> *January, 1897, pp. 1-3.*

### HARRY THURSTON PECK  (essay date 1898)

Mrs. Stetson is a woman of much originality, of very pronounced opinions which she expresses with vigour, and from a literary point of view she is worthy of serious consideration. Her verse shows an improvement in technique during the past three years until now both in the aptness of her thought, the terseness of her phrase, and the general compactness of her style as a whole, she stands head and shoulders above any of the other minor poets of her sex. In fact, did we not know the author's name, we should have selected many of the poems collected in this volume as having been written by a man.

Mrs. Stetson is most interested in life and its various problems. She does not deal very much in sentiment, but she goes out among men and women and looks at them from a semi-sociological point of view and hammers away at what she thinks she sees. Almost everything that she writes is strong and effective, from the way in which she has dealt with it. In her milder moods (which are not frequent) she sometimes shows a touch that is truly poetical. She is at her best, however, and also most at her ease, when she is dealing with questions that are partly ethical. (pp. 50-1)

It is not, however, with Mrs. Stetson in the light of a poet-at-large that we are now especially concerned. . . . What we wish to discuss at the present time is one particular theme to which she continually reverts, so often, in fact, as to excite in us a mild degree of irritation. This theme is, broadly speaking, the inferior position which married women occupy; and, more specifically, what may be styled (after the Stetsonian manner) the Curse of the Cook-Stove. Mrs. Stetson in a general way, regards the American wife as a person who is very sadly put upon; in the first place because she is obliged to spend so much time at home looking after her household duties, while her husband roves around and mingles with the wise and great and improves his mind; in the second place, because she has no corresponding pleasures or advantages; and in the third place, because she is remorselessly sacrificed to the Cook-Stove over which she has to spend so many weary and overheated hours. (p. 51)

We are inclined to suspect that the sort of woman whom Mrs. Stetson pictures as so dominated by the Cook-Stove is the sort of woman who would snarl and complain over anything else that fate had given her to do. She is probably a sad slattern who goes around with slippers down at heel in a greasy old wrapper, and with her hair up in curl-papers at five o'clock in the afternoon when her husband is coming home. Instead of finding fault with the Cook-Stove and telling the young wife that it is a horror and a blight upon her life, we for our part should try to give her some ideas of how to be happy even with the Cook-Stove. . . .

[We] think that she ought to keep the Cook-Stove nicely polished and to have the kitchen neat as wax to match it. Next we should instill into her mind the momentous truth that it is really just as easy to cook food in a dainty and wholesome and artistic way as it is to cook it like a savage. . . . She would find . . . that cooking would become an artistic pleasure rather than a ''slavish service,'' and that it could be done in half the time that she had spent pottering around in making dishes fit only for a barbarian. Thus she would have plenty of time to herself, and could put on her prettiest dress in the afternoon and meet her husband with a flower in her hair and delight his soul by her dainty looks and by an equally dainty dinner. . . .

Finally, we really do not see but what she would have time enough to cultivate her mind if she desired to. She would probably take out books from the circulating library, and perhaps in the course of time she would come upon Mrs. Stetson's volume of dynamic verse. If so, she would take it home and read the fiery denunciations of the Cook-Stove; and, being a sensible person, she would derive from their perusal just the same amount of pity and amusement that they have recently afforded us. (p. 53)

> Harry Thurston Peck, ''The Cook-Stove in Poetry,'' in The Bookman, New York (copyright, 1898, by George H. Doran Company), Vol. VIII, No. 1, September, 1898, pp. 50-3.

### ARTHUR B. WOODFORD (essay date 1899)

[Many economics] books are written from what might be called the masculine point of view, if a point could be said to have life; ''**Women and Economics**'' shows us the woman's side of the case in an entirely new light. The author is not arguing a case in court, but stating a profound social philosophy; and she does this with enough wit and sarcasm to make the book very entertaining reading, and with such a wealth of illustration from the study of man's development from primitive conditions, and of the sex relations of animal life, as to make her theory seem almost startling in the vividness of its truth. . . .

We are the only animal species in which the female depends on the male for food, the only animal species in which the sex-relation is also an economic relation. Mrs. Stetson's book is written to offer a simple and natural explanation of this fact, to show its present significance, and ''to reach in especial the thinking women of to-day, and urge upon them a new sense, not only of their social responsibility as individuals, but of their measureless racial importance as makers of men.'' Herein her book embodies the idea which marks perhaps the most pronounced tendency of recent thought along economic lines, namely, that social progress is more and more becoming a conscious process, and that, while it is perfectly true that there is a natural and physical basis for society and for social institutions, it is equally true that in a large measure man is as he thinks he is and as he wills he shall be. (pp. 85-6)

> Arthur B. Woodford, ''Present Tendencies in Economic Thought,'' in The Dial (copyright, 1899, by The Dial Publishing Company, Inc.), Vol. XXVI, No. 303, February 1, 1899, pp. 83-6.*

### [H. A. CLARKE] (essay date 1899)

In her book '**Women and Economics**,' Mrs. Stetson has not only unduly emphasized, as it seems to me, certain series of facts which make for the strength of her argument, but she is not altogether free from a floating sex bias, which makes her, when dealing with facts, too hard on women and too lenient toward men for their respective shortcomings, growing out of lack of consciousness and development, at the same time that her general conclusions exalt women at the expense of men, whose good qualities she attributes almost entirely to the fact of woman's past subjection, through which alone man has become human. Furthermore, she places the responsibility of future development entirely in the hands of woman. Thus, the self-respecting man might well ask, ''Are my good qualities the result only of your incapacity in the past, and am I to have no active part in bringing about those better social ideals for which awakened humanity is struggling?''

Her chief contention is that women have had no economic relation to society, which, though true in part, is not the whole truth; since history and society are full of marriages sought on the man's part for wealth's sake, inherited if not earned, and of many more, made for the sake of the social influence of the woman, who, through her extensive acquaintanceship brings business opportunities to her husband. Woman has certainly had an economic *value* to man if not an economic relation to society. . . . Whether the women of America regard their husbands so exclusively in the light of bankers as Mrs. Stetson seems to make out, is however to be doubted. Frequently, if it were not for the good advice and economy of the wife the husband would not be able to keep himself, let alone his family.

The truth is, there are other elements at work to develop the human race besides economic relations, and while it is no doubt probable in the long run that man has an economic value for woman which woman has not for man, yet this material accident of life has been so overlaid with love and devotion in innumerable cases that the economic relation has been quite swallowed up in the more exalted spiritual relations. Does not Mrs. Stetson overlook the fact that under any social phase there is an infinite variation of personal ideal, and therefore any sweeping generalization as to the state of society is not only unjust to large masses of individuals but is unscientific? All that should be claimed is that the tendency of any social system is increasingly toward certain bad results, which may be illustrated by constantly accumulating facts, and a social phase which has in it the seeds of injustice is one to be reformed as fast as possible, its evils dropped and whatever beauties it may have retained. . . . (pp. 124-25)

Mrs. Stetson has not classified her groups of facts with sufficient care to be thoroughly scientific, and the result is a certain amount of muddle and inconsistency in her arguments which is much to be regretted in a book so earnest and in the main so liberal and progressive.

When it comes to the constructive part of her work, she guides her rudder with a steadier hand. Though her facts have been pitch-forked too recklessly into one basket, and her arguments at times lack in balance, she has, by her wit, and her intuitive wisdom convinced every open mind that there has been something radically wrong in the social phase beginning even now to pass away, and in presenting her ideal of future social life she opens up many delightful possibilities, households whence all domestic work has been banished, professional cleaners to come in and do all the work with a precision and expertness unknown at present, meals to be served either at home from a central café, or the family to proceed thither for meals according to taste, babies to spend a large part of the day in company with other babies in a delightfully appointed nursery watched over by a cultivated lover of children, where they can enjoy each others society, instead of being confined to the adoring and over sentimental environment of "mamma's" arms. There is something quite pathetic in the thought of the millions of babies who have never been permitted to enjoy the society of their equals, other babies near the same age, and the possibilities for development in a baby society are immense. These arrangements will, of course, free the time of the mother, and she will be able to follow her own career, by means of which she will secure her own economic independence and contribute to the maintenance of her child.

When the economic independence of woman becomes an understood thing, there will also disappear all those evils from society which result from what Mrs. Stetson calls our oversexedness.

We pray that she may be right, and that the future young woman may exhibit a frank and friendly nature without laying herself open to the suspicion that she has "designs," and that contrariwise, the future young man may show his friendly interest without anybody supposing he has "intentions." (pp. 126-27)

We should hope, too, that in this new dispensation the unmarried man or woman would not be regarded as an abnormal being, but a natural differentiation who finds individuality better developed by remaining in that state,—a sort of added seventh, in musical parlance, giving contrast and piquancy to the social music. Upon this point Mrs. Stetson is not perfectly sound. She seems to think unmarried people remnants of social material left over. However, she kindly makes provision for them.

Assembly rooms where men and women can meet for social converse and the exchange of ideas on the subjects of the day are among Mrs. Stetson's beautiful dreams. May humanity soon develop to the point where they will know how to respect and appreciate such a social possibility!

The coming in of this Utopia of Mrs. Stetson's is doubtless bound up with other social problems which she does not go into, but to the solution of which she has made a valuable contribution in the construction of so wise and pleasant an ideal of social life.

The same note sounds in her poetry, which will reach the understanding of many through its emotional force, who would not be touched by the arguments of the philosopher. It also comes out in her poetry that she is a believer in socialism or something allied to it, as well as in the economic independence of woman. She gives in some of her poems vivid and dramatic pictures of the wrongs growing out of present conditions, and in others points her moral in witty parables, that make one think as well as smile. In such poems as these she is at her best, her style having an emphasis and distribution of climaxes which seals every piece into the memory.

Others of her poems upon themes with which she was probably less possessed show roughness and a decided lack of musical perception In fine, she is not a lyricist by nature and reveals her strength rather in satiric and dramatic verse. . . . (pp. 127-28)

> [*H. A. Clarke,*] *"Charlotte Perkins Stetson As Social Philosopher and Poet,"* in Poet Lore *(copyright, 1899, by Poet Lore, Inc.), Vol. XI, No. 1, January-March, 1899, pp. 124-28.*

## ANNIE L. MUZZEY (essay date 1899)

For a number of years the original verse of Mrs. Stetson has been floating about in the newspapers, which, with all their faults, are more or less fair records of the upward thought and movement that show at what point of recognition we are in our march of human progress. It did not matter that the now world-famed poem, **"Similar Cases,"** was first printed in a periodical of limited circulation among a few radical thinkers who dared to aspire to a higher order of life than is possible in the existing state of things. (p. 263)

Other poems of equal force and brilliancy, over the same signature, have, from time to time, appealed to our slumbering sense of truth and justice in respect to common customs which we had accepted without thought; as things to be regretted, perhaps, but still endured. The keen, delicate lance that with one dart pierces to the very center of sores that we have kept covered, has been felt many times through the poems, under various familiar titles, which have come to us in fragmentary ways during the last half dozen years. To find them collected . . . was a real delight. . . .

But just now our business is with Mrs. Stetson's latest work, **"Women and Economics,"** a philosophic study of the economic relations between men and women. . . . (p. 264)

The primal evil which Mrs. Stetson points out in our social life, is the economic dependence of woman on the sex-relation. From this false and unnatural position, sanctioned by human law and sustained for centuries as an inviolable custom, has proceeded the multitude of social perversions which the present age has set about eradicating by this, that, and the other so-called reform. While granting that the sexuo-economic relation has had its use in the earlier evolutionary stages of humanity, the time has come, in the view of Mrs. Stetson, for a radical change in the status of woman who can no longer find her sole environment in man. (pp. 264-65)

It must not be supposed that Mrs. Stetson's clear and sustained argument militates at any point against marriage in its truer and diviner sense. On the contrary, the whole trend of her reasoning is towards such freedom, such independence, as shall make possible between the individual man and woman a union based on the highest sentiment of love and social use, rather than on the low, common plane of selfish passion and economic dependence. None too scathing is the scorn and shame with which the lower and baser motives of marriage, so-called, are held up to our view by this bold, logical thinker who fearlessly strips the illusion of false sentiment from what passes in the world as love and wedlock. (p. 266)

It is not a fair treatment of **"Women and Economics"** to give its bald, bare statements, wrested from the chain of argument that harmonizes and shows the logical sequence and consistency of its conclusions. The best that can be done is to ask every reader to lay aside all preconceived views and prejudices on the particular subject in hand, and to bring to the study a calm, impartial spirit of inquiry that does not shrink from admitting truths even when they undermine the long-cherished theories and beliefs of heredity and education.

The conventional thinker will inevitably be shocked by Mrs. Stetson's ungloved handling of a relation which has been from time immemorial regarded as, on the one hand, sacred and beautiful, or, on the other, wanton and unmentionable. But it is sometimes necessary to be shocked before we can be moved to that dispassionate, unbiased consideration which will qualify us to distinguish between the real and the fictitious value of time-honored customs and institutions. A great step is gained by the woman who reads this book, if she catch a glimpse of larger horizons, and begins to realize that any personal love which limits her vision to mere temporal ends and fills her life with doubt, anxiety, anguish, fear, dissatisfaction, and unrest, is unworthy of the name of love, and must either be lifted to a higher plane or be set aside altogether. (pp. 266-67)

Mrs. Stetson herself, is giving a fine example of free womanhood in following her own high ideals, with a sincerity and directness that wins the admiration of even those who do not agree with her.

As a masculine critic [Harry Thurston Peck] remarks, "No one can easily overpraise the vigor, the clearness, and the acuteness of her writing." And he adds, "She writes, indeed, like a man, and like a very logical and very able man."

This is a mistake. She writes simply like Charlotte Perkins Stetson, a woman who, in the school of experience, has learned her lessons, not automatically from the text-books of custom and tradition, but with spiritual insight and a keen analytical sense that penetrates to the heart of things. . . . (pp. 268-69)

To some persons—perhaps to the majority—there appears a certain hardness and rudeness of touch in Mrs. Stetson's treatment of wifehood and motherhood, which is instinctively resented. But a closer study of her attitude toward these relations will reveal an unusual reverence for all that is deepest, purest, and holiest in them. It is only the false sentiment that is riddled and cast out in her keen analyzing process. As a revelation of the spirit of true motherhood turn to the not too familiar [poem, **"Mother to Child"**]. . . . (p. 269)

When we have a race of mothers entering fully into the spirit of this poem, then we shall have taken indeed a long step toward that divine order of love which is the end of all our human striving. So far from undervaluing the vocation of maternity, which has been conceded as the one unquestioned right of womanhood, it must be acknowledged by even her severest critics, that Mrs. Stetson exalts and broadens the office and

power of motherhood. But there must be the condition of free, brave womanhood to insure such a race of mothers.

However distant may appear the day when the principles of **"Woman and Economics"** shall be put to a practical test, we may congratulate ourselves on the impulse to thought which has been given by the book. . . . It remains to be seen whether women, more than men, will resist this relentless attack on the time-honored institution of marriage as a means of livelihood, vested as it is, with the sacred rites of the holiest of compacts. But all changes from lower to higher levels are pushed by the power of thought, and if the sex relation is lifted, in common perception, from the sensual plane, and made to stand in its true character for something greater than mere worldly considerations, then the author of **"Women and Economics,"** by her bold stroke, will have contributed her share to the upward impetus. (pp. 271-72)

> *Annie L. Muzzey, "'The Hour and the Woman',"*
> *in* The Arena *(copyright, 1899, by Stephen C. Cook,*
> *Trustee for Albert Brandt), Vol. XXII, No. 2, August,*
> *1899, pp. 263-72.*

**FLOYD DELL** (essay date 1913)

[In] this book of verse, **"In This Our World,"** Mrs. Gilman has so completely justified herself that no man need ever be afraid of her—nor any woman who, having a lingering tenderness for the other sex, would object to living in a beehive world, full of raging efficient females, with the males relegated to the position of drones.

Of course, I do but jest when I speak of this fear; but there is, to the ordinary male, something curiously objectionable at the first glance in Mrs. Gilman's arguments, whether they are for coöperative kitchens or for the labor of women outside the home. And the reason for that objection lies precisely in the fact that her plans seem to be made in a complete forgetfulness of him and his interests. It all has the air of a feminine plot. The coöperative kitchens, and the labor by which women's economic independence is to be achieved, seem the means to an end.

And so they are. But the end, as revealed in Mrs. Gilman's poems, is that one which all intelligent men must desire. I do not know whether or not the more elaborate coöperative schemes of Mrs. Gilman are practical; and I fancy that she rather exaggerates the possibilities of independent work for women who have or intend to have children. But the spirit behind these plans is one which cannot but be in the greatest degree stimulating and beneficent in its effect upon her sex.

For Mrs. Gilman is, first of all, a poet, an idealist. She is a lover of life. She rejoices in beauty and daring and achievement, in all the fine and splendid things of the world. She does not merely disapprove of the contemporary "home" as wasteful and inefficient—she hates it because it vulgarizes life. In this "home," this private food-preparing and baby-rearing establishment, she sees a machine which breaks down all that is good and noble in women, which degrades and pettifies them. The contrast between the instinctive ideals of young women and the sordid realities into which housekeeping plunges them is to her intolerable. And in the best satirical verses of modern times she ridicules these unnecessary shames. (pp. 23-5)

Mrs. Gilman is not under the illusion that the conditions of work outside the home are perfect; she is, indeed, a socialist, and as such is engaged in the great task of revolutionizing the basis of modern industry. But she has looked into women's souls, and turned away in disgust at the likeness of a dirty kitchen which those souls present. (p. 26)

> Floyd Dell, "Charlotte Perkins Gilman," in his *Women As World Builders: Studies in Modern Feminism (copyright, 1913, by Forbes and Company), Forbes, 1913, pp. 22-9.*

## WILLIAM DEAN HOWELLS  (essay date 1920)

[*Howells' inclusion of "The Yellow Wall Paper" in his 1920 anthology* The Great Modern American Stories *provided Gilman with her first broad exposure as an author. It marked the first of many times the story was anthologized; however, it was not until Elaine Hedges's 1973 explication of "The Yellow Wall Paper" (see excerpt below) that it was interpreted as a feminist story and not a horror story.*]

Horace Scudder (then of *The Atlantic*) said in refusing [Mrs. Perkins Gilman's story **The Yellow Wall Paper**] that it was so terribly good that it ought never to be printed. But terrible and too wholly dire as it was, I could not rest until I had corrupted the editor of *The New England Magazine* into publishing it. Now that I have got it into my collection here, I shiver over it as much as I did when I first read it in manuscript, though I agree with the editor of *The Atlantic* of the time that it was too terribly good to be printed. (p. vii)

> William Dean Howells, "A Reminiscent Introduction," in The Great Modern American Stories: An Anthology, *edited by William Dean Howells (copyright, 1920, by Boni & Liveright, Inc.; copyright renewed © 1948 by Liveright Publishing Company), Boni and Liveright, 1920, pp. vii-xiv.*

## ZONA GALE  (essay date 1935)

[*Gale provides an overview of Gilman's major ideas for social and economic reforms, including food services, day-care centers, and specific women's rights.*]

In the long, slow development of our social consciousness, Charlotte Perkins Gilman has flamed like a torch. This seems the right simile, for she has burned her way about the world, one message blazing from her spoken and written words, and from her living:

"Life is growth."

Anything which hampers or thwarts the growth, the expanding consciousness, the increasing coöperation of The Social Body, that Unit of Life, has been to her the sin not so much unpardonable as incredible. For life is growth. That is the brilliant common sense of her enormous awareness of the human scene.

Set against the simple tragedy, the simple ambition, even the simple aspiration of the individual life, this interpretation of hers raised living to new riches. It's not new to us now. We know about it. But when Charlotte Perkins began to understand it, most ethical concepts in America still had to do with individual morality and the hope of personal reward after death. (p. xiii)

Especially the stunted development of women roused her passion and her pity and her protest. Women, "specialized to sex and to housework"; women, "confusing marriage with domestic service." She saw in women half the human race, moth-

ers of all of it, cut off from their great work of world-raising by their position as private servants. . . .

In the rich and shared living into which certain men and women have entered now, all this is a commonplace;—and in certain bizarre extremes of to-day, such a picture as she draws has long since passed. But in the 1870's this was heresy to which every sort of opprobrium was attached. The idea of any life for women besides that offered by sex and housework was then unthinkable, and the larger integration could not be visualized at all. That women had many another contribution to make which would enrich society and human growth . . . ; that women's share in living is as limitless as that of man—all this was new and heretical—as to-day it remains heretical to millions.

To her all this was but newly revealed interpretation of age-old facts, and her beliefs were rooted in the story of the race. (p. xv)

To those who marvel at the vitality and one-pointedness of Mrs. Gilman's interest down the years, the obvious rejoinder is that this interest *was* her life. From the days of the '70s and '80's when she was a pioneer in America in this thinking, the integration of her ideas into her living and writing and talking never flagged.

One wonders where Charlotte Perkins got it. Even she does not know, though in her autobiography she tried to recall. Inherited wisdom explains something; and already the air was being charged for the new day. But her mind was one of the first in America to catch the fire. Incidentally, she never thought of suffrage for women as anything more than one iron in that fire. Useful, expectable, inevitable. That, of course. Then more, more! She had a thousand suggestions no less vital. . . . College education was just opening to women. But she longed for more. She longed for the release of the married through professionalized house service. (p. xxiii)

It took a long time. Even yet the cooked food service has but begun. Nor, though tractors and harvesting machinery are coöperatively owned and used, are realized her brigade of expert house-cleaners, to enter the home in spring and autumn, with proper equipment. . . .

She was intensely sad about women, about their lost opportunities, their lost advantage and for the millions who had gone down to the breast of earth with no knowledge that they were not the inferiors of the men who had taught them so well that they were so. (p. xxiv)

In the 1870's already she was as scornful of the woman who had to be "protected"—who dare not walk alone on the streets at night, as is the woman of to-day. And once, when she had refused a man's "escort" to her home, he cried, in bewilderment:

"But any man would be glad to protect a woman. Man is a woman's natural protector!"

And she asked him: "Against what?"

She was one of the first to stand for the use of her own name by the professional woman after marriage—or by any woman, if she so prefers; and one of the first to note that there exists no law whatever against this, but only a convention. (pp. xxiv-xxv)

One of her greatest social contributions is her interpretation of the needs of childhood. In her youth, no one had ever heard of a nursery-school. Kindergartens had not long arrived in this country. The whole duty of a mother was to give entire *and ungraded* instruction to her children. How did she know enough to do this? Well, wasn't she a mother? Did not God-given wisdom in how to do these things arrive with the baby? And so on. It seems strange now, in the light of the enormous literature on child psychology, on understanding children, on their development—to realize that "train" and "discipline" were the two words then most often applied to the growth of children. Human growth again. This hope, always in her thought, taught her that children were everywhere misunderstood and lied to and inhibited and repressed and crippled in mind and in energy by the terrible impress of the adult upon a consciousness of which, in a large measure of cases, that adult knew next to nothing. (pp. xxv-xxvi)

So she preached that a majority of children under school age were being ruined in their homes. At this women, of course, turned to rend her. She advocated great airy nurseries where small children could be taken and developed, taught to *grow,* by women specialized and trained in this wisdom. Women called her an unnatural creature. Now, in the days of pre-kindergarten care, of the books on "newer ways with children," of the definite knowledge that children may be mentally scarred for life before they are five years old, all this objection to child development takes its place with the old cry against college education for women. (p. xxvi)

*Women and Economics,* probably her greatest book, acclaimed in England even more favorably than in America where it became a great textbook, will stand for many as the sum of her life-work. It lit to energy many thousands of the unaware, the indolent, the oblivious, and made of them socially-conscious beings. You cannot say for a book more than this, unless you can also say that it kindled a spiritual energy. And the book did both. It does both now, and will continue to do so. It is a clear call to all women. (pp. xxxi-xxxii)

[*In This Our World*] shakes the complacence, the self-righteousness, the self-sufficiency of to-day, even as it did when it was published. If you want to be interpreted, like a dream, this book is your gentle Daniel—who bites, too, sometimes. *His Religion and Hers* performs for many a service like unto that of *The Green Pastures,* since it tells to a man and a woman his and her individual absurdities, while innocently imputing them to a type—or a race. All Mrs. Gilman's books are, for the greater part, of and for to-day. Like her quatrain aimed so laughingly at youth ["**The Front Wave**"]. . . .

We shall hardly outgrow her in long, long lives to come. In time to come, they will be saying: "How She Knew!" and there is an epitaph.

Her greatest single achievement was the *writing* and publishing for seven years, of the *Forerunner,* a monthly magazine all of which she wrote herself. These seven volumes are a treasury of the advanced development of the social awareness of our own time. These are "Gilman, in seven volumes." Fiction, essay and poetry in the magazine were all written by her, and there was the serial use of several of her later books. (p. xxxii)

One of the great women of the two centuries, she has the supreme reward of standing, in the mind of to-day, for that for which she has striven. She has sought to give out the sovereign knowledge that life has meaning; and that human growth—which is to say, the current of awareness of brotherhood, resulting in conduct—is the chief flow of the spirit to awareness of what that meaning may be. (pp. xxxvii-xxxviii)

*Zona Gale, in her foreword to* The Living of Charlotte Perkins Gilman: An Autobiography *by Charlotte Perkins Gilman (copyright © 1935 by Katharine Beecher Stetson Chamberlin; reprinted by permission of Radcliffe College), D. Appleton-Century Company, 1935, copyright renewed © 1963, (and reprinted by Arno Press Inc., 1972), pp. xiii-xxxviii.*

## CHARLOTTE PERKINS GILMAN (essay date 1935)

Besides "**Similar Cases**" the most outstanding piece of work of 1890 was "**The Yellow Wallpaper.**" It is a description of a case of nervous breakdown beginning something as mine did, and treated as Dr. S. Weir Mitchell treated me with what I considered the inevitable result, progressive insanity.

This I sent to Mr. Howells, and he tried to have the *Atlantic Monthly* print it, but Mr. Scudder, then the editor, sent it back with this brief card:

> Dear Madam,
>
> Mr. Howells has handed me this story.
>
> I could not forgive myself if I made others as miserable as I have made myself!
>
> Sincerely yours,
>
> H. E. Scudder

This was funny. The story was meant to be dreadful, and succeeded. I suppose he would have sent back one of Poe's on the same ground. Later I put it in the hands of an agent who had written me, one Henry Austin, and he placed it with the *New England Magazine.* (pp. 118-19)

I never got a cent for it till later publishers brought it out in book form, and very little then. But it made a tremendous impression. A protest was sent to the Boston *Transcript,* headed "Perilous Stuff"—

> To the Editor of the Transcript:
>
> In a well-known magazine has recently appeared a story entitled "**The Yellow Wallpaper.**" It is a sad story of a young wife passing the gradations from slight mental derangement to raving lunacy. It is graphically told, in a somewhat sensational style, which makes it difficult to lay aside, after the first glance, til it is finished, holding the reader in morbid fascination to the end. It certainly seems open to serious question if such literature should be permitted in print.
>
> The story could hardly, it would seem, give pleasure to any reader, and to many whose lives have been touched through the dearest ties by this dread disease, it must bring the keenest pain. To others, whose lives have become a struggle against an heredity of mental derangement, such literature contains deadly peril. Should such stories be allowed to pass without severest censure?
>
> M. D.

Another doctor, one Brummel Jones, of Kansas City, Missouri, wrote me in 1892 concerning this story, saying: "When I read '**The Yellow Wallpaper**' I was very much pleased with it; when I read it again I was delighted with it, and now that I have read it again I am overwhelmed with the delicacy of your touch and the correctness of portrayal. From a doctor's standpoint, and I am a doctor, you have made a success. So far as I know, and I am fairly well up in literature, there has been no detailed account of incipient insanity.'' (pp. 119-20)

But the real purpose of the story was to reach Dr. S. Weir Mitchell, and convince him of the error of his ways. I sent him a copy as soon as it came out, but got no response. However, many years later, I met some one who knew close friends of Dr. Mitchell's who said he had told them that he had changed his treatment of nervous prostration since reading **"The Yellow Wallpaper."** If that is a fact, I have not lived in vain.

A few years ago Mr. Howells asked leave to include this story in a collection he was arranging—*Masterpieces of American Fiction.* I was more than willing, but assured him that it was no more ''literature'' than my other stuff, being definitely written ''with a purpose.'' In my judgment it is a pretty poor thing to write, to talk, without a purpose. (p. 121)

> *Charlotte Perkins Gilman, in her* The Living of Charlotte Perkins Gilman: An Autobiography (*copyright © 1935, copyright renewed © 1963, by Katharine Beecher Stetson Chamberlin; reprinted by permission of Radcliffe College*), *D. Appleton-Century Company, 1935 (and reprinted by Arno Press Inc., 1972), 341 p.*

**CARL N. DEGLER** (essay date 1966)

[*Degler provides the first significant criticism on Gilman since Zona Gale's 1935 introduction to* The Living of Charlotte Perkins Gilman, *Gilman's autobiography. Degler was instrumental in the reprinting of* Women and Economics, *which was in use as a college economics text in the 1920s.*]

Today [Charlotte Perkins Gilman's] name is almost unknown, even among historians of American social thought. Yet in the first two decades of the twentieth century her books ran through numerous editions and were translated into half a dozen foreign languages. (p. vi)

The explanation for this transformation in Mrs. Gilman's reputation is linked with the fate of the women's movement. (Charlotte Gilman did not like to be known as a feminist—she preferred ''sociologist''—but the cause that she served best and most consistently was the women's movement.) The vicissitudes of that movement account for her dropping beneath the horizon of public awareness. In the minds of most Americans, the history of the women's rights movement is summed up by merely one of its aspects, the struggle for the suffrage. Yet it is evident from the writings of Mrs. Gilman and most particularly from **Women and Economics** that the vote was only a peripheral part of the revolution she both prophesied and advanced. Between 1910 and the adoption of the Nineteenth Amendment in 1920, the broad and important question of the place and destiny of women in a modern industrial society was swallowed up in the struggle for the vote. Since Mrs. Gilman wrote very little that was directly concerned with the achievement of the suffrage, her work has been lost sight of because historians have also defined the women's rights movement as primarily a drive for the suffrage. Moreover, simply because the woman question became politically defined, the achievement of the suffrage for women marked the end of concern for most Americans. (pp. vi-vii)

More recently, however, a growing number of students of American life have recognized that the achievement of the suffrage did not settle the question of women any more than the adoption of the Fourteenth and Fifteenth Amendments settled the question of the Negro in American life. The denial of the vote was only one sign of women's inferior position and exclusion from equal opportunity; hence, the achievement of suffrage left other aspects untouched. The question that engaged the interest of Charlotte Gilman was how to achieve full equality for women in an industrial society. Today this concept is once again a live one. . . . A half century before Simone de Beauvoir wrote [in *The Second Sex*] that woman has been ''a being apart, unknown, having no weapon other than her sex . . . ,'' Charlotte Gilman explored the idea in **Women and Economics.** Sixty years before Betty Friedan argued for outside interests for married women and Morton Hunt reminded us of the diverse potentialities of woman, **Women and Economics** canvassed the same issues. (pp. vii-viii)

[With **Women and Economics** Gilman] established her reputation in the United States and Europe. . . . *The Nation* went so far as to pronounce **Women and Economics** ''the most significant utterance on the subject [of women] since Mill's *Subjection of Woman,*'' which had appeared over thirty years earlier. Although she published four other books in the next ten years, none achieved the acclaim of **Women and Economics.** Part of the reason was that her subsequent books had all been adumbrated in that first effort; those that followed largely elaborated a position already clearly staked out, even if not thoroughly explored. (p. xiii)

[For the] seven years between 1909 and 1916 she edited and published a monthly magazine, *The Forerunner,* devoted to subjects that interested her—primarily the question of women's place in a new industrial and urban world. Actually, she was more than editor and publisher, for almost the entire contents of the magazine were written by her—unimpeachable testimony to her industry if not her scholarship. Often she filled the magazine with anything that came to hand, including three of her novels and other books before they were published separately, some of her verse, and rewritings of **Women and Economics.** Since the enterprise never really paid for itself, she continued her lecturing and writing for other organs in order to support herself. Characteristically, after keeping *The Forerunner* going for seven years, she abandoned it on the ground that lack of success showed that enough people did not want the magazine ''and it is sociologically incorrect to maintain an insufficiently desired publication.''

Aside from her autobiography, she published only one book after the First World War. *His Religion and Hers* . . . is the only one not clearly anticipated in **Women and Economics**; it explores the effects upon religion of the separation of the sexes in past time. Like most of her thought it is iconoclastic, for it finds contemporary religion poorer for lacking the influence of women. Modern religion, she points out, would show less preoccupation with death and damnation, if women had more to do with its origin and development. Her reason for believing this was related to her conviction that women are the bearers of the life-principle by virtue of their biological role in reproduction. Her conception of religion was as social bond and moral force rather than as theological truth; indeed she never belonged to an established denomination. . . . (pp. xiv-xv)

Her religious views may have been in line with the new intellectual currents of the 1920's, but in other respects she found herself in an unfriendly time. The new-found interest in Freudian psychology and sex she thought excessive. Freud she described as a throwback to ancient phallic worship, and psychoanalysis she equated with ''mind-meddlers.'' In several places she made it clear that she thought sex was intended by nature only for procreation, not for ''recreation,'' as she scornfully summed up her view of the sexual revolution of the 1920's. . . . Since the mainspring of her own life had been social service and subordination of the individual to society, she had little patience with the new freedom that stressed individual happiness and satisfaction, whether in sexual relations or in anything else.

Like many Progressives of pre-war years, Gilman also exhibited in the 1920's a nativist strain, as when she deplored the large number of immigrants in the cities of the eastern seaboard. Yet it should be added that in the 1890's she had been one of the few leaders in the women's movement who refused to accept the nativists' argument that the influx of new immigrants from eastern Europe should be limited by the introduction of a literacy test.

She could only feel vindicated, however, by the progressive thought of the twenties on child-rearing. In her books and articles she had long been preaching the need to grant the maximum freedom to children in order to teach responsibility and self-reliance. In her book *Concerning Children* . . . , for example, she had urged parents to explain to their children the reasons behind their commands or requests. She also counselled against the use of corporal punishment or condescension in the raising of children. (pp. xv-xvii)

Gilman's candor, forthrightness, and non-conformity make her seem a ''typical'' feminist, strong-minded, aggressive, and somewhat over-bearing. Perhaps for that reason, her lecture audiences were frequently taken aback to find that she was in fact a slight person who spoke rather softly and effortlessly, and with a light voice that nevertheless reached the back rows. On the platform, one auditor reported, she appeared to be a ''militant madonna.''

Despite her slight appearance, determination and self-discipline were the dominant forces in her character. Her success in controlling herself brought her perilously close to self-righteousness at times. . . . Later in life she was saved by a sense of humor and utter honesty with herself. Her humor was witty and satiric, bubbling through in her prose and poetry alike.

As a writer she was remarkably fluent and lucid, doing very little or no revising. Even her difficulties in concentrating did not interfere with her writing, which proceeded as easily, she asserted, as walking or breathing. Despite her feeling for words and the easy flow of language on paper and tongue, she showed little talent for imaginative writing. She tried her hand at several feminist novels, but they are worth reading today only for historical purposes. Although she read widely, especially on social questions and in biology, her interest in literature tended to be commonplace and traditional, as her references in *Women and Economics* make evident. (pp. xvii-xviii)

The purpose of *Women and Economics* was to show that a common humanity was the cardinal fact about both sexes and that the few biological differences were never in any danger of being overlooked.

*Women and Economics* is an easy book to read. In keeping with the pamphleteering tradition, it is forthright and easily comprehensible. Its message is stated several times, yet the author's aphoristic style is both quotable and readable. The

importance of *Women and Economics* does not lie in any sweeping originality, for other women and feminists had set forth many of her arguments over the years. However, no one in her time focussed the arguments so sharply and stated them so cogently and lucidly as she did. Moreover, at a time when most feminists were talking about the ideal of equal rights as the primary justification for women's claims, Mrs. Gilman raised the more fundamental question of the nature and potentialities of the sexes. She challenged the Victorian assumption that men and women were so different that their social activities ought not and could not overlap. Convinced of the molding power of environment, she stressed the plasticity of human nature. The Victorian woman, she pointed out, was socially created, and as a type was neither universal nor eternal. In her book *The Man-Made World* . . . she developed this theme at length, pointing out that from the earliest years young girls were encouraged, if not forced, to act, think, look, and talk differently from boys, though their interests and capabilities at that age might be identical. (pp. xxi-xxii)

Despite her obvious and deep concern for equality of opportunity for women, Gilman argued for neither the superiority of women nor their complete similarity to men. The two sexes she always envisioned as more human than either male or female. In an early issue of the *Forerunner,* for example, she wrote ''. . . *women* are not undeveloped *men,* but the feminine half of humanity is undeveloped human.'' She was never very specific about the precise differences between the sexes, probably for fear that to be so would help arm the anti-feminists, but she did see the sexes as making different contributions to society. . . . [She] would deny Freud's dictum that ''anatomy is destiny,'' but she never denied the differences between the sexes.

Charlotte Gilman's feminism, in short, was not shrill. In fact, her argument that women were different from men came perilously close to the traditional masculine argument that the difference between the sexes justified the conventionally prescribed roles for women. But Gilman stood on its head the traditional defense of a limited sphere of activity for women. Yes, she agreed, women are different, but to keep them out of the world is to make the world a poorer place. As a socialist who viewed society as highly interdependent, she was not satisfied to justify reform in the name of the individual, or even in the name of a whole sex. She objected, for example, to Ibsen's solution to Nora's problem in ''The Doll's House'' because it was too individual; Nora's family was sacrificed to her independence. Gilman's principal defense of unrestricted opportunities for women, as *Women and Economics* makes clear, was that the denial of those opportunities deprived the world. (pp. xxiii-xxiv)

The phillipic against men that appears in some feminist literature is not to be found in Gilman's work. In *Man-Made World,* for example, she denies attributing ''a wholly evil influence to men, and a wholly good one to women; it is not even claimed that purely feminine culture would have advanced the world more successfully.'' It is true that in her view the dominance of man was coming to an end, but that development she considered to be the result of the changes in the economy and social evolution. (pp. xxiv-xv)

Sometimes she is careless or wrong in her use of the early history of society in pleading her case, but in seeing the changing position of women as the result of historical forces she was generally right. . . . *Women and Economics* had a wide appeal because it addressed itself to a change already in full swing.

Modern industrial and urban life brought millions of American women to work outside the home; its urgent recommendation that women seek economic independence was simply taking notice of a social fact. (p. xxv)

She refused to be doctrinaire as to what kinds of jobs or careers women in the future would follow. (p. xxviii)

Fundamental to Gilman's feminism, as *Women and Economics* makes evident, was her conviction of the redeeming qualities, or, as she would put it, the human necessity, of work. With arduous, fatiguing, and onerous labor done by machines, modern work could now be appreciated as the highest of human activities. In 1904 she devoted a whole book, *Human Work,* to the elaboration of this theme. Significantly, she always thought of that book as her best and most important. (pp. xxviii-xxix)

In reading *Women and Economics* it is easy to be beguiled into thinking it is a scientific study rather than the reform tract that it is. Gilman had long been impressed by the certainty of science and wanted to find a similar certainty in social affairs. (p. xxix)

[*Women and Economics*] is not the result of elaborate or new research. In fact, in some portions of her analysis she is clearly incorrect by the standards of modern knowledge. . . . Her information is drawn from common knowledge and her own unsystematic, but wide reading. She was not a careful scholar checking her sources; in fact, she probably wrote from memory. Her method of attack is logic, her target the inconsistency between the pretensions and practices of society. Mercilessly she picks up every social idiocy that supports the conventional wisdom about women, subjecting it to witty ridicule. (pp. xxx-xxxi)

Aside from its feminist argument, *Women and Economics* is a veritable compendium of the dominant intellectual currents of the late nineteenth century. Socialism, democracy, Darwinism, and the belief in progress are all here. Gilman's public and life-long commitment to socialism is only implicit in this book, but she was an important figure in the general movement, though apparently never an active member of the Socialist party. (pp. xxxii-xxxiii)

The most obvious intellectual source upon which she drew in writing *Women and Economics* was Darwinism. Almost from the first page of the book it is evident that she lived in the post-Darwinian age. To her, man was a part of the animal kingdom, as her analogies between animal and human behavior make evident. Her whole argument, in fact, rested upon an evolutionary scheme of things, in which women's new role was defended as a natural outgrowth of social evolution, not simply of natural rights in the eighteenth century sense of the term. (p. xxxiii)

The immediate source of her intellectual inspiration, however, was not Darwin, but Lester Frank Ward . . . , the American sociologist who is usually credited with being the founder of his discipline in the United States. Ward's popular article in *Forum* magazine in 1888, ''Our Better Halves,'' sets forth the biological and anthropological position that Gilman was to base her book upon. . . . Ward's point was that woman ''is the unchanging trunk of the great geneological tree'' upon which the male is simply grafted. ''Woman *is* the race and the race can be raised up only as she is raised up. . . . True science teaches that the elevation of woman is the only sure road to the evolution of man.'' (p. xxxiv)

Gilman reflected the intellectual outlook of her time in her undeviating commitment to progress; part of this belief derived naturally from her acceptance of Darwinism, but part came also from her personal optimism and *joie de vivre*. History, progress, and nature itself, in Gilman's mind, were emancipating women. She was not doing much; she was merely calling attention to the direction in which things were moving and to the inevitability of it all. Actually, of course, she and the other feminist agitators of her time were doing a great deal to bring a new era into being. (pp. xxxiv-xxxv)

> *Carl N. Degler, ''Introduction to the Torchbook Edition'' (copyright © 1966 by Carl N. Degler; reprinted by permission of Harper & Row, Publishers, Inc.), in* Women and Economics: A Study of the Economic Relation between Men and Women As a Factor in Social Evolution *by Charlotte Perkins Gilman, edited by Carl N. Degler, Harper & Row, 1966, pp. vi-xxxv.*

**ELAINE R. HEDGES**   (essay date 1973)

[*Hedges provides the first lengthy analysis of ''The Yellow Wallpaper.'' She employs a highly biographical form of criticism, inferring that the events in the story closely parallel the facts of Gilman's own breakdown. This approach is criticized by Beate Schöpp-Schilling (see excerpt below).*]

''**The Yellow Wallpaper**'' is a small literary masterpiece. For almost fifty years it has been overlooked, as has its author, one of the most commanding feminists of her time. Now, with the new growth of the feminist movement, Charlotte Perkins Gilman is being rediscovered, and ''**The Yellow Wallpaper**'' should share in that rediscovery. The story of a woman's mental breakdown, narrated with superb psychological and dramatic precision, it is, as William Dean Howells said of it in 1920, a story to ''freeze our . . . blood.''

The story was wrenched out of Gilman's own life, and is unique in the canon of her works. Although she wrote other fiction— short stories and novels—and much poetry as well, none of it ever achieved the power and directness, the imaginative authenticity of this piece. Polemical intent often made her fiction dry and clumsily didactic; and the extraordinary pressures of publishing deadlines under which she worked made careful composition almost impossible. (pp. 37-8)

''**The Yellow Wallpaper**'' has resurfaced in several anthologies. However, tucked away among many other selections and frequently with only brief biographical information about its author, the story will not necessarily find in these anthologies the wide audience it deserves.

Yet it does deserve the widest possible audience. For aside from the light it throws on the personal despairs, and the artistic triumph over them, of one of America's foremost feminists, the story is one of the rare pieces of literature we have by a nineteenth-century woman which directly confronts the sexual politics of the male-female, husband-wife relationship. In its time . . . the story was read essentially as a Poe-esque tale of chilling horror—and as a story of mental aberration. It is both of these. But it is more. It is a feminist document, dealing with sexual politics at a time when few writers felt free to do so, at least so candidly. (p. 39)

[The story] was greeted with strong but mixed feelings. Gilman was warned that such stories were ''perilous stuff,'' which should not be printed because of the threat they posed to the relatives of such "deranged" persons as the heroine. The implications of such warnings—that women should "stay in their place," that nothing could or should be done except maintain silence or conceal problems—are fairly clear. Those who praised the story for the accuracy of its portrayal and its delicacy of touch, did so on the grounds that Gilman had captured in literature, from a medical point of view, the most "detailed account of incipient insanity." . . . [However,] no one seems to have made the connection between the insanity and the sex, or sexual role, of the victim, no one explored the story's implications for male-female relationships in the nineteenth century. (p. 41)

By the time she was in her late teens Charlotte Perkins had begun seriously to ponder "the injustices under which women suffered." Although not in close touch with the suffrage movement (with which indeed she never in her later career directly associated herself, finding its objectives too limited for her own more radical views on the need for social change), she was becoming increasingly aware of such current developments as the entrance of some young women into colleges—and the ridicule they received—of the growing numbers of young women in the working population, of a few books being written that critically examined the institution of marriage. . . . She began to write poems—one in defense of prostitutes—and to pursue her own independent thinking. (pp. 43-4)

A year after [her] marriage she gave birth to a daughter and within a month of the birth she became, again in her own words, "a mental wreck." There was a constant dragging weariness. . . . "Absolute incapacity. Absolute misery."

It would seem that Charlotte Perkins Stetson felt trapped by the role assigned the wife within the conventional nineteenth century marriage. If marriage meant children and too many children meant incapacity for other work; if she saw her father's abandonment and her mother's coldness as the result of this sexual-marital bind; if she saw herself as victimized by marriage, the woman playing the passive role—then she was simply seeing clearly.

It was out of this set of marital circumstances, but beyond that out of her larger social awareness of the situation of women in her century, that **"The Yellow Wallpaper"** emerged five years later. (p. 46)

[**"The Yellow Wallpaper"**] is narrated with clinical precision and aesthetic tact. The curt, chopped sentences, the brevity of the paragraphs, which often consist of only one or two sentences, convey the taut, distraught mental state of the narrator. The style creates a controlled tension: everything is low key and understated. The stance of the narrator is all, and it is a very complex stance indeed, since she is ultimately mad and yet, throughout her descent into madness, in many ways more sensible than the people who surround and cripple her. As she tells her story the reader has confidence in the reasonableness of her arguments and explanations.

The narrator is a woman who has been taken to the country by her husband in an effort to cure her of some undefined illness—a kind of nervous fatigue. Although her husband, a doctor, is presented as kindly and well meaning, it is soon apparent that his treatment of his wife, guided as it is by nineteenth-century attitudes toward women is an important source of her affliction and a perhaps inadvertent but nonetheless vicious abettor of it. Here is a woman who, as she tries to explain to anyone who will listen, wants very much to *work*. Specifically, she wants to write (and the story she is narrating is her

desperate and secret attempt both to engage in work that is meaningful to her and to retain her sanity). But the medical advice she receives, from her doctor/husband, from her brother, also a doctor, and from S. Weir Mitchell, explicitly referred to in the story, is that she do nothing. The prescribed cure is total rest and total emptiness of mind. While she craves intellectual stimulation and activity, and at one point poignantly expresses her wish for "advice and companionship" (one can read today respect and equality) in her work, what she receives is the standard treatment neted out to women in a patriarchal society. Thus her husband sees her as a "blessed little goose." She is his "little girl" and she must take care of herself for his sake. Her role is to be "a rest and comfort to him." That he often laughs at her is, she notes forlornly and almost casually at one point, only what one expects in marriage. (pp. 48-50)

[He chooses] for her a room in the house that was formerly a nursery. It is a room with barred windows originally intended to prevent small children from falling out. It is the room with the fateful yellow wallpaper. The narrator herself had preferred a room downstairs; but this is 1890 and, to use Virginia Woolf's phrase, there is no choice for this wife of "a room of one's own."

Without such choice, however, the woman has been emotionally and intellectually violated. In fact, her husband instills guilt in her. They have come to the country, he says "solely on [her] account." Yet this means that he must be away all day, and many nights, dealing with his patients.

The result in the woman is subterfuge. With her husband she cannot be her true self but must pose; and this, as she says, "makes me very tired." Finally, the fatigue and the subterfuge are unbearable. Increasingly she concentrates her attention on the wallpaper in her room—a paper of a sickly yellow that both disgusts and fascinates her. Gilman works out the symbolism of the wallpaper beautifully, without ostentation. For, despite all the elaborate descriptive detail devoted to it, the wallpaper remains mysteriously, hauntingly undefined and only vaguely visuable. But such, of course, is the situation of this wife, who identifies herself with the paper. The paper symbolizes her situation as seen by the men who control her and hence her situation as seen by herself. How can she define herself?

The wallpaper consists of "lame uncertain curves" that suddenly "commit suicide—destroy themselves in unheard-of contradictions." There are pointless patterns in the paper, which the narrator nevertheless determines to pursue to some conclusion. Fighting for her identity, for some sense of independent self, she observes the wallpaper and notes that just as she is about to find some pattern and meaning in it, it "slaps you in the face, knocks you down, and tramples upon you."

Inevitably, therefore, the narrator, imprisoned within the room, thinks she discerns the figure of a woman behind the paper. The paper is barred—that is part of what pattern it has, and the woman is trapped behind the bars, trying to get free. Ultimately, in the narrator's distraught state, there are a great many women behind the patterned bars, all trying to get free.

Given the morbid social situation that by now the wallpaper has come to symbolize, it is no wonder that the narrator begins to see it as staining everything it touches. (pp. 50-2)

[But this woman] never does get free. Her insights, and her desperate attempts to define and thus cure herself by tracing the bewildering pattern of the wallpaper and deciphering its meaning, are poor weapons against the male certainty of her husband. . . . (p. 52)

It is no surprise to find, therefore, that at the end of the story the narrator both does and does not identify with the creeping women who surround her in her hallucinations. The women creep out of the wallpaper, they creep through the arbors and lanes and along the roads outside the house. Women must creep. The narrator knows this. She has fought as best she could against creeping. In her perceptivity and in her resistance lie her heroism (her heroineism). But at the end of the story, on her last day in the house, as she peels off yards and yards of wallpaper and creeps around the floor, she has been defeated. She is totally mad.

But in her mad-sane way she has seen the situation of women for what it is. She has wanted to strangle the woman behind the paper—tie her with a rope. For that woman, the tragic product of her society, is of course the narrator's self. By rejecting that woman she might free the other, imprisoned woman within herself. But the only available reaction is suicidal, and hence she descends into madness. Madness is her only freedom, as crawling around the room, she screams at her husband that she has finally "got out"—outside the wallpaper—and can't be put back.

Earlier in the story the heroine gnawed with her teeth at the nailed-down bed in her room: excruciating proof of her sense of imprisonment. Woman as prisoner; woman as child or cripple. . . . These images permeate Gilman's story. If they are the images men had of women, and hence that women had of themselves, it is not surprising that madness and suicide bulk large in the work of late nineteenth-century women writers. "Much madness is divinest sense . . . Much sense the starkest madness," Emily Dickinson had written some decades earlier; and she had chosen spinsterhood as one way of rejecting society's "requirements" regarding woman's role as wife. One thinks, too, of Edith Wharton's *The House of Mirth,* with its heroine, Lily Bart, "manacled" by the bracelets she wears. (pp. 53-4)

Such suicides as that of Lily, or of Kate Chopin's heroine [in *The Awakening*] . . . , as well as the madness that descends upon the heroine in **"The Yellow Wallpaper,"** are all deliberate dramatic indictments, by women writers, of the crippling social pressures imposed on women in the nineteenth century and the sufferings they thereby endured: women who could not attend college although their brothers could; women expected to devote themselves, their lives, to aging and ailing parents; women treated as toys or as children and experiencing who is to say how much loss of self-confidence as a result. (pp. 54-5)

The heroine in **"The Yellow Wallpaper"** is destroyed. She has fought her best against husband, brother, doctor, and even against women friends (her husband's sister, for example, is "a perfect and enthusiastic housekeeper, and hopes for no better profession"). She has tried, in defiance of all the social and medical codes of her time, to retain her sanity and her individuality. But the odds are against her and she fails. (p. 55)

> *Elaine R. Hedges, "Afterword" (copyright ©1973 by Elaine R. Hedges), in* The Yellow Wallpaper *by Charlotte Perkins Gilman, The Feminist Press, 1973, pp. 37-63.*

## BEATE SCHÖPP-SCHILLING   (essay date 1975)

[*Schopp-Schilling attacks what she considers to be two mistaken conceptions of literary criticism "the intentional and biographical fallacy," which Ann Douglas Wood, Gail Parker (see entries in bibliography), and Elaine Hedges (see excerpt above) utilize in their criticism of "The Yellow Wall Paper." Schopp-Schilling discusses the story in relation to the principles of Adlerian depth psychology. Alfred Adler (1870-1937) was an Austrian psychiatrist who theorized that human behavior stems from an attempt to compensate for feelings of inferiority caused by physical, psychological, or social deficiencies—the inability to overcome feelings of inferiority leading to neurotic behavior. Adler's is considered one of the first theories to emphasize the role of environmental influences on human behavior.*]

Most of Charlotte Perkins Gilman's rather didactic literary productions were written between 1890 and 1916 and can be characterized as "realistic" in the sense defined by literary critics of that period. **"The Yellow Wallpaper,"** however, a short story written in a highly expressionistic manner, can be seen within the framework of a specific kind of "psychological realism" that so far has not been sufficiently appreciated. With the help of an interdisciplinary combination of Adlerian depth psychology and literary criticism, I want first to give an interpretation that explores the relationship between Gilman's life and this specific literary work from a psychological point of view. In a second step, I will evaluate the story as a psychologically realistic account of the causes and the progressive stages of mental illness.

Published in 1892 and read by contemporary readers and reviewers as an effective tale of incipient insanity, the story is seen today by feminist scholars primarily in the light of Gilman's own life. Ann Douglas Wood and Gail Parker accept Gilman's motives for writing the story as expressed in her autobiography, where she speaks of her desire to convince Dr. S. Weir Mitchell, famous for his rest-cures, of the errors of his medical treatment, which she herself had to undergo. . . .

Elaine Hedges, who has written the most detailed critical discussion of the story so far [see excerpt above], also sees it partly as an indictment of the medical advice Gilman received from Mitchell. But beyond that she praises it as a feminist document "which directly confronts the sexual politics of the male-female, husband-wife relationship." She, too, has recourse to Gilman's autobiography. (p. 284)

[These] critics do not avoid two pitfalls of literary criticism, i.e., the intentional and the biographical fallacy. Especially in the case of Hedges the method of reading Gilman's life into her story is particularly deceptive since she relies exclusively on Gilman's own interpretation of her life. This sort of information can never be taken at face value for autobiographical statements combine fact *and* fiction, the latter being an expression of the individual's unconscious need to justify his lifestyle.

After having decoded the autobiography with the tools of Adlerian depth psychology, one has to disqualify Gilman's own interpretation of her breakdown as just this sort of rationalization. Beneath the self-sacrificing attitude which places her work, "the elevation of the race," above her "more intimate personal happiness," one senses an extreme fear of entering into close personal relationships due to her utter lack of confidence in her ability to succeed in them. When confronted with the demands of marriage and motherhood, she helplessly escaped into a serious depression, using the role-conflict as a convenient cover. Seeing her breakdown in these terms allowed her to ask for the freedom to realize herself in the realm of work, where she felt more secure, though even there she was plagued by feelings of inferiority. Viewed in the light of these psychic processes, a more complex connection between author and work than the usual *l'homme et l'oeuvre* approach achieves is established: Gilman's gruesome relentlessness in depicting the sado-masochistic relationship between husband and wife can be explained as her unconscious attempt to cope with her fears and to justify her decision to leave her husband.

If looked at aside from Gilman's life and interpreted with the help of Adlerian depth psychology, the story itself reveals an intuitive grasp of psychological processes which so far has not been sufficiently acknowledged by the critics. The story's heroine, after having been forbidden by her husband to exercise her creative powers in writing, defies him by turning to a different kind of paper, the hideous wallpaper with which he forces her to live. Through her exclusive preoccupation with its design, she descends into madness, which ultimately enables her to creep triumphantly over her husband. Here Gilman reveals a fundamental truth about interpersonal relationships, hinting at the active, protest-like characteristics of mental illness, which represents the continual though completely perverted attempt of a human being to overcome his feelings of inferiority.

Beyond this, Gilman succeeds with high artistic perfection in the realistic depiction of the progressive stages of her heroine's psychic disintegration, which starts with depression and feelings of guilt and aggression, then develops into increasing withdrawal from reality, a persecution complex, odor hallucinations, synaesthesia and ends in the complete breakdown of her ego. She objectifies this through her ingenious use of the image of the wallpaper with its multiple function as part of the setting, as objective correlative to the heroine's repressed emotions, and finally as the symbol of her life. (pp. 284-85)

> Beate Schöpp-Schilling, "'The Yellow Wallpaper':
> A Rediscovered 'Realistic' Story," in American Literary Realism 1870-1910 (copyright © 1975 by the Department of English, The University of Texas at Arlington), Vol. 8, No. 3, Summer, 1975, pp. 284-86.

**ANN J. LANE**  (essay date 1978)

[*In this introduction to the first book publication of* Herland, *originally published in* The Forerunner *in 1915, Lane discusses Gilman's life and her economic, social and feminist theories as they relate to her utopian novels:* Moving the Mountain, Herland, *and* With Her in Ourland.]

Charlotte Perkins Gilman is not ordinarily thought of as a humorist, but her feminist utopia, *Herland,* is a very funny book. . . . [Much] of her fiction, the least known of her work, relies on humor for its social commentary. Ideologues—and Gilman was one of the best—rarely can establish sufficient distance between themselves and their cause to laugh and make others laugh with them. The women's movement is only now coming to recognize the power of humor as a device for social criticism, a power which, as with Gilman, is located essentially in imaginative work. Gilman appealed to an assortment of our comic sensibilities—the satiric, the whimsical, the sardonic, the rousing belly laugh—all in the interest of exposing the absurdities of accepted pieties, particularly as they applied to woman's "eternal place" or "eternal nature." She used the marginality forced upon her as a woman in Victorian America to shape a distinctly woman's humor. *Herland* is an example of Gilman's playful best.

What makes Gilman's skill even more special is the facility with which she moved back and forth from humor to serious social and historical analysis, and the setting in which *Herland* appeared well illustrates her virtuosity. (p. v)

She came of age during a time of struggle over the ideas of Charles Darwin and their application to society. . . . Lester Frank Ward, an American sociologist, rejected this interpretation of Social Darwinism, as it was called. He insisted that it was possible for humans, who, unlike other animals, possess a Mind and therefore a Culture, to shape the social laws under which they operate. Gilman early identified herself with the ideological camp of Ward in believing that human beings were the key to determining their own destinies and in using evolutionary theory as a weapon in the movement for social change. Convinced of the plasticity of human nature, she vehemently sought to destroy the molds into which people, especially but not only, female people, were forced. Her specific contribution to this wing of Social Darwinist thought was her assertion that women, as a collective entity, could, if they so chose, be the moving force in the reorganization of society.

Gilman's ideas matured at the turn of the century. Like most other intellectuals of her time, particularly those in the new social sciences, she struggled to create a theory and to envision a world that relied neither on class violence nor on uncontrolled individualism. Unlike other social scientists . . . she did not seek explanations for social problems or solutions to them from experts in these newly created disciplines. (pp. ix-x)

Gilman was determined to package her social vision in terms attractive to the mass of the population and at the same time to make socialism a legitimate, appealing, and reasonable idea. The literary genre she selected was the utopian novel, and she wrote three of them: [*Moving the Mountain; Herland;* and its sequel, *With Her in Ourland*]. . . . Although *Moving the Mountain* and *With Her in Ourland* are more earth-bound, a look at them can nonetheless provide the reader with a deeper sense of the texture and meaning of the world of Herland.

*Moving the Mountain* is set in the United States in 1940. John Robertson, traveling in Tibet in 1910, falls over a precipice and loses all memory until he is found by his sister thirty years later. During the long trip home and afterward, he studies the enormous changes that have taken place in his country. He finds, in Gilman's words, "a short-distance Utopia, a baby Utopia," a society brought about by "no other change than a change of mind, the mere awakening of people, especially the women, to existing possibilities." (p. xii)

In *Moving the Mountain* men and women learn to live together in a humanist-socialist world. In *Herland* women have created a utopia without men at all. Again this world is unfolded through male eyes and a male consciousness, not in the traditional manner of a dialogue, but through the dramatic confrontation that occurs when three American men stumble on an all-female society. Most utopias create worlds that are elevating but bland, a paradise without sparkle. *Moving the Mountain* creates such a place, but *Herland* soars. Gilman romps through the game of what is feminine and what is masculine, what is manly and what is womanly, what is culturally learned and what is biologically determined male-female behavior. Her belief in the power of humans to alter their societies and to control nature in their own interest is carried out literally in *Herland,* where parthenogenic births producing only girl children demonstrate that where there's a will, there's a way.

The focus of the new society is the New Motherhood, children being the central most important fact. As in *Moving the Moun-*

**tain,** child-rearing is an honored profession permitted only highly trained specialists. Women like Gilman herself, who had difficulty with mothering (though she loved her daughter), could live comfortably in such a place. (pp. xiii-xiv)

*Herland* opens with its three male adventurers in full agreement that such a superior society inevitably presupposes men. With a characteristic mischievousness, Gilman makes the man of reason, Vandyck Jennings, a sociologist by profession. Van uses his scientific knowledge to argue "learnedly" about the well-known physiological limitations of women. It is Van who says, at the start, "This is a *civilized* country. . . . There must be men." Noting the agility of the women scampering up trees, he establishes the absolute truth: "inhabitants evidently arboreal." So much for Gilman's belief in both the neutrality and the wisdom of science. Van's conversion is almost complete by the end of the story, when he admits that he is now "well used to seeing women not as females, but as people; people of all sorts, doing every kind of work."

The women of Herland have no way of relating to the men other than as friends. They do not understand the words "lover" or "home" or "wife," and the process by which they learn the meanings of these concepts is filled with good humor. . . . Indeed, the women have no interest in the men sexually except as potential fathers, which distresses the men. Sexuality is subjected to the same treatment as are all other social values, as part of our primarily cultural, not biological, package.

With wide-eyed innocence and simple reason, the Herland women expose the hideousness of much that to us is commonplace. The possibilities for cavorting are unending, and Gilman delightfully ridicules much conventional wisdom through the twelve chapters. The women of Herland do not understand why someone else's name should be taken after marriage; why dead bodies should be put in the ground to decay; why long hair is considered womanly by men when only male lions and male buffaloes have manes . . . ; what women in the outside world do all day long if they do not work; why women with the fewest children seem to have the most servants; why a God of love and wisdom has left a legacy of sacrifice, the devil, and damnation; why God is personalized at all—they do not believe in a Big Woman somewhere but rather a Pervading Power, an Indwelling Spirit, a Maternal Pantheism; why people who are emotionally ill, such as criminals, are punished, when people who are physically ill are not; why ideas from thousands of years ago should be cherished and honored.

The men find it odd being treated not as men, but as people; and we realize, by contrast, how much of human behavior is sex-oriented. In their "marriages," the men miss not sex so much as the sense of possession. Terry, the super-macho exploiter of women, complains that even the young and beautiful women are unfeminine because they lack qualities of deference. . . . To Van also these women are without seductive appeal, because femininity, he realizes for the first time, is a creation meant to satisfy men's wishes. (pp. xiv-xvi)

With time and some pain, Van discovers that the comradeship and intimacy he establishes with Ellador does indeed reduce the mystery of sexual allure. When their relationship is finally consummated, their love is so deep that sexual pleasure becomes simply a part of their larger feeling. Gilman was not alone among feminists in asserting that the strategy of sexual freedom led to another form of female subordination.

*With Her in Ourland,* the sequel, follows Van and Ellador as they tour our world just after the outbreak of the Great War.

She, with her disarming logic, causes Van, and presumably the reader, to see the world afresh. But where *Herland* skips and sprints, *Ourland* trudges. Didacticism often seems inevitable in the genre of utopia. Still, as a vehicle for Gilman's opinions, *Ourland* is interesting. (p. xvi)

On the home: "A man does not have to stay in it all day long in order to love it; why should a woman?" . . . "Motherhood is venerated in your world, as it is in Herland, but with you it is used to confine women and children, not help them grow." (p. xvii)

One might wonder what prompted Ellador to leave her home in the first place. Her mission was twofold: eventually, to spread news of the "local exhibit" that Herland represents; more immediately, to educate Herlanders about what they call the "bisexuality" of the outside world. "It *must* be best or it would not have been evolved in all the higher animals," reasons Ellador, with unfaltering Darwinian logic. The women of Herland have "made a nice little safe clean garden place and lived happily in it." But it is the men of the outside, driven by greed, lust, and aggression, who have nevertheless built, explored, discovered, and "gone all over the world and civilized it." When both strains—the male and the female—are balanced properly, then truly will the world be a glorious place.

Gilman's views of immigrants, blacks, and Jews, however typical of her time and place, are sometimes unsettling and sometimes offensive, though characteristically clever. The Jewish people, Ellador explains to Van, "seem not to have passed the tribal stage," as demonstrated by their inability to establish a separate nation. . . . Ultimately, Ellador feels, assimilation is probably the best solution. As for the "race prejudice" to which Jews are subjected, Ellador tells Van that "you will have to bring up your children without that," just as the Jews will have to eliminate their characteristics which the whole world dislikes.

On the matter of immigrants, Gilman is just this side of xenophobic, and sometimes her foot slips badly. Genuine democracy will not be achieved in the United States, Ellador comments, on the basis of an "ill-assorted and unassimilable mass of human material," not immigrants, "but victims, poor ignorant people scraped up by paid agents, deceived by lying advertisements, brought over here by greedy American ship owners and employers of labor." From a reasoned objection to the exploitation of unskilled immigrant workers, Ellador moves to a notion of stages of development, suggesting that "only some races—or some individuals in a given race—have reached the democratic stage."

Ellador's hope for America's future rests with the "swift growing" women's movement and labor movement, which will ultimately lead the people to socialism, "the most inclusive forward-looking system." Gilman's utopian fantasies are addressed not only to the population at large, but to the socialist and women's movements in an attempt to persuade each other to alter its strategy to encompass the goals of the other.

While Van's conversion is a major theme in *Herland* and its sequel, even Ellador, splendid as she is, grows with new experiences. By the end of *Ourland*, Ellador proudly announces: "At first I thought of men just as males—a Herlander would, you know. Now I know that men are people, too, just as much as women are."

Several utopias have espoused the rights or exposed the plight of women . . . but few utopias were written by women. Even those few rarely view women's situation in any special way. (pp. xvii-xix)

The utopian novel as a literary form seems to be going through a rebirth as a uniquely feminist expression at the present, with such books as Marge Piercy's *Woman on the Edge of Time* (1976), Joanna Russ's *The Female Man* (1975), Ursula Le Guin's *The Dispossessed* (1974), Dorothy Bryant's *The Kin of Ata Are Waiting for You* (published in 1971 as *The Comforter*), and Mary Staton's *From the Legend of Biel* (1975). Many of the ideas in these books are reminiscent of notions expressed in *Herland:* class equality; some kind of communal child-rearing; absence of privilege by sex; freedom from fear of male violence; elimination of sex-linked work; the mother-child relationship and the idealized home as models for social institutions; and the use of persuasion and consensus to maintain social order. But the contemporary fictional worlds are so much in the arena of the fantastic, in the genre of science fiction, that as a new kind of feminist expression they are in important ways not comparable to the classic utopian form. (p. xx)

Utopian works often assume that [human] institutions can be changed without explaining how it is possible—not literally possible but humanly comprehensible—to change the habits and create the people by whom and for whom these institutions had been formed. *Herland* and *Moving the Mountain* offer an answer, and that makes them unusual. Gilman's transition rests with marginal people—women. Because women are nurturers of the young and bearers of the cultural values of love and cooperation, and because women have been excluded from the sources of power, they are in an ideal position to create an alternative social vision. By the early twentieth century, women also had decades of sophisticated collective action and a trained leadership to call upon. Most utopias neglect the central role of education in reconstructing their worlds. In Gilman's work education—not formal education but the process by which values permeate an entire social fabric—evolves as a natural device in the creation of new people, especially the young.

Since Gilman's concern is with changing consciousness, she is free to create a material world that encompasses science and technology, on the one hand, and the beauty and simplicity of a pastoral life, on the other, and to avoid the major errors of both. Her technology does not dominate; it serves human needs. In addition, artificial wants are not created by scientific elites, for there are no elites, scientific or otherwise. The pastoral qualities are not linked to a pre-industrial world; nor is man—in this case, woman—re-created in a state of innocence, because to Gilman innocence is the first chain women must discard if they are to be free. Women's innocence has served only men's needs. (pp. xxi-xxii)

In Gilman's work it is not the scientist, the warrior, the priest, or the craftsman, but the mother, who is the connecting point from present to future. In her utopia, Charlotte Perkins Gilman transforms the private world of mother-child, isolated in the individual home, into a community of mothers and children in a socialized world. It is a world in which humane social values have been achieved by women in the interest of us all. (p. xxiii)

*Ann J. Lane, "Introduction" (1978; copyright © 1979 by Ann J. Lane; reprinted by permission of Pantheon Books, a Division of Random House, Inc.), in* Herland *by Charlotte Perkins Gilman, Pantheon Books, 1979, pp. v-xxiii.*

**MARY BETH PRINGLE** (essay date 1979)

First published in 1957, Gaston Bachelard's phenomenological study, *La Poétique de l'espace*, ably illustrates relationships between "exterior space" (so-called "objective reality") and "interior territories" (subjective perceptions of the "external"). Bachelard argues that external space exists only through our perceptions of it. Central to any examination of such space—a house, for example—are the "real" houses of the memory and the ideal house, the prototype embedded in each person's unconscious. . . . One's mind and soul can be better understood by analyzing that person's real and imagined abodes. . . . (p. 15)

Bachelard's "topo-analyse" is a valuable critical tool for interpreting literature because it emphasizes the subjectivity of the fictional, physical setting as presented by a narrator. Charlotte Perkins Gilman's **"The Yellow Wallpaper,"** now considered a classic feminist piece, lends itself especially well to such a tool of analysis. (pp. 15-16)

[Most] criticism of **"The Yellow Wallpaper"** has been biographical and intentional, two approaches that fail to point out the symbiosis of the narrator's mental state and her perceptions of her environment. . . . A phenomenological approach to **"The Yellow Wallpaper"** such as Bachelard proposes begins with the assumption that the world of the nursery is a microcosmic representation of the world that imprisons the narrator. With Bachelard in mind, one can easily detect connections between the narrator's state of mind and her portrayal of her entire "experience" of the family's vacation site.

"Ancestral halls," "a haunted house" . . . are chilling phrases used by the narrator to describe her family's rented summer home. Once, early in the story, she calls it "a most beautiful place" . . . , but elsewhere she belies this claim by her description of it. "It is quite alone," she writes in a journal kept secret from her family. "It stands well back from the road, quite three miles from the village. . . . There are hedges and walls and gates that lock, and lots of separate little houses for the gardeners and people." . . . At first reading, one is struck by the narrator's fear and hatred of the ancient home, especially since others seem to like it. When she confesses to her husband that "there is something strange about the house—I can feel it" . . . , he tells her that she is feeling a draft and closes a window near where she is sitting. No one in the family understands why she detests the yellow wallpaper in her attic bedroom.

In analyzing such details in the story one must beware of forming equations of meaning. . . . Space (a house) does not exist independent of the past, present, and future dreams of its inhabitant. When one moves into a new home, one totes along as baggage the past and its inhabited spaces and dreams of future rooms. When the narrator of **"The Yellow Wallpaper"** first moves into the "ancestral halls" of the summer house, she feels acutely out of place. The estate, she writes, is "hereditary," but she is not descended from the family that owns it. As a representation of her life on several levels, the inhabited past of the house is alien to her. The narrator is a city woman, an artist, whose life, whose experience of space, has been shaped elsewhere. The old house coincides in no way with the house of the woman's daydreams, the protective maternal/paternal home of her imagination. It is cold, "long untenanted" . . . , and subject to some kind of legal trouble, "something about the heirs and coheirs". . . . The place is beyond her experience, real or imagined.

In a flashback, the narrator even provides a glimpse of her imagined house, of the protective home of her childhood: "I used to lie awake as a child and get more entertainment and terror out of blank walls and plain furniture than most children could find in any toy store. . . . I remember what a kindly wink the knobs of our big, old bureau used to have, and there was one chair that always seemed like a strong friend. . . . I used to feel that if any of the other things looked too fierce I could always hop into that chair and be safe.'' . . . The sense of inhabited space carried about by the narrator is protective. Within it are places to hide, sites in which to seek succor. (pp. 16-17)

[The] narrator's bedroom in the summer house does not afford protection, nor is it the room that she would have chosen. . . . Instead, she is coerced into accepting an attic bedroom. Although it is large, airy, and light, it has been first a nursery, then a gymnasium for children. Its windows are barred ''and there are rings and things in the walls.'' . . . In a sense, the narrator's room reflects her position within the family. She is shunted aside, placed upstairs beyond familial activity. She is situated in a child's bedroom and playroom, befitting her role as child to her husband. . . . The relative position of the narrator's room to the rest of the house also reflects her mental situation. She is locked into the ''attic'' area of her brain; she is locked away from its main floor and out of its basement. . . . Because the narrator wishes to write and because she depends on her unconscious, mystical impulses as a creative source, she is spiritually slaughtered by being kept out of the basement. Because she also depends on interaction with people as a creative source, she is damaged by imprisonment in the top of the house. (p. 18)

The husband's and narrator's differing reactions to the house illustrate the subjectivity of their separate perceptions. She responds immediately and emotionally to her surroundings; he mocks what he considers her irrational behavior. When the narrator first mentions the attic wallpaper, she confesses that ''I never saw a worse paper in my life . . . one of those sprawling flamboyant patterns committing every artistic sin.'' . . . In response the husband promises to repaper the bedroom, ''but afterwards he said that I was letting it get the better of me, and that nothing was worse for a nervous patient than to give way to such fancies.'' . . .

Give way she does. In the wallpaper the narrator seems to concentrate all of her aversion toward the house. Besides its ugliness . . . the wallpaper reminds her that the summer house bears small resemblance to the intimate, protective house of her childhood that Bachelard writes is a part of each person's unconscious repertoire of past ''spaces.'' Her bedroom in the earlier house had blank walls and furniture to protect a frightened child. The summer house bedroom walls are alive: ''Up, down and sideways they crawl, and those absurd, unblinking eyes are everywhere.'' . . . Casually, at first, the narrator mentions that the wallpaper ''is stripped off'' . . . in patches within arm's reach of her bed. The narrator uses the passive voice, however, to avoid naming the person who has scratched the paper off the wall. Five pages later she refers to the paper's being ''torn off in spots'' and incriminates herself by adding ''it sticketh closer than a brother.'' . . . She also studies its pattern and coloring. . . . The wallpaper—embodying the hideousness of ''present space''—becomes an ever-increasing obsession with her.

The narrator focuses on furnishings in the house that correspond with her situation as she perceives it. Although windows in her attic bedroom provide her with a view that might distract others, she picks up on the fact that the window is barred. Someone else under other circumstances might enjoy looking out on the estate's luxurious gardens, a bay that sprawls before her, and a wharf out over the water. Since, however, the distance of wharf and garden confirms her isolation in the attic, she focuses on the bars. And the wallpaper. Not only does she write down her reactions to it, but she imagines how children (in particular, her own new infant whom she is not allowed to see) might also respond to it. . . . She obliquely associates herself with the children whom she mentions. Referring to the wallpaper that the reader later learns the narrator has torn, she claims that ''I never saw such ravages as the children have made here.'' . . .

That she should think of herself as a child and eventually attempt to restore ''past space'' (to make of the attic her childhood bedroom) is not surprising in view of her husband's treatment of her. The narrator wishes to practice an adult craft: writing. She wishes to pour out the ideas overflowing in her mind, to live in full harmony with the ''present space'' (attic to basement) in her soul. She cannot because her husband and her physician will not allow her to write. She must hide her notebook whenever they come near. . . . [She wishes to return] to the blank walls (the unwritten pages, the safety of ''past space'') of her childhood.

The narrator's childlike status in her marriage is represented by the house and, in particular, by her husband's choice of the attic bedroom for her. He chooses that bedroom so that they can have two beds instead of one. . . . Otherwise, he treats her with condescending neglect. He laughs at her, she notes in her journal, and, because he is a doctor, frequently sleeps overnight in town ''when his cases are serious.'' . . .

In fact, the narrator is often left alone with the house and wallpaper. Close to the beginning of the story, she says that she cannot think about her sickness because her husband has told her not to. ''So I will let it alone,'' she writes, ''and talk about the house.'' . . . In talking about the house she discusses her condition, since the two, in Bachelardean terms, are much the same. Gradually, however, the images of space representative of the narrator's life become even more focused. Like the house itself, the yellow wallpaper becomes a complex representation of the author's life and mind. The shift in focus from house-space to wallpaper-space is predictable. As occasionally happens to captives, the narrator begins to enjoy what she has formerly despised. In her journal she writes, ''I'm getting really fond of the room in spite of the wall-paper. Perhaps *because* of the wall-paper.'' . . . Formerly, as writer and captive, the narrator has tried to understand the forces and space that have imprisoned her. Now she tries to see a pattern in the wallpaper. Her efforts are unsuccessful. . . . The ''pointless pattern'' is exactly that: the life of the narrator is as randomly designed.

Perhaps that is why the pattern comes to life for her. First, it seems as if eyes are following her. Then its designs seem to shift and its colors change in certain lights. It begins to smell. . . . The odor, like the house that contains it, she regards as pervasive and enveloping. Little wonder that the narrator discovers a woman caught, yet able to slip around, between the crazy paper and the blank walls of the narrator's childhood. Attempting to free herself, she tears the paper from the walls. The creeping women multiply; the narrator is simultaneously one and all of them. At the end of the story, the narrator has recreated the blank walls of her childhood, at least to her satisfaction, and herself a child again, crawls around on the floor of her prison, imagining that she is free.

Because the narrator sees with an artist's eyes, her houseless-ness, her "spacelessness," is particularly distressing. . . . The ancient, ancestral halls of another family are impossibly re-strictive. . . . Nor does she have a future home to dream of. She is told by her husband that they cannot return to their usual residence for three weeks because it is being repaired. He threatens to send her to another future home—a sanitarium called Weir Mitchell . . .—if her condition does not improve by fall.

Working from a Bachelardean perspective, one can understand why the narrator begins her story by describing the "external space" of the summer house, but focuses instead on the wall-paper in one of its rooms. She discovers that, as with her illness, the house-as-prison image is too large, too difficult to cope with. Wallpaper is smaller but not more manageable. Out of yellow wallpaper the narrator shapes the only thing she knows: a cage. Bachelard allows us a full understanding of her im-prisonment. (pp. 18-21)

> Mary Beth Pringle, "'La poétique de l'espace' in Charlotte Perkins Gilman's 'The Yellow Wallpa-per'," in The French-American Review (copyright © 1979, The French-American Review), Vol. III, Nos. 1 & 2, Winter, 1978 and Spring, 1979, pp. 15-22.

## ANN J. LANE (essay date 1980)

[*Lane provides a survey of the most important themes in Gilman's fiction, and discusses the formulas, the plots, and the characters which she employed to illustrate her iconoclastic ideas.*]

Gilman's fiction is part of her ideological world view, and therein lies its interest and its power. We read her books today because the problems she addressed and the solutions she sought are, unhappily, as relevant to the present as they were to her time. Several themes appear persistently. (p. xiv)

In Gilman's stories, certain characters break out of limiting places with the help of intervening others. There is a formula and there are stock characters who work out the formula. The young girl-woman, restricted by her traditional view of parental obligation or social place, or endangered by an innocence that does not protect her from a cruel libertine, is offered the model of an older woman, frequently a doctor, who presents her with options she never knew existed and knowledge she did not have. Middle-aged and older women, having done their service to husband and children, often extract from their own previ-ously unexamined experience possibilities for new opportu-nities that point out the pleasures and powers available in our last years. Support for the young does not usually come from within the immediate family, neither from parents nor from siblings. Indeed, the young frequently need to reject their im-mediate families to seek help from others, sometimes a grand-father or an aunt, more often not a relative at all. Men who are redeemable, and Gilman does offer many such examples, are decent, sensitive, and well-meaning, though conventional; but they are capable, when pressed, of changing, a quality of conversion without which they are lost.

Although Gilman was a socialist, and identified herself as such, and although her utopian fiction creates an ideal socialist so-ciety, the strategies she offered in her realistic fiction were often strangely conservative. There were many cooperative ventures scattered throughout the nation; yet her short-term, immediate suggestions for individual or social reform took women out of the home and into capitalistic business activities,

not into producer or consumer cooperatives. Gilman evaded the issue of class by examining women's issues alone and resolving women's problems without reference to class. Most of the employed women of her time were servants, and yet Gilman's solutions, for individuals or projected onto a larger social screen, very rarely addressed the concerns or needs of a servant class in a way that could be expected to win them over to her point of view.

Gilman gave little attention to her writing as literature, and neither will the reader, I am afraid. She wrote quickly, care-lessly, to make a point. She always wrote fiction to meet a deadline. Still, she had a good ear for dialogue, was adept at sketching within a few pages a familiar but complicated set of relationships, and knew well the whole range of worries and joys women shared. She wrote to engage an audience in her ideas, not in her literary accomplishments. (pp. xv-xvi)

[In her] entire body of published and unpublished fiction . . . , Gilman examines, clearly and pointedly, a variety of problems women share and a variety of proposed ways of dealing with those problems. Although Gilman later ascribed a didactic rea-son for writing it, **"The Yellow Wallpaper"** came from a deep and private part of her that she ordinarily kept well protected from the public, and perhaps from herself. She may have taken the risk with the hope that writing **"The Yellow Wallpaper"** would purge her of the demons she so feared would one day claim her permanently. However, the debilitating depressions never did disappear entirely and for many years neither did the frightening specter of insanity. Never again did she publicly plumb her emotions with the intensity and honesty that per-meate **"The Yellow Wallpaper."** (p. xvii)

Gilman used fiction as a device to offer an answer to the question she always posed: "But what if . . .?" What if she wants a family and a career, and her husband-to-be objects? What if her children are grown up and she is bored? What if her husband is abusive and she wants to leave him, but she does not know how? What if her vacuous life causes her to make impossible demands upon her caring husband? . . . Ex-cept in **"The Yellow Wallpaper,"** there is always a feasible, positive alternative, and there is always a happy, or at least a moderately happy, ending. The questions, in one form or an-other, came from Gilman's own experience, either because she had herself come to a satisfactory resolution or, more often, because she had not and suffered the consequences, which she wished to spare subsequent generations. If there were not many models after which young women could fashion a new way of life, then Gilman would create them in fiction. (pp. xvii-xviii)

Many Gilman enthusiasts do not much like her fiction. They consider it too ideological, too didactic. Gilman mischievously used the commonly shared forms and structures of her day— farces, domestic novels, mysteries, adventure stories—and in-fused them with her own brand of feminism and socialism. Her work is ideological, but she implies that all literature is ideological, only its familiarity, its "naturalness" to us, makes it appear to reflect all possible world views. Although she does not challenge all the conventions of her day, she introduces a new sense of intellectual play when she poses her "What if" questions in the arena of traditional male-female relations, thereby exposing the absurd pieties embedded in domestic life. (p. xviii)

Gilman was determined to package her social vision in ways persuasive to a general audience. [Her] short stories are written in the style and with the simplicity common to women's mag-azines of the day. Each story is a lesson. Each focuses on a specific problem, usually but not always a problem shared primarily by women, and each has a happy resolution. The happy ending, however, comes about as a result of a good deal of intelligence, resourcefulness, and, most important, a willingness to defy convention, to look afresh at an old situation. What each story requires is the shaking off of traditional ways of doing things, especially as they relate to accepted male or female behavior. (p. xix)

**"When I Was a Witch"** has a wishes-come-true technique that is used, not to turn everything touched to gold, but to improve the quality of collective life. . . . But what do you imagine would happen to our cities if the homilies to which we pay lip-service were acted upon with sincerity: if people told only the truth in their pulpits, in their newspapers, in their stockholders' meetings? What would happen if the pain we inflict on others we felt in their place? The point she makes is droll, because we, in fact, would be astonished if truth, decency, courtesy, and generosity ruled our public life.

**"If I Were a Man"** applies the same sport to a husband-and-wife switch. When Mollie Mathewson, a "true woman," suddenly finds herself Gerald Mathewson, she discovers what it feels like to be a man: the quiet superiority; the pleasure of his large size; the comfort of his sensible clothing and shoes; the sense of power from controlling his own, earned money. In the body and mind of a man with the "memory of a whole lifetime," Mollie sees the world as a big place, a place of business and politics and action. Most startling of all, she learns what men really think about women.

Gilman felt strongly that innocence was a device through which girls and women were victimized, so innocence is the moral villain of **"The Girl in the Pink Hat."** An effort to seduce an innocent is foiled, partly because the young lady, though naive is not without courage and determination, and partly through the interference of a woman who is a combination of Nancy Drew and Miss Marple. . . . In this story the villain can be recognized by the smell of his breath and by his attempts to "assert a premature authority" over the woman he claims to love. Gilman frequently created a particular kind of man who is successful in winning women and then mistreating them. Trust, if not rooted in knowledge and experience, is dangerous, we learn.

In **"The Cottagette"** we see how to catch a man and how (almost) to lose one, if we accept without thinking the standard canons of female wiles. Malda follows the advice of her friend Lois because Lois, who is thirty-five and divorced, claims to know the real route to marital success. . . . [Malda is prepared] to sacrifice her time, her pleasures, her work, to make that home for the man she loves, who, fortunately wants her the way she was, "wild and sweet . . . truly an artist" not a household drudge. We discover that gratifying and beautiful work need not be esoteric; that there are men who value women as individuals, not as domestic servants. . . . (pp. xix-xx)

**"The Unnatural Mother"** comes out of Gilman's private pain, for it was a phrase often used against her in the press. In this story the mother is considered unnatural because she willingly sacrifices her own child to save the community, Ironically, the child survives, the town inhabitants survive, and only she and her husband perish. . . .

The tension between career and family, a problem in Gilman's time as in ours, is a frequent theme in her fiction. **"Making a Change"** is a typical piece on the subject. Julia, a wonderful musician and an exalted beauty, has neither the patience for

unrelieved mothering nor the abilities for household management. She tries only because it is her duty. Everybody is miserable: the baby cries, the wife is distraught, the husband sulks, and the mother-in-law wrings her hands. Then the women conspire to change it all. On the roof of the apartment house they set up a baby-garden with fifteen babies, run by Julia's mother-in-law. Julia returns to her music and thus relieves Frank of his obligation to be sole breadwinner. Everybody does what he/she is best suited for, and the children are happy because they are with other babies while being cared for by a competent person, who is not their mother.

**"An Honest Woman"** is a "fallen" woman who gets up. Deserted by the man she loved and lived with (though he could not marry her), Mary Cameron puts her life together, defying the conventional notion that, as one person observes, "you can't reform spilled milk." She is Gilman's answer to Nathaniel Hawthorne. Unlike Hester Prynne, who carries her humiliation with dignity, Mary Cameron refuses to carry it at all. She feels grief but no shame, for she is an honest woman. . . . (p. xxi)

Adultery was a subject genteel folk avoided talking about, except to denounce the women who engaged in it. In **"Turned,"** Mrs. Marroner (a Ph.D. formerly on a college faculty) discovers that her husband has seduced and impregnated their docile, trusting servant girl, Gerta. Initially enraged at the girl's disloyalty, Mrs. Marroner soon turns her fury on the husband who took advantage of the girl's innocence without even loving her. . . . It is the seduction she cannot forgive, the use of power against a helpless victim. It is an "offense against all women and against the unborn child." The two women unite and together confront the villainous man. . . . (p. xxii)

In **"The Widow's Might"** the mature woman, having spent her adult life devoted to husband and children, decides it is time to go off and play, to run her own business, to do whatever she chooses. Not a helpless, broken, distraught woman after her husband's death, she discovers resources within herself never before explored.

Mr. Peebles in **"Mr. Peebles' Heart"** is a fiftyish, grayish, stoutish man who has spent his life doing his duty, which meant essentially supporting women—his mother, his wife, his daughters—by running a store that he detested. He is persuaded by his sister-in-law, who is a doctor and a "new woman," to take off and travel. He does, and returns "enlarged, refreshed, and stimulated." His wife, left to take care of herself, also changes and grows in his absence. As a result, a tired and conventional marriage, built on unarticulated assumptions that did not help either party develop, gains a new life when the people involved learn that their possibilities are limitless.

Gilman's message is essentially just that: our possibilities for change are limitless, if we want them. How to achieve those changes is examined on a small scale in the short stories, and in a considerably more complicated way in the novels. . . . The first three "realistic" novels are followed by . . . her only detective story. The last three are her utopian visions. Together they constitute her strategy for getting from the realistic present to the feasible future.

***The Crux*** . . . takes another look at innocence betrayed—or almost betrayed. (pp. xxii-xxiii)

The novel is about the growing up of Vivian Lane, a sheltered, smothered, New England girl, who defies her parents by leaving home to go West. A group of women, including her zesty grandmother, are inspired to move to Colorado by a woman doctor, who is tough, breezy, powerful, and unmarried. Vivian is torn between her attraction to this model and to that offered by Adela St. Cloud, who flutters, is soft and misty, sinks into cushions, and is entrancing to young men—the embodiment of conventional feminine qualities. Then there are the men. Morton, whom Vivian has promised to marry, is fast, racy, wild, "practiced in the art of pleasing women." . . . Gilman skillfully draws the appeal of that kind of man, showing how a woman can choose to thwart her own needs and talents by focusing on her role as his helpmate. The other major male character is Dr. Richard Hale, independent, slightly cantankerous, somewhat misogynistic.

The crux of the story is that Morton has venereal disease. . . . [There is a] confrontation between the two doctors, the conventional male and the socially conscious female, on the question of Morton's disease and the subsequent painful disclosure made to Vivian. (pp. xxiii-xxiv)

Gilman created a woman doctor who refuses to be bound by tradition, although as author she shied away from direct challenge to medical protocol. . . .

Slowly Vivian rebuilds her world. She discovers the pleasures of the outdoor life in the West. She establishes a kindergarten and is gratified by her work. (p. xxiv)

[*What Diantha Did*] juxtaposes the ordinary way of doing things, that is, the irrational way, against the sensible, useful way, which is unconventional and therefore shocking. Diantha Bell also escapes her home, leaving behind a "virtuous" mother, a good, self-sacrificing New England woman, and her father, who is a run-of-the-mill tyrant. (pp. xxiv-xxv)

She begins her career as an apprentice-housekeeper in the home of a young couple with a child. The lady of the house is an architect, who loves her husband and loves her child, but does not love keeping house. . . .

Eventually Diantha puts her domestic skills and her business head to professional use in what Gilman calls domestic specialization. Diantha elevates domestic service to "world service" by treating it as any other kind of specialized skill. (p. xxv)

Eventually Diantha manages an entire hotel complex, complete with housekeeping cottages, child-care facilities, and food service.

*Benigna Machiavelli* . . . creates a special Gilman character, a kind of female Huck Finn, but one with a social conscience and a large view; one who ultimately agrees to grow up, but on her own terms. She is bright, mischievous, manipulative, and not especially honest, but she is essentially good, a good Iago, a good Machiavelli.

There is very little coming-of-age literature written for and about women. In this short novel Gilman offers a model of girl-into-womanhood, a road to autonomy, a system to develop independence and courage, a way to handle difficult parents without irreconcilable tensions. (p. xxvi)

Gilman's fiction can end cheerfully because she ordinarily presents problems that can be resolved by individual will. Firmly believing that we can, in some fashion, shape our lives, she had to avoid creating situations that lacked that fundamental possibility. Inevitably her people are middle or lower-middle class, and primarily of Northern European background. Most of the seemingly hopeless situations involve people with some

maneuvering space: they are widows, or are secure financially, or are young and without responsibilities, so that with reason and enterprise and lots of hard work, they can triumph. (pp. xxvi-xxvii)

*Unpunished,* Gilman's only detective novel, was completed by 1929 and, despite Gilman's effort and interest, was never published. Her attempt to write a racy, clever piece is not successful. She is not comfortable with the language or structure of suspense stories. *Unpunished* suffers, more than does most of her fiction, from hasty writing. It is not a bad first draft, which is probably what it was, but she had no patience to work at it persistently. Still, its ideas are intriguing, and the manuscript presents the culmination of a number of key themes in her writing. (p. xxx)

Bess and Jim Hunt, a detective duo like Dashiell Hammett's Nick and Nora Charles, are the narrators through whom the story takes form. Their friend, Dr. Ross Akers, physician to Vaughn and friend to the family, introduces the Hunts to the problem. The problem is that Vaughn has been murdered—many times. He has been shot, garroted, smashed on the head, and poisoned.

Vaughn is Gilman's embodiment of all conceivable villainy, although he appears to the world as a benevolent protector of a crippled woman and two defenseless children and as a reliable criminal attorney, defender of those in legal trouble. In reality he is a hideous and depraved tyrant. . . . The questions are: Who killed him first? Is it a crime to kill a man already dead? And is it morally acceptable to kill a person so wicked and corrupt? To begin with the last, Charlotte Gilman, in the tradition of Agatha Christie's *Murder on the Orient Express,* asserts that Vaughn's murder was morally justifiable. Initially it is only Bess Hunt who insists that "if any people had a right to kill a man, they had," while her husband accuses her of having lost her moral sense. But when Vaughn's base and diabolical qualities are disclosed, even Jim is convinced. "I regret that Mr. Vaughn is dead," he says, ". . . so I cannot have the pleasure of killing him." (p. xxxi)

Never in her fiction, and this was her last fictional work, did Gilman remove her villain with such direct violence. Destruction replaced persuasion. *Unpunished,* written when Gilman was in her last years, perhaps voices the frustration she experienced at having devoted a life to struggling for changes that did not occur. (p. xxxiv)

For Gilman, in fiction as in life, a favorite place of flight is the West. Gilman's West is a metaphor, an idea, a process, and a place. It is not Frederick Jackson Turner's West, the frontier where the trappings of a decaying civilization are discarded and a new, essentially male and capitalist American culture is reshaped. Gilman's is an urban West. Western cities are a place for the new, the untried; rules there are stretchable. Men far outnumber women, so women can select their mates from competing males, which Gilman believed to be the traditional way in nature. The West is the great leveler, and its cities, a powerful source of community and civilization. The West is where Gilman went to regain her emotional strength, where her daughter lived her long life, where Gilman chose to die. The West is also an idea, not just for Horace Greeley's young men, but for Charlotte Gilman's young women, and middle-aged women, and elderly women; in fact, for anyone struggling to escape confining convention. (p. xxxviii)

The women in Gilman's fictional world struggle to reach a new sense of themselves, but not through sexual awakening, not as Kate Chopin's heroine or Anna Karenina or Emma Bovary relates to her world, by defying conventions that define women's sexual place. Gilman's women, through struggle and hardship, ultimately achieve autonomy, usually through their work. With that autonomy, they are then complete enough to love and to be loved. Gilman's heroines often do not marry the most sympathetic men. They come to love the men who have to change; and those men do change ultimately, a hint to women readers that it is possible to persuade men to think and to behave differently.

In general, male authors are naturally concerned primarily with problems faced commonly by men. Female writers tend to create female characters who respond, more often than not tragically or painfully, to the male world. Gilman created models of women who do all sorts of things; they do not exclusively react to the men in their lives. . . . One can read Gilman's fiction as an effort to create a literary genre where woman's business is the business of the story, and that business ironically is often narrated through male characters. In her fictional writing Gilman tried to create a consciousness that defines and defends values and a projected society that is yet to be realized. It is the imaginative demands, not the literary skill, that make reading her fiction informing. (pp. xxxix-xl)

> *Ann J. Lane, "The Fictional World of Charlotte Perkins Gilman" (copyright © 1980 by Ann J. Lane; reprinted by permission of Pantheon Books, a Division of Random House, Inc.), in* The Charlotte Perkins Gilman Reader: The Yellow Wallpaper and Other Fiction *by Charlotte Perkins Gilman, edited by Ann J. Lane, Pantheon Books, 1980, pp. ix-xlii.*

**PETER LEWIS**  (essay date 1981)

Charlotte Perkins Gilman's novels, whether realistic (like ***The Crux*** and ***What Diantha Did***) or utopianly fantastic (like ***Moving the Mountain*** and ***Herland***), are a working-out of her ideas and theories in fictional form. Indeed, her sequel to ***Herland, With Her in Ourland,*** is little more than a series of dialogues with a minimum of narration and dramatic interplay. In the main extract from ***What Diantha Did,*** the eponymous and rebellious heroine, determined to free herself from her expected role at home, quantifies financially what her parents regard as her filial duty and presents her father with a bill for her household labour over the years. For Gilman, the Victorian concept of "duty" is a *bête noire,* enslaving both sexes (but especially women) and preventing a raising of consciousness. Her story, **"Mr. Peebles' Heart",** is about the stifling effect of duty on a marriage, and about the regeneration of the couple through the imaginative sympathy of a liberated woman who frees both husband and wife from their moribund relationship by changing their ideas.

Virtually all Mrs. Gilman's stories, like her novels, are essentially attempts to give her philosophy human expression, and were conceived to make polemical points rather than to explore experience in depth. The rather melodramatic **"The Widow's Might"** deals with a newly-widowed, middle-aged woman who after a lifetime of duty and service finally asserts her independence to the amazement of her children. **"Turned",** also tending to melodrama, is about male duplicity and female solidarity in the face of it. . . . All this fictional work of 1909-16 was written at great speed and is not notable for verbal, formal, or psychological subtlety. Some of it has dated badly, some is heavy-handed, some is morally dubious; her wittier or fantastic

vein, as in **"When I Was a Witch"** and **"If I Were a Man"**, is more effective.

None of this work, however, is in the same class as **"The Yellow Wallpaper"**. Written before her involvement in political and feminist activities, this chilling study . . . contrasts markedly with the Fabian evolutionary optimism underlying her later work. . . . The taut, economical idiom and the sustained symbolism combine to make it an important literary achievement. It suggests that she could have turned out to be a fiction writer of considerable significance if she had not channelled most of her creative energy into the women's movement from the mid-1890s on.

> *Peter Lewis, "Herland and Ourland," in* The Times Literary Supplement *(© Times Newspapers Ltd. (London) 1981; reproduced from* The Times Literary Supplement *by permission), No. 4074, May 1, 1981, p. 484.*

---

## ADDITIONAL BIBLIOGRAPHY

Hill, Mary A. *Charlotte Perkins Gilman: The Making of a Radical Feminist, 1860-1896.* Philadelphia: Temple University Press, 1980, 362 p.
>  The first of a two-volume biographical study. In this volume Hill traces Gilman's feminist convictions and explains "some of the patterns of her early life." By contrasting excerpts from Gilman's private letters and journals with her published works, Hill suggests that Gilman's idealistic, intellectual goals conflicted with her personal needs and the practical demands of her life.

Holden, David F. "Three Literary Sources for *Through a Glass Darkly.*" *Literature/Film Quarterly* II, No. 1 (Winter 1974): 22-9.*
>  Cites Anton Chekhov's *The Seagull,* August Strindberg's *Easter,* and Gilman's "The Yellow Wall Paper" as the literary sources for the Ingmar Bergman film *Through a Glass Darkly.* Holden reveals that the working title for the film was *Wallpaper,* and that the central character, her doctor-husband, and the old house with an upper room are all elements borrowed from Gilman's story.

Hough, Eugene. "The Work and Influence of Charlotte Perkins Stetson in the Labor Movement." *The American Fabian* III, No. 1 (January 1897): 12.
>  Account of Gilman's selfless efforts to further trade unions and labor reform.

Kolodny, Annette. "A Map for Rereading: or, Gender and the Interpretation of Literary Texts." *New Literary History* XI, No. 3 (Spring 1980): 451-67.*
>  Discusses "The Yellow Wall Paper" as a story which "anticipated its own reception." Kolodny indicates that the noncomprehending husband of the story symbolizes male readers who would not understand the depth of meaning in "The Yellow Wall Paper."

Lovecraft, H. P. "Introduction" and "The Weird Tradition in America." In his *Super-Natural Horror in Literature,* pp. iii-viii, pp. 60-75. New York: Dover Publications, 1973.*
>  Early standard interpretation of "The Yellow Wall Paper." Lovecraft mentions "the impulse which now and then drives writers of totally opposite leanings to try their hands at" horror stories, and cites "The Yellow Wall Paper" as an example of such a story.

MacPike, Loralee. "Environment as Psychopathological Symbolism in 'The Yellow Wallpaper'." *American Literary Realism 1870-1910* 8, No. 3 (Summer 1975): 286-88.
>  Concise analysis of the symbolism Gilman employed in "The Yellow Wall Paper." MacPike defines the importance of the deteriorating wallpaper, the barred windows, and the immovable

bed as symbols of the narrator's position in society and her relationship with her husband.

Parker, Gail. Introduction to *The Oven Birds: American Woman on
Womanhood, 1820-1920*, edited by Gail Parker, pp. 1-56. Garden City,
N.Y.: Doubleday & Co., 1972.*

Provides a brief history of American feminism and feminists in
the 1890s. Parker details the ''rest cure'' which both Jane Addams
and Gilman underwent, and how each reacted to it.

Wood, Ann Douglas. '' 'The Fashionable Diseases': 'Women's Complaints and Their Treatment in Nineteenth-Century America.'' *The
Journal of Interdisciplinary History* IV, No. 1 (Summer 1973): 25-
52.*

Thoroughly documented study of common medical treatments for
''woman's complaints'' in the middle to late 1900s, including
examination of S. Weir Mitchell's ''rest cure'' and its effect on
two of Mitchell's well-known patients, Gilman and Catherine
Esther Beecher.

# (Patricio) Lafcadio (Tessima Carlos) Hearn

## 1850-1904

(Also wrote under pseudonyms of Fiat Lux and Ozias Midwinter; also known as Yakumo Koizumi) American short story and novella writer, critic, essayist, journalist, and translator.

Considered one of modern America's leading prose impressionists, Hearn produced a large body of work that is more closely related to nineteenth-century European than American literature. His sketches, short stories, and novellas demonstrate a vision of evil and the supernatural reminiscent of Edgar Allan Poe and Charles Baudelaire. Hearn is also recognized as a perceptive literary critic whose readings and theories reflect his devotion to the beautiful and the bizarre. His lectures on American and European literature, published in collections such as *Interpretations of Literature,* are exceptional for their break with the conventions of Victorian criticism, and his essays on Japanese culture long influenced Western perceptions of the Orient. In both his criticism and his fiction Hearn emphasized the emotional effects of art rather than its social and ethical functions. Although he has long been a subject for biographers and critics, Hearn remains an enigmatic figure—a sensitive and painfully shy man with a penchant for the exotic and an enthusiasm for the macabre.

Hearn was born on the Ionian Island of Levkas, off the coast of Greece. His parents, a British army surgeon and his Greek wife, separated six years later and placed Hearn with an aunt in Ireland. He attended St. Cuthbert's College, and there suffered a mishap that resulted in the loss of sight in his left eye. This injury, coupled with Hearn's severe myopia, caused the abnormal enlargement of his right eye, giving him a deformed appearance which commentators often use to explain his lifelong sense of estrangement and, consequently, his affinity for subjects outside the mainstream of human experience. Hearn emigrated to the United States in 1869 and eventually settled in Ohio. There he met an English printer, Henry Watkin, who trained him as a proofreader and encouraged his literary ambitions. Hearn began his career as a feature writer for *The Cincinnati Enquirer,* gaining notoriety for his stories on slum and riverfront life. He received national attention with his report of the sensational "Tan Yard Murder." Hearn's account, written after viewing the coroner's autopsy, contains vivid descriptions of the gruesome crime and the victim's charred corpse. In the late 1870s Hearn moved to New Orleans, where he wrote for local newspapers and contributed to national magazines. His writings included editorials, book reviews, short stories, local color sketches, adaptations of Creole and foreign folktales, and translations of Spanish and French works. During this period Hearn pledged himself "to the worship of the odd, the queer, the strange, the exotic, the monstrous." In 1887 he traveled to the West Indies. Two years later, under commission to *Harper's Magazine* for a series of articles, Hearn left for Japan. There he remained for the rest of his life, lecturing in English and comparative literature at schools and universities and recording his impressions of the Orient for Western readers.

Hearn's work is divided into three periods, each corresponding to a juncture in his life. The first consists of the sketches, short stories, and journalism that appeared in New Orleans news-

papers and various national magazines. These works, collected in *Exotics and Restrospectives, Fantastics and Other Fancies,* and *Leaves from the Diary of an Impressionist,* focus on the bizarre, the supernatural, and the sensuous. Set in New Orleans, they offer colorful, romantic descriptions of Creole society conveyed in an ornate and consciously affected style. *Stray Leaves from Strange Literature* and *Some Chinese Ghosts,* also of this period, are volumes of obscure fables freely adapted from eastern legends.

Hearn's second period, encompassing material based on his life in the Caribbean, comprises the book of sketches *Two Years in the French West Indies* and the novellas *Chita* and *Youma.* Extravagant diction and lush imagery pervade these efforts, as do the motifs of death and ruin. Moreover, these works, which depict the interrelationship of nature and humankind and the struggle for survival between civilized and primitive peoples, manifest Hearn's interest in the evolutionary philosophy of Herbert Spencer.

The Far East, particularly Japan, is the dominant subject of Hearn's third period. Although the author's predilection for the grotesque is still evident, his style is now more subtle and controlled. Hearn's first impressions are recorded in *Glimpses of Unfamiliar Japan,* a series of vignettes that extol the land and its people. *Out of the East* and *Kokoro* contain similar sketches, while *In Ghostly Japan* relates traditional ghost stories and fairy tales. Hearn's final book on the Orient, the posthumously published *Japan, an Attempt at Interpretation,* stands in contrast to his earlier volumes, which were largely uncritical of Oriental culture. In this collection of essays Hearn, warning against the trend towards westernization, expressed his disillusionment with contemporary Japan and his concern for its economic and cultural independence.

Critics find that at his best Hearn was an exacting author whose work displays craftmanship and integrity. At his worst he appeared a flowery, mannered stylist, rather than a creative artist. He has been praised for his ability to arouse the senses but criticized for the lack of variety in his sketches and short stories. Critics contend that, with the exception of *Japan, an Attempt at Interpretation,* he sentimentalized and misrepresented various aspects of Eastern culture. Yet these works are credited with familiarizing Western readers with the people and traditions of the Orient. Despite the unevenness of his work, most reviewers agree that Hearn is an important prose stylist, a perceptive albeit unconventional critic, and an intriguing literary personality.

(See also *Dictionary of Literary Biography,* Vol. 12: *American Realists and Naturalists.*)

PRINCIPAL WORKS

*One of Cleopatra's Nights* [translator]　(short stories) 1882
*Stray Leaves from Strange Literature*　(legends and fables) 1884
*Gombo Zhebes*　(dictionary)　1885
*Some Chinese Ghosts*　(short stories)　1887
*Chita*　(novella)　1889
*Two Years in the French West Indies*　(essays and sketches) 1890
*Youma*　(novella)　1890
*Glimpses of Unfamiliar Japan.* 2 vols.　(essays and sketches)　1894
*Out of the East*　(essays and sketches)　1895
*Kokoro*　(essays and sketches)　1896
*Gleanings in Buddha-Fields*　(essays and sketches)　1897
*Exotics and Retrospectives*　(essays, sketches, and prose poems)　1898
*In Ghostly Japan*　(folklore, legends, and prose poems) 1899
*Shadowings*　(short stories, essays, and sketches)　1900
*A Japanese Miscellany*　(short stories, folklore, essays, and sketches)　1901
*Kottō*　(short stories, prose poems, and sketches)　1902
*Japan: An Attempt at Interpretation*　(essays)　1904
*Kwaidan*　(short stories and essays)　1904
*The Romance of the Milky Way, and Other Studies and Stories*　(short stories and essays)　1905
*The Life and Letters of Lafcadio Hearn.* 2 vols.　(letters) 1906
*The Japanese Letters of Lafcadio Hearn*　(letters)　1910
*Leaves from the Diary of an Impressionist*　(sketches) 1911
*Fantastics and Other Fancies*　(short stories, prose poems, and sketches)　1914
*Interpretations of Literature.* 2 vols.　(essays and criticism) 1915
*Appreciations of Poetry*　(essays and criticism)　1916
*Life and Literature*　(essays and criticism)　1917

*The Writings of Lafcadio Hearn.* 16 vols.　(sketches, journalism, essays, criticism, letters, novellas, short stories, folklore, prose poems, and legends)　1922
*Essays in European and Oriental Literature*　(essays and criticism)　1923
*A History of English Literature.* 2 vols.　(criticism)　1927
*Essays on American Literature*　(essays and criticism) 1929
*Articles on Literature and Other Writings from "The Cincinnati Enquirer"*　(essays and sketches)　1974

---

CHARLES W. COLEMAN　(essay date 1887)

"**Stray Leaves from Strange Literature,**" inspired by some words of Baudelaire—*"le miracle d'une prose poétique, musicale sans rhythme et sans rime"*—a happy description of the book, by-the-way—is an interpretation of certain Eastern stories and legends in English poetical prose. From exhaustive studies in Oriental literature, a subject which has always possessed for [Mr. Hearn] a strong fascination, resulted this volume of exquisite exotics, gathered from the rich treasures of ancient Egyptian, Indian, and Buddhist literature. . . . The weird and beautiful myths, as interpreted by Mr. Hearn, though lacking the metrical form, are veritable poems, heavy with the perfume and glamour of the East, delicate, fragrant, graceful. A second effort in the direction of poetical prose is a little volume . . . entitled "**Chinese Ghosts.**" In his treatment of the legend lore of the Celestial Empire Mr. Hearn has, if possible, been even more delicate and charming than in the stories which go to make the previous volume. . . . (p. 855)

> *Charles W. Coleman, "The Recent Movement in Southern Literature," in* Harper's Monthly Magazine *(copyright © 1887 by* Harper's Magazine*), Vol. LXXIV, No. CCCCXLIV, May, 1887, pp. 837-55.*

---

*THE NATION*　(essay date 1890)

'Chita' is the slightest possible melody set to an elaborate accompaniment. Off the coast of Louisiana lies an archipelago of islands, approached by a course through a half-drowned marsh country, and populated by a motley collection of races, where Malays, Spaniards, and Chinamen may be found. . . .

The story of '**Chita**' is laid in this island region, and has to do with the demolition of Last Island, the subject fitting itself, with a grim appropriateness, to many tragedies of the year just elapsed. A more uniquely picturesque scene for a romance, this side of the Atlantic does not afford. The romance, as already hinted, is not less than the islands themselves (perhaps for the sake of analogy), so overwhelmed by the real subject of the book—the sea—as to be a mere incident in the great ocean spaces. Possibly it is the Greek half of Mr. Hearn's ancestry crying out, "Thalatta!" At all events, he feels the sea like a poet, and summons to its portrayal in every phase a wild, hypertropical language which is the blemish of the book. Such words as "ivorine," "gracile," and "blattering"; such phrases as "a vibrant lifting up" (of the sea), "a fluttering and scattering of rose-leaves of fire," "a jewel light as of vaporized sapphire," "the stridulous telegraphy of crickets," "scudding mockeries of ridged foam," "imageries multi-colored of mountain frondage," occur till one has a feeling of having dined on lucent syrup tinct with cinnamon. On the whole, the impression left by the book is that of an ill-treated opportunity, a rarely fine subject made tiresome by a lush style.

*"More Fiction: 'Chita, a Memory of Last Island',"*
*in* The Nation *(copyright 1890 The Nation magazine, The Nation Associates, Inc.), Vol. 50, No. 1286, February 20, 1890, p. 159.*

### THE SPECTATOR   (essay date 1894)

Most travellers who have recorded their impressions of Japan, have written rather in the spirit of the lover who can see no defect in the object of affection, and [in **Glimpses of Unfamiliar Japan**] Mr. Hearn is no exception to the rule. His impressions however, in spite of his own manifest bias in favour of all things Japanese, are more valuable than those of the ordinary traveller inasmuch as he has been at some pains to get below the external grace and beauty of the country, and to explore its less familiar depths. . . . But the picture which he now presents as the result of his investigations is, we fancy, too uniformly charming and delightful to be absolutely true to fact. If Japan is all that he says; if the Japanese are so compounded of all the virtues, and so innocent of the ugly failings that mar our Western civilisation, then the poet's dream of a Golden Age has actually been realised in the remote East. Much as we should like to believe that such a land and such a people actually exist, we cannot altogether conquer our doubts, or avoid the suspicion that the author's feelings sometimes get the better of his judgment. . . .

The author has a charming style and a very pretty and felicitous taste in language; he writes so prettily, in fact, that it is difficult not to fancy that he sometimes sacrifices ugly facts to preserve the harmony of his tale. We may be wronging him, but that is the main impression that his account of Japan leaves upon our minds. The fault, however, is one upon the right side, and though a too persistent rose-colour may detract from the accuracy of his picture, it does not impair our pleasure in regarding it. . . .

To know and understand the Japanese it is necessary . . . to understand the simpler faiths of the country-people. Our author has been at some pains to put these clearly before us; and although it is difficult to fit together the scraps that he has collected into anything like a coherent scheme of religion, we can at least catch the spirit that generally seems to underlie them. His descriptions of the many shrines and temples that he visited would be just a little monotonous, were it not that he contrives to discover in each some trace of the unseen life of the country. But some of his chapters—notably, those upon Household Shrines, upon Jizo the guardian of children, upon the mysteries of the Bon-Odori, and that which is entitled "At the Market of the Dead," have quite a special charm and interest for a thoughtful reader. Not less pleasant in their way are his experiences as a schoolmaster among Japanese scholars. . . .

The most curious and suggestive of Mr. Hearn's disquisitions is that upon the Japanese smile. In this chapter, as in most of the others, the fanciful form in which he expresses his thoughts somewhat detracts from their force. Indeed, the chief fault that we have to find with the author is a rather obvious struggle for effect in all that he writes. His style is too persistently picturesque; after a time it begins to cloy upon the palate. Nevertheless, one must still confess that these two volumes upon Japanese life are not only more interesting, but also in-

finitely more readable than many works of a similar character.

*"The Inner Life of Japan," in* The Spectator *(© 1894 by* The Spectator*), Vol. 73, No. 3464, November 17, 1894, p. 698.*

### PAUL ELMER MORE   (essay date 1903)

[*More is one of the most important American literary critics and one of the most favorable commentators on Hearn's work. In the following excerpt, More examines Hearn's fusion of Oriental and Western thought.*]

[Mr. Hearn's work is] one of the most extraordinary artistic achievements of modern days. For it is as an art of strange subtlety that we must regard his literary work, an art that, like some sympathetic menstruum, has fused into one compound three elements never before associated together.

In the mere manner and method of this art there is, to be sure, nothing mysterious. One recognizes immediately throughout his writing that sense of restraint joined with a power of after suggestion, which he has described as appertaining to Japanese poetry, but which is no less his own by native right. There is a term, *ittakkiri*, it seems, meaning "all gone," or "entirely vanished," which is applied contemptuously by the Japanese to verse that tells all and trusts nothing to the reader's imagination. Their praise they reserve for compositions that leave in the mind the thrilling of a something unsaid. . . .

Now these ghostly reverberations are precisely the property of the simplest of Mr. Hearn's pictures. (p. 204)

Had it been that Mr. Hearn's art sufficed only to reproduce the delicacy and the ghostliness of Japanese tales, he would have performed a notable but scarcely an extraordinary service to letters. But into the study of these byways of Oriental literature he has carried [a third] element, the dominant idea of Occidental science; and this element he has blended with Hindu religion and Japanese aestheticism in a combination as bewildering as it is voluptuous. In this triple union lies his real claim to high originality.

Now it is a fact well known to those who have studied Buddhism at its genuine sources that our modern conception of evolution fits into Buddhist psychology more readily and completely than into any dogmatic theology of the West. It is natural, therefore, that the only Western authors quoted freely by Mr. Hearn in support of his Oriental meditations should be Huxley and Herbert Spencer. For the most part these allusions to Western science are merely made in passing. But in one essay, that on **The Idea of Preëxistence,** he endeavors with something of philosophic system to develop the harmony between evolution and the Buddhist conception of previous existences, a conception which, as he shows, has little in common with the crude form of metempsychosis embodied by Wordsworth in such poems as *Fidelity* and *Intimations of Immortality.* (p. 208)

[Mr. Hearn] quotes from Herbert Spencer to show how the notion of impermanence also invades our Western evolutional philosophy. But the parallel in this respect is at once apt and misleading. To Mr. Spencer and all the spokesmen of science, it is the impermanent sphere of phenomena that is alone knowable, whereas the permanent Reality hidden from the eyes is the great Unknowable. To the Buddhist, on the contrary, all impermanence is wrapped in illusion, as indeed the very meaning of the word would seem to imply; whereas the permanent

Reality, though inexpressible, is alone knowable. The difference is of great importance when we come to consider the effect of interpreting Japanese ideas in Occidental terms. It even seems that Mr. Hearn himself is not aware of the gulf set between these two methods of viewing the world, and that consequently he has never measured the full originality of this realm of sensation which his art has opened by spanning a bridge between the two. In the fusion of Mr. Hearn's thought the world of impermanent phenomena is at once knowable and unknowable: it is the reality of Western cognition, and therefore is invested with an intensity of influence and fullness of meaning impossible to an Oriental writer; and at the same time it is the unreality of Eastern philosophy, and hence is involved in illusion and subtle shadows into which it threatens momentarily to melt away. It is a realm of half reality, this phenomenal world, a realm of mingled spirit and matter, seeming now to tantalize the eyes with colors of unimaginable beauty that fade away when we gaze on them too intently, and again to promise the Soul that one long sought word which shall solve the riddle of her existence in this land of exile. It is a new symbolism that troubles while it illumines. It leads the artist to dwell on the weirder, more impalpable phases of Japanese literature, and to lend to these subconscious motives a force of realism which they could not possess in the original. From this union with science the Oriental belief in the indwelling of the past now receives a vividness of present actuality that dissolves the Soul into ghostly intimacy with the mystic unexplored background of life. As a consequence of this new sense of impermanence and of this new realism lent to the indwelling past, all the primitive emotions of the heart are translated into a strange language, which, when once it lays hold of the imagination, carries us into a region of dreams akin to that world which our psychologists dimly call the subliminal or subconscious. The far-reaching results of this psychology on literature it is not easy to foresee. (pp. 208-09)

Beauty itself, which forms the essence of Mr. Hearn's art and of all true art, receives a new content from this union of the East and the West. . . . The emotion of beauty, like all our emotions, is certainly the inherited product of unimaginably countless experiences in an immeasurable past. In every aesthetic sensation is the stirring of trillions of trillions of ghostly memories buried in the magical soil of the brain. And each man carries within him an ideal of beauty which is but an infinite composite of dead perceptions of form, color, grace, once dear to look upon. (p. 209)

We are indeed living in the past, we who foolishly cry out that the past is dead. In one remarkable study of the emotions awakened by the baying of a gaunt white hound, Mr. Hearn shows how even the very beasts whom we despise as unreasoning and unremembering are filled with an inarticulate sense of this dark backward and abysm of time, whose shadow falls on their sensitive souls with the chill of a vague dread,—dread, I say, for it must begin to be evident that this new psychology is fraught with meanings that may well trouble and awe the student.

In the ghostly residuum of these psychological meditations we may perceive a vision dimly foreshadowing itself which mankind for centuries, nay, for thousands of years, has striven half unwittingly to keep veiled. I do not know, but it seems to me that the foreboding of this dreaded disclosure may account for many things in the obscure history of the race, for the long struggle of religion against the observations of science which to-day we are wont to slur over as only a superficial struggle

after all. . . . [In Mr. Hearn's] essays and tales, whose substance is so strangely mingled together out of the austere dreams of India and the subtle beauty of Japan and the relentless science of Europe, I read vaguely the interpretation of many things which hitherto were quite dark. (p. 211)

> *Paul Elmer More, "Lafcadio Hearn: The Meeting of Three Ways," in* The Atlantic Monthly *(copyright © 1903, by the Atlantic Monthly Company, Boston, Mass.; reprinted with permission), Vol. XCI, No. DXLIV, February, 1903, pp. 204-11.*

### BASIL HALL CHAMBERLAIN   (essay date 1905)

[*Chamberlain was a scholar of Japanese language and literature, an Englishman who had lived in Japan since 1873 and taught at Tokyo Imperial University. His friendship with Hearn is chronicled in* Letters from Basil Hall Chamberlain *and* More Letters from Basil Hall Chamberlain.]

Lafcadio Hearn understands contemporary Japan better, and makes *us* understand it better, than any other writer, because he loves it better. Japanese life, manners, thoughts, aspirations, the student class, the singing-girls, the politicians, the delightful country-folk of secluded hamlets who still bow down before ancestral gods, Japan's attitude in time of war, Buddhist funeral services chanted by priestly choirs in vestments gold-embroidered, not men only but ghosts and folk-lore fancies, the scenery of remote islands which Hearn alone among Europeans has ever trod,—not a single thing Japanese, in short, except perhaps the humorous side of native life, but [Hearn's] wonderful books shed on it the blended light of poetry and truth. Our only quarrel is with some of Lafcadio Hearn's judgments:—in righting the Japanese, he seems to us continually to wrong his own race. The objectionable character in his stories is too apt to be a European. However, Europe is well-able to take care of herself; and if this be the price demanded for so great a gift to literature and ethnologic science, we at least will pay it uncomplainingly. (p. 65)

> *Basil Hall Chamberlain, "Books on Japan," in his* Things Japanese; Being Notes on Various Subjects Connected with Japan for the Use of Travellers and Others, *revised edition, John Murray, 1905, pp. 64-73.*

### GEORGE M. GOULD   (essay date 1906)

[*Gould was an ophthalmologist with an interest in literature. He corresponded with Hearn and was privileged to gain his confidence and personal insights. For a time Hearn went to live and work in Gould's Philadelphia home. Ultimately Gould formed the deprecating theory that Hearn's bad eyesight was both the symbol and physical cause of his flawed artistic vision. This theory has been widely attacked or dismissed.]

Clearly and patently, [Lafcadio Hearn's] was a mind without creative ability, spring, or the desire for it. It was a mind improcrant by inheritance and by education, by necessity and by training, by poverty internal and external. To enable its master to live, it must write, and, as was pitifully evident, if it could not write in obedience to a creative instinct, it must do the next best thing. This residual second was to describe the external world, or at least so much of the externals of all worlds, physical, biological, or social, as romance or common sense demanded to make the writing vivid, accurate, and bodied. Any good literature, especially the poetic, must be based on reality, must at least incidentally have its running obbligato of reality. For the poet, . . . vision is the intermediary, the broad, bright highway to facts. Prosaically, local colour requires the local seer. Barred out [by his defective eyesight] from this divine roadway to and through the actual universe, the foiled mind of Hearn could choose but one course: to regarment, transform, and colour the world, devised and transmitted by others, . . . for in Hearn's alembic the solidest of flesh was "melted" and escaped in clouds of spirit; it was indeed often so disembodied and freed that one is lost in wonder at the mere vision of the cloudland so eerie, so silent, so void, so invisibly far, and fading ever still farther away. But, chained to the *here,* Hearn could not march on the bright road. He could never even see the road, or its ending. If freed to go, *there* became *here* with the intolerable limitation of his vision, the peculiarity of his unvision. The world, the world of the *there* must be brought to him, and in the bringing it became the *here.* In the process, distant motion or action became dead, silent, and immobile being; distance was transformed to presence, and an intimacy of presence which at one blow destroyed scene, setting, and illumination. For, except to passionate love, nearness and touch are not poetical or transfiguring, and to Hearn love never could come, leastwise never did come. (pp. 885-86)

With creative instinct or ability denied, with the poet's craving for open-eyed knowing, and with the poet's necessity of realising the world out there, Hearn, baldly stated, was forced to become the poet of myopia. His groping mind was compelled to rest satisfied with the world of distance and reality transported by the magic carpet to the door of his imagination and fancy. There in a flash it was melted to formless spirit, recombined to soul, and given the semblance of a thin reincarnation, fashioned, refashioned, coloured, recoloured. There, lo, that incomparable wonder of art, the haunting magical essence of reality, the quivering, elusive protean ghost of the tragedy of dead pain, the smile of a lost universe murmuring *non dolet* while it dies struck by the hand of the beloved murderer.

For with Hearn's lack of creative ability, married to his inexperience of happiness, he could but choose the darksome, the tragical elements of life . . . as his themes. His intellect being a reflecting, or at least a recombining and colouring faculty, his datum must be sought without and it must be brought to him; his joyless and even his tragic experience compelled him to cull from the mingled sad and bright only the pathetic or pessimistic subjects; his physical and optical imprisonment forbade that objectivation and distinctive embodiment which stamps an art-work with the seal of reality and makes it stand there wholly nonexcusing, or offering itself as its own excuse for being. True art must have the warp of materiality, interwoven with the woof of life, or else the coloration and designs of the imagination cannot avail to dower it with immortality.

Working within the sad limits his Fates had set, Hearn performed wonders. None has made tragedy so soft and gentle, none has rendered suffering more beautiful, none has dissolved disappointment into such painless grief, none has blunted the hurt of mortality with such a delightful anaesthesia, and by none have death and hopelessness been more deftly figured in the guise of a desirable Nirvana. The doing of this was almost a unique doing . . . and constitutes Hearn's claim to an artist's "Forever." He would have made no claim, it is true, to this, or to any other endless existence, but we who read would be too undiscriminating, would be losers, ingrates, if we did not

cherish the lovely gift he brings to us so shyly. Restricted and confined as was his garden, he grew in it exotic flowers of unearthly but imperishable beauty. One will not find elsewhere an equal craftsmanship in bringing into words and vision the intangible, the far, fine elusive fancy, the ghosts of vanished hearts and hopes. Under his magic touch unseen spirit almost reappears with the veiling of materiality, and behind the grim and grinning death's-head a supplanting smile of kindness invites pity, if not a friendly whisper.

As to literary aim, Hearn distinctly and repeatedly confessed to me that his ideal was, in his own words, to give his reader "a ghostly shudder," a sense of the closeness of the unseen about us, as if eyes we saw not were watching us, as if long-dead spirits and weird powers were haunting the very air about our ears, were sitting hid in our heart of hearts. It was a pleasing task to him to make us hear the moans and croonings of disincarnate griefs and old pulseless pains, begging piteously, but always softly, gently, for our love and comforting. But it should not be unrecognised that no allurement of his art can hide from view the deeper pathos of a horrid and iron fatalism which to his mind moved the worlds of nature or of life, throttled freedom, steeled the heart, iced the emotions, and dictated the essential automatonism of our own being and of these sad dead millions which crowd the dimly seen dreams of Hearn's mind. (pp. 886-87)

If we look upon Hearn as a painter, almost the sole colour of his palette was mummy brown, the powdered flesh of the ancient dead holding in solution their griefs, their hopes, their loves, their yearnings, which he found to sink always to pulselessness, and to end in eternal defeat! But the pallor and sadness for the brief moment of their resuscitation was divinely softened and atoningly beautified. Then they disappeared again in the waste and gloom from which love and poesy had evoked them. (p. 892)

*George M. Gould, "Lafcadio Hearn: A Study of His Personality and Art," in* The Fortnightly Review, *Vol. LXXXVI, No. CCCCLXXIX, November 1, 1906, pp. 881-92.*

## FERRIS GREENSLET (essay date 1911)

In conveying the flavor of a strongly-flavored writer [Hearn's translation of Théophile Gautier's "One of Cleopatra's Nights and Other Fantastic Tales"] was singularly successful. It was dedicated 'To the lovers of the loveliness of the antique world, the lovers of artistic beauty and artistic truth.' A dedication to the lovers of *macabre* would have been more appropriate. In his choice of tales, in his gusto in the rendering of certain passages, in the 'flowers of the yew' which he thought best to add in an appendix, Hearn showed himself more macabresque than his master. (pp. 7-8)

As we look at the decade of his life [in New Orleans], the notable thing now is the growth of his artistic, and still more of his intellectual, power. At first his imagination was captured by the strange, tropical, intoxicating beauty of the old Creole city, its social and ethnological contrasts, its mysterious underworld, and barbaric cults. He felt it to be his artistic duty, he writes, 'to be absorbed into this new life and study its form and color and passion.' (p. 8)

[He] 'pledges himself to the worship of the Odd, the Queer, the Strange, the Exotic, the Monstrous,' which, as he writes, 'suits my temperament.'

The chief literary expression of this impulse in its early phase was his **'Stray Leaves from Strange Literatures,'** chiefly written before 1883, and published two years later. This, a series of reconstructions of what impressed him as most fantastically beautiful in the most exotic literature he was able to obtain, shows a remarkable growth in mere craftsmanship over his translations from Gautier. The cadences are surer, the weird or gorgeous pictures built up from simpler words, and the exotic atmosphere is more enveloping and persuasive.

But the handful of arabesques that Hearn brought together in his **'Stray Leaves from Strange Literatures'** was only a drop in the bucket that came up brimming from that deep well of 'the Odd, the Queer, the Strange, the Exotic, the Monstrous.' In the first five years of his work for the 'Times-Democrat,' he made and printed in the paper no fewer than two hundred translations of French stories and striking chapters or passages from the French books that engaged his eager attention. When we remember that the bulk of these versions were from the writings of the greatest contemporary masters of French prose,— thirty-one were from Maupassant,—we become aware of at least one of the sources of that extraordinary growth in Hearn's mastery of his instrument that can be seen when we compare the suave and luminous current of the prose of **'Some Chinese Ghosts'** in 1887, with the volume from Gautier, or even with the **'Stray Leaves.'**

It was at this time, too, that Hearn, forsaking translation for original work, began to follow the leading of his imagination into characteristic paths. . . . He printed, even apparently with a certain *réclame*, curious, condensed, personalized paraphrases of out of the way books, like Perron's 'Femmes Arabes,' and other curious investigations of the Exotic, and passed easily from this into such excursions in aromatic impressionism as those that record his vacation in Florida, colored by his reading of Gaffarel's 'Floride Française,' or his studies of the Creole life and language. (pp. 10-13)

The year 1883, as readers of his letters know, marked an epoch in Hearn's intellectual life. Then for the first time he read Herbert Spencer, and by a singular paradox conceived a passionate adoration for that passionless philosopher who, we may think, had the peculiar advantage of knowing so much about the 'Unknowable.' . . . [The] philosophy of Spencer came to him with something of the power and unction of an evangelical religion, bringing with it not only conversion, but 'conviction of sin,' and 'regeneration.' From this time on, there was a new seriousness in his life and a new gravity in his work. Henceforth he was concerned about the Exotic and Monstrous chiefly as they could be employed as parables of the gospel according to Herbert Spencer.

A year or two later there came into his work another strain that was to remain potent,—the tropical. (pp. 15-16)

In 1884 he made the visit to Grande Isle in the Mexican Gulf that resulted in his **'Chita,'** which is still in many respects his most astonishing *tour de force* in word-painting, though in it we see how far away he was from the English tradition of creative art in fiction. The only logic in the harrowing conclusion is the emotional logic of a temperament immitigably macabresque, that must make a tale of terror intensify in poignancy to the end.

In 1887, he went to the French West Indies, and found there a theme perhaps more in consonance with the full richness of his vein than any he afterwards encountered. In **'Youma,'** his West Indian novelette, the note is certainly falsetto, but in his

**'Two Years in the French West Indies'** the luxuriant leafiness of his style, heavy with tropical perfumes, subtly interpenetrated with the sense of tropical terror, rarely goes beyond the bounds of faithful depiction. And underneath it all we begin to see that impressive Spencerian perception of the fatal unity of the world. (pp. 16-17)

As one who reads Hearn's writings chronologically passes from the West Indian books to the Japanese, there is evident a remarkable change, not only of atmosphere but of tone, and, despite the continuity of the Spencerian preoccupation, of what we may perhaps call 'soul.' The tropical luxuriance of his earlier manner has been replaced by quieter tints and subtler cadences, and henceforth he gives free rein to his faculty only in rare heightened passages, which rise above the narrow, quiet stream of his habitual prose with an effect incomparably telling. In part this was the result of his sensitive perception of the peculiar color of Japanese landscape, 'a domesticated Nature, which loves man, and makes itself beautiful in a quiet gray-and-blue way like the Japanese women'; which must in consequence be reproduced in water-color rather than in the oils in which he had been working. In part it was the result of his greater maturity, and that assured control over his medium, which left him no impulse to mere virtuosity. (pp. 18-19)

Lafcadio Hearn has been called a 'decadent'; the word does not signify, but if by it is meant, as sometimes seems to be, a humanist without physique, there is a considerable measure of truth in its application. If one symptom of decadence be the love of words for their own sake, it was, as we have seen, not lacking in his earlier work. (p. 20)

The final estimation of Hearn's work is impeded by its scattered bulk, but when in the fullness of time it is finally brought together in a collected edition it will be seen to stand very high in the second class of English prose, the class of the great *prosateurs*, Sir Thomas Browne, Thomas DeQuincey, Walter Pater.

Had he lived longer his rank might have been higher still. He had outgrown his old decadent conception of style as separable from substance, as an end to be attained in itself, to be arrived at by miners' work in dictionaries and thesauri. His work never ceased to be conscious art, but in his very latest writing there is a perfect fusion of his vigorous imaginative thought in the melancholy music of his cadenced prose. (pp. 25-6)

[The last of his work] shows both a broadening and a deepening of what, despite the artifice of his method, we may justly call his inspiration. Had he lived to complete the imaginative autobiography of which fragments are printed in his **'Life and Letters,'** it might have proved his masterpiece. The fragments have a sincere and haunting poignancy, and his prose was never more vivid and musical. For all that 'population' within him, his own intellectual and imaginative life had been marked by a unity that would doubtless have induced a corresponding unity in the book, with striking artistic results.

The integrity of Hearn's intellectual life consisted in his strangely single-hearted devotion to both artistic beauty and scientific truth. And precisely in this, I believe, lies the significance of his work. He was, in a certain sense, the most Lucretian of modern writers. It has been said that, as Spinoza was 'a man drunk with God,' so Lucretius was 'a man drunk with natural law.' Well, Hearn was a man drunk with Herbert Spencer, and in all save the accident of form he was the poet of Spencerian evolution. As Lucretius, preaching his tremendous doctrine of the monstrous, eternal rain of atoms through the world, wove into his great poem the beauty of the old mythology, the tragedy of passionate humanity, so Hearn, in his gentler fashion, steadily envisaged the horror that envelops the stupendous universe of modern science, and by evoking and reviving ancient myths and immemorial longings, cast over the darkness a ghostly light of vanished suns. (pp. 27-9)

> *Ferris Greenslet, in his introduction to* Leaves from the Diary of an Impressionist: Early Writings *by Lafcadio Hearn (Copyright 1911, renewed 1939 by Houghton Mifflin Company. Reprinted by permission of Houghton Mifflin Company.), Houghton Mifflin, 1911, pp. 3-31.*

## WARREN BARTON BLAKE  (essay date 1912)

[There] is something baffling about everything that [Hearn] put his hand to—if we except his journeyman's work (and very good work, too) as a newspaper writer. His interpretation of Japan has been fairly described as the most remarkable attempt at the interpretation of an alien race ever made, in any language; and yet it was produced by one who never himself mastered the Japanese tongue. This is not the chief difficulty, however. For what are we to think of his interpretation of the elder civilization of Japan—not merely in the book which he calls **"Japan: An Attempt at Interpretation,"** but as we find it in all his volumes of studies and legends? What are we to think of it, that is, now that certain documents of an intimate sort have been recently published in the so-called **"Japanese Letters"** . . .?

One may learn here how melancholy was the man. "I am absolutely unproductive now," he writes in one letter of depression; "hovering between one thing and another,—sometimes angry with men,—sometimes with the Gods." But we were already aware how pathetic was this figure, best likened (in the simile of a Japanese poem of the people) to

The water-weed drifting, finding no place of attachment.

The first value of the **"Japanese Letters"** lies, not so much in the insight they give us into Hearn's personality, as in the light they throw—or seem to throw, since we are for the moment left in no little perplexity—on Hearn's later writings. What are we to think when the author of **"Kwaidan"** and **"Kokoro"** writes:

> The finale of my long correspondence with you on the Japanese character is frankly this . . . I hate and detest the Japanese . . .

adding, wistfully, "There's a nice confession"; then, with more vigor, "D—n the Japanese!"

Before deciding what to think of it all, one may read further. A letter to his American friend, W. B. Mason, is instructive. "Professor Chamberlain spoke to me about the variablity of one's feelings toward Japan being like the oscillations of a pendulum: one day swinging towards pessimism, and the next to optimism. I have this feeling very often, and I suppose you must have had it many times. *But the pessimistic feeling is generally coincident with some experience of New Japan, and the optimistic with something of Old Japan. . . .* With what hideous rapidity Japan is modernizing after all!"

For one who has read Hearn with either thoroughness or sympathy, there is no suspicion that he was to an appreciable degree insincere in his writings about the Japanese. He was at first radiantly happy in achieving his life-dream: the study of the Oriental mind at close range; life in a wonderful exotic kingdom of flowers and singing cicada. But, apart from the fact that Japan is itself in transition,—apart from the fact that the student of Japan must oscillate, as Hearn says Professor Chamberlain put it, between optimism and pessimism, admiration and repulsion, there is the personal element to be taken into account. Hearn was Hearn. That means, in part, that he was one of those who have set up "Whim" over their portals. It means, too, that he was a victim of romantic nostalgia—literally, as well as in critics' cant, a native of No-man's Land. To quote this man himself, he suffered from "the nostalgia which is rather a world-sickness than a home-sickness"—"like an unutterable wish to flee away from the Present into the Unknown." It was not in him to be lastingly happy anywhere. Earlier, in New Orleans, his imagination, captured at first by the tropical and intoxicating beauty of the old Creole city, with all its contrasts, was soon sated, and we find him writing to Mr. Krehbiel, at New York, "I am very weary of New Orleans. The city of my dreams . . . has vanished." Philosophically, morally, and aesthetically, no less than nationally, he was a hybrid—and hybrids are notoriously unhappy. (pp. 266-67)

Knowledge of those who have wrought exquisite things is not always to be had with impunity. It is not always even desirable. There were dark places in the career of this elusive genius—who, without belonging to the family of the greater geniuses, succeeded as no one else in retelling the tales of Old Japan in the English tongue, and in imparting to what Mr. [Yone] Noguchi described as his "Spencerian-Buddhistic Studies" a charming and penetrating accent of mystery. Hearn's Japanese critic lays emphasis, however, on the retold tales: and here we must follow him. Hearn's later work, done in the gray and blue coloring of his adopted country, though it wants the fire and enthusiasm of his first impressions, receives the highest praise of the Japanese, as shining with Hearn's "golden light, which was as old as a spring in Horai; its slowness was poetry and its reticence was a blessing." No longer did this writer practise style for style's sake. Let us then be content with the knowledge that his best poetry, his "blessings," have an appeal truer and deeper than that of mere exoticism, skilfully managed—like the *japoneries* of Pierre Loti. Their beauty is not wasted even upon the critic born in the land of whose myths and elder traditions they are the treasury. (p. 267)

> *Warren Barton Blake, "The Problem of Lafcadio Hearn," in* The Dial *(copyright, 1912, by The Dial Publishing Company, Inc.), Vol. LII, No. 619, April 1, 1912, pp. 265-67.*

## JOHN ERSKINE  (essay date 1915)

In substance if not in form [the lectures collected in *Interpretations of Literature*] are criticism of the finest kind, unmatched in English unless we return to the best of Coleridge, and in some ways unequalled by anything in Coleridge. Most literary criticism discusses other things than the one matter in which the writer and the reader are interested—that is, the effect of the writing upon the reader. It is hardly too severe to say that most critics talk around a poem or a story or a play, without risking a judgment on the centre of their subject; or else, like even Coleridge at times, they tell you what you ought to read into a given work, instead of showing you what is waiting there to be seen. Lafcadio Hearn is remarkable among critics for throwing a clear light on genuine literary experience—on the emotions which the books under discussion actually give us. Himself a craftsman of the first order, he wasted no time on the analysis of technique, knowing that the emotional substance of literature must become a personal and conscious possession of the reader before the discussion of technique can be profitable. Where he seems to be analysing technique, as sometimes in the second volume of these lectures, he is still helping the student to realise the emotional experience, rather than the device that produced it. (pp. ix-x)

[His] letters show that Lafcadio Hearn knew he was unusual in his emphasis upon the emotional content of literature, and realised that his sympathetic knowledge of the Japanese temperament was of unique advantage in his teaching. But in another direction he probably was not aware of his sharp divergence from the Anglo-Saxon approach to English literature. Perhaps because he had the good fortune to know French and Greek literature, perhaps simply because he had a genius for broadmindedness, he included in his definition of literature the master-pieces of historical, of philosophical, and of scientific writing. (p. x)

Lafcadio Hearn lectured upon English literature in Japan as we should like to see it taught in America and England,—as a total expression of racial experience, in which ideas, however abstract, often control emotions and conduct, and in which conduct and emotions often explain or modify ideas.

Even a casual reading of these lectures will suggest that Lafcadio Hearn was under a peculiar debt to the writings of Herbert Spencer, and in his letters he speaks of himself as a devoted Spencerian. Yet it was not a particular philosophy which illuminated his interpretation of books, so much as the fact that he had a philosophy at all. To have a philosophy of life is the prime requirement, if one would understand literature; for a great poem or drama is only an expression of life, and will become intelligible only as life does, when examined under the lens of experience and reason. Lafcadio Hearn's equipment here was greater than he realised. His wide contact with life and his philosophising temperament gave him a weird power to assimilate books; and though the knowledge of Anglo-Saxon might have helped him to a different historical horizon, it could hardly have improved his insight into the universal content of art—the problems and the aspirations of living men.

Even the briefest comment on these lectures must speak of their very noble tone. Was it Lafcadio Hearn's intelligence or his temperament that flooded this unique service of his with a spirit of dignity, of largeness, of devotion to ideals? We must think it was the whole man who was speaking, an artist whose brain and heart were both great. It is not the least of our debt to him that in his classroom he illustrated day by day, before young men who might have been critical of the civilisation he represented, the noblest attitude which that civilisation has learned to take toward the things of the mind. (pp. xi-xii)

> *John Erskine, in his introduction to* Interpretations of Literature *by Lafcadio Hearn, edited by John Erskine (reprinted by permission of Dodd, Mead & Company, Inc.; copyright 1915 by Mitchell McDonald; copyright renewed 1942 by Kazuo Koizumi), Dodd, Mead, 1915 (and reprinted by Kennikat Press, Inc. 1965, pp. v-xii).*

## JAMES HUNEKER (essay date 1915)

[The major portion of *Life and Letters of Lafcadio Hearn*] is devoted to the letters of this exotic and extraordinary writer; he was both, without being either a great man or a great artist. The dominant impression made by his personality, so much and often so unhappily discussed, is itself impressionistic. Curiously enough, as he viewed the world, so has he been judged by the world. His life, fragmentary, episodic, restless, doubtless the result of physical and psychical limitations, is admirably reflected in his writings with their staccato phrasing, overcoloured style, their flight from anything approaching reality, their uneasy apprehension of sex, and their flittings among the folk-lore of a half dozen extinct civilisations. His defective eyesight was largely the cause of his attitude toward life and art—for with our eyes we create our world—and his intense sufferings and consequent pessimism must be set down to the inevitable tragedy of a soul that greatly aspired, but a soul that had the interior vision though not the instrument with which to interpret it. Lafcadio Hearn was a poetic temperament, a stylist, but an incomplete artist.

His biographer, Miss [Elizabeth] Bisland, speaks of him as a "stylist." Unfortunately this is not far from the truth; he was a "stylist," though not always with an individual style. The real Hearn had superimposed upon him the débris of many writers, usually Frenchmen. He began his literary life as a worshipper and translator of Théophile Gautier and died in the faith that Pierre Loti had said the last word of modern prose. Gautier attracted him by his sumptuousness of epithet, the perfectly realised material splendours of gold, of marble, of colour. To the neurasthenic Hearn, his brain big with glorious dreams, the Parisian pagan must have seemed godlike in his half-smiling, half-contemptuous mastery of language, a mastery in its ease not outrivalled even by Flaubert. Gautier was a gigantic reflector of the visible world, but without genuine sympathy for humanity, and he boasted that his periods, like cats, always fell on their feet, no matter how high or carelessly he tossed them. And then he was Greek in his temperament, Greek grafted upon a Parisian who loved form and hue above all else, and this appealed to Hearn, whose mother was Greek, whose tastes were exotic. It was only after he had passed the half-century mark and when he was the father of three sons that some apprehension of the gravity of Occidental ethical teaching was realised by him.

When M. Loti-Viaud, that most exquisite of French prose artists and sentimental sensualists, made his appearance, Lafcadio was ravished into the seventh heaven. Here was what he had sought to do, what he never would do—the perfection of impressionism, created by an accumulation of delicate details, unerringly presented, with the intention of attacking the visual (literary) sense, not the ear. You can't read a page of Loti aloud; hearing is never the final court of appeal for him. Nor is the ear regarded in Hearn's prose. He is not "auditive"; like Loti and the Goncourts, he writes for the eye. Fr. Paulhan calls writers of this type rich in the prédominance des sensations visuelles. Disconnected by his constant abuse of the dash—he must have studied Poe not too wisely—infinitesimal strokes of colour supplying the place of a large-moulded syntax, this prose has not unity, precision, speed, euphony. Its rhythms are choppy, the dabs of paint, the shadings within shadings, the return upon itself of the theme, the reticent, inverted sentences, the absence of architectonic and the fatal lack of variety, surprise, or grandeur in the harmonic sense, these disbar the prose of Lafcadio Hearn from the exalted position claimed for it by his admirers.

Yet it is a delicate prose; the haunted twilight of the soul has found its notations in his work. With Amiel he could say of a landscape that it was a state of soul. His very defects became his strength. With normal eyesight we should not have had the man of ghostly reveries, the patient, charming etcher on a miniature block of evanescent prose, the forger of tiny chords, modulating into Chopin-like mist. His mania for the word caused him to neglect the sentence; his devotion to the sentence closed for him any comprehensive handling of the paragraph; he seldom wrote a perfect page; never an entire chapter or book. At his best he equals Loti in his evocation of the mystery that encompasses us, a mystery that has been sounded in music, seldom in language. His cast of mind was essentially romantic. Hearn does not mention the name of Goncourt in his letters, and yet it is a certain side of the brothers, the impressionistic side, that his writings resemble. But he had not their artistry. Nor could he, like Maupassant, summon tangible spirits from the vasty deep, as did the Norman master in Le Horla. . . . Hearn seldom pinned down to the paper his dreams, though he had a gift of suggestion, of spiritual overtones, in a key of transcendentalism, that, in certain pages, far outshines Loti or Maupassant. Disciple of Herbert Spencer—he was forced because of his feminine fluidity to lean on a strong, positive brain—hater of social conventions, despiser of Christianity, a proselyte to a dozen creeds, from the black magic of Voodooism to Japanese Shintoism, he never quite rid himself of the spiritual deposits inherited from his Christian ancestry. This strain, this contradiction, to be found in his later letters, explains much of his psychology, all of his art. A man after nearly two thousand years of Christianity may say to himself: "Lo! I am a pagan." But all the horses from Dan to Beersheba cannot drag him back to paganism, cannot make him resist the "pull" of his hereditary faith. The very quality Hearn most deplored in himself gives his work an exotic savour; he is a Christian of Greek and Roman Catholic training, a half Greek, half Celt, whole gipsy, masquerading as an Oriental. The mask is an agreeable one, the voice of the speaker sweet, almost enticing, but one more mask it is, and therefore not the real Hearn. He was Goth, not Greek; he suffered from the mystic fear of the Goth, while he yearned for the great day flame of the classics. Even his Japonisme was skin-deep. (pp. 240-44)

Shy, complex, sensuous, Hearn is the real Lafcadio Hearn in [his] letters. Therein we discover the tenderness, the passion, the capacity for friendship, the genuine humanity absent in his books. His life, his art, were sadly misfitted with masks—though Nietzsche says: "All that is profound loves the mask"; and the symbolism of the Orient completed the disintegration of his baffling personality. (p. 248)

> James Huneker, "The Cult of the Nuance: Lafcadio Hearn," in his Ivory, Apes and Peacocks: Joseph Conrad, Walt Whitman, Jules Laforgue, Dostoïevsky and Tolstoy, Schoenberg, Wedekind, Moussorgsky, Cézanne, Vermeer, Matisse, Van Gogh, Gauguin, Italian Futurists, Various Latter-Day Poets, Painters, Composers and Dramatists (copyright © 1915 by Charles Scribner's Sons; copyright renewed © 1943 by Josephine Huneker; reprinted with permission of Charles Scribner's Sons), Charles Scribner's Sons, 1915 (and reprinted by Charles Scribner's Sons, 1922), pp. 240-48.

## JOYCE KILMER (essay date 1921)

What was the matter with Lafcadio Hearn? No American has written prose more delicate and vividly beautiful than his, nor has any one else—not even Yone Noguchi—put into English so clear a revelation of Japan's soul. Yet after an hour with "Kwaidan" or "Glimpses of Unfamiliar Japan" the normal reader is wearied and, instead of being grateful to the erudite and skillful author, regards him with actual dislike.

Why is this? Is it because Hearn had a morbid fondness for the tragic, and loved to dwell on mental, physical and spiritual disease? This is partly the reason, yet De Quincey and Edgar Allan Poe inspire no such aversion. Is it because Hearn's style is too rich, exquisite and precious? Walter Pater had the same fault, but Walter Pater is read with delight by Hearn's enemies. Is it because of Hearn's ridiculous religious prejudices—his hatred for the Jesuits, for example? No, Hearn's hatred for the Jesuits is simply a bad little boy's impudence toward his schoolmaster. He had none of George Borrow's fiery, romantic passion against the "Man in Black." And Borrow's "Lavengro" and "Romany Rye" were loved even by so un-Protestant a writer as Lionel Johnson.

No, the reason lies deeper, and is simpler, than any of these. Hearn failed, not because he was precious, not because he was morbid, not because he was prejudiced, but because he had no imagination.

Lafcadio Hearn was, in the worst sense of the word, a realist. He had thoroughly the materialistic attitude toward life; he could see only the dull outside of things, not the indwelling splendor. . . . Hearn was so prosaic and matter-of-fact that he saw only the forms and outlines of the things about him, and so sentimentally credulous that he believed that Japan contained greater wonders than Louisiana. Dr. George M. Gould, in his interesting but unpleasant work, "Concerning Lafcadio Hearn," blames many of his dead friend's faults on his defective vision. But Hearn's myopia was spiritual as well as physical: he could not see the soul. (pp. 159-61)

Lafcadio Hearn might have been a great writer. If proof of this were needed, it would be found in a posthumously published book of singular interest—**"Fantastics and Other Fancies."** This is a collection of Hearn's earliest writings. . . .

The brief essays in this book are as charmingly phrased as anything this master of charming phrases ever wrote, and they are—unlike his later work—imaginative. That is, they are interpretations and idealizations of the things naturally familiar to Hearn. He had not yet committed the artistic heresy of confusing strangeness with beauty. He was not yet deluded into the belief that romance belongs exclusively to Nippon. (p. 161)

The literary value of Hearn's work is not to be questioned. No living writer (not even Algernon Blackwood) has so great and fiery an imagination as had this quondam reporter of the New Orleans *Daily Item;* no living writer (except Alice Meynell) understands so thoroughly the art of putting together a few hundred words so as to form a structure of enduring loveliness. (p. 162)

Any trivial incident of his daily round, any quaint bit of history or legend that he came upon in his amazingly extensive reading, would furnish this strangest of newspaper men with a theme. He saw in some antique shop a faun and dryad pictured in enamel on a little golden case, and, sitting at his littered, ink-stained desk in his noisy office, he wrote the exquisite **"Idyl of a French Snuffbox."** (p. 163)

He was not always absolutely original, this obscure hack whose genius was one day to surprise and delight the world. Subconsciously, he remembered his spiritual brother, Edgar Allan Poe, when he wrote those tales of the grotesque and arabesque, **"The Black Cupid"** and **"The One Pill Box."** Also there are echoes of Coleridge, and of those Parnassian Frenchmen whose methods and ideals Hearn always shared.

But no Frenchmen of his time could match the tender humor of **"The Post Office,"** nor were Poe and Coleridge standing at his elbow when he wrote **"Hiouen-Thrang."** These were written by Lafcadio Hearn himself, by that strange nomad who called no one race his own, who looked at life with huge and perilous curiosity. . . . (pp. 163-64)

Already, the **"Fantastics"** show, Hearn was hearing the Orient's alluring voice. (p. 164)

There are sketches in this extraordinary little book, notably **"Les Coulisses"** and **"The Undying One,"** which remind the reader, strangely enough, of certain prose fancies of another son of Ushaw, Francis Thompson. A healthier Lafcadio Hearn, with a broader vision and a tradition more clearly English, might have written "Finis Coronat Opus." And the thought makes one, perhaps, a little regretful that Hearn was so sincerely a gypsy, that he was drawn away from the scenes of his young manhood to a lovely but wholly alien land. Of course, he wrote beautifully of Japan. But these youthful sketches show that Japan was not necessary to his artistic expression. And to take on that strange new culture he had to give up some heritages of thought and belief that he could ill spare, the loss of which, it may be, is the cause of that melancholy, shading sometimes into despair, which permeates even his richest and most sympathetic Japanese studies.

Hearn did not ruin himself as a writer by writing about Japan. He ruined himself by trying to be a Japanese. (pp. 164-65)

Hearn has been held up by the sentimentalists as a shining example of humanity's cruelty to great artists. He is instead a shining example of the minor artist's cruelty to humanity. He was not rejected of men. His was not "divine discontent," his was the pernicious "desire for new things." Therefore he became merely the maker of fair and futile decorations, and he who might have been a poet, a creator, became a clever wordsmith. (p. 166)

> Joyce Kilmer, "Japanese Lacquer," in his The Circus and Other Essays and Fugitive Pieces, *edited by Robert Cortes Holliday (copyright, 1921, by George H. Doran Company; copyright renewed © 1948 by Kenton Kilmer and Christopher Kilmer; reprinted by permission of Doubleday & Company, Inc.), Doran, 1921, pp. 159-67.*

## PERCY H. BOYNTON    (essay date 1927)

In the life that surrounded [Hearn] as a journalist he saw no more to admire in New York than in London, or in Cincinnati than in New York. Even in New Orleans the human city of the day was buried under a lava flood of sordid chicane. The golden sunlight of eternal summer shone for him on a charnel-house of corruption. He was ready to abandon himself to cynical skepticism—was, in fact, abandoned to it—when he found himself under the spell of Herbert Spencer, thenceforth his literary superman.

The experience of Spencerolatry is a common one in literary history, but in Hearn's case it was an experience with a difference. Often the effect was to deprive the young believer of a comfortable faith. "The 'Data of Ethics' and 'First Principles,'" said Theodore Dreiser, for example, "nearly killed me, took away every shred of belief from me, showed me that I was a chemical atom in a whirl of unknown forces. . . . I went into the depths and am not sure that I have ever got entirely out of them." But for Hearn, who was deep in the

center of indifference, the effect was more like a positive redemption: "I . . . learned what an absurd thing positive skepticism is. I also found unspeakable comfort in the sudden and, for me, eternal reopening of the Great Doubt which renders pessimism ridiculous, and teaches a new reverence for all forms of faith." In a word, what Hearn derived from Spencer was an approach to the study of human experience and a stimulus to pursue the study for himself.

The result of the study was a new artistic trinity of romanticism, idealism, and moralism. The mind, wearied by toil and strife, could be recreated only in escape from reality; the escape should be to an ideal world; but this was not pre-eminently a sensuously beautiful world, it was rather a morally beautiful world. As surely as there was a low of progress a new idealism must arise. The morals of the present world are avenues to the fulfilment of human possibilities. It is for this sound reason that the common sense of the mass always condemns any attempt to overthrow the moral code. Yet for the educated the new teaching of ethics should substitute a rational for an emotional morality, though it is fitting that for the mass the old emotional reactions toward the virtues should preserve the moral balance of the world. In the ideal world, however, this balance will be preserved through inherited instinct, and only in a social order where this prevails can the consciousness of the code be allowed to sleep. Short of this millennium, therefore, Hearn concluded, moral idealism must be sought and practiced because of its necessity as a regulating force.

In arriving at these conclusions, though he never strayed far from the trail blazed by his teacher, Hearn was not wholly preoccupied with following the marks. His eyes were open to the whole path and his imagination reached on to the end of the journey. So it developed that Spencer's dicta interested him not as finalities so much as reopenings of the Great Doubt. He saw what otherwise intelligent people are continually failing to see—that any doubt may lead the way to fine adventure, and that it is anything but a doubt that precludes all but one possibility. As a consequence, without clearly articulating his procedure, he moved on to the scientific theory of multiple hypotheses. He was already on guard against the Jack Horner type of philosophizing that leaps to fond conclusions derived from a single plum. He was willing to admit that to human vision truth is an iridescent thing, changing hues as the light plays upon it; that an old principle may turn out to be not quite true, and yet to contain an evident measure of truth that may not be rejected; that in the explanations of life an order of ideas, temporarily out of fashion, may come back into favor if it is found to offer a better explanation than the set which is in vogue.

Herbert Spencer might very likely have seemed to his new disciple an approach to infallibility even if Hearn had lived out his life in America; but the influence was doubled when Hearn found in the history of Japanese culture a multitude of confirmations for what Spencer had derived from other sources on the nature of individual and social life. His whole volume, ***Japan: an Attempt at an Interpretation,*** is interspersed with allusions to Spencer's generalizations and the corresponding facts in Japanese life. Near the beginning is the acknowledgment that "the evolutional history of ancestor worship, much the same in all countries, offers in the Japanese cult remarkable evidence of Herbert Spencer's exposition of the law of religious development." There are citations of Spencer in reference to the spirits of the dead, the longevity of religious dynasties, the intensity of patriotism in militant societies, the vague character of the Shinto hierarchy, the theory that the greater gods of a people represent the later forms of ancestor worship, even the thesis that elaborate pronominal distinctions prevail where subjection is extreme. The chapter on ,"The Higher Buddhism" is a running commentary on Spencerian doctrines, the book is appended with Spencer's advice to the Japanese nation on the proper policy toward occidental intruders, and the last reference to him in the text calls him "the wisest man in the world."

Hearn's sex philosophy, if it deserves so formal a name, was not unrelated to the Spencerian influence and was interwoven with his Japanese experience. It was not until he had attempted to think life through that his instinctive reactions became convictions and his convictions were translated into words. Until then his impulse seems to have led him to shroud in reticence every phase of sexual emotion or sexual experience. His reticence was not because the subject was holy, and not because it was base, but simply because it was intimately personal. It belonged to himself—though perhaps not quite as normally as the appetite for food and drink—but it was no more to be dwelt on than were the details of the digestive process.

Just this reticence he found in Japan; and as a teacher he found himself under the necessity of explaining to his students the depth and width of the difference between Eastern and Western thinking when he attempted to give them some understanding of the prevalence of love as a theme in English literature. "It is all very unfamiliar to you," he said in substance to them, "English literature is permeated with references to romantic love. You don't talk about such matters over here. You will be surprised, but you needn't be horrified. It is actually respectable enough, if only you understand it. You see, women in the occident. . . ." To these boys he did not express himself as freely as to one of his old New Orleans friends: "We live in the murky atmosphere of desire in the West;—an erotic perfume emanates from all that artificial life of ours;—we keep the senses perpetually stimulated with a million ideas of the eternally feminine, and our very language reflects the strain. The Western civilization is using all its arts, its science, its philosophy in stimulating and exaggerating and exacerbating the thought of sex. . . . It now seems, even to me, almost disgusting." (pp. 59-64)

Yet withal Hearn felt that the golden mean was to be found somewhere between where he was and where he had been. There was something of himself in the Western life that he almost abhorred. There was something negatively unsatisfactory in the ruthlessly regulated life of the East. An overstimulated sense of sex "cultivates one's aesthetic faculty at the expense of all the rest. And yet—perhaps its working is divine behind all that veil of vulgarity and lustfulness. It is cultivating also, beyond any question, a capacity for tenderness the Orient knows nothing of." (p. 65)

Throughout his career Hearn, the artist, was pulled by rival forces. He wanted to prepare himself for writing and to write what would last. He had had enough of making copy under pressure for newspapers. At the same time he entertained none of the illusions of the lazy-inspired. He must fill his mind and plan his work and lay out ambitious programs and submit to the "Foul Fiend Routine." And always he must keep his sensibilities alert and wait patiently for the flash of perception that would reveal a broad prospect or thrill him with the inevitable word. Nothing that could be known or felt was inexpressible— but the right expression might come—and for subtle feelings should come—as a happy surprise. He must be an aeolian harp or a sensitized plate, a medium prepared with slow solicitude to respond to the gentlest zephyr or the first gleams of dawn.

His journalistic writing, to judge from the best of it . . . , was facile and fluent and obvious in its effects as such writing should be. At that it was strikingly literary for the columns of the daily press, even for the unyellowed American press of the eighteen eighties. Hearn's contributions passed from horrors to oddities and from oddities to fantasies. There was a measure of scrupulous translation from the French and an element of leaves from stranger literatures—Egyptian, Persian, Indian, Chinese, Finnish. There was a good deal of erudition in some of the papers. It sounds encyclopedic and some of it may have been drawn from thesauruses; but the titles in his own exotic library go far toward proving that he was a genuine delver in quaint lores. His liking for the recondite cropped out all through his career, sometimes as in the charming chronicle of Pere Labat, the Martinique pioneer, and sometimes as in the perfunctory literary and entomological summaries for which a Japanese student had done the preliminary drudgery. But the best of his writing, the part that is beyond chance of confusion with anyone else's, is the writing in which out of his vivid first-hand experience, or out of his delicately sympathetic interpretation, he preserves the evanescent charm of scenes and episodes and cultural traditions that are alien to Anglo-Saxondom. (pp. 67-8)

*Percy H. Boynton, "Lafcadio Hearn," in his* More Contemporary Americans *(reprinted by permission of The University of Chicago Press; copyright 1927 by The University of Chicago), University of Chicago Press, 1927, pp. 51-74.*

**FRED LEWIS PATTEE** (essay date 1930)

A full half of [Hearn's] work belongs to the period before the nineties, most of it to the eighties. The man's life was in two distinct chapters, divided sharply by the year 1890, as sharply indeed as if he had died and had transmigrated into another existence which we have been enabled to know. (p. 218)

The gathering into volumes of all Hearn's American writings, including even the scraps of his newspaper work, has permitted for the first time a critical study of the man's personality and his early sources. First, we note the influence of Poe, the Poe of the horrific and the morbidly ghastly areas. . . . Everywhere horrible subjects like **"The Utilization of Human Remains,"** or **"The Poisoners"**; or murder tales like the news story that first made him famous in Cincinnati—**"The Tan-yard Cremation,"** ghastly in its realistic details. He delighted too, in this early period, in essays implying much curious research— ghost studies, essays in bizarre linguistics, nightmare legends, picturings of New Orleans uniquenesses, studies of negro life, the sensations of steeple-climbers and the like. Everywhere the unusual, the unique, the extreme.

From Poe it was but a step to Baudelaire, the French Poe, and then to Gautier, whom he translated in all his voluptuous bareness, a translation impossible of publication in the America of the eighties. A part of it, savagely "Comstocked," he finally did publish as **"One of Cleopatra's Nights,"** but he was ahead of his times.

It was New Orleans and later the French West Indies that awakened to the full his De Quincey-like, his Gautier-like, imagination. Nowhere else in English such a jungle of exotic flora—in diction, in imagery, in startling impressionism. (pp. 219-20)

His novel **"Chita"** and his **"Two Years in the French West Indies,"** a throwing of the Gulf islands and the Caribbean tropics into pastels drenched with vermilion and ochre, are like nothing else in English. They add color and Gautier-like brilliance to our all-too-drab American literature. In our Puritan age Hearn was a man emotional, unanchored, a bundle of jangling nerves, moody, sullen, sensuous, with little of vision save for physical beauty and the voluptuousness of external colorings. . . . Surfeited with the Nordic and the blond, he escaped at last into the strangeness of an alien race—alien even to him, foreign indeed to every shred of inheritance within him—and began again with new eagerness, newly aroused emotion, to record his impressions. (p. 222)

His books of this last period belong on a different shelf from those created during his American apprenticeship. He was seeking now the soul not of a place but of a people and a race, and so far as it was in him to do so he succeeded. (p. 224)

Pity and tenderness came now into the art of the man, so far as he was permitted by his nature to feel it. So incurably was he a romantic, however, that everything he touched he romanticized. . . . Yearningly he analyzed for inner meanings, for the soul of Japan, even for the mystery of the unfathomable East, but always his quest led him into romantic emotionalism. It is not the East we see: it is Hearn projected against the East. (p. 225)

There were moments when he penetrated deeply—more deeply, perhaps, than any other Occidental—but his ten Japanese volumes must on the whole be classed as intuitive impressionism. (p. 226)

In his efforts to make a Japanese of himself he had erased so much that it was impossible ever to return to the Occidental world of his birth and training. He had obliterated his very self: he was neither Occidental nor Oriental. (p. 227)

Such men leave no posterity, found no schools, establish no system. And yet his genius, more eccentric in its way even than Poe's, his uniqueness, his De Quincey-like word-buildings, make him a borealis illumination that streams with fantastic waverings, pallid light, without heat, and yet one that does not fade out nor die. (pp. 227-28)

> *Fred Lewis Pattee, "The Émigré Writers," in his* The New American Literature 1890-1930 *(copyright, 1930, by* The Century Co.), *Century, 1930 (and reprinted by Cooper Square Publishers, Inc., 1968), pp. 215-32.\**

## MATTHEW JOSEPHSON  (essay date 1930)

[Lafcadio Hearn] was one of the rebels of art who multiplied in the closing years of the nineteenth century. Hating the cold north, he had found an 'island' for himself in New Orleans—one of the regions in America that resisted longest the harsh new influences. He could earn a living writing short pieces, odd sketches, even translations of his beloved Gautier and Nerval, for a press that was not yet yellow. He could live an unhampered life of his own among the tropical and somewhat sinister elements he preferred, and under their influence his talents for a romantic and musical prose could take an exotic and lonely growth.

Hearn scarcely impresses us at this time as an original thinker; he is rather an egoistic, almost an adolescent, one. It is with an air of deliberate eccentricity, of overcoming a quite marked sense of physical inferiority, that he seeks distinction by wor-

shiping the 'Esoteric, the Odd, the Strange, the Queer, the Monstrous.' He announces himself a pagan, ruled by the Greek conception of 'beauty, nudity, fate.' Passion was the inspiring breath of Greek art, and the mother of language: its gratification, the act of a creator, and the divinest rite in Nature's Temple (*sic*). 'Virginity, Mysticism, Melancholy—three unknown words, three new maladies brought to us by the Christ. . . .' His Epicureanism is systematic: unless he can enjoy 'mad excesses,' he tells us, he cannot think, work, write; his mind remains arid and desolate!

It is interesting to note the dangers which Lafcadio ran in uttering at random, even in letters and newspaper sketches, such notions as belong rather to the post-Freudian era with its progressive dissolution of moral values. Everywhere at that time, social pressure, social contagion, stamped men with the same traits; youth was brought up on Miss Louisa Alcott and the *Rollo* books; at the worst it read the moderated Byronism of Thomas Aldrich, and was warned even by Howells against the brutal Zola. It was a time when a moral conformity of the utmost rigor and of an unruffled surface was strenuously imposed upon all men. The eccentricity of Hearn seems like a retort to the repressions and ostracisms he felt himself victim of. And in turn we expect him, as naturally occurred, to be isolated and condemned as a sort of moral plague-spot.

The dangers of a half-articulated dissent, of eccentricity almost for its own sake and subject to no discipline, no system of values which replaces the rejected one, are implicit in Lafcadio Hearn's career. He becomes a solitary, derided figure; he must conceal his mode of life, lie away his godless beliefs. His existence is unstable, torn between the need for limitless sensations and the need for order. He finds no medium in which he may express himself completely through a labor of patience and resolution. He is a lesser Swinburne with no band of Pre-Raphaelites to explain or defend him; and the French romantics or symbolists who might have welcomed or taught him are equally far away. All of his work is fragmentary, scattered, now inept, now touched with perfection. He wrote essays, sketches, critiques, fantasies, based on the folk-lore of Hindus, Chinese, Creoles, Africans, Japanese, and a great volume of letters which yield us the wavering line of his life. And so we have no single masterpiece, no Complete Works, but their torso: fragments that compose a character—a character of the sinful, rebellious type met with in older literatures—who flourishes secretly and stubbornly for a time in the inhospitable atmosphere of America's Gilded Age, and offers himself always in the ornate over-colored and rhythmic prose of the romantics whom he adores and emulates. (pp. 205-07)

[Hearn's] later books, such as *Glimpses of Unfamiliar Japan, Out of the East, Japanese Fairy Tales,* and *Kokoro,* which painted an exotic world with great sensitiveness and with a rare sympathy, had gathered a certain fame. The imaginative writings, including tales, fantasies, and ghost stories based on folk-lore, were quietly enjoyed by the aesthetic '90s; for us they have 'dated,' and we must taste their fragile charms in despite of an over-cloying sweetness and a prevailing lyricism. *Japan: An Interpretation,* which Hearn completed before his death, is more reasoned, more complete, than his previous essays in Oriental civilization, and retains after a quarter of a century the deepest interest for those who would compare our own forms of life with those of the East.

Lafcadio Hearn was a minor artist; he contributed no invention, no energizing principle of form, that could give his work a significant order and force. None knew this better than he, or contended more with his own limitations. (p. 230)

Matthew Josephson, "An Enemy of the West: Lafcadio Hearn," in his Portrait of the Artist As American (reprinted by permission of Harold Ober Associates Incorporated; copyright 1930, 1958 by Matthew Josephson), Harcourt, Brace and Company, 1930, pp. 199-231.

## DANIEL STEMPEL  (essay date 1948)

[While] it is true that Hearn sentimentalized and misrepresented certain aspects of Japanese culture, his works as a whole present a detailed and informative picture of Japan during the latter part of the Meiji Era. Hearn's colorful career, the history of an erratic and impulsive personality, has imparted an aura of romance to his writings on Japan, but he was not a mere rhapsodist over things Japanese. His love for Japan did not prevent him from being a clear-sighted reporter of Japanese customs, and, on occasion, a capable analyst of Japanese culture. (p. 1)

Hearn's books were written between 1890 and 1904. During this period the success of Japanese military power in the Sino-Japanese and Russo-Japanese wars raised Japan to the status of a world power. Because Hearn witnessed the development of Japanese power, his writings display an increasing interest in political and social problems. His last book, *Japan,* contrasts significantly with his first, *Glimpses of Unfamiliar Japan* . . . , in subject and attitude. The *Glimpses* are impressionistic travel sketches; *Japan* is a dispassionate and clear-sighted study of the dangers inherent in the social and political structure of Japan.

Hearn's writings cover an enormous range of subjects, from studies of Japanese insects to an analysis of the Japanese industrial system. These essays were usually written for publication in American periodicals; each book is therefore a collection of separate articles on specific topics. Despite the multiplicity of subjects, however, there are certain basic attitudes and ideas in his work which constantly recur, and these color his observations of Japanese life.

First, Hearn was not an unbiased judge of the relative values of Japanese and Western civilizations. He was always a champion of Japan against the West, even when his disillusionment had reached the point where he could write to a friend: *"I hate and detest the Japanese. . . .* I fear the missionaries are right who declare them without honor, without gratitude, and without brains." When his first enthusiasm had vanished, he transferred his approbation to feudal Japan, and, like Miniver Cheevy, mourned that he had been born too late. He blamed the unpleasant elements of modern Japanese society on the corrupting influence of Western civilization, and so absolved traditional Japanese culture. (pp. 2-3)

Second, Hearn's attempt to establish the parallelism of the philosophical background of modern science and the doctrines of Oriental religions is closely connected with his belief in the superiority of Japanese culture. Hearn had studied Oriental religions before he came to Japan, and had come to the conclusion that Buddhist metaphysics were similar to the metaphysics of Herbert Spencer. That correspondence was sufficient proof to him that Buddhism was the only faith that could be reconciled with science, since he believed implicitly in the scientific accuracy of Spencer's *Synthetic Philosophy.* (p. 3)

Finally, not all of Hearn's work was descriptive or expository; he collected and retold traditional Japanese tales and expanded incidents of contemporary life into short stories. Hearn's interest in the ghostly and macabre determined the selection of these narratives; his stories usually treat of ghosts, goblins, murders, and suicides. Often, however, they are used as illustrations of the Japanese acceptance of the interdependence of the material and spiritual planes, and perhaps Spencer's view of animism as the primary stage in the development of religion influenced Hearn's treatment of these subjects.

Three motifs which are omnipresent in Hearn's books on Japan, then, are the defense of Japanese civilization against Western influence; the alliance of Spencer's philosophy, viewed as the essence of modern science, with Buddhism; and a predilection for the macabre.

His sources were varied: for his narratives he utilized collections of Japanese tales; the poems which he translated for **"Old Japanese Songs," "Frogs,"** and **"Semi"** were taken from classical Japanese literature or from the folk songs of his day; his articles on Buddhism imply a broad knowledge of the rituals and doctrines of Japanese, Chinese, and Indian Buddhism. (p. 4)

*Glimpses of Unfamiliar Japan,* Hearn's first book on Japan, . . . covers the period from 1890 to 1893. (p. 5)

The sketches in [*Glimpses of Unfamiliar Japan*] are the reports of a sensitive observer. Hearn's impressions are not vague; he notes the sounds and smells of Japanese streets, the cries of street vendors, and he attempts to record Japanese folkways. The area covered by these studies, however, is limited to Izumo and the surrounding provinces; it is not a survey of Japan but of a provincial and mostly rural culture.

The conversation of the Japanese is often given a touch of the "quaintness" which is associated with the romantic view of Japan. Hearn translates literally, even keeping the exact order of the ideographs in a Chinese compound. (p. 7)

Several of the articles, such as **"Kitsune,"** a study of the fox cult, are of special interest to the student of Japanese customs. Hearn makes few personal judgments. His primary purpose is to observe and report, and his observations are detailed and accurate.

Despite the scarcity of overt evaluations, however, Hearn's prejudices and predilections are quite evident. He includes an article on Japanese ghosts, **"Of Ghosts and Goblins,"** the first of a long series of studies of Japanese ghost folklore. The article **"Of Souls"** is an explanation of the Buddhist doctrine of multiple souls within a single ego. This doctrine was later worked into Hearn's theory of the parallelism of Buddhism and science. In the final paper, **"Sayonara,"** Hearn reprints a significant letter of farewell to his students at Matsue, written on the occasion of his departure for Kumamoto. The letter, thanking the students for the gift of a sword, urges the necessity for absolute loyalty to the Emperor. . . .

[Hearn's next two books on Japan, *Out of the East* and *Kokoro,*] display a change from general description to exposition and evaluation of the spiritual side of Japanese life. (p. 8)

Several of these essays are indicative of the range and depth of Hearn's early observations of Japanese social patterns and religion. In **"With Kyushu Students"** he records the Japanese attitude toward family obligations, as explained to him by his students. One of his conclusions is that "childhood in Japan is certainly happier than in other lands, and therefore perhaps is regretted earlier in adult life.'' Dr. Benedict, a well-known anthropologist, corroborates this opinion. . . . (p. 9)

*Kokoro* extended the study of Japan's spiritual life which Hearn had begun in *Out of the East*. In it he continued to draw political and social corollaries. The preface reflects his increasing preoccupation with the spirit of Japanese culture: ''The papers composing this volume treat of the inner rather than of the outer life of Japan,—for which reason they have been grouped under the title *Kokoro* (heart).''

In ''**The Genius of Japanese Civilization**'' Hearn declares that the adoption of Western technology has not changed the physical appearance of Japan. The corollary which he draws from this observation is significant: ''The strength of Japan, like the strength of her ancient faith, needs little material display: both exist where the deepest real power of any great people exists—in the Race Ghost.'' This is an argument which was repeated over and over again by Japanese propagandists during the war. Hearn was rephrasing a widespread Japanese belief in terms more plausible to the Western reader. (pp. 9-10)

In ''**A Glimpse of Tendencies**'' Hearn predicts correctly the extension of Japanese control over foreign capital in Japan and the growth of resentment against the Western powers. He warns that ''Japan must develop her own soul: she cannot borrow another.'' The essay is an exposition of the conservatism which Hearn supported, but it is backed by a perceptive analysis of the dominant factors in the development of Japan. It is not a mere polemic against Western civilization.

''**By Force of Karma**'' is a variation on the theme of the parallelism of modern science and Buddhism, and the same theme is introduced into a sentimental study of the education of ''**A Conservative.**'' ''**The Idea of Preexistence**'' and ''**Some Thoughts about Ancestor-Worship**'' are attempts to link the two major religions of Japan to modern science. Hearn sought to correlate the nineteenth-century concept of heredity with the Buddhist doctrine of Karma and with the Shinto belief in the influence of the dead upon the living.

The first complete statement of Hearn's characteristic themes and attitudes, then, appears in *Out of the East* and *Kokoro*. The pattern which had been formed in these studies of Japanese ''inner life'' remained as the core of his later books which covered an increasingly wider area of Japanese life and culture. (p. 10)

Hearn's last book, *Japan: An Attempt at Interpretation*, is his most comprehensive and definitive analysis of Japan. It draws on the store of knowledge which had been accumulated in the preparation of the preceding books. Moreover, there is little trace of the sentimentality which appears in much of the earlier work; the tone of the book is scholarly and balanced. (pp. 13-14)

[Hearn's knowledge of Japan] had increased to the point where he could discern the errors in his earlier writings. He had learned that Japan had a long history of rigid control and oppression, and that life in feudal Japan was not as idyllic as he had believed. Hearn condemned ''**The Genius of Japanese Civilization**'' as a ''failure'' and admitted that it contained ''some very serious sociological errors.''

The primary purpose of *Japan*, as explained in a letter written in 1903, was to treat of Japanese religious life. Hearn intended to point out similarities between the early Greek and modern Japanese civilizations. In the final version, however, he took pains to emphasize that this comparison did not imply the complete identity of their cultural patterns, but was made to illustrate the survival in modern Japan of customs common to societies in an early stage of development.

*Japan* is not merely a study of Japanese religion; it is an exposition of the policies of Japanese conservatism. Hearn's acceptance of this political doctrine was not based on an emotional reverence for Japanese tradition, as it had been in his earliest writings. He had accepted Herbert Spencer's analysis of the modernization of Japan, and he concurred with Spencer in urging the Japanese to resist the economic and cultural domination of the West. (p. 14)

In attempting to estimate the ability of the Japanese to preserve their independence, Hearn achieved, more than in any other of his works, a dispassionate view of the faults and virtues of Japanese society. Some of his cherished theories were dropped completely, and others were modified. (p. 15)

[Hearn's] writings reveal the progressive stages of his education in things Japanese. *Glimpses of Unfamiliar Japan* was composed of essays recording the reactions of an enthusiastic traveler to the beauty of a strange new world. In his later books Hearn attempted to gain some understanding of the pattern and spirit of Japanese culture, but his judgments were often premature and warped by his reliance on Spencer's philosophy, by his irrational love of Japan, and by his hatred of the West. In his last book, however, although he still wrote as a conservative Japanese subject, he was able to divest himself of his prejudices and presented a balanced analysis of Japan. His analysis was accurate in many respects, and it can hardly be termed ''romantic.'' (p. 19)

Daniel Stempel, ''Lafcadio Hearn: Interpreter of Japan,'' in American Literature *(reprinted by permission of the Publisher; copyright © 1948, copyright renewed © 1976, by Duke University Press, Durham, North Carolina), Vol. XX, No. 1, March, 1948, pp. 1-19.*

**MALCOLM COWLEY**   (essay date 1949)

It was a surprising experience to reread Hearn's work volume after volume. Some of it seemed as mannered and frilled as the fashions of sixty years ago, and not always the best fashions; at times it might have been copied from Paris models by an earnest but awkward provincial dressmaker. Perhaps I was expecting all of it to have this end-of-the-century air, this charm of the faded and half-forgotten; what surprised me was that so much of it remained new and genuine. (p. 100)

Rereading his work after many years, one is impressed by its limitations as well as by its workmanship and integrity. It is narrow in scope, as if his smallness and shortsightedness had been moral as well as physical qualities. Sometimes it deals with general ideas, but in an apprentice fashion and with continual nods of deference to Herbert Spencer, who was Hearn's only schoolmaster in philosophy. It is full of moods, colors, and misty outlines, but lacking in pictures of daily life. Hearn complained in a letter that he knew nothing about the smallest practical matters: ''Nothing, for example, about a boat, a horse, a farm, an orchard, a watch, a garden. Nothing about what a man ought to do under any possible circumstances.'' In short, he knew very little about the experiences of other human beings, and that is only one of his disabilities as an author. He was never able to invent a plot and often begged his friends to tell him stories so that he would have something to write about.

He had little power of construction beyond the limits of a short essay or a folk tale. Of the sixteen books he published during his lifetime only one—*Japan: An Attempt at Interpretation*—is a book properly speaking. The others are either loose novelettes like *Chita* and *Youma,* in which the atmosphere is more important than the story; or else they are collections of shorter pieces that appeared or might have appeared in the magazines. (pp. 109-10)

The great weakness of his early sketches is that they aren't sufficiently odd or monstrous or differentiated from one another. The best of them are folk tales adapted from various foreign literatures. The others keep reverting to the same situation, that of a vaguely pictured hero in love with a dead woman or with her ghost (just as Hearn was in love with the memory of his mother, who disappeared from his life when he was seven years old). They are obsessive rather than exotic; and they are written in a style that suggests the scrollwork on the ceiling of an old-fashioned theater.

After his death Hearn's reputation suffered from the collections that others made of his early newspaper work, most of which should have been allowed to sleep in the files of the Cincinnati and New Orleans press. Even the books he wrote in his later New Orleans years—*Stray Leaves from Strange Literatures, Some Chinese Ghosts,* and *Chita*—though they all contained fine things are not yet his mature writing. *Two Years in the French West Indies* . . . is longer and richer and shows how Hearn could be carried out of himself by living among a people with whom he sympathized. Still, it was not until after his first years in Japan that he really mastered a subject and a style.

He wrote to [Basil Hall] Chamberlain in 1893, "After for years studying poetical prose, I am forced now to study simplicity. After attempting my utmost at ornamentation, I am converted by my own mistakes. The great point is to touch with simple words." That is exactly what he did in the best of his later writing. Instead of using important-sounding words to describe events that were not always important in themselves, he depended on the events to impress the reader and looked for words that would reveal them as through a clear glass. Here, for example, is a crucial paragraph from "**The Story of Mimi-Nashi-Hōïchi,**" a Japanese legend retold in *Kwaidan:*

> At that instant Hōïchi felt his ears gripped by fingers of iron, and torn off! Great as the pain was, he gave no cry. The heavy footfalls receded along the verandah,—descended into the garden,—passed out to the roadway,—ceased. From either side of his head, the blind man felt a thick warm trickling; but he dared not lift his hands.

Today we don't like the exclamation point after the first sentence, or the commas followed by dashes in the third; but Hearn was following his own theories about punctuation as a guide to the reader's voice. Primarily he was writing for the ear, not the eye; and the passage in its context sounds exactly right when read aloud. He almost always found the right words. . . . (pp. 110-11)

In his best work one never finds the fault of less scrupulous writers, who proclaim one emotion by the meaning of their words while suggesting another by the color and sound of their words. What they usually suggest is an absence of emotion and a disbelief in what they are saying. Hearn's writing was true not only on the surface but in depth; not only to his conscious thinking but also to the submerged feelings that gave

their rhythms to his prose. It wears well because it is all of a piece.

Besides his sense of language and his patient integrity he had something else in his later years that larger talents have often lacked: a subject. Of course the subject was Japanese culture in the broad sense, and a question still being argued is whether his picture of it was true by factual standards or was dangerously romanticized. That question we can let the experts decide, but not before we have noted that each of them seems to have a different notion of the truth. To another question, whether Hearn knew Japan, there can be only one answer.

He knew Japan, not as an observer, but as a citizen, the adopted son of Japanese parents and the father of Japanese children. He knew the faults of his countrymen by adoption, although he preferred to emphasize their virtues when writing for Western magazines. He foresaw the conflict between Japan and the West. He knew what arguments would touch the Japanese mind and what explanations were necessary before English poems could be understood by Japanese students. . . . Some of the students took down his lectures word for word; and after his death a whole series of volumes—four in this country, five others in Japan—was compiled and published from their notes. The volumes do not prove that Hearn was a great critic or that he always preferred the best to the second-best. What they do prove is that he was a great interpreter who, belonging to English literature, could still explain it as if he formed part of a Japanese audience.

More important for us than the lectures, which have their place in the history of Japanese thought, are the eleven books in which he performed the opposite task of interpreting Japan to the West. . . . [He] had a householder's knowledge of Japanese life, a scholar's knowledge of religious customs, and something more than that, an intimate and sympathetic grasp of Japanese legends. (pp. 113-15)

Long before coming to Japan he had shown an instinct for finding in legends the permanent archetypes of human experience—that is the secret of their power to move us—and he later proved that he knew which tales to choose and which details to emphasize, in exactly the right English. Now that so much of his work in many fields has been collected in one volume [*The Selected Writings of Lafcadio Hearn*], I think it will be apparent that his folk tales are the most valuable part of it and that he is the writer in our language who can best be compared with Hans Christian Andersen and the brothers Grimm. (p. 115)

> *Malcolm Cowley, in his introduction to* The Selected Writings of Lafcadio Hearn *by Lafcadio Hearn, edited by Henry Goodman (copyright, 1949, copyright renewed © 1977, by The Citadel Press), Citadel Press, 1949 (and reprinted as "Lafcadio Herun-san," in his* A Many-Windowed House: Collected Essays on American Writers and American Writing, *edited by Henry Dan Piper, Southern Illinois University Press, 1970, pp. 100-15).*

**EARL MINER** (essay date 1958)

The question of where exactly Hearn's enormous popular appeal lay is one for which hindsight has few advantages. Perhaps one explanation is that his peculiar talent came at a propitious time. The movement of art for art's sake and the growing protest in many circles against the ideas of Progress and Respectability and what they connoted in social and economic terms came to a climax in the years between 1885 and 1905. The public as a whole was scarcely ready to endure what Whistler, Wilde, Symons, Beardsley and their fellow radicals were demanding be done in England and America, but the popular imagination was sufficiently attuned to the Aesthetic Revolt to welcome enthusiastically what Hearn had to say about Japan. He may have made a great deal of bother about Oriental refinement which treated of realms above the popular mind, but it was all very quaint and pretty. He may have proclaimed the superiority of Buddhism to Christianity and science, but all of this protest against the ideals of the age was safely off in faraway Japan, and not in London or Boston. He offered aestheticism and unorthodoxy to his large audience at an easy remove, and flights into the strange or the exotic which were a welcome escape from the strenuous life of the late nineteenth century in England and America. The age seems to have found in Hearn a compromise with Whistler, the French, and unorthodoxy.

There was in addition the sop of exoticism, a taste whose appeal seems to be proportional to its ineffability. People who turn with warm expectations to a book called *Exotics and Retrospects* have tastes which the sober-minded find difficult to explain. But exoticism runs closely parallel to cultural relativism, and the popular imagination seems to have discovered both at this time, without of course ever really losing hold of the absolute of Protestant orthodoxy.

For his part, Hearn contributed an element which was essential to capture the taste of his time. Although he was orthodox in no common acceptance of the term, he was idealistic, and intensely so. This idealism echoes in the tone of every paragraph he wrote. Impelled by Percivall Lowell's *Soul of the Far East* (1888), he seems to have gone to Japan as if he expected to find a Utopia, and in any case wrote as if he had. The characters who float through his stories are either very good or very bad, and although the criteria by which we are to judge them are often not Western standards, this is only part of the secret between the author and us—we are never in doubt about the nature of heroism or villainy. It is also significant that he idealized the people of Japan and their culture, not simply or blindly, but in the terms in which the Japanese themselves like to think they excel. (pp. 62-4)

Lafcadio Hearn is in part a symbol, then—to the West of the exotic, of the ideal, and of that which is safely heterodox because it is in a far-off land. And to Japan he is a symbol of true appreciation of the Japanese spirit. The West and Japan have shared the idea that he has understood Japan as no Westerner ever had before or is likely to again and, in certain rather limited senses, this is true. With the help of a sensitive personality which was akin to Japanese aestheticism and with the aid of the sentimental image of Japan which the travelers had established before him, he more than any other man gave Japan an appeal that it had never before exercised over the imagination, especially the popular imagination, of the West. When people thought of the ideally strange, they thought of Japan; and when they thought of Japan, they were sure to glow with a warm feeling for Lafcadio Hearn. There is scarcely another man in history who has become to such an extraordinary degree a sympathetic symbol to two different cultures, who could appeal so much to the nation he visited, or create as warm an image of that nation in his own culture—at the very time that his writings were only half understood. (p. 65)

[The popular image of Hearn the exoticist] was not so much wrong as superficial, as a closer examination of his develop-

ment will show. His career as a wandering journalist, which ended in Japan, stopped momentarily at an earlier date in New Orleans where he discovered two elements which he sought throughout his lifetime—the unusual and a rich historic past. His taste for the unusual was really a taste for the exotic in both the cultural and chronological senses, but it also directed him to his métier as an Impressionist. . . . He had learned to trust to his own responses for inspiration, and this meant that the fine shades of perception of which his sensitive personality was capable were more important than the perceived object itself. This theory might well have been a pernicious stylistic influence had he not taken Flaubert as his literary model and had he not always sought to convey the quality of his own impressions to his reader. As he said of his more macabre writing, he wished to make his reader feel "a ghostly shudder."

Hearn's mature style was formed by the time he had written *Chita*. . . . It is a periodic style which is typically formed of units with complex sentence structure, slight inversions, or series; these units are loosely co-ordinated by semicolons or co-ordinating conjunctions. He achieved a style of seeming simplicity and freedom and of real ease in these rhythms of loosely joined complex units. The reader proceeds on wave after wave of the small, qualified, and controlled vibrations of Hearn's fine sensibility. Stylistically, he is reminiscent of Hawthorne, but he lacks Hawthorne's tough-mindedness and the necessity, which goes beyond technique, of holding evil and pessimism at bay with his style. (pp. 87-8)

[Hearn's] literary accomplishment is difficult to judge. Most of his readers wrongly assumed that he was the creator or at least the translator of the stories with which he charmed them. Actually, he only adapted and rewrote stories he heard from others—lacking any real knowledge of the language and with only an indifferent inventive gift, he had to have them translated into English before he could begin to work. And, as he recognized himself, he had no poetic genius. He did have a talent approaching genius for that rhythmical prose which is frequently and mistakenly called poetic, but it is easy to see that concentrated and brief poems like the Japanese forms cannot be adequately translated by a writer of periodic prose. The popular image of Hearn the translator remains, however. . . . Another limitation of his literary accomplishments has already been suggested. His Impressionistic method was ill suited to sustained writing. His usual piece is picture, an Impression, or a reflection; and his only treatment of a single subject throughout a book is his last, most laborious work, *Japan, An Attempt at Interpretation,* which is political and philosophical rather than literary.

Hearn's chief claim to literary fame lies in his style and his finely adjusted tone. The style varies as his purpose changes from reflection to description and from narration to analysis; the tone is more consistent—such typical words as "fleeting," "death," and "shadows" suggest the note of anguish which the falling cadence of a period often conveys. He undoubtedly belongs to the foremost group of nineteenth-century American prose stylists and, while he is no Thoreau or Henry Adams, it is true of him as of all superior stylists that his style reflects his ideas. Paul Elmer More [see excerpt above] was perhaps the first to observe that Hearn's thought involved Buddhism and evolutionary science and that this combination determined his whole mode of expression and thought. But there is a third element as well, the Impressionism which taught him that truth is made up of varying perceptions and is relative to the perceiver. Evolutionary science told him that there is little scope for mere sentience in the struggle for survival which goes to the fittest, and Buddhism declared that all of what science calls the objective world is illusory, a vanity and striving after wind. These three different, one might say dissident, elements in his thought produce a certain tension which makes Hearn something other than a mere stylist. (pp. 90-2)

In accepting Buddhism, and by uniting it with Western knowledge, Hearn brought Impressionism full circle to one of its origins, Japan. The movement which had begun with Japanese art as its shibboleth found its finest expression in English prose when Lafcadio Hearn went to Japan. Although Impressionism was antithetical to Buddhism both in its psychological theory and in its veneration of the block prints which Buddhists held in contempt for their celebration of the fleeting, ''unreal'' world, Hearn reconciled the two at least for his own satisfaction. That he did this in a prose style of very real beauty is his personal accomplishment as a writer, an accomplishment which cannot be dismissed by exposing the half-errors of the image of him which have arisen in the popular imagination. (p. 96)

> Earl Miner, ''New Images and Stereotypes of Japan'' and ''From 'Japonisme' to Impressionism: The Change from Nineteenth to Twentieth-Century Artistic and Poetic Modes,'' in his The Japanese Tradition in British and American Literature *(copyright © 1958 by Princeton University Press; reprinted by permission of Princeton University Press), Princeton University Press, 1958, pp. 25-65, 66-96.**

### BEONGCHEON YU   (essay date 1964)

[*Yu's study, from which this excerpt on Hearn's Carribean sketches and fiction is taken, is one of the most thorough and critically sophisticated examinations of the author's art and philosophy.*]

Only in a general sense could *Leaves from the Diary of an Impressionist* be called a book of travel, being a collection of sketches about Florida, essays on Creole women in New Orleans and the West Indies, and Arabian subjects. (p. 85)

[Each sketch] has its central concern. But when they are taken together we may discover the continuation of Hearn's old theme, the search for paradise in the heart of nature under the shadow of time, and something of its consequence. **''To the Fountain of Youth''** is a hymn to the divinity of nature and the holiness of beauty, a hymn recited by a pilgrim in search of the legendary Fountain of Youth—in the sanctum of nature. It is Hearn's version of man's eternal quest for the garden of Hesperus, as he aptly named it. Its logical sequel, so to speak, **''A Tropical Intermezzo,''** is a tale told in the form of confession by a dying wanderer from the Spanish Americas. As a young warrior, he wanders one night alone into ''the dale of fountains,'' where he becomes a lover of the woman of the dale. ''Verily,'' says he, ''it was the Eden-garden, the Paradise of Eve.'' . . . In both pieces there is seen the fate of man seeking ''sweet pantheism.'' The lost Eden symbolizes the fate of every Rip van Winkle who returns to the human world, the world of time.

Time remains supreme in **''Vultur Aura.''** Through the eyes of a divine vulture circling high above Saint John of the Pines, the ancient Spanish fort, Hearn muses on the passing caravan of races, nations, and civilizations. Man may, Hearn seems to suggest in **''A Name in the Plaza,''** transcend time only by discovering where time begins. . . . This dream-piece is concerned with the mystery of our memory, whose origin must be traced back beyond our human realm. It anticipates his later

belief that time crosses many bournes of existence. The center of **''Floridian Reveries''** has as its theme man's search for the Garden of Eden, where man and nature are one, and his tragedy when they are divorced. That which both harmonizes and divorces them is the mystery of time. In this, **''Floridian Reveries''** already foreshadows his *Two Years in the French West Indies.* (p. 86)

[What] separates *Two Years* [from *Leaves from the Dairy of an Impressionist*] is its appreciable degree of structural unity. The book begins and ends in New York Harbor, the voyage coming full circle. As expectation yields to ecstasy, and then to apprehension, the whole voyage turns out to be a sort of pilgrimage. Besides this cyclic pattern, there is structural grouping among the chapters. The early ones are altogether concerned with descriptions or sketches, whereas the narrative quality comes to dominate the later chapters, such as ''''Ti Canotié'' (VIII), ''Ma Bonne'' (XI), '''Pa combiné, chè!'' '' (XII), ''Yé'' (XIII), and ''Lys'' (XIV). The gradual shift from the descriptive to the narrative or dramatic corresponds with that from the ''visual'' to the ''emotional.'' As this change develops, the narrator also emerges from that impersonal realm, and now more personally weaves sketches, legends, and episodes into one fabric of his own reflection. The tropical world steals into the mind by way of the five senses. (p. 87)

Structurally, the initial piece, **''A Midsummer Trip to the Tropics,''** a complete account of Hearn's first West Indian voyage in 1887, serves the total effect of the book by contrast with the ensuing **''Martinique Sketches.''** A travel sketch done by a sensitive observer, it is open-eyed but never emotionally involved. Certainly this is one way of writing travel sketches, but Hearn seems sceptical of its merit. We almost suspect that it is his real intent to demonstrate what a travel sketch could be without one's growing awareness and emotional commitment. Hearn seems to believe that the emotional approach must complete the intellectual, if travel writing is to be genuine art. In this respect **''Martinique Sketches''** is the main part of the drama, whereas the opening piece serves as a prolog. Their combined effect is that of appearance and reality juxtaposed. (pp. 87-8)

On the surface, the theme of *Two Years* is predominantly sociological, being concerned with the tragic contact between the colored natives and the white colonists, and also between the primitive and the civilized worlds. But going a step further, we recognize something more fundamental. Hearn's ultimate interest centers on the antipodal relationship between nature and man. One approach is represented by the natives; the other by the whites. The first half of the book is primarily a study of the native approach toward nature, whereas the second half presents a dramatic conflict between nature and the civilized race. Quite contrary to our expectation, Hearn becomes more and more hesitant about judging between these two approaches. Having come to know something of nature's destructive force, he seems to feel no longer comfortable with his earlier romantic pantheism. (pp. 89-90)

The struggle between man and nature cannot be so easily won; for it is at heart the drama of temptation, which, as usual with Hearn, must come in the guise of a Circe rather than a Mephistopheles. All his senses, one after another, become inert before her mesmerism. He becomes oblivious to his burden of knowledge and his world of civilization. This final moment of temptation is personally and yet symbolically dramatized in the twelfth chapter, '''Pa combiné, chè!'' '' To Hearn's friend

Félicien, an ailing white youth, his native lover whispers: *"Si ou ainmein moin, pa combiné—non!"* . . .

Earlier she had implored Hearn ". . . you are his friend! why do you let him think? It is thinking that will prevent him getting well." The youth's illness is a familiar symptom accompanying his total conversion to the world of nature. It is a soul's struggle for all or nothing, a struggle which knows no compromise. Once out of this drama of temptation, one has no choice. He must return to the world he is destined for. This seems to be the real meaning of Hearn's own flight from the tropics.

The very fact that the whole drama reaches its climax near the end of *Two Years* may suggest the book's thematic design and Hearn's climatic obsession. In the closing chapter, "Lys," both combine so as to create a sense of dramatic irony. There the author's return home coincides with Lys's visit to New York. This West Indian maiden is leaving her homeland forever to be a governess! No matter how absurd the whole situation sounds, it is going to be surely another rehearsal of that bitter dilemma from which he has narrowly escaped. (p. 91)

His southward flight finally proved to be a pilgrimage, but when this pilgrimage terminated as a drama of temptation, Hearn had to bid farewell to the heart of the tropics. His farewell, however, was no more than a gesture of flight, because it meant simply the beginning of another flight. In his "twilight only,—but the Twilight of the Gods! . . ." there is already a shadow of uncertainty. As his truce with his own world turned out to be only temporary, his presentiment came true also. To settle in America, Hearn must have felt, would be a compromise, not a reconciliation. He had to continue pursuing the destined pattern for "the civilized nomad." No sooner was *Two Years* published . . . than he was on his long journey to the East across the Pacific. (p. 92)

> *Beongcheon Yu, in his* An Ape of Gods: The Art and Thought of Lafcadio Hearn *(reprinted by permission of the Wayne State University Press; copyright © 1964 by Wayne State University Press), Wayne State University Press, 1964, 346 p.*

**LEWIS LEARY**   (essay date 1967)

[During his] apprentice years Hearn steeped himself in the writings of European contemporaries, especially those who probed beyond convention toward controlled description of passionate joys or aspirations. . . . Pierre Loti, Jules Le Maître, Gerard de Nerval, Villiers de l'Isle-Adam, Maupassant, Zola, Daudet, Flaubert, and Gautier all attracted him, and many others, including Dostoevski, Tolstoi, and Sienkiewicz. (p. 147)

Thousands of Americans first read these foreign writers in the anonymous translations by Lafcadio Hearn. While during the 1880's America was discovering itself in the writings of Mark Twain and Howells, Edward Eggleston and Cable and Parkman, Mary Murfree, James Whitcomb Riley, and many another who dwelt on the local scene, Hearn was more than any native contemporary extending literary horizons toward new themes and bold transatlantic notions of the proper substance of art. His contribution to the cultural expansion of his adopted country has sometimes been made to seem Hearn's whole and sufficient claim to being remembered, and praise has rightly been given New Orleans as the only city in the United States which at that time would have fostered so strange a talent. But New Orleans had more than that to offer, and translating was not in itself an end: "I see beauty here all around me,—a strange tropical, intoxicating beauty. I consider it my artistic duty to let myself be absorbed into this new life, and study its form and colour and passion."

Wandering through the Vieux Carré, listening to street cries and street brawls, "the melancholy, quavering beauty and weirdness of Negro chants," absorbing sights and sounds and odors, listening to and reading of strange "traditions, superstitions, legends, fairy tales, goblin stories, impossible romances," blending them, he attempted a new form, based on brief impressions of scene fleetingly glimpsed or conversation overheard, and then painstakingly embellished—"moulded," he said, "and coloured by imagination alone." He called these writings "Fantastics," and some thirty of them appeared through 1881, telling "of wonders and of marvels, of riches and rarities": in **"Aphrodite and the King's Prisoners,"** of a captive kept in luxury, but alone with only an ebony statue of the Goddess of Love for company, until he kills himself at the foot of the statue in **"Love which is brother to death"**; in **"El Vómito,"** which celebrates beauty and death, and **"The Name on the Stone,"** in which a Ligeia-like maiden returns from the grave to inform her lover that "Love is stronger than death"; or in **"The Fountain of God,"** a parable of eternal youth and love and happiness secured in death and dream.

Many of the Fantastics are slight indeed, like **"The Idyl of the French Snuff-Box,"** from the enameled cover of which a nymph and faun come briefly but charmingly to life, or like **"Spring Phantoms,"** which reminds man of visions of luscious ladies which may come to him as winter wanes. One borrows the semiscientific manner made popular by Oliver Wendell Holmes as a doctor at a boarding-house table holds forth on **"Hereditary Memories"**—a theme obsessively intriguing to Hearn; another spoke in **"A Dream of Kites,"** of children's windswept toys entangled in a web of telegraph wires, lost and tattered like the dreams of youth. Most of them are too fragile for quick retelling, and Hearn admitted them trivial. But he was right in refusing to be ashamed of them as unworthy of his talents. "I fancy the idea of the fantastics is artistic," he said. "They are my impressions of the strange life of New Orleans. They are dreams of a tropical city. There is one idea running through them all—love and death."

"I live forever in dreams of other centuries and other faiths and other ethics," he said then, as he gathered from Brahmanic, Buddhistic, Talmudic, Arabic, Persian, Chinese, and Polynesian legend a collection of twenty-seven tales . . . [published] as *Stray Leaves from Strange Literatures*. Adapted from translations by other men, these fables, Hearn explained, are "reconstructions of what impressed me as the most fantastically beautiful in the exotic literature which I was able to obtain." Though he learnedly discussed sources, he made no claims to scholarship: he wished simply to share with others the delights which he had experienced among "some very strange and beautiful literatures."

The tales are brief, and often bold; they speak of passion, especially the passion of love, and of wisdom which may, but does not always, bring comfort or calm. Weirdness is their keynote: spectral lovers and enchantress wives, and love which leads to death. "The wise," he wrote in introduction to one tale, "will not attach themselves unto women; for women sport with the hearts of those who love them," and women die, even as love dies, so that memories are best, and sad, strange tales not shrouded in reality. He told of Polynesian lands "where garments are worn by none save the dead," of youth which might be eternal, and of dreams despoiled by phantoms, of intelligence greater than wisdom, and faith superior to truth.

Each tale is carefully chiseled, and meant to be enchanting. Each is frankly derivative, a retreat to ancient quietness. The language is honeyed with Biblical phrasing, cloyed sometimes with alliterative rhythm, as Hearn strove to attain what Baudelaire had described as ''le miracle d'une prose poétic.'' They were exercises done by a young man who trained for something beyond virtuosity; ''veritable poems,'' Charles W. Coleman thought them, ''heavy with the perfume and glamour of the East, delicate, fragrant, graceful.'' Hearn was, however, to reach closer to an idiom of his own three years later in *Some Chinese Ghosts*. . . . Having wandered, he said, through ''vast and mysterious pleasure-grounds of Chinese fancy,'' he presented in this, his second volume, ''the marvellous flowers there growing, . . . as souvenirs of his curious voyage.'' He spoke again of spectral lovers, of nocturnal meetings, of passion sublimated to beauty, with no habitation in time or place, only in the questing spirit of man. Myth and legend, and the unlearned yearning of people, contained unchanging essences. He prefaced the book with an epigram from a Chinese poet: ''If ye desire to witness prodigies and to behold marvels, / Be not concerned as to whether the mountains are distant or the rivers far away.''

But there were marvels also in New Orleans and the bayou country beyond it. . . . In 1885 he published *La Cuisine Creole,* an assembly of culinary recipes ''from leading chefs and noted Creole housewives who had made New Orleans famous,'' and *Gombo Zhèbes,* a dictionary of Creole proverbs. And he had begun a collection of **''Ephemerae''** or **''Leaves from the Diary of an Impressionist,''** which included **''Floridian Reveries''** written on a journey to that peninsular coast in the summer of 1885. No publisher for this or for the Creole sketches was found during Hearn's lifetime, but they contain his most impressive insights into the life and character of the tropical South. . . . (pp. 148-52)

Even more than George Washington Cable, who Hearn finally decided was handicapped by a Sunday-school compulsion to do something about things, he caught the lush languor of old New Orleans, its Mardi Gras, its Creole girls, its proud but purse-pinching lodging-house keepers, its tales of voodoo and ghostly apparitions, of women tantalizingly lovely, calculating, and bitter. He had a surer ear for words than an eye for exact detail, spoke more confidently of color and shadow than of particularities of place. His people are less often remembered as appearances than as voices, often Hearn's own voice, but often also in dialect which caught nuances of character. (p. 152)

These Hearn did briefly best, renderings of people through what they said and how they sounded. But he did them seldom, preferring instead to turn his ear for tone and modulation to continuing re-creation of tales which came to him at second hand. His writings suggest that he knew few people well, and that what he observed of people was how they talked or what they thought, seldom how they looked or acted—except that he was curiously fascinated by eyes, by sparkling or furtive eyes, Venetian eyes challenging from behind a carnival mask. In telling a story or sketching a street scene, a seascape, or a sunrise, he seems at ease with words, evoking color and movement and sound; but people, unless overheard, eluded him. He was as bookish as he was sensually perceptive, and was finally most comfortable with the rhythm of words skillfully arranged to capture atmosphere or mood.

When Cable told him a sad story of storm and death which years before had visited an island on the Gulf coast, Hearn wove words around it to produce a novelette called *Chita: A*

*Memory of Last Island,* in part a magnificent tour de force, in part briefly evocative character portrayal, and in part pathos shaded toward sentimentality. In attempting a longer story, Hearn did not build well; he could decorate a plot better than he could resolve a situation, and so *Chita,* his single attempt at sustained narrative during his years in New Orleans, fails to please. However clear his intention to present man as part of, but caught relentlessly within, the power of nature, and to demonstrate that simple men who know and respect nature's force live cleaner, more satisfying lives than dwellers in cities to whom nature is hidden ''by walls, and by weary avenues of trees with whitewashed trunks,'' the result is distorted more than Hearn could have meant it to be. As a child of nature, young Chita is never seen as clearly as the sea and sky, whose color may be thought of as in itself a major theme. (pp. 153-54)

Hearn was later, he said, ashamed of *Chita* as overworked and overstylized, but he could not have been thinking of the first section, which is heightened surely, but which in tone and substance is almost exactly right. Word and mood and rhythm advance confidently side by side. Hearn's sea is a cradle endlessly rocking, but not by the hand of an elemental crone-mother. Mystery and beauty and menace there are one, not to be defined by eyes sharpened for daily use, or ears attuned to pleasing waltzes.

No Southern writer, except perhaps Sidney Lanier, had composed with more exulatant fervor. (p. 157)

Hearn had almost every minor literary virtue; he succeeded in minor genres, but he is real, as person and artist, and bold enough to stand, however unsteadily, alone. When the critic or literary historian forgets him, something of literary heritage is lost, for he has added, said Paul Elmer More, ''a new thrill to our intellectual experience,'' and people who care for writing as art will not pass him by, even when they are sure that he may finally disappoint them. (p. 158)

> Lewis Leary, ''Lafcadio Hearn: One of Our Southern Writers,'' in Essays on American Literature in Honor of Jay B. Hubbell, *edited by Clarence Gohdes (reprinted by permission of the Publisher; copyright © 1967 by Duke University Press, Durham, North Carolina), Duke University Press, 1967 (and reprinted in his* Southern Excursions: Essays on Mark Twain and Others, *Louisiana State University Press, 1971, pp. 142-58).*

## ARTHUR E. KUNST (essay date 1969)

[*Kunst's discussion of Hearn's early fantastic writings is taken from his important critical overview,* Lafcadio Hearn.]

The reveries and imaginative fragments collected under the name of *Fantastics and Other Fancies* . . . are, to say the least, decadent. For Lafcadio Hearn, who thought the way to express his new-found happiness with Louisiana was to call it ''a dead face that asked for a kiss,'' decadence was a natural humor. Occasionally these selections are merely unsuccessful experiments; occasionally they pass over the line from decadence to sentimentality, as in the nauseating archness of **''The Little Red Kitten.''** But other times, when by accident or design a sketch manages to hold back from the seductions of profundity, the decadence achieves that willful denial of reality that marks the dying century's flight toward the dream and the unconscious. At these moments, Hearn's ''dreams of a tropical city'' have all the unexplained and fixated beauty that no amount of invocations and cosmic metaphorings could otherwise provide. The heavy burden which figuration and eternities place on such brief narratives can be observed in **"The Vision of the Dead Creole."** . . .

The leading sentence of the opening paragraph makes thoroughly consistent and satisfying decadence combine with metaphors which we must either find beyond the range of the narrator who is making his way onto the shore, or hold to be the blathering of the dreariest kind of *poseur:* "The sea-ripples kissed the brown sands silently, as if afraid; faint breezes laden with odors of saffron and cinnamon and drowsy flowers came over the water;—the stars seemed vaster than in other nights;—the fires of the Southern Cross burned steadily without one diamond-twinkle;—I paused a moment in terror;—for it seemed I could hear the night breathe—in long, weird sighs." (pp. 46-7)

Nothing, of course, is wrong with fiery stars or sighing nights. The difficulty lies in trying to reconcile the feeling of the narrator's terror with a simultaneous feeling that the author is blandly handicrafting the sentences before our eyes. Moreover, none of these possibilities lasts for long—we begin to perceive a deeper explanation for these distracting paradoxes, and then the story turns and leaves us with an expectation that goes nowhere. We have, for instance, the odd but incredible image of blood from his torn hands "dripping with a thick, dead sound, as of molten lead, upon the leaves" at his feet. Such a metaphysical conceit does not belong to a world where flowers open their hearts to the moon. (p. 47)

Although **"All in White"** uses the garrulous I-narrator device, it . . . has one who is more direct, less "refined." "No," he starts, "I did not stay long in Havana." The body of the story is taken up with events so isolated and so insistently sketched that their conjunction maddeningly suggests some undetectable relevance: a narrow, walled street; an iron window behind which one can see the reclining body of a girl in white; the passing battalion of Spanish soldiers which presses him against the wall. Instead of these events for a plot, the story devotes itself to a frightened clarification of details: "candles were burning at her head and feet; and in the stillness of the hot air their yellow flames did not even tremble." But there is not so much clarification of details as to convey a sense of disinterest in the moment. (pp. 47-8)

The story, a nightmare, has the meaningfulness of one; with or without dream analysis, it characterizes the dreamer. The "Americano" does not survive to offer us his free associations; still, insofar as we can respond to these vivid symbols, the effects of association are left to us. Such a presentation of Lust and Death together is the main theme of the *Fantastics* (Hearn would say, Love and Death). (p. 48)

[**"The Ghostly Kiss"**] lacks the courage of its insane convictions. Just before the end, the monstrous hallucination disperses, and what the narrator had seen as a vast auditorium is revealed, rather disappointingly, as a mere hazy graveyard. Kissing a corpse is all very well, even in the context of all these other corpse-kisses in surrounding tales; but in *this* tale everything has been focussed on the horror of the public kiss—for the narrator's perspiring, trembling body in the midst of the unreasonably large audience, his heart beating so loud he is aware that it drowns out the sounds of the actors, provides the essential terror of the story. To suddenly deprive it of the source of this paranoid embarrassment is to rid the tale of all its terror: to be alone with a corpse comes as a sort of mock-

relief. Almost anything else which would hold onto the scene—feeling her mouth give way beneath his, a deafening volume of noise or silence, finding himself unable to breathe or to pull his mouth from her kiss—might be better, so long as it offered a different kind of final twist to his uncontrollable urge to accept the doom she represents.

Some of the imagery is quite adequate to the ambiguous tone of graveyard within apparent theater: "crests of palms casting moving shadows like gigantic spiders" through "far distant oriel windows" and her lips "humid, as with the kisses of the last lover." The narrator's extravagant euphemisms on the charms of the woman seated before him are reasonable because he does show himself to be at once a babbler and a repressed, terrorized rapist. Hence his fascination with the curls against the soft movements of her neck becomes his appropriated and perverted sensuality. (pp. 48-9)

[In the opening section of **"The One Pill-Box"**], Hearn calls upon images from many other sketches of New Orleans to create a plague scene: an awesome, metallic furnace-heat that blisters the wood and iron of the dusty city. Nothing in the rest of its narrative, carefully (and capably) restricted to the stream-of-consciousness of a dying, plague-stricken mill-master, quite achieves the level of the beginning. But in it Hearn's cataloguemania becomes realistic, obsessional impressions in the mind of a delirious patient. Even the images chosen are appropriate to the experience of a mill-man. The paragraphs are used to suggest both stages of the disease and the jumbled, fragmentary mood of a conscious moment. (pp. 50-1)

The style of **"One Pill-Box"** is clean until the end; and there, in the vivid awareness of death, the sudden emergence of gross metaphors—"the fathomless purple of the night, and the milky blossoms of the stars"—corresponds to a mute, momentary terror felt for the first time by this man of contracts. But this is not, in fact, the last image or impression: from the heavily colored visual oppression, the narrative turns once again to the thinking man within—this time to a sentence whose bitter objectivity conveys far better than any thrill or moral the disappointment of dying.

Others of the *Fancies* concentrate upon the love aspect of the theme rather than on that of death. **"The Idyl of a French Snuff-Box"** . . . utilizes a realistic outer framework to enclose two types of fantasy within. The outside frame is simplicity itself: an old gentleman leaves behind his snuffbox and later returns to pick it up again. The two fantasies neatly illustrate the two ways, one objective and the other plotted, in which Hearn is currently experimenting. Both present a "dream of Theocritus": the first, through contemplation of the ivory relief scene on the snuffbox; the second, through substitution of an actual dream of Arcadia in which the carved figures are made to become characters in a story. The dream-story created is much less convincing, primarily because it is too sweetly idyllic and too coy—the dreamer is awakened just before the nymph can yield. (pp. 51-2)

The first version, like some antinovel of the 1950's, calculates its verbs so closely as to let description tremble on the verge of motion. The discoveries of the narrator, as his eyes pass over the parts of the scene, only just hold themselves back from actual succession in time. The opening view is summary: "a slumbering dryad; an amorous faun." The following view expands the initial impression, reinforces the illusion of life: "The dryad was sleeping like a bacchante weary of love and wine, half-lying upon her side; half upon her bosom, pillowing her charming head upon one arm.'' The next view starts to use the ambiguous verb, noticeable because of the slight shift in tense: ''Above her crouched the faun . . . he lifted the robe . . . gazed. . . .''

This use of a series of impressions to convey a sense of time into the relationships among unmoving objects is most apparent in the consideration of the snake: ''But around her polished thigh clung a loving snake, the guardian of her sleep; and the snake raised its jeweled head and fixed upon the faun its glittering topaz eyes.'' Then, having set up this spurious historical dimension, the narrator provokingly frustrates the suspended scene, and returns to frigid immobility: ''motionless the lithe limbs of the dryad and the serpent thigh-bracelet and the unhappily amorous faun holding the drapery rigid in his outstretched hand.'' No sentimental poetry here, no coy doves cooing in the myrtles, only the paradox of life lurking in gracefully motionless figures.

At the beginning, we know that the narrator of ''MDCCCLIII'' . . . is a speculative man. This tale is another in the series which works upon the manner in which the style of a man's mind and his inner experience characterize him as an object removed from time. (p. 52)

The story moves off the plane of the old theme of lost love to the larger one of an awakened dead-faith. That the man is shown to be meditative, uneasy with death; that the man is confronted on the bare, gleaming corridors by the apparitions of winged-capped Sisters and not the Woman whose name he utters; that the Sister, taking his hand, leads him onward, repeating strangely, ''You are not afraid?''—these elements lead toward the man's confrontation with a religion and a death he prefers to believe he has put behind him. (p. 53)

Another personage who talks himself into reality is portrayed in ''A Mephistophelian,'' in which skeptical outrage is neither humorous nor expository, only subtly cynical, as slowly this portrait of a didactic unbeliever is unveiled. The tone of the responses—the piece is structured into dialogue form—is consistently self-confident and urbane. Indeed, it is almost as if the answers had been rehearsed long ago; the questions have become so familiar through either boredom of repetition or long, defensive anticipation that every attack or amazement ceases to be upsetting. Love, honor, pleasure come up again and again; and, as the smoothly ready replies dispose of the problems, the very life being described somehow comes to seem less fully experienced. It is not that the refutations seem so unfair or sophistic, but that, as the conversation proceeds, the Mephistophelian seems to content himself with less and less of vividness, liveliness. The more he finds human habit to be ''mere . . . ,'' the less emotional quality his own leftover existence can lay claim to.

For this reason the concluding lines seem to point logically towards suicide: and it is on suicide that the piece does indeed come to an end. The tone has not altered; suicide is spoken of with the same sophisticated indifference—but his life appears already so close to complete unimportance that a boredom without scruples would be an almost imperceptible change, a slight movement toward the momentary whim of weariness that chooses death. The language has never been supercilious, or suave enough to make us suspect a compensation; we get only a sense of regretful waste. . . . (pp. 53-4)

The last of the New Orleans *Fantastics* to be treated in this discussion also marks a pause in Hearn's original (if we may make any such crude distinction) output, in the tradition of Poe, Baudelaire, Gautier, and the larger ranges of the Gothic story. Easily discontented with these associations, however peripheral they may be in fact to the real significance of his stories, Hearn absorbs, with voracious appetite, huge volumes of materials from the literatures of the world; for he is still searching for structural materials of plot and action suited to his elaborative and emotive talents.

The first results of this extended and zealous literary exploration are collected under the modest title of *Stray Leaves from Strange Literature*. We must say *results*, because these are emphatically not translations; they are as original and as perceptibly Hearnian as the *Fantastics*. If the *Fantastics* occasionally show their clear membership in some part of the Gothic genre, the *Stray Leaves* also fall by locale or persons or events into some corner of the world's traditions. Hearn borrows plots and ideas from Egyptian, Polynesian, Eskimo, Indian, Buddhist, Finnish, Muslim, and Talmudic legend; and he frequently alters, recombines, or abridges. (pp. 54-5)

*Stray Leaves from Strange Literature* might better have been titled *Strange Leaves from Stray Literature*. At least half of the tales concern a devastating love for a woman; most also make use of some quaint supernatural belief. Other prominent themes include nakedness, beautiful youths, and the death of a son. In other words, the stories are carefully selected to appeal to the then current taste for the mildly decadent, the prettily exotic, and the vapidly sentimental. Additional evidence for their being done more to satisfy market expectations than a true search for the foreign is given by Hearn himself in his introduction: the tales, he says, are ''the most fantastically beautiful in the most exotic literature I was able to obtain.''

If the tales seem more familiar than exotic, this effect is no doubt because of the touchstone of ''fantastic beauty.'' If they seem to show a considerable lapse in Hearn's already demonstrated ability to work within the tradition of fantastic beauty, it must be because they are essentially unsuited to Hearn's peculiar talent. A merely cursory consideration of the sort of tales gathered reveals one inevitable structural pattern—almost without exception they are ''well-made,'' plot-aligned stories. Simple tales, yet not merely episodic, their simplicity lies in the linking of simple causes to simple effects: the attention is neither to the complex of influences at any one moment nor to the multiple consequences upon the mind of any one character. The attention is given to a single chain of events, one following probably upon another (however fortuitous their entrance may be).

Such overwhelming emphasis on the time scheme—at the expense of description, character, and mood—is utterly inimical to the kind of fiction practiced and developed by Lafcadio Hearn. Although a glance at his future work shows us that these experiments in plot did help Hearn to deal with plot-form, they do not belong to the mainstream of his creative talent. (pp. 55-6)

One sure sign of false yearnings for acceptance exists: vain pretense of language. And *Stray Leaves* (except for the stark honesty of the Kalevala tales) is full of it. *Yea*, and *verily*, and *lo*, cries the narrator again and again, in his pompous ''olde Englishe.'' Sentences begin with *and* or *for* or *now there was*; things do not happen, they come to pass; the kings do not speak to their wives, they speak *even unto* them. Persons are not upon intimate terms; they converse stiltedly through *thee* and *thou*. The quaint people in these stories are very much like the quaint people in the Bible, only less important. (p. 56)

The interesting pieces from *Stray Leaves* are few in number. Chiefly, they are those in which the original tale has a minimum of significant content: **"The Fountain Maiden," "The Bird Wife," "Yamaraja."** Upon occasion they become noticeable through some probably fortuitous oddity, like the lesbian attraction the weary courtesan feels in **"Pundari"** for the Buddha in the form of a beauteous woman. (p. 57)

The exceptional piece in the *Stray Leaves* is the collection of fragments from the *Kalevala*. Unusual for its crudity of style (a merit in this instance), it is also restrained in being a translation from the French and little more. Most of the power derives from the repetition of incident, the striking images, and the play between narrative image and magical subject— all qualities found in Hearn's source. Each of the three translated segments . . . contains plot and a suitable suggestion of atmosphere through mythical exaggeration. . . . Everything seems appropriate because Hearn neither improves nor responds to the text. (p. 58)

> *Arthur E. Kunst, in his* Lafcadio Hearn *(copyright © 1969 by Twayne Publishers, Inc.; reprinted with the permission of Twayne Publishers, a division of G. K. Hall & Co., Boston), Twayne, 1969, 146 p.*

## KENNETH REXROTH   (essay date 1977)

[*Rexroth brings his expertise as a poet and noted translator of oriental literature to the following discussion of Hearn's writings on Buddhism.*]

Hearn's Japanese writings demonstrate economy, concentration, and great control of language, with little stylistic exhibitionism. Their attitude of uncritical appreciation for the exotic and the mysterious is as unmistakably nineteenth century as the fine prose idiom with which it is consistent.

In spite of the incredible changes that have taken place in Japan since Hearn's death in 1904, as an informant of Japanese life, literature, and religion he is still amazingly reliable, because beneath the effects of industrialization, war, population explosion, and prosperity much of Japanese life remains unchanged. (pp. xi-xii)

There is no interpreter of Japanese Buddhism quite like Hearn, but he is not a Buddhologist. Far from it. Hearn was not a scholar, nor was he in the Western sense a religious believer. What distinguishes him is an emotional identification with the Buddhist way of life and with Buddhist cults. Hearn is as good as anyone at providing an elementary grounding in Buddhist doctrine. But what he does incomparably is to give his reader a feeling for how Buddhism is *lived* in Japan, its persistent influence upon folklore, burial customs, children's riddles, toys for sale in the marketplace, and even upon the farmer's ruminations in the field. For Hearn, Buddhism is a way of life, and he is interested in the effects of its doctrine upon the daily actions and common beliefs of ordinary people. (p. xiii)

The only peculiarity in Hearn's Buddhism is his habit of equating it with the philosophy of Herbert Spencer, now so out of date. However, this presents few difficulties for the modern reader, as his Spencerianism can be said to resemble Buddhism more than his Buddhism resembles Herbert Spencer. Also, it is not Spencer's Darwinism, "red in tooth and claw," but Spencer's metaphysical and spiritual speculations that have influenced Hearn's interpretation of Buddhism. (pp. xiv-xv)

Hearn's role in the spread of Buddhism to the West was a preparatory one. He was the first important American writer to live in Japan and to commit his imagination and considerable literary powers to what he found there. Like the "popular" expressions of Buddhist faith that were his favorite subject, Hearn popularized the Buddhist way of life for his Western readers. And he was widely read, both in his articles for *Harper's Magazine* and the *Atlantic Monthly,* and in his numerous books on Japan. Hearn's essays, with their rich descriptions and queer details, almost never generalizing but staying with a particular subject, always backed by the likeable and enthusiastic personality of Hearn himself, and always factually reliable, satisfied the vague and growing curiosity of his American readers about the mysterious East. (p. xxvi)

Hearn never became a Buddhist, and he remained skeptical about certain of Buddhism's key doctrines—such as the relationship of *karma* and rebirth—but he passionately believed that Buddhism promoted a far better attitude toward daily life than did Christianity. It would be up to more scholarly and less imaginative writers to begin to translate and preach specific Buddhist doctrines, but Hearn has done much to translate the spirit of Japanese Buddhism and to prepare Western society for it. (p. xxvii)

> *Kenneth Rexroth, "Introduction" (copyright © 1977 by Kenneth Rexroth), in* The Buddhist Writings of Lafcadio Hearn *by Lafcadio Hearn, Ross-Erikson, Inc., Publishers, 1977, pp. vii-xxvii.*

## ANNE ROWE   (essay date 1978)

Hearn's search for his own "field for fiction" had its first success in New Orleans, gateway to the tropical South. Drawing on the South for material was, of course, nothing new, and Hearn's early use of the material he found there was not unlike that of other writers. . . . [Although] his style could never be confused with that of local color fiction such as Constance Fenimore Woolson's, for example, the two writers shared a deep admiration for the beauty of the South, unfettered by political and moral concerns. (p. 79)

[Like John De Forest, Albion Tourgée, and Woolson], Hearn wrote about the people he encountered in the South, but for him the importance of individuals in their own right is greater. His southerners are neither reduced to foils or backdrops for northerners nor used to illustrate a point. The author's concern with their human qualities distinguishes his writings from the works previously discussed, where even when characters are more extensively developed they are usually exploited for thematic purposes. Hearn, for example, explores the life of a black voudoo purely for the interest it generates in itself, and in his sketch of a Creole servant girl he depicts the mysterious ways of the Negroes who lived closely with whites but whose private thoughts remained always a mystery to their masters.

To a much greater degree than the other writers Hearn sought to present black men in their own milieu, as a valuable source of literary material in their own right. The sketch **"Les Porteuses"** included in *Two Years in the French West Indies* carefully and lovingly describes the girls who carry merchandise on their heads and thus serve as a major means of commerce in islands such as Martinique. The opening chapter of *Youma* describes the "da" who served as foster-mother and nurse to Creole children and stayed with the child more than did the real mother: "She alone satisfied all his little needs; he found her more indulgent, more patient, perhaps even more caressing, than the other." In *Youma* Hearn's portrayal of the "da" is such that the girl achieves heroic stature when she gives her life for her Creole charge. "Her special type was a product of slavery, largely created by selection: the one creation of slavery perhaps not unworthy of regret—one strange flowering amid all the rank dark growths of that bitter soil." Hearn's treatment of this special sort of Negro, the Creole servant, achieves a reality that goes beyond the stereotype.

The same is true with his other characters. In his sketches treating the Creole working class he does not criticize them as society's failures; instead they have color and life and diversity. He saw humor and even virtue in the situation of four Creole carpenters taking three weeks to put up an awning at a corner grocery when "two stout Irishmen would have done it in twenty-four hours." After all, "they did not propose to work themselves to death. Life was too short." (pp. 81-2)

The Creoles of Hearn's sketches share the qualities hinted at by De Forest and Tourgée and lavishly praised by Woolson: dignity, grace, refinement, and above all, an adherence to noble old ways that set them apart from the rest of the world.

Although the idealized aspect of the South was presented in the works of the other writers in their depiction of the noble classes, only Hearn seems to have been fully aware of the appeal of this idealization. (p. 84)

Not only does Hearn indicate a greater awareness of the fascination of the South, but his liberation from restrictions on how to deal with it enabled him to pursue his interests in directions not open to the other writers. For Hearn the literary evocation of the South was an end in itself. In writing about southern people, lifestyles, and ideals, he directed his energies toward the development of a style which, he felt, was in harmony with his subject matter. Both in his articles for New Orleans newspapers in which he examined the style of contemporary writers and in the letters to friends in which many of his own attitudes toward style were formulated, there is evident a much greater concern with style than Tourgeé, De Forest, or Woolson showed. His translations and critical reviews reveal some of his prejudices—an admiration for characteristics of impressionism, such as concern with color and the relationship between the receptor and the shapes and forms of the material conveyed by a work, and a dislike for some of the tenets of naturalism. (pp. 85-6)

Hearn's expressed conviction that the picture and the feeling it conveyed are most important perhaps explains the two prevailing characteristics of his works that further distinguish them from the other writers. These are the prevalence of sensual, especially visual, imagery and the absence of moral commentary. (p. 87)

These distinctions—an impressionistic style that placed content above thesis in importance paralleled by an intensity of sensual perception and an absence of moral commentary (Hearn could even lament the passing of a social system that produced octoroons as a gain for morality but a loss for art)—represent key differences between Hearn's southern writings and those of De Forest, Tourgée, and Woolson. But although he developed a unique style, he also developed most fully the portrayal shared by the others of the South as an idealized place. (p. 88)

[Because] Hearn's major concern was with the presentation or evocation of the material itself, the style he found most appropriate reduced the writer to the role of mere observer. The sketches in *Two Years in the French West Indies*, which begin with description and then intensify until the reader shares with the narrator his feelings of wonder and awe, show the effects of the author's method. Another example of this approach is found in Hearn's best-known American work, *Chita.*

This novelette, recounting the destruction of Last Isle and the fate of two of its survivors, may be seen as the culmination of Hearn's concern with the exotic, of blending form with content. . . .

Hearn uses the techniques of impressionism, stressing the effect of the material upon its receptor, to evoke from the subject that intensity of feeling he often stated was the goal of this writing. Thus, the seven sections in the first part of the novel, "The Legend of L'Ile Derniere," each repeat a pattern of heightening the effect of description at the conclusion. (p. 89)

[There] is in *Chita* little stress upon self-determination; the focus is on an account of things simply happening to people, of people swept along by forces greater than themselves. Thus, the characters must make only a few moral choices—notably the choice of Julien La Brierre not to commit suicide; and Hearn deemphasizes this by remarking that whether a man lives or dies is of little consequence to society. The simple elements of plot—the storm that sweeps away the vacationers at Last Isle, the rescue of a small girl by a fisherman, and a final meeting between father and daughter—are events that are not planned by the characters but simply happen to them.

The dwindling away of plot allows more room for what Hearn considered more important—the presentation of the locale and the people, heightened by the use of symbolism. The first apparent symbol, that of the steamer compared to a white bird, sets up a predominant thesis of the close relationship between man and nature. (pp. 89-90)

Another major symbol for Hearn is the sea, which represents an abyss, an ambiguous mixture of good and evil, source both of life and destruction of life. (pp. 90-1)

Although the sea is the strongest single symbol, other aspects of nature also become symbolic. As elsewhere in Hearn's work the colors of sea and sky are dominant throughout. In contrast to the North where "rarely, in the paler zones, do earth and heaven take such luminosity," a summer day on the islands becomes "a caress of color . . . a spirituality, as of eternal tropical spring. It must have been to even such a sky that Xenophanes lifted up his eyes of old when he vowed the Infinite Blue was God." . . .

In a sense, the symbolism of sea, sky, and color are inseparable. They merge and blend together, the changes of one reflecting the shifting of another. And this connection reflects a unity of meaning, for the natural elements and their colors represent for Hearn the beauty and divinity sought by all men. . . . (pp. 91-2)

The key to the premise that Hearn is presenting an idealized place in *Chita* is the predominance of the color blue. Further, the novel contains two variations of this ideal. First, there is the passing grandeur represented by Last (constantly evoking "lost") Isle, the destruction of the gentle, noble Creoles being a metaphor for the passing of the old order in the South. And those who do survive, like Julien, find that nothing will ever be the same. When he returns to New Orleans there is no place for him in society, and Hearn comments on Julien's action in taking up as a profession the medicine he had studied only as an accomplishment: "After the passing of that huge shock, which left all the imposing and splendid fabric of Southern feudalism wrecked forever, his profession stood him in good stead." . . .

But in place of the ideal evoked by the other writers—of the days of splendor and chivalry—Hearn suggests the beauty of tropical nature. The transition from one to the other is embodied in the metamorphosis of Chita (formerly Zouzoune) from small, elegant Creole to a child of nature. (pp. 92-3)

[For Hearn] there was in nature some measure of chance for stability. In the divine blue of the sea and sky he found hope of a lasting paradise. Consequently, in **Chita** the lives of the main characters remain always subordinate to the forces of nature, and in the face of the power and greatness of the tropical surroundings man's actions are displaced in importance. For Hearn the importance of man is as a receiver of impressions, not as a judge. His reason for writing such a novel was to reflect and mirror the beauty revealed to man, to blend form and content in projecting the intensity of feeling evoked by the splendor of the South.

It has been suggested, with justification, that **Chita** is a flawed work, that Parts Two and Three fail to meet the promise of the opening section. Hearn attempts too much in the third part when he compresses ten years of Chita's life into a brief section. . . . But if **Chita** ultimately fails, it is perhaps because Hearn violates his own principle of dealing with only a single theme and paring away all that is not necessary. For this reason Part One is the novel's best part. In the picture of the Gulf Coast, the description of the confrontation between man and nature and the struggle among natural forces, Hearn achieved his dream of a poetical prose, of word pictures as poetical jewels. (pp. 93-4)

> Anne Rowe, "Lafcadio Hearn's Southern Paradise," in her The Enchanted Country: Northern Writers in the South 1865-1910 (reprinted by permission of Louisiana State University Press; copyright © 1978 Louisiana State University Press), Louisiana State University Press, 1978, pp. 74-95.

## ADDITIONAL BIBLIOGRAPHY

Bisland, Elizabeth. "Introductory Sketch." In *The Life and Letters of Lafcadio Hearn, Vol. I,* by Lafcadio Hearn, pp. 1-162. London: Archibald Constable & Co., 1907.
First lengthy biography. Bisland initially met Hearn in New Orleans, where they both wrote for the *Times-Democrat,* and she became a life-long acquaintance and correspondent.

Gould, George M. *Concerning Lafcadio Hearn.* Philadelphia: George W. Jacobs & Co., 1908, 416 p.
Notorious biograhy by a physician who once befriended but later quarreled bitterly with Hearn. Characterizing Hearn as unlearned and amoral, Gould sparked a controversy that ultimately furthered the author's literary reputation.

Hicks, Granville. "Hearn and Bierce." In his *The Great Tradition: An Interpretation of American Literature since the Civil War,* rev. ed., pp. 148-56. New York: The Macmillan Co., 1935.*
Examines Hearn's contempt for capitalism and its effect on his career.

Kennard, Nina H. *Lafcadio Hearn: Containing Some Letters from Lafcadio Hearn to His Half-Sister, Mrs. Atkinson.* New York: D. Appleton and Co., 1912, 356 p.
Sympathetic critical biography.

Mais, S.P.B. "Lafcadio Hearn." In his *Books and Their Writers,* pp. 242-76. New York: Dodd, Mead and Co., 1920.
Survey of the lectures collected in *Interpretations of Literature* and *Appreciations of Poetry.*

McWilliams, Vera. *Lafcadio Hearn.* Boston: Houghton Mifflin Co., 1946, 464 p.
Comprehensive and objective biography.

Mordell, Albert. *Discoveries: Essays on Lafcadio Hearn.* Tokyo: Orient/West, 1964, 240 p.
Biographical and critical essays that first appeared in *Today's Japan* (later *Orient/West*) and as introductions to Hearn's books. Mordell focuses on the author's early articles and translations.

Noguchi, Yone. *Lafcadio Hearn in Japan.* New York: Mitchell Kennerly, 1911, 177 p.
Responding to Gould's caustic biography, an informative though somewhat idealized portrait of Hearn as an artist and teacher.

Stevenson, Elizabeth. *Lafcadio Hearn.* 1961. Reprint. New York: Octagon Books, 1979, 362 p.
Insightful biography that attempts to remedy the personal and critical bias often present in Hearn commentary.

# Georg (Theodor Franz Arthur) Heym

## 1887-1912

German poet, short story writer, dramatist, and diarist.

Heym's lyric poems and short stories were an important contribution to the development of German Expressionism. Like many of his contemporaries, Heym attacked the banality of middle-class existence, and his works are often concerned with the horrors of the modern metropolis. Throughout his writings Heym employs vivid images and macabre allusions to evoke the nightmarish qualities typical of early Expressionism.

Heym was born to a middle-class family, but his early adolescent security was shaken when he moved from a small, quiet village to the urban bustle of Berlin. Heym's school years were a time of severe loneliness, and his isolation and misery are recorded with poetic imagination in his diaries of this period. In his desperation, Heym repeatedly entertained thoughts of suicide and death, a fascination that later appeared in his creative works. He studied law at the universities of Würzburg, Berlin, and Jena in an attempt to conform to the family tradition of civil service. However, Heym's feelings vacillated between serving what he considered a loathsome society and following his artistic inclinations toward a less conventional life-style. His acceptance into the Expressionist Neue Club in 1910, and the recognition of his unperformed drama *Atalanta oder die Angst!* by other Berlin writers did not relieve his despondency and self-doubt, but it did encourage him to adopt their bohemian way of life. A literary career that was just beginning ended when, at twenty-four, Heym fell through the ice and drowned while skating on the Havel River.

Heym began writing in his early youth. He developed rapidly from the extreme subjectivity of his first attempts at verse to the much-noted objective voice of his mature work, as represented by *Umbra Vitae* and the short stories of *Der Dieb*. Bridging these two phases are the dramas *Der Athener Ausfahrt* and *Atalanta oder die Angst!* These works display Heym's progress from a poet of private anguish and shifting moods to one who was sure of his attitude toward himself and the world around him, and just as sure of how he would portray these attitudes in his work. Heym's major works express a somber pessimism and fatalistic view of life which disparages human values and denies individuals control of their destinies.

Typical of Heym's mature phase are the "city" poems in *Umbra Vitae*, including "Die Stadt," "Der Gott der Stadt," and "Die Dämonen de Städte." These lyrics display his vision of the industrialized city as a hostile environment where man is merely part of a faceless mass in the grip of menacing forces. These forces are both concrete and abstract—they embody not only the process of moral and material decay in urban life, but also humanity's persecution by the biblical God, whom the atheist Heym depicts as a Satanic rather than a righteously vengeful deity. Together, these forces destroy modern culture, annihilating all aspects of order and stability. Some critics contend that Heym's grotesque visions form a plea to end materialistic society and return to a simple existence; others claim that for Heym there was no meaningful existence. Critics believe that some of Heym's works presaged the First World War, especially the catastrophic scenario of his most famous war poem, "Der Krieg."

In his posthumously published short story collection, *Der Dieb*, Heym uses the horrific and the bizarre to express his somber themes. Critical analysis of his short stories suggests that they are similar to his poetry in their representation of society's suppression of the individual. The short story "Der Irre" is representative of Heym's depiction of madness in his tales. It has been praised for sustaining a detached narrative voice which abandons the reader to the grotesqueries of the work, deprived of the comforting sense of an authorial presence.

Heym was often overlooked as a shaper of early twentieth-century Expressionism, and it was only long after his death that his status was reevaluated. According to his biographer Egbert Krispyn, "Heym's poetry now appears to be one of the most valuable manifestations of the Expressionist movement in any literary genre."

## PRINCIPAL WORKS

*Der Athener Ausfahrt* [first publication]   (drama)  1907
*Atalanta oder die Angst* [first publication]   (drama)  1911; published in journal *Die Aktion*
*Der ewige Tag*  (poetry)  1911
*Umbra Vitae*  (poetry)  1912
*Der Dieb*  (short stories)  1913
*Marathon*  (poetry)  1914

*Dictungen*   (poetry and short stories)   1922
*Gesammelte Gedichte*   (poetry)   1947
*Dictungen und Schriften.* 4 vols.   (poetry, short stories,
   dramas, and diary)   1960-65

*This work was not published in its entirety until 1962.

---

### WALTER H. SOKEL   (essay date 1959)

The world beckons as a vision of triumph to the youthful poet
Georg Heym, whose apocalyptic visions belong to the most
striking work of the Expressionist revolution. Heym rebelled
furiously against the compulsions and restrictions which family
and school imposed on him. One of his schoolmates committed
suicide, and Heym envied him the courage for a deed which
he himself continuously contemplated. Heym's fascinated
preoccupation with death, a conspicuous element in his work,
can be traced partially to his early wretchedness and isolation.
A skull decorated with vine leaves graced his desk as a constant
memento.

Heym's somber meditations on death provide the foil to his
yearning for glory, enjoyment, and triumph, his dream of a
wild exuberant life in years to come. This brooding introvert
is at the same time possessed by a fierce vitality, a hunger for
love, experience, physical and emotional fulfillment. He has
the reputation of being a wild student, an instigator of "orgies"
in outlawed fraternities, a leader among his classmates, and a
horror to his teachers. The impression he makes on the Berlin
Bohemians among whom he later moves is that of "life itself. . . . He was the boldest, sunniest, least self-conscious [of
us]: his vitality broke through all barriers of convention" [ac-
cording to Helmut Greulich]. It strikes his literary friends as
incongruous that this sports-lover and "nature boy" should be
the poet of the most macabre visions and miasmic scenes. The
strange combination of melancholy pessimism and exuberant
extroversion, of *Weltschmerz* and *Kraftnatur*, is strongly reminiscent of Storm and Stress; it suggests that similar forces of
repression caused similar reactions of anarchic individualism
in the late eighteenth and early twentieth centuries. In a diary
entry Heym analyzes the relationship between his melancholy
death-bound self and his restlessly ambitious life-bound self.

> The strangest thing is that no one has yet no-
> ticed that I am the most delicate . . . but I have
> carefully concealed it *because I have always
> been ashamed of it.*

This conflict between a surface brutality and an inner delicacy
which the surface brutality covers is symptomatic of Expressionist vitalism. (pp. 97-8)

> *Walter H. Sokel, "The Thorn of Socrates," in his*
> The Writer in Extremis: Expressionism in Twentieth-
> Century German Literature *(with permission of the
> publishers, Stanford University Press; copyright 1959
> by the Board of Trustees of the Leland Stanford Ju-
> nior University), Stanford University Press, 1959,
> pp. 83-118.*

### URSULA R. MAHLENDORF   (essay date 1961)

[Under] the influence of Nietzsche, Georg Heym wrote his
**"Versuch einer neuen Religion,"** an essay in which he rejected

Christianity as a religion for weaklings and advocated a new
religion, a mixture of hero and nature worship. . . . Yet despite
this rejection of Christianity we find in Heym's work a large
number of allusions to Biblical literature and to the Christian
tradition, as well as direct treatments of Biblical and Christian
themes. These allusions and thematic treatments show a profound concern with man's relationship to god, though it is
expressed negatively; this interest appears also in Heym's diaries which reveal a deeply religious temperament. (p. 180)

The use of a Biblical theme or allusion in Expressionist letters
can be seen from two aspects. The author connects the contemporary event with an ancient parallel occurrence or else
roots the subjective experience in an age-old expression of
emotion. In the attempt to overcome the incidental, subjective
and insignificant, and to envision the essential and the eternal,
"die Wurzeln der Dinge," the Judaic-Christian tradition was
but one, even though the most important, employed by the
Expressionist poet. Then, after the author has established the
link with tradition, he may reevaluate it from his private, modern standpoint. From the individually different reevaluations
of the Judaic-Christian tradition emerge basic differences in
regard to views of life.

Georg Heym's work shows both facets of the use of the Judaic-
Christian tradition. He gives depth and color to his contemporary settings or private visions primarily by allusion. He
recreates Biblical themes or reevaluates allusions and references to express his view of God, man, life, and death. Yet,
unlike many other Expressionists, Heym explores only the somber aspects of the Judaic-Christian tradition.

It is necessary first to outline briefly the extent of easily recognizable influence of the Bible and the Christian tradition on
Heym. Only eight of the approximately one hundred and fifty
published poems of Heym bear a title announcing a Biblical
or Christian theme. Even though Heym was brought up as a
Protestant, three of the titles suggest a Catholic background,
**"Fronleichnamsprozession," "Die Messe,"** and **"Savonarola."** . . . Two other poems refer to general Christian ritual
or custom—or its reversal, **"Das infernalische Abendmahl"**
and **"Allerseelen."** Two poems belong to the world of the New
Testament, **"Judas"** and **"Pilatus";** title and inspiration for
one, **"Simson"** (Samson), is taken from the Old Testament.
A theme from or a reference to the Judaic-Christian tradition
plays a major role in **"Das Fieberspital," "Der fliegende Hol-
länder," "Die Morgue," "Der Baum," "Der Garten," "Die
Nacht," "Die Irren," "Hymne," "Gewölke gleich,"** as also
in the tales **"Der fünfte Oktober," "Der Irre," "Jonathan,"
"Der Dieb,"** and in the drama **"Atalanta."** The Biblical quotations in Heym's work and diaries are almost all taken from
the New Testament. In many other poems can be found allusions to ecclesiastic tradition or references to Biblical literature.
(pp. 181-82)

A direct Biblical influence is most clearly seen in the descriptions of war and catastrophe. Heym found in Biblical literature,
especially in the books of the prophets, an abundance of somber
images well-suited to his imagination. The combination of classical or Biblical traditions and images from the modern city
makes Heym's poems of war and catastrophe powerful in impact. During and after the First World War, other Expressionists gave similar apocalyptic visions of war. A holy war, as in
the prophetic books, their war was to purify mankind and to
make possible a new and higher existence. Heym gives no such
indication that he considers the catastrophe he envisions as a
meaningful one; into the midst of a modern metropolis, with

church towers and factory chimneys, suddenly falls the hand of a cruel god. Ancient images of catastrophe awaken age-old fears.

Biblical place names and proper names give to Heym's poems a wealth of associations. Often a few images used in the description of a city suggest whole chapters from the Bible. . . . (pp. 183-84)

The names of Biblical figures are frequently used without any change in meaning. . . . [A crane in **"Ophelia"**] becomes a "Moloch," a god of a materialistic civilization. Twice the author identifies himself with New Testament characters. In **"Gewölke gleich"** . . . , he sees himself as Judas, betraying by a kiss a woman he no longer loves. . . . The poem treats a bacchantic procession through a wasteland of ruins and thorns, a chaotic and turbulent nature. The author includes himself in the group, participates in their violence, until he realizes their fear, impotence, and bestiality, and distances himself. . . . Through his identification with Christ he attains a sanity and objectivity that is reflected in a clarity and simplicity of expression contrasting sharply with the foregoing confusion of language and imagery. In Expressionist literature analogies between the fate of the artist and that of Christ frequently represent the artist as a saviour of mankind. . . . Heym identifies himself with a forsaken and helpless Christ, who regards with a compassionate but objective eye the madness of his fellow men. Heym's Christ is not a saviour. The distance from the historical Christ is provided by the two adverbs, "dereinst," and "nun" ["at some future time" and "at present"]. The modern Christ is not crucified, he is a prophet in the wilderness, poverty-stricken and forever without glory.

While allusions to names do not permit drastic alterations and only a Biblical reminiscence can be given, other references to the Bible, though recognizable, have undergone considerable changes. The city of death which Heym describes in **"Schwarze Visionen II"** calls to mind a Biblical source, the vision of the New Jerusalem in the Revelation of Saint John xxi, 11-25. Heym creates his own vision from the Biblical elements. . . . As in the Revelation of St. John, the city is of noble metal, but of silver instead of gold. Only the last and most precious of the jewels of the Biblical description is mentioned. In contrast to the Revelation, it is not a foundation stone but forms the gates of the city. While in the heavenly city shines neither sun nor moon, since it is lit by the glory of God, the heavenly bodies in Heym's city play an important role. They are mentioned so closely together that they seem to exist together. Time is suspended as in the heavenly city, but by different means. (pp. 184-85)

Almost all instances of allusion to the Bible or the ecclesiastical tradition discussed above show Heym's preference for their macabre aspects; but Heym uses these references without giving a value judgment. He may make changes in order to achieve a more dramatic expression, yet he is interested mainly in the evocative power of these references. He often combines allusions to the Judaic-Christian tradition with elements from Greek and Roman antiquity, inferring that the boundaries of civilizations and time are insignificant to the visionary poet.

Like other Expressionists, Heym reinterpreted and reevaluated the Judaic-Christian tradition. . . . By his transformation the poet not only shows his attitude to the tradition but also to the question of the relationship between man and God. It must be kept in mind that to alter this tradition Heym had to be intensely concerned with it. (pp. 186-87)

Heym gives a pejorative meaning to references and themes. Images referring to the clergy may be depreciated by the objects they are compared to. . . . By the comparison of a tonsure with a prison court yard Heym works out only negative aspects, isolation and barrenness, of monastic life. . . . Heym frequently uses such gradual distortions that terminate in complete devaluation. From the numerous interpretations that can be given to religious practices and symbols Heym frequently chooses a pejorative one. Asceticism he regards only from its austere side, as an enforced deprivation. . . . Heym associates religious symbols like the cross exclusively with death and with the color white. . . . Kurt Mautz in his essay on Heym's use of color metaphors has pointed out that white (or pale) is employed to suggest horror and fear of death and demonic powers. (p. 187)

Pejorative use of allusions to the Christian tradition tends to become devaluation. The tradition's complete reversal reveals most clearly Heym's position. In ever new transformations he explores all possible evil aspects of the Church, of Christ, and of the divine. One could call Heym's violent accusations a negative testimony to the power of his god. A description of church symbols in **"Fronleichnamsprozession,"** a poem that in its beginning portrays the splendor of the Church, reevaluates the symbols basically; not Christ but Mary, the human being, bears the stigmata. . . . Heym's accusation against the church concentrates on its ministers, their role as mediators of the divine and their function in society. A priest coming to the "Fieberspital" is seen as the emissary of a dreaded death. The priest gives the extreme unction impersonally and cruelly, not heeding the pain he causes the sick. . . . The priest's prayer is not solace but an insult. He remains indifferent to suffering, sure of his office and his God. . . . Small wonder that the sufferers rise up and slay him. Not only does the clergy fulfill the opposite of its function, it exploits the miserable and poor. (pp. 188-89)

In **"Savonarola"** Heym comes to the climax of his reinterpretation. Savonarola is an agent of hell celebrating a black mass. . . . [A] pun in the last line indicates not only that Savonarola begins the mass with the sign of the cross, but also that he becomes a cross for mankind; he tortures and sacrifices men. . . . The last, somewhat inaccurate image [in **"Savonarola"**] probably refers to a spider killing its victim. It is clear, though, that the priest by the performance of the ritual satisfies his lust for power and gains strength, becomes a giant, by sucking man's lifeblood.

Even more violent are Heym's dithyrambs against Christ as saviour and divinity. Christ may appear as a weakling who gloats in lascivious suffering and who mocks man. . . . Heym considers Christ's suffering on earth meaningless and even an insult to man because Christ ascends to God. In **"Pilatus,"** one of the most finely balanced and memorable poems, this and other accusations against Christ find their most valid expression. . . . (pp. 189-90)

The step to seeing man as a plaything of a cruel god is short. Two grotesque tales, **"Der Irre"** and **"Der Dieb,"** give a diabolic twist to the idea of insanity as divine possession. (p. 191)

Nowhere in his work except in these grotesque tales does Heym make man a tool and plaything of an evil god, an instrument that destroys and is destroyed. . . .

The process of the transformation of Biblical allusions and themes and the reevaluation of ecclesiastic references can perhaps best be summarized as follows: Heym came to regard God as an evil power. This view determines his reinterpretation of the role of Christ. The son of the demon can only increase man's suffering. The clergy function as emissaries of Satan. With such a view of religion Heym works out the pejorative aspects of allusions to the Judaic-Christian tradition. Where he found that this tradition supplied him with apocalyptic and evocative images he felt no need to alter it. Yet he does change perspective, for instance, in his poems on war and catastrophe. Heym's god of war is only that. He lacks Jehovah's other qualities. Heym's catastrophe occurs with no suggestion of a deserved punishment. (p. 192)

[In Heym's work,] not only the Christian God becomes an evil demon. By endowing his divinities with the attributes of different Greek deities, Heym suggests that there is a host of nefarious gods. . . . Out of Greek and Judaic-Christian elements Heym creates a hierarchy of demons, a myth of evil. K. L. Schneider has pointed out that by means of verbal metaphor and hyperbole Heym achieves a demonization of the world, but he does not point out that the world view standing behind this stylistic phenomenon is a basically demonic one.

Heym's myth of a host of demons surrounding man has no precedent in German letters. His reading of Baudelaire and Rimbaud probably acquainted him with Satanism. Heym shares with them the rejection of contemporary Christianity. Yet he neither pays tribute to the demonic for the sake of knowledge of the unknown, nor does he regard man as evil. He accuses the mysterious divine to whom he attempts to give shape. He sees these forces degrading and destroying man. His sympathy is always with man. Heym's view of the demonic as torturer of mankind is similar to Kafka's portrayal of an Old Testament god, the old commander in the "Strafkolonie." Unlike other Expressionists, Heym regards human suffering neither as ennobling man nor as purifying him for a higher existence. Death, which for other Expressionists is the step to this new life, is for Heym only a different existence with its own tortures and terrors. With violent expression, Heym cries out in anguish his accusation of the divine; with an almost insane fury he explores the different faces of his evil god. (pp. 192-94)

[Heym's] diaries prove that his religious questioning never ceased. As an entry on November 10, 1911, two months before Heym's death, shows, the god remained an evil mystery. . . . Two undated letters of 1910-11 state his wish to become acquainted with the mysteries of occult sects. The tone of the letters reveals the desperate urgency of his search. . . . Finally, according to Helmut Greulich, the day before his death, Heym wrote the poem "Die Messe," in its tone and in its use of ecclesiastic imagery strikingly at variance with his earlier treatment of such themes. The poet sees death not as before, as a voyage to lands of dread or uncertainty, but as repose. The ritual performed by monks is treated with reverence. In glad welcome the dead stretch out their hands to angels.

Perhaps the last entry in the diary and the poem "Die Messe" are an answer to Heym's questioning and crisis. It remains conjecture what his concept of a god would have been and how he would have treated it, had he lived. It seems quite certain to me though that Heym wanted his poetry interpreted as a rebellious quest into the darkness beyond the world. . . . (p. 194)

*Ursula R. Mahlendorf, "The Myth of Evil: The Reevaluation of the Judaic-Christian Tradition in the Work of Georg Heym," in* The Germanic Review *(reprinted by permission of Joseph P. Bauke), Vol. XXXVI, No. 3, October, 1961, pp. 180-94.*

## WERNER VORDTRIEDE (essay date 1963)

Georg Heym's **"Morgue,"** one discovers, has both theme and exaltation in common with the nearly fifty stanzas of Andreas Gryphius' "Gedanken," the thoughts "about the churchyard and the resting place of the dead." If Heym wants to shock a sophisticated reader into a sceptical view of his epoch, so Gryphius, describing at length the "fleshless skeletons, cranes without hair or ornament, faces without nose and lip" and "the yellowish-green feet" wants to shock the proud Christian into humility. The resulting stench in both poems is not that of Zola, but has rather a metaphysical origin. And Heym's is, with all the poet's professed defiance, his reminiscences of Rimbaud and the *poètes maudits,* still a Christian stench, which tries to educate our souls while offending our noses. And Gryphius certainly goes much farther even than Heym in this malodorous practice. Certain words, the classical allusions of one who flaunts his humanist education, which are almost forbidden in contemporary poetry, as are the reversed position of adjective and noun, the loud pathos and the direct confession, are still permissible for Heym. . . . (pp. 284-85)

Yet, certain new themes and new combinations of images have found an echo in what was to follow: the demonization of the great city, the drowned man who continues to move in a private universe, the deromanticized suicide. Bertold Brecht's famous poem about the floating Ophelia continues Heym's Ophelia poems, an echo of which we find in stanza fifteen of the **"Morgue."** (p. 285)

**"Umbra Vitae,"** not the description of a war-threatened city, but written before the First World War, reads like the text to some expressionist picture, as indeed expressionism, vague and simplifying as the term may be, was an art form in which poetry and pictorial art went hand in hand more closely than in many other artistic movements. Both forms of expressionism often seem direct translations of each other, the poem painting the world in vast images of a non-natural coloration and in a crowded and floating disequilibrium, and the picture telling a visionary story.

The first stanzas of **"Umbra Vitae"** put in all those oblique lines and sloping masses which give a picture by Franz Marc or Lyonel Feininger its crystalline transversals. The static right angles of observable reality have been abolished in favor of a tremendous movement of obliqueness. The people in the streets of the city are "standing forward" (stehen vorwärts), leaning in improbable and dangerous angles, oppressed by the impending ruination of the city. In the sky the comets have "fiery noses" (Feuernasen), irregular protuberances of light in all directions. They creep around towers whose shape no longer is straight like that of reliable bastions, but "craggy" (gezackt), lending their contours to the inexorable geometrical arrangement. All the roofs are covered with star gazers. The "tubes" (grosse Röhren), which they push into the sky are surely not erect and seen at a straight angle with the roofs which themselves are certainly gabled, adding the triangle to the apocalyptic crystal. And to undo the straightness of the walls of houses, magicians trying to move or exorcise the threatening stars grow "athwart in darkness" (im Dunkel schräg), long sloping bodies, out of attic windows. The large crowds of suicides go with a "stooped" posture (gebückt). With an appropriate palette one can follow the poet's every direction and paint an unmistakable expressionist picture.

When the last war was over no new expressionism arose, indeed could arise; pathos, rhetoric, the tremendous confession in sounding phrases seemed, fortunately, a thing of the immediate past which now demanded a sober, almost silent re-interpretation of the world. But a new interest in expressionist painting and literature became visible almost at once. . . . Yet, in the process, the term "expressionism" tends to become more and more diffuse. Should Brecht and Kafka, Walser and Else Lasker-Schüler all be seen as members of the same literary school? What have Däubler and Benn in common? One will have to look for family relations, genealogical trees, as it were. There, one line of relationship clearly emerges. One might call them the black line of writers, those whose visions evoke the anti-life, the poetic dangers, the unpoetic terrors, and whose ecstasies spring from despair: Büchner, Grabbe, Strindberg, Rimbaud, Benn, and the early Brecht. Georg Heym is in a line with these. His poems and his few short pieces of prose might serve as the very yardstick with which to measure this particular aspect of expressionism. (pp. 285-87)

> *Werner Vordtriede, "The Expressionism of Georg Heym: A Note and Two Translations," in* Wisconsin Studies in Contemporary Literature *(© 1963, Wisconsin Studies in Contemporary Literature), Vol. IV, No. 3, Autumn, 1963, pp. 284-97.*

## CLAIRE JUNG   (essay date 1965)

After the Impressionist poetry of resignation, whose most beautiful works were verses of a deeply melancholy nature by Hugo von Hofmannsthal or poems of weary renunciation such as can often be found in Rainer Maria Rilke, a new form of art attempted to bring about a revolution in style by activating all man's powers. Not only would a transformation be achieved in artistic form, Expressionism also intended to evoke a revolution in the general attitude to life. To German literature of the prewar period the poet Georg Heym seemed to be one of the white hopes of early Expressionism. (p. 39)

Although Georg Heym could often be youthfully gay and full of boisterous high spirits, nevertheless none of his works are free of the shadows cast by events that were to come. The soul of Heym the poet was filled with a consuming and constant unrest. His heart was with the suffering and the rejected, the poor of this world. In his poems he spoke of the mad, the blind and the deaf, the captive, the sick and the dead. He foresaw all the torments of war as well as the destruction of cities. His poems *War* or *The City of Torment* could have been written in our own time. And that's what still links his poems with us to this day. It's as if they spoke of our suffering, as if their author had experienced in one vast vision all the horrors of our days and their shadows cast a spell of sadness over his art, even where it speaks of love. The tone his powerful, picturesque language prefers is always the sombre, the dark colours, their rhythm filled with passionate drama. His dreams were linked to the time of the French Revolution, which he felt to be a turning-point in the history of mankind. This is how he expressed it in a letter: "I have been depressed for several days— a kind of apathy had settled over me. Now I know my sickness: nothing to stir the soul, no great activity. If only I had been born during the French Revolution. Nowadays there is nothing you can get enthusiastic about, nothing you can make your life's work."

Heym's poetic models were the French poets Verlaine, Rimbaud, Baudelaire and Flammarion.

The last of his poems written the day before his death bears the title *Mass* and is filled with a premonition of death; the voice of the Beyond can already be heard in it. Already, in his earlier poems, Georg Heym had experienced and suffered death by drowning: in the *Death of the Lovers* and in *Ophelia* the vision of the eternal grave in the watery depths is a painful enticement towards that shadowy forest he conceived to lie at the bottom of the sea. (pp. 40-1)

> *Claire Jung, "Memories of Georg Heym and His Friends," in* The Era of German Expressionism, *edited by Paul Raabe, translated by J.M. Ritchie (translation copyright © 1974 Calder & Boyars Limited; reprinted by permission of The Overlook Press, Lewis Hollow Road, Woodstock, NY 12498; in Canada by John Calder (Publishers) Ltd.; originally published as* Expressionismus: Aufzeichnungen und Erinnerungen der Zeitgenossen, *Walter Verlag, 1965), The Overlook Press, 1974, Calder & Boyars, 1974, pp. 37-42.*

## EGBERT KRISPYN   (essay date 1968)

[*Krispyn's study is the most comprehensive biocritical work in English on Heym.*]

[Georg Heym's dramatic attempts] reveal the indirect subjectivity typical of the transitory phase between egocentric soul-searching and mature writing. (p. 56)

[The plays "**The Sicily Campaign**" ("**Der Feldzug nach Sizilien**") and "**Atalanta**" ("**Atalanta oder die Angst**")] reveal that Heym, in his second phase as a writer, had the same attitude toward historical and literary source material as he displayed toward nature scenes in [his early love poems to Hedy Weissenfels]. These dramas, too, reflect his own preoccupations and personal problems in the treatment of the subject matter. In "**The Sicily Campaign**" Heym's overpowering feelings of homelessness and helplessness have, somewhat inappropriately, been attached to the figure of Alcibiades. At the same time, this character represents Heym's adolescent ideal of the beautiful, brave, reckless, and irresistible young man. In the tense relationship between Alcibiades and the old, diseased, superstitious, and reactionary Nikias, the intergeneration conflict of the Wilhelmian era as experienced by Heym finds thinly disguised expression. Gylippos, of "**The Sicily Campaign**," in his ugliness embodies Heym's fixed idea about his own appearance and in his ruthlessness, the quality of mind on which the youthful author occasionally prided himself. . . . (pp. 56-7)

Gylippos' counterpart in "**Atalanta**" is Sigismondo Baffi. He too was condemned by birth to the ugliness which made his heart evil and barren until Atalanta "cured" him temporarily with her kisses. In the same period Heym wrote in his diary, with reference to his own supposed physical and moral shortcomings, that he knew love would "cure" him. . . . His private despair over the insoluble disparity between his supposed ugliness and his thirst for beauty was superimposed on the action of "**The Sicily Campaign**." Some of Gylippos' utterances correspond almost literally to the frequent complaints in Heym's diaries about this obsessive notion. . . . [Heym's] completed plays are on the borderline of his mature literary work. From the beginning they contained elements which anticipated the characteristics of the best writing of Heym's last years. (pp. 57-8)

These elements of maturity amount primarily to the representation of a specific world view. In the dramas the reflection of private moods and feelings began to be supplanted by the postulation of a philosophy of life. This development is, of course, concurrent with Heym's systematization of his incidental grievances and sorrows. . . .

His pessimistic fatalism determined his poetic universe. This is very directly revealed in **"The Sicily Campaign,"** in which fate plays the decisive role. By negating all the calculations of the Greeks who failed to consider it, fate "gruesomely proved its majesty." . . .

Man's helpless subjugation to a tyrannical power beyond his ken or control is strikingly demonstrated in the very prominent death motif of Heym's mature work. Walter Sokel points to the connection between the personal experiences from which Heym's fatalistic outlook was derived and his literary obsession with death: "Heym's fascinated preoccupation with death, a conspicuous element in his work, can be traced partially to his early wretchedness and isolation." In both **"The Sicily Campaign"** and **"Atalanta"** death not only forms the ever present background to the action, but is also invoked in its most desolate aspects by the personages. (p. 58)

Heym's fatalistic world view has also left its mark upon the dramatis personae themselves, whose characterizations exemplify their abject subservience to the arbitrary, unknowable force which rules the universe. Interesting in this context is a letter from a publisher to whom Heym had submitted **"The Sicily Campaign."** This document furthermore testifies to the keen eye of the publisher's reader, who made an entirely accurate assumption about the genesis of the piece: "Your play gave us the impression that a project which goes back to a very early date had been taken up again by you and brought to a conclusion, but that the weaknesses of the first plan could not be overcome. With the sole exception of the passage of Nikias' death nothing in the piece affects us forcefully and directly; the action is always ponderously political ("es ist immer eine Haupt- und Staatsaktion") and the problem of Gylippos cannot disguise this. But what is most fatal for the play is, we think, that nothing has been made out of Alcibiades. He is in word and action such a weak figure that the deviation from history therefore seems to be particularly unmotivated." . . . (p. 61)

The weakness for which this report criticizes the figure of Alcibiades is, of course, the very aspect of his personality which reflects Heym's views on mankind. Alcibiades' weakness symbolizes the utter passivity with which humanity submits to the fatal powers. This fatalism also appears clearly in the case of Nikias, who, like a parody on Wallenstein, is in all his actions guided by the stars. His death, which the publisher's reader singled out for praise, actually shows a close affinity with Alcibiades' character as a symbolic expression of Heym's fatalism. (pp. 61-2)

The other major figure in **"The Sicily Campaign,"** Gylippos, at first sight seems to contradict the conception of mankind embodied in Alcibiades and Nikias. Gylippos in the course of the action seems to control his own destiny and the destinies of the others. The final scene makes it clear, however, that he has been blindly driven onward by the demonic force of his jealous hate-love for Alcibiades. When he finally has the latter in his power, he reluctantly kills him, because he has devoted his entire life to this purpose. But at the same time that he achieves his end, his own existence becomes meaningless, and he sits down, caressing the face of his victim, to wait for his own death. Thus, in the end, all the humans are defeated by fate.

In many respects, **"Atalanta"** is the radical opposite of **"The Sicily Campaign."** The latter has a very extensive cast, which includes masses of soldiers and citizens; it is divided into four acts placed respectively in Athens, Sicily, Sparta, and Asia,

and covers an unspecified, but considerable length of time. The one-act play **"Atalanta,"** which is less than one-quarter as long as **"The Sicily Campaign,"** has only three characters, is set in one room, and covers less than one hour in its action. This tendency toward general condensation is a vast step forward compared with the prolixity of **"The Sicily Campaign"** and shows Heym's greater awareness of the nature of his talent. (p. 62)

Since Heym's plays to some extent project into his creative maturity, they do open up certain literary historical perspectives. As a dramatist, Heym stood on the borderline of two periods. His choice of subject matter reveals a strong preference for classical and Renaissance themes which lend themselves to the portrayal of a unique individual. . . .

[Heym], as a survey of his completed dramas indicates, having chosen his protagonists from history's store of great and exceptional individuals, treated them in a very unhistorical manner. He did not bring out their uniqueness, but depicted them as weak-willed victims and tools of fate—that is to say, representatives of general, amorphous humanity as he saw it. This discrepancy between his subject matter and his approach was probably the main reason why Heym's dramatic attempts, with but two exceptions, remained unfinished. (p. 65)

[Heym's **"The Sicily Campaign"** and **"Atalanta"**] are qualitatively and quantitatively quite insignificant compared to his prolific creation of poems and short stories.

These works are entirely dominated by the fatalistic view of mankind which Georg Heym abstracted from his lifelong, unavailing struggle against loneliness and isolation. His mature work is entirely devoted to the expression of the view that humanity is in the relentless grip of fatal forces bent on terror and annihilation. As in the dramas, so in his poetry and prose, the theme of death is very prominent among the symbolizations and manifestations of man's dismal lot.

In the poems three main approaches to the theme of death can be distinguished. First, the phenomenon of death itself may be referred to in any manner, varying from the simple mention of the word "death" to such extensive allegorizations of a classical-mythological nature as those found in the poem **"The Land of the Dead"** (**"Die Heimat der Toten"**). (pp. 71-2)

Second, the state of death may be dealt with either in speculations about its nature or in repeated visions of the realm of the dead [as in **"The Morgue"** (**"Die Morgue"**)]. (p. 72)

The works dealing with the realm of death can take the shape of turbulent erotic visions of the underworld of antiquity, as in the poem **"Styx."** More commonly, however, the land of the dead is described in terms similar to those used for the world of the living. (p. 74)

Heym's fascination with death and decay as signs of man's "mute misery" indicates affinity with the French symbolists. This is confirmed not only by certain diary entries in which he praises them . . . , but also by the evidence of their influence on his work. This is clearest in **"Ophelia"** which is an adaptation and expansion of the first section of Rimbaud's "Ophélie." But the way in which he changed his model indicates the narrow limits of his dependence on the Frenchman. Heym consistently stressed his concept of death as the exemplary state of passivity in which the human being is the defenseless prey of forces bent on his destruction. (p. 78)

Unlike the French symbolists' transfigurative animation of nature, Heym's visions of nature tend toward the grotesque, as indicated by their similarity to the prints of Alfred Kubin, in which plants, trees, shrubs, implements, and buildings receive a sinister life. Yet very few of Heym's poetic visions could unreservedly be classed as grotesque, not only because of the complete absence of humor, but also because he alters the concept of the grotesque, which typically dissolves and disintegrates every vestige of order in the universe. (p. 80)

Like his poem **"Ophelia,"** Heym's [**"The Suburb" ("Die Vorstadt")**] in its approach to the city theme shows his affinity with the French symbolists. Here too, however, important differences reveal themselves between his attitude and that of the French poets. Baudelaire was fascinated in a positive sense by the decaying, evil, disgusting aspects of metropolitan life. It was to him the absolute antithesis to nature which he detested as "a great tepid and abundant force which penetrates everywhere." Heym's attitude as expressed in **"The Suburb"** is the radical opposite of this. But the poem itself shows many similarities of form and mode of expression with the works of the symbolists. (pp. 84-5)

Heym dealt with the modern metropolis in a more typical, independent manner in his poem **"The God of the City" ("Der Gott der Stadt").** (p. 85)

[In this poem the] use of allegory enables Heym to employ the most graphic terms in referring to the demonic forces which terrorize the modern industrial metropolis. The first line of **"The God of the City"** indicates the demon's oppressiveness in a simple but highly effective image. (pp. 86-7)

In **"The God of the City"** the reference to the teeming millions serves Heym not only to reduce humanity to an anonymous, amorphous mass, but also to stress that mankind universally owes worship and homage to the god of the city. After the traditional Christian and pagan allusions, the religious aspect of the relations between the people and Baal is expressed in an image typical of the modern industrial city. The factory chimneys, like the church steeples, are directed towards him and glorify him with the "incense" of their smoke. (p. 88)

When the city as the collective manifestation of human existence is subjected to the terror of the supernatural force allegorized by God or demons, it exemplifies the fate of mankind. With the wars and rumors of wars in the years before 1914, the depiction of the city destroyed by military force, as in **"The War" ("Der Krieg"),** would seem an obvious variant of this motif. . . . Yet Heym used the war motif very sparingly. This must be due to the fact that human combat and his poetic purpose are basically irreconcilable. He wanted to express the notion that all of mankind is the helpless victim of the metaphysical forces of fate. The losers of a battle, however, are in the first instance the victims of other humans, and these, the winners, must have displayed an activity and self-assertion quite incompatible with the passivity and apathy of Heym's figures.

Heym could not overcome the discrepancy between the war motif and his creative attitude by invoking established mythological personifications of war. He did, in fact, only very seldom resort to traditional allegories of any kind. Their familiarity would weaken the impact of his visions and deprive them of their essential quality of uniqueness. (pp. 88-9)

The consequences of the war motif are largely responsible for the difference in tone between Heym's mature work and the very early *Marathon* cycle. . . . (pp. 89-90)

[Although] Heym's prose is on the whole rather limited in the range of its subject matter, and on Heym's own evidence represents only a passing phase in his development as an author, the stories in [*The Thief (Der Dieb)*] are not without literary merit. They are, moreover, in form and content highly indicative of Heym's world view. In both respects, the work entitled **"The Fifth of October" ("Der fünfte Oktober"),** which opened the original collection, is the most important of the seven stories concerned. (p. 106)

This story is based on the historical events leading to the march of the Parisian masses on the royal palace at Versailles, which took place on October 5, 1789, and which *The Cambridge Modern History* describes as follows:

> On the morning of October 5 a crowd, in the first instance chiefly of women, although afterwards supported by men, assembled in the Place de Grève and began an assault on the Hôtel de Ville. Feebly resisted by the National Guards on duty, they forced their way in, seized a quantity of arms and were about to hang an Abbé whom they chanced to find there, when a certain Stanislas Maillard, who had taken part in the attack on the Bastille, raised the cry "To Versailles." The women followed him, and on the march were joined by crowds of male rioters.

Beside the historical source, **"The Fifth of October"** also reflects the influence of two authors Heym greatly admired. There are some similarities with Grabbe's play *Napoleon or The Hundred Days (Napoleon oder die hundert Tage),* in which the crowds are as antagonistic to bakers as those in **"The Fifth of October."** In both works allegations are made that the famine has been brought about intentionally by those in power. The Parisian market-women are designated as "Damen der Halle" in the play as well as in the story. The episode of the baker in **"The Fifth of October,"** which replaces the historic incident with the cleric in the Hôtel de Ville, is further reminiscent of a scene in Grabbe's play, in which a tailor is murdered by ruffians from the faubourg St. Antoine. It lacks a "happy ending," but otherwise the circumstances are comparable. Concrete evidence of the connection between the two works lies in the fact that the coal-carriers who wanted to kill the baker also hailed from St. Antoine.

But this episode from **"The Fifth of October"** shows a still closer resemblance to the scene from Büchner's play *Danton's Death (Dantons Tod)* in which the mob threatens to hang a young aristocrat. In view of Heym's great admiration for Büchner there is little doubt that his baker was a direct descendant of this figure. However, the similarity of **"The Fifth of October"** with *Danton's Death* goes beyond such details and extends to the underlying fatalistic outlook of the respective authors. (pp. 113-14)

Deviating from his historical source, Heym used Maillard to demonstrate the individual's subjection to the law of historical necessity. Actually, this Bastille veteran took the initiative in the march on the royal residence, and placed himself at the head of the marchers. According to Heym, however, Maillard was a prophet of gloom and a defeatist. When the demonstrators got under way he vainly tried to halt their march by arguments and action, but he and his handful of helpers were swept away by the people. Maillard is shown to be utterly incapable of influencing or guiding the course of events. His impotence in the face of the people's decision to march on Versailles implies that in the storming of the Bastille he had been a mere tool of fate, a puppet manipulated by the unknown forces that rule the universe. If Maillard in the story **"The Fifth of October"** is thus a clear and straightforward embodiment of Heym's basic outlook on the world, the role of the people in this work is much more complicated. Almost up to the last page the misery and hopelessness of life in the Parisian proletarian quarters are depicted with ever increasing penetration. But when Captain Maillard shatters the people's last hope of a better future, an almost forcible turn takes place in the action of the story. Instead of showing definite resignation, the people allow themselves to be stung into action by an anonymous shout.

The fact that from this turning point on the people are attributed with the power and the will to revolt against their fate may seem at first sight to be inconsistent with Heym's conception of humanity as a creature driven passively by demonic forces. On closer consideration it appears that the discrepancy is limited to the surface, because the turn in the development of the action affects the function of the collective protagonist. Initially the Parisians by their misery and helplessness demonstrate the absolute subjection of humanity to a gruesome fate. In the last sections of the story they offer the same demonstration, for they themselves represent the forces of fate in their relations to Maillard and his people.

The apparent optimism of the closing images is, moreover, ironically ambiguous. The people are compared with Prometheus who brought fire from the gods, but was afterwards chained to a rock where an eagle devoured his liver. As the people marched on Versailles, they "knew" the years of suffering were over. History proved them wrong. In the years of revolution and terror which followed, their lot became even worse, and with the advent of Napoleon—for whom Heym had limitless admiration—the revolution was virtually abrogated. But the story does not merely indirectly show the fatuity of the hopes which moved the Parisian masses at the outset of the French Revolution. Like all individuals who appear in Heym's work, they represent the whole of humanity. The glaring unhistoricity of the concluding scene therefore unmasks the illusiveness of all idealistic dreams of a better world to come. Thus, **"The Fifth of October"** does indeed in every respect appear to be most typical of the pessimistic, fatalistic conception of human existence to which Heym subscribed.

Of the other works in Heym's collection of prose, the most interesting is the title story **"The Thief"** (**"Der Dieb"**) which concludes the book. Like **"The Fifth of October,"** **"The Thief"** is based on an actual occurrence, although in this case it was a contemporary rather than a historic event. The theft in August, 1911, of the "Mona Lisa" from the Parisian Louvre provided Heym with the basic idea and the setting of the story. But of the actual incident, only the broadest outline went into the making of Heym's work. (pp. 114-16)

**"The Thief"** is not only much longer than the other works in the collection, but also much more complicated in structure. The development and prehistory of the mania which incites the protagonist to the theft of the "Mona Lisa" are, after a brief introductory passage, depicted in the form of an extensive flashback. When the thief has stolen the painting, the poet quite literally passes over an interval of three years by means of a dash. The original religious mania which caused the protagonist to see in the portrait the embodiment of evil has in the meantime given way to a passionate love for the painting. But Mona Lisa seems to mock the thief on account of his

feelings, and thus provokes him to the act of revenge through which the final catastrophe is brought about.

The thematic transition from the religious to the erotic sphere is a consistent and psychological development of the action. His hatred of the feminine sex, which in the first part causes the thief to see in the portrait of La Gioconda a symbol of evil, is only a religiously disguised aspect of his ambivalent attitude toward the opposite sex. It is very much to the point here to refer to Freud's theories, according to which religion belongs to those phenomena which have their origin in the Oedipus complex. Thereby religion is closely related to such difficulties in the libidinal economy as manifest themselves in the fetishistic and ambivalent attitude of the thief to the "Mona Lisa." Heym obviously knew something about psychoanalytic theory. It is significant, for instance, that in **"The Thief"** typical symbols like snakes and umbrellas occur. Moreover, the thief protects himself against the regard of La Gioconda through phallic gestures or by carrying a silver phallus. His initial religiously disguised hatred of the painting thus in many ways reveals itself as a perverted love, which in the second part of the story appears in a more direct form.

But whether it appears as love or hate, the maniac's attitude to the painting is the outcome of his condition, in which his human reason and judgment have been superseded by a demonic force. How completely he is enslaved and possessed by this power, which he believes is divine, becomes clear in the description of his final acceptance of his mission: "He lay before God in the dust, he humiliated himself, he tore his entire soul apart and let God stream in like smoke, like a fluid. . . . And on the tips of his hands which he swung in the dark a weak blue light gleamed like a St. Elmo's fire, as if God's power entered into him like an electric current to fill him with ecstasy." The dehumanizing effect of the thief's submission to a superior force is accentuated in his animal-like behavior and appearance when he is about to steal the painting: "He let himself down on his hands, and so he crawled on all fours like an animal through the anteroom. . . ."

In **"The Lunatic"** Heym makes much more extensive use of this animalization motif. An irresistible force takes possession of the human being and determines his actions so completely that he at last seems to lose his human shape and begins to embody this demonic force. . . . (pp. 118-19)

A brief survey of the other stories collected in *The Thief* indicates that they, too, in different ways express Heym's pessimistic fatalism concerning mankind's position in the universe. In the story **"Jonathan"** the poet's conception of human fate is illustrated by a fatally injured ship's engineer. The fact that this man is the passive toy of higher powers is made clear through his life story, the course of which has completely eluded his own will or control. Moreover, sickness and death are depicted in a way, and with the aid of a terminology, which accentuates human passivity, helplessness, and subjugation to fate. (p. 120)

In **"The Ship"** (**"Das Schiff"**) the inexorable, inescapable fate of the crew of a small sailing ship appears to them in the form of a plague. Throughout the story the author stresses the mental and physical paralysis which overcomes the crew when confronted with its fate. The theme of the absolute subjection of humanity by demonic forces is expressed with particular clearness in the following sentences: "Immediately they all realized in the same moment that they were lost. They were in the merciless hands of a terrible invisible foe. . . ."

"**An Afternoon**" ("**Ein Nachmittag**") distinguishes itself from these works in that this "contribution to the biography of a small boy" in no way deals with extreme characters or situations. . . . In this story Heym shows that mankind's passive sufferance of fate does not occur only in such extraordinary cases as he represents in his other works. Even in the everyday realm of childish hopes and disappointments and against the banal background of a bourgeois seaside resort, the human existence is shown to be guided by forces which are completely beyond the influence of the creature.

In "**The Dissection**" ("**Die Sektion**") the passivity of the main figure is of course already determined by the given situation, namely that a corpse is being dissected. The dehumanization which is derived from this is further stressed in the description of the doctors' activities: "Over their hands the blood ran, and they dipped them ever deeper into the cold corpse and took its contents out, like white cooks who gut a goose." The dead man "patiently let himself be pulled to and fro, be jerked to and fro by his hair." Fritz Martini has expressed the opinion that the occurrence of the motif of love in this story amounts to a departure from Heym's customary absolute pessimism because it introduces a force capable of conquering death and decay. This interpretation is not entirely convincing. Rather than adding a new dimension to the story, the motif of love seems to be a consistent development of the theme which in the first half of the story is deployed in its physical aspects. The first part of this very short work describes how after death the human body seems to come to life once again—on a sub-human level—through the process of decay: "Beautiful red and blue colors" cause the corpse to resemble "a shimmering calyx, a mysterious plant from Indian jungles."

In the second half of the story the apparent blossoming of the corpse extends to the brain. The distortion of the putrifying lips suggests smiling and kissing. This description offers a means of attributing to the macabre revitalizing effect of decay the spiritual expression demanded in this context through the vehicle of a dream of love. "**The Dissection**" thus appears to be entirely consistent with Heym's characteristic use of death and decay to demonstrate his fatalistic world view. (pp. 120-21)

[In] Heym's collection *The Thief,* it becomes clear that his prose does not offer much basis of comparison with his contemporaries. His stories are a highly personal literary sublimation of the sociological conditions common to all representatives of the expressionist generation. The peculiar composition of Heym's personality and the particular nature of his creative talent account for the unique qualities of these works which distinguish them from other prose *oeuvres* springing from the same substratum. (pp. 121-22)

The quintessence of Georg Heym's work may be summarized . . . as a denial of the anthropocentric conception of life. Heym created a universe in which man is not the supreme force capable of dominating and exploiting the world for his own materialistic purposes through his rational powers. In his works, a deanimated humanity, reduced to utter insignificance in the cosmic order, is the passive victim of demonized natural and metaphysical phenomena. This hopeless pessimism determines the tone of practically all his writings. There are, to be sure, occasional images of great beauty and serenity in his work. . . . Such instances of relief from the gloom and horror of Heym's customary poetic visions are relatively rare, and they do no more than hint at the possibility of some ideal in which mankind could free its existence from the misery and horror of fate's

absolute domination. Yet these restrainedly positive passages are a very essential part of his work and establish his relationship with the expressionist movement. However, in the overall effect of his *oeuvre* these proto-idealistic elements tend to be completely overshadowed by the much more prominent and characteristic atmosphere of dismal hopelessness. (pp. 123-24)

*Egbert Krispyn, in his* Georg Heym: A Reluctant Rebel *(copyright © 1968 by the Board of Commissioners of State Institutions of Florida), University of Florida Press, 1968, 135 p.*

**ALLAN BLUNDEN**   (essay date 1975)

[An instructive comparison] is that between Heym and Poe, surely most eminent of 'horror story' writers. Poe's narrative manner is quite different, for he is generally talking *with* his readers, dictating that his perspective shall also be theirs. Poe's narrative voice registers the shock and horror of a sensitive mind confronted by the ghastly; he anticipates our own reactions—fashions them, rather—and when we read Poe we are consoled, ultimately, by a common consent as to what is and what is not acceptable among civilized men. Not so with Heym. *Der Irre* is more horrible than Poe's tales because Heym himself has deserted us, because Heym himself no longer believes in the civilization which the madman offends. . . . [In his diary], Heym goes on to deny that an artist has any 'responsibility'. . . . Nowhere in Heym's work is this bleak conviction more drastically exemplified than in *Der Irre.*

We see the absence of such 'responsibility' in Heym's persistent desire to speak 'the hitherto unspeakable', to bring before his readers new or ignored tracts of experience. Heym wrote *Der Irre* in the very year that the term 'schizophrenia' was coined, and what we have here is not a study or a description of the schizophrenic mind, but an immediate evocation of what it is like to be like that. . . . [It] is the artist's privilege, sometimes his duty, to show things from a different point of view, free from stereotyped opinions and accepted standards. A reading of *Der Irre* disposes us neither to condemn nor to condone. The errant individual is not educated towards integration into society, as in the Bildungsroman tradition, nor is his rebellion glorified as a heroic gesture of defiance, as it is, magnificently, in Kesey's novel [*One Flew Over the Cuckoo's Nest*]. In Heym's story there are no heroes. We see a man, and we see the world through the man's eyes. Where Woyzeck [in Georg Buchner's drama *Woyzeck*] saw in every man an abyss, Heym sees in every man an animal, a pathetic caricature of the ideals cherished by humanistic Western civilization. In that memorable scene where the madman *recognizes* the insanity which overcomes him, there occurs the only rent in the veil of his illusion, the moment when he looks into the abyss and feels the very same giddiness which Woyzeck also speaks of; and what he finds there is 'das Tier' ['the beast'] the creature of destruction that is his own true nature.

As for the world—well, it is recognizably our own, and the mind that perceives it is not wholly alien. We know that if the world is an ugly, depressing, and hostile place in the madman's eyes, then that is because the world is like that. We understand that madness is not necessarily an aberration, a 'wrong' way of seeing the world, but a way of seeing which the world itself engenders. On the surface, *Der Irre* describes a conflict between the individual and society; in fact the conflict is an instrument of exorcism in the hands of society, a witchhunt that affirms the innocence of the hunters by proclaiming the guilt of the victim. There is, after all, something gladiatorial about the shape of the story, from the man's release into the world, to his public execution by the authorities; there is even, in the scene where he visits his apartment, a description of him battering down the door which is couched in exactly the language one would use of a bull. If the violence in the story shocks us, if the final act of 'justice' leaves a nasty taste, if the dying man's bliss somehow offends us, it is because Heym has shown us our world naked and demythologized. Social organization is not the opposite of individual brutality, but a precarious refuge from it. If, therefore, we don't feel quite so safe at the end of the story, if we don't like what we have seen, that is not Heym's fault: on the contrary, it is his merit. (pp. 117-19)

Allan Blunden, "Notes on Georg Heym's Novelle 'Der irre'," in German Life & Letters, n.s. Vol. XXVIII, No. 2, January, 1975, pp. 107-19.

## FRANCIS MICHAEL SHARP (essay date 1978)

The diaries of Georg Heym, the German poet of the demonic city, regularly erupt into tirades against the banality of his age, a setting which he felt was too tepid for the extremes of experience he craved. Only a time of wars and revolutions, he asserted, could satisfy his experiential hunger. In an entry on May 28, 1911, he describes his brain as a prisoner battering itself against its cell door: "I need convulsions, storms, torrents." . . . His litany of complaints returns constantly to the main themes of boredom and lack of stimulation. "If I could only be continually inspired, then what I would accomplish," he writes on the 16th of October 1911. . . . There is undoubtedly an element of rhetorical excess in these outbursts, an element which fed on the undercurrent of vitalistic thought endemic to expressionism as a whole. Yet they are too persistent and vehement to be fully accounted for by intellectual influence. Heym's experience of Berlin adds a further dimension to this account. Already in 1903, Georg Simmel had remarked on the "blasé state" ("Blasiertheit") of the city dweller, the attitude of apparent indifference which he had been forced to acquire towards the sights and sounds that threatened him with a sensory overload. Heym's vigorous reactions to a tepid age must at least partially be seen as an attempt to counter this natural mechanism of adaptation, to resist the indifference and satiety of experience in one of the world's fastest growing cities. To the apathy which he felt threatening his senses, Heym responded with a rebellious cry for convulsive experiences. . . . (pp. 61-2)

A year after his death in 1912, a selection of Heym's short prose appeared under the title *Der Dieb (The Thief)*. A motto from Baudelaire precedes the title story. An early reviewer found Heym's prose to be as much in the debt of Baudelaire, Rimbaud and Poe as his poetry. . . . Another reviewer sought to distinguish Heym from conventional literary "satanists" who aimed chiefly to make such material as Heym dealt with palatable for an aristocratic and bourgeois reading public. Heym's prose, on the other hand, showed scant trace of such consideration for squeamish readers: "Here however the reader is shocked by the spectacle of a character which is compelled by an inner drive toward atrocities with the inevitability of fate." . . . Heym would have been flattered with the reviewer's reaction to his prose, especially with his choice of "erschüttern" (shock) to describe its effect. Fifty years later, the author of an article commemorating his prose turned to the same word to characterize the effect on the reader of Heym's negative

heroes: "The apparent eccentricity of his general negative heroes—who, if not clinically mad are in most cases subject to delusions—it shocks us." . . . (pp. 62-3)

Madmen populate the prose and poetry of expressionism in abundance. Various suggestions have been made about the factors behind the repeated appearance of the figure as well as its representational function. For Heym's prose however, madness was more than a theme and the madman more than a carrier of implied meaning. The figure of the madman was a means to an end, a formal vehicle by which the shock of his prose could be conveyed. Nowhere does this become clearer than in **"Der Irre" ("The Madman")**, one of the stories from *Der Dieb* in which Heym's refusal to make his material 'palatable' shows up in the distinct, yet detached presence of a narrator. The ultimate shock of **"Der Irre"** lies in the narrator's silent presence, his refusal to comment and psychologize.

**"Der Irre"** depicts the escapades of an asylum inmate just released and on his way home. His one goal is to now take revenge on his wife whom he holds responsible for his incarceration. Although he never finds her, he commits several wanton murders along his homeward journey, all reported in a journalistically detached style. As he leaves the gates of the asylum behind him, he seems to announce in his thoughts the havoc which he intends to wreak on the unsuspecting world: "So, now the world should experience something" ("So, und nun sollte die Welt etwas erleben" . . .). Yet the source and goal of these thoughts are ambiguous. They belong in the first place to the protagonist, but they can also be read as a direct statement of the narrator to the reader. As the thoughts of the madman, they have their point of reference in the fictional world about to experience his rampages. Read as the narrator's thoughts, they aim at a reader whose appetite for stimulation Heym takes to be the equivalent of his own, particularly the reader who in 1910 was already jaded by journalistic writing that reaped profit from sensationalism.

The madman himself is repeatedly subject to the most vivid of experiences, hallucinatory states in which external stimuli can no longer be distinguished from internal ones. The reader however is kept well aware of the difference between the "real" fictional world of the narrator and the protagonist's hallucinatory flights beyond it. In most cases the narrator mediates between these two worlds with a variation of a telltale "as if." The protagonist's first hallucination begins: "It seemed to him as if he were walking across a broad square" ("Es war ihm, als wenn er über einen weiten Platz ginge" . . .). Yet at other points, this most obvious sign of mediation disappears. "Now he was himself the animal" ("Jetzt war er selber das Tier" . . .), the narrator remarks as the madman begins to track down an old woman whom he imagines may laugh at him. Metaphor here becomes reality as Kurt Mautz points out, but clearly for the madman alone. The story's linear structure—the madman moves along a narrative path from one gate, door or wall to another—as well as its consistent perspective and tense do not allow the reader to forget the presence of a sane narrator. He has privileged access to the spectacle of the madman's mind, displays it for the reader, and never loses control of his presentation. Even in Heym's various poems dealing with the insane, the cycle entitled **"Die Irren" ("The Madmen")**, for example, the reader experiences madmen hallucinating rather than unmediated hallucinations like those characteristic of Trakl's prose poems.

The hallucinating protagonist of **"Der Irre"** shocks in quite a different way than Gregor Samsa [in Franz Kafka's *The Meta-*

*morphosis*] whose hallucination, as the only fictional reality, convinces his family as well as himself. The presence of Heym's narrator with a foot anchored in a sane fictional reality, doubles the alienated distance between the reader and the protagonist. The latter is a specimen impaled and exhibited by the narrator, a species apart from him and thus doubly removed from the reader; that is, once by his madness and again by the narrator's icy objectivity. Heym's detached method of depicting his madman conforms to Döblin's advice to avoid what he called a "basic defect of today's writer of prose," that is, "his psychological style." Döblin recommends the cold eye of the psychiatrist over the sympathetic eye of the psychologist anxious to explain and understand: "One should learn from psychiatry, the only science which concerns itself with man as a psychic whole. It long ago recognized the naiveté of psychology and confines itself to making note of processes and movements with a shake of the head and a shrug of the shoulders for anything else, the 'Why' and the 'How'." Without the framework of a narrative psychology between Heym's protagonist and the reader, there is no buffer to cushion the shock of the atrocities which the madman commits. The break in the dialogue between reason and madness, exemplified by the relationship between narrator and protagonist, is thereby doubled between protagonist and reader.

Lacking even a name, the madman is so totally in a no-man's land that his alienation becomes tangible experience to a readership for whom alienation had become commonplace. As he begins his ostensible journey back to a home he had left several years earlier, the garden gate of the asylum closes behind him. He moves unhindered through open country until he comes to a garden wall on the outskirts of the city where he had formerly lived. At precisely the point where he first comes into contact with city life—an electric tram and a street crowded with indifferent people—he experiences an "unbounded solitude" ("grenzenlose Verlassenheit") and a powerful feeling of homesickness for the asylum. He cannot return however and moves mindlessly on until the next barrier confronts him—the locked door of the house that had once been his home. Although he forcibly enters the premises, his wife is gone and the rooms are vacant. He no longer is at home in the rural asylum or in the house that had been his home in the city. He belongs neither among the insane nor among the sane.

Two doors remain to be passed through however until his murderous rampage is finally halted by a bullet in the back of the head. The first is a revolving door which leads into a wide hall filled with people and tables of merchandise. The protagonist never realizes that he has entered a modern department store and although his initial assumption that he has entered a church may be a delusion on his part, it is a barely concealed comment on Heym's part about the materialistic orientation of his age. The protagonist moves through this spectacle until he reaches the enclosed door of an elevator that then carries him to the final site of his execution. Although he has surmounted all the barriers that confront him along his path, he has never reached a goal because there simply is no goal or home for this outcast. In the last throes of death, his heart opens in an "immeasurable bliss." . . . (pp. 64-6)

The sane world finally answers the madman with a violence equal to his own, yet even here the narrator's cold eye does not perceive him as a victim. His madness is, in the best and worst sense of positivistic psychiatry, one of the many "clinical cases of true insanity" in modern literature. He is not "explained" in either psychological or sociological terms. Al-

though the materialism of the sane outside the asylum walls is implicitly criticized and the asylum's staff is remembered as violent and stupid by the madman himself, his own violence initially brought him behind the asylum walls. To say with Thomas Anz that the madman's deeds are a "reaction and protest against the inhuman treatment and coercion which he has experienced" is to overlook the wife-beating that went on before the story began. An interpretation of madness which blames society or social conditions overtaxes the slim evidence in the text. The narrator is almost as restrained with sociological conjecture as he is with psychological explanation. He reports without comment the protagonist's psychopathological shift of moods from murderous fury to pity to indifference. These shifts are entirely unpredictable and stem from the reason of madness which Heym's narrator makes no attempt to reach. Finally, Heym's madman possesses no trace of that Nietzschean inversion of madness into a higher form of rationality that sees through the hypocrisies of the sane. His actions arouse no sympathy either in the fictional world to which he belongs or in the reader. The psychical and physical shock which he sets up in the fictional world is translated into an aesthetic shock for the reader by the detached narrator.

Over twenty years ago, Karl Ludwig Schneider suggested that Heym's "cynical metaphors" paradoxically forced the reader to actively defend the distorted values of his imagery. Although there is little that a reader can defend in **"Der Irre,"** its shock is only superficially alienating as Schneider realized. Only as shock could it infringe upon and remain indelibly etched in the hypertrophied consciousness of its readership. It repels in order to bind. (pp. 66-7)

> *Francis Michael Sharp, "Georg Heym and the Aesthetics of Trauma," in* Review of National Literatures *(copyright © 1978 by St. John's University), Vol. 9, 1978, pp. 59-69.*

### HERBERT LEHNERT (essay date 1979)

There are some beautiful poems in Heym's work, but more often, he was less interested in overcoming nihilism and alienation or in withdrawing to artifacts as an occasion for transformation, than in depicting macabre senselessness. Death is not so much a part of life or a symbol of the permanence of the work of art, as a force which invalidates untrustworthy reality. Some of Heym's poems consist of long rambling sequences of death-images; in others, such as [the draft form of **"Die Stadt"**], he imposed a strict form to the composition. Heym used the sonnet form much less playfully than Rilke, who tended to dissolve it, and in **"Die Stadt,"** Heym subjects his succession of images to a formal strictness. There is no subordinate clause in the whole poem (the "die" in line 13 is demonstrative; it summarizes the four subjects in line 12). The rhymes lack variety, their sounds are only *ei* and *a*. This consistency of form, followed to the point of monotony, is the heritage of Stefan George, a heritage which Heym denies in vain. Six times the conjunction "und" stresses the concatenation of images, echoing Hofmannsthal's poem *Ballade des äußeren Lebens,* which also presents a succession of images flowing into the unanswered question of the purpose of life. Hofmannsthal's poem ends with the evocation of the poetic quality of a word, Heym's with the cloud image of liberating destruction. While Hofmannsthal's *Ballade* is written in the terza-rima-form which corresponds to the succession of incoherent images, Heym's sonnet-form counteracts the successive flow by imposing finality. But the finality does not have a redeeming quality. The poem does not humanize the world, does not unlock it, does not make it more bearable, as was Hofmannsthal's intention. (pp. 29-30)

The vision of fire and destruction at the end carries an apocalyptic allusion which remains only a threat since there is neither God nor a heavenly Jerusalem and not even a revolution promising a better world. The beauty which the poem nevertheless evokes depends on the liberalizing effect of the detachment, as empty as it is. The poem depicts dissociation, or alienation, but the poet, by imposing form on it, transposes alienation into its positive aspect so that it becomes an act of freedom. Heym does not present a religious, aesthetic or political utopia; he does not present a morally better way, not even by implication. The joy of the poem is in the freedom of its images, in the triumph of form which spellbinds, while it speaks of destruction. Its message, if there is one, is that doom will end a senseless world.

Heym's images of death and destruction have a provocative intention. The freedom they offer for enjoyment is not supposed to be integrated in the bourgeois world. George's and Rilke's poems are not intended to either, really, but they are conceived by Heym as compromises because they violate the traditional sense of beauty less than he finds necessary. If a specific difference to bourgeois alienation is to be identified as the root of the Expressionist experience, it is this provocation which constitutes a more violent detachment from society. (p. 30)

In September 1911, after months of severe tension in European foreign relations associated with the second Marocco-crisis, Heym wrote a poem called "Gebet," a veritable prayer for war, battle, death, fire, rain, winter, starvation, and acres full of corpses, because, he felt, the barrenness, the sickness of the times ought to be overcome. Heym's famous poem "Der Krieg," which begins "Aufgestanden ist er, welcher lange schlief . . ." was also written in September of 1911. It was never fully completed by Heym, probably abandoned in favor of another one by the same title also written in September 1911, which is almost unknown. The better known poem is not, as good-natured critics liked to tell us, a warning of the horrors of war, nor does it miraculously prophesy World War I. Everybody discussed war in the summer of 1911. The poem-draft is an imaginative experience of an end to the oily and barren peace. To be sure it does not depict war heroically. The last stanza of the second war poem, the one that Heym obviously considered more valid, betrays the attraction that death, dying, destruction and apocalyptic downfall hold for Heym. . . . (p. 31)

If we cannot in good conscience consider Heym a prophet, if his alienation leads to a rebellion which is politically suspect, in what sense do we read his poetry? Since Heym, in many ways, is a prototype of the Expressionist rebellion, in what way do we enjoy his work, teach it, pass it on? Value judgments stemming from Expressionism are continued today, and sometimes are considered progressive, especially if they are directed against bourgeois literature. Yes, Goethe and Thomas Mann were bourgeois, but that does not make them mere advocates of exploitation, and reification. Bourgeois literature is inseparable from its origins in the 18th century. It is literature as an exercise of freedom in the imagination. Alienation, as in Heym's *Stadt*-Sonnet, is freedom with a negative accent. (p. 33)

*Herbert Lehnert, "Alienation and Rebellion in the German Bourgeoisie: Georg Heym," in* Expressionism Reconsidered: Relationships and Affinities, *Vol. 1, edited by Gertrud Bauer Pickar and Karl Eugene Webb (© 1979 Wilhelm Fink Verlag), Fink, 1979, pp. 25-34.*

---

## ADDITIONAL BIBLIOGRAPHY

Blunden, Allan. "Beside the Seaside with Georg Heym and Dylan Thomas." *German Life and Letters* n.s. XXIX, No. 1 (October 1975): 4-14.*

Compares Heym's "Ein Nachmittag" and Dylan Thomas's "One Warm Saturday."

Brown, Russell E. "Time of Day in Early Expressionist Poetry." *Publications of the Modern Language Association* 84, No. 1 (January 1969): 20-8.*

Discusses the time motif in the poetry of Heym, Georg Trakl, and Ernst Stadler. Brown points out Heym's use of night references are fitting to his nightmarish and grotesque poetry, and that he also "uses the images of night to proclaim the end of a long 'enlightened' European day."

Mahlendorf, Ursula R. "Georg Heym's Development As a Dramatist and Poet." *Journal of English and German Philology* 63 (1964): 58-71.

Insightful comparison between Heym's *Atalanta oder die Angst*, which brought him to the attention of other Expressionists, and his earlier version, *Die Hochzeit des Bartolomeo*.

Viereck, Peter. "On Georg Heym's 'War'." *Michigan Quarterly Review* XVIII, No. 3 (Summer 1979): 403-04.

Short introduction to a translation of "Der Krieg." Viereck views this war poem as a prophecy of the mass-killing of World War II.

# Zinaida (Nikolayevna) Hippius (Merezhkovsky)

## 1869-1945

(Born Zinaida Gippius; also wrote under the pseudonyms of Anton Krayny, Anton Kirsha, Comrade Hermann, Roman Arensky, and Lev Pushchin) Russian poet, critic, essayist, dramatist, short story writer, novelist, and biographer.

A major poet and critic of her era, Hippius was one of the most controversial figures of prerevolutionary Russia. Some critics have called her Russia's greatest woman poet, while others have condemned the poet and her work as "diabolical, feline and entirely without tenderness." Although Hippius is often misrepresented as a decadent, her poetic quest for belief in something beyond the self reveals that she was actually one of the first Russian Symbolists. Simon Karlinsky has written that Hippius was to modern Russian poetry what Fyodor Dostoevsky was to the modern Russian novel.

Hippius was born in St. Petersburg to a family of Swedish descent. Although her formal education was curtailed by weak health, she felt that she belonged to the last generation of Russians to be educated in the great Russian cultural tradition. Her marriage to the poet Dmitry Merezhkovsky in 1889 thrust her into the forefront of intellectual life in St. Petersburg. The Merezhkovskys' circle included all of the prominent writers and thinkers of *fin de siècle* Russia. Andrey Bely, Fyodor Sologub, and many highly placed officials of the Russian Orthodox Church participated enthusiastically in the salons and Religious-Philosophical Meetings organized by the pair during 1902 and 1903. Hippius's influence within this group was widely felt, for by this time she was writing and publishing poetry that her contemporaries recognized as innovative and brilliant. Unfortunately, her delight in shocking people with at times provocative attire, a supercilious manner, and blunt speech offended many, and earned her the reputation of a decadent and a "white she-devil." Throughout her lifetime her flamboyant personality competed with her poetry for attention, and often influenced critical opinion of her work.

One aspect of the Merezhkovskys' interest in religion was their involvement with "The Cause," a group formed by Hippius, Merezhkovsky, and Dmitry Filosofov for the purpose of promoting Neo-Christianity. This was a philosophy based on the concept of spiritual renewal through the sanctification of the flesh as well as the traditional exaltation of the spirit. Hippius viewed the androgyne as the ideal being, a concept she incorporated into her religious philosophy. The theme of sexual ambiguity appeared in such short stories as "Ty-ty" and "Perlamutrova trost." The Merezhkovskys' "Religion of the Third Testament," as it was called, gave impetus to the religious renaissance among the Russian intelligentsia of the early twentieth century. During this period, Hippius also founded a journal called *Novy put'* *(The New Road)* in which many gifted Russian writers made their literary debut.

After the October Revolution of 1917, the Merezhkovskys fled from Russia to Paris, where they lived the rest of their lives. Hippius wrote many articles denouncing the Bolsheviks, urging other Russians to join her in opposing their regime, which she considered to be more brutal than that of the czars. She published her essays in the expatriate Russian journals that

proliferated in Paris at that time. Hippius also founded a literary-philosophical society for Russian emigres called Zelyonaya lampa (The Green Lamp) that exerted a significant influence on emigre Russian literature. At these meetings she instructed young Russian writers in the techniques of poetry, and urged them to master their native language and literature, fearing that otherwise they would lack the background in Russian culture necessary to preserve the Russian literary tradition.

Hippius's writings reveal an intense religious fervor; Hippius believed, as did Dostoevsky, that the purpose of art is the affirmation of life, and the purpose of life is the search for God. Her poetry, fiction, and drama provide the record of a personal search for belief. Valery Bryusov believed that Hippius's poetry "formulates, as it were, in concise and expressive words the whole of the contemporary soul's experience." Hippius's principal collections of poetry include two volumes of *Sobranniye stikhov, Stikhi,* and *Siyaniya.* The poems in these collections, written in her epigrammatic style, provide a concise statement of her ideas on God, the transcendent effects of love and justice, and the hatefulness of mundane existence. They also reveal her great technical expertise. In them she explored metric innovations that opened up new possibilities for the development of Russian poetry. Her virtuosic technical ability has led more than one scholar to proclaim many of her poems untranslatable.

Hippius's short stories and novels, notably *Lunnye muravye* and *Chortova Kukla*, are most often described by critics as Dostoevskian in their psychological explorations of the human psyche. Dostoevsky's work moved her profoundly, and he assuredly influenced her approach to literature. Unlike Dostoevsky, however, Hippius often could not refrain from turning her protagonists into mere spokesmen for various abstract concepts. Critics consider this the main flaw of her fiction. The literary memoir *Zhivye litsa* is also one of her most important works. Because it contains candid, first-hand portraits of the many renowned writers with whom she was acquainted, it preserves a part of Russian literary history that might otherwise have been lost. As a critic, Hippius was fervently subjective. Many critics have condemned her critical tone as being "too spitefully cold," while others have praised her wit and insight. Hippius's style of criticism, like her poetry, was unique in her day, and inspired much imitation.

Because of the influence of their Religious-Philosophical Meetings, Hippius and Merezhkovsky are credited with restoring vitality to an otherwise "stagnating and reactionary" period in Russian intellectual life. Although Merezhkovsky is commonly regarded as the author of Neo-Christian doctrine, many scholars maintain that Hippius was the more original thinker of the pair, and that she was often the source of ideas commonly attributed to her husband. Many critics believe that the initial inspiration for this fusion of paganism and traditional Christianity was hers, and that the fiction resulting from her allegiance to "The Cause" anticipated the sophisticated complexity of Russian Symbolism. As her work is gradually rescued from obscurity, contemporary critics are becoming increasingly aware of the extent of her contribution to modern Russian literature.

## PRINCIPAL WORKS

*Novye lyudi*   (short stories)   1896
*Sobranie stikohov: 1889-1903*   (poetry)   1904
*Makov tsvet* [with Dmitry Merezhdovsky and Dmitry
      Filosofov]   (drama)   1905
*Aly mech*   (short stories)   1906
*Le Tsar et la Révolution* [with Dmitry Merezhkovsky and
      Dmitry Filosofov]   (essays)   1907
*Literaturny dnevnik: 1889-1907* [as Anton Krayny]
      (criticism)   1908
*Makov tsvet*   (drama)   1908
*Sobranie stikhov: Kniga vtoraya*   (poetry)   1910
*Chortova kukla*   (novel)   1911
*Lunnye muravyi*   (short stories)   1912
*Roman-Tsarevich*   (novel)   1913
*Zelyonoye kol'tso*   (drama)   1916
      [*The Green Ring*, 1920]
*Poslednie stikhi: 1914-1918*   (poetry)   1918
*Stikhi: Knevnik, 1911-1922*   (poetry)   1922
*Zhivye litsa*. 2 vols.   (essays)   1925
*Siyaniya*   (poetry)   1938
*Dmitry Merezhkovsky*   (biography)   1951
*Posledny Krug: I novyi Dant v adu*   (poetry   1968;
      published in journal *Vozrozhdenie*
*Between Paris and St. Petersburg*   (diaries)   1975

## ANDREY BELY   (essay date 1906)

[*Bely was a frequent guest at the Merezhkovskys' many salons, and a key figure in the mystical Russian Symbolist movement. He expresses his great admiration for Hippius in the following review of* Aly mech.]

Hippius is equipped with everything that forms the basis and strength of refined culture. In this lies her abiding significance. By confronting us with the most complex antinomies in life, she stirs up our consciousness, [revealing beauty and harmony in artistic form and word.] . . . This harmony is based on the regularity of dissonances in her verse. Hippius' method points to her intellect, taste, and refinement. Her dissonant notes and lack of unity enthrall us—like everything else which is graceful and delicate—in the same way as Scriabin's music. . . . If there is any integrity in the poetry of Z. N. Hippius, it is her intellect, taste, and refinement. Everything else is based on contradictions. . . . But we can see in the mosaics of these heterogeneous elements . . . outlines of wondrous beauty and words which are profound in their religious clairvoyance.

> *Andrey Bely, in his excerpt in "Beginnings" (originally published in "Z. N. Hippius: 'Aly mech. Rasskazy'," in Zolotoe runo, No. 9, 1906), in* Zinaida Hippius: An Intellectual Profile *by Temira Pachmuss (copyright © 1971 by Southern Illinois University Press; reprinted by permission of Southern Illinois University Press), Southern Illinois University Press, 1971, p. 21.*

## LEON TROTSKY   (essay date 1924)

[*In sharp contrast to Bely, Trotsky attacks Hippius, offering an appraisal of the politically noncompliant artist which is typical of Bolshevik literary criticism during the regime's early years.*]

[In *Poslednie stikhi: 1914-1918*, Zinaida Hippius wrote], "And swiftly you will be driven to the old stable with a club, O people, disrespectful of holy things." . . . This, of course, is not poetry, but nevertheless, what natural journalism! What an inimitable slice of life is this effort of the decadent mystic poetess to wield a club (in iambics!). When Hippius threatens the people with her whips "for eternity", she is, of course, exaggerating, if she wants it to be understood that her curses will shatter hearts in the course of the ages. But through this exaggeration, fully excusable under the circumstances, one can see her nature quite clearly. Only yesterday she was a Petrograd lady, languid, decorated with talents, liberal, modern. Suddenly today, this lady, so full of her own subtleties, sees the black outrageous ingratitude on the part of the mob "in nailed boots", and, offended in her holy of holies, transforms her impotent rage into a shrill womanish squeak (in iambics). And indeed, if her squeak will not shatter hearts, it will arouse interest. A hundred years hence the historian of the Russian Revolution will perhaps point out how a nailed boot stepped on the lyrical little toe of a Petrograd lady, who immediately showed the real property-owning witch under her decadent-mystic-erotic Christian covering. Because of the real witch in Zinaida Hippius, her poems tower above the others and are more perfect, though they are more "neutral" and therefore dead. (pp. 29-30)

> *Leon Trotsky, "Pre-Revolutionary Art" (1924), in his* Literature and Revolution, *translated by Rose Strunsky (reprinted by permission of The University of Michigan Press, originally published as* Literatura i revoliutsiia, *Gosudarstvenoye izdatelstva, 1924),*

*Allen & Unwin, 1925 (and reprinted by Russell & Russell, 1957), pp. 19-55.\**

## VLADISLAW KHODASEVICH  (essay date 1925)

*Living Faces* [*Zhivye litsa*] is beautifully written from the literary point of view. . . . In her descriptions Hippius does not attempt to be impartial and non-biased. It appears that she herself wishes to be a writer of memoirs, rather than a judge. She is endowed with a power of keen observation; she portrays everything from her own viewpoint, not concealing her sympathies and antipathies, not veiling her genuine interest in her evaluations of people and events. . . . Besides the portrayals of the people in this book, Hippius' own, authentic, and very "living" face appears before the reader of its own accord. . . . *Living Faces* is a work which, even at this early stage, has the compelling power of a novel.

> *Vladislav Khodasevich, in his excerpt in "The Parisian Period" (originally published in "Z. N. Hippius, 'Zhivye litsa'," in* Soviemennye zapiski, *Vol. XXV, 1925), in* Zinaida Hippius: An Intellectual Profile *by Temira Pachmuss (copyright © 1971 by Southern Illinois University Press; reprinted by permission of Southern Illinois University Press), Southern Illinois University Press, 1971, p. 235.*

## D. S. MIRSKY  (essay date 1926)

> [*A widely respected scholar of Russian literature, Mirsky offers a concise overview of Hippius's career to-date.*]

The most remarkable of [the] early metaphysical symbolists is Zinaída Híppius. . . . Like Konevskóy and Dobrolyúbov, she avoids rhetoric and prettiness. She considers her matter more important than her manner, and she works at her form only to make it more flexible and adequate to the expression of her ideas. She is a Slavophil also, inasmuch as she proceeds not from any French example, but from the Russian traditions—from Baratýnsky, Tyútchev, and Dostoyévsky. The wife of D. S. Merezhkóvsky, she is a more original and significant writer than her somewhat overrated husband. Her activity was almost as many-sided as his; she wrote short stories and longer novels, plays, critical and political articles—and poetry. The most salient feature in all her writings is intellectual power and wit, things rare in a woman. In fact there is very little that is feminine in Mme Híppius, except a tendency to be oversubtle and a certain willfulness—the capriciousness of a brilliant and spoiled coquette. This last quality gives a peculiarly piquant flavor to her work, which is, on the whole, intense and serious. Like Dostoyévsky, she "feels ideas" as living entities, and all her literary life is a life "among ideas." Her imaginative prose is voluminous—but inferior in quality to her verse. It consists of several volumes of short stories, two longer novels, and one or two plays. All these are with a "purpose"—to give expression to some idea or to some subtle psychological observation. The ideas are the real characters in her stories, but she does not possess Dostoyévsky's power of giving them an individual and complete existence. Her characters are abstractions. Her most ambitious works, the two novels [*The Devil's Doll (Chortova Kukla)* and *Román-Tsarévich*] . . . , are weak offshoots of a great trunk—Dostoyévsky's *Possessed;* they are mystical studies in political psychology. A fair example of her manner may be had in her play *The Green Ring* . . . , which is available in English.

Her poetry is much more important. Some of it is also abstract and merely intellectual. But from the very beginning she made her verse a wonderfully refined and well-tempered instrument for the expression of her thought. She went on refining it and making it more obedient to every twist and turn of her subtle musings. Like Dostoyévsky's people, she oscillates between the two poles of spirituality and earthliness—between burning faith and apathetic skepticism—and it cannot be denied that her skeptical and nihilistic moods found more memorable expression than her moments of faith. She has an intensely acute feeling of the "stickiness," of the slime and ooze, of everyday life, and she feels her most intimate self in thrall to it. . . . [Her] most characteristic poem in this order of ideas [is] *Psyche.* In *Crime and Punishment,* Svidrigáylov wonders if eternity is not but a "Russian bath-house with cobwebs in every corner." Mme Hippius took up the idea, and perhaps her best poems are variations of this theme. She has created for them a sort of quaint mythology, of filthy, "sticky," and quite morbidly attractive little demons.

In 1905 Zinaída Híppius, like her husband, became an ardent Revolutionary, and after that time she wrote much political verse, which is certainly the best of its kind—unrhetorical, unexpected, fresh, and often biting. She excels in sarcasm: a splendid example is *Petrográd,* a satire on the renaming of St. Petersburg. In 1917, like Merezhkóvsky, she took a violently anti-Bolshevík attitude. Her later political verse is often as good as the earlier, but in her later prose writings she does not show up very attractively. Her *Petersburg Diary,* describing life in 1918-19, is inspired by spiteful hatred rather than by noble indignation. However, her prose must not be judged by such examples. She is a brilliant literary critic, the master of a wonderfully flexible, expressive, and unconventional style (her critiques appeared over the signature of Antón Kráyny—Anton Extremist). Her judgment is swift and sure, and her sarcasm had a glorious time when she dealt with the swollen reputations of the early years of the century. Her criticism is frankly subjective, almost capricious, and is more valuable for its manner than its matter. (pp. 439-41)

> *D. S. Mirsky, "The Symbolists," in his* Contemporary Russian Literature: 1881-1925 *(copyright 1926 by Alfred A. Knopf, Inc., reprinted by permission of the publisher), Knopf, 1926, G. Routledge & Sons, 1926 (and reprinted in his* A History of Russian Literature Comprising: "A History of Russian Literature" and "Contemporary Russian Literature," *edited by Francis J. Whitfield, Knopf, 1973, pp. 430-84).\**

## OLEG A. MASLENIKOV  (essay date 1960)

> [*Maslenikov explores Hippius's poetry for images conveying the theme of nothingness and naturalistic meaninglessness.*]

On the literary Olympus of Russian modernism one of the most important places indisputably belongs to Zinaida Nikolaevna Hippius-Merežkovskaja. . . . As befits a genuine Modernist poet, Hippius in her verses seeks to break away from the canons of established traditions—to embrace the extremes in her striving to "transvaluate all values." Her attitude is typical for a Russian writer of the 1890's-1900's, and in this respect Hippius stands close to such "coryphees" of Symbolism as Brjusov, Ivanov, and Belyj.

Hippius, in her technique, which reflects an implied adherence to a dualistic, anti-positivist world view, may be placed with

Blok, Belyj, Ivanov, and their teacher Vladimir Solov'ev (as well as with Bal'mont, Sologub, and the early Brjusov) among the Symbolists. She usually selects her poetical images and figures from the world of sensate and emotional experiences, and so presents them as to imply that some mysterious bond exists between the world of external reality and that of another, invisible, vague and mysterious immanency.

Her attitude toward all phenomena of the physical world resembles that of a superstitious savage. Chance, as an abstract causation, almost does not exist for her. On the contrary, every phenomenon, every physical aspect of what we commonly regard as ''reality,'' holds for her a hidden significance that derives from another existence. And in her dualistic view, Hippius is a genuine symbolist.

In her thematics, Hippius stands apart from most of her fellow poets, and may be regarded as an outstanding representative of the ''decadent'' component of Russian Symbolism.

Her poetry abounds in themes that strongly differentiate it from that of, say, Andrej Belyj. The distinction is seen in her partiality for such elements as the demonic, evil, and the morbid. It is seen also in her repeated reference to her own isolation, impotence, insignificance, and in her awareness of paralyzing inertia and dispassion, and in her penchant for lightless, sullen hues. It is to the province of the thematic element, therefore, that Hippius's greatest original contribution to Russian poetry belongs.

The poetry of Hippius, especially [**St. Petersburg**] . . . , presents an eerie picture of her poetic world.

It is a world of damp, shadowy whispers that melt into silence; it is a realm of heavy, bitter odors that evaporate into the nocturnal abyss; it is a domain of chill, bleak joylessness that blends with inescapable pain; it is a Manichean world in which the visage of the Evil One looms larger and more significant than does the image of the Creator, or the Savior. Despite the number of poems in which the religious motif is dominant, the reader is not impressed by any real depth of Christian feelings in Zinaida Hippius, whereas when she records that ''Someone greedy, dark-visaged'' visits her at night . . . one has no doubts that for her (as for Vladimir Solov'ev) the Devil is a reality and no mere figment of the imagination. This demonic element, reflected in some of her finest verses, lends them a peculiar intensity and pathos. (pp. 299-300)

In her poetry one feels a renunciation of life, of any desire for light, joy, love, excitement. In other words, much of her verse reflects the truly modernist rejection of Ivan Karamazov in his offer to return to his Creator his ''ticket of admission'' to life. In my present paper I shall attempt to show how this rejection of life is reflected in the poetry of Hippius in the form of what we may refer to as [the] Phantom of Nothingness.

Perhaps the most important single motif that recurs in the early poetry of Hippius is that of privativism. It is symbolized by what I have called the Spectre of Nothingness, which seems to haunt her everywhere. Her verses are filled with negative constructions and references to voids that seem to engulf her very existence. (p. 301)

The first manifestation of the Void that encompasses Hippius is a realization of her own isolation. She finds herself alone, with no deity and no companions. She has no one to turn to for solace or aid. Her attitude toward her Creator is typical of the *fin de siécle* intellectual. She feels both that God has re-

jected her . . . and that despite her yearning to pray, she is aware of a frustrating inability to do so. . . .

Lacking in spiritual satisfaction, she feels, as befits a genuine Decadent, that life is meaningless, all the more so since she cannot accept the companionship of human beings. She can find no reflection of the divine spirit in the people who surround her. The human race seems pitiful and colorless and completely alien to her . . . She therefore can make no attempt to adapt herself to their environment. . . . Finding thus that she has no desire to associate with people, she confesses that she is of a different breed . . . and finds isolation from the mob, now in her ivory tower high above the rest of the world . . . , now in a monastery cell among the silent, black-robed monks, its quiet broken only by the measured dripping of waxen tears from the glowing candles.

She realizes that isolation is sinful and diabolic, yet finds its temptation irresistible. . . . Finally she seeks solitude in the motionless woods by the still waters of an abandoned pond.

Hope, however, is short-lived, for the poet is suddenly struck by the certainty that the mob will invade her privacy even here. . . . And now Hippius is almost willing, Ophelia-like, to obey the tempting voice which she hears whispering to her that escape lies at the bottom of the pond. . . . (pp. 302-03)

The other phantoms that comprise her all-embracing spectre seem to emerge out of the theme of solitude. As we have already seen, solitude goes hand in hand with *silence,* which to Hippius, a Symbolist, possesses some mysterious and evil link with the other world. It is the stillness of a pond that urges the poet to seek escape from people in its depths. This stillness, moreover, is not unlike the quiet of the slough that teems with black leeches. . . . But the real element of the stillness is Night. Hippius listens to the silence as one listens for the inaudible footsteps of an enemy moving stealthily in the dark. . . . The same silence of the night is broken eerily by the inaudible movement of falling rain. . . . (p. 303)

On occasion, Hippius finds the black silence broken by someone's mysterious voice (undoubtedly that of the Devil) . . . ; or by the symbolic, Poesque thumping of the heart and by the ticking of the clock as though to convey the poet's belief that a bond exists between the world of earthly sounds and another world. . . . Even the halting, stuttering beat of the very *dol'nik,* which occurs . . . in the second and fourth lines and breaks the regularity of the expected amphibrach pattern of the first and third lines, seems to suggest a supernatural connection with something vague, mysterious, and—evil.

Silence and solitude are the lot of a true Decadent poet. In the poetry of Hippius, silence and solitude are no mere incidental chord that resounds occasionally, by chance. Silence and solitude are a *leitmotif,* almost a major theme, throughout her early verse.

In one of her poems, **"Ograda"** . . . , Hippius combines several of her privative motifs in one symbolic reference. The poet, after a long and torturous journey, during which he has significantly abandoned his two companions, finds himself standing alone outside the gates of his walled-off paradise. As he waits, no one will come to let him inside. His shouts, entreaties, and demands seem to rouse no one who might open the gate to him, and his expectations and hopes, like those of many heroes of stories by Leonid Andreev, are repeatedly met only with a devastating *silence, darkness,* and *quiet.* . . . Thus we find ourselves confronted with yet another of Hippius's phantoms—that of *darkness*. Darkness in her poetry is an over-powering debilitating element: it is the natural habitat of the Devil. The nocturnal gloom, broken only occasionally by the faint rays of a waning moon, symbolizes the immobility and the paralysis of a complete cessation of life. . . . (pp. 303-04)

Absence of light suggests the absence of life and absence of motion. From the nocturnal darkness thus arises another of Hippius's phantoms; it is the spectre of *immobility,* as seen when the poet stands chained to the earth above an abyss, yearning to soar into the beyond and yet unable to move. . . . It again looms in the stagnant slough with leeches clinging motionless to the roots of equally still rushes. Even the shadows of the night stand still and motionless as death itself. . . . (pp. 304-05)

When dealing with abstract negative concepts, Hippius frequently resorts to the simile in order to give them greater substance—to tie them more closely to the world of everyday experience. Here, too, the privative aspect of her poetry becomes all-important. In depicting her soul, for example, Hippius speaks of its immobility, as though it were encased in the visous, heavy slime of a stagnant pond. . . . Life itself seems as stifling as the unyielding coils of a serpent. . . . The symbol of her sightless sky presses down like a sepulchral slab. . . . I am not implying that all her images are devoid of motion; nevertheless, when Hippius does portray movement, it is quiet, measured, and almost imperceptible. It is almost like the breathing silence that the poet detects in the dark. . . . In her **"Flowers of Night"** she depicts the same deliberate movement, when the poisonous drops are recorded falling rhythmically onto the carpet. . . .

Time and again Hippius characterizes her phantom of immobility by the epithet "heavy." It is as though the very air had suddenly become weighted down with lead. . . . The weight of the blanket of night is an apt symbol for the absence of motion, or for the deathlike stillness of the heavy casket which she portrays. . . . Even the very landscape reflects the static quiescence seen in the glimpses of the pond and slough. . . . (p. 305)

All nature in its quiescence assumes a strangely lifeless aspect. Small wonder, then, that the still-life tableaux that Hippius occasionally depicts should seem even less alive. **"The Clock Has Stopped"** affords one such example. . . . The table with its unremoved dishes, its tablecloth drooping "shroudlike" to the floor, and the lamp standing dark, as well as the motionless clock, suggest the immobility of death. (pp. 305-06)

The silence and the immobility of the images taken from Hippius's verses undeniably remind one of the Dragon of Death that haunted Tolstoj (to borrow Professor Lavrin's term) and the death theme that recurs time and again in the writings of the Modernists. The fact of its appearance in the poetry of Hippius is therefore not surprising. She is in good company.

Yet, where some writers are terrified by the thought of death, and others (like Sologub) see in it a hopeful escape from life, Hippius, who implies that life is onerous at best, does not anticipate in death any change either for the better or for the worse. Her poem **"In the Beyond"** . . . in the spirit of fatalistic resignation, expresses complete apathy toward death. Charon is portrayed ferrying the poet across the Styx. The stony sky above is immobile, and the heavy boat glides through the leaden waters of the dark silence into nothingness. And the poet, as though echoing a previous fear that no fear exists in his souls . . . admits that the only emotion he feels in the face of one

of the most significant events in man's conscious life is that of empty boredom. . . . And yet to call Hippius's poetry unemotional would be to do her a great injustice. One needs to recall only her incantations addressed to Petersburg. They are charged with emotional undercurrents. Apathy—lack of emotion—nevertheless, plays an important role in her decadent verse.

Although a rebellious strain does occur in her poetry, it is usually less convincing than is the motif of resignation. This indifference to everything, this unemotional submission to an unknown higher will (whether good or evil), resembles a similar attitude toward life by Feodor Sologub, and stands in contrast to the self-assertions of such of her contemporaries as Brjusov, Bal'mont, and the early Belyj. The emotional void that she portrays is seen in her reference to the emptiness of everyday existence, symbolized by the gray room, and the repeated use of the negative particle *ne*. . . . (pp. 306-07)

Even in a scene which one might expect to be filled with pathos, as that in which the poet listens mutely to "love dying" . . . Hippius, maintaining a complete indifference, does not admit feeling any emotion. . . . In view of this indifference (which is nevertheless basically romantically emotional, rather than classically dispassionate), the use of such symbols as cold, snow, wind, fog, absence of fire, cannot be unexpected.

A hearth without its fire . . . is a setting typical for Hippius. It leads logically to the spiritual frustration of the scene in which the poet seeking and expecting martyrdom, in being burned at the stake, discovers that his sacrifice is suddenly unwanted . . . and the suffering for which he had hoped is rejected. Instead of self-sacrifice, in place of a deed of heroism, he is met with frustration; instead of claiming love and compassion as his reward, he finds only an unresponsive cold.

When viewed in historical perspective, the privative motifs in the poetry of Hippius resemble similar elements in the works of Gogol' and Tjutčev. (p. 307)

An important distinction, however, must be observed between Hippius's treatment of nothingness and that of Gogol'. Gogol''s images of the void are usually connected with the physical, tangible world. They are materially concrete. Hippius's images of nothingness relate usually to the province of emotion and the intellect. They are symbolically abstract. And in this respect, a veritable chasm separates Hippius's post-realistic images from Golgol' "naturalistic" sketches.

In the abstractness of her world view Hippius is closer to another nineteenth century Russian literary figure—Tjutčev, than she is to Gogol'. Her vision of the void leads her to employ a number of symbols used commonly by Tjutčev. One of his favorite images is that of the nocturnal *abyss*, which yields a glimpse of the transphysical universe. . . . Tjutčev's penchant for the privative is seen, moreover, in his image of the *fleshless, invisible* world swarming in the nocturnal chaos. . . . For Tjutčev, Chaos is a primordial, unbridled, sightless and naked living creature, at once awesome and dear. . . .

Since Hippius's lightless realm . . . like that of Tjutčev, also breathes mystery and dread, the revelations of the two poets seem parallel.

Nevertheless, as with Gogol', an important distinction must be observed between Tjutčev's poetic world and that of Hippius. (p. 308)

Her universe, as we have seen, is basically a negative, lifeless realm. Her chief images are privative; they suggest the absence of an element that is usually expected. Her domain is one of isolation and solitude (absence of beings); of silence (absence of sound); of immobility (absence of motion); of darkness (absence of light); of death (absence of life); of indifference and apathy (absence of emotion); of chill and cold (absence of life-giving warmth). Her world is quiet, mysterious, and motionless.

Tjutčev's poetic realm, on the other hand, is a living, breathing albeit sightless, invisible force, and is, above all, a constantly moving power engaged in an eternal struggle. . . . It is precisely this dynamism which characterizes Tjutčev's night, that is absent in Hippius's dark. Her Spectre of Nothingness is motionless. Hers is a world of vacuous stillness, and its spectre though pregnant with an inner tension is essentially one of static immobility. (p. 309)

> Oleg A. Maslenikov, "Spectre of Nothingness: The Primitive Element in the Poetry of Zinaida Hippius," in Slavic and East European Journal (© 1960 by AATSEEL of the U.S., Inc.), n.s. Vol. IV, No. 18, 1960, pp. 299-311.

**RENATO POGGIOLI** (essay date 1960)

Gippius' most important work of fiction is a novel, *The Devil's Puppet*. . . . Its literary importance is not great, yet it proves that even as a novelist Gippius was more gifted than her husband. The story conveys a tragic vision in the manner of Dostoevskij's *The Devils*. Like the latter it is a political novel, even though it is written from a different ideological standpoint. Its theme is the fatal failure, on the part of the political and spiritual leaders of the Russian Left, to help to build, during the ordeal of 1905, the new society and the new church of which they had been dreaming and preaching for so long. It is this failure that makes of those would-be angels and apostles not tragic "demons" but pathetic "devil's puppets."

The novel now has hardly more than historical interest, and there is perhaps more lasting merit in Gippius' lesser pieces of fiction, where she often shows a keen insight into the psychology of her sex. Her prose reaches its high point, however, in her excellent, although too subjective, critical essays, which are mainly psychological profiles and individual critiques, always lucid and often acid, for which she chose the masculine pen name Anton Krajnij ("Anthony the Extreme"), and which she collected in a two-volume work significantly entitled *Living Faces*. . . . (p. 112)

The best of Gippius' poetry is included in *Collected Poems*, published as early as 1904. In these lyrics, as well as in those written later, the poetess handles the commonplaces of the poetry of her time, generally suggested by a pessimistic conception of life and by an idealistic vision of the world. The central fable of her poetry is the ordeal of the spirit in its attempts to break away from the jail of reality, and to fly heavenward. Gippius treats this motif with great originality, but in impersonal accents, and with a kind of detached serenity. Naturally enough, she succeeds better when she describes the defeat of the spirit rather than its triumphs; not so much the soul's flight as its downfall. It is with repelling metaphors and drastic words that she depicts the vulgarity of daily life, the prosaic coarseness of our existence on earth. Nothing is more significant in this regard than the poem **"Psyche,"** where she develops for her own purposes the image of the little, dark,

empty room, with only cobwebs in its corners, by which Svidrigajlov, in Dostoevskij's *Crime and Punishment*, conveys his own nihilistic notion of the idea of eternity. The poem reveals Gippius' ability to express her own experience in terms of an abstract, cerebral wisdom, and to suggest her view of life in aphoristic and epigrammatic form. She converts images into ideas, and ideas into images, with no effort, almost at will. A perfect example of this is the poem **"Electricity,"** where, by metaphorically using the scientific terminology connected with the phenomena of electric polarity, she translates the mechanical antitheses of her husband's nebulous metaphysics into a popular allegory, into a familiar myth. (pp. 112-13)

> Renato Poggioli, "The Decadents," in his The Poets of Russia 1890-1930 (copyright © 1960 by the President and Fellows of Harvard College; excerpted by permission), Cambridge, Mass.: Harvard University Press, 1960, pp. 89-115.*

**VLADIMIR ZLOBIN** (essay date 1970)

[Author of the impressionistic biography Zinaida Gippius: A Difficult Soul, Zlobin was Hippius's private secretary for more than twenty-five years. Here, he examines Hippius's perceptions and poetic treatment of Satan.]

Gippius first mentioned the Devil in the poem **"Griselda,"** written in 1895. Griselda, in a castle awaiting the return of her husband from war, suffered "unheard of misfortunes." The "Lord of Evil" himself tried to tempt her. . . . And Gippius exclaims:

> O, tell me, Wisest Tempter,
> Dark Spirit—could you be
> The misconstrued Preceptor
> Who teaches us Beauty?

But in 1895 she was not the only one to exclaim like that. Russian poets of the Silver Age were tied to the French Symbolists by more than their name. The question of the Devil and the problem of evil had been raised already by Baudelaire and Verlaine. Their influence on the Russian Symbolists in this area is undeniable. The seed fell on fertile soil.

The following quatrain deserves special attention:

> Griselda is triumphant,
> Her soul is shining bright.
> But still, how strong the spirit
> Of lies and darkest night.

Here, in the last two lines, we see the change from contemplation to action, still timid, not fully realized, but already fatally irrepressible. But then, the poison worked slowly. Seven years were to pass before she expressed with her usual, utmost clarity her feelings about the Devil in a poem called **"God's Creature."** (pp. 134-35)

[Here,] she shares the Devil's suffering with him fraternally—it is the result of their joint madness. We will find out later just what that madness was. Let us now speak of her three encounters with the Devil. The first one is described in the poem **"Into a Line,"** dated 1905. (p. 136)

What is immediately striking here is that the Devil comes to her not as a tempter, for her fall took place before his arrival, but merely to draft something like an official record. Speaking modern Russian, what he does is "establish the facts." Furthermore, it should also be noted that he behaves not in the least diabolically. He tries to wound her pride, obviously in order to help her "break the ring," i.e., to escape from an unpleasant predicament for which she is herself responsible. Who he really is, is not known. However, there is every reason to assume that hiding under that cape is an angel, not the Devil.

The second encounter took place thirteen years later in September, 1918, in St. Petersburg (please note the date). She described it in the poem **"The Hour of Victory."** (pp. 136-37)

And so the Devil returned [as predicted in **"Into a Line"**]. Gippius's premonition did not deceive her. But it was no longer a "decadent" devil in a romantic cape, but a devil of 1918 in a stylish caped overcoat, with gloves (black ones, what else?), an *agent provocateur* of the Cheka. She defeated him with the magical word "blood" (yet why should he fear blood? Wasn't he wearing gloves because his hands were covered with it?). Like his predecessor he also "sank into a void." But Gippius's victory was only on paper. The Devil "sank into a void" solely out of respect for her literary status. Otherwise there would have been no need for him to appear for the third time.

The third encounter took place after she had emigrated. The date is not indicated (it can be dated approximately between 1925 and 1930). Gippius described this encounter with her usual mastery in the poem **"Indifference."** . . . (p. 138)

Now, for the first time, he is behaving as a devil should. He is actually a tempter, even though he appeared in the form of a "trembling creature." In spite of his degraded, wretched state he does not give up until the last moment. She pretended she didn't notice him, as if he weren't there, and because of her scornful indifference he melts and dissolves into dust.

But Gippius's indifference was a sham. Actually it was she and not the Devil who was consumed by a secret fear and she tried to hide it from him with all the means at her disposal. But the Devil was also pretending. He only pretended to tempt her because, as her poetry testifies, she had long since yielded to the temptation of looking into the souls of her fellow men in order to see the insignificance of the people around her (especially of those closest to her). (pp. 139-40)

Let us return for the moment to the problem of the Devil as **"God's Creature."** Gippius was not only not in conflict with this "second" Devil, but on the contrary she shared with him fraternally his suffering, the result of their joint madness. . . .

What is meant, however, by the "madness" of the Devil, the madness which Gippius so imprudently shares with him? It is not so easy to answer that question and it is possible that my somewhat amateurish approach to such an important topic may seem superficial to the enlightened reader. I ask the reader's forbearance in advance. What the Devil wants, has always wanted, both before and after his fall (it was the cause of his fall), is to enjoy eternal bliss alone with God. Outside of that, he wants nothing else to exist. (p. 142)

For the modern-day Devil, man, mankind, and world history are but a barrier between himself and God. He tries to destroy that barrier and is tireless in his destructiveness. But the more he tries to draw near God, the farther God is from him. The contradiction is irreconcilable and that irreconcilability is the cause of the Devil's suffering and madness. He exists in a state akin to eternal falling. Many of the poems by Gippius that seem to us obscure become clear in light of this. One need not search [further than the poem **"All the Same"**] for an example. (p. 143)

[Gippius] seemed to be and indeed was an extremely balanced person. But her spiritual equilibrium was not really an equilibrium, but only the immpossibility of inner conflict. Her soul was peculiarly constructed: good and evil alternated in it but did not clash. When an angel made an entrance, the Devil would vanish and vice versa. More and more it began to seem to her that it was one and the same person, one who could change costumes in the wings with the agility of a Fregoli. (p. 144)

The pendulum continued to sway. Only its sweep was gradually growing shorter. In 1934, fifteen years after she had secured her victory over the Devil, she wrote the following four lines in the poem **"November 8"** (her birthday):

> It smells of roses and inevitability.
> Who will help and how can they help?
> Eternal changes, eternal contiguities,
> Summer and fall, day and night.

In those simple, sparse lines, which are like tearful children's faces to which no one pays any attention, lies the whole tragedy of her soul. And the pendulum still swings. Now it is hope:

> I believe in the happiness of liberation,

now it is fear:

> It's frightening because I do not live, I sleep.
> And everything splits into two, into four.
>
> (p. 145)

[There] is nothing new about this self-contradiction. It has always been there to a lesser or greater extent and it was reflected in her poetry perhaps not in such a categorical form, but every bit as expressively. For example, here is the beginning of her poem **"The Earth,"** written in 1908:

> And the deserted orb in empty desert,
> Like meditation of the Devil,
> Suspended always, still hangs there . . .
> Madness! Madness!

At that time she still realized that to see the world as she sometimes depicted it was madness. Now, however, when she was actually sinking to the bottom, she did not realize her madness, or, at any rate, she did not call it by its name. [**"The Last Circle"**] is perhaps the most terrifying of all her poems. (p. 148)

It would appear that Gippius had looked deeper into hell than Dante. But she remained silent about what was revealed to her in the last circle. That is not such a great secret, though, because the Devil is a logician and a mathematician and his goal is always the same. There, at the bottom of hell, in the last circle, she could see with her own eyes that *God was the Devil*. Her madness was the Devil's logic carried to its ultimate conclusion. (p. 149)

How was she saved? Several days before November 8, 1918—her birthday (I remind you, she was born on the day of Archangel Michael and all the heavenly hosts)—when she was in Bolshevik-occupied St. Petersburg, she wrote a poem called **"Days"** [containing the lines]

> The sword of the Archangel touches me
> With burning flame and I'm alive again!

That flame was an eight-line poem titled **"8"** which she wrote on November 8 of that same year, on her birthday. But she did not write down the last two lines of the second stanza, each line containing four words. Instead she used dashes. (pp. 149-50)

We will never know those words. Their exact meaning is irrevocably lost to us. But if we possess an ounce of imagination and try to imagine her life at the end of 1918 in Bolshevik St. Petersburg, try to understand her spiritual condition at the time, and the problem that tormented her most of all just then, and if we add to all that some audacity, to say nothing of personal intuition, then these are approximately the eight words she did not write down:

8

Eight words burn in my heart,
But I will never dare to say them.
There is a line which no one ever mentions
Because this line cannot be crossed.
And all the same, no one will understand
That through these words there courses human blood:
"But God calls freedom
What we call love."

But what is the power of these seemingly simple, ordinary words? It resides in the following: "To him that overcometh will I give to eat of the hidden manna, and will give him a white stone, and in the stone a new name written, which no man knoweth saving he that receiveth it" (Revelations 2:17). That new name is FREEDOM, the new name of love and the ultimate revelation of the Divine Triunity. This name is given to "him that overcometh" together with "hidden manna"—the source of indestructible spiritual power—and it enables him who partakes of the manna to achieve communion with divine nature.

But why eight words? It was more important to her in that poem than anywhere else to emphasize that she was born on the day the Archangel Michael was victorious over the Devil and that she was under his protection. But that reason was not the chief one.

The chief reason is this. The number of the cross is four; the eight words burning in her heart were like a burning cross becoming two in the quivering flames, symbolizing in essence the double sacrifice—of God for the sake of the world and of the world for the coming of the Holy Ghost: "Thy Kingdom come."

And when the storm of death descended upon her from the depths of eternity, when the forces of hell come crashing down upon her and for the first time she found herself face to face with the enemy without his mask, then even the Archangel Michael with his hosts, who were aiding her in her battle, could not have saved her if at that moment she had not held in her hands an invincible weapon: a Cross of Flame. (pp. 151-53)

> *Vladimir Zlobin, "Gippius and the Devil," in his* A Difficult Soul: Zinaida Gippius, *edited and translated by Simon Karlinsky (translation copyright © 1980 by The Regents of the University of California; reprinted by permission of the University of California Press; originally published as* Tyazhelaya dusha, *Victor Kamkin, Inc., 1970), University of California Press, 1980, pp. 134-53.*

## TEMIRA PACHMUSS (essay date 1971)

[*The most important of Hippius's modern critics, Pachmuss has written numerous essays on the poet's work. Zinaida Hippius: An Intellectual Profile, from which the following survey is taken, is considered the definitive biography.*]

The early work of Hippius, in the 1890's, reveals her as a poet of aestheticism and supreme individualism, voicing her nostalgia for "that which is not of this world." She denounced the vulgarity and boredom in human existence. Only occasionally did Hippius take delight in nature and life, having been inspired by Italian Renaissance and Hellenic concepts concerning the sanctity of the flesh. Such views she shared with Merezhkovsky, Minsky, and A. Volynsky. Her prevailing moods of melancholy, a desire for solitude, and an acute feeling of alienation from her fellow men became especially prominent toward the end of the century. With this emphasis the tenor of Hippius' creative work (1899-1905) changed—aware of her own will, strength, and calling, she became preoccupied with religious matters. At this time her ideas took a more definite shape as she continued to resist the positivism and primitive utilitarianism of the radicals. To her former concept of God she added a new idea of freedom and a desire to attain profound faith in God. Abandoning the Greek notion of the sanctity of the flesh and the Christian concept of the sanctity of the spirit, she expressed, together with Merezhkovsky, a hope that these two would be synthesized and later merged into a religion of the Holy Trinity. Theirs was an "apocalyptical" Christianity which believed in the Second Coming of Christ in the same way that historical Christianity believed in His First Coming. Neo-Christianity formulated as its objective the synthesis of the Holy Flesh and the Holy Spirit in their equality and wholeness, and Hippius vindicated this religious renaissance in her poetry. Her poems of this period can be called a discourse on abstract ideas in rhyme and verse.

Hippius' mystical and religious sophistication gradually led her to the conviction that the Russian Orthodox Church should be reorganized, and that a "new religious consciousness" should replace the dogmas of the Church. Opposed to the subservience of the Russian Church to the state, she wished to reform both the Church and Russian socio-political affairs of that time. During this period in her creative work (1905-14) her religious, mystical, and philosophical ideas became linked with plans for achieving social and political order. (pp. 22-3)

Her poems of the period 1889-1903 are reminiscent of pious hymns or chants in praise of God, such as the Gloria in Excelsis, and of the ecstatic presentiments and expectations of Ephrem Syrus, the "Harp of the Holy Ghost." The homilies of Andrew of Crete and especially his great penitential Canon, which is sung on Thursday before Passion Sunday, appear to have exercised an influence upon Hippius' poems. They also resemble solemn religious odes based on the principal beliefs of Manichaeism, with its concept of duality in the structure of the world, and there is a resemblance to Gnosticism with its doctrine that an emancipation of the spirit comes through knowledge.

The salient features of Hippius' early work can be seen also in her prose. The first two volumes of her short stories, *Novye lyudi* (**New People** . . .) and *Zerkala* (**Mirrors** . . .), convey Hippius' rejection of conventional morals and norms of behavior. Her heroes search for new outlooks in life. They indulge in lengthy conversations about the beauty of the world, harmony, and love as an abstract idea. The feverish atmosphere is reminiscent of Dostoevsky's novels, especially *The Idiot.* Although Hippius' verse shows no obvious indebtedness to foreign models, her prose reveals the influence of several Western writers. Her early short stories, for example, employ the descriptive method of the Belgian poet Georges Rodenbach, his "aristocratic cult of solitude giving rise to an adoration of *lonely canal waters,* of the solitary moon, of everything that is secluded, reserved, and silent." Hippius' Val'tsev, the hero of her short story **"Luna"** (*The Moon . . .*), roams the deserted streets of Venice at night thinking about the loneliness of the moon, of canal waters, of his hotel room, and about man's isolation in general. Like Rodenbach's protagonists, he complains of the terrible pain caused by calumny from the blasphemous crowd. (pp. 52-3)

Some of Hippius' novels and short stories of this early period display the positive aspect of her religious outlook, which . . . distinguishes her from the attitudes of "decadent" writers. Her heroes vindicate "enlightened love" in God, a subliminated flesh, and the importance of love and understanding between people. "Love must be infinite," says Hippius' Shadrov to Margaret in a novel entitled **Sumerki dukha** (*The Twilight of the Spirit . . .*). "It must be an open window, a light in one's consciousness." Some other short stories, for instance in the volume **Aly mech** (*A Scarlet Sword . . .*), are tendentious. Whereas religious clairvoyance and considerations of beauty and harmony occupy the central place in her earlier narratives, social ideas and a candid preaching of neo-Christianity and ecumenity ("sobornost'") are emphasized in *A Scarlet Sword.* Since Hippius' themes are too extensive and too complex to be incorporated in the texture of a short story, their inclusion impairs the artistic value of *A Scarlet Sword.* This volume may be described as a collection of articles in which the author develops her thought in a certain sequence. Hippius soon realized that the short-story form was too limited for an expression of her social and political concerns. So she turned her pen to the writing of novels on these subjects. Two of them, **Chortova kukla** (*The Devil's Doll . . .*) and **Roman-Tsarevich . . . .**, are patterned after *The Possessed.* There is a difference, however, in that the protagonists are less enigmatic and less important in the context of Hippius' novels than is the mysterious Stavrogin in Dostoevsky. The code of behavior of Yury Dolgoruky, the hero of *The Devil's Doll,* is based on his precept: "Man should love only himself." In the image of Dolgoruky, Mikhail Artsybashev's crude and instinctive Sanin has transformed himself into a refined aesthete. Even the title of Hippius' novel suggests a deadly vacuum in the soul of this young man. He is a convinced individualist, guided in all his actions by the selfish dictates of his Ego. He protests against the pessimistic outlook of his generation and affirms the supremacy of life. His "truth" is entirely rational, devoid of all traces of intuition and religious feeling; he pleads the cause of rationality in human deeds, feelings, and desires. Yury, in this rational approach to life, is an entirely different man from the "intuitive" predecessors of Hippius' earlier narratives. In his persistent striving to deprive life of all its holiness, of all its "lofty meaning," Yury profanes life and human destiny on earth. Since he does not believe in God, he is certain to become a monstrosity. (pp. 54-5)

[In **"Zhenskoe"** (**"The Feminine"**) and **"Net vozvrata"** (**"There is No Return"**)] something new appears in Hippius' artistic method. The straight narrative technique previously characteristic of her prose is now subordinated to a figurative mode of narration. Hippius' dialogue is effective; her portrayal of prostitutes, servants, and particularly of housemaids is excellent in its psychological veracity and its gentle Goncharovian humor. Her "educated" characters, on the other hand, again lack verisimilitude, involved as they are in complex situations and engaging in conversations that abound in philosophical

ideas. Again they concentrate on searching for a "new religious consciousness," for a new path toward the attainment of God.

The religious orientation of Hippius' poetry and prose of this first formative period remained the salient feature of her entire work. She never deviated from the premise she had formulated at the turn of the century—art is real only when it strives toward the spiritual and merges with God. (pp. 55-6)

With Merezhkovsky and Filosofov as coauthors, Hippius conveyed [her socio-political] views to her Western readers in a volume of articles entitled *Le Tsar et la Révolution* in 1907. Here they denied both the concept of the autocrat and the concept of the state and rejected the possibility of a theocratic society established on the existing governmental forms. Theocracy, the Kingdom of God on earth, was not possible; autocracy and the state, both symbolizing externally enforced powers, represented the kingdom of the devil. Consequently religious anarchy became the ideal of the three. (pp. 166-67)

Hippius' interest in socio-political ideas during 1904-5 can be seen in her prose and in such poems as **"Petersburg"** . . . and **"14-oye dekabrya"** (**"The Fourteenth of December"** . . .), which begin and conclude her *Sobranie stikhov: kniga vtoraya* (*Collection of Verse: Second Book . . .*). Her heroes discuss various social topics and reflect Hippius' view that only a religious revolution could succeed in Russia. During the years following the suppression of the Revolution she wrote a drama entitled **Makov tsvet** (*The Red Poppy . . .*), allegedly with Merezhkovsky and Filosofov, and two volumes of short stories, **Chornoe po belomu** (*Black on White . . .*) and **Lunnye muravyi** (*The Moon Ants, . . .*). In 1908 she published a volume of her literary essays and articles under the title of *Literaturny dnevnik: 1889-1907* (*Literary Diary: 1889-1907*). Hippius' novels, *The Devil's Doll* and *Roman-Tsarevich,* intended to be the first and third parts of a trilogy, were also written during this time. The second part, *Ocharovanie istiny (The Charm of Truth)* was never finished. Despite the tendentiousness and artificiality of the events described in these writings, their texts exhibit Hippius' superb sense of style and humor.

The drama *The Red Poppy,* which was written in response to the Revolution of 1905, reveals a changed attitude of the "trio." It portrays the effect of the Revolution on a well-to-do family, the Motovilovs, from the day of the October Manifesto in 1905 to the following October. The Motovilov family is symbolic of all Russia. Some of its members participate in the Revolution, while others oppose it; the Revolution has a positive effect on some, and a negative one on others. Blank, a dogmatic Marxist who entirely lacks the romantic views and attitudes characteristic of the Motovilov family, is contrasted with them. This contrast emphasizes the unity and the affinity of the Motovilovs. They symbolize Russia as a nation which can shed its blood, accept suffering, recognize its common guilt, and sacrifice the best, most idealistic members in the name of love and future harmony. The drama illustrates the Merezhkovskys' disagreement with Marxist views, their rejection of the Revolution of 1905, and their disappointment and frustration over its outcome. Disappointment and increasingly negative feelings toward the revolutionary movement may be seen in other works by Hippius, as well as in her religious activities, which show a deeper interest in the concept of God as the spiritual and philosophical Beginning of All.

An analysis of the style of *The Red Poppy* indicates that in all probability Hippius was the sole writer of the drama. She listed three authors in order to convince readers that the expressed views were not of a single individual, but of a group. The work contains many of Hippius' typical expressions and ideas, such as "eto samoe strashnoe-to i est': nikogo nikto ne lyubit" (this is the most frightful thing: nobody loves anybody) or "molodezhi prezhde vsego uchit'sya nado" (before everything else, youth must study). Similar expressions may be found in several of Hippius' earlier works. (pp. 173-75)

As her introduction to *The Devil's Doll* indicates, Hippius was concerned here with the reactionary trends which followed the ill-fated liberation movement. Her artistic objective was to examine the roots of any reaction, independent of a particular historical moment. She believed it was her task to oppose the regressive forces which threatened to assert themselves after the failure of the revolutionary movement. These regressive forces, in her opinion, operated everywhere in Russian society; they were not visible, but they were omnipresent and dangerous. She also wished "to bring into focus all the traits of the sluggish and self-centered human personality," hoping to stimulate a transformation of man into a conscious being who would be able to affirm and to justify his *Weltanschauung*. Everything else in *The Devil's Doll* only serves to intensify the portrayal of the main hero, Yury Dolgoruky.

Life as Hippius presents it in *The Devil's Doll* and in *Roman-Tsarevich* is a solipsistic melodrama of a single person, of a Yury or of a Roman, who manages to drag many other people into his personal misfortunes, ruining them at his whim. In the figure of Roman, Hippius wished to reveal the psychology of a man whose heart mysteriously harbors both lofty idealism and base treachery, the heights of selflessness and a desire to shed innocent blood. The basic idea of the novel affirms the author's belief that a simple Russian's faith in God is sacred and that no one should use it for his own purposes, even for an elevated goal, namely, the freedom of the people. Any abuse of this intuitive faith in God will inevitably lead to punishment—this is the solemn message of the book. Roman takes the place of God; he wishes to incite the Russian peasantry to rebel and commit bloodshed and conflagrations in the name of God. God Himself takes vengeance on him. This theme of pseudo-religious revolution links Hippius' novel with Dostoevsky's *The Possessed*. Like Dostoevsky's novel, *Roman-Tsarevich* contains an artistic presentation of revolution and reaction, Russian *émigrés* and their provocations, and the prostration and tedium which follow.

Hippius availed herself in this novel of yet another opportunity to express her idea that at its core revolution is identical with universal movement into the future. Hippius always associated revolution with the eternal questions of the meaning of human existence and God and His Creation. In *The Devil's Doll* she presented Mikhail Rzhevsky as attempting to impart purely religious, even prophetic meaning to the revolutionary movement. *The Devil's Doll* manifests Hippius' interest in the socio-ethical problems of the time; a political emphasis is noticeably absent. Her short stories, written after the suppression of the Revolution of 1905, treat temporal events and display the pessimistic attitudes characteristic of the post-revolutionary period in Russia. However, the writer's main concern still remained with God and His Creation. This is particularly true of her volume *The Moon Ants* which touches upon contemporary topics. (pp. 175-76)

[During World War I, Hippius] wrote poems, articles, and a play *Zelyonoe kol'tso (The Green Ring* . . .), which was produced at the Alexandrinsky Theater of St. Petersburg. (p. 189)

*The Green Ring* portrays the Russian younger generation, the "offspring of Russia's harrowing years," who intensely experienced "days of war" and "days of freedom," as the Epilogue explains. In their hearts, once animated by freedom, there is now a "fatal emptiness," a "fatal boredom." Their only salvation lies in their forming a "togetherness," almost a clan, in which every member is morally responsible for others. The central idea, the "secret of *The Green Ring,* is *the joy of sociality,*" says the author, true to her religious and socio-political philosophy. The young people in the play plan to create new human relationships based on freedom, equality, and brotherhood. They will reject the past, but without crude and senseless actions; they will fight against the past "mercifully" to attain a bright future. They will select from the past only what they need for the creation of a new life, a new society, new spiritual values. The young generation nudges its "fathers" out of the way compassionately, while the "fathers" refuse with a stubborn hard-heartedness to understand their "sons." The "children" in Hippius' play are lenient toward their parents; unlike Chatsky and Bazarov, they neither mock nor scorn them. *The Green Ring* challenges the attitudes of the older generation—its callousness, inertia, and mental cruelty to the young—and praises the hopes and "togetherness" of Russian youth.

The ending of the play expresses the love and "sociality" of these Russian high school students and their ardent faith in the future. . . . Hippius assures her reader that the conflict between the old and new generations, between "fathers and sons," will eventually disappear and the "people of the future, who are merciful, yet merciless, will win."

*The Green Ring* is a forceful play, although there is hardly any action or developed conflict. There is no struggle, because the young protagonists lack experience and depend on their parents in a material way. In their thoughts and feelings, however, they are independent. As in all of Hippius' writing, the language is refined and rich in nuances. (pp. 189-90)

Hippius welcomed only the initial phase of the Russian Revolution, which abolished autocracy and promised freedom. . . . [Later, she] vehemently opposed the Soviet regime, the "Kingdom of the devil," the "Beast-people." This was a negative period in Hippius' creative work. The verse **"Tak est'"** ("So It Is") is a tragic poem of the time in which she laments that her Russia belongs to the irrevocable past. (p. 201)

In 1925 Hippius published her "literary portraits," *Zhivye litsa (Living Faces).* In these portraits, as Khodasevich perceptively commented, "People and events are presented with remarkable vividness and perspicacity—from general characteristics to the minutest details, from descriptions of events of foremost significance to small but typical scenes." (p. 235)

All these descriptions and portrayals are lifelike miniatures, memorable and unique in their color, outlines, and dialogue and imbued with a poetic atmosphere. The people, indeed, appear as living personalities, with all their individual characteristics. Their artistic presentation is graceful; the style is lucid and smoothly flowing. The work occupies an unparalleled position among all literary reminiscences in Russian. (p. 236)

Hippius' concern with the Russian *émigrés* in France precluded her writing much poetry. Only one volume of her poems, entitled *Siyaniya (Radiances),* appeared in 1938, although much of her verse was published in the Russian periodicals and newspapers in Paris. Unfortunately, her poems have not yet been anthologized. With the exception of the book *Nebesnye slova*

*(Heavenly Words)*, which contains exclusively her narratives published previously in Russia, no other volume of her short stories appeared in exile. There is no collection of her prose works of the period 1920-39.

*Radiances* is written in a "minor key." It lacks the joyous and belligerent notes characteristic of Hippius' earlier poems. Fatigue, disenchantment, and her failure to oppose Bolshevism successfully seem to have finally affected her spirits. . . . Lyricism, irony, religiosity, spiritual search, and reflection may be found in the poems of *Radiances*. Life goes on, taking away color and passion, making everything gray and dull, and promising only tears. (pp. 249-50)

There is no sentimentality or melodrama in *Radiances*. Hippius' temperance, her unwillingness to indulge in tears, and her contempt for childish dreams are evident everywhere. With restrained, yet pointed words the poems reveal a lonely spirit trying to come to grips with reality. (p. 256)

Among her works in prose of the Parisian period Hippius herself attached importance to *The Memoirs of Martynov* and "The Pearl-Handled Cane." . . . *The Memoirs of Martynov* is a series of stories with one common narrator, Ivan Martynov, who tells various episodes from his childhood, adolescence, and youth. Martynov's love experiences form the plot. . . . Perhaps the most interesting of all these short stories is "You—You" with its portrayal of Martynov's "vlyublyonnost'," which overwhelms the rational and sceptical hero for the first time. This feeling is his first real passion; a young and handsome Frenchman in Nice become his "only 'you' in the entire world." (pp. 272-73)

Another story by Hippius places the same hero in yet another unusual situation. In "The Pearl-Handled Cane" Martynov is in Sicily, surrounded by strange young men and women. Ivan's friend, Franz von Hallen, is in love with Otto, who lives in Berlin with his wife. Nino and Giovanni, two handsome Sicilians, are likewise infatuated with von Hallen. Ivan, too, succumbs to homosexual love. . . . "The Pearl-Handled Cane" is based on Hippius' own observations in Taormina in 1896, where she witnessed a variety of psychological entanglements in the people who surrounded her at the time.

"He is White" is a remarkable work which Hippius selected from her *Moon Ants* for publication in *The Latest News*. Like the short stories "Ivan Ivanivich and the Devil" and "They are Alike," "He is White" utilizes an esoteric myth about the devil as a bewitcher, the difference here being a revelation of his seraphic nature. (p. 273)

Among Hippius' new literary undertakings were her unfinished poem *Posledny Krug (The Last Circle)* and an incompleted biography of Merezhkovsky. She began to write both of them after her husband's death in 1941; the biography was published posthumously. . . . [These] memoirs, like *Living Faces*, are of inestimable value to a historian of Russian literature, even though *Dmitry Merezhkovsky* is inferior to *Living Faces* from the artistic viewpoint. (p. 276)

*The Last Circle*, which Hippius wrote shortly before her death, portrays the poet's last years and reveals her ultimate views on human life and its end—in Hell. She had dreamed of a miraculous merging of Heaven and earth throughout her life, but now, near the end, Hippius envisioned herself being cast into a frightful darkness beyond the grave. The work is rich in philosophical ideas, and it is a poignant presentation of Hippius' own death agony. The indisputable value of *The Last*

*Circle* lies in the final elucidation of the poet's basic metaphysical concepts concerning Love, Faith, Time, and Death.

*The Last Circle* is certainly not one of Hippius' masterpieces, nevertheless all her works deserve attention because of their significance in the Age of Russian Symbolism. The poem lacks the craftsmanship, vitality, and euphonious refinement of expression which characterize Hippius' earlier work. There are some serious artistic faults in *The Last Circle*—abstract theorizing, colorless prosaisms, and annoying schematism and sermonizing. Rhyme and meter are not always perfect. Also missing is that aphoristic quality which Bryusov valued so highly in Hippius' verse. In several passages, however, she transcends her critical and somewhat contemptuous attitude, breaks through the bounds of intellect, and attains her former artistic perfection. One should also keep in mind that the poem was never completed—Hippius' illness and subsequent death prevented her from finishing and polishing the work. Hippius herself described her initial concept of *The Last Circle* in a letter to Gerell dated June 5, 1943: "I wrote a long poem recently—for myself, for myself alone, alas! The subject amused me: I wanted to imagine a *modern* Dante, a descendant of the real one. The *modern* Dante enters the deepest circle of Hell, and there he finds people whom he had once known. At the end he goes to Paradise. But I stopped here, for what do we know about Paradise?"

*The Last Circle,* then, is modeled on Dante's *Divine Comedy*. The four parts describe the wanderings of the "new Dante" in the Inferno and in Purgatory. In the Inferno he meets two "sinners," two contemporaries of Hippius who were at one time close to her—a "half-friend" and a real friend. The two "sinners" give Dante personal accounts of their lives and confess their transgressions against Love, Friendship, and Time. The two stories are told in an ironic and often disdainful manner, yet the tone changes whenever the author touches upon her philosophy. (pp. 287-88)

[*The Last Circle*] reveals that Hippius did not deviate from her basic religious and philosophical beliefs even at the end of her life. The poem may be considered an artistic *résumé* of her metaphysical philosophy—Love is supreme in human life; it draws Heaven and Earth together into One Whole; it reconciles all conflicts and eradicates all hostilities. The way to Love is through the gamut of life experiences and through humble acceptance of suffering in Time. (p. 304)

Hippius wrote many unconventional essays in which she expounded her artistic views, using a "special style, a style of intimate conversation." Her manner of expression—ironically serious, paradoxically casual, unaffectedly elegant—is unprecedented in Russian literary criticism. It attracted the attention of other Russian prose writers, and some of them attempted to imitate it, with occasional success; but in the history of Russian criticism this humorous, yet highly artistic manner of stating her views has remained uniquely hers. (p. 305)

Hippius' essays on Russian literature must be valued for their perspicacity, originality, and wit—characteristics rarely found in the criticism of belles-lettres at the time. Her ability to express her opinions eloquently in clear, vivid images testifies to her cultured taste and artistic prowess. (p. 383)

Without Zinaida Hippius the Silver Age of Russian poetry and the Russian religious renaissance would have been unthinkable. She was one of the most stimulating minds of her time, a sophisticated poet, an original religious thinker, and an inimitable literary critic. In her work the four chief aspects of the Russian cultural tradition—art, religion, metaphysical philosophy, and socio-political thought—receive their harmonious embodiment. (pp. 409-10)

*Temira Pachmuss, in her* Zinaida Hippius: An Intellectual Profile *(copyright © 1971 by Southern Illinois University Press; reprinted by permission of Southern Illinois University Press), Southern Illinois University Press, 1971, 491 p.*

## OLGA MATICH   (essay date 1972)

If one must classify Gippius the poet, one should consider her together with the second generation symbolists, who in contrast with the decadents associate their art with religion rather than pure aestheticism. In attempting to overcome the loneliness and total self-centeredness of the decadents, the second generation poets wish to find meaning outside of themselves by reaching out to God in their poetry. . . . Gippius's poetic visions are more akin to the younger generation's in that she hopes and attempts to escape the spiritual loneliness of her existence by finding her own path to God. (p. 15)

Since Gippius's poetry is highly abstract and philosophical, it is difficult on the whole to relate it to her biography. In 1895, she noted in her diary that while writing a poem she never dedicates it to any earthly relationships or to any particular individual. Baluev feels that this abstractness allowed Gippius to express her strong feelings about such universal themes as God, love and death without becoming intimate. In this respect Gippius is closer to the classicists than to the neo-romanticists of her generation. Probably it is this abstractness which created the erroneous impression of impersonality, a characteristic frequently mentioned in connection with Gippius. Actually she was a very personal poet, recording her innermost philosophical and metaphysical conflicts in a somewhat detached, intellectual manner.

Another peculiarity of Gippius's poetry is the lack of chronological development. Zlobin writes that chronology does not play a significant role in her art and life. Her original attitudes remained with her always, as she so frequently emphasizes by poetically asserting her absolute faithfulness. The fact that the arrangement of her books of poetry is not strictly chronological reinforces this general observation. Already her first well known poem **"Pesnja"** contains the basic theme of all of Gippius's poetic works—the search for that indefinable, never fully attainable, faith in God. (This, however, does not mean that Gippius's poetry lacks movement; movement in a metaphysical sense represents the cornerstone of the poetic vision.) From the point of view of technique and form, it can also be stated that Gippius develops her specific poetic style in the very beginning of her career. Consequently her early poems are already formally mature, reflecting her characteristic unadorned, yet expressive, conciseness. (pp. 33-4)

Although the poet was definitely concerned with the expression of ideas, she was at the same time a master craftsman, in fact, an innovator in matters of poetic form. . . . [She] experimented with rhyme in spite of her stated attachment to the cliché rhymes of the nineteenth century (See **"Banal'nostjam"**). Becoming a master of homonymic and internal rhymes, Gippius also created certain "revolutionary" rhyme patterns which predated the futurists and later Russian poets. Thus in **"Verili my v nevernoe,"** she rhymes the first words in each line instead of the last. In **"Neumestnye rifmy"** Gippius gives an even more unusual rhyme pattern in which the sound correspondence oc-

curs in the stressed vowels and consonants preceding them. . . .

There is no doubt that Gippius is a cerebral poet. Her verse lacks a light touch and is completely devoid of sentimentalism. However, one cannot deny the presence of passion, a Dostoevskian passion of feeling philosophical ideas, produced by an ever present poetically expressed metaphysical conflict. (p. 36)

[The] desire for attainment and its simultaneous fear lie at the core of Gippius's religiosity. We are confronted with a logical paradox (paradox is basic to the understanding of Gippius's "ideology"): lasting attainment is unfulfilling because it means spiritual death. At the same time nonattainment causes the poet to doubt the divine, often leading her to great despair. This constitutes the tragedy and difficulty of Gippius's metaphysical position, which she held throughout her life. However, let us not consider this statement as absolute, for paradoxically or absurdly Gippius at the same time found boundless satisfaction in this conviction. . . . [The] struggle was more gratifying than the realization. Perhaps Gippius took upon herself the task of Sisyphus in her willful struggle of pushing the rock up the hill while consciously knowing that the rock will always roll back down. Camus writes in the "Myth of Sisyphus": "The struggle itself toward the heights is enough to fill man's heart. One must imagine Sisyphus happy." The resolution of Gippius is similar to that of Camus's Sisyphus except that she puts it into a religious perspective.

In her early poems (primarily in the 1890's), Gippius expresses a desire for "that which does not exist," for the unattainable. . . . In part, such statements can be explained in terms of Gippius's bombastic and capricious willfulness, which contributed to the poet's notorious reputation. However, in view of Gippius's general spiritual development, the desire for that which does not exist represents an early manifestation of the spiritual paradox inherent in the poet's religiosity. The desire for the unattainable is in this case really the same as fearing the attainment of the possible. (pp. 45-6)

While desiring to transgress the bounds of phenomenal reality in order to merge with the divine, she is at the same time bound to this earth and to its basic principle of movement. . . . The transcendental sphere is timeless in essence, consequently static. This emphasis on the notion of becoming, rather than being, points to the real vitality of these concepts as far as Gippius is concerned. She actually lived these ideas, and therefore the time element is very significant for her. It is not by accident that Gippius uses the term *vljublennost'* to denote a higher form of love, for it refers to an active state of being in love, which requires a constant willful striving for the coming of a "new man."

It is in this context that we must interpret some of Gippius's love poems which deal with the theme of "non-merging." Lundberg writes that her love poetry represents the "poetic dogma of non-merging." There is no final real merging between the two in love—a note of separation or of being separated is always present. This should not lead to the simple conclusion that the poet was incapable of becoming involved in any love relationships. The fact of non-merging is rather associated with Gippius's fear of finally realizing her life's goals, in this case a love which will transform the nature of man. It is rather the possibility of achieving such a love which gives the poet spiritual satisfaction. The poet glorifies the state of being in love, a state in which there has been no final merging of the two involved in the relationship. (pp. 74-5)

Basically Gippius has two conflicting attitudes toward death: she is attracted to death and at the same time fears its coming.

This ambivalence is related to the poet's philosophically paradoxical view of time. The desire for death (death-wish) reflects her attraction to the timeless, which is the attribute of eternity. The fear of death, on the other hand, reveals the poet's love for the temporal or earthly existence. . . . Gippius was never able to reconcile these two opposite longings within herself. In addition to this philosophical dualism in the poet's attitude, there is also a psychological reaction to death in Gippius's poetry. It is manifested in the already mentioned themes and especially in the motif of indifference toward the inevitability of dying.

The poet's death-wish has two related sources: a decadent feeling of exhaustion, a desire to flee from earthly existence; and the wish to enter the sphere of eternity. (p. 100)

Death is not always simply an escape for the poet; it also brings liberation. Like Kirilov *(The Possessed)*, Gippius associates death with true freedom. Unlike Kirilov, however, she does not desire freedom from God but from the earthly life. . . . (p. 101)

Gippius's concern for the eternal can also be seen as desire for immortality. (p. 102)

The long narrative poem ***The Last Cirlce*** (*Poslednij krug*, subtitled *I novyj Dant v adu*) is Gippius's most elaborate statement on death. . . . The realm of death, in this case hell, is presented in totally pessimistic hues. It is depicted as an indescribable "nauseous black ocean," characterized by the "dull spinning motion of eternity." . . . (p. 108)

The notion of time again plays an important role. The inhabitants of hell have renamed their realm, calling it "Infinity" rather than using the earthly epithet. It is this infinity or the lack of time which makes hell so terrifying. The first two sinners whom young Dante encounters during his travels through hell speak of the frightening timelessness which is the attribute of their existence. Having sinned against time in their earthly life, they hope for forgiveness and desire to return to the world which is ruled by the spectre of Time. In contrast to the earthly death-wish, the dwellers of the underworld want to return to life. The poet thus confronts us with the paradox of the final circle from which there is no escape: on earth man desires death, hoping that it will provide a solution; in death the human spirit longs for earthly existence. . . .

Patterned on Dante's *Divine Comedy*, *The Last Circle* describes young Dante's journey through hell and on to paradise. The fictional descendant of the medieval poet, he is a well known Italian pilot during the Second World War, who out of intellectual curiosity descends into the underworld in order to learn about life after death. The evildoers whom Dante meets there confess their sins to him, which in some cases are reminiscent of the activities and attitudes of the Merežkovskijs and the people surrounding them. Among these sins are indifference to others, inability to love, contempt for man, lack of humility, self-centeredness, deceit and self-deception, preoccupation with the flesh and sexual perversion, etc. By indicating, e.g., that the lack of humility is sinful, the poet is rejecting her earlier position on this issue (see section on humility). In another passage, Gippius ridicules her lifelong preoccupation with physical and spiritual movement. Or she mocks the symbolists' belief that they were prophets, not only poets. (p. 109)

Gippius seems to refute or at least question some of her lifelong convictions and aspirations. In *The Last Circle* the poet comes to the realization that a very severe punishment awaits people like herself. However, this pessimism does not mean that she categorically rejects the possibility of spiritual fulfillment after death. Even in hell there is hope for forgiveness. . . . And the Shadow, who embodies many of Gippius's characteristics, is finally allowed to enter beyond the gates of this paradise. It is curious that the first being she meets there is her dog Bul'ka, who is very happy to see her master. The immortalization of the poet's dog adds a light, whimsical note to the narrative. (pp. 109-10)

Like Dante's *Divine Comedy*, Gippius's poem is an allegory of a human soul's journey from the spiritual bottom to the celestial realms. ***The Last Circle*** portrays the religious idea of *de profundis*—that the journey upwards must begin in the lowest depths of spiritual degradation. The Shadow, who is one of the inhabitants of hell, has been granted the right to move freely throughout the circles of the underworld in search for her beloved partner in life. They had lived together half a century without ever parting from each other, [as had Gippius and Merežkovskij]. The Shadow had been given the great gift of love, a force which allows her to overcome all obstacles in finally reaching paradise, the apparent dwelling of her loved one. Again love conquers all; it compensates for the sins which initially condemned the Shadow to the underworld. (pp. 110-11)

In spite of the frightening picture of hell, there is . . . a ray of hope. At the same time, it is true that the narrator of the poem presents a very forceful vision of the underworld but is unable to depict paradise. . . .

Analyzing Gippius's poems about death, one is amazed by the variety of emotions that the poet experienced in the face of the last parting. This variety reflects the complexity of Gippius's meditations on this subject and underscores the basic paradox of her philosophical thought. (p. 111)

> *Olga Matich, in her* Paradox in the Religious Poetry of Zinaida Gippius *(© 1972 Wilhelm Fink), Wilhelm Fink, 1972, 126 p.*

## OLGA MATICH (essay date 1975)

[*Matich examines the role of androgyny in Hippius's beliefs and work.*]

The outstanding symbolist poetess Zinaida Gippius was a leading figure of the so-called Russian religious renaissance at the turn of the twentieth century. Together with her husband Dmitrij Merežkovskij, she initiated the metaphysical searchings of a portion of the Russian intelligentsia. During this very tumultuous historical period, when Russians were seeking new solutions in many spheres of life, the Merežkovskijs attempted to create a new religion, which they called *Neo-Christianity* or *the Religion of the Third Testament*. In very general terms, their religion was to be the result of the necessary synthesis of paganism, with its emphasis on the flesh, and historical Christianity, which affirmed the value of the spirit only. . . .

Historical Christianity [to be distinguished from apocalyptical Christianity] equates the spiritual with the incorporeal, which is *pure, good, sacred,* and *divine;* the carnal is seen as *impure, evil, sinful, demonic*. The Merežkovskijs' synthesis proposes a religion in which the spirit and flesh will merge into one indivisible whole, thus consecrating and disincarnating the flesh and at the same time corporealizing the spirit. They saw this as an absolute prerequisite for humanity's progress and salvation.

Gippius's interest in androgyny is in part a reflection of her religious preoccupations which emphasize universal order by eliminating the disharmony caused by the age-old conflict between the spirit and the flesh. The "unisex of heavenly existence, where the processes of reproduction are no longer necessary," hopes to overcome the equally important conflict between the male and the female. Gippius maintained that much of the discord in man's existence has been caused by the traditional sexual differentiations imposed by nature and especially society. The transformation of life, in which the Russian symbolists wanted to believe, is clearly associated with the androgynous ideal in Gippius's metaphysics, as revealed in her poetry, prose fiction and philosophical essays. (pp. 98-9)

It is not so much the androgyne explicitly as androgynous love which plays a central role in Gippius's religious thought. . . . Love, according to Gippius, is the only divine element in man's human existence, and it is only through the divine that man can approach divinity. At the same time true love, the one which breaks down the barriers between the spirit and the flesh, is inherently androgynous. The difference in sex is not so important for those experiencing the passion of sublimity. Her essay *Vljublennost'* deals with the dissolution of sex once the stage of sublime love has been achieved. In the poem *Esli* . . . Gippius maintains that the desired transfiguration and consequent resurrection of the lovers cannot be reified without their androgynous similarity. In accordance with the utopian interpretation of androgyny, the poet also concludes that the love which merges the masculine and feminine into a unisex will come some day, even if the lovers in *Esli* have not been able to achieve it. At the same time resurrection implies the realization of perfection which would bring to an end the dynamism of life's forward movement. The notion of androgyny in *Esli* is further underscored by the usage of the hermaphroditic symbol of the circle, both thematically and in the formal structure of the poem. . . . (pp. 101-02)

Believing in the intrinsic meaning of numerals, Gippius chose the figure eight, the traditional symbol of infinity, to indicate man's androgyny. The numeral eight is comprised of two loops of unequal size, one indicating the masculine element in man, the other the feminine. Like Otto Weininger, whose *Sex and Character* she read with great interest, Gippius maintained that one of the sexes, masculine or feminine, must prevail in each human being. Every person has his own particular masculine and feminine combination, which in turn seeks out its "correspondingly-reversible" partner. For example, the smaller feminine loop seeks to unite with an identical masculine one, and the larger masculine portion of the eight searches for a feminine loop of equal size. This is the corresponding reversibility of sex, bringing about the desired state of sublime love, of which Gippius writes in her *Arithmetic of Love*.

Gippius also uses the mythically traditional symbolism of the moon in her androgynous poetry. Believed to be a bisexual being in ancient Greece, the moon is the source of the androgyne according to Aristophanes's tale in the *Symposium*, while the sun gave rise to man and the earth to woman. The moon shares the qualities of the sun and the earth and is thereby the originator of bisexuality. In the untranslatable love poem *Ty* . . . , the poet is addressing his beloved who is the moon. The Russian language has two words for the moon—the masculine *mesjac* and feminine *luna*, both of which are used in the poem. Playing with this untranslatable grammatical gender difference, the persona is emphasizing the androgynous nature of the lover.

Equally interesting is the fact that the *lyrical I* of the poet alternates between the masculine and feminine, which indicates the persona's androgyny. The sexual duality is further underscored by the consistent alternation of lines dominated by the masculine and feminine gender respectively. . . . The same kind of alternation, although less pronounced, appears in the much later poem *Večnoženstvennoe,* written already in emigration.

Although man's unisexual aspirations have their roots in ancient cults and philosophies, Gippius's reinterpretation of the meaning and function of sexuality has anticipated the development of the psychological unisex in contemporary Western society. The causes for today's rejection and transformation of the traditional sexual roles and distinctions seem to be analogous to the motivating forces which gave rise to the androgynous ideal at the turn of the century. (pp. 102-04)

> Olga Matich, *"Zinaida Gippius and the Unisex of Heavenly Existence," in* Die Welt der Slaven: Halbjahresschrift für Slavistik *(reprinted by permission of Böhlau Verlag, Köln, Wein), Vol. XIX-XX, 1974-75, pp. 98-104.*

**TEMIRA PACHMUSS**   (essay date 1977)

To borrow Brjusov's pertinent description, Hippius was . . . "an outstanding *maître* of poetry" in that she created a harmony based on the regularity of dissonances and different emotional keys in her ever-changing moods. In order to see how the heterogeneous elements in her verse blend into one organic, well-integrated mosaic, it will suffice to analyze only a few of her poems written in exile and randomly selected. The careful distribution of words, colors, rhymes and metrical irregularities, all of which lead logically to the often paradoxical final statement is evident, for example, in *"Zvezdoubijca."* . . . (p. 121)

This verse can certainly be recognized as Hippius's own creation. There are her familiar mannerisms—the proverbial quality of diction, the Bal'montain repetition and "song" elements. The alternating masculine and feminine rhymes help to bring the ever-changing appearances of the eternal in the imperfect, physical world into more relief. The central image, the moon, with its nocturnal light which "kills" the mysterious and everlasting light of stars and illuminates only the seemingly disconnected and evanescent reflections of the absolute on the earth, reappears in all three stanzas. The poet creates an effective contrast between the moon as the *leitmotif* portraying all that is passing and illusory, on the one hand, and the stars, as the symbolic mystery of superior significance and imminence, on the other. In Hippius's poems, the last line almost invariably carries the whole semantic and emotional load. The degree of emphasis (emotional force) is achieved through the isolation of this single line from the rest of the final quatrain and the disruption of the repetition and the position of the words and syntagmas in the last two lines of the first and second stanzas. In fact, it is precisely in the last line of the poem that Hippius appeals to her reader to mistrust the deceptive light of the moon, for the beauty of the transcendental world, in her opinion, can also be realized on earth. . . . (p. 122)

Another device which Hippius often used to contrast the spiritual world of God and Platonic ideas with the material world is the compound epithet. Her epithets describing the spiritual world usually glorify the divine order and perfection that are lacking on earth. They portray the poet's aspirations to attain love in and with Christ. The epithets related to the empirical world, on the other hand, bewail its emptiness and immobility. The compound epithet [translated as "idly bright"] in **"Zvezdoubijca"** expresses the poet's vision of the insipidness and futility of all human endeavor on earth, which is symbolized by the central image of the moon with its deceptive light. The epithet, connected with the motifs of inactivity, impotence, loneliness and coldness, becomes a philosophically rich symbol which helps to open up the poet's *Weltanschauung.*

The concept of the dual universe is amplified in another poem of the period, **"Ne za mnoj."** . . . (p. 123)

The *persona* realizes that she belongs simultaneously to two worlds—the spiritual, in which she is free, and the physical, in which she is restricted. She "feels" and sees the ideal world, but is bound to earth. Availing herself of these devices, Hippius makes here a full, rounded poetic statement of her philosophy by producing rich, contrastive associations on several levels. The symbolic plane, the emotional aspect, the "semantic" level, and the rhyming pattern, are organically interrelated, resulting in a refined example of symbolic poetry. . . . (p. 124)

**"Ne za mnoj"** employs four colors: two are explicitly named (red and white), and two are implied ("green" valleys and "gray" steep slopes). They uphold the prevailing mood and amplify the philosophical and religious thought at the center of the poem. White almost always appears in Hippius's poetry as a symbol of the ideal, supranatural world, purity, love in Christ and eternity. A curious deviation from these meanings is found in her short story **"On belyj,"** . . . in which the devil emerges as a fallen angel of God who will ascend His throne while wearing white garments. The emphasis, however, even here is on the seraphic nature of the devil as a great sufferer, an angel grieving over man's spiritual torment.

The gray color in **"Ne za mnoj"** denotes anguish and hopelessness, among many other associations within the "negative" semantic field. The red stands for the love of Christ, His suffering and sacrifice. The green is linked with the beauty of nature, birth and life. We can see that the four colors, used in their symbolic meaning, form an integral part of the verse structure, for they establish the ties between the world of ideal love and perfect harmony and the world of finite experience. Although imperfectly mirrored on the earth, the spiritual world imparts meaning and unity to human life.

The most ingenious of the three poems selected for this study is perhaps **"V starom zamke."** . . . Everything in the poem is geared toward producing an impression of something extraordinary and unexpected at the end of the verse, when the reader learns that it is only the *persona's* heart which continues to beat, even though barely alive. At this point, Hippius's linguistic paradox becomes resolved into an existential paradox, revealing that this still, nocturnal world begins to affect even the *persona* herself. . . . The night, overpowering the *persona,* begins to draw her towards her death, all this only gradually coming to the self-awareness of the poet as a personal entity. This unanticipated revelation imparts a poignancy to the poem as a whole. The last cadence is also one of the shortest ones within **"V starom zamke."** Thus, as frequently happens in Hippius's verse, the climax is achieved at the end of the poem. The content and the meaning of the whole are again amplified and deepened by the subtle arrangement of imagery, rhythm, rhyme, parallels, and repetitions of words and syntactical units. . . . (pp. 125-26)

Another poem of the period, **"Domoj!"** . . . , which concludes the volume *Sijanija* and from which Hippius was often re-

quested to recite at various *soirées,* expresses the maximum degree of the poet's characteristic alienation and withdrawal from the visible and tangible world. . . . The former "negative semantic field" permeates the texture of the poem—life on earth is no more than disguises, masks, evil deeds, lies and bloodshed. With her strong and proud personality, the poet willfully rises above the exterior world, which is empty, cruel and tedious, and enters her own realm. It is noteworthy that the poem lacks epithets, for the empirical world, in its inanity, vulgarity and stagnation, needs no descriptive adjectives for its portrayal. There are no "cosmic" elements in **"Domoj!"** because the *persona,* with her feelings of disgust and disenchantment, is no longer involved in any struggle. Only the color red is implied here, but it is not used as a powerful symbol of Christ's love, suffering and sacrifice—it denotes bloodshed and war. . . . (pp. 127-28)

The climax is reached in the ending line of the poem—the *persona,* deceived by the promises given to her at her birth, is going "home." She is determined to escape this world of triviality and crime. . . . (p. 128)

The content and the symbolic meaning are magnified and rendered more intense by the artful collocation of words, syntagmas, images, rhythm and rhyme.

The foregoing analysis has revealed that, in exile, Hippius continued to experiment with new metrical possibilities and new means of organizing material. Her poems display their own individual forms and combinations of freedom and restriction. The *persona's* loneliness and isolation, which are the *leitmotifs* of her entire poetry, are expressed not only through images, but also through other poetic devices, such as colors, oxymoron constructions, contrasts, parallelisms, similes, abstract and "cosmic" vocabulary. . . . Rhyme, rhythm and alliteration add to the cumulative effect on the thematic level. The purely technical aspect of her poetry, therefore, discloses the magnitude of the situation at the center of the verse. Hippius explored all the latent potentialities of the Russian language to express the spiritual, universal struggle and to affirm the divine order of the universe, both of which are at the focus of her aesthetics. (p. 130)

*Temira Pachmuss, "Zinaida Hippius: A Russian Poet in Exile," in* Russian Language Journal *(copyright © 1977 by Editor of the* RLJ*), Vol. XXXI, No. 108, Winter, 1977, pp. 121-31.*

**HAROLD B. SEGEL** (essay date 1979)

[*Segel discusses Hippius's three dramas.*]

The first evidence of a movement away from realism and naturalism in Russian drama appeared in the 1880s and 1890s. (p. 59)

Merezhkovsky's wife, Zinaida Gippius . . . , an important literary figure in her own right and, like Merezhkovsky, a passionate disseminator of mystical Christian beliefs, . . . became interested in the drama and wrote three plays. Two of these, *Makov tsvet* (*The Red Poppy* . . . allegedly written together with Merezhkovsky and their friend D. V. Filosofov) and *Zelyonoe koltso* (*The Green Ring* . . .) deal with contemporary themes: the first with the impact on an affluent Russian family of the Revolution of 1905 with which Merezhkovsky and Gippius soon became disenchanted; the second, with young people (members of the "Green Ring Society," an obvious allusion to the Merezhkovskys' own "Green Lamp Society") attempting to assert their independence often in conflict with the older generation.

Gippius' first play, *Svyataya krov* (*Sacred Blood* . . .), anticipates a folkloric current in Neo-Romantic drama and at the same time dramatizes the transfigurative power of mystical Christianity with which much Symbolist thought was informed. Distantly echoing Gerhart Hauptmann's famous *The Sunken Bell*, *Sacred Blood* tells the story of the water sprite (*rusalka*) who yearns to acquire a human soul. In Gippius' version, the folk motif assumes a distinctly Christian aspect. The water sprite has heard of the sacrifice of Christ because of which man thereafter enjoys immortality of the soul and it is the beauty of Christ's Passion and Resurrection which inspires her. Eventually she learns that she can acquire a soul only by killing the old monk Pafnuti who has befriended her and whom she has come to love. . . . The murder, kept as an offstage action in the play, embodies two central concepts of Gippius' mysticism, namely love and sacrifice. It is only through love that life acquires meaning, death is vanquished, and man gains true immortality. The water sprite is finally able to kill Father Pafnuti because her love for Christ transcends her repugnance at the means she must use to unite with Him. By the same token, it is his love for the water sprite and his compassionate understanding of the love that motivates her that enables Father Pafnuti to offer himself in sacrifice. Both characters suffer but can accept their suffering as they perceive the love in which it is rooted and the spiritual perfection to which it gives rise. Although it has never been produced, *Sacred Blood* is by far the most interesting of Gippius' plays. The prose of the dialogue has the appealing quality of the *naïf* while the two water sprites' songs in the first and third acts provided Gippius with an opportunity to engage in novel experimentation with free unrhymed verse. (pp. 59-60)

> *Harold B. Segel, "The Revolt Against Naturalism: Symbolism, Neo-Romanticism, and Theatricalism," in his* Twentieth-Century Russian Drama: From Gorky to the Present *(copyright © 1979 Columbia University Press; reprinted by permission of the publisher), Columbia University Press, 1979, pp. 50-146.*

**SIMON KARLINSKY**   (essay date 1980)

[*Karlinsky surveys Hippius's career, finding her a seminal figure in Russian literature.*]

[Zinaida Gippius] was one of the main initiators of the poetic renascence known as Russian Symbolism, the originator of the verse forms and thematic concerns that helped shape the poetics of Alexander Blok, Andrei Bely, and numerous other poets. Anna Akhmatova . . . was central to the sober-minded, neo-realistic poetics of Acmeism. Marina Tsvetaeva . . . , who never joined a literary school in her life and would have bristled at being termed a Futurist poet, nevertheless summarized in her work all that was finest in the lexically and structurally innovative literary art of the Russian Futurists.

As a poet, Zinaida Gippius is the equal of these two great younger contemporaries. As a historical phenomenon, she is probably more important than either of them. (p. 1)

In any other country, the value of her achievement as a poet, the originality of her social, sexual, and religious views, and the impact of these views on the intellectual trends of her time would have by now resulted in a wide array of critical and biographical studies of Gippius, assessing her significance and

influence. But her violently anti-Bolshevik stance after the Revolution made her an un-person in the Soviet Union in post-revolutionary times, while her religious and political radicalism did not sit well with the growing conservatism of both Soviet and émigré literary scholarship from the 1930s on. (p. 2)

For a poet and thinker of such complexity, the formative influences on Gippius were surprisingly few. The essential ones were her reading of Dostoevsky at an early age, as Zlobin suggests, an equally early exposure to Lermontov's narrative poem "The Demon." Her enthusiasm for Dostoevsky determined her subsequent literary tastes and sympathies. . . . Like most other Symbolists, she fell under the spell of the idealistic and mystical teachings of Vladimir Solovyov. Apart from this, Gippius seems to have arrived at her theology, philosophy, and poetics on her own or in collaboration with Merezhkovsky. (p. 4)

Both Gippius and Merezhkovsky published their earliest poetry in the 1880s. It was a time when several decades of domination over literature by dogmatic, utilitarian-minded, radical critics, who tolerated poetry only when it preached elementary morality or contained social criticism, had brought poetic taste and understanding to its lowest point in modern Russian history. The decade of the eighties was dominated by the maudlin poetaster Semyon Nadson, acclaimed as a new incarnation of Pushkin merely because he wrote mainly of the evils of oppression and tyranny. Merezhkovsky's poetry never quite managed to shake off all traces of Nadsonism, but Gippius liberated herself from it, quickly and triumphantly. The poems she wrote in 1893 and 1894, initially rejected by some of the best literary journals of the time, marked the beginning of modern Russian poetry. In her verse of those years, Gippius expanded the boundaries of traditional Russian metrics, popularized the use of accentual verse (previously found in a few exceptional poems by such earlier figures as Vasily Zhukovsky and Afanasy Fet) and initiated the use of assonance rhymes. All these features were later developed and perfected by other important twentieth-century poets, among them Blok, Akhmatova, and Osip Mandelstam. But Gippius led the way. Without her pioneering example, neither Alexander Blok nor Vladimir Mayakovsky could have been what they later became.

Equally essential for the development of twentieth-century poetry in Russia were the themes of her poetry of the early 1890s. Some of her poems addressed themselves to social topics, but Gippius was primarily a philosophical and religious poet, possibly Russia's most profound religious poet of all time. She was one of the first to take up in her poetry the themes that were to become the central ones of much of Russian Symbolism as a whole: humanity's need for religious faith, the problem of achieving freedom in a necessity-bound world, the ambiguities of sex roles in most love relationships, the evil forces present in this world, and the inevitability of death as an ever-present factor in our lives. It is not an exaggeration to say that Gippius confronted in her poetry many of the basic themes that Dostoevsky treated in his novels and gave them her own original solutions or that, in a sense, she occupies in Russian poetry the position that Dostoevsky occupies in the Russian novel. (pp. 5-6)

While a governmental policy prevents Soviet scholars from according Gippius the attention she so obviously merits, the affinity of some of her views and interests with cultural trends in the West during the 1960s has led to the rediscovery of her work by some Western scholars. (p. 18)

Temira Pachmuss was responsible for the recent appearance of previously unpublished writings of Gippius such as her diaries and her correspondence, both in separate books and in excerpts and selections in various Russian émigré journals in Paris and New York. Professor Pachmuss's own detailed study, *Zinaida Hippius: An Intellectual Profile . . .* , while informative and containing important documentation, suffers, as do her numerous introductory essays to recent publications on Gippius, from this scholar's unwillingness to see the religiously heretical, politically radical, and sexually unconventional aspects of her subject. The constant desire of Professor Pachmuss to render Zinaida Gippius as conventional and innocuous as possible has led her not only to play down the very things that make Gippius the unique writer she is, but also to delete and censor in her editions of the diaries in English (*Between Paris and St. Petersburg*) and of the letters in Russian (*Intellect and Ideas in Action: Selected Correspondence of Zinaida Hippius*) the passages that apparently shock her notions of propriety.

A careful reading of the entire *oeuvre* of Zinaida Gippius that has now been made available in Russian in the West will confirm that her contemporaries at the turn of the century were right to place her in the front rank of Russian poets of that or any time. Her ability as a playwright is also beyond dispute. Her dramatic fantasy **Sacred Blood** and the more realistic **Poppy Blossoms** (written jointly with Merezhkovsky and Filosofov, but very much of a piece with her other works in conception and style) hold up remarkably well. Her play **The Green Ring,** which in a brilliant production by Vsevolod Meyerhold was the major event of the 1916 theatrical season, remains to this day one of the finest genuinely revolutionary and genuinely poetic plays in the Russian language.

In her prose writings, Gippius was at her weakest in the area where Merezhkovsky was at his best and most enduring: in literary criticism. The very qualities that made her such an original thinker and poet also made her blind as a critic. Her single critical feat—her early recognition of the genius of Osip Mandelstam—was never recorded in her essays and is known to us only through the accounts of others and a brief mention in her memoirs. By and large, as a critic she expected her own kind of metaphysical subtlety from all other writers and was incapable of taking an interest in any writing that did not derive from Dostoevsky. This *parti pris* led her to condemn as frivolous and insignificant prose writers of the caliber of Anton Chekhov (who was for Gippius a provincial dullard able to describe only the animal side of human existence and devoid of any understanding of women) and Vladimir Nabokov ("a writer who has absolutely nothing to say"), and to treat with contempt almost all the important Russian post-Symbolist poets, including Mayakovsky, Sergei Esenin, Pasternak, Akhmatova, and Tsvetaeva. In the case of Tsvetaeva, the attitude of Gippius (as revealed in her recently published letters to Nina Berberova and Vladislav Khodasevich) could on occasion take the form of irrational hatred that verged on the paranoid.

Nor was Gippius able to compete with Merezhkovsky in the field of the novel. Her two big political novels, **The Devil's**

**Puppet** and **Tsarevich Roman,** for all the knowledgeable and sympathetic glimpses they offer of life among turn-of-the-century revolutionaries, remain pallid and ineffectual imitations of Dostoevsky's *The Possessed*. But in the prose genres where Merezhkovsky did not leave his mark, the short story and the memoir, Gippius comes into her own and produces work that is superior to anything by Merezhkovsky and as good as anything written by the Symbolist prose writers of her generation. Her book of literary memoirs **Zhivye litsa** (reprinted by Professor Pachmuss as **Living Portraits,** although either *Living Persons* or *Lifelike Faces* would have been closer to the multi-levelled meaning of the Russian title) and her biography of Merezhkovsky (published in 1951 as **Dmitry Merezhkovsky;** her original title for this book was *He and We*) are basic documents for the study of the momentous literary epoch during which Gippius lived and to which she so prominently contributed. Together with her poetry, her plays, and her diaries, these two books add up to one of the more valuable literary treasure troves of our century. (pp. 19-21)

> *Simon Karlinsky, in his introduction to* A Difficult Soul: Zinaida Gippius *by Vladimir Zlobin, edited and translated by Simon Karlinsky (translation copyright © 1980 by The Regents of the University of California; reprinted by permission of the University of California Press), University of California Press, 1980, pp. 1-21.*

---

## ADDITIONAL BIBLIOGRAPHY

Maslenikov, Oleg A. "Disruption of Canonical Verse Norms in the Poetry of Zinaida Hippius." In *Studies in Slavic Linguistics and Poetics in Honor of Boris O. Unbegaun,* edited by Robert Magidoff, George Y. Shevelof, J.S.G. Simmons, and Kiril Taranovski, pp. 86-96. New York: New York University Press, 1963, 287 p.
      Technical analysis of the poetic forms employed by Hippius.

Pachmuss, Temira. Introductions to *Svjataja krov'*, *Makov cvet*, and *Zelënoe kol'co*. In *Collected Dramatical Works,* by Z. N. Hippius, pp. IX-XIII, I-XII, I-XI. Centrifuga: Russian Printings and Reprintings, edited by Karl Eimermacher and others, vol. 19. Munich: Wilhelm Fink, 1972.
      Examines each of Hippius's dramas as they reflect her changing religious and political attitudes.

Pachmuss, Temira. Introduction to *Between Paris and St. Petersburg: Selected Diaries of Zinaida Hippius,* by Zinaida Hippius, edited and translated by Termira Pachmuss, pp. 3-55. Urbana: University of Illinois Press, 1975.
      Biocritical essay, providing a detailed description of Hippius's religious philosophy.

Zernov, Nicolas. *The Russian Religious Renaissance of the Twentieth Century.* New York: Harper & Row, 1963, 410 p.*
      An intellectual history of the Russian religious renaissance, with reference to the roles played by Hippius and Merezhkovsky.

# (Friedrich Karl) Georg Kaiser

## 1878-1945

German dramatist, novelist, short story writer, essayist, and poet.

Kaiser is considered the most gifted and prolific dramatist of the German Expressionist movement. Extremely skillful and inventive, he did more than any other writer, except perhaps Bertolt Brecht, to transform German theater in the twentieth century. Kaiser wrote over seventy plays and two novels; between 1917 and 1933 he was the most frequently performed playwright in Germany. Though the majority of his plays were critically successful, his reputation rests specifically on three important works: *Die Bürger von Calais (The Burghers of Calais), Von Morgens bis Mitternachts (From Morn to Midnight),* and the *Gas* trilogy. Each of these dramas demonstrates the norms of pure expressionism in their emphasis on social issues and ideas rather than psychological concerns, and in their use of character types instead of individuated characters. They also display Kaiser's concept of the "New Man"—an individual who sacrifices himself for the common good of society and for new ideals of nonviolence and peace.

Kaiser was born in Magdeburg, Germany, the son of wealthy parents. When he was twenty-one he was sent to Argentina to serve as an official of a large German electric company in Buenos Aires. The climate disagreed with him, and after an attack of tropical fever he returned to Europe. Ill for a number of years, Kaiser resided in Spain and Italy and began to write as a means of passing the time. During this period he wrote his first plays, which were mainly satirical comedies, and included *Rektor Kleist* and *Die judische Witwe.* After his return to Germany, Kaiser enjoyed success with his first produced play, *The Burghers of Calais.* This work revealed his outstanding gift for constructing a close-knit drama, expressed in tense and impassioned language. *The Burghers of Calais* was followed by a series of social plays—including *From Morn to Midnight,* the *Gas* trilogy, and *Der Brand im Opernhaus (Fire in the Opera House)*—which quickly established his position as leader of the expressionist movement. As Kaiser continued his writing, his dedication to art began to assume a single-minded intensity. After the war and the collapse of the German economy, he illegally sold the furnishings from a house he did not own and used the money to maintain his luxurious lifestyle. He was arrested and served six months in prison. During his trial Kaiser had argued that as an artist he was above the law. Upon his release from prison he quietly returned to work with the same intensity and commitment, producing a variety of German dramas which embody social issues, personal conflicts, and classical themes. With the advent of Naziism, Kaiser's works were banned for their antimilitarism and subversive championing of the individual. In 1938 he barely managed to escape Nazi Germany and fled to Switzerland. There he continued to write until his death.

Nearly all of Kaiser's plays repeat the same themes: the fear of dehumanization; hostility to war, militarism, and industrialism; the conflict between intellectual and physical life; and the need for spiritual regeneration. *The Burghers of Calais*— based on the medieval chronicle by Jean Froissant—expresses Kaiser's conception of the "New Man." The drama also dem-

*Courtesy of the German Information Center*

onstrates the playwright's talents as a formalist: its structure is delicately composed of a series of patterned tableaux. *From Morn to Midnight* deals with the escape of an ordinary man from humdrum reality and his search for meaning in his life. Not only does the play reintroduce Kaiser's vision of the "New Man," but it also presents new techniques—such as rapid dialogue and fast-changing scenes—which served to establish the expressionistic form. The *Gas* trilogy—consisting of *Die Koralle (The Coral), Gas I,* and *Gas II*—is a symbolic portrayal of the disintegrating effects of industrialism on modern civilization. In the trilogy Kaiser argues that only individual spiritual renewal, and not social or economic reforms, can bring about the salvation of civilization. In his later works Kaiser strove for a more intimate view of humanity, one embodying a deep experience of love. Such plays as *Oktobertag (The Phantom Lover), Rosamunde Floris,* and *Alain und Elise* stress the need for sacrifice and love as a means of transcending human suffering. Kaiser's last work, the trilogy *Griechische Dramen,* is even more inward than his dramas of love. Loosely based on Greek mythology and written in iambic verse, *Griechische Dramen* reasserts the need for love and devotion in a hostile world.

Critics have consistently praised Kaiser's work for a number of different reasons. Some, such as B. J. Kenworthy, have lauded the originality of his language and stressed the importance of his contributions to the expressionist movement. Others, like R. W. Last, have praised the author for his subtle use of symbolism and setting. Perhaps what most sets Kaiser apart from his contemporaries is his acute feeling for dramatic form. It is this aspect of his writing which transforms the chaos of his plays into a drama which is both understandable and effective. However, Kaiser's work has also received its fair share of negative criticism. Certain commentators—such as Roderick Seidenberg, Ronald Peacock, and Ian C. Loram— have criticized his inability to empathize with his characters, or to create even a single sympathetic figure. Others have argued that he was more of a stage craftsman than a thinker, and that the success of his work is due to its daring expressionism rather than to the significance of its content. But despite the differences in critical opinion, Kaiser remains one of the most significant figures in German literature. In the words of Ernst Schurer, Kaiser "is not only an outstanding figure in twentieth-century German literature, he also occupies a focal position in the development of modern drama."

## PRINCIPAL WORKS

*Die Bürger von Calais* (drama) 1917
  [*The Burghers of Calais* published in *Five Plays*, 1971]
*\*Die Koralle* (drama) 1917
  [*The Coral* published in *Modern Continental Plays*, 1929]
*Von Morgens bis Mitternachts* (drama) 1917
  [*From Morn to Midnight* published in journal *Poet Lore*, 1920]
*Der Zentaur* (drama) 1917
*Der Brand im Opernhaus* (drama) 1918
  [*Fire in the Opera House* published in *Eight European Plays*, 1927]
*Das Frauenopfer* (drama) 1918
*\*Gas, I* (drama) 1918
  [*Gas*, 1924; also published as *Gas I* in *Modern Continental Plays*, 1929]
*Rektor Kleist* (drama) 1918
*Hölle Weg Erde* (drama) 1919
*\*Gas, II* (drama) 1920
  [*Gas II* published in *Modern Continental Plays*, 1929]
*Der gerettete Alkibiades* (drama) 1920
  [*Alkibiades Saved* published in *An Anthology of German Expressionist Drama*, 1963]
*Die jüdische Witwe* (drama) 1921
*Kanzlist Krehler* (drama) 1922
*Der Protagonist* (drama) 1922
  [*The Protagonist* published in journal *Tulane Drama Review*, 1960]
*Nebeneinander* (drama) 1923
*Gats* (drama) 1925
*Zweimal Oliver* (drama) 1926
*Gesammelte Werke*. 2 vols. (dramas and essays) 1928
*Oktobertag* (drama) 1928
  [*The Phantom Lover*, 1928]
*Es ist genug* (novel) 1932
*Villa Aurea* (novel) 1940
  [*A Villa in Sicily*, 1939; also published as *Vera*, 1939]
*\*\*Zweimal Amphitryon* (drama) 1944
*Das Floss der Medusa* (drama) 1945
  [*The Raft of the Medusa* published in journal *First Stage*, 1962]
*\*\*Bellerophon* (drama) 1953
*\*\*Pygmalion* (drama) 1953
*Rosamunde Floris* (drama) 1953

*Alain und Elise* (drama) 1954
*Stücke, Erzählungen, Anfsätze, Gedichte* (dramas, novels, short stories, essays, and poetry) 1966

*These works are collectively referred to as *Gas*.

**These works are collectively referred to as *Griechische Dramen*.

---

## LUDWIG LEWISOHN (essay date 1922)

Georg Kaiser, who has gained an international reputation more rapidly than Hauptmann did in his day, is not a great writer. Nor is he a small man borrowing glow and splendor from a great period; he is the small man of a violent period. But he has made that period or, rather, that moment—for it is already over—intelligible and vocal. And he has done so primarily in this piece "From Morn to Midnight." I have been rereading his other plays. There is a great, unclarified idea and a tinge of human warmth in "Die Bürger von Calais"; there is a force and turmoil like the contention of icy storms in "Gas"; in his comedies—"Die Sorina," "Der Zentaur,"—in his pseudo-historical plays—"Die jüdische Witwe," "König Hahnrei"— there is but one monotonous attitude, one frozen gesture. The moment in the history of the drama which will, not only in Germany, be connected with the names of Kaiser and Sternheim was a moment of unutterably cold disgust. It said to its predecessors, to Hauptmann, Shaw, Schnitzler, Galsworthy: "You whined about justice, compassion, rectitude, understanding, tolerance, beauty. Here is the war. This is what Europe is like. Man is a filthy beast; life is slime and ordure; let us whine no more." That mood is gone. In Ernst Toller, in Franz Werfel there sounds the voice of the eternal, bloodless revolution, the voice of love, of that tireless hope that "creates from its own wreck the thing it contemplates." Kaiser's hour of moral nihilism belongs to the past. "From Morn to Midnight" is its most memorable work.

The outer form of ["From Morn to Midnight"] is new—seven discontinuous episodes that merge into a final oneness of effect; the inner form is old as parables and legends. This bank cashier who, dazed by a woman's glow and fragrance, embezzles a small fortune and flees, what is he, at his core, but a pilgrim seeking salvation? It is only the name of salvation that changes. In one age it is submission of the human will to the divine will; in another it is the submergence of the will and so of pain in ecstasy. Ecstasy—that is the salvation the cashier seeks. The price is death. He shrinks no more than the martyrs did. He is not without scruples. He tests himself and his home; he tests natural pieties and griefs. They have no power to save him. He flees to the mob and finds tameness, to the flesh and finds no flame, to the soul and finds money-changers in her temple. There is no salvation whose name is ecstasy. He dies unsaved; the world is empty and the universe is empty. He is the crucified one of that emptiness. His dying lips moan an "Ecce homo!" This is, obviously, no vulgar fable, no vulgar work. In its small, narrow, unbeautiful way it has its faint kinship with the "Divine Comedy," "The Pilgrim's Progress," "Faust." . . . The snow scene, which is purely symbolical, is devised with astonishing skill, perhaps with too emphatic a virtuosity. The scene in the cashier's house strikes an imperfect note. What has the Germany of idyllic quaintness, of porcelain pipe and silken cap to do with this debased machine-made environment? The other scenes are magnificent. That in the hall of the Salvation Army is a triumph. Vulgarity, mystery, terror, the gloom of the spirit—all are here.

These racing visions must remain visions yet be real; every indication must have its sharp concreteness yet its symbolical power. The world is this actual world but it is in the fevered brain of one creature. (p. 726)

*Ludwig Lewisohn, "The Empty Road," in* The Nation *(copyright 1922 The Nation magazine, The Nation Associates, Inc.), Vol. 114, No. 2971, June 14, 1922, p. 726.*

## ASHLEY DUKES   (essay date 1923)

For Georg Kaiser the theatre is a rearrangement of intellectual particles. His personages are not in themselves interesting; we have no desire to know them, though we admit their reality. They are wholly creatures of habit and desire, filling a place in the *schema* of the dramatist. We are reminded of the working of a dynamo. It is indeed a perfect piece of mechanism that functions in his dramas, though it is not the smooth mechanism of the mechanical playwright. Rather is it the intricate interplay of two forces, on the one hand a naked but shameless instinct, and on the other a sharp intellectual faculty that penetrates to the core of the subject without touching either the heart of emotional response or the deepest sense of poetry. The utterance is felt to be unequal to the importance of the subject. The illumination is intense and intermittent, flash upon flash.

All these qualities are seen in *From Morn to Midnight (Von Morgens bis Mitternachts),* the drama of a bank cashier who embezzles money under the spell of the *beaux yeux* of a client at his counter, and is thereafter driven from pillar to post in mingled disillusionment and exaltation, casting his stolen money to the winds, until at last he shoots himself in a Salvation Army hall. The conception is distinguished, the technique masterly. A throng of nameless characters hurries across our field of vision, and if one of them pause but for an instant, the outline of his character remains fixed in the memory. But Georg Kaiser's imagination turns most of all to the sinister possibilities of his subject—the deadly and deadening satire of the cashier's home life, the flashy excitement of the crowd at the cycle races, the prostitute with a wooden leg at the cabaret, the lyrical salvation-seekers in the midst of "a city of asphalt." (pp. 121-22)

Rapid and sure characterisation, graphic gesture, concentration of dialogue into key-words and phrases from which thought is crystallised—these are the qualities of Kaiser's drama as a whole. Exaltation is there, but ecstasy fails. The art that transfigures reality is yet to seek. (p. 125)

*Ashley Dukes, "Expressionists," in his* The Youngest Drama: Studies of Fifty Dramatists *(reprinted by permission of the Literary Estate of Ashley Dukes), Ernest Benn, Limited, 1923, pp. 107-40.**

## WILLIAM A. DRAKE   (essay date 1928)

Two decades ago, it was Frank Wedekind. To-day, it is Georg Kaiser who shocks and astounds the multitude and confounds the critics into terminological inexactitudes. In considering the work of Georg Kaiser, one should not lose sight of the fundamental paradoxes which he, as an artist, represents. He has become the acknowledged leader of a movement to which he does not properly belong. In his plays are indistinguishably

mingled the impulses of a pure craftsman with those of an obstreperous pamphleteer. His emphatic individualism is not egoism at all, but the desperate assertion of a prophet who cries with his solitary voice in a wilderness of ruined social forms. And finally, the considerable achievements which have already placed Georg Kaiser in the first rank of the dramatists of modern Germany, are merely the beginning of the greater work in which he may justly still be expected to consummate his unique and erratic genius. Far from having, as some of his critics pretend, exhausted his talent by producing thirty plays in half as many years, he gives evidence of a still broader development along the lines so admirably introduced in **Die Koralle** and the twin plays of **Gas.** Consequently, any criticism which may now be made of Georg Kaiser must needs be preliminary, for the masterpiece which ought logically to culminate his labors is apparently still to be written.

In the brief period of its ascendancy, the genius of Georg Kaiser has been adorned with a variety of descriptive titles, none of which is quite exact. The truth is, that his is an eccentric talent, ordered by a certain constancy alike of technique and social focus, but in its nature largely outside the prevailing manners of the day. Bernhard Diebold, in that exceedingly intelligent discursion upon the contemporary German playwrights, *Anarchie im Drama,* insists that Kaiser is a Cubist. So far as the point of specific technique is concerned, he is doubtless more nearly right than those other critics who have secured the author of **Von Morgens bis Mitternachts** in the position which he now holds, by common consent, at the head of the Expressionist movement. But this is a minor distinction. Cubism, at least as far as literature is concerned, has by now become a department of a larger, more systematic, and more consequential effort toward a vigorous, original, and compact art for the new age, which has long since outgrown the original significance of the name, but is still referred to by the convenient tab of Expressionism.

But these considerations have to do with movements and with deliberate technical expedients. Kaiser, except incidentally, does not concern himself with either. He is an instinctive artist, writing in the form best suited for the interpretation of his peculiar message. If, in his work, he has been able to make a considerable contribution to the dramaturgy of Expressionism, this has come about because the spirit of his art, its content, and his instinctive approach to its expression, are charged with a force of conviction and a dynamic contemporaneity which have provided their own genius. . . . (pp. 87-8)

Kaiser has frequently been called a philosophical dramatist, and the absurdity of the epithet is patent in the great images of Goethe and Schiller which it evokes. Kaiser is, in fact, more free from the taint of philosophy than any serious dramatist since the loquacious days of Weimar. He is a man who has felt life bitterly without having lost his faith in life, but who has arrived at certain disturbing convictions with regard to the present course of human society. Perhaps the strongest impression which one has after reading the whole medley of Kaiser's plays, is that their author is a man who knows almost more than is decent of the meanness of his fellow-creatures, but loves them all with an impetuous commiseration that transcends finite judgment. In a curious sense, it is the insistence of this love that makes Kaiser appear more significant, as a social prophet and reformer than as an artist. His social vision is not sufficiently comprehensive and coherent, nor analytical enough, to let him see wherein his world is out of joint and how he may prevail to set it right. His social consciousness is, in fact, singularly shallow. But it is passionately earnest, and is consecrated to the sole desire of humanity's advancement through the survival of its superior types. The pure passion of fellow-love and of resentment of social wrong has taken Kaiser closer to actual significance than either such a limited art as his or a far sounder social theory could have done. (p. 89)

The influence of Strindberg, and especially of Wedekind, is emphatic in Kaiser's earliest plays; it was not until afterwards that the lighter influences of Shaw and Sternheim came to qualify their rigors. Kaiser himself claims Schopenhauer, Dostoevsky, Nietzsche, Plato, and Hölderlin as his chief inspirers. *Rektor Kleist, Die Sorina* and *Der Zentaur* are light satirical comedies, strongly influenced by the author of *Die Büchse der Pandora,* and distinctly social in character. For a time after these early efforts, Kaiser attempted a curious revamping of legendary scenes and characters to modern situations. In *Die Jüdische Witwe,* he satirizes the legend of Judith and Holofernes; in *König Hahnrei,* that of Tristan and Isolde; in *Der Gerettete Alkibiades,* the apocryphal exploit of Sokrates in rescuing the Greek general, and his subsequent sentence. These are plays full of deliberate anachronisms, wherein, with the most delightful malice, Kaiser flays modern institutions and prejudices. Wedekind had attempted the same feat in *So ist das Leben* and *Simson,* but without anything of Kaiser's lightness and his complete success. Beneath the dexterous hand of his successor, these allegorical satires become as lucid and incisive as Shaw's *Man and Superman.*

The best and most serious of Kaiser's pseudo-historical dramas is *Die Bürger von Calais.* In this magnificent play, Kaiser for the first time . . . establishes the sociological orientation of his maturer work. The plot is founded upon the familiar legend of the six citizens of Calais demanded by the English as hostages for their city in 1347, after the rout of the French armies at Crécy. The story hinges upon the determination of all the men of Calais to possess this perilous honor, and the suicide of old Eustache de Saint-Pierre because he fears to arrive too late at the place of meeting. The thesis, punctuated in the play by much discussion of social problems, is obvious: that the good of the community surpasses all other benefits, and that the individual must, at all times, be prepared to offer himself for the community, and to covet that sacrifice as the highest possible consummation of his existence.

With *Die Bürger von Calais,* the plays of Georg Kaiser become significant as social documents. The erotic persiflage of the earlier comedies has entirely disappeared, and the social satire becomes sharper and more aggressive. In *Europa,* Kaiser returns for a moment to his Dionysian Spiel und Tanz, to preach the gospel of a new Superman. Then, in *Von Morgens bis Mitternachts,* he contrives the most savage satire in recent literature upon the money-lust of the modern world and the fallacy of its reduction of all values to a common denominator of gold. In *Kanzlist Krahler,* that pathetic tragedy of the old man whose single day of freedom, after forty years of humdrum labor, leaves him with a hatred of work, he as severely arraigns the capitalistic system which, by its incessant pressure, incapacitates the individual for the enjoyment of life. In the three-part play *Hölle Weg Erde,* he relates an effective allegory of each man's responsibility for his brother's good; and in *Der Brand im Opernhaus,* he recites the more somber and melodramatic tale of a weary man of the world who seeks a new life in the bosom of innocence, only to have that innocence become smirched by the ineludible cynicism of the metropolis.

One might with profit pause to examine all of Kaiser's plays and playlets, observing in *Das Frauenopfer,* the wife who sac-

rifices herself for her husband; in *Claudius,* the knight who recognizes his responsibility in his wife's guilt, yet kills her to keep his honor and their love untarnished; in *Friedrich und Anna,* the man whose resentment against his wife's early seducer is changed to gratitude when he learns that she has had joy of him; in *Juana,* the involuntarily bigamistic wife who poisons herself to preserve the friendship which unites her erstwhile husbands; in *Die Flucht nach Venedig,* the amorous regurgitations of George Sand and Alfred de Musset; in *Gilles und Jeanne,* the reaction of an unsatisfied and historically non-existent passion upon a violent character. But we must hasten to the great dramatic sequence composed of *Die Koralle* and the two parts of *Gas.* This trilogy was published in 1920, but it remains, in its entirety, decidedly Kaiser's finest dramatic achievement, and the instrument in which his art and his ideology at once reach their highest and most complete expression. (pp. 90-3)

[Kaiser] is too acutely conscious of life to be impassive about it, and he loves his fellow-man too well not to be ferociously jealous of his destiny. Georg Kaiser is exclusively a dramatist of ideas, and a strenuous crusader for those ideas. But these intellectual qualities do not detract from his effectiveness or his dexterity as a dramatist; and therein he is revealed, not as a philosopher at all, but as a practical reformer in action. He perceives, with devastating clarity, the drama inherent in ideas, because ideas present themselves to him much more dramatically than ever the eternal puppet-play of life.

And in carrying out this instinctive dramatization of ideological values in the theater, Georg Kaiser has accomplished a particular goal which sets him in a place apart from his alleged school and all his contemporaries. Although he is one of the first and most clever practitioners of the Expressionist dramaturgy, he has adopted an objective and scientific approach in the point where his contemporaries are most subjective and mystical. A dramatist entirely born of and absorbed in his epoch, he has transposed the exact tempo of that epoch in his art. His is a mechanized universe, as cruel and stark as structural steel and as curt and matter-of-fact as the telegraph: a universe of intense compression, frigid economy, and complete materialism. Here even men have ceased to exist as individuals, but disclose themselves as abstractions symbolizing the types of their various social appearances. So, from allegory to allegory, Georg Kaiser arranges his symbolical figures and plots against the background of factory smokestacks, and, by the pure passion of his conviction, makes them live, beneath their masks, a tragedy as bitter and significant as that which Hamlet designed to accuse the guilty King. Not all of this may be art. But it is something finer and more deadly. (pp. 96-7)

> William A. Drake, ''Georg Kaiser,'' in his Contemporary European Writers (copyright, 1927, by William A. Drake), The John Day Company, 1928, pp. 87-97.

**MOSES JOSEPH FRUCHTER**   (essay date 1933)

[*In the opening chapter to his study of Kaiser, excerpted below, Fruchter explains Kaiser's oeuvre as a diverse body of works unified by their efforts to define a moral stance for the individual confronted with an immoral society.*]

Georg Kaiser's amazing productivity has been subject to some speculation and much comment. He has been called a man of scattered interests, a kind of literary Janus, a dramatic juggler, a skilful craftsman with a nose for the possibilities of the stage, a dealer in problems, an eccentric stylist, a dramatic mechanic, a cinematographic author. In short, a playwright whose enormously prolific output bore witness to the fact that birth was not connected with great spiritual pain. Thus various negative critics have represented him as deficient in what is doubtless the most essential element of all significant literature, namely true human warmth, sincere interest in human life, consequently as lacking in poetry, in lyricism; above all, the harshest of indictments, as lacking in a central philosophy of life, a definite attitude to the problems of existence. (p. 5)

The denial of a central philosophy of life which seems to be the upshot of these criticisms must be considered the gravest of possible charges. To have no definite philosophy of life is to have no form, no soul. For soul is nothing but what James Joyce terms it in *"Ulysses,"* the form of forms. Consequently to be found guilty of this charge is to be formless, inconsequential, of no significance whatever.

In the face of the problem of Kaiser's prolific literary output, purely from the external aspect of the matter and without inner evidence from his work, obviously the thought suggests itself that:

1. Kaiser's works did not flow from a deeply unified conception of life; since to express a profound and crystallized philosophy superproductivity would be anomalous, shallow, superfluous, and

2. That consequently Kaiser must be a man of many themes which are perhaps only feebly connected by a common thread of whatever nature: style, mannerism or what not.

Such contentions are, to be sure, in part correct. Single instances may be brought to illustrate and qualify these judgments. But as a generally applicable dictum such a criticism would be exaggerated and entirely unjust. (pp. 6-7)

[It is important to prove by positive results] in the first place, that within the apparent diversity Kaiser shows clearly singleness of purpose, and secondly, that, with rare exceptions, his works point to a definite philosophy of life underlying the treatment of each theme, no matter how widely separated some of them may appear. (p. 7)

Bearing in mind that it was left to Expressionism to pierce through the individual to the social conscience, and having accepted the generally undisputed classification of Kaiser as an expressionist, nothing remains more logical than the choice of what must be the most typical and essential in his work: man's conscience or the ethical theme.

In an article by Georg Kaiser entitled *"Dichtung und Energie"* one finds certain theoretical utterances which are strongly self-revelatory. In it Kaiser appears pre-eminently as the apostle of Platonic perfectionism positing the proposition that happiness consists in a harmonious development of all human faculties, and that the root of all social evil lies in society's frustration of this effort.

"Man," he says, "is perfect from the very beginning. He is, so to speak, a finished product from the very moment of his birth. The limitations to which he finally succumbs are not part of his inner nature," but "imposed upon him from without, as a result of the distorted forms to which his destiny is subjected."

This sounds like the familiar voice of Rousseau. It exonerates the individual from guilt in his own fate and places the burden of responsibility upon the faulty social organization which forces him from the straight path, predestined by Nature, into fatal maladjustments. The problem of guilt and responsibility here touched upon in a cursory manner will be treated again, more fully, at a later stage, as one of the crucial moral interests in Kaiser's social system. The tragedy of the individual who is designed by Nature to lead a harmonious life, consists in the fact that the individual is thrown off his course and that he is condemned—living within an unnatural scheme of things—to a slow and inexorable corrosion of his creative powers which leaves no hope of personal happiness.

Thus we can conceive of the tragedy of thwarted faculties of life of the Millionaire in *"Koralle,"* of the Cashier in *"Von Morgens bis Mitternachts,"* of Krehler in *"Kanzlist Krehler";* such is the tragedy of chained existence and imprisoned instincts of life in *"Noli me tangere."* This is also one of the problems, if not the dominant problem in a series of other plays.

Against this crippling of life the victims of this tragic fate revolt: the Cashier doomed to the deadening monotony of counting bills behind the barred window of his cage; Krehler whose whole course of life consists in the inanimate routine of office work; the Millionaire who is horrified by the misery and the degradation which are to him synonymous with poverty. And in this unequal struggle they are doomed to inevitable crushing defeat. For opposing them is a world-system blind and deaf to the outcries, to the unutterable longings of wounded souls. From the constricting grip of this mechanized, unfeeling, fixed world-system there appears to be no escape, save—in death. It clutches man with a machine's iron teeth and there is no return.

To understand Kaiser's condemnation of present-day society, it is necessary to recognize that at the very foundation of his ethical system lies *the principle of the individual's positive moral obligation in relation to society.* This concept works itself slowly through his comedies and rises to the height of clarity and conviction in his social dramas. It is caricatured as an aberration in *"Konstantin Strobel";* its distorted forms are satirized from varying aspects in *"Die Versuchung," "Der Geist der Antike," "Der Präsident";* it is treated from a peculiar angle in *"Claudius."* It manifests itself with growing force of belief in the Sixteenth Prisoner of *"Noli me tangere,"* the Captain of *"Gats,"* the Millionaire's descendants in the *"Koralle"*—*"Gas"* cycle, in the luminous figures of the Pawnbroker in *"Nebeneinander",* Spazierer in *"Hölle, Weg, Erde",* Eustache in *"Die Bürger von Calais".*

This consciousness of moral responsibility, carried a step further, becomes *the sense of individual guilt,* inherited by each through the mere act of belonging to the common body of humanity, the sense of guilt from which none can be exempted. This thought is given expression most emphatically in *"Nebeneinander"* and *"Hölle, Weg, Erde",* but it can be seen in its embryonic stage of development already as early as *"Rektor Kleist",* in the figure of Kornmüller. These ideas are aspects of what may be termed Kaiser's *dynamic conception of social ethics.*

If society is a collective body composed of individuals, the whole cannot transcend its units of composition. This is one of the strongest tenets of Kaiser's moral philosophy. As in Greek tragedy, man bears upon his shoulders the guilt in the commission of which he may have had no definitely direct part. But what in Greek tragedy was the sin of the fathers, a fatalistic curse, becomes in Kaiser the sin of society, consequently an outgrowth of human factors and thus controllable by force of reason. The transcendent divine force of Greek tragedy is in Kaiser devoid of any theological or metaphysical connotation; it is the recognition of the universality of man and of the interdependence of individuals on the one hand, and the individual and society on the other.

The antithesis to Kaiser's ideal of a *positive ethics* is contained in the *negative moral principles* of present society. According to Kaiser, human misery and suffering is due to this absence of a social sense of responsibility on the part of the individual, either because of a lack of understanding, or because of hard-heartedness, callousness, selfish indifference to the rights and interests of others—the great sin of present-day society, the only great immorality.

This immorality, however, is the officially sanctioned practice of modern society. Organized society does not recognize the great moral *crime of omission*. It punishes and defends exclusively against certain forms of positive criminal offences. Perpetration of a damaging act against another individual is a crime, but to stand by indifferently and suffer your next to perish without the slightest attempt to intercede, to assist—is legal. Therein consists the antithesis of the ethical code of the state to the positive dynamic morality of the coming humanity, of the *New Man*.

Present social morality is negative in its very foundation and in its principles. (pp. 7-10)

As early as in the play, *"Die jüdische Witwe,"* Kaiser exposes this negative spirit against which Judith attempts to assert her natural human rights, but it is not until the later plays, especially in *"Nebeneinander"* and in *"Hölle, Weg, Erde"*, that this thought finds its fullest expression. In these two dramas the dialectic clash between the negative ethics of society and the dynamic conception of ethics of the New Man is portrayed vividly through the encounters between the Pawnbroker and Spazierer and the various forms of organized society. (p. 10)

According to Kaiser a new world can be created, the regeneration of humanity can be brought about only by a transvaluation of moral values from a static and negative to a positive and dynamic force. To make morality the true Messiah of a new and happy form of existence, it must crush the top-crust of sterility and stereotypy and become natural and positive. Not until then can it become a progressive and enriching force. (pp. 11-12)

> *Moses Joseph Fruchter, in his* The Social Dialectic in Georg Kaiser's Dramatic Works *(reprinted by permission of the Literary Estate of Moses Joseph Fruchter; originally a thesis presented at The University of Pennsylvania in 1933; copyright 1933), 1933, 89 p.*

## HORST FRENZ (essay date 1946)

Kaiser is considered one of the chief exponents of Expressionism (defined by Lothar Schreyer as "the spiritual movement of a time that places inner experience above external life"), the best known example of which, in his repertoire, is *From Morn to Midnight,* the story of man's futile attempt at realizing his ideals, compressed into the events of a single day. The drama depicts such typical scenes of modern life as a sport palace, a cabaret, a bank, all symbolizing various human activities. Most of the characters are nameless abstractions or types—a bank cashier, a lady, a stout gentleman, a mask. No

attempt is made to have us know his characters; their features, Desmond MacCarthy declares in *The New Statesman*, "are apprehended in the same vivid, perfunctory way that a man in a desperate hurry at a crowded railway station, looking for somebody or something, takes in the faces of other travellers."

Kaiser's language is factual, concise, at times even brutal, his style laconic, staccato, emphasizing with telegraphic brevity the haste and tempo of the action. As in all his plays, he evinces a deep understanding of theatrical contrasts, stage effects, and dramatic tension. Always an eager student of the scenic and staging techniques of modern stage designers—particularly the stylists and constructionists—he makes extensive use of such striking technical devices as the revolving stage, cyclorama, platforms, and masks. (pp. 363-64)

More interesting than *From Morn to Midnight* is the loosely connected trilogy of *Gas, I* . . . . Here and in most of his serious plays Kaiser paints an extremely pessimistic picture of modern society, a society in which energy is the driving force and man emerges impotent and enslaved by a civilization for which he himself is responsible. But—and this is very significant for an understanding of many of Kaiser's plays—there is a glimmer of hope, the hope for a rejuvenated, regenerated race, for a "new man." In the gigantic struggle between mechanical forces and man there is, in the words of Barrett H. Clark, "always some idealist ready to be crucified, some woman who will bear a son to carry on the struggle with that energy which the dramatist believes to lie at the root of all human endeavor." (p. 365)

Of special significance is the fact that Kaiser not only exerted great influence upon the European drama and stage but stimulated American playwrights. In many ways, Elmer Rice's *The Adding Machine* reminds one of *From Morn to Midnight*. There is an affinity, also, between Kaiser and Eugene O'Neill, both of whom consider Strindberg their spiritual father. Clara Blackburn, in the March, 1941, issue of *American Literature*, for instance, pointed out similarities in dialogue and stage directions between the third scene of *From Morn to Midnight*, "in which The Cashier trudges across a snow-covered field through a tangle of low-hanging branches," and the scenes of *The Emperor Jones* in which Brutus Jones wanders in the jungle. Their visions are almost alike, "the skeleton with grinning jaws which The Cashier sees in a tree, and the ghosts of murdered victims which Jones sees in front of him." (p. 366)

Although Kaiser has become known as an Expressionist, his plays have never been really popular on the American and British stage; which is surprising, for there is a quality in Kaiser's style and technique which Herman G. Scheffauer in his book, *The New Vision in the German Arts*, calls the expression and efflorescence of the American spirit—Scheffauer speaks of the early twenties—"as this is seen idealized by a European artist . . . and given power, voice, direction as an element in art." Unfortunately, as far as his reputation in this country is concerned, Kaiser has been classified almost exclusively as the member of the Expressionist school, a school in which there was only a passing interest. He has never been considered for what he really is—one of the most versatile of modern playwrights, one who has made a serious attempt at finding a new form of dramatic expression and has tried his hand at tragedies, tragicomedies, social problem plays, satires, entertaining comedies, and even detective plays.

In the turmoil of the late thirties the world heard little of Kaiser, but he continued to write plays that should be made known to the American public: *Adrienne Ambrossat,* for instance, which had its premiere in Vienna in 1935, and which, although unsuccessful, proved Kaiser's real poetic abilities. (pp. 366-67)

[A] play which, in scenes filled with emotion, brings out the cruelty and quiet suffering of which man is capable, is *Rosamunde Floris*. . . . In order to keep her real love preserved from shame and public smear, Rosamunde names a man who died in an accident of having been the father of her child, then forces his brother to marry her, and finally kills him, his fiancée, and the child. Although she is cleared of all suspicion, her conscience makes her break down and confess. In this drama Kaiser performs the difficult task of creating a woman character who, in spite of her crimes, arouses pity and toward the end even sympathy.

Here is a timeless human conflict between love and moral guilt.

[In *Alain und Elise*] Kaiser reveals the depths of feelings man can reach and describes his complete submission to them. Alain, a sensitive artist, who has painted a picture of Elise, the wife of a wealthy industrialist, rejects her love. He has discovered that his life belongs to his art. Through intrigues of every kind Elise tries to bring Alain closer to her—by inventing a story of his abuse of her husband's hospitality, by falsely accusing him of the murder of her husband, by preventing the court from showing clemency during the trial. In a remarkable final scene Kaiser shows Alain on his way to the prisoners' island and Elise watching him from a window. Although they are separated, although they know that they will never see each other again, the drama ends on a note of almost triumphant happiness. At last, Elise's irresistable love finds response in Alain who, at the very end of the play, expresses the belief that, beyond time and space, there is "an eternal power which balances joy and suffering."

*Der Soldat Tanaka* shows, perhaps better than any other play by Kaiser, the fusion of high thinking and deep emotion of which the German playwright is capable. . . . Tanaka is one of the Emperor's best soldiers, obedient and content because he believes that the Emperor feeds and clothes him and pays for his maintenance out of his private funds. However, when he realizes that the utter poverty and desolation of his family is the result of the Emperor's splendor, and particularly when he discovers that his parents had to sell their daughter to a brothel in order to meet the payment of taxes and rent, he becomes the murderer of his sister and of one of his superior officers. When he is promised some consideration by the military court on the condition that he apologize to the Emperor, Tanaka makes an extraordinary speech in which he denounces the Emperor, blames him for the outrageous conditions of the country, and finally asks him for his apologies. Tanaka is immediately led from the court room and put to death.

While in these plays Kaiser seems to be primarily interested in the individual's feelings, his hopes and disappointments, he has by no means given up certain expressionistic techniques. There is much symbolism in *Alain und Elise,* as, for instance, the court scene which might be called a new dramatic interpretation of the dance of death, or the recurrent motif of the tolling of the bell. Kaiser makes extensive use of the pantomime, particularly in the group scenes. The protagonist in *Der Soldat Tanaka* is not only the Emperor's soldier, he is any man turning against political systems and doctrines which advocate and perpetuate poverty, ignorance, and suppression. The prostitutes, who have lost their identity, are symbolic of the crushed and suppressed members of society, while the military court

stands for indisputable authority and military might. And so Kaiser, who in his earlier years showed the effect of the cruel forces of machinery, trusts, and industries upon man, in one of his last plays advanced to an indictment of the most recent enslaver of mankind—dictatorship. (pp. 367-69)

> *Horst Frenz, "Georg Kaiser" (reprinted by permission of the author), in* Poet Lore, *Vol. LII, No. 4, Winter, 1946, pp. 363-69.*

### RONALD PEACOCK (essay date 1953)

*Gas* is not a great play; it suffers from stridency and overemphatic style, and the feeling about "humanity" that makes it a violent rhetorical protest against certain tendencies in modern society remains crude and sentimental. Yet it is a very remarkable play because, using a bold and incisive method for the theatre, it projected an original vision of the society that was fast developing within the liberal bourgeois framework which was still what the surface showed. In the general development of this century the date of the play—1918—has significance as marking the end of World War I and therewith of the first stage of the transition from the liberal capitalist society of the nineteenth century to the socialized states and planned centralized societies of the following era. Kaiser's theme is the dehumanizing influence of technocratic social organization. His method is to portray such a society, bring catastrophe upon it from one of its own elements, and use a main character as a foil to point his moral. His picture shows a factory community, producing the most up-to-date form of energy, not only run with maximum scientific efficiency but also completely socialized, since its head, the Billionaire's Son, has renounced his wealth for the sake of the new ideal, by which the profits are shared. In this perfectly, even idyllically, arranged life an explosion occurs which by all the laws of science should not. Kaiser makes great play with the symbolic "formula" that represents the limit of scientific exactitude and yet still leaves something to the unexplainable and uncontrollable; so that there is a dangerous flaw not only in the formula but in the nature of the society which is built on the idea behind it. The Billionaire's Son learns his lesson from the destruction and suffering and turns away from a society and a philosophy that are at the mercy of such a catastrophe. If the factory with its formulae and machines is liable to such a breakdown why be enslaved to it? He recovers for himself the human sense of values of the pre-technological life and, finding a new ideal for his philanthropy, imagines a farming community in which men can be natural and human again. This vapid return-to-nature or agrarian philosophy is as weak as the picture of the futuristic worker-technician-factory culture is incisive. (pp. 62-3)

Toller was to say in connection with his own technique that you can see men as "realistic human beings" but you can also see the same men, in a flash of vision, as puppets which move mechanically in response to external direction. The people in Kaiser's picture of society are puppets in this sense, with their meaning withdrawn from their humanness and concentrated in their function, for which one part of them may be alone of significance, their hand, or eye, for instance. In a sullen way these people are indeed aware that they are distortions; but great pathos (in spite of the overemphasis) derives from their inability to revolt and liberate themselves; so long as someone is "punished" for the explosion they are satisfied to let the process start again. . . . (p. 63)

One realizes [in *Gas*] that Kaiser has taken several steps beyond the simple protests at the misery of underpaid workers, uninteresting factory jobs, and slums, consequent on the industrial revolution. These were familiar to the later nineteenth century, both in literature and sociological writing. In drama the humanitarian protest at social misery is well seen in Hauptmann's *Die Weber*. Kaiser's protest is not against misery of that kind, held in abhorrence as an affront to human beings. His socialized world has removed those things. He protests against the loss of human status. The shrill nostalgia of the Billionaire's Son for "den Menschen" ["mankind"] would not be so excessive if it were a case simply of suffering, for that brings human qualities and virtues into play. He fights his battle against men who have lost the knowledge of what man is. They are morally destitute because the private world is gone. A wholly public world engulfs the human one. Every person is chained to a function in a closely articulated mechanism; and when human creatures exist as no more than a function within a whole, the whole itself is not human.

The nature of Kaiser's vision of society in this play has not to my knowledge been explicitly related to the conditions of 1917-18 in Germany, when, under the stress of a war no longer offensive but desperately defensive, the country was converted into a military machine. . . . If *Gas* is based on German society of 1917-18, as I think it is, it gives, however "expressionistic" in method, a vision of reality. Clearly a process of generalization is involved; but the play presents an image of the skeletal structure of a certain kind of society. Although simplified, it is logical and analytically true. And on this truth to something real rests its power, because that provides some justification for an emotional atmosphere so intense as to border on hysteria. The pessimism is strong; and with reason, when the end of the individual and his moral independence is involved. (pp. 64-5)

[If] "society" for Ibsen was the herd with its fears and stupidities, but still a human herd, here in Kaiser it is the product of economic and industrial forces which transcend the individual will. His drama is in consequence a *critique of society*, or social structure, in the twentieth century sociological meaning of the words. His picture, with its unnamed persons representing classes or functions, its elimination of the private man and his private life (the daughter and her officer husband who runs into debt and commits suicide are the faintest echoes of "bourgeois" life), its sharp stylizations streamlining the features of the technocratic culture, and its clipped, pounding verbal style, shows an adjustment of dramatic form not only to some extraneous principle of style or subjective expression but to the new social realities.

It is a noticeable feature of *Gas* that the nature and quality of *Menschentum* remain obscure. Kaiser's feeling is all concentrated in his protest, in the name of something referred to as humanity, against its elimination. Hence on the one hand we have a stark, metallic, glinting picture of the system criticized, and on the other an explosion of rebellious sentiment. The former we see to be analytically correct; the indignation and pity we take as a sign of good faith. But we are not given to feel in our minds or senses some quality of living, or thought, or sensibility, or character, recognizable as belonging to what we mean in an ideal sense by "humanity." In short, the play, although a strained expression of human resentment and nostalgia, contains no person, or situation, or words that vibrate, if only for a moment, with the ideal so constantly evoked in name. (p. 65)

*Ronald Peacock, "Public and Private Problems in Modern Drama," in* Bulletin of the John Rylands Library (*reprinted by permission*), *Vol. 36, No. 1, September, 1953 (and reprinted in* The Tulane Drama Review, *Vol. 3, No. 3, March, 1959, pp. 58-72)**

### IAN C. LORAM  (essay date 1957)

The last three plays which Georg Kaiser wrote as a trilogy are a strange combination of pessimism and optimism. They have in common a mythical background—the legends of Pygmalion, Amphitryon, and Bellerophon, and testify at some length to their author's pessimistic belief that mankind is incapable of managing its affairs. The element of optimism also lies in this conclusion, because it seems clear from the ending of *Bellerophon* that some kind of mystical union with a greater power behind the world is Kaiser's final solution to the problem, which he felt so deeply, of the weakness and brutality of man's relationship to man.

There is much that is personal in the plays, particularly *Pygmalion*, and Kaiser never tired of speaking out against tyranny, violence, and war in all their various forms, as he does in *Zweimal Amphitryon*. But the emphasis, so vehemently expressed in many of the earlier plays, on the necessity and ability of the individual to fight his way through, even though he be destroyed in the process, is missing here. In none of these dramas is the protagonist literally destroyed, and yet Kaiser makes it perfectly obvious that without the help of a higher power man is frustrated and defeated. He is no longer capable, as he once was for the expressionist Kaiser, of taking upon himself the sins of the world. What he needs now is the assistance of grace.

Pygmalion seems to be Kaiser's version of the now familiar theme of the "problem of the artist," and quite possibly of the author himself. Kaiser's persecution complex, his conviction that the artist cannot and should not be judged by ordinary standards, and the belief, not necessarily applicable only to himself, that the artist is a man unappreciated by his philistine fellows, all come into focus in the first part of the trilogy. Despite the fact that the persons of the drama have names and specific physical attributes, Kaiser is still working here, as he was in his early days, with types. Konon, the fig dealer of Athens, for whom Pygmalion has created his statue, is the representative of materialism and philistinism; Korinna, the widow of Corinth, who has supported Pygmalion in return for a half promise of marriage, is the picture of hypocrisy and all that is unpleasant in sex; Alexias, the elegant aristocrat from Thebes, appears as "high society," concerned only with the preservation of its reputation and "good name." All three appear as Pygmalion's enemies and accusers, and all have one trait in common—self-interest. (p. 23)

[The idea that the artist is destined to suffer] is an old expressionist idea, and one that Kaiser himself used more than once. The cashier in *Von Morgens bis Mitternachts* dies with his arms outstretched against the cross in the Salvation Army meeting hall, an obvious symbol for Kaiser's belief that the individual (in this case, to be sure, not an artist) is taking upon himself the sins of the world. But whereas in the heyday of expressionism Kaiser was convinced that this could be done by the individual alone, in 1944 this is only possible with the aid of grace, and even then the redemption of mankind is by no means assured. The artist will inevitably pay the price for his presumptuousness, justified though it may be in the eyes of the divine. He may momentarily experience the ultimate, but this experience is self-destruction.

Pygmalion comes up against the first sign of the ignorance and misunderstanding of the world when Konon, the merchant for whom he has created his statue, appears to claim it. Unwilling to admit that his work of art has come to life, Pygmalion attempts to lie his way out of his predicament, and succeeds only in compounding his difficulties. That the artist is a dreamer Kaiser has already told us, but here he seems to be saying that he is also naive and ill-equipped to compete with the selfish materialism of the world. With each of his three visitors, Konon, Korinna, and Alexias, Pygmalion finds himself in a more frustrating and agonizing situation. As an artist, he is unable to forego the pleasure of consorting with a creation which is part of him, and yet, as a human being, he cannot avoid the dilemma in which he finds himself. Nor can he actually comprehend it, despite the fact that he has been warned by the goddess what to expect. Even fate turns against him. When he tells Konon and Korinna that the girl whom they glimpse in his studio is the niece of a fine Theban gentleman, the man whose name he has chosen at random appears to call him to account. . . .

By the time Pygmalion is brought to trial in the market place of Athens he has begun to realize that if he tells the truth about his statue he will be ridiculed as a fool and a dreamer, and so he is forced to continue to perjure himself. Only when Chaire, the name he has given to the living statue, is threatened with torture does he blurt out the real story. In his love and fear for her he repeats what the statue meant to him and tells the truth. . . . (p. 25)

The realization of art is something that only the artist himself can experience and understand—and then only with divine help. The world will never understand it. It will ridicule the creator and plunge him into misery. Pygmalion, like Kaiser, comes to see this. . . . This is, then, the fate of the artist in Kaiser's eyes. There is no lasting reward on earth for him. He cannot find the middle way of [Thomas Mann's] Tonio Kröger, but he does not go the way of Sappho either. He has a hint of something better in eternity, but in return for this hint and for a brief moment of ecstasy on earth he must, if he can, put up stoically with all the scorn and misunderstanding of his fellow man. We never really know what happens to Pygmalion. Kaiser leaves unanswered the question of whether he can continue to be creative. In spite of his promise to Athene to carry on in return for the last glimpse of Chaire before she is returned to stone, one has the feeling that because he has poured his life into this one inspired work, he will, as he says at the beginning of the play, remain forever "leer" ["empty"]. . . . It is true that Zeus has postponed the destruction of mankind once because of Pygmalion's talent, and it is likewise true that Athene tells him that divine suffering will be his lot and his greatest treasure for the remainder of his life, but from the tone of Pygmalion's final monologue and the dull "ich komme" ["I am coming"] as he follows Korinna at the end, one has the unpleasant feeling that the artist is not strong enough to resist the pressures put upon him. The one positive conclusion to which Pygmalion does come is that the artist's dream and his life can never be fused.

*Zweimal Amphitryon* has none of the wit or humor of Molière, Kleist, or Giraudoux. It is from beginning to end deadly serious, despite the seemingly absurd ending. Here again, in the person of the military leader, Kaiser attempts to prove his point that the individual has no future except through the intervention of divine power. Amphitryon, loved—one could almost say idolized—by the beautiful Alkmene, has been so wrapped up in his desire for fame and power that he has never even consummated their marriage, having left Alkmene on their wedding day on a campaign to raze Pharsala. His self-effacing wife is comforted by Zeus. . . . The humanity of Alkmene lies simply in the fact that she is a woman who loves. She is in no way an Iphigenie or Charlotte von Stein. It is not Alkmene who transforms her husband, it is Zeus. True, Amphitryon is forgiven because of the impression she has made upon the god . . . but there is none of the power of personality in Alkmene that one feels in Iphigenie. Kaiser may have intended us to feel it, but it is not there. The mere fact that Alkmene appears so infrequently in the play is an indication that Kaiser was not primarily interested in her effect upon her husband. His concern in all of these plays is not so much with "Menschlichkeit" ["humanity"] as it is with "Gnade" ["grace"]. It is Amphitryon who is saved by divine intervention, just as is Pygmalion. Alkmene and Chaire may be looked upon as catalysts in this refining process, but in the final analysis Kaiser's emphasis lies in the fact that humanity alone is not enough. (pp. 26-7)

Although *Zweimal Amphitryon* was the first play of the trilogy under consideration, it appears in printed form as the second. In a way this makes for a more logical sequence. *Pygmalion* ends on a vague and puzzling note—we do not quite know how his life will shape itself. Amphitryon has a more definite destiny: he is to remain in exile until the birth of Hercules, and then presumably will return to educate him and reap the benefits of the young man's feats. We will see in *Bellerophon* that Kaiser carries the tentative beginnings of a solution to man's problem to a definite conclusion. (p. 28)

*Bellerophon* is perhaps the least satisfying unit of the trilogy. At the same time it can be considered the most pessimistic. Here Kaiser gives up completely the attempt to have man save himself by his own efforts or by any virtue that may be inherent in him. Direct and final intervention by the divine is the last hope. Pygmalion remains on earth to do—what? Amphitryon has hopes of seeing a better world, but only through the efforts of a demigod. Bellerophon and Myrtis, his beloved, are removed directly to the beyond with the help of the winged horse. . . . What [Kaiser] attempts to show here is that a good man cannot compete with this world. (p. 29)

Kaiser has chosen to write this trilogy in verse. One can exercise the same criticism of his verse as of the overall effect of many of his plays—it is cold, and for the most part, hard. There are occasional flashes of sensuous beauty, but Kaiser vacillates too frequently between a simple, straightforward style and one which is so concentrated as to be distorted. The exclamation point and the dash—so beloved by the expressionists, are still part of his technique. The constant parallelism, at which Kaiser admittedly is a past master, becomes wearying in plays as long as these. Inversions are heaped one upon the other, and one begins to wonder whether Kaiser's style comes naturally to him or whether there is always a searching for effect, a conscious effort on his part to make the reader puzzle over what is being said. What he is probably trying to do is to formulate his ideas in as concise and sharp a manner as possible, but this often has an adverse effect, so that his succinctness leads him into ugly distortions.

We have said that this trilogy is pessimistic and optimistic. It can not be claimed that an interest in religion and mysticism is something entirely new for Kaiser. Such interests are part and parcel of much of expressionism and even of Kaiser's later, less obviously expressionistic work. But the conclusion to which he comes in these three plays goes far beyond anything he has said before. It still revolves around the theme of "the new man," but now the "Erneuerung" ["renewal"] can come only through grace. There is no longer the emphasis on the "flight from reality into illusion." Rather, one must see here the flight into the only true reality—away from the illusion of the world. Those who feel that this is the solution for mankind will praise the optimism of **"Griechische Dramen."** Those who are convinced that man must work out the problem for himself, here and now, will regret that Kaiser has given up his faith in the potential of the human race. (pp. 29-30)

> Ian C. Loram, "Georg Kaiser's Swan Song: 'Griechische Dramen'," in Monatshefte (copyright © 1957 by The Board of Regents of the University of Wisconsin System), Vol. XLIX, No. 1, January, 1957, pp. 23-30.

## B. J. KENWORTHY (essay date 1957)

[*Kenworthy's is considered the most important single work on Kaiser in English. The following excerpt presents Kenworthy's premise, developed throughout his study, that although Kaiser's works may be divided into discrete periods and styles—early dramas, dramas of regeneration—certain contradictions and paradoxes remain unresolved.*]

The earliest work of Georg Kaiser, the tragi-comedy *Rektor Kleist* of 1905, introduces a theme which not only reflects a prevailing intellectual attitude of the time, but also gives expression to a problem which touched him very closely. For eight years, between the ages of twenty-one and thirty, he was a semi-invalid, as a result of the malaria he had contracted on his journey into the South American interior. His physical weakness brought with it a compensatory quickening of mental activity: the will to live grew stronger with the body's infirmity. It is in this contradictory reciprocal relationship of mind and body that Kaiser found his first real dramatic material; and it continued to engage him intellectually and emotionally throughout his life.

To a generation beginning to emancipate itself from the mechanistic determinism that dominated the thought of the later nineteenth century, Nietzsche's Dionysian vitalism and Schopenhauser's assertion of an immanent will to life proved invigorating stimuli; the vital forces had been sapped by the dogma of the scientist and the theoretician; against this the twentieth century, in its first three decades, revolted. . . .

Thus the problem of the conflict between the urges of the flesh and the volition of the intellect presents itself to Kaiser, in the first instance, as a synthesis of his immediate experience and the popularized philosophy of the day. Perhaps his personal situation, at least in the earlier plays, leads him to find here material for comedy or tragi-comedy; he explores the question ironically, sometimes even with a certain bitterness. (p. 19)

In *Der gerettete Alkibiades* Kaiser's early preoccupation with the problem of the interrelation of mind and body achieves its finest expression; it also acquires a broader significance than it has in the other works [of Kaiser's early period, including *Der Geiste der Antike, Die jüdische Witwe, König Hahnrei,* and *Europa*]. Generally the problem has been presented in the figures of individuals like Judith or Marke, who are extreme cases, depending for their effect upon their very singularity. At the same time, even in the earliest play, *Rektor Kleist,* the effect upon the school community of the tension in the headmaster's mind is indicated; and in *Europa* the dramatist is concerned to show the social implications of over-civilization. The thematic

unity of this group of plays is exemplified in the parallel between Kleist and Kornmüller on the one hand and Socrates and Alcibiades on the other; but the latter are integrated into a larger community than the former; their names bear the weight of history, their authority—one as a general, the other as a teacher—is greater. And each acts in the consciousness of social responsibility. Socrates, especially, once he has fully appreciated the danger which his rationalism holds for Alcibiades and the life of which he is the highest representation, is content to sacrifice himself for the communal good. (p. 20)

*Der gerettete Alkibiades,* then, with its fusion of the individual fate and the vital needs of the community, is the culmination of Kaiser's considered affirmation of life. It is only one of the paradoxes in this most contradictory of writers that he makes sovereign use of the intellect to assert the pre-eminence of the flesh.

Towards the middle of the period . . . (1905-1920) a new element in Kaiser's work begins to emerge. It is embryonic in the two one-act plays, *Claudius* and *Friedrich und Anna* (both 1912), and in a third, *Juana,* which Kaiser added to them when they were published in 1918 as *Drei Einakter.* Each presents a variation on the same theme; and this theme develops out of Kaiser's preoccupation with the body, for their common point of departure is the adjustment of the sexual impulses which is necessitated by marriage: a problem, then, already adumbrated in the childless union of Rektor Kleist, in the efforts of Judith and in the morbidity of king Marke. But each of these three plays marks a stage in the emancipation of the mind from the flesh, through the conquest of possessive sexual jealousy. (pp. 21-2)

Kaiser moves away from his examination of the various manifestations of the sexual impulse to a consideration of its idealization. Incidentally, he condemns a moral code which prescribes violence, and not love, as the arbiter between a man's reason and his irrational jealousy.

A very similar transition can be seen within the compass of a single play—*Von Morgens bis Mitternachts* . . . , perhaps Kaiser's most expressionistic work, yet one that was conceived in the very early days of the Expressionist movement. Here, again, the initial impetus of the dramatic action originates in sexual desire; but almost at once the issues grow wider, and the sexual becomes only one aspect incidental to others. For the stress is now laid on the social background of the drama: the tension arises out of the friction between the individual and the whole of his environment, which Kaiser seeks to compress into seven loosely-connected scenes, whose only unity is the presence in each of the central figure, and the fact that each attempts to present in its barest essentials a particular but representative aspect of modern life.

*Von Morgens bis Mitternachts* is Kaiser's first *Stationsdrama,* depicting the stations of the martyrdom of modern man—a dramatic technique whose popularity with the Expressionist writers was due largely to Strindberg's use of it in *Till Damaskus* (*The Road to Damascus,* 1898). Here a highly-developed drama looks back to its medieval origins in the mystery and passion-play, where the figure of Christ unifies the various scenes of his suffering.

That Kaiser intends here to represent the fate of modern man, and not of one specific man, is clear from a glance at the dramatis personae: we find, for instance, Kassierer; Mutter; Frau; Herren im Frack; Mädchen der Heilsarmee and a host of other nameless figures, who bear only the label of their social function. This accepted expressionist device of typification is intended to strip from the drama all that is merely contingent, and to achieve a maximum concentration of significance. Thus the bank-clerk stands for any bank-clerk; indeed, for any man who is condemned by social conditions and his passive acceptance of them to the monotonous drudgery of competitive bread-winning. (pp. 24-5)

In the early plays it is clear that the decisive stimulus to action lay in the body, although, as with Marke and Socrates, the mind may subsequently continue autonomously, and eventually itself become the impelling force. The *Drei Einakter* show the progressive emancipation of the mental from the physical, while an intellectually recognized truth, deriving in the first instance from an urge of the body, drives the clerk in *Von Morgens bis Mitternachts* to suicide. In *Die Bürger von Calais,* however, it is the mind that conquers the body: Eustache sacrifices himself to an idea; and similarly, the motivating force of *Hölle Weg Erde* is the universal acceptance of an ethical concept. The physical appetites of man give place to the moral aspirations of the New Man.

So emerges the theme to which Kaiser devoted much of his work: the proclaiming of an ideal and its propagation in concrete, plastic form. His dramas of regeneration are all directed to one end—the inculcation of the idea of the New Man. For it is his conviction that man can properly express his thoughts only through their translation into action, by doing and making; and the product of this action in its turn modifies the original thought or promotes a fresh one. It is certainly this realization that prompted Kaiser to choose almost exclusively the drama as a medium of self-expression. . . . (pp. 40-1)

[Starting] out from the reality of the vital urge and its manifestations in the physical world, Kaiser arrives at a consideration of the potency of the idea. But in every play belonging to this group, with the exception of the quietly argued *Friedrich und Anna* and the Utopian *Hölle Weg Erde,* the ideal explicitly or implicitly proclaimed must await its realization at some future time. In each play, the individual who suddenly sees new, untried possibilities in the world, or who seeks to break away from the customary round of his life, is faced with an opposing force stronger than himself; the clash nearly always results in the death—most often by suicide—of the individual. Thus the material reality prevails over the ideal, and yet at the same time the refusal to compromise with an imperfect world preserves the ideal inviolate: it is carried over with the death of its advocate into another world. Not, however, into a spiritual life beyond the grave—but into the mental life of the spectators of the conflict which Kaiser has presented in his play; for his figures are designed to appeal primarily to the mind, their function being to expound or exemplify a thesis. They embody an idea. . . . (pp. 41-2)

Kaiser recognizes the power of myth, and uses it with conscious deliberation in the creation of his social dramas: the New Man is a mythologue. But the forms in which the dramatist presents his conception are many—yet they are all united by three fundamental and universal considerations, which proceed necessarily from the nature of social organization. An individual can be considered from three general aspects: as a member of a community; as one of a family; and as a bread-winner, upon which function the claims of family and community converge. Kaiser's social dramas are directed to an examination of these three basic aspects. They have been seen combined in, for instance, *Von Morgens bis Mitternachts;* sometimes, however, one of them is emphasized and treated in detail.

The dramatic tension in these plays arises out of the conflict of an individual with the society in which he lives. But this society imposes its values—and it is the false values which Kaiser is concerned to expose—upon the individual, thus turning him from the course he should best follow. (pp. 42-3)

Kaiser confronts the dreamer in himself with the opposite side of his creative personality—the critical observer of the world.

To resolve this conflict—even provisionally—Kaiser summons up his faith in man's potentialities: the advent of the New Man can be hoped for only in some remote future; the poet is concerned to prepare the way for him. In this, he has the figure of Christ before him—not as one around which a body of dogma has accumulated, but as an ideal projection into the superhuman of human aspirations to perfection. Like Christ, the New Man is crucified, and so removed from the material world to live on in man's consciousness. . . . [Kaiser's *Erneuerungsdramen* ("dramas of regeneration")], in which he seeks to realize his vision, are the product of an attempt to reconcile the haphazard compromises of everyday life with these ideal values; to reconcile heaven and earth, and to discover the 'heavenly, earthly man' of the expressionist dream. . . . (pp. 100-01)

The quest for the New Man represents Georg Kaiser's attempt to come to grips with the real world about him, with its problems and its people: but it is only an attempt. His own hatred of reality is reflected in the rejection of life by the majority of the main figures in these dramas; with only a few exceptions, such as Spazierer, Jean, Ossian Balvesen and Olim, they seek 'beyond human things' the ultimate logical refuge from the material world in death. For Kaiser, the idealist, makes absolute demands upon the world, and is hence bound to be disappointed and disillusioned in it; the individual may be good, but the state—man in the mass—can never be. . . .

Thus in the dramas of regeneration, an individual is confronted with an objective world with which he must come to terms; yet most often the final settlement is reached not in a compromise with the world of objective reality, but in a retreat into a mental world, culminating generally in the self-annihilation of the individual; less frequently (and then only in the comedies) a compromise is made for the sake of an ideal—and only once is the ecstatic utopianism of *Hölle Weg Erde* offered as a solution. (p. 102)

Although there are, in general, few coherent lines of development through the course of Kaiser's work, one clear change in his thought can nevertheless be seen from a comparison of some of the plays in this group with earlier ones which also deal with this theme of love. Perhaps the most striking example among his early work is *Die jüdische Witwe*, where every action of Judith is dictated by a primitive erotic urge. In two plays written some ten years later, *Das Frauenopfer* . . . and *Der Brand im Opernhaus* . . . , a strong erotic element persists; but it is finally outweighed by an idealized conception of love; this, again, is further emphasized in *Oktobertag,* in which the physical aspect of the sexual relationship is only expositional, and becomes relatively insignificant beside the 'mystical union' of Catherine and Marrien. The same is true of *Rosamunde Floris,* where the mystique of love grows out of the three weeks that Rosamunde spent with William—of which only the last moments are actually shown on the stage. In *Alain und Elise* there is no physical contact between the couple; the whole action is directed to a spiritual development. The flesh, the material reality, is completely abnegated in favour of the idealized, mental realization of an overwhelming passion: it represents the final sublimation of the theme announced in *Die jüdische Witwe.*

These plays written during the years between the seizure of power by the National Socialists and Georg Kaiser's emigration to Switzerland reflect the conditions under which they were conceived and composed; there is something oppressive, almost forced, in them. Although, at this period, their theme is not new in Kaiser's work, it is developed to a logical extreme—a change matched in the compact structure of the plays, in which the conventional unities are skilfully preserved, and only traces of the Expressionism of the nineteen-twenties remain. Their logic, however, is still expressionistic: the objective realities of the material world are consistently translated to a subjective world, whose laws are created by and subject to the will of the dramatist. This constant examination and reinterpretation of the everyday phenomenon of love, moreover, repeatedly uses the expressionist technique of abstraction: the love that Kaiser shows us is absolute, it seeks to escape the restrictions and compromises of this world. (pp. 130-31)

The plays which Kaiser wrote during his voluntary exile in Switzerland, in spite of a certain bitterness, make an impression of greater freedom; even the play that he wrote during his first year there has less constraint and greater immediacy: with *Der Soldat Tanaka*—published in the same year as *Rosamunde Floria* and *Alain und Elise,* but, unlike them, finished only in that year . . .—Kaiser again turns to contemporary social and moral problems. The rather cloying effect of these other two plays is no longer felt. This is true also of *Der englische Sender* . . . , a play in which Kaiser portrays the general degradation brought by the Hitlerites upon the country he had recently left. *Der englische Sender,* together with the comedy *Klawitter* and parts of some few other plays, in his reckoning with the political system which had closed the German theatres to him; but neither this play nor *Klawitter* deals directly with the system, and there is no stylized representation of the masses that marked some of the plays written during and immediately after the First World War. Here he is concerned rather to expose the actual people who made the system possible: the lascivious sneak-thief, the morally irresponsible opportunist. The former of these plays shows the ordinary man, a simple peasant, in conflict with the petty representative of the Nazi tyranny in a small village; the latter supplements this picture with a presentation of the clash between Nazism and the intellectually and emotionally cultivated artist. (p. 131)

Around the year 1940 Kaiser was preoccupied with the figure of Napoleon; and out of this interest arose two plays. The first, *Pferdewechsel,* introduces Napoleon at the time when he has been condemned to live in the shadow of his former glory as the ruler of the tiny island of Elba: it is essentially a study of fallen greatness. The second is based on a legend which attached itself to Napoleon, and shows him only through the distorted vision of a hero-worshipper blinded by a ludicrous reverence for the power he embodied; it is a study of an ill-founded and fanatical devotion to a lost cause, with a side-glance at the supporters of Hitler. (p. 135)

Just as there is a dualism in the content of Kaiser's work and within Kaiser himself, so, for all his versatility and dramatic virtuosity, there are discernible in the form of his work as a whole two broad patterns of drama. On the one hand are the plays which centre upon the fate of a single individual, and consist of a series of scenes showing how this is worked out rather than developing a conventional plot; they are the 'Stationsdramen', whose unity depends upon the presence of the

central figure, for whom the other figures provide only the context. Of this kind are such plays as *König Hahnrei, Von Morgens bis Mitternachts, Hölle Weg Erde,* even *Nebeneinander* (although the Pawnbroker does not appear in every scene). (p. 190)

Contrasting in manner with these plays are those having a compact, taut structure, built round a more precisely-defined plot. Almost always they are divided conventionally into acts, yet, as in all Kaiser's work, there is no retarding moment: the action moves forward logically and swiftly. These plays, dealing generally with the validity of subjective truth—the escape from or the modification of the outer world by the mind — have, in contrast with the crowds which so often fill the stage in the 'social' dramas, a small cast; and the unities of place, time and action are strictly observed. To this group, modelled on the French *pièce de chambre,* and set usually in France, belong such works as *Das Frauenopfer, Der Brand im Opernhaus, Die Flucht nach Venedig, Der Präsident, Oktobertag* and *Der Gärtner von Toulouse.* And closely akin to them are the satirical comedies (set in Scandinavia) *David und Goliath, Der mutige Seefahrer, Kolportage* and *Das Los des Ossian Balvesen.*

It is, or course, impossible to confine Kaiser's dramatic production completely within one or other of these two groups; they represent rather the limits between which there is a rich and varied intermingling of the two types. But all have one element in common: their motivation depends upon the clearly-defined and often dialectically worked out clash of opposites. His own restless, inquiring mind showed him a world continually changing, as the contradictory forces which shape it seek a precarious equilibrium. Yet these changes generally affect the world of a single person or of a couple; the community, the great world outside, remains unchangeably indifferent or hostile, breaking in upon the private world or threatening its security.

From his earliest to his latest work we find figures representing such forces, of which the following may serve as instances: those of mind and body in Rektor Kleist and Kornmüller, in Socrates and Alcibiades; of the individual and the community in *Von Morgens bis Mitternachts, Hölle Weg Erde,* and *Gas* plays, *Mississippi* and *Pygmalion;* the opposition of the sexes—which, when it becomes reconciled, sets the lovers, secure in their world of emotion, over against the instrusive material world—in such plays as *Rosamunde Floria, Alain und Elise, Zweimal Amphitryon* and, again, *Pygmalion.* (pp. 190-91)

[There] was for many years a half-resolved conflict in Kaiser himself—between the observing, analysing critic and the visionary creative writer, between the classicist and the romantic, the admirer of Plato on the one hand and of Büchner, Kleist and Nietzsche on the other—has already been sufficiently shown. Besides this acute awareness of a duality in life, he was filled with a sense of its insecurity: a trifling incident may bring momentous consequences, or a coincidence may determine a fate. These are the sources of Kaiser's thought and feeling—and an inner necessity compelled him to give them expression and form; and the natural vehicle for their immediate and concise formulation is the drama. (p. 191)

Georg Kaiser's production, viewed as a whole, shows an astounding compass and variety: it ranges from romantic—occasionally even lyrical—plays to carefully contrived dialectical pieces; from the satirical to the ecstatic; from comedy and revue to tragedy. Its material is drawn from such divers sources as Greek legend, the Platonic Dialogues, the events of history, the problems of the modern industrial world and Kaiser's own fertile imagination. In the form of his drama there is such variety as to suggest that a resourceful talent was for ever experimenting with new methods of expression, while the language, though it always retains its own distinctive note, catches the raciness of colloquial speech, argues and reasons with cool detachment or explodes in outbursts of emotion. Work follows upon work in a bewildering stream, and with a prolificness that can have few parallels; differing and often contradictory solutions are offered to the same problem, as the approach to it shifts. (p. 198)

Kaiser's art revolves round these two opposing poles, sometimes falling within the field of the one, sometimes within the field of the other, and occasionally wavering between them. Kaiser was the 'Denkspieler' who made romantic love the theme of many of his plays; he was a social reformer who denied any wish to appear as a 'benefactor of mankind', and at the same time a dreaming escapist with an uneasy social conscience: his Socrates, impelled by his reason to affirm the supreme value of life (and even to die in its defence), nevertheless 'parted from life as from a long sickness'.

This division of Kaiser against himself accounts for the dichotomy that emerges clearly from nearly all his work; it explains the division of his work on the one hand into dramas of regeneration and on the other into dramas of escape from the material world—just as it also explains the presence, in greater or lesser degree, of both these elements in almost every one of his works. Here, too, is to be sought the source of Kaiser's dialectical thought, and of the inner contradictions in both content and form which a study of his work continually reveals. Even his own life presents a paradox: as a writer he devoted much of his energy to advocating the fullest living of life, the savouring of 'Erlebnis', and he condemned any sort of specialization as a mutilation of the human spirit and of man's multifold capacities; and yet Kaiser, who wrote in *Die Flucht nach Venedig*, 'das Wort tötet das Leben', dedicated a lifetime to the single-minded creation of literature. The plays that he devoted to the problems facing the artist indicate the way in which he himself sought to resolve this conflict between the world about him and the world within him: by artistic creation, whose product partakes of the ideal and yet has its existence in the objectively real world. The volume of his production, and the fact that much of it promises to outlive the transient literary movement out of which it first grew, serve to underline the intensity of the inner conflicts from which his work, with its many paradoxes, sprang. (p. 199)

> *B. J. Kenworthy, in his* Georg Kaiser, *Basil Blackwell, 1957, 217 p.*

**WALTER H. SOKEL** (essay date 1959)

[*Sokel's* The Writer in Extremis, *from which the sections on Kaiser are excerpted below, is a major comprehensive study of Expressionism in twentieth-century German literature.*]

While the Expressionist intellectual sees himself as an outcast and inhuman monster, he likewise views himself as a martyr, a pioneer, and a savior of his fellow men. The work in which this ambivalence receives its most consummate treatment is Kaiser's Socrates drama, *Der gerettete Alkibiades (Alcibiades Saved)* . . . , a masterpiece of tragic irony.

Kaiser's hero Socrates, a sculptor—a character based on the historical Socrates—is a wretched hunchback who compensates

for his physical deformity by developing his reflectiveness. . . . [In] one of his first works, *Rektor Kleist,* Kaiser had defined the intellect as the sublimation of physical shortcomings; and *Rektor Kleist* foreshadows the contrast between the extrovert physical hero Alcibiades and the deformed intellectual Socrates in the coach Kornmüller and the classical-humanist school principal Kleist. In an argument with Kornmüller about the principles of education Rektor Kleist exclaims, "The greatest Greek was Socrates!") "My hump," Socrates says, "is a detour for my blood so that it cannot rush to the head too fast and flood my reason." He is an intellectual artist, a *Denkspieler,* who works in stone as his creator works with words. For Socrates, as for Kaiser, the head, not the heart, is the guide in art, the creative principle. "Writing a drama amounts to thinking out a thought to its conclusions," says Kaiser. His Socrates makes hermae, images of heads resting on stone pillars. His art is "head-art," a metaphoric visualization of Kaiser's own art. Socrates' images lack a body. As the work is, so is the artist. Alcibiades compares him to a herma "with a head that is alive over the foundation of dead stone!" . . . A chill emanates from Socrates and no one feels at ease with him. His probing mind disturbs good fellowship and upsets the carefree spirit of Athenian society. At his appearance, a novel shadow seems to fall over the habitual games of poetry and love. However, the decisive fact about Socrates' startling intellectuality is not an external but an invisible informity. A secret debility sets him completely apart from all other men and forces him to adopt a unique and revolutionary behavior. This secret wound is a symbol of the inhibiting, isolating, and revolutionary nature of the intellect; it opens Socrates' eyes to the meaninglessness of the world and the absurdity of human destiny; it compels him to develop a behavior monstrously different from the mores of his society; and finally it enables him to transcend his nihilism and isolation and to evolve new values which save his society from disintegration and despair. The same infirmity which reduces Socrates to a cripple and a monster also permits him to become a hero. (pp. 104-05)

Socrates' aesthetics, so contemptuous of the personality of the artist, so exclusively concerned with the work, is Kaiser's own. . . . Both the humility and the functionalism of these views reveal the modernist's contempt for himself as a personality, as a growing and living human being. The continuous personality of the artist, his experiences, his individuality, his "soul" command no interest. The artist is to be nothing more than an executive organ for the record production of works. His greatness is measured by the quantity of his achievements. The writing of a drama is "a geometric problem." It has nothing to do with the writer's character. This production engineer's view of the creative process derives from the Expressionist's self-hatred. What this view implies is something like this: "My personality is hateful and unendurable, if it can be said to exist at all. The less said about it the better. Fortunately there exists an escape from my humanity (or rather lack of it) into a world of pure forms and abstract ideas. When I write I escape into this world, which is as pleasantly impersonal as mathematics." Kaiser's reduction of literature to a geometry of ideas is the exact opposite of the view of Goethe, who regarded the work of art as part of his personal growth, and who viewed personality as of supreme importance, as "the highest bliss of earth's children." The impersonal, self-hating Expressionist is opposed to Goethe, the genius of life, as the coldly ironical thinker Socrates in Kaiser's play, from whom everyone shies away, is opposed to the Poet, whom his grateful people feasts. In Kaiser's antipersonal functionalism we see another aspect of the "musicalization" of the arts, which replaces the ideal of character portrait by the ideal of composition. We also recognize now beneath this fundamental principle of modernism a certain self-hatred, a vengeance, as it were, on those who still possess a definite individuality, a character, and believe in its value. (pp. 106-07)

Kaiser's dramatic practice closely conforms to his theory. Like Strindberg, he does not write dramas of character, but dramas of ideas. But in contrast to Strindberg's, Kaiser's drama is not patterned on the existential journey and the splitting of the self into leitmotiv aspects. It is not a "musicalization" of the miracle play. Neither is it based on dream and visualization. It grows out of aphorism, anecdote, and debate. Kaiser's model dramatist was Plato. It is also a further development of Wedekind's and Sternheim's aphoristic, epigrammatic dialogue. Kafka's stories are extended metaphors; Kaiser's dramas are extended aphorisms. The aphoristic parable, the anecdote with a sharply formulated twist, form the basis and strength of Kaiser's dramas. Early works like *The Jewish Widow* . . . , a parodistic version of the Old Testament subject treated by Hebbel, show this tendency very clearly. Judith kills Holophernes and liberates the Jewish people accidentally, motivated not by heroism but by sexual frustration. She wants to sleep with the Babylonian king, the first potent man she has met; when the general Holophernes interferes with her lustful desire for the king, she simply slays the famous general and thus liberates the besieged Jewish town. Babylonian king and army flee in panic. The disappointed heroine is brought back to her people in triumph and finally satisfied by the potent High Priest sent from Jerusalem. We note the parodistic irony as in Wedekind. The parodistic idea determines the plot. The characters are neither personalities in the traditional sense nor Strindbergian projections of subconscious states; they are carriers of the "joke," the ironic trick effect of the work.

The kinship between Wedekind, Sternheim, and Kaiser lies in their tendency to unmask "the essence" of social reality not by naturalistic imitation, which would still lull us in illusions, but by crass and shocking formulations. Their drama seeks to demonstrate in pure and, therefore, necessarily abstract and distorted conditions (in the experimental laboratory, as it were) the true nature of existential or social problems. In *The Jewish Widow,* for instance, Kaiser unmasks by his "joke" the true nature of heroism as frustration. In his *Burghers of Calais,* probably his greatest work, he demonstrates by two highly dramatic surprise effects the true nature of heroism as pacifism and self-sacrifice. In his *Alcibiades Saved* he demonstrates by a highly ironic tour de force the true nature of the intellect as both a wound and a heroic fraud. Here the trick, Kaiser's basic dramatic form, merges with the dramatic content and idea. *Alcibiades Saved* is the dramatic formulation of its author's form of existence. (pp. 107-08)

The depersonalizing, deadening cleverness in Socrates' pain-inspired views outrages Alcibiades, the hero of physical vitality and *joie de vivre,* even as Kaiser's, Sternheim's, Brecht's, and George Grosz' provocative, unmasking "cleverness" outraged and infuriated the German "romantic" *bourgeoisie.* Alcibiades' last weapon against Socrates is Woman. The charms of the beautiful courtesan Phryne will surely undo the cold reasoner. But the intellectual cannot love. The thorn in Socrates' flesh prevents him from approaching Phryne and making love to her. Pain has destroyed desire in him. His aloofness, on the other hand, converts Phryne to asceticism. The first man to disdain her impresses her as the true human being, the

godlike man. Like everyone else, she mistakes Socrates' infirmity for strength. His incapacity for love raises him to the level of the gods.

Nietzsche saw the historical Socrates as the initiator of Greek decadence and the pioneer of the Christian "slave revolt"; Kaiser sees in Socrates the fateful innovator who ends the age of naïve self-assurance and ushers in a self-conscious, i.e., guilt-ridden, civilization. The mind replaces the muscles. Reflection drives out spontaneity. The cripple wins out over the athlete. But Socrates' revolutionary philosophy does not result from the cripple's resentment of the strong and healthy; it results from his compassion for them. Although it was necessary, Socrates regrets his victory:

> I had to invent what should have remained un-
> invented!!—I had to blanket the sky—and wither
> the earth—!!

He takes Alcibiades' guilt for overturning the sacred hermae upon himself and suffers the death penalty in his stead.

Kaiser-Socrates' intellectualism reveals itself as a protective barrier against nihilism. Only Socrates, the intellectual, knows the trivial accident to which the hero Alcibiades owes his life; if he had disclosed it, Alcibiades would have become a laughingstock, Greek faith would have been shattered, and the *meaninglessness of greatness* would have been brutally obvious. Civilization could not have withstood such a shock. Better to interpose new values between the traditional hero worship and the banal truth than to allow the truth to destroy all values. Chilling and subversive as these new values of abstract intellect may be, they still serve as a screen between man and the devastating insight into the absurdity of the universe and human existence. Thus Socrates suffers his thorn and sacrifices his life to save Alcibiades, and with him Greece, from the despair of nihilism. (pp. 108-09)

> *Walter H. Sokel, "The Thorn of Socrates" (origi-*
> *nally published in a different form in* The Germanic
> Review, *Vol. 30, No. 1, February, 1955), in his* The
> Writer in Extremis: Expressionism in Twentieth-Cen-
> tury German Literature *(with the permission of the*
> *publishers, Stanford University Press; copyright 1959*
> *by the Board of Trustees of the Leland Stanford Ju-*
> *nior University), Stanford University Press, 1959,*
> *pp. 83-118.**

### WALTER H. SOKEL (essay date 1959)

The intellectual-turned-leader must be willing to sacrifice himself for mankind and thus is akin to Prometheus and Christ. The self-sacrifice of the new type of leader is the theme of one of the most powerful dramas of Expressionist pacifism, Kaiser's *Die Bürger von Calais (The Burghers of Calais),* written in the year that the First World War broke out. The French city of Calais is besieged by the king of England. The king wants to spare the city, because of its excellent harbor, if the city will surrender and, as token of defeat, deliver six citizens who will be put to death by the English. The powerful patriotic party inside the city urges a fight to the finish; they would rather see the city destroyed than surrender. (pp. 172-73)

Kaiser's *Burghers of Calais* is a synthesis of the abstractionist and the activist—or the aesthetic and the ethical—revolution of Expressionism. Both abstractionism and activism assert and indeed deify the intellect in opposition to nature and "the natural." In complete opposition to vitalism, both uphold the rational planning capacity of the mind and its ever-ready originality over instinct, habit, convention, and tradition. They affirm that which has been "made" against that which has "grown." Both believe in artifice.

The conflict between artifice and instinct is the central issue in Kaiser's drama. The national enemy is willing to spare the city for the sake of its great "artifice," the excellent man-made harbor. This harbor is beautiful and intelligently planned—a work of artful design. In addition, however, it is extremely useful. In this synthesis of the artful and the useful the antithesis between aesthetic idealism and ethical-humanitarian idealism is resolved. The patriots, however, would rather see the harbor destroyed than betray their country's "honor." They act from an irrational, "natural" instinct, an inherited belief. Their response is unreflective and traditional. Such behavior, so Kaiser reasons in his drama, is not only unworthy of human beings, but it also jeopardizes human life as well as human artifice. For in the patriotic fight to the finish not only the harbor but also the lives of the citizens will be destroyed. Life cannot be separated from artifice. It is not instinct, but, on the contrary, the artifice of intellect that saves and enhances life. With this complete reversal of the vitalist position Kaiser shows that there can be no conflict between vitality and intellect, even as there is no cleavage between the aesthetic and the ethical. Life to survive must foster and protect artifice; the protection of artifice is also the protection of life. (pp. 174-75)

> Walter H. Sokel, "The Revolt," in his The Writer in Extremis: Expressionism in Twentieth-Century German Literature (with the permission of the publishers, Stanford University Press; copyright 1959 by the Board of Trustees of the Leland Stanford Junior University), Stanford University Press, 1959, pp. 164-91.*

**VICTOR LANGE** (essay date 1963)

Kaiser's career is not easily summarized. . . . In more than seventy plays—thirteen of them produced in 1917-18 alone—ranging from brittle comedies to savage attacks upon the delusions of his age, from modern farces to sustained tragedies in the Greek manner, he deals again and again with the forces of unreason and delusion that threaten contemporary man. Kaiser is first and foremost a moralist: his theme is the "renewal of man," the search for those authentic qualities in the human being that will prove durable and creative beyond the paralysis of judgment.

Like Gerhart Hauptmann, Kaiser is a social dramatist without doctrinaire convictions; but, different from Hauptmann, he limits the scope and mobility of the individual and subjects it to the inexorable logic of circumstance and technical realities. In one of his early plays, *From Morn Till Midnight* . . . , Kaiser examines, in a series of highpitched scenes, the pathetic efforts of a bank teller who breaks out of his routine existence to find meaning and integrity. No familiar form of social life can provide it for him: he can in the end assert it only for himself. He dies a martyr in a sacrificial act of self-destruction. (pp. vii-viii)

[*Gas*] is a dramatic project of greater scope and intensity. It consists of three plays, *Die Koralle, Gas I,* and *Gas II.* (p. viii)

[In *The Coral*], the first of the three plays, the theme of integrity—the utopian vision of the "new man"—is elaborated in the context of an individual life. Kaiser shows in a series of carefully contrived scenes the climax of a harassed life: the

millionaire (or, as Kaiser with characteristic overemphasis calls him, the billionaire) has all his life been in flight from poverty and exploitation. Now he has at last achieved immense wealth and, through it, something like protection against the terrors of his childhood, terrors from which he hopes to spare his son. But the son turns against the life of power through exploitation and joins the workers. Through a curious and effective theatrical conceit Kaiser provides the billionaire with a double who acts as his secretary—an alter ego whose happy childhood distinguishes him from his employer. In order to "adopt" his identity, the billionaire kills his secretary, and the coral fob which the secretary wore on his watch chain becomes the symbol of an authentic life. For the sake of this symbol he is willing to die as a murderer: "We are forever driven; we are exiles from our paradise of silence, pieces broken loose from the coral tree of life, wounded on the very first day." A state of mind beyond fear and anguish Kaiser seems here to argue, must remain a dream embodied in the token of the coral.

The execution of the tycoon is, of course, no resolution of the sense of futility in which, as Kaiser sees it, his furious capitalistic struggle has engulfed him; it is merely the gesture of renunciation so characteristic of many expressionist plays by which an intolerable life is canceled out and a return to a state of nirvana is achieved.

*Gas I* advances the argument from a private issue to a group experience: the son of the "billionaire" has become a social revolutionary, dedicated to the realization of the "new man." He offers his workers the opportunity of a humane life if they will agree to abandon the production of gas upon which the huge machinery of capitalism depends but which threatens from time to time to destroy the workers' community. At the risk of their happiness the workers prefer the "system" to "life": the new man is not yet. (pp. viii-x)

[In *Gas II*] the world is engulfed in apocalyptic destruction: the impact of fanatical technological thinking upon the human being is demonstrated most dramatically. The great-grandson of the billionaire is now one of the workers in a state run plant; in an effort at preventing imminent total war he proclaims the ideals of meekness and brotherly love instead of self-ambition and battle. He fails. Not victory but radical destruction of both warring sides is the inescapable result. The voice of the visionary cries in a wilderness of inhumanity: beyond the evidence of barbarism he can only project a dream of peace in another world.

The three plays, each artistically and intellectually complete in itself, may at first sight seem profoundly skeptical of the very idealism that constituted the chief impulse of the German expressionist poet. Yet they provide in fact the poetic elaboration, in extreme images and situations, of the economic and social implications of capitalism as Kaiser and the German revolutionary intelligentsia saw them after the First World War. The exploitational character of money and the concomitant paralysis of the individual leaves the billionaire in *The Coral* with only the essentially romantic desire for self-extinction; in *Gas I* his son proclaims an ethical socialism which is doomed to failure in the face of collective blindness and the compelling or persuasive interests of the state; in *Gas II* state socialism itself leads to a holocaust in which the "blue figures" of capitalism and the "yellow figures" of socialism extinguish one another. None of these forms of economic and political organization seem tolerable: the billionaire-worker in *Gas II* is the "new man" who accepts the inevitable "eccentricity" of an absolute conviction of human integrity. He knows that he must continue to proclaim it as a platonic truth, an "inner realm" of meaning, to which any future must refer.

Thus the central motif of these three plays is the clash between a stubbornly maintained vision of truth and the seductive and often overwhelming compulsions of power—the power of individual satisfaction, the power of wealth, and power in its harshest and most technical modern form, exercised for its own sake.

It is true that Kaiser insists that "the deepest wisdom is found only by a single mind. And when it is found it is so overwhelming that it cannot become effective." Yet, the issue which Kaiser argues concerns all of us, it is not a private one; its moral impact cannot therefore, as in the plays of Ibsen and Hauptmann, be shown in a series of individual experiences with which we as spectators might identify ourselves. Indeed, Kaiser is not primarily concerned with the alternatives of action or judgment that might be open to a well-defined character; his purpose is altogether the unraveling of the implications of an intellectual position. Each turn of events, every sentence that is uttered, is, therefore, in Kaiser's plays, a key to an essentially dialectical intention. His plots are exactly developed elaborations of his central ideas. This is to say that the dramatic structure of the *Gas* trilogy is determined not so much by the logic of individual, or group, psychology, as by the logic—we might almost say, logistics—of an idea. All of Kaiser's works are masterpieces of deduction: "To write a play," Kaiser himself suggested, "is to pursue an idea to the end."

This deliberate narrowing of the dramatic intent has its striking consequences for the form of Kaiser's plays. Where intellectual and emotional tensions are to be stated with the utmost concentration a high degree of abstraction becomes inevitable. Instead of the ample and detailed setting of the naturalistic theater, Kaiser employs few but emphatic properties in an otherwise bleak and pointedly inhuman stage space. (pp. x-xii)

Deliberate sparseness and economy of setting, figure, and language corresponds to the precision with which the play as a whole is designed. We need only analyze with some care the fourth act of *Gas I* to recognize Kaiser's craftsmanship, his use of the fugal structure, and his skill in organizing, through sound and light and a careful manipulation of group movements, a slowly rising crescendo of urgency.

Kaiser's incomparable instinct for the theatrical effect is one of his greatest assets. Indeed, it saves his plays on the one hand from becoming mere intellectual exercises in the hands of an accomplished "Denkspieler"; and on the other from that excess of exclamatory feeling which is typical of much expressionist writing. Kaiser's passion is directed toward the illumination of rational and, therefore, arguable human alternatives; his utopian vision of the "new man" is not vague and sentimental but amounts to a calculated appraisal of the energies of heart and mind and action which the human being must marshal for his own salvation. We cannot read the final speech of the "billionaire," or the second act of *Gas II*, without being moved by the superb pathos of the moralist. Here, as in the plays of Lessing or Schiller, with whom Kaiser has in form and in substance so much in common, the work of art offers us a most articulate and compelling assertion of the humanistic faith. (pp. xiii-xiv)

> *Victor Lange, in his introduction to* The Coral: A Play in Five Acts *by Georg Kaiser, translated by Winifred Katzin (translation copyright 1963 by Fred-*

*erick Ungar Publishing Co., Inc.), Ungar, 1963, pp. v-xiv.*

## R. W. LAST (essay date 1969)

Kaiser had so successfully and deliberately distanced himself from his works that it seemed impossible to refer them all back to a single common point, one source from which they could all have derived their inspiration. Even now that the dust has settled—some of it, regrettably, on Kaiser's work—it is still not easy to reconcile many contradictions. However, in an essay, *Vision und Figur* . . . , Kaiser himself sought to define his mission as an artist—which he saw as overriding all other considerations in life—and to penetrate through the confused exterior to the guiding principles beneath. . . . [This essay], in which he typically conceals himself behind a rhetorical mask, is more descriptive than explanatory, for the range and nature of his "Vision", like that of the Expressionists at large, seems to shift abruptly from one work to the next: in *Zweimal Oliver* . . . , the New Man born of the Vision becomes a Mad Man; in *Von morgens bis mitternachts* . . . , he gets nowhere at all, and keeps returning to his point of departure; in *Rosamunde Floris* . . . , the New Man is a woman, who destroys all about her—and ultimately herself—in a grotesque black comedy which seems to pour scorn on the very idea of "Newness". Perhaps Kaiser's vision can more adequately be interpreted as an attempt to establish contact between transcendent and immanent, between "heaven" and "earth", to render the "figure" transparent so that the Vision behind can be observed, to erect a kind of slippery pole reaching up into infinity, on various parts of which he places his central figures, and observes their struggles. The "turmoil" arises in the mind of the observer, not only at the spectacle of the embattled participants, but also because they are most frequently making only a partial comment on the Vision from a narrow standpoint: some, like Oliver, have their eyes fixed upon the sky, but it is either heavily overcast or dazzling with the blinding light of the sun; others, like Rosamunde and the bank clerk in *Von morgens bis mitternachts,* stare at the ground, fearfully clawing away from the morass beneath them. The earth too takes on many forms: contemporary urban society, an abstracted battleground, a small family group, an industrial monolith. And the Vision also is seen variously as a brave new era, or total destruction, or as a primitivist retreat; it may seek to encompass the whole of humanity or offer release in eroticism just to two lovers.

Only rarely is the whole length of the slippery pole explored, in an attempt to translate into dramatic terms the totality of the Vision in all its implications. The work which makes that attempt in its fullest and most "classical" form is *The Burghers of Calais* . . . , thereby giving the most comprehensive picture of its author's Expressionist Vision. (pp. 248-50)

Kaiser was first drawn to the subject by Auguste Rodin's sculpture, *Les bourgeois de Calais (1884-6),* and his second source was Jean Froissart's *Chroniques de France* covering the period of the siege (1946-7). But, if Kaiser treats his sources here in anything like the same way as he does in plays like *The Jewish Widow* . . . or *Alkibiades Saved* . . . , a study of such extrinsic material can offer little guidance towards an understanding of the intentions of *The Burghers of Calais*. And so it seems to be at first sight.

The statue by Rodin, as one critic has been at some pains to point out, has virtually nothing in common with the play, at least as far as content is concerned. . . . The statue depicts the six about to set forth for the English camp, despondent and overwhelmingly weary: the whole composition evokes both their reluctance and the supreme effort required to overcome it and submit the self to the greater need of the community. It demands the utmost critical ingenuity to correlate even some of the figures with Kaiser's volunteers, even ignoring the awkward fact that he swelled their ranks to seven, and that, when they set out in the play—already calmly and positively accepting their fate—the bearded old man of the statue (Eustache) is not present among them.

Froissart, too, offers only a welter of contradictions. According to him Jean de Vienne was leader of the garrison—in Kaiser, it is Duguesclins, who by all accounts was nowhere near Calais at the time of the siege, and was anyway far too young then to have been entrusted with a position of such importance. . . . The French chronicler insists that the volunteers numbered six, that they set off immediately, and were saved by the pleadings of the English Queen. . . . In *The Burghers of Calais,* they are increased to seven, they do not set off, once they have been trimmed down to the right total, until the following morning, and are spared by the actual birth of a son (in fact, it was a daughter) to the Queen. The play ends on a note of resounding triumph, whereas the prospect for the actual citizens of Calais was far from pleasant: mass expulsion to provide accommodation for the English army of occupation. Besides all this, Kaiser also changes the cause of the siege to the construction of the harbour. So, apart from minor considerations like the names of some of the characters, and the motif of the bell which Kaiser takes up and extends, Froissart seems to offer about as much by way of illumination as Rodin's sculpture.

But Kaiser was not primarily concerned with subject-matter when he saw the Rodin group: he was seeking means of rendering his Vision of man into dramatic terms, and he recognized a similarity of method and intention in the statue: Rodin was not interested in the historical sacrifice of six late mediaeval burghers, but in the Idea of sacrifice. He sought to penetrate through the specific event in order to arrive at a general and universally valid statement about sacrifice. He tried to portray, not one historical sacrifice, but Sacrifice. (pp. 250-52)

This was what drew Kaiser to Rodin's sculpture: although Rodin is by no means as ruthless, and works rather from the specific to the Idea, Kaiser noted the affinities between them, and from this grew his intention to impose upon the historical events of the siege of Calais his Expressionist Vision of regeneration, as Rodin had imposed to some degree on the historical moment his more timebound insight.

The domination of Kaiser's will over his material can readily be seen at work in the "characters" of the volunteers.

Of the volunteers, only the Fifth Councillor remains silent throughout the first act. Even when he comes forward to join Eustache, striding resolutely and with the formalized posture of a man deep in concentration, he utters no word. He takes leave of his business associate with the same calm deliberation: only for a brief instant does his inner turmoil rise to the surface, but almost immediately he regains his self-discipline. Such is the extent of his characterization. He is neither explored in depth, nor is he a mere cipher. He is not a businessman; he is The Businessman. He is the essence, the Idea of Business become flesh. Similarly, the Fourth Councillor is the incarnation of The Husband, the Third The Son, Jean d'Aire is Age, and the brothers de Wissant Youth. Severally and collectively they become The Old Man. They are the representatives of the common mass of mankind, lost in the maze of existence, darkly aware of their own humanity, but shackled by a dread of losing their tenuous hold on life. They demand certainty (*Gewißheit*), a selfish security in a world which they do not comprehend and which they regard as essentially hostile. When threatened, they seek desperately for a leader, and fine one in Duguesclins. He, too, is The Old Man, but where they are fearful, he is aggressive: he strikes out blindly at the enemy in his frenzy (*Rausch*). Where they cling on to their lives, he rushes into an orgy of self-destruction. His code of conduct is likewise founded on the superior claims of the individual in conflict with society; it is a code of honour and shame, attack against counter-attack, an eye for an eye, and is the mirror image of the craving for certainty.

This is the vicious circle which Eustache seeks to break, by recognizing and acting upon the necessity of man's collective responsibility for his destiny, and his ability to control and master his environment. The two concepts are irrevocably bound together: the man who is afraid of the world about him either strikes out blindly at the dark forces he imagines are conspiring to overwhelm him, or shrinks into himself to create a semblance of security within his narrow circle of family and acquaintances. (pp. 252-53)

On the level at which Kaiser's dramas are acted out, it is frequently the case that logical progression is subservient to the driving thrust of the individual's urge towards renewal, and the Expressionist writer forces chance into an "inevitable" path towards renewal. Thus it is, in *Oktobertag (The Phantom Lover)*, that Catherine turns fantasy into reality by an act of will: she determines that the child she is carrying is not that of the butcher's boy Leguerche from whom she conceived it, but of the officer—Jean-Marc Marrien—whom she once saw fleetingly, and now loves with overwhelming passion. The logic which render this true is not that of an external law, but stems from the inner impulse of the individual. It is a real victory of mind over matter, in which the Vision imposes its pattern through an individual upon the material world. And such is the case also in *The Burghers of Calais;* for Eustache recognizes that it would be impossible for him to execute his plan with five other volunteers only, five Old Men who would undergo no fundamental change, but simply substitute the certainty of death for that in life for which they yearn.

Eustache must therefore break the vicious circle within them, must first convert them into New Men before he can use them as agents in the regeneration of mankind as a whole. It is for this reason that Kaiser causes Eustache to "will" seven volunteers in all to come forward, outwardly motivated by the fact that, after Jean d'Aire, who is so near to death that he feels he might as well die in a good cause as on his sickbed, comes forward to make the total five, his two prospective sons-in-law dash forward simultaneously in a protective gesture that is at the same time an expression of youthful rashness as a counter to Jean d'Aire's worn-out fatalism. And when the seven are gathered together, there is general consternation, but Eustache reacts *almost joyfully;* for he has now drawn up a group of men ready for the process of renewal; when they realize what has happened, their personalities will become fluid as they founder in a half-world of uncertainty, and he will then be able to mould them into a new and higher state of certainty.

The opening act of *The Burghers of Calais* can be seen as the first step in this direction, the exposing and discrediting of the Old Order, of contemporary society, and the hope that something new might emerge. In this situation Kaiser has fastened on two of the principal social targets of Expressionism: the selfishness and self-destructiveness of capitalism; and war, the inevitable constituent of a culture founded on the sanctity of private property and the stubborn separateness of the individual.

The second act sees Eustache preparing the volunteers for their sacrifice.

The initial leave-taking scene is a kind of anticipatory parody of those that follow: in it, Jean de Vienne, the leader of the council, expresses to Eustache his fears as representative of the people. . . . Throughout Jean de Vienne's long speech, Eustache remains *silent,* as he had been also at the commencement of the previous act. But now the reasons are different. Instead of the situation having run away from him as before, he now says nothing because he is no longer thinking on the same kind of plane as Jean de Vienne: his eyes are fixed on the Vision; he has left behind him the vicious circle of certainty and frenzy, which still torments the other citizens.

Silences such as this are characteristic of the Kaiser New Man in similar circumstances, and demonstrate the magnitude of the aspirations of the Expressionist Activist. Between the Old and the New the gulf is vast; it can only be bridged by an instantaneous, revolutionary change from fear to confidence, from blind panic to total mastery. Eustache has now already become the New Man—he is not, as has been argued, a superhuman figure from the outset—and has undergone the process he is about to induce in the other volunteers: ridding himself of the dross of *idées reçues* which have shackled him in the past, and determinedly facing the supremely difficult task that lies before him. Hence his mood is one of (very) quiet optimism as he patiently listens to Jean de Vienne's tale of woe. (pp. 254-56)

The grotesque is one of the strongest moral and satirical weapons of the Expressionists; and, in Kaiser's work, physical deformity and disability as a reflection of man's imprisonment within his body in contrast to his boundless aspirations is extensively used. (p. 258)

[In *The Burghers of Calais*] the Idea of deformity is generalised to represent the total incapacity of man to exceed himself. The New Man—he who is to lead the world to regeneration and rebirth—is no ardent youngster, but Eustache, a greybeard of three score years and ten, worn out by the cares of life, who can hardly stagger to his feet to face the immense effort that lies before him.

This second part of the central act has many overtones of Christian tradition and ceremonial, underlining both the eclecticism of the Expressionists, who borrowed themes and motifs from any and every source that would give a greater impact to their Vision; and also the ecstatic, quasi-religious nature of their search for moral regeneration. Here Christianity is used both as a point of reference, and also to demonstrate its inadequacy in the face of the problems confronting the twentieth century. . . .

But *The Burghers of Calais* can by no stretch of the imagination be termed an orthodox religious drama, in spite of such overtones, and others like the church in the background of the third act, or the magic numbers of three (acts) and seven (volunteers). Kaiser is simply taking over from the Christian tradition, as he took over from Froissart's chronicles, those things useful to his purpose.

*The Burghers of Calais,* it is true, is religious in the sense that it seeks a bond between transcendent and immanent, but the Christian legend is not essential to it: it could equally well be described in Platonic terms, a drama depicting man moving out from the flickering light of the cave by an arduous educational process into the brilliant sunlight of the realm of Forms. What differentiates *The Burghers of Calais* from Christianity is its Expressionist anthropocentricity: Eustache is not promising a new life in Heaven; he is promising to bring Heaven here and now down to earth. (p. 259)

[Confronted] with the gulf between world and Vision, man has to commit himself to one or the other; it is impossible to effect a compromise between the two. The warning signs of this are clear from the commencement of the drama, particularly in the powerful symbolism, which parallels and develops together with events on the stage. The first act debate between Eustache and Duguesclins, for example, is in many ways a clash of symbols. On the one hand, there is Duguesclins' armour, on the other, Eustache's robes. Duguesclins' visor is mocked by Eustache as cutting him off from the environment, instead of offering protection; the loose robes of the citizens, in contrast, far from leaving them open to attack, play quite a different rôle. . . . The robes allow receptivity to the environment, whereas armour cuts Duguesclins off from his surroundings. And this emphasis on the oneness of all things, the bonds between man and man, and humanity and the universe, runs through all of Eustache's symbols. Duguesclins is seen as a flickering, smoky flame that excludes the world from view. . . . The central symbol of the play, the circle, seems at first to corroborate the opening up of man's range of understanding that the other symbols brought forward by Eustache suggest: it represents in the first instance the creation of order and confidence out of fear and chaos. . . . Circle becomes sphere in the balls used for the lot-drawing; and at the same time, too, it is the vicious circle of the Old, and the closed ring of the volunteers. This alternation from circle to sphere, from closed to open ring, underlines the impossible dilemma which confronts Eustache. His aim is perfection, a realm sufficient unto itself, but he realises that, unlike the Platonic sphere of the sun, it is unable to radiate light and enlightenment upon humanity. It is not the fulfilment, but the negation of life. Eustache attains the Ideal, but discovers that the Ideal is death. The "message" of *The Burghers of Calais*—and Expressionist drama has a moral purpose—is, therefore, that, in spite of Eustache's Herculean efforts, regeneration in reality is possible only for the individual: for mankind as a whole it is a lost dream.

That Kaiser is content to leave the paradox unresolved underlines the acutest problem of Expressionism: the gulf between the temporal and the absolute. Kaiser takes the Activist path, plotting out the stages—chaos, purification, setting off, struggle, Ideal—in a vain attempt to reconcile them. For the Expressionist the moral purpose of art lies in expounding this tension: either in satirical, negative terms, or unwordly flights of ecstatic fancy, or with the positive, missionary fervour of Kaiser. (pp. 261-63)

*R. W. Last, "Kaiser's 'Bürger von Calais' and the Drama of Expressionism," in his* Periods in German Literature: Text and Contexts, Vol. II, *edited by J. M. Ritchie (© 1969 Oswald Wolff (Publishers) Ltd.), Wolff, 1969, pp. 247-64.*

**LEROY R. SHAW** (essay date 1970)

[In *Von morgens bis mitternachts*] Kaiser has obviously rejected the notion that the best way to reveal reality is through the conscientious depiction of actuality. Although the play pulsates with the spirit of World War I Germany, nothing in it refers directly to historical circumstances, and none of its events or scenes or characters are meant to suggest actual counterparts in life. On the contrary, Kaiser has broken the frame of illusionism and thrown away the principles which held it together. Instead of verisimilitude we have improbabilities and distortions; instead of objective reportage, an arbitrary and obvious fiction; instead of a careful record of everyday speech, we get a flood of rhetoric. Nothing reveals this new dramaturgy more graphically, perhaps, than Kaiser's boldness in depicting the undepictable—the ultimate reality of death. . . . Kaiser, unrestrained by any consideration except his symbolic purpose, conjures up death at will in a shape and form devised solely by imagination. The playwright's manipulating hand is everywhere visible in *Von morgens bis mitternachts,* flaunting his virtuosity, insisting that the play is sheer artifice and that only artifice makes the game worthwhile.

Like many early Kaiser plays, this one complicates its presentation of situation and strategy by elaborate linguistic conceits and blatant theatrical effects. Too much never seems enough in Kaiser's opinion, and where other playwrights are content to disarm their audiences with sporadic shocks, he discharges a constant barrage of words, images, sights, scenes, noises, and colors in a tempo rapid enough to send most spectators reeling. The meaning in the mélange usually clusters around a key metaphor—in *Von morgens bis mitternachts* it is the metaphor of money, chosen because it stands ambivalently for a real as well as a symbolic medium of exchange and also because of the opportunities it offers for punning on the problems of value. . . . Kaiser wittily traces a parallel set of implications in the metaphor, placing one in counterpoint to the other until a new perspective on both eventually emerges. Hence the ever present contrast between material and spiritual "goods," and the strong hints throughout the play that the cashier's real goal is his salvation through the *imitatio Christi*. Just before tossing his money to the crowd, he refers to the various steps in his search as *Stationen,* a clear echo of the Christian stations of the cross, and Kaiser supports this suggestion by his staging of the cashier's death. As he dies, he is made to fall "with arms stretched out wide" against a cross sewn on a curtain behind the altar. (pp. 71-2)

The intent of all this seems obvious enough, and in fact most interpretations of *Von morgens bis mitternachts* differ in only minor respects. As one critic words it, the play is concerned with "the existential buying power of money," asking "whether it is possible with money to acquire the essence of life." The answer, of course, is that money has no such power, and the cashier reacts to this insight by rejecting his materialist orientation for a spiritual (or is it an other-worldly?) one, thereby setting an example for us all to follow. He becomes, in effect, another embodiment of Kaiser's much-lauded Vision of the New Man (*der neue Mensch*), a self-sacrificing martyr for humanity.

Now it would be difficult to quarrel with this interpretation. It accords with most of the evidence and provides the play with a social-moral message corresponding to Kaiser's own brief against the predominantly money-oriented society of his day. Still, as a statement of situation and strategy, the interpretation sounds a bit simplistic, and I for one am reluctant to believe that Kaiser would have constructed such an elaborate work only to demonstate a truism. Further doubts arise in reflecting on the link between the cashier's conscious search for value

and his unconscious need to save his soul. Most interpretations accept this connection as "inspirational" rather than "logical," thereby sparing it further (and possibly damaging) scrutiny. Yet can we really take the cashier's search as a secular version of Christ's passion and crucifixion? If so, then why do Kaiser's parallels diverge more often than they coincide? On the other hand, if this notion is rejected, how are we to understand the playwright's cryptic *ecce homo*? Does the cashier stand for Everyman, as most critics seem to assume, or is he a unique and very singular martyr? And if a martyr, in what sense, for what values does he sacrifice himself, and how can these be recommended seriously to those who are still among the living?

Questions like these have been left unanswered; indeed, they are not usually even raised—perhaps because the message is deemed moral enough to justify treating them as irrelevant, perhaps because the impression still persists that this *Denkspieler,* as Bernhard Diebold called Kaiser, is just frivolously playing with an idea instead of thinking it through to the end. Be that as it may, I suspect that the questions might not exist if the interpretation of the play were of a different sort. My own feeling is that Kaiser did not write *Von morgens bis mitternachts* simply to propound an exemplary moral or social message; on the contrary, I believe that his burden here was primarily personal—conditioned by historical circumstances, to be sure, and even arising in part from them, but ultimately distinct and independent—and that the strategy he devised was intended to release him from that burden symbolically without exposing its nature to others. (pp. 72-4)

[A dialectical] process is clearly taking place in *Von morgens bis mitternachts,* even if it is still imperfectly worked out, so that at the end of the play things do look different from the way they looked at the beginning. "Value" has been redefined; the sense of the words Kassierer uses has changed from his initial conception of them; the role of "cashier" has another meaning for Kaiser than the one he set out with. Even the tripartite division so much favored by dialecticians (and the later Kaiser) may be discerned in the way Kaiser-Kassierer has transcended the original situation. If the scheme has not been perceived as such until now, it is because the formal structure of the play does not reflect it. Kaiser has asked us to assume the first step and left us to deduce the last one. With respect to the problem of "not counting," for example, the first step in the scheme shows Kaiser-Kassierer's awareness of being impersonally used in the rationalized world of the bank, the second his attempt to use its power personally for his own ends in the chaotic world of mundane experience, and the third his transcendence of both conditions by identifying himself with a larger impersonal purpose, thereby proving his usefulness by electing to be of use to others. A similar progression can be detected for solving the problems of change, creativity, and alienation. In each instance, the situation is transformed by dialectic, the meaning of events is remade by thinking them through. Kaiser admits in essays that accompany his later work to having derived the method from Socrates. He seems also to have taken the further Platonic step of believing that dialectic is not only the means to the good or valuable in life, but the way of the good life as well. (p. 116)

*Leroy R. Shaw, "The Strategy of Exchange: Georg Kaiser's 'Von Morgens bis Mitternachts'" (a revision of a lecture delivered at Trinity College in 1967), in his* The Playwright & Historical Change: Dramatic Strategies in Brecht, Hauptmann, Kaiser & Wedekind *(copyright © 1970 by the Regents of the Uni-*

*versity of Wisconsin), University of Wisconsin Press, 1970, pp. 66-116.*

## J. M. RITCHIE (essay date 1971)

In [*The Burghers of Calais*] Georg Kaiser stretched the resources of the German language to their utmost, exploiting all the linguistic techniques of the Expressionist Telegram style and more. The play ranges from one extreme of vast expansiveness to another of extreme concentration, from stylized gesture and mime to unnaturally long monologues. But even the latter, of which there are many, are built up from small speech units of extreme precision. Definite and indefinite articles are eliminated, subjunctives avoided, rhetorical questions, alliterations and exclamations heaped one on top of the other. The level of address constantly reaches an incredible height as the proliferating punctuation indicates, yet at the same time the vocabulary is utterly basic. The result is a combination of Nietzschean Zarathustra-pathos and the simplicity of the Luther Bible. As in *From Morning to Midnight,* though the play is non-Christian, Christian parallels are constantly being invoked, culminating in the final tableau before the steps of the cathedral. At no time is there any suggestion that this is the normal everyday speech of real people in an historical setting. The language is deliberately stylized, not in the direction of 'poetic' drama, but in that of mannered Expressionist diction. There is simply nothing like this in English.

In the same way as the language of the play is strikingly non-naturalistic, so too the structure of the play is a deliberate departure, despite its apparently traditional three-act form. The stage directions at the beginning of the play would seem by their very length to indicate a wealth of localizing detail. In fact the opposite is the case. Despite the 'Gothic' setting so beloved of the Expressionists and despite the choice of a famous incident from the Hundred Years' War in the 14th century, the work does not rely on historical accuracy. Instead of conjuring up a picture of a past age every aspect of the play conspires to free it from one particular frame of reference, and make it relevant for any time. Instead of historically accurate clothing or geographically precise details, it revels in all the purely theatrical possibilities of geometric stage-design, choreographic crowd scenes, stylized colour sequences, special lighting and sound-effects, exaggerated gestures, mimes and movements. The total effect is that of a pageant, a series of tableaux or set pieces, but one in which the static quality of such a form is counterbalanced not only by the sheer theatricality of the staging, but also by the dynamic presentation of the dialectic. As always Kaiser makes the clash of speech and counter-speech, argument and counter-argument dramatically gripping. Since plot has been virtually eliminated or at least reduced to a basic situation, the heart of the matter is the decision that has to be taken. Hence only the leading figures in the conflict, like Eustache de Saint-Pierre and Duguesclins, need be named, the rest are designated simply as Third, Fourth, Fifth Councillor, Father, Mother, Nurse, Daughter, English Officer etc.

It is clear that Kaiser was not attempting anything like the traditional historical drama when in 1913 he turned from the famous Rodin group of figures to Froissart's Chronicle for the theme of this work. His aim was to write a visionary play and the dedication he gave it—*ad aeternam memoriam*—indicates not so much a desire to perpetuate the *names* of the individuals concerned as to reveal the symbolic significance of their act for all ages. Important too in this connection is the date of the play's conception, expressing *before* the outbreak of the Great World War the message of peace and conciliation and a readiness for self-sacrifice in the cause of constructive communal achievement, rather than the traditional blind militarism. All in all, therefore, the play is completely Expressionistic in its themes: the idea that a new start has to be made; the readiness for sacrifice; the longing for salvation; the idea of a brotherhood of man; the vision of a rebirth of mankind; the manifestation of an aggressive pacifism. Man, it is argued, is conditioned no more by history and tradition than he is by milieu, race or psychological makeup. He is at all times free to make a break with the past, free to abandon antiquated ideas of honour and heroism which lead only to open aggression. He can turn to new paths. Hence this, too, is a play of ideas along the lines of a Platonic dialogue in which a case is argued out publicly by the main protagonists before the people. But of far greater importance than any of the many ideas expressed through the play is the process of purification which it exemplifies. The decision to accept the extreme demands of the King of England and to face death is not enough in itself. Each of the six must come to realize *why* he is prepared to do so and must arrive at the point where he makes this sacrifice for the right reasons. This is why the simple situation is complicated by the extra man, the choosing of lots, the walk to the square. These are not extraneous elements or unnecessary repetitions, they demonstrate that the choice is not something done in the heat of the moment to 'get it over with': the choice must be constantly repeated. The old way was characterized by simple responses to clear-cut situations. Now there can be no such certainty.

While in *The Burghers of Calais* some at least of the main protagonists were named and historically identifiable, the antinaturalism of Kaiser's *Gas* trilogy is obvious from the start of *The Coral.* Now all have become generalizations: father, son and daughter; or are differentiated only by colour; The Gentleman in Grey ( = Socialist), The Man in Blue ( = Worker), The Lady in Black ( = Widow), The Yellow Stoker, The Coloured Man-servant etc. (pp. 8-11)

Whatever interpretation is given to this play it is certainly not a social drama in the normal sense of one dealing with the fate of the masses or class-hatred. (p. 11)

[In *Gas I*] Kaiser is concerned not with a naturalistic picture of modern life, but with fundamental questions: what is it all for? what does this mean in terms of the quality of human life? how can a rebirth of mankind be brought about and what are the forces resisting such change? As in *The Coral* the characters are unnamed though the colours are significant. Where the millionaire has been aware of the 'horror' of poverty and the capitalistic system, the millionaire's son, who has identified himself with the workers, must be made to see the 'white terror' reached when technology arrives at its ultimate limits. There is no flaw in the mathematical formula and yet the gas inevitably explodes. While the millionaire's son sees the white terror and the vast devastation caused by it as 'what was needed to give us the impetus,—violently—to hurl us forwards by a thousand years' this insight is reserved for him alone and he meets immovable resistance to change in everyone from the clerk and the engineers to the workers, men, women and children. (pp. 11-12)

In *Gas II* the destruction of humanity predicted in *Gas I* now seems imminent. Apart from the millionaire-worker and the chief engineer all characters are reduced to Blue Figures, Yellow Figures and workers. The world is completely denaturalized into concrete hangars, electronic panels and radar screens. The war is global and the balance of terror a simple calculation. . . . The stage is now set for the final twilight of mankind when the chief engineer offers the 'automata' release from serfdom by the ultimate technological triumph—a poison gas capable of annihilating the tyrant. 'Now there is triumph in a thin glass membrane that shatters and at once eats away the flesh, leaving bleached brittle bones!' The final discussion between the chief engineer and the millionaire-worker on whether to use this ultimate weapon or not is argued out in public. The millionaire-worker has only a mystic appeal akin to the vision of the millionaire in *The Coral* that the end is the beginning: 'Widen your vision for the new that intermingles with the primal.' The kingdom is not of this world, he claims, mankind has to be the kingdom. But this still proves an unattainable ideal. Like Eustache de Saint-Pierre he asks the people to return to the work, not to thoughts of military greatness. But his appeal, like all appeals of his family before him, has been in vain: man is not ready to change, and he himself drops the bomb and unleashes the final orgy of total destruction.

Georg Kaiser's three plays, written fifty years ago, were to prove a prophetic vision of the balance of nuclear terror in the world today. (pp. 13-14)

> *J. M. Ritchie, in his introduction to* Five Plays *by Georg Kaiser, translated by B. J. Kenworthy, Rex Last, J. M. Ritchie (translation © Calder and Boyars 1971), Calder and Boyars, 1971, pp. 7-14.*

**ERNST SCHÜRER** (essay date 1971)

[*Schürer's* Georg Kaiser, *from which the following is excerpted, is a comprehensive introduction to Kaiser's works.*]

Kaiser's first work to be published, *Die jüdische Witwe (The Jewish Widow* . . .), is also his first wholly successful and satisfying comedy. The biblical legend of Judith has always held a strong fascination for playwrights, the last serious treatment having been Hebbel's *Judith* (1843). Nestroy had parodied Hebbel's version in his *Judith und Holofernes* (1849), and now Kaiser adds his own ironic treatment. His *Judith* has no qualms about anything she does; she dispenses with all morality. Following only her nature and vitality—her sex drive—she never considers herself an instrument of divine providence for the rescue of the city. She is as amoral and strong-willed as Lulu in Wedekind's *Erdgeist,* and like Lulu she does not have any parents. She is always convinced of her innocence and maintains: "I have no sins!" Kaiser's comedy is a parody of the biblical version of the story, not of Hebbel's play. (p. 72)

The play displays a remarkable use of language, pantomime, symbolism, and structure. Judith is a vital but silent character, who uses her body more than her tongue. When being led into the temple to marry Manasse, she offers determined resistance, not because she wants to retain her virginity, as [Wolfgang] Fix maintains, but because she considers the match unnatural. All she answers to the persuasion of her relatives is a "No!" repeated nine times in the first act. In the last act, this action is duplicated because Judith does not want to remain a virgin eternally, and her resistance only ceases when she recognizes the high priest's intentions. . . . The identical beginnings of Acts I and V show the circular structure of the play, which could be extended indefinitely since it can consist of any number of episodes in Judith's quest for a man. The ring is closed, however, with Judith's wish being fulfilled. (pp. 72-3)

The stage, still realistic, . . . has symbolic function. In the first act, the towering structure of the temple, with its huge pillars, symbolizes the might of the conventions and laws of Jewish society, which Judith must obey. This society is represented, on the one hand, by her family, the house of Uz, which Kaiser takes great care to show with all male members, who carry on the tradition. Secondly, there are the priests and scribes representing church and state. They abide by the letter of the law and despair when they cannot follow the rules of purification during the siege. Their actions are determined by a code of belief and by ordinances, while Judith does not proceed according to plan. She lets circumstances determine her steps. However, it is not the futile actions of the elders but Judith's unconventional behavior which saves the town. She does not tolerate the unnatural restraint of her impulses which Manasse tries to impose on her. (pp. 73-4)

The play is witty and full of irony resulting from the contrast between appearance and reality. This is already evident in the title: Judith is not a widow, nor is she a patriotic Jewish woman. Kaiser no longer takes recourse to coarse language, as in some of the earlier comedies. Although formally influenced by Naturalistic historical dramas like Hauptmann's *Florian Geyer* (this is evident in the list of characters) and immersed in a neo-Romantic atmosphere, the play is nevertheless a savage attack on traditional heroism and the historical drama. As far as this aspect is concerned, Kaiser was later joined by Brecht and Sternheim, who also saw Judith with fresh eyes. [B. J.] Kenworthy points out some Expressionistic features: Kaiser's "social criticism emerges in broader terms" and "his technical skill is increasing, notably in the dramatic exploitation of the crowd. Both the gathering of merchants and the throng of Jewish women awaiting the spectacle of Judith's wedding and of her dedication fulfil the choric function of commenting on the action and supplying expositive detail in their snatches of conversation."

The dichotomy between body and mind, life and the intellect, receives its most illuminating treatment in Kaiser's play *Der gerettete Alkibiades (Alkibiades Saved* . . .). Stylistically, it belongs to his most Expressionist dramas. . . . The play consists of three parts, proceeding from thesis to antithesis, and finally arriving at a synthesis. (pp. 74-5)

After completing the play, Kaiser wrote to a friend: "It contains all of Plato—and all of Nietzsche—and everything is transformed into scenes of the liveliest construction. I have created Greece anew—and toppled that of Goethe—Winckelmann. Humanity must thank me, or it does not exist." Kaiser contrasts the positive picture of Socrates given by Plato in the *Symposion* and in *Phaidon* with the negative opinion of the late Nietzsche, who wrote:

> The common development in the history of Europe since *Socrates* is the attempt to make the *moral values* rule over all other values: . . . three forces are hidden behind it:
>
> 1. the instinct of the herd against the strong and independent;
>
> 2. the instinct of the suffering and have-nots against the happy;
>
> 3. the instinct of the average people against the exceptional ones.

Kaiser rejects [Johann] Winckelmann's view embracing Greek culture as a period of "noble simplicity and serene grandeur," while he envisions the Greek people as wrestling with problems very similar to those he detected in the German culture of his times. Kaiser also rejected the Greek ideal which Goethe presents in his *Iphigenie* and, indeed, Goethe's world view in general. This becomes especially evident in the scene in which Sokrates develops his new esthetics. (pp. 77-8)

The influence of Schopenhauer's idealistic philosophy on Kaiser can also be detected in the play. Sokrates' will to live has been undermined, since he has recognized the meaninglessness of reality and of human existence. But he tries to overcome his pessimism and nihilism by constructing a new system of philosophy. This he does out of compassion for humanity. Following Schopenhauer, this compassion with humanity, which shows the unity of all existence, also leads to the denial of the will to live, to the release of the individual from life and his salvation in death. But although the individual is destroyed, the species continues to live. Therefore Sokrates admonishes Xanthippe, who is a midwife, to continue bringing forth new life. (pp. 78-9)

In the fate of Sokrates, Kaiser actually portrays the dilemma of the Expressionists and their mission: they would have liked to save the world by establishing a new "religion" in order to hide the knowledge of the meaninglessness of man's existence, of nihilism, from mankind, but they also reveal it. The contradictory actions are caused by a schizophrenic state of mind. Just as Athens is destroyed in spite of Sokrates' sacrifice, so the Expressionists' vision could not save modern society, nor divert it from its suicidal course. What did Kaiser do when he recognized this fact? He turned away from life and escaped into the spheres of the spirit, accepting the isolation this entailed. He no longer used the metaphor of the "thorn in the flesh" with its negative meaning; for him, the intellect was no longer a sickness but "the highest development of energy in nature" and the source of his talents. In 1928 he said in an interview: "I discovered the highest form of health—spiritual health, in Plato's sense—that same Plato to whom I dedicated my earliest passion and whom I determined to follow—here, today, more strongly than ever before." But although he still maintained that the intellect was the force which could give shape to the chaotic world and determine the course of history, in many of his plays he elevated it into the realm of the stars, thereby severing any connections to the world of reality and losing the chance to apply his reason to the problems of existence waiting for solutions. (pp. 79-80)

The tragicomedy *Kanzlist Krehler* is generally considered an appendix to *Von morgens bis mitternachts*. Kenworthy states that it "extends to three acts the theme of the short domestic scene" in the latter play. This creates the impression that Kaiser was trying to repeat the success of the former play by writing a similar one. But this is not the case. To be sure, the starting point is the same in both dramas: Krehler is also suddenly thrown out of his accustomed existence when he receives an unexpected day off after his daughter Ida's wedding. But here the similarity ends. The Cashier runs from station to station, looking for a new life and finally shoots himself because the world is not as he imagined it to be. He blames it for his failure, never realizing that it was his own inner lack of substance which caused his destruction. The clerk Krehler, on the other hand, has time to have a good, hard look at himself and comes to the conclusion that he will never be able to start a new life. The structure and the setting of the play are tailored to its purpose: *Kanzlist Krehler* is not a *Stationendrama* but a conventional family tragedy in three acts and, therefore, takes place in Krehler's apartment. Krehler and his daughter Ida are contrasted with his wife and son-in-law Max. (pp. 88-9)

[In *Nebeneinander*] Kaiser gives dramatic expression to the agony and misery brought on by inflation as well as to the opportunism and corruption that mushroomed in the fetid atmosphere of post-World War I Germany, causing economic and moral degradation. He shows how the struggle for survival brings about the desolation of souls who hunger for a more human atmosphere yet are completely isolated, although they live side by side. The play is especially interesting because of its structure, which attempts to express this alienation of human beings from each other in the big cities. Each act of the play consists of three scenes, the central one being devoted to the Pawnbroker and the two supporting scenes to the fate of Luise and Neumann. (p. 91)

*Hölle Weg Erde* has often been hailed as Kaiser's only positive Expressionist drama. It was preceded by his outline for a drama, *Die Erneuerung* (*Regeneration*), dating from 1919. (pp. 93-4)

The play discloses its tripartite division in the title. *Hölle* gives a picture of people living in the hell of a capitalist society, where everybody cares only for himself. *Weg* portrays the sudden recognition by all that they themselves are responsible for the present conditions. *Erde* shows them crossing the bridge to a new life of brotherhood and love. Kaiser dedicated the drama to his two infant sons, Dante Anselm and Michael Laurent, who represented the new time for him. Written after the armistice of 1918, the play represents the high point of Kaiser's hopes for a better world. The Russian Revolution, the end of the senseless slaughter of World War I, the proclamation of Wilson's Fourteen Points—all these events seemed to indicate that a turning point in the relations between people had come. (pp. 94-5)

[Kaiser] later realized the shortcomings of *Hölle Weg Erde*. It is, indeed, one of his weakest plays. Like Jhering, one gets the feeling that Kaiser himself did not believe in his own words. He uses his usual stage symbolism; the language is as mechanistic and impersonal as its speakers, but it does not change in the last part of the play, where it should convey to us the ecstasy and totality of a new world. *Hölle Weg Erde* and *Gas II*, written about the same time, give the impression of being exercises in symmetry rather than dramas. If the play is to show the birth of a new ethical responsibility, a moral awakening and regeneration, this aim gets lost in an ocean of words. It only demonstrates the failure of abstract language to convince and change people. . . .

[*Kanzlist Krehler, Von morgen bis mitternachts, Nebeneinander,* and *Hölle Weg Erde*] present a picture of society in which man is merely an economic factor. It is possible and even probable that the Cashier's and Krehler's work is of value to society, but to them it is only routine and void of any meaning. It has denatured them and left them floundering in the vacuum of a senseless world: they are truly alienated. Discovering the limitations of their existence, they rebel against the society which has condemned them to such a life. But they are too weak to fight successfully. Their cry of rage soon turns into a death rattle which cuts short their protests. The Pawnbroker and Spazierer, however, are creatures of conscience who try to assist their fellow men. Their criticism of society is not purely emotional; they attack specific ills, such as the ideal of abstract justice which does not serve the individual the way it should. They force society to review its values. While the Pawnbroker gives up, Spazierer finally reaches his utopia. In all cases, the impetus is a basically insignificant event, and the decision to help is an instinctive and emotional reaction. The characters strive not so much for a reform of society, but they really want to reform human nature and create a world in which love is possible, in which egoism is replaced by altruism. Kaiser seems to believe in the basic goodness of man, which has been perverted by society and must only be rediscovered. (p. 97)

Not without justification, [Kaiser] has been called a *Denkspieler,* and his plays cold constructions of reason and intellect, top-heavy with theorizing.

This assertion is especially applicable to a group of nine plays [including *Das Frauenopfer (Sacrifice of a Woman), Der Brand im Opernhaus (Fire in the Opera House), Rosamunde Floris, Der Gärtner von Toulouse (The Gardner of Toulouse), Agnete, Alain und Elise (Alain and Elise),* and *Pferdewechsel (Horse-Relay)*] centering round a leading female character, aptly entitled *Frauenstücke.* They are designed for a small cast in an intimate theater. All except *Der Gärtner von Toulouse* have three acts. Kaiser purposely places the plays in an artificial setting; it is often a greenhouse or a winter garden, a place of constant high temperature separated from the world around it by glass plates, locked doors, or water. The exotic characters are cut off from society and live in a fantasy world. They cling to an abstract idea, on whose altar they sacrifice their feelings and sometimes their humanity. They even go so far as to commit murder to save the inner world of their dreams—for them the ideal reality which allows for no compromise. Kaiser poses the problem of illusion and truth, and it is characteristic that in most cases the illusion emerges victorious. While in real life the illusions of the Expressionist writers had been defeated and trampled in the dust, at least they could come to life on stage. But even here they only disclose that it is not always the happiness of his human brother Kaiser is concerned about, but often his own abstruse intellectual problems, his spiritual world which, in many cases, shows all the signs of psychopathic deviation.

The plot of these plays is constructed around the personal relationship between a man and a woman. It is the purity of love, and the purity of the woman, which is seen as the ideal. (pp. 140-41)

The most characteristic element of Kaiser's [*Frauenstücke* dramas] . . . is the growing isolation discernible in the characters, the plot, and even the style of the dialogue. In the earlier plays, this isolation is already expressed by the fact that all male and female characters, who are usually orphans, are lone individuals. But while in these dramas the two main characters at least try to create a world for themselves, they remain separated in the later ones. William and Rosamunde, Alain and Elise are not united, as the conjunction of their names in the titles would indicate, but remain alone. Kaiser's Expressionist plays, like *Von morgens bis mitternachts* and *Hölle Weg Erde,* are significant because they portray the isolated individual within his social environment, on the road which takes him to the homes of the bourgeois family, to shops, bank, and churches, to the Salvation Army, sports events, and army barracks, to restaurants, cabarets, and hotels, to brothels, police stations, and prisons. . . . Because of the exclusion of an environment, they have lost their sense of political urgency and protest and manifest a growing sterility and artificiality. Kaiser used the basic elements of certain plots over and over again; he repeated himself and often used formulations which appeared in earlier plays. His last plays especially make it evident that Kaiser was tortured by growing doubts about his artistic abilities. His powers had actually been on the decline since about 1920. Although he was looking for new forms and means of expressing himself, he was not successful in finding them. After the intermezzo

of the Expressionist plays, he actually returned to his own beginnings, the classical form of the three-act play. (pp. 151-52)

[*Zweimal Amphitryon* is the first of Kaiser's] three so-called Greek dramas, the other two being *Pygmalion* and *Bellerophon.* In these plays, Kaiser reverted not only to classical themes but also to the traditional five-act structure and to the blank-verse form. Stylistically, the retreat of the Expressionist had ended in the safe haven of traditional forms, but Kaiser's message remains the same: the play, inspired by Molière and Kleist, is his final protest against militarism. (p. 170)

In *Zweimal Amphitryon,* some of Kaiser's main themes are intertwined: first, his protest against war; second, the salvation of the world by a pure woman; and third, the promised birth of a child as the future redeemer. The curse of war destroys all that is good in man; it can only be overcome if love, as exemplified by Alkmene, rules the world. And a new world can only be created by individuals; therefore it must be started by a single man, the child. (p. 171)

In *Pygmalion* the work of art and the woman whom the artist loves become one. An ideal situation is created, in which Pygmalion thinks that he will be able to create perfect works of art easily and intuitively. (p. 188)

Pygmalion is the artist who attempts to fuse art's illusions and life's realities. He achieves this first by creating the ideal statue as a symbol of a higher being and then by bringing it into this world through his love. But society rejects art and the artist, since people cannot understand the artist, and the work of art is incomprehensible to them. Completely disillusioned, Pygmalion finally realizes that art and life cannot be united; he no longer believes that his art will change man's nature since he is completely isolated from him. He is now convinced that his works do not spring from happiness but from suffering. Indeed, during his period of happiness with Chaire, Pygmalion does not work. Since he has created his ideal, since his dream has become true, and since he already lives in paradise, he does not feel the urge to devote himself to art. Because he is living with his work, he no longer feels the emptiness which seizes the artist after the completion of a work. Only after he has lost Chaire does Pygmalion return to his artistic calling. (p. 189)

Pygmalion works for his own self-satisfaction, protecting himself against the attacks of the world. Indeed, Kaiser considered the play a defense and an attack: "In *Pygmalion* I have told everything I still had to say. I believe that I have spoken for all of us—probably never before has the reviled artist been defended so passionately and justly as with the power of my wrath and my art. The play is my bequest to the world, which now has one more reason to be red with shame."

The theme of the loneliness of the artist is carried to its logical extreme in *Bellerophon,* which ends with the two lovers being placed among the stars. . . . Bellerophon is a naïve artist; he is completely innocent and, free of fear, is able to overcome the world's pitfalls. But although pursued by the evils of the world, Bellerophon is never confronted with them. He walks through life completely isolated from its realities. Since art has been powerless in this world, at the end he and his beloved Myrtis are placed among the stars and Bellerophon is presented with a divine instrument, on which he will delight the gods with his music. The artist, the chosen one among the herd of the common people, has now become part of divinity. Kaiser's hybris once more becomes apparent through the fact that he wanted only one word engraved on his tombstone—"Bellerophon.'' To a friend he wrote: ''Yesterday I finished my third Hellenistic play: *Bellerophon.* My swan song. I have placed myself among the stars.'' He might have done well to read the Greek myth to its end: Bellerophon was *not* placed among the stars, although he attempted to fly up into heaven on Pegasus. His pride and presumption angered the gods, and Jupiter sent down a gadfly which stung Pegasus, causing him to throw his rider, who became lame and blind, wandering alone across the face of the earth until he died miserably. (pp. 190-91)

Although written at different times, Kaiser's two completed novels [*Es ist genug (It Is Enough)* and *Villa Aurea*] are closely related to each other. They have the same basic structure and are highly subjective, thematically as well as formally. In both, the hero, who is also the first-person narrator of the novel, lives a happy life in an intact world. When this existence ends abruptly with a catastrophe, he is unable to cope with the situation and attempts to save himself by rejecting his former identity, taking on a new name, and building a new life. Although he believes that he has cut all strings to his past and would like to erase its memory as well, he is still tied to it by his guilt and by his sense of failure. His endeavors to find new happiness cause him to commit crimes until, finally, he realizes that only by accepting his destiny can he master his fate. In the course of his process of recognition, he comes to a better understanding of himself. Yet, even in the end, he does not return to society but remains imprisoned in the happy memories of his former love, or in the hell of his conscience.

The novels take the form of a long letter written by the protagonist. The action revolves around him, and subplots are used to comment upon his behavior. His qualities, feelings, and thoughts are similar to those of the heroes of Kaiser's plays. The economic and social circumstances of the characters are of little importance, and the world of politics is completely excluded, since the hero lives in a world of his own. The settings and events have a highly symbolic value and serve to elucidate the subjective experiences of the hero. The style is abstract and concentrated; the sentences, short and precise. In short, Kaiser, the dramatist, is very much in evidence in his epic works.

*Es ist genug* is divided into two parts: in the first, the narrator tells about his experiences in the twelve years from the death of his wife until he meets his daughter again; in the second, he relates how he won and lost his daughter. In the end, he recognizes that he has been fleeing all his life. But unlike Aldo, one of the supporting characters, he is not destroyed by his guilt. He returns to the glacier to find a new life, for he knows that he once possessed Isa's love and that he can never lose this treasure. It was real, while the incestuous passion, which made him believe in an enforced resurrection of Isa in Doris, was a bad dream, from which he is finally awakening. (pp. 192-93)

In this novel, as well as in *Villa Aurea,* the hero is loved and admired by all women while, basically, he loves only himself. With Doris, his own daughter—an extension of himself—he withdraws from the world, separated from it by the sea and by a mountain which can only be reached by a dangerous cable car, which could carry its occupants to death at any moment. The symbolism of the novel betrays the author and verifies Sokel's words: ''To the obscure private symbolism of the Expressionist's work corresponds the narcissism of his life, the withdrawal of love from the world to the self. In this withdrawal we shall find the root of the Expressionist's feeling of guilt.''

Many other motifs from Kaiser's plays reappear in the novel: first, the clash between illusion and reality; second, the predilection for identity and name-changing. (pp. 193-94)

[*Villa Aurea*] is a novel in the form of a long letter, written by Boris Tscherski to his former wife, Vera. (p. 194)

The novel's three main characters try to save themselves from destruction at the hands of cruel reality: Vera by fleeing into illusion, Pere Lot by substituting Boris for his sons, and Boris by taking on another identity and marrying Marie. But, in the final analysis, none of these attempts succeeds: Vera will learn from Boris's letter that her picture of the shining knight was false; Pere Lot suffers the most when Boris leaves him and his daughter drowns herself in the river; and Boris realizes that he cannot escape the consequences of his actions by simply changing his identity. In this respect, he differs markedly from most of the characters in Kaiser's plays, who find their happiness in illusion and do not experience guilt for deeds committed in the world of reality. (pp. 195-96)

> *Ernst Schürer, in his* Georg Kaiser *(copyright ©1971 by Twayne Publishers, Inc.; reprinted with the permission of Twayne Publishers, a Division of G. K. Hall & Co., Boston), Twayne, 1971, 256 p.*

### J. L. STYAN (essay date 1981)

[*Von Morgens bis Mitternachts (From Morn to Midnight]* is a regeneration play, a morality play, made up of seven scenes or 'stations' (*Stationen*). The idea is borrowed from the stations of the cross, and the scenes trace the Cashier's progress through the day. Each scene is an expressionistic statement more stylized than the last. His life in the bank is that of a caged robot which moves in jerks to resemble a piece of machinery. On his way through a field covered in snow, he sees the figure of death formed by the snow in the branches of a tree like a giant skeleton. The scene at the races is like a madhouse, the promoters in identical silk hats behaving like automata. In the orgy of the cabaret, the beautiful girls he wants get drunk, fall asleep or turn out to be old and ugly; even the dancer has a wooden leg; and they all wear impersonal masks. At the end, the Cashier punctuates his speech with blasts on a trumpet, and as he shoots himself, 'all the light-bulbs explode' and he 'sinks with outstretched arms against the cross'. 'His death-rattle sounds like an Ecce—his final sighed expiration like a Homo.' (pp. 49-50)

Kaiser's plays have a machine-like precision, but his sense of the stage is always strong and he is always concerned to channel the excitement of expressionism into workable theatre. He is conscious of space and the opposition of forces upon it, and he makes good use of lighting and perspective effects and different levels. And for all the feverishness in performance, the devices of expressionism produced a cold, logical drama, and threw the weight on to the play's thesis. Kaiser's plays of ideas are therefore never 'discussion plays', and in dramatic method they stand diametrically opposed to the plays of Bernard Shaw and Bertolt Brecht. (p. 54)

> *J. L. Styan, ''Expressionism in Germany: Kaiser and Toller,'' in his* Modern Drama in Theory and Practice: Expressionism and Epic Theatre, Vol. 3 *(© Cambridge University Press 1981), Cambridge University Press, 1981, pp. 47-61.*

ADDITIONAL BIBLIOGRAPHY

Frenz, Horst. "Eugene O'Neill and Georg Kaiser." In *Eugene O'Neill: A World View,* edited by Virginia Floyd, pp. 172-85. New York: Frederick Ungar Publishing Co., 1979.*

    Comparative study. Frenz develops a comparison between O'Neill's *The Emperor Jones* and Kaiser's *From Morn to Midnight* to "ascertain if and to what extent O'Neill could have known Kaiser's work."

Garten, H. F. "Georg Kaiser." In *German Men of Letters: Twelve Literary Essays, Vol. II,* edited by Alex Natan, pp. 157-72. London: Oswald Wolff Publishers, 1963.

    Discussion of the influence Plato and Nietzsche had on Kaiser's work. Through a survey of Kaiser's major plays Garten reflects on the dialectic character of his dialogue and the duality of "spirit" and "life" which forms the basis of his work.

Jetter, Marianne R. "Some Thoughts on Kleist's *Amphitryon* and Kaiser's *Zweimal Amphitryon.*" *German Life and Letters* XIII, No. 3 (April 1960): 178-89.*

    Comparative study. Jetter compares and contrasts Kaiser's treatment of the Amphitryon legend in *Zweimal Amphitryon* and Heinrich von Kleist's treatment of it in his *Amphitryon.*

Kauf, Robert. " 'Schellenkönig': An Unpublished Early Play by Georg Kaiser." *The Journal of English and Germanic Philology* LV, No. 3 (July 1956): 439-50.

    Examination of Kaiser's "Schellenkönig." Through a detailed study, Kauf attempts to demonstrate a "clear continuity and consistency of development in Kaiser's work."

Kauf, Robert. "Georg Kaiser's Social Tetralogy and the Social Ideas of Walter Rathenau." *PMLA* LXXVII (June 1962): 311-17.*

    Comparative study. Kauf outlines the similarities between the social ideas of Walter Rathenau and the concepts presented by Kaiser in his *Gas* trilogy.

Reichert, Herbert W. "Nietzsche and Georg Kaiser." *Studies in Philology* LXI, No. 1 (January 1964): 85-108.*

    Discussion of the possible influence Nietzsche had on Kaiser's work.

Scher, Steven P. "Georg Kaiser's *Von Morgens bis Mitternachts:* Isolation as Theme and Artistic Method." In *Theatrum Mundi: Essays on German Drama and German Literature Dedicated to Harold Lenz on His Seventieth Birthday, September 11, 1978,* edited by Edward R. Haymes, pp. 125-35. Munich: Wilhelm Fink Verlag, 1980.

    Critical analysis. Scher illustrates the validity of the assertions in Georg Lukacs's essay "Große und Verfall' des Expressionismus" as it pertains to Kaiser's "treatment of the typically expressionistic theme of the isolation of the individual" in his *Von Morgens bis Mitternachts.*

Tunstall, George C. "Light Symbolism in Georg Kaiser's *Die Bürger von Calais.*" *Journal of English and German Philology* LXXVIII, No. 2 (April 1979): 178-92.

    Structural examination. Tunstall suggests that a structural analysis of *Die Bürger von Calais,* from the perspective of language and symbolism, can lead to a better understanding of the way in which Kaiser composed his play.

# Valéry Larbaud

## 1881-1957

(Also wrote under pseudonym of L. Hagiosy) French poet, novella and short story writer, novelist, essayist, critic, translator, and journalist.

Larbaud is best remembered for his creation of the eccentric millionaire-poet A. O. Barnabooth. This famous persona, who first appeared in *Poèmes par un riche amateur,* was the prototype of the modern, cultured individual, both in his quest of the absolute and in his search for a common bond among human beings. Both Larbaud's *Poèmes par un riche amateur* and the later *A. O. Barnabooth, ses oeuvres complètes (A. O. Barnabooth, His Diary)* were influential in shaping the vogue for a "new cosmopolitanism" in European literature. In his later works, such as *Fermina Márquez* and *Enfantines,* Larbaud became one of the first French writers to successfully depict the world of adolescence from the internal perspective of the child. Larbaud was also influential in developing the stream of consciousness technique. He attempted to break down the barriers between poetry and prose and, according to John L. Brown, this liberation of language "may well be one of Larbaud's essential achievements."

Born of wealthy parents in the cosmopolitan city of Vichy, France, Larbaud was a delicate child who loved books and solitude. Though he often felt isolated because of his family's economic status, Larbaud enjoyed the luxuries of the rich, including a private education and a tour through Europe and Russia at the age of seventeen. As a result of his early exposure to a variety of cultures, he soon became proficient in a number of languages and literatures, particularly Spanish, Italian, and English. After he obtained his *licencié ès lettres* he decided to become a translator and was the first to translate Samuel Butler, G. K. Chesterton, Joseph Conrad, Thomas Hardy, Robert Louis Stevenson, James Joyce, and many others into French. Larbaud received his first recognition as a writer with the publication of *Poèmes par un riche amateur.* Though there were only two hundred copies of the collection printed, a number of critics, including André Gide and Paul Claudel, immediately sensed the extent of Larbaud's talent. But it was not until the publication of *A. O. Barnabooth, His Diary* that Larbaud was widely recognized as a major writer of his generation. One of the most important literary alliances for Larbaud was his friendship with Joyce, who at that time was still an unknown writer. Joyce's stream of consciousness technique had a profound influence on the Frenchman's work, especially *Amants, heureux amants.* Larbaud's career as a writer was cut short when, at the age of fifty-five, he was incapacitated by a cerebral hemorrhage. As a result, he was confined to his home for the last twenty years of his life.

The characters, techniques, and themes which eventually became Larbaud's fictional and poetic trademarks were already evident in his early publications, *Poèmes par un riche amateur* and *A. O. Barnabooth.* The latter depicts the young and restless Barnabooth as he travels across Europe in search of self-knowledge. Endowed with an ardent idealism and a diversified cultural background, Barnabooth constantly uproots himself physically and morally in a vain effort to join his life to the rich variety of human experience. In *Enfantines* and *Fermina*

*Culver Pictures*

*Márquez,* Larbaud demonstrated his skill in capturing the subtle, yet poignant, shades of childhood and adolescence. His innovative way of writing about children greatly altered the adolescent novel. In his collection of novellas, *Amants, heureux amants,* Larbaud experimented with the interior monologue and advanced that technique towards the total "inwardness" Joyce later achieved in *Finnegans Wake.* All of these works develop Larbaud's recurring concerns: a sensuous delight in this world, the necessity of love, work, and pleasure, and the inevitability of death.

Larbaud has been compared to the masters in nearly every genre he attempted. Critics have noted his affinity with Walt Whitman in the hymn-like character of his free verse, and many have compared him to Marcel Proust and Gide for the sensual evocations of childhood, adolescence, and young erotic love in his fiction. As a translator, Larbaud has been praised for his conscientious workmanship and for his attempts to make an art of the translator's craft. And as a critic Larbaud succeeded in introducing many foreign authors to French readers and in promoting an understanding of the unity of European literature. It is for this reason that critic Justin O'Brien labeled him "a citizen of Europe."

## PRINCIPAL WORKS

*Les portiques*   (poetry)   1896

*Les archontes; ou, La liberté religieuse* [as L. Hagiosy] (satire) 1900

*Poèmes par un riche amateur* (poetry) 1908; also published as *Le livre de M. Barnabooth*, 1908

*Fermina Márquez* (novel) 1911

*\*A. O. Barnabooth, ses oeuvres complètes, c'est-à-dire: Un conte, ses poèmes, et son journal intime* (novel, poetry, and fictional diary) 1913

    [*A. O. Barnabooth, His Diary* (partial translation), 1924; also published as *Poems of a Multimillionaire* (partial translation), 1955; and *The Poems of A. O. Barnabooth* (partial translation), 1977]

*Enfantines* (short stories) 1918

*Amants, heureux amants* (novellas) 1923

*Ce vice impuni, la lecture. Domaine anglais* (essays) 1925; also published as *Ce vice impuni, la lecture. Domaine anglais* [enlarged edition], 1936

*Jaune bleu blanc* (essays and sketches) 1927

*Allen* (fictional dialogues) 1929

*Aux couleurs de Rome* (essays) 1938

*Ce vice impuni, la lecture. Domaine francais* (essays) 1941

*"Rachel Frutiger"* (short story) 1945; published in *The Best of Modern European Literature: 1920-1940*

*Sous l'invocation de Saint Jérôme* (essays) 1946

*Oeuvres complètes*. 10 vols. (poetry, short stories, novellas, novels, essays, fictional diary, and fictional dialogues) 1950-55

*Journal, 1912-1935* (journal) 1955

*Le coeur de l'Angleterre* (essays) 1971

*This work includes a revision of the earlier *Poèmes par un riche amateur*.

---

**RENÉ LALOU** (essay date 1924)

Valéry Larbaud's books keep the clinging fascination of a perfume. To analyse him would be useless had all rendered justice to the writer who has so subtly resolved the conflict of the ego and the universe as it presents itself to the novelist. Larbaud's work is situated at what Proust would call "a seam." He is capable of being at once in the ark and out of the ark. The author of *Enfantines* has really tasted the joys of "the great epoch," he has poetized even its vacation tasks. In Elaine and Milou he has indicated its perverse imaginings like a delicate painter whose hand trembles neither with admiration nor with indignation. The author of *Fermina Marquez* has really lived school life with its troubles, its immediate ambitions, its immense dreams. . . . The translator of Butler, the poet-storyteller of *A. O. Barnabooth*, became like his hero, "from the standpoint of culture, a great European." (p. 355)

"Had I also my part to play, I could not be attentive. And I want to lose nothing." Thus speaks Barnabooth; but how well this sentence defines Larbaud's attitude! *A. O. Barnabooth, ses oeuvres complètes, c'est-à-dire un conte, ses poésies, et son journal intime* is a book which, to borrow still another of his formulas, "one must not only have read, but know," a compendium of the aspirations of our epoch. If some stiffness is remarked in it, this is because men, in Larbaud's universe, are good for little but to express ideas, women alone provoking them without moreover expressing them. Barnabooth, a mul-

timillionaire escaping from his caste, made up of cruelties and of pities, sinks to kleptomania without finding attraction in vice, attempts to be charitable without succeeding in not hating the poor, tries love without acquiring a taste for women, defiles himself without transcending the literature of the *Borborygmes*. . . . (p. 356)

Too indiscreet to knock at half-open doors, Larbaud has, since Barnabooth, drawn no great, virile figure, Marc and Réginald in **Beauté, mon beau souci** . . . being merely awkward screens between the artist and his model; but, warned "not to try to extend the long adventure," having learned from Larbaud that "liaisons begin in champagne and end in camomile," with what a sentiment of deliverance we welcome the women with whom he peoples his novels! Blessings on these creatures who heal man of man, awakening in his intelligence a new sensual vision of the world! For with Larbaud women all play this part of helping to free the mind. The ardours of Fermina, noble and triumphant in mystic or amorous exaltation, "the Geneifese gentleness" of Rachel Frutiger, the equivocal coldness of Gertie "smiling and showing her small teeth under her heavy lips," leave in the imagination the same many-coloured wake as the ambiguous friends, Rose Lourdin and Rosa Kessler, as the sisters of the doomed women, Inga and Romana locked in each other's arms. (p. 357)

There are two sorts of lovers in Larbaud: those moved merely by the ambition "to have" a certain woman, by "the difficulty of the undertaking"; the others, the "happy lovers," those between whom everything happens . . . , those who can separate while love is still a lovely ripe fruit at their lips and who go away without bitterness. . . . [Let] one reread the opening paragraph of **Amants, heureux amants,** that paragraph of a dozen long pages where the light of the mind plays on the inner monologue like the ray on Inga's throat, and one will recognize the originality of an art which, without impoverishing the multiple modern universe, reflects all its play of colour in the mirror of a French intelligence. (pp. 357-58)

René Lalou, "Some Tendencies," in his Contemporary French Literature, translated by William Aspenwall Bradley (copyright 1924, copyright renewed 1952, by Alfred A. Knopf, Inc.; reprinted by permission of the publisher; originally published as Histoire de la littérature française contemporaine—1870 à nos jours, revised edition, G. Crès et Cie, 1924), Knopf, 1924, pp. 336-69.*

**EDMOND JALOUX** (essay date 1924)

[*Jaloux's essay is one of the earliest available surveys of Larbaud's work.*]

The journal of Barnabooth is the key to Valery Larbaud, as the *Notes from the Underground* is the key to Dostoevsky. Our taste for the classical composition of the novel, against which it is time to show ourselves justly severe, has too often deprived us of one of these typical books, in which we can discover the almost total figure of a man with all its irregularities. . . . I do not say that Valery Larbaud is Barnabooth, but that by mixing the imaginary with the real (the one and the other equally authentic and meaningful), he has created an almost complete character, seen from the inside, offering the conflicts and complexities of a real man; a man seen in a latent state, in an almost complete inaction, that is to say himself and not in the least transformed by outer necessities. (pp. 126-27)

The slow undulatory progress of Barnabooth's life, the meanders of his thought which advances and turns back on itself, his vague expectation, his scrupulous researches, his discussions, his fits of anger, his innumerable contradictions—that is the whole subject of one of the most important works of recent years. In this semi-stagnation, produced by immense leisure, can grow and bloom all the natural flowers that are germinated by intelligence, metaphysical anxiety (which is certainly distinct from it), liking for adventure, desire for love, and sensuality. Thus we have a portrait of a man who may well be for the beginning of the twentieth century as representative as Werther or René would have been a century ago if only Goethe and Chateaubriand had not done just the opposite of what Larbaud does: that is to say, fixed a single aspect of themselves in a frozen attitude, and limited to a too well defined type the enormous and complex central movement of their own characters.

There are in Barnabooth two quite distinct elements, although they sometimes merge into one another; one is this very detailed study of a young man who is too rich, the heir of a billionaire businessman; the other is the moral analysis of the man of the years 1900-1915. (pp. 127-28)

Barnabooth contains indeed in embryonic state the special mysticism which preceded the war of 1914 and which the group of the *Revue Critique* had more or less systematized. (One must not forget that **Barnabooth** appeared in 1913.) The need of giving oneself to something bigger than oneself is its fundamental theme. And it is therein that the dilettantism of Larbaud (for, after all, there is dilettantism in Barnabooth, however old-fashioned and spurned this word may be) is so different from the dilettantism of the men of 1880. The latter seek only to protect themselves against strong emotions . . . ; the characters of Barnabooth are on the contrary tortured by the need to give themselves body and soul to strong emotions or to a great Idea. . . . (pp. 128-29)

That Larbaud was not able to create an environment for his Barnabooth is a rather regrettable flaw in this beautiful book, and it is even his most serious fault as a novelist in general. Whatever the circumstances with which he surrounds his creations, we never find more than one man, surrounded by an immense solitude and always more or less the same, facing a woman who is more or less identical and equally alone (or divided in two, but she is still the same; the mother and daughter in **Beauté, mon beau souci,** the two friends in **Amants, heureux amants**).

Thus, on the one hand, an unbridled epicureanism, and on the other, a latent and all the more irrepressible mysticism, such is the moral formula of **Barnabooth.** . . . This mysticism is sometimes religious in nature, sometimes social, but it is especially moral; it is a kind of mysticism of life; it is a need to take on oneself the greatest possible quantity of suffering, of humiliation, of experience, not for the purpose of redemption, but for the knowledge, as if knowledge, the first and last faith of the true modern man, demanded of its faithful almost as many bloody sacrifices as the old oriental theogonies. (pp. 129-30)

I emphasize this side of Valery Larbaud because it is the one that is least often brought to light. The cosmopolite and the traveller are too generally seen in him, and not this burning spirit, tormented by a desire for truth. (p. 130)

[In] the whole of his work Valery Larbaud has drawn above all one central figure, to which each one of his works adds

some new features. The problem which rises before him now is to know whether he is going to dig deeper and develop this central figure, or whether he is going to oppose him to different individualities, in a word, whether he will remain an analyst or will become a true novelist. But if he renounces being one, he will nevertheless have created a type of man who, as I said before, will remain inseparable from the knowledge of the years 1900-1915. I should be happy, however, to have him send that man forth into conflicts more revealing of his resources and his limits. . . . [Barnabooth shows] us principally vague impulses and aspirations—just what fills the lives of all of us. But it is another problem that presents itself: this man called Barnabooth,—what will he do in the face of reality? Will he try to realize his mystical ideal? Or if life permits him to do so will he not always prefer the *status quo* and his state of eternal aspiration? What would he do in the presence of sickness, of poverty? What will he do in the presence of other men; I mean men different from him and not Putouarey, Claremoris, and Prince Stéphane? Without leaving his principal hero, a considerable source of subjects is open to Valery Larbaud. If he has the strength to deal with them, he could make of Barnabooth (under whatever name he presents him and no longer making a millionaire of him) one of the most considerable figures of our time. He is already that in part, but his limits are still too vast and too ill defined. (pp. 134-35)

> *Edmond Jaloux, "Valery Larbaud," translated by Vincent Milligan (1924), in* From the N.R.F.: An Image of the Twentieth Century from the Pages of the "Nouvelle revue francaise", *edited by Justin O'Brien (reprinted by permission of Farrar, Straus, and Giroux, Inc.; copyright © 1958 by Justin O'Brien), Farrar, Straus and Cudahy, 1958, pp. 125-35.*

## JUSTIN O'BRIEN (essay date 1932)

[*O'Brien is considered one of the foremost experts on the works of Larbaud.*]

[Larbaud made his literary debut] with a thin volume of poems purporting to be written by a South American millionaire who "sings Europe, its railways and its theaters and its constellations of cities." These vivid images of continental capitals and small towns untouched by tourists are like a series of delicate etchings remarkable for their economy of line and the evocative power of a few significant and well-chosen details. Caviar to the general, these exercises in free verse nevertheless profoundly influenced the poets of Larbaud's generation: Paul Morand, Jules Romains, etc.

Five years later, in 1913, the *Poèmes d'un riche amateur* were reprinted together with the *Journal d'A. O. Barnabooth,* their imaginary author. . . . *A. O. Barnabooth* is nothing more nor less than a picture of a twenty-three-year-old millionaire suffering a progressive loss of illusions in an effort to find himself (unlike Brulard, however, he begins with "the cult of hotels" and ends by settling down in domesticity). This is why the younger generation saw in Barnabooth the prototype of the modern man: endowed with an ardent idealism, a solid cultural background, and a fabulous income, he tears himself free from all social obligations and wanders alone throughout Europe striving to solve his spiritual problems. And every time he approaches a decision or a judgment he interrupts himself to dissect his thought and determine just what percentage of vanity, of self-deceit, or of affectation has entered into it. . . . (pp. 197-98)

Barnabooth constantly uproots himself physically and morally, experiencing every possible change of milieu, of habits, and of outlook in a vain effort to dissociate his true personality from fortuitous influences. Love, friendship, wealth, poverty, the various countries he lives in and the adventures he plunges into, constitute a series of laboratory experiments from which he emerges without having been able to isolate the one element that remains constant throughout them all, without having been able to determine, in fact, that such an element exists. . . .

[Just before the war, Larbaud, with Proust,] sounded the keynote of a new literature that was to dominate the postwar period in France. At about the same time Pirandello was doing likewise in Italy. Since everything in the world of physical phenomena is in a state of flux and exists only in relation to something else, these writers directed their attention to the intangible world of the spirit to find certainty and stability. Withdrawing into themselves, they sought reality through a dissociation of the personality; introspection became their tool, and utter sincerity toward oneself, the chief postulate of their art. As we now know, their search resulted only in greater uncertainty and the carrying over into literature of the relativistic attitude prevalent in scientific circles, but their example became the most conspicuous force in the ten years of intellectual restlessness following the cataclysm of the war. (p. 199)

[This] creation of a new literary method based on introspection and glorifying sincerity inevitably led to a desire to trace one's memories back to childhood and to record the spontaneous impressions and desires of a virgin mind: hence the overwhelming popularity of the novel of adolescence.

In this respect too Valery Larbaud was a precursor. His *Fermina Márquez* . . . served as an inspiration, if not a model for Jacques de Lacretelle, Jean Cocteau, Roger Martin du Gard, Raymond Radiguet, and others who have distinguished themselves in the recapturing of the first fine careless rapture. An extremely delicate portrayal of life in a lycée, this novel concentrates upon reproducing the tenuous atmosphere of those years between fifteen and nineteen spent within the shelter of an aristocratic institution just outside of Paris. (pp. 199-200)

Besides its original subject, *Fermina Márquez* introduced an innovation into the form of the novel, for it is written in a series of episodes whose common denominator is the heroine herself. But the factor that really binds this novel into a whole is far less tangible than this; it is to be found in an extremely subtle unity of atmosphere, a device, if device it be, particularly dear to Larbaud. Because of its novelty *Fermina Márquez* produced a great impression when it appeared; it is doubtful, however, whether anyone would now consider it as successful as Larbaud's subsequent works. (pp. 200-01)

[The stories collected in *Enfantines*] clearly indicated the path Larbaud was to follow to his greatest advantage. As the title suggests, he is still dealing with children but this time instead of writing an episodic novel he has given each episode its full value and left it as a short story. Besides, *Enfantines* suffers from no overdelicacy of touch: here the portraitist has abandoned pastels for oils and developed a vigorous, confident handling of the brush so that he never fails to achieve his effect. More than anyone else, Larbaud has penetrated that other world in which children live and been able to evoke its ingenuously fanciful charm. The characters are traced with the same psychological method and the same truth to detail as those in *Barnabooth*: a taciturn, unhappy little girl has a violent "crush" on one of her schoolmates and years later tries to analyze her

emotions at that time; a boy, in love with a young shepherdess whose finger happens to be badly cut, spontaneously cuts himself in the same way and is shocked when another of his playmates guesses his motive; three children create a dream world and people it with fantastic creatures; another little boy while waiting for his music lesson discovers a face in the veined marble of the fireplace and endows it with a personality and an existence; and above all that faultless **"Portrait of Eliane at Fourteen"** in which the author traces step by step the painful awakening of adolescence.

In four of these eight stories Larbaud most vividly recreates that dreamworld that imaginative children elaborately construct as an escape from the adult world surrounding them: the complicated games they play with imaginary companions, the fictitious confidants more real than the parents in whom the child cannot confide, and formed, as it were, by a projection of the child's personality, and finally the inanimate objects that suddenly assume a life of their own. Just as Cocteau did . . . in his *Enfants terribles,* Larbaud recognized that no picture of childhood could be true which did not begin with glimpses into this mysteriously supernatural realm. (p. 201)

[*Amants, heureux amants*] is Larbaud's masterpiece. Though they are less ambitious than *Barnabooth,* these three long stories, or short novels, have yet to be surpassed for compactness of composition, lyric beauty, and vivid characterization. Here for the first time Larbaud uses the interior monologue form exclusively in two of the stories, **"Amants, heureux amants"** and **"Mon plus secret conseil."** . . . (p. 202)

In **"Amants, heureux amants"** Larbaud dares to ignore conventions and tell a story *altogether* from the inside by suppressing the hand of the author and letting everything be expressed through the mind of the character himself. The interior monologue is an unspoken, unheard flow of thought caught on the threshold of consciousness and *supposedly* set down before it has passed from the crude state to that of organized speech. It is nothing more than a literary form, according to Larbaud's definition, by means of which the reader penetrates the thoughts of a given character and thus learns, from within, the series of circumstances and the atmosphere in which that character is living. But since art implies selection and composition, some organization of this amorphous stream of consciousness must take place before the resulting document can have anything more than a scientific interest. It is in this most subtle composition that Larbaud shows his skill, for while keeping always literally *in character,* he gives life not only to the one who speaks in the first person but also to the other characters and the world in which they live as seen through the eyes of the involuntary narrator. (pp. 203-04)

The manner in which Larbaud evokes the scene of his action in each of these stories is very characteristic; he had already developed the technique in *Barnabooth:* the setting gradually forms itself as its details, for one reason or another, rise to the surface of the stream of consciousness; the device is similar to Browning's in his dramatic monologues, but less artificial. Moreover, the setting, together with the theme, determines the atmosphere of the story much as in a poem, so that these stories, laid in Montpellier and Naples, are vastly different in the total impression each produces.

A few of those who have appreciated the advantages offered by this new form of writing *from the inside out* have wisely insisted upon the fact that it is by no means suitable to all subjects. Larbaud has always limited its use to stories or passages whose subject called for such a treatment: the portrayal of a child's mind (and occasionally of an adult but childlike mind) in which dream and reality are inextricably confused; or the realization of the complex and contradictory aspirations of a sensitive young man in whom several natures are constantly struggling for supremacy.

Since *Amants, heureux amants* Larbaud has published but one story, *Deux Artistes lyriques* (1929), in which he employs a more conventional style of exposition. The slightness of its theme and the rich development he has given it, together with its brilliantly sketched south Italian setting, incline one to link it with the essays of *Jaune, bleu, blanc* . . . rather than with the earlier stories. The latter volume presents, as it were, a group of samples of Valery Larbaud, so many facets of his personality does it reflect. A traveler's notes and letters from Italy, England, Spain, and Portugal interspersed with essays on Paris and what it means to be a true Parisian, philological digressions, humorous *divertissements,* and a delightful dramatic monologue in prose. Many of these literary *hors d'oeuvres* are taken almost directly from his notebook, which always travels with him, but all, no matter what the value of their subject, are finished, polished products. Nevertheless these sketches give us an intimate picture of the author at work and reveal his varied interests. We see here the literary craftsman applying himself to linguistic problems and questions of style, the modern cosmopolitan and his voluptuous manner of identifying himself with the life of a foreign country while still maintaining enough perspective from which to judge it, the discriminating critic and discoverer of talent, and finally the sincere and self-effacing scholar.

A reading of this one volume (though it is by no means advisable as the best way to approach his work) would convince anyone that Valery Larbaud is a worthy counterpart of the Renaissance humanists. (pp. 205-06)

[In] seeking a deeper interpretation of his entire scholarly activity—his excellent translations, his patient explorations, and his profound critical studies—one cannot but discern that Larbaud is striving to bring into closer communication the intellectual aristocracies of the various races that inhabit Europe. Whether one considers it from the point of view of this attempt to create an enlightened cosmopolitanism by unifying that scattered spiritual *élite* to which he has always addressed his works or from the point of view of his manifold enrichment of French literature, Valery Larbaud's career follows a single direct course. Though he already belongs to the great French tradition, he will also live as the internationally recognized founder of a new intellectual commerce. (pp. 207-08)

> *Justin O'Brien, "Valery Larbaud: Complete Man of Letters" (reprinted by permission of Isabel O'Brien), in* The Symposium: A Critical Review *(copyright © 1932 by Syracuse University Press), Vol. III, No. 3, July, 1932 (and reprinted in his* The French Literary Horizon, *Rutgers University Press, 1967, pp. 193-208).*

## MELVIN FRIEDMAN (essay date 1952-53)

[*In the following excerpt, Friedman discusses the theme of erotic love in Larbaud's fiction.*]

Larbaud's creative works, as several critics have already pointed out, are almost completely concerned with the three earliest stages of man: childhood, adolescence, and young manhood. The book about childhood, *Enfantines,* would seem scarcely

to be of interest to us here. Yet Larbaud shows us, in almost everyone of the stories, a certain perversion growing out of too intense love. It is perhaps a commonplace to say that love is born of the obstacle and nourished on anxiety. The obstacle in at least two of the stories, found in *Enfantines,* is the love a child displays for another child beneath his social station. (This is one of the important problems in Proust, where both Charlus and Swann seek love "au-dessous d'eux.") In *le Couperet,* the eight-year-old protagonist cuts his hand so as to share the affliction of a young shepherdess he believes that he loves. In *la Grande Epoque,* the social hierarchy of the child is threatened by the admiration the owner's son displays for the children of a common laborer. (p. 93)

[In the stories of *Enfantines* there] is a certain biological and intellectual rhythm, nearly imperceptible, which seems to approximate the physical longings of the child. After reading some of these stories, one no longer finds it impossible to conceive of a book composed of the interior life of a child, free from anecdotes and other supernumeraries, concerned only with the circulation of the blood and the lymph, the race of nervous excitations towards the centers, the twisting of emotion and thought through the cells. *Enfantines* would seem to support the belief in a tonal scale residing in the soul of the child, beyond any precise form, which is to reveal itself during special moments when the subconscious mind is at work. Joyce said once to Larbaud, in conversation, that "the soul, in one sense, is all which exists." *Enfantines* applies this dictum to the internal physical existence of the child, caught up in the pangs of desire. (p. 94)

[*Amants, heureux amants,*] is a collection of three stories, all about young dilettantes who mix philosophical speculation with love making. (p. 96)

The title story of the collection is nurtured on immediate sensation rather than developed reflection. It is entirely a monologue, partaking of the form of Joyce's *Ulysses* and Dujardin's *les Lauriers sont coupés.* It begins in a whirlpool of erotic sensation, felt and voiced subconsciously by the young Francia who peers out of a hotel window at midnight, and who is constantly diverted by the two nude female figures stretched out on a nearby bed in his room. . . . Francia's monologue, which continues through 50 pages, outlines elaborately his feeling for the two women on the bed, Inga and Romana, and how his erotic impulse received satisfaction in various of the encounters with them. This recalls somewhat Molly Bloom's long monologue at the end of *Ulysses,* which likens her to the Gaea Tellus of the domain of Eros. Francia's obscenity is often couched in foreign expressions, generally Italian, a luxury Joyce never affords his heroine. (pp. 96-7)

The hero of the third story of the collection, *Mon plus secret conseil,* is also a "monologueur," and receives the same delight as Francia in speaking of amorous intrigues. Unlike Francia, however, Lucas Letheil speaks only of one love affair, which he expands as a series of concentric circles about a common center. There are frequent breaks in this imperfect monologue, which were nowhere evident in *Amants, heureux amants,* but this merely adds to the consistency of the account—told completely from a train, carrying Lucas away from his mistress. Lucas continually contrasts this mistress, Isabelle, with another woman whom he scarcely knows, Irène. This is again part of the technique of the *Amants.* . . .

The use of foreign expression, usually as a veil for eroticism, is even more frequent here, and is used quite systematically.

We can trace it with considerable ease: Italian is used when Lucas recalls an erotic moment with Isabelle, English when Irène's sophistication gains the upper hand, and finally Greek (used very infrequently) when Lucas' feeling for literature supersedes his love for woman. (p. 97)

Another observation we might make about the *Amants, heureux amants* and *Mon plus secret conseil* is the consistent failure to rely on the metaphor for stylistic effects. We found this to be the handmaid of sexual fusion in Proust, and we saw the opposite effect achieved by its limited use in Joyce. Larbaud takes heed of the message of *Les Nourritures terrestres,* in his last two stories, "to banish from them (it) all metaphor." His expression is of the utmost simplicity, consistently avoiding difficult grammatical constructions. . . . This carefully condensed style, cleansed of all extraneous matter, seems to have the effect of intensifying the erotic experience. Nothing is quite so bare of metaphorical content and so suggestive of the mood created by Eros as the last passage of *Mon plus secret conseil.* This is appropriately placed at the end of the story, as the story itself is the last in the collection. One finishes the reading of Larbaud's creative writing (*Mon plus secret conseil* is his last story) with the often bitter taste of too strong sensuality. Artistically, however, this last passage is perhaps the most successful piece Larbaud has written to date. . . . Each line is measured as a breath group for a person falling asleep. This passage expresses the erotic sentiment of the entire story synthetically. The language seems to recapture this biological rhythm which Larbaud appeared so intent on approximating elsewhere in his writing, particularly in the *Enfantines.* The arrangement of the diverse properties of this passage is not a matter of chance. A careful glance will reveal an analogy with music. I am thinking especially of the fugue. We find in this passage a relatively complex theme—a fugual theme is rarely simple—of relating a young women, Irène, whom Lucas has infrequently seen, to the best known parts of his past life. All the parts appear to overlap, they are juxtaposed in curious combinations, often deserting French for polyglottal relationships, and closely produce the effect of a chord of music. Words are truncated, phrases are clipped and interlocked, often with faulty punctuation. This is the same effect Joyce produced in the prologue to the Siren episode in *Ulysses,* which is also, as you may recall, built on the fugue analogy. (pp. 98-9)

In his own life, Larbaud was constantly torn between a mild mysticism and an erotic impulse. His conversion seemed clearly to decide in favor of the former. Yet his writing, after *Barnabooth,* is unmistakably in the direction of the latter. It is not always true that the sentiments of a work of art are determined by the details of the artist's personal life. In the case of Larbaud, we have seen that the presence of Joyce, and to a lesser extent Proust, has directed his books towards the two traditions of Eros. (p. 100)

> *Melvin Friedman, "Valery Larbaud: The Two Traditions of Eros," in* Yale French Studies *(copyright © Yale French Studies 1953), Spring-Summer, No. 11, 1952-53, pp. 91-100.*

## WILLIAM JAY SMITH (essay date 1955)

In Paris in 1908 appeared a slim volume of poems entitled *Poèmes par un riche amateur* in an edition of one hundred copies. The book, which purported to be the work of a South American multimillionaire Archibaldo Olson Barnabooth, might have passed gently into oblivion had it not been what Charles-Louis Philippe called "one of the most astonishing and original books to appear in France in years," and had it not been the work of a writer of the first rank whose name was, in reality, Valery Larbaud.

Writing to Larbaud at the time, Charles-Louis Philippe said he did not bear the multimillionaire any ill will, but would simply like to join him from time to time in order to experience a form of happiness with which he was unfamiliar. "You have created Barnabooth because you contained him." André Gide wrote of the work later in the newly-founded *Nouvelle Revue française*: "This book is calculated to irritate some people, and to amuse others all the more; let us put ourselves among the latter. . . . Barnabooth has roamed every country. I love his haste, his cynicism, his gluttony. These poems, dated from here, there, and everywhere, are as thirst-making as a wine list. . . . In this peculiar book, each picture of sensation, no matter how correct or dubious it may be, is made valid by the speed with which it is superseded."

When the poems were reissued in 1913, together with the *Journal* of Barnabooth, fifteen of them were eliminated and a number considerably shortened. The *Journal,* a fitting prose accompaniment to the poems, relates the struggle of Barnabooth, in his travels throughout Europe, to come to terms with life. The book cannot be called a novel: there is little plot, and yet it is filled with action; it is the record of a conflict between the inner and outer self. Gide suggested that it be called the journal of a "free man"—and one can see how he drew upon it in his own writing. The mind of Barnabooth acts as a mirror held up to people and places; what results is a series of acute observations on manners and, in its way, a judgment on life itself. In addition to the poems and the journal, the book contained *"Le pauvre chemisier,"* a parody of eighteenth century tales, a morality whose moral is itself double-edged. The biography, which Gide had found contrived and out of place in *Poèmes par un riche amateur,* was dropped; and Valery Larbaud appeared simply as the literary executor. This edition, containing the complete works of A. O. Barnabooth in their final form, has been reissued many times since. Witty and wise, paradoxical and profound, it has influenced many writers in France, and still attracts discerning readers today as one of the truly original books of the century. (pp. ii-iv)

Barnabooth, in his *poésie des départs,* is the spiritual descendant of des Esseintes, the hero of Huysmans' novel, *A Rebours,* who perfumed his room with tar so that he might imagine he was at sea, and papered its walls with advertisements of voyages, timetables of the Royal Mail Steam Packet Company and other shipping lines. To des Esseintes the pleasures of travel are imaginary: one enjoys the anticipation and the recollection of a journey rather than the actual experience itself. In spirit, also, Barnabooth is a follower of that earlier traveler, Xavier de Maistre, who, when confined to his barracks for forty-two days in 1790, produced his celebrated *Voyage autour de ma chambre. . . .* While de Maistre carries the world into his room, Larbaud-Barnabooth carries his room into the world. . . . It amounts to the same thing, a triumph of the individual over time and space. And it is the carefully circumscribed point of observation—the bridge of the yacht—that makes the vista imposing. Each place to which Barnabooth journeys opens for him a new life; and yet in memory each place is reduced to a name so that the name itself . . . becomes a symbol, a sign, leading the mind on. Countries open before one, infinite and infinitely varied, and yet borne always in miniature projection, like the contour of a map reproduced on a postage stamp.

People are places and places are people; Barnabooth, above all, directs our attention to a humanized landscape.

In creating Barnabooth, Larbaud had in mind a very definite character with a precise background and distinct tastes. The poems as presented were intended to be those that only a man in his social, economic, and cultural position could write. While Larbaud was surely right to exclude the biography eventually, he made no mistake in putting it down in the first place; in doing so, he delineated, more for himself than for his reader perhaps, clearly the man he had in mind. It is significant, first of all, that Barnabooth is a South American, one who sings of Europe, "her railroads and theatres," and yet brings to his poems the "spoils of a new world." He can love Europe, all of it, more intensely than the European because he does not belong to it. He writes always as if he were at the edge of Europe, approaching it on an ocean liner, dallying in one of its outlying provinces, and yet in spirit at its very heart. It is one of Valery Larbaud's favorite ideas that history and art must be approached not always directly, but often obliquely. One will know the main road all the better for having wandered off from time to time along lanes and bypaths. In what is discarded or cast off one may find something to give meaning and dimension to the whole. The work of a little-known or neglected writer may illuminate an entire era, as Rome is defined by its periphery. The creation of Barnabooth was for Valery Larbaud a way out, a means of approach to the centers of London and New York. For us he is a way back: if the poet began with Walt Whitman, he ended with Henry James, and his hymn to a civilized Europe is more rewarding today than ever. (pp. vii-ix)

Larbaud is careful to put in the mouth of Barnabooth expressions appropriate to a Peruvian-born gentleman. It is impossible in English to convey the full undertone of comedy in all this; the author, in any case, gets away with more than he would under ordinary circumstances.

Perhaps the real force of *Poems of a Multi-millionaire,* as I have chosen to call them in English, lies in the fact that Barnabooth, for all his gaiety, knows that the price demanded for the possession of the world can never be paid in full; it is the price of human suffering. . . . . He sees the full horror of the room brightly lit by the raw electric bulb. That lighted room has grown larger with time, the shadow outside ever more menacing. Larbaud often looks at things through the innocent eyes of a child, through the wrong end of a field glass, as it were, which he does again in the charming stories of *Enfantines* . . . ; but if innocence exists, it is always because of experience. Barnabooth is youthful and ebullient, but old beyond his years.

Often in these poems, bearing as they do the unmistakable imprint of American poetry and speech, I have the feeling that something has shifted—perhaps not out of, but into, focus. The author catches remarkably well, it seems to me, that note of nostalgia inherent in the American character, the heart quickening at night to the sound of a train whistle, the vision responding to the beam of headlights cutting across broad plains. But the emphatic gestures of Whitman he has subtly tempered with wit; and he has added something the American has always sorely needed: the ability not to take himself, even in seriousness, too seriously. (pp. ix-x)

*William Jay Smith, "Poems of a Multimillionaire" (revised by the author for this publication; originally published as his introduction to* Poems of a Multimillionaire *by Valery Larbaud, translated by William*

*Jay Smith, Bonacio & Saul, 1955), in his* The Streaks of the Tulip: Selected Criticism *(copyright © 1954, 1955, 1957, 1958, 1959, 1960, 1961, 1962, 1963, 1964, 1965, 1966, 1967, 1968, 1969, 1970, 1972, by William Jay Smith; reprinted by permission of the author), Delacourte Press, 1972, pp. 349-57.*

**BENEDETTO FABRIZI**　(essay date 1966)

[*Fabrizi evaluates Larbaud's success in utilizing the interior monologue, or stream of consciousness technique, in his fiction.*]

[Larbaud was] the first and perhaps the most accomplished user of the interior monologue in modern French literature. . . . Governed as he liked to be by the norms of proportion and moderation of his admired classics, he realized that this form could not be used indiscriminately nor could it suit all subjects. Accordingly, he limited it to two short stories, "**Amants, heureux amants . . .**" and "**Mon plus secret conseil. . . .**"

In "**Amants, heureux amants . . . ,**" the interior monologue allowed Larbaud to reveal the confusion existing in the soul of a man of twenty. . . . (p. 24)

The rambling incoherence of [Francia's] thoughts gives one the impression that the author himself has lost his train of thought; at first glance, it seems that Labaud is marking time and filling pages until the flash of inspiration again visits him. And for one brief moment one is tempted to skim over, if not omit entirely, what seems to be wordy window dressing. The fact is, however, that by the use of this medium the author is allowed to slip into the person of the hero and record his mental action. Also the reader has the opportunity to penetrate more directly into his floating thoughts, which superimpose themselves upon the sensations aroused by the external world. On deeper reflection, and from an artistic point of view, how better could inner thought be presented? How more verisimilarly? Foreign expressions, such as *"Pieno il capo"* and *"Belle,"* are not set apart because they, too, constitute an integral and natural part of the thought process. Larbaud's painstaking adherence to objective fact is realistically true; inner thoughts *are* swiftmoving, far-reaching, unconnected, wandering.

In "**Mon plus secret conseil . . . ,**" the interior monologue serves to place on the same level reality and the imaginary elements in which the hero takes pleasure. Here we find Lucas, the hero, deliberating on the most efficacious means of separating himself from his mistress, Isabelle. (pp. 25-6)

It is in this story that Larbaud's ability in the use of the interior monologue attains full scope, for it is here that he exploits, to good advantage, all the intriguing possibilities of the form. Among the pleasures he allows himself is the use of pronouns other than the customary first singular; in fact, he makes use of several pronouns, alternating them with remarkable skill. . . . Where this procedure passes from mere technical virtuosity to meaningful artistic achievement is in Larbaud's ability to give it some logical coherence, a form, and to bring to life through it not only the person of the narrator himself, but also the other characters who are seen through the mind and the eyes of the narrator.

In a work published nine years after "**Mon plus secret conseil. . .**" . . . , Larbaud seems to make another attempt at using the interior monologue. "**Le Vaisseau de Thésée**" an article-story (difficult to classify as to genre, as are many of Larbaud's other writings), is considered by some to be written as interior monologue and by others to be no more in this form than, say, the unrecognized probings of some of his earlier works, such as the *A. O. Barnabooth* of 1913. What is clear, in any case, is that in it Larbaud reverts to the single pronoun *je* and that the zest and verve manifest in **"Mon plus secret conseil . . ."** have become somewhat inconspicuous. In this account of the emotional crises and of the aspirations of a hotel manager who would like to see his son acquire the erudition which he himself had lacked the time and opportunity to attain, a good portion of the monologue merges with the semi-diary of the hero, Monsieur Bonsignor. The form of this inner confession comes close to that of a narrative in the first person. The effective short, simple, direct and bone-bare sentences by which Dujardin was able to distinguish his monologue from the interminable verbal convolutions of Proust are hardly existent. . . . (pp. 26-7)

In spite of the limitations in quantity and content that he imposed on himself, Larbaud immersed himself into this new-found form and, by exploiting its manifold possibilities, enriched it and gave it new vitality. (p. 28)

[Larbaud] seems to have achieved analytical and artistic heights with his use of the interior monologue. This new formula made its way easily and naturally into his manner. As a matter of fact, he had already the habit of insinuating himself into the person of his male heroes, often identifying himself with them. It is not unexpected, then, that the monologues of Francia, Lucas, and even Bonsignor turn out to be essentially a revealment of the sensibility of Larbaud himself. Moreover, they became models of imitation and inspiration for other men of letters—Jean Schlumberger, Léon-Paul Fargue and Jacques de Lacretelle, to name only a few—exercising, as many believe, a large influence on French literature. If any such influence was felt, it was due primarily to the fact that Larbaud, as Joyce in the English langauge, had advanced the interior monologue to a high degree of perfection and that he gave it literary status in France. (pp. 28-9)

> Benedetto Fabrizi, *"Valery Larbaud and the Interior Monologue," in* Kentucky Foreign Language Quarterly *(© University of Kentucky), Vol. XIII, No. 1, 1966, pp. 20-9.*

### JOHN KENNETH SIMON   (essay date 1968)

[With] *Fermina Márquez,* we find ourselves reading an introduction to Valery Larbaud and, at the same time, a poised little chef d'oeuvre. . . . Larbaud's novel was a precursor for many books of adolescence. Still, however early its appearance, it contains none of the unchecked and un-nuanced reliance upon autobiographical material, the heavy-handed self-analysis, the propounding of a thesis or pleading of a cause which seem to characterize the genre. While the theme of adolescence has become a commonplace, perhaps overworked, a reading of Larbaud's novel continues to raise important problems of form and style. For all the praise and affection which *Fermina Márquez* has inspired, the workings of its charm have never been studied in more than a passing way. (p. 543)

Larbaud's delicate, indirect approach is suggested from the beginning by the way in which the reflection of light on the ground catches and focuses the attention. Similarly, the form of the novel is based upon a reflection originating elsewhere than within the actions and thoughts of the principal characters. The narrator's first-person plural is drawn into the event, unobtrusively, with the swing of the door. Finally, there is the simple, awe-inspired acknowledgmement of the nubile intrud-

ers, provoking a reverential silence on the part of the onlookers, magically charmed.

For these are the unsensational, poetic memories of the effect produced on the members of a cosmopolitan boys' boarding-school outside of Paris by the sudden presence of a young Columbian girl. Fermina is one of the sisters of a homesick student, and her afternoon visits at the approach of summer are a catalyst for new adolescent emotions among the teenage boys. Mainly, Valery Larbaud's preoccupation is with Joanny Léniot, a lonely, hard-working introvert from Lyon, whose daydreams of a dispassionate genius's glory are undercut, in a way reminiscent of Julian Sorel, by his meetings with the passionate Latin-American. . . . [Our] interest is aroused not in the outcome of the plot—for the various characters are scattered and vanish at the end (as they do earlier in the very narration of the novel)—but rather in the arabesque phase of adolescence. This is the composite portrayal of a moment of transformation, demanding a commensurate, whimsical tone and form. (pp. 543-44)

Fermina, the center of the story, its pretext and stimulus, is not particularized until the end. Like the reflection in the courtyard at her first entrance, refracted through the consciousness of the narrator, Joanny Léniot and Camille Moûtier, she is "girlhood," "la jeune fille," and evokes an unknown world of happiness. . . . (p. 546)

It is through Joanny Léniot that the confrontation between masculine and feminine characteristics is enacted: rational plans on the one hand; passionate feelings on the other. The former are undercut by the latter, and this constitutes the basic development in the novel, Joanny's indirect awareness of the complex emotions stimulated by Fermina.

The form of the novel is dependent upon this emotional evolution. The concentration in the second part upon Joanny, our close but still measured identification with him and his train of thought, and the sequence of dialogues between Joanny and Fermina grow out of the central theme. Chapter VI having defined *la jeune fille* and outlined the antithetical but overlapping traits in each of the sexes, Chapter VII, one short paragraph, selects and isolates Joanny Léniot as the sole companion of Fermina for a period. . . . Later on, through a narrative technique which is really quite radical, but *quietly* so, Joanny's point of view will be dropped, taken up once again and finally abandoned for good. As at the beginning, now explicitly he will be considered, in retrospective, one among many; the news of his death in a sudden epidemic years later as another sort of boarder—in a casern during military training in the east of France—will be announced in passing at the end. The bittersweet pathos of this world of life is suggested precisely by the episodic quality with which the adolescent feelings described are themselves fleeting, bringing into focus now one, now another of the characters, like the fickleness of our affection. The tone of ephemerality is created also by the unequal length of the chapters, the flexibility of a movement in time which avoids any fixed, determined direction. (pp. 549-50)

[The situation in this novel] and the emotional terms in which it is posed are not without recalling the last part of *Notes from Underground.* I am not calumniating Fermina by comparing her with the prostitute Liza, but, from the point of view of Joanny, there is the same deliberately abstract, literary, adolescent mind, intent upon storybook seduction, plagued by a desperate fear of ridicule. The narrator of Dostoevsky's novella—which Larbaud read at a particularly crucial moment, an event which encouraged him in a literary career—fails the test through an excess of self-consciousness. Faced with a similar stimulus for the warm, passionate, *feminine* expression of feeling, Joanny, amazed and charmed, tried to keep up somehow. Hoping to create some kind of communion between equals, he tries to adapt his bookish articles of faith. When he realizes that these integers for a male sensibility, phrased in the language of school themes about the empire of Rome, its dead language and buried history, are inadequate, he can do nothing but abandon himself to a declaration of love. But in Joanny's case, there has been no emotional development to sustain the transition. This will only come now with the failure and its aftermath. The lack of reciprocality in Fermina is a reflection of Joanny's immaturity, witness to the fact that he is still a child. Realizing his powerlessness in this domain, he must pull back immediately to the cold-genius pose with which he began, shaken in his confidence and ready, eventually, to learn. (p. 553)

The description of setting in Larbaud's novel is no more traditional than the narrative structure. Like the unfolding of plot, the sense of place has an improvisational spontaneity recalling that of Stendhal. From the beginning, the rarefied atmosphere of a cosmopolitan *collège* on the outskirts of Paris permits us to assign a figurative value to the physical displacement of the boarders, foreign and domestic alike. . . . The surrounding perspectives sighted from the terrace or through the windows mingle with internal matters and produce a bittersweet melancholy. Paris remains an unseen reality in the distance, but the reminder of its proximity together with the peaceful, ordered countryside coincides with a transitional stage of development, close to and in touch with the complicated world, yet protected from it.

Rather than a confrontation of the real and the imaginary, as in the province of Alain-Fournier, there are opening vistas, like those of the French gardens, with no infinite beyond. In the school itself, a graduated relationship with adulthood exists: some of the younger masters are still within the emotional bounds of adolescence, feeling jealous of Fermina, being unable to cope with the complex situation of the study hall. The Spanish language, spiritually dominant at Saint-Augustin, helps in the creation of an autonomous country whose people are sensitive to the evocative effect of words and names, the ritual of school awards, the colors of a national flag. (pp. 556-57)

To suggest the way that Larbaud communicates a common language of adolescence, equal to the vocabulary of South American geography and history for the imagination, we must study the difficult matter of style. Like the fragrance of Saint-Augustin which is situated neither wholly in the surroundings nor in the minds of those who daydream looking out, there is a constant balance held between irony and empathy. If the setting is deliberately in an interim realm and the point of view shifts casually to suggest an episodic phase, the author maintains with his reader a similar delicate relationship of guarded intimacy.

The use of indirect discourse is frequent. We effortlessly follow the development of thought of each character successively. This technique is particularly apt for capturing both the creation of an expression and its effect upon the listener, as when Fermina's guardian Mama Doloré tells stories of her homeland and her first impressions of Paris. . . . Always grazing the interior monologue which he will later practice in a more exclusive form, Larbaud seems intent upon placing us just on the periphery of identification. Here we are witnessing, as we will

later with Joanny, Fermina, Camille and Santos, the process by which certain personal forms of expression are put between quotation marks. They seem actually suspended in that intermediate position. The words and thoughts neither remain wholly private and inviolate, nor do they become conventional dialogue. The usual ironic distance of indirect discourse characteristic of its use in Flaubert does not cancel out the sentimental content. The emotional effect of hearing what was said, its memory, is kept alive without naive over-indulgence.

After all, there could hardly be a more sentimental subject. Larbaud wishes to convince his reader that there exists an intangible mystery in our initiation to the troubled feelings of adolescence. He must create a sense of astonishment checked but undiminished by the adult perspective. The responsibility for keeping the balance is entrusted to the indirect art of narration and a certain style of expression. . . . [Certain quotations] may easily give the impression of excess, and no doubt there are obvious stylistic *tics* in the habit of enumeration, the accumulation of adjectives, and the repetition of *et* as they are added, the frequent use of exclamatory adverbs (*si, tellement*), the emphatic terms enlivening the inflection with a childlike enthusiasm. . . . Yet these efforts to recreate convincing examples of the precise feelings inspired by the unique experience of adolescence are balanced by the context. A constant restraint is present in the manner of narration. The pill is coated with the bittersweetness of gentle irony.

Underneath it all there is of course the intention of suggesting the authenticity of a child's speech. Here it is that Larbaud should be compared with Charles-Louis Philippe for whom he had such deep affection. The resemblance is even more precise in a number of passages where Larbaud has sought, like Philippe, to express a precise emotional discovery by materializing the emotion, making it a weight or some other measurable quantity. . . . Or else the feeling is grasped through a metaphor relating to the most ordinary (and therefore the most dangerously banal) of common experiences. . . . Larbaud's style is part of a lineage. The head of the family apparently was Philippe, Giraudoux being the youngest and today the most well known of the name. The author of *Intermezzo* of course shared with Larbaud a number of themes, principal among them the mystery of adolescence, a purity localized in the charming, intransigent *jeune fille*. Giraudoux was responsible for creating a Fermina-type in *Tessa,* the French version of Margaret Kennedy's young heroine. The dramatist's famous *préciosité* is related to just such a pretext for sustained metaphor as the theme of the hours of night.

In Larbaud, however, the rhetoric has not yet become a separate and almost autonomous end in itself. In a sense he occupies an intermediary position between the personalism of Charles-Louis Philippe and the rather detached stance of Giraudoux. His first person singular is neither totally immersed in real memories nor a more or less transparent rhetorical device. As with the other elements of style, the author's use of *vous, nous* and *je* helps keep an equilibrium—both a bridge and a screen—between his evocations of the past and the reading experience. The narrative voice is on familiar but not intimate terms with the reader; it keeps its distance. (pp. 557-60)

Throughout the book we are learning of a generalized adolescence when the narrator was, like Léniot and Moûrier too, one of the crowd. But figuratively—and, at the end literally—it is alone that he visits the scene of his childhood. Quietly, we are being told that it must be so for us too. The real grounding of Larbaud's autobiographical inspiration is included in the narrator's presence, his flexible use of personal pronouns inform-ing the novel with an unstressed feeling of intimacy. Visiting his memory, like the ruins of Saint-Augustin, Larbaud creates a style which modulates between complicity and melancholic isolation. (p. 562)

With the appearance of Fermina at the beginning of the novel, we remember that the "esperance" [hope] that each boy felt inside was *lourde* [awkward] as well as *belle* [beautiful]. As in Proust, there is the desire to recapture the essence of some-thing intangible, with the child often aware of the process. . . . As it is still more apparent perhaps in **Enfantines,** the child's world, like the writer's, is one of absence, however beautiful the style conceived to fill that absence, to anticipate the future or substitute for the past.

It would be a pity to reduce the spirit of the novel to simple nostalgia. Rather there is a basic vulnerability, not concerned with the passage of time alone. According to the old caretaker this is a period piece, a special caste has disappeared. But adulthood brings its own democratic leveling off; adolescence is itself an aristocracy of mind. (p. 563)

No question that **Fermina Márquez** is a minor work; no ques-tion, either, that it epitomizes both adolescence and a literary era characterized by the analysis of that period of life. In fact, it is hardly controversial to suggest that a significant moment in the history of letters may be best defined in a minor key. Certainly, this is true of much that we admire in eighteenth-century art, for example. It is rather a just measure of himself and the nature of his preoccupations, rather than merely per-sonal modesty, which led Larbaud to conceive of his works as he did, and to accomplish them with such perfection. (p. 564)

*John Kenneth Simon, "Valery Larbaud's 'Fer-mina'," in MLN (© copyright 1968 by The Johns Hopkins University Press), Vol. 83, No. 4, May, 1968, pp. 543-64.*

**ALLISON CONNELL**   (essay date 1974)

Translators, according to Larbaud, may be divided into two types: translators as artists and translators as craftsmen. The first, like Baudelaire, are great writers in their own right. The craftsmen, 'translators of the second order,' are characterized as displaying the qualities necessary for any conscientious work: patience, skill, self-sacrifice and honesty, to which Larbaud adds the literary sense. They are able to achieve the honour of being worthy 'sons-in-law' of the original writer.

It is in this second order that Larbaud too modestly places himself. . . . That he belongs in fact to the first is acknowl-edged by his peers. Charles Du Bos reminds us that there are translations in which nothing is omitted but in which nothing of the spirit of the original is expressed, whereas Larbaud's translations of Butler convey the immense impact of Butler's irony and humour. There were plaudits for Larbaud from other quarters: G. K. Chesterton thought he sounded better in Lar-baud's French than in his own English and Archibald MacLeish made virtually the same remark on Larbaud's translation of *Train Stop.*

There are lines in the translation which so far surpass the English form as to leave it quite insignificant, if that is not true of the whole translation.

What then were the principles of translation Larbaud actually followed? His article **'De la Traduction'** in *Effort Libre . . .* was his first 'manifesto' on the subject. Essentially, he opposes translations that are too 'academic' in favour of those that express *'l'esprit, l'intention, le génie'* even at the expense of the literal. It is interesting to note that he binds translation to his Europeanism in this article by making a number of thrusts at the absurdly exaggerated nationalism of the period which thought the translation of Dostoïevski, Hardy, and Ibsen a danger to French culture.

In his major essay on translation in **Sous l'Invocation de St Jérôme,** which is also entitled **De la Traduction,** Larbaud agrees in all essentials with A. Fraser Tytler, defining his position against the background of Tytler's, which he sees as a turning point. The eighteenth century had put 'beauty' before 'preci-sion'; Tytler in 1791 had begun the trend in which precision is put before beauty when necessary. In Larbaud's view trans-lation should first of all be precise. If possible it should also be as 'beautiful' as the original. But at the same time it should possess 'toute l'aisance d'une composition originale ['all the fluency of the original essay']. The last point is important because it suggests that the texts of Larbaud's translation could themselves be studied as original compositions.

Transposition is a term Larbaud often uses for the technique of translation. The real debate revolves around the question of the liberties that may be taken in this transposition. Larbaud sees in Tytler's revolt against the extreme liberties allegedly taken in the seventeenth century the beginnings of a more scientifically scrupulous translation theory.

Surprisingly enough, he does approve of Joseph De Maistre's formula to the effect that a translator may replace one proper name by another (for purely ethetic reasons), replace one noun by another for the same reasons, and suppress whole passages if they appear 'ridiculous.' Larbaud prefers the term 'useless' here. Thus it is the translator's 'right' to substitute or suppress. (pp. 183-85)

The technique of transposition, in the mind of Larbaud, is a weighing process on an imaginary pair of scales. . . . This process of establishing a balance between the two texts is not a simple one for Larbaud. He prefers the consultation of un-ilingual dictionaries in each language and his own experience of both languages to the use of bilingual dictionaries. (p. 185)

The scales will occasionally yield differing values for the same word: a noun may become a verb or a verb a noun as in the translation of the title of *The Way of All Flesh (Ainsi va toute chair)* in which the noun *way* assumes its corresponding verbal form *va* in a pattern known to have been inspired by Nietzsche's title *Thus Spake Zarathustra.*

Larbaud really translates conceptual relationships rather than words. This is clearly seen in a clause from *The Book of the Machines* in *Erewhon.* Higgs is reading the revolutionary trea-tise proposing to abolish machines, written by an Erewhonian 'Rousseau' five hundred years before his arrival in Erewhon. In this treatise are the prophetic words: 'Our bondage will steal upon us noiselessly and by imperceptible approaches.' Larbaud rearranges the conceptual pattern while still translating the clause faithfully. The words, however, indicate each other's translated forms in a balance that is admirable indeed: 'Notre esclavage s'approchera de nous sans bruit et à pas imperceptibles.' (p. 186)

Butler himself says little about the art of translation, but he has a good deal to say about art in general, and his words sometimes seem strangely applicable to Larbaud's translations:

> The great thing is that all shall be new and yet nothing new at the same time; the details must minister to the main effect and not obscure it . . . This holds just as true for literature and painting and for art of all kinds . . .

The details and effect of Butler's text are possessed by Larbaud to an extraordinary degree, 'to the point of drawing it from its own form and investing it little by little, cell by cell, with a new form that is our own handiwork.' (pp. 189-90)

> Allison Connell, "Forgotten Masterpieces of Literary Translation: Valery Larbaud's 'Butlers'," in Canadian Review of Comparative Literature (© Canadian Comparative Literature Association), Vol. 1, No. 2, Spring, 1974, pp. 167-90.

## JOHN L. BROWN (essay date 1981)

[Brown's study is the most comprehensive examination of Larbaud's work available in English.]

[Much of Larbaud's] poetry was written when he was a very young man, a good deal of it before 1908, when *Poèmes par un riche amateur* appeared. He made his debut as a poet at the age of fifteen with a slim volume of thirty pages, entitled *Les Portiques* and, with a schoolboy's parading of erudition, subtitled in Greek. . . . The collection consists of some fifteen very derivative, sub-Parnassian *pastiches*, clearly written under the influence of Leconte de Lisle, with echoes of Hugo, Hérédia, and occasionally even of August Barbier. . . . For Larbaud, these poems were probably a thing of the past by the time they had appeared. He had left Parnasse behind him and was now attracted by the Symbolists and especially by Verlaine. (pp. 50-1)

[Four years later he published] another youthful effort entitled *Les Archontes.* Presented as a "comedy translated from the Greek of L. Hagiosy" . . . , it was, of course, an original work, expressing all Larbaud's youthful disdain for the "Republicanism," the materialism, and the bourgeois complacency of his family's milieu. There are even deliberately "shocking" passages, composed in Latin, designed doubtless to "épater la bourgeoisie." (p. 51)

Larbaud subsequently disowned both of these *juvenilia,* which were never reprinted.

But the poems in his next collection [*Poémes par un riche amateur*], in spite of their obvious and often deliberate reminiscences (especially of Whitman and of Henry J.M. Levet) reveal that he had found a voice of his own. . . . In fabricating the mask of "Barnabooth, le riche amateur," Larbaud may have been following the example of Whitman, an inveterate wearer of many different masks, as were Yeats and Pound (one of whose volumes is entitled *Personae*) and especially of the bilingual Portuguese poet, Fernando Pessoa, who created some nineteen different identities or "voices" to express diverse and contradictory attitudes in his verse. (pp. 51-2)

A certain flippancy, a certain tone of self-mockery runs through the volume. Both Claudel and Gide sometimes deplored this side of Larbaud, although Gide in reading the poems expressed regret that he had not been "plus cynique" in *Les Nourritures terrestres.* But it is precisely this tone, a combination of *persiflage* with "seriousness," of lyricism with cynicism which confers on the work of Larbaud its very personal charm. Clearly,

he admired the spirit of "the rich amateur" who couldn't care less about acquiring literary fame or about competing successfully with those "professionals" whom he disdained. Larbaud, too, was writing "pour son déplaisir" and for his own amusement. But his amusement did not exclude all the seriousness of "homo ludens" nor a sincere but discretely concealed sensibility. Barnabooth-Larbaud is often writing very much in earnest and we should not be put off by the surface frivolity of some of the poems and especially of the texts of Tournier de Zambie. Underneath their flippancy, they provide clues about the nature of the very original enterprise upon which Larbaud had embarked. (p. 53)

The poems included in *A. O. Barnabooth: Ses Oeuvres complétes,* some fifty in number . . . , are organized in two sections: "Borborygmes" ("Intestinal Rumblings") and "Ievropa" ("Europe"). On the most obvious level, they constitute a record of Larbaud's travels. But they also testify to a triple liberation. A spiritual liberation, encouraged by his ardent reading of Whitman which incited him to reject the prudery and the restraints of his milieu in Vichy, to accept the physical side of life, to recognize the importance of the body. They also record an esthetic liberation, a breaking away from a "refined" Symbolist tradition, which preferred an abstract "otherworldliness" to daily reality. (p. 55)

[The "author," Barnabooth,] is represented as immensely wealthy and one of the recurrent themes of the poems is the problem of being rich and consequently of being cut off from others. The rich man is able "to buy everything except the essentials. But the attitude of Barnabooth-Larbaud toward the problem of the relationship between the rich and the poor, as in so much else, always remains ambiguous. It reflects one of Larbaud's basic convictions that man is never "all of a piece," never reaches definitive solutions, but always remains "divers et ondovant" ["diverse and inconsistent"]. (pp. 55-6)

These poems testify to the efforts of "the author," a man imprisoned in self, to turn outwards and embrace the exterior world, even the world of contemporary technology, with something of the extrovert exuberance of Whitman. These efforts were rarely successful. For although Barnabooth might proclaim his longing to embrace the universe, to identify himself with the crowd, as in "Europe, III" . . . , he never is able to pull it off. A younger cousin of Mr. Prufrock, he always remains the spectator, rich and privileged, viewing the tumult of daily existence from a favored vantage-point: from the bridge of a yacht, as in "Nuit dans le port" . . . , from the window of a luxury train, from the balcony of a room in an international *palace.* (pp. 56-7)

[For Larbaud, man] remained always the measure of all things and the works of man delighted him more than the marvels of nature. In many, most of these "poems of places," the human visage, especially the feminine visage, is seldom lacking. . . . Here the great, modern city sheds the hard impersonality that others, like [Emile] Verhaeren, found in it; in these poems of Larbaud, it is constantly humanized, constantly eroticized. (pp. 58-9)

[*Le Journal intime de A. O. Barnabooth*] ranks as Larbaud's most ambitious work, the one in which he risked the most, in which he took chances, chances he would no longer hazard in his later, smaller scale, more cautious writings. It has usually been approached on the surface level as a pioneer example of a "new cosmopolitanism" in French literature. It is very much more than that.

In spite of its originality (the creation of the *persona* of Barnabooth, the pre-Joycean use of a form of *monologue intérieur*, among other innovations), the **Journal intime** continues the European tradition of the *Bildungsroman*, the novel of initiation, of which *Wilhelm Meister* and Flaubert's *Education sentimentale* are two outstanding examples. It records Barnabooth's "education" through travel, through his experiences with women, and most particularly through his conversations. . . . Barnabooth recounts the drama of a young man—very much the drama of Larbaud himself when he was writing the **Journal intime**—in search of an identity, a man cut off from normal everyday life by his vast wealth, a man who is haunted by the fear that he has no real existence of his own . . . , a man tempted by the adventure of the absolute.

*Barnabooth* is a "big" book, a youthful book (although the author was thirty-two, he had had a prolonged and protected adolescence) which dares to confront the insoluble questions; never again, as we shall see, does he attempt such an audacious enterprise. He resigns himself, he takes in sail, he navigates closer to the safety of the shore. (pp. 69-70)

*Enfantines* constitutes an homage of Larbaud to childhood. The texts comprising this collection—eight in all—first appeared in little magazines (beginning with **"Dolly"** in *La Phalange* in 1909) before publication as a volume. . . .

The techniques employed in them are varied, ranging from early, almost unconscious experiments with the interior monologue to more conventional third person narrative (**"La Grande Epoque"**), although each one has elements of originality that set them apart from most "short stories" of the period, notably a quasi-identification of the author with the children about whom he is writing. Works about children in the nineteenth century (and the child really entered literature only with Romanticism) usually viewed the subject from outside. In France more than in England (and this was one of the reasons why Larbaud was attracted to the Anglo-Saxon world), they were often patronizing, sounded like accounts written by a dominant ruling class concerning the curious habits of an underdeveloped minority. Larbaud in **Enfantines** entered as an equal into the universe of the child, a universe from which the adult is usually excluded because of his own insensitivity. (p. 87)

Such an intimate identification of the narrator with the children who people **Enfantines** produces a tone of ambiguity, of uncertainty, of shifting roles. Often the "moi" of these stories is a double, but indivisible one—the fusion of the child participating in the action and of the adult remembering it, seeking to recreate it. (p. 88)

Technically, the very brief text, **"La Paix et le salut"** (originally written in 1914 as an epilogue for **Enfantines**) is one of the most intriguing in the collection. It is essentially an extended poem in prose and reveals how Larbaud was moving, in the course of his development as a writer, farther and farther away from any vestige of "story" or linear narrative. Composed of impressionistic evocations of Dublin, of Marienlyst in Sweden, of London, it suggests more than it "tells." It lends itself to a variety of interpretations, depending on the angle of vision of the reader, who, in a sense, must create for himself the "meaning" of the text. The author apparently has no precise "message" to convey. The prose suggests a late Monet, where clear delineation has been sacrificed to shifting effects of light and color, to sensual stimulation. . . . It begins enigmatically, with a phrase of delicately erotic implications: "To the youngest rosebud, so tender and so hard, and so firmly closed . . ." . . . .

"So tender and so hard": this phrase reveals, perhaps, an essential feature of the overall structure of **Enfantines** which might be described in terms of polarity between "tenderness" and "hardness." The tenderness of Milou towards Justine, for example, is paralleled by the cruel harshness of Julia. The "tenderness" of all those English "kiddies" is matched by their thoughtless abandonment of the "pauvre, vieux garçon," their lonely, rather pathetic adult admirer. And this alternation between tenderness and hardness is also established within a larger context in the opposition of the world of childhood (a world of "gentleness," of "douceur," a key word in **Enfantines**) and the harsh, insensitive world of adults. (p. 93)

The casual reader might be inclined to dismiss **Enfantines** as fragile sketches of little substance. Those who expect to find the "well-made" short story in the manner of Maupassant will be disappointed. There is no "plot," no "surprise ending," in fact really no "ending" at all. Many of them read like fragments from a journal. But the rare, really attentive reader, so beloved of Larbaud, the reader who reads "little but well," will soon find in them much more than meets the eye. Nowhere is Larbaud's gift of making "something of nothing," or rather of capturing profound but fleeting sentiments rarely expressed in conventional narrative, more richly apparent. To achieve his purpose he experimented with new techniques, but experimented with them so unobtrusively that their truly innovative character is often not immediately apparent. He employs in certain **Enfantines** a *proto-monologue intérieur* long before he heard of Joyce or Dujardin. He breaks down the traditional patterns of French prose into irregular cadences of poetry as in **"La Paix et le salut."** And as we have said, in **Enfantines** Larbaud explored a new area of expression: the life of the child as seen from within. He opened up a whole new domain, later to be exploited by Alain Fournier, Cocteau, Jacques Cheneviére, and others after them. (p. 94)

From the world of the child in **Enfantines**, Larbaud, in **Fermina Márques**, moves on to explore another *terra incognita*—that of adolescence. And just as **Enfantines** was the first of many subsequent books on childhood, so **Fermina Márquez** launched the vogue for the novel of adolescence, as exemplified in works of Raymond Radiguet, Jacques de Lacretelle, Roger Martin du Gard, and many others of lesser talent. (p. 95)

Its structure clearly indicated his distaste for the conventional realistic novel. In one passage, he comments pointedly that the young Fermina, as she read popular novels, could not realize how "insignificant and artificial" they were. . . . There is no "plot"; Larbaud offers us rather a series of episodes poetic, impressionistic, and presented with an artful absence of "logical progression," which describe the impact of a beautiful Colombian girl of 16 on the students of the cosmopolitan College of St. Augustin, where her little brother, Paquito, is a *pensionnaire*. (pp. 95-6)

From the opening paragraphs, Larbaud creates a shimmering, shifting verbal atmosphere which has affinities with the visual atmosphere of post-impressionist painting, with Bonnard and Vuillard. . . . The boys first perceive Fermina not directly, realistically, "face to face," but rather as a reflection on the glass door of the *parloir* of the school. (Larbaud has a predilection for such effects, for "images in a mirror," which were more suggestive for him than "concrete," directly observed reality.) (p. 96)

Larbaud is not essentially interested in telling a story of the innocent raptures of young love. The stellar role in the *récit* is reserved for an unlikely candidate—Joanny Liénot. Liénot, always the first in the class, vain, ambitious, calculating, obsessed with power and fame even to the point of being somewhat unbalanced, is of the same family as Lucien, in Sartre's short story, ''L'Enfance d'un chef.'' He coldly decides that he must ''win'' Fermina, as he would win the first prize in Latin composition. (p. 97)

[The] central chapters (XI-XVIII) are the least convincing of the *récit*. Joanny becomes more and more incredible in his ranting, his eccentric brilliance, his virtuosity in handling unusual ideas. The mask of Liénot slips and reveals the face of the author himself. (p. 99)

*Fermina,* unlike so many of the ''novels of adolescence'' that came after it, is no passionate defense of youth against adulthood. There is no perceptible ''message'' except perhaps that in our lives, human passions and feelings are more important than reason and abstract intelligence. Youth passes, everything passes and there is no bitterness about it, only a certain Larbaudian melancholy. Finally, if we can say that *Fermina* is ''about'' anything, it is about being young and growing older. (pp. 99-100)

*Fermina Márquez,* although a youthful work, is already a supremely ''finished'' one, possessing the essence of Larbaud's art and sensibility. Technically, it testifies to his dislike of straight, realistic narration. To cite his own words: ''Narration and action have been relegated to the background and have been replaced by the description of states of conscience.'' . . . And such ''description of states of consciousness'' leads us here, as in *Enfantines,* to experiments, perhaps unconsciously, and still unsystematically, with the use of the *monologue intérieur* which he will employ so brilliantly in *Amants, Heureux Amants.* The style is of an accomplished grace and suppleness, uniting, with characteristic skill, tenderness and irony. But occasionally, here as elsewhere, sensibility sometimes softens into sentimentality and produces passages worthy of an archly refined, very ''literary'' maiden lady. As in *Enfantines,* several passages testify that he had abolished—indeed, if he had ever admitted them!—any absolute distinction between poetry and prose. (p. 100)

[*Amants, heureux amants* is] a collection of three of Larbaud's *récits:* ''**Beauté, mon beau souci,**'' ''**Amants, heureux amants,**'' and ''**Mon plus secret conseil.**'' These texts incorporate the principal ingredients which he so artfully combined in his narratives: autobiography, the personal essay, psychological analysis, plus a slender, usually very slender, thread of plot to hold things together in a well-formed package. Well formed, certainly, but not of any conventional shape nor of any strictly definable content. (p. 101)

It is in this volume that Larbaud makes his first deliberate and systematic use of the ''stream of consciousness'' technique, in which he had become deeply interested after his discovery of *Ulysses* and his close friendship with its author. (pp. 101-02)

In his own use of it, visible already in the monologues of *Barnabooth* and of *Fermina Márquez,* he discreetly refrains from plunging too deep into the murk of the subconscious, from exploiting ''free association'' to the full. His Latin instincts (allied with his distaste for Freudian theory) impelled him to remain on the conscious surface of the mind. Of course, he was fully aware that the *monologue intérieur* was an instrument which could well serve his own strategy in freeing fiction from the constraints of a conventional plot, in fostering that process of the ''inwardization'' of narrative, in which he

himself was engaged and which he identified with the future of prose writing. (p. 102)

''**Beauté, mon beau souci,**'' once the surface grace has been stripped away, is a sad and disillusioned tale that illustrates some of the melancholy of Larbaud's complex approach to love and sexuality. Certain Freudian overtones (although Larbaud disliked Freud's theories) keep recurring, such as ''Queenie's desire ''to carry the cane'' of Marc and Reggie. The ambiguities with which Larbaud confronts us are never resolved. Are we to see in Marc a condemnation of those callous upper middle-class Don Juans for whom women (particularly women ''of the lower orders'') are simply disposable objects of pleasure? Was Marc being outrageously cynical or simply honest when he admitted that when he heard of Edith's death he was ''sad for a quarter of an hour''? Or is Marc less unfeeling than he would like to appear? Does the mask of callous Don Juanism conceal a nostalgia for genuine emotion? But perhaps Larbaud is simply telling us once again that people are complicated and contradictory, neither as good nor as bad as we think or as they would like to appear.

One aspect of ''**Beauté . . . ,**'' however, poses no problems. The descriptions it contains of London are among the most graceful prose-poems Larbaud ever wrote, particularly the opening paragraphs describing Chelsea, where ''tout est solitaire et discret: les couleurs mêmes se taisent. . . .'' [''everything is deserted and subdued; even the colors are quiet . . .'']. . . . More than Mrs. Crosland, more than Queenie, London itself is the heroine of the *récit*, the object of ''**mon beau souci. . . .**'' (p 107)

[''**Amants, hevreux amants**''] opens as Felice watches Igna and Romana] still sleeping and ruminates on the pleasures of the night before. We follow the ''inner monologue'' of Felice throughout the day, as he takes his guests to lunch, walks with them in the public gardens, escorts them to the train, and then resumes his life of studious solitude, having resisted the temptation of following the girls to Nice or of returning to still another mistress who lives in Spain. Two themes preoccupy him in his musings: the various kinds of love and the inevitable human solitude which love, always doomed to end in boredom or disappointment, can never conquer. Felice knows that finally he wants solitude more than anything else and that he must be willing to pay the price for it. (p. 108)

''**Amants . . .**'' has a Proustian flavor in its subtle psychological probings, its speculations about the mystery of love and about the impossibility of ever really ''knowing'' the beloved object. . . . Felice concludes, ''it's really useless to try to see those whom we love or even those who interest us, as an indifferent third party would see them.'' He is also constantly aware of the complex interplay between ''individuality'' and universal human traits. . . . Aware, too, of the comparable interplay between the ''male'' and ''female'' present in every individual and of the impossibility here, as elsewhere, of making sharp distinctions, of establishing well-defined frontiers. . . . Such observations recall the classical moralists, with whom Larbaud felt such a close affinity. (p. 110)

[Technically, ''**Mon plus secret conseil**''] represents Larbaud's most ambitious and consistent use of the stream of consciousness technique; he introduces, moreover, an innovation in its application by employing all three persons in close association to achieve shifts in perspective and changes in ''lighting.'' Lucas may first address himself as ''vous,'' then shift to ''moi'' as he speaks of himself directly, finally changing to ''il'' to refer to himself in the third person. As Patrick McCarthy has pointed out, this device was well adapted to express the various "voices" that struggle within each character. (pp. 111-12)

The text is composed of twenty-one brief sections, some bearing the names of towns between Naples and Taranto, along the route of Lucas Letheil's "flight from love." It introduces us into "the stream of consciousness" of this very young man of twenty-two (the age of Larbaud himself when he embarked on his first "serious" affair) who has run off to Italy with an older married woman, Isabelle. (p. 112)

Lucas emerges as probably the least sympathetic and least convincing of the young *dandys* who figure in [*Amants, heureux amants*]. He is callow and immature, but astonishing riches of the spirit and of the intellect incongruously float to the surface in the course of his *monologue intérieur*. Many passages—like the one of the beauty of Naples in the morning light . . . or the Proustian reflections on time . . . —strike us as quite "out of character." (p. 114)

Larbaud was quite willing to admit . . . that his "essays" could be called almost anything the reader liked: "essays, treatises, divagations, sketches, fantasies, epistles, remarks, conversations, promenades. . . ." They reflect his old and deeply-rooted distaste for "genre distinctions," for trying to put things (as he felt that French academicians were all too prone to do) into neat pigeonholes, to halt the flow, to falsify by categorizing. He increasingly wanted (and in this he announced future literary trends) to break down these distinctions and "put it all in," even though the Cartesian might feel that logically it all didn't belong together. But when he got through with them, these apparently random remarks, these apparently incongruous juxtapositions did really go together, orchestrated as they were by his own very individual talent. In spite of their often offhand tone, their "slightness," even the briefest and the least pretentious of them, woven together with a subtle art and a deceptive modesty, are "serious" without being solemn, take up once again with a smiling gravity some of his obsessive themes: the sensuous delight of this world, the importance of love and work and pleasure, the persistence of continuity even in the midst of apparent change, the inevitability of death. Technically, they testify to his rare verbal virtuosity, his intense (but almost clandestine) effort to cast aside artificial formal distinctions, to write the text and the the antitext, to approach "l'oeuvre totale," the total work of which his Symbolist predecessors, like Mallarmé, were always dreaming. (p. 116)

*Allen* is more interesting, perhaps, as literary experiment than as a restatement of Larbaud's ideas on European unity and the revival of the Empire. In spite of its surface randomness, the notes make it clear that the various themes and the various tones were artfully orchestrated. For example, in note IX . . . , he points out that the chapters of "movement" (2-6) had been placed between two chapters of "immobility." This arrangement illustrates once again Larbaud's penchant for "gliding" for "oscillation"—from repose to motion and then back to immobility again. A similar "oscillation" is established between the diversity of small principalities and the unity of Empire; between Paris and province—an oscillation between the small scale and the large, a continuous movement back and forth between opposing states. He was also trying an experiment in recording conversation in such a way that, as we have said, it would approximate the randomness, the abruptness, the *non sequiturs,* the modifications of tone of actual speech. To do this, he rejected the usual literary conventions of dialogue, the repetition of the "he says," the identification of

speakers, the maintenance of a certain "logical" sequence in the discourse. (p. 120)

[The eighteen texts of *Jaune Bleu Blanc*] offer an excellent introduction to the various manners and tones of Larbaud's work, sum up, so to speak, his varied interests as a writer and scholar. They include notes on travels in Portugal, Spain, Italy, England, essays on Paris and what it means to be "a true Parisian," a dramatic monologue, philological *divertissements*. They form an artfully arranged tray of literary *hors d'oeuvres,* all exquisitely fashioned, of unique savor, and presented with the confident modesty of an artist sure of his craft. An artist content to create on a small scale—but determined to create impeccably within self-imposed limits. (p. 122)

The entire text is peppered with "incongruities." And given the self-consciousness of Larbaud's art, we must assume that they are calculated incongruities. In attempting to catch in words the fleeting, variegated, contradictory stuff of life, then you put everything in. . . . Human existence is incongruous, he seems to be hinting quite openly, as Sterne did before him, and the "little" things are perhaps as important as those the world considers as "big" ones, particularly if you are trying "to make, from truth and dreams, a little French prose." . . .

But occasionally one longs for more solid fare. One cannot make a dinner of *hors d'oeuvres.* And Larbaud, over-concerned with the *bienséances,* too discreet, too entertaining, too well bred, often sends us with relief to the unwashed, the uncombed, the savage elemental writers like Melville, or Dostoyevsky, or Whitman, a youthful enthusiasm which Larbaud later sacrificed to his need for elegance and *mesure.* (p. 127)

*Jaune Bleu Blanc* revolves (as Larbaud indicated in his letter to Jean-Aubry) about the axis of Paris, the point of departure and the point of return. *Aux Couleurs de Rome* is a celebration of Italy and especially of Rome ("O Roma nobilis") which, in the course of the years, had become Larbaud's favorite city, the center of his personal universe as well as the center of that unifying Latin civilization of which he had been the ardent lifelong advocate. . . .

This collection, the gravest of Larbaud's works, affirms once again the Protean quality of his art. The "essay" is constantly turning into "fiction," fiction into personal reminiscence, prose into poetry. Nothing is fixed, everything is flowing, gliding, imperceptibly shifting from one form, from one mood into another. One genre is rarely sustained throughout the entirety of a text, but the transitions are so skillfully manipulated that only the very attentive reader is wholly aware of what is happening. (p. 128)

Larbaud, a painstaking craftsman, always reluctant to publish any text that had not been "aged" and scrupulously revised, had little patience with colleagues who were proud to bring out a book every year. His friends, indeed, sometimes chided him for not producing more. However, each of his major works, although not numerous, marks a new departure, often established new trends. (p. 186)

The texts of *Amants, heureux amants* . . . experimented brilliantly with various forms of the stream of consciousness technique, advanced even further towards that "inwardness" which, in reaction against naturalistic fiction, has characterized the major lines of development of the modern novel. All of [his] works, disregarding conventional genre distinctions, broke down the frontiers between poetry and prose, between fiction and nonfiction. In the essays of the latter part of his career, Larbaud goes even further in his effort to make French prose more supple and more fluid, to liberate it from formal constraints, from Cartesian logic, from the strait-jacket of "la dissertation." . . . This liberation of language, the invention of new forms of expression capable of capturing the ceaseless "oscillation" which marked his own sensibility, may well be one of Larbaud's essential achievements. (p. 187)

> *John L. Brown, in his* Valery Larbaud *(copyright ©
> 1981 by Twayne Publishers, Inc.; reprinted with per-
> mission of Twayne Publishers, a Division of G. K.
> Hall & Co., Boston), Twayne, 1981, 217 p.*

---

## ADDITIONAL BIBLIOGRAPHY

Carl, Ralph F. "The Early Critical Writings of Valery Larbaud." *Kentucky Foreign Language Quarterly* V, No. 1 (1958): 1-11.
    Descriptive essay about the criticism Larbaud wrote for the French publication, *La Phalange*. Carl focuses upon Larbaud's articles about English and American authors, including H. G. Wells and Jack London, as well as obscure authors like Herman Knicker-bocker Viele.

Champigny, Robert. "Spatial Anxiety in the Poems of Barnabooth." *Modern Language Quarterly* 16, No. 1 (March 1955): 78-84.
    Detailed study of Larbaud's poetry. Champigny focuses on the theme of spatial anxiety in the poems of *A. O. Barnabooth*.

Connell, Allison B. "Saint-John Perse and Valery Larbaud." *The French Review* XLI, No. 1 (October 1967): 11-22.*
    Comparative essay. Connell examines the influence of Perse on Larbaud's poetry.

Grace, Jane Opper. "Geography as Metaphor: Larbaud's Fiction Revisited." *Romanic Review* LXVII, No. 4 (Nov. 1976): 300-07.
    Takes issue with "excessively literal readings" of Larbaud's fiction as autobiography. Grace suggests that a metaphorical interpretation of Larbaud's work leads to a richer, as well as a more accurate, reading.

McCarthy, Patrick. "The Valery Larbaud-Marcel Ray Correspondence 1899-1908." *Revue de Litterature Comparee* XLII, No. 3 (1968): 431-43.*
    Traces Larbaud's development through his correspondence with Marcel Ray who was the author's confidant and mentor.

O'Brien, Justin, "Lafcadio and Barnabooth: A Supposition." *Symposium* VII, No. 1 (Summer 1954): 33-41.*
    Discusses the themes common to Larbaud's *A. O. Barnabooth, His Diary* and Gide's *Les Caves du Vatican*.

Stansbury, Milton H. "Valery Larbaud." In his *French Novelists of Today*, pp. 69-82. 1935. Reprint. Port Washington, N.Y.: Kennikat Press, 1966.
    Biocritical examination of Larbaud's major works, including relevant biographical material which helps to explain this author's identification as a "cosmopolitan."

# D(avid) H(erbert) Lawrence

## 1885-1930

(Also wrote under pseudonym of Lawrence H. Davison) English novelist, novella and short story writer, poet, essayist, critic, translator, and dramatist.

Lawrence was one of the first novelists to introduce themes of modern psychology into his fiction. In his lifetime he was a controversial figure, both for the explicit sexuality he portrayed in his novels and for his unconventional personal life. Much of the criticism of Lawrence's work revolves around his highly individualistic moral system, which is based on absolute freedom of expression, particularly sexual expression. Human sexuality was for Lawrence a symbol of the Life Force, and is frequently pitted against modern industrial society, which he felt was dehumanizing. His most famous novel, *Lady Chatterley's Lover,* was the subject of a landmark obscenity trial in Great Britain in 1960, which turned largely on the legitimacy of Lawrence's inclusion of hitherto forbidden sexual terms.

The fourth child of an illiterate coal miner and his wife, a former school teacher, Lawrence was raised in the colliery town of Eastwood, Nottinghamshire. Temperamentally alienated from his environment, he grew to hate the debilitating mine work which he felt was responsible for his father's debased condition. He shared from boyhood a close relationship with his mother. Lawrence won a scholarship to the local grammar school and later to Nottingham University College. He taught school at Croyden for three years, during which time Ford Madox Ford published some of Lawrence's poems in the *English Review.* The onset of tuberculosis forced Lawrence to resign from teaching in 1911, and that same year he published his first novel, *The White Peacock,* which was critically well received. When he was twenty-seven, Lawrence eloped with Frieda von Richthofen Weekly, the wife of one of his college professors. The couple's first years together are chronicled in the poems contained in *Look! We Have Come Through!* After they married, the Lawrences lived briefly in Germany, Austria, Italy, Sicily, England, France, Australia, Mexico, and in the southwestern United States, where Lawrence hoped to someday establish a Utopian community. The varied locales provided the settings of many of the novels Lawrence wrote in the 1920s, and also inspired four books of travel sketches: *Twilight in Italy, Sea and Sardinia, Mornings in Mexico,* and *Etruscan Places.* In 1930 Lawrence entered a sanatorium in Vence, France, in an attempt to cure the tuberculosis which afflicted him throughout his life. He died soon after.

Lawrence's first major work, the largely autobiographical novel *Sons and Lovers,* made an important contribution to the development of the psychological novel. *Sons and Lovers* contains some of Lawrence's most characteristic themes: the complexity of human relationships, especially that between a mother and son; the experience of first love; and the emotional dominance of one person by another. *The Rainbow,* Lawrence's second major novel, is a more complex narrative than *Sons and Lovers,* and introduces psychological themes into the family-chronicle saga format. The novel focuses on relationships between men and women, and especially those of marriage. In *The Rainbow* Lawrence sought to develop a specialized vocab-

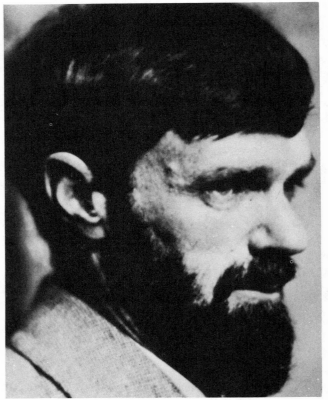

ulary to describe sexual experience. For this explicit discussion of sexuality the novel was judged obscene and suppressed in England. This began Lawrence's bitter struggle with social orthodoxy, and, some critics believe, his seeming obsession with portraying sexuality in his works. *Women in Love* followed *The Rainbow* chronologically and thematically. The later novel has been compared to T. S. Eliot's *The Waste Land,* for in both works the decadence of an entire culture is symbolized by representative figures. *The Rainbow* and *Women in Love* are generally regarded as Lawrence's best works. He originally conceived of the two works as a single novel, to be called *The Sisters,* and some continuity is preserved between the novels. *The Rainbow* is concerned with three generations of the Brangwen family, and *Women in Love* examines the two men with whom Ursula and Gudrun Brangwen fall in love.

In his later novels, such as *Aaron's Rod, Kangaroo,* and *The Plumed Serpent,* Lawrence dealt more extensively with themes of power, dominance, and leadership. He also began to focus in these later works on the relationships that men form with one another, rather than with women. Lawrence formulated a concept of *blutbruderschaft* ("blood brotherhood"), which he felt was essential to men as a complement to "right relationships" with women. This precept is developed in *The Plumed Serpent,* along with the concept of "blood consciousness," a religion of intuition and instinct which was the product of his lifelong search for a new mystical expression of life's meaning. In his last major novel, *Lady Chatterley's Lover*, Lawrence returned to some of his earlier themes, such as the dehumanizing effect of industrialization on the Life Force. *Lady Chatterley's Lover* is also the most blatant of Lawrence's novels since *The Rainbow* for the use of words commonly considered obscene and was available only in an expurgated version until 1959 in the United States and 1960 in England. A 1960 obscenity trial, *Regina vs. Penguin*, eventually vindicated *Lady Chatterley's Lover* as a work of literature, and not pornography. Many literary critics testified on behalf of the book simply because they opposed literary censorship. While most critics did and still do decry the bowdlerization to which Lawrence's novel was subjected, some are now finding fault with his attempt to redeem words primarily thought of as obscene. It is felt by some that in his attempt to bring taboo words and phrases into general usage, he was ignoring the social connotations the words had acquired.

Lawrence's novels are notable for beautifully descriptive passages. The obscenity trial which vindicated *Lady Chatterley's Lover* also brought extensive critical attention to other facets of Lawrence's writing, including his unsurpassed nature prose. In his best work, Lawrence utilized imaginative symbols for his ideas; in his weaker writing, Lawrence attempted to describe and define meaningful experiences, especially sexual experiences, in a specialized vocabulary which often led to obscure, almost unintelligible prose. A more common fault of Lawrence's writing is a tendency toward didacticism. This tendency to preach increased during his career, so that his last major work, *Lady Chatterley's Lover*, is heavily burdened by frequent sermonizing. Lawrence's short stories present a contrast to his novels. They are economical in style and structure, and differ from the novels in that they present Lawrence's themes in terms of literature and not homily, avoiding the didacticism that pervades almost all of his novels. The psychological themes Lawrence explored in his fiction were further elaborated in his essays *Psychoanalysis and the Unconscious* and *Fantasia of the Unconscious*.

Like his fiction, most of Lawrence's poetry is intensely personal. In fact, as Sigrid Undset noted, "It may safely be said that the whole of Lawrence's production was autobiographical." Lawrence's earliest poetry adhered to traditional poetic forms and is not as highly regarded as his later works in this genre. It is in the free forms of his nature poems, especially those in *Birds, Beasts and Flowers*, that Lawrence achieves his best poetic effects. In addition to his fiction and poetry, Lawrence wrote eight dramas. Most of these have never been produced. They are of interest primarily as a reflection of Lawrence's effort to present his basic literary ideas in a different medium than fiction.

Lawrence has come to be regarded as one of the twentieth century's most important novelists. In his innovative use of psychological themes he produced the first, and some critics still believe finest, modern psychological novels. He remains a significant force in modern fiction, both for the artistic example of his style and the continued influence of his vision.

(See also *TCLC*, Vol. 2, and *Dictionary of Literary Biography*, Vol. 10: *Modern British Dramatists, 1900-1945*.)

## PRINCIPAL WORKS

*The White Peacock* (novel) 1911
*The Trespasser* (novel) 1912
*Love Poems and Others* (poetry) 1913
*Sons and Lovers* (novel) 1913
*The Prussian Officer* (short stories) 1914
*The Rainbow* (novel) 1915
*Amores* (poetry) 1916
*Twilight in Italy* (essays) 1916
*Look! We Have Come Through!* (poetry) 1917
*New Poems* (poetry) 1918
*The Lost Girl* (novel) 1920
*Women in Love* (novel) 1920
*Psychoanalysis and the Unconscious* (essay) 1921
*Sea and Sardinia* (essays) 1921
*Tortoises* (poetry) 1921
*Aaron's Rod* (novel) 1922
*England, My England* (short stories) 1922
*Fantasia of the Unconscious* (essay) 1922
*Movements in European History* [as Lawrence H. Davison] (essays) 1922
*Birds, Beasts and Flowers* (poetry) 1923
*Kangaroo* (novel) 1923
*Studies in Classic American Literature* (essays) 1923
*Reflections on the Death of a Porcupine* (essays) 1925
*The Plumed Serpent* (novel) 1926
*Mornings in Mexico* (essays) 1927
*The Collected Poems of D. H. Lawrence*. 2 vols. (poetry) 1928
*\*Lady Chatterley's Lover* (novel) 1928
*The Woman Who Rode Away* (short stories) 1928
*Pansies* (poetry) 1929
*The Escaped Cock* (novella) 1930; also published as *The Man Who Died*, 1931
*Love among the Haystacks* (short stories) 1930
*Nettles* (poetry) 1930
*The Virgin and the Gipsy* (novel) 1930
*Etruscan Places* (essays) 1932
*Last Poems* (poetry) 1932
*The Lovely Lady* (short stories) 1933
*The Ship of Death* (poetry) 1933
*A Modern Lover* (short stories) 1934
*The Spirit of the Place* (essays) 1935
*Phoenix* (essays and criticism) 1936
*Fire* (poetry) 1940
*The First Lady Chatterley* (novel) 1944
*The Complete Short Stories of D. H. Lawrence*. 3 vols. (short stories) 1955
*The Collected Letters of D. H. Lawrence*. 2 vols. (letters) 1962
*The Complete Poems of D. H. Lawrence*. 2 vols. (poetry) 1964
*The Complete Plays of D. H. Lawrence* (drama) 1966
*Phoenix II* (essays and criticism) 1968
*John Thomas and Lady Jane* (novel) 1972

*This work is the third of three different versions. The other two were posthumously published as *The First Lady Chatterley* and *John Thomas and Lady Jane*.

---

**THE TIMES LITERARY SUPPLEMENT** (essay date 1911)

The merit of this rather odd book [*The White Peacock*] is its feeling for and descriptions of nature on its pathetic side. Perhaps we may add, what is often a merit, its studied neglect of a well-knit plot. But it is not easy to feel much enthusiasm about people of Nethermere—the Beardsalls of the "Cottage," the Tempests, mineowners in the lone house across the lake, and the farming Saxtons, though George Saxton, who takes to public-house keeping, its a good attempt at character study. But the tale meanders through much that is trivial, and one gets an impression of aimlessness. A good deal of the conversation is quite banal, despite its suggestions of advanced culture; for when such names as Ibsen, Gorki, Schopenhauer, Maupassant, Clausen, Debussy, and others startle the stillness of the woodland, as they frequently do, we have a feeling that it is not the characters but the author who is uttering them. And the reader is annoyed by the unsubstantiality of Cyril Beardsall, in whose mouth the whole story is put. He appears to have poetic thoughts, to sketch from nature, and to work in the fields; but for much of the book he is a wraithlike kind of person who appears to be present without being seen.

> "'The White Peacock'," in The Times Literary Supplement (© Times Newspapers Ltd. (London) 1911; reproduced from The Times Literary Supplement by permission), No. 472, January 21, 1911, p. 35.

### THE NEW YORK TIMES BOOK REVIEW (essay date 1913)

There is probably no phrase much more hackneyed than that of "human document," yet it is the only one which at all describes this very unusual book ["**Sons and Lovers**"]. It is hardly a story; rather the first part of a man's life, from his birth until his 25th year, the conditions surrounding him, his strength and his numerous weaknesses, put before us in a manner which misses no subtlest effect either of emotion or environment. And the heroine of the book is not sweetheart, but mother; the mother with whose marriage the novel begins, with whose pathetic death it reaches its climax. The love for each other of the mother and her son, Paul Morel, is the mainspring of both their lives; it is portrayed tenderly, yet with a truthfulness which slurs nothing even of that friction which is unavoidable between the members of two different generations. . . .

It is wonderfully real, this daily life of the Morel family and the village wherein they lived as reflected in Mr. Lawrence's pages; the more real because he never flaunts his knowledge of the intimate details of the existence led by these households whose men folk toil underground. They slip from his pen so unobtrusively that it is only when we pause and consider that we recognize how full and complete is the background against which he projects his principal characters—Mr. and Mrs. Morel, Paul, Miriam, and Clara.

Paul himself is a person who awakens interest rather than sympathy; it is difficult not to despise him a little for his weakness, his constant need of that strengthening he sought from two other women, but which only his splendid, indomitable little mother could give him—a fact of which he was constantly aware, though he acknowledged it only at the very end. And it is not easy upon any grounds to excuse his treatment of Miriam, even though it was a spiritual self-defense which urged him to disloyalty. Mr. Lawrence has small regard for what we term conventional morality; nevertheless, though plain spoken to a degree, his book is not in the least offensive.

It is, in fact, fearless; never coarse, although the relations between Paul, Miriam, and Clara are portrayed with absolute frankness. And one must go far to find a better study of an intense woman, so over-spiritualized that she has almost lost touch with ordinary life and ordinary humanity, than he has given us in the person of Miriam. . . .

Clara is less remarkable than Miriam only because she is necessarily more obvious—a woman in whom the animal predominates, certain after a brief time to weary one like Paul. And better than either, strong of will, rich in love and sympathy, holding her place in her son's heart against even Miriam, who so nearly took him from her, reigning at last supreme over every rival stands the heroic little mother—the best-drawn character in a book which contains many admirable portrayals. . . .

Although this is a novel of over 500 closely printed pages the style is terse—so terse that at times it produces an effect as of short, sharp hammer strokes. Yet it is flexible, too, as shown by its success in depicting varying shades of mood, in expressing those more intimate emotions which are so very nearly inexpressible. Yet, when all is said, it is the complex character of Miriam, she who was only Paul's "conscience, not his mate," and the beautiful bond between the restless son and the mother whom "his soul could not leave" even when she slept and "dreamed her young dream" which makes this book one of rare excellence.

> L.M.F., "Mother Love," in The New York Times Book Review (© 1913 by The New York Times Company; reprinted by permission), September 21, 1913, p. 479.

### SOLOMON EAGLE [J. C. Squire] (essay date 1915)

Last Saturday, at Bow Street, Mr. D. H. Lawrence's new novel *The Rainbow* was brought before the bench and sentenced to death. Who lodged an information against the book I don't know. It is conceivable at a time when the patriotism of our criminals must leave our policemen plenty of leisure, that some cultured constable may have got hold of the work and rushed to his superiors with it. But it is likelier that the prosecution was the work of some Society or individual set upon Mr. Lawrence's track by one of the violent attacks upon the book which appeared in the Press. Two of these attacks figured in court, those of Mr. James Douglas and Mr. Clement Shorter. The prosecution attached much importance to them and the magistrate blamed the publishers for not withdrawing the book as a direct result of these gentlemen's criticisms. And both these critics as well as counsel for the prosecution and the magistrate himself talked a good deal of hyperbolical nonsense.

Some qualification must be made with regard to Mr. Douglas and Mr. Shorter. Mr. Douglas is a man with a genius for invective which I myself heartily appreciate when it is aimed at politicians whom I don't like—and who, incidentally, are never impounded and destroyed by the police as the result of his attacks. It is a weakness of Mr. Douglas to turn sometimes his powers of epigrammatic vituperation against books which he considers obscene. . . . On the present occasion he was irritated by seeing a man like Mr. Lawrence wasting his powers, and fairly let himself go about the obscenity of *The Rainbow*. Mr. Shorter, again, to do him justice, appears to be hostile to censorship, and, in the middle of his abuse, remarked that Mr. Lawrence's book would have "served one good purpose" in that "the next writer of a piece of frank, free literature who is an artist will assuredly run no risk of a police prosecution." All the same both critics carried their language to an indefensible pitch. Mr. Shorter said that "Zola's novels are child's food compared with the strong meat" in the book. He did not personally charge Mr. Lawrence "with a deliberate attempt to provide nastiness for commercial purposes''; but he had unfortunately said quite enough to put the hounds upon the scent. His reservations were little good in court. The prosecuting counsel, Mr. Muskett, referred to the book as "this bawdy volume''; and the magistrate, Sir John Dickinson, described it as ''utter filth'' and said that he had ''never read anything more disgusting than this book.''. . .

I am quite unacquainted with Sir John Dickinson's antecedents. For all I know he may have been Mother-Superior of a Convent before he was translated to the more lucrative but less secluded position that he now graces. But if he has never seen anything more disgusting than *The Rainbow,* all I can say is that he cannot be familiar with many books that are sold in this country and that he must be abysmally ignorant of the literatures of our two Allies, France and Great White Russia. For the critics the excuse of ignorance cannot be advanced. That influential critics, with the interests of literature—not to speak of the livings of authors—in their charge should let loose as Mr. Shorter did is unpardonable. . . .

Now, I am not arguing the whole question of censorship. Most people will agree that there is a point at which the police must interfere: we can all imagine things, in our heads, which certainly ought not to be written down and exposed for sale. And I am not maintaining that *The Rainbow* is a great work of art. Its author has a strain of genius, but in this novel he is at his worst. It is a dull and monotonous book which broods gloomily over the physical reactions of sex in a way so persistent that one wonders whether the author is under the spell of German psychologists, and so tedious that a perusal of it might send Casanova himself into a monastery, if he did not go to sleep before his revulsion against sex was complete. I think it a bad novel: and it contains opinions unpalatable to me and tendencies that I personally believe to be unhealthy. But in the first place it is very much to be doubted whether, the good faith of the book being evident, censorship in this case was desirable; in the second place if *The Rainbow* is to be interfered with there are scores of other books that demand prior attention; and in the third place it is doing Mr. Lawrence common justice to protest against the way in which his name has been dragged through the mud. How many of those who read the criticisms and gloated over the police court proceedings will realise that he is an uncommercial young writer who, whatever he may write, writes it as he does because of an earnestness which is almost awe-inspiring? It will be no consolation to him that many people, who look on in smug silence whenever a distinguished writer is stigmatized as bawdy, will treasure up his name and rush to buy his next novel when it appears. Critics really should try to keep their sense of proportion.

*Solomon Eagle [pseudonym of J. C. Squire],* "Books in General: 'The Rainbow','' *in* New Statesman *(© 1915 The Statesman Publishing Co. Ltd.), Vol. VI, No. 137, November 20, 1915, p. 161.*

## *NEW STATESMAN* (essay date 1918)

Mr. D. H. Lawrence's new volume, with its somewhat terrifying title [*Look! We Have Come Through*], is, he informs us, not to be taken ''as so many single pieces,'' but as ''an essential story, or history, or confession,'' the component parts of which unfold ''one from the other in organic development.'' It is, that is to say, a lyrical novel resembling Richard Dehmel's *Zwei Menschen* both in its method of seizing on salient crises without giving any intervening narrative or working in any

background, and its story, which tells how a young man ran away with a married woman and how their ''conflict of love and hate'' ended in ''some condition of blessedness.''. . .

What emerges most clearly, however, from an examination of the book is that Mr. Lawrence has in a high degree many of the poet's gifts without the one essential gift, a specifically poetic temperament. He has a prose mind and a prose ear; his ecstasy is the long, detailed, self-possessed ecstasy of prose, and his visual power, strong and vivid as it is, is a little too slow to be properly rendered in verse. His images and pictures are often very fine. . . . But it is hard not to think that [his descriptive] passages would have had a greater effect in their proper place as prose descriptions in a novel. Mr. Lawrence has suffered too often and too much (and made his readers suffer), in attempting the simplest metre, for him ever to pretend that he has adopted the ''free verse'' form for any reason but that it is easy. But his ''free verse'' is artificially cramped and cut up without gaining anything in brevity, intensity or solidity. It is prose moving in an affected manner; and Mr. Lawrence's prose at its best is not affected. So far as the psychology of this book goes, it seems to prove that Mr. Lawrence's earlier sensuality has been transformed into a sort of metaphysical lust, the aches and pleasures of which reside wholly in the spirit. And we might warn the reader (or reassure him) that the *Hymn to Priapus,* which is the seventh piece in the book, has no discoverable connection with Priapus.

*"Recent Verse: 'Look! We Have Come Through','' in* New Statesman *(© 1918 The Statesman Publishing Co. Ltd.), Vol. X, No. 251, January 26, 1918, p. 406-407.*

## [VIRGINIA WOOLF] (essay date 1920)

Perhaps the verdicts of critics would read less preposterously and their opinions would carry greater weight if, in the first place, they bound themselves to declare the standard which they had in mind, and, in the second, confessed the course, bound, in the case of a book read for the first time, to be erratic, by which they reached their final decision. Our standard for Mr. Lawrence, then, is a high one. Taking into account the fact, which is so constantly forgotten, that never in the course of the world will there be a second Meredith or a second Hardy, for the sufficient reason that there have already been a Meredith and a Hardy, why, we sometimes asked, should there not be a D. H. Lawrence? By that we meant that we might have to allow him the praise, than which there is none higher, of being himself an original; for such of his work as came our way was disquieting, as the original work of a contemporary writer always is.

This was the standard which we had in mind when we opened **''The Lost Girl.''** We now go on to trace the strayings and stumblings of that mind as it came to the conclusion that **''The Lost Girl''** is not an original, or a book which touches the high standard which we have named. Together with our belief in Mr. Lawrence's originality went, of course, some sort of forecast as to the direction which that originality was likely to take. We conceived him to be a writer, with an extraordinary sense of the physical world, of the colour and texture and shape of things, for whom the body was alive and the problems of the body insistent and important. It was plain that sex had for him a meaning which it was disquieting to think that we, too, might have to explore. Sex, indeed, was the first red-herring that crossed our path in the new volume. The story is the story of

Alvina Houghton, the daughter of a draper in Woodhouse, a mining town in the Midlands. It is all built up of solid fabric. If you want a truthful description of a draper's shop, evident knowledge of his stock, and a faithful and keen yet not satiric or sentimental description of James Houghton, Mrs. Houghton, Miss Frost, and Miss Pinnegar, here you have it. Nor does this summary do any kind of justice to the variety of the cast and the number of events in which they play their parts. But, distracted by our preconception of what Mr. Lawrence was to give us, we turned many pages of very able writing in search for something else which must be there. Alvina seemed the most likely instrument to transmit Mr. Lawrence's electric shock through the calicos, prints, and miners' shirts by which she stood surrounded. We watched for signs of her development nervously, for we always dread originality, yet with the sense that once the shock was received we should rise braced and purified. The signs we looked for were not lacking. . . . [We believed] that sex was the magnet to which the myriad of separate details would adhere. We were wrong. Details accumulated; the picture of life in Woodhouse was built up; and sex disappeared. This detail, then this realism, must have another meaning than we had given them. Relieved, yet a trifle disappointed, for we want originality as much as we dread it, we adopted a fresh attitude, and read Mr. Lawrence as one reads Mr. Bennett—for the facts, and for the story. Mr. Lawrence shows indeed something of Mr. Bennett's power of displaying by means of immense industry and great ability a section of the hive beneath glass. Like all the other insects, Alvina runs in and out of other people's lives, and it is the pattern of the whole that interests us rather than the fate of one of the individuals. And then, as we have long ceased to find in reading Mr. Bennett, suddenly the method seems to justify itself by a single phrase which we may liken to a glow or to a transparency, since to quote one apart from the context would give no idea of our meaning. In other words, Mr. Lawrence occasionally and momentarily achieves that concentration which Tolstoy preserves sometimes for a chapter or more. And then again the laborious process continues of building up a model of life from saying how d'you do, and cutting the loaf, and knocking the cigarette ash into the ash tray, and standing the yellow bicycle against the wall. Little by little Alvina disappears beneath the heap of facts recorded about her, and the only sense in which we feel to be lost is that we can no longer believe in her existence.

So, though the novel is probably better than any that will appear for the next six months, we are disappointed, and would write Mr. Lawrence off as one of the people who have determined to produce seaworthy books were it not for those momentary phrases and for a strong suspicion that the proper way to look at **"The Lost Girl"** is as a stepping stone in a writer's progress. It is either a postscript or a prelude.

> [*Virginia Woolf*], *"Postscript or Prelude?" in* The Times Literary Supplement *(© Times Newspapers Ltd. (London) 1920; reproduced from* The Times Literary Supplement *by permission), No. 985, December 2, 1920, p. 795.*

## J. MIDDLETON MURRY   (essay date 1921)

[*The following two essays, and Murry's 1931 essay on Lawrence (TCLC Vol. 2), illustrate the varying judgement Murry made on Lawrence's writing. The two men shared a close relationship, fraught with serious rifts, until Lawrence's death. The characters of Rupert Birkin and Gerald Crich in* The Rainbow *and* Women

in Love *are based upon Lawrence and Murry, with whom Lawrence expressed a desire to form a blood brotherhood.*]

[Mr. Lawrence] is the outlaw of modern English literature; and he is the most interesting figure in it. But he must be shown no mercy. (p. 713)

**"Women in Love"** is five hundred pages of passionate vehemence, wave after wave of turgid, exasperated writing impelled towards some distant and invisible end; the persistent underground beating of some dark and inaccessible sea aura in an underworld whose inhabitants are known by this alone, that they writhe continually, like the damned, in a frenzy of sexual awareness of one another. Their creator believes that he can distinguish the writhing of one from the writhing of another; he spends pages and pages in describing the contortions of the first, the second, the third, and the fourth. To him they are utterly and profoundly different; to us they are all the same. And yet Mr. Lawrence has invented a language, as we are forced to believe he has discovered a perception for them. The eyes of these creatures are "absolved"; their bodies (or their souls: there is no difference in this world) are "suspended"; they are "polarized"; they "lapse out"; they have, all of them, "inchoate" eyes. In this language their unending contortions are described; they struggle and writhe in these terms; they emerge from dark hatred into darker beatitudes; they grope in their own slime to some final consummation, in which they are utterly "negated" or utterly "fulfilled." We remain utterly indifferent to their destinies, we are weary to death of them.

At the end we know one thing and one thing alone: that Mr. Lawrence believes, with all his heart and soul, that he is revealing to us the profound and naked reality of life, that it is a matter of life and death to him that he should persuade us that it is a matter of life and death to ourselves to know that these things are so. . . . It is of no avail for us to declare and protest that the things he finds are not there; a fanatical shriek arises from his pages that they are there, but we deny them.

If they are there, then indeed it is all-important that we should not deny them. Whether we ought to expose them is another matter. The fact that European civilization has up to the advent of Mr. Lawrence ignored them can prove nothing, though it may indicate many things. It may indicate that they do not exist at all; or it may indicate that they do exist, but that it is bound up with the very nature of civilization that they should not be exposed. Mr. Lawrence vehemently believes the latter. It is the real basis of his fury against the consciousness of European civilization which he lately expounded . . . in a paper on Whitman. He claims that his characters attain whatever they do attain by their power of going back and re-living the vital process of pre-European civilization. (pp. 713-14)

Is Mr. Lawrence a fanatic or a prophet? That he is an artist no longer is certain, as certain as it is that he has no desire to be one. . . .

The essential crisis of the book occurs in a chapter called, mystically enough, "Excurse." In that chapter Rupert and Ursula, who are said to reach salvation at the end of the history, have a critical and indescribable experience. It is not a matter of sexual intercourse, though that is, of course, incidentally thrown in; but it has a very great deal to do with "loins." They are loins of a curious kind, and they belong to Rupert. Mr. Lawrence calls them "his suave loins of darkness." These Ursula comes "to know." It is, fortunately or unfortunately, impossible to quote these crucial pages. We cannot attempt to paraphrase them; for to us they are completely and utterly unintelligible if we assume (as we must assume if we have regard to the vehemence of Mr. Lawrence's passion) that they are not the crudest sexuality. Rupert and Ursula achieve their esoteric beatitude in a tea-room; they discover by means of "the suave loins of darkness" the mysteries of "the deepest physical mind." They die, and live again. . . .

We have given, in spite of our repulsion and our weariness, our undivided attention to Mr. Lawrence's book for the space of three days; we have striven with all our power to understand what he means by the experience *x;* we have compared it with the experience *y,* which takes place between the other pair of lovers, Gudrun and Gerald; we can see no difference between them, and we are precluded from inviting our readers to pronounce. We are sure that not more than one person in a thousand would decide that they were anything but the crudest kind of sexuality, wrapped up in what Mr. S. K. Ratcliffe has aptly called the language of Higher Thought. We feel that the solitary person might be right; but even he, we are convinced, would be quite unable to distinguish between experience *x* and experience *y.* Yet *x* leads one pair to undreamed of happiness, and *y* conducts the other to attempted murder and suicide.

This *x* and this *y* are separate, if they are separate, on a plane of consciousness other than ours. To our consciousness they are indistinguishable; either they belong to the nothingness of unconscious sexuality, or they are utterly meaningless. For Mr. Lawrence they are the supreme realities, positive and negative, of a plane of consciousness the white race has yet to reach. . . .

If the experiences which he presents to us as part of this process mean nothing, the book means nothing; if they mean something, the book means something; and the value of the book is precisely the value of these experiences. Whatever they are, they are of ultimate fundamental importance to Mr. Lawrence. He has sacrificed everything to achieve them; he has murdered his gifts for an acceptable offering to them. Those gifts were great; they were valuable to the civilization which he believes he has transcended. (p. 714)

> *J. Middleton Murry, "The Nostalgia of Mr. D. H. Lawrence," in* The Nation and The Athenaeum, *Vol. XXIX, No. 20, August 13, 1921, pp. 713-14.*

**J. MIDDLETON MURRY** (essay date 1923)

About two years ago I wrote in an essay in an English review that 'Mr. D. H. Lawrence is the outlaw of English literature, and he is the most interesting figure in it' [see excerpt above]. In substance that opinion of mine may still stand. But a nuance of modification is necessary. Mr. Lawrence during the last two years has become a little less of the outlaw, and a little more perceptibly the most interesting figure among the writers of his generation. (p. 55)

Lawrence—with whom we are quickly compelled to drop the polite prefix—is primarily a novelist. . . . He is also a notable poet; but it is a long while now since he published a volume of verses. In the last year, however, he has presented to the world two volumes which contain an exposition of his beliefs [*Psychoanalysis and the Unconscious* and *Fantasia of the Unconscious*]. Of these, the more important by far is the latter one, *Fantasia of the Unconscious.* . . .

I must content myself for the moment with pointing out the significance and indicating the context of two perfectly commonplace facts concerning this remarkable book. The first of these may seem almost puerile. The book has been published

in America, and not in England. For the time being, if we desire to read it, we have to procure it from the United States. And the meaning of this is that Lawrence—an Englishman of the English, born in a Midland mining village, where the grim Black Country fades into some of the most beautiful rural scenery that England possesses—is, or has been, in a state of rebellion against his native land. By a monstrous abuse of the law in 1915 one of the most significant of his novels, *The Rainbow,* was suppressed on a fantastic charge of immorality. Shortly after, so soon, in fact, as the material opportunity offered—the suppression of the one book made publishers fearful of accepting work from him—he shook the dust of England from his feet and began a slow and haphazard journey round the world, which has ended temporarily in the south of the United States. This was the period of his outlawry in spirit and in fact. He was anathema to English criticism. (pp. 55-6)

I felt, and I said, that he was an enemy of civilisation. It was perfectly true. He is the conscious and deliberate, yet passionate and potent, enemy of modern civilisation. If our modern life, our modern civilisation, is fundamentally good and true and valuable, then indeed the cry must be raised against Lawrence: 'Écrasez l'infâme!' It is war to the knife between them, and two years ago the attack and the defence were alike angry and embittered. I do not wish to suggest that, at that or any other time, I was the equal antagonist of Lawrence. He has a sheer creative power that is completely beyond my range. But at that time I was the only English critic who took Lawrence with the impassioned seriousness he deserved: the rest had washed their hands of him long ago, or, if they wrote of him at all, wrote only of his early novels and poems in a tone of mild regret that he should wilfully have forsaken such comparatively mild and flowery paths. (p. 56)

Well, I changed. I came to believe that Lawrence was right and I was wrong. In reviewing his next novel, *Aaron's Rod,* I published my recantation, with these words: '*Aaron's Rod* is the most important thing that has happened to English literature since the war. . . . To read it is to drink of a fountain of life.' For the bitterness had gone out of Lawrence's hostility to modern life. No less, nay, even more profoundly the enemy of modern 'civilisation,' he was no longer an angry and venomous enemy. He had reached the gaiety and serenity of a man who has come, through bitter struggles, into the secure possession of his truth. He had lived out life to an issue.

That brings me to the second of my simple facts, in order to explain, as briefly as I can, the nature of Lawrence's challenge to modern life. Both of Lawrence's expository or philosophical volumes start from a psycho-analytical basis. Lawrence was the first man in England, and I believe the first man in Europe, truly to realise the scope, the *envergure,* of the problems of which psycho-analysis has touched the fringe. This knowledge he had not as a student of Freud or Jung, but directly and instinctively by his own intuitive apprehension of life. The language and conceptions of the psycho-analysts were useful to him sometimes in giving expression to his own discoveries; but his discoveries were his own: they were also far in advance of anything the professional psycho-analysts had reached. (pp. 56-7)

The professional psycho-analysts had discovered that in modern 'civilisation' some great primal urge—'Sex' for Freud, something less simple, *Libido,* for Jung—was thwarted and contorted with disastrous results to the individual. They began, clinically, to elaborate a subtle technique for liberating these suppressions. They have only just begun to see that when the suppressions are liberated, the problem of life remains, only more conscious and urgent than before. For the victim of neurosis, the man who cannot live in modern life, has at least a *modus vivendi* in the framework and among the compulsions of our industrial 'civilisation'. If he becomes a machine, he also acquires some of the numbness of a machine. To make him aware of his own deep discomfiture, his lack of true satisfaction, his poverty of being, is only to increase his pain and his impotence, unless you can give him something new and true to live by. Psycho-analysis, without knowing what it is doing, has assumed the responsibilities of a religion without having religious duties to impose or religious satisfactions to offer.

This then is the cardinal issue which Lawrence has faced continuously and unflinchingly during his life as a writer, in moods that have passed through anger, embitterment, dismay, to a final serenity and insouciance. Men must enter into a new order of being. It is the conclusion of the great minds of modern times—of Dostoevsky, of Tolstoy, of Nietzsche, of Whitman. But how? In *Fantasia of the Unconscious* Lawrence gives, with a joyful spontaneity of language which is itself an augury of the newness of life he proclaims, his answer to the question. And, for my own part, I will declare my faith that it is essentially a true one; that D. H. Lawrence is the only writer of modern England who has something profoundly new to say; and finally that he must inevitably become a figure of European significance. (pp. 57-8)

> *J. Middleton Murry, "D. H. Lawrence" (1923), in his* Reminiscences of D. H. Lawrence *(reprinted by permission of The Society of Authors as the literary representative of the Estate of John Middleton Murry), J. Cape, 1933 (and reprinted in his* Selected Criticism 1916-1957, *edited by Richard Rees, Oxford University Press, London, 1960, pp. 55-8).*

**ALYSE GREGORY** (essay date 1924)

In *Son and Lovers*, in *The Rainbow*, in *Twilight in Italy*, and in a few of his poems Mr Lawrence is, we believe, at his best. Here his febrile and tortured genius flows richly and turbulently. Every passing stir upon his sensitiveness is passionately or beautifully recorded. The mother-complex in *Sons and Lovers* is artistically convincing without being obtrusive, the picture of the old miner, his father, done with sharp and restrained veracity, and even if the author himself as the hero seems a trifle priggish, no one could read this book through without feeling in its pages something wholly new and vital in the literature of our day. Perhaps *The Rainbow* is less integrated as a work of art, but it also contains passages of greater beauty, passages in which every seed and flower in the English landscape seem to share that same vibration of life which moves so inscrutably in the frames of men. As animals prey on each other in order to sustain life to which every passing hour is a recurrent threat, so Mr Lawrence showed us men and women in their obscure destructive combats for empire, in their isolations and irremediable woes and curative returns to the soil.

Not until the appearance of *Women in Love* did we begin to detect the real trend of his developing philosophy. And then what a sorry—what a very pitiful and unexpected spectacle met our startled eyes! The very tiger that he had loosed so magically with his own hands, the tiger of sex was slowly turning and driving him back, inch by inch, into the hermetic cell of dogma. Birkin and Gerald are but two aspects of Mr Lawrence himself, just as Gudrun and Ursula are animated

dolls set up to play off his theories one against the other. Gerald must be destroyed by Gudrun because he has sunk all his capital in sex and thereby lost his power to dominate her. Birkin struggles to find his necessary *manly* connexion with the outside world while Ursula seeks to imprison him for ever in the stultifying circle of their intimacy. Only the feverish Hermione in spite of artistic distortion has reality; and perhaps Mr and Mrs Crich, who are presented with that narrowed percipient power of Lawrence's for probing straight through to the essential and mute differences between certain associated couples.

If *Women in Love* left us with a residue of doubt in our minds *The Lost Girl* corroborated our worst fears and in spite of some lovely passages toward the end of the book it is as a whole boring and unconvincing, a shell of the Lawrence we have honoured. And *Aaron's Rod* continues the disillusion. Here Birkin and Gerald are replaced by Aaron and Lilly. It is Lawrence hypnotizing himself, ceding his ground step by step to the avenging tiger, scattering his messages through the pages as would a prisoner about to be entombed and already beginning to lose direct communication with the outside world. Always the *dénouement* is the same. It recurs in *Lady-Bird*, in *The Captain's Doll*, in *The Fox*. "Away, oh women, out of the world of disturbing ideas, of politics, of men's activities! Seek your salvation and ours in the dark caverns of *willing* obedience! Up, men, and assert your power. The only way you can keep your women docile is by seeking out some male purpose greater than sex." It is as absurd to think of a clever English girl like Alvina Houghton submerging herself for ever in her Italian husband as for March in *The Fox,* an eager, intelligent, modern young woman, once clear of the fog of sensuous desire, submitting her soul to the limited, murdering bully she married.

It is not, however, until Mr Lawrence steps clean out of the field of fiction into that of metaphysics that he delivers himself over completely into our hands. But perhaps if, as Mr Bertrand Russell says, "Metaphysics is the attempt to conceive the world as a whole by means of thought," Mr Lawrence cannot even be termed a metaphysician; for it is rather with the "brutish sting" of his inflamed sensibilities than with the pen of reflection that he traces his manifestos and slips with them into that exalted area where are usually assembled the most profound and imaginative minds of the day—scientists, poets, philosophers. Yet it is hardly a case of slipping, either. For not reverently, with no deprecatory bow, no indeed, but with one great whirling leap in hobnailed boots Mr Lawrence lands squarely on his two feet in the midst of this grave and eclectic company, apparently oblivious to the fact that he is not alone in the universe. It is hardly necessary to say that from the pens of mystics have come truths beautiful and eternal, and science is for ever resolving the world for us into new and liberating shapes and sequences. But it is, we feel, when these two aspects of insight are artistically fused that the greatest literature is written. In Mr Lawrence's *Psychoanalysis and the Unconscious,* and *Fantasia of the Unconscious* there is neither the exquisite intimate discovery of a poet like Blake nor the passionless appeal to intellect that one demands from a scientific statement. There is only Mr Lawrence looking about him with slightly dilated and belligerent eyes. . . . To try to understand the divagations and recoils of Mr Lawrence's logic in its eccentric movements is as difficult as to follow the zig-zag flight of a snipe disturbed on a frosty morning. He is one of those very familiar writers on the complexities of sex, who, starting with the assertion that men and women are for ever and ever *ad infinitum* different—mentally, morally, biologically different—and can never therefore hope by the barest possibility to understand each other, forthwith proceeds to devote endless pages to instructing this mysterious other sex as to its own secret desires.

He cries out pugnaciously that man is alone, alone, alone, for ever isolate and adrift upon this planet and then hems him in on all sides with dangerous currents, "dynamic flows," "blood polarities," each with subtle and puissant commands upon his balance.

He disposes of Freud's *Interpretation of Dreams* as "insulting to the integrity of the human soul" and in its place sets up another of his own which may be pleasing to the soul, but certainly pays small attention to the reason.

Of course, it would be impossible for Mr Lawrence to write a book without saying many shrewd and illuminating things, but in this case they are vitiated at the root by his obsession to attain security and control in the sexual relation. (pp. 66-9)

In *Studies in Classic American Literature* we see this versatile Englishman in still another attire, that of interpretive critic of literature. Like some of the scientists he takes such pleasure in deriding he has always a new thesis up his sleeve, or rather the old thesis in some new form. America is, as it were, suffering from a father complex. She ran away, bolted, in fact, from the domination of Europe, only to find herself unable to establish a separate life of her own. (pp. 69-70)

Benjamin Franklin was the arch rationalizer. It was he who set up "the first dummy American," invented a list of virtues "which he trotted inside like a grey nag in a paddock." He is the *practical* type of American, while Crèvecoeur [author of *Letters from an American Farmer*], on the other hand, is the emotional, the first of his countrymen to transcribe with veracity the savagery and strangeness of the animal life about him, a savagery which the upper levels of his mind refused to accept and so subverted into spurious idealism. Here according to Mr Lawrence is the typical American artist whose real insights are for ever being betrayed by the falseness of existing ethics. But perhaps this dualism remarked by the author is even more clearly illustrated in the case of Fenimore Cooper's *Deerslayer*, where the hunter says "Hurt nothing unless you are forced to" and yet exults in the hunt and exists only by killing. For, says Mr Lawrence, "Idealism in America is a sort of byplay. The essential American soul is hard, isolate, stoic, and a killer. It has never yet melted." And so with a chance cunning he thrusts his finger straight through the flimsy draperies of our public pretences and touches the sharp and jagged blade beneath. For can any one deny that this is not true of America? (pp. 70-1)

In writing of Edgar Allan Poe Mr Lawrence connects his lively theories about sex with his no less active interpretation of America to the great detriment of the author of "Ligeia." But what a light one gets on his own limitations when he tells us that "The Fall of the House of Usher" is "an overdone vulgar fantasy" and that Poe's "so-called" style is false and meretricious.

Perhaps in the end what emerges from this book as most interesting, most significant, is the indestructibility of man's craving for worship. (p. 71)

One wishes that one might close here and cancel for ever from one's mind the memory of Mr Lawrence's latest novel, *Kangaroo*. Would that he himself had remained uncorrupted by the

disease of ideology which so exasperates him in others and in the throes of which he likewise now lies prostrate. . . .

In spite of his vigorous honesty and his insight [Mr Lawrence] has not the kind of background or information that could justify even so fragmentary a venture into the fields of sociology, economics, or psychology. Nor has he those temperamental qualities of reverence and detachment which are necessary if a fact, most delicate and evasive of all things in life, is to be convincingly established and lucidly interpreted. But though the construction of *Kangaroo* is bad, the characters unreal, the dialogue and reflections vulgar and wearying beyond belief, we are every now and then reminded by a passing phrase that Mr Lawrence is still living and still potential. And even if he should never write a sentence again penetrated with that quality of mobil response to the savage and destructive beauty of life at its foundation which has been so uniquely his gift to our literature, but should turn gradually into an inflammable and churlish fanatic whom everyone hastens for the sake of peace to placate, we shall still continue to revere and respect him. For have we not, to balance against his worst literary indecorums, certain other transcendently revealing pages; and to have written even two books and a few poems that contain flashes of pure genius, that most sacred of all gifts which life has to offer, is to have done more than enough to justify the acclaim he has received in a disoriented age with many bogies and few gods. (p. 72)

*Alyse Gregory, "Artist Turned Prophet," in* The Dial *(copyright, 1924, by The Dial Publishing Company, Inc.), Vol. LXXVI, No. 1, January, 1924, pp. 66-72.*

### D. H. LAWRENCE   (essay date 1929)

[*This is Lawrence's explication of his most controversial novel,* Lady Chatterley's Lover. *Lawrence discusses modern attitudes toward human sexuality, and he describes at some length the various editions of the book.*]

I put forth [*Lady Chatterley's Lover*] as an honest, healthy book, necessary for us today. The words that shock so much at first don't shock at all after a while. Is this because the mind is depraved by habit? Not a bit. It is that the words merely shocked the eye, they never shocked the mind at all. People without minds may go on being shocked, but they don't matter. People with minds realize that they aren't shocked, and never really were: and they experience a sense of relief.

And that is the whole point. We are today, as human beings, evolved and cultured far beyond the taboos which are inherent in our culture. This is a very important fact to realize. Probably, to the Crusaders, mere words were potent and evocative to a degree we can't realize. The evocative power of the so-called obscene words must have been very dangerous to the dim-minded, obscure, violent natures of the Middle Ages, and perhaps is still too strong for slow-minded, half-evoked lower natures today. But real culture makes us give to a word only those mental and imaginative reactions which belong to the mind, and saves us from violent and indiscriminate physical reactions which may wreck social decency. In the past, man was too weak-minded, or crude-minded, to contemplate his own physical body and physical functions, without getting all messed up with physical reactions that overpowered him. It is no longer so. Culture and civilization have taught us to separate the reactions. We now know the act does not necessarily follow on the thought. In fact, thought and action, word and deed, are two separate forms of consciousness, two separate lives which we lead. We need, very sincerely, to keep a connection. But while we think, we do not act, and while we act we do not think. The great necessity is that we should act according to our thoughts, and think according to our acts. But while we are in thought we cannot really act, and while we are in action we cannot really think. The two conditions, of thought and action, are mutually exclusive. Yet they should be related in harmony.

And this is the real point of this book. I want men and women to be able to think sex, fully, completely, honestly and cleanly.

Even if we can't act sexually to our complete satisfaction, let us at least think sexually, complete and clear. All this talk of young girls and virginity, like a blank white sheet on which nothing is written, is pure nonsense. A young girl and a young boy is a tormented tangle, a seething confusion of sexual feelings and sexual thoughts which only the years will disentangle. Years of honest thoughts of sex, and years of struggling action in sex will bring us at last where we want to get, to our real and accomplished chastity, our completeness, when our sexual act and our sexual thought are in harmony, and the one does not interfere with the other.

Far be it from me to suggest that all women should go running after gamekeepers for lovers. Far be it from me to suggest that they should be running after anybody. A great many men and women today are happiest when they abstain and stay sexually apart, quite clean: and at the same time, when they understand and realize sex more fully. Ours is the day of realization rather than action. There has been so much action in the past, especially sexual action, a wearying repetition over and over, without a corresponding thought, a corresponding realization. Now our business is to realize sex. Today the full conscious realization of sex is even more important than the act itself. After centuries of obfuscation, the mind demands to know and know fully. The body is a good deal in abeyance, really. When people act in sex, nowadays, they are half the time acting up. They do it because they think it is expected of them. Whereas as a matter of fact it is the mind which is interested, and the body has to be provoked. The reason being that our ancestors have so assiduously acted sex without ever thinking it or realizing it, that now the act tends to be mechanical, dull and disappointing, and only fresh mental realization will freshen up the experience.

The mind has to catch up, in sex: indeed, in all the physical acts. Mentally, we lag behind in our sexual thought, in a dimness, a lurking, grovelling fear which belongs to our raw, somewhat bestial ancestors. In this one respect, sexual and physical, we have left the mind unevolved. Now we have to catch up, and make a balance between the consciousness of the body's sensations and experiences, and these sensations and experiences themselves. Balance up the consciousness of the act, and the act itself. Get the two in harmony. It means having a proper reverence for sex, and a proper awe of the body's strange experience. It means being able to use the so-called obscene words, because these are a natural part of the mind's consciousness of the body. Obscenity only comes in when the mind despises and fears the body, and the body hates and resists the mind. (pp. 489-90)

[Thousands of women today] know nothing, they can't think sexually at all; they are morons in this respect. It is better to give all girls this book, at the age of seventeen. . . .

In contrast to the puritan hush! hush!, which produces the sexual moron, we have the modern young jazzy and high-brow person who has gone one better, and won't be hushed in any respect, and just "does as she likes". From fearing the body, and denying its existence, the advanced young go to the other extreme and treat it as a sort of toy to be played with, a slightly nasty toy, but still you can get some fun out of it, before it lets you down. These young people scoff at the importance of sex, take it like a cocktail, and flout their elders with it. These young ones are advanced and superior. They despise a book like *Lady Chatterley's Lover.* It is much too simple and ordinary for them. (p. 491)

So, between the stale grey puritan who is likely to fall into sexual indecency in advanced age, and the smart jazzy person of the young world, who says: "We can do anything. If we can think a thing we can do it," and then the low uncultured person with a dirty mind, who looks for dirt—this book has hardly a space to turn in. But to them all I say the same: Keep your perversions if you like them—your perversion of puritanism, your perversion of smart licentiousness, your perversion of a dirty mind. But I stick to my book and my position: Life is only bearable when the mind and body are in harmony, and there is a natural balance between them, and each has a natural respect for the other. (p. 492)

[In] *Lady Chatterley's Lover* we have a man, Sir Clifford, who is purely a personality, having lost entirely all connection with his fellowmen and women, except those of usage. All warmth is gone entirely, the hearth is cold, the heart does not humanly exist. He is a pure product of our civilization, but he is the death of the great humanity of the world. He is kind by rule, but he does not know what warm sympathy means. He is what he is. And he loses the woman of his choice.

The other man still has the warmth of a man, but he is being hunted down, destroyed. Even it is a question if the woman who turns to him will really stand by him and his vital meaning.

I have been asked many times if I intentionally made Clifford paralysed, if it is symbolic. And literary friends say, it would have been better to have left him whole and potent, and to have made the woman leave him nevertheless.

As to whether the "symbolism" is intentional—I don't know. Certainly not in the beginning, when Clifford was created. When I created Clifford and Connie, I had no idea what they were or why they were. They just came, pretty much as they are. But the novel was written, from start to finish, three times. And when I read the first version, I recognized that the lameness of Clifford was symbolic of the paralysis, the deeper emotional or passional paralysis, of most men of his sort and class today. I realized that it was perhaps taking an unfair advantage of Connie, to paralyse him technically. It made it so much more vulgar of her to leave him. Yet the story came as it did, by itself, so I left it alone. Whether we call it symbolism or not, it is, in the sense of its happening, inevitable. (pp. 513-14)

*D. H. Lawrence, "A Propos of 'Lady Chatterley's Lover'" (1929; originally published as* A Propos of "Lady Chatterley's Lover," *M. Secker, 1931), in his* Phoenix II: Uncollected, Unpublished, and Other Prose Works by D. H. Lawrence, *edited by Warren Roberts and Harry T. Moore (copyright © 1959, 1963, 1968 by the Estate of Frieda Lawrence Ravagli; reprinted by permission of Viking Penguin Inc.), Viking Penguin, 1968, pp. 487-515).*

**ANDRÉ MAUROIS**   (essay date 1935)

If ever there was a writer who longed to preach a gospel, to offer men a faith, it was Lawrence. But to define that faith is not easy. "You ask me about the message of the **Rainbow**. I don't know myself what it is: except that the older world is done for, toppling on top of us: and that it's no use the men looking to the women for salvation, nor the women looking to sensuous satisfaction for their fulfilment. There must be a new world."

What must this new world be? According to Lawrence, it should apparently be, first and foremost, a return to an older world. The society which he likes and praises is the Mexican tribe, or the poorest of Italian villages. He had liked Cornwall in so far as it had remained primitive; when he was in Italy he became interested in the Etruscans, and when in Mexico in the Axtec civilizations. He turned always to the oldest, the most aboriginal things he could find. The modern world, he felt, had substituted for the real and natural man, an artificial being, inevitably unhappy and unbalanced because he has denied his instincts. (p. 266)

Lawrence's natural man lives mainly through the body. The modern sporting youth, the Boy Scout camping out in the open, are nearer to the natural man than were their fathers. The renaissance of the body is perhaps the only feature common to the new civilization which is springing up around us. But the body is not enough. Lawrence wants men to listen also to their hearts. (p. 269)

[Two isolated characteristics of Lawrence are] the effort to transcend the civilized man and reach again the natural man and communion of bodies; and the hope of achieving this through the senses and thanks to the intercession of woman. A third point would be a strong awareness of class warfare, not in the Marxist and economic sense, but in a Lawrencean, psychological way.

In all his books Lawrence contrasts the aristocrat with the common people. He realizes the conflict better because it is within himself. He is the son of a working man, but his culture is that of the favoured classes. And he was acutely conscious of the clash. As one of the working class, he declared, he could feel the middle classes cutting some part of his vitality when he found himself in their company. . . . Working-class people were deeper and more profoundly emotional than the others, but they were also narrow-minded, prejudiced, unintelligent. (p. 278)

Perhaps the solution of this conflict, also, should be sought in sensuality? Lawrence delights to show women of high birth finding happiness, moral and, even more, physical, in the love of a man of the people. His own marriage with Frieda was a symbol of this. But the solution is not perfect. Love and conflict are coexistent. (p. 279)

And what of equality? Where is there equality in nature? There everything is at war, and the most vital have to win their place in the sun at the expense of the less vital. Consider the striking *Reflections on the Death of a Porcupine*. Lawrence tells how in Mexico, in the depths of a forest, he comes across a porcupine, as big as a small boar, a strange, rather beautiful creature. A few days later the dogs come home from the woods, injured by the porcupine. What is to be done? The porcupine must be killed. And Lawrence, who has never taken life, takes a gun and, with repugnance, destroys this form of life. Then he thinks it all over. Nobody can start a ranch in New Mexico unless he is resolved to kill the porcupine. No porcupine can live unless it resists the dogs, and the dogs in their turn destroy and are destroyed. Even so with men and with peoples. The leader is the man who is strong enough to be leader.

There is an element of despair in this; but how could Lawrence feel other than despairing once he began to reason consciously? Foe to intellect though he is, he is too intelligent not to discern the futility of some of his precepts. To become natural, to become spontaneous? But man is never spontaneous in the sense that the vulture and the sparrow are spontaneous. Man cannot live by instinct alone, because he has a mind. The most savage of men has his ideas. . . . [What] must be done in the face of this conflict which is rending every man?

First and foremost, replies Lawrence, do not seek a solution. Be simpler, far simpler; do not worry about the whole universe; never wonder to what end the world has been created. There is no such end. Life and love are life and love; a bunch of violets is a bunch of violets, and to push an idea of finality with it is utterly destructive. Live and let live. Love and let love. Follow the natural curve of blossoming and fading. . . .

Such is the gist. And hence comes his doctrine of heedlessness. (pp. 279-80)

[Wisdom lies] in losing oneself in contemplation of man wielding the sickle, of animals and plants. Nothing is so genuine in Lawrence as this mute communion with nature. He knows animals like brothers, loving to spy upon their lives, their lovemaking, their footprints in the snow. He imagines the sensations of the strangest among them, and has written moving poems about a couple of tortoises, an essay on the death of a porcupine. A fine black stallion symbolizes for him all the male forces, and in the story entitled **St Mawr,** man and horse live on the same plane and are jealous of each other. We may picture Lawrence crouching in the forest grass, with his faun's beard, patiently watching the movements of a squirrel, a rabbit, a stag-animal himself, a creature "without frontiers, a piece of nature." For a moment, in the quietude of intuition, all conflicts then stand resolved. The poet has brought to birth again a virgin world. (p. 281)

To save us, ideas, like gods, must become incarnate. Lawrence strove to make his doctrine visible in works of art. In his poems and in his stories he succeeded, but not always in his novels. By an odd paradox, the advocate of the unconscious was a too conscious novelist. Too weak to submit to laws, he believed he was freeing himself by denying the conventions: whence **Lady Chatterley's Lover,** and, on the social plane, the flights to Italy and Australia and Mexico. If Lawrence had been a whole and full man, the true Lawrencean hero, he would have accepted society and the conventions as the complete poet (like Baudelaire or Valéry) accepts rhyme and fixed metre. But the partial failure of a prophet does not refute his prophecy, nor does the martyrdom of Lawrence belie his faith. (pp. 282-83)

*André Maurois, "D. H. Lawrence," in his* Prophets and Poets, *translated by Hamish Miles (translation copyright © 1935 by Harper & Brothers; reprinted by permission of the author and the author's agents, Scott Meredith Literary Agency, Inc., 845 Third Avenue, New York, New York 10022; originally published as* Magiciens et logiciens, *B. Grasset, 1935), Harper & Row, 1935, pp. 243-84.*

### T. S. ELIOT (essay date 1951)

We have had a number of books about Lawrence by people who knew him; we need books about him by critics who know him only through his works. To have been associated with Lawrence was, evidently, for those who were attracted, or alternately attracted and repelled, by that dominating, cross-grained and extreme personality, a very important part of their lives, an experience which had to be recorded in print. But perhaps one of the reasons why Lawrence's books are now less read by young people than they were twenty and thirty years ago, is that the books about him give the impression that he is a man to read about, rather than an author to read: a Johnson surrounded by a shoal of Boswells, some of them less tender towards the great man than was Johnson's biographer.

This is not the only reason why Lawrence's work needs to be examined from a new perspective. He was an impatient and impulsive man (or so I imagine him to have been; for . . . I never knew him). He was a man of fitful and profound insights, rather than of ratiocinative powers; and therefore he was an impatient man: he expressed some of his insights in the form least likely to make them acceptable to most of his contemporaries, and sometimes in a form which almost wilfully encouraged misunderstanding. If the foolish or the ill-disposed chose to regard him as a blasphemer, a ''fascist,'' or a pornographer, Lawrence would not put himself out to persuade them. Wrong he often was (I think) from ignorance, prejudice, or drawing the wrong conclusions in his conscious mind from the insights which came to him from below consciousness: and it will take time to dissociate the superficial error from the fundamental truth. To me, also, he seems often to write very badly; but to be a writer who had to write often badly in order to write sometimes well. After being misunderstood, he is in danger of being ignored. As for his religious attitude . . . we can now begin to see better how much was ignorance, rather than hostility; for Lawrence was an ignorant man in the sense that he was unaware of how much he did not know. His strictures upon Christianity (and indeed upon Buddhism) are often ill-informed; at other times they go straight to the heart of the matter; and no Christian ought to feel sure that he is religious-minded enough, to ignore the criticism of a man who, without being a Christian, was primarily and always religious. (pp. 93-4)

> *T. S. Eliot, in his foreword to* D. H. Lawrence and Human Existence *by W. Tiverton, Philosophical Library, 1951 (and reprinted in* The Achievement of D. H. Lawrence, *edited by Frederick H. Hoffman and Harry T. Moore, University of Oklahoma, 1953, pp. 93-4).*

**FRANK AMON**   (essay date 1953)

Lawrence, like Chekhov, stands for a distension in the form of the [short] story. Like Chekhov, he had the genius for portraying the intimate feeling of a place, a landscape, a conversation, or a character. Like Chekhov—but in a manner peculiar to his technique—he crystallized vacancy, frustration, inertia, and futile aspiration. We see that all of Lawrence's stories share one characteristic: all depend, as stories, upon subtle psychological changes of character.

With Lawrence's characters (as with Chekhov's) the subconscious seems to come to the surface and they communicate directly without the impediment of speech. Naturally the most interesting point for Lawrence is that at which the interplay of psychic forces is incomplete, where the adjustment is difficult, where the emphasis is on discord rather than on harmony. Consequently, Lawrence focused his attention, as Frederick Hoffman has said, ''on the subtle complexity of an emotional state which a character assumes in a crisis.''

The significance of this is that Lawrence has accomplished a transfiguration of experience. He lifts his characters from the surface experience of the concrete world onto new and immediate levels of psychic consciousness, and then returns them, sanctified and altered, to the concrete world in which they must continue. Inevitably this is the symbolic *rites de passage,* the ceremony or initiation or baptism, which ushers an individual into a new way of life; and in this, too, it is the spiritual death and rebirth motif of Lawrence's chosen symbol, the Phoenix.

If we take, for example, **''The Odour of Chrysanthemums,''** one of Lawrence's earliest stories, . . . this *rites de passage* aspect comes out quite clearly.

The autobiographical setting of Lawrence's youth—the lower-class colliery family—is of course common to many of his early stories and novels. But the theme, too, is central to Lawrence: the inviolable isolation of the individual psyche, the utter separateness of those with whom we share physical intimacy.

The revelation of the theme (of which for us the entire story is the qualifying and modifying symbol) comes to the wife through the death of her husband. Revelation through death then is the means of objectifying the theme. However, it is the *moment* of revelation with which we are concerned here and with the peculiar means of objectifying that moment.

Gradually, as the story unfolds, our interest in the chrysanthemums increases. At first, they hang dishevelled, ''like pink cloths.'' A little later, Elizabeth's small son tears at the ''ragged wisps of chrysanthemums'' and drops the petals in handfuls along the path: '''Don't do that—it does look nasty,' said his mother. He refrained, and she, suddenly pitiful, broke off a twig with three or four wan flowers and held them against her face.'' . . . [Later] Elizabeth's daughter wants to smell the flowers:

> ''Don't they smell beautiful!''
>
> Her mother gave a short laugh.
>
> ''No,'' she said, ''not to me. It was chrysanthemums when I married him, and chrysanthemums when you were born, and the first time they ever brought him home drunk, he'd got brown chrysanthemums in his button-hole.''

Here then is their significance: they are talismans of change, transition into a new way of life—a tragic way of life. They are markers of marriage, birth, and—inevitably—death. The chrysanthemums, we might say, are the omens, and it is through them that a great part of our interest is aroused and focalized; and it is through them (but not through them alone) that the father's death is foreshadowed. (pp. 222-24)

[Lawrence was able to] throughly incorporate into his art the most appropriate action—literal and symbolic—to objectify his theme.

We find incipient in this story such other patterns and motifs as the *Mater Dolorata*, possessive motherhood, lack of rapport between the sexes, and father-hatred-envy, which were to occupy Lawrence the rest of his life. (pp. 225-26)

By the time he was twenty-five he had written one of the world's masterpieces of short fiction, **''The Prussian Officer.''** Lawrence recognized its worth in a letter to Edward Garnett at the time: ''I have written the best story I have ever done—

about a German officer in the army and his orderly.'' It is this of course—and much more.

For the pattern of the Handsome Soldier and his tragic death has a mythic counterpart. It suggests that universal motif, the fable of the Fall of Man, the loss of Paradise. For the orderly is, on one level at least, Primal Man. Indeed, it is said of him that he seemed ''never to have thought, only to have received life direct through his senses, and acted straight from instinct.'' (p. 226)

If the orderly is the Adam of this Eden, the Captain is its Satan. Maleficent as he is, the Captain, like the arch-fiend in *Paradise Lost,* has a certain nobility of stature, an aura of the Fallen Prince about him (''He had ruined his prospects in the Army, and remained an infantry captain.'') . . . In contrast to his orderly, he is a man completely ''dominated by mind,'' a man of ''passionate temper who had always kept himself suppressed.'' He had never married, for his position did not allow it, and ''no woman had ever moved him to it.'' ''Whereas the young soldier seemed to live out of his warm, full nature, to give it off in his very movements, which had a certain zest, such as wild animals have in free movement.'' And it is precisely this guileless nature that the Captain hates and tempts to action.

The Captain's predisposition to iniquity is innate in him, however, not the product of training or intellect but a trait hitherto repressed. It takes the form of an instinctive hatred for innocence and good, but a hatred so obsessive and even paranoid as to suggest the perversion of a still more deep-rooted love.

And if there are mythic overtones of the Biblical temptation and fall (the youth's limitations as a human being lead him to commit in fact a capital crime), there are also psychological undertones of homosexuality. For it is in effect the story of a courtship. From the first, the orderly feels that he is ''connected'' with the figure of the Captain—''and damned by it.'' While rubbing his Captain down, he admires the ''amazing riding muscles of his loins.'' (pp. 226-27)

As for the Captain, he had ''become aware of his servant's young, vigorous, unconscious presence about him.'' And it was like a ''warm flame upon the older man's tense, rigid body.'' He is attracted to the youth's ''strong young shoulders'' and ''the bend of his neck.'' We have the feeling throughout the story of a homosexual courtship: the older man, in spite of himself, wooing the younger; and the youth, sensing the advances, repudiating the Captain.

And with the soldier's denial, it becomes more difficult for the Captain to restrain himself: ''As yet, the soldier had held himself off from the elder man. The Captain grew madly irritable. He could not rest when the soldier was away, and when he was present, he glared at him with tormented eyes. . . . he was infuriated by the free movement of the handsome limbs. . . . And he became harsh and cruelly bullying. . . .'' And it would seem impossible to ignore this homosexual aspect in such a statement as ''The officer tried hard not to admit the passion that had got hold of him. He would not know that his feeling for his orderly was anything but that of a man incensed by his stupid, perverse servant. So, keeping quite justified and conventional in his consciousness, he let the other thing run on.''

Finally, the officer's passion culminates in an outburst of rage when the soldier in confusion ignores a question. As the orderly is crouching to set down a load of dishes before a stairway, the captain kicks him, sending the dishes tumbling; and as the soldier clings to the bannister pillar for support, the captain kicks him repeatedly. . . . And afterwards, when the orderly confesses that he had been writing some poetry:

> ''Poetry, what poetry?'' asked the Captain, with a sickly smile.
>
> Again there was the working in the throat. The Captain's heart had suddenly gone down heavily, and he stood sick and tired.
>
> ''For my girl, sir,'' he heard the dry, inhuman sound.
>
> ''Oh!'' he said, turning away. ''Clear the table.''

Here, on one level, is the Captain's realization that he can never succeed. The sinking of his heart and the curt dismissal of the orderly would seem to indicate his acknowledgment of a rival and the futility of the pursuit. In fact he erases the incident from his mind, denies it to himself—and is ''successful in his denial.''

With the soldier it is a different matter. He feels that he has been violated emotionally and physically, and he is filled with ''one single, sleep-heavy intention: to save himself.'' The maneuvers are the following morning; and the combination of his bruises, the marching, the hot sun, and the violation of his inner self moves him—when he and the officer are alone—to attack the Captain and choke him to death. (pp. 227-29)

In one sense, this is a victory—a victory over and a release from the evil dominance of the Captain. But, in another sense, it is a capitulation, for this is what the orderly has been continuously fighting against. It is foreshadowed earlier in the story with the statement that ''in spite of himself the hate grew, responsive to the officer's passion.'' And it is for this surrender to the Captain, as well as for the criminal act, that the orderly pays with his life.

I have postponed until now a consideration of the nature imagery in this story. For although it is intimately related to—and is in fact a part of—both the mythic and sexual patterns, it serves a wider and, if possible, more profound purpose. I refer specifically to the emotional significance of the valley-garden-mountain imagery which is wrought into the pattern of the story. . . . We perceive in terms of spatial contrasts the life of the body, down in the hot suffocating valley, challenged by the allurement of mountain heights. The contending opposites communicate a distinctive sense of the life of the earth in tension with the heaven of the spirit. The flux and heat of the soldier's sensuous experience—intoxicating and soporific—becomes at once a challenge and a bondage: a challenge because of the strange allurement of the mountain snows and a bondage or crucifixion because he cannot escape—or can escape only through death.

This theme—the conflict of the flesh and the spirit—is of course common to many of Lawrence's works, and the valley-mountain cluster with the same connotations can be found in such of his novels as **Women in Love** and **The Lost Girl,** in the poem **''Meeting in the Mountains,''** and in the first pages of his travel essays (with a valuable commentary), **Twilight in Italy.**

In the story the theme becomes more and more explicit after the fateful beating. The orderly feels that the snowy peaks, radiant in the sky, and the ''whity-green glacier river,'' in the valley below, seem almost supernatural, but at the same time he is going mad with fever and thirst. And near the end of the story, when he is in a delirium of fever, he sees "the mountains in a wonderlight, not far away and radiant. Behind the soft, grey ridge of the nearest range the further mountains stood golden and pale grey, the snow all radiant like pure, soft gold. . . . And like the golden, lustrous gleaming of the snow he felt his own thirst bright in him. And everything slid away." He remains in a state of delirium throughout the night, but in the morning, straight in front of him are the mountains: "He wanted them—he wanted them alone—he wanted to leave himself and be identified with them." And he does attain his realization—through death:

> There they ranked, all still and wonderful between earth and heaven. He stared till his eyes went black, and the mountains, as they stood in their beauty, so clean and cool, seemed to have it, that which was lost in him.

No one would suppose that the mythic, the psychological, and the image function separately, alternating perhaps from one level to the other like the negative and positive charges in a flow of electric current. One in fact *is* the other, and all operate more or less simultaneously while we follow the literal level. And we must never forget that the literal is there, for if it is not there, we have no story. It is important to note, however, that, regardless of levels of meaning, the distinctive characteristic is the flow and conflict of *opposites*: officer-soldier, aristocrat-peasant, evil-innocence, homosexual-heterosexual, mind-instinct, flesh-spirit, valley-mountain; and Freudians would see a father-son dichotomy. (pp. 229-31)

Lawrence has a special and unique contribution to offer in the art of the short story. I have not considered to any extent Lawrence's prose style, which serves its subject consummately. Rather I have dealt with his subject, the discovery under the social surface of more opulent realms of being.

For the effect of D. H. Lawrence's art, and it is also its value, is that it gives a new meaning to our experience. Lawrence's command of life, significant life, was such that we discover in his fiction a new content—an immediacy and relevance that was not previously perceived. An emotion with Lawrence is an apotheosis. Through its elemental and seminal processes of action it is a transition into another sphere of being, a *rite de passage*. And once having experienced this, a character is never quite the same. . . . Lawrence has captured this moment of transition, reinforced it with an emotionally charged symbol (chrysanthemums, valley-garden-mountain . . .), and perpetuated it on the printed page.

Lawrence commanded his art so completely as to suggest less discipline than it had. There is in him an uninterrupted communication between his thought and his senses. This deceptive ease of style has contributed to a myth concerning his method of composition: that he preferred not—as most authors do when dissatisfied with what they have written—to file, clip, insert, and transpose . . . , but rather to rewrite entire new drafts straight off the pen in new bursts of spontaneity and intuition. (pp. 233-34)

This method attributed to Lawrence, however, has served several critics as a point of departure in attacking his "looseness" and "diffuseness." No doubt—like all great artists—Lawrence's first conception of an idea was involuntary, a "vital fortuity"; and perhaps his *first* drafts were written in bursts of spontaneity. But his revisions were certainly voluntary and meticulous.

My interpretations would argue that few artists could be more consciously and pertinently preoccupied with problems of method, technique, and form. (p. 234)

*Frank Amon, "D. H. Lawrence and the Short Story," in* The Achievement of D. H. Lawrence, *edited by Frederick J. Hoffman and Harry T. Moore (copyright 1953 by the University of Oklahoma Press; copyright renewed © by Beatrice Moore), University of Oklahoma Press, 1953, pp. 222-34.*

**RONALD P. DRAPER**    (essay date 1964)

[*Draper's* D. H. Lawrence *examines all of Lawrence's major works, including novels, short stories, and poetry. A concluding chapter assesses Lawrence's literary reputation and his influence on the modern novel. The following excerpt is taken from a chapter dealing with Lawrence's early novels.*]

Lawrence's early novels, except for *The Trespasser,* are about his native area. He writes about what he knows well, and this is evident in the realism with which he describes people and places, especially in *Sons and Lovers.* But he is not content with this limited aim. His Romantic inheritance makes him also wish to transform the familiar—not to give it a falsely enchanted glamour, but, in Wordsworth's phrase, to throw over it "a certain colouring of imagination, whereby ordinary things should be presented to the mind in an unusual way." The effect can be summarized in this sentence from *The White Peacock:* "I looked down on the blackness where trees filled the quarry, and the valley bottoms, and it seemed that the world, my own home-world, was strange again." . . .

Because of Lawrence's experimenting with the combination of realism and romanticism, these early novels form a deeply interesting prelude to his most important novels, *The Rainbow* and *Women in Love,* but they are also of great interest in themselves. Indeed, where *Sons and Lovers* is concerned, it is unjust to allow the two later novels to obscure what is already a very fine achievement. *Sons and Lovers* is an autobiographical work, and this gives it the extraordinary inwardness which is its unique feature; but it is also a remarkable picture of English working-class life and Lawrence's first major study of personal relations.

Lawrence's first novel, *The White Peacock* . . . was described by Ford Madox Ford as "a rotten work of genius," and Lawrence himself was well aware of its faults. In a letter of April 15, 1908, he says:

> In the first place it is a novel of sentiment—may the devil fly away with it—what the critics would call, I believe, an 'erotic novel'—the devil damn the whole race black—, all about love—and rhapsodies on Spring scattered here and there—heroines galore—no plot—nine-tenths adjectives—every colour in the spectrum descanted upon—a poem or two—scraps of Latin and French—altogether a sloppy, spicy mess.

This letter refers to an early version, later revised. The published version is not such "a sloppy, spicy mess," but the weaknesses are still apparent. The "rhapsodies on Spring," and the nature descriptions generally, are lyrical excrescences, often beautiful in themselves and full of an intensely personal feeling for nonhuman life; but they are only loosely related to the novel as a whole.

The "scraps of Latin and French" are mostly used by the educated and socially superior characters. Their effect is pretentious, and this is not altogether accidental. Already *The White Peacock* anticipates, as it does so many other developments in Lawrence's work, the antipathy to "accursed human education" expressed in the poem **"Snake."** . . . If the theme of "accursed human education" forms a serious part of the novel's purpose, it is, one suspects, because the novelist himself is struggling with a tendency which he dislikes, but cannot wholly escape—nor, as yet, see clearly for what it is. As in the poetry which Lawrence writes at this time, there is evidence of a struggle going on between the literary pretensions of a highly self-conscious young man and the "demon" of the true artist. (pp. 30-1)

[Despite] its rawness and over-adolescent sensibility, *The White Peacock* makes a deep impression. It provides a mirror of English provincial life, and yet suggests that something far more penetrating is at work in the author's mind. From any point of view, it is a remarkable first novel.

The setting of Lawrence's second novel [*The Trespasser*] is the Isle of Wight and South London. These derive from his schoolmastering at Croydon and a holiday spent on the Isle of Wight in August, 1909. His friendship with Helen Corke, the Helena of the novel, is, however, the most important source. Helen Corke had undergone a disastrous emotional experience similar to that recorded in *The Trespasser*. . . . (pp. 33-4)

Lawrence began writing his novel in 1910, shortly after Helen Corke's actual experience occurred, but he rewrote it in 1912, feeling distaste for its "fluid, luscious quality," and making an effort at form. ("I hope the thing is knitted firm—I hate those pieces where the stitch is slack and loose.") These comments are very relevant to what the reader feels about the finished novel. There is an element of callowness in the book, by no means dominant, but reflecting perhaps the youthfulness of the earlier draft which Lawrence did not succeed in completely revising away. More positively to the credit of the book is its tightness of structure—the main action takes place within a week; the retrospective frame gives it a certain distance, without detracting from the immediacy of the love idyll; and the overflowing variety of description, incident, and character that is so marked in *The White Peacock* is kept very much more under control. Yet the "fluid, luscious quality" remains an inescapable weakness, and a serious one; for it is as an attempt to render erotic experience that at least half of *The Trespasser* must be judged. Lawrence is making his first real attempt to communicate through poetic prose the powerful, baffling, elusive emotions of sexual experience. He has to cut through the inhibitions imposed in 1912 on any attempt even to imagine seriously what such experience might be, and it is evident in the vagueness of certain passages that Lawrence is not yet so defiant of public taboos as he was to become. . . .

In *The Trespasser* Helena has an affair with a married man, Siegmund, which ends in the latter's suicide. They steal five days on the Isle of Wight away from the sordid complications of Siegmund's wife and children. It is here that the erotic interest of the novel arises. Helena "belonged to that class of 'dreaming women' with whom passion exhausts itself at the mouth." She loves Siegmund, but she cannot respond to his physical passion. (p. 34)

Siegmund is fairly well realized as a character, and this fact makes it possible to see that his failure is also due to weakness within himself. He lacks the toughness of mind necessary to suppress qualms and to make unpleasant decisions that must be carried through by strength of will. But the essential blow, given unwittingly by Helena, is the blow to his male self-respect. Their relationship is thus more destructive than creative. (p. 35)

In the train that takes the two lovers back to London, Siegmund begins to reckon the complications of his adultery; and, from the moment he reaches his home, the atmosphere is completely changed. The novel becomes a bitterly realistic treatment of the misery of a defecting husband, the coldly self-righteous anger of an injured wife, and the repercussions of their behavior upon the children.

The shock caused by this change in the novel must not be underestimated. Lawrence no doubt knew what he was doing. Intensely romantic a writer as he was, he was also, even in his very earliest work, not only a realist but also a sardonic antiromantic. He pitches his readers almost brutally from the idyllic world of the Isle of Wight into the grating realism of Siegmund's domestic life. This transfer does not, however, toughen the story in quite the way that Lawrence intended. Instead, it seals off the island experience as a cruelly temporary escape from reality. The imaginative devices that have already been discussed provide a connection between the two halves of the book, but not one that is strong enough to overcome the shock of the sudden and complete transition that takes place in Chapter 22. The extremely difficult problem of welding together romanticism and realism is left unsolved. . . .

*Sons and Lovers* begins with a fine historical and geographical sweep of the Nottinghamshire and Derbyshire coal field. The beginning also contains within it the criticism of industrialism which Lawrence was to develop so much more fully later. (p. 37)

The toughness of mind and the strength of will that are the driving force of industry are given less hostile treatment in *Sons and Lovers* than in the rest of Lawrence's novels. Mrs. Morel above all has these qualities; they are evident not only in her painfully prolonged resistance to death, but also in her heroic determination to resist the spiritually deadening effect of life in a mining community. Her unconscious tyranny over her sons, the primary theme of the novel and what makes it a tragedy, is perhaps to be connected with the evil influence of industrialism; but the grit which her life develops in her, and which she hands on to her son Paul, is also part of working-class life as Lawrence displays it in the Morel home. (pp. 38-9)

Lawrence said that *Sons and Lovers* would be "a novel—not a florid prose poem, or a decorated idyll running to seed in realism." In other words, it would avoid the faults of both *The White Peacock* and *The Trespasser.* One way in which it does this is by being solidly embedded in the working-class life that Lawrence thoroughly understood. He does not attempt this time to transpose his relatives and friends into a higher social class. They are as they were in real life. The result is an exceptionally vivid portrayal of the ordinary surface of working-class life in the English Midlands as it was near the beginning of the twentieth century. The first part of the novel breaks out again and again into little dramatically alert scenes of common life that remain in the memory as captured glimpses of an intense and intimate domestic existence highly charged with passionate feelings which those who share them could not normally articulate. This is the great difference between working-class and middle-class life. There are subtleties of relationship, though nothing like the subtleties of a cultured middle-class world; and they are unconscious pressures toward conformity that are possibly even stronger than those of the middle class. At the same time there is a large, crude mold into which all life is forced. (p. 41)

[There is] general refusal in *Sons and Lovers* to retreat from tough realities into attitudes of romantic escape. As already indicated, this is a great novel of naturalistically presented working-class life, "probably the only one written completely from the inside." The sordid and brutal features are accepted as well as the "life itself, warmth" that Paul claims is the heritage of "the common people."

Yet romance penetrates to the humblest details of this life—as in the Wordsworthian quality of the pot scene. In *The Trespasser* realism and romance had split the novel into two parts, but in *Sons and Lovers* they come much nearer to coalescing. At the very least, the novel moves between the two easily, without a jolting change of gear. (pp. 49-50)

[The] romantic element in *Sons and Lovers* has an intricate relationship with character, especially the character of Miriam. An extremely sensitive girl, she has been reduced by her mother's mistaken high-mindedness to a semineurotic condition; and, as the love affair between her and Paul develops, her terror of sex becomes a serious barrier between them (though one might also add that Paul's clumsiness and selfishness create an even greater block). There were, perhaps, didactic implications here for Lawrence about the rights of the body as against the spirit. (p. 51)

Perhaps most of all, the peculiar way in which [Miriam] responds to flowers communicates the quality of her romantic sensibility. This for example, is how she treats the daffodils at Willey Farm:

> Miriam went on her knees before one cluster, took a wild-looking daffodil between her hands, turned up its face of gold to her, and bowed down, caressing it with her mouth and cheeks and brow. . . .
>
> 'Aren't they magnificent?' she murmured.
>
> 'Magnificent! it's a bit thick—they're pretty!' . . .

Paul's rough answer emphasizes the author's detachment from this religious attitude. Though, as he is forced, often reluctantly, to admit, Miriam's sensibility stimulates him into brilliant conscious activity, he rejects her disembodied religious ecstasy in favor of a plainer, grittier determination. (p. 52)

It is clear how this difference of sensibility, and criticism of Miriam's sensibility, connects with the struggle in personal relations which is the major theme of the novel. Not only is Miriam defeated by Paul's mother, but she is to some extent crippled by her own romanticism. Like Helen's fancifulness in *The Trespasser*, this romanticism is something which is at odds with commonplace reality. Paul, and Lawrence through him, by no means rejects the romantic, but he needs to disentangle himself from Miriam's kind. The novel as a whole shows how a more vital romanticism is being developed, and one of the fine effects of the work is the balancing and contrasting of these two kinds. But there is no mere advocacy of the one and rejection of the other. They both form an integral part of the novel as a rich and complex reflection of life. Even the unreal is real in such a setting, for it is part of vital human experience. The finest achievement of *Sons and Lovers* is this

quickening truthfulness to actual life—"the shimmering protoplasm" which Paul tries to capture in his paintings, and which is "the real living." Without the romantic element it would simply be, to quote Paul again, "a dead crust." (pp. 52-3)

> *Ronald P. Draper, in his* D. H. Lawrence *(copyright © 1964 by Twayne Publishers, Inc.; reprinted with the permission of Twayne Publishers, a Division of G. K. Hall & Co., Boston), Twayne, 1964, 194 p.*

## SANDRA M. GILBERT (essay date 1972)

"In England people have got that loathsome superior knack of refusing to consider me a poet at all." D. H. Lawrence wrote to his friend A. W. McLeod in February, 1914. " 'Your prose is so good,' say the kind fools, 'that we are obliged to forgive you your poetry.' How I hate them." Now, over half a century later, though Lawrence's genius as a novelist is even more widely recognized than it was in 1914, his poetry has still received comparatively little attention. Somehow, the prose has always stood in the way. For one thing, it *is* "so good," and, for another, it more obviously falls into a clearly defined and widely accepted tradition. Thus most commentators treat the poetry as a merely interesting, if not embarrassing, by-product of the novel-making process. (pp. 1-2)

Yet Lawrence did, after all, begin his literary career as a poet, producing in his lifetime ten books of verse. . . . Lawrence's dual production certainly suggests that he himself must have made at least a pragmatic distinction between the two forms, a distinction which, if we can discover it, may not only illuminate his aesthetic theories but also aid in an appreciative understanding of his too often neglected poems in verse. (p. 3)

[Though Lawrence] had much to say about poetry and poetic theory, in letters, essays, and introductions, his most important attempt at a general definition of poetry occurs in the preface to Harry Crosby's *Chariot of the Sun,* which he wrote toward the end of his life. He began this essay by demolishing some of the vaguer, more conventional definitions of poetry. . . . "The essential quality of poetry," he asserts, introducing his crucial definition, "is that it makes a new effort of attention, and 'discovers' a new world within the known world." Poetry, in Lawrence's view, is visionary: "Man and the animals, and the flowers all live within a strange and forever surging chaos. The chaos which we have got used to we call a cosmos. The unspeakable inner chaos of which we are composed we call consciousness, and mind, and even civilization. But it is, ultimately, chaos, lit up by visions or not lit up by visions." And those visions are poems. (pp. 4-5)

Perhaps a major reason for the prolonged neglect of Lawrence's verse is that while his theory of the novel falls within a definable and acceptable tradition, his view of poetry was the exception rather than the rule in the earlier part of this century. He himself was well aware that as a poetic theorist he consistently opposed contemporary critical opinion and, to a lesser extent, prevailing poetic practice. For one thing, his view of a poem as a pure act of attention, an act of absolute surrender to the visionary image, was very much at odds with the emerging belief of critics—and of many influential poets—that the essential qualities of poetry are irony, ambiguity, and paradox. (p. 9)

While he never rejected irony, ambiguity, and paradox as literary techniques, he did not regard them as essential, especially not in poetry. For him, poetry, unlike the novel, did not involve elaborated relationships. On the contrary, he believed that its essence was single rather than double vision or, as he put it, "naiveté." For the act of attention was not only an act of intensity but, more important, an act of "the intrinsic naiveté without which no poetry can exist, not even the most sophisticated." . . . But Lawrence's advocacy of naiveté is more than a stand against the kind of double vision that was coming to seem to many poets and critics the essence of poetry. It becomes clear in the Crosby preface that he is directing his definition of poetry against what he considers false sophistication in verse. Such sophistication appears chiefly in a preoccupation with form rather than substance ("the fear of chaos is in their parade of forms and techniques") in empty traditionalism, and in foolish "flippancy" or irony. In all cases it is in Lawrence's view a sign of the poet's failure to submit himself with almost religious humility to the single demonic vision that should be the wellspring of poetry. (p. 10)

Lawrence's poet of naiveté, then, consciously choosing the path of visionary awareness, must be "sufficiently sophisticated to wring the neck of sophistication." He must be anti-formal and anti-traditional, as well as anti-ironic, not out of ignorance or literary incapacity—two faults of which Lawrence himself has often been accused—but because he deliberately chooses to go beyond or beneath technique to the naiveté at the heart of the artistic impulse. "Thought, I love thought," wrote Lawrence in one of his *Pansies,* perhaps replying to those critics who accused him of anti-intellectualism, but "not the jiggling and twisting of already existent ideas. / I despise that self-important game." "Thought"—and we may take poetry to be one of the highest forms of thought—should not be "a trick or an exercise or a set of dodges." It is, rather, "the welling up of unknown life into consciousness." Thus the effort of attention is finally not crassly anti-intellectual or boorishly irrational, but a sophisticated striving for innocence; and to be a poet, to be able to *attend,* is to be in a state of grace.

Such a poetic, though it contradicts much early twentieth-century aesthetic theory, is obviously Romantic in its origins, and Romantic in several ways. To begin with, Lawrence's advocacy of organic or anti-formal form can be traced back through Whitman and Ruskin to Coleridge. In repudiating the artifice of premeditated form, Lawrence recommends and, at his best, writes a kind of unpremeditated process poetry that discovers its form both in its content and in the process of its composition. . . . Moreover, in advising that the poet yield himself to the visionary process of attention, Lawrence clearly participates in the anti-traditional tradition of originality, spontaneity, and sincerity that was first fully articulated by Wordsworth in his Preface to *Lyrical Ballads,* and Lawrence's sense that the poet must be skillfully passive, like his belief in sophisticated innocence, recalls Wordsworth's advocacy of "wise passiveness." (pp. 11-12)

As a poetic theorist, then, Lawrence is a Romantic in modern dress; and he expresses his visionary Romanticism metaphorically as well as directly. In his **"Song of a Man Who Has Come Through,"** for instance, he makes use of the central Romantic metaphor for creativity, "the metaphor of the correspondent breeze." Like Shelley in the "Ode to the West Wind," Coleridge in "Dejection: An Ode" or Wordsworth in *The Prelude,* he longs to "yield" himself and be "borrowed / By the fine, fine wind that takes its course through the chaos of the world"; he longs, paradoxically, for the strength to be passive, to be "keen and hard like the sheer tip of a wedge / Driven by invisible blows." Only so, in the Romantic tradition, can he "come at the wonder," at the visionary guardians of creative renewal within his own soul.

But even in his use of this Romantic metaphor Lawrence was violating what we might call the ordinary usage of modern English poetry, for to many of the British and American poets who were his contemporaries the wind had become a symbol of futility rather than of creative vitality. (p. 13)

[In studying Lawrence's poetry we] see that, like most poet-novelists, he went through phases of greater or lesser interest in the different forms in which he worked. When he was in what we might call a fictional phase, his poetry frequently suffered as much from a blurring of distinctions, a failure to bear in mind his own definition of lyric poetry, as from anything else. When his interest in writing novels waned temporarily, as it did around 1920, his poetry gained in intensity and distinction, as though all his creative energy had flowed for the time being into this other channel. In short, while many of his weaker poems do usurp prose ideas and consequently have formal as well as substantial problems, his best poems deal with matters which, according to his own definition, are the special province of poetry. At his best, then, Lawrence is not a poet in prose but a poet in "poetry," for in his best poems, to quote [Vivian de Sola] Pinto, he "said something . . . that he could never have said in prose." (p. 15)

*Sandra M. Gilbert, in her* Acts of Attention: The Poems of D. H. Lawrence *(copyright © 1972 by Cornell University; used by permission of the publisher, Cornell University Press), Cornell University Press, 1972, 327 p.*

## SCOTT SANDERS   (essay date 1973)

In his essay of 1914 on "The New Novel" Henry James complained that contemporary practitioners of the art of fiction—among them the Lawrence of *Sons and Lovers*—had become obsessed with the depiction of environment and the notation of consciousness, to the neglect of those virtues of selection, emphasis and design which characterized the works of Austen, Dickens, Trollope, Thackeray, and, implicitly, James himself. These new novels by Wells, Bennett and Lawrence seemed to James fairly saturated with naturalistic details, without any discrimination, without any overall imaginative control, as if they had been transcribed from experience rather than composed. Amidst such jumble, James further complained, the critic looks in vain for a centre of interest or a sense of the whole. . . . [This criticism points] to an important difference between the novel form as handled by Austen, Eliot, Thackeray and James, and the novel form as develped by the author of *Sons and Lovers.*

In his rendering of the formation of Paul Morel within the concentric circles of family, colliery village and industrial Midlands, Lawrence followed the best nineteenth century realist tradition of representing the development of consciousness and affection within a particular social context, at a particular time. Where he differs from his predecessors, however—even from Emily Brontë, Dickens and Hardy whom he most nearly resembles in this respect—is in the degree to which he treats that social context as alien, as something neither created nor sustained nor comprehended by those who are forced to live within it, something imposed from without upon the Bestwood community, upon the Morel family and upon young Paul. The world of *Sons and Lovers* seems *given,* to the novelist as to the protagonist. (pp. 206-07)

[The] ties between environment and psyche are indeed closer than Lawrence was at that time prepared to acknowledge. The activities and pressures of Bestwood life are not some pictur-esque backdrop for the human drama, but rather form the sub-stance of that drama itself, they mold personal relations and direct the growth of character. The shaping and connecting role of social forces is everywhere implicit in *Sons and Lovers,* demonstrating an historical awareness which rivals that of Dickens and George Eliot. Like those Victorian critics of so-ciety, Lawrence underwent a social dislocation which made him sensitive to the determining influences of education, wealth, class position and sexual roles. Yet because, to his mind, he had escaped the confines of Eastwood, he tended to overesti-mate the power of the individual to struggle free of community. In other words his awareness of the determining influence of social forces was accompanied by an exaggerated appraisal of individual freedom. Hence the contradiction one often en-counters in Lawrence's fiction: a character who appears en-meshed in society on one level of the novel may appear on another as a free agent. Man is governed by culture: man is freed by nature. . . .

[The] given-ness of the fictional world in *Sons and Lovers* may be accounted for in part as a sign of his temperamental anti-formalism. But this anti-formalism, which has annoyed many critics besides James, was only one expression of Lawrence's general suspicion of reason. (p. 207)

The earlier Victorian novelists presented both community and individual as knowable, either by the narrator, as in Scott, or by a central observer, as in Austen; and the same novelists treated the social order, however imperfect, as the product of human reason and desire. The fictional world appears pro-gressively less rational and intelligible after 1848, particularly in the later works of Dickens, Eliot and Hardy, and in Gissing and Conrad. Lawrence reproduces this century-long evolution within the space of his own career. He starts from the earlier position in *The White Peacock,* assuming intelligibility; but already in *Sons and Lovers* he is uncovering wild zones within the self and inhuman zones within society; and by the writing of *Women in Love* he is depicting contemporary society as so irrational and destructive, so utterly alien to all human reason or desire, that it must be escaped altogether if the individual— who is himself already unstable—is to survive. Just as *The Rainbow* continues and develops the work of George Eliot, so *Women in Love* extends the work of Hardy, taking up the moral issues where they were left tangled at the end of *Jude the Obscure.* Although in that novel Hardy several times blames the suffering of Jude Fawley and Sue Bridehead upon indif-ferent nature, the deeper implication of their story—as Law-rence pointed out in his analysis of the novel and as Hardy certainly intended—is that the social code itself is at fault. . . . What was implicit in *Jude the Obscure* becomes explicit in *Women in Love.* Birkin and Ursula pursue their passion in solitude; sex becomes a region which they inhabit instead of society. Their fulfillment is to be sought no longer through activity in the world, but through more and more private, in-tense physical experience. Hence Birkin's assumption that the first step towards ''completeness of being'' was to drop all social responsibilities and quit his school inspector's job. There is nothing whatsoever triumphant about this alienation in Law-rence's work, nothing of the defiant exile we have come to expect as a stock feature of twentieth century literature; rather there is a deep sense of loss, not simply of the knowable community, but of the inhabitable community.

Adrift, the isolate self, like Ursula alone in the horse pasture at the close of *The Rainbow,* is subject to incomprehensible influences from within and from without. So far as Lawrence can see, there is no longer any ''cultivated field'' of human activity which will guarantee an authentic existence, no longer any settled community in which the self can discover its iden-tity, no longer any agreed code by which the self can gauge its conduct. Thus he cannot provide that sense of the whole which James desired, that impression of a range of life wholly encompassed within the artist's organizing vision, for Law-rence's subject stretches obstinately beyond his ken; outward, into the destructive realm of social forces, and beyond that to the enveloping process of nature; inward, into the irrational recesses of the self, where the divine life impulse stirs with unpredictable motions. There is no still centre from which this can all be measured, no circumference within which it can all be contained.

The indeterminacy of character and of community are clearly inter-related: if the individual is subject to irrational influences, then society, multiplying this effect a thousandfold, may act irrationally on a vast scale, as in the First World War; on the other hand, if community disintegrates, as it does in the tran-sition from Marsh Farm to industrial Wiggiston in *The Rain-bow,* then character must also fragment. This is the meaning of Lawrence's celebrated warning, with reference to early drafts of *The Rainbow,* that ''You mustn't look in my novel for the old stable *ego*—of the character.'' The stable ego is product of a coherent society, and the unstable ego of an incoherent society. Beginning with the wartime novels, Lawrence no longer presents character as a developing psychic continuity, but rather as a variable, discontinuous, unpredictable manifestation, al-most a form of energy. The demands such a reconception of character made upon language were extreme, particularly no-ticeable in *Women in Love.*

In conscious opposition to his nineteenth-century predecessors, Lawrence was unwilling or unable ''to conceive a character in a certain moral scheme and make him consistent.'' The impres-sion of self-sufficiency and solidity created by *Emma, David Copperfield, Middlemarch* or *The Portrait of a Lady* depends in large part upon the assumption of a shared moral scheme linking narrator and audience, and upon the futher assumption that the fictional world is essentially knowable. Lawrence could no longer make those assumptions, for the inherited moral schemes seemed to him bankrupt, while life itself seemed too vast and mysterious for reason to comprehend. Victorian novels could generally get by without God, without seriously invoking any superhuman order, because the social code itself seemed adequate for defining personal relationships and for assessing individual lives. Specific faults within society were of course denounced, notably by Dickens; but they were denounced through appeal to a set of assumptions, a scale of values, which the writer held in common with his audience. Whereas the Vic-torian novelist typically spoke with the moral force of the first person plural, Lawrence speaks in the first person singular. As J. Hillis Miller has argued in *The Form of Victorian Fiction,* the narrator of Dickens, Eliot, Thackeray or Hardy plays the role of a generalized social consciousness, speaking for the whole community. Lawrence more nearly appears to speak *against* the community, from the solitary prominence of his own conscience.

His abandonment of the stable, coherent, knowable character of Victorian fiction coincided with economic and social de-velopments which during his lifetime were undermining that cornerstone of bourgeois ideology—the autonomous individ-ual, who was theoretically free to pursue his own ends and who therefore bore the responsibility for his own destiny. Throughout the nineteenth century, as commodity relations—the buying and selling of products on the market—displaced other forms of human intercourse, as the power of financiers, governors, industrialists and bureaucrats grew, society increasingly thwarted the free development of the individual. . . . Lawrence's unstable, frustrated characters, prey to irrational impulses and thwarted by society, clearly reflect these vast, gradual changes in the real world. Like every great inventive artist, he developed new literary forms to express a changed historical content. (pp. 208-11)

[For Lawrence] the problems of character and community [were] so acute, that he had to devise what was practically a new language in order to express his altered conception of man, and he had to radically modify the novel form in order to express his altered perception of society. *Sons and Lovers* still follows the pattern of much nineteenth century fiction: a child grows to young manhood within the context of family life, in organic relation to a richly evoked community; his personal relationships and his psychological development are inextricably woven out of that common life, even when he is in conscious opposition to his surroundings. *The Rainbow* begins on very much the same pattern, but over the course of three generations personal relations are progressively isolated from community. This development is then carried to its extreme in *Women in Love,* where four individuals appear as atomic units, fully developed at the opening of action, independent of family, cut off from all social involvement (with the partial exception of Gerald, whose involvement is wholly predatory). Problems of meaning, value and relationship have been *abstracted* from the social context, and the offered solutions, such as they are, appear in almost algebraic form. Birkin's ultra-individualistic love-ethic seems to be a last desperate attempt to salvage the self in face of a uniformly destructive society, and to defend the self against all claims, either personal or communal.

In the early novel, identity was still to be found in community; in the later it was to be found, if at all, in isolation. This change of perspective is graphically displayed in *The Lost Girl.* The first half of that novel, written before the War, represents the petit-bourgeois upbringing of Alvina Houghton within a shopkeeper's home in a Midlands mining town, all of it rendered with Dickensian gusto and concreteness; the second half of the novel, written after the War, dispenses with family and community, and drives the heroine (in dubious partnership with a vaudeville performer) to the desolate, remote and defiantly inhuman wastes of a mountain settlement in southern Italy; at the end Alvina is cut off even from her improbable husband, who is called away to battle. The difference between the first and second halves of *The Lost Girl,* like the difference between the first and third versions of *Lady Chatterley's Lover,* like the difference between *Sons and Lovers* and *Women in Love,* is a measure of Lawrence's disillusionment with the available forms of community. (pp. 211-12)

Stronger than [Lawrence's] inclination to reject society as irredeemably corrupt and corrupting, was his belief in man's capacity to conceive and create a more humane social order. His fictions and essays continually pose the question, "What is the underlying impulse in us that will provide the motive power for a new state of things . . .?"

In agreement with Blake, indeed with all revolutionary thinkers, Lawrence maintained that the impulse is *there,* inherent in man. Like Blake in particular he identified that impulse with Eros, the creative force which prevailing social forms had per-

verted to acquisitive or destructive ends. Individually, this meant the repression of spontaneous desire. Socially, it meant the repression of particular classes. . . . Lawrence insists upon the connection between repression on the personal and on the social level. He was convinced by direct experience that an entire class had been repressed, a class represented by the industrial communities of Bestwood in *Sons and Lovers,* Wiggiston in *The Rainbow,* Beldover in *Women in Love,* and Tevershall in *Lady Chatterley's Lover.* He showed that the power to shape these communities had passed from the people themselves, and had been alienated to landowners, industrial magnates, planners, engineers and politicians. This identification between the cause of the id and the cause of the working people gave to Lawrence's protests a force and significance that has not been surpassed in the work of any other modern writer. By comparison the social views of Proust, Joyce, Eliot, Mann and even Gide seem the expression of a narrower class interest, a more private frustration. Although Lawrence offered no program for the recovery of that alienated power which had been lost from the enslaved body and from the laboring community, he continually witnessed, both in the activity of his own mind and in the vitality of his characters, to the creative energy potential in all men. (pp. 214-15)

> *Scott Sanders, in his* D. H. Lawrence: The World of the Major Novels *(© 1973 by Scott Sanders; reprinted by permission of Viking Penguin Inc.; in Canada by Vision Press Ltd.),* Vision, *1973 (and reprinted by Viking Press, 1974), 224 p.*

## JOSEPH C. VOELKER (essay date 1979)

[*In the first major study of utopianism in Lawrence's novels since Eugene Goodheart's 1963 study,* The Utopian Vision of D. H. Lawrence, *Voelker finds that* Lady Chatterley's Lover *exhibits the "motifs and structural devices of the ironic utopian tradition of Plato, More, Rabelais, and Swift."*]

D. H. Lawrence's critics have frequently observed a strain of utopianism in his thought. Their tendency, however, has been to perceive that utopianism as "oppositional" rather than "ironic," a program for social reform rather than an alternative world poetically conceived. Evidence, gathered equally and without distinction from his novels, travel books, and social writings, indicates that Lawrence, as a social philosopher, held a vision of an ideal community which he strove to actualize on earth. (p. 223)

[It] is not immediately apparent that *Lady Chatterley's Lover* is a classical utopia, nor do we place it next to *The Republic* or *Gulliver's Travels* in our acts of mental shelving. Perhaps the reason lies in this: there is a kind of permanence in the ironic utopian perspective, but the rhetorical posturings of its individual practitioners are subject to the changes of history. The classical perspective operates in *Lady Chatterley's Lover,* but in a new manner. The watershed between Lawrence's utopia and its forebears is the Romantic movement. From Shelley to Norman Mailer, political poetry has replaced Erasmian equivocation with advertisements for the self. To uncover Lawrence's irony, one must turn his famous dictum concerning "art-speech" upon its author. The modern posture of the political artist is one of loud unconstraint. But the truth, despite authorial opinion, is the province of the imagination:

> Art-speech is the only truth. An artist is usually a damned liar, but his art, if it be art, will tell you the truth of his day. And that is all that

matters. Away with eternal truth. Truth lives
from day to day, and marvelous Plato of yesterday is chiefly bosh today.

In short, the reader must consider the poetic structure of *Lady Chatterley's Lover*—its vision of two antithetical worlds—alongside Lawrence's shrill expostulations. No doubt he meant every word of them, but, they do not constitute the center of his artistic/political apprehension. It is possible to find in the novel a genuine imaginative balance, in spite of the fact that the book's most rabid passages (unlike those in Swift or More) are attributable to the author himself. Irony is no longer dramatic—the discrepancy between Mellors' opinions and Lawrence's. It is topographical—the symbolic distance between Wragby Hall and Wragby wood.

Only the third version of *Lady Chatterley's Lover* finds its structure and significance in a consistent exploitation of a symbolic topography. The two earlier drafts record Lawrence's attempts to postulate a vital life in the face of his own vivid and honest apprehension of the reality of class warfare in modern industrial England. Rather than entertain an alternative vision, the first two versions portray futility. They are tentative and realist (or naturalist) in attitude, and, despite brilliantly rendered scenes and trenchant social criticism, both bog down in their own awareness of "circumstance." While their concerns are occasionally (and in a broad sense) utopian, neither *The First Lady Chatterley* nor *John Thomas and Lady Jane* is a utopia. In the third draft, Lawrence got free of the quagmire of circumstance. Most important among his final revisions is his abandonment of the noble, inarticulate, physically and psychically battered Parkin for the quasi-divine prophet Mellors. Parkin could occupy and comprehend only one world; Mellors' knowledge of two is the key to their structural opposition in the novel. A result of this central alteration is that numerous utopian elements that had an inchoate presence in the first and second drafts come into sharp focus in the third. (pp. 224-25)

The novel opens on an anti-Platonic note. Young Constance and Hilda Reid toured the continent in search of education and soon found themselves "not the least daunted by art or ideal politics." Their attendance at socialist meetings gave them an education at once superficial and misdirected. The means to truth for Glaucon and John Clement has become, in the twentieth century, a deadly cerebralism. Philosophical eros has degenerated into an evasion of the vital centers of consciousness. For Connie and Hilda, "it was the talk that mattered supremely: the impassioned interchange of talk. Love was only a minor accompaniment." . . . Lawrence identifies the novel's first delusory utopia specifically: "The paradisal promise: thou shalt have young men to talk to." . . . Genuine education constitutes the central theme of the novel. But for Lawrence, it is the Platonic progression in reverse, a radical movement away from dialogue.

The meretriciousness of Connie's verbal love affairs on the continent characterizes the scenes of pseudo-philosophical dialogue at Wragby Hall as well, and there, utopian topics abound. At one conversation, a woman indulges in futuristic speculation—her daydream of a society in which sex will have become obsolete and babies will be bred in test tubes. . . . [Aldous] Huxley's dystopia may or may not have benefited from Lawrence, but there is a clear anticipation of the theology of *Brave New World* in Connie's exasperated response to her husband's intellectual arrogance as he puffs along in his motorized wheelchair. . . . (pp. 226-27)

Not all of Lawrence's utopian borrowings are set into the dialogues at Wragby. If the conversations in *Lady Chatterley's Lover* anticipate the witty horrors of Huxley, Connie's private meditations on Tevershall and Stack's Gate approach the fantastic dystopian visions of Lawrence's contemporary, H. G. Wells. (p. 227)

Numerous other topical borrowings from utopian literature are to be found in *Lady Chatterley's Lover;* however, they demand more thorough analysis in terms of the book's structure. There is Mellors' Rabelaisian community, with red clothing, dormitories, and Epicureanism. There is a recurrent use of medieval motifs, indicating Lawrence's sympathy with such medieval-revivalist utopias as [William] Morris's *News From Nowhere* with its recommendations of decentralization and a craft economy. Finally, there are echoes of the Alice books of Lewis Carroll, which exploit mirror-metaphysics and satirize social rigidity and repression.

*Lady Chatterley's Lover* inverts the classical utopia as defined by Plato and More. The traditional elements of dialogue, mirror-geography, education, and play have been turned upside down. For instance, the ironic use of mirrors (Socrates' Republic looks suspiciously like barbarous Sparta; Utopia has the dimensions, cities, and waterways of England) remains, but its impact is reversed. Instead of locating perfection in an "ideal" setting, a cerebral nowhere the reality of which is purely linguistic, Lawrence places it in a clearing in a remnant of Sherwood Forest. He evokes the clearing sensuously: it is a physically and historically actual place at England's center. Conversely, the corrupt "here" of the book, corresponding to Socrates' Athens and Hythlodaeus' portrait of England, is Wragby Hall. The house is a metonymy for modern England in its passional emptiness and worship of material wealth. It is characterized in terms of blankness, boredom, and vacuity. Materialism has fulfilled itself in an imaginative *topos* wherein the identifying factor is an absence of phenomena. (pp. 228-29)

[The Chatterley's world] is an artificial paradise, anticipated in the hookah dreams of Baudelaire and Poe and the cerebral, game-based fantasies of Lewis Carroll. Described as a metaphysical void, it is stuffed with the paraphernalia of non-being: behavior ritualized into futile games, suffocating physical comfort without joy, and interminable talk. Connie Chatterley's route, however, is directly antithetical to that of Carroll's Alice. She finds herself trapped and bored in a looking-glass world and journeys into immediate biological experience. . . .

A product of leisure-class education, Connie is the victim of defunct Platonism, or "image-consciousness." Her world is governed by a weird, self-critical reflectiveness. At Wragby Hall, Tommy Dukes carries the practice to a point of infinite regression by criticizing himself and the group for their self-criticism. His speech allows Lawrence to attack the Platonic epistemology, wherein education is a measurement of self in the mirror of perfection, attained by participating in a game Lawrence derisively entitles "the life of the mind." (p. 229)

Wragby Hall, then, is an anti-utopia, a satirically exaggerated fantasy portrait of modern England. Its antithesis is the world of Oliver Mellors, the "gamekeeper." For Lawrence there are good games as well. They are spontaneously inventive, erotic, and unruled. They bring to their participants a deep awareness of the uniqueness of the moment in which they occur. Existence, rightly perceived, is a cosmic game, played, for instance, by the newly hatched chick Connie finds at Mellors' coop. (p. 233)

Since the erotic utopia of Connie and Mellors is based in the real, their language is an actual spoken variant of English, not an intellectual fabrication. It is richly physical and free of adulteration by the self-criticizing faculty. Striclty speaking, though, it is not Midlands dialect that they speak, for, while dialect can express brutality as easily as tenderness, the language of Connie and Mellors is a gentle, fancifully ribald argot, filled with sensual awakening and characterized by spontaneous, unruled play. One might better call it "Rabelaisian." Lawrence said that Rabelais, like other erotic writers of the Renaissance, was not obscene; he did not offer "insult to the human body." He asserted that Rabelais had a startling, warming effect upon the consciousness, and he strove to synthesize a language for *Lady Chatterley's Lover* that would imitate Rabelais' effect and awaken the reader's passionate nature.

Rabelaisianism in the talk of Connie and Mellors resides, for the most part, in the fanciful naming of their sexual organs and in their comic personification as John Thomas and Lady Jane, Sir Mortar and Lady Pestle. The personification, both in its attribution of an autonomous will to the sexual organs and its exploitation of folk motifs, is Rabelaisian (the medieval flavor of the names stems from Lawrence's desire to link utopia with the "old England"). . . . At its center, *Lady Chatterley's Lover* re-enacts Lawrence's most crucial artistic decision. It moves from pseudo-philosophical verbiage to a kind of language which the common reader will inevitably condemn as obscene. In Wragby Wood "Rabelaisian" is a nearly perfect tongue; it is alive and of the body. But in the publishing world of England and America in the late 1920s, Lawrence's "Rabelaisian" was everyone else's "pornographic." (The fact that it is *legal now* does not mean it is understood.) Lawrence's situation is peculiarly modern. His attack upon what Susan Sontag calls "secular-historical" self-consciousness took the form of an aggressive stance toward his reader, a use of language deliberately designed to offend its audience rather than participate in its "talk." Besides its modernity, however, Lawrence's response to his plight reduplicates that of the classical writer. By definition, his reader is a loyal citizen of an alien and barbarous country. Authorship is an act of diplomacy, but its goal is to maximize strain.

Rabelais provides more than the utopian language of *Lady Chatterley's Lover.* Mellors' dream of a regenerated England owes its "Land of Cockayne" quality to Rabelais' Abbé de Thélème. Mellors' ideal society contains a number of traditional utopian elements. Like Thélème and More's Utopia, it is dedicated to pleasure. Its citizens are spontaneous in their behavior, and there is an absence of arbitrary convention and provision for unruled play. It borrows directly from Rabelais in the vision of collective housing and the wearing of red (Lawrence dresses the men in red, Rabelais the women) to symbolize physical pride. (pp. 236-38)

Lawrence performed severe alterations on the utopian format. Most significantly, he wrote a novel and not a dialogue in order that he might locate his ironic mirrors in lived experience. His irony resides in the measurable difference between the quality of life at Wragby Hall and in the wood. He would have his reader perform that measurement on his pulse, not in a syllogism. Irony is less a part of the verbal artifice of the novel than of the texture of its spatial imaginings. It is only by means of such power that Lawrence maintained his fervent dream across a lifetime of disappointment in the human capacity for community. (p. 239)

*Joseph C. Voelker, "The Spirit of No-Place: Elements of the Classical Ironic Utopia in D. H. Law-*

*rence's 'Lady Chatterley's Lover',"* in Modern Fiction Studies (© *1979 by Purdue Research Foundation, West Lafayette, Indiana 47907, U.S.A.), Vol. 25, No. 2, Summer, 1979, pp. 223-39.*

## JEROME BUMP (essay date 1982)

The poetry of nature is no longer as popular as it once was, but it remains an invaluable index to the spirit of our age, especially our response to the age-old dialectics of man and nature, objectivity and subjectivity, intellect and emotion, fact and fiction, prose and poetry, the sciences and the humanities. Besides taking up traditional conundrums such as the status of external reality and the functions of metaphor, literature, and literary criticism, the nature poetry of Wallace Stevens and D. H. Lawrence, for instance, asks us to determine the significance of the shift in the humanities from the traditional values of "humane letters" to the imitation of science's apparent objectivity, abstraction, and rationality. Their lyrics also suggest the origins of our new environmental ethic and of the increasing dominance of ennui in the humanities, that is, the infatuation of much of modern literature and criticism with solipsism, decreation, nihilism, and death. (p. 44)

The narrator of *Lady Chatterly's Lover,* one of the most un-Victorian works of this century, speaks of novels, but his remarks apply to all of literature and literary criticism: "It is the way our sympathy flows and recoils that really determines our lives. And here lies the vast importance of the novel, properly handled. It can inform and lead into new places the flow of our sympathetic consciousness, and it can lead our sympathy away in recoil from things gone dead. . . . But the novel . . . can also excite spurious sympathies and recoils, mechanical and deadening to the psyche; the novel can glorify the most corrupt feelings. . . . Then the novel . . . becomes at last vicious and . . . all the more vicious because it is always ostensibly on the side of the angels." The essential argument is that literature and literary criticism are better when they lead us away from what is "mechanical and deadening," when they serve the forces of life rather than death, of Eros rather than of Thanatos.

What this means in practice may be seen in Lawrence's own nature poetry. It is no doubt ironic to turn to British poetry for an example of true intimacy with nature. Previously, the British were supposedly the overly civilized ones, and we Americans were closer to nature. Compare Frost and Yeats, for instance. Now, despite or perhaps because of our vast stretches of untamed wilderness, it could be argued that we are the ones trying most desperately to escape from nature, especially in such mushrooming growths of ultramodern steel and glass as Houston and Dallas. Lawrence stands out as the one prophet who most effectively opposed this attempt to escape from nature in our century.

"Lawrence's rank as a poet is still unsettled," [Robert Langbaum observes in his *The Modern Spirit*]. "But Lawrence had the genius to see the way things were tending and, in his animal poems, sets the style for the new nature poetry." (p. 54)

Ruskin defined poetry of the first order as poetry in which "the intellect also rises, till it is strong enough to assert its rule against, or together with, the utmost efforts of the passions.". . . [In his poem **"Fish"**], Lawrence does communicate the utmost effort of his passion to love all animals, even a creature as alien as a fish. Keats had said, "If a Sparrow comes before my Window, I take part in its existence and pick about the Gravel.'' Lawrence extrapolates this concept of the sympathetic imagination, generated by eighteenth-century ethics and developed in the Victorian novel, and extends it to other living creatures. The result is the suggestion of a modern environmental ethic in his description of catching the fish, as well as in poems such as **"Snake"** and **"Mountain Lion":** ''And my heart accused itself, / Thinking: *I am not the measure of creation*.'' In this new approach to nature the aim is to love the fish for its own sake rather than for what it can do for us. . . . Despite the rejection of the pathetic fallacy, parallels with man are developed at length, including fear, *joie de vivre*, the desires for sex and food, and in conclusion the fish is compared explicitly to one particular man, Jesus.

Moreover, while in **"Fish"** we feel Lawrence's intellect ''asserting its rule against'' his desire to love even a fish, in his other animal poems we experience his intellect ''together with'' the utmost efforts of his passions. **"Fish"** is an anomaly for Lawrence. He is able to identify more fully with virtually all other creatures, even a bat (**"Man and Bat"**) and any number of tortoises. The personifications in his tortoise poems especially illustrate Ruskin's assertion that ''if we think over our favourite poetry, we shall find it full of this kind of fallacy, and that we like it all the more for being so.'' ''Pathetic fallacies'' do seem to be quite effective in Lawrence's tortoise poems, as when he describes the tortoise with the symmetrical design on its shell as ''The first little mathematical gentleman / Stepping, wee mite, in his loose trousers'' (**"Baby Tortoise"**), or the ''arrogance'' of the tortoise in **"Tortoise Family Connections,"** or the male tortoise making ''an intolerable fool of himself'' before the sardonic female in **"Lui et Elle,"** or the ''gallant'' little ''gentleman'' in **"Tortoise Gallantry."** (pp. 55-6)

Lawrence's most famous animal poem is about another reptile, **"Snake."** Again, Lawrence is aware of the fundamental difference, the active antagonism even, between man and nature, in this case between himself and a poisonous snake. Yet, by trying to love rather than hate, by extending his sympathetic imagination or ''blood consciousness,'' he becomes aware of the ultimate bond between himself and the snake: their membership in something that dwarfs their differences, namely the communion of all living beings. He knows that intuition of this ancient wellspring of unity can help him save himself, help him get in tune with the nature within him as well as without. Lawrence's approach to the snake, treating it as if it were an equal, another personal presence, a ''Someone'' who had stopped and ''mused a moment'' in his presence, is thus not a sign of ignorance, some kind of pathetic fallacy, but an indication of his love and respect for this creature, ''one of the lords of life,'' a ''king of the underworld.'' After he threw the log at the snake he immediately regretted it. . . . (p. 57)

[**"The Wild Common"** is] a more convincing expression of what Lawrence was trying to say in the scene in *Women in Love* where Birkin leaves Hermione to run naked through the plants on the hillside. . . . Lawrence is not afraid of confronting the void in this poem: ''What if the gorse-flowers shrivelled, and I were gone? / What if the waters ceased, where were the marigolds then, and the gudgeon?'' Yet instead of nothingness, Lawrence emphasizes the glorious substance of all of creation, including himself, in the ''here'' and ''now.'' Their triumph over the ages is the victory of life itself, of themselves, over the world of shadows. . . .

Lawrence seems to glory in the pathetic fallacy. The ''screamings'' of the peewits ''proclaim'' that they are ''exultant.''

The turf that the rabbits have bitten down to the quick is ''mournful.'' The ''common flaunts bravely.'' And ''the lazy streamlet pushes / His bent course mildly; here wakes again, leaps, laughs, and gushes.'' Lawrence's God is ''substantially here'' and thus for him ''the wilful fountain sings,'' to use Ruskin's term. (p. 58)

Admittedly, few readers will accept the notion that the willful fountain ''sings'' in Lawrence's poetry. . . . ''Lawrence's rank as a poet is still unsettled,'' as Langbaum tactfully puts it. T. S. Eliot, R. P. Blackmur, D. S. Savage, and others have stated bluntly that much of Lawrence's poetry is so deficient in rhythm, rhyme, and music generally that it is not poetry at all, merely prose. . . . Yet I think it is important to realize that we are brought closer to nature by Lawrence's music as well as his metaphors, his parallelism in sound as well as in thought.

Blackmur's complaint that Lawrence was incompetent in the ''ordering of words in component rhythms'' is belied by the first poem in Lawrence's *Collected Poems*, **"The Wild Common."** Lawrence could adapt the traditional rhythms of English poetry if he chose as in his trochaic ''There the lazy streamlet pushes'' and ''Little jets of sunlight texture imitating flame,'' and he could sing in sprung rhythms—''The quick sparks on the gorse-bushes are leaping''—but he was best in the larger phrasal rhythms he developed in his fiction. The rhythm of word and phrase repetition is obvious in the first and fifth stanzas and there is often a medial caesura in his lines, after which the second half seems to repeat the rhythm of the first. . . . The unity of nature is conveyed in the sounds of the syllables as well as in their rhythms, moreover. (pp. 59-60)

Most of the criticism is focused on Lawrence's later poetry, however. Hence it is more significant that the music of creation is heard still more clearly in the later poem, **"Snake."** Again, Lawrence's mastery of the traditional falling rhythm of English poetry is evident, in the ending, ''And depart, peaceful, pacified, and thankless,'' for instance. (p. 60)

[Lawrence used consonance] to organize and unify his poem as a whole. His early alliteration in **"Snake,"** for instance, of the sound ''s,'' the characteristic sound of a snake, prepares us for the description of the snake's drinking: ''He sipped with his straight mouth, / Softly drunk through his straight gums, into his slack long body / Silently.'' Onomatopeia is implied not only by the ''s'' alliteration (though here the snake is silent) but also by the line itself stretching out to describe the snake's long body. ''F'' alliteration also returns as a refrain in the coda to this drinking episode, itself integrated by ''dr'' alliteration: ''He drank enough / And lifted his head, dreamily, as one who has drunken, / And flickered his tongue like a forked night on the air, so black.'' ''H'' alliteration then unifies the representation of the speaker's horror as the snake returns to the underworld.

These and other musical patterns are obviously not as pervasive in Lawrence's poetry as they are in Hopkins' or Tennyson's, but if the Romantics revived the traditional belief that harmonious word-music, *musica humana*, can make us receptive to the *musica mundana*, the music of our world, it is sign of hope for nature poetry in our century that both kinds of music can still be heard, even in Lawrence's poems, considered by many to be all too characteristic of the dissonance of our age. (p. 61)

*Jerome Bump, ''Stevens and Lawrence: The Poetry of Nature and the Spirit of the Age'' (copyright, 1982,* by Jerome Bump), in The Southern Review, *Vol. 18, No. 1*, January, 1982, pp. 44-61.*

---

## ADDITIONAL BIBLIOGRAPHY

Aldington, Richard. *D. H. Lawrence: Portrait of a Genius, But. . . .* New York: Duell, Sloan and Pearce, 1950, 432 p.
  Standard biography of Lawrence. The critic frequently employs passages from Lawrence's works to illustrate a biographical point.

Bertocci, Angelo P. "Symbolism in *Women in Love*." In *Modern British Fiction*, edited by Mark Schorer, pp. 267-84. New York: Oxford University Press, 1961.
  Views *Women in Love* as a work originating "in religious vision, as any drastic proposal for destruction and re-creation . . . is the translation of religious vision into action."

Cornwell, Ethel F. "The Sex Mysticism of D. H. Lawrence." In her *The "Still Point": Themes and Variations in the Writings of T. S. Eliot, Coleridge, Yeats, Henry James, Virginia Woolf, and D. H. Lawrence*, pp. 208-41. New Brunswick, N.J.: Rutgers University Press, 1962.
  Analyses Lawrence's belief, as put forth in some of his novels and nonfiction works, in the need to "expand emotional consciousness" and attain "totality of consciousness" through perfect physical union.

Goodheart, Eugene. *The Utopian Vision of D. H. Lawrence*. Chicago: The University of Chicago Press, 1963, 190 p.
  Study of Lawrence's social thought, his utopianism, and his affinities with Fourier, Nietzsche, and Freud.

Hazlitt, Henry. "Bowdlerized Lawrence." *The Nation* CXXXV, No. 3505 (7 September 1932): 214-15.
  Brief article deploring the extensive expurgations in the 1932 "authorized abridged edition" of *Lady Chatterley's Lover*.

Hough, Graham. "*Sons and Lovers*." In *Modern British Fiction*, edited by Mark Schorer, pp. 225-43. New York: Oxford University Press, 1961.
  Analysis of the autobiographical elements in *Sons and Lovers*.

John, Brian. "D. H. Lawrence and the Quickening Word." In his *Supreme Fictions: Studies in the Work of William Blake, Thomas Carlyle, W. B. Yeats, and D. H. Lawrence*, pp. 231-309. Montreal: McGill-Queen's University Press, 1974.
  Compares and contrasts the tradition of Romantic vitalism in the works of Lawrence and the other authors of the title.

Lawrence, D. H. Introduction to *Chariot of the Sun*, by Harry Crosby. Paris: Black Sun Press, 1931.
  Important attempt by Lawrence at a general definition of poetry.

Lawrence, Frieda. *Not I, But the Wind. . . .* 1934. Reprint. St. Clair Shores, Mich.: Scholarly Press, 1972, 297 p.
  Lengthy reminiscence interspersed with letters from Lawrence to his wife and members of her family.

Lawrence, Frieda. Introduction to *The First Lady Chatterley*, by D. H. Lawrence, pp. v-xiii. New York: Dial Press, 1944.
  Personal recollection by Lawrence's wife of their life together and of the circumstances surrounding the writing of the first draft of *Lady Chatterley's Lover*.

Moore, Harry T. *The Intelligent Heart: The Story of D. H. Lawrence*. Rev. ed. New York: Grove Press, 1962, 560 p.
  Lengthy biography making use of previously unpublished reminiscences by acquaintances of Lawrence.

Mudrick, Marvin. "The Originality of *The Rainbow*." In *Modern British Fiction*, edited by Mark Schorer, pp. 244-66. New York: Oxford University Press, 1961.
  Characterizes *The Rainbow* as "a *really* great English family-chronicle novel" of manners.

Nahal, Chaman. *D. H. Lawrence: An Eastern View*. New York: A. S. Barnes and Co., 1970, 304 p.
  Study of "the deep affinities, irrespective of what Lawrence might or might not have known of Hinduism, that exist between Lawrence's approach to life" and traditional Hindu thought.

Nehls, Edward, ed. *D. H. Lawrence: A Composite Biography*. 3 vols. Madison: The University of Wisconsin Press, 1957.
  "Composite biography" primarily comprised of excerpts from letters, journals, diaries, and memoirs written by Lawrence, members of his family, and his friends.

Schorer, Mark. "On *Lady Chatterley's Lover*." In *Modern British Fiction*, edited by Mark Schorer, pp. 285-307. New York: Oxford University Press, 1961.
  Traces, through the three extant versions of *Lady Chatterley's Lover*, the changes Lawrence made in the text.

Spivey, Ted R. "Lawrence and Faulkner: The Symbolist Novel and the Prophetic Song." In his *The Journey Beyond Tragedy: A Study of Myth and Modern Fiction*, pp. 72-93. Orlando: University Presses of Florida, 1980.*
  Characterizes Lawrence and Faulkner as the two novelists who "more than any others in this century have achieved the power of the prophetic song" in their novels, utilizing techniques of symbolist fiction while retaining a sense of nature and mythic community.

Stoll, John E. *The Novels of D. H. Lawrence: A Search for Integration*. Columbia: University of Missouri Press, 1971, 263 p.
  Study of Lawrence's imagery and how it relates to his "theory of consciousness . . . a manifestation at once of the author's self-division and his attempt to overcome duality through art. . . ."

Tindall, William York. *D. H. Lawrence and Susan His Cow*. New York: Cooper Square Publishers, 1972, 231 p.
  Discusses D. H. Lawrence's cow as "a symbol in which Lawrence's life and work are conveniently expressed."

Walker, Ronald G. "The 'Dark Blood' of America." In his *Infernal Paradise: Mexico and the Modern English Novel*, pp. 28-138. Berkeley: University of California Press, 1976.
  Assessment of the fascination that Mexico held for Lawrence, and of the role his stays in Mexico played in the writing of *The Plumed Serpent* and some of his minor works.

Widmer, Kingsley. *The Art of Perversity: D. H. Lawrence's Shorter Fictions*. Seattle: University of Washington Press, 1962, 258 p.
  Explores apparent contradictions in Lawrence's short stories and novellas, discussing his "negative ways to his affirmations," ways which drew upon the demonic and presented a negation of modern woman.

Williams, Raymond. "Social and Personal Tragedy: Tolstoy and Lawrence." In his *Modern Tragedy*, pp. 121-38. Stanford: Stanford University Press, 1966.*
  Contrasts *Anna Karenina* and *Women in Love*, calling them modern literature's two most important novels focussing on the crises of the individual and society.

# (Percy) Wyndham Lewis

## 1882(?)-1957

Canadian-born English novelist, essayist, critic, short story writer, editor, poet, autobiographer, and dramatist.

T. S. Eliot has called Lewis the greatest prose stylist of the twentieth century. Together with Eliot, Ezra Pound, and T. E. Hulme, Lewis was instrumental in establishing the anti-Romantic movement in literature during the first decades of the 1900s. He also emerged as a leader of the Vorticist movement, founded by Pound. However, critical and popular recognition of Lewis has been limited, for a variety of reasons. Early in his career he alienated the literary establishment with his merciless and savage satires of its members, particularly in the novel *The Apes of God*. He then antagonized those intellectuals and radicals who were inclined to support him when, in *Hitler*, he strongly favored the growth of National Socialism in Germany. Today, however, Lewis's work is being reevaluated, and many critics now consider him one of the most individual and influential forces in modern literature.

Lewis was born on his family's yacht off the North American coast and spent his first years in Canada and Maine. When he was very young, his parents moved to England, where his father abandoned the family. Lewis received a public school education, including two years at Rugby, and from 1898 until 1901 studied at the Slade School of Art in Paris. A sporadic allowance from his father enabled him to travel extensively in France, Germany, Spain, and Holland before returning to England, where he sought to establish himself as a painter. By 1909 Lewis's radical post-Impressionist paintings were finding some success, and Ford Madox Ford began publishing several of his short stories in *The English Review*. Although he originally subscribed to the Futurism of Filippo Marinetti, Lewis found the tenets of Vorticism, a movement which began as a reaction against Futurism, more akin to his artistic temperament. Though its principles are vague, a critical consensus exists that Vorticism is related to Imagism in poetry and to Cubism in painting, and that one of its primary characteristics is a belief in the total impersonality of art, achieved by fragmenting and reordering the elements of experience into a new and more meaningful synthesis. Together, Pound and Lewis established the periodical *Blast*, to give the new movement a voice and a rallying point. *Blast*, however, appeared for only two issues.

Between the years 1926 and 1930, Lewis, subsidized by several wealthy admirers, "went underground," as he phrased it, and produced "an unspeakable amount of work." These works include *Time and Western Man*—an important summation of his Cartesian philosophical beliefs—as well as the controversial essays in *The Art of Being Ruled*, one of the key works in his political canon. During this time Lewis also wrote his famous satirical novel *The Apes of God*, and began another periodical, *The Enemy*. At the outbreak of World War II, Lewis was traveling to Canada to deliver a series of lectures, and he remained there until the war ended. Upon returning to England, he began and completed perhaps his most remarkable work, *The Human Age*, and worked as an art critic for *The Listener* until his eyesight failed.

Lewis's savage, satiric fiction has been compared to that of Swift and Pope. His best-known novel, *The Apes of God*, is a long and aggressive satire on the cultural life of England in the 1920s. In it he presents thinly-disguised lampoons of such literary figures as Marcel Proust, James Joyce, Gertrude Stein, D. H. Lawrence, and members of the Bloomsbury Group. England's literary establishment responded by virtually ignoring Lewis thereafter. In the massive trilogy *The Human Age*—which includes *The Childermass, Malign Fiesta,* and *Monstre Gai*—Lewis created one of the most unique novels in modern literature. Set in the immediate afterlife, *The Human Age* is a surrealistic and obscure examination of the sufferings of the artist, who must remain detached from human experience in order to portray it.

Lewis published several volumes of short stories, *The Wild Body, Rotting Hill,* and *Unlucky for Pringle,* and one of poetry, *One-Way Song*. The stories are for the most part satires; and while his poetry, too, was satiric and frequently vitriolic, his work in this genre is less impressive than his prose. Of Lewis's nonfiction, *The Art of Being Ruled* and *Time and Western Man* contain the most inclusive general statements of his philosophy. *The Art of Being Ruled* is an almost totally negative commentary on society, human relations, and political systems. In this book, Lewis contrasted democracy—which he believed forced conformity upon human beings—with his ideal of individual growth and creative freedom. *Time and Western Man* began as a study of the linear and cyclical time theories of Henri Bergson and Oswald Spengler, but ultimately developed into an assault on almost all contemporary schools of philosophic, artistic, and literary thought. It contains Lewis's most aggressive attack on the forces of subjectivism. Lewis also wrote a highly unusual book of Shakespearean criticism, *The Lion and the Fox: The Role of the Hero in the Plays of Shakespeare*. The book has been interpreted by some critics as a polemic demanding that people make conscious decisions instead of abandoning themselves to unconscious desires and the influence of the masses.

Early critical reaction to Lewis was for the most part favorable. T. S. Eliot in 1918 wrote that it was "a commonplace to compare Mr. Lewis to Dostoevsky"; and even those critics, such as Conrad Aiken and R. P. Blackmur, who found fault with Lewis's highly idiosyncratic fiction and his frequently polemical nonfiction, praised him as an incomparable literary stylist. In the early 1930s, Lewis's reputation suffered a serious critical and popular decline. But the primary reason for this decline was the publication of *Hitler*, a sympathetic and approving study of National Socialism and of Adolf Hitler's rise to power. During the course of the 1930s Lewis's views on this matter changed completely, and in 1939 he renounced his earlier support of National Socialism in *The Hitler Cult* and in *The Jews, Are They Human?* Despite his renunciation, Lewis was long considered a Fascist. In recent years, however, critical attention has once again focused on Lewis's skills as a literary stylist. Some critics, such as Cyril Connolly, believe he will eventually be ranked with Eliot, Pound, and Joyce as one of the most influential writers of the early twentieth century.

Lewis is one of the most fascinating and controversial writers in twentieth-century literature. Few artists can match the range of his talents as a satirist, novelist, essayist, and painter. In the words of W. G. Constable: "Not only his work, but his personality makes Mr. Wyndham Lewis one of the most interesting figures in contemporary British Art."

(See also *TCLC*, Vol. 2.)

PRINCIPAL WORKS

*Tarr* (novel) 1918; also published as *Tarr* [revised edition], 1928
*The Caliph's Design* (essay) 1919
*The Art of Being Ruled* (essays) 1926
*The Lion and the Fox: The Role of the Hero in the Plays of Shakespeare* (criticism) 1927
*Time and Western Man* (essays) 1927
*The Wild Body* (short stories) 1927
*\*The Childermass* (novel) 1928
*Paleface: The Philosophy of the 'Melting Pot'* (essays) 1929
*The Apes of God* (novel) 1930
*The Diabolical Principle and the Dithyrambic Spectator* (essays) 1931
*Hitler* (essay) 1931
*The Doom of Youth* (essays) 1932
*Enemy of the Stars* [first publication] (drama) 1932
*Snooty Baronet* (novel) 1932
*Engine Fight Talk* (poetry) 1933; also published as *One-Way Song*, 1960
*Men without Art* (criticism) 1934

*Left Wings over Europe; or, How to Make a War about Nothing* (essays) 1936
*Blasting and Bombardiering* (autobiography) 1937
*Count Your Dead: They Are Alive! or, A New War in the Making* (essays) 1937
*The Revenge for Love* (novel) 1937
*The Hitler Cult* (essay) 1939
*The Jews, Are They Human?* (essay) 1939
*Wyndham Lewis the Artist, from "Blast" to Burlington House* (essays and criticism) 1939
*America, I Presume* (essays) 1940
*The Vulgar Streak* (novel) 1941
*America and Cosmic Man* (essays) 1948
*Rude Assignment: A Narrative of My Career Up-to-Date* (autobiography) 1950
*Rotting Hill* (short stories) 1951
*The Writer and the Absolute* (essays) 1952
*The Demon of Progress in the Arts* (criticism) 1954
*Self Condemned* (novel) 1954
*\*Malign Fiesta* (novel) 1955
*\*Monstre Gai* (novel) 1955
*The Red Priest* (novel) 1956
*Letters* (letters) 1962
*Wyndham Lewis on Art* (criticism) 1969
*\*\*The Roaring Queen* (novel) 1973
*Unlucky for Pringle* (short stories) 1973
*Enemy Salvoes* (criticism) 1976
*\*\*\*Mrs. Duke's Million* (novel) 1977

\*These works were published as *The Human Age* in 1955.

\*\*This work was written in 1936.

\*\*\*This work was written in 1908.

---

**THE TIMES, London (essay date 1914)**

The art of the present day seems to be exhausting its energies in "manifestoes." The latest of all is that contained in a large quarto magazine, edited by Wyndham Lewis . . . , bound in purple paper, with nothing on its cover but the five letters—printed in type just under 1 in. thick and stamped transversely from the left-hand top to the right-hand bottom corner—which form the word *Blast*. There is a suggestion about it of the "lightning campaign" which is to sweep away all accepted doctrines, and for which futurism is already a mere "sensational and sentimental mixture of the aesthete of 1890 and the realist of 1870." The fine frenzy of the authors of *Blast* has made havoc of its printing press, and we do not remember seeing in a publication of its size so many misprints. Perhaps this is an assertion of the Individualism which is the main gospel of the coterie who join in the *Blast*. . . .

We readily acknowledge that there is in this document a great deal more matter and meaning and originality than is to be found in the Futurist Manifesto—and, if one can shut one's eyes to their violent gesticulations, one may peruse with some profit their notions as to the art of the South and the art of the North; as to the English character "based on the sea" as to the new age of machinery, chiefly Anglo-Saxon in origin, which gives us a new scope for art. . . .

[The] one thing, of course, is to be in a state of revolt, and for England, so these gentlemen think, this is the normal state.

For the rest the reader may make what he can of "the great art vortex sprung up in the centre of this town"; of a great many papal statements about art, life, nature, the present, the past, the future, and other, matters; of some poetry—by Mr. Ezra Pound—of no particular merit, and some of no merit at all. . . .

*"The Vorticists' Manifesto," in* The Times, *London (© Times Newspapers Limited 1914), July 1, 1914, p. 8.\**

## T. S. ELIOT   (essay date 1918)

[*Eliot, who was a close friend of Lewis's for over forty years, was one of the first critics to recognize and praise his talents as a stylist.*]

The fact that Mr. Wyndham Lewis is known as a draughtsman and painter is not of the least consequence to his standing as a prose writer. To treat his writing as an outlet for his superabundant vitality, or a means on his part of satisfying intellectual passions and keeping his art healthy, cannot lead to accurate criticism. His prose must be judged quite independently of his painting, he must be allowed the hypothesis of a dual creative personality. (p. 65)

It is already a commonplace to compare Mr. Lewis to Dostoevsky, analogy fostered by Mr. Lewis's explicit admiration for Dostoevsky. The relationship is so apparent that we can all the more easily be mistaken in our analysis of it. To find the resemblance is nothing; several other contemporary novelists have obviously admired Dostoevsky, the result is of no importance. Mr. Lewis has made such good use of Dostoevsky— has commandeered him so efficiently for his purposes—that his differences from the Russian must be insisted upon. His mind is different, his method is different, his aims are different.

The method of Mr. Lewis is in fact no more like that of Dostoevsky, taking *Tarr* as a whole, than it is like that of Flaubert. The book does not comply with any of the accepted categories of fiction. It is not the extended conte (**"Cantelman's Spring Mate"** is not on the pattern of either Turgenev or Maupassant). It is not the elaboration of a datum, as *Madame Bovary*. From the standpoint of a Dostoevsky novel *Tarr* needs filling out: so much of Dostoevsky's effect is due to apparent pure receptivity, lack of conscious selection, to the irrelevances which merely happen and contribute imperceptibly to a total impression. In contrast to Dostoevsky, Mr. Lewis is impressively deliberate, frigid; his interest in his own personages is wholly intellectual. This is a peculiar intellectuality, not kin to Flaubert; and perhaps inhuman would be a better word than frigid. Intelligence, however, is only a part of Mr. Lewis's quality; it is united with a vigorous physical organism which interests itself directly in sensation for its own sake. The direct contact with the senses, perception of the world of immediate experience with its own scale of values, is like Dostoevsky, but there is always the suggestion of a purely intellectual curiosity in the senses which will disconcert many readers of the Russian novelist. And there is another important quality, neither French nor Russian, which may disconcert them still more. This is Humour.

Humour is distinctly English. No one can be so aware of the environment of Stupidity as the Englishman; no other nationality perhaps provides so dense an environment as the English. The intelligent Englishman is more aware of loneliness, has more reserves, than the man of intelligence of any other nation.

Wit is public, it is in the object; humour (I am speaking only of real humour) is the instinctive attempt of a sensitive mind to protect beauty against ugliness; and to protect itself against stupidity. The older British humour is of this sort; in that great but decadent humourist, Dickens, and in some of his contemporaries it is on the way to the imbecilities of *Punch*. Mr. Lewis's humour is near to Dickens, but on the right side, for it is not too remote from Ben Jonson. In *Tarr* it is by no means omnipresent. It turns up when the movement is relaxed, it disappears when the action moves rapidly. The action is in places very rapid indeed: from the blow given by Kreisler in the cafe to the suicide is one uninterrupted movement. The awakening of Kreisler by the alarum-clock is as good as anything of the sort by Dostoevsky; the feverish haste of the suitcase episode proceeds without a smile. (pp. 65-6)

It is always with the appearance of Tarr, a very English figure, that Humour is apt to enter; whenever the situation is seen from Tarr's point of view. Humour invests him. . . . Humour, indeed, protects Tarr from Bertha, from the less important Anastasya, from the Lipmann circle. As a figure in the book, indeed, he is protected too well: "Tarr exalts life into a Comedy," but it remains his (private) comedy. In one scene, and that in contact with Kreisler, Tarr is moved from his reserve into reality: the scene in which Tarr is forced out of Kreisler's bedroom. Here there is another point of contact with Dostoevsky, in a variation on one of Dostoevsky's best themes: Humiliation. This is one of the most important elements in human life, and one little exploited. Kreisler is a study in humiliation.

I do not understand the *Times* when it remarks that the book "is a very brilliant *reducto ad absurdum* not only of its own characters, but of its own method." I am not sure that there is one method at all; or that there is not a different method for Tarr, for Kreisler, and for Bertha. It is absurd to attack the method which produced Kreisler and Bertha; they are permanent for literature. But there is an invisible conflict in progress all the time, between Tarr and Kreisler, to impose two different methods upon the book. We cannot say, therefore, that the form is perfect. In form, and in the actual writing, it is surpassed by **"Cantelman's Spring Mate."** And **"Inferior Religions"** remains in my opinion the most indubitable evidence of genius, the most powerful piece of imaginative thought, of anything Mr. Lewis has written.

There can be no question of the importance of *Tarr*. But it is only in part a novel; for the rest, Mr. Lewis is a magician who compels our interest in himself; he is the most fascinating personality of our time rather than a novelist. (pp. 67-8)

*T. S. Eliot, "Wyndham Lewis, Two Views: 'Tarr'" (originally published as "Tarr," in* The Egoist, *Vol. V, No. 8, September, 1918), in* Shenandoah, *Vol. IV, No. 1, Spring, 1953, pp. 65-8.*

## W. G. CONSTABLE   (essay date 1920)

[*Constable was one of the first critics to comment on the self-consciousness of Lewis's writing. This point is further developed by such later critics as Conrad Aiken and Northrop Frye (see excerpts below).*]

Not only his work, but his personality makes Mr. Wyndham Lewis one of the most interesting figures in contemporary British Art. He is a journalist, a novelist, a revolutionary and a painter; and in all these activities he shows a vigorous facility after a manner quite his own. He has edited *Blast;* his contributions to the Press are stimulating and provocative; he is a violent and able controversialist, whose favourite weapon is the bludgeon; his pamphlet, *The Caliph's Design,* is one of the most entertaining I have read for a long time; and *Tarr* is a really important novel. Thus Mr. Lewis belongs to the small group of artists, such as Rossetti and William Morris, who have adequately expressed themselves in two mediums. The translation of a painter's conception of the world into terms of another art is always interesting. . . . Mr. Lewis stands alone to-day as both a serious painter and writer, and his methods in the two arts he practises cast light upon each other. . Take his writing first. His literary style is extremely self-conscious. Every sentence seems inspired by the thought, "Will it tell; will it go home?" and he constantly uses strange epithets and piquant neologisms to catch the reader's attention. The general effect is that of a succession of hammer-blows, each aimed to secure the maximum effect irrespective of its relation to the others. At the same time, values are wilfully distorted—not as a necessary and inevitable outcome of the whole design, but as a result of conscious straining after singularity—so that there is a complete neglect of relative significance in what is said. This lack of proportion and of a necessary inter-relation of parts gives Mr. Lewis's writing a hard, mechanical, jerky quality, characteristics which are also conspicuous in his drawings. (pp. 73-4)

The desire to impress, which is a conspicuous quality of Mr. Lewis's work, is likewise reflected in the characters in *Tarr.* They constantly seem to be dominated by the thought "Have I made my point? Have I really downed the other fellow?" It comes to this, that Mr. Lewis is a striking instance of the egoist in art. It is tempting to compare him with Whistler in his anxiety to make his personality felt at any cost. But Whistler's egotism was of a different quality. He reacted to hostile criticism much as a wasp resents an ineffectual attempt to kill him—he became offensive only when offensively treated. . . . [But Mr. Lewis's] is an egotism which not merely resents criticism, but is eager to provoke it; for criticism enables him to make his personality felt. No sooner does a movement with which he is connected become accepted, than he heads a secession, and thus reasserts his individuality. . . . Thus, Mr. Lewis is in a constant state of protest against his age; and if he could to-day remodel the world, to-morrow he would be in revolt against it. If he has been dubbed a poseur and charlatan, his desire for self-assertion is the cause. I have no doubt myself of his sincerity; but "Sois belle si tu peux, sage si tu veux; mais sois considerée, il le faut" ["Be beautiful if you can, be wise if you will; but don't fail to be considered"] is his motto.

*The Caliph's Design,* which contains Mr. Lewis's latest profession of faith, bears this out. It is a series of vicious and vigorous attacks upon everything and everybody Mr. Lewis dislikes, with a too unobtrusive undercurrent of eulogy upon the little he approves. Mingled with shrewd abuse of such diverse things as the modern architect, the public school product, the infant prodigy, the naïve in art, Italian futurism, and conscious aesthetes, is some approval of what seems to Mr. Lewis vital and expressive of modern life. He prefers Mr. George Robey to Mr. Roger Fry. Reacting against a tired and disillusioned society seeking for refuge from realities which it finds intolerable, he is anxious to discover the essential nature of things, and to know life as it is. *The Caliph's Design* is an interesting diagnosis of the maladies of modern society in general, and of modern art in particular; but Mr. Lewis is singularly elusive when it comes to suggesting a remedy. Every page contains something

amusing or suggestive; but the book is a collection of bricks, not a coherent and logical structure. Mr. Lewis is tantalising. When you think he is just going to hand you the key to the whole muddle, he turns and instead flings down yet another idol. Still, something constructive does emerge, though it is neither very new nor remarkably important. Mr. Lewis emphasises (and here no one will differ from him) that it is the artist's first duty to create, to bring something new into the world. To do this he must thoroughly grasp the essential character of phenomena in the world around him, and determine what constitutes significant mass, line and colour. These in turn are to be combined into an independent reality. . . .

When an artist expresses himself in two mediums, his use of the technique of the one is apt to influence his use of the technique of the other. Rossetti imported into his painting literary methods, using forms and suggestions which appealed to the understanding rather than the eye. It might seem at first the most outrageous of paradoxes to accuse Mr. Wyndham Lewis's pictures of being literary, since the essence of the literary picture is to work upon our imaginations through the associations roused by the objects represented, and the casual observer is reminded often of. nothing in the world by his work. . . . But, for all that, there is a quality in his work which, if one examines it, discovers itself to be proper to the literary medium. . . . [The] pleasure one derives from his pictures [is] principally an analytical pleasure and not one inspired by the whole; . . . he turns facts into symbols which he cleverly arranges, so that an attentive person can translate them back into facts as though they were symbols of another kind—namely, words. In short, he is also, in a more cryptic, subtle way, himself a "literary" artist and, for my part, I cannot help concluding that the truth about Mr. Lewis is that he is really a writer who paints rather than a painter who writes. (p. 74)

> *W. G. Constable, "Wyndham Lewis," in* New Statesman *(© 1920 The Statesman Publishing Co. Ltd.), Vol. XV, No. 367, April 24, 1920, pp. 73-4.*

### R. P. BLACKMUR   (essay date 1928)

[*Blackmur reviews* Time and Western Man.]

Mr. Lewis is an artist in two kinds—painting and literature—and we might make a fable that the circuit of our times caught him up and tangled his talents in a hard knot from which he has been trying to extricate himself, and incidentally the rest of us, for the last ten years. Hence there is a prophetic earnestness and a prophetic confusion and hurry about much of his critical writings. In [*Time and Western Man*] he displays with great fervour and seriousness, with an almost self-foundering weight of knowledge and thought, the full intricacy and essential nature of the knot.

This book is such a tumult of doctrine, observation, insight and aside, that anything like a fair resolution of its contents would swell a volume and baulk the reader's appetite. Mr. Lewis has ransacked so much disorder and confusion for his subject-matter, it is no wonder the critical order he attempts sometimes strains and gasps, often overtakes and hides itself in an avalanche, and on occasion obfuscates itself entirely in polemic and distortion. But—and this is a very important but—nothing in the book, whether true or untrue, apt or irrelevant, lacks interest. Mr. Lewis has superlatively the talent for starting hares in the reader's mind; and some of them run in otherwise trackless warrens. That is, as a philosopher, he is a new type; the type of the artist; with a sensibility, a method of intelligence largely his own. But he is thus individual not from a love of self (which would have made him common) but from the necessities of the problems which strike him. (p. 270)

His main thesis has to do with the concepts of time and space, the oppositions which current ideas round these concepts furnish, and particularly with the contemporary misapplications of the concept of time in literature and art. He points out with veracity and much detail that many of our most important attitudes towards experience have been radically altered by what he calls the time-philosophy. And Mr. Lewis' contention is that the resulting shift of emphasis destroys the validity of these attitudes themselves; especially attitudes towards art and common sense.

What the time-philosophy is Mr. Lewis does not wholly define, but, among others, the names of Spengler, Whitehead, Russell, Alexander, and Bergson are intended to be representative. And the element in the various philosophies of these gentlemen to which Mr. Lewis most objects is the faculty for construing ordinary experience as bits, events, relations in the flux of time *only,* at the expense of concreteness and qualification. He does not object, I think, to the application of such a structure, however mathematical, to the realm of physical, in the scientific sense, matter, but only opposes its conversion to other fields. Or perhaps the real objection is still further away: to the results of such a false conversion in the minds of "Popular" thinkers. (pp. 270-71)

Lewis is an individualist of the Aristotelian order. Hence his feeling against the time-philosophy amounts to the drive of terror; as if his own mind suffered under it constant irreparable injury. The time-philosophers become villains, bugaboos and nightmares; and the amazing insight into life of any sort offered by the current concept of space-time, when disciplined to relevance, is ignored.

The problem may be otherwise stated. Inspection of both Mr. Lewis and his antagonists shows that the object of his terror is only a form of dialectic. . . . The dialectic in question is an excellent technique for physics and mathematics—for the world as a series of relations; and has issued in a way of thinking amounting to an elaborate faculty. This faculty postures as a philosophy, whereas it is only one element of a philosophy; and that is what frightens Mr. Lewis—the success of its posture. It has been used as a philosophy where the kinds of measurement it affords are either insignificant or give a grossly false emphasis—as in history, politics, art, religion, and commonsense. (pp. 272-73)

Mr. Lewis is concerned to restore the intelligence and the sensibility by adverse criticism of any such misapplications of science; and all that he objects to as the result of time-philosophy may be laid to the practice of an insufficient dialectic. Which does not diminish the difficulty but makes it easier to handle.

As to Mr. Lewis' judgments on James Joyce, Ezra Pound and company, they are valid only from Mr. Lewis' attitude; are reversible from even a slightly different attitude. But that is no matter; good art sometimes exists in spite of the artist and what he thinks about it; and it doesn't follow that imitation be recommended. What Mr. Lewis is judging is the *kind* of literature, the *kind* of idea, and the *kind* of technique. He is not, in this essay, primarily interested in the works themselves. What the reader has to decide is whether he can accept the total attitude which makes these criticisms possible; when he will make his own minor corrections.

Mr. Lewis is interested in making art possible and in making good society possible from the point of view of the artist. The attitude which he attacks—the romantic-scientific, sensational, and naturalistic habit of soul—is also suffering adverse inspection in other quarters [by Ramon Fernandez and Henri Massis]. . . . Mr. Lewis' *Time and Western Man* may be correlated with the work of these authors with the result that a very definitely "intelligent" attitude emerges, at least tentatively, upon which to erect thorough-going critical structure. (p. 273)

> *R. P. Blackmur, "The Enemy" (reprinted by permission of the Literary Estate of R. P. Blackmur), in* The Hound & Horn, *Vol. I, No. 3, March, 1928, pp. 270-73.*

## CONRAD AIKEN    (essay date 1928)

[*Aiken argues that Lewis could be "one of the most brilliant of contemporary writers of fiction" if it were not for his "self-consciousness" and desire to shock his audience. This conclusion is also reached by other critics, such as W. G. Constable (see excerpt above) and Northrop Frye (see excerpt below).*]

Mr. Wyndham Lewis is something of a cornac himself—he is not without curious resemblances to his admirable portrait of a showman in the story called **"The Cornac and His Wife."** In this story we are presented with a melancholy creature who is in a sense a victim of his own audiences. His audience *works* him, just as he, too, in turn works his audience; a queer kind of reciprocal puppetry. The public expects, demands, *extracts* from the sad cornac the kind of humor it wants. . . . The cornac thus becomes something which is not exactly himself: a current passes through him, or a string pulls him, and he is drastically changed. He behaves to something outside himself. He is thus two people (at least): a man, and also a man whom an audience has contorted to a particular end. (pp. 268-69)

[In *The Wild Body*] Mr. Lewis is very much in that plight. He is on the one hand a very original observer of human nature, a brilliant chronicler of its small beer, with a queer, angular, muscular, awkward and sometimes ungrammatical prose at his command—a prose which despite its lapses is astonishingly effective. He strikes one as being a very independent creature. . . . One feels also that he has the power to survey this curious world into which we are born with a very remarkable degree of detachment—a detachment so complete as almost to amount to genius in itself. There is something of the behaviorist in him: he habitually see emotions as actions, ideas as responses to stimuli, and takes an almost sadistic delight in pursuing a character through rigidly logical sequences of cause and effect. He has, in short, a very keen mind, and a very vigorous imagination, and one can at first discover no good reason why he should not be one of the most brilliant of contemporary writers of fiction.

But there is also, on the other hand, that aspect of Mr. Lewis which makes one think of the cornac being acted upon by his public. One gradually becomes aware, as one reads these delightful and highly idiosyncratic stories, that Mr. Lewis is perpetually adopting a role: he is, in fact, being *forced* into a special part. His awareness, whether vague or definite, of an audience there in the background—an audience waiting to see whether Mr. Lewis is clever or not (and, if so, *how* clever)—is an unresting one and an uneasy one. It gives him a nervous manner, a high degree of self-consciousness; it takes away from him precisely that pure freedom of mind with which he appeared to be starting out. His detachment is swallowed up in this other reaction: he remembers that something unusually dexterous is expected of him, and in his anxiety to produce a startling effect he begins, now and then, when he suspects he is not being too closely observed, to indulge in a questionable sleight or two.

Thus, in the present book, he appears in two lights. He is a first-rate narrator of psychological short stories; and he is also, less fortunately, a theorist with an ax to grind. His ax is the theory, not especially original, of the comic; and throughout [The Wild Body] he is periodically taking this out and giving it a polish, and then burying it again, or simply forgetting it in the pleasure of creation or observation for its own sake. This is the clever side of Mr. Lewis, and one cheerfully enough admits that it is clever.

But wouldn't it be a relief to Mr. Lewis, as well as to his audience, if he were told that after all he needn't bother to try to impress us in this fashion? One needn't be a crank to be interesting—and there are moments when one sees Mr. Lewis well along the road to crankiness. (pp. 269-70)

[With the stories in The Wild Body] we are on solid ground. They are brilliant, and they show everywhere a psychological astuteness of a high order. They are at the same time actual and queer. They have that consistence in oddity for which the only convenient word is genius. If only Mr. Lewis would content himself with this admirable tale-bearing as regards the foibles of human behavior and forget for a while that he thinks he has a philosophical mission, one feels certain that he could write fiction that would make any living writer green with envy. (pp. 270-71)

> Conrad Aiken, "Wyndham Lewis" (originally published as a review in New York Evening Post, Sec. III, April 14, 1928), in his Collected Criticism (copyright © 1935, 1939, 1940, 1942, 1951, 1958 by Conrad Aiken; reprinted by permission of Oxford University Press, Inc.), Oxford University Press, New York, 1968, pp. 268-71.

## FRANK SWINNERTON  (essay date 1934)

[Swinnerton reaches a conclusion similar to Conrad Aiken's (see excerpt above) when he argues that Lewis might have received the recognition that the author felt he deserved if it were not for his obsession with "unimportant" writers and issues and his tendency to inflate everything "to the proportions of sensational intrigue or monstrous perversion." This has become a standard assessment of Lewis's work, and it is taken up by such later critics as Timothy Materer and Roger B. Henkle (see excerpts below).]

Wyndham Lewis began writing character sketches long before the War, brief and vivid ironic studies: those are his forte. If one could pick them out from among the verbiage of his longer books and bring them together in series, they would reveal better than anything else could do the strength and liveliness of his talent. Just before the War began, he was at work upon an ambitious novel of which all sorts of people heard and of which several people had glimpses; but the War arrived, Lewis was ill, and it was July, 1918, before Tarr was published. . . . Tarr had its great admirers, mostly among young artists and writers from Chelsea and the Café Royal, who were personally acquainted with the author; but outside these it made little stir, and the larger public never heard of it. The larger public never hears of anything until it has a united push behind it, and Lewis

has always missed the united push, for a reason which I shall give in a moment. (p. 455)

Tarr remained an only visible child for some time. Then, on the wings of the newer modernism Lewis shook a little shower of works upon the public, from The Art of Being Ruled and Time and Western Man to the first part of The Childermass (so far uncompleted), at last publishing The Apes of God from his own address and a number of smaller pamphlets, polemics, and diatribes with various adventurous firms free of commitments to persons whom Lewis attacked. All these works were written with the utmost freedom and ebullience of style, and were either greatly and properly admired as invective or shunned as tiresome vehemence or set aside as incomprehensible nonsense. They were mostly in the nature of denunciations, in the expression of which the author excels; and while, following Joyce, he frequently abstains from the use of punctuation he has never been designedly gnomic, and as a rule becomes incomprehensible only when one misses the point through ignorance of the people he is lambasting.

The people themselves, no doubt, understand only too well who is portrayed and what is intended. Some of them, in obscure sheets or in counterblasts, hit back. Most of them ignore what has been said of them. That is their best offensive weapon; for if Lewis is unanswered he has to pass on to another subject, which is distinctly hard on one who means no harm but who must fight or sink into gloomy inaction. . . .

The standpoint of genius is apt to make a man egotistical and aggressive, and Lewis is egotistical and aggressive. He is afraid that if he were otherwise he would be overlooked. As it is, he is looked at askance. (p. 456)

I have not the heart to attack any man's belief in his own genius. . . . Besides, I am not sure that Lewis is quite wrong about himself. If egotism and ebullience, a multitudinous vocabulary and a capacity for the grotesque which (among moderns) only Joyce surpasses, are enough to make a man a genius, he is one. He certainly has extraordinary talent. He has a furiously energetic brain, full of fire and odd knowledges and scraps of profundity which bob among the general gas; sometimes he can quite brilliantly execute a scene in a book or tear the inside out of a man in a polemic. But he must all the time, so tiresomely, melodramatize everything, enlarge it to the proportions of sensational intrigue or monstrous perversion, proclaim a betrayal or a disaster, and denounce all who are not of his party. Since that party consists of Lewis alone, he is never done with mares' nests and dirty linen.

Furthermore, he is much too much concerned in his fiction— e.g., Tarr and The Apes of God—with the silly little tribe of unimportant artists and writers, the unpublished, the barely publishable, the half-known, the eccentric, the homosexual, and the dilettantish. He may bowl them over like ninepins, a fearful slaughter; but he has to pretend, as another famous fighter did, that they are more dangerous as opponents than in fact they are. . . . (p. 457)

The windmills with which Lewis is so furiously engaged for a good part of his time are unimportant windmills. He is mistaken in thinking that he is attacking essentials. He could attack essentials if he chose, but what with the small life he has led among pettifogging artistic sets and in his own company, and what with his apparent admiration for Joyce as an artist; what with his sense of genius and genius denied and that nervous excitability which causes him to reach for a pen as soon as he sees or hears of something he does not like, he is forever producing work which irritates without angering, and which amuses without producing the admiration which is its due. He has a manner of glorious flamboyance; sometimes rhetorical, sometimes pretentious, sometimes magnificent. He has a gift for uproarious farce and another gift for superbly savage irony. With such gifts you would imagine him sure of the applause of all who know how rare are any gifts at all in the realm of modern literature.

It is not the case. He has admirers; but unless they say the right word every time he imagines them to have joined the other windmills. One must praise him very hard indeed to have a chance of his endorsement. And the truth, which must be told, however disagreeable it may be to all of us, is that Lewis's matter is so often commonplace. I do not here refer alone to the little aesthetes of whom he makes such hay, but to the social and political ideas which he sets forth with so much eloquence. Some of this matter has been dead for some time; much of it is without foundation; most of it, stripped of the enchanting heat and fun of the author's vituperation, is seen to be nothing but Café Royal chit-chat and back-chat, unworthy of such gorgeous apparel. The standpoint of genius as an excuse for irresponsible polemic is very well in its way. I think Lewis has literary genius. But what he writes about seems to me to be very nearly worthless.

That is a question the reply to which must vary with the individual; for Lewis could quite well say (if he has not done so already) that what I write about and what everybody else writes about is worthless. I mean, however, that genius has no concern with the little, and that I think Lewis himself wastes his great talent upon the trivial, the scrap, the denunciation, and the mare's nest. With such gifts as his, he might be demonstrating to our astonished eyes and minds the greater world as it is and constructing a greater future for that world as it might and, under the guidance of genius, surely would be. Instead, he makes up his mind too quickly, and trusts to genius to give worth to what is no more than hasty judgment such as you or I, less gifted, might make, though in our case with less ferocious zest. The result, though often exciting, is not good enough. (pp. 458-59)

*Frank Swinnerton, "Post-War Pessimism," in his* The Georgian Scene: A Literary Panorama *(copyright 1934, © 1962 by Frank Swinnerton; reprinted by permission of Holt, Rinehart and Winston, Publishers), Farrar & Rinehart, 1934, pp. 433-59.**

## THE TIMES LITERARY SUPPLEMENT (essay date 1941)

Mr. Wyndham Lewis's latest novel ["**The Vulgar Streak**"], like most that have gone before, is a fierce and provocative performance. Savage in humour, vehement in argument and rather melodramatic in gesture, the book is fairly to be described, for all its un-Meredithian manners, as a modern "Evan Harrington." Mr. Lewis's theme is class, class discrimination, "the relentless pressure of the English class incubus." Class is not only the theme, indeed, but the plot and the villain of the plot. Evan Harrington, the son of a tailor, though a tailor Above Buttons—Evan Harrington by his accomplishment and virtue brought polite society to heel. In Mr. Lewis's version of the way things happen today, polite society, into which Vincent Penhale tried to thrust himself, drives talent and merit outside to perdition. For there is no crime, it seems, to match the crime of having been born a rank outsider. Cursed are the lowly who aspire in England, for they shall be found out. . . .

It is an intense, angry, pointed but curiously uneven piece of work. The passion and the penetration of Mr. Lewis's social criticism are always telling, and the characteristic mixture of the ribald and the mordant in satire likewise has its effect. Nevertheless Mr. Lewis's headlong rush is a little too much of a good thing. It gives, if we may say so, too pronounced an air of amateurishness to his novelist's way of writing, so indifferent is he to intellectual consistency on the one hand and to finish of style on the other. And it leads him to confuse his own vehement case through lack of imaginative discrimination. That Vincent, convinced as he is that he has been wronged by society, should be so blatant and unprepossessing an exhibitionist is no doubt reasonable; having assumed an imaginary class personality, he is, as he confesses, never quite real to himself. But, unless the plea is that only crime cancels out privilege, why mix up forgery and its penalties with all this? However, Mr. Lewis has never yet written a book that did not invite argument. He is free from the sterility of far too many of our intellectuals, and in Vincent's heart-to-heart talk with the Viennese psychiatrist, Mr. Humbert Perl, he diagnoses the English cult of class with searching brilliance.

*"Cult of the Class," in* The Times Literary Supplement *(© Times Newspapers Ltd. (London) 1941; reproduced from* The Times Literary Supplement *by permission), No. 2082, December 27, 1941, p. 653.**

## NORTHROP FRYE (essay date 1957-58)

[*Frye is perhaps Lewis's harshest critic. In the excerpt below, he disputes critical opinion and argues that Lewis was a poor stylist because he neglected the structural rhythm of his writing. Frye also attempts to explain the contradictions in Lewis's work by calling him a "solipsistic writer." This idea is a further development of the position put forth by W. G. Constable and Conrad Aiken (see excerpts below) that Lewis was a "self-conscious" writer.*]

Lewis's painting usually makes sense; much of his writing does not, partly because writing with Lewis was a hobby, as painting was with D. H. Lawrence, though a hobby which he cultivated with such energy that it came to overshadow the main art. Many features of his writing are those of the amateur. He never mastered—never tried to master—the art of expository prose, and the insincerity in his journalism is mainly due to the fact that he does not have the technical equipment to be sincere. He cannot make words express a precise meaning: he showers his reader with a verbal offensive, with what the accurate schoolboy phrase calls shooting a line. . . . [Much] of Lewis's prose is couched in the huff-snuff rhetoric which is a nonoccult form of automatic writing. . . . In reading even the best of expository works, one feels in contact with an acute, witty, and erudite mind, yet [Lewis's] books are unusually difficult to finish. There are two reasons, I think, for this. One is their inconclusiveness: they never seem to make a memorable or rounded point except when they are attacking some other writer. The other is their lack of rhythm: one bores one's way along a deafening, unaccented clatter of words until one can stand the noise no longer.

Such a style, though largely useless for exposition, has its points as a style for satire, founded as it is on invective and parody, and Lewis's theory of writing is chiefly a rationalization of his satiric style. The theory is that his approach is external and spatialized, in contrast to that of Joyce (whom he considers only as a stream-of-consciousness writer) and, more particularly, Gertrude Stein, who writes "like a confused, stammering, rather 'soft' [bloated, acromegalic, squinting, and spectacled, one can figure it as] child,'' and who is ''just the german musical soul leering at itself in a mirror, and sticking out at itself a stuttering welt of swollen tongue.'' The difference in kind from his own style implied by such remarks does not, of course, exist: his is simply another highly mannered rhetoric, and it would be easy to think up similar epithets for it. Lewis maintains that his own approach is consistently concerned with the outsides of people, paying attention only to the visible ''ossatures,'' in contrast to the emotional and temporal fumblings for a dark and soft interior. His definitions of his own aims, however, in the flat, antithetical form in which they are presented in *Men Without Art,* are sheer idiocies: space is better than time; the outside is better than the inside; painting is better than music, and so on, and so on. Besides, the human body not being crustacean, its ossature is inside anyway.

Even Lewis, however, can hardly be unaware of the badness of his metaphors: he adopts them because they give a general idea of his tradition. This is the line of intellectual satire represented by Petronius (one of the nearest to him technically), Rabelais, certain aspects of Dickens, and the Flaubert of *Bouvard et Pecuchet,* which he imitates to some extent in *The Human Age.* Satire is based on a moral attitude—there is a halfhearted effort in *Men Without Art* to argue that satire need not be moral, but it soon breaks down—and the basis of this attitude is frequently an assumed contrast between a moral norm that is pragmatically free and flexible, and behavior that appears grotesque because it is obsessed, or bound to a single repeated pattern of action, like Jonson's ''humor.'' The obvious metaphor for the latter is the machine or puppet, and Lewis's characterization deliberately reduces his characters to mechanisms. . . . In the light of this, the image of the external ossature makes more sense: a machine does have such a thing, and, in studying a machine, only its external behavior need be examined; it has no inner essence or soul stuff. Lewis, in contrast to Lawrence, associates mechanical behavior with the primitive, the ''wild body'' which cannot attain the disciplined freedom of civilized man.

When we compare Lewis with other satirists in his tradition we notice that his metaphor has in one respect led him astray. One element in writing is the rhythm of narrative, the inner pulsation and continuity in the style that keeps one turning the pages. Lewis's theory would doubtless oblige him to condemn this as an internal or temporal quality in writing, but unfortunately for the theory, structural rhythm is the real skeleton or inner ossature of writing. His neglect of it brings the defects of his expository style into his satires. If we look at *The Apes of God,* we see a use of catalogs and set repetitive passages, like the splitman's litany, that remind us of similar things in Rabelais. But in Rabelais there is a sweeping rhythmical power that carries them off, and Lewis has no power of rhythm. . . . The exuberance of Rabelais (and Swift and Joyce) results from a rigorous discipline which is also a professional competence in their art. Lewis has this discipline as a painter, but writing he has approached externally; and when his theory extends from a technique of satiric presentation to a technique of writing satire, caricature becomes self-caricature, and the book as a whole resembles a Cartesian ghost caught in its own machine, trying to break out of a closed circle of parody. Lewis speaks of D. H. Lawrence's painting as incompetent Gauguin: partisans of Lawrence might retort that much of Lewis's writing reads like delirious Dickens. For one is often reminded of the way in which Dickens allows his facility in caricature to take

over the style of writing and produce the prodigies of unplausible melodrama that mark his lapses. (pp. 178-81)

Lewis appears to think of the role of the artist in terms of an anti-Communist redefinition of a proletariat, anti-Communism being one of the few attitudes that Lewis has consistently maintained. The genuinely declassed person, for Lewis, is the detached or withdrawn observer. Such an observer has a continuity in his attitude that most people, stampeded as they are by the pressures of news and propaganda, lack; he is more radical than the crowd, yet he is deeply conservative too, for the crowd, being plunged into the time-spirit, is restless for constant change, this being what Lewis calls the attitude of the ''revolutionary simpleton'' in the arts. The crowd wants the kind of art that reflects itself: art which glorifies the primitive, the child, or the ordinary or inarticulate common man, as in the Chaplin films and in Hemingway's ''dumb ox'' characters; art which follows the endless associative burble of the inner consciousness, as in the interior monologues of Joyce and Stein; art which tends to approximate, in one way or another, the communal dance, the art which encourages a sense of participation by the untrained, or of what Lewis calls the ''dithyrambic spectator.'' All this is in contrast to the detached contemplation necessary for the Egyptian and Chinese art that Lewis (like Gauguin) prefers to the modern West, where we realize that art is not self-expression but the expression of something disinterested, a ''not-self.'' . . . The true artist thus becomes the ''enemy'' of society, for he must either declare war on it or be crushed by its hostility. (pp. 181-82)

In Lewis, as in others of the neoclassical group, antiromanticism seems to be a late romanticism fouling its own nest. The romantic decadence glanced at in Lewis's *Diabolical Principle* seems merely to expand into a more political form of experimenting in sadomasochism. The genuine statements in neoclassical theory are mainly of romantic origin. . . . Lewis's theory of satire is lifted almost bodily from Bergson's *Le Rire*— an excellent place to go for a theory of satire, except that Bergson is one of the two philosophers most violently attacked in *Time and Western Man.* In any case, the contrast between organism and mechanism is a romantic commonplace, going back to Goethe and Coleridge. The other target of *Time and Western Man* is Spengler, and the framework of Lewis's pronouncements on contemporary culture comes straight out of Spengler. Lewis's polemical writings are in a relatively modern genre—Spengler calls it the diatribe—which was largely created by Victorian romanticism, though Milton and Swift had practiced the form earlier. It was romanticism that brought to Lewis's notion of a special type of creative man, superior to others not simply in his particular expertise, but in general, in his whole attitude to life. (pp. 183-84)

[As] a satirist, one would expect Lewis to lampoon the popular ideals of the English, their devotion to sport and fair play, their pride in having a sense of humor, and so on. The villain of *The Human Age* is a cliché expert known as the Bailiff, whose appearance, recorded on Michael Ayrton's jacket design, recalls *Punch.* Yet this attitude exists beside another which is its direct opposite, apparently motivated by some feeling of guilt at being declassed by art, and which at every stage has followed a Colonel Blimp line. *Tarr* reflects the popular anti-Germanism of the First World War; in the twenties Lewis is explaining that Stein, Joyce, and *transition* are really ''shams,'' that there are too many homosexuals in modern art, and that cubism is largely humbug; as the political situation darkens, he becomes pro-fascist and ridicules the color cult which is part of the reaction against white supremacy; in 1939 he abruptly takes a democratic line on Nazis and Jews; in 1941 he completes the circle by writing *Anglo-Saxony: A League that Works.* Even in religion, on which he says little, we still find him sucking his own blood, like the Ancient Mariner. He believes in Something Upstairs, rejects Catholicism with some respect, and treats Protestantism with great contempt, as was usual in diatribes of his generation. (pp. 185-86)

If these diatribes formed, as Lewis is not unwilling to suggest, a deliberate masquerade, behind which the serious writing of the "Not-Self" takes place, or if the diatribes could in any other way be separated from the serious writing, their inconsistencies would not matter. They cannot—*The Childermass,* in particular, is a diatribe in fictional form—and the inconsistencies of the one become a kind of split creative personality in the other. The masquerade theory ascribes an impossible degree of subtlety, in any case, to a most unsubtle writer. Lewis ridicules the archetypal approach to fiction, yet his most memorable characters are culture-myths, some of them, like Kreisler in *Tarr,* largely of newspaper origin. He nags at homosexuals, yet shows a curious distaste for the normal relation, and his women resemble Asiatic mother-goddesses as they might have been described by the prophet Elijah. One would expect his "external" approach to have some affinity with realism, as in Flaubert; but anything like a setting in a Lewis satire becomes a fantasy of Grand Guignol proportions. The Parisian left bank in *Tarr,* the Bloomsbury-Chelsea London of *The Apes of God,* the Toronto of *Self Condemned* (if the reader will accept the opinion of a reviewer who lives there) are all as far out of this world as the limbo of *The Human Age.*

What is one to make of a writer who hates everything, with the unvarying querulousness of a neurotic, that his own writing represents? The easy way out is to decide that Lewis must be some kind of phony. . . . Certainly one cannot study Lewis in detail without exasperation, but that is true of many writers, and though he has uniformly substituted cleverness for wisdom, still no one can read *The Human Age* carefully and feel that its author has no real place in literature. The better solution is to take all Lewis's theories as projections, realizing that he is an almost solipsistic writer, whose hatreds are a part of him because he understands nothing of what goes on outside his own mind. . . . No one better manifests Yeats's dictum that we make rhetoric out of the quarrel with others, poetry (read satire) out of the quarrel with ourselves. Lewis's temporary admiration for Hitler thus becomes intelligible: here was someone else lost in a dream, yet with a medium's power of animating and imposing his dream. . . . Lewis is the satirist of an age whose drama is a flickering optical illusion in a darkened room, whose politics is an attempt to make clichés into axioms of automatic conduct, whose spiritual discipline is a subjective exploring of the infantile and the perverted. Such books as *The Apes of God* or *The Human Age* can hardly be written without a personal descent into the hell they portray, and Lewis has made that descent, and taken the consequences of making it, with a perverse but unflinching courage. (pp. 186-87)

*Northrop Frye, "Neo-Classical Agony," in* The Hudson Review *(copyright © 1958 by The Hudson Review, Inc.; reprinted by permission), Vol. X, No. 4, Winter, 1957-58 (and reprinted in* Northrop Frye on Culture and Literature: A Collection of Review Essays, *The University of Chicago Press, 1978, pp. 178-87).*

**JOHN R. HARRISON** (essay date 1966)

[Lewis] has described himself as "a writer who is a novelist, a critic, a political pamphleteer . . . who has been engaged in the analysis of what is obsessional in contemporary social life . . . expressing abuses in art-politics; celebrating in fiction picturesque parasites; in weighing, to the best of his ability, contemporary theories of the State . . . who has often found himself in conflict with the inveterate prepossessions of his age and country". He has also been one of the most misinterpreted and misrepresented. *The Art of Being Ruled . . .* is mainly responsible for this, and yet the ideas contained in this book are fundamentally the same as those expressed in *Time and Western Man . . .* , which was considered one of the best literary-sociological books of the time. In the former book, Lewis stated his principles more forcibly and applied them more directly to social and political questions. *Time and Western Man,* on the other hand, is an attack on Joyce, Gertrude Stein, Bergson, Spengler and Einstein. But the principles behind the two books are the same.

Lewis has been accused of writing *The Art of Being Ruled* as a justification of oppressive forms of government. What he did do in this book was to describe how, to his mind, the great mass of people had no interest in what form the government of their country took, and were incapable of deciding by whom, or how, they should be ruled. . . . In *The Art of Being Ruled,* he recognises himself as liable to make a mistake about democracy: "I feel that I slighted too much the notion of 'democracy' by using that term to mean too exclusively the present so-called democratic masses, hypnotised into a sort of hysterical imbecility by the mesmeric methods of Advertisement." But, after correcting this, he is vigorously opposed to the democratic system itself, not merely to certain symptoms which may or may not be inherent in it. . . . Lewis objected to the uniformity and standardisation that moulds separate individuals into indistinct masses. This hatred of the mass of people has often been stressed in Lewis's sociological writings, and has no doubt been compared with Nietzsche's concept of the botched masses. These two attitudes are very different, however. For Nietzsche, the mass of people did not deserve any consideration in themselves; he thought them intrinsically futile. Lewis, on the other hand, believed the mass had been degraded by the advance of technology and the growth of democracy. He probably had no great faith in their capabilities in any period of history, but thought they had been made worse by these agents. (pp. 77-8)

In *The Art of Being Ruled,* Lewis adds a rider to the belief that the same principles hold good both in aesthetics and politics. This is that political problems had better be solved on aesthetic lines. In other words, art is the measure of all things, and political problems should be worked out by applying the same principles as one would in judging a work of art. . . . Before 1940, Lewis had very little human sympathy, either for individuals or for the mass of humanity. Like T. E. Hulme, he rejected humanitarian standards, but did not accept what Hulme called "absolute" ethical standards provided by religious dogma. He created his own "absolute" aesthetic standards, and said that any problem can be judged according to these standards. Problems concerning human behaviour, however, man's treatment of man, ought not to be solved according to aesthetic principles. The belief in absolute standards, whether aesthetic or religious, can cause and has caused the most atrocious human suffering. Lewis believed in the paramount importance of the arts; that artistic principles should govern one's attitude to moral and social problems. Such is the relation between his own artistic and political beliefs. (pp. 88-9)

Lewis wrote *Time and Western Man* to try to counteract the influence of Bergson's philosophy of "Creative Evolution", and Einstein's Relativity Theory. He believed the whole movement to be democratic in essence, political in impulse and not genuinely speculative. . . . Lewis was right in finding a close relation between the political concept of "Progress" and Bergson's "Creative Evolution". Bergson's version of evolution differs from Lamarck's in that he believed life has within it some driving force towards the highest forms, while Lamarck said it produces the forms which its environment makes it need. Indeed the political idea of progress was derived from this by analogy. But the whole of Bergson's philosophy is anathema to Lewis. His belief in the value of stability . . . is the antithesis of Bergson's "eternal flux". For Bergson, time is the essence of living things, and somehow part of the reality of all material things; Lewis rejects all this completely. With a touch of persecution mania, he describes an extremely widespread movement, including "time-philosophy", Einstein's theory of an expanding universe, and the idea of "Progress", which is fundamentally a political plot. (pp. 92-3)

To explain his opposition to Bergson, Lewis says that time has no existence apart from things. It is not an absolute, and cannot be separated from change; indeed, the infinitesimal time-lag between a stationary object and a moving object will finally prove the downfall of the time-philosophers. In the meantime, however, the time doctrine is connected with action and violence; fascists have the word "action" always on their lips, and violence is their god. This is in *Time and Western Man*, written shortly after *The Art of Being Ruled*, and before *Hitler*, both of which are pro-fascist. Lewis, therefore, saw the dangers inherent in fascism right from the start, but this did not stop him from supporting it. In the late nineteen-thirties, Lewis said that he had not recognised the violent nature of German fascism in its early years. But these quotations show that he had. It was not until he saw the mass-hysteria which fascism aroused that he changed his mind about it. In fact, it was not the coercion or the atrocities of the Nazi regime that made Lewis withdraw his support. He did so when he saw that it had certain characteristics in common with what he called democracy.

What concerns Lewis even more than the effect of the "time-philosophers" on society, is their effect on the arts. They have not only destroyed an ancient, traditional culture, but have tried to undermine all those artistic ideals which Lewis upholds. . . . He believes that the influence of Bergson's philosophy on literature is to make language imprecise. "Hostility to the word goes hand in hand with propaganda for the intuitional, mystical chaos." By "hostility to the word", he means indifference to the precise use of language; having no interest in, or knowledge of, semantics and philology; using words for their evocative power rather than their intellectual power; and taking no account of their use and associations in literature and science. . . . Lewis's "classical" bias, his preference for the concrete, the clearly defined, the "hard", makes him reject writing of this kind. . . . (pp. 93-4)

In *Time and Western Man*, there is a lengthy criticism of Behaviourism, which Lewis sees as the counterpart in Psychology of the ideas of Bergson and the time-philosophers. The physiological explanation of psychological states, the idea that glandular action determines personality, is responsible for the destruction of the self, the ego, the personality, the mind, the psyche, or what Lewis calls "the thinking subject". He sees these psychological theories as pseudo-scientific evidence trumped up by the agents of this destructive force in art, politics and science. Consequently the brain emerges not as the "master tissue", but merely as the servant of the "vegetative apparatus", with the stress always placed on the primitive. . . .

Lewis says that Nietzsche and Bergson share the responsibility for the poor state of the arts in twentieth-century society. They have caused a perversion of the artistic ideal, which has resulted in extreme and worthless movements. (p. 95)

In an attempt to uphold the principles by which he believes art flourishes, and to create conditions suitable for artistic production, Lewis [in *Time and Western Man*] sets up his "classical" ideal against Bergson's ideals. The contrast lets us see more clearly what he is aiming at. First, he is concerned with the concrete reality, and the "hard exact outline" of things. He calls the arts "the science of the *outside* of things". This is the exact opposite, he says, of Bergson's concern with "Life" which cannot be properly defined. . . . This is the view of the artist—the writer and painter—who is concerned with trying to communicate his observations of the external world as accurately as possible, as opposed to the view of the philosopher. But Lewis believes that the only hope for the arts and for society in general lies in a return to the ideals of the classical tradition. . . . The "neo-classic" movement in literature and the fine arts which included Lewis, Pound, Eliot and Yeats was the development he talks about. . . . The fact that very few writers have been affected by this formal enthusiasm might be said to show how deep Bergson's influence had gone. I think, however, it is the result of political causes. The search for authority in the arts was conducted side by side with a search for authority in society. An extreme form of political authoritarianism, fascism, appeared at the right time to attract these writers. It had the added attractions of appearing to be a benevolent despotism, and to have an interest in the arts and the function of the artist in society. The political system as it developed in Germany and Italy under fascism, and in the Second World War, however, was sufficient to make most writers reject Lewis's ideas, even writers who might otherwise have agreed with him. (pp. 95-6)

> *John R. Harrison, "Wyndham Lewis," in his* The Reactionaries: A Study of the Anti-Democratic Intelligentsia *(reprinted by permission; copyright © 1966 by John R. Harrison), Gollancz, 1966, pp. 77-108.*

## ROBERT T. CHAPMAN (essay date 1973)

[*Chapman's* Wyndham Lewis: Fictions and Satires, *from which the following excerpt is taken, is an important survey of Lewis's entire career as a writer.*]

Lewis's reputation evolved from that of the *infant bizarre* (of the *Blast* days), through the "author of *Tarr*" stage, until, in the early twenties, he was increasingly accepted as a "serious" intellectual. Hand in hand with the seriousness of such works as *The Art of Being Ruled, The Lion and the Fox,* and *Time and Western Man,* went an iconoclasm which could be both intellectually violent and playful. Lewis's "enemy" *persona* was not limited to his journal of that name, and *One-Way Song* suggests one of the public masks he presented to the world at this time:

> Good fighters
> When-driven-in-corners are common: but here's a fellow
> Who does not wait to be trapped—an aggressive fellow.
>
>                                                        (p. 99)

_The Apes of God,_ published in 1930 but begun in the early twenties, continues both these Lewisian traits in what was to be the biggest _succès de scandale_ of a very controversial career. . . . _Tarr_ was a preliminary sketch for what Pound called this "smashing big canvas for what ole England's neck." In the earlier novel, the _milieu_—the artist-quarter of Paris—is extremely vividly achieved, but is essentially the back-cloth against which the action unfolds. In _The Apes of God,_ however, the evocation and analysis of the cultural scene is the _raison d'être_ of the novel. In _Rude Assignment_ Lewis describes the novel thus: "The social decay of the insanitary trough between the two great wars is its subject, and it is accurate. . . . The extreme decay of the bourgeois era preceding the present socialist one was what I depicted. It was in its last sickly saraband." . . . (pp. 99-100)

The peregrinations of Dan Boleyn (a young "queen" of exceptional beauty) through the drawing-rooms of Bloomsbury and Mayfair form the central section of the novel. Dan is cast in the traditional rôle of the _naif_ whose experiences are the medium of the satire, and whose innocence highlights the vices, hypocrisies and stupidity of the satiric victims. But here the convention is given a typically Lewisian twist—Dan is "innocent" to such an extent as to be moronic, and represents one of the principle forms of the pervasive "anti-intellectual campaign" that Lewis anathematized in _The Art of Being Ruled._ . . . Dan conveys a satirical judgement upon certain of the characters, only to be implicated himself in a more comprehensive satiric vision. The only character who is free from attack is Pierpoint. By means of Horace Zagreus, Pierpoint masterminds Dan's entry into society with the intention of having him accepted as a "youthful genius." On his travels, Dan stumbles across the full range of Lewis's _bêtes noires:_ Bloomsbury pseudo-artists, sham intellectuals, homosexual poseurs, psychoanalysts, ignorant aristocrats, nymphomaniacs, cunning _nouveaux riches,_ sycophantic critics, braggart flagellants, the Irish, Oxford poets, lesbians, socially exclusive coteries, pseudo-Prousts, jazz, militarism, youth cults, primitive cults, genius cults, and many, many more. Lewis is not always general: James Joyce, Roy Campbell, Aldous Huxley, Gertrude Stein, Gide, Cocteau, and many others, both by name and allusion, are implicated in the virulent and incisive attack. This great blast of punitive satire forms the central section of the novel, and it is framed by two sections about Lady Fredigonde, the "ex-gossip-column belle." These form a prologue and epilogue to the knockabout satirical farce. (p. 100)

There are obviously two types of satirical attack being made in _The Apes of God:_ the first is the sarcastic reduction of certain recognizable individuals (or coteries) to what Lewis sees as their proper size. Secondly, by means of Lady Fredigonde, Lewis comments, not upon the follies and vices of individuals, but upon qualities inherent in life itself. (p. 101)

In _Tarr,_ Lewis used the protagonist as a _persona,_ embodying many of his own ideas in his conversation and actions. In _The Apes of God,_ however, he uses impersonal statements (called "broadcasts") to underline, stress and elucidate elements of his fictional world. These broadcasts are an infallible touchstone to judge the validity of statements and actions in the novel. They are, in fact, Lewis's voice filtered through Pierpoint and through Zagreus, but still pure Lewis.

There are several well-defined levels of awareness in the novel. Lowest of the low is the "youthful genius," Dan Boleyn, who is even more ludicrous than the main butts of the punitive satire, the Finnian-Shaws. Zagreus is above them, Blackshirt com-

ments upon Zagreus and, above all, reigning supreme, invincible, untouchable, unseen, is Pierpoint. . . . In the novel Pierpoint functions as disembodied mind: Tarr was always embarrassed by his body and its needs—Pierpoint is Tarr without such physical handicaps. He is both pageant master and chorus. . . . He sits in the wings, observing, commenting, and attempting to make sense of the chaos—but is powerless to change anything, since to act in the pageant would mean abdicating the role of outsider. Again, like so many of the ideas in _The Apes of God,_ this could almost be a fictionalization of one of the central concepts of _The Art of Being Ruled:_

> The intellect is more removed from the crowd than is anything: but it is not a snobbish withdrawal, but a going aside for the purposes of work, of work not without its utility for the crowd. . . .
>
> (pp. 104-05)

Pierpoint's status in the novel, and the relationship with Zagreus, his mouthpiece, also dramatize an important Platonic concept. Just as Tarr/Kreisler dramatize the Cartesian dichotomy of intellect/emotion, so Pierpoint/Zagreus represent the dualism between the perfection of the word and the limitation of the deed. Perfection is only possible in the mind of the philosopher or the artist; once there is movement from the realm of ideas, and there is introduced an element of human action, any notion of the ideal must be dismissed. (p. 105)

For Lewis, fiction was forever pulling in opposite directions: either away from reality into pure fantasy (e.g., _The Human Age_), or away from an imaginatively created universe to actual events in the contemporary world (as in his non-fiction short stories in _Rotting Hill_). The "broadcasts" in _The Apes_ point the reader away from the fictional world towards the everyday world, and the effect of these reality-interpolations may be compared to the use of newsreel in an imaginative film: the juxtaposition of real and fictional creates an ambiguous plane of unreality which modifies our response both to "fact" and fiction—we are forced to look at the cavortings of the apes in the light of Pierpoint-Lewis's intellectual standards. . . . (p. 106)

The oracular broadcasts cover three main areas: ideas about satire, the relationship between "truth" and fiction, and the reason for the decline in aesthetic standards. The first of these declarations of aesthetic policy comes in discussion with Lionel Kein, the "pseudo-Proust":

> How is it that no one ever sees _himself_ in the public mirror—in official Fiction. . . . Everyone gazes into the public mirror. No one sees himself! What is the use of a mirror if it reflects a world always without the principal person— the Me? . . .

This statement is very Swiftean, and the image of the mirror is also used by Swift in The Preface to _The Battle of the Books._ . . . The ideas are identical: satire has become debased and, instead of being virulently anti-establishment, it is now part of the establishment of bourgeois art. Lewis again follows Swift in formulating a solution to revivify pusillanimous satire: it must be made more cruel and the victims should be made to feel its lash. . . . When considering these affinities in satiric theory, it is important to remember one of Lewis's early "blesses": "Bless Swift for his solemn bleak wisdom of laughter." This solemn laughter is antithetical to the "simple laughter" of humour: it is the satirical laugh which, as Zagreus says, contains "the harsh metallic bark that kills." It is the mirthless, sardonic laugh of the intellect, occasioned by what is true rather than what is comic. This is the laughter caused by Fredigonde and the black, inhuman vision of the death-in-life framework of *The Apes of God.* The novel suggests its own exegesis, and the broadcasts forever prod the reader towards a deeper understanding of why he is laughing, and what his laughter implies.

The second part of the broadcast goes on to explore the relationship of art to objective reality. . . . [The] aesthetic criterion is most obviously seen to be fulfilled in Lewis's painting: his "geometrical art" being an attempt to bring stasis to the flux, to tame life and capture the form beneath the flesh. At first sight *The Apes of God* seems antithetical to this principle: the sprawling formlessness of the novel appears to be an impressionistic rendering of the formlessness of life, and not at all "creating gentle order in place of natural chaos." However, as Lewis himself stressed in *Rude Assignment,* the novel does adhere to his "two worlds" aesthetic: "It is not portraiture. A new world is created from the shoddy material of everyday, and nothing does, or could go over into that as it appeared in nature." . . . The extravagant grotesqueries of *The Apes of God* are, indeed, nearer Ben Jonson's characters of humours than anything in "the real world"—closer to a Gerald Scarfe sketch than a photograph—but as an absolute statement about fiction, this principle must be seen in a wider context. One of the major aesthetic evils brought about by the merging of the real world with the fictional world is, according to Lewis, the reduction of the novel to "a dramatized social news-sheet." Proust—"for years the gossip-column writer upon the staff of the Figaro"—is specifically mentioned as "one of the high priests of gossip," who do not create, but merely "edit" their material. (pp. 106-08)

The other major theme in these critical interpolations is concerned with the lowering of aesthetic standards (to "Lyon's level") in every facet of contemporary popular culture. . . . There is a general *exposé* of the perverted and untalented literary world, from the "litero-criminal circles of New York" to the "sex oddities" (like Gide) of France. Gide's *The Counterfeiters* (1925) is the *roman à clef* in this literary decadence: written by a homosexual about an author with homosexual tendencies, the plot concerns the clandestine activities of a group of child criminals. It even has "social interest" (in Lewis's derogatory sense), in that Duchamps, Cocteau, and Alfred Jarry are all "in it." These, and other asides in this broadcast, have the effect of throwing the mind outwards—away from twenties London, to similar art-worlds of America and France, suggesting that this novel is a paradigm for the state of Art in the modern world. As Lewis wrote in *Men Without Art:* "Art will die, perhaps. It can, however, before doing so, paint us a picture of what life looks like without art. That will be, of course, a satiric picture." . . . This is, in fact, the picture we have in *The Apes of God.* (pp. 108-09)

> *Robert T. Chapman, "Satire, Apes and Behaviour," in* Contemporary Literature *(© 1971 by the Regents of the University of Wisconsin), Vol. 12, No. 2, Spring, 1971 (and reprinted in a different form in his* Wyndham Lewis: Fictions and Satires, *Barnes & Noble, 1973, pp. 99-121).*

## TIMOTHY MATERER (essay date 1976)

[*Materer is considered one of today's foremost experts on the works of Wyndham Lewis. The excerpt below is drawn from his* Wyndham Lewis the Novelist, *a major survey of the author's novels.*]

[*Tarr*] is a novel in spite of itself. The conception of an experimental fiction that Lewis brought to the writing of his first novel set two obstacles to its artistic success. First, he began writing in the heavy-going style of the *Enemy of the Stars;* second, he tried to force *Tarr*'s major character into a minor role.

The first, stylistic obstacle was quickly turned to advantage. Lewis found that the lapidary style of his play was inappropriate for narrative. . . . He modified his prose because "[he] grew more interested with every page in the life of [his] characters." (p. 52)

The clipped style of the original *Tarr* as well as its rapid juxtaposition of scenes enforce the harsh, satiric view Lewis takes of his characters. The finest example of this technique occurs in one of the novel's key scenes. Bertha Lunken, Tarr's former mistress, has been using a German artist to make Tarr jealous and so win him back. When Bertha naively arouses the German, Otto Kreisler, he rapes her. . . . The effect Lewis's style achieves in this scene is indirectly described as he explains Bertha's state of mind. . . . The novel affects us much as the juxtaposed images of Kreisler affect Bertha. Lewis communicates the mystery and bewildering suddenness of human actions. It was this quality that earlier reviewers, especially Rebecca West, were observing when they compared Lewis to Dostoevsky [see excerpt in *TCLC*, Vol. 2].

Yet the references to Dostoyevsky were prompted by the character of Kreisler—not by the novel's hero, Tarr. This brings us to the second and more serious obstacle that Lewis's preconceptions set for the novel. Lewis wavers between concentrating upon Tarr as a satiric commentator and Kreisler as a tragic protagonist. This obstacle is more serious because Lewis never modified his conception of Tarr's character, in the way he did modify his style, to make it appropriate to the life of the novel. (pp. 53-4)

Since Tarr is Lewis's spokesman, he never seems to break free of his creator's discursive needs and live a dramatic life of his own. Otto Kreisler, on the other hand, who is neither Lewis's spokesman nor his persona, becomes a vital character almost against Lewis's will. (p. 57)

It is not surprising that Kreisler won the spotlight from Tarr. Although Tarr talks about the "abyss" as if he has just been reading Baudelaire and is showing off a new enthusiasm, Kreisler's hysterical and nearly masochistic sufferings vividly dramatize his awareness of the abyss he inhabits. In one sense, he is the conventional comic German: stiff and boorish, ferocious although ordinarily harmless, a "Captain of Koepenich." . . . Yet Kreisler is comic only because the despair beneath his "layers of putrefying tragedy" . . . motivates his reckless antics. (p. 58)

However inconsistent or unpleasant Tarr's character may seem, he is clearly Lewis's hero. The central contrast between Kreisler's absurd devotion to Anastasya and Tarr's dedication of his best energies to art alone is wholly favorable to Tarr. Tarr's relationships with the bourgeois Bertha and the artistic Anastasya, and the later, corresponding one with Rose Fawcett and Prism Dirkes, suggests that he is able to reconcile opposites—rather like Thomas Mann's Tonio Kröger. . . . The way Lewis speaks of Tarr's "message" [in the prologue] suggests that, although he needs Tarr as a spokesman for his ideas, he finds it difficult to show any human being actually applying those ideas. If Tarr is a "figure of health," it follows, as one critic concludes, that "Tarr goes on from mistress to mistress to a long creative life." Yet Tarr has violated his own rules by taking up with Anastasya; and by fathering children by Rose Fawcett, he certainly wastes his creative energies on "life." . . . Here one glimpses the theme of the *Enemy of the Stars.* Perhaps Kreisler is an aspect of Tarr in the way that Hanp is of Arghol. In this view, the intellectual Tarr has succumbed to the same emotional weakness (the mind/body duality again) that has destroyed Kreisler. But as in the *Enemy of the Stars,* Lewis cannot quite hold to this balanced, ironic view of the artistic temperament. (pp. 63-4)

As I have suggested, Tarr's character seems to retain the mark of the harshly theoretical approach Lewis first took to his novel. Originally he meant Tarr to be a triumphant Arghol—the artist who has learned to live among the Hanps of the world. When Tarr claims that he is a "new sort of person; the creative man," he asserts Lewis's belief in an artistic *übermensch.* But when the demands of the novel forced Lewis to show this superior being associating with other people, he saw that Tarr would look more like a boorish young man than an artist who transcends the petty frustrations of everyday life. Lewis tries to obscure this flaw by allowing occasional criticism of Tarr and through Tarr's marriage with Bertha. The flaw is nevertheless obvious because Tarr, as Lewis conceives him, cannot interact with other characters.

Although Tarr fails to carry the significance Lewis would like, this deficiency leaves much of the novel untouched, and not only the Kreisler sections. Lewis is often at his best when he forgets his theory of art and writes in a conventional comic style. When Lewis allows Tarr to be simply the cocky young artist, he is always amusing. The novel has a number of successful minor comic characters, such as Anastasya, Bitzenko, and the painters in Tarr's circle. (pp. 64-5)

Like *Tarr, The Apes of God* is a work which strains against itself. Its intense but almost eccentric power may recall Swift's *A Tale of a Tub* or Flaubert's *Bouvard et Pécuchet.* Although individual passages are unquestionably great, and its vast scope is masterly, too often it seems labored or even tedious. This problem is severe in *The Apes* because, as in the *Enemy of the Stars,* the brilliant style never gathers narrative momentum, nor does it create significant characters. Yet many passages and even entire sections at times give *The Apes* the power of a modern *Dunciad.*

Wyndham Lewis's great achievement in *The Apes of God* was to invent a prose style appropriate to the violent, mechanized life of the modern era. In his satiric portrait of England between two World Wars, he exposes a culture that is not creative enough to control its immense powers. Without this control, the forces of the machine age move in destructive circles. . . . The subtitle Lewis gave his magazine *BLAST* fits *The Apes* as well: "Review of the Great English Vortex."

The Vortex begins and ends at the estate of Lord and Lady Follett. When Lady Follett's nephew arrives there to safeguard his claim to the Follett fortune during a conference with the family lawyer, Lewis displays the first of his "apes of God"— or imitators of the god-like artist. But the interest here is in the mechanical rather than the animal images associated with the nephew, Dick Whittingdon. (pp. 83-4)

[In the] descriptions of Dick Whittingdon, the principle of Lewis's style is to transform his victim into a violently unstable object. With the same satiric logic, he also makes inanimate objects, chairs for example, seem more vital than people. (p. 84)

Lewis's concern with people who seem less vital than the things they use is significantly paralleled in the contemporary cinema. Jean-Luc Godard, who often lets the garish plastic and glass surfaces of life dominate his films, could be explaining Lewis's technique when he explains his own: "Objects exist, and if one pays more attention to them than to people, it is precisely because they exist more than these people. Dead objects are still alive. Living people are often already dead." (pp. 84-5)

This parallel of his style with contemporary film technique reveals how vital Lewis's perceptions are today. It also indicates, however, a weakness in his style that must be considered in any evaluation of *The Apes of God.* The problem is that Lewis approaches literature with the portrait painter's devotion to the details of appearance. . . . He places his victims in what Ezra Pound called a "Kleig light of ridicule" to reveal their mindless, mechanized natures. Yet the very vividness of these descriptions hampers the return to the narrative pace and the progression to the next description. A brief cut to inanimate objects in a film need not disturb the narrative flow. In a film, the object is immediately present; in prose, the object emerges only as the writer assembles its parts. (p. 85)

[The] descriptive weakness of Lewis's style is that it sometimes blurs the object it seeks to define. Its narrative weakness is that it occasionally moves in slow motion.

Through the middle episodes of the satire, Lewis attempts to breathe life into his narrative with a picaresque plot. The picaresque episodes begin as Horace Zagreus, another nephew of the Folletts, introduces his hulking young protégé Dan Boleyn (the picaro) to the world of artistic apes in order to alert him to the danger they pose for the true artist. Since Zagreus is a fool himself, he cannot recognize the pretensions of his brother apes—it's a case of the blind leading the blind. However, Zagreus can make Dan follow the program that his own master, Pierpoint, once set for him. The mysterious Pierpoint (whose private life and opinions correspond to Lewis's) never appears in the satire. He is the observer at the still center of the Vortex— in it but not of it. (p. 86)

Like identically programmed automata, these dilettantes repeat the same inanities. They provoke neither sympathy nor contempt. Through this uniformity, the apes avenge themselves on their creator. Their dull unoriginality often destroys the reader's interest in Lewis's satire.

His utter contempt for his characters prevents him from making any one of them an absorbing focal point for the narrative. Because he makes Dan almost mindless, even Lewis's descriptive powers do little to make Dan's lugubrious presence more bearable. He rarely opens his mouth, unless to say something like "'I am *so terribly unhappy!*'" . . . In the description of Dick Whittingdon, his words appear comically idiotic. But descriptive brilliance cannot animate Dan's stupidity; he dominates so many pages of the satire that description quickly becomes repetitive. (pp. 86-7)

In the more than six hundred pages of *The Apes,* virtually nothing happens. Although the Folletts have died, their lives were too self-centered for anyone, except the predatory Zagreus, to miss them. A new young protégé replaces Dan, but Zagreus's young men are so characterless that the replacement, like that of an interchangeable part in a machine, alters nothing. Despite the near anarchy of the General Strike, the apes refuse to see it as a portent of the political and economic disasters their irresponsibility foments. After the Vortex engulfs the Bloomsbury scribblers and the Chelsea canvas daubers, it swings out further still to include the whole country. But the Vortex begins and ends at the Follett mansion, where nothing happens because the Folletts are spiritually and, finally, physically dead. The Vortex has moved in a destructive circle. (p. 93)

Lewis creates his satiric Vortex with a seriousness and gusto that, as Yeats and Pound attest, rivals Swift's. Yet one can discover the weakness in Lewis's satiric vision as well as its strength by examining the Vortex image more closely. The Vortex implies a still center where the artist, at the heart of experience and the master of it, retains the repose essential for great art. By keeping Pierpoint—Lewis's surrogate—out of the book's action, Lewis implies that he himself is the cool, objective observer at the center of the Vortex the apes create. Nevertheless, the prose style of *The Apes* communicates so overpowering and sometimes so oppressive a sense of Lewis's personality that one cannot believe in his objectivity. Even in the portrait of Dick Whittingdon, his anger tends to turn satire into mere denunciation. In such a portrait, Lewis's presence is felt because his anger, in excess of the object that provoked it, suggests that he is too personally involved with his characters—or rather with the real life models for them. Far from creating a nonemotional art, he has still not escaped the kind of personal animus that limits *Tarr*. (pp. 93-4)

[In the novels following *Snooty Baronet*] one detects Lewis pushing the troublesome Enemy aside and speaking in his own voice. The Enemy, like Tarr, becomes more of a spokesman than a persona. As Lewis drops his ironic mask, satire degenerates into personal complaint. A similar weakness can be found even in *Snooty Baronet*. Kell-Imrie's character is based on the Enemy persona, and the ironic first-person narrative eventually unmasks him as a dehumanized killer. Yet there are times, as in Chapter 5, when Lewis uses Kell-Imrie to state his own political attitudes and thus undercuts his ironic detachment.

In *The Revenge for Love,* Lewis overcomes this failure of detachment. Rather than using his persona as a spokesman, Lewis involves him in a plot that fully dramatizes the novel's theme. Since *The Revenge,* unlike *The Apes* or *Snooty Baronet,* reveals more concern with people than with ideas, there is no need for a spokesman. As Lewis moves his persona, Percy Hardcaster, through the contrasting worlds of art and politics, his theme and emotional tone attain a control and complexity unprecedented in his fiction.

*The Revenge for Love* recreates the period of Communist and Fascist agitation that preceded the Spanish Civil War. Since Lewis opposed Communism even to the point of praising Fascist movements that tried to destroy Russian influence, some critics read *The Revenge* as an anti-Communist tract. (pp. 113-14)

Because Lewis is more concerned with the characters in *The Revenge* than in the political movements they represent, he detaches himself from any specific political commitment. As he describes the human suffering that they cause, all violent political programs seem equally abhorrent to him. A sign of this deeper human involvement with his characters in *The Revenge* is that the fate of Victor Stamp, an artist who is killed after being betrayed by a political profiteer, is evidently inspired by the death of Henri Gaudier-Brzeska. Lewis's fellow Vorticist, a young sculptor of genius, was killed in World War

I. Like Victor Stamp, Gaudier-Brzeska was driven to forging "masterpieces" in order to earn a living. His death at the age of twenty-three shocked Lewis (as it did Ezra Pound) into political consciousness. Lewis wrote that Gaudier-Brzeska "was so preternaturally *alive,* that I began my lesson then; a lesson of hatred for this soul-less machine, of big-wig money-government. . . ." He illustrates this lesson in *The Revenge for Love.* (p. 116)

As Lewis's persona, Percy Hardcaster dramatizes rather than states the novel's political theme. Hardcaster's denunciation of the "*salon*-revolutionaries" expresses Lewis's deepest feelings about prewar politics in London. But much as his comic treatment of Hardcaster's beating controls the scene's emotional tone, Lewis controls his temptation to drop Hardcaster's mask and use him, as he uses Kell-Imrie and the "Enemy," to defend his own personality. . . . Instead of using his persona for self-justification, he uses it for self-criticism. . . . Hardcaster has acquired the piercing gaze that Bestre uses to confound his enemies. In *The Revenge,* unlike *The Wild Body,* Lewis sees the danger of this satiric outlook. The dehumanized wasteland of *The Apes* was the result of this intellectualized treatment of human experience. By the thirties Lewis himself understood the danger. No longer does he believe, as he seemed to when he wrote the *Enemy of the Stars,* that a severely intellectual approach to life, like Arghol's, is heroic. He no longer ridicules his characters, as he does in *The Apes,* solely because they are unable to think. In *The Revenge for Love,* he instead shows the aridity of the intellectual values of Hardcaster's world. (pp. 125-26)

In *The Revenge for Love,* Lewis no longer relies on the sheer force of his prose style to drive home his theme. With no loss of satiric insight, Lewis controls his dehumanizing impulse enough to create sympathetic human beings who dramatize the novel's meaning. Within the novel's political sphere, Hardcaster's sincerity contrasts with the triviality of "parlour pinks" like Gillian and with the hypocrisy of Abershaw, the political profiteer. Once Hardcaster enters the artistic sphere, we in turn see his limitations. Next to Victor's devotion to art, Hardcaster's revolutionary ideals are violent and destructive. . . . Art is one of the two values (the other is love) that Lewis affirms through his characters. Of all the characters in the artistic sphere, Abershaw—who exploits both artistic and political movements—is again the falsest. (pp. 130-31)

Because his characters and not his prose style carry the weight of his theme, Lewis at last writes an objective novel. The plot of *The Revenge* directs our attention away from his prose (which keeps Lewis the stylist too much in view in *The Apes*) and to the characters. His success in keeping his own personality out of view in *The Revenge* is also the result of a deeper understanding of his characters. This greater depth can be measured by recalling Tarr's callous treatment of Bertha. In his first novel, Lewis is so absorbed in his persona that he cannot recognize Tarr's callousness. When Hardcaster is trying to convince Mateau that Margot's love for Victor is not genuine, he is virtually trying to acquire Tarr's insensitivity. Hardcaster does have Tarr's cold, intellectual approach to human experience, but in *The Revenge for Love* Lewis is no longer so uncritical of this excessive rationality. His insight into Hardcaster opens up the world of Margot and Bertha to his art. (p. 131)

Lewis achieved some major artistic goals in *The Revenge.* His ambition to write an impersonal work in a clear, visual style is realized without sacrificing the reality of his characters. The juxtaposition of scenes dramatizes his theme without risking the blurred, flowing qualities that he feared in narrative art. *The Revenge for Love,* however, does not fulfill Lewis's tragic vision. For this fulfillment, one must look to his greatest novel, *Self Condemned.* (p. 133)

The finest sections of *Self Condemned* recreate Lewis's sense of helpless anger at the course of the [second world] war. The sympathetic exploration of the disordered mind of his protagonist, René Harding, gives the book the "almost unbearable spiritual agony" and "high tragedy" that T. S. Eliot praises. . . . In this novel Lewis finally creates what is essential to any great novel, a character that can involve the reader in his life. . . . Although *The Revenge* does involve one in Margot's life, its satiric tone severely limits any sympathy for her. In *The Vulgar Streak,* on the other hand, the sympathy for Vincent is excessive and uncritical. *Self Condemned* attains a balance between these extremes.

In his earlier novels, Lewis's interest in his characters at best matches his intent to dramatize a thesis. In *Self Condemned,* he is wholly absorbed in his protagonist, and the development of the thesis is firmly subordinated to that of his characters. This novel seems inspired, whereas the others seem planned. Next to the carefully-placed recurrent "nothings" of *The Revenge,* for example, the animal images of *Self Condemned* seem to come from depths Lewis had not sounded before. Through the consciousness of René Harding, one enters a jungle of distorted animal shapes. . . . Many of the novel's fine portraits use animal imagery to mix the comic with the menacing. (pp. 139-40)

If these images dehumanize the characters, they do so without creating a sterile landscape like that of *The Apes of God.* For these images are organic rather than mechanical, and they are firmly anchored in René's consciousness. They dramatize his personal nightmare. Although he too is sometimes described through animal images ("a hairy faun" and "a bearded rooster"), his suffering is a constant reminder of his humanity.

It is of course ironic that Lewis, who so prided himself on his impersonal objectivity, should create his finest character when he writes a nearly autobiographical novel. One finds the same paradox in Ezra Pound's *Pisan Cantos.* . . . Pound and Lewis, however, also share a similar autobiographical flaw. Both *The Pisan Cantos* and *Self Condemned* are shot through with self-pity and bitter anger. Although Lewis criticizes the cold intellectuality of René's character (much as Pound admits to a lack of compassion), he often seems to view the same frigid quality as heroic. Like Pound in *The Pisan Cantos,* Lewis sometimes seems to admit his protagonist's faults and the extremity of his views, and sometimes tries to justify them. (p. 140)

Lewis's descriptive powers are as acute in this novel as they were in "Bestre" or *The Apes of God.* But now Lewis's characters are not lost in the flashy brilliance of his style. He has total confidence in what his prose can accomplish and never strains after virtuoso effects. (p. 141)

*Self Condemned* is a war novel even though it does not show the agonies, heroic or otherwise, of combatants. Modern war affects whole populations but usually indirectly. *Self Condemned* is a war novel about people who are denied the combatant's, or even the military bureaucrat's, opportunity to act. The Hardings can only wait out the war, hardly knowing what is happening thousands of miles away. (p. 146)

René's tragedy recalls Margot's and Victor's in *The Revenge for Love.* Their love and René's intellectual honesty cause their respective downfalls. Unlike Vincent in *The Vulgar Streak,* they are destroyed through their noble qualities. René's fall, however, traces a more convincing tragic pattern than Margot's and Victor's. First, because Lewis respects René more, he enters more deeply into his character's life. Secondly, Margot and Victor are victims of Abershaw rather than of their own characters and to this extent are more pathetic than tragic. René contributes to his own destruction. René's fate shows how even those who struggle against violence and evil can be corrupted by it. The pity of his life is that, in Bertolt Brecht's words, "Even hatred of vileness / Distorts a man's features." The irony of his character is that, because his sensitivity is so acute, he must go to extremes to protect it. By setting up defense mechanisms, René becomes a kind of mechanism himself— incapable of human sympathy. Because he hoped so much for man, his rage at the war descends into misanthropy. René fits Lewis's conception of characters like Othello, "whose tragedy is that they are involved in a real action; whereas they come from, and naturally inhabit, an ideal world." René's ideal world is that of the mind. Before the war, he could thrive while isolated from the world of average people. When he is forced from this noble though artificial world, his inflexible intellect cannot survive. Like Oedipus, Othello, or Conrad's Nostromo, he rages at the evil in the world, looks for its source without, and is shattered when he finds it within. (pp. 150-51)

[Both his late stories and *Self Condemned*] show that Lewis's power to fix a mordantly accurate eye on the externals of experience remained undiminished as he entered his seventieth year. In *The Human Age,* he unfortunately allows his gaze to wander from external reality. He now creates a fantasy world in which supernatural beings (angels, demons, even dragons) mingle incongruously with humans. (p. 155)

The main character of *The Human Age,* James Pullman, was a famous writer (a satirist) before his death. When alive, he believed that his life expressed a disinterested love of art; in the afterlife, he learns that he had deceived himself. . . . Pullman dimly understands his guilt in the first world he experiences (Third City), and when he is transported to the next (Matopolis) he finds himself involved in a plot to attack God himself by humanizing the divine and thus bringing about a Human Age. The meaning of his life is now clear even to Pullman himself. Although the pessimistic works Pullman once wrote may have been great art, the man who wrote them led a coldly intellectual, selfish life that now aligns him with the diabolical. Lewis involves us with Pullman as closely as he does with René Harding, whom Pullman closely resembles. Through his consciousness, we search for the meaning of his new world and of his past life. Pullman's fantasy world, however, does not support the drama of his character as René's densely realistic one supports his.

In *Monstre Gai,* when Pullman and his childish friend Satters enter the city, instead of finding the Paradise the Bailiff (the "monstre gai" of the title) has promised, they find a travesty of the welfare state. Passive, unnaturally youthful crowds file through the streets or sit idly at the cafés that line them. Lewis's description of the city's sterile architecture is effective; but where other creators of dystopias (Orwell, Huxley) would give us a score of details to authenticate the city, Lewis gives us one or two. (p. 156)

Whatever the precise nature of [Lewis's] religious beliefs, they do not fire his imagination in *The Human Age.* The destructive power in Pullman's strange new world, as revealed in *Malign Fiesta,* is Satan himself. Lewis's Satan, suave, witty, a trifle bored, might have stepped out of the "Don Juan in Hell" section of Shaw's *Man and Superman*. As we listen to Satan complaining that it was he who left God, that there are so many sinners nowadays that punishing them scarcely seems worth the effort, and that God is a disagreeable old autocrat, we could say of Lewis's ideas (as Samuel Johnson said less justly of Milton's in *Paradise Lost*) "Being therefore not new, they raise no unaccustomed emotion in the mind: what we knew before, we cannot learn; what is not unexpected, cannot surprise." Surprise is the life-giving quality *The Human Age* lacks.

Yet *The Human Age* has been compared to the works of Swift by critics such as Hugh Kenner and Walter Allen. John Holloway thinks that it "is perhaps the most memorable picture, in the form of fable rather than realistic fiction, that we have of our own time." One can understand how the work could be so highly praised. Allen writes that "in grandeur of conception and of execution it obviously transcends anything written by an Englishman during the past twenty years." He may be right about the conception of the work. Individual scenes refer back powerfully and disturbingly to our own world. In Lewis's version of Purgatory, Third City, the ghetto-dwellers are quieted by drugs and the ordinary citizens by fashionable clothing. In his version of Hell, Matapolis, Satan stops the cry of an infant with a hypodermic needle. . . . (pp. 157-58)

The problem is that these fine scenes are not integrated into a coherent vision of the afterlife. Lewis's powers of execution do not match his conceptions. His inconsistent characterization of his angels, some treated comically and some with reverence, suggests that Lewis was toying with a theological system that needs the intellectual commitment of a Milton to present convincingly. The relationship of God to the world that the book presents is especially weak. Satan claims that he is God's equal and that he tortures sinners only as a favor to his former divine associate. It is obvious that Satan has been lying when God, after Satan provokes him with the "malign fiesta" held to celebrate his followers' decision to join their angelic natures to the human, effortlessly destroys Satan's forces. But if Satan was lying, and if as Pullman concludes "God values man," why did God tolerate Satan's sadistic treatment of man? The basic problem, and perhaps the one from which all the others spring, is that although Lewis uses a Christian framework, and was even drawn to the Christian religion, the spirit of his work is far from Christian. Satan is condemned for trying to do exactly what Christians believe Christ has done: join the divine with the human. Lewis would have done better to discard the Christian framework and invent a new metaphor for the relationship of the human and the divine, as Franz Kafka did in *The Castle*. The uninspired use of the Christian scheme shows that Lewis's religious insights were not sufficiently developed to support so ambitious a work. (p. 158)

> *Timothy Materer, in his* Wyndham Lewis the Novelist *(reprinted by permission of the Wayne State University Press; copyright © 1976 by Wayne State University Press), Wayne State University Press, 1976, 189 p. [some portions of this essay were originally published in a different form in Materer's essay "Apes of God," in* Agenda, Special Issue: Wyndham Lewis, *Vols. 7 & 8, Nos. 3 & 1, Autumn/Winter, 1969-70].*

## FREDRIC JAMESON (essay date 1978)

[*Jameson's* Fables of Aggression: Wyndham Lewis, the Modernist As Fascist, *from which the following excerpt is taken, is an important study that focuses on the differences between Lewis and* his contemporaries. Jameson combines a Marxist-structuralist and psychoanalytic critical approach in an attempt to determine why Lewis adopted the social and political viewpoints that he did. Jameson is one of the few critics who praises Lewis for those qualities which others find detestable: his aggressiveness, his elitism, his proto-fascism, his racism, and his dislike of women and homosexuals.]

Wyndham Lewis is surely the least read and most unfamiliar of all the great modernists of his generation, a generation that included the names of Pound and Eliot, Joyce, Lawrence and Yeats; nor can it be said that his painting has been assimilated any more successfully into the visual canon. Lewis was a presence for his contemporaries, but we have forgotten their admiration for him. (pp. 1-2)

Yet it has been my experience that new readers can be electrified by exposure to *Tarr*, a book in which, as in few others, the sentence is reinvented with all the force of origins, as sculptural gesture and fiat in the void. Such reinvention, however, demands new reading habits, for which we are less and less prepared. Anglo-American modernism has indeed traditionally been dominated by an impressionistic aesthetic, rather than that—externalizing and mechanical—of Lewis' expressionism. (p. 2)

There were of course excellent and objective reasons for Lewis' neglect: reasonable motives, which it would be naive to ignore, for the resistance of sophisticated modern readers to that particular brand of modernism he had in store for them. A consistent perversity made of him at one and the same time the exemplary practitioner of one of the most powerful of all modernistic styles and an aggressive ideological critic and adversary of modernism itself in all its forms. Indeed, *Time and Western Man* . . . diagnostically attributes the aberrant impulse of all the great contemporary artistic and philosophical modernisms to what he called the "Time Cult," to the fetishization of temporality and the celebration of Bergsonian flux. However illuminating this diagnosis may have been, it had the unfortunate effect of forcing his readership to choose between himself and virtually everything else (Joyce, Pound, Proust, Stein, Picasso, Stravinsky, Bergson, Whitehead, etc.) in the modern canon.

Meanwhile, at the very moment in which the modernisms of the mainstream discovered their anti-Victorian vocation and developed a battery of onslaughts on moral taboos and repressive hypocrisies, an analogous gesture finds Lewis affirming the oppressiveness of the sexual instinct and unseasonably expressing a kind of archaic horror at sexual dependency. The polemic hostility to feminism, the uglier misogynist fantasies embodied in his narratives, the obsessive phobia against homosexuals, the most extreme restatements of grotesque traditional sexist myths and attitudes—such features, released by Lewis' peculiar sexual politics . . . , are not likely to endear him to the contemporary reader.

This *esprit de contradiction* of Lewis' polemic and aesthetic production alike is but another face of that aggressivity which was a lifelong constant of both the form and the content of his works, and of his own characterological style. To the aggressive impulses Lewis found within himself we are of course indebted for the astonishing pathology of figures like Kreisler (in *Tarr*). But there is no point denying the oppressiveness with which such impulses gradually become dominant, are generalized and projected outwards as a global hostility, not merely to his own characters, but also to the quasi-totality of his contemporaries as well, not excluding his own readership. (pp. 3-4)

Ideologically, Lewis' brief flirtation with Nazism—celebrated in the notorious *Hitler* . . .—stands as a symptom somewhere in between his deep misogyny and his violent anti-Communism. The episode itself may have been no more (but no less) serious than the comparable enthusiasms of Pound, Yeats, Shaw and others. . . . The stance of the postwar polemics—see, for instance, *The Writer and The Absolute* . . . , a blistering attack on Sartrean *engagement* and the concept of a political vocation for literature—only reconfirmed his sterile and chronic oppositionalism, his cranky and passionate mission to repudiate whatever in "modern civilization" seemed to be currently fashionable. The more sombre and dramatic turns in Lewis' personal destiny—his forced and impecunious exile in Canada during World War II, the blindness visited on the great painter during his final years—do not necessarily redeem the querulous posture of the nay-sayer or make it any more immediately attractive to the unfamiliar reader.

In spite of all this—yet in some deeper sense, surely, because of it—Lewis' intellectual, formal, and ideological trajectory was marked and monumentalized by a series of remarkable novels, each one utterly unlike the next, and all of them without analogy among the production of his contemporaries. We have already mentioned his "artist's novel," *Tarr*. . . . The mid-thirties Graham-Greene-type thriller, *The Revenge for Love* . . . , invests Bolshevik conspiracies with a characteristic and unmistakably personal resonance. The autobiographical *Self Condemned* . . . , bleakest of all Lewis' works, records the dark night of the soul in the icy dreariness of exile in wartime Canada. Finally, spanning thirty years, the immense unfinished *Human Age* (whose first volume, *The Childermass* . . . constitutes a veritable summa of Lewis' narrative modernism) unexpectedly confronts us with the supreme realization of what has to be called theological science fiction.

Such texts, which reveal Lewis to have been among the most richly inventive of modern British writers, merit unapologetic rediscovery and can sustain enthusiastic reading as well as the closest critical scrutiny. (pp. 5-6)

> Fredric Jameson, "On Not Reading Wyndham Lewis"
> (1978), in his Fables of Aggression: Wyndham Lewis,
> the Modernist as Fascist *(copyright © 1979 by The
> Regents of the University of California; reprinted by
> permission of the University of California Press),
> University of California Press, 1979, pp. 1-25.*

## ROGER B. HENKLE (essay date 1979)

Lewis loved to cast himself in his fiction—or at least husks of himself—and one of the protagonists of [*Tarr*], Frederick Tarr, is a Lewis persona: harsh, brooding, angular in his relationships, prickly, somewhat detached. Throughout the book Tarr tries to ease himself out of a romantic entanglement with Bertha, a fleshy German lover whose agreeable yielding passiveness enchants and yet irritates Tarr. (p. 97)

A novel, particularly by an author as programmatic as Lewis, who likes so much to project himself into fictional situations, will often reveal because of its broader context, a fuller insight into the nature of an aesthetic position than will any number of manifestos. *Tarr* proves that: we can see that Lewis' insistence on a cold, impersonal art arises as much from his disgust with the way one becomes emotively involved with objects

and relationships as it does from the artist's need to see things clearly. (p. 98)

*Tarr,* for many of us Lewis' most intriguing novel, is not properly a satire, although its portrayal of two would-be artists, Frederick Tarr, and an inept German named Otto Kreisler, is highly ironic. Kreisler is a fat, slothful, moody Bohemian, who lives by sponging off his friends and eking out an allowance from his disapproving father, and who nurtures his dull Angst by cultivating sordid love affairs. . . . Kreisler might be a bourgeois refugee from Joseph Conrad's *The Secret Agent:* the idiot half-brother of Ossipon and Verloc. A self-consciously "experimental" novel, *Tarr* explores the strange rhythms and disjunctures of what Lewis considers to be the nature of the human mind. Frederick Tarr—and to a lesser extent Otto Kreisler—always find themselves in states of curious detachment. They are both elaborate schemers, but when they are in the midst of acting upon their schemes, their attention wanders in the most disconcerting ways. . . . As a result, all human encounters disintegrate into ludicrous farces. Tarr cannot break clean from Bertha and instead spends his late afternoons every day in her apartment, answering his mail while she sobs softly in the background. Kreisler arranges a duel with a Pole, Soltyk, whom he thinks to be his "double," and at the moment of truth, in a meadow in the Bois de Boulogne, Kreisler outrages everyone by offering to settle the dispute without arms if Soltyk will kiss him. (pp. 99-100)

Kreisler's bizarre behavior has a pathological "truth" to it; bourgeois degeneracy frequently takes on the shape of sexual deviation, particularly homosexuality, for Lewis. Similarly, Tarr's predicament is familiar to us all—the way in which, in moments of tension we find ourselves unable to control or account for our thoughts and impulses. Lewis believes, however, that his protagonists' comic behavior has a more fundamental implication; there is only the flimsiest correlation between outward behavior and the workings of consciousness. And there seems to be no accounting for the patterns that the consciousness takes. Tableaus of attitude and feeling appear suddenly in the mind; they burst into full and elaborate shapes, like fireworks in the sky, slowly exfoliating, freezing into images on the dark space, and then as quickly disappear. (p. 100)

Sex is the great distraction of life, as far as Lewis is concerned, because one cannot control how one feels; one doesn't know what the nature of romantic or lustful impulses is. *Tarr* essentially documents Kreisler's and Tarr's ludicrous confusions on this score, as the two men haplessly circle around the two women they share, Bertha and Anastasya, unaccountably being attracted to and repulsed by each, as if they were magnetic bars turning positive and negative poles toward each other. . . . Women in this and other works of Lewis' are reduced mercilessly to bourgeois commodities, to symbols of the softness and inertia of the culture—to Gaudier-Brzeska's Mona Lisa. But Lewis' sexism may be another symptom of the same difficulty he has in *knowing* people—or, more important, knowing his real feelings about people. Sexuality seems to fuddle one's perceptions. In his later book of cultural philosophy, *Time and Western Man* . . . , Lewis complains that the "sex-nuisance" has made it impossible for modern Western cultures to make any clear moral or social statements. Sex is the great distraction of cultural debate; it has been the foolish concern of all reactions against middle class morality. . . . Admittedly, this is a very important idea, but one wonders if Lewis' position on this matter, also, stems in part from the same problem that underlies so much of his analysis of human nature: that we cannot know how or why we feel as we do.

Lewis' own sense of "psychology," then, is the first and most crucial source of his satirical mode of rendering character by external appearances. *Tarr* furnished him a kind of fictional laboratory for the revelation and analysis of individual psychology, and it demonstrates the difficulty—the impossibility—of knowing the courses of human emotion and thought. "What is 'the truth' regarding any person?" Lewis asks rhetorically in his chapters on satire in *Men Without Art*. . . . *Tarr,* Lewis' first "mimetic" novel, demonstrates the inadequacies of mimesis, especially in the context of the later nineteenth-century and early twentieth-century art, which sought to show the workings of the mind reflecting upon itself. Indeed, the form is culturally insidious, distracting us not only with romantic "truths" about ourselves, but also inducing us to believe that we cannot break off the process of culturally-informed self-expression—that we are in the Bergsonian, Jamesian "stream of consciousness," lost, like a Proustian character, in the flows of our memories and our tastes. On the contrary, the intelligent human being acknowledges the erratic course of the mind, and the way it disgorges great shreds of indistinctive, associative matter from the imperfect digestions of a sensuously over-rich culture. Consequently, such a man is aware that most people operate in a kind of random way; whatever consistency of "personality" they develop is very likely an *assertion,* a program of behavior and attitudes. (pp. 101-03)

Lewis conceived of himself . . . as an "advertisement of self." His character Arghol, in the Vorticist short story, **"The Enemy of the Stars,"** concludes cynically that one can create the persona of his false self of social excrescence by repeating his name "like a sinister word invented to launch a new Soap in gigantic advertisement—toilet-necessity, he." Lewis had a properly jaundiced appreciation of the power of self-promotion in this newspaper world. . . . He became a master of what we have come to call "media events" or "happenings": commotion-filled grand openings, carefully staged walkouts, salon gatherings with impressionable old dowagers, blizzards of manifestos. . . . And when Lewis discovered after the War that people were not attending to him any more—*enfants terribles* are not as captivating when all the boys are dead—he unleashed a veritable "media blitz" of publications. . . . (p. 103)

He that lives by the advertisement may fall by it, however, and this appears to be largely the problem that besets *Apes of God,* Lewis' "purest" satire, and the book by which he is best known. The novel is a ruthless anatomy of triviality in the upper reaches of English art society. Opening with a description of an angry old woman, Lady Fredigonde . . . , the novel takes its protagonist, a young man named Daniel Boleyn, on a grand tour of specimens of the dry rot in the English Establishment. *Apes of God* has its fine moments—usually when desperate old women are frantically cuddling young men in a struggle to seduce them—but it is a curiously nerveless production: Eliot's etherized body. For Lewis' diagnosis seems to be that the culture has been made impotent by its own cultural sensationalism. (p. 104)

The use of Horace Zagreus as spokesman of his ideas proves rather telling, for Zagreus emerges as a strangely ineffectual man. The reader discovers that Zagreus rarely articulates his own ideas; he is a word-perfect mimic of the pronouncements of a sage named Pierpoint, who never appears in the novel, and whose observations on the Gossip-Society (published in an "encyclical" or recounted by Zagreus) are orthodox Wyndham Lewis. (Particularly ironic, incidentally, is Lewis' pre-

sentation of Pierpoint's political secretary in the guise of a "fascist"—at a time when Lewis was still making fun of Mussolini and had not reached his German-apologist stage.) Zagreus, like Lewis, has a penchant for outraging people, especially those in the upper class "art" circles. But can Lewis be thinking of his own position, when other characters in the novel dismiss Zagreus as a man whose obsession with being a kind of cultural gadfly has superseded his artistic interests, and whose chief reputation is that of an elaborate practical joker? Curiously apropos to Lewis is Zagreus' fate: after he has spouted his unfashionable philosophies to a shocked luncheon party, the hostess—a wealthy commercial supporter of the arts—asks that he leave the premises. Instructions will be left with the butler; he will no longer be admitted to the house.

The mentality of the advertising age may alienate Lewis, and he may feel that others are using its premises and methods to vulgarize art, but that mentality must surely be another impulse behind Lewis' satire in *The Apes of God.* For it is the spirit of the polemicist/sensationalist that pushes him to extremes; that assumes that all the other people he deals with are tendentiously exaggerating their positions; that they are "advertising" or promoting themselves (or the false personas that are all they can call "selves"); that their ideas are commodities which they bought from cultural supersalesmen, usually in the cheapest, most vulgar editions, and which they are proceeding to "consume" and use in the most meritricious sort of way. Fredric Jameson in his recent book on Lewis contends that Lewis, for all his intellectual elitism, seemed to share the outlook of Western petit bourgeois ideology. That ideology assumes that the aspirations and values of large segments of the middle class are oriented by their commercial desires, and framed always in material terms. Lewis' satiric position is predicated on that sort of debasement of the tastes of the people.

The characters in *Apes of God* accordingly cherish their reified personas as if they were prize possessions. The vagueness of "self" that plagued Otto Kreisler has been replaced by carefully nurtured personas that are polished and displayed like favorite pieces of garish furniture. (pp. 105-06)

Lewis' vision of a society of false, culturally programmed personas, of people with masks, is a familiar one in English literature of the turn of the nineteenth century and the early decades of the twentieth. One thinks of Wilde and Yeats and George Moore and even Joyce. None of these, however, treats the phenomenon with the hard, satirical disdain of Lewis. *Apes of God* invites comparison in fact, with Wilde's *The Picture of Dorian Gray,* for both novels focus upon the "education" of an impressionable, physically beautiful young man by a cynical older man. In both the overtones of homosexual influences are clear. Yet *Apes of God* has none of the psychological intensity of the earlier novel. Wilde clearly believes in the power of one personality to shape another, and he considers the concept of role-playing an important one, for it can be used—*was* frantically used by Wilde himself—to liberate one from the formulaic behavior and morality of the dominant culture. In Wilde, the homosexual aspect of the relationship is not perversion, as it is for Lewis; it is an opening up to human perversity, to the dark corners of the psyche. For all the melodrama, for all the flippancy, Wilde's book transmits the intensity of a deeply felt concern—of something he must explore and must bring to light. In *Apes of God,* on the other hand, the relationships and the implications they may have are simply allowed to fade away. Just as no character in the novel is worth bothering about, neither, one feels, are the issues raised by the characterizations. And this, one suspects, is the mentality of the publicist/advertisement-monger at work. Lewis is a ferocious critic of his time and place, and an indefatigable hawker of ideas, but he is not (at this stage) a writer driven by the passion of his needs of self-expression, nor is he a true propagandist, for he has no ideology or program to which he is committed. Perhaps this is the reason why he could readily become an apologist for many unpopular and offensive ideas in the next decades, and why he could so readily change specific positions. (p. 107)

> *Roger B. Henkle, "The 'Advertised' Self: Wyndham Lewis' Satire," in* Novel: A Forum on Fiction *(copyright © Novel Corp., 1979), Vol. 13, No. 1, Fall, 1979, pp. 95-108.*

### BERNARD BERGONZI   (essay date 1980)

In the nineteen-twenties Wyndham Lewis presented himself to a philistine world as the Enemy. The enmity was duly returned. Twenty-three years after his death he is regarded with unenthusiastic respect as one of the "men of 1914" and a pioneer English modernist in art and letters; theses are written about him and . . . he is becoming the subject of academic studies. But people find it difficult to speak well of Lewis: he is thought of as a fascist, a racist, a sexist, a man whose opinions, delivered with brutal provocativeness, were repugnant to the liberal consensus. Nevertheless, extreme and uncompromising controversialists seem, by some law of intellectual life, to attract passionately devoted followers. Accordingly, there are Poundians and Leavisites; and a small but articulate band of Lewisites, working hard to get due recognition for the Enemy. Still, it would be idle to pretend that he is very widely read, even if his novels are easier to obtain than they once were.

Some major modernist texts, once thought difficult and subversive, have been quite easily assimilated and incorporated into the general practice of novel reading, and subsequently canonized by academic syllabuses. Young readers can now respond very comfortably to, or, as they put it, "relate to", *A Portrait of the Artist* or *The Rainbow*. It is difficult to imagine them feeling in the same way about the hard, aggressive, seemingly inhuman comedy of *Tarr*, which was written at the same time as those novels. (p. 1215)

Lewis is now being increasingly written about; whether he is being any more widely and appreciatively read remains uncertain. Particular puzzles and contradictions recur throughout them. Lewis's contempt for the exaltation of the ego and for Romantic self-expression went along with an essentially Romantic egoism and cult of the artist in his own writings. Indeed, one might argue that an assertive literary neo-classicism, of the kind that Lewis flaunted in the 1920s, is, in our century, a further version of Romanticism. Lewis disliked modern civilization because it reduced men to the status of puppets and machines, yet depicted them as such in his own painting and fiction. There seems to be a division between importance and value in Lewis, which is implied by several of his critics but not brought clearly into focus. That is to say, Lewis was without doubt a major modernist innovator; in painting and design with the abstraction and near-abstraction of the years 1912 to 1915; in prose with *The Wild Body, Enemy of the Stars,* and *Tarr;* and in cultural politics with *Blast* and Vorticism. These works and activities imply an anti-humanist attack on bourgeois order, which . . . has affinities with the iconoclasm and radicalism of the proto-fascism which emerged from the First World War.

But what most writers about Lewis . . . seem to value, to "relate to", are those works of the late 1930s and after where he returns to a humanistic mainstream; the serene paintings of Eliot, Pound and his wife; *The Revenge for Love* and the powerful but traditional realism of *Self Condemned*. A sufficiently flexible and pluralistic criticism can come to terms with these paradoxes. But Lewis remains what he always was, a very difficult man to deal with. (p. 1217)

> *Bernard Bergonzi, "An Artist and His Armour," in* The Times Literary Supplement *(© Times Newspapers Ltd. (London) 1980; reproduced from* The Times Literary Supplement *by permission), No. 4048, October 31, 1980, pp. 1215-17.\**

---

## ADDITIONAL BIBLIOGRAPHY

*Agenda* 7, No. 3 (Autumn-Winter 1970): 224 p.
> Special Wyndham Lewis issue. Included are articles by Julian Symonds, Ezra Pound, Rebecca West, Hugh Kenner, and C. H. Sisson, among others. Several articles by Lewis are included, as well as extracts from his longer works. A bibliography is also included.

Ayrton, Michael. "*Tarr* and Flying Feathers." *Shenandoah* VII, No. 1 (Autumn 1955): 31-43.
> Informal account of Ayrton's acquaintance with Lewis.

Gawsworth, John. *Apes, Japes and Hitlerism: A Study and Bibliography of Wyndham Lewis*. London: Unicorn Press, 1932, 100 p.
> One of the few positive appraisals of Lewis's work during the 1930s.

Glicksburg, Charles I. "Wyndham Lewis: The Reactionary Artist and His Commitment." In his *The Literature of Commitment*, pp. 84-99. Lewisburg, Pa.: Bucknell University Press, 1976.
> Discussion of Lewis's fascism and anti-Semitism as they relate to his writing.

Handley-Read, Charles, and Newton, Eric. *The Art of Wyndham Lewis*. London: Faber and Faber, 1951, 109 p.
> Discussion of Lewis's painting, with some commentary on his writing. Newton's essay demonstrates which artists and writers, as well as which social, political, and artistic movements influenced Lewis's painting and writing.

Materer, Timothy. *Vortex: Pound, Eliot, and Lewis*. Ithaca: Cornell University Press, 1979, 231 p.\*
> Examination of the Vorticist movement and of Lewis's contributions to it. Materer details the close relationships between Lewis, Pound, and Eliot.

Meyers, Jeffrey. "Wyndham Lewis and T. S. Eliot: A Friendship." *The Virginia Quarterly Review* 56, No. 3 (Summer 1980): 455-69.\*
> Recounts the forty-year friendship between Lewis and Eliot, focusing on the later years of Lewis's life.

Meyers, Jeffrey. *The Enemy: A Biography of Wyndham Lewis*. London: Routledge and Kegan Paul, 1980, 391 p.
> Major biography of Lewis, well-documented and especially thorough in recounting his childhood.

Meyers, Jeffrey, ed. *Wyndham Lewis: A Revaluation*. London: Athlone Press, 1980, 276 p.
> Contains essays by Meyers, John Holloway, Marshall McLuhan, E.W.F. Tomlin, Bernard Lafourcade, Valerie Parker, and Timothy Materer.

Pritchard, William H. "On Wyndham Lewis." *Partisan Review* XXXV, No. 2 (Spring 1968): 253-73.

Study of Lewis's literary criticism. Pritchard also examines Lewis's influence upon and relation to Pound, James Joyce, Eliot, and D. H. Lawrence.

Pritchard, William H. "Satire and Fiction: Examples from the 1930s." In his *Seeing through Everything: English Writers 1918-1940*, pp. 178-228. New York: Oxford University Press, 1977.*
Compares Lewis with Evelyn Waugh, Anthony Powell, and George Orwell in his use of moral and satire.

Russell, John. "Wyndham Lewis: *Tarr, Self Condemned*." In his *Style in Modern British Fiction: Studies in Joyce, Lawrence, Forster, Lewis, and Green*, pp. 123-57. Baltimore: The Johns Hopkins University Press, 1978.

Examination of Lewis's style as evidenced in *Tarr* and *Self Condemned*. Russell demonstrates that many of Lewis's stylistic devices remained unchanged from his first novel to his last.

Wagner, Geoffrey. "Wyndham Lewis (1886-1957)." In *The Politics of Twentieth-Century Novelists*, edited by George A. Panichas, pp. 52-64. New York: Hawthorne Books, 1971.
Describes Lewis as "an extreme case of the contemporary aesthetic infatuation with politics." Wagner discounts the validity of Lewis's political writings because of the frequency with which he contradicts himself.

# Jack London

## 1876-1916

(Born John Griffiths London) American novelist, short story writer, essayist, journalist, and dramatist.

London was a popular Naturalist whose work combined high adventure, socialism, mysticism, Darwinian determinism, and Nietzschean theories of race. Of the fifty books he published during his short career, *The Call of the Wild* is the most famous and widely read. London's fiction, particularly *The Call of the Wild*, *The Iron Heel*, and the short stories "Love of Life," "Lost Face," and "To Build a Fire" are considered classics in American literature, and have often been compared with the stories of Joseph Conrad and Rudyard Kipling.

Born in San Francisco and abandoned shortly after birth by his father, London took the name of his stepfather. Because of his family's poor financial condition, London was forced to leave school at the age of fourteen and find work. He labored for several years as a cannery worker, a longshoreman and as a nocturnal scavenger of San Francisco Bay, becoming the self-styled "Prince of the Oyster Pirates." In his spare time, he attempted to further his education by reading the works of Herbert Spencer, Karl Marx, Rudyard Kipling, Friedrich Nietzsche, and others. He joined the Klondike gold rush of 1898, returning to San Francisco penniless, but with a wealth of memories which provided the raw material for his first stories. *The Son of the Wolf*, containing stories of the colorful, violent adventures of men and animals who fight for survival in the pitiless Yukon wilds, proved immensely popular. Several other short story collections and novels set in Alaska followed, written, like all of London's work, in a simple, vigorous style. *The Call of the Wild* and *White Fang* are the most highly regarded of these books—like all the Alaskan stories, they explore the struggle between the conflicting calls of barbarity and civilization. As a correspondent for various magazines, London traveled to the Far East during the Russo-Japanese war, through the South Pacific in a leaking ketch, and to the slums of England disguised as a derelict. These experiences provided the material for many of his books. London became the highest-paid writer of his day, earning more than a million dollars. He was an extremely disciplined craftsman and each day he wrote at least one thousand words. During his last years, London purchased ideas for stories from other writers when his own imagination failed him, but he did so infrequently, and critics often overemphasize this aspect of his career. Ill health and alcoholism, brought on by financial difficulties and the demands of his work, led to London's premature death which, it is widely believed, was by suicide.

The wide variety of readings and experiences that fed London's imagination produced the two seemingly contradictory world views found in his work. Adventure tales, such as *White Fang* and *The Sea Wolf*, reflect the doctrines of rugged individualism and of the amoral *ubermensch* (superman), which London had learned from reading Darwin and Nietzsche. In later short story collections such as *South Sea Tales*, London's evolutionary theories took on the more sinister aspect of white supremacy, reflected in his characterizations of Nordic or Anglo-Saxon heroes as the conquerors of "inferior" island races. Yet, at the same time that London was writing these celebra-

tions of the Blond Beast, he was also producing thoughtful socialist novels and essays, in which he advocated the solidarity of the working class for the betterment of humanity. *The Iron Heel*, a futuristic dystopia, is the most notable example of his political fiction; here, London drew upon his own experiences as a laborer and upon his reading of Marx to portray a vision of the rise of fascism in America. The author injected his own political sympathies into the novel, making his hero a dynamic socialist leader who champions the cause of labor reform. The paradoxes of London's fiction mirrored the contradictions of his personal and political life; he once told a reporter, "I am a white man first and a socialist second." London also declared that such works as *The Sea Wolf* and the autobiographical *Martin Eden* were written to refute the doctrines of individualism and the superman, an argument which many critics have been unable to reconcile upon examination of the texts.

Most critics agree with H. L. Mencken's estimate that London's "too deadly industry" produced a "steady emission of half-done books" which the author never took time to rework. However, most also agree that despite their flaws, there remain in all of London's works moments of brilliance which prove, again in Mencken's words, "that London, at bottom, was no fraud." His innovative, simple style, descriptive skill, and adherence to the principles of Realism and Naturalism laid the groundwork for such later writers as Sherwood Anderson,

Ring Lardner, and Ernest Hemingway. In Earle Labor's estimation, London's stature as an artist derives from "his 'primordial vision'—the mythopoeic force which animates his finest creations and to which we respond without fully understanding why." He is an important figure in American literature for establishing "a middle ground," in Labor's words, "between the gutter and the drawing room."

(See also *Dictionary of Literary Biography*, Vol. 8: *Twentieth-Century American Science Fiction Writers;* Vol. 12: *American Realists and Naturalists.*)

## PRINCIPAL WORKS

*The Son of the Wolf*   (short stories)   1900
*The God of His Fathers and Other Stories*   (short stories) 1901
*A Daughter of the Snows*   (novel)   1902
*The Call of the Wild*   (novel)   1903
*The Kempton-Wace Letters* [with Anna Strunsky]   (novel) 1903
*The People of the Abyss*   (essay)   1903
*The Sea-Wolf*   (novel)   1904
*The Game*   (novel)   1905
*War of the Classes*   (essays)   1905
*White Fang*   (novel)   1906
*Before Adam*   (novel)   1907
*Love of Life and Other Stories*   (short stories)   1907
*The Road*   (essays)   1907
*The Iron Heel*   (novel)   1908
*Martin Eden*   (novel)   1909
*Lost Face*   (short stories)   1910
*Revolution and Other Essays*   (essays)   1910
*The Cruise of the "Snark"*   (essays)   1911
*South Sea Tales*   (short stories)   1911
*John Barleycorn*   (autobiography)   1913
*The Valley of the Moon*   (novel)   1913
*The Mutiny of the "Elsinore"*   (novel)   1914
*The Strength of the Strong*   (short stories)   1914
*The Scarlet Plague*   (novella)   1915
*The Star Rover*   (novel)   1915
*The Little Lady of the Big House*   (novel)   1916
*The Turtles of Tasman*   (short stories and drama)   1916
*The Red One*   (short stories)   1918
*Island Tales*   (short stories)   1920
*Letters*   (letters)   1965

---

## NINETTA EAMES   (essay date 1900)

In "The Son of the Wolf" the author gives his testimony of Alaskan life through actual sojourn in the country he describes. This personal contact, as it were, with his subject gives the book a unique charm and value. The reader feels that he is following the footsteps of one familiar with the trail but in no wise servile to bald fact; for here and there interspersed are bits of delicious fantasy with more than a hint of frank and wholesome sentiment. There is, nevertheless, little of the ethereal idealist in Jack London's work. We find him always human—a humanness which the spiritual-minded can share with profit. (p. 423)

Mr. London's adroit but graphic portrayal of character suggests scope and symmetry of thought rather than limitation and indefiniteness. His magnetic ardor and earnestness of thought move even the most stolid, notwithstanding an undercurrent of protest against certain inadvertencies—false syntax and the flagrant misuse of an occasional word—which are the result of inexperience or carelessness. In justice to the author, however, it must be admitted that these errors—most of which are not serious—are not of a nature to beget a distrust of his genius.

If this youthful California writer makes a study of literary style, it is not apparent, so simply and unaffectedly does he relate a story. There is, indeed, small showing of that painstaking polish so dear to the academic mind; this young man of twenty-four has something more virile to offer than finish. Crude as is his diction, he has learned the ways out of prescribed literature into a spontaneity and freedom that charm and invigorate. One sees no straining after effect, no circumlocution; he reaches the humanity of his readers by direct course. (p. 424)

It may be permitted to the writer of this sketch to express the belief that London's genius will long continue to present the world with literary products that must delight and edify a constantly growing circle of readers. His youth, his robust health, his assiduous application, his indomitable purpose, his rare discrimination in the choice of literary materials, and the facility and felicity of his style—these all give promise and prophecy of exceptional achievement. (p. 425)

> *Ninetta Eames, "Jack London," in* The Overland Monthly, *Vol. XXXV, No. 209, May 1900, pp. 417-25.*

## FREDERIC TABER COOPER   (essay date 1905)

[*Cooper praises the power of London's writing, while acknowledging the horror and violence of his subject matter.*]

[Jack London] is by instinct a realist of such brutal strength that at times he is repellent. Yet even when you shrink from him, you are forced to concede his power. Sometimes one is forced to question whether he writes as he does because such themes appeal to him, or whether he does not rather do so from sheer delight in his mastery over words—a perverse satisfaction in ringing the changes upon some one of the baser human passions, hatred, cruelty, or revenge, and making his reader shrink and wince. You read a book like *The Sea Wolf* very much as you gaze upon some ghastly accident, in a sort of horrified fascination that holds your eyes against your will. His technique is not always of the best; but he is always emphatically, splendidly, triumphantly himself. Whether it was necessary that such a book as *The Sea Wolf* should ever have been written is quite a separate question; but at least there is not another American writer of to-day to whom we could point and say, "He might have written it."

As already said, Jack London's technique is by no means above criticism. But he has produced at least one story which of its kinds seems to the present writer very nearly flawless—*The Game*. Some writers, of the school of Henry James and Paul Bourget, dwell so persistently upon the psychological side of life, that one comes to think of their characters as scarcely more substantial than so many disembodied spirits. Jack London, on the contrary, portrays his men and women as vital, passionate, human animals; and when he takes his characters from the higher walks of life, there is something incongruous in his insistence upon the animal side. But in *The Game* his two principal characters, the man and the girl, are both taken from the masses, the people at large. There is nothing of the artistic temperament about him, nor of the over-sensitive, neurotic woman about her. They are simply types of the normal, healthy, human male and female. In him, rather more than in the average man, there dwells a lust of combat, handed down from generation to generation since the stone age. And in the girl there slumbers, unknown to her, that instinctive pride in the victories of her chosen mate which the woman of primordial times shared with the tigress in the jungles. In short, the hero of *The Game* is a born prize-fighter. . . . The pleasure of a prize-fight, like most of Mr. London's themes, is largely a matter of individual taste. But one may say with confidence that to read *The Game* is quite as good, or quite as bad, according to the way you look at it, as though you had seen the fight yourself. (pp. 35-6)

> Frederic Taber Cooper, "The Individual Note: 'The Game'," in The Bookman, *New York (copyright, 1905, by George H. Doran Company), Vol. XXII, No. 1, September, 1905, pp. 35-6.*

### CHARLES A. SANDBURG [Carl Sandburg]   (essay date 1906)

[*Sandburg finds the struggle of the individual with the "System" to be a common motif in London's work.*]

London's fame as a writer has of recent days been hard pushed by his notoriety as an agitator. Howells, "the dean of American literature," Bliss Carman, Richard Le Galliene, Edwin Markham, and other literary men are socialists, but they have made no noise about it. London, however, has neglected no occasion to boom his theories. He has gone up and down the land talking to thousands urging the need of a new "System." For the upper and middle classes he has tried to picture the hellishness of the social pit that forever yawns for the man and woman out of work. His book, *The War of the Classes* is a vivid presentation of the facts of the class struggle.

But towering above these transitory events are his works in the way of fiction. . . . They dealt with the Klondike regions, experiences of the hardy gold-hunters, so many of whom left their bones in the shadow of the Arctic circle. It has been his part to interpret the fear of "the white silence," that vast and awesome loneliness of the far north.

Among his various studies in the north, none shows a higher appreciation of the present "System," none will set you thinking about how far the human race has progressed, the gulf between savagery and civilization, than the tale of **"Nam Bok the Unveracious."** . . . I cannot name a piece of literature in which the contrasts of civilization and savagery are more livingly set forth. It should be a part of the reading-course of every school.

*The Call of the Wild* and *The Sea-Wolf* are his masterpieces. Of these not a great deal may be said that is not repetitive. *The Call of the Wild* is the greatest dog-story every written and is at the same time a study of one of the most curious and profound motives that plays hide-and-seek in the human soul. The more civilized we become the deeper is the fear that back in barbarism is something of the beauty and joy of life we have not brought along with us. (pp. 36-8)

*The Sea-Wolf* bore down on me for all my brain-traffic would bear. I read it first as it appeared in cereal form and found it wholesome and nutritious. Had I not held a policy in the Equitable and felt certain I was going to live, I would surely have written the publishers to tell me how it was all going to end. The reviews of *The Sea-Wolf* were fun. Almost every man-jack of the hired scribes missed the allegory of the book, the lesson. Wolf Larsen is one in whose character revolve the motives of ambition and domination in their most terrible form. He is a ship-captain and absolute master of the vessel's crew. What gets in his way goes overboard, be it scullion or first mate. Do you know of any Thing that relentlessly crushes whatever gets in its way, be it a frail child, a tender woman, or a strong man? Wolf Larsen is The System incarnate. London has him die of a slow, pathetic paralysis. No wonder the well-sleeked critics thought his end was not artistic! (pp. 38-9)

I am not a prophet and I don't like to dabble in futurities, but I know London to be a tremendous worker and of simple habits, so I put him down as X, a dynamo of unguessable power.

If he were not a Common Man I would call him a Great Man. (p. 39)

> Charles A. Sandburg [pseudonym of Carl Sandburg], *"Jack London: A Common Man," in* Tomorrow *(copyright by Creative Age Press, Inc., 1906), Vol. 2, No. 4, April, 1906, pp. 35-9.*

### AMBROSE BIERCE   (essay date 1908)

[*Bierce admired most of London's works. This sarcastic review of* The Iron Heel, *however, offers little evidence of the critic's admiration.*]

Jack London's titanic exaggerations may be obvious enough when he writes of social and industrial conditions, but mark his accuracy and moderation in relating (in **"The Iron Heel"**) the things that he knows about:

"The mob came on, but it could not advance. It piled up in a heap, a mound, a huge and growing wave of dead and dying. Those behind urged on, and the column, from gutter to gutter, telescoped upon itself. Wounded creatures, men and women, were vomited over the top of that awful wave and fell squirming down the face of it till they threshed about under the automobiles and against the legs of the soldiers."

As an authority on the effects of gun-fire Colonel London stands foremost among the military men of his period.

Colonel London's book is supposed to be written in the year 419 B.O.M. (Brotherhood of Man), and following the cheerful incident related above come three centuries of similar controversy between the people and their oppressors, the mound-builders and wave-makers. Then—a natural and inevitable result of tempers and dispositions softened by slaughter—behind this frowning providence the Brotherhood of Man reveals its smiling face and the book "ends happily," its gallant author in receipt of a comfortable pension.

> Ambrose Bierce, "Small Contributions," in Cosmopolitan (© 1908 by The Hearst Corporation), Vol. XLV, No. 2, July 1908, p. 220.*

### PHILO M. BUCK, JR.   (essay date 1912)

[*In* "The American Barbarian," *Buck charged that, London's popular success was based on appeals to his readers' taste for uncultured, rough-and-tumble barbarity. The article angered London, and brought about an exchange of letters which are collected in* Creator and Critic: A Controversy between Jack London and Philo M. Buck, Jr.]

Jack London began by imitating Kipling, who perhaps more than any other English author has best written in praise of the English Barbarian—witness the stories of India and the early stories of Alaska; only Kipling's Barbarians wear khaki, and on occasion dress uniforms, while London's are seldom seen except in fur or the miner's blue of our polar territory. There is more than one point of similarity besides that of style between *My Own People* and the **Children of the Frost.** Again, when Kipling drew the picture of a society of partly civilized barbarians in the jungle, under the leadership of Bagherra, the Black Panther; Baloo, the Bear; and Mowgli, the Man Cub; London followed with an equally well-drawn picture of a slightly less civilized—and a trifle more strenuous, to be sure, as befits our Western ideal, but no less individualistic—life in the wilderness, Buck's atavism in the **Call of the Wild.** (p. 22)

Return to nature—how often have we heard that expression. This is the cry of each of London's stories from **The Call of the Wild** to his latest, **Burning Daylight.** To be sure, the nature that he makes too strong in its appeal for the thin veneer of Buck's civilization is a very different nature from that of Kipling's Jungle stories. In India even nature has long been steeped in an antique civilization; here in the rude Northwest it is all crude, mysterious, harsh, full of primeval unrest, force, and elemental rage. The English Barbarian, as expounded by Arnold and pictured by Kipling, long subject to the softer influence of a settled civilization and hereditary possessor of the goods of civilization, has in much become conservative. With him the call to nature is a mild flutelike note that seldom invites to more than a lawn party, or the hunter's whistle that calls for dog and gun, or, at the loudest, the bugle that summons to war. With London it is the clamorous demand for the pitting of a man's whole strength and cunning against the fiercest assaults of a worthy foeman armed at all points and eager for the battle. For it is London's creed that it is only by the severest of conflicts with the most truthful and worthy foeman a man can meet that a man's highest and best nature may be developed. (p. 23)

London's barbarian is no new type in the world's history. He is the recrudescence of a type long since dead in Western Europe, the purely primitive individualist of the age when society was in the making. He is an atavism. But it is this very return to the primitive in the present, like the romantic stories of the strenuous days of the past, that arouses the enthusiasm of hero-worshiping youth. It is this that explains the huge popularity of such stories as **The Sea Wolf, The Call of the Wild, Burning Daylight,** and even **Martin Eden.** Their "elemental strength," as a critic phrases it, their war against the conventions of society, their love of combat, their delight in pure physical existence—in a word, their essential barbarity is cause sufficient for their magnetic hold upon our imaginations. The same half fearful eagerness which drew the exhausted heirs of the rationalizing and philosophic eighteenth century to the romantic heroes of Scott's novels again draws us, the exhausted heirs of the socializing, scientific, inventive, and industrial nineteenth century, with less art, to be sure, to the romantic heroes of our age of chivalry.

London's heroes feel the tingle of life . . . , that electric thrill with which man goes forth to combat, perchance even to pay life's penalty. The greatest lovers of life are those who hazard it most freely, who most open-breasted brave its dangers; not those who hoard, to spend it moment by moment like precious grains of gold, but those who gamble, staking their whole upon the turn of a card. . . . [His] heroes are successful so long,

and only so long, as they employ this delight in life in a conflict with nature and with men in natural surroundings. In the field of their own choice, and with this fair and even-handed opponent, their success is assured. No difficulty apparently is great enough to cause them a moment's apprehension; no game is so strenuous that they are forced to withdraw before the desired end; no stakes are so high that they do not meet them willingly; in craft, in skill, in courage, in strength, they are equal to any emergency. (p. 25)

Naturally, as the exuberance of their first conflicts with nature wears off, these barbarians throw themselves against that arch foe of all supermanism—settled society. There they find no even-handed, good-natured justice, and free play for all their energies. Society is not to be conquered by pure muscular strength and agility. Nor is a man's cunning or skill always a match for the many wiles of a man trained in the smooth ways of the street or the market place. Society to the individualists is a mass of mildewed tradition and convention, materialistic and false to the core. Into this they plunge. They are astonished that it never directly attacks them, but seemingly ignores all blows. It has strange powers of giving way when attack is directed against one point, but closing in behind and, once the pressure is released, of slowly flowing back to its first position. It is soft, elastic, fluid; no impression, be it made with ever so much energy, is lasting. It wears out its antagonist by the very weight of its listlessness. To triumph over this is to triumph only during the victor's life time, no more, and then the viscous mass slowly settles, covering its victim and all his spoils. (pp. 26-7)

[In] this new conflict, with a foe whom he has painted in all the gloomy colors of a cynic's rainbow, there comes as surely the melancholy loosening of the underpinning of physical, mental, and moral manhood; muscles become soft and flabby, the mind needs by strong stimulants to be aroused to its day's work, for the strong ideal of industry remains; and the moral fiber—there remains no need for moral fiber when man's faith in man has once vanished. This is the tragedy of Martin Eden and of Elam Harnish. . . . [Both] are forced to the great renunciation: the former, with no ties to hold him, seeks rest in self-destruction; the latter, with the one tie of a reciprocated affection, retires to solitude and communion with nature. This seems the fate of purely selfish individualism which remorselessly pits itself against the settled order of society.

But, we ask, what is the essential flaw in these American Barbarians? What are the symptoms of a diseased imagination, intellect, or will, that bring the catastrophe? . . . If the Barbarian is . . . utterly lacking in the necessary passive virtues he is no less flawed by the utter selfishness of his aims. (pp. 27-9)

It is because the stories of Jack London stimulate in us of America our best virtues, which, because he stimulates also our worst vices—our thoughtless, reckless, inconsequential energy, our love of a blind conflict, our man and institution-baiting, our love of change, our caprice, our so-called reform and progressiveness; because he, like us, adores big men who set traditions at naught, who set culture at naught—it is because of all this that Jack London is probably the most popular author in America to-day. But it is also because he lacks true culture that Jack London fails at the test, for without true culture neither a man nor a nation may truly be called great and cause succeeding ages to rise up and call him blessed. (p. 29)

*Philo M. Buck, Jr., "The American Barbarian"*
*(originally published in* The Methodist Review, Vol.

XCIV, No. 5, September-October, 1912), in Creator and Critic: A Controversy between Jack London and Philo M. Buck, Jr. *by Jack London and Philo M. Buck, Jr., edited by King Hendricks, Vol. VIII, No. 2, March, 1961, pp. 20-9.*

## JACK LONDON (Interview with EMANUEL HALDEMAN-JULIUS) (interview date 1913)

[*The following statement was made during the difficult last years of London's life.*]

I assure you that I do not write because I love the game. I loathe it. I cannot find words to express my disgust. The only reason I write is because I am well paid for my labor—that's what I call it—labor. I get lots of money for my books and stories. I tell you I would be glad to dig ditches for twice as many hours as I devote to writing if only I could get as much money. To me, writing is an easy way to make a fine living. Unless I meant it, I wouldn't think of saying a thing like this, for I am speaking for publication. I am sincere when I say that my profession sickens me. Every story that I write is for the money that will come to me. I always write what the editors want, not what I'd like to write. I grind out what the capitalist editors want, and the editors buy only what the business and editorial departments permit. . . . (pp. 11-12)

I am weary of everything. I no longer think of the world or the movement (the social revolution) or of writing as an art. I am a great dreamer, but I dream of my ranch, of my wife. I dream of beautiful horses and fine soil. I dream of the beautiful things I own up in Sonoma County. And I write for no other purpose than to add to the beauty that now belongs to me. I write a book for no other reason than to add three or four hundred acres to my magnificent estate. I write a story with no other purpose than to buy a stallion. To me, my cattle are more interesting than my profession. My friends don't believe me when I say this, but I am absolutely sincere. (p. 12)

> *Jack London, in an excerpt from an interview with Emanuel Haldeman-Julius (originally published in "The Pessimism of Jack London," in* Western Comrade, *Vol. 1, June, 1913), in* Creator and Critic: A Controversy between Jack London and Philo M. Buck, Jr. *by Jack London and Philo M. Buck, Jr., edited by King Hendricks, Vol. VIII, No. 2, March, 1961, pp. 11-12.*

## WILLIAM LYON PHELPS (essay date 1916)

[*Like Frederic Taber Cooper, Phelps was impressed by London's skill, in spite of what Phelps saw as gratuitous depictions of violence.*]

The flannel-shirted novelist, Jack London, has never written anything nearly so good as his *Call of the Wild* . . . , though the early chapters of *The Sea Wolf* . . . are brilliantly executed. When I began to read that story, the scenes at the start, the tumbling into the icy waters of the bay, the helplessness of the critic of Poe's literary style in the presence of the Wolf, I thought I was at last reading the great American novel—but when I came to the love scenes and the seal scenes, then I knew I was not. During the great and fleeting popularity of the "red-blood" school, an intense love of which is a sure indication of effeminacy, Jack London stood high in favour. Such phrases as "red corpuscles" (whatever that may mean), "male ardour," "sheer brutality," were quite in fashion; in-

deed they were the dying kicks of a pseudo-romanticism—instead of being a sign of vitality, they were evidences of the last convulsion. To read a book like *White Fang* is to feel like a cannibal, crunching bones and bolting blood. Yet Jack London is a man of letters; he has the true gift of style, so rare and so unmistakable; if he would forget his social and political creed, and lower his voice, he might achieve another masterpiece. Meanwhile let us be grateful for *The Call of the Wild,* a story that no other man could have written. (pp. 282-84)

> *William Lyon Phelps, "Twentieth Century American Novelists" (originally published as "The Advance of the English Novel," in* The Bookman, *New York, Vol. XLIII, No. 5, July 1916), in his* The Advance of the English Novel *(copyright, 1915, 1916, by Dodd, Mead and Company, Inc.), Dodd, Mead, 1917, pp. 267-301.**

## OLIVER MADOX HUEFFER (essay date 1916)

[*Hueffer stresses the eternal youthfulness of London and his writings.*]

Jack London was the ideal yarn-spinner—his spoken stories were even better than his written—and one reason why I think him likely to be numbered as among the writers of real mark was that he was perfectly unconscious of it. Like Peter Pan, he never grew up, and he lived his own stories with such intensity that he ended by believing them himself. (p. 206)

We have got so accustomed to that misused word "literature" and all the horrors of pose and insincerity that its unchecked ravages have come to stand for in this country, that we cannot understand the possibility of a man writing merely because he cannot help it. So it was with Jack London; so one hopes it may be with the future writers of the Pacific Slope, where, if anywhere, we must look for the "great American School," which can never find birth until its upholders have finally cast off the shackles of European "literature." When they do, it will be to Jack London that they will owe no small share of their freedom. The *mot juste,* and similar trappings had no share in Jack London's work. In his forty-one years of life he turned out an amazing amount of work; he was as industrious as that other great story-teller Alexandre Dumas—and there is nothing among it which cannot rank as a story. Almost invariably it is also a good story, though, like other men, he turned out his fair share of pot-boilers. . . .

I shall always think of him as the most lovable child I ever met. As a writer, I believe that also he will not grow old quickly. It is a good sign that, already, he is loved—as is perhaps no other contemporary writer—by the simple-minded. Wherever you find soldiers and boys and those that prefer the story to the setting, there Jack London is read and loved. (p. 207)

> *Oliver Madox Hueffer, "Jack London: A Personal Sketch," in* New Statesman *(© 1916 The Statesman Publishing Co. Ltd.), Vol. VIII, No. 191, December 2, 1916, pp. 206-07.*

## UPTON SINCLAIR (essay date 1917)

[*A famous socialist and reformer, Sinclair was a friend of London and shared many beliefs with him. Sinclair depicts London as a near-saint in this elegiac article.*]

Jack London was a man with a magnificent mind, and a giant's will. He fought tremendous battles in his own soul—battles fought in spite of his own false philosophy, battles which he was fighting even while he was quarreling at other men's self-restraint. He went on a trip around the Horn, which lasted several months and drank nothing all that time; and he wrote that shining book, **"John Barleycorn,"** assuredly one of the most useful as well as one of the most entertaining books ever penned by a man. . . .

Jack London had a dream . . . of a strong, free proud woman, the mate for a strong, free, proud man. This dream came into his writings at the start in **"A Daughter of the Snows,"** his third novel—the very name of it, you perceive. This story published in the second year of the present century was crude, and boyish, but it had the promise of his dawning greatness, and was the occasion of my first letter to him, and the beginning of our friendship. Afterwards he told this story, over and over again; he continued to tell it long after he had ceased to believe in it himself. (p. 18)

I suspect that his real attitude towards women was expressed in **"Martin Eden,"** his most autobiographical novel, whose hero gives his final conclusion about life by dropping himself out of the porthole of an ocean steamer at night. This hero is a working boy, who makes a desperate struggle to rise from poverty, but the girl of the world of culture, whom he has idealized and worshipped, proves a coward and fails him in his need. . . .

This **"Martin Eden"** is assuredly one of Jack London's greatest works; he put his real soul into it; and the fact that it is so little known and read, compared with other works, must have been of evil significance to him. It taught him that if an American writer wants to earn a living with his pen—especially an extravagant living—it is necessary above all things that he should avoid dealing in any true and vital way with the theme of sex. Either he must write over and over again the dream of primitive and perfect mating, a phenomenon unreal and unconvincing to people who are not primitive, but who have intellects as well as bodies to mate with: or else, if he deals with modern life, he must give us details of the splendid and devastating passions of the prosperous—the kind of perfumed poison made fashionable by Robert W. Chambers. One saw the beginning of that in **"The Little Lady of the Big House,"** and I count this book the most sinister sign in the life of Jack London. A man can hardly have a thirty-six thousand dollar a year contract with William Randolph Hearst and still keep his soul alive! . . .

If I have written of him here severely it is because I believe in rigid truth, as I know he did; I have written just as I would have men write of me, if they had it worth while to write anything at all when I am dead. But I would not leave any one with the idea that I do not appreciate the greatness of Jack London that I do not realize that I am dealing with one of the greatest writers and one of the greatest souls that America has given to the world. . . .

Jack had a divine pity, he had wept over the East End of London as Jesus wept over Jerusalem. For years afterwards the memories of this stunted and depraved population haunted him beyond all peace; the pictures he wrote of them in **"The People of the Abyss"** will be read by posterity with horror and incredulity and recognized as among the most powerful products of his pen. Those with his vivid and intensely felt Socialist essays, constitute him one of the great revolutionary figures of our

history. In that role he is of course doubly precious to the present writer. I know that he kept that sacred light burning to the very end, for a little over a year before his death. I tried him with the manuscript of a revolutionary anthology, "The Cry for Justice." The preface he wrote for it is one of the finest things he ever did. (p. 19)

I recall the inscription he put in the copy of **"Martin Eden"** which he sent me; I have not the book at hand, and cannot quote it literally, but the substance was that without exception the critics of the book had missed his point. He had meant it for a refutation of the philosophy of individualism; the story of a man who won success, but found that this triumph brought him nothing. After reading the book I replied that it was easy to understand the befuddlement of the critics; for he had shown such sympathy with his hard-driving individualist that it would hardly occur to any one that the character was meant to be a warning and a reproach.

You feel that same thing in all his books—in **"The Sea Wolf,"** for example, or **"The Mutiny of the Elsinore"**; the Nietzschean all conqueror has conquered London's imagination, in spite of his reason and his conscience. (pp. 19-20)

If you wish to know the message of his life, as he himself wrote it, take that essay in **"The Cry for Justice,"** the last word he wrote upon ethical matters, so far as I know: "He, who by understanding becomes converted to the gospel of service will serve kindness so that brutality will perish; will serve beauty to the erasement of all that is not beautiful. And he who is strong will serve the weak that they may become strong. He will devote his strength not to the making of opportunity for them to make themselves into men rather than into slaves and beasts."

These words are from a new Bible, "this humanist Holy Book," as London called it. Such words and actions based upon them make precious his memory and will preserve it as long as anything in American literature is preserved. (p. 20)

> *Upton Sinclair, "About Jack London," in* The Masses,
> *Vol. 10, Nos. 1 & 2, November-December, 1917,*
> *pp. 17-20.*


## H. L. MENCKEN (essay date 1918)

[*A critic who reserved some of his sharpest barbs for socialists and reformers, Mencken perceived in London a true artist smothered under socialism and commercialism.*]

[Jack London] in truth, was an instinctive artist of a high order, and if ignorance often corrupted his art, it only made the fact of his inborn mastery the more remarkable. No other popular writer of his time did any better writing than you will find in **"The Call of the Wild,"** or in parts of **"John Barleycorn,"** or in such short stories as **"The Sea Farmer"** and **"Samuel."** Here, indeed, are all the elements of sound fiction: clear thinking, a sense of character, the dramatic instinct, and, above all, the adept putting together of words—words charming and slyly significant, words arranged, in a French phrase, for the respiration and the ear. (pp. 236-37)

That great thinking of his, of course, took color from the sordid misery of his early life; it was, in the main, a jejune Socialism, wholly uncriticised by humor. Some of his propagandist and expository books are almost unbelievably nonsensical, and whenever he allowed any of his so-called ideas to sneak into an imaginative work the intrusion promptly spoiled it. . . . The materialistic conception of history was too heavy a load for him to carry. When he would create beautiful books he had to throw it overboard as Wagner threw overboard democracy, the superman and free thought. A sort of temporary Christian created "Parsifal." A sort of temporary aristocrat created **"The Call of the Wild."**

Also in another way London's early absorption of social and economic nostrums damaged him as an artist. It led him into a socialistic exaltation of mere money; it put a touch of avarice into him. Hence his too deadly industry, his relentless thousand words a day, his steady emission of half-done books. The prophet of freedom, he yet sold himself into slavery to the publishers, and paid off with his soul for his ranch, his horses, his trappings of a wealthy cheese-monger. His volumes rolled out almost as fast as those of E. Phillips Oppenheim; he simply could not make them perfect at such a gait. There are books on his list—for example, **"The Scarlet Plague"** and **"The Little Lady of the Big House"**—that are little more than garrulous notes for books.

But even in the worst of them one comes upon sudden splashes of brilliant color, stray proofs of the adept penman, half-wistful reminders that London, at bottom, was no fraud. He left enough, I am convinced, to keep him in mind. There was in him a vast delicacy of perception, a high feeling, a sensitiveness to beauty. And there was in him, too, under all his blatancies, a poignant sense of the infinite romance and mystery of human life. (pp. 237-39)

> H. L. Mencken, *"Jack London"* (originally published as *"Literae Humaniores—II,"* in The Smart Set, *Vol. LIV, No. 3, March, 1918), in his* Prejudices, first series *(copyright 1919 by Alfred A. Knopf, Inc.; renewed 1947 by H. L. Mencken), Knopf, 1919, pp. 236-39.*

## WALDO FRANK   (essay date 1919)

[*Like Mencken, Frank decries London's selling his talent for quick, easy, commercial gain. His essay below, with its comments on London's youthfulness, offers an interesting contrast to Oliver Madox Hueffer's article (see excerpt above).*]

[The background of Jack London] was the background of America. He had gone back to primal stratum: stolen and labored and adventured. Finally, he had learned to write. Criticism grew in him. He pierced the American myths. He no longer believed in the Puritan God. He no longer believed in the Constitution. He signed his personal letters "yours for the Revolution." But what of this experience and passion and exploration lives in his books? Precisely, nothing. London became a "best-seller." He sold himself to a Syndicate which paid him a fabulous price for every word he wrote. He visited half the world, and produced a thousand words a day. And the burden of his literary output was an infantile romanticism under which he deliberately hid his own despair. Since the reality of the world he had come up through was barred to his pen, he wrote stories about sea-wolves and star-gazers: he wallowed in the details of bloody combat. If he was aware of the density of American life, of the drama of the conflict of its planes, he used his knowledge only as a measure of avoidance. He claimed to have found truth in a complete cynical disillusion. "But I know better," he says, "than to give this truth as I have seen it, in my books. The bubbles of illusion, the pap of pretty lies are the true stuff of stories."

Of course, a man so at odds with his experience could not compose a true autobiography. But in one of London's later volumes, **John Barleycorn,** there is the essence of confession. To the psychologist, a lie is as true a testimony as a consciously stated fact: for it is the word of the unconscious wish. So in this book, London professes to trace the growth of his love for drink under the guise of setting himself forth as an object lesson to the world, and merely portrays the bully and the playboy. (pp. 35-6)

Like his country, Jack London was corporeally mature, innerly a child. He mastered the outward circumstance of life—and then played with toys. The world was his, by physical and intellectual possession: but he preferred to live in a nursery, and blamed his excess drinking on the fact that no Nurse was there to keep the liquor from his lips. (p. 37)

> Waldo Frank, *"The Land of the Pioneer," in his* Our America *(copyright, 1919, by Boni & Liveright, Inc.; copyright renewed © 1947 by Waldo Frank), Boni and Liveright, 1919, pp. 13-58.*

## KATHERINE MANSFIELD   (essay date 1920)

[*In this review of* Island Tales, *Mansfield sees London's sentimentality and his ego as a combination deadly to his fiction.*]

[Jack London] is one of those writers who win the affection of their readers—who are, in themselves the favourite book. But this very affection which he inspired is a something sentimental. That which prevented Jack London from ever being one of the real adventurers, the real explorers and rebels, was his heart; there was always the moment when his heart went to his head and he was carried away by passions which were immensely appropriate to the occasion, but which suffered from a histrionic tinge. Then his simplicity, smothered under a torrent of puffed-up words, obscured the firm outlines upon which his story relied, and we were left with the vaguely uncomfortable sensations of those to whom an 'appeal' has been made.

Jack London at his best was the author of **'White Fang.'** From the first chapter we step straight into the book. There is the immense snowy landscape, spread out unruffled, empty as far as they can see except for the sled, the straining dogs, the two tiny creatures who urge them on, and, as the quick dusk thickens, the moving shapes of shadow which howl after them. In describing at length the hateful fight that went on and on, in making us watch with the tiny creatures and fear for them, in keeping the issue so uncertain that we cannot afford to take our eyes off those starving beasts for a second, the author prepares us for his story. For the first chapter is only a prologue—a taste of what wolves are like, a 'now you know what wolves can be,' which precedes the life-story from the birth to the fulness of years of that most beguiling animal, White Fang. . . . (p. 256)

When we turn to **'Island Tales'** we cannot help regretting that the gleaners have been so busy in the field where such a teeming crop has been reaped. For there is not a single story in it which is better than the average magazine supplies. True, his admirers would recognize them as having come from the Jack London shop; but they are machine-made, ready-to-read tales which depend for their novelty upon the originality of the Hawaiian ornament. It is a little sad to notice the effect of this ambrosial climate upon his style of writing. Words became hyphenated, bedecked, sentences were spun out until the whole reminded one of the wreaths—the 'Leis' or love-tokens—that the gentle savages love to hang about their necks. And then the Hawaiian greeting, 'Arms around,' as he describes it so often and with such delight, was no antidote to his sentimentality. It would not, however, be fair to judge him by this book. But it does confirm us in the opinion that his salvation lay in wolves, snow, hardship and toil. (p. 257)

> *Katherine Mansfield, "Hearts Are Trumps" (origi-nally published in* The Athenaeum, *No. 4713, August 27, 1920), in her* Novels and Novelists, *edited by J. Middleton Murry (copyright 1930, copyright re-newed © 1958, by Alfred A. Knopf, Inc.; reprinted by permission of The Society of Authors as the lit-erary representative of the Estate of Katherine Mans-field), Knopf, 1930, pp. 255-57.*

## C. HARTLEY GRATTAN  (essay date 1929)

[*Grattan's essay includes all the major negative criticisms of London's work as of 1929.*]

The active life and the primitive life were the two dominant concerns of London. In them he found his only satisfactions. And, like most Americans, he felt no high admiration for the intellectual life. His intensity was physical, muscular. (p. 667)

Jack London was a man of action to whom, deep down, learn-ing was a fraud and a delusion. The energy he communicated to his heroes, *l'énergie américaine,* was in a large part his own and was physical or coarse. Even the intellectual labors are recounted in physical terms. He made a great show of loving knowledge, but it is significant that all his heroes, including himself as the archetype, who got much of it, voluntarily sought death. With the primitives whom he portrayed it was not so. They had a firm "love of life". It was civilization that brought on mental sickness. For London, the man of civilization, all was glory or despair, and despair was death. Ideas were very real to him, as real as things. He concreted them so thoroughly, and the spectres he conjured up were so gruesome, that in the end he had an intellectual nightmare. Being essentially unso-phisticated, he took no joy in the free play of ideas. There was no humor, nor irony, nor subtlety in his intellectual life. He demanded, as a man of action, the finality which is necessary to action and made no concessions to relativity. He judged truth by its workability and held to it with a table-pounder's finality.

This hard positivity measurably weakened his fiction. There is in London none of that awe and wonder which has so much to do with the quality of Theodore Dreiser and Joseph Conrad. It is curious, too, that he should have victimized himself in this fashion in his studies of civilized life, for in his stories of the Alaskan natives he could render their bafflements vividly. He could see, apparently, their strange incomprehensions of the universe and of the white man's ways only as so much appealing ignorance, and his superior attitude would not allow him to believe that civilized man is only more ingenious, and not more penetratingly final, in his explanations. It is, there-fore, aimless to compare him to Maxim Gorki, to whom in social origin he roughly corresponds, for much of Gorki's at-traction is precisely his capacity for wonder—for scepticism.

This inability to assume a saving scepticism led London to entertain certain cheap ideas which either subtly flattered his intelligence or rationalized his activities. For instance, in 1915 he shouted, almost, at a harmless correspondent, "God abhors a mongrel. In nature there is no place for a mixed breed"

London was a proponent of the Nordic nonsense, and wrote *The Mutiny of the Elsinore* to show that the inferior races were crowding the Nordic blondes out of America. In *The Valley of the Moon* he harps on the transcendent virtues of the old Amer-icans, too. And in the same book he rationalized elaborately his own back-to-the-land activities. London was always going back to something, and his only satisfying intellectual orien-tation was in a large measure retrospective.

The ability, or necessity, to make ideas concrete was of great value to London, the writer, however much it may have dam-aged him as a thinker. The extroverted personality always de-mands a close relation to things. It does not grasp abstractions easily. Without invidious intent, attention may be called to London's success in giving a great air of plausibility to his studies of the primitive mind in *The Children of the Frost*. He must have found it easy to think in terms of concrete objects rather than in abstractions. A direct, uncomplicated relation to the world was balm to his spirit. These considerations give point to the idea that *The Call of the Wild* is his spiritual autobiography—and his best work. Concreteness is character-istic of his style also. It is organic to an astonishing degree. Each sentence has direct reference to a thing—often to more than one thing. Progression in his stories is from object to object, from act to act. In none of them is there any elaborate exposition of mental states. No one can discover the intellectual basis of Martin Eden's career. His acts are there, but where are his mental activities? London could not portray them, for such things eluded him. The result is that the novel lacks plausibility, however true to the facts of London's life it may be.

To be sure, not all facts got equal attention from London. He fumbled the matter of sex as badly as anyone of his generation. It is more than usually interesting to dig into the matter for, though he could with great frankness detail his alcoholic career in *John Barleycorn,* he never brought himself to the compo-sition of the projected *Jack Liverpool* which would have de-tailed his sexual career. (pp. 668-69)

"Absurd suppressions" characterizes the love element in all the novels. The sex attraction of Martin Eden breaks through all class barriers and leads to his engagement to Ruth Morse against her own class judgment. But when later, after they have been separated and he has tasted success—and disillusion—she offers her person without resort to clergy, he refuses and coldly escorts her home. His attitude is the same toward a working girl who makes a similar offer.

Perhaps London meant to convey by these episodes the depths of Eden's despair, but more likely the explanation of this strange course is to be found in London's enslavement to the editors. (p. 609)

He was not interested in writing as writing, but in writing in so far as it gave access to money with which he could acquire and control things. He was not, fundamentally, an artist and thinker at all; he was a man of action, a doer. Here we touch the quick of the problems of Jack London. He tried to realize his personality *through* literature, not *in* literature. His course was through words to things. . . . The man of thought and art clashed with the man of action, the lover of things. The latter won, and art was subverted to cash. (pp. 669-70)

Jack London found no final satisfaction in socialism—or in anything else, for that matter. It is undoubtedly accurate to say that his most satisfying orientation was retrospective and so unrealizable. He got great joy out of his studies of primitive life, primitive peoples—he constantly heard the call of the wild. In fact his novel, *The Call of the Wild,* epitomizes his ideals and aspirations. On the dog Buck is lavished all his admiration. . . . Here we have London's struggle for domination. We have his sadistic delight in punishing his opponents and his masochistic delight in punishing himself by devastating labor. We have his belief in the healing power of love. He epitomized his rejection of civilization—the call of the wild. He fictionized his spiritual aspiration. (pp. 670-71)

> C. Hartley Grattan, "Jack London," in The Bookman, *New York (reprinted by permission of the Literary Estate of C. Hartley Grattan), Vol. 68, No. 6, February, 1929, pp. 667-71.*

## GRANVILLE HICKS   (essay date 1935)

[*From the pages of* The Great Tradition, *a Marxist interpretation of American literary history, Hicks attacks London for consistently burying the socialist elements of his books under a mass of high adventure, overshadowed by the superman.*]

London believed that he was a socialist and that his work showed the influence of his creed. *The Sea-Wolf,* he said, was to prove that "the superman cannot be successful in modern life. The superman is antisocial in his tendencies, and in these days of our complex society and sociology he cannot be successful in his hostile aloofness." Who, reading the book, can fail to see that Larsen's defeat is not due to "our complex society and sociology," and that the wolf of the sea has London's sympathies and is intended to win ours. *Martin Eden,* he declared, was a protest against the philosophy of Nietzsche, and Martin was deliberately made a thoroughgoing individualist for the greater glory of socialism. What reader, one wonders, would ever guess it? Even *The Iron Heel* can scarcely be called a socialistic novel: it contains, in Everhard's speeches, many arguments for socialism, and it deals with the revolution, but Everhard, far from being a typical socialist, is a typical London superman, and the revolution, which is unsuccessful, is the occasion for description of the typical red-blooded variety. *The Valley of the Moon* uses London's own experiences as a manual laborer, and the first third gives a fine authentic account of the life of the proletariat in such a city as Oakland. Yet if one had never heard of London's devotion to the revolution, one might easily suppose that the book was written by an opponent of socialism: the only socialist in the book is a weak dreamer, ineffectual, hen-pecked, and unhappy; the hero, on the other hand, deserts the working class in the midst of a crucial strike, goes back to the land like a good pioneer, and achieves success as a scientific farmer, exploiting the labor of others. (p. 192)

If Jack London had had a disciplined mind, if he had understood all the implications of socialist theory, his outlook on life would have changed, and, if he had written at all, he would have written very different books. As it was, his mind could function on two levels and he could both be a socialist and cultivate what his widow calls a princely ego. It was on the egotistic level that his books were conceived, and in each of them that princely ego is projected in the creation of the hero. The discussion of his socialism indicates that we are not to expect in his work the virtues we had hoped to discover in the novels of a socialist, for his socialism scarcely entered into the conception of his fiction. The discussion still further defines the nature of his writing. We must not expect fine character portrayal, for there is only one character London could depict,

and that one character is so much a product of his dreams, so nearly a personal myth, that we cannot find it convincing. We must not expect sound and beautiful structure: London, thanks to the lack of discipline, thought in episodes and, thanks to his impulsiveness and his eagerness for money, wrote in haste. We must not expect a subtle and dignified style; he had neither the sensitiveness nor the patience to create it. We can expect to feel vigor, the driving energy of Jack London, surging through the action, the characterization, the movement of the words. We can expect to find descriptions that, however much they may be overwritten, do evoke their scenes. And we can expect to respond, with whatever atavistic qualities we may have, to tales of brutal men and their heroic adventures. (pp. 195-96)

For millions of men whose lives industrial society has made dull and ugly and narrow, London provided the relief of vicarious adventure. He could take these people into a dreamland of heroic opportunity. He could not give them a sharp awareness of the kind of world in which they live, an understanding of the minds of their masters and their fellows, a sense of the power and destiny of their class, those things that we might expect to be the gifts of a socialist novelist. (p. 196)

> Granville Hicks, "The Years of Hope," in his The Great Tradition: An Interpretation of American Literature since the Civil War *(copyright © 1933, 1935 by Macmillan Publishing Co., Inc.; originally published in 1933 by The Macmillan Company, New York; new material in the revised edition copyright © 1969 by Granville Hicks; reprinted by permission of Russell & Volkening, Inc., as agent for the author), revised edition, Macmillan, 1935, Quadrangle Books, 1969, pp. 164-206.\**

## LEON TROTSKY   (essay date 1937)

[*A prominent Marxist critic, Trotsky judges* The Iron Heel *to be a work of genius.*]

[*The Iron Heel*] produced upon me—I speak without exaggeration—a deep impression. Not because of its artistic qualities: the form of the novel here represents only an armor for social analysis and prognosis. The author is intentionally sparing in his use of artistic means. He is himself interested not so much in the individual fate of his heroes as in the fate of mankind. By this, however, I don't want at all to belittle the artistic value of the work, especially in its last chapters beginning with the Chicago commune. The pictures of civil war develop in powerful frescoes. Nevertheless, this is not the main feature. The book surprised me with the audacity and independence of its historical foresight. (p. 221)

Jack London not only absorbed creatively the impetus given by the first Russian Revolution but also courageously thought over again in its light the fate of capitalist society as a whole. Precisely those problems which the official socialism of this time considered to be definitely buried: the growth of wealth and power at one pole, of misery and destitution at the other pole; the accumulation of social bitterness and hatred; the unalterable preparation of bloody cataclysms—all those questions Jack London felt with an intrepidity which forces one to ask himself again and again with astonishment: when was this written? Really before the war?

One must accentuate especially the role which Jack London attributes to the labor bureaucracy and to the labor aristocracy in the further fate of mankind. Thanks to their support, the American plutocracy not only succeeds in defeating the workers' insurrection but also in keeping its iron dictatorship during the following three centuries. We will not dispute with the poet the delay which can but seem to us too long. However, it is not a question of Jack London's pessimism, but of his passionate effort to shake those who are lulled by routine, to force them to open their eyes and to see what is and what approaches. The artist is audaciously utilizing the methods of hyperbole. He is bringing the tendencies rooted in capitalism: of oppression, cruelty, bestiality, betrayal, to their extreme expression. He is operating with centuries in order to measure the tyrannical will of the exploiters and the treacherous role of the labor bureaucracy. But his most "romantic" hyperboles are finally much more realistic than the bookkeeperlike calculations of the so-called sober politicians. (pp. 222-23)

The chapter "The Roaring Abysmal Beast" undoubtedly constitutes the focus of the book. At the time when the novel appeared, this apocalyptical chapter must have seemed to be the boundary of hyperbolism. However, the consequent happenings have almost surpassed it. And the last word of class struggle has not yet been said by far! The "Abysmal Beast" is to the extreme degree oppressed, humiliated, and degenerated people. Who would now dare to speak for this reason about the artist's pessimism? No, London is an optimist, only a penetrating and farsighted one. "Look into what kind of abyss the bourgeoisie will hurl you down, if you don't finish with them!" This is his thought. Today it sounds incomparably more real and sharp than thirty years ago. But still more astonishing is the genuinely prophetic vision of the methods by which the Iron Heel will sustain its domination over crushed mankind. London manifests remarkable freedom from reformistic pacifist illusions. In this picture of the future there remains not a trace of democracy and peaceful progress. Over the mass of the deprived rise the castes of labor aristocracy, of praetorian army, of an all-penetrating police, with the financial oligarchy at the top. In reading it one does not believe his own eyes: it is precisely the picture of fascism, of its economy, of its governmental technique, its political psychology! The fact is incontestable: in 1907 Jack London already foresaw and described the fascist regime as the inevitable result of the defeat of the proletarian revolution. Whatever may be the single "errors" of the novel—and they exist—we cannot help inclining before the powerful intuition of the revolutionary artist. (pp. 223-24)

> *Leon Trotsky, "Jack London's 'The Iron Heel'" (1937; originally published in* New International, *April, 1945), in his* Leon Trotsky on Literature and Art, *edited by Paul N. Siegel (copyright © 1970 by Pathfinder Press, Inc.), Pathfinder Press, 1970, pp. 221-24.*

**ALFRED KAZIN**  (essay date 1942)

[*In a survey of London's career, Kazin expands upon the contentions of Granville Hicks (see excerpt above): that in London, the socialist is always far less in evidence than the Blond Beast.*]

The clue to Jack London's work is certainly to be found in his own turbulent life, and not in his Socialism. He was a Socialist by instinct, but he was also a Nietzschean and a follower of Herbert Spencer by instinct. All his life he grasped whatever straw of salvation lay nearest at hand, and if he joined Karl Marx to the Superman with a boyish glee that has shocked American Marxists ever since, it is interesting to remember that he joined Herbert Spencer to Shelley, and astrology to philosophy, with as carefree a will. (p. 111)

It is the man of power, the aspirant Superman, who bestrides London's books, now as self-sacrificing as Prometheus, now as angry as Jove, but always a "blond beast" strangely bearing Jack London's own strength and Jack London's good looks. His Socialism was in truth an unconscious condescension; he rejoiced in the consciousness of a power which could be shared by the masses, a power that spilled over from the leader, as in *The Iron Heel*. (pp. 112-13)

[If] London is remembered as one of the first Socialist novelists of the modern age, he should also be remembered as one of the pioneers of the *Argosy* story tradition. By 1913 he could boast that he was the best-known and highest-paid writer in the world, and he had reached that eminence by cultivating the vein of Wild West romance. Yet in his many novels and stories of adventure he was not always writing as a deliberate hack. He never believed in any strength equal to his, for that strength had come from his own self-assertion; and out of his worship of strength and force came his delight in violence. He had proved himself by it, as seaman and adventurer, and it was by violence that his greatest characters came to live. For violence was their only avenue of expression in a world which, as London conceived it, was a testing-ground for the strong; violence expressed the truth of life, both the violence of the naturalist creed and the violence of superior men and women. Needless to say, it was London himself who spoke through Wolf Larsen, that Zolaesque Captain Ahab in *The Sea Wolf*, when he said: "I believe that life is a mess. It is like yeast, a ferment, a thing that moves or may move for a minute, an hour, a year, or a hundred years, but that in the end will cease to move. The big eat the little that they may continue to move, the strong eat the weak that they retain their strength. The lucky eat the most and move the longest, that is all." So all his primitive heroes, from Wolf Larsen to Martin Eden and Ernest Everhard, the blacksmith hero of *The Iron Heel*, came to express his desperate love of violence and its undercurrent of romanticism: the prizefighter in *The Game*, the prehistoric savages in *Before Adam*, the wild dog in *White Fang*, the gargantuan Daylight in *Burning Daylight*, and even the very titles of later books like *The Strength of the Strong* and *The Abysmal Brute*.

What his immediate contemporaries got out of London, it is now clear, was not his occasional Socialist message, but the same thrill in pursuit of "the strenuous life" that Theodore Roosevelt gave it. No one before him had discovered the literary possibilities of the Alaskan frontier, and he satisfied the taste of a generation still too close to its own frontier to lack appreciation of "red-blooded" romance, satisfied it as joyfully and commercially as he knew how. How much it must have meant, in a day when Nietzsche's Superman seemed to be wearing high boots and a rough frontiersman's jacket, to read the story of Buck in *The Call of the Wild*, that California dog-king roving in the Alaskan wilderness whom London had conceived as a type of the "dominant primordial beast"! How much it must have meant to polite readers, shivering with delight over "the real thing," to read a sentence like: "Buck got a frothing adversary by the throat, and was sprayed with blood when his teeth sank through the jugular"! Socialism or no Socialism, London appeared in his time as a man who could play all the roles of his generation with equal zest and indiscriminate energy—the insurgent reformer, the follower of Darwin and Herbert Spencer, the naturalist who worked amid romantic scenes, and especially the kind of self-made success, boastful and dominant and contemptuous of others, that at the same time appealed to contemporary taste and frightened it.

For if it matters to us, it did not matter to London or his time that intensity is not enough. There was an apocalypse in all his stories of struggle and revolt—it is that final tearing of the bond of convention that London himself was to accomplish only by his suicide—that satisfied the taste for brutality; and nothing is so important about London as the fact that he came on the scene at a time when the shocked consciousness of a new epoch demanded the kind of heady violence that he was always so quick to provide. (pp. 113-15)

> *Alfred Kazin, "Progressivism: The Superman and the Muckrake," in his* On Native Grounds: An Interpretation of Modern American Prose Literature *(copyright 1942, 1970 by Alfred Kazin; reprinted by permission of Harcourt Brace Jovanovich, Inc.), Reynal & Hitchcock, 1942, pp. 91-126.**

### JAMES T. FARRELL  (essay date 1946)

[*Farrell praises* The Iron Heel, *finding London to have masterfully captured the spirit of the 1905 Russian Revolution.*]

I have many favorite forgotten books. One of these is Jack London's novel, *The Iron Heel,* a rare and prophetic kind of novel which concerns the contemporary struggle between labor and capital. The work purports to be derived from a document discovered in "the fourth century of the era of Brotherhood which dates the final triumph of socialist democracy." It tells the story of Ernest Everhard's contribution to the struggle of socialism and freedom in the early part of the twentieth century, and is written by his "gently nurtured wife," Avis. It concludes with an unfinished sentence which restates the theme of this story: "the magnitude of the task" of creating a free and democratic socialist society. (p. 63)

History has not unfolded precisely, and in a detailed manner, as it was forecast in this novel. The Iron Heel, anticipated in America, developed under the name of fascism or nazism in Germany, Italy, and Spain; and a parallel Iron Heel developed as a counterrevolution in the Soviet Union after the October Revolution. And while there are many precise differences between what happened and what is pictured in this work, it is, on the whole, one of the most amazing prophetic works of the twentieth century.

*The Iron Heel* is not a work of characterization in the sense that so many modern novels are. It is written in the form of a document, as the political biography of a man who was a leader in a period of pitiless struggle. The characterization of the hero, Ernest Everhard, is a political and a historical one, rather than an intimate and personal creation. His character is revealed in his political acts, his political courage, his loyalty, comradeship, and his political decency.

The masses of the people, reduced to slavery, and the workers who revolt and go into the underground are all portrayed in a similar fashion. But this is no mere journalistic work. Only a truly great artist could handle this social theme as imaginatively and with such profound insight as did London. London never worked with a greater vigor; his description of imaginary civil war in Chicago is masterly and unforgettable.

It seems paradoxical that London, a young American socialist artist, should have had much keener insight into the mechanisms of capitalist society than did many of the leading theoreticians of the Second International. But one of the factors which helps to resolve this paradox is to be seen in the world-wide repercussions of the Russian Revolution of 1905. Behind

*The Iron Heel* stands this historic event; and London was helped to draw his conclusions because of this revolution. Also, London, a self-educated American writer, one with wide experience and a passionate love of life, had read Marx, Spencer, Nietzsche. From these men he drew hypotheses which helped him to organize his insights. He caught on the wing, as it were, tendencies in motion in modern society. To have achieved this is to have performed a truly great feat of the imagination. (pp. 63-4)

> *James T. Farrell, "My Favorite Forgotten Book" (reprinted by permission of the Literary Estate of James T. Farrell), in* Tomorrow, *Vol. VI, No. 3, November, 1946, pp. 63-4.*

### VAN WYCK BROOKS  (essay date 1952)

[*Brooks offers a thoughtful overview of London's works and discussion of his vision.*]

In his Alaskan stories [Jack London] sounded the note of the "strenuous life" that Roosevelt had struck in a speech one year before him, the theme that life is a struggle for survival in a world that is cruel and grim but in which the fighting will has a chance to triumph. In the title story of *The Son of the Wolf* the daughter of an Indian chief in the North is captured, in the teeth of her suitors, by a white lover, and most of the stories, with their Kiplingesque swagger, abounded in scenes of violent death and the conflict of man with the "white silence" and the savagery of nature. This second, wilder Bret Harte world of miners' cabins, bars and flats, of Russian fur-traders, Eskimos, half-breeds and squaw-men, was the last corner of the Western frontier that bordered on a wilderness where only the caribou and the wolf were able to survive; and one felt that the stories had been somehow lived,—that they were not merely observed,—that the author was not telling tales but telling his life.

In later stories, long or short, *The Call of the Wild, The Faith of Men, A Daughter of the Snows, Children of the Frost,* Jack London continued to recreate this world of the long arctic night in which men fought with men and with hunger and cold. (pp. 229-30)

As a writer, Jack London had announced his revolt against the "poor young American girl" who was not allowed anything "less insipid than mare's milk," and one felt in all his compositions, good or bad as they might have been, a vehement and even a brutal affirmation of life. Veritable waves of force seemed to rush out of him,—the fresh sea-breeze of personality that Ruth observed in Martin Eden; and there was, in fact, an uncommon vitality in these tales of pluck and enterprise, of the triumph,—and sometimes the tragic defeat,—of the will. One could understand why Lenin, as he lay dying, rejoiced in Jack London, as hundreds of thousands of Americans had rejoiced before him; for these stories of strong men, bully-boys, prizefighters and traders who dreamed of rivalling Cecil Rhodes suggested, in their glorification of courage, the true heroic ordeals and toils that complex modern writers had largely forgotten. For instance, there was *Love of Life,* in which the sick miner, lost in the north, dragged his way back to safety, followed by the wolf, and *The Mexican* about the little boxer who won the fund for the revolution by beating the big popular, hated, gringo bruiser. . . . These stories, as George Orwell later said, were paradoxically not "well written,"—for they abounded in worn and obvious phrases,—while, on the other hand, they were "well told"; and sometimes, as in *The Seed of McCoy,*—the story of the governor of Pitcairn island who pilots the burning ship through a hundred perils,—they were moving in a human and even in a spiritual way. One felt, moreover, as a rule, behind them the passionate intellectual earnestness of the former "boy socialist" of Oakland, the student who had been ready to rush to any town about the bay where he could start a furious discussion of anthropology or economics. Many of his characters were avid readers, even Frona, who quoted Browning and carried a copy of Wordsworth in her clothes-bag in Alaska, or "Burning Daylight," who bought a grammar and toiled through it when he made his pile, or the "intellectual swashbuckler" Everhard in *The Iron Heel.* (pp. 231-32)

Alive, imaginative, alert, Jack London became within four or five years the best-known younger writer in the country, not only with readers of popular books but among the intelligentsia, who were struck by his dramatization of serious ideas. For his stories had a philosophical bearing,—they were illustrations of the theories of Darwin, or of Karl Marx, Nietzsche or Herbert Spencer,—and they made battles of the mind as actual and thrilling as prize-fights, adventures in the gold-fields or scenes of war. . . . But Jack London, the hero of romance, was also an imperialist who had swallowed Kipling whole,—along with Karl Marx,—and delighted in the "primitive brutality" of the "salt of the earth." For this was his phrase for the Anglo-Saxons, in whom Norris had exulted in a similar way before he matured emotionally and outgrew this nonsense, while Jack London continued to glorify the "great race-adventure of the Anglo-Saxon" who was destined to rule the red, the yellow and the black. He was all for the "race-egotism" of Vance in *A Daughter of the Snows,*—not to mention the flaxen-haired "typically Saxon" Frona,—for whom "Nature's chosen people," the "Angles and Saxons and Normans and Vikings" were "zone-conquerors," fit to "survive and inherit the earth." In his belief that "the world belongs to the strong," Jack London agreed with Nietzsche as well as with Kipling.

Thus, for one reason or another, Jack London was a success in every camp until this confusion of ideas led to his undoing, while his own thirst for money and power destroyed the artist in him and he wrote what he called the "pap of pretty lies." (pp. 233-34)

[Jack London] saw life as the most primitive kind of struggle for survival. To him, without doubt, it actually seemed like the struggle of the wolf-pack in *The Call of the Wild;* and did he not picture himself in a sense in the dog that "reverted" on the Klondike and became the leader of the wolf-pack? Buck, who had been kidnapped and sold in Alaska, soon found that his fastidious ways would never do in this world of the club and the fang where there was no fair play and the only law was the ruthless "kill or be killed, eat or be eaten." Buck, who saw a dog destroyed that would neither conciliate nor obey, was bent on surviving himself, so, ceasing to be bound by man and his claims, he learned to run down the living meat and wash his muzzle to the eyes in the blood of his prey.

This was, in a manner, Jack London's story, symbolically told,—which explained why *The Call of the Wild* was perhaps his best book, written directly from his unconscious while the transparent *Martin Eden,*—good in parts,—abounded in rationalizations. For like Buck, the California dog, he suppressed the more sensitive side of his nature in his effort to beat the magazines and get up in a world in which you did not prosper if you had scruples, observing that "morality is only an evidence of low blood-pressure" and acting as if he believed this

to be true. . . . It was not that Jack London did not have the "delicate sensitive spirit" within that he imputed to his Everhard, the labour-leader, the "ingenuous boy" with the bulging muscles and the prizefighter's throat that were like Jack's own, together with the "smashing sledge-hammer manner of attack." But, whatever could be said for *The Iron Heel* as socialist propaganda, the psychology of the book was as crude as Upton Sinclair's, and the "beaming brotherliness" of Everhard ill befitted the "superman . . . the blond beast such as Nietzsche has described." The sensitive spirit existed in London or he would never have been a writer; and he was, after all, a writer with an unconscious *to write out of,*—which could not have been said for his followers in the pulp-magazines. But he had repressed this spirit too effectively, too long. Was not this the reason for the "long sickness" that killed him at last? (pp. 235-37)

> *Van Wyck Brooks, "Frank Norris and Jack London," in his* The Confident Years: 1885-1915 *(copyright, 1952, by Van Wyck Brooks; copyright renewed © by Mrs. Van Wyck Brooks; reprinted by permission of the publisher, E. P. Dutton, Inc.), Dutton, 1952, pp. 217-37.\**

**MAXWELL GEISMAR**    (essay date 1953)

[*Geismar, one of America's most respected nonacademic literary critics, provides, in the following essay, a survey of London's work.*]

London's first collection of Arctic tales, *The Son of the Wolf,* in 1900, was dedicated to the last of the frontiersmen "who sought their heritage and left their bones among the shadows of the circle." (p. 144)

Against the background of abstract splendor, there were the deeds of men's heroism, or cruelty, or the meticulous descriptions of moral and physical deterioration as in the scurvy, when muscles and joints began to swell, the flesh turned black, and gums and lips took on the color of rich cream. In **"In A Far Country"** two tenderfeet from the Southland lose their sanity in the silent space of an Arctic winter—are betrayed finally by nature's apparitions. (pp. 144-45)

[The second collection, *The God of His Fathers,* offered] writing that was completely fresh in its time, offering a contrast to the sweetness and goodness of popular fiction in the 1900's. The cadence of [the] prose only became completely familiar to us, indeed, in the work of the postwar generation of the 1920's. The frenzied epic of the gold rush was summarized in a vista of broken and dying animals (beside which the famous horses in Stephen Crane's work were almost untouched). In these tales of cupidity, of fear, of hunger, of the grim humor of murder and death, too, the will to survive—all that was left here of men's appetites and joys—was often viewed as another kind of phobia, ironical, insane. And in the lament of a northern gambler who was bankrupt and pursued by the shapes and forms of his crimes, merely waiting for death in the same unchanging position, London made his theme explicit. "Life's a skin-game. . . . I never had half a chance. . . . I was faked in my birth and flimflammed with my mother's milk. The dice were loaded when she tossed the box, and I was born to prove the loss."

But there were few instances in the short stories where London's sense of character was up to the level of the emotions he described, or where in fact the excellent material was not finally circumscribed by a shallow set of moral values. After the hero of "**The Great Interrogation,**" like many northern adventurers, had taken an Indian wife, he was urged by his former sweetheart, Mrs. Sayther, to renounce a debased form of marriage. . . . And this anthropological widow couching her love call in the clichés of popular Darwinism, expressed the central point of view in London's collection of Indian stories, *Children of the Frost,* in 1902. Although Sitka Charley, the half-breed, had been one of London's heroes in the earlier series of tales, even he, respecting, almost venerating the white man's power, had yet to divine its secret essence, so we are told—the honor of the trail, and of the 'law.'

Whose law, what law? The white man's law, of course, or at least the law in Kipling's romances of the white man's fate, as adapted to an imperial American audience of the 1900's. (pp. 145-46)

[In "**The League of Old Men,**" an] aboriginal chieftain recorded a desperate compact to kill off the whites before the tribal life had disappeared completely. The judge, listening to this confession of crime and frustration, also has another view of race—his steel-shod, mail-clad race, the lawgiver and worldmaker among the families of men. "He saw it dawn redflickering across the dark forests and sullen seas; he saw it blaze, bloody and red, to full and triumphant noon; and down the shaded slope he saw the blood-red sands dropping into night."

Darwin's grand principle of natural selection had been cut down here, even from the Anglo-Saxon 'law' of conquest and empire to a single law of slaughter in the progress of Nordics whose horizon was bathed in a river of blood. Nevertheless, the boss of the Yukon in London's first novel, *A Daughter of the Snows,* in 1902, was another economic strong man and empire builder. Jacob Welse is a robber baron of the Arctic shore, a raw individualist of the icy waste, who combines private enterprise with the code of the frontier. . . . The Yukon scene of *A Daughter of the Snows* contained Bonanza Kings who were adventurers, outcasts, misfits, scoundrels from the four corners of the world; the life in the dance halls of Dawson with their gamblers and gay women; the odd democracy of the northern frontier with its extremes of fantastic wealth, gained overnight, and of ruin, suffering and death; the mixed society of miners, tradespeople, guides, badmen, hunters, trappers and police; the mixture and jumble of national types from the Americans, Russians and Scandinavians to the Indians, Eskimos and half-breeds. But all this—the true material of the novelist—was used only for 'local color,' a trite romance, a meretricious philosophy.

And London himself had realized his first novel was a failure while he was writing it. In the movement of a talent which was itself a mixture of extremes, spontaneous, poetic, erratic, unchartable, even while it had already been confined to the standards of popular fiction, he was on the edge of his first memorable work. (pp. 147-49)

[*The Call of the Wild*] was in fact a sort of prose-poem, a novella of a single mood, admirably sustained. The sketch of the great Chilkoot Divide, which stood between the salt water and the fresh, "and guards forbiddingly the sad and lonely North," set the tone; just as the early episode in which Buck was 'broken' into the "reign of primitive law," the first step in his education as a pack dog, starts his reversion to the wild. One notices how delicately London kept his story within the limits of credible animal behavior. The human beings are good or bad, efficient or useless, only to the degree that they affect the well-being of the dogs—and here indeed the brutes often rose to a stoic dignity not granted to the humans. (p. 149)

London carried us back—with an ease and sureness of perception that appeared also to be "without effort of discovery"—through the ages of fire and roof to the raw beginnings of animal creation. . . . The theory of racial instinct, of memory as inherited habit, that was at the start, through long aeons, a very conscious and alert process of behavior indeed—this theory, as developed by such figures as Samuel Butler, Bergson or Jung, was very clear here, of course. Similarly, the scene in which Buck finally deposed Spitz as the leader of the team, surrounded by the ring of huskies waiting to kill and eat the vanquished king, was a perfect instance of the 'son-horde' theory which Frazer traced in *The Golden Bough,* and of that primitive ritual to which Freud himself attributed both a sense of original sin and the fundamental ceremony of religious exorcism. But what is fascinating in *The Call of the Wild* is the brilliance of London's own intuitions (quite apart from any system of psychology) in this study of animal instincts which are the first, as they are the final biological response to the blind savagery of existence. (pp. 150-51)

If *The Call of the Wild* celebrated the animal instincts, indeed, *The Sea Wolf,* in 1904, still one of London's best known or best remembered novels, was the study of a cruel and to a large degree corrupt 'natural man.' The writer himself claimed the story was an argument against a rapacious individualism, and was one of his most widely misunderstood books. But there was a certain ambiguity between the 'conscious' moral of the artist and the true emotional center of his work. The popular audience at least was concerned with the portrait of a savage and tyrannical sea captain. Wolf Larsen was really a sort of nautical Nietzsche or a Lucifer of the sealing trade—vicious and proud spirit that he was, condemned by his own excess of vitality. He had "the mechanism of a primitive fighting beast," he was perfectly at home in the welter of violence that marked the sailing life of his period; he took pleasure and almost drew his life breath by tormenting and mastering the crew.

In addition, he has read Herbert Spencer and theorizes at some length about the meaning of life, immortality, social reform. Larsen is today, of course, through modern eyes, an empty and inflated figure; without the myth of the superman to bolster his rhetoric, his original fascination has collapsed. (p. 153)

[Heroes] and villains alike in the story all became puppets in a continuous play of shocks and horrors. The true theme of *The Sea Wolf* was simply the reversion of a higher form of intelligence not so much to an animal as to a subhuman level. The consciousness of evil is the corrupting element; the novel's tone in the end is curiously close to that of entertainment. . . . Did the evidence of virility flow really through these channels of brutality? There was a practically schizophrenic split here between brutal Darwinian mating (or coupling) and the spiritual love, attendant upon a world of art and culture in London's mind, which was attributed to the novel's two upper-class figures, Humphrey Van Weyden and Maude Brewster. The closing sections of *The Sea Wolf* marked, indeed, the victory of a false idealism over what was essentially a false, and to some degree perverted materialism, and this was also a central issue in *The Kempton-Wace Letters,* which London had published a year earlier, in 1903.

The book was written in collaboration with Anna Strunsky, gifted daughter of a Russian Jewish family in San Francisco, who was herself a memorable personality in the intellectual life of the west coast and a strong influence on London's early work. She was Kempton in the exchange of letters, while London was Wace, and the theme of their argument was ostensibly that of love. But their discourses included Science, Socialism, Art and Life in a curious fusion of Victorian morals and frontier values in the 1900's. *The Kempton-Wace Letters* was an interesting record of the period—the climax of the Yellow Nineties on the Gold Coast—and in no other book of this period did London reveal his own 'program' and personal beliefs quite so clearly. (p. 155)

[One] realizes that throughout *The Kempton-Wace Letters* human behavior, . . . in London's mind was reduced, at best to an animal, but often to a merely mechanical level. Was the post-Darwinian view of man based on the main functions of nutrition and reproduction, and life itself a blind expression of an infinite fecundity? In London's own thought "the mere passion of begetting" and "the paltry romance of pursuit" had been reduced even further to a continuous letting-off steam, as it were—by a more or less inefficient valve system. (p. 157)

[*The People of the Abyss*] was the first of London's social documents. . . .

The book was a running account of experiences in such places as the "sweat-dens" of Frying-pan Alley, the casual ward at Whitechapel workhouse, or Spitalfields Garden where, in the shadow of Christ's Church, he found families of paupers and women who would sell themselves "for thru'pence, or tu'pence, or a loaf of stale bread." It was a diseased lung of England's capital, "an abscess, a great putrescent sore." Though the writing was light, breezy, human-interest stuff—a typical muckraking document, a catalogue of human misery—*The People of the Abyss* was an illuminating document. (p. 158)

London's next book of social criticism, his *War of the Classes*, in 1905, dealt in part with an impending battle for world supremacy among the nations. (p. 159)

[The book] was actually a collection of articles and socialist talks which had been written during the period of London's apprenticeship and early literary success. The tone of the volume was an odd mixture of the abstract or conceptual, and the evangelical or hortatory vein. But the tenets of London's revolutionary socialism were very different from the intellectual or 'leisure class' socialism in, say, the later work of William Dean Howells, and he was the first major fiction writer to proclaim these beliefs not only so clearly but so loudly. (p. 160)

In the moral underworld that was described in the pages of *War of the Classes*, the strike and the boycott, the black list and the lockout, led the way only to suborned judges and armies of private militias; and these in turn were the support of an industrial system whose primary condition of existence was that there should be less work than there were men to do work. (p. 161)

*The Iron Heel* was a blueprint for fascism in which London had joined the Freudian social pathology, as it were, with the evangelical Marxist dialectic; and compared with his instinct for the propagation of mass terror and consolidation of social barbarism in the native scene, a novel like Sinclair Lewis's *It Can't Happen Here* would appear naïve. Two years later, moreover, during the richest creative period in London's career, *Martin Eden* was another book famous in its own time.

The story was based on his early romance with Mabel Applegarth in San Francisco, a fatal romance for London at least. It

was one of London's most completely personal works of fiction, authentic in tone from the opening scene of the suffering 'proletarian' hero in a drawing room of (to him) pure beauty and luxury. (pp. 168-69)

[The] coarse grain of the writing in *Martin Eden,* quite different from the prose of *The Iron Heel,* was exactly right for the emotional texture of the story. The best literary comparison is with the early D. H. Lawrence in *Sons and Lovers.* There is the same mixture of anger, frustration and sexual desire—but the theme of the novel is a typical one in our own letters. "Never had he been at such an altitude of living," Martin Eden says, in almost the same phrases that Thomas Wolfe used to describe the effect of Park Avenue society—that "enfabled Rock" of wealth and beauty and art—upon a later provincial hero; and there was the same confusion of the heroine's temperament with the values of her milieu. He did not think of her flesh as flesh, London said, but as an emanation of her spirit; and her spirit is, at the outset, almost purely that of the cultural environment which she represents. What was different, though, and lent power to *Martin Eden*—a power of definition—was the sharp stress on social class in this drama of social ambition. (pp. 169-70)

*Martin Eden* is one of the angry books in American literature, very much in the manner of Richard Wright's *Black Boy,* and as in Wright's case, too, there were curious personal undertones in this acrid and feverish story of what appeared to be purely a social—or even a class—struggle. (p. 172)

The final volume in this phase of London's work, *Revolution and Other Essays,* in 1910, was an interesting contrast to his first collection of socialist essays, five years earlier. One notices the harsh tone of London's polemics. "Our statesmen sell themselves and their country for gold. . . . The world of graft! the world of betrayal!" Yet in **"The Yellow Peril,"** the economic issues of Asia were described in almost purely racist terms. (There was also his notorious remark of this period, when he was attacked for these views: "I am a white man first, a socialist second.") The true meaning of this increasingly dominant strain in his thinking was revealed in his praise of Kipling as the poet of the Anglo-Saxon race and the English empire. (p. 173)

The history of increasing corruption in a genuine talent is both painful and fascinating. . . . Some of London's most brilliant passages of prose will describe the sensations of drawing steadily closer to a moral, if not now a social abyss.

It was interesting, too, that in *The Game,* a story of boxing which London published in 1905 (along with *War of the Classes*), his view of the working classes for popular consumption stressed their sexual purity to the point of incredulity.

The hero was a champ; the heroine a soda fountain girl. They were altogether unreal, wooden characters in the middle class vein, very different from the working class people whom London knew and wrote about in his serious work. The high point of their tedious romance, very much like the barely disguised strip-tease act that London had used to redeem the faltering action in *Theft,* was when the peeping girl, smuggled into a boxing match, saw her young proletarian lover "naked save for the low canvas shoes and narrow hip-cloth of white."

As in some of Ellen Glasgow's early novels—in the fashion of the times—the Victorian taboo on direct sexuality led to a veiled sexuality, or a sexual sublimation that verged on pornography, almost everywhere in the story, despite the fact that

London's athlete was presented as an absolutely pure young boy with an honest pride in his muscles. . . . There was the glorification of physical prowess and virility, the adulation of the masculine body, or the symbolic use of that "looking-glass" into which Martin himself, like any young Scott Fitzgerald figure, gazed and conversed with his own image so consistently—and was "both onlooker and participant." (pp. 178-79)

[*White Fang*], a converse to *The Call of the Wild,* dealt with a wolf-dog who was finally domesticated. But, more accurately, the earlier parable dealt with the rebirth of primitive instincts in the wilderness, the true life impulses. This one was concerned quite literally with the death impulses which apparently, in London's case as in Freud's, were dominant in nature itself—or at least were primary in the key episodes and prevailing imagery of London's second animal fable. (p. 181)

The cry of a brokenhearted youth—of an outcast in a world of horrors—is a familiar refrain in London's work. It was illuminating that the last memorable episode in the wolf-dog's apprenticeship should be that of the bulldog's grip on his throat. ("It made him frantic, this clinging, dragging weight. . . . It was like a trap.") While the bulldog's stumpy tail, in the blind horrors of nature and civilization alike, continued to wag vigorously. . . . The Clinging Death indeed! It was only when White Fang was rescued from these extremes of cruelty and terror, to become "the blessed wolf" of a gracious California estate in the Southland, a perfect pet of an aristocratic gentry, that London succumbed to the sentiment which spoiled another beautiful little parable of the instinctual life.

"From my earliest recollection my sleep was a period of terror," said the hero of *Before Adam,* published in the same year . . . , and this fantasy of prehistoric man carried on and developed the dark vein in London's middle period. (p. 183)

This portrait of childhood in the childhood of the race—the Lost Eden—is an Eden of Horrors, viewed ironically. In his evocation of an age of "perpetual insecurity," London tied together all the terrors of primitive life with the fears and terrors of childhood itself, which he attributed indeed to racial memory—and Weismann's germ-plasm theory—more than to personal neurosis. *Before Adam* is a prime instance of the Darwinian unconscious, so to say, rather than the Freudian. But Freud, as well as Marx owed much to the central revelation of evolutionary thinking; and we should not miss the brilliance of intuition which London himself used to transform the embryonic anthropology of his own period into the insights of art.

The central mood in [*Love of Life and Other Stories* and *Lost Face*], two more collections of tales, was also one of inhuman, but almost mechanical misery. (p. 187)

*Burning Daylight,* in 1910, was another bit of hack work, a poor novel about Alaska; and the romance of the Northland which had established London's fame was in its way the real trap of his literary career. The hero, Burning Daylight himself, was another explicit example of the Superman of the Snows, the Blond Brute of the North Pole, and later, returning to the California scene, the Lone Wolf of Western Finance. (p. 190)

"He had become cynical, bitter, brutal," London said about this spokesman for a central line of heroes. His enemies "feared and hated him, and no one loved him." As in the career of Martin Eden also, his single motivation was merely "lust for power in order to revenge." He was described as an enemy

of his society and, though the novel has been praised by some left critics as authentic proletarian writing, the summary of American finance, of the press, politics, civic responsibility, and the masses of the people, was intended only to justify the views of London's hero. It was not so much social criticism as the reflection of a consuming sense of personal corruption. The guiding influence wasn't Marx but, so to speak, Narcissus; and from the prophet of the social abyss this was in the end an abysmal view of society. . . . "When all was said and done, it was a scurvy game. The dice were loaded. Those that died did not win, and all died. Who won? Not even Life, the stool-pigeon, the arch-capper for the game—Life, the ever flourishing graveyard, the everlasting funeral procession." (p. 191)

That was the underlying philosophy of the novel, and it was of course a more direct statement of the dominant symbolism and imagery in his fiction of this period. (p. 192)

In the beginning, [London's] realism, however circumspect in the final analysis, had revolutionized the tone of popular fiction in the 1900's. Now he capitulated cynically to the standards of the mass mind, and to the new vulgarity of a lower middle class audience that had been reached by the low-priced journals. . . . *Adventure,* in 1911, the first of London's South Sea stories, was a popular romance in this vein. The contrast in London's work was not merely between the Arctic scene and the warm, lush tropics; but, as almost always, between what he could have done with this material, and what he did do.

The hero of the novel ran a slave plantation in the Solomon islands. The blacks on whom he depended for profits were head-hunters, cannibals, savages of the lowest order, adorned with barbaric ornaments and endowed with a native cunning and cruelty. A wonderful scene for a storyteller (as Alaska was, too), granted the ways of the world, and balanced here by the savages' own methods of revenge. But one realizes that London compressed this material, too, into a stereotyped version of the white man's burden and the wily 'niggers.' There was the sadistic humor he extracted from the spectacle of the dog Satan, who had been trained to attack the Negro slaves; and the underground sexuality he suggested when the virtuous white heroine watched the naked black being whipped in public. (pp. 199-200)

*The Night-Born,* in 1913, took its title from Thoreau's lines. "The Society Islanders had their day-born gods, but they were not supposed to be of equal antiquity with the night-born gods." Most surely London himself was an example of primitive and supernatural strains in the artist—of the darker and ancient side of life, of the buried instincts that in his case hardly rose to the human level. Yet these stories of pathology, insanity, or crime, were for the most part converted into popular tales, again with false or sentimental endings. They were hardly so revealing as *John Barleycorn,* a key document in London's personal history that was published in the same year. The book was written ostensibly as a sermon on alcoholism. It is actually a close and illuminating kind of spiritual autobiography, and, as in all more or less personal statements of this writer, the drums rolled in a somber overture of disaster. (pp. 202-03)

[In] this twisted and tortured *apologia pro vita sua*—so remarkably honest and penetrating in parts to the point of narcissistic self-abasement—there were evasions and lacunae. And there were certain developments, still. *The Valley of the Moon,* also published in 1913, and received with higher critical acclaim than the "alcoholic memoirs," is less impressive today. Often described as an example of London's later proletarian fiction, it is actually another phase of his languishing interest in social problems, or his antipathy to them. The hero was a teamster; the early part of the novel was centered around a trucking strike in San Francisco, but the description of this area of society was vulgar and trite. The heroine's name was 'Saxon' and almost from the story's start there was a continual stress on the Anglo-Saxon Nordic White Supremacy of native American stock that seemed not only to be threatened (in London's mind) but practically extinct. . . . The novel was a weird concoction of a sexuality that verged on pornography, of distorted chauvinism, and of social-economic crises that were interpreted as racial phenomena. The real theme of *The Valley of the Moon* was indeed race, blood and soil. (pp. 206-07)

London's own model farm had become the center of his literary cosmos, in a tradition which extended to other prosperous literary hinds like Louis Bromfield, and from the center of his Ovidian meadows he threw out a strange melange of bucolic fears and superstitions. . . . Though he transferred the scene to an old-fashioned clipper ship in his next novel, *The Mutiny of the Elsinore*, in 1914, the central mood was identical, when he forced this story, too, into a procrustean mold of race and class. The decline of the clippers became a parable of "these degenerate sailing days." The "mass of human wreckage" that London found in the crew was another instance, not of an outmoded style of transportation, but of biological differentiation. (p. 208)

[The] theme of a diseased life force was repeated in *The Scarlet Plague*, in 1915, where the artist saw the source of evolutionary development only as "the abysmal fecundity." In *The Strength of the Strong,* a collection of stories published a year earlier, a new China, "rejuvenescent, fruitful, and militant," that had dominated Asia by the sheer force of her massive population, was annihilated by the methods of bacterial warfare. "Hundreds of millions of dead remained unburied and the germs multiplied themselves, and, toward the last, millions died daily of starvation." And the main action of *The Star Rover*, in 1915 also, took place within a strait jacket—from which the hero continued to defy the prison authorities who had, he thinks, wrongly condemned him. One of the last novels London wrote before his death, it was disorganized and broken in structure, an incredibly bad novel, but interesting in its descriptions of a curious psychological state. Supine, prostrate in the bosom of the strait jacket, London's Last Superman still proclaimed his innate superiority over those who were slowly breaking down his body but who are themselves the victims of his fantastic will to survive. He has perfected a form of trance and self-hypnotism during his periods of torture. He learns to make his body die, while in his delusionary fantasies he roves through the central epochs of history as the perfect egomaniac in a series of cruel and bloody catastrophes. (pp. 209-10)

In a literary cosmos that was now a world beyond pain, the final triumph was that of invincible, untouchable paranoia. . . .

[The style of *The Star Rover*]—an absolute frenzy of hyperbole and capital letters—was admirably suited to the grandiloquent thesis, the insane ecstasy. (p. 211)

*The Little Lady of the Big House*, in 1916, the last novel published before his death, had some autobiographical interest, too, in the final stage of London's life. Here, as in "**The Kanaka Surf**" in *On the Makaloa Mat*, a collection of tales published posthumously in 1919, the theme was the break-up of a marital relationship through the wife's infidelity. . . . The record of the rest of London's posthumous books is brief. (*The*

*Turtles of Tasman*, 1916, contained an almost Lardnerian tale of "a high-grade feeb" who emphasized his superiority to the low-grade droolers and epileptics in a state mental institution.) *The Human Drift*, in 1917, was a collection of minor essays and sketches London had written earlier. *Jerry of the Islands* and *Michael, Brother of Jerry*, in the same year, were two supposed juveniles which concerned the adventures of "a nigger-chasing, adorable Irish terrier puppy" *(sic)* in the familiar setting of the Solomon islands. (pp. 212-13)

The broken tone of the stories in London's final period, the uneven style of his later work as a whole, with bad and good jumbled together, showed the haste and recklessness with which he had poured out this virtuosity. (p. 216)

> Maxwell Geismar, "Jack London: The Short Cut," in his Rebels and Ancestors: The American Novel, 1890-1915 (Copyright 1953 by Maxwell Geismar. copyright renewed © 1981 by Anne Geismar. Reprinted by permission of Houghton Mifflin Company.), Houghton Mifflin, 1953, pp. 139-216.

**SAM S. BASKETT** (essay date 1958)

[*Baskett analyzes the similarities between London's work and that of Joseph Conrad.*]

Although there are certain obvious similarities in the fiction of Jack London and Joseph Conrad—both wrote tales of the sea as well as stories set in exotic lands, and frequently both peopled their fiction with rough characters engaged in violent action—Conrad's different emphasis, surer craftsmanship and more profound insight into the psychological motivations of his characters have made these similarities seem relatively inconsequential. London is often, even within the same book, an exponent of the cult of raw meat and red blood and a political expounder using fiction as a means of advancing the doctrines of socialism. This blatant dichotomy is in obvious contrast to Conrad's characteristically subtle investigations of states of mind. Conrad himself bridled at being regarded "as literarily a sort of Jack London":

> I don't mean to depreciate in the least the talent of the late Jack London, who wrote me in a most friendly way many years ago at the very beginning, I think, of his literary career, and with whom I used to exchange messages through friends afterwards; but the fact remains that temperamentally, mentally, and as a prose writer, I am a different person.

Thus London's biographers and critics have given what seems to be the proper emphasis to the London-Conrad relation when they merely note in a sentence or so that London read the English author and that at one point or another their literary interests coincided extrinsically. Actually, however, it is as misleading to minimize their similarities as to exaggerate them; and to say that London exhibits *only* a superficial likeness to Conrad obscures a basic correspondence which is of some significance in an over-all consideration of London's fiction. (p. 66)

Walter F. Wright has commented on the similarity of theme in London's "**To Build a Fire**" and [Conrad's] "An Outpost of Progress," noting that London in the physical realm as Conrad in the mental "has illuminated the mystery of existence," as he portrays a civilized man freezing to death in the arctic wastes. Actually, the earlier "**In a Far Country**" is much closer to Conrad's story in the description of characters, as well as in situation and incidents.

In "An Outpost of Progress," "Two perfectly insignificant and incapable individuals," Carlier and Kayerts, are left in charge of a trading post on the upper reaches of an African river. Since their existence had been "only rendered possible through the high organization of civilized crowds," the isolation of this outpost and "the contact with pure unmitigated savagery, with primitive nature and primitive man, brings sudden and profound trouble." They gradually deteriorate morally, emotionally and physically, eventually one kills the other and then commits suicide. In London's story, two "ordinary" men, the "Incapables" London repeatedly terms them, rather than undertake a hazardous thousand-mile journey with the remainder of their party, choose to spend the winter in an abandoned cabin on a tributary of the Yukon. Weatherbee and Cuthfert, "hardened to the ruts in which they were created," find the "pressure of the altered environment is unbearable, and they chafe in body and spirit" as they "face the savage youth, the primordial simplicity of the North. . . ." The story is a record of their quarrels, their concomitant disintegration. Finally each is successful in killing the other. (pp. 67-8)

It is difficult to say, of course, whether London consciously borrowed from Conrad's story. It is apparent, however, that both the situation and the theme of the two stories are the same and that the theme of **"In a Far Country"** is much closer to Conrad than that of any of London's previous stories. London had handled each of his first four stories (**"To the Man on Trail," "The White Silence," "The Son of the Wolf,"** and **"The Men of Forty-Mile"**) as a tour de force. An unusual situation in each instance brings one of the central characters to confront violence and perhaps death. But once London has delineated the situation, sketched the characters briefly and indicated the turn of action, the story is finished. **"In a Far Country"** also contains many of these elements. The theme, however, is not catastrophe (surmounted or not) but disintegration. **"In a Far Country,"** like "An Outpost of Progress," goes beyond the description of nature, and of man trying to exist on the "natural" physical level: Two unexceptional men, neither particularly good or bad, placed in isolation in an unfamiliar and unfriendly environment, reach a point of complete moral and emotional as well as physical breakdown. (p. 69)

**Martin Eden** is usually said to be about a writer torn between working-class and bourgeois standards; and **John Barleycorn** is considered a semi-accurate autobiography giving principal stress to London's alcoholic experiences. A comparison of these two books with "Youth" and "Heart of Darkness" focuses attention on the fact that there is a level of meaning beneath their obvious statements. (p. 70)

The twenty-year-old Marlow and young Jack London in his autobiographical writings both feel that a glamorous life of romantic adventure at sea is unfolding before them, that each is on the verge of discovering his essential nature, and both experience the intoxicating sense of accomplishment of the youth just beginning to find himself. Marlow thrills to the thought of a voyage to the mysterious East, even in a "rattletrap" of a ship: "Youth and the sea. Glamour and the sea! The good, strong sea, the salt, bitter sea, that would whisper to you and roar at you and knock your breath out of you." (pp. 70-1)

A corresponding picture of youthful exuberance is presented in **Martin Eden** and **John Barleycorn**. To young Jack London

in the latter book, "the winds of adventure" blew up and down San Francisco Bay where "the afternoon sea breeze blew its tang into my lungs, and curled the waves in mid-channel. . . . There it was, the smack and slap of the spirit of revolt, of adventure, of romance, of the things forbidden and done defiantly and grandly." Like Marlow, London is half apologetic about the actual facts of the adventure. "And now, of all this that is squalid, and ridiculous, and bestial, try to think what it meant to me, a youth not yet sixteen, burning with the spirit of adventure. . . . Came the whisper to range farther. I had not found it yet. There was more behind." Of course the themes of alcohol and lawlessness in **John Barleycorn** introduce some facets of youthful experience with which Conrad does not deal, but for the most part these two aspects of London's life merely heighten the mood of adventure which permeates both "Youth" and the parts of **John Barleycorn** describing London's early life. In **Martin Eden** the experiences of the protagonist as a sailor are not stressed, but he has the same zest for experience, the same compulsion to realize his identity that the youthful Marlow has. The tone of the first part of the book is set by Martin's radiant enthusiasm as he discovers a new social and intellectual world. As he begins to feel at home in that world, his confidence in his own ability mounts. (p. 71)

In the first parts of these books, then, London, like Conrad in "Youth," gives a vivid picture of the spiritually undefeated youth exulting in his new-found powers. But twenty-two years have passed and Marlow must now say, anticipating the more somber mood of "Heart of Darkness," that even while we are "looking anxiously for something out of life, that while it is expected is already gone—has passed unseen, in a sigh, in a flash—together with the youth, with the strength, with the romance of illusions. . . . Youth, strength, genius, thoughts, achievements, simple hearts—all die. . . ." The central characters of **Martin Eden** and **John Barleycorn** have also experienced the passing of time, and the tone of the concluding portions of both books coincides with the tone of this statement and with the even darker expression of "Heart of Darkness." In the conviction that "the so-called truths of life are not true," but are "illusions" by which one lives, the drunken protagonist of **John Barleycorn,** as he sinks into "fuddled sleep," recites "Yea, I am Youth because I die." (pp. 71-2)

[When **Martin Eden** and **John Barleycorn**] are considered together, then, the pattern of experience which London has delineated is made clear. The progression has been from almost animal gusto to satiety, from the eager quest of experience to the center of indifference. Self knowledge has led to skepticism. Marlow's experience in "Heart of Darkness" is of the same pattern. At first he is a comparatively unreflecting young sailor, occupied with the world of "straightforward facts," eager for adventure. (Conrad remarked, "Before the Congo I was just a mere animal.") But Marlow-Conrad like Eden-London is led to a reassessment of himself, of his values, of life itself; and this similar experience the two writers often describe in much the same terms.

By his experience on the African river and by his "loyalty" to Kurtz, Marlow is brought to the "ordeal of looking into myself," and he is thus led to the "threshold of the invisible." . . . London, during "this long sickness of pessimism . . . meditated suicide coolly," struggling in "the dusk of my soul" as he discourses with the White Logic which, under "a mask of hedonism," is the "Noseless One . . . whispering his whispers of death," and which "undefeated has never left me." "John Barleycorn sends his White Logic, the argent messenger of truth beyond truth, the antithesis of life, cruel and bleak as interstellar space, pulseless and frozen as absolute zero. . . ." (p. 73)

The level of experience as well as the respective attitudes of the two writers toward [their experiences], in these and similar passages, is manifestly different. Eden-London's "long sickness" is apparently in part the result of reading "too much positive science" and of a somewhat immature reaction to the fact that life had not turned out as he had wished—in contrast to Marlow's pessimism which seems to be the result of a sensitive and mature individual becoming aware, philosophically as well as emotionally, of the terrors of hell. London makes no attempt to use the traditional imagery and symbolism of the voyage to Hades which Conrad, like Virgil and Dante, employed "to create that otherwise formless region into which not only the artist but every man must descend if he wishes to understand himself." And perhaps because of this very formlessness London's characters are less able to withstand their experience. Even so, London and Conrad in these works are writing about the same problem. Their characters achieve knowledge of themselves and their world, a knowledge which leads them to an awareness of man's capacity for and affinity to evil. This awareness is directly expressed by both authors in their frequent use of terms referring to physical and spiritual darkness. (pp. 74-5)

This similarity of expression is made more emphatic by the almost identical summations of life made by the two writers. Marlow remarks: "Droll thing life is—that mysterious arrangement of merciless logic for a futile purpose." In *John Barleycorn* London says, "on every hand I see the merciless and infinite waste of natural selection. The White Logic insists upon opening the long-closed books, and . . . states the beauty and wonder I behold in terms of futility and dust." The "truths" here stated were, of course, in part the truths of all writers who contemplated the post-Darwinian cosmology from a certain point of view. Marlow confounds the beating of the savages' drum with the beating of his own heart; Eden's ambitions and reactions are principally shaped by his social environment. But neither writer in these books is unremittingly a naturalist, depicting his characters as animalistic drones rigidly controlled by biological and sociological forces. Although Marlow and Eden-London are confronted by these forces, the principal emphasis is on their *conscious* reaction to them. These protagonists consider that the world is a dark and futile place, but even as they investigate this insight they struggle with that darkness and futility. In these works London and Conrad coincide in differing from strict naturalists, for they both present the struggle from the side of the human antagonist. If one of London's "long-closed books" was "Heart of Darkness," he found a view of life fundamentally in keeping with the one he had expressed in the last parts of *Martin Eden* and *John Barleycorn*. (pp. 75-6)

*Sam S. Baskett, "Jack London's Heart of Darkness," in* American Quarterly *(copyright, 1958 Trustees of the University of Pennsylvania), Vol. X, No. 1, Spring, 1958, pp. 66-77.*

## MORDECAI RICHLER (essay date 1963)

[*Richler acknowledges London as a basically noncontemplative writer and a bigot, but also as a writer whose work occasionally glimmers with brilliance.*]

[London] rode the rods over the United States and Canada, he wandered as far off as Korea, he was in Alaska in the Gold Rush of 1898; and everywhere he went he seemed to come back with a story. I'm not saying that London's vitality or his reckless appetite for adventure made him a better writer than today's cautious fellowship-seeker, but it does—for my money anyway—suggest a man of enviable size. Unfortunately a lot of the stories London came back with are superficial, only fool's gold, but I doubt that he would have been a better writer had he stayed home. London was not a contemplative man. Indeed, it's generally when he thinks hard or angrily that he is embarrassing.

Some of Jack London's best stories, the adventure yarns and the rhetorical tales of man against nature, as well as that little gem, *The Call of the Wild,* are collected in *The Bodley Head Jack London.* . . . London's militant socialism makes for some of his most honourable but heavy-handed writing. At best his ideology was muddled, at worst, it was condescending, arrogant, and ridden with bigotry. . . . The one Jew who appears in these stories, and appears only briefly enough to be identified as a 'Polish Jew,' is the first to take a lifeboat when a ship is threatened by a hurricane. With him flee four native divers. All the wogs together.

In '**South of the Slot**,' one of his more obvious socialist stories, a strike action is saved only by the timely, rather comic-strip-type intervention, of the dashingly handsome middle-class hero of the piece, Freddie Drummond. Even Buck, the dog, almost overcome by sleighs and symbolism in *Call of the Wild,* is, so to speak, an Anglo-Saxon dog. Yes, children, it's true that like Freddie Drummond he gives up the good but tame life in California to lead (and breed with) the wolf pack, that is to say, workers, but don't you ever forget that Buck, like most of our very own socialist leaders, comes of a solid background and has been to the right man or dog schools. He isn't *really* smelly.

Occasionally over-laden with confused symbolism, *Call of the Wild* also suffers from wooden dialogue. London's French-Canadians here, as in the other stories in this collection, are outrageously caricatured. ('T'ree vair' good dogs,' François told Perrault. 'Dat Buck, heem pool lak hell. I tich heem queek as ant'ing.') All the same *Call of the Wild* is a delight. Full of convincing detail, it pulls the reader along by its sheer narrative drive. In fact, it is the Yukon stories in this collection—especially '**To Build a Fire**' and '**Batard**'—that seem to flow most easily. Possibly Jack London despised these romantic adventure stories and favoured his more 'serious' work ('**The Unparalleled Invasion**,' it's true, is alarmingly prophetic about germ warfare), but they remain, to my mind, his most enjoyable writings. *Call of the Wild,* at its best, is thrilling. And some of the stories share this same rare quality.

*Mordecai Richler, "Dogs and Wogs," in* The Spectator *(© 1963 by The Spectator; reprinted by permission of* The Spectator*), Vol. 211, No. 7045, July 5, 1963, p. 28.*

## TONY TANNER (essay date 1965)

[*Tanner discusses London's inner struggle between the call of the wild and the call of domesticity, and the expression of this conflict in his work.*]

Two of Jack London's most famous novels are about dogs: taken together they reveal a great deal about the author. In *The*

*Call of the Wild* we see Buck, snatched from the security of his master's home, adjusting to the brutal conditions of the northern wastes, and gradually responding to a lurking instinct for wildness which, dormant at the start, finally commands his whole being and obliterates the last traces of civilised training. Buck's story is a release, a sloughing off of bonds: it starts in the sobriety of the judge's house and ends with Buck running wild, 'his great throat a-bellow as he sings a song of the younger world, which is the song of the pack.'

The other dog, *White Fang,* reverses the process. He starts life in the heart of the wilds and ends up in a judge's home (i.e., claimed and tamed by 'law'). Where Buck used to dream of a world of prehistoric violence and woke to answer the primordial call of the wolf-howl, White Fang dreams of camp fires and the communities of man, and although he is 'ferocious, indomitable, and solitary,' he hears a different call, an instinct to submit to man in exchange for food and companionship. Freedom is fine—but it involves great loneliness: the camp is constricting—but it means warmth and rewards. White Fang ends like an Horatio Alger hero. Transported from the wilds to civilisation, he saves the judge's life and though he does not quite marry the judge's daughter, he mates with the judge's dog—a snooty collie who fits the usual stereotype. He is now called 'Blessed Wolf' and we last see him dozing in the sun with his progeny climbing all over him—the very image of domesticity, all wildness gone. Take the two books together and I think you get a very clear indication of Jack London's own deeply ambivalent attitudes towards the call of the camp and the call of the wild. . . .

These twin pulls—towards culture and social achievement, and again to the savage freedom of the wild—are blatantly apparent in some of his stories. Whichever world Jack London was in, he was drawn to the other. This is very clear in *Martin Eden,* . . . a distorted and selective account of his struggle up from brutalising poverty to successful authorship, and his first love affair, with Mabel Applegarth. Despite some execrable writing, it does convey with genuine power the emotional and intellectual turmoil of a young struggling writer. But more revealing, to me, is London's practice of constantly juxtaposing the worlds of gentility and savagery by what he calls 'memory pictures.' The book opens with Martin's stumbling, awed entry into a cultured middle-class home—he longs to find a place in this world. But whenever he is at some cultured social gathering we read that 'Martin kept seeing himself down all his past'— a past of fighting, drinking, and generally roughing it. At elegant dinners he dreams of brawls. Although he enjoys the struggle to break into cultured society, once he gets there he finds he has lost reality somewhere along the way. He is a genuine case of alienation. His vitality ebbs, a great torpor settles over him, and he commits suicide.

I have not mentioned the oft-remarked paradox of London's avowed socialism and his strenuous temperamental individualism ('The ultimate word is I LIKE') or the contrast between his humanitarian democratic feelings (see his warning against totalitarianism in *The Iron Heel*) and his shameless racism ('I am first of all a white man and only then a socialist'), because it seems to me that the most important struggle in his work is not between Superman and the mob, but between energy and inertia. His best stories are set in the frozen north, because there the battle between organic life and inorganic non-life was pursued with elemental simplicity. . . . Thus it is that his greatest single piece of writing, **'To Build a Fire,'** is simply about a man fighting a losing battle with the frost. For a man to

succumb to the glacial immobility of 'the white silence' was to 'sleep off to death.' Martin Eden thrives on the struggle for accomplishment and recognition, but when he has achieved it, he, too, sleeps off to death. Indeed, his last delight is to swim vigorously *downwards* to a deep-sea death, just as he had relished the struggle to climb *upwards* to a successful literary life. London seems to have sensed that at the heart of any great energy for life there is a reversible quantity—an energy for death, and that these twin hankerings somehow provided the most elemental struggle of all.

Although London exalted physical vitality to an abnormal degree ('I'd rather win a water-fight in a swimming pool . . . than write the great American novel'), he was deeply preoccupied with suicide and what he called 'the instinct for death . . . the will to die when the time to die is at hand.' The phrase comes from **John Barleycorn,** to my mind one of London's two great books. In describing with unforgettable vividness his gradual involvement with alcohol past the point of no return, London gives an almost archetypal clarity to a tragically familiar pattern in the lives of many American writers. His realisation that the attractions of drink and death are subtly intermingled is graphically revealed in his account of a night when he gets drunk, falls into the water and decides to swim out to sea and death—until he sobers up and directs his energy to a desperate and barely successful fight for life. As he says, this incident showed him 'abysses of intoxication hitherto undreamed'; abysses to which he finally returned at the age of forty. I think he comes close to the secret when he says that he found drink often appealed, not to the mediocre and timid, but to those people of 'superabundant vitality,' for as he demonstrated by his own life, an excess of life-hunger often contains its own principle of self-destruction.

It was from another abyss that he drew his other great book— the East End of London in 1902, which became *The People of the Abyss.* He found, indeed, that 'all human potentialities are in it,' but 'the Abyss is literally a huge man-killing machine,' 'a vast shambles.' The book is not merely an assemblage of appalling facts (though the facts are shocking enough to silence critics of the welfare state): what gives it its force is the way Jack London acquaints himself with 'the ferocious facts of life,' exposing his superb health and resilience to routines which thousands of homeless unemployed people went through daily— and finding he cannot take [it]. . . . The book is accurate and unanswerable. That civilisation could produce societies which were worse to live in than any of nature's wildnesses was not only a sociological truth but, for Jack London, a lived truth.

Perhaps he was not a great writer (though he is underrated), perhaps, like Martin Eden, he suffered from 'the clumsiness of too great strength.' But much of what he called his 'impassioned realism' still has an amazing power, and there are moments when he seems to have a hold on profound elemental issues. I see him as he saw White Fang, poised unhappily between civilisation and wildness: 'He could not immediately forgo all his wild heritage and his memories of the Wild. There were days when he crept to the edge of the forest and stood and listened to something calling him far and away. And always he returned, restless and uncomfortable. . . .' (pp. 80-1)

*Tony Tanner, "The Call of the Wild," in* The Spectator *(© 1965 by* The Spectator; *reprinted by permission of* The Spectator), *Vol. 215, No. 7151, July 16, 1965, pp. 80-1.*

**EARL WILCOX** (essay date 1970)

[*Wilcox examines* White Fang *as a Naturalistic novel.*]

Previous discussion of the major tenets of London's naturalism can be enlarged upon but little in an examination of *White Fang*. For the novel is hack work in its artistry and uninspiring in its philosophy. Nevertheless, it stands in central importance as evidence of the almost thoroughgoing naturalistic peak which London reached at this point in his writing. The familiar story of a survival-of-the-fittest animal, characterized by numerous animal impulses, in a bleak and pessimistic setting, accounts for major themes. To quote passages from the novel, it will be apparent, is but to echo nearly all that London has previously said.

The deliberateness with which London parallels his two animal fables may be noted in the ending of *The Call of the Wild* and the beginning of *White Fang*. One recalls that Buck is certain that he belongs with the wild when he tracks down and kills a bull moose, the clinging terror of the wolves being detailed. . . . It is into this world with all its primordial and savage splendor that Fang is born. It is not a new setting for London's fiction, this land of the White Silence, delineated so thoroughly in London's early stories and novel. Here is nature, which London personifies throughout as the "Wild," both man's and beast's great enemy. Nature is the inscrutable force that must be fought against day and night for survival. And the beasts are part of a world which the naturalists called the "hostile environment" where pressures from every side dictate its creatures' survival. (pp. 42-3)

But life does exist here, and the kind of life London intends to examine he has detailed before. Yet somehow characteristically, it seems, this is a land too of hunters and trappers—and dead men, men "whom the Wild had conquered and beaten down until [they] would never move or struggle again." These overtures which contain the implicit assumption that man is destined but to seek his own manner of death, present a strong materialistic creed, harking back even to classical thought. (p. 44)

Almost half way through the novel London finally introduces his central character. The "milieu" has been detailed, the "moment" is right, and as representative of his "race," Fang enters the world. And it is a world dominated by creatures of instinct who recognize that happiness is momentary, and in their recognition the inhabitants frequently voice a pessimistic attitude because of the lack of something more permanent. Yet, paradoxically, their materialism also spurs the citizens to live life to its fullest capacity. To be sure, this is London's world, thinly disguised in the study of a wolf's progression to a dog. Indeed based on London's assertions in *The Cruise of the Snark* . . . there is no doubt that whatever conclusions London draws about Fang's world, he also draws about his own. . . . And in the worlds, both existence itself and the meaning of existence are gauged by the extent to which one does to fullest capacity that which he is capable of doing. Parallel passages stressing this fusion of the biological and philosophical principles recur with regularity when one looks at Buck's "ascent" to the Wild with Fang's "descent" from the Wild. Weighing the final experience which convinces him of his affinity with the Wild, Buck's philosophy, London explains, is that there is an ecstasy that marks the summit of life. And beginning his first day of adventures with the same materialistic outlook, Fang learns that in killing a ptarmigan, "He [is] justifying his existence, that which life can do no greater; for life achieves its summit when it does to the uttermost that which it was equipped to do."

The description of White Fang's initial experiences as a cub are elementary adventures in their quality, despite Maxwell Geismar's claim that the tone of the battles with the ptarmigan chicks and the hawks is "lyrical." Compared with the terse, succinct manner in which London describes Buck's return to the Wild, Fang's experiences are over-drawn and padded. Yet the psychology of the cub's learning of the laws of survival is centrally important. As Dreiser's Carrie, Crane's Maggie, and London's own Buck all had learned how environment treats people and how to adjust to that hostile environment, Fang also learns his lessons well. But Fang is schooled not only for survival; he also lustfully relishes the idea of finding meat and of battling with the birds. Parallels with Buck's gluttony are obvious. (pp. 47-9)

Fang's initiation into the ritual of his world is arduously labored in the inflated chapter, "The Law of Meat." Here London reiterates the naturalistic concern with physical survival. The instinctive, nonreasoning law of the universe, Fang learns in going on the meat hunts with his mother, is to kill or be killed. This is the law of life. . . . (p. 49)

[The] survival tactics [Fang learns] make his body strong, just as precisely, London argues with Darwin, as the environment had made the bodies of the people of the abyss weak, puny, and diseased. Fang "became quicker of movement than the other dogs, swifter of foot, craftier, deadlier, more lithe, more lean with ironlike muscle and sinew, more enduring, more cruel, more ferocious, and more intelligent." And when the dogs are put into the traces, White Fang's obvious superiority brings the wrath of his peers upon him. After long journeys the dogs are always well fed, wasting nothing lest their share be taken by another. But none dare cross Fang, for he is the plunderer—and the wise servant of law: "White Fang knew the law well: *to oppress the weak and obey the strong*." One feels that the entire assessment London makes of Fang's development often hinges not so much on Fang's need for strength for survival as on his egotistical, rebellious nature with which his Creator, London, has endowed him.

It is clear that the same strictures which have been noted in Buck's "adaptability" must be leveled against London here too. It is not possible to consider Fang as a typical product of environment because he quickly becomes a superior type—the evolved, dominant race, among dogs. Consequently the naturalistic concern with the idea of survival of the fittest serves only an initial thematic configuration, not a philosophical reality. Indeed in a famine that grips the Indian tribe, while the other dogs perish (and are eaten), because they cannot find food, Fang survives. The law of natural selection would seem to be at work—the strong becoming stronger and the weak becoming weaker. But not so with Fang. It is the old nemesis of the naturalists, the inscrutable world which defeated Hurstwood but developed Carrie. In Fang, the Darwinian "accident" proves his salvation. . . . At last when Fang is fully developed and the "gods" have recognized his superiority, he becomes a monstrous tyrant who has been exposed to (and survived) the pitiless struggle for life.

But his outlook is not a happy one. Few clearer statements of the naturalistic paradox of joy in momentary and sensuous pleasure being clouded by a pall that shrouds even the happiest summits can be found in London's fiction than his summary of Fang's outlook at the moment of realization:

. . . it would have seemed that his mental development was well-nigh complete. He had come to know quite thoroughly the world in which he lived. His outlook was bleak and materialistic. The world as he saw it was a fierce and brutal world, a world without warmth, a world in which caresses and affection and the bright sweetnesses of the spirit did not exist.

Structurally, the reason for this insertion is clear enough. This comment permits London later to explore the ostensible differences in the Northland and the Southland. For all the while Fang's destiny leads to a luxurious life in California. There he will find life, apparently, different.

The erratic Part IV reiterates the parallels between Buck's and Fang's life. In this section Fang is sold to a "mad god," Beauty Smith, who uses Fang in dog fights. . . . Becoming famous as "The Fighting Wolf," he regards all other dogs as enemies, despite his earlier love for some of his comrades. And London quips, "It was another instance of the plasticity of his clay, of his capacity for being moulded by the pressure of environment."

From this point in the narrative to the end of the book it is only too obvious that London is merely rounding out an already padded novel. In rapid order Fang is finally defeated, being nearly killed by a monstrous bull dog, and then quickly rescued by Scott, the love-master. With Scott, "it was the beginning of the end for White Fang—the ending of the old life and the reign of hate." The new way of life is meant to convince one of the power of environment again, for Fang adapts. . . . (pp. 51-4)

Here he achieves "staidness, and calmness, and philosophic tolerance. He no longer lived in a hostile environment." To London's credit he does not end his propaganda pamphlet at the point of Fang's dreams of love and humanity. For this too is a land of evil doers, and the good must be protected from the evil. So a beast—"a human beast, it is true, but nevertheless so terrible a beast that he can best be characterized as carnivorous,"—Jim Hall, an escaped convict, invades Fang's Edenic world. Hall is bad because of "the treatment he had received from the time he was a little pulpy boy in a San Francisco slum—soft clay in the hands of society and ready to be formed into something." He is formed into a bad "thing" and is captured by Fang, who earns the approbation of all as "The Blessed Wolf." The novel fades out with Fang drowsing in the sun with puppies at his feet.

The naturalistic tendencies in the novel seem clear. Obviously London is still intent on using his fiction to present a popularly acceptable adventure story buttressed by a thin philosophical background rather than arguing in any systematic way for the philosophy. For the Darwinian and Spencerian motifs are clearly not discussed either in forceful or clear terms, except as London wishes to impress his audience with the plasticity of the individual. The strengths of the novel, in a larger sense, lie not in the book itself, but in its parallels with the much superior work, *The Call of the Wild*. The episodic structure here, as in *The Call of the Wild*, indicates more than any other feature London's almost total disregard for assimilating and integrating with depth either the philosophy or the style of the naturalists. Yet the dominant themes in the novel, one feels, are more naturalistic in concept than with any other genre in which the novel can be classified. (p. 55)

> Earl J. Wilcox, "Le milieu, le moment, la race: Literary Naturalism in Jack London's 'White Fang',"

*in* Jack London Newsletter, *Vol. 3, No. 2, May-August, 1970, pp. 42-55.*

### EARLE LABOR   (essay date 1974)

[*In this part of his critical study* Jack London, *Labor states his conclusions about the various sides of London and his work.*]

There is no gainsaying the genuine weaknesses in London's fiction. He can seldom sustain a long narrative structure. His best novels are occasionally marred by didacticism and sentimentalism. His female characters tend to be too flat, and his heroes are often too tall. Though he exalted content over form, he was too busy to be a philosopher; and he could seldom grasp a new idea without squeezing it into dogma. Compared with the great fictionists in American literature, London appears consistently lacking. He lacks the innovative brilliance of Poe, the encyclopedic vision of Melville, the great tragi-comic scope of Twain, the psychological sensitivity of James, the cultural responsibleness of Howells, the penetrating social insight of Fitzgerald, the stylistic integrity of Hemingway, and the magnificent artistic insouciance of Faulkner. Judged by their standards, his work does, indeed, seem to be "of minor importance in the development of our modern fiction."

However, the New Critical hegemony fell into fragments a decade ago because it could not measure the writer by any other than its own narrow rule. In the more tolerant 1970's it has become commonplace that no great writer can be accurately gauged by his shortcomings. A proper assessment of Jack London's work must therefore focus on his palpable achievements, which may be summarized as follows:

1. THE SOCIAL CRUSADER. He was a "born protestant." Writing for the working class directly from his own experiences, he spoke with authority about the "Submerged Tenth." He was the first writer to depict the hobo with genuine understanding. He also pioneered in the sympathetic, realistic treatment of the convict. Such works as *The People of the Abyss* and *The Road* possess social and historical significance apart from any literary considerations. The same may be said of much of London's fantasy and "social science fiction"—*e.g.*, *The Iron Heel* and *The Star Rover*. As often happens with dystopian fiction, London's apocalyptic prophecies may have been self-defeating in that most of the social ills he decried have been subsequently remedied. His protests against the enormities perpetrated by capitalist overlords sound as foreign to modern America as the term "proletarian" itself. Nevertheless, the social and economic inequities he attacked were as immediate to his age as pollution and the demands of the Third World are to our own. And some of his concerns for reform—alcoholism, the rape of the wilderness, and the senselessness of the penal system—still demand our attention.

2. THE FOLK WRITER. Jack London is the archetypal "kosmos" envisioned by Walt Whitman—the poet/seer embraced as lovingly by his people as he has embraced them. He has achieved a popularity so wide and so long-standing that he seems to have become a permanent legend in the American heritage. Other popular writers have become household words in the American common culture—*e.g.*, Horatio Alger, O. Henry, Zane Grey. But in the combining of a sustained popular appeal with serious literary merit and heroic personal stature Jack London is comparable to only one other figure in American literature—Mark Twain—and even that great writer did not excite the American yearnings for romantic adventure as profoundly as London—in short, theirs are complementary ap-

peals. London's variations on the complex theme of the American Dream place much of his work in the mainstream of our cultural history. *Martin Eden* anticipates the disenchanted success novels of Theodore Dreiser, Sinclair Lewis, and Scott Fitzgerald. *Burning Daylight* and *The Valley of the Moon* dramatize the archetypal tensions between civilization and the wilderness, the machine versus the garden.

3. THE LITERARY CRAFTSMAN. Guided by the principles of sincerity, functionalism, and imaginative Realism, London ushered in a new prose for the modern fictionist—clear, straightforward, uncluttered, imagistic—that is particularly well suited to the short story and to the depiction of violence and physical action. He was a major force in establishing for fiction a respectable middle ground between the gutter and the drawing room, and his efforts prepared the way for the new generations of Hemingway, Ring Lardner, and Norman Mailer. A consummate storyteller, he is gifted with the power to modulate narrative tempo so that his reader is often spellbound. While even his best work suffers from stylistic lapses, even his worst work is readable. If he is sometimes clumsy, he is seldom dull. He is capable of moments of lyric intensity. He possesses, moreover, an exceptional feeling for irony, cosmic as well as dramatic. Such stories as **"To Build a Fire"** and **"The Law of Life"** are masterpieces of short fiction. And even such longer works as *The Sea-Wolf* and *White Fang* have become, to the embarrassment of the critics, popular classics.

But London's ultimate greatness derives from his "primordial vision"—the mythopoeic force which animates his finest creations and to which we respond without fully understanding why. This is the secret of the immediate and lasting appeal of a work like *The Call of the Wild,* which remains fresh and vital over the years while our critical humming and hawing grows stale. (pp. 148-50)

> *Earle Labor, in his* Jack London *(copyright © 1974 by Twayne Publishers, Inc.; reprinted with the permission of Twayne Publishers, a Division of G. K. Hall & Co., Boston), Twayne, 1974, 179 p.*

**JAMES I. McCLINTOCK**   (essay date 1975)

[*In this excerpt, McClintock explores the development of London's story-writing technique.*]

When London began dissecting the magazine fiction in order to find "the proper trend of style and literary art" which led to the publication of the Northland stories, one of the first techniques he discovered was the use of the reliable, omniscient narrative point of view. He dropped the loose first person point of view that allowed his stories like **"Typhoon," "In the Time of Prince Charley," "A Thousand Deaths"** and **"The Rejuvenation of Major Rathborn"** to ramble in chronicle fashion and began to utilize more narrative control in the Alaskan tales. Switching to the third person narrator brought him into line with the most commonly used narrative method employed by his contemporaries. But with it, he inherited its legacy of authorial intrusion, even though writers were learning to restrict narrative privilege. Many of his stories, particularly in his first two volumes, *The Son of the Wolf* and *The God of His Fathers,* employ an essay-exemplum type of construction reminiscent of earlier writers who prefixed rambling sermons to their stories. . . . He thought of his short stories as having a block form of introduction-story rather than as a single entity.

In these introductory essays, in order to give the text, London would pose as an Alaskan social historian (**"The Wife of a King," "The God of His Fathers,"** and **"At the Rainbow's End"**); a modern philosopher (**"In a Far Country"**); or psychologist (**"The Son of the Wolf"**) among other roles. Then the illustrative story would follow. No doubt, this was the simplest method for presenting unequivocally the peculiarities of life in surroundings unfamiliar to the readers. Since London's first loyalty was to ideas and values, this uncomplicated form allowed him to present them so clearly that no reader could misunderstand. He never forgot his audience, and in these essay-exemplum stories, his didacticism led him to present views rather than to merely use them. Often the essays are superfluous, detachable moralizations whose import is implicit in the stories themselves. (pp. 15-16)

By discovering the omniscient narrator, London did improve beyond his early first person experiments. Although he sometimes rambled or padded his materials in these introductory essays which characterize many of his early Klondike tales, he generally used only those ideas which were germane to his story. Still, he was violating the primary concern of the short story theorists, the movement towards a more dramatic story. But call as they would for economical story-telling, the critics were not fully understood by London or other practicing magazine writers. Theory remained, to some extent, divorced from practice. The omniscient narrator did not move unobtrusively behind stories; instead, the narrator continued to impose his personality upon the fiction. He was privy to his characters' minds and hearts, had access to all knowledge and cavalierly interrupted at will to pass judgment upon his characters, situations and life in general.

London's first Northland stories demonstrate that he was not an innovator in this regard. Even after the introductory essays, the narrator insistently performs many functions. The characters do not reveal themselves through their actions and speech; instead, the narrator intrudes to comment and evaluate. . . . Often these intrusions are epigrammatic summaries used to resolve one section of the story before going on to the next. Rather than being inconspicuous, they draw attention to themselves and exist for their own sakes as well as for structural purposes—for example, this aside to the reader from **"The Priestly Prerogative,"** one of the most flagrantly non-dramatic stories he ever wrote: "Some people are good, not for inherent love of virtue, but from sheer laziness. Those of us who know weak moments may understand." . . . Besides the precious, epigrammatic language, the intrusions are often particularly noticeable because of their exuberant, emotional or moralizing tone that draws attention to the highly personalized narrator who is indistinguishable from the author. (pp. 17-18)

[London] was learning "the art of omission" which he found most difficult but realized that its mastery meant the difference between a powerful story and one whose strength was dissipated. . . . [Dialogue] does begin to replace the narrator in some stories, but often it is a mere transplantation of the narrator's essay into the mouths of the characters, as, for example, Karen's discussion of "race affinity" in **"The Great Interrogation."** . . . But no matter how amateurishly executed, this is a step towards depersonalizing the narrator. Furthermore, London began to find techniques which would eliminate the author, or, at least, camouflage his operations. (pp. 19-20)

London hit upon a form of which Kipling was the master—the frame story. In these stories the narrator provides some kind of setting that permits a character to elicit a story from another, recalls some story told to him, or provides some motivation for a character to recall a personal experience. These frame stories represent London's first major movement towards a more dramatic form of story-telling. They begin early in his work, while he continued to produce the essay-exemplum form, and became a significantly large portion of his total canon. Significantly there are more frame stories in the second volume of his short stories than in the first, and more in the third than in the second. They are a modification of the essay-exemplum type since the frame takes the place of the essay, and the story-within often illustrates some idea that is discussed in the frame section.

"**An Odyssey of the North**" is a well known London story which exemplifies his experimentation with this more dramatic type of story. An omniscient narrator begins by introducing the characters, familiar from earlier stories, and establishing the setting. The Malemute Kid and Prince take over the narrative functions through their dialogue and provide the frame. They discuss the various Northland types of men who are in their cabin, especially the mysterious visitor who is later revealed as Naass, the central figure who narrates the odyssey in the title. The initial part of the frame ends here. Finally, the tale within the story is told by Naass in the long first person narrative passage which is the central interest of this story. After Naass' tale, the "Odyssey of the North" concludes with the final part of the frame as the Kid and Prince ponder what they have heard. (pp. 20-1)

In his movement from the essay-exemplum form to the frame story, London was not only responding to a general dramatic trend reflected in the construction of magazine stories, but revealing his indebtedness to Kipling's example. Rothberg and other critics have documented the themes and materials shared by Kipling and London, and Joan London mentioned that Jack attempted to imitate Kipling's style. But no one has noticed the remarkable similarity of their short story structures. Moreover, Jack London's testimony that he studied the magazines when Kipling was in the first rank in order to find the proper short story form and techniques, his open and frequently mentioned admiration of Kipling, and the striking correspondences between the two authors' short story patterns, even plots, are strong evidence that London used Kipling's stories as models for his own. (pp. 21-2)

[London learned] to use the frame story adequately, and it allowed him to explore his ideas more thoroughly than the essay-exemplum type. In the essay-exemplum stories the narrator was constrained to speak in what can only be the author's authoritative voice rather than through a *persona*. Most of the explicit comments made by the narrator are awkwardly overbearing and dogmatic in their attempts to force ideas upon the reader and commit the story-teller to arriving at definite conclusions. But London's frame stories, using a teller who is clearly distinguishable from London himself, allowed him to present more complicated social and moral situations. For example, in "**An Odyssey of the North**" Naass, an admirable and complex character-narrator, comes into conflict with two other idealized characters. The situation is morally complex since Naass's suffering and loyalty are emotionally equivalent to Unga's and Axel's love for each other, and equally justified. Yet the two sets of emotions are incompatible, and the story rightly remains unresolved. Because the point of view is not that absolutely omniscient and reliable author's, the dilemma can be left without final auctorial redress and pontifical judgment, making artistic uses of ambiguity and irony. And in the

Northland tales as a group we find that the frame tale becomes a frequently employed form for presenting stories which deal with the conflict between civilization and primitive culture, the white man and the Indian, topics complex in their moral overtones. (pp. 24-5)

Sometime in late spring, 1900, only a year and a half after beginning his serious apprenticeship and after composing most of the stories eventually collected in *Son of the Wolf* and *God of His Fathers* and beginning to work on the *Children of the Frost* stories, Jack London began to recognize the need for a more satisfactory dramatic form that would encompass an entire story, rather than being limited to the story within another story. In the course of the next few months he developed his most sophisticated theory and practice of dramatic fiction. . . . (p. 25)

[In "**The Law of Life**"] London discovered that he could use a limited, rather than fully omniscient, third person point of view for a dramatic effect powerful in its simplicity. There is no essay in the beginning, and the setting is established in terms of the old man's awareness so that there is no awkward shift from narrative landscaping to action; therefore, the reader is not conscious of a direct bid for his attention. . . . The comments made by the narrator are tailored to the demands of character rather than inappropriately out of the range of the character's perceptions and are so appropriate in tone and style that no unusual emphasis draws attention away from the character's point of view.

Although none of the stories following "**The Law of Life**" in *The Children of the Frost* . . . are as rigorous in point of view nor in artistic simplicity, stories like "**Nam-Bok the Unveracious**," "**The Sunlanders**," and "**Keesh, the Son of Keesh**," (told "from the Indian's point of view, through the Indian's eyes as it were") do demonstrate that London was avoiding direct philosophical, social or psychological evaluations of character or setting in the voice of the narrator appealing directly to his audience.

London, then, was learning techniques which allowed him to be more economical and dramatic. The logical extension of this movement toward depersonalizing the narrator voice is a scenic method which uses a stage-manager narrator who merely records what can be seen and heard but who does not enter the characters' minds, analyze their motives, nor explain the source and implications of the scenes. The product of such a method would be similar to a painting, a pictorial representation of a situation. (pp. 27-8)

[There] is an extremely important basic correlation between London's theory and his actual practice. From the beginning of his Klondike stories, he had relied upon dramatic scenes as the core around which the rest of the story coalesced. Although the story might contain narrative essays and other authorial interference, an evocative scene lay at the center of dramatic interest in the best of these stories. Even an early critic recognized the visual quality achieved in the *Children of the Frost* as a mark of distinguished writing and wrote that in "**The Master of Mystery**," "the subject is so interesting and the treatment so powerfully simple and sincere that the picture stands out clear and flawless." The poorer stories, the ones that London himself disliked, such as "**The Wife of a King**" and "**A Priestly Prerogative**," fail to focus upon a single dramatic scene or central image. London did realize though that such scenes replace the author, or, more accurately, become the author in the sense that his emotional and intellectual experience can be embodied more compactly and forcefully through scene than through exposition. (p. 29)

Throughout the rest of his career, London continued to rely on the three major short story forms and the evocative style that he learned during these early, apprenticeship years. His social criticism stories and South Seas stories, the good ones as well as the pot-boilers, are cast in these familiar molds. At their best, the stories wed form, content and style while transcending formal and technical deficiencies by emphasizing central, powerful scenes. The essay-exemplum form remained a staple for presenting ideas dogmatically, particularly when introducing new ideas about strange lands or situations whether in the Northland, the South Seas, or among the "submerged tenth" in America. The frame stories allowed him to develop more complex ideas. The more dramatic forms and techniques were used for statements about basic human experiences which needed no explicit introduction, but demanded emotional impact, especially if the perspective were ironic. (p. 32)

> *James I. McClintock, in his* White Logic: Jack London's Short Stories *(copyright © 1975 by James I. McClintock), Wolf House Books, 1975, 206 p.*

**GORDON MILLS** (essay date 1976)

*[Mills considers London's successes and failures in transferring his self-perceptions to the pages of* Martin Eden.*]*

One of the materials London incorporated into *Martin Eden* was himself. "I was Martin Eden," he wrote, defending himself against the charge that Martin Eden could not possibly have achieved so great a success so rapidly. The nature of their great energy and the chronology of their success are indeed much the same for the author and his fictional character, as is the chronology of their subsequent despair. (p. 12)

In pondering the effectiveness of the work, we therefore seem to be at once confronted with the question of whether its appeal lies in its autobiographical factuality or in its illusional power as a work of art. Reasonable though it appears, however, this question is somewhat misleading. Illusional power is no stranger to the pages of either history or autobiography. Surely everyone would agree that long stretches of the historical works of Francis Parkman or Arthur M. Schlesinger, Jr., move with the intensity of fiction. . . . Our problem in *Martin Eden* is not factuality but what was done with factuality; it is not whether readers see glimpses of the real Jack London in the story but what is done with the real Jack London they see.

From this point of view it becomes apparent that the presence of the real Jack London in the story sometimes lends power to the illusion but at other times constitutes a flaw. The author was not uniformly successful in the transformation of the material constituted by his own experience.

Let us consider first one of the successful transformations. For this purpose, no part of the novel is more interesting than that initial section in which Martin first becomes aware of the world of the Morses and strives to make himself worthy of it. The dominant movement of this section, its wholeness, can be initially formulated as the relationship between the two concepts of vitality and a transcendent reality. Out of the vital force embodied in Martin Eden emerges a vision of a transcendent reality, initiated by his sudden introduction to the Morses; the early part of the novel is a depiction of the movement of this vital force in the direction established by the vision. The entire process can be understood as a transformation of the material of London's personal experience. At its simplest this trans-

formation is only an idealizing, a romanticizing, but in the end it is much more complex than that.

So far as mere animal vitality is concerned, little transformation appears to have been needed. Tributes to London's own superabundant spirits and contagious enthusiasm are found everywhere. . . . In the novel, London's need was simply to give this vitality its necessary direction toward the love and beauty contained in his vision rather than toward, or not only toward, the mere acquisition of wealth. In actuality, London's feelings were evidently mixed. He contributed his time and effort freely to the cause of socialism, for instance, but meanwhile asserted his willingness to sell himself outright to the magazines. . . . Martin Eden, on the other hand, regarded wealth as an inadequate motive for undergoing severe privation as an apprentice, in contrast to the motive of "the love of a woman, or . . . attainment of beauty." . . . (pp. 13-14)

A full apprehension of the transformation of London's vitality into that of Martin Eden cannot be separated from the vision associated with that vitality. Martin's vision of a world of love, beauty, and intellectuality was of course false, and a particularly interesting question is the degree to which London had ever himself experienced such a vision. The power of the novel is heavily dependent on the great gap between the seaman's world of Martin Eden and the gentility of the Morse home on which Martin centers his vision. Had London himself ever undergone the full impact of an encounter involving so great a disparity as that between Martin Eden and the Morses? . . . London faced a very concrete problem. He had to establish the greatest conceivable distance between the actual circumstances of his protagonist and the supposed embodiment of his protagonist's vision. Given enough distance, the fact that the real Morse household was by no means isomorphic with his vision could go unnoticed by the protagonist. Anything which unnecessarily lessened the gap between Martin's own situation and what he mistakenly believed to be the situation in the Morse home had to be rejected as unsuitable material. Were London to have allowed Martin the status of a student in the University of California when he first entered the Morse home, for instance, the illusion sought would have vanished, or at best would have lost much of its intensity. In fact, Jack London was a student at the University of California within months of his first visit to the real-life original of the Morse home and was, unlike Martin Eden, at the age of nineteen enrolled in the Oakland High School when this first visit was made. It was through his membership in the Henry Clay Debating Society, a club for people with intellectual interests, that London became acquainted with Edward Applegarth, who took him home and introduced him to his sister Mabel, on whom Ruth Morse was modeled.

These facts from London's personal experience were not suitable material; they would have brought Martin Eden much too close to the Morse life-style. Their transformation would have required a quite different totality. On the other hand, many of the events of London's past were indeed readily adaptable: his life at sea; his decision, while a hobo, to acquire an education; the nature of his relationship with Mabel Applegarth; his prodigious efforts to learn to write. It should be remembered, however, that although these events may have a certain interest in themselves, it is only when they are integrated into the "wholeness" of *Martin Eden* that they take on the intensity of art.

Yet it is generally agreed that London was by no means uniformly successful in transforming his personal experience into the illusional quality of art. The meaning of transformation is, in fact, clarified by examination of an instance or two of failure. We might begin by considering one of the mirror scenes. Martin repeatedly talks to his image in a mirror. . . . His first such talk is very brief, but is preceded by a long and thoughtful examination of his reflected appearance. Possibly the face he sees in the mirror is not that of Jack London; the trouble is, if it is not London's face, there is no way to prove it is not and every reason to suspect that it is. The features described bear a remarkable resemblance to photographs of London: high forehead, mop of brown hair, blue eyes, square chin. (pp. 15-16)

The difficulty is not that Martin Eden is Jack London but that it is so hard to avoid regarding Martin's absorbed contemplation of his image in the mirror as a narcissistic compulsion of the author's ego. Had the structural wholeness of the illusion the novel creates required that the features described resemble London's features, as the structural wholeness clearly requires that the intensity of Martin's efforts to learn to write resemble London's own efforts, there would have been no transformational problem. The illusion would have been unimpaired. Unfortunately, no such requirement is evident as far as Martin's personal appearance is concerned, and the reader is forced into an unpleasant choice he would much rather not have to make. Is he witnessing an emotionally effective element in the esthetic illusion of Martin Eden's movement toward his vision, one in which Martin first truly confronts the question, ''Who am I?''— or is he witnessing a compulsive narcissistic ritual on the part of Jack London? Of course, the reader should never have been presented with such a dilemma.

A fundamental principle seems to be involved. A writer can make use of his personal experience so long as that experience is unquestionably subordinate to the totality of the illusion. It is when a reader unavoidably begins to feel that an author's intrusion of himself into the story is directly self-serving in some way, a begging for sympathy or for admiration, that the illusion is damaged. A rather obvious intrusion may go virtually unnoticed if it seems to be entirely subservient to an appropriate structural totality, as with the obvious presence of London himself in the learning-to-write scenes. To feel ourselves in the presence of a truly great literary work, we must at no time doubt that the author is thinking of the illusion he is creating as a means of exploring human experience rather than as a direct outlet for his personal emotions. The writer must evidently perceive himself only as one of the materials to be transformed into an esthetic illusion if he is to make effective use of his own feelings in the process. (pp. 17-18)

It would seem, it must in fact be, impossible for any mature and thoughtful reader to escape occasionally being jarred out of his absorption in the story. On formalistic grounds we must give **Martin Eden** some low marks. We are forced into ambiguity, however, by the disparity between this novel's failure to meet formalistic demands and its demonstrated power to grip the attention of sophisticated readers. Logic seems to demand postulation of a wholeness which is more than the sum of the individual transformations contained in the work, although how this wholeness could be articulated is at present beyond the resources of literary theory. Psychoanalytic theory offers one attractive possibility, but the essentially static character of psychoanalytic interpretations has not yet been shown capable of responding effectively to the requirements of those dynamics of the reader-text relationship which can be observed daily by any thoughtful person. (p. 21)

[Many] sophisticated readers do testify to the affective quality of **Martin Eden** and do indicate their intellectual assent to its

import—grimacing, meanwhile, over its flaws. And so in the end we seem forced to stand our initial proposition on its head and seek a more comprehensive literary theory than we yet possess. If the mere absence of flaws is no assurance of greatness, neither does the presence of serious flaws preclude enjoyment and the granting of intellectual assent. (p. 22)

*Gordon Mills, ''The Transformation of Material in a Mimetic Fiction,'' in* Modern Fiction Studies *(© 1976 by Purdue Research Foundation, West Lafayette, Indiana 47907, U.S.A.), Vol. 22, No. 1, Spring, 1976, pp. 9-22.*

**SUSAN WARD** (essay date 1976)

[*Ward's discussion of the female heroines in London's fiction is the most thorough treatment of a subject to which many other critics allude only in passing.*]

Jack London's fictional heroines are divisible into three types. The first of these is the blonde, blue-eyed, virtuous heroine of late nineteenth century romance. She is beautiful, often rich, and always respectable. She surrounds herself with books, music, and beautiful clothes and serves as the embodiment of ''culture'' to London's heroes. She probably served as the embodiment of culture to London's readers and to London as well. To mid-twentieth century readers, she is infinitely boring.

Heroines of the second type are not quite so inimical to modern tastes. Along with Frank Norris around the turn of the century, London did much to popularize the convention of the ''comrade woman'' who took part in adventures with her man instead of sitting home with her embroidery. A large number of London's heroines fall into this category. Frona Welse in **A Daughter of the Snows** introduces her man to the art of survival in the Yukon, Joan Lackland in **Adventure** helps her hero to quell a native uprising, and even fragile Maud Brewster, the poetess-heroine of **The Sea-Wolf,** trades her pen for a club to help Humphrey Van Weyden hunt seals when the larder runs low on their deserted island. These heroines, however, are a far cry from the ''liberated'' woman mid-twentieth century readers might wish for. Frona does not admit to love until the man in question is as good as she is on snow shoes, Maud cures extra seal skins so that Van Weyden can build her a separate hut to preserve her maiden privacy, and Joan Lackland, after showing the strength of mind to subdue restless natives and reorganize the plantation, allows David Sheldon to bully her into a marriage which negates all of her former life plans. After reviewing plots like these, one feels that London sells the ''comrade woman'' short to some late nineteenth century concept of respectable womanhood. That concept is more than a little wooden, and, as many critics have pointed out, so are the heroines.

The heroines of the third type are not respectable, but they are less wooden and more admirable than any other of London's women. They are the dance-hall girls and Indian wives and mistresses of London's Alaskan heroes, and they are more admirable because they possess virtues which the ''respectable'' heroines often lack. (pp. 81-2)

The most important dance-hall girl in London's short fiction is Freda Moloof, a Greek dancer in the Dawson saloons whose beautiful face has, according to London, ''overmuch strength in it.'' She is joined in **Burning Daylight** by another dancer named Freda and by a young woman ''comely of face and figure'' who is known simply as ''the Virgin.'' Lest anyone doubt their profession, London notes that Freda is denied entrance to all respectable gatherings after wives and sister arrive in Dawson and that the Virgin has to give up the dance-hall and work at washing clothes, sewing parkas, and clerking in the first Yukon bank once she decides to "straighten up." Both are acutely aware of their low social position. This is seen most clearly in Freda's refusal to allow the most respectable lady in Dawson to enter her cabin though she would like, in fact, to entertain her. "Freda could worship such a woman, and she could have asked no greater joy than to have had her into the cabin," we read in **"The Scorn of Women."** "But her respect for Mrs. Eppingwell . . . prevented her." She suffers from this, but that is beside the point. London is not about to allow either Freda or his readers to forget the dance-hall girl's low social standing, even on the frontier.

Beyond the humility which this recognition brings, the dance-hall girls are good-hearted, proud, and possessed of a knowledge which their respectable sisters lack and which the dance-hall girls often use to someone else's advantage. Freda, for example, shames one young man into remaining with the native whom he had determined to set aside and forestalls another young man's secret elopement in the face of his former fiance's impending arrival in the Yukon, her knowledge of men enables her to carry off these incidents successfully. (p. 82)

Humility, good-heartedness, pride, and success at the man game are all standard characteristics of frontier prostitutes. What becomes interesting in London's fiction is not that London endows his dance-hall girls with these traits but that he sets at least one who possesses them above a respectable heroine. In **"The Scorn of Women,"** Freda is able to keep Floyd Vanderlip by her side and thus to forestall his elopement when Mrs. Eppingwell is not; her ability to do so allows her to play a more important part in the salvation of Floyd than a respectable Colonel's lady. Although London does not exactly exonerate Freda for her ability to play to a dishonest man's weakness for women ("One cannot understand defilement without laying hands to pitch" London writes), he nevertheless gives Freda the better role. He further arouses our sympathy for Freda by letting Mrs. Eppingwell misjudge her. Though he freely forgives Mrs. Eppingwell for so doing, he notes that respectable ladies often "fall short of universality." This places greater worldly knowledge as well as greater humility in Freda's corner. We are not asked to choose between the two in this story, but we cannot help seeing that Freda is in many ways the stronger and more admirable woman.

The Indian women in London's frontier stories share the dubious social status of Freda and the Virgin. Like the dance-hall girls, Indian common-law wives and mistresses are frowned upon by "respectable" women. This attitude results in many stories in the abandonment of Indian women by their white husbands and lovers. London's attitude toward this mass abandonment is ambivalent. In some stories, like **"The Wife of the King,"** he calls those men who participate in it "cowards," and in others, like **"The Story of Jees Uck,"** he simply asserts that kind must marry kind and that the white man's abandonment of the Indian girl is inevitable. For the most part, the Indians accept their low status uncomplainingly. This is illustrated most forcefully in the story **"Siwash"** in which a dying Indian woman makes her white husband promise not to take another Indian girl as his wife because "Your people call you 'squawman,' your women turn their heads to one side on the street, . . . you do not go to their cabins like other men. . . . And this is not good." Therefore, she proposes to die so that her husband can marry a white woman and be accepted back

into white society where, according to his Indian wife, he belongs.

Like the dance-hall girls the Indian women possess several admirable character traits. They are loyal, self-sacrificing, stoical in the face of pain or disappointment, and possessed of a natural sexuality which London does not allow to operate in "respectable" white heroines. The Indian girls do not demand separate huts, even when white men suggest cohabitation on less than deserted islands. They are loyal above the law of kind, and the law of kind is an important principle throughout London's fiction. They are self-sacrificing to the point of jeopardizing their own lives to save the lives of their husbands or lovers. They are also possessed of a quality which London names "elemental simplicity" and which is in large part responsible for their attractiveness. This is brought out most clearly in **"The Story of Jees Uck"** as London describes the beneficial effects which Neil Bonner, a young white man, derives from his relationship with an Indian girl on a lonely trading post in the Yukon. "Not alone was she solace to his loneliness," London writes "but her primitiveness rejuvenated his jaded mind. It was as though, after long wandering, he had returned to pillow his head in the lap of Mother Earth." The "primitive" comfort is partly sexual, of course, but London also refers to a special kinship with nature and a simpler way of looking at the world which are the attributes of the "good savage" throughout nineteenth and twentieth century American fiction.

Though London's Indian women do possess several admirable character traits, we cannot assume, simply on the basis of this fact, that London admires them more than his "respectable" heroines. Comparisons of his fiction treating Indian women with his fiction treating white heroines, however, lead us to two further observations which can be used to support this conclusion. First, many of the traits which London assigns to the Indian women are noteworthy for their absence in the white heroines of other stories. And, second, certain stories featuring both an Indian girl and a white woman lead us in the direction of admiring the Indian girl more completely. This second observation is based on our noting the pattern in stories about Indians which we noted earlier in stories about white prostitutes: that is, in certain stories London pits a "respectable" against a not so respectable heroine and allows the not so respectable heroine to win in the contest for reader admiration.

The list of Indian virtues for which London depicts corresponding white women's vices is a long one. Indian women are loyal. White women, like the heroine of **"Flush of Gold,"** desert lovers for no good reasons. Indian women do not interfere in what they consider to be men's affairs. White women, like Genevieve in *The Game* and Ruth Morse in *Martin Eden,* try to turn men away from what eventually becomes their life work. Indian women do not try to be masterful. (pp. 82-4)

Indian wives and mistresses are also sometimes set against white heroines in a single story, and, like the dance-hall girls, they sometimes emerge as victors. Again, Jees Uck is an Indian girl who lives with a young white man and bears him a son and who is deserted after three years time when her lover returns to his native San Francisco. When she journeys south in search of him and learns of his marriage, she elects not to reveal their relationship or the identity of their son to his society wife. Instead, she returns to the Yukon and opens a school for Indian girls, "to show them the way of their feet in the world." We have no cause to dislike Kitty Bonner, the wife of the story, but, again, we cannot help but feel that the least respectable is the more admirable woman.

We cannot simply assert that all Jack London's respectable white heroines are a pallid and uninteresting lot—Saxon Roberts in *The Valley of the Moon* for example, is fairly admirable—but we can conclude that London accorded his dance-hall girls and Indian squaws a sneaking admiration which he did not bestow on their genteel sisters. (p. 84)

> Susan Ward, "Jack London's Women: Civilization vs. The Frontier," in Jack London Newsletter, *Vol. 9, No. 2, May-August, 1976, pp. 81-5.*

## PAUL STEIN  (essay date 1978)

[*Stein examines the literary and sociological elements of* The Iron Heel, *finding the book a worthy accomplishment.*]

Friedrich Engels would probably have expressed some reservations regarding the merits of Jack London's *The Iron Heel* as a work of art. It was not that he was finicky about the use of literature as an instrument of social commentary and instruction, but that he expected something more than overt didacticism and exposition from the literary artist. . . . Engels, writing to Margaret Harkness about her play *Franz von Sickingen,* warned her that she should "Shakespearize more, while at present I consider Schillerism, making individuals the mere mouthpieces of the spirit of the times, your main fault."

From Engels' point of view, then, it would not be difficult to find *The Iron Heel* both artistically deficient because of its clearly labeled, flatly dimensioned characters and politically injudicious because of its unhesitating prediction of the coming destruction of the very social class to which most of its putative readers belonged. On the other hand, it is hard to believe that Engels would have been unsympathetic to the ideological assumptions that London brought to bear when he came to write the novel and which dictate its structure. For *The Iron Heel,* London's most deliberate transmutation of political vision into artistic statement, represents in its analysis of the state of society and of the imperatives of social and economic change, a consistent exposition of revolutionary Marxist thought. A *Tendenzroman* whose hero is an idea, the novel is a call to understanding and action and can be viewed as London's literary version of the *Communist Manifesto* with which Marx and Engels addressed the proletariat of Europe in 1848. As such, *The Iron Heel* provides a synthesis in most concrete and coherent terms of London's grasp of Marxist ideology and demonstrates the extent of his ability to use literary device for programmatic purpose. (pp. 77-8)

Central to [London's] social thought was his unqualified endorsement of the theory of the class nature of pre-socialist society with its concomitant recognition of class conflict as a manifestation of the absolutely opposed interests of capitalist and worker. This conflict he saw rooted in the material conditions of life which, in turn, were determined by the mode of organization of the means of production by which society sustained itself. And he was convinced that only through revolutionary change, the overthrow and destruction of resistant capitalistic modes and attendant social values, could those conditions be fundamentally altered and a truly new order established. It is this Marxist foundation upon which his novel rests. As Philip S. Foner has pointed out, in *The Iron Heel* "London presented his ablest application of Marxist theory to American conditions."

This presentation takes its most explicit form in a series of expository statements made by Ernest Everhard during the first half of the novel. . . . Physically and mentally powerful, fearless and dedicated, Everhard is the epitome of the revolutionary hero, and it is not difficult to see him as London's alter ego. But the revolutionary commitment of the novel is not expressed through Everhard alone. In addition to London's depiction of Everhard and the other characters in the novel, his construction of narrative structure is also shaped by a consistent and pervasive Marxist vision. Characterization, plot, and form are parts of an integrated whole, with Everhard's speeches providing the statement and the novel's action and structure the demonstration of London's theme.

Everhard first appears in the opening chapter at a dinner party given by [his wife's] father, a professor of physics at Berkeley. The professor had invited the young radical in the hope of stimulating intellectual controversy, the other guests being conventional and orthodox churchmen. By setting up this confrontation between the crusading socialist and the comfortable men of the cloth, London brings into direct conflict two faiths, two versions of reality, of which only one, in his view, can reflect the truth of human existence. . . . London, through Everhard's words, presents to the reader a basic aspect of his argument, that reality resides in what actually is and not in what should or is believed to be, that the anchor of truth is embedded in the material world.

The nature of that material world is delineated comprehensively in a follow-up set-piece in which Everhard faces the Philomath Club, an exclusive group of the wealthiest members of society who gather periodically to hear guest speakers discourse on the latest developments in science, art, and politics. He has been invited as a sort of curiosity from the underworld, but he intends to use the opportunity to challenge the very basis of their existence, to "shake them to the roots of their primitive natures." . . . And indeed he does. (pp. 82-4)

The eagle-like Everhard, magnificent in his fiercely physical individuality, yet as well as manifestation of a class ethos, arouses in each of his opponents the age-old instinct for survival. They, in turn, driven by common purpose into a pack-like response, join together to face the common foe. London, in this respect, is not far in his formulation from Karl Marx. "Man," wrote Marx in rather more moderate terms, "is in the most literal sense of the word a *zoon politikon,* not only a social animal, but an animal which can develop into an individual only in society." Individual behavior, for London, is determined by the biological imperative for sustenance and survival conditioned by sociological circumstance. Given the appropriate conditions, that is to say through the rational ordering of social relationships, that imperative can be channeled in a communal way, in a way beneficial to an entire people. Under other conditions, it can produce social disaster, stemming either from willful selfishness or an organized minority, the Iron Heel, or desperate rebellion by a disorganized majority, the People of the Abyss. The crucial struggle, then, as London sees it, at this stage of history, is taking place between a capitalist class keenly aware of its privileges and determined to keep them and a slumbering working class slowly awakening under the prodding of its most advanced political elements to an understanding of its epochal mission to reshape the world.

Everhard's charges evoke an outraged response from his audience. They shout and jeer at him and excitedly attempt to argue with him, but to no avail; London has placed fact and logic at his side. Only one of Everhard's opponents remains cool, and he at the end of the evening goes calmly to the heart of the matter. It is not, he declares, a question of morality or justice that justifies the maintenance of the status quo, the resistance to change, it is a question of power. . . . London, in this dialogue, makes clear his understanding of the possibilities for major social change and progress. They will not come about with the voluntary cooperation of the present owners of the means of production, but through their forcible overthrow. The reorganization of society will require revolution.

In this schematic of the social order and the dynamics of its movement into the future projected by London, the capitalist and working classes are thus seen to be the primary combatants in the war that will end only with the achievement of a classless society, or perhaps more precisely a one-class society, a working-class society. Though doomed to extinction, the capitalists, prompted by a class instinct for survival, fight on. . . . The middle class, neither fish now fowl, caught in an economic no man's land, is doomed to be an early casualty of the intensifying conflict.

Again, London uses the setting of a dinner or a formal meeting to provide a platform for Everhard to speak on the role and destiny of the middle class. (pp. 84-6)

These three scenes, the dinner parties with the churchmen and the middle class businessmen and the meeting with the Philomaths, state the ideological theses of the book in a straightforward and overtly expository way. As novelistic devices in the usual sense, they do not seize the imagination. Telling rather than showing, they are flat and undramatic, as exciting for the reader as watching a marksman shoot sitting ducks, for not only has London designed them as set-pieces, he has made the outcome of the three confrontations a foregone conclusion. In disputation, Everhard invariably carries the day. In command of all the facts, rigorously logical, fiercely articulate, and physically overwhelming, he demolishes the arguments, mocks the hypocrisies, and exposes the self-deceptions of his opponents. Yet, these scenes are more than merely vehicles for ideological demonstration; they serve in addition a twofold thematic function. For Avis, who observes and records them, they provide moments of high exhilaration as she witnesses the unfolding of a great and unassailable truth. Through her, London promises the reader a similar experience if the reader's mind opens to this message of the future. She is energized into a fuller life of understanding and action, and her experience stands as an example of the power of theory to affect the course of human events. On the other hand, in the context of the novel as a whole, these scenes reveal as well the limitations of theory. As a debater in dining room or public hall, Everhard is unconquerable, but as a revolutionary on the field of battle he is not. He perishes like so many others in the Second Revolt against the Iron Heel. The correct political theory may be all-powerful on an intellectual plane, but, as London shows, it must be implemented and made effective in the ordering of society by human action engaged in the arena of real events and hazards. (pp. 86-7)

Everhard's death, in the light of the ultimate triumph of socialism centuries later, illustrates the comparative insignificance of individual action in an historical context. Yet the change, London is convinced, cannot be brought about without the joining together of many single efforts and contributions, unimportant as each alone may be in the larger sense. What the business of the novel illuminates, then, is London's view of the relationship between individual effort and evolutionary sweep. Insofar as the former is concerned. he shows how first there

arises on various levels of society a new awareness of the reality of the social scene. This awareness may well trigger individual protest and revolutionary-like acts and stimulate the organization of reform-oriented social groups like labor unions, but it alone cannot bring about a fundamental change in the social structure. What is required is a revolutionary movement, comprised of individuals with highly advanced political understanding, consciously dedicated to an entirely new arrangement of the building blocks of society. Even then, the evolutionary moment must be right for the revolutionary movement to succeed. (p. 87)

London's description of the emergence of the Iron Heel in all its brutal strength as a defensive measure by which the ruling class attempts to solve the repeated crises faced by capitalism exemplifies his conviction, as stated by Everhard, of the severity of the struggle faced by the proponents of socialism. The narrative line of the novel traces the polarization of social forces as the long battle is joined. On one side is the Iron Heel, the tightly organized oligarchy of ruling capitalists, with its retinue of mercenaries and specially privileged workers; on the other are the Fighting Groups, revolutionary cells whose members are drawn from all walks of life, united in common purpose, the eventual overthrow of their enemies. And in between, surging helplessly like the tide torn between moon and earth, are the People of the Abyss, the great mass of the common people, living in despair, brutalized by ceaseless exploitation, laboring like beasts of burden at the beck and call of their overseers. (p. 89)

What London offers the revolutionary is the conviction of inevitable triumph, despite immediate defeat. What he calls for from his audience are recruits for the struggle so that the victory he envisages may come all the sooner.

Avis Everhard answers that call. She moves from acceptance to rejection of what society is and determines to give her life to the cause of its refashioning. Though her husband is her tutor, and he is the spokesman who enunciates the theoretical basis of the novel, it is she who is at the center of the novel's account of the terrible events taking place at the time of the rise of the Iron Heel. As the action intensifies, the reader quickly loses sight of Everhard, who fades into the background and takes a position of distant eminence. The effect, again, is to diminish the centrality of the individual in history, no matter what leading role that person may play in any given period. . . .

[If] conventional novelistic criteria are applied to *The Iron Heel,* London's failure to Shakespearize, to return to Engels' term, can be seen as a fault. Avis, her husband, her father, the encircling cast of characters are not fully drawn in any interior sense. As psychological portraits they fall flat, and as a consequence the novel may be dismissed as a didactic exercise. (p. 90)

Yet, if the terms of criticism are altered, and *The Iron Heel* is taken for what it is, a fictional presentation utilized for programmatic purpose, London's achievement is of a high order. Notwithstanding the superficiality of characterization and the over-simplified analysis of economic process, the novel succeeds in projecting in Marxist political terms a gripping view of future possibilities, a view that has not turned out to be entirely inaccurate. (p. 91)

*Paul Stein, "Jack London's 'The Iron Heel': Art as Manifesto," in* Studies in American Fiction *(copy-*

*right © 1978 Northeastern University), Vol. 6, No. 1, Spring, 1978, pp. 77-92.*

**JOHN BRAZIL** (essay date 1979)

[*Brazil studies London's integration of art and politics.*]

London's ultimate goal was the realization of his intertwined personal and social ideals. To be sure, that took intellect: one had to understand how man and society worked. But to appeal to man's mind alone, London realized, to merely expose psychological and sociological truth for his consideration, was nugatory. The artist's ultimate goal was to induce his reader's emotional assent to the societal implications of the social vision in his fiction. London not only had to convince his readers that, for example, Darwin's theory of natural selection was valid. He further had to convince them of what that theory implied about how society *should* be structured. He had to compel, in other words, his readers' belief in the value system that conditioned his use of Darwin's ideas in his social criticism.

As a result, London could not be merely descriptive, merely pedagogic. . . .

Controlled drama and ideas in emotional context—both of which necessitate a literary expression subjected to formal aesthetic control—were the artist's goal. From early in his writing career, London implicitly argued for such a definition of literature. "I doubt if even you," he wrote a pedantically inclined friend, "would consider the novel avowedly with a purpose to be real literature. If you do, then let us abandon fiction altogether and give the newspaper its due, for fixing or changing public opinion especially on lesser things."

One concluding point will consolidate our understanding of the interanimation of London's aesthetic and political ideas. At the core of his social and political ideology was an environmentalism. The thought of the men London had submerged himself in—Spenser, Darwin, Freud, Marx—grew from perceptions of the importance environment plays in individual and social development; and, to name but one manifestation of their influence on him, central to London's socialist credo was the notion that the economic environment determines social forms and human behavior.

It is not surprising, therefore, that the theme most pervasive in London's fiction is the impact environment, particularly a radically altered environment, has on an individual's character. Permutations of this theme fill his work from *Son of the Wolf* to *Little Lady of the Big House.* Nor, for the reasons I have been describing, is it surprising that one of London's aesthetic dicta was to "develop your locality. Get your local color." Locality, the specific environment of a drama was, in his words, a "germane part of the story." (p. 5)

At bottom, London's view of the political nature of literature was also tied to a tenet central to most environmentalist thinking: that is, that the causal flow between man and environment is not one way. By conscious effort, man—the artist—can rise above environmental determination and become a self-determining cause. He can purposefully change the environment so that it will conduce to his chosen ends. Through the newly expanding mass literary markets of the late nineteenth and early twentieth centuries, London hoped his fiction would become a new element in the experiential environment of his society, altering its substance and form. Once altered, that new envi-

ronment, it was London's unspoken desire, would mean new experience, and new experience would induce new patterns of response and behavior: a consciousness structured on a new set of operative cultural values.

Although journalistic in many ways, London's fiction was not disinterested reportage. "Contrary to his own belief," as F. L. Pattee has observed, "he was not a realist at all. His tales were not written on the spot, but after they had mellowed for years in his imagination." For London realism did not mean eidetic reproduction. Situation, character, and setting were imaginative constructs, projections of self and society that tried, while adhering to the present and actual—to the "real"—to program the future and possible. They were London's dream vision, and their creation his ultimate aesthetic and political acts. For as Joseph Campbell has argued, if dream, in this sense, is personalized myth, myth is depersonalized dream, and one of the purposes of London's art was the creation of a new depersonalized dream—a new aesthetic and political mythology. . . .

Clearly, in the mind and experience of London the artist and London the reformer, art and ideology were fused and inseparable.

Once this thesis has been accepted, the obvious failures of London's life—the aesthetic, the political, and the personal— become more comprehensible. Take, for example, the central, singly most informative book London wrote in his later years, *Valley of the Moon.* . . . Its protagonists, Billy Roberts and Saxon Brown, are caught and slowly mangled by the pressure of urban existence. Ultimately, even their ability to produce children is affected. Industrial violence, a teamster's strike, results in Saxon's stillborn child. Nature was not at fault, the city was. (p. 6)

In *Valley of the Moon,* London expressed what he termed his "heart toward the land." Clearly this search for severed natural connections and the restoration that they implied was intimately related to his heart toward the past and the restoration that reestablishment of continuity with it implied. The land and the past were the same "real, one and only spot." One was historical and the other geographical, but each was a counterbalance to the urban present.

To anyone who requires thematic consistency or formal integrity, however, *Valley of the Moon* is profoundly dissatisfactory. Billy and Saxon's final happiness is not the result of intimate concord with nature, successful small scale farming, nor the recapturing of the pioneer past. Saxon runs a "scientific" (read "commerical" and "intensive") farm from her accounting office. She employs dirt cheap convict labor to do the actual farming. Billy has virtually nothing to do with the farm. He supervises his own teamsters' business. Indeed, the Roberts' ultimate spiritual and financial salvation is neither their farm, escape from the city, newly reclaimed pioneer virtue, nor Billy's business. It is the discovery of a clay deposit that can be mined and sold to a "brick yard at twenty cents a yard—may be more." . . . (p. 7.)

London spends most of this novel (and a great deal of his own life) describing the pernicious effects of urban life and searching for a suitable alternative. The solution is not what he intended, what his characters say it will be, nor what he says it is. It is also in itself unsatisfactory. The clay pit will, as Billy and Saxon realize, bring people to the valley, the surrounding town will grow, new businesses will spring up (which, they are pleased to note, will provide markets for their farm produce) and soon the railroad will build an extension to service the community. Their economic-growth mentality will result in exactly the conditions they sought to escape, with the single exception of their being on top rather than on the bottom of the social ladder. For Billy and for London the only preventative, the only act aimed at inhibiting a recurrence of urban growth, is to build the mine and the hauling road on the other side of the hill. This solipsistic out-of-sight-out-of-mind tergiveration is patently inadequate. Billy and Saxon are starting the cycle again, reinvigrating the burgeoning modern ''man-world that was wrong, and mad, and horrible.''

These confusions in *Valley of the Moon* are dynamically interelated to similar inconsistencies in London's political thought. (p. 8)

Concurrently with his ideational and psychological attachment to Darwinism, London held to the version of historical causality in which progress resulted not from the actions of the superior individual but through the ineluctable Marxian dialectic and the confrontation of groups, specifically, the proletarian masses with the capitalist elite. The end product of this clash of impersonal forces was to be a collectivist state in which cooperation would replace individualism. Since there would be no contest for nature's or society's rewards, there would be no inequitable distribution of wealth or status. The superior individual, London himself, would be superfluous, would, in fact, be atavistic. Pursuit of self would be supplanted by subjugation to society.

The pride in personal achievement and the ''scientific'' theories of Spencer that reinforced London's individualism were at odds with his ''scientific'' socialism and his undeniable sympathy for those who could not escape poverty, the Billies and Saxons of the first half of *Valley of the Moon*. Analogous confusions percolated through his fiction, muddying his thematic point, causing him to lose aesthetic control. (pp. 8-9)

> John Brazil, ''Politics and Art: The Integrated Sensibility of Jack London,'' in Jack London Newsletter, Vol. 12, Nos. 1-3, 1979, pp. 1-11.

## RICHARD W. ETULAIN  (essay date 1979)

[*Etulain provides an appraisal of London's works on hoboing.*]

Most of the nine sections of [London's] *The Road* deal with enough specific incidents that they could have been arranged chronologically to give the full impact of his travels. But when the book was published, London was satisfied to have the episodes placed in the unplanned order that he wrote them rather than to have them organized in such a manner as to give the full impact of his experiences. Two essays, **''Road-Kids and Gay Cats''** and **''Confession,''** deal primarily with his earliest tramp travels in 1892. Two others, **''Hoboes That Pass in the Night,''** and **''Two Thousand Stiffs,''** center on his escapades with Kelly's Army. **'''Pinched'''** and **''The Pen''** treat his days in the Erie County jail. His travels from Buffalo to Washington, D.C. and northward to New York City are delineated in **''Pictures''** and **''Bulls'';** and **''Holding Her Down''** is a lively account of his outwitting train crews while on his way westward across Canada.

It is not surprising that the individual sections of *The Road* are primarily narrative and anecdotal in form. London, who seemed unable to cast his hobo materials in an extended narrative, chose to lard the individual essays with episodes and yarns to illustrate a few generalizations. This approach gives *The Road*

a folksy appeal but also contributes to its lack of unity. For example, the first section of the book, ''Confession,'' opens with a story about London's lying to a woman in Reno in 1892. Then he tells of his experiences in Reno, returns to the woman, relates his failures to land a handout, describes a man who stubbornly refuses to give him food, reverts to the Reno woman, goes on to points about his story-telling abilities, and finally back to the woman in Reno. All of the nine segments are organized in similar fashion: London begins with an idea, gets sidetracked on different stories or experiences, and then returns to where he began. (pp. 17-18)

But these criticsms can be carried too far. Although *The Road* lacks unity and contains surprisingly little social commentary, it is an entertaining book. London knows how to tell a story, and *The Road* illustrates his abilities as a raconteur. He catches the joy, the adventure, and the youth of his tramp days. (p. 19)

[London] was unable to produce a full-bodied tramp character. None of his works includes a convincingly-portrayed hobo. And the notes that he left behind for other tramp projects indicate his future tramp stories might have suffered from the same weakness. London's hoboes philosophize, speak in dialect, and spin yarns; but they are not actors. They do not live the characteristics ascribed to them, and their actions do not personify the ideas that London claimed to have garnered on his road trips. If London's contemporaries were reluctant to accept the tramp as a hero, he never proved that he could create a persuasive hobo figure. His failure to turn out powerful tramp fiction, then, seems as much the result of his artistic shortcomings as the result of his bucking a culture hostile to tramp fiction. (p. 22)

When London turned out his most extensive work on tramps—*The Road*—he did not choose to include lengthy commentary on social issues. Except for a brief section on prison life, London stressed primarily the colorful and entertaining details of tramp life rather than material dealing with social and economic problems. (p. 24)

Despite the artistic shortcomings of much of London's work about tramps, these writings are important for other reasons. First of all, even though London's tramp experiences brought about less sensational and less abrupt changes in his life and thinking than he indicated, they did bring recognizable modifications. As Earle Labor has pointed out, London's hobo days ''sharpened his storytelling ability,'' they ''tempered his naively individualist attitude and started his questioning of the American socio-economic system,'' and finally they helped him to realize that he must ''use his brain rather than his brawn to make his way in the world.'' Generally, his eyes were opened to sights and experiences that had previously escaped him, and he realized that some of the purposes of his life would have to be rethought and probably redirected.

London's works about tramps also demonstrate his life-long tendency to dramatize his personal experiences in his fiction and essays. His adventures in the Northland with miners and natives were worked into such novels as *A Daughter of the Snows, The Call of the Wild, Burning Daylight*, and numerous short stories. He drew upon his voyages aboard the *Sophia Sutherland* and the *Snark* for *The Sea-Wolf* and the *South Sea Tales*. . . . (p. 25)

In addition, London was the first major American writer to deal with hoboes. Later, John Dos Passos, John Steinbeck, and Jack Kerouac, among others, wrote about migrant workers and tramps. (pp. 25-6)

The largest contribution of London's tramp writings is their revelation of some of the cultural and intellectual changes that were sweeping through America in the years surrounding 1900. As many Americans became conscious of the closing frontier of the 1890s, they sought means of escaping the circumstances slowly encircling them. . . . [For some], the road beckoned— the leaving of jobs, the fleeing from family responsibilities and pressures, and the taking to the adventure of the road. Not all who became tramps did so as a means of escape. As London makes clear, many men were forced into hobo life because they lost their jobs or were not physically able to hold positions available to them. When London dealt with tramps, he was writing about a portion of a society experiencing a closing frontier and searching for a new one. And he was the first American author to treat the hobo as a by-product of a culture gradually moving from frontier status to an urban industrial society. (p. 26)

> Richard W. Etulain, in his introduction to Jack London on the Road: The Tramp Diary and Other Hobo Writings, *edited by Richard W. Etulain (copyright © 1979 by Milo Shepard; reprinted by permission of the Trust of Irving Shepard, I. Milo Shepard, Trustee and the publisher), Utah State University Press, 1979, pp. 1-28.*

**DAVID A. MORELAND**   (essay date 1982)

[*Moreland traces London's common themes as they appear throughout* The Cruise of the "Snark."]

Jack London's South Pacific is a typhoon-ravaged paradise. The chaos, contradictions, and conflicts that tormented its creator often churn its waters, devastate its islands, and decimate its inhabitants. If one is to navigate these seas, a helmsman with local knowledge is required, consequently, *The Cruise of the Snark* . . . , London's autobiographical travel narrative of his voyage through Polynesia and Melanesia (1907-1909), is a valuable preface to his South Sea canon. It is important both as a source of factual information regarding this exotic last frontier and, more significantly, as an introduction to those themes and motifs of the author's South Sea fiction which demonstrate his distinctive blending of romantic, realistic, and naturalistic elements.

Although modern critics consider him a mainstream naturalist, Jack London termed himself a realist. He viewed man as circumscribed by powerful hereditary and environmental forces, and he was emphatic in his rejection of a dualistic universe. . . . And since it is a truism of London scholarship that the author strove to dramatize his "ideas" through his fiction, one might assume that London's South Sea stories and novels dramatize a necessitarian ideology, probably through documentary slice-of-life technique. One also expects to find the tenets of the realistic mode adhered to with some fidelity, especially verisimilitude of detail an emphasis on "the norm of experience," i.e., "the representative rather than the exceptional in plot, setting, and character," and an effort by the writer to "achieve objectivity, rather than a subjective or idealistic view of human nature and experience." However, this is seldom the case in any of Jack London's fictive realms, and never so in the South Sea narratives. For in his utilization of the exotic and the unusual in setting, plot, and action and in his creation of powerful, idealized protagonists whose struggles in a hostile universe are sympathetically treated, London blended traditionally romantic elements with aspects of realism (his

verisimilitude of detail) and naturalism (his deterministic bias). (pp. 57-8)

Andrew Sinclair has suggested that London's entire career was an acting out of this role of rugged individualist with the *Snark* cruise, taken in the face of such overwhelming odds, merely the "hazarding [of] his own life and the lives of his crew to satisfy an image of himself as master of his own ketch and dream. . . ." *The Cruise of the Snark* illustrates that "for London the living and writing became almost one. . . ." In this work he did not have to create an alter ego; the adventure was his and he recorded it as he lived it. Consequently, the themes and motifs found in this narrative are particularly significant for they arose from his quintessential self and became the foundation for his subsequent stories and novels of the South Seas. Those to be noted and analyzed in detail are the most pervasive—the ironic motif of anticipation and disillusionment, the theme of the testing of the individual against the various manifestations of a hostile universe, and an emphasis upon race and racial characteristics. (p. 60)

It is remarkable that a work . . . conceived in segments with apparently less conscious concern for overall organization than a picaresque novel, and written at sea or upon tropical islands as the author strove to keep boat and crew together and afloat should be as unified and artistically successful as it is. The explanations for this achievement are several. The most obvious is London's ability to bring the reader into the adventure of the Pacific traverse, whose romantic quest motif is, in itself, a unifying element. The self-image which the writer conveys is one with which the reader willingly identifies—that of the intelligent adventurer, the man of action and self-knowledge, willing to test himself against the elements while acknowledging, with ironic detachment, his own weakness and fallibility. From the opening description of the struggles and frustration of building the *Snark* to the final chapter's record of the author's battles against debilitating tropical maladies, London's popular appeal in its purest form is evident. Such experiences as the learning of navigation as the *Snark* gropes toward the Hawaiian Islands; the mastering of "the royal sport," surfing at Waikiki; a visit to the dreaded leper colony on Molokai; a horseback climb up magnificent Haleakala, "the House of the Sun," and back down along the dangerous Nahiku Ditch Trail; the "impossible" traverse from Hawaii to the Marquesas; and a recruiting voyage for plantation labor along the coast of Malaita, the most savage of the Solomons, possess a common denominator—the author's obsession with measuring his ability to meet the forces of nature and man arrayed against him. Like the speaker in Stephen Crane's poem, Jack London strove to force the universe to recognize him. "Sir, I exist!" is the statement embodied in his every action. (p. 61)

"Chapter IV: Finding One's Way About" . . . introduces this thematic test motif which runs throughout the narrative. A comic tone pervades this chapter as the author possesses sufficient self-confidence and sense of achievement to laugh at himself and the "mystery" of navigation by sun and stars. (p. 62)

The four following chapters deal with the Londons' Hawaiian experiences. The first that requires consideration is "Chapter VI: A Royal Sport." . . . It is significant in two respects. First, it presents the reader with another dramatic example of the motif of fragile man versus his environment. London finds in the sport of surfing the same allure as the mastering of navigation offered—the chance to test himself. And, secondly, this chapter contains an excellent example of the author's ability to blend subjective romantic description (that of the surfer riding the waves) with coolly objective, scientific discussion of natural phenomena (the physics of a wave). The author's handling of these two paradoxical aspects of his vision of reality conveys the essence of his romantic naturalism. (p. 63)

London goes on to relate in detail his surfing tutelage. And as the chapter draws to a conclusion, one is led to expect a dramatic description of the author's mastery of the sport, perhaps the conquest of Waikiki's biggest wave; however, as will be the case in incident after incident in the *Snark* narrative, London undercuts the reader's expectations. The "insidious, deceitful" Hawaiian sun blisters his fair skin, and instead of rising from the sea like a white god, he is forced to a painful exile in his bungalow. Probably there was a smile on London's face as he wrote the chapter's last sentence: "Upon one thing I am resolved: the *Snark* shall not sail from Honolulu until I, too, wing my heels with the swiftness of the sea, and become a sun-burned, skin-peeling Mercury." In a light vein the writer has reminded his readers of his recognition of his vincibility and has introduced the physical weakness which will ultimately force him to end the cruise—his inability to handle the effects of the tropical sun.

"Chapter VII: The Lepers of Molokai" . . . was of such importance that alone it justified the *Snark* cruise. For the first time an American writer with a large audience spoke out to debunk the lurid myths of horror and degradation that enshrouded leprosy and its treatment on the Hawaiian island of Molokai. (p. 64)

"The chief horror of leprosy," he wrote, "obtains in the minds of those who do not know anything about the disease." While London did not gloss over the gravity of the disease or its terrible aspects, he made his point effectively. . . .

The chapter concludes with the author's projection of the future elimination of the disease: "Once an efficacious serum is discovered . . . leprosy, because it is so feebly contagious, will pass away swiftly from the earth. The battle with it will be short and sharp." The language of conflict and the basic idea that through action based on knowledge victory would be obtained are emblematic of London's whole approach to life. In this case leprosy is merely another manifestation of that harsh and indifferent universe with which man struggles.

The last of the Hawaiian episodes is "Chapter VIII: The House of the Sun." . . . This chapter relates London's horseback excursion to the crater atop Haleakala, the Hawaiian Islands' most majestic volcanic peak, whose name translates as "House of the Sun." Because it was off the beaten track and spectacular in its grandeur, Haleakala appealed to London's temperament. His description of the crater's floor possesses that atavic ambience which he reveled in and fully expressed in such works as *Before Adam*. (p. 65)

As London naturally turned to the metaphor of battle to describe the waves of Waikiki and to forecast the destruction of leprosy so, once again, he resorted to the language of violence to describe the collision of Ukiukiu and Naulu, the tradewinds whose accompanying clouds clash as armies on the slopes of the House of the Sun. In a most effective Homeric simile, which extends for two and a half pages, this "mighty battle of the clouds" is dramatized. . . . For most viewers this scene would be regarded as majestic but certainly benign. For Jack London nature is "red in fang and claw."

Subsequent to the battle simile, London retells an Hawaiian myth of the demigod Maui, a story of great symbolic signif-

icance for him. With his feet firmly planted on Haleakala, Maui roped the sun's beams and forced the sun to show down in its journey through the sky; thereby Maui extended the day and allowed mankind (herein represented by Maui's mother) more time to complete the day's labors. This symbolic portrayal of the individual's triumph over nature, London's "sternly exacting environment," is another example of this motif and is clearly related to the countless other incidents of individual achievement which the author records in the course of the narrative.

On October 7, 1907, the *Snark* sailed from Hilo, Hawaii; its destination was Nuka-hiva, in the Marquesas, which was reached on December 6, 1907. This segment of the *Snark* adventure most pleased the author, and he recorded it in glowing detail in "Chapter IX: A Pacific Traverse." . . . (p. 66)

Through the twenty pages of this chapter, Jack London's pride of accomplishment permeates every line. The possibly catastrophic loss of half their fresh water is described as "our most exciting event" and the "sordid and bloody slaughter" of flying fish by bonitas, dolphins, and crewmen alike dramatizes the writer's conception of man's natural position is a world governed by Darwin's law of life. . . .

Earlier in this essay it was mentioned that along with the theme of the testing of the individual the ironic motif of anticipation and consequent disillusionment runs as an undercurrent through ***The Cruise of the Snark***. This pattern first surfaces in the narrative's second chapter, "The Inconceivable and Monstrous," . . . as London describes the time and money invested to insure that the *Snark* would be the best of its kind. . . . [He] discovers that the *Snark* will not heave to in heavy weather. Despite a thirty-five-thousand-dollar investment, "[t]hat beautiful bow of hers refused to come up and face the wind." (p. 67)

However, this motif is most successfully employed in "Chapter X: Typee." . . . London opens this most interesting episode of the narrative by relating that as a boy he had spent many hours dreaming over Herman Melville's *Typee*. "Nor was it all dreaming. I resolved there and then . . . come what would, that when I had gained strength and years, I, too, would voyage to Typee." So that when the traverse was accomplished and London stepped ashore at Taiohae Bay, some part of himself still expected to enter a world of Kory-Korys and Fayaways. But instead of Melville's paradise, he found the dying remnants of a once proud culture. . . .

What survived were "half-breeds and strange conglomerations of different races," or rather "a wreckage of races at best."

While this discovery was a shock to London the romantic adventurer, London the scientist-sociologist found in it support for his racial theories, particularly the superiority of the white man—a thesis that finds expression in many of the South Sea tales. (p. 68)

This chapter contains many of London's experiences among the Typeans and concludes with one of those remarkably lyrical passages that demonstrate the quality of his better prose and remind the reader of his Keatsian sensitivity to the intermingling of beauty and mortality, pain and promise, the paradoxes of existence. . . . "Typee" demonstrates London's recognition of the vast chasm separating the ideal and the real and extends the motif of anticipation and disillusionment.

"Chapter XI: The Nature Man," . . . is at first glance an artistically unjustifiable insertion into the work. (pp. 68-9)

[The] author devotes the body of this essay to a character study of Ernest Darling, an eccentric American socialist-hippie, who had made Tahiti his home. (p. 69)

Jack London interrupted the narrative of his own adventures to relate the story of Ernest Darling because he, like the Kanaka surfer and the demigod Maui, came to stand in the writer's mind as a personification of triumphant individualism—"The golden sun-god in the scarlet loin-cloth, standing upright in his tiny outrigger canoe." Darling was tested and not found wanting. This is merely a variation on that theme which runs through *The Cruise of the Snark*. While ironically qualifying any assertion with the parallel motif of failure and disillusionment, London continues to express the conviction that despite the harsh realities of existence, marginal salvage is possible— the strong man is capable of winning victories.

As the *Snark* sailed westward from Tahiti, a lull set in which is reflected in the subsequent three chapters: "The High Seat of Abundance," "Stone-Fishing of Bora Bora," and "The Amateur Navigator." Because of a paucity of material, it was essential that London fall back on all the reserves of the professional writer. "To sustain creating from almost nothing implies a powerful talent," which is amply demonstrated in these essays.

"Chapter XII: The High Seat of Abundance" . . . relates London's impressions of Raiatea, in the Society Group of French Polynesia, and the neighboring island of Tahaa. In particular he emphasizes the *natural* kindness and hospitality he finds among the uncorrupted natives of Polynesia. . . . Set in contrast to him will be the other natural man of the South Pacific, the black man of Melanesia, whom London usually presented as a cross between demon and beast. (pp. 69-70)

Thematically "Chapter XV: Cruising the Solomons" . . . is the climax of *The Cruise of the Snark*. In this chapter Jack London picks up the topic of racial characteristics and combines it with the theme of the testing of the individual and the motif of anticipation and disillusionment. For all practical purposes the *Snark* adventure ended in the "terrible Solomons"; consequently, the author uses this chapter to bring together those elements which give thematic unity to the narrative.

"If I were king," writes London, "the worst punishment I could inflict on my enemies would be to banish them to the Solomons. (On second thought, king or no king, I don't think I'd have the heart to do it.)" The Solomons' oppressive climate, its indigenous diseases, and its native population were equally horrifying to him. But it is the Melanesians themselves that draw most of his attention. Their animal-like physical ugliness and total inability to grasp, let alone live by, the white man's code of civilized conduct amazed him. Only in his wildest speculations regarding primitive man in *Before Adam* had London conceived of such men. Now he walked among them. One cannot fail to note the bitter, heavy-handed irony which pounds through this chapter. (pp. 70-1)

Tropical diseases were now taking their toll, and the Solomons were beginning to teach London "how frail and unstable is human tissue." He concludes "Cruising the Solomons" with a full-page verbatim catalogue of the various illnesses ravaging the crew of Captain Keller's *Eugenie* "to point out that we of the *Snark* are not a crowd of weaklings." Then he devotes an entire chapter "The Amateur M.D." . . . to citing the maladies that turned the *Snark* into a hospital ship. His purpose is clear: He felt compelled to justify to his audience (and to himself) his decision to terminate the voyage. . . . His remarkably re-

silient constitution and physical prowess, in which he had taken much pride, had . . . begun to fail him. This was the ultimate disappointment and disillusionment. Until this time, London had theoretically recognized his weakness and mortality; now the reality was upon him. Ironically, the voyage intended to demonstrate the author's triumph over "ferocious environment" had become his *memento mori*. . . .

Like kaleidoscopic fragments of colored glass, London's chaotic, eclectic beliefs take on a semblance of order when viewed from the perspective of his romantic egotism. *The Cruise of the Snark* records his most spectacular, if unsuccessful, attempt to master "the face of life" and is a valuable introduction to this paradoxical man's South Sea fiction. (p. 72)

> *David A. Moreland, "The Author As Hero: Jack London's 'The Cruise of the "Snark"',"* in Jack London Newsletter, *Vol. XV, No. 1, January-April, 1982, pp. 57-75.*

---

## ADDITIONAL BIBLIOGRAPHY

Ahearn, Marlie L. "'The People of the Abyss': Jack London As New Journalist." *Modern Fiction Studies* 22, No. 1 (Spring 1976): 73-83.
  Proposes that London's style in *The People of the Abyss* has affinities to that of the New Journalism. The critic bases this conclusion upon the immediacy of the scenes London draws, and his personal involvement in the situations described.

Baskett, Sam S. "*Martin Eden:* Jack London's Poem of the Mind." *Modern Fiction Studies* 22, No. 1 (Spring 1976): 23-36.
  A study of Martin as a portrait of the artist.

Foner, Philip S. "Jack London: American Rebel." In *Jack London, American Rebel: A Collection of His Social Writings, Together with an Extensive Study of the Man and His Times,* by Jack London, edited by Philip S. Foner, pp. 3-132. New York: The Citadel Press, 1947.
  A thoughtful, introductory survey of London's thought and work.

Geismar, Maxwell. Introduction to *Short Stories,* by Jack London, pp. ix-xx. New York: Hill and Wang, 1960.
  Discussion of the major critical issues pertaining to London's fiction, especially those in *Martin Eden, The Call of the Wild,* and *The Iron Heel.*

Giles, James R. "Jack London 'Down and Out' in England: The Relevance of the Sociological Study *People of the Abyss* to London's Fiction." *Jack London Newsletter* 2, No. 3 (September-December 1969): 79-83.
  Discusses the concept of atavism in London's work, most specifically in *The People of the Abyss.*

Lacassin, Francis. "Upton Sinclair and Jack London: A Great Friendship . . . by Correspondence." *Jack London Newsletter* 9, No. 1 (January-April 1976): 1-7.
  Traces the conflicts that developed between Sinclair and London, focusing primarily upon their views of socialism and their attitudes toward alcoholism.

London, Charmian. *The Book of Jack London.* 2 Vols. New York: The Century Co., 1921.
  An intimate portrait of Jack London written by his second wife. His personal life is the focus of this biography, which includes extensive quotations from private conversations and numerous excerpts from London's correspondence.

London, Joan. *Jack London and His Times.* Seattle: University of Washington Press, 1939, 385 p.
  Describes the economic and political backdrop against which Jack London pursued his literary career. The author, London's daughter, concentrates upon the rise of industrialism, the concomitant

popularization of socialist and labor politics, and the influence of both upon London's work.

Mumford, Lewis. "The Shadow of the Muck-rake." In his *The Golden Day: A Study in American Experience and Culture*, pp. 233-72.*
  Attacks London's nihilistic vision and his depiction of the Nietzschean superman as a common, musclebound thug.

Noel, Joseph. *Footloose in Arcadia*. New York: Carrick and Evans, 1946, 330 p.*
  Details the personal, political, and literary fabric of the alliances among London, Ambrose Bierce, and George Sterling.

Orwell, George. Introduction to *Love of Life, and Other Stories*, by Jack London. London: Paul Elek, 1946.
  Explores London's ambivalent attitude toward socialism and power as these themes appear in his fiction. Orwell concludes, of London and his work, that "if he had been a politically reliable person he would probably have left behind nothing of interest."

Orwell, George. "Forces Educational Broadcast: Jack London." *Jack London Newsletter* 11, Nos. 2 and 3 (May-December 1978): 33-40.
  Radio script of a broadcast about London. Orwell uses lengthy quotations from the author's published works to illustrate personal and political issues that were pertinent to London's literary development.

Ownbey, Ray Wilson, ed. *Jack London: Essays in Criticism*. Santa Barbara, Salt Lake City: Peregrine Smith, 1978, 126 p.
  A collection of critical essays by Clarice Stasz, Sam S. Baskett, Earle Labor, and others.

Pankake, Jon. "Jack London's Wild Man: The Broken Myths of *Before Adam*." *Modern Fiction Studies* 22, No. 1 (Spring 1976): 37-49.
  Examines London's failure to consistently integrate Freud's, Darwin's, and his own concepts of primitive humanity in *Before Adam*.

Perry, John. *Jack London: An American Myth*. Chicago: Nelson-Hall, 1981, 351 p.
  Attempts to strip away the myths that surround London in order to present a clear narrative of his life and work.

Rexroth, Kenneth. "Jack London's Native Sons." In his *With Eye and Ear*, pp. 167-70. New York: Herder & Herder.
  Fierce denunciation of London's fiction.

Riber, Jørgen. "Archetypal Patterns in 'The Red One'." *Jack London Newsletter* 8, No. 3 (September-December 1975): 104-06.

Identifies the archetypes of the quest motif, the wise old man, and the Great Mother in this short story.

Rothberg, Abraham. "Land Dogs and Sea Wolves: A Jack London Dilemma." *The Massachusetts Review* XXI, No. 3 (Fall 1980): 569-93.
  A Freudian analysis of London's novel, *The Sea Wolf*, which suggests that the main characters, Larsen and Van Weyden, represent conflicting aspects of London's own personality.

Shivers, Alfred S. "Jack London's Mate-Women." *American Book Collector* XV, No. 2, (October 1964): 17-21.
  Proposes that London's female characters fall into two distinct categories, namely, primitives and white-skinned American. Shivers uses examples from London's fiction to illustrate the traits these women share with male characters.

Spangler, George M. "Suicide and Social Criticism: Durkheim, Dreiser, Wharton, and London." *American Quarterly* XXXI, No. 4 (Fall 1979): 496-516.*
  Discusses the use of suicide as a "social fact or literary image" in the writings of London, Theodore Dreiser, Edith Wharton, and Émile Durkheim. In the case of London, Spangler uses the novel *Martin Eden* to illustrate the author's concept of death as a logical conclusion to personal isolation and empty success.

Stone, Irving. *Sailor on Horseback: The Biography of Jack London*. Cambridge: Houghton Mifflin Co., 1938, 338 p.
  A sympathetic biography.

Van Doren, Carl. "Toward the Left: Naturalism." In his *The American Novel: 1789-1939*, pp. 256-71. Rev. ed. New York: Macmillan Publishing Co., 1940.*
  A discussion of London's career, similar in content to Mencken's appraisal [see excerpt above].

Walcutt, Charles Child. *Jack London*. American Writers Pamphlet, no. 57. Minneapolis: University of Minnesota Press, 1966, 48 p.
  An excellent biocritical essay, covering most of London's work.

Walker, Franklin. *Jack London and the Klondike*. San Marino, Calif.: The Huntington Library, 1966, 288 p.
  Relates London's Klondike adventures to their fictional counterparts in his Arctic tales.

Ward, Susan. "Toward a Simpler Style: Jack London's Stylistic Development." *Jack London Newsletter* 11, Nos. 2 and 3 (May-December 1978): 71-80.
  Examines London's work for evidence of the author's role as an innovator of a new, simpler, American prose style.

# George MacDonald

## 1824-1905

Scottish novelist, short story writer, poet, homilist, essayist, critic, and translator.

MacDonald was a key figure in shaping the fantastic and myth-opoeic literature of the nineteenth and twentieth centuries. Such novels and fantasy stories as *Phantastes, Lilith, The Princess and the Goblin, At the Back of the North Wind,* and *The Golden Key* are considered classics of fantasy literature. These works have influenced C. S. Lewis, Charles Williams, T. S. Eliot, J.R.R. Tolkien, and other seekers of divine truth, adventure, and escape from mortal limitations. During his long, prolific career, MacDonald also wrote in several other genres, achieving particular success with his novels of British country life. These, like his work in all genres but fantasy, are nearly forgotten today.

MacDonald was raised and educated in rural Aberdeenshire, and attended the University of Aberdeen. There, he discovered and delighted in the literature of E.T.A. Hoffmann, Novalis, and other German Romantics. MacDonald served two years in England as a Congregationalist minister, resigning his pulpit in 1853 because of protests against his universalism and pantheistic view of nature—he believed that the spirit of God is manifest in all beings and things, and preached that, after death, all souls will be united in fellowship with God. After his resignation, MacDonald resolved to spread his beliefs through writing. He spent several impoverished years dependent upon the patronage of Lady Byron—the poet's widow—before he enjoyed commercial success. This came in 1864 with MacDonald's first realistic novel, *David Elginbrod,* written in Scottish dialect and inspired by a homely Highland epitaph. Thereafter, MacDonald's books found a ready audience, although the author was still occasionally denounced in the press for his unorthodox Christianity. MacDonald was the friend of nearly all of Great Britain's noted nineteenth-century literary figures, among them Lewis Carroll, Lord Tennyson, and John Ruskin, whose troubled affair with young Rose La Touche is fictionalized in *Wilfrid Cumbermede.* Throughout his career, MacDonald was a beloved and much-sought public speaker, attracting enthusiastic crowds to his readings throughout Britain and the United States. Because of poor health—he suffered from asthma and bronchitis—MacDonald spent his last years in near silence, waiting for death.

"Death is the theme that most inspired George MacDonald," wrote Tolkien. C. S. Lewis defined this recurring theme as "good death," or release from mundane reality and physical or spiritual limitations into a dimension of beauty, fulfillment, and unending wonder. Death and evil are seen as tools used by God to chasten and discipline humanity into renewing the search for the divine. The theme of the spiritual quest runs through much of MacDonald's fiction, reflecting the author's deep admiration for John Bunyan's *Pilgrim's Progress.* MacDonald's treatment of the search takes its best-known form in his fantasy literature. Here, his protagonists are led through unexpected doorways into a supernatural realm of faerie inhabited by talking animals, mythical sylvan creatures, biblical characters, and spiritual beings. MacDonald's works share affinities with those of other nineteenth-century fantas-

ists, including Carroll, Hoffmann, and Novalis, who is acknowledged as MacDonald's strongest influence. One of Novalis's aphorisms is often cited as MacDonald's credo: "Our life is no dream, but it should and perhaps will become one."

During his career, MacDonald published several volumes of poetry, each marked by a Wordsworthian religious spirit. MacDonald worked in this genre throughout his professional life, often sprinkling verse into his prose works. *At the Back of the North Wind* contains his best-known lyric: the oft-anthologized "baby poem," which begins "Where did you come from, baby dear?" This poem, which echoes Wordsworth's "Immortality Ode," is emblematic of the pervasive theme of *At the Back of the North Wind*—that, in the everyday world, reality is seen "through a mirror, dimly," but that worldly problems find their justification in another dimension. In this and all of MacDonald's other fantasy works, commonplace objects and beings are at once recognizable as such, while also conveying intimations of timelessness and a corresponding existence in the supernatural realm. MacDonald's stories and fairy tales for children, including *The Princess and the Goblin,* 'The Golden Key,' and "The Light Princess," are informed by unobtrusive symbolism and delicate fancy. *Phantastes* and *Lilith* which stand, respectively, at the beginning and end of MacDonald's career, are deeper explorations of the quest theme, and emphasize the biblical paradox which states: "He who loves his life loses it, and he who hates his life in this world will keep it for eternal life.''

This theme is also presented, in varying degrees, in Mac-Donald's realistic character novels of Scotland and England, of which *Alec Forbes of Howglen* is usually deemed the best. The dialectical Scottish novels, including *David Elginbrod, Alec Forbes,* and *Robert Falconer,* exhibit a strong skill in characterization and portray the quiet dignity of honest rural labor. The moralistic English novels, such as *Annals of a Quiet Neighborhood* and *Wilfrid Cumbermede,* often draw upon elements of the author's personal experience. Today MacDonald's realistic novels are familiar to readers primarily through excerpts included in *George MacDonald: An Anthology,* a collection of aphorisms compiled by his most direct literary descendent, C. S. Lewis.

In his seminal essay prefacing that anthology, Lewis acknowledges the weaknesses of MacDonald's fiction. These include the Victorian tendency toward meandering wordiness, endowing his child characters with sickly-sweet baby talk, and the inability to draw villains as interesting and believable as his heroes. Other critics believe MacDonald's writing is spoiled by a bent towards moralizing, while his admirers see his sheer imagination and his ability to create and sustain a sense of awe as redeeming strengths. Regardless, MacDonald's role as an influence, rather than an artist in his own right, is emphasized by critics today. His themes of transdimensional travel and joyous spiritual rebirth are found throughout Lewis's *Chronicles of Narnia* and Ransom Trilogy, and evidence suggests that *Phantastes* and the story "Cross Purposes" may have inspired Carroll's *Alice in Wonderland.* "Surely George MacDonald is the grandfather of us all," wrote Madeleine L'Engle, "—all of us who struggle to come to terms with truth through imagination."

## PRINCIPAL WORKS

*Within and Without*  (poetry)  1855
*Poems*  (poetry)  1857
*Phantastes*  (novel)  1858
*David Elginbrod.* 3 vols.  (novel)  1863
*Adela Cathcart.* 3 vols.  (novel)  1864
*A Hidden Life and Other Poems*  (poetry)  1864
*The Portent: A Story of the Inner Vision of the Highlanders, Commonly Called the Second Sight*  (short story)  1864
*Alec Forbes of Howglen.* 3 vols.  (novel)  1865
*Annals of a Quiet Neighborhood.* 3 vols.  (novel)  1867
*Dealings with the Fairies*  (short stories)  1867
*Unspoken Sermons*  (sermons)  1867
*Robert Falconer.* 3 vols.  (novel)  1868
*The Seaboard Parish.* 3 vols.  (novel)  1868
*At the Back of the North Wind*  (short story)  1871
*The Princess and the Goblin*  (novel)  1872
*Wilfrid Cumbermede.* 3 vols.  (novel)  1872
*Malcolm.* 3 vols.  (novel)  1875
*The Wise Woman*  (novel)  1875; also published as *The Lost Princess,* 1895
*Thomas Wingfold, Curate.* 3 vols.  (novel)  1876
*Sir Gibbie*  (novel)  1879
*A Book of Strife in the Form of the Diary of an Old Soul*  (poetry)  1880
*The Gifts of the Christ Child and Other Tales*  (short stories)  1882
*The Imagination and Other Essays*  (essays)  1883

*The Princess and Curdie*  (novel)  1883
*Unspoken Sermons, second series*  (sermons)  1886
*Unspoken Sermons, third series*  (sermons)  1889
*A Dish of Orts*  (essays)  1893
*Lilith*  (novel)  1895
*Salted with Fire*  (novel)  1897
*George MacDonald: An Anthology*  (aphorisms)  1946
*The Golden Key*  (short story)  1967

---

## THE ATHENAEUM  (essay date 1855)

[*Within and Without*] has a purpose and a plan, and a profound meaning which, on the first perusal, we cannot pretend to fathom. . . .

There is frequently a sportiveness in [MacDonald's] thoughts and imagery which, like an iris above a cataract, over-arches, as it were, the soul-agony that rages in the deeps of his genius. Seldom have spiritual abysses been more thoroughly sounded,— seldom has despair had a more eloquent voice,—seldom has mystic sentiment been more beautifully interpreted. We find, too, in this poem what for the most part is wanted in such ideal compositions—a story. There is enough of fable to form the basis of a tolerably long romance, in which the feelings here treated in essences would be vastly expanded. There is, however, no attempt at an acting drama;—all is pure poetry, meant for the closet, for quiet and reflective perusal, in which the reader is his own actor. The aim indicated in the title, to contrast the inner and outer life, is subtly shadowed,—with not enough of outline and colour for the popular perception, but with sufficient suggestion to the select student whose imagination is willing—perhaps proud—to meet half way that of the poet. Many of the scenes consist of a single line or so, yet embody more than a chapter of ordinary narrative. There may be some affectation in this,—but the effect must be judged of by feeling, not by dry rules of criticism. . . .

There is deep tenderness in many passages of this poem;—and the incident of the deserted father being evermore accompanied with his orphan child is most delicately imagined and deliciously touched. Much, too, is set to sweet music;—the whole, nevertheless, is inexpressibly painful. It would seem as if, in the author's opinion, a happy life were inconsistent with the purpose of living. "Love," says the poor child, "hurts so": to which replies her father, "Yes, darling; love does hurt. It is too good never to hurt." Such is the moral of the poetic action,—thus, as with a diamond pencil, cut in on the crystal of the soul, wounding that it may indite a memorable legend. There is an intensity in the state of emotion thus indicated, which will operate as a charm on sensitive spirits. But at the same time, it must be maintained that there is in this new poem a want of comprehension. The poetical view taken is not sufficiently large. The highest poetical spirits are also the most cheerful. Nature and existence are not all clouds and rain, but attended with sunshine and honest pleasures.

*"Reviews: 'Within and Without: A Dramatic Poem',"*
*in* The Athenaeum, *No. 1445, July 7, 1855, p. 783.*

## LEWIS CARROLL  (essay date 1866)

I read *Alec Forbes* . . . and *The Hillyars and Burtons* [by Henry Kingsley]. The former is very enjoyable and the character of

Annie Anderson one of the most delightful I have ever met with in fiction. The Scotch dialect, too, is pleasant enough when one gets a little used to it. (p. 238)

> *Lewis Carroll, in an excerpt from his diary entry of January 16, 1866 (reprinted by permission of the Estate of C. L. Dodgson) in* The Diaries of Lewis Carroll, Vol. 1, *edited by Roger Lancelyn Green, Oxford University Press, New York, 1954, pp. 238-39.\**

## A[NDREW] LANG   (essay date 1877)

The world of novel readers owe a debt of gratitude to Mr. George Macdonald, for more than one touching picture of Scottish peasant life, for many refined examples of religious thought, and above all for one of the most moving ballads that ever caused a superstitious shudder. It is therefore with pain and diffidence, that one is obliged to admit the very unpleasant impression left after reading **Thomas Wingfold, Curate.** A work more likely to encourage unhealthy feeling, and the taste for the feverish rhetoric of religious sentiment, one has rarely seen. The author loses the sense of humour which in the beginning of the book he displays, and commits himself to passages which it is pitiable to read in cold blood. This impression, it must be said, is entirely an impression in taste, it is entirely the result of reaction against mistaken methods in art, and a want of dignity and fitness in expression. Mr. Macdonald has a perfect right to advocate any religious views—he has often done so before with measure and sobriety—as long as he writes in conformity with the natural moderation and refinement, which we expect even in a three volume novel, offered by a poet and a man of letters. (p. 93)

> *A[ndrew] Lang, "Three New Novels," in* The Fortnightly Review, *Vol. XXI, January 1, 1877, pp. 88-96.\**

## A. P. PEABODY   (essay date 1883)

> [*Peabody, who stresses MacDonald's spirituality and ability to illuminate the inner being, was a Unitarian clergyman and professor of Christian morals at Harvard University.*]

[MacDonald] is best known by his novels, and they furnish the most genuine test of the quality and strength of his intellectual fibre. As stories, they are by no means faultless. They often have ill-constructed plots, awkward *denouements,* unnatural incidents, and impossible characters; and the conversations, though never dull, are abnormally prolix, and when the person speaking can be supposed to have a provincial dialect, its vocabulary is aired to the reader's utter weariness. Yet with all these drawbacks MacDonald clenches the heart and soul of his reader with an iron grasp; the interest, strong at the outset, grows with every chapter; the personages brought upon the stage seem, if not our near kindred, at least our next-door neighbors, and we part from them as from old acquaintance,—from some of them as from very dear friends. Yet the power thus exerted, though the story is its vehicle, is independent of the story. It is in the man himself, and in the medium through which he beholds the world and its Creator,—things seen and things unseen. He is preeminently realistic; not in the material, but in the spiritual sense of the word. He looks directly and always into the soul of things, and that soul is to him the imminent God. (pp. 3-4)

We are afraid to associate the Divine image with paltry things, with every-day affairs, with trivial needs, vexations and enjoyments; to him the least things seem great, because he sees God in them. In like manner he brings us, as it were, into the interior presence of the human beings that he portrays; gives us the inmost physiology of emotion, purpose, will, self-congratulation, penitence, remorse; shows us his personages, not as they look or talk for the eye or ear of the outside world, but as in their moments of deepest introspection they know themselves to be. In religion, he deals not with dogmas or their verbal drapery, but with the actual relations of beings which, in his apprehension, are not typified, but literally described by the terms of the closest and tenderest human kindred as applied to God and man, and to man and man. It is in accordance with this tone of representation that duty, conscience, obligation, sin, in fine, all ethical concepts, are treated not as matters of formal law and statute, but as phases of the human soul turned to or averted from the present God.

The same characteristics mark his sermons and religious essays, which are a handling of realities, and not of their symbols. His words have a transparency which belongs to very few writers of any age. One looks through them, instead of seeing things by means of them. His literary criticisms have a similar directness and translucency. They manifest keen insight rather than appreciation. He does not look at his author as from a distance, but rather for the time assumes his personality, thinks and feels with him, and almost in him.

With these traits MacDonald might seem better furnished as an essayist than as a novel-writer, and I certainly should say so were I not more delighted with his novels. But as an essayist he would have won distinguished reputation, had he not eclipsed himself in this department by his eminent success in another. I have before me two volumes of his essays, one on **The Miracles of our Lord,** the other—**England's Antiphon**—on English religious poetry, either of which would have given a new writer a very high place in the esteem of the best minds. In the former of these especially, are all the elements of thought and feeling which give character to his novels,—the near approach to sacred verities, the vivid sense of their reality, and their familiar presentation with a loving tenderness that is more than reverence.

What has been said may in a good measure describe [**The Imagination and Other Essays**]. . . . Its subjects are various, and they show the several aspects of the author's genius; but in all of them the reader is brought into the closest relation with the author, and he, in a sense almost peculiar to him, literally, rather than metaphorically, "enters into" his subject. (pp. 4-6)

> *A. P. Peabody, in his introduction to* The Imagination and Other Essays *by George MacDonald (copyright, 1883, D. Lothrup and Company), Lothrup, 1883, pp. 3-6.*

## GEORGE MacDONALD   (essay date 1893)

> [*MacDonald's essay "The Fantastic Imagination" is considered the author's most important discussion of fantasy literature, providing insight into his own work in the genre.*]

Were I asked, what is a fairytale? I should reply, *Read* Undine: *that is a fairytale; then read this and that as well, and you will see what is a fairytale.* Were I further begged to describe the *fairytale,* or define what it is, I would make answer, that

I should as soon think of describing the abstract human face, or stating what must go to constitute a human being. (p. 313)

Many a man, however, who would not attempt to define *a man,* might venture to say something as to what a man ought to be: even so much I will not in this place venture with regard to the fairytale, for my long past work in that kind might but poorly instance or illustrate my now more matured judgment. I will but say some things helpful to the reading, in right-minded fashion, of such fairytales as I would wish to write, or care to read.

Some thinkers would feel sorely hampered if at liberty to use no forms but such as existed in nature, or to invent nothing save in accordance with the laws of the world of the senses; but it must not therefore be imagined that they desire escape from the region of law. Nothing lawless can show the least reason why it should exist, or could at best have more than an appearance of life. (pp. 313-14)

[Man] may, if he pleases, invent a little world of his own, with its own laws; for there is that in him which delights in calling up new forms—which is the nearest, perhaps, he can come to creation. When such forms are new embodiments of old truths, we call them products of the Imagination; when they are mere inventions, however lovely, I should call them the work of the Fancy: in either case, Law has been diligently at work.

His world once invented, the highest law that comes next into play is, that there shall be harmony between the laws by which the new world has begun to exist; and in the process of his creation, the inventor must hold by those laws. The moment he forgets one of them, he makes the story, by its own postulates, incredible. . . . Suppose the gracious creatures of some childlike region of Fairyland talking either cockney or Gascon! Would not the tale, however lovelily begun, sink at once to the level of the Burlesque—of all forms of literature the least worthy? (pp. 314-15)

"You write as if a fairytale were a thing of importance: must it have a meaning?"

It cannot help having some meaning; if it have proportion and harmony it has vitality, and vitality is truth. The beauty may be plainer in it than the truth, but without the truth the beauty could not be, and the fairytale would give no delight. Everyone, however, who feels the story, will read its meaning after his own nature and development: one man will read one meaning in it, another will read another. (p. 316)

A genuine work of art must mean many things; the truer its art, the more things it will mean. If my drawing, on the other hand, is so far from being a work of art that it needs THIS IS A HORSE written under it, what can it matter that neither you nor your child should know what it means? It is there not so much to convey a meaning as to wake a meaning. If it do not even wake an interest, throw it aside. A meaning may be there, but it is not for you. If, again, you do not know a horse when you see it, the name written under it will not serve you much. At all events, the business of the painter is not to teach zoology.

But indeed your children are not likely to trouble you about the meaning. They find what they are capable of finding, and more would be too much. For my part, I do not write for children, but for the childlike, whether of five, or fifty, or seventy-five.

A fairytale is not an allegory. There may be allegory in it, but it is not an allegory. He must be an artist indeed who can, in

any mode, produce a strict allegory that is not a weariness to the spirit. (p. 317)

The best thing you can do for your fellow, next to rousing his conscience, is—not to give him things to think about, but to wake things up that are in him; or say, to make him think things for himself. The best Nature does for us is to work in us such moods in which thoughts of high import arise. . . . Nature is mood-engendering, thought-provoking: such ought the sonata, such ought the fairytale to be.

"But a man may then imagine in your work what he pleases, what you never meant!"

Not what he pleases, but what he can. If he be not a true man, he will draw evil out of the best; we need not mind how he treats any work of art! If he be a true man, he will imagine true things; what matter whether I meant them or not? They are there none the less that I cannot claim putting them there! (pp. 319-20)

If a writer's aim be logical conviction, he must spare no logical pains, not merely to be understood, but to escape being misunderstood; where his object is to move by suggestion, to cause to imagine, then let him assail the soul of his reader as the wind assails an æolian harp. If there be music in my reader, I would gladly wake it. Let fairytale of mine go for a firefly that now flashes, now is dark, but may flash again. Caught in a hand which does not love its kind, it will turn to an insignificant, ugly thing, that can neither flash nor fly.

The best way with music, I imagine, is not to bring the forces of our intellect to bear upon it, but to be still and let it work on that part of us for whose sake it exists. We spoil countless precious things by intellectual greed. (pp. 321-22)

If any strain of my "broken music" make a child's eyes flash, or his mother's grow for a moment dim, my labour will not have been in vain. (p. 322)

> *George MacDonald, "The Fantastic Imagination,"*
> *in his* A Dish of Orts: Chiefly Papers on the Imag-
> *ination and on Shakespeare, Sampson Low and Mar-*
> *ston, 1893 (and reprinted by Norwood Editions, 1977),*
> *pp. 313-22.*

## G. K. CHESTERTON   (essay date 1924)

[*Chesterton highlights MacDonald's successful transformation of the seemingly mundane into the magical, a skill Chesterton adopted and polished in his own fiction. His remarks on MacDonald's liberal Christian beliefs are expanded upon by Eric Rabkin (see excerpt below).*]

I for one can really testify to a book that has made a difference to my whole existence, which helped me to see things in a certain way from the start; a vision of things which even so real a revolution as a change of religious allegiance has substantially only crowned and confirmed. Of all the stories I have read, including even all the novels of the same novelist, it remains the most real, the most realistic, in the exact sense of the phrase the most like life. It is called *The Princess and the Goblin.* (pp. 163-64)

When I say it is like life, what I mean is this. It describes a little princess living in a castle in the mountains which is perpetually undermined, so to speak, by subterranean demons who sometimes come up through the cellars. She climbs up the castle stairways to the nursery or the other rooms; but now and again the stairs do not lead to the usual landings, but to a new room she has never seen before, and cannot generally find again. Here a good great-grandmother, who is a sort of fairy godmother, is perpetually spinning and speaking words of understanding and encouragement. When I read it as a child, I felt that the whole thing was happening inside a real human house, not essentially unlike the house I was living in, which also had staircases and rooms and cellars. This is where the fairy-tale differed from many other fairy-tales; above all, this is where the philosophy differed from many other philosophies. I have always felt a certain insufficiency about the ideal of Progress, even of the best sort which is a Pilgrim's Progress. It hardly suggests how near both the best and the worst things are to us from the first; even perhaps especially at the first. And though like every other sane person I value and revere the ordinary fairy-tale of the miller's third son who set out to seek his fortune (a form which MacDonald himself followed in the sequel called *The Princess and Curdie*), the very suggestion of travelling to a far-off fairyland, which is the soul of it, prevents it from achieving this particular purpose of making all the ordinary staircases and doors and windows into magical things.

Dr. Greville MacDonald, in his intensely interesting memoir of his father which follows, has I think mentioned somewhere his sense of the strange symbolism of stairs. Another recurrent image in his romances was a great white horse; the father of the princess had one, and there was another in *The Back of the North Wind.* To this day I can never see a big white horse in the street without a sudden sense of indescribable things. But for the moment I am speaking of what may emphatically be called the presence of household gods—and household goblins. And the picture of life in this parable is not only truer than the image of a journey like that of the Pilgrim's Progress, it is ever truer than the mere image of a siege like that of The Holy War. There is something not only imaginative but intimately true about the idea of the goblins being below the house and capable of besieging it from the cellars. When the evil things besieging us do appear, they do not appear outside but inside. Anyhow, that simple image of a house that is our home, that is rightly loved as our home, but of which we hardly know the best or the worst, and must always wait for the one and watch against the other, has always remained in my mind as something singularly solid and unanswerable; and was more corroborated than corrected when I came to give a more definite name to the lady watching over us from the turret, and perhaps to take a more practical view of the goblins under the floor. Since I first read that story some five alternative philosophies of the universe have come to our colleges out of Germany, blowing through the world like the east wind. But for me that castle is still standing in the mountains and the light in its tower is not put out.

All George MacDonald's other stories, interesting and suggestive in their several ways, seem to be illustrations and even disguises of that one. I say disguises, for this is the very important difference between his sort of mystery and mere allegory. The commonplace allegory takes what it regards as the commonplaces or conventions necessary to ordinary men and women, and tries to make them pleasant or picturesque by dressing them up as princesses or goblins or good fairies. But George MacDonald did really believe that people were princesses and goblins and good fairies, and he dressed them up as ordinary men and women. The fairy-tale was the inside of the ordinary story and not the outside. One result of this is that all the inanimate objects that are the stage properties of the story retain that nameless glamour which they have in a literal

fairytale. The staircase in *Robert Falconer* is as much of a magic ladder as the staircase in the *Princess and the Goblin;* and when the boys are making the boat and the girl is reciting verses to them, in *Alec Forbes,* and some old gentleman says playfully that it will rise to song like a magic Scandinavian ship, it always seemed to me as if he were describing the reality, apart from the appearance, of the incident. The novels as novels are uneven, but as fairy-tales they are extraordinarily consistent. He never for a moment loses his own inner thread that runs through the patchwork, and it is the thread that the fairy great-grandmother put into the hands of Curdie to guide him out of the mazes of the goblins.

The originality of George MacDonald has also a historical significance, which perhaps can best be estimated by comparing him with his great countryman Carlyle. It is a measure of the very real power and even popularity of Puritanism in Scotland that Carlyle never lost the Puritan mood even when he lost the whole of the Puritan theology. If an escape from the bias of environment be the test of originality, Carlyle never completely escaped, and George MacDonald did. He evolved out of his own mystical meditations a complete alternative theology leading to a completely contrary mood. And in those mystical meditations he learned secrets far beyond the mere extension of Puritan indignation to ethics and politics. For in the real genius of Carlyle there was a touch of the bully, and wherever there is an element of bullying there is an element of platitude, of reiteration and repeated orders. Carlyle could never have said anything so subtle and simple as MacDonald's saying that God is easy to please and hard to satisfy. Carlyle was too obviously occupied with insisting that God was hard to satisfy; just as some optimists are doubtless too much occupied with insisting that He is easy to please. In other words, MacDonald had made for himself a sort of spiritual environment, a space and transparency of mystical light, which was quite exceptional in his national and denominational environment. He said things that were like the Cavalier mystics, like the Catholic saints, sometimes perhaps like the Platonists or the Swedenborgians, but not in the least like the Calvinists, even as Calvinism remained in a man like Carlyle. (pp. 164-68)

[MacDonald] wrote nothing empty; but he wrote much that is rather too full, and of which the appreciation depends rather on a sympathy with the substance than on the first sight of the form. As a matter of fact, the mystics have not often been men of letters in the finished and almost professional sense. A thoughtful man will now find more to think about in Vaughan or Crashaw than in Milton, but he will also find more to criticize; and nobody need deny that in the ordinary sense a casual reader may wish there was less of Blake and more of Keats. But even this allowance must not be exaggerated; and it is in exactly the same sense in which we pity a man who has missed the whole of Keats or Milton, that we can feel compassion for the critic who has not walked in the forest of Phantastes or made the acquaintance of Mr. Cupples in the adventures of Alec Forbes. (pp. 171-72)

> *G. K. Chesterton, in his introduction to* George MacDonald and His Wife *by Greville M. MacDonald, George Allen & Unwin, Ltd., 1924 (and reprinted as "George MacDonald," in his* G.K.C. As M.C.: Being a Collection of Thirty-Seven Introductions *by G. K. Chesterton, edited by J. P. de Fonseka, Metheun & Co. Ltd., 1929, pp. 163-72).*

**GREVILLE MacDONALD** (essay date 1924)

[*Greville MacDonald was George MacDonald's eldest son. Since each thought very highly of the other, the biography* George MacDonald and His Wife—*from which the following survey is drawn—is favorably biased, though by no means uncritical.*]

[It] will be apparent to some who see human love as offshoot of the Divine, that *Within and Without* just *had* to be written. For it brought direct from God to my father a message which he must give to my mother also—hardly less direct from God for that. For my mother's earlier trouble was simply this: seeing this man of her own heart so much absorbed in adoration of Him—and those letters of his which has denied us sight of must have constantly revealed this to her—she felt that his love for her fell short of what it might have been, had she been gifted as some other women were. . . . He was all Heaven and Earth to her; she, she feared, but a possible earthly-paradise to him. If the poem is actually pertinent to my parents' rarely troubled courtship, it suggests very plainly that my father had long since discovered this truth—that in bringing the firstfruits to his wife he was still rendering to God the things that were God's. (p. 224)

If some do not care for [the work's] poetical metaphysics, they will admit its lyrical beauty and power. In the latter its author had discovered his higher art. (p. 225)

If in *Within and Without* we have some reminders of his youth's passionate immaturity, of a spiritual gloom contrasting strangely with the songs and sonnets that flash out like stars for an enduring glory, perfect in form and clarity of utterance, [his next] volume was of the day-spring purely. (p. 278)

*Poems* manifests an increasing freedom in blank verse, particularly in *A Hidden Life.* Its poetical vision into the life of sweet common things makes it ring truer and simpler than *Within and Without,* even though it has none of the matchless songs of the dramatic poem. In *The Lost Soul* there is such obvious tragic power that, once read, it can never be forgot, even if some reviewers stigmatized it as belonging to the "spasmodic school." (p. 280)

*Phantastes: A Faerie Romance for Men and Women,* to give its full title, was a new adventure, and one into the highest realm of imaginative literature, that of symbolic presentation. (p. 296)

But *Phantastes* is more than symbolic, even though the *Athenœum* stigmatized it as no more than "a confusedly furnished, second-hand symbol-shop." Through its beauty it does something more than appeal to our feelings: it rouses them from sleepy contentment, sets us first wondering, then thinking, and at last awakens the resolve to set about some husbandry of life, or some defying of death. (pp. 296-97)

*Phantastes,* with its grace, its wit, its irony, makes us conscious of real magic in the air we breathe: it is a "candle of the Lord, searching all the inward parts." More, its symbolism appeals not only to the light within a man's own soul, but shows him his own shadow spreading over the world if ever he looks upon poesy as a mere anodyne to the chatter of facts that will not let him sleep. (p. 297)

We have but to compare the opening of Hoffmann's [*The Golden Pot*] with the manner in which, in *Phantastes,* Anodos steps from his own bed into the daisied grass to see how both Celtic and German poet would have us understand that quite easily and unexpectedly we also may step—not *if we will,* but rather *if we are led*—out of the common tangible world into that truer land of faerie and imagery; and that having once set foot in it, we can never quite leave it, even though shadows of the tangible overwhelm the gentler beings of impalpable beauty. (p. 298)

*Phantastes,* in a word, is a spiritual pilgrimate out of this world of impoverishing possessions into the fairy Kingdom of Heaven. . . . (p. 299)

[It] is curious that no book was produced between [*Phantastes* and *David Elginbrod*]. . . . The one-volumed story, *The Portent,* appeared serially, . . . but it did not appear in book form till 1864. The story is different from almost any other of his books, but it at once convinced friends and publishers of his art in simple narrative. It deals with the Highland belief in second-sight—of which gift my father would reluctantly admit he had himself no trace. It is weird, yet strangely convincing, and has no touch of the didactic. My mother once told an admirer, that when she asked my father for the story's meaning, he said, "You may make of it what you like. If you see anything in it, take it and I am glad you have it; but I wrote it for the tale." (p. 318)

We now find my father in touch with literary society, although he made intimates with but a few. . . . One evening at an informal supper of oysters, beefsteak pudding and bottled stout, . . . my father and others were consorting, when George MacDonald's attention was arrested by hearing Manby Smith, the gifted journalist, then writing regularly for the *Leisure Hour, Chambers' Journal,* etc., reciting a certain Scotch epitaph he had read somewhere. . . .

> Here lie I, Martin Elginbrodde;
> Hae mercy o' my soul, Lord God;
> As I wad do, were I Lord God,
> An' ye war Martin Elginbrodde!

My father caught and held it—the thing that grew in stature and favour till its story was written. (pp. 320-21)

[The] just and sensitive portraiture [of *David Elginbrod*], rather than its story—which yet is vigorous and profluent—its pictures of simple life in Highland cottage, of dull respectability in English Squire's home or suburban tradesman's, its imaginative treatment of unfathomed possibilities in telepathy and suggestion, its advocacy of individualism in education, all contributed to the building of a novel unlike anything ever attempted before. But its chief claim upon those who study its author's own life will be the portraiture of his own father in David Elginbrod. It introduces us, moreover, to Robert Falconer, perhaps more definitely a creation than a facsimile or amplification of any one friend's temperament. In this book, too, there is an arresting sketch of Frederick Denison Maurice. (pp. 322-23)

[It must] have been quite in the early sixties that my father discovered his gift for lighter, imaginative narrative. For now and again, in place of a lecture he would read or recite a fairytale—particularly *The Light Princess.* All the fairy stories comprised in the little volume, *Dealings with the Fairies* . . . , had been written before the end of 1863, and appeared first in the novel, *Adela Cathcart* . . . , as setting for them. *The Light Princess,* written on a long scroll, perhaps with some idea of making its form accord with vocal delivery, should be defined rather as a *jeu d'esprit.* It hardly compares with the other fairy stories which were expressly written for little people. . . . (pp. 324-25)

The year 1865 was one of considerable events. It saw the publication of *Alec Forbes of Howglen,* a novel that fully justified George Smith's opinion as to his gifts in fiction: it is perhaps the most successful, *quâ* fiction, of all his efforts. It had so fine a reception that it encouraged the development of a book even nearer his genius. *Robert Falconer,* though between these two came *Annals of a Quiet Neighbourhood,* running through a year of the *Sunday Magazine.* The latter story is based . . . upon his life at Arundel; his success with *Alec Forbes* having led him to write more definitely for the English reader. But not even in *Thomas Wingfold* or *Paul Faber*—which latter my father once told me he thought the best of all his novels, though emphatically it is not so—did he reach the level of his finest Scotch writing, even granting the possible inferiority of some later ones dealing with the North. (p. 353)

*Good Words for the Young* made its first appearance in 1869. . . . [The magazine] was too good to succeed, in spite of contributors such as Charles Kingsley, William Gilbert, W.R.S. Ralston, and George MacDonald. It reawakened, however, my father's surest gift of faerie-allegory, and produced *At the Back of the North Wind,* with like-inspired illustrations by Arthur Hughes. Of all my father's works, this remains the "best seller." Its secret here again lies in its two-world consciousness. A child no more grasps intellectually its exalted symbolism than he reflects upon Form's relation to its indwelling Idea when he runs to his mother with a primrose because of its beauty. Yet in both cases a lasting impression of the story's and the flower's place in the Divine Economy remains, consciously or not. One need not ask what the rose means if its sweetness pierces the veil and gives taste of the joy that "will never pass into nothingness." (p. 361)

*The Seaboard Parish* is not one of the strong novels, neither story nor characters being very convincing. The incident of the drowned man was actually witnessed by us, and the incredible incident of a storm when two men leapt from the life-boat at the top of a wave to the main shrouds of a small schooner riding at anchor in the harbour, was told to my father by a coastguardsman with whom we hatched an invigorating intimacy. The description of the storm itself is worthy of Clark-Russell or Dickens in its detail and grandeur; but I do think my father's ingrain capacity for discovering the "spot of red" in every man he came in contact with tended to make him believe many a story that to others would be incredible. (p. 370)

Perhaps the ten years from 1870 to 1880 were fuller of enterprise and hard work, of contest with sickness and sorrow, than any in George MacDonald's life. The industry of his pen was unremitting. In 1871 appeared an important contribution to the publishing world, namely his *Works of Fancy and Imagination,* in ten small 8vo. volumes. They contained most of his poetry and all the fairytales and short stories that had so far appeared, including *Phantastes* and *The Portent.* They were rapidly followed by [*At the Back of the North Wind, Ranald Bannerman's Boyhood, The Princess and the Goblin, Wilfrid Cumbermede, The Vicar's Daughter, Gutta Percha Willie, Malcolm, The Wise Woman, Thomas Wingfold, St. George and St. Michael, Exotics, The Marquis of Lossie, Sir Gibbie,* and *Paul Faber*]. . . . (p. 409)

*Malcolm* [is] a story whose matchless characterization of the piper, Miss Horn, Barabara Catanach, Phemy Mair, and the fisher-lad heir to the marquisate, sets it among his best Scotch novels. (p. 466)

[*Sir Gibbie*] marked a renewal of my father's powers. In some ways it is the most picturesque of his Scottish stories, full of his belief in the peasantry and their power of seeing deep truths in common things. (p. 488)

[*A Book of Strife in the Form of The Diary of an Old Soul*] seems the most inspired of all his utterances. During my father's lifetime it interested only his exceptionally understanding readers, but now has a steady and increasing circulation. Ruskin, in his Oxford Lectures on "The Pleasures of England," spoke thus of it: "The generation which has seen *Hiawatha* and George MacDonald's *Soul's Diary,* and Keble's Hymns might fairly claim to be an age not destitute of religious poetry." (p. 496)

My father was never what mere schoolmen consider a first-rate academic critic, perhaps just because he was so very much more. In [*A Dish of Orts*] we sometimes even miss his genius—particularly, perhaps, in that on the *Imagination,* for, as already suggested, it falls short of his other references to the subject, both in prose and verse. But none the less we may well claim his gift of criticism to be profound and enthusiastic. All who remember his minutely learned critique on Hamlet—"the noblest character in all fiction"—or any of his lectures, must admit this: they were unlike anything else ever given to the world. I believe that his *Hamlet* will yet be recognized as the most important interpretation of the play ever written. But the writer's power lay rather in the consanguinity of his mind with Shakespeare's and every other poet's. It is his intuitive understanding—like a mother's of her children, a son's of his father—rather than learned analysis—of which there is yet overwhelming evidence—that makes it so splendid. It is his special pleading for the play's revelations, rather than his criticism, that gives his *Hamlet* a place quite apart from all other writings on this subject. The honestly passionate advocate is a greater man than the most honest judge: what the former must have, namely *fire,* the latter must do without. (p. 540)

[The] final years of [my father's] active life gave the world some of his greatest writing. If, to some, certain books suggest waning powers, as much might be said of several written in his prime. *The Elect Lady* . . . , with its captivating church—of three children and a broken-legged chicken—in contrast with a repellant miser, perhaps did not reach the highest level; but *There and Back* . . . , the last of his novels published in three volumes, was fresh and strong; some friends, among them conspicuously Carey Davies, thought it the best of the English novels. In another, *The Flight of the Shadow* . . . , the author dismisses his didactic and returns to the simple narrative style of *The Portent,* in a surprising and fantastic tale.

*Lilith,* the greatest, some think, of all his purely imaginative books, appeared in 1895, and was followed two years later by his last book of all, *Salted with Fire,* where he once more handles Scottish material and shows us the grim conscience of an erring minister.

Among prose writings, *Phantastes* . . . was the first essentially imaginative message, and *Lilith* the last. *Phantastes* was quite simple. It dealt with the eclipse of truth by the Shadow, whom yet the sun may set speeding away into nothingness. *Lilith* is more complex in its superb, if odd imagery; and it tells of a viler Shadow more awful, who had "himself within him," and, from the selfish use of celestial gifts, became so Satanic that only Hell Fire could drive "himself" out. (pp. 546-47)

William Blake has said: "God is within and without, even in the depths of Hell"; and *Lilith* tackles the eternal paradox of, on the one hand, Beauty, inspiring in power, evoking man's worship; and, on the other, its profanation, persuasive in equal power, but to man's utter undoing: the paradox of passion, which is but "heavenly hunger" and its prostitution to greed; of the god-like becoming devil-incarnate.

It is in the boldness of this paradox that the book's note of prophecy rings. It spells for the reader, as mutually revealing, the wrath and the pity of God enshrined together in that creation which was once the most lovely but becomes most accursed of all—Lilith, the Angel-vampire. In it we perhaps seem to understand how it comes to pass that, though man is created to uphold the Kingdom of Heaven within him, he generates Hell in his heart and belches its flames to scorch the Heavens beyond him. We find too, symbolic suggestion of a word uttered at the close of the noblest sermon of my father that I remember, "Who, then, shall ever dare to say, 'God has done all He can'''? (pp. 552-53)

Towards the end of **Lilith,** some are congregated in the Cemetery.

> "What is that flapping of wings I hear?" I asked.
>
> "The Shadow is hovering," replied Adam; "there is one here [Lilith] whom he counts his own! But ours once, never more can she be his!"
>
> (p. 553)

The writing of this strange chapter will give many a reader some sense of that infinite hope which may burgeon into faith; it is an utterance in art that transcends all creeds or rhetorical arguments. (p. 554)

> *Greville MacDonald, in his* George MacDonald and His Wife *(reprinted by permission of The Mac-Donald Family), Dial Press, 1924, 575 p.*

## C. S. LEWIS  (essay date 1933)

[*Lewis is considered one of the foremost authorities on Mac-Donald's work.*]

I have just re-read **Lilith** and am much clearer about the meaning. The first thing to get out of the way is all Greville Macdonald's nonsense about 'dimensions' and 'elements'—if you have his preface in your edition. That is just the sort of *mechanical* 'mysticism' which is worlds away from Geo. Macdonald. The main lesson of the book is against secular philanthropy—against the belief that you can effectively obey the 2nd command about loving your neighbour without first trying to love God.

The story runs like this. The human soul exploring its own house (the Mind) finds itself on the verge of unexpected worlds which at first dismay it (Chap. I-V). The first utterance of these worlds is an unconditional demand for absolute surrender of the Soul to the will of God, or, if you like, for Death (Chap. VI). To this demand the soul cannot at first face up (VI). But attempting to return to normal consciousness finds by education that its experiences are not abnormal or trivial but are vouched for by all the great poets and philosophers (VII . . .). It repents and tries to face the demand, but its original refusal has now rendered real submission temporarily impossible (IX). It has to face instead the impulses of the subconscious (X) and the slightly spurious loyalties to purely human 'causes'—political, theological etc (XI). It now becomes conscious of its fellow men: and finds them divided into 'Lovers' . . . and 'Bags' or 'Giants.' . . . But because it is an unconverted soul, has not yet died, it cannot really help the Lovers and becomes the slave of the Bags. In other words the young man, however amiably disposed towards the sweet and simple people of the world,

gets a job or draws a dividend, and becomes in fact the servant of the economic machine (XII-XIII). But he is too good to go on like this, and so becomes a 'Reformer', a 'friend of humanity'—a Shelley, Ruskin, Lenin (XIV). Here follows a digression on Purgatory (XV-XVII).

With the next section we enter on the deepest part of the book which I still only v. dimly understand. Why do so many purely secular reformers and philanthropists fail and in the end leave men more wretched and wicked than they found them? Apparently the unconverted soul, doing its very best for the Lovers, only succeeds first in *waking* (at the price of its own blood) and then in becoming the tool of, *Lilith.* Lilith is still quite beyond me. One can trace in her specially the Will to Power—which here fits in quite well—but there is a great deal more than that. She is also the real ideal somehow spoiled: she is not primarily a sexual symbol, but includes the characteristic *female* abuse of sex, which is love of Power, as the characteristic male abuse is sensuality (XVIII-XXIX). After a long and stormy attempt to do God's work in Lilith's way or Lilith's work in God's way, the soul comes to itself again, realises that its previous proceedings are 'cracked absolutely' and in fact has a sort of half-conversion. But the new powers of will and imagination which even this half conversion inspires (symbolised in the horse) are so exhilarating that the soul thinks *these* will do instead of 'death' and again shoots off on its own. This passage is v. true and important. Macdonald is aware how *religion itself* supplies new temptations (XXX-XXXI). This again leads to another attempt to help the Lovers in his own way, with consequent partial disaster in the death of Lona (XXXII-XXXVII). He finds himself the *jailer* of Lilith: i.e. he is now living in the state of tension with the evil thing inside him only just held down, and at a terrible cost—until he (or Lilith—the Lilith-part of him) at last repents (Mara) and consents to die (XXXVIII-end). (pp. 459-61)

> *C. S. Lewis, in his letter to Arthur Greeves on September 1, 1933, in* They Stand Together: The Letters of C. S. Lewis to Arthur Greeves (1914-1963), *edited by Walter Hooper (© The Estate of C. S. Lewis 1979; reprinted by permission of William Collins Sons & Co Ltd), Collins, 1979, pp. 459-62.*

## C. S. LEWIS  (essay date 1946)

[*In this key essay, Lewis discusses MacDonald's skill as a myth-maker, ranking him above Novalis and Kafka in this genre.*]

In making [**George MacDonald: An Anthology**] I have been concerned with MacDonald not as a writer but as a Christian teacher. If I were to deal with him as a writer, a man of letters, I should be faced with a difficult critical problem. If we define Literature as an art whose medium is words, then certainly MacDonald has no place in its first rank—perhaps not even in its second. There are indeed passages, many of them in this collection, where the wisdom and (I would dare to call it) the holiness that are in him triumph over and even burn away the baser elements in his style: the expression becomes precise, weighty, economic; acquires a cutting edge. But he does not maintain this level for long. The texture of his writing as a whole is undistinguished, at times fumbling. Bad pulpit traditions cling to it; there is sometimes a nonconformist verbosity, sometimes an old Scotch weakness for florid ornament (it runs right through them from Dunbar to the Waverly Novels), sometimes an oversweetness picked up from Novalis. But this does not quite dispose of him even for the literary critic. What he does best is fantasy—fantasy that hovers between the allegorical and the mythopoeic. And this, in my opinion, he does better than any man. The critical problem with which we are confronted is whether this art—the art of myth-making—is a species of the literary art. (pp. xxv-xxvi)

Most myths were made in prehistoric times, and, I suppose, not consciously made by individuals at all. But every now and then there occurs in the modern world a genius—a Kafka or a Novalis—who can make such a story. MacDonald is the greatest genius of this kind whom I know. But I do not know how to classify such genius. To call it literary genius seems unsatisfactory since it can coexist with great inferiority in the art of words—nay, since its connection with words at all turns out to be merely external and, in a sense, accidental. Nor can it be fitted into any of the other arts. It begins to look as if there were an art, or a gift, which criticism has largely ignored. It may even be one of the greatest arts; for it produces works which give us (at the first meeting) as much delight and (on prolonged acquaintance) as much wisdom and strength as the works of the greatest poets. . . . It gets under our skin, hits us at a level deeper than our thoughts or even our passions, troubles oldest certainties till all questions are reopened, and in general shocks us more fully awake than we are for most of our lives.

It was in this mythopoeic art that MacDonald excelled. And from this it follows that his best art is least represented in this collection. The great works are *Phantastes,* the *Curdie* books, *The Golden Key, The Wise Woman,* and *Lilith.* From them, just because they are supremely good in their own kind, there is little to be extracted. The meaning, the suggestion, the radiance, is incarnate in the whole story: it is only by chance that you find any detachable merits. The novels, on the other hand, have yielded me a rich crop. This does not mean that they are good novels. Necessity made MacDonald a novelist, but few of his novels are good and none is very good. They are best when they depart most from the canons of novel writing, and that in two directions. Sometimes they depart in order to come nearer to fantasy, as in the whole character of the hero in *Sir Gibbie* or the opening chapters of *Wilfrid Cumbermede.* Sometimes they diverge into direct and prolonged preachments which would be intolerable if a man were reading for the story, but which are in fact welcome because the author, though a poor novelist, is a supreme preacher. Some of his best things are thus hidden in his dullest books. . . . I am speaking so far of the novels as I think they would appear if judged by any reasonably objective standard. But it is, no doubt, true that any reader who loves holiness and loves MacDonald—yet perhaps he will need to love Scotland too—can find even in the worst of them something that disarms criticism and will come to feel a queer, awkward charm in their very faults. (But that, of course, is what happens to us with all favorite authors.) One rare, and all but unique, merit these novels must be allowed. The "good" characters are always the best and most convincing. His saints live; his villains are stagey.

This collection, as I have said, was designed not to revive MacDonald's literary reputation but to spread his religious teaching. (pp. xxviii-xxx)

[In] MacDonald it is always the voice of conscience that speaks. He addresses the will: the demand for obedience, for "something to be neither more nor less nor other than *done*" is incessant. Yet in that very voice of conscience every other faculty somehow speaks as well—intellect, and imagination, and humor, and fancy, and all the affections; and no man in

modern times was perhaps more aware of the distinction between Law and Gospel, the inevitable failure of mere morality. The Divine Sonship is the key-conception which unites all the different elements of his thought. I dare not say that he is never in error; but to speak plainly I know hardly any other writer who seems to be closer, or more continually close, to the Spirit of Christ Himself. Hence his Christ-like union of tenderness and severity. Nowhere else outside the New Testament have I found terror and comfort so intertwined. The title "Inexorable Love" which I have given to several individual extracts would serve for the whole collection. Inexorability—but never the inexorability of anything less than love—runs through it like a refrain; "escape is hopeless"—"agree quickly with your adversary"—"compulsion waits behind"—"the uttermost farthing will be exacted." Yet this urgency never becomes shrill. All the sermons are suffused with a spirit of love and wonder which prevents it from doing so. MacDonald shows God threatening, but (as Jeremy Taylor says) "He threatens terrible things if we will not be happy."

In many respects MacDonald's thought has, in a high degree, just those excellences which his period and his personal history would lead us to expect least. A romantic, escaping from a drily intellectual theology, might easily be betrayed into valuing mere emotion and "religious experience" too highly: but in fact few nineteenth-century writers are more firmly catholic in relegating feeling to its proper place. . . . [His whole philosophy of Nature] with its resolute insistence on the concrete, owes little to the thought of an age which hovered between mechanism and idealism; he would obviously have been more at home with Professor Whitehead than with Herbert Spencer or T. H. Green. . . . All romantics are vividly aware of mutability, but most of them are content to bewail it: for MacDonald this nostalgia is merely the starting point—he goes on and discovers what it is made for. His psychology also is worth noticing: he is quite as well aware as the moderns that the conscious self, the thing revealed by introspection, is a superficies. Hence the cellars and attics of the King's castle in *The Princess and the Goblin,* and the terror of his own house which falls upon Mr. Vane in *Lilith.* . . . Perhaps most remarkable of all is the function—a low and primitive, yet often indispensable function—which he allows to Fear in the spiritual life. . . . Reaction against early teachings might on this point have very easily driven him into a shallow liberalism. But it does not. He hopes, indeed, that all men will be saved; but that is because he hopes that all will repent. He knows (none better) that even omnipotence cannot save the unconverted. He never trifles with eternal impossibilities. He is as golden and genial as Traherne; but also as astringent as the *Imitation.*

So at least I have found him. In making this collection I was discharging a debt of justice. I have never concealed the fact that I regarded him as my master; indeed I fancy I have never written a book in which I did not quote from him. . . . It must be more than thirty years ago that I bought . . . the Everyman edition of *Phantastes.* A few hours later I knew that I had crossed a great frontier. I had already been waist-deep in Romanticism; and likely enough, at any moment, to flounder into its darker and more evil forms, slithering down the steep descent that leads from the love of strangeness to that of eccentricity and thence to that of perversity. Now *Phantastes* was romantic enough in all conscience; but there was a difference. Nothing was at that time further from my thoughts than Christianity and I therefore had no notion what this difference really was. I was only aware that if this new world was strange, it was also homely and humble; that if this was a dream, it was a dream in which one at least felt strangely vigilant; that the whole book had about it a sort of cool, morning innocence, and also, quite unmistakably, a certain quality of Death, *good* Death. What it actually did to me was to convert, even to baptize (that was where the Death came in) my imagination. (pp. xxx-xxxiv)

The quality which had enchanted me in [MacDonald's] imaginative works turned out to be the quality of the real universe, the divine, magical, terrifying, and ecstatic reality in which we all live. I should have been shocked in my teens if anyone had told me that what I learned to love in *Phantastes* was goodness. But now that I know, I see there was no deception. The deception is all the other way round—in that prosaic moralism which confines goodness to the region of Law and Duty, which never lets us feel in our face the sweet air blowing from "the land of righteousness," never reveals that elusive Form which if once seen must inevitably be desired with all but sensuous desire—the thing (in Sappho's phrase) "more gold than gold." (p. xxxiv)

> *C. S. Lewis, in his preface to* George MacDonald: An Anthology by George MacDonald, *edited by C. S. Lewis (copyright © 1947 Macmillan Publishing Co., Inc.; copyright renewed 1974 by Arthur Owen Barfield and Alfred Cecil Harwood; reprinted by permission of William Collins Sons & Co Ltd), G. Bles: The Centenary Press, 1946 (and reprinted by Macmillan, 1947), pp. xxi-xxxiv (and to be reprinted in a Fount Paperback in 1983).*

## W. H. AUDEN (essay date 1954)

[*Auden writes favorably of MacDonald's power to successfully and artfully translate his inner life into the elements of his fiction, a strength noted also by Chesterton (see excerpt above).*]

For the writing of what may comprehensively be called Dream Literature, though it includes many works, like detective stories and opera libretti which are, formally, "feigned histories," the primary requirement is the gift of mythopoeic imagination. This gift is one with which criticism finds it hard to deal for it seems to have no necessary connection with the gift of verbal expression or the power to structure experience. . . .

A genuine "mythical" character like Sherlock Holmes can always be recognized by two characteristics: his appeal, at least within a given culture, transcends all highbrow-lowbrow, child-adult differences of taste, and his nature is independent of his history. . . . (p. v)

George Macdonald is pre-eminently a mythopoeic writer. Though he has very considerable literary gifts in the usual sense, his style sometimes lapses into Ossian Gothic and Victorian sentimentality (the baby talk of The Little Ones in *Lilith* is, frankly, shy-making, though partly redeemed by the fact that they represent not real children but people who, afraid of the risks and suffering involved in becoming adult, refuse to grow up) and, in reissuing *Phantastes,* the editors have been wise, I think, in their decision to omit most of the hero's songs, for George Macdonald was not endowed with that particular verbal gift which the writing of verse requires. In his power, however, to project his inner life into images, events, beings, landscapes which are valid for all, he is one of the most remarkable writers of the nineteenth century: *The Princess and The Goblin* is, in my opinion, the only English children's book in the same class as the Alice books, and *Lilith* is equal if not superior to the best of Poe.

The Scylla and Charybdis of Dream Literature are incoherence and mechanical allegory. Without some allegorical scheme of meaning—it is not always necessary that the reader know what it is—the writer has no principle by which to select and organize his material and no defense against his private obsessions; on the other hand, if he allows the allegory to take control so that symbol and thing symbolized have a mere one-to-one correspondence, he becomes boring. . . . If *Lilith* is a more satisfactory book than *Phantastes,* one reason is that its allegorical structure is much tighter: there seems no particular reason, one feels, why Anodos should have just the number of adventures which he does have—they could equally be more or less—but Mr. Vane's experiences and his spiritual education exactly coincide. The danger of the chain adventure story is that perpetual novelty gives excitement at the cost of understanding; the landscape of *Lilith* becomes all the more vivid and credible to the reader because he is made to repeat the journey Adam's-Cottage to Bad-Burrow to Dry-River to Evil-Wood to Orchard-Valley to Rocky-Scaur to Hot-Stream to Bulika-City several times.

In comparison with his colleague, the novelist of our social waking life, the novelist of dream life is freer in his choice of events but more restricted in his choice of characters, for the latter must all be variations on a few "archetypes," the Wise Old Man, the Wise Old Woman, the Harlot-Witch, the Child-Bride, the Shadow-Self, etc., and it is no easy matter to present these types in unique and personal figures. George Macdonald, however, almost invariably manages to do so: there is a clear affinity between Lilith and the Alder Witch, between Eve and the old woman in the cottage with four doors, yet each is herself, and not a mere repetition.

But his greatest gift is what one might call his dream realism, his exact and profound knowledge of dream causality, dream logic, dream change, dream morality: when one reads him, the illusion of participating in a real dream is perfect; one never feels that it is an allegorical presentation of wakeful conscious processes. Nobody can describe better that curious experience of dreaming that one is awake. . . . To describe how a dreamer reasons without making him sound either too arbitrary or too logical is not easy, but Macdonald's characters always argue like real dreamers. . . . Like real dreamers, too, their consciences are aware of ambiguities of feeling and motive before and during their actions in a way that, when we are awake, we can only become aware, if at all, after we have acted.

> But a false sense of power, a sense which had
> no root and was merely vibrated into me from
> the strength of the horse, had, alas, rendered
> me too stupid to listen to anything he said.

In waking life, it would be psychologically false to make the rider so aware of his self-deception at the moment of choice; in a dream it is true. (pp. v-viii)

In addition to the dream stories for which he is best known, he wrote a number of realistic stories about Scotch peasant life some of which, like *Alec Forbes* and *Robert Falconer,* deserve to be better known. . . .

If unorthodox on certain points—for example, he believed, like Origen, in the ultimate salvation of the Devil—he never, like many "liberals" of his day, abandoned the Christian doctrines of God, Sin and Grace for some vague emergent "force making for righteousness" or a Pelagian and secular belief in "Progress." *Lilith* is a surprisingly tough book. Bulika, its *civitas terrenae,* where all human beings are born, is a nightmare of suspicion, greed, sterility and cruelty, and, if in Mr. Vane's dream it is captured by the innocent, it is, one feels, only in his dream; the reader is not left with the impression that Bulika has ceased to exist for others. The life-giving waters are restored to the Waste Land, but evil is not thereby abolished. . . . (p. ix)

*W. H. Auden, "Introduction" (copyright © 1954 by W. H. Auden; reprinted by permission of Curtis Brown, Ltd.) in* The Visionary Novels of George MacDonald: Lilith, Phantastes, *edited by Anne Fremantle, Noonday Press, 1954, pp. v-x.*

## ROBERT LEE WOLFF (essay date 1961)

[*Wolff's* The Golden Key: A Study of the Fiction of George MacDonald, *from which the following study of* Wilfrid Cumbermede *is taken, is an important—albeit controversial—Freudian interpretation of MacDonald's novels and short stories.*]

[*Wilfrid Cumbermede* is] a *Bildungsroman* like *Alec Forbes* or *Robert Falconer,* set, like them, in the early nineteenth century but told in the first person. Long ago Greville MacDonald suggested that his father had written this novel under the influence of the emotions aroused in him by his involvement in John Ruskin's love affair with Rose La Touche. But Greville never pursued his own suggestion further, nor has anyone else apparently read *Wilfrid Cumbermede* with this in mind. Yet because it does indeed represent MacDonald's effort to make in fictional form a statement about the Ruskin affair, this novel takes on an interest all its own.

Its first fourteen chapters, about a third, move with economy and charm, and without preaching, but with certain ominous overtones not heard unless one listens for them. As a child, Wilfrid, an orphan, lives with his uncle, a well-educated farmer. Though the family seems of humble origin, there is a secret about Wilfrid, symbolized by an ancient sword that hangs on the wall, and by a splendid watch given him by his ninety-five-year-old great-grandmother, who lives upstairs, eager for death. During a great storm one night, the child overhears his uncle refusing the offer of a mysterious visitor to take him away and bring him up and pay for his education. Wilfrid feels great relief when his uncle rejects the plan.

But the whole episode has aroused feelings of guilt and terror. Some time before, Wilfrid had discovered in the lumber room a mechanical toy invented by an ancestor:

> It had a kind of pendulum . . . my fancy concerning it was that if I could keep the pendulum wagging long enough, it would set [the] trees [outside the window] going too; and if I still kept it swinging, we should have such a storm of wind as no living man had ever felt or heard of. . . . I had not . . . had the courage to keep up the oscillations beyond ten or a dozen strokes; partly from fear of the trees, partly from a dim dread of exercising power whose source and extent were not within my knowledge. I kept the pendulum in the closet . . . and never spoke to any one of it. . . .

[Sometime later when Wilfrid sets the pendulum in motion], the wind actually does rise and grows steadily into a gale. Wilfrid decides he must stop the pendulum: "I seized hold of the oscillating thing, and stopped it; but to my amaze and consternation, the moment I released it on it went again." He

decides he must take it to bed with him "and stifle its motions with the bed-clothes." But, as a horseman gallops up outside, it stops. This is the man who wants to take Wilfrid away. Wilfrid is sure that his playing with the pendulum has brought on the storm.

Can we doubt that we have been reading a description of masturbation? Once we accustom ourselves to the shock of thinking of it in this way, and contemplate the possibility that MacDonald himself so thought of it, we understand why he imagined and set down the episode. MacDonald was Ruskin's confidant. Ruskin himself regarded his youthful masturbation as a dreadful sin, and confessed it as such to Mrs. Cowper-Temple and MacDonald. Tormented as he was by Ruskin's difficulties, was not MacDonald, an experienced worker with symbols, trying to tell the story of an oversensitive and deeply imaginative boy? At school, where Wilfrid is very happy, he has a fantasy, "the family romance," as psychologists call it: "Aware of the humbleness of my birth, and unrestrained by pride in my parents—I had lost them so early—I would indulge in a daydream of what I would gladly have been." (pp. 268-70)

Wilfrid's uncle pledges him to try not to learn the secret [of his birth] until he is old enough, and meanwhile gives him for his own the great sword, overt symbol of a noble ancestry, but also a phallic symbol of manhood, like Mossy's golden key.

The housekeeper of a neighboring great house, Moldwarp Hall, which belongs to Sir Giles Brotherton, a Baronet, shows Wilfrid the great library there. Here he meets Clara, a charming girl of thirteen, a little older than he. On one of his visits to the Hall, he brings his sword to compare it with those in the collection there, and is invited to spend the night. . . . During the night the sword is mysteriously taken from him. He has somehow been unmanned. Wilfrid discovers that Clara's father is an attorney, the very man who had offered to adopt him and caused his fright. His uncle now warns that this man is a former friend of Wilfrid's father, but "dangerous" and "worldly." Up to this point in the story, the Ruskin-character is Wilfrid himself.

Now, with the hero in his teens, the story enters a new phase, in which struggle and passion predominate. Wilfrid goes off to school in Switzerland with a boy his own age, Charley Osborne, deeply sensitive, the son of a clergyman. Charley's father is "severe, pure, and irritable . . . an *Evangelical* of the most pure, honest, and narrow type," who is "overlaying and smothering" his son's life. As for Charley, "A tremulousness about the mouth betrayed a nervous temperament." At the first sight of the Jungfrau,

> "Oh, Charley!" was all I could say. Our hands met blindly and clasped each other. I burst into silent tears. . . . His eyes too were full of tears, but some troubling contradiction prevented their flowing. . . .

Here MacDonald quite explicitly introduces a new theme: the conflict between strict evangelical piety as embodied in Mr. Osborne, and the Wordsworthian pantheism that sees God in nature. . . . The Ruskin personality is now split, Wilfrid representing the attractions of Wordsworthian pantheism and Charley the unfortunate impact of evangelical narrowness on the spirit.

Wilfrid and Charley room together at the school. Their relationship leaves little doubt in our minds: they are lovers. Lost and wet through after an Alpine walk, Wilfrid takes refuge at a mountain inn, where the lady of the house and her daughter offer him the girl's clothes while his own are drying. They put her jewelry on him as well as her garments, and he himself asks them to comb his hair as much like the girl's as possible. . . . "'One girl may kiss another,'" he says, and does so. (pp. 271-73)

When Wilfrid is sick, Charley nurses him "more like a woman than a boy." . . . Wilfrid dreams that both are dead; in the dream, Charley urges him to take courage; Wilfrid begs Charley not to leave him, and finds himself "floating half reclined on the air. We met midway each in the other's arms." (p. 274)

It would be futile to debate the precise degree of MacDonald's awareness of homosexual relationships, or of his intention to portray one. But even if one sets aside as sentimental Victorian hyperbole the terms that the young men use about each other, one can hardly miss the implications of Wilfrid's dream or of his transvestitism. We must inevitably regard the boys as having a homosexual relationship, and we can easily understand the circumstances in Charley's and Wilfrid's lives that led to it.

MacDonald, like Ruskin, had himself experienced an Alpine revelation, but in middle age, not in youth, and long after he had already undergone great influence from Wordsworth. Wilfrid and Charley undergo the same emotional experiences, in that same, deliberately chosen, Swiss environment so conducive to discussions of the true relationships between God and Nature. But there is more in these episodes of *Wilfrid Cumbermede* than that. Ruskin's love for the beautiful young neurotic Rose La Touche had deeply involved the MacDonalds. (p. 276)

MacDonald could not of course deal with the affair directly or introduce into his novel recognizable portraits of the real personages. But, in his portrait of Mr. Osborne, and in his account of Mr. Osborne's impact on Charley, MacDonald was thinking of the tragedy that—so he believed—evangelical Christianity had made of Ruskin's life: first that of his over-possessive parents, and then that of Mr. and Mrs. La Touche, one of whose main objections to Ruskin was that in their narrow view he was not a believer. MacDonald says of Charley: "Gifted with the keenest perceptions, and a nature unusually responsive to the feelings of others, he was born to be an artist." He is describing a nature precisely like Ruskin's own. No doubt, he also wanted to use the hint (or more) of sexual abnormality in the relations between Wilfrid and Charley as a substitute for what he could not possibly say about the peculiar sexual constitution of Ruskin.

In the final third of *Wilfrid Cumbermede,* MacDonald shows himself unable to resolve simultaneously the two sets of themes: that of a lost heir, and that of religious and sexual tensions and abnormal passion. The book collapses hopelessly. Sir Giles Brotherton offers Wilfrid the chance of restoring the books in the library at Moldwarp Hall. But, although Clara is often present, MacDonald does not revert to his usual theme of love in the library: indeed, Wilfrid, though attracted by Clara, keeps from falling in love with her because he resents her friendly conversations with Geoffrey Brotherton. Instead, it is Charley Osborne who falls in love with Clara, while Wilfrid is more and more attracted to Charley's sister, Mary Osborne. (pp. 277-78)

On one occasion, when he is spending the night at the Hall, Wilfrid dreams of love and death and wakes to find his own lost sword lying on the bed, restored to him as mysteriously as years before it had been taken. Even more astonishing and

disturbing: Mary Osborne in all her beauty is asleep on the neighboring pillow. The sword lies between them (as between Tristram and Iseult). . . . Wilfrid steals out in the early morning, clothes and sword in hand, without waking Mary or revealing to her the embarrassing position they are in. (pp. 278-79)

[Let] us consider the obvious phallic significance of Wilfrid's sword. After it had been stolen from him at the Hall, we almost immediately saw him dressing in girls' clothes and embarking on a love affair with a boy. It is mysteriously returned to him at the Hall, and simultaneously the boy's sister, his true ladylove, is in bed with him, and he is unbearably excited, but inhibited. Soon after, a maid—knowing that the room was Wilfrid's—brings him a ring left there; she assumes it is his. It is, however, Mary's ring which she has left there; and he accepts it to save her embarrassment, and then puts it on the third finger of her left hand, begging her to ask no questions. This is more than symbolic marriage; it is to all intents and purposes marriage. (p. 279)

If George MacDonald seldom wrote anything more effective on its own level than the first third of *Wilfrid Cumbermede,* he never wrote anything more ludicrously inept than the last third. He had set himself in the central third the problem of portraying deep emotional conflicts, and it defeated him. In real life, he helped Ruskin pursue the desperate courtship of Rose La Touche, but he never seems to have stopped to consider that, even if not impotent, Ruskin was at least peculiar: he had lived for years with a beautiful wife, whom he had certainly loved before his marriage to her, and he had refused with horror to consummate the marriage. Nor did it seem to trouble MacDonald that Ruskin was thirty years older than Rose; nor did he face the supreme irony that it was precisely those sexual relations of marriage which Ruskin insisted he could and would offer to Rose that horrified and repelled her: had Ruskin been willing to admit impotence or to agree to abstain from physical intimacy, he might well have won the girl. Like the knight in his own *Phantastes* who can look on at evil without recognizing it because his soul is so pure, MacDonald failed to appreciate sexual abnormality, and so helped to renew the agonizing relationships that within a few years would drive Rose to death and Ruskin to madness. *Wilfrid Cumbermede* is in part at least his effort to try to deal in disguised form with the forces that he saw at work in the affair of his friend. Its failure as a novel therefore becomes almost irrelevant, since it stands as a small and hitherto unnoticed monument to one of the most shocking human tragedies of the entire century. (pp. 281-82)

*Robert Lee Wolff, in his* The Golden Key: A Study of George MacDonald *(© 1961 by Yale University Press, Inc.), Yale University Press, 1961, 425 p.*

## TONY TANNER (essay date 1962)

In *The Nineteenth Century* for April 1895 a critic named B. A. Crackenthorpe inveighed against minor writers who had been adversely influenced by the dubious merits of such books as George Moore's *Esther Waters*. This is how he words his complaint: 'Instead of walking on the mountain-tops, breathing the pure, high atmosphere of imagination freely playing around the truths of life and of love, they force us down into the stifling charnel-house, where animal decay, with its swarms of loathsome activities, meets us at every turn.' (p. 51)

The idea that truths might be discrete and hostile, the feeling of chasmic separation between the truths of the heights and those of the depths, and a feeling of revulsion from the latter—this I take to be a characteristic Victorian syndrome. We can detect this characteristic dualism expressing itself in a variety of ways throughout the century. . . . [To illustrate], let us consider a fairy story which enjoyed a great vogue at the end of the century—*The Princess and the Goblin* by George Macdonald. The opening setting is immediately suggestive:

> There was once a little princess whose father was king over a great country full of mountains and valleys. His palace was built upon one of the mountains, and was very grand and beautiful.

The Princess's situation is, however, not so immune. She is being brought up in a castle-house on the side of the mountain, 'about halfway between its base and its peak'. She often looks yearningly up the mountain—the realm of her pure origin and absolute safety—but she is at least half involved in the life of the lower parts of the mountain, and 'these mountains were full of hollow places'. The caves are inhabited [by "a strange race of beings, called by some gnomes, by some kobolds, by some goblins."] . . . Hideous inhabitants of dark caves clearly invite a Freudian interpretation, particularly in this case where excessively authoritarian actions have driven them underground where they have become deformed and ugly. The inflexible banishment of base urges by an imperious conscience—this description fits the story just as it fits the age in which it was written. But banishment if not extermination, the 'id' will out, the goblins plan revenge on the people who live in the light of day, particularly on the vulnerable representative of the mountain-top, the Princess. And in the temporary absence of the king (the super-ego perhaps) the goblins lay two plots. First their ugliest member, Harelip, plans to abduct the Princess and force her into an ugly and defiling marriage. So the goblins tunnel under the palace and then rise up suddenly and overcome all who dwell there (surely the strategy of all irrational impulse), at which moment the abduction should be irresistible. When this fails they put into operation their second plan—to flood the palace. 'The goblins had, in pursuance of their designs, let loose all the underground reservoirs and streams. . . .' The palace of reasonable harmonious living (the image is employed in *Othello*) is threatened by a flood of murky underground water, the pressure of which has been building up since the goblins were banished underground—the schematic location of the hostile parties could hardly have clearer implications. The story as a whole need not concern us: the Princess, not surprisingly, is saved by the forces of goodness, the goblins are thwarted. But one or two incidental points merit attention. The goblins, for instance, can always be rendered impotent and harmless by poetry—art, that is, is on the side of the truths and virtues of the upper-air. Then again, living very high up in the castle is a benevolent lady with magic protective powers which are responsible for bringing the princess safely through her encounters with the goblins—in fact a magic thread connects the princess with this supernatural lady, thus ensuring a safe return to her elevated sanctuary. The frisson of the book is provided by the Princess's adventures within the caves where she nearly succumbs to the goblins; the happy ending is her victorious return to the top of the mountain in the very safe keeping of her father.

There is one incident in the book which brings to mind another popular fairy tale of the age in which a similar type of dualism is clearly in evidence. When the Princess Irene finally makes her way to the sanctuary of the good lady's room she is covered with dirt because of 'creeping through narrow places'. The lady [bathes her]. . . . The magic lady throughout the book represents a cleansing agency, a purifying power capable of eradicating all traces of any grimy involvements with the goblins. 'Any time you want a bath, come to me' she says to the Princess. (pp. 51-4)

In what is no more than an introductory hint I have suggested that the Cartesian dichotomy of mind and matter [as evidenced in the work of MacDonald, Kingsley, and Conrad] has become part of the landscape of the nineteenth-century mind; that an acute, at times almost schizophrenic, awareness of the realms of the spirit and the claims of the flesh and their mutual hostility and exclusiveness can dominate the profound as well as the superficial mind of the age (Jekyll and Hyde, Dorian Gray, etc., comprise another revealing and recurring theme); that in particular a threat from below was challenging the easy unquestioned reign of the most revered truths of the time. The common people and the official culture preferred, like our reviewer, to keep their eyes desperately fixed on the mountain-top and to deny-by-ignoring the truths from below. (pp. 60-1)

> *Tony Tanner, "Mountains and Depths—An Approach to Nineteenth-Century Dualism," in* A Review of English Literature *(© Longmans, Green & Co. Ltd. 1962), Vol. 3, No. 4, October, 1962, pp. 51-61.*

## LOUIS MacNEICE (essay date 1965)

MacDonald's writings are not to everyone's taste—I myself find much of *Phantastes* unpalatable—partly because he is not essentially a writer. Both Chesterton and Lewis admit that he often writes badly [see excerpts above]—most of his verse is deplorable—and Lewis explains that the sort of myth which MacDonald creates so lavishly 'does not essentially exist in *words* at all'; this is similar to what Miss [Kathleen] Raine maintains of Blake, that his dream figures are drawn from a layer that lies below words. If this premise is accepted, it follows, as Lewis points out, that MacDonald's myths might come over just as well in some other medium such as the film. However, as he happened to write them, let us consider them as literature, for in the realm of parable writing no one went further than MacDonald in the whole of the nineteenth century. MacDonald is thought of today as a children's writer; but his first and last books of fantasy, [*Phantastes* and *Lilith*] . . . , far from being intended for children, are the parable equivalents of the intimate journals of someone who is basically a mystic but also constitutionally melancholy. It is significant that both of these books are written in the first person. Technically, MacDonald's main problem was that of the mystical poets, how to express the Ineffable, and like many mystical poets he tries to do this by piling up sensuous detail (notice particularly the use he makes of precious stones). But even in MacDonald, especially in the children's books, we find, as in Bunyan and Andersen, the dry aside, the flat prosy statement or the touch of humour which serve as correctives to what might seem overlush or overjewelled. Thus the Bunyanesque note is struck in *The Princess and the Curdie* when he is describing a corrupt society: 'There were even certain quacks in the city who advertised pills for enabling people to think well of themselves, and some few bought of them, but most laughed, and said, with evident truth, that they did not require them.' And in *The Golden Key,* where the hero and heroine, Mossy and Tangle, are enabled to communicate with the beasts, birds and insects, we hear the Andersen note: the squirrels, for instance, turn out to be kind, 'but the bees were selfish and rude, justifying themselves on the ground that Tangle and Mossy were not subjects of their queen, and charity must begin at home, though indeed they had not one drone in their poorhouse at the time'. But these are minor matters: what is unique in MacDonald is his passionately spiritual attitude to the universe and his prolific invention of symbols to embody it. It should be noted that with him, as with [Charles] Kingsley but much more so, the stories involve very serious moral issues, which are contingent not on Law but on Grace.

MacDonald was a great admirer of *Pilgrim's Progress,* but Bunyan's story is traditional homespun in comparison with his own fantastically novel and highly complicated embroideries. This complexity reaches an extreme in his last fantasy *Lilith.* I can here do no more than mention some of his basic themes and symbols, and I doubt if this will convince anyone that Chesterton was not mad when he wrote that of all the stories he had read *The Princess and the Goblin* was 'the most like life'. It will be remembered that C. S. Lewis said something similar about *The Faerie Queene.* The life that these two critics discover in these two works is human life as seen, or felt, or divined from the inside. All MacDonald's fantasies are spiritual explorations, and he could not have written them, any more than Bunyan could have written *Pilgrim's Progress,* if he had not held certain beliefs. The orthodox Christian belief in personal immortality is complicated in him by an individual and mystical vision of a universe which can only be understood by the assumption of extra dimensions, a universe where, regardless of time and space, two or more worlds are continually superimposed. This special vision MacDonald, like the mystical poets, could only attempt to convey through physical imagery, but with him, as his son pointed out, it is essential to remember that such images are never mere algebraic symbols. 'The rose,' he explained in a conversation reported by his son, 'when it gives some glimmer of the freedom for which a man hungers, does so because of its *substantial* unity with the man, each in degree being a signature of God's immanence.' MacDonald's son says that, when his father wrote *Lilith,* 'he was possessed by a feeling . . . that it was a mandate direct from God'.

This being so, it is worth noting that MacDonald does not talk about God, let alone Christ, in his parable writing. . . . MacDonald's course requires a very unusual gift of sheer invention, which fortunately he possessed. A few of his minor creations appear arbitrary and therefore fail to pull their weight—some of his monsters, for instance, might have been knocked up by Hieronymus Bosch on an off day—but on the whole the stream of invention flows astonishingly fresh without any sign of failing: compare the last scene of *Faust* either with the last scene of *The Golden Key* or with the Ascent to the City near the end of *Lilith.* As for Goethe's speciality, *das Ewig-Weibliche,* I think MacDonald's extraordinary supernatural females compare very well with either Gretchen or Goethe's Virgin Mary. It would be more appropriate to compare the mysterious powers known as 'The Mothers', except that Goethe has not really told us enough about them. They are the conferrers of magical gifts, and so are these strange creations of MacDonald's such as the Old Lady in *The Princess and the Goblin* who can be seen only by those who have faith and who then sometimes appears as a beautiful young lady. Other examples are the beautiful old women in *Phantastes* and *The Golden Key,* and Mara, the daughter of Adam and Eve, in *Lilith.*

These creatures, who are neither goddesses nor angels nor enchantresses nor fairies but something of all four, exist in a way outside normal time but slip into our time or allow us to slip into theirs, in order to do their good works—and they are all indefatigable workers. The other world to which they belong seems to be ruled by the two great principles of Love and Death—what C. S. Lewis rightly calls 'a good death'. These worlds are entered from ours by something in the nature of a conjuring trick. In both *The Princess and the Goblin* and *Lilith* the approach is made through an attic reached by a long flight of stairs. MacDonald himself wrote in a letter, 'I have a passion for stairs,' and our man with a smattering of Freud, who connected stairs with coition, could of course have a field-day with this as with many other of MacDonald's symbols. Anyhow these attics are the counterpart to the cellars in the former book and to the subterranean passages, especially those inside mountains, which are always appearing in MacDonald. Both sets of images represent things outside the compass of the normal reasoning mind. . . . (pp. 95-9)

Psychologically, MacDonald is as rich as Spenser. He is also as moral as Spenser. But, unlike Kingsley, there is nothing facile about his morality. He sees that the problem of evil really *is* a problem. Thus in *Phantastes* he creates a macabre creature called the 'Alder Maiden' who, like Spenser's Duessa, leads or rather *is* a double life: the hero, who has fallen into her clutches from which he never fully recovers, is left reflecting: 'How can beauty and ugliness dwell so near?' There are similar false females in Malory and, more relevantly, in Shelley's *Epipsychidion.* . . . Immediately after the encounter with the Alder Maiden, and partly because of it, the hero is saddled with something described as his 'shadow' which throws a blight on everything he meets. In *Lilith* we meet another and far greater Shadow who stands to the whole of humanity as the earlier shadow stood to the hero of Phantastes. He can be equated with Satan and he is closely in league with Lilith herself. (p. 100)

On a less cosmic scale MacDonald's moral view of the universe means that his heroes and heroines have to develop and they usually do it the hard way. MacDonald talks about Fairies and Fairy Land as freely as Barrie but in attitude as in vision he is poles apart from him: MacDonald would never tolerate Peter Pan or, for that matter, Wendy. There are indeed Peter Pan-like children in *Lilith* but the hero sees that their growth has been arrested and feels that it is his mission to cure this. MacDonald's heroes have not only to prove themselves through action, like Tom in *The Water Babies,* they have also to achieve a spiritual evolution. This involves paradoxes which are nearly all variants on the Christian paradox that one must lose one's life to save it. In *Lilith* when we first meet Adam he is in the form of a librarian, but he promptly turns into a raven and this raven is also a sexton, but a creative sexton. Thus he suddenly plunges his beak into the earth 'drawing out a great wriggling red worm. He threw back his head, and tossed it in the air. It spread great wings, gorgeous in red and black, and soared aloft.' The raven explains: 'When you have nothing to bury, you must dig something up!' In the next chapter he tells us: 'But indeed the business of the universe is to make such a fool of you that you will know yourself for one, and so begin to be wise!' And here I will leave MacDonald. In this particular kind of parable writing I think no one could go much further. (p. 101)

*Louis MacNeice, "The Victorians," in his* Varieties of Parable *(© Cambridge University Press 1965), Cambridge University Press, 1965, pp. 76-101.*

**MAURICE SENDAK**  (essay date 1966)

[*A noted children's author and illustrator, best known for* Where the Wild Things Are, *Sendak notes the growing darkness of MacDonald's vision in the later fantasy works. Sendak also illuminates the importance of MacDonald's dream-imagery and its successful transferal from the creator's mind to the printed page.*]

George MacDonald was a novelist, poet, mythmaker, allegorist, critic, essayist, and, in everything, a preacher. One of the towering and mystifying figures of Victorian literature, he wrote well over 50 books, of which only two, *At the Back of the North Wind,* and *The Princess and the Goblin,* are still widely read. His main forte was fantasy—his remarkable power, in the words of W. H. Auden, to "project his inner life in images, events, beings, landscapes which are valid for all" [see excerpt above]. For admirers of MacDonald, such as myself, his work has something of the effect of an hallucinatory drug. Finishing one of his stories is often like waking from a dream—one's own dream. The best of them stimulate long-forgotten images and feelings—the "something profound" that borders frustratingly close to memory without quite ever reaching it. . . .

*The Lost Princess* strikes a very different note from Mac-Donald's earlier fairy tales. There is a falling off, not of creative power but rather of his faith in moral power. This is a harsh, angry tale whose magic, unlike the pure crystal fantasy of MacDonald's earlier stories, is black, erratic, and appears finally to be nearly impotent against the forces of evil. (p. 14)

*The Lost Princess* and *The Princess and Curdie* are the last major fairy tales MacDonald wrote for children, and in both of them joyfulness of the early tales has been replaced by a grim, apocalyptic gloom. Magic is powerless against evil, which partially triumphs in *The Lost Princess* and at the end of *The Princess and Curdie* sweeps everything before it. The two heroines of *The Lost Princess* are the very opposite of the lovely Princess Irene of *The Princess and the Goblin.* Unlike Rosamond and Agnes, Irene believes completely in her great-great-grandmother, who lives at the top of the staircase; she puts herself unquestioningly in her care and follows wherever her magic thread leads. Those who admire MacDonald for Irene and for Diamond, the gentle boy of *At the Back of the North Wind,* might very well be put off by the harshness of *The Lost Princess.* That would be a pity, for despite the sharp change of mood from the earlier fairy tales, *The Lost Princess* abounds in MacDonald's wildly beautiful imagery. There are the familiar unearthly landscapes, the subtlety and seriousness with which he analyzes his characters' thoughts and feelings.

Best of all, there is MacDonald's extraordinary evocation of the dream, as astonishing and as true as ever. Beyond providing the personal motif of his works, the dream offered MacDonald freedom to examine his emotions behind a screen sufficiently remote and fantastic to safeguard his mid-Victorian audience from shock. Even more important, he shared the views of the early German Romantic writers, particularly Novalis and E.T.A. Hoffmann, whom he most admired. These pre-Freudian artists rebelled against the prevalent attitude that dreams were merely the meaningless rumblings of the brain. They equated dreams with emotional truths and imagination, and Novalis contended that life would have meaning only when it attained the spiritual, poetic truth of the dream. Rosamond, the lost princess, only begins to find herself in the mood—or dream—chambers of the Wise Women.

MacDonald might have ended *The Lost Princess* with one of his favorite questions, from Novalis, a quotation he used as an epigraph for his first great fairy tale for adults, *Phantastes,* and which make up the closing words of his last book, the dream romance *Lilith:* "Our life is no dream, but it should and will perhaps become one." (p. 15)

Maurice Sendak, "The Depths of Fantasy," in Book Week—The Washington Post (© 1966, Washington Post Co.), July 24, 1966, pp. 14-15.

**IFOR EVANS**  (essay date 1966)

Macdonald's whole work shows him as a child of Victorian circumstance and opportunity: the emergence from strict religious discipline, with early educational struggles; the religious doubt, solved by rejecting old faiths for an amalgam of Browning, Carlyle, and such German philosophy as is within reach, and the cheerful but unsupported assumption that God approves of the change. He had passed through the whole of this spiritual saga and had an unusual talent for describing it in verse. Indeed, he possesses such metrical fluency that at moments one might suspect the presence of great poetry, but in reality both thought and verse possess a swollen wordiness. In his religious poems there appears rather the voice of exhortation than of experience, with some flavour of the enthusiasms of the 'confessional bench', while the lyrics, though bright with rhetorical phrases, are never illuminated by images that arrest and satisfy. Macdonald's popularity in his own age lay in his subject-matter and general metrical competence. While poetry was withdrawing away from life he was busy contriving readable verses on most of the important problems both of this life and of the future.

*Within and Without,* his one attempt at dramatic poetry, deals with such problems as the secular and religious life, love and marital fidelity, sin and the consciousness of sin, the possibility of the survival of good and of the reconciliation of divine elements in the future world. Quite naturally he finds that he has overcrowded his drama, and its numerous and disjointed scenes may be better described as a collection of dramatic episodes than as a play. Further, the thought is somewhat incongruously allied to the narrative basis: it is as if one of Byron's heroes had found himself in a Calderon play which had been finished by Browning in one of his more sentimental moods. Despite all inadequacies, the early scenes which describe Count Julian's desertion of the monastery have a sense of power in exploring spiritual dilemmas, and nothing in his later work equals the best passages in this play. *Poems* . . . , apart from the well-contrived verse autobiography, *A Hidden Life,* contains a series of poems on the women of the New Testament. This metrical presentation of Biblical narrative is a device as old as Anglo-Saxon poetry, when its practical value was more obvious. In Macdonald these pieces have the qualities that an uneducated reader of simple piety would appreciate, but they lack any revelation of blood and tears in fresh-found words and melodies. Though this religious verse remains a dominant element in Macdonald's later poetry, it is varied with many other interests. In *The Disciple* . . . he writes a number of Scots songs and ballads which have heartiness and rollicking movement seldom discoverable in his English verse. Like Stevenson, he seems, in his own tongue, to penetrate to some parts of his nature, humorous, satiric, which he can never release in English. His Jacobite ancestry seems to take possession of him in such a full-blooded ballad as *The Yerl of Waterydeck,* while there is a roguish humour which did not appear in the English verses in *The Waesome Carl.* . . . His last and most ambitious poem was *A Book of Strife, in the form of The Diary of an Old Soul* . . . , where he attempts in rime royal to trace a spiritual experience, month by month for a year. Rhetorically competent, these verses have a sermonizing quality that infects their value as a record of poignant religious anguish. In 1876 he had published a volume of verse translations, possessing the same interests and sources of suggestion which govern many of his own poems. Schiller, Goethe's lyrical poetry are here, and Novalis, who had contributed to the conception of *Phantastes,* also a translation of Luther's *Hymn Book,* which reads exactly like Macdonald's own religious poems.

In his poetry one always seems to be on the threshold of great things, but his thought is ever giving way to self-caressing complacency. Even in his religious poems, when there is thunder and storm on the stage we feel that he is already in the wings preparing the inevitable and happy conclusion. His lyrical verses rise at times into short passages that have the compelling power of the imagination, but he does not maintain this strenuousness. . . . One wishes that the Jacobite ancestor could have dominated him more often and allowed him, in writing more Scottish ballads, to have grown into a greater poet. (pp. 308-11)

> Ifor Evans, "Minor Poets, I: George Macdonald, Robert Buchanan, David Gray, Gerald Massey, Alexander Anderson, Joseph Skipsey," in his English Poetry in the Later Nineteenth Century *(by permission of Barnes & Noble Books, a Division of Littlefield, Adams & Co., Inc.), revised edition, Barnes & Noble, 1966, pp. 307-25.\**

## DENIS DONOGHUE  (essay date 1967)

George MacDonald and Lewis Carroll were friends, but their writings have little in common. . . . Carroll's art is Nonsense, MacDonald's is fairy-tale: the difference is fundamental. In *The Field of Nonsense* Elizabeth Sewell gives the rules of the Carroll game. The first rule is that Nonsense is a closed system, which delights in minding its own business. Part of this business is to exclude many respectable considerations and values which, outside the system, are properly acknowledged. In Nonsense, Miss Sewell observes, "all the world is paper and all the seas are ink." So the touch of nature which makes the whole world kith and kin destroys, in Nonsense, the whole pack of cards . . . . The aim of Nonsense is "to make the mind create for itself a more orderly universe," more like symbolic logic, that bachelor science, to be precise. Telegrams and anger are replaced by numbers, progressions, one and one and one and one and one. The effects are bound to be insidious, subversive, considered from any standpoint in the sensual world, and the perpetrator is bound to be manic. . . . [In MacDonald's] fiction there are numbers, but they are always amenable to other persuasions, love, fear, the desire and pursuit of the good. There are also dreams, but dreams are important in MacDonald's fiction only for their influence upon the quality of the dreamer's waking hours, his decisions and actions thereafter. . . .

So the motive for fairy tale is the motive for metaphor, the exhilaration of change. You like metaphor, Wallace Stevens says in an exemplary poem, when you want things to change, when you particularly want them to change to you, as if a cripple were to sing. The particular change that MacDonald wanted was a change of character, as he wanted people to be different by being better. This is the flow of feeling between his sermons, metaphors, novels, and fairy tales. Metaphor is

the shortest way of getting out of Manchester, the quickest answer to the Industrial Revolution. Some of the evidence is contained in **"A Manchester Poem,"** one of his most revealing compositions. "Slave engines utter again their ugly growl," he says, but every "marvellous imperfection" points ahead to "higher perfectness than heart can think." The strange feature of the poem is that it is so deeply committed to metaphor and change that Paradise itself, because it is the End, is deemed to be improper. To MacDonald it was far more important, because far more human, to travel hopefully than to arrive. He turns away from first and last things, preferring drama to eschatology. . . . The problem is to endow the Good Life with the right metaphors of action. In several stories we hear of "the place where the end of the rainbow stands," clearly the same place as "the back of the North Wind" and "the country from which the shadows come," but there is always a suggestion that this place is worthy because of the aspiration, the energy, it engenders; and that its finality is its defect. Heaven is inferior to Nature, MacDonald goes to the brink of implying, because Heaven is changeless and Nature is always changing. His parishioners were right, MacDonald's sermons are short of doctrine.

Emerson is relevant. . . . The supernatural tinge which Emerson gives to his descriptions of Nature is more evident in him than in MacDonald, but even to MacDonald the strongest justification of a change of character is featured in the constantly changing appearances of Nature. Magic is the equivalent of all the possibilities of ethical change, brought together in a single dramatic power. . . . Darwin is good medicine. In Emerson and in MacDonald Nature is also featured as discipline, because she contains and therefore presumably knows all the answers. MacDonald's *The Lost Princess* is often read as a moral tract, the point being that children should never be pampered. But its power as a story depends upon MacDonald's sense of natural forces working behind or beneath the maxim; forces far in excess of the moral occasion, but working in its behalf. North Wind has more business in hand than merely to push Diamond or Old Sal in the right direction. The point about Princess Rosamond and the shepherd-child Agnes in *The Lost Princess* is only incidentally that they are both spoiled brats. Rather it is that their young lives are perverse and unnatural, because deprived of the discipline of natural power. This is what the Wise Woman knows, so she takes the children away for their own good. Nature is a foster parent, better than the original. MacDonald's stories reach far and wide and deep because, especially in *The Golden Key* and the Curdie books, they imply a lively set of forces which can get out of hand, at least for a time.

Here again MacDonald differs from Lewis Carroll. William Empson, as usual, makes a good point about the Alice books. Carroll shared the Wordsworthian feeling that children are wiser than us because they are "in the right relation to Nature"; being right about life, the young girl can afford to be independent. Perhaps we might add that this independence is Carroll's way of urging a certain disengagement from Nature's apron-strings. If the child is right, to start with, there is no need to keep fussing. MacDonald was inclined to fuss. He believed that adults are better than children because they have been active longer. Lying in Abraham's bosom is not enough. The narrator is a good teacher because he is gifted in reading natural signs, alive to the metaphorical possibilities and the force they contain. The only advantage children have is that the likelihood of becoming adults still stretches ahead of them. There is a right way, there is a wrong way, children must be taught the difference. So MacDonald saw his work as the collusion of an adult with Nature for the guidance of children, bringing them along. "The whole system of the universe," he says in one of his sermons, "works upon this law—the driving of things upwards towards the centre." Everything in his books is on the move, because to stop is to despair. Battles are great occasions, especially in *The Princess and Curdie* where the King's forces include the great Uglies and the birds, all striving for the Good. The books are Sermons on the Mount. Diamond reaches for the sky. Curdie, attacked by a flock of birds, is defended by Lina, an animal on its way to become a child. The worm strives to be man. Much of MacDonald's symbolism is based on this figure: stairs, winding paths, mountains, excelsior, excelsior. The only way to live, moment by moment, is in aspiration. With the right metaphors, conspiring with natural change, we can then enjoy what he calls in *Sir Gibbie* "the holy carelessness of the eternal *now*." Magic is Faith. When Curdie has let himself become stupid and insensitive, killing harmless things like pigeons, Nature rebukes him:

> Suddenly everything round about him seemed against him. The red sunset stung him; the rocks frowned at him. . . .

There is a passage in *The Princess and Curdie* which seems to refute this symbolism but, in fact, confirms it. When Curdie reaches the castle he sees the great staircase and he knows that to reach the tower he must go further. The narrator takes the occasion to say that "those who work well in the depths more easily understand the heights, for indeed in their true nature they are one and the same. . . ." The goblins are evil and their home is underground, but the miners are good because they work well in the depths, the King's servants. If the King's palace is at the top of the mountain it is necessary to redeem the lower places. MacDonald does this by an ethic of content, Christian humility. Curdie is a good miner, so "from knowing the ways of the king's mines, and being able to calculate his whereabouts in them, [he] was now able to find his way about the king's house." The social equivalent comes later when the Lady of Light says to Peter: "I am poor as well as rich . . . I, too, work for my bread. . . ."

Mostly, this pastoral consolation is given in familial images. There is an especially ingenuous poem called **"The Golden Key,"** in MacDonald's *Parables,* about a boy, caught in a storm, trying to find the golden key. Darkness falls, he goes home, his mother kisses him, and

> Soon, things that are and things that
>                    seem
> Did mingle merrily;
> He dreamed, nor was it all a dream,
> His mother had the key.

The available force is called Love, a word which MacDonald pays extra because, like Humpty Dumpty, he makes it do a lot of work. North Wind is Mother. "Love makes everything lovely," MacDonald writes in *Alec Forbes;* "hate concentrates itself on the one thing hated." To Emerson the spirit of Nature is Father; to MacDonald, Mother. Either way, there can be no final evil. In MacDonald's stories the local evils are considerable, especially when they are our own construction, like Mr. Vane's house which falls upon him in *Lilith. At the Back of the North Wind* is particularly keen in its suggestion of the power of darkness. Among MacDonald's stories it is the one which most vigorously implies the world of Industrial Revolution, crying for Love, metaphor, and the Factory Acts. Sal

the gin-crone and the drunken cabman stay in the mind longer than North Wind's ostensible cruelties, which are rationalized in the usual way. When North Wind is rebuked by Diamond for sinking the ship, she tells him that behind the cries from the drowning ship she hears the sound of a far-off song in which every cry is reconciled. Diamond does not protest. At the end of *Phantastes* MacDonald says that "what we call evil is the only and best shape which, for the person and his condition at the time, could be assumed by the best good." Ideally, evil consumes itself; as the goblins, trying to flood the King's palace, are drowned in the flood. When the people in *The Princess and Curdie* choose a bad King, he plunders the mountain for gold, and the mountain, caving in, destroys the palace. Then there is nothing. The country is given back to the wild deer, "and the very name of Gwyntystorm . . . ceased from the lips of men." But the deer will strive upward, presumably, in their season.

It is customary to say, with Professor Tolkien, that "Death is the theme that most inspired George MacDonald." But it is a hard point to establish. His work is not very Grimm. Besides, he could always treat death as he treated evil, taking the harm out of it. *The Golden Key* is the classic text. The action of the book is the convergence of the boy Mossy and the girl Tangle. For a long time their stories are separate. They meet, about halfway through the book, only to lose each other again. Tangle's adventures bring her to meet an air-fish, then the Old Man of the Sea, the Old Man of the Earth, and a naked child who turns out to be the Old Man of the Fire. "Follow that serpent," the Man of Fire says, "He will lead you the right way" . . . to the country from which the shadows come. Meanwhile Mossy, who has found the key, is searching for the appropriate lock. After sundry incidents he meets the same Old Man of the Sea. "You have tasted of death now," the Old Man says, "Is it good?" "It is good," Mossy answers, "It is better than life." "No," the Old Man says, "it is only more life." . . . True, the story can be glossed as MacDonald's refusal to think of his favorite metaphors languishing in the Fortunate Fields, their work done. If life loses the name of action it loses itself, and to MacDonald no prize, however Elysian, is worth the loss. So it is natural for him to think of death as merely more life, carrying the figures of action beyond the grave. The Old Man of the Sea is the guardian of this idiom.

Of the other books, *The Princess and Curdie* is unusual in its impression of finality, writing "Finis." More often we are meant to hear: "To be Continued in our Next." This is the impression of *The Golden Key,* as of *North Wind* and *The Lost Princess.* MacDonald is happiest, after all, in the "sensuality of the shade," working, acting, choosing. His most characteristic work is a form of cooperation, participation in natural energies which are deemed to be already working in the field. Think of that serpent, in *The Golden Key,* which the Man of Fire creates to lead Tangle to the shadowy place. The dramatic invention at that point in the story, so easy and fluent, implies full confidence in the metaphorical resources of Nature and confidence, hardly less full, in the poetic imagination, Metaphor, metamorphosis, invention, Nature as the Aeolian lyre: the imaginative unity of MacDonald's work relies upon these fictions. Thinking of these figures we think of literature according to Coleridge, who in "The Aeolian Harp" invokes *"the one Life within us and abroad, / Which meets all motion and becomes its soul."* The idiom is sufficiently active to suit MacDonald, and may be allowed to stand as another gloss. (pp. 35-6)

Denis Donoghue, "The Other Country," in The New York Review of Books *(reprinted with permission from* The New York Review of Books; *copyright © 1967 Nyrev, Inc.), Vol. IX, No. 11, December 21, 1967, pp. 34-6.*

**GLENN EDWARD SADLER** (essay date 1971)

[*The editor of several recent collections of MacDonald's stories, Sadler examines the specific elements of MacDonald's work which mark him as a progenitor of the twentieth-century Christian Romantic tradition.*]

Because I believe MacDonald to be the nineteenth-century innovator of the current revived interest in fantasy literature, represented by the Oxford Christians and others, I should like to trace the emergence of his Christianized Romantic idea, so admirably rediscovered by C. S. Lewis. In MacDonald's ten-volume **Works of Fancy and Imagination** . . . we have, it seems to me, the modern beginnings of a fantasy school—if we can suppose that one now exists—which has its mimetic roots in the Blue Flower tradition of the English-German Romantic poets. (p. 216)

In *Surprised by Joy* Lewis tells us that before he was six years old he was seized by an insatiable longing which seemed, like the deep pain of incurable Delight, endless. Following Novalis and MacDonald, he later became "a votary of the Blue Flower." Novalis, describing this romantic sensation, calls it "homesickness, an impulse to be at home everywhere." . . . This religious syndrome of Desire or *Sehnsucht* gave birth to the imagination of all three men. They envisioned it simply as Nature's maternal "home-centre," where lived the Landlord and his Son, feared by John in Lewis's *Pilgrim's Regress.* MacDonald depicts this archetypal image well in his verse-parable **"The Hills"**:

> For I am always climbing hills,
>     From the known to the unknown—
> Surely, at last, on some high peak,
>     To find my Father's throne. . . .

To objectify the spiritual implications of this common Christian scene through natural images and symbols is the central purpose of everything MacDonald and Lewis wrote; it is what kept Anodos in Fairyland.

**Phantastes,** like most dream romances, is peopled by the disguised inhabitants of the imagination. Its title, taken from Canto vi of Phineas Fletcher's *Purple Island,* and the two lines which MacDonald extracts from it—

> Phantastes from "their fount" all shapes deriving,
>     In new habiliments can quickly dight

—hint at a seething array of semi-material beings, all of which "can quickly dight" themselves before us. We discover a colorful cosmology of talkative (sometimes ornery) garden flower-fairies, greedy and kind tree-spirits, a voluptuous marble maiden, dancing statues, a beautiful-wise old woman, an ominous Shadow, and other lively citizens of Faerie. The eye-catching power of **Phantastes** is derived, at the start, from the speed and smoothness of the transformations and from its teasing symbolism throughout. With wide sweeps MacDonald crosses in Chapter i the "peach-colored" horizon of morning slumber and manages in three short pages in Chapter ii to skillfully shift Anodos ("pathless") from his Victorian bedroom, with its green marble washbasin and heavily carved black oak dresser, to the timeless "path into Fairy Land." Thus Anodos—followed by Lewis's John—leaves the land of Puritania. Both are overcome, however, like Novalis's Hyacinth, by the sickness of the young man's quest: "'I must away to a foreign land!' he said: 'the strange old woman in the wood has told me what I must do to get well. . . .'" (pp. 217-18)

Perhaps every poet, especially a writer of fairytales, has his own symbolic vision of life's tale with which he delights young and old alike. The Romantic poets cradled theirs in dreams. . . . Perhaps the greatest dream of all . . . is the *Märchen* of Eternal Youth. Without it Romanticism could not exist. It is difficult, in fact, to think of any dream-world in which a handsome youth does not eventually meet and wed his Rosebud. This Romantic ideal, with its optimistic longing, nurtured the imagination of the Blue-Flower offspring. Sexual desire pursued them all. Alastor, for instance, is driven to destruction by the "veiled maid" who in a dream sequence confronts him with the poet's ideal of relentless satisfaction. She appears, fleetingly, to Anodos as his "white lady" and, also in a dream, to Lewis's John as his "divinely fair" Media. . . . The pursuit of her is the theme of **Phantastes**.

MacDonald's **Phantastes** is a poet's artistic diary of youthful dreams. Like Lewis's *Pilgrim's Regress,* it is the record of a young man's spiritual contest with the "false objects" which taunt his thirst for the fulfillment of "Sweet Desire." Both Anodos and John search bravely for a realization in their actual life of dream-world aspirations. Both must forsake parental ties. (pp. 219-20)

MacDonald's imagination was, Lewis notes, haunted by "the image of a great house." It became his Cosmic Image of life. Within this lofty "half castle, half farmhouse" (or sometimes in a magical hut) an inquisitive, lonely, and spiritually orphaned child learned some of life's hardest lessons. A certain Norman castle was, I believe, the boyhood source of MacDonald's imaginative house of instruction. Frequently as a bairn in Huntly, Aberdeenshire, he had visited it. (p. 221)

Consistently we sense in MacDonald's best poems and tales of fantasy a certain Scottish clannishness—"a warm atmosphere," as he defined it in his parable **"The Castle,"** "like the children of a household when the mother is at home." The vision of his own family always securely "at home" continued to be MacDonald's source of literary inspiration. Whenever he wrote fairytales, there were children at his feet or sleeping nearby. (p. 222)

MacDonald's literary career is marked by periods of spiritual introspection and unrest. **Phantastes** is, as I have suggested, an imaginative journey into MacDonald's poetic consciousness. In a sense it is his fortress of dreams. Anodos's fear of his shadow-self and at the end his heroic fight against the worshippers of apostate religion reflect conflicts dating from MacDonald's own student days at King's College. . . . [Though] the natural and intellectual austerity at King's sparked his active imagination, neither his mastery of chemistry and natural philosophy nor the dissenting sermons he heard on Sunday adequately filled his need for spiritual kinship with the universe. There rose in him waves of melancholy and anxiety which never totally subsided. . . . Later, in a suicidal moment MacDonald would send Anodos into the deep. . . . (pp. 222-23)

Death, its sensations and significance, drives Anodos onward. Through dying he learns "that it is by loving, and not by being loved, that one can come nearest to the soul of another." . . . MacDonald's Shelleyan sea-flight produced, however, unlike

Alastor's, deep religious commitment; it fostered Anodos's unguarded belief "that good is always coming; though few have at all times the simplicity and the courage to believe it." . . . In poetry, MacDonald told of his call to discipleship.

MacDonald's first published poem **"David,"** in 1846, typifies his early excitement over religious themes, this time the theme of a broken family. In a blank-verse narrative of 114 lines he describes the grief-stricken King David who, having lost his son Absalom, wanders aimlessly through the "desolate streets" of dark conscience. Finally David sees in a vision the restored filial scene. . . . In 1855, after his marriage to Miss Louisa Powell, MacDonald repeated the child-son-ship theme in his verse-drama *Within and Without,* a five-act operatic poem in which he treats the inner strife between dedication to an active intellectual life and outward duty to his wife and child. . . . This vigorous search for a balance between intellectual aspiration and filial duty continues as the mainspring of MacDonald's poetic imagination.

In 1857 MacDonald published his first collection of poems. Included in it are narratives on love, age, and death, parables of fanciful excursions (one to find the Grail), other lyrics on traditional subjects, sonnets on the nature of Jesus Christ, and sixteen devotional poems on New Testament women. In its diversity of themes and versification, *Poems* is what one would expect from a beginning poet. By far the best poem in the collection is MacDonald's semi-autobiographical narrative on his student days, **"A Hidden Life,"** in which he returns to his family theme: a Scottish farmer's son discovers the world of thought and aesthetics through his visionary encounter with a beautiful lady. Aside from its poetic merits, **"A Hidden Life"** has sections revealing what I think is MacDonald's greatest talent, his childlike fascination with the spirit of living things. All of MacDonald's major poems (and frequently passages in his prose) have in them Wordsworth's universal spirit and Shelley's windblown child. It is the visionary and moralist perfectly balanced: the "hidden life" of the imagination speaking without offense. . . . And it is this emergent myth of Christian cosmology proliferated through Romantic symbolism which, I believe, dominated Lewis's mind and imagination as he read *Phantastes.* (pp. 223-25)

Every fairytale must have, I suppose, some kind of ending. MacDonald's is graphically given in *Lilith,* his "A Tale of the Seventh Dimension," as it was subtitled in its shortened manuscript version. The theme of *Lilith* is conversion. We are introduced to Mr. Vane (Anodos on his return journey through Fairyland), this time to rescue the Little Ones from their depraved giant kin and from Lilith the night queen, snatcher of babies and Adam's rebellious first wife. Throughout the tale MacDonald interweaves his strong belief in the immortality of all creation. At the end, in "The Waking," Adam exults:

> Hark to the golden cock! Silent and motionless
> for millions of years has he stood on the clock
> of the universe; now at last he is flapping his
> wings! now will he begin to crow! and at in-
> tervals will men hear him until the dawn of the
> day eternal. . . .

Such golden passages are balanced by equally fine scenes of Dantesque grotesqueness; for example the glittering moonlit "Gruesome Dance" of the skeletons in the pinewood hall or Lilith's struggle against repentance, symbolized by her tightly ingrowing hand which Adam severs. Admittedly *Lilith* is overcrowded with religious symbols (at times so is Dante's *Divine Comedy*); and yet, there is nothing written in the nineteenth century to equal, I think, its rapturous portrayal of resurrection life. There are passages in it, in fact, which almost break into poetry. To awaken into the *real* life was MacDonald's fairytale ending; thus he quoted from Novalis: "Our life is no dream, but it should and will perhaps become one."

I have taken considerable space to discuss MacDonald's poetry, because it is there and in his fantasies that one finds the sources of his genius. What Lewis has defined as MacDonald's "pure vision" appears only occasionally in his novels—although there are sections there which sparkle with it—but MacDonald's greatest literary claim is not, I am convinced, that of a novelist. Primarily he is, as Louis MacNeice has suggested, a "parable writer" [see excerpt above]. ". . . In the realm of parable writing no one went further than MacDonald," says MacNeice, "in the whole of the nineteenth century." He will be remembered, I think, as the founder of a modern circle of fantasy writers all of whom use, in varying degrees, the parable form. *Phantastes* and *Lilith* will stand as touchstones of the fantasy craft in fiction. Finally, MacDonald gave to Lewis, Charles Williams, and Tolkien their simple definition of the function of the imagination—the definition he quoted in his *A Cabinet of Gems* . . . from Sir Philip Sidney:

> With a tale forsooth the poet cometh unto you,
> with a tale which holdeth children from play,
> and old men from the chimney-corner; and pre-
> tending no more, doth intend the winning of
> the mind from wickedness to virtue.

(pp. 226-27)

*Glenn Edward Sadler, "The Fantastic Imagination in George MacDonald," in* Imagination and the Spirit: Essays in Literature and the Christian Faith Presented to Clyde S. Kilby, *edited by Charles A. Huttar (copyright © 1971 by William B. Eerdmans Publishing Company; used by permission), Eerdmans, 1971, pp. 215-27.*

**RICHARD H. REIS**   (essay date 1972)

From time to time, MacDonald produced short fairy tales for children, mostly to be featured in *Good Words for the Young,* a magazine which he edited for a while early in his professional career. Some of these little stories are rather wooden and trivial in both conception and execution, written as they were under the pressure of printers' deadlines and without waiting for inspiration to strike; but the fact is that most such works are very good indeed of their kind; for, even with a deadline looming over him, MacDonald was capable of astonishing brilliance, charm, and subtlety. Most of these shorter works for children were, in time, collected into anthologies, of which the earliest was entitled *Dealings with the Fairies.* . . . (pp. 75-6)

**"The Light Princess,"** longest and one of the most fascinating of MacDonald's shorter fairy stories, is remarkable both for its humor and for what appears to be, in the humorous context, a rather incongruous sexual motif. In this tale, a princess is deprived at birth by a nasty witch of her "gravity." MacDonald puns on the word by having the princess lose both her weight and the ability to take anything seriously. Her chief pleasure is to swim in a lake nearby, where she seems to have weight of a sort and to be free of the inconvenience of forever floating up to the ceiling unless held down. When a prince falls in love with the princess and joins her in her swims, the witch resolves to spoil the girl's new-found happiness. With the aid of a snake, the witch tunnels beneath the lake and begins to drain its water through a hole in the bottom that has been drilled by the malevolent serpent. Simultaneously, all the springs and rivers of the kingdom stop giving water, all rain ceases, and a drought threatens. Indeed, the drainage of the lake can be stopped only if some man will plug up the hole with his body; and, in the manner of all fairy-tale heroes, the prince volunteers. As the lake begins to refill, it threatens to drown the hero. For a while, the princess cannot take even this martyrdom seriously; but, just as the prince is about to drown, she screams in terror and pulls him from the hole. Her action breaks all of the spells: she regains her weight, she weeps for days, and the springs are restored.

As Robert Lee Wolff remarks, "some psychoanalysts would no doubt have a field day with this story." Sexual symbolism is easy to unearth and impossible to ignore—the phallic snake, the man's plugging the hole with his body, and so forth—but it need not be insisted upon. The Wasteland motif, so familiar to the twentieth-century consciousness since Eliot's poem was written, is also present, with its implicit equation between vegetative and sexual sterility. Here, the drought is identified with the absence of tears, and thus with the child's inability to face the troubles of life with the "gravity" of adulthood.

The entire story is, in fact, a parable of puberty. When the princess has married her prince, MacDonald pictures her looking back nostalgically to her gravityless childhood: "It was a long time before she got reconciled to walking. She had always drifted lightly through the air until that time. But the pain of learning was quite counterbalanced by two things, either of which would have been sufficient consolation. The first was that the Prince himself was her teacher; and the second was that she could tumble into the lake as often as she pleased." Perhaps this reference is to the relative sexual license of the married state, just as the entire story is designed to convince children that sooner or later childhood's frivolity must be abandoned for the sake of mature seriousness, which has its own rewards, as Wordsworth's "Immortality Ode" points out. (pp. 76-7)

[Several] of the motifs in **"The Light Princess"** reappear in several of MacDonald's later fantasies. The equation between the infertile Wasteland and a child's reluctance to grow up into a world of tears crops up again, most notably in *Lilith*. (pp. 77-8)

In another remarkable story for children, **"The Golden Key,"** a boy and a girl set out separately on journeys to fairyland, meet on the way, go through a series of odd adventures both together and apart, and at the end are apparently united in the Other World. Mossy, the boy, finds a golden key at the foot of a rainbow and searches through fairyland for the lock which it will fit. Wolff's Freudian orientation leads him to insist that the key is Mossy's phallus, and he concludes that the fairy wise woman of the story is only being practical when she assures Tangle, the heroine, that it is safe to accompany a man who has a key—who is potent. But Wolff adds: "If this were all . . . would we not find the story banal? We must read **'The Golden Key,'** however, at other levels: the key may stand for the poetic imagination, for warmth and kindness, for religious faith, for love: any or all of these are talismans which a man may not fully know how to use, but whose mere possession makes it safe for a woman to accompany him." (p. 78)

The important point about **"The Golden Key"** is not its sexual undertones but its vastness of scope. In it, MacDonald manages to incorporate a great many of the salient ideas which he expresses in his sermons and essays and to utilize nearly every device in the repertoire of symbolic technique.

The tale lacks the coherence of **"The Light Princess"**; instead, it is what Auden calls a "chain adventure story." From an apparently vast store of invention, MacDonald throws into the story many incidents which are intriguing in themselves but which would not subvert the plot (if it can be called that) if one or the other were omitted, and which are related to each other only by the fact that they happen to the same two characters, Mossy and Tangle. Each such adventure is described in a delicate, evocative, haunting style which contrasts remarkably with that of the pedestrian, conventional novels. (pp. 78-9)

In addition to the two superb stories I have outlined above, MacDonald wrote other short works for children which are of nearly equal brilliance, though perhaps not of equal subtlety and evocativeness. **"The Carasoyn"** is a delightful trip through a world of toy ships and brownies into which a child is suddenly projected. In **"The History of Photogen and Nycteris"** the symbolism of light and darkness is developed at some length and with considerable, if somewhat labored, metaphysical subtlety. The hero, Photogen (*phos, genea:* light-bearing), and the heroine, Nycteris (*nyktos, eris:* night-striving), represent the opposites of knowledge and ignorance, respectively. Nycteris is especially well named in that she illustrates the proper attitude of the ignorant: to *strive* amid darkness, in accordance with MacDonald's educational imperative to the effect that in ignorance a person must *do* the little he knows to be right, in confidence that in so doing the next step will become clear.

Others of the short children's stories are similarly suggestive but are less inspired. . . . Although most of these works are entertaining enough, none ever reaches the brilliance of **"The Light Princess"** or **"The Golden Key."**

MacDonald wrote four book-length fairy stories for children, and all but one of them continue to be popular in the twentieth century. Of *The Princess and the Goblin*, which is generally considered the best of these, Auden says that it is "the only English children's book in the same class as the Alice books" [see excerpt above]. (pp. 80-1)

Neither the plot nor the particular incidents can be regarded as very remarkable; but the image of the castle with underground chambers and with a holy force in the attic stays with the reader. The transformation which this typical setting undergoes when the reader passes from the novels to this story for children is astounding: the setting becomes a powerful symbol rather than a mere piece of Gothic claptrap full of spooks and fiends or of hidden family secrets. The Freudian hierarchy of ego (the Princess), superego (the Fairy Grandmother in the attic), and id (the Goblins in the basement) is obvious enough; and their presence reflects MacDonald's independent discovery of these phenomena. But, when symbolically presented, the triad becomes more compelling and convincing than in either Freud's tomes or in MacDonald's own essay, **"A Sketch of Individual Development,"** where the same concepts are presented in straightforward terms.

Apparently encouraged by the success of *The Princess and the Goblin*, MacDonald wrote a sequel to it, *The Princess and Curdie*. . . . Like most sequels, *The Princess and Curdie* lacks the power of its predecessor, although its picture of a corrupt society is penetrating and effective. The work's chief symbolic significance lies in its implicit treatment of political and civic corruption and in the cellars of the capital which equal the underground labyrinths of other MacDonald books in their sinister quality. (pp. 81-2)

[*At the Back of the North Wind* is] one of MacDonald's most impressive works for children, and one which I am in the minority in somewhat preferring even to *The Princess and the Goblin*, excellent as the latter is. Unlike the other full-length children's stories, this one has a very real setting, though the events are not "realistic" in the ordinary sense of the word. The setting is London sometime during the middle of the nineteenth century, and the characters are mostly poor people.

Little Diamond, the child-hero, is so very good and innocent that most worldly folk think him absent-minded or even feeble-minded. . . . Among Diamond's London friends is a little girl who sweeps crossings for the gentry, and whose earnings are stolen by her mother to buy gin. . . . The setting in general is comparable to the first part of Charles Kingsley's *Water Babies*, which was published eight years earlier and which may have suggested the idea to MacDonald; but, whereas Kingsley's chimneysweep suffers the cruelties of slaving for the owners of English country houses, Diamond and the little girl undergo the complementary cruelties of the city. As does Kingsley, MacDonald takes his child from a bitter life in this world to another, better existence through the door of ostensible "death."

Perhaps the most remarkable thing about *At the Back of the North Wind* is that MacDonald is trying, in fact, to justify death, that most inscrutable of the ways of God, to children. Diamond falls ill and nearly dies when exposed to the North Wind in winter through a crack near his bed over the stable. His coma is explained as the result of the fact that his spirit is journeying to the "hyperborean regions," an idea taken from Herodotus. The North Wind, personified as a woman who takes Diamond on a sort of guided tour through her domains, is also the force which brings death. (pp. 82-3)

MacDonald tries to explain to his child readers that death is not an end but a departure to another place which is a good deal more pleasant than the poverty in which Diamond had "lived." Here we have, perhaps, a seminal difference between the children's classics of the nineteenth century and the wishy-washy stories fed to the children in our own time: a hundred years ago a MacDonald *faced* the bitter fact of death and made his readers face it, while the authors of children's stories today seem, with a well-meaning but rather fatuous effort, to avoid subjecting their readers to "traumas"; and they expend their efforts in *denying* the reality of life's grimmer side.

And *At the Back of the North Wind* has a most peculiar attribute of plot, besides its bluntness of implicit content, to distinguish it from most saccharine books for children. Diamond, perhaps uniquely among the child-heroes of fairy tales, comes back again into this world after having had a glimpse of the Other World after death. This oddity is something present in *At the Back of the North Wind* that is absent from the otherwise similar *Water Babies* of Charles Kingsley (in which there is likewise a dual this-world, other-world setting and a blunt facing of death). The idea of trips to the other world sandwiched between returns to this is . . . typical of MacDonald and of some symbolic significance. (p. 84)

MacDonald's masterpieces are the two full-length, thoroughly symbolic fantasies for adults, *Phantastes* and *Lilith*. In these books, as in *The Princess and the Goblin, The Princess and the Curdie, At the Back of the North Wind*, "The Light Princess," and "The Golden Key," his symbolic techniques reach their

fullest realizations. Both *Phantastes* and *Lilith* are serious, exciting, richly textured, and crammed with astounding imaginative strokes. Because of their excellence, I draw most heavily upon these two works for examples of the typical devices found throughout MacDonald's imaginative fiction. Yet the two stories are in some respects very unlike each other, as might be expected from the fact that *Phantastes* was published in 1858 and *Lilith* in 1895. *Lilith* is darker and less triumphant, *Phantastes* more in the tradition of the heroic Romance whose hero succeeds in the end. They are even more different in plot: *Phantastes* is looser, less integrated, like "The Golden Key"; *Lilith* is more tightly constructed, like "The Light Princess." (pp. 86-7)

The word "Phantastes" is taken from the name of a character in Phineas Fletcher's early seventeenth-century Spenserian pastiche, *The Purple Island* (1633), but I have been able to discover no particular resemblance between Fletcher's work and MacDonald's. . . .

The protagonist and narrator of *Phantastes* is named Anodos, a Greek word usually interpreted as meaning "a way back." Wolff, however, states in *The Golden Key* that it means "pathless;" . . . either significance seems to fit the story, in that Anodos is a young man who does not know where he is going, and in that the story indicates his unknown goal as finding "a way back" to the guiltlessness of childhood. I personally suspect that MacDonald had "a way back" in mind, since that phrase occurs a couple of times in the text. (p. 87)

[Anodos enters] fairyland, where he undergoes a great many . . . dreamlike experiences. What may be called the "shape" of the plot is remarkably unstructured: episodes succeed one another without apparent causal relationship or interconnection (except insofar as they all happen to the same protagonist). The reader feels that the order of Anodos's adventures might often be shuffled without loss of coherence. The protagonist is generally traveling eastward, but a spatial as well as temporal rearrangement of his encounters would not be disturbing; we feel that he is not so much making progress in his spiritual education as simply adding to the *number* of his experiences. Along the way he stops overnight at a succession of houses, huts, cottages, and palaces which he conveniently arrives at just as the sun is setting. Many of these buildings are inhabited by middle-aged and old women who give Anodos advice and explain the nature of fairyland to him; he usually fails to heed or understand what they tell him, and then departs the next morning, none the wiser. *Phantastes* is what Auden calls a "chain adventure story," full of events which are strung out like beads on a string (the string being the central character, who alone connects the episodes) rather than interconnected into a tight network with every event and character connected by causality and relationship to every other. (p. 89)

Despite its loose organization, the plot of *Phantastes* does have a certain degree of coherence, provided by several devices. For one thing, it may be read as an allegorical representation of the first twenty-one years of Anodos's life. The story begins just after his twenty-first birthday, and at the end Anodos makes a significant remark upon returning to the real world and to his family: "I had been gone, they told me, twenty-one days. To me it seemed twenty-one years." Presumably, therefore, we are to read *Phantastes* as if each of its episodes corresponds to a childhood or youthful experience of its narrator—but this is not easy to do, since we have little information about the first twenty-one years of Anodos's life to compare with his possibly corresponding adventures in fairyland. Furthermore, as Professor Wolff insists, the story may possibly be read not merely as an analogical biography of Anodos but as an auto-biography of MacDonald himself. . . . At one point, Anodos forms an alliance with two other young men, sons of a local king, who "adopt" Anodos as a third brother. The three enter into a pact to rid the countryside of three giants who have been harassing the kingdom. Each kills a giant in the ensuing battle, but Anodos survives while the other two die as the giants do. This otherwise detached episode is, to anyone who has read the biography of George MacDonald, clearly an allegorical representation of the fact that George and his brothers Alec and John all contracted tuberculosis in their youth, and only George survived it. . . . But reading *Phantastes* as an auto-biographical allegory throughout would no doubt be unwise. MacDonald frequently expressed his distrust of mere allegory as sterile equation-mongering, and he could hardly have had an emotional experience precisely equivalent to *each* adventure of Anodos. . . . Nevertheless, the allegorical-autobiography aspect of the story does provide a suggestion of unity in a plot otherwise rather incoherent.

Another unifying aspect of the plot lies in the fact that several characters do reappear in different episodes, although most are met only once. The two most important of these are Sir Percivale, taken from the late medieval Arthurian Romances, and a young woman whom Anodos awakens into life and falls in love with. (pp. 90-1)

A third unifying factor is a rather frightening being called the Shadow. When visiting one of the many cottages inhabited by old women, Anodos is warned not to open the door of a mysterious-looking closet, but he neglects the warning. At once the Shadow engulfs him, and thereafter becomes a constant, sinister companion, blackening his view of the world. In *The Golden Key* . . . , Robert Lee Wolff equates it with the Doppelgänger of German folklore and traces several parallels in German Romantic literature. Whatever its origin, the Shadow becomes a symbol of great and sometimes rather confusing complexity, as it seems to acquire different meanings in different contexts. (pp. 91-2)

[Although] its symbolic meanings are multifold, there is a subtle unity among the significances of the Shadow; it comes to represent the complex relationships between guilt and innocence, humility and pride, courage and cowardice, living life and fleeing from it. Yet, since it is really a part of Anodos's self, the Shadow imparts only a minor unity to *Phantastes,* complementary to that provided by the fact that all the adventures happen to the same central character.

The loose, episodic plot of *Phantastes,* then, is not really tied together very well by the reappearance of characters like Percivale and the alabaster maiden, or of the symbolic Shadow. In many episodes, MacDonald appears to "forget" these unifying factors—even the Shadow—and seems to have included some incidents for the sake of mere excitement. I have mentioned several adventures which have considerable suggestiveness, imaginativeness, and symbolic resonance; but I have not mentioned many others which lack these qualities. The looseness and unevenness of *Phantastes* must be counted as defects, though in most respects the work is surely an excellent one. (pp. 93-4)

As *Phantastes* is the story of a young man, so *Lilith* is the old man's reemphasis of the same teachings found in the earlier work, colored more darkly now with the repeated disappointments and sufferings of MacDonald's long life. (p. 94)

The story of *Lilith* has a number of remarkable characteristics. The retracing of steps, including repeated visits to the "real world" and to the world of the children, the Bad Giants, and the Evil City, gives the plot a remarkable flavor, integrating it tightly. The Kabbalistic substratum makes it resonant with the echoes of immemorial legend. The repeated motifs—cats, skeletons, vampirism, water—are likewise resonant and echoing, acquiring added ominous significance with every recurrence. And perhaps the most striking attribute of *Lilith* is the fact that, at the end, its narrator has *not* attained ultimate transcendence; he only knows that there is such a thing after death, which he awaits patiently. There is no apotheosis—only an awaiting, a partial arrival at wherever Mr. Vane is destined to go.

Robert Lee Wolff is offended by this longing for death—which appears elsewhere in MacDonald—and condemns *Lilith* as a sermon of despair. But it is clear that MacDonald is advocating acceptance of *both* life and death, the latter as the God-given if bitter way to enlightenment and salvation. His very recognition of life's bitterness is, as it was for Kierkegaard, the absurd reason for his leap of faith. The very incompleteness of the ending is consistent with MacDonald's view that enlightenment is never complete in this life, though we may have dreams and fleeting visions of the better world, as Mr. Vane does. If *Lilith* fails (I do not think it does), it is not through discouraged pessimism but with the "failure" of Milton, who, like MacDonald, portrayed willful pride with such sympathy that he made himself, in Blake's words, "of the devil's party without knowing it." (p. 102)

*Richard H. Reis, in his* George MacDonald *(copyright © 1972 by Twayne Publishers, Inc.; reprinted with the permission of Twayne Publishers, A Division of G. K. Hall & Co., Boston), Twayne, 1972, 161 p.*

### ERIC S. RABKIN (essay date 1976)

To the Victorians, who saw children as the innocently wise, the notion that a person might regain childlike innocence, a notion approved by scripture, was a consoling thought indeed. MacDonald, even when writing for actual children, offers this consolation to the great mass of adults. . . . To assert in one's fiction, as MacDonald does, that a person can be redeemed through God's infinite Grace by a single acceptance of humility might be viewed not as the antinomian heresy but as a new substantiation of gospel truth. (pp. 101-02)

MacDonald's writings were and are popular, especially with the devout. For such people, [*At the Back of the North Wind* and *Phantastes*] . . . offer an escape from the dogma of their religion, but do not require a slackening of faith. As Thomas Gunn Selby, [a] theologian contemporary to MacDonald, wrote:

> To know the chief characters of George MacDonald's . . . books is a means of grace, although we may demur to some of the things in the theology taught.

The chief character of *At the Back of the North Wind* is a waif named Diamond who would gladden the mushy heart of Dickens. Diamond just plain doesn't understand bad language and he automatically makes up songs that calm the savagery of alcohol and quiet crying babies. The central question of the book is that of theodicy, and MacDonald's answer is simple: the North Wind (whose other name is never mentioned but we know it is Death) is revealed as a perfect servant of some higher good (again unnamed, again we know: God) and therefore the narrative action (in which the North Wind, personified as a lady, becomes Diamond's best friend) justifies the doctrine of the fortunate fall. The Hyperborean region is gotten to by going through death, and one dies into a better life of perfect communication, a fantastic reversal of human fears that echoes St. John of Patmos and predicts the later poetry of T. S. Eliot. As the narrator says in an interpolated original fairy tale called "Little Daylight," "I never knew of any interference on the part of a wicked fairy that did not turn out a good thing in the end." MacDonald is fully aware of the conventions of his fantastic genre and uses them to escape the difficult theological problem of evil: he takes the bold step of calling death the best thing in the world. If man does not see it that way, he has the wrong perspective. . . .

The consolation of MacDonald came from fantastic reversals and was an escape both from a world of social turmoil and the rigors of a religion that did not help to make that turmoil bearable. "'Surely,'" Diamond suggests, "'it is good to be afflicted.'"

One must make two points clear concerning MacDonald: first, he is a good writer; second, his theology has nearly won the day. MacDonald's style is characterized not only by a comforting, preaching kind of mysticism, but extraordinary description and ringing psychological insight. (pp. 104-05)

[MacDonald] had more theological strength than Lewis. He seemed, in going from books for adults to books for children, not to vary his underlying theology. *Phantastes* offers the same kind of consolations against death that we find in *At the Back of the North Wind*. Again we find that these consolations depend upon fantastic reversals of our normal perspectives: . . .

> With a presence I am smitten
> Dumb, with a foreknown surprise. . . .
>                                                    (pp. 106-07)

Like *At the Back of the North Wind*, *Phantastes* too has an interpolated fairy tale; *Phantastes* too has a main character (Anodos: he who finds the way up) whose powers are Orphic; *Phantastes* too takes consolation from the idea of dying into life. In the use of fairy tale, of the Orpheus myth, and of mystic rebirth, both these works are fantastic. The difference between the adult and the child literature does not reside in the uses of the fantastic. In the book intended for children, the main character is a boy who is innocent. His innocence is shown to be all powerful, and when at the end others think he is dead, the narrator says approvingly, "I knew that he had gone to the back of the north wind." In the book for adults, the main character, following his twenty-first birthday, undergoes a series of humbling visions that take twenty-one days. In the course of these he dies and is reborn childlike, not to the back of the north wind but into his non-visionary life. *Phantastes* implies that a person may regain blessed innocence. From a theological perspective, the books are the same. Since the escape from religion is offered most dramatically by the fantastic elements of the narrative, it is wholly fitting that the fantastic elements are not different in the two genres: MacDonald merely shows the adult and child version of the same thing. . . . Just as William Morris had offered an escape from history, both for children and for adults who would be as children, George MacDonald's Fantasies offered the Victorians an escape from their religion. (pp. 107-08)

> Eric S. Rabkin, *"The Fantastic and Perspective,"* in his The Fantastic in Literature *(copyright © 1976*

*by Princeton University Press; reprinted by permission of Princeton University Press), Princeton University Press, 1976, pp. 74-116.**

**FRANCIS RUSSELL HART** (essay date 1978)

For all their rich regional particularity, MacDonald's "novels" are actually theological romances, where the fantastic and the normal, the ideal and the real, are separated only by semivisible and shifting boundaries. Their characters are best described in his defense of Robert Falconer: "Those who are in the habit of regarding the real and the ideal as essentially and therefore irreconcilably opposed, will remark that I cannot have drawn the representation of Falconer faithfully." . . . Their subject, both romantic and theological, is the mystery of inheritance. As elsewhere in Victorian romance, the orphan and the disinherited are seeking their true fathers; but in MacDonald the search for the hidden father is the way of crisis and conversion that reveals the fatherhood of an immanent, hidden God. The innocence of the child—or more accurately, the childlike—preserved in older natures such as David Elginbrod embodies an ideal of fidelity to one's childhood simplicities, social, natural, intellectual, and linguistic (that is, northeast Scots). But the providential role of the incarnate childlike must be played in time in that place of deprivation, darkness, sin, and yet love, the city; and MacDonald's redeemers—Falconer, Gibbie, Malcolm, and David—are missionaries there. The role is perilous, but the loving Father is always nearby. Evil and suffering are necessary but unreal, hence uninteresting. Villainy lacks character, "for all wickedness tends to destroy individuality." This precept from *Alec Forbes* is an essential principle, both of MacDonald's theological morality and of his narrative characterology.

Those with the most character in his novels appear evil initially; they are the stern natures, fruits of a vigorous peasant tradition but victims of a corrupt pseudo-Calvinism, who must be overthrown by the divine vengeance of love. Such problematic characters give MacDonald's fiction its moral interest but also its modal ambiguity; they must play roles at once in a theological romance and in a drama of cultural process. They are spiritual archetypes and at the same time cultural-historical representatives, a mixture we see often in Scottish fiction. Moreover, in such a mixture the narrator must play both chronicler and prophet. His historical intentions are strongly homiletic, and he is vulnerable to the charge leveled at Malcolm in *The Marquis of Lossie:* "'You are like all the rest of the Scotch I ever knew,' said Lady Clementina: 'the Scotch are always preaching! I believe it is in their blood. You are a nation of parsons'." . . . (pp. 101-02)

His romances envision the transformation of stern natures by the providential agents of divine love and the assimilation of all hells on earth into a design for universal redemption. Such a vision is sure to offend at least two kinds of readers: neo-Calvinists, for whom it is theologically "soft," sentimentally liberal; and radical humanists, for whom it is socioeconomically conservative, neofeudal, even reactionary. (pp. 102-03)

*David Elginbrod* introduces themes and images that will become prominent in later, better novels. It rests, for example, on a vision of pastoral nature that is traced to Wordsworth but seems inspired more by Carlyle and German Romanticism. It celebrates and appeals to the childlike, though here the childlike is found in an old peasant whose wisdom is higher innocence. David serves as a spiritual archetype, but also as a cultural representative—the simple, learned Scots peasant—and as a literary type as well: "One evening, while reading *The Heart of Midlothian,* the thought struck [Hugh]—what a character David would have been for Sir Walter." . . . But the essential David is spirit. His influence is spiritual, even ghostly, for he functions in the book's Gothic parts as the benign ghost, whose spectral counterpart, the false mesmerist and magician Funkelstein, underlines by negative contrast the truth of David's influence. Though David is culturally representative, his example transcends cultural identity. Paradoxically, the book attacks "Scotch metaphysics" while celebrating the true metaphysical in David, distinguishes the truth of Calvin from a corrupt, sabbatarian Calvinism, and defends the cultural beauty of the Scots language against those in whom it is ugly or vulgar. For MacDonald the restoration of Scotland to its cultural truth demands a freeing of its theology and its culture from false idols. And the central figure in this process is one of MacDonald's stern natures.

The stern nature in **Robert Falconer,** . . . natural successor to **Elginbrod,** is Robert's grandmother, and she too is drawn with characteristic ambivalence—presented with cultural sympathy to an English audience and with theological disapproval to a Scottish one. . . . Her false religion condemns Robert's father and cuts Robert off from his natural inheritance. Robert moves through village and pastoral boyhood to an educational interlude in Aberdeen and finally to London, where his search for his father leads to a career as saintly, secular missionary of the streets.

His final wisdom is rooted still in "what lay at the root of his character, at the root of all he did, felt, and became . . . childlike simplicity and purity of nature." But, in this insistently typological book, his childhood is merely the type of a higher one. For a time his kite and his grandfather's violin are "full globated" symbols of a wondrous and deep glory; but his stern grandmother burns the violin, and the kite must be cut loose—and with it his childhood, a "feeble and necessarily vanishing type" of a "deeper and holier childhood." He loses his ideal lady to a more poetic soul, and must enter upon the "desert" of Teufelsdröckhian wanderings, where he is subject once more to the despair of his grandmother's theology. But the romance of his inheritance drives him to seek his lost father in London, where her false vision must give way to a new sense of humanity, and he learns to judge human nature "from no standpoint of his own, but in every individual case to take a new position whence the nature and history of the man should appear in true relation to the yet uncompleted result." . . . And now the quest for his own inheritance transcends all merely cultural identity: "His whole countenance bore self-evident witness of being a true face and no mask, a revelation of his individual being, and not a mere inheritance from a fine breed of fathers and mothers." . . . (pp. 103-05)

The paradox is central to MacDonald's transcendental nationalism, and after him to the transcelticism of the fin de siecle Highland novel and of twentieth-century Highland novelists such as Neil Gunn and the Compton Mackenzie of *The Four Winds of Love.* It envisions a tearing away of the false, of the cultural overlay, a winnowing to the true and essential in language and "manners." The truth thus restored is a type of an emergent higher truth. To have his full force as a cultural exemplar, Robert, like Elginbrod, must die in his local self and be translated in spirit (Robert dies en route to India) to far-off places. His cultural inheritance is celebrated—"for the latter had ancestors—that is, he came of people with a mental

and spiritual history" . . .—but only in the course of movement toward its transcendence. His local language survives the prudent impulse to learn English; but the rugged tongue of his cultural childhood is reinstated only to be transcended in death. The same must be true for his Scottish manners. . . . A restored and purified Scottish culture is merely a type of a higher reality.

It is impossible to undertake here a full survey of MacDonald's eleven "Scottish" novels. But the broad, general strokes I have just drawn can be tested specifically against two of the novels. Consider the two that stand up best as narratives: [*Alec Forbes of Howglen* and *Sir Gibbie*]. . . . (p. 105)

Coming between *Elginbrod* and *Falconer, Alec Forbes* is a more sustained effort at narrative realism than either. Coming a decade after all three, *Sir Gibbie* is a fuller adaptation of novelistic elements to romance and fantasy. Yet they have much in common, and both illustrate the unity and modal tension characteristic of MacDonald's novels. The transvaluation of Scottish culture through exile and death to a transcendent realm, which we have seen in *Elginbrod* and *Falconer,* is not evident in them, for both end triumphantly with the young laird reinstated in his local inheritance. The reinstatement can take place only after both have survived the trials of great but false expectations, Alec Forbes by error and redemption and Gibbie by providential suffering and active faith.

The differences between the heroes are symbolized in differences of attitude toward language. In *Alec Forbes,* the novel of manners, vernacular Aberdonian is given, characteristically, to the good characters; and a rejection of Scots—as with Alec's mother, Kate the false heroine, and Beauchamp the Byronic villain—is associated with social and cultural falseness. But Alec is effectively bilingual. . . . [He] is educated accordingly in conciliation and accommodation. (pp. 105-06)

Gibbie, on the other hand, cannot speak at all. There is a physiological reason, but we never learn what it is. Speechless Gibbie, with his smile, his eyes, his strange singing, wins out over men of words. The heroine Jenny, redeemed from her father's false values (social and theological), returns to her love of nature and speaks broad Scots to Gibbie; but their betrothal scene is carried on in sign language. The book consistently mocks affected English speakers, such as the pharisaical minister Sclater and Jenny's father the false laird. Donal the sensitive poet speaks Scots. But Scots is justified as a child-speech, a special poetic medium. . . . (p. 106)

As the contrast suggests, Alec Forbes is a hero of experience, learning and growing through influence and error, enlightenment and penance. Gibbie is a hero insulated against experience, living his providential destiny, testing and restoring faith in others. He is the incarnate childlike, while Alec is never quite a child. Yet the lesson Alec must learn is the same Gibbie symbolically enacts, and it leads both heroes to the same inheritance.

For Alec, the lesson centers on the familiar romance pattern of false heroine and true. The false heroine is his romantic, deluded, anti-vernacular cousin Kate, with whom he falls in love at Aberdeen. The true is little orphan Annie Anderson, who idolizes him as her protector at rural school, worships him quietly, and wins him in the end when false Kate, finally deserted by the Byronic Highland cad Beauchamp, goes mad and drowns herself. The book is organized according to Alec's and Annie's parallel fortunes. Alec is natural goodness untried, a "great handsome good natured ordinary-gifted wretch," courageous, just, but a somewhat thoughtless schoolboy, capable of cruelty and violence—an unusually plausible protagonist for Victorian romance. Annie the orphan plays the sacramental role of the childlike, elsewhere given by MacDonald to a boy. While Alec struggles chiefly with romantic folly and the temporary youthful sins of drunkenness "and worse," Annie is caught in a war of sects and faiths, susceptible to the influence of natures stern and false. She is devoted to the established minister Cowie—who is spiritually a mere child to her—and yet drawn half in fear to more severe missionaries. It is Annie who has the awakening religious sensibility and providential influence, and Annie whose inheritance, so crucial a symbol for MacDonald's theological romance, is the more problematic. Alec is a dynamic and "realistic" protagonist, but Annie is the symbolic or philosophical center.

They are touched by the same forces. Alec's inheritance, through his mother's debt, is vaguely threatened by the same falseness that imperils Annie's. When her father dies, her kinsman the mean shopkeeper Robert Bruce takes her to live in his shop and garret to control her little inheritance. He is a petty miser-hypocrite who moves from church to church to improve his business and is finally expelled for stealing Annie's five-pound note from the old Bible left her by the minister. MacDonald makes a caustic cultural joke of his name: is this "Robert Bruce" what has become of heroic Scotland? But MacDonald is no novelist of manners; social issues and values are important only as they are types of theological and spiritual ones. Robert Bruce is of little interest; his creator finds trivial wickedness uninteresting, just as he does in the case of the stereotyped fraud Beauchamp.

More interesting, because closer to the center of MacDonald's imagination, are the stronger, sterner natures, the traditional types of peasant elder, schoolmaster, and scholar: Crann the stonemason, Malison the brutal schoolmaster, and Cupples. All must be saved from their own excesses by the divine vengeance of love, the influence of Annie, the perseverance of poor crippled Truffey. In Malison's tyranny over children is personified "the God of a corrupt Calvinism," but he is defended by MacDonald as the type and victim of this cultural disease. In Crann the same doctrinal harshness is at war with more loving religious impulses. Cupples is saved from a lonely and alcoholic academicism by his suffering devotion to Alec, which leads him back to the exhilaration and sobriety of nature. All are saved, and their salvations matter more than Alec's redemption from the foolish romantic excesses of his young manhood. And at the center of the marvelous, often visionary world where their struggles and salvations occur is the divinely childlike Annie.

Sir Gibbie is a male version of that ideal, and more. He is almost a force of nature and a fabulous one. To come into the inheritance lost to him by his degenerate forebears, he must go back to the archaic vitalities of nature—the mountain, the river, shepherds and beasts—but also to his foster parents, old peasants once the glory of Scotland, where he can learn a simple, pretheological Bible Christianity. He becomes a legend. He plays fabulous roles as local sprites; the natural springs of his true inheritance are inseparable from the springs of faith and wonder. Both bring him into conflict with the false Thomas Galbraith, usurper of his inheritance, who personifies the two cardinal temptations to Scottish disinheritance as MacDonald sees them: anglicization and atheism, both representing the denial of local tradition and belief.

There is a further stage to Gibbie's inheritance, and it carries him back to the city where he began. MacDonald's city seems akin to Dickens's—preindustrial, crowded, labyrinthine, a place of fear, sin, and violence. But unlike Dickens's innocents—Oliver, David, Esther, and Pip—Gibbie is perfectly at home there, an innocent protector of those who wander in hunger or drunkenness in its streets. He has no consciousness of humanity's fall. But when his father's death sets him loose and when the Negro Sammbo is murdered before his eyes, his faith in humanity fails, and he follows his drunken father's "vague urging up Daurside" to his natural inheritance. The same river, in spate, causes his return to the city, but this time as the recognized heir, a mute but resistant Pip with expectations, in the hands of Sclater the pharisee. A corrupt church now plays his foster parent and tries in vain to make him a "gentleman," but he returns to play the missionary of the city streets, a literal Christian, and ultimately uses his money to restore the Auld Hoose of Galbraith as a settlement house. Here he lives winters to care for his outcasts and strays, and summers he spends up Daurside as the kindly laird-baronet, married to the old laird's daughter. It is a curious and interesting variant on the Waverley pattern of cultural redemption.

It is also a mythic revision of *Robert Falconer,* a movement back toward the visionary or fantastic, where MacDonald is at his best and most unique. Cultural types are transposed into archetypes of theological romance, and thus the local realism of the nineteenth-century idyll is present only to be transcended. (pp. 107-09)

> *Francis Russell Hart, "Mid-Victorians," in his* The Scottish Novel: From Smollett to Spark *(copyright © 1978 by Francis Russell Hart; excerpted by permission of the President and Fellows of Harvard College), Cambridge, Mass.: Harvard University Press, 1978, pp. 93-113.\**

**ROSEMARY JACKSON**  (essay date 1981)

[*In her* Fantasy: The World of Subversion, *from which the following is excerpted, Jackson explores fantasy literature as an expression of subconscious drives, composed of hidden images of longing and disenchantment.*]

[Stephen] Prickett discerns a continuous line of Platonic idealism sustained through the works of Carroll, MacDonald, Kingsley, Morris, Kipling, E. Nesbit, defining their fantasies in terms of their transcendentalism. They all manifest 'a desire for something *more,*' for a 'magic city' or a visionary dream land. This is analogous, argues Prickett, to that vision of Paradise which consummates Dante's *Divine Comedy,* as an image of the cosmic harmony towards which the whole creation moves. (p. 146)

But it is possible to see contradictions within the writings of MacDonald and Kingsley, which suggest that their embrace of Platonic idealism was less of a transcendental movement, and more of a displacement of psychological and social issues, for their fantasies betray a dissatisfaction with their own idealism. This is particularly so with George MacDonald's work. . . . [His novels] were influenced by German Romanticism, especially by Novalis, and they construct a 'dream' world, but one which is never entirely satisfactory.

*Phantastes*, 'A Faerie Romance for men and women', is told as a distant dream, insufficiently incongruous to really disturb the reader. Yet it has several qualities of a fantastic mode. Its hero, Anodos (Greek for 'the way upwards'), discovers his room inexplicably transformed into a woodland scene. It becomes peculiarly quiet, without life or noise. . . . Entering the wood, Anodos comes to 'the house of the ogre', where he opens a forbidden cupboard, to discover it has no back. . . . Anodos is staring into an infinite void, a place with no shape or name, until he sees (projects) there a figure which he reads as signifying his own death. . . . Anodos names this dark figure 'an evil demon'. The narrative focuses upon its exorcism, producing a magical romance of (supernatural) good against evil. Yet these early scenes suggest that Anodos is facing his double in that dark recess, similar to Brydon's encounter in James's *Jolly Corner,* or Stevenson's Jekyll mirrored by Hyde. MacDonald's fantasy *begins* as psychological projection, as an uncanny tale, and only later is developed into a moral allegory. Initially, the 'other' is beyond good or evil: it is self *as* other, as its own death. 'The strangest figure; vague, shadowy, almost transparent (. . .) the face reminded me of what I had heard of vampires; for the face resembled that of a corpse.' Its eyes 'were alive, yet not with life. They seemed lighted up with an infinite greed. A gnawing voracity, which devoured the devourer, seemed to be the indwelling and propelling power of the whole ghastly apparition.'

*Lilith* repeats this fantasy of a rehearsal with death. (Most fantasies of a 'double' or 'devil' can be interpreted as the self rehearsing his/her own death, own absence.) Its narcissistic hero, Vane, ceases to feel 'at home' in the world. His room changes into a wood and he experiences objects and people as distanced, alienated. Parallel to Dostoevsky's and Kafka's representations of the real, MacDonald's hollows out the familiar world. Vane's ordinary home is dis-covered to be a house of the dead. (pp. 146-48)

Throughout *Lilith,* a topography of labyrinthine passages, wasteland, doors opening to emptiness, graveyards, mirrors, constitutes the internal 'space' which Vane occupies. It is a dead landscape, inhabited by ravens, eagles, black cats, ghosts, the un-dead. 'Everywhere was the same as *nowhere*! I had not yet, by doing something, made *anywhere* into a place.' As his name suggests, Vane's world is inseparable from his self-absorption. Like Dorian Gray, he is trapped by his narcissism. 'I was not yet alive; I was only dreaming I lived.' 'I saw that man alone is but a being that may become a man.' . . . Yet MacDonald's tale of movement away from this 'paraxial' realm, as a place for a kind of death-in-life, is one which replaces one unreality for another.

As with *Phantastes, Lilith* develops into a magical narrative: its 'death-in-life' is projected on to the 'evil' figure of Lilith from whom sterility has been supposed to derive. According to Assyrian mythology, Lilith precedes Eve, and is produced not from Adam's rib, but simultaneously, from the dust of the earth, generated as an equal. Lilith refuses a passive maternal role and is cast into hell, becoming the figure behind female succubi and vampires through many folk legends. MacDonald reawakens this tradition by making of Lilith a protean evil shape, 'indestructible evil, the heart of horror essential', manifesting herself as leopardess, leech, vampire, bat, owl, demon. On to Lilith are placed all Vane's life-denying instincts. She becomes a malign cosmic force operating against goodness and vitality. 'Something was gone from her.' 'The source of life had withdrawn itself.' 'I saw the face of a live death.' . . . By destroying Lilith, the romance moves towards an assertion of cosmic goodness, where evil is no more. 'There is a light that lightens the darkness. . . .' Vane does achieve a reflection of Dante's paradisical vision, 'Love possessed me! Love was my life! Love was . . . all in all! . . . The world and its being, its life and mine, were one. The microcosm and macrocosm

were at length atoned, at length in harmony. I lived in everything; everything entered and lived in me,' but it is no resolution of his narcissism. Instead of concentrating upon himself, he transfers his love to the cosmos internalized, asserting a magical faith in goodness, as some transcendental entity. MacDonald's fantasies betray dissatisfaction with the real and seek something other. They fill emptiness with a magical, divine plenitude. Yet a strange melancholy remains, as his hollow characters arrive at their ideal visions. Their ideals lie beyond the mirror, or through the north wind, in a landscape of death.

*Phantastes* and *Lilith* are not dissimilar to *Dracula* and *The Lair of the White Worm* in their ideological effects. An apprehension of something *without* signification is rewritten as 'evil' and into that evil category are exiled forms of social deviancy and subversion. Here . . . it is woman, under the sign of Lilith: woman as threat, as a demanding, desiring, angry and violent presence. MacDonald's other tales also equate female sexuality with immorality. His story *The Princess and Curdie* . . . repeats a frequent post-Darwinian fantasy of regression to bestiality. Several characters are incompletely human: their hands have retained animal features, as the paws of a bear, claws of a dragon, scales of a snake and scorpion. The most notable monster is Lina, 'a woman that was naughty', a hybrid of dog, snake, dragon and bear. (pp. 149-50)

> *Rosemary Jackson, "Victorian Fantasies," in her* Fantasy: The Literature of Subversion *(© 1981 by Rosemary Jackson), Methuen & Co., Ltd., 1981, pp. 141-56.\**

---

## ADDITIONAL BIBLIOGRAPHY

Benson, A. C. "George MacDonald." In his *Rambles and Reflections,* pp. 145-54. New York: G. P. Putnam's Sons, 1926.

> Biocritical essay examining *Phantastes* and finding it a bizarre, powerful work whose power overrides its weaknesses. Nevertheless, Benson sees little future interest in MacDonald's books, pointing to their unevenness and moralizing as fatal characteristics.

Betham-Edwards, Matilda Barbara. "George MacDonald." In her *Friendly Faces of Three Nationalities,* pp. 173-81. London: Chapman and Hall, 1911.

> Acknowledges MacDonald to be the "second Emerson" of his epoch, but by no means a first-rate writer or thinker.

Bulloch, John Malcolm. "A Bibliography of George MacDonald." *Aberdeen University Library Bulletin* V, No. 30 (February 1925): 679-747.

> Exhaustive catalogue, listing the publishing history of MacDonald's books and stories, the books and magazines he edited, anthologies and devotionals gleaned from his writings, his poems set to music, photographs and paintings of him, the sites of centenary celebrations, and critical articles and books—many of them difficult to obtain today.

Chamberlain, Robert L. "George MacDonald's 'A Manchester Poem' and Hopkins' 'God's Grandeur'." *Personalist* XLIV, No. 4 (Autumn 1963): 518-27.

> Compares MacDonald's "A Manchester Poem" to Gerard Manley Hopkin's "God's Grandeur," noting the poems' similarity in the thesis that God's presence yet shines on the Earth, though humanity has blighted the Earth in the name of progress.

Chesterton, G. K. "George MacDonald." *Daily News* (23 September 1905): 6.

> Article praising MacDonald as "one of the three or four greatest men of the nineteenth century." Chesterton compares Mac-

Donald's literary expression of mysticism favorably to that of W. B. Yeats.

Fadiman, Clifton. Afterword to *At the Back of the North Wind,* by George MacDonald, pp. 309-10. New York: The Macmillan Co.; London: Collier-Macmillan, 1964.

    Short sketch of MacDonald's life and its effect on his work. This afterword is intended to help children appreciate *At the Back of the North Wind.*

Hein, Rolland. *The Harmony Within: The Spiritual Vision of George MacDonald.* Grand Rapids, Mich.: William B. Eerdmans Publishing Co., 1982, 163 p.

    An insightful critical study of MacDonald's beliefs as revealed in his fiction.

Hutton, Muriel. "George Eliot, George MacDonald and the Muckle Speat." *Scottish Literary Journal* 2, No. 2 (December 1975): 36-46.*

    Compares the language of the flood scene in *Sir Gibbie* with the flood account given in Sir Thomas Dick Lauder's *An Account of the Great Floods of August 1829 in the Province of Morayshire and Adjoining Districts,* and with the flood descriptions in George Eliot's *The Mill on the Floss.*

Lewis, C. S. *They Stand Together: The Letters of C. S. Lewis to Arthur Greeves (1914-1963).* Edited by Walter Hooper. London: Collins, 1979, 592 p.*

    Contains numerous references to and brief comments on Mac-Donald's books. Of particular interest is the letter of 7 March 1916, in which Lewis records his initial impressions of *Phantastes.*

MacDonald, Ronald. "George MacDonald: A Personal Note." In *From a Northern Window: Papers Critical, Historical, and Imaginative,* edited by Frederick Watson, pp. 55-113. London: James Nisbet & Co., 1911.

    Sympathetic critical essay, tracing the development of Mac-Donald's works. The essayist was one of MacDonald's sons.

Manlove, C[olin] N. "George MacDonald (1824-1905)." In his *Modern Fantasy: Five Studies,* pp. 55-98. Cambridge: Cambridge University Press, 1975.

    Excellent in-depth study of MacDonald's fantasy literature.

Manlove, Colin [N]. "George MacDonald's Early Scottish Novels." In *Nineteenth-Century Scottish Fiction,* edited by Ian Campbell, pp. 68-88. New York: Barnes & Noble Books, 1979.

    Discussion of *David Elginbrod, Alec Forbes of Howglen, Robert Falconer,* and *Malcolm.* Manlove acknowledges their weaknesses, but concludes that "the evocation of Aberdeenshire characters that they contain shows a power of vivid portrayal, the equal of which is only to be found in the finest of Scottish novels."

Paladin [pseud.]. "George MacDonald." In *Glances at Great and Little Men,* pp. 187-94. London: Sampson Low, Marston, Searle, & Rivington, 1890.

    Biographical and critical sketch by an unknown friend of MacDonald. Paladin takes issue with the intrusion of Mac-Donald's religious beliefs into his books, rendering them "philosophical treatises rather than studies of life."

Power, William. "The Years Between." In his *Literature and Oatmeal: What Literature Has Meant to Scotland,* pp. 116-27. London: George Routledge and Sons, 1935.*

    Appraisal of MacDonald and his place in nineteenth-century Scottish literature. Power says that MacDonald, "with a far finer mind and personality than [John] Galt, is not in the same street with him as an artist" because of the former's preoccupation with religious matters.

Prickett, Stephen. "Adults in Allegory Land: Kingsley and Mac-Donald." In his *Victorian Fantasy,* pp. 150-97. Bloomington: Indiana University Press, 1979.*

    An examination of the vision behind MacDonald's fantasies, a study of the fantasies themselves, and a comparison of Mac-Donald's allegorical technique with that of Charles Kingsley.

Sigman, Joseph. "Death's Ecstasies: Transformation and Rebirth in George MacDonald's *Phantastes.*" *English Studies in Canada* II, No. 2, (Summer 1976): 203-26.

    Jungian interpretation of *Phantastes.*

Simmons, Charles L. "George MacDonald and His Writings." *Universalist Quarterly* n.s. XXI (January 1884): 54-63.

    Discusses MacDonald's novels as expressions of the author's universalism. Simmons cites the evocations of Scottish life as one of MacDonald's strongest skills.

Wolff, Robert Lee. "An 1862 Alice: 'Cross Purposes'; or, Which Dreamed It?" *Harvard Library Bulletin* XXIII, No. 2 (April 1975): 199-202.*

    Discusses MacDonald's "Cross Purposes," a short story similar, in several notable features, to *Alice in Wonderland.* Wolff suggests the possibility that "Cross Purposes" may have influenced Carroll.

# (Luiz) Heinrich Mann

## (1871-1950)

German novelist, short story and novella writer, dramatist, essayist, journalist, and critic.

Considered the father of the German intellectual left, Mann is best known for *Professor Unrat (The Blue Angel)*, his satirical novel about the abuses of power which was popularized in this country in Josef von Sternberg's film version. Both in his fiction and nonfiction, Mann criticized the authoritarian mentality and examined its social and psychological effects. Today, Mann is considered one of the major practitioners of the social novel. This literary form was originated in France to serve as an impersonal, quasi-scientific document of the workings of society. In Germany, Mann adapted its technique to serve more personal and ethical aims. His facility with the social novel has led critics to call him the Zola of Germany.

Mann was born in Lubeck, Germany, the eldest of five children. His parents did little to encourage his early literary interests; instead, he was sent to Dresden to learn the book trade and subsequently worked in the Berlin publishing house of Samuel Fischer. When Mann's father died in 1893, leaving behind a substantial estate, Heinrich was able to devote himself to his writing. Over the next decade he wrote several works of fiction and literary criticism. He also traveled extensively during this period, especially in Italy, where he studied the southern European culture which he later used in his novel *Die Kleine Stadt (The Little Town)*. In these years of apprenticeship Mann studied the writings of Friedrich Nietzsche, whose philosophy the young author integrated into his own thought. As a writer, Mann always worked in the shadow of his younger brother, Thomas, whose literary reputation surpassed his own. The relationship between the brothers was always strained, but the first serious break between the two came when Heinrich, in his 1915 essay *Zola*, criticized Germany's misguided nationalism in World War I. Thomas had long defended his country's cause in that war. Ten years later, when Heinrich fell seriously ill, the brothers finally reached a reconciliation, although their relationship was riddled with difficulties until the end. When the Nazis came to power, Heinrich, one of the strongest and most respected critics of the new regime, fled to France where he continued to work for a German popular front. In 1940, Hitler's invasion of France forced him to join other German exiles, including his brother Thomas and Bertolt Brecht, in California. The German Democratic Republic invited Mann to return to his country as president of the Academy of Arts, but he died before he could return home.

Mann's work is often divided into three distinct periods which reflect a gradual shift from aesthetic to political concerns. Mann's earliest successful novel, *Im Schlaraffenland (In the Land of Cockaigne)*, reflects his interest in art and the artist. In this realistic satire, Mann presented a comic exposure of the literary coteries among Berlin's new bourgeoisie. In his second period, Mann achieved a closer balance between art and politics. *The Blue Angel*, a novel about an authoritarian Gymnasium teacher who tries to assert his power beyond the classroom, illustrates Mann's concern with the attitude of intellectuals toward power and violence. At about the same time

Mann also wrote *The Little Town*, in which he maintained that the most effective kind of art serves a social function and is actually strengthened by being a part of life. In the final period of Mann's career, political themes dominated his work. With the *Kaiserreich* trilogy, Mann began to analyze the weaknesses of the German empire, placing responsibility for Germany's problems squarely upon the shoulders of intellectuals whose factionalism prevented their political effectiveness.

Because Mann expressed his political views so passionately in both fiction and nonfiction, critics have frequently paid more attention to the content of his social criticism than to the quality of his prose. The majority of scholars, in commenting upon the elder Mann, have noted considerable unevenness in his work. They criticize *In the Land of Cockaigne* for its disjointed style, and *Der Kopf* for its historical inaccuracies. They also point out that the author's caricatures and satires, like those found in *The Blue Angel*, were sometimes so harsh and distasteful that they marred the final effect of Mann's work. However, his *Der Untertan (The Patrioteer)* has been praised for its life-like characterizations, and his *Henri Quatre* novels are considered masterpieces of historical fiction.

In his writing Mann sought to convey his social and political insights. While his works vary greatly in artistic quality, Mann always believed that "the language used in a book is the unmistakable sign of the author's mental attitude and ability—and of the length of time they will endure." Throughout his works, Mann often achieves a level of artistry sufficient to ensure the endurance of his socially committed thought and to preserve his identity as an author who ably advocated the responsibilities that artists and intellectuals have to society.

## PRINCIPAL WORKS

*In einer Familie*  (novel)  1894
*Im Schlaraffenland*  (novel)  1900
  [*In the Land of Cockaigne*, 1929; also published as *Berlin: The Land of Cockaigne*, 1929]
*Die Göttinnen*  (novels)  1903
  [*Diana* (partial translation), 1929]
*Die Jagd nach Liebe*  (novel)  1903
*Flöten und Dolche*  (novellas)  1905
*Professor Unrat*  (novel)  1905
  [*The Blue Angel*, 1931; also published as *Small Town Tyrant*, 1944]
*Eine Freundschaft. Gustave Flaubert und George Sand*  (essay)  1905-06
*Schauspielerin*  (novel)  1906
*Zwischen den Rassen*  (novel)  1907
*Die Bösen*  (novellas)  1908
*Die kleine Stadt*  (novel)  1908
  [*The Little Town*, 1930]
*Die Rückkehr vom Hades*  (novellas)  1911
*Die grosse Liebe*  (drama)  1912
*Madame Legros*  (drama)  1913
  [*Madame Legros* published in *Eight European Plays*, 1927]
*Die Armen*  (novel)  1917
*Der Untertan*  (novel)  1918
  [*The Patrioteer*, 1921; also published as *Little Superman*, 1945; and *Man of Straw*, 1947]
*Macht und Mensch*  (essays)  1919
*Abrechnungen*  (novellas)  1925
*Kobes*  (novel)  1925
*Der Kopf*  (novel)  1925
*Mutter Marie*  (novel)  1927
  [*Mother Mary*, 1928]
*Eugénie*  (novel)  1928
  [*The Royal Woman*, 1930]
*Sieben Jahre: Chronik der Gedanken und Vorgange*  (essays)  1929
*Die grosse Sache*  (novel)  1930
*Geist und Tat: Franzosen 1780-1930*  (essays)  1931
*Ein ernstes Leben*  (novel)  1932
  [*The Hill of Lies*, 1934]
*Das öffentliche Leben*  (essays)  1932
*Das Bekenntnis zum Übernationalen*  (essay)  1933
*Der Hass: Deutsche Zeitgeschichte*  (essays)  1933
*Die Jugend des Königs Henri Quatre*  (novel)  1935
  [*Young Henry of Navarre*, 1937; also published as *King Wren: The Young of Henri IV*, 1937]
*Die Vollendung des Königs Henri Quatre*  (novel)  1938
  [*Henry, King of France*, 1939; also published as *Henri Quatre, King of France*, 1938-39]
*The Living Thoughts of Neitzsche*  (essay)  1939
*Lidice*  (novel)  1943
*Ein Zeitalter wird besichtigt*  (autobiography)  1945
*Der Atem*  (novel)  1949
*Empfang bei der Welt*  (novel)  1956

*These works are collectively referred to as the *Kaiserreich* trilogy.

## OTTO EDUARD LESSING  (essay date 1912)

[*At the time the following critical evaluation was written, Mann's pre-World War I fiction had established him as an author whose works primarily treated themes of social and artistic decadence. Following the war, as David Roberts documents in his study [see excerpt below], Mann moved away from fiction examining the lives of artistic personalities and began to produce novels and essays concerned with political issues.*]

The first and prevailing impression of Heinrich Mann's writings is that of an unbridled and disgusting sensuality which appears in the garb of an overheated, romantically embellished pathos. The reader is constantly reminded of Heine's Ardinghello, of Tieck's William Lovell, of Freidrich Schlegel's Lucinde, of Gabriele D'Annunzio. It is the ennervating atmosphere of a society which, without vital aims, without the necessity of work, leads a life, not "beyond good and evil" but in the very midst of vice; a society which, remote from the brisk air-currents of progressive humanity, enclosed within a dream-world of voluptuous fancies, knows of only one struggle: the paralizing vacillation between the affectations of an over-refined culture and barbaric lusts. (p. 169)

Heinrich Mann first attracted attention in 1897 with a small volume of short stories the style of which showed the influence of Paul Heyse and Theodor Storm, while its dreamy suggestiveness recalled older romanticists like Eichendorff.—The best of these stories "**The Wondrous**" ("**Das Wunderbare**") the author surpassed later in the mastery of technique but not in its uniformly enrapturing poetry. "The wondrous" is a perfectly spiritualized love, a singular experience in the life of a man of affairs, an experience so free from all earthly disturbances, so heavenly that it remains for ever the resting place of his aspirations, the paradise of his dreams. . . . This story is a lyric poem, a song of grief and longing and renunciation, but of a renunciation that makes man wise and efficient in the struggle for the attainable.

There followed—an almost incredible contrast—a series of erotic novels and stories that shared, to a deplorable degree, the superficial sensationalism of Sudermann's *Song of Songs*. It is only in his very latest works that Heinrich Mann showed himself once more worthy of serious attention, even if he extended the range of his subjects but little, preserving his preference for erotic motives. The titles of his recent books are: *The Bad* (*Die Bösen*), *The Heart* (*Das Herz*), two collections of short stories, and *The Small Town* (*Die kleine Stadt*), a novel. . . . One of the two stories in *The Bad* is "**Branzilla**," the other "**The Tyrant**". "**Branzilla**" is a great Italian singer who makes her art the moloch of her life, to whom she sacrifices the happiness of others and her own soul.

This story is composed in a technique that Heinrich Mann had gradually acquired in former works of his, going back partly to Flaubert, partly to Holz-Schlaf's Papa Hamlet. The action rests entirely upon the dialog. The narration, limited to the smallest possible space, produces the effect of stage-directions. Separate periods of time are, in the manner of scenes, put together without direct connections so as to make the impression of perspective continuity. Since the narrating transitions are lacking and the changes of time and space are indicated in the dialog only, the author's personality being entirely eliminated, the reader's imagination is forced to a most intense co-operation. He has, therefore, at the end an image in his mind of all happenings as plastic, as if he had been watching a theatrical performance. (pp. 170-71)

Similar remarks may be made concerning **"The Tyrant."** . . . With great force, audacity, and psychological subtlety "the eternal contest between the sexes", as Hebbel put it, has been treated in this story. The whole of it is an ingenious, if indeed satanic, play with the noblest and purest sentiments of the human heart, a gloomy, yet magnificent, picture of the Italian Renaissance when mankind pendulated between the lofty ideal of the superman and the savage ferocity of beasts of prey.

The collection *The Heart* is of uneven value. Beside a trivial piece of citizen-life and a balladesque tale of jealousy in Paul Heyse's style, beside two romantic stories suggesting the bizarre method of Hoffmann, there is a masterpiece of perfect originality: **"The Innocent One"** (**"Die Unschuldige"**). (pp. 172-73)

While this story is written in the style of **"Branzilla"**, another in the same volume is of an older date and technique: **"The Actress"** (**"Die Schauspielerin"**). This contains an analysis of the author's own character, his two principal traits being represented by the heroine and her counterpart Mr. Rothaus. The actress longs for a full enjoyment of life through the happiness of love. Mr. Rothaus, the refined the sensitive man, is condemned to asceticism chiefly by his esthetic delicacy. (p. 174)

The same discrepancy of feeling is the subject of an earlier story **"Pippo Spano"** where the author portrays both himself and D'Annunzio in the same character. His self-scrutiny is as keen and icy as Strindberg's, when he confesses to a bewildering mixture of genuine sentiment and studied pose, of real self-control and morbid ambition which, instead of rating men and things according to their original and individual values, views them exclusively as material for "artistic" purposes. (p. 175)

*The Small Town (Die kleine Stadt)* again represents the struggle between life and asceticism. The chief motives of his earlier works are all united here, as Felix Stoessinger has pointed out: the artist who keeps himself apart from life, and his contrast, the man who enjoys life; the egotistically ambitious woman of Branzilla's type, and the woman who throws herself away. (pp. 175-76)

Various critics praised this novel in the most extravagant terms, one going so far as to declare it the greatest literary accomplishment since Flaubert. Indeed, there is a technical skill, a control of the linguistic means of expression which can hardly be surpassed. The language is so completely adapted to the Italian environment as to make the impression of a masterly translation from that tongue. It is full of metallic sonority, fill of melody and rhythm, reflecting, as it were, Italy's blue sky and brilliant colors. There are few works in German literature like this: young Heyse's best stories and K. F. Meyer's "The Temptation of Pescara" and "The Monk's Wedding". But otherwise the technique, however well it is handled, seems problematical. What in the short story leads to dramatic scenes, here leads to chaos. Dialog replaces narration to such an extent as to make it often impossible to understand the buzz of voices. Too much happens before our very eyes. The novel knows of no presuppositions or secondary motives that might be disposed of by means of brief narration. We are forced to ascend all stairs, to count all windows, to know all costumes, and all gossip. The grandiose effect of concentration in **"Branzilla"** is here given up for a minute enumeration of details which, as with Zola, distract our attention from essentials. The short

stories are distinguished by their harmonious proportions; here everything is disproportionate, exaggerated, confusing.

Having finished the book, we think that we are very familiar with "the small town". But life in this town is badly monotonous and quite unreal. Its people are mere shadows appearing only in a single and strangely spectral relation to life. Such onesidedness, the emphasis being laid upon one remarkable character-trait or one remarkable event, is the nature of the short story; it decomposes the novel. (pp. 176-78)

Heinrich Mann makes one of his self-portraits say: "The tenor of my life is barrenness, as though nothing ever had happened." And another: "He loved things chiefly for their aftertaste, the love of women only for the bitter solitude following, happiness, if at all, for the choking yearning which it leaves in one's throat." In this he represents the decadent phase of romanticism. Indeed, since, as a young man, he experienced the beautiful "wonder" in which he believed, nothing happened to him to create a harmonious impression. His world is the sham of the theater, the artist with half-true feelings, the cynical epicurean. (p. 178)

In a fine analytical study of Flaubert's relation to George Sand (perhaps his best work) Mann himself ascribes to his great master a fervid love of life which over-sensitiveness forbade him to admit. If his own apparent hatred is such a love in disguise, he is guilty of the same fatal deception which is Heine's great sin, a deception more pernicious than the most radical negation. (pp. 178-79)

> *Otto Eduard Lessing, "Heinrich Mann," in his* Masters in His Modern German Literature, *Verlag Von Carl Reissner, 1912 (and reprinted by Books for Libraries Press, 1967; distributed by Arno Press, Inc.), pp. 167-79.*

**HARRISON SMITH**   (essay date 1928)

Compared to a great deal of recent German fiction, the British and our own home grown product seems as pastoral as a woolly lamb and as naive as a child sucking its thumb. Our one-time enemies have been dealing since the war with sorcery, devils, crimes, incest, lust, death and other spooky things dragged out of humanity's drainpipe.

There is a horrid fascination about this kind of novel, and at its best it can rise to the heights of [Thomas Mann's] "The Magic Mountain," which, as you will recall, dealt with the diseased, the moribund and the dead in a tuberculosis sanitarium.

But the book which has occasioned these prefatory remarks ["**Mother Mary**"] is not by Thomas, but by Heinrich Mann, and I am afraid that it is somewhere at the other end of the scale of merit. It is worth reading because Mr. Mann does not lack the power to hypnotize his readers, and also because it is an interesting experiment to see how far from the bright light of day your intelligence can be drawn. Consider the situation which is revealed in **"Mother Mary."** You will find it difficult not to think at the same time of three or four dime novels you may have had the temerity to read in your youth. . . .

After one has read this novel and reason once more assumes her wonted sway, it seems incredible that this nonsensical plot, this accumulation of fictional insanities, should have been tolerable. I can only state that it is tolerable and that one reads the book with fascinated and somewhat feverish attention.

*Harrison Smith, "A German Thriller," in* New York
Herald Tribune Books *(© I.H.T. Corporation; reprinted by permission), November 4, 1928, p. 11.*

## FÉLIX BERTAUX (essay date 1931)

In an age of illusions and blissful optimism, [Heinrich Mann]
was a disillusionist, seeking to sharpen the senses of his public.
Yet his criticism does not exclude generosity; his bitterness is
that of conviction mingled with sympathy. His thinking, in
spite of its severity, has flashes of passion. One example is
the reproach, in *Schauspielerin,* to the uncertain lover who
could never express "his final word, his truest thought." Like
his favorite heroine, Heinrich Mann has a hot scorn for the
lukewarm, the tepid. His is an art of hyperbole; he avoids
subtleties; his passionate logic shuns distinctions which are
merely relative. He strips his material bare, with a hurried,
clean, direct movement. His mood is always imperative, even
when he is reserved or persuasive. His satire is accompanied
by panegyrics. For everything he destroys he has a substitute
ready, piping hot. Destructive or constructive, he is always
radical. His is the vehemence of over-lively sensibilities, of a
mind which sees too clearly, knows too much and cannot withhold it. At least he makes no effort to withhold it. He is at
once a Schiller—with all the pathos of *Die Räuber* and *Don
Carlos,* though without the dreamy quality; colorful; taking his
themes as willingly from the French Revolution as from modern
Berlin—and a Roman senator. He instinctively seeks out the
public of the forum. Literature offers him not a pulpit from
which to philosophize, but a tribune from which to impose his
ideas upon the people—ideas not alone political but esthetic,
psychological, moral as well.

Heinrich Mann was destined to give Germany the social novel
which neither Gutzkov nor Freitag nor Spielhagen had succeeded in creating. He is passionately desirous of asserting
himself, scornful of mere self-reminiscence or egoism and even
of introspection. His inmost thought is turned outward; his
whole work is oriented toward contemporary society. His chief
function, he believes, is to seek out the springs of power in
that society. It may be added that he seeks also to introduce
into that society power in another, the spiritual, form.

His first conception of that power was that it sprang from the
dynamism of the individual. The ego is power. He felt this
power in all the characters with which he filled his novels—
bourgeois, artists, poor worthless wretches as well as exceptional personalities. He thus broke with the tradition of the
novel of individual development and attached himself to the
naturalist tradition, substituting for the single hero the num-
berless mass, for the author's ego the thousand egos of contemporary reality. At the same time he cast off the German
habit of turning the novel into lyric effusions and descriptions.
No more of those confidences in which the author pours out
his soul, those "confessions of a noble spirit." Heinrich Mann's
objectivity recalls both that of the experimental novel of Zola
and that of the *Wahlverwandtschaften.* He looks upon individuals as so many objects with which to experiment. But he
surpasses the observation of the naturalists, does more than
express exterior states. He attempts also to seize upon and to
express the reactions which take place within the individual,
to uncover the properties of each element which goes to make
up that individual, emphatically rejecting the complacencies
of a dishonest psychology.

Even in the most mediocre of his characters he discovers an
astonishing dynamism of instinct. He carried his investigations

into the least known regions of sensibility and sensuality. "One
must unlearn modesty before one can learn life," says Jean
Guignol in *Die Göttinnen.* During his Italian period Heinrich
Mann reintroduced sensuality into Protestant literature; but at
the same time he overcame what there was in him of the
d'Annunzio type of estheticism. His was the task of the amoral
moralist who must himself remain cold if he is to comprehend
the human soul. Then forced optimism ceases; man wherever
he appears is a beast of prey and pleasure, sometimes bursting
civilization open, sometimes turning civilization into a lie. In
every adventurer there is a bourgeois who ultimately recognizes
himself; in every bourgeois there is an adventurer who is unconscious of his own existence. In every man there is a demon
which alternately sleeps and wakes, and it is the activity of
this demon which Heinrich Mann describes. (pp. 127-29)

The type of individual represented in his books is filled with
contradictory passions superimposed one upon the other. There
is an apparently insoluble conflict between the concept of a
reasonable humanity and the concept of a demonism ever
brooding in its depths. Heinrich Mann's originality lies in the
fact that he does not attempt to eliminate the one in order to
strengthen the other, but accepts the coexistence of forces of
order and forces of destruction in the human soul, seeing in
their antagonism the true mystery of life. Victory for Heinrich
Mann would not be a victory in which the opposing armies are
destroyed and the field of battle cleared; he comprehends the
opposing forces, but for him the conflict never ends. It gives
us power enough that we should understand it. (p. 134)

*Félix Bertaux, "The Novel," in his* A Panorama of
German Literature from 1871 to 1931, *translated by
John J. Troustine (originally published as* Panorama
de la littérature allemande contemporaine, *Editions
du Sagittaire, 1931), Whittlesey House, 1935 (and
reprinted by Cooper Square Publishers, Inc., 1970,
pp. 61-162).*

## HEINRICH MANN (essay date 1944)

[*Mann wrote the letter excerpted below to be read at a gathering
of exiled writers from Germany, Austria, and Czechoslovakia who
had assembled on the occasion of Mann's seventy-third birthday
to honor his work.*]

[Generally], if not always, in giving creative expression to my
own life I subordinate it to contemporary events and social
conditions. When an author writes "social" novels, he looks
upon himself as a part of his environment or as reacting against
it. (pp. 239-40)

By and large the public paid no attention to the first fifteen
years of my literary work. I was loved, I was hated in silence.
This helped make me impartial and sure of myself. So long a
period of apprenticeship is never to be regretted. I am only
sorry that it came so long ago.

When the friendly pre-war times were behind us (they were
not entirely friendly, it is only that they seem so in retrospect—
the first of our glorious wars had already been thoroughly
rehearsed) my work rose from the ashes of the epoch like a
Phoenix. I don't mean to overestimate its value. Even a Phoenix
can be modest. But it is a fact that novels which had previously
been without readers suddenly had millions of them. People
discovered that they were understandable; for a long time they
had been considered esoteric. It was plain that they told the
truth. Up to the time when the prevailing picture was rudely
demolished by war, my picture was condemned without a hear-

ing as wicked. The lesson of a lost war is unmistakable. The Germans changed this and that, their form of government, the things they read. But their changes were not profound or lasting, as you know. They made them unwillingly. They sulked from the very beginning. The whole Republic was hostile to the honest facts, to the world as it is. So, through awkwardness or malice, they steered straight into the second war. That is why Hitler was their successful tribune. He owes everything he became to the Republic, to its tolerance, its complicity. And now he is a miserable figure just as the defeated Republic once was.

During that fourteen-year interval, everything returned to the former rut, reading along with the rest. My books were still read, I even represented literature officially. The Republic kept up appearances, it permitted me to become chairman of the literary section of the Academy of Arts. But in the enemy camp, Hitler's disciples were read by millions. There were old writers and young ones. The former, whose traditional sympathies had not changed, accommodated themselves to circumstances, and when everything was safe, they spoke out again. The young recruits, too, fitted beautifully into the dawning millennium of the Third Reich which in its twelfth year is falling in ruins.

Will the Germans try to change their reading again? I must confess that that is the least of my worries. They must be taught a lesson first: they have not known where God lives. They must be basically re-educated, and this, of course, can only be accomplished by German teachers.

Then if they want to read books which in their time mirrored life faithfully, and which therefore might still be true, I shall be at their service. Perhaps they will want something cheerful. My writings are all cheerful. The one with the saddest subject, **Der Untertan,** is spiritually the most cheerful.

If they never want to see my books again, it doesn't matter. There will always be books that encourage the depressed, shake up the unthinking, and bring smiles to the lips of the weary. Like Max Reinhardt, who believed in the immortality of the theater, I know that literature is immortal. (pp. 240-41)

> *Heinrich Mann, "A Word About My Work," in* Books Abroad *(copyright 1944 by the University of Oklahoma Press), Vol. 18, No. 3, Summer, 1944, pp. 239-41.*

## HARRY SLOCHOWER  (essay date 1945)

Heinrich Mann has been called the Zola of Germany. He continues the realistic tradition of Lessing, Heine, Hebbel and Dehmel—that is, of those who fought against the Romantic orientation in German letters. Back in 1914 and again in 1933, Heinrich Mann clearly indicated that the problem of the German people is bound up with that of human beings everywhere, with the people of France, of England, of Russia, of America. His novels around King Henry of France are the first positive counterstatement to fascism in mature artistic form. They suggest the continuity in man's struggle for emancipation and are a foreshadowing of the organic harmony between the great personality and the common man.

Mann depicts Henry as the first king who sought to represent the interests of the people. His politics aimed at a united Europe consisting of nations enjoying equal rights. Henry's collective representation is here joined to his own heroic personality. Henry breaks with the feudal idea of the divine ruler, where

the king was conceived as standing above classes, embodying a higher principle of justice due to his native, personal character. Yet Mann's Henry does not become a democratic "delegate" who merely carries out the instructions of his people. His sense of responsibility to others is wedded to personal responsibility and initiative. In short, Henry the democrat was a *personality.* He vanquished his enemy, "not only with his hands, he showed them his face, which spoke of majesty and power." In King Henry, majesty has been made manifest from within and without. He stood for the unity of the King and the Kingdom, which was more than "a territory and a domain, it was the very essence of freedom and justice." Henry was both prince and people.

Yet Mann's narrative does not quite succeed in making this point through its story. In the first novel, **Henry of Navarre,** Henry is pictured as impetuous, reckless and irresponsible in his personal dealings, especially with women. Moreover, Mann's story deals in the main with Henry's heroic biography and not with the masses. Now, the sequel is the story of **Henry the King.** Henry has matured. He abandons his earlier light-o'-loves, marries Gabrielle d'Estrée and would raise her to the status of queen over court and church opposition to her lower descent. Henry is ready to organize and husband his energies in his own and his people's interest.

But his time, just as ours, knew no rest. The peace Henry achieved was no peace, and his victory brought no stability. . . . Mann writes that Henry's violent death was to be expected, for he combined, as Lenin did, the spirit of reconstruction with an active temper. Daring and innovation court disaster. "Did not Henry himself foresee that . . . his active humanism consecrated him toward a tragic death?" These are questions which arise from a *complete* consideration of human issues. And they are resultants of the inner misgivings which come with exile. The way toward emancipated humanity must be taken through the No-Man's-Land of estrangement.

Yet despite these difficulties, Heinrich Mann has produced a great anti-fascist novel, the first work in our exiled literature which does not merely inveigh but points the affirmative direction. One may question Mann's choice of the particular character as a historical analogy; one may feel that he has not quite succeeded in showing the development of King Henry toward his humanistic perspective; one may note that in this novel it is again Henry the individual rather than the people's leader who stands out. What remains, however, is the promise and the hope in the hearts of men like Heinrich Mann that history and the myth provide an approximation of our social hope: the state in which men will act as personalities with a sense of individual and communal responsibility. In the French epilogue, King Henry prophetically encourages us against the enemies who have arisen today in another guise. For Mann, his King did not die: "We do not die. As is made very clear in sleep. We end indeed; but the shadow of our consciousness passes over into other brains, and thence into others again. What we stood for will think and act." In this sense, Heinrich Mann's novel takes its place with the great body of literature which is a foreshadowing of the organic harmony between man and the masses. (pp. 283-85)

> *Harry Slochower, "Toward the Communal Personality," in his* No Voice Is Wholly Lost . . . Writers and Thinkers in War and Peace *(reprinted by permission of Farrar, Straus and Giroux, Inc.; copyright, 1945, copyright renewed © 1972, by Harry Slochower), Creative Age Press, Inc., 1945, pp. 261-306.\**

## LEWIS MUMFORD   (essay date 1946)

[*The following consideration of Mann's* Der Untertan *is written in the form of a letter to a fictional German author whom Mumford calls Alfons F.*]

During the last century two writers stand out, among a bare handful one might name: Heinrich Heine and Heinrich Mann. These men dared to challenge Germany. When they attacked they did not graze a few hairs: they aimed at the fatty tissue around the heart. I wonder if you recall that it was Heinrich Mann that you yourself used as a symbol of the impure artist, whose work was unpleasantly discolored by his democratic political opinions?

You had the advantage of me at this point. At the time I had not read Heinrich Mann; I somehow had even escaped *Der Untertan,* though it had been translated into English shortly after the first World War, under the title, *The Patrioteer.*

There are novels and plays that tell one more about the character of a nation than more systematic works. If one wants to know the essence of England, one must read Shaw's *Pygmalion;* it is a clue both to the oligarchical structure of English society and to its democratic foundations. If you want to know the heart of America, read Sinclair Lewis's *Main Street;* it is a caricature of our life and it treats of the small country town rather than the city; yet the caricature tells something important about the kind of community and the kinds of personality we have developed here: while he winces at the picture, every American recognizes its truth. You in Germany have such a modern novel: it is a piece of merciless criticism, coarse in its outlines, with few qualifying touches: certainly, dear Alfons, it is very plainly colored—I would not use your word discolored—by the writer's political opinions, his hatred of caste, servility, militarism, cold deceit, and brutality: his outrage at all the traits and habits that have made democracy impossible in Germany. But in *Der Untertan* Heinrich Mann touched precisely those aspects of your character as a people that are hardest for a foreigner to describe without seeming prejudiced: indeed, if a foreigner painted a similar portrait today you would accuse him of malignant Vansittartism. Obviously, it is hard for you to dissociate yourself from the crawling, materialistic, decadent Germany that Mann presented. It was easier to dissociate yourself from Mann, by saying that he was not a pure artist.

Yet if your countrymen had taken that novel seriously, that is, if they had been capable of Heinrich Mann's kind of self-criticism, their entire life after the defeat of 1918 might have taken a different course. If the rest of the world had understood its essential truth, they would have remained on guard, and would never have indulgently over-looked the rearming of Germany, which took place even under the Republic. For remember: the Germany Mann described was not Nazi Germany: it was the "good" and "enlightened" Germany of the eighteen-nineties, when German music, German philosophy, and German science were at the height of their reputation if not of their power. Diederich, the "hero" of the book, lacked only one qualification for being a Nazi: a brown shirt. *Everything else was there.* Diederich's cringing fear of his father is only equaled by his masochistic love of being beaten by him; as he grows up he becomes an informer, just as Hitler was in the days before the Beer Hall Putsch; and Diederich's mixture of sadism and sentiment prepares one's mind for equally revolting spectacles in our own day—the entrance to one of your extermination camps, *neatly gardened,* or the sign on the walls of one of your human abattoirs, reminding attendants, in the interest of health, to keep their hands clean.

Here is an answer to the old question, so often discussed in Germany, *What is German?* Do you dare now to admit the terrible answer? *Diederich* is German; what *Diederich did* was German. The life he led in his student union needed only to be organized on a wholesale scale, covering the whole country, to become the life of storm troopers and SS men and the bureaucracy and the Wehrmacht. The brutality, the servile loyalty to the leader, his absolute devotion (in theory) to war, were all of the same order. In its plot, the book was prophetic. Anyone who read *Der Untertan* in 1918, when it came out, would have been fully prepared for all that happened in 1933, including the gullibility and the paralysis of the Social Democrats. He would have been prepared, provided he accepted Heinrich Mann's satire as the expression of an essential truth—admittedly not the whole truth or the best truth—about German society. You were not prepared, dear Alfons: you attributed to Heinrich Mann's political philosophy the discoloration that actually existed on the face of Germany. All that Hitler changed was to enable his followers to do openly, boastfully, shamelessly the same things that the Diederich of the Second Reich did slyly and underhandedly. Even there the change was not of a radical nature: for did not Diederich beat up a Jewish classmate with the tacit approval of his teachers? (pp. 275-78)

> Lewis Mumford, "To Alfons F., a German Writer in Austria," in his Values for Survival: Essays, Addresses, and Letters on Politics and Education (*copyright, 1946, 1974, by Lewis Mumford; reprinted by permission of Harcourt Brace Jovanovich, Inc.*), Harcourt Brace Jovanovich, 1946, pp. 270-84.

## GEORG LUKÁCS   (essay date 1947)

[*Lukács, an important Marxist literary critic, interprets* Henri IV *as a compromise between literature and political history.*]

[Heinrich Mann] is the most progressive and determined leader of anti-Fascist writing. He traces with a clairvoyant attention the human, the heroic, the significant cultural and humanist qualities which the revolutionary anti-Fascist struggle of the German people reveals more and more clearly from day to day. (p. 269)

Heinrich Mann, as an essayist and publicist, has always pointed out the contrast between the political development of France and Germany and held up the more democratic development of France as a model for the progressive bourgeoisie of Germany. . . . [His] novel *Henri IV* follows on from his publicist writing and pursues the same aim of popularizing French democracy for the German intelligentsia; in the history of German revolutionary democracy this novel constitutes a modern revival of the great ideological struggles of the thirties and forties of the previous century. (p. 271)

Since Henri IV is presented as the eternal emissary of reason and humanity it is natural that he should occupy the central position in the novel. His character, problems, historical importance and political-human physiognomy do not grow concretely out of the definite antagonisms of a definite phase in the life of the French people. On the contrary the problems of French popular life appear to be no more than a—in a certain sense accidental—sphere in which these eternal ideals may be realized.

Of course, Heinrich Mann's *Henri IV* is not constructed throughout on this principle. If it were, it could not be a work of art which breathed real life. It, too, has a transitional character: a concrete historical conception of the problem of popular life at a particular stage of historical development conflicts with an abstractly monumentalized, eternalizing conception of an exaggerated Enlightenment kind.

From a literary-historical point of view the influence of Victor Hugo can be felt here in Heinrich Mann. This is important and noteworthy, because Victor Hugo's development led him away from Romanticism and made him into a forerunner of the humanist revolt against the growing barbarism of capitalism. (pp. 279-80)

Mann's conception of humanity as something that is real and triumphant starts from the same premise as we find in all really important realistic writers. The premise, namely, that the really great features of humanity are present in life itself, in the objective reality of society, in man, and are only reproduced by the writer in a concentrated artistic form. (p. 281)

But *Henri IV* in this respect, too, is a transitional product. Conceived originally under the influence of Hugo, with a monumentalized hero as the eternal champion of an ideal, it won through in many directions to a concrete and straightforward richness of life. However, the framework of the original conception stood in the way of a really concrete portrayal of this richness of life in its simplicity and humanity. . . . Mann's dilemma of belittling and magnifying insight . . . is not an invention of aesthetics, but proceeds from life itself into aesthetics.

Nevertheless, it proceeded from a phase which life itself—and with it Heinrich Mann—has already left behind. Heinrich Mann's present artistic struggle is with the legacy of a past which he has overcome both politically and humanly. The substance of the struggle is to find a fully appropriate form for his new sense of life. If we call *Henri IV* a transitional product, this does not lower its literary significance, on the contrary, only emphasizes it. It is a product of the transition of the best section of the German intelligentsia, and the German people, to the decisive struggle against Hitler's barbarism and to the revival of revolutionary democracy in Germany. (pp. 281-82)

> *George Lukács, "The Historical Novel of Democratic Humanism," in his* The Historical Novel, *translated by Hannah Mitchell and Stanley Mitchell (translation copyright © 1962 by Merlin Press Ltd; originally published as A történelmi regény, 1947), Merlin Press, 1962, pp. 251-350.**

## R. TRAVIS HARDAWAY   (essay date 1954)

[*Hardaway's essay, excerpted below, is considered the standard reading of Mann's* Kaiserrich *trilogy, especially among English-language critics.*]

Recognizing much earlier than his brother Thomas the dominance of authoritarianism in the German empire and its evil manifestations in German society, Heinrich Mann began his merciless exposure of it . . . in the novel *Im Schlaraffenland.* His literary portrayal of it reached its climax in the trilogy which he termed *Das Kaiserreich.* . . . These novels—obviously influenced by Zola's great series on French life during the Second Empire—constitute a representative and particularly important segment of Heinrich Mann's social-political literary production, and give prominence to questions of democracy

vs. authoritarianism. . . . In the first of the novels, *Der Untertan,* we have Mann's picture of the bourgeoisie of Wilhelminian Germany and its bitter internal conflict. On the one side are arrayed the liberal democratic forces of the small Prussian city of Netzig. . . .

A combination of opposing forces, with a certain Diederich Hessling as its instigator and leader, rises to challenge and, in the event, utterly to defeat the liberals. Blindly worshipping and imitating all of Wilhelm II's worst qualities, aping his mannerisms and even his mustache, avidly mouthing melodramatic, bombastic, and belligerently nationalistic utterances, Hessling is one of the most pitilessly drawn figures in all modern literature. He is a vivid caricature of the professional "loyal subject" in the worst authoritarian sense. It is now generally recognized also, in view of recent German history, that Heinrich Mann has here created one of the most prophetic literary figures of all time. (p. 320)

Heinrich Mann obviously wished to induce strong nausea at a social philosophy which he regarded both as the essence of evil and as the dominant force in Wilhelminian Germany. And the personalities and actions of Diederich Hessling and his cronies match their words. Obsessed with the worship of success and power by any means, preferably foul, each follows as a matter of natural law the principle of "dog eat dog," with only contempt for any opponent who is weak enough to place his self-respect, his sense of decency, his "degenerate" ideas of democracy or of the common welfare above his own selfish interests. . . . Through clever maneuvers, which incidentally impoverish and slander many of his fellow citizens, Diederich himself, at the close of the novel, becomes the most powerful financial and political figure in the community. His bliss is crowned when he receives two imperial decorations. (pp. 322-23)

In the second novel, *Die Armen,* Geheimrat Diederich Hessling is the master of the paper-manufacturing community of Gausenfeld. In his mansion in the woods above, Villa Höhe, he is spared the sight and smells of the valley in which his mills and workers' barracks are located and in which his riches continue to pile up. (p. 323)

Hessling's workers live without hope. Although they vaguely yearn for the Marxist revolution which will reverse the existing order and give them power and wealth, it is for them only a dream. Except in occasional flare-ups of hatred, they have no thought of taking action to change their existence as instruments for the production of more wealth for their masters. (p. 324)

Karl Balrich rises to challenge Hessling's position and to rouse the workers briefly from their fatalistic resignation. . . . But the outcome is from the beginning a foregone conclusion. The combination of economic and governmental power is too much for the workers, and after their strike is broken, they lapse into their former passive hatred and misery. Balrich becomes again an ordinary worker and is one of the first to be drafted for World War I from Gausenfeld, now converted into a munitions plant.

*Der Kopf,* the last unit of the trilogy, is essentially the portrayal of a bizarre, almost singlehanded attempt by one Claudius Terra to trick the leaders of Germany before World War I into the application of a more democratic and humanitarian spirit and into the avoidance of the war which he sees approaching ever closer. (p. 325)

One of the authoritarian forces against which Terra wages his futile battle is the Pan-German League, with its rabid nationalism and imperialism and its arrogant advocacy of an ever mightier German navy. Another is the Junker caste, with its scornful hatred and contempt for democracy and its reliance upon a supremely strong army. Still another is the powerful and aggressive class of industrial magnates, led by the munitions manufacturer Knack, with their jealousy of the ancient predominance and prestige of the Junkers, their insatiable appetite for expansion of domestic and foreign power, their almost open wholesale bribery of government officials and legislators, and their alternate willingness and eagerness to plunge their country into war for their own aims. . . .

The foregoing analysis demonstrates sufficiently that Heinrich Mann, with a pen dipped in acid, has here held up to scorn the spirit of authoritarianism and totalitarianism. Its living representatives are sometimes pitiable, sometimes terrifying in their viciousness. The basic motivations governing their lives are ruthless self-interest, with complete disregard for the rights or welfare of others. (p. 326)

The strongest effect of the novels is to awaken or to intensify contempt for the spirit of authoritarianism. In picturing this system in all its nuances, in showing its debasing effect upon the individual and upon human society, Heinrich Mann has helped to clear the way for something better. He has aided in removing some of the obstacles which stand in the way of a more civilized humanity, an improved society.

The question now arises as to the positive aspect of the novels. Do they contribute not only to the necessary destruction of a system of jungle law but also to the building up of something to take its place? Do they contain a message of faith in the democratic way of life, in the name of which Heinrich Mann so often spoke and wrote? . . .

Let us consider briefly the personalities and characters of those whom Mann arrays against the authoritarian forces in Wilhelminian Germany.

That figure which in the entire trilogy most nearly represents the democratic ideal is old Herr Buck, in *Der Untertan.* He is on the whole an attractive and strong personality, possessing personal integrity, selfless devotion to the common welfare, and understanding of the meaning of democracy. . . . At the same time, however, he feels that he is an outdated relic of the better, more civilized days of the Revolution of 1848, one who is foredoomed to failure in the rising generation in Germany; and he ends broken not only financially and politically but also spiritually; he dies utterly without hope for the cause for which he has lived. (p. 327)

In the second novel—reminiscent of, but not so powerful as, Zola's *Germinal*—the workers are bitterly aware that the social and economic system under which they exist cries out to heaven for revision; but they are primarily actuated in their forlorn revolt not by the democratic principles of freedom, justice, and equality for all, but rather by class hatred stemming from Marxist doctrines. They hold together for a time in the wild dream of taking over for their own exclusive enjoyment the wealth and power of their hated oppressor, the capitalist Hessling; yet they cannot be steadfast even in their strongest feeling. (p. 328)

The last work of the trilogy, *Der Kopf,* offers no more inspiration or hope for democracy than the first two. Here there is not a single figure of any importance, except Claudius Terra, that has any strong desire for a more civilized society. (p. 329)

It is thus apparent that the reader who might approach *Das Kaiserreich* in the hope of finding a portrayal of inspiring, living examples of democracy, or a positive message of faith in the ultimate victory of the democratic philosophy, will come away with empty hands. (p. 330)

It should be stated at once that we cannot, of course, demand of Heinrich Mann that he should necessarily, either in *Das Kaiserreich* or in any of his other works, have painted a positive picture of inspiration and hope for the democratic way of life. A writer has the privilege and the duty to create according to his own particular imagination and interpretive faculties. At the same time, in view of Heinrich Mann's consistent intellectual interest in questions of democracy and his expressed admiration and active personal support of it, the absence of such a positive message should be pointed out. (p. 331)

In *Das Kaiserreich,* Heinrich Mann definitely concerns himself with democracy by constantly holding up democratic ideals as preferable alternatives to the absolutistic spirit; his chief success, brilliantly achieved, is to arouse abhorrence for this spirit; to this extent, by helping to clear the way for democracy, he has made a highly valuable contribution to it; he does not, however, whatever the reasons, present a constructive, inspiring message. (p. 333)

> R. Travis Hardaway, "Heinrich Mann's 'Kaiserreich' Trilogy and the Democratic Spirit," in Journal of English and Germanic Philology (© 1954 by the Board of Trustees of the University of Illinois), Vol. LIII, No. 3, 1954, pp. 319-33.

**ROLF N. LINN** (essay date 1955)

[*Linn traces Mann's development from his earliest novels* Im Schlaraffenland *and* Die Gottinnen *to his final novels and memoirs written while he was living in the United States.*]

Two poles, among others, between which flowed the current of Mann's creativity were his ideas on freedom and the various forms of human bondage by which he found himself surrounded. It was, however, less the compassionate description of subjugated men that intrigued him than the analysis of those who wield power, for to find the mainsprings of power in contemporary society was one of the tasks he had set for himself. It was natural that such a preoccupation should lead him to discuss and depict both despotism and individual despots.

Tyrants of various types occur in many of Mann's works, but only in a few did he deal exclusively with political despots and at the same time grant precedence to the personal over the sociological aspects of tyranny. . . . Two novellas in particular invite the study of their despotic characters, namely *Auferstehung* and *Der Tyrann.* They are not the only ones dealing with pathological egocentricity and the abuse of power, but in them, more clearly than in his other works, the author delineates his concept of the tyrant and reveals the close relationship of tyranny to decadence.

Both these novellas are contained in *Die Rückkehr vom Hades,* a collection of short narratives originally published in 1911. There was at that time no ruling prince who could have furnished the combination of traits which make up the characters in the works under consideration. Mann created a composite, drawn in part from Italian history, and in part invented; the result was nevertheless a detailed and plausible portrayal of a despot, a portrayal which served Heinrich Mann in his studies of Wilhelminian Germany undertaken at about the same time.

From these facts arise several questions that are to be answered here: What kind of man is the decadent tyrant whom the author depicts in these two novellas? What attitude does he display toward his own creation? And finally, by what traits is his decadent despot related to other literary works of decadence?

In *Auferstehung* not one but two figures must be considered: Don Rocco Ascani and the Duke of Lagoscuro. The latter, though not the protagonist, is the tyrant of the tale; a part of the present study will be focussed on him. The former, however, cannot be ignored, for his life constitutes the plot of the novella, and thus an acquaintance with his development is necessary for the understanding of the duke's role in it. Moreover, Don Rocco spends most of his years in the service of tyranny. He acts like a despot and is regarded by the people as one, without being one in Mann's sense of the word. For this reason the contrast between the two characters is an aid in the interpretation of Mann's ideas.

Don Rocco Ascani is the leader of the people in their fight against the oppressive government of the Duke of Lagoscuro. Their rebellion—reminiscent of the spontaneous uprising in Modena in 1796—is about to be quelled, when Napoleon arrives, fresh from his triumph at Lodi, and conquers the duchy. But the intervention of the French, which means victory for the people, marks also the end of Don Rocco's idealism, for through Bonaparte Don Rocco learns that his best friend is the lover of his wife, Donna Carla. Crushed by this double betrayal—and coincidentally made aware of Napoleon's personal ambitions—he renounces his past and helps Napoleon in the exploitation of the populace. After the eclipse of the great Corsican he is retained as prime minister by the reinstated duke. In this capacity he rules the little country with an iron hand for more than thirty years. Then a new liberator appears, Garibaldi; and with him Donna Carla comes back. Throughout her lifetime Donna Carla has preserved her democratic ideals. Her unshakable faith inspires Don Rocco with new confidence in the cause of liberty. At peace with himself, and ready to receive Garibaldi who is a ''purer hero than Bonaparte was'' he dies.

Don Rocco is at all times an impetuous man, both in his actions and his emotions. First he is a courageous leader in the crusade for freedom; his devotion to justice is as boundless as is his love for his wife. Then, when he is undeceived about her and his best friend, his despair leads him to the brink of madness. And from this experience, finally, he emerges as a cold, calculating scoundrel, determined to destroy the world and himself.

But even during this period of degrading tyranny, which lasts until a few moments before his death, Don Rocco is not a real despot. To be sure, the people of Lagoscuro regard him rightly as a crook, pander, killer, and oppressor. But to act his part Don Rocco is compelled to invent a pseudophilosophy for himself. In order not to relent he reasons as follows: Lagoscuro was liberated at the very moment his love had to die. This was not fortuitous. Freedom is always purchased at a price, and the price, any price, is too high. Furthermore, Napoleon became a tyrant eventually, proving that freedom cannot last because neither leaders nor followers are made for it. Consequently one serves the design of the universe best by serving men like the duke. And sending idealistic rebels to the gallows is not merely an act of obedience to the divine will but also a kindness to the victims; for were they to live on, they would sooner or later be disabused, just as he was, and would experience the death of their ideals within themselves.

These are the attempts at self-justification of a person who has been hurt rather than those of a fundamentally cruel character. (pp. 125-27)

Since *Auferstehung* is primarily the story of Don Rocco's faith lost and faith regained, the duke quite properly recedes into the background for a large portion of the novella. However, when he is reintroduced, the reader has no difficulty in recognizing an old acquaintance who has aged but has not basically changed. (p. 127)

The fact of which the duke is proud is his isolation from society. . . . Not making common cause with the people means, of course, dominating and torturing them, which in his better moments appears childish to the duke, and inferior to other courses of action a ruler might take. He recalls that he has toyed with ideas of a different way of life. . . . But he toyed with them only to reject them, since putting them into practice would have meant unendurable loss of prestige. He is certain that he would have harvested nothing but disdain from the people, had he chosen decency and anonymity, so he tells Don Rocco. Heinrich Mann's despot, one may say, is a man who spreads horror because of a distorted conception of human nature and an insane desire to be exalted. He cannot help doing so, although he recognizes his baseness for what it is. (p. 128)

Turning from *Auferstehung* to *Der Tyrann* the reader has little difficulty in recognizing the relationship of these two novellas, since Heinrich Mann obviously meant the Duke of Lagoscuro in the former and Duke Alessandro in the latter to be one and the same person at different stages of his life. For instance, when Alessandro mentions one of his former ministers by the name of Vampa, one recalls that at the beginning of *Auferstehung* a ducal minister by that name is killed in the struggle for the freedom of Lagoscuro. And when Signora Raminga Guidati, Alessandro's antagonist, is brought before him, she is led to his chamber through the ruins of an old theater reminiscent of that in which Don Rocco's master hoped to find refuge from Garibaldi. (pp. 130-31)

When Alessandro ascended the throne, he banished his mother from the court, but he did not alter the government of the country. Being the scion of a family of despots, he felt that he, too, had to be a despot; and his pusillanimous silence at a strategic moment was generally regarded as tacit acceptance of the role he was supposed to play. In the eyes of friend and foe he was committed to despotism. Subsequent events merely made matters worse. Liberals who had escaped the wrath of the duchess now made attempts on Alessandro's life. He had to execute them to maintain himself. After that there were no more links between him and the people of his state. He remained the tyrant that inner weakness and family pressure had made of him. (p. 131)

[In *Der Tyrann*] Heinrich Mann naturally leads the reader deeper into the recesses of the despotic mind than was necessary in *Auferstehung*. Four aspects in particular add substantially to the picture of the tyrant drawn by the author: (1) the relationship of Alessandro to his forbears, (2) his obsession for camouflaging his weakness by means of cruelty, (3) his fears and suspicions, and finally, (4) the realization of his impotence in spite of his power. (p. 132)

As regards his ancestors Alessandro feels very strongly that by expending heroic efforts uprooting all goodness on earth they determined his own manner of ruling the state. Their legacy of tyranny is a burden he cannot shake off. . . . Merciless conquest and brutal administration established the dynasty and set the pattern for all later rulers; and even more important, conditioned the populace to despotism. The young duke's much lauded forbears, one may say, relegated to him a task and the tools for the task, but they failed to transmit their gusto and their ability to accomplish it. (pp. 132-33)

The only thing to offset the burden of Alessandro's heritage is the temporal power given to him. But the weak young ruler rarely derives genuine pleasure from his power, since most of the time it merely serves him to defeat attacks against his person and his regime. To be sure, he finds some satisfaction in outwitting his opponents and destroying them. To be sure, he sees some cosmic purpose in the preservation of his self. . . . But in the final analysis this rationalization crumbles, and Alessandro must admit that the self he preserves is of little value, and that in every other respect his power is sterile. . . .

The picture of the despot as drawn by Heinrich Mann is complete. It is the portrait of the weakling in power, sketched deftly by an implacable observer to whom his subject is most unsavory. Convincing as they are in their role as despots, Alessandro and the Duke of Lagoscuro are also decadents, and this fact is most impressive. It shows that Heinrich Mann experienced and explored decadence so deeply that he discovered the elements of tyranny latent in it long before flesh-and-blood dictators appeared on the contemporary political scene. When they did rise to prominence in our own time, they demonstrated their resemblance to the portrait drawn by Heinrich Mann in 1911 clearly enough for the best known interpreter of decadence, Thomas Mann, to say of Hitler: "This man is my brother." (pp. 134)

*Rolf N. Linn, "Portrait of Two Despots by Heinrich Mann," in* The Germanic Review *(reprinted by permission of Joseph P. Bauke), Vol. XXX, No. 1, February, 1955, pp. 125-34.*

## THOMAS MANN  (essay date 1955)

[*The following is excerpted from a letter to Guido Devescovi, an Italian professor of German literature.*]

I was especially moved by your remark: "*La figura di Heinrich Mann, oscurata dalla grande ombra del fratello per tanto tempo, appare oggi sempre più nella sua giusta luce e grandezza.*" ["The figure of Heinrich Mann, obscured by the great shadow of his brother for such a long time, is today appearing more and more in its true light and greatness."] May that be true! His status is officially very high in the Communist part of Germany; but with few exceptions, one of which you cite, the West is silent about him. Even his beloved Italy and his still more beloved France show little receptivity to his life work, entirely Latin in schooling and character though it was, for all the peaks of sheer genius in it, such as *Die kleine Stadt, Professor Unrat, Henri IV,* and the late masterpiece, *Ein Zeitalter wird besichtigt.* I can assure you that a chariness concerning the obscuring "grande ombra" has marked my whole life since *Buddenbrooks.* Granted, I too have contributed to the Europeanization of the German novel, but my way of doing it was more traditionally German and closer to music, sounding a more ironic note than his—a dubious advantage, but a real one precisely in the eyes of the Germans and of Latin students of German literature. At the same time, my basic attitude toward him and his somewhat formidably intellectual work was always that of the little brother looking up at the elder. It is expressed autobiographically in *Royal Highness,* where Klaus Heinrich says to his brother, the Grand Duke: "I have always looked

up to you because I always felt and knew that you were the more distinguished and superior of us two and I am only a plebeian compared with you. But if you deem me worthy of standing at your side and bearing your title, *and representing you to the people,* although I do not consider myself so very presentable and have this hindrance here with my left hand, which I must always hide—then I thank you and am yours to command."

I represented "Albrecht" to the people *per tanto tempo,* with all that feeling for family which both of us had. Harold Nicolson once wrote something about "that amazing family," and this gave me more pleasure than any praise of me alone. For the rest, I feel quite sure that posterity will establish justice insofar as the hierarchy in this *family* is concerned. But it was an indescribable shock to me, and seemed like a dream, when shortly before his death Heinrich dedicated one of his books to me with the words: "To my great brother, who wrote *Doctor Faustus.*" What? How? He had always been the great brother. And I puffed out my chest and thought of Goethe's remark about the Germans' silly bickering over which was greater, he or Schiller: "They ought to be glad that they have two such boys." (pp. 679-80)

*Thomas Mann, in his letter to Guido Devescovi on May 1, 1955, in his* Letters of Thomas Mann, 1889-1955, *edited and translated by Richard Winston and Clara Winston (translation copyright © 1970 by Alfred A. Knopf, Inc.; reprinted by permission of the publisher), Knopf, 1971, pp. 678-80.*

## ROGER A. NICHOLLS  (essay date 1960)

Echoes of Nietzsche may be found throughout most of Heinrich Mann's writings, but it would perhaps be most useful to concentrate on the early trilogy *Die Göttinnen,* where the influence seems most explicit, to attempt to find what it is in Nietzsche that is important to Heinrich Mann and how Mann made use of Nietzsche's thought and experience. . . .

[*Die Göttinnen*] was among the most ambitious of Mann's earlier works and one that today seems particularly revealing of his inmost concerns. (p. 165)

Mann attempts nothing less than an exploration of the whole reigning morality, observing in contrast with the Duchess the extravagances and weaknesses of the present. Nietzsche's contribution may be felt in both these aspects. As a chronicler of decadence, he provided Mann with a means for interpreting and understanding his own deeply felt sense of degeneration. At the same time, the Duchess reflects that longing for human grandeur that Nietzsche believed possible only in periods free from the rational and moral restraints of the present.

For the portrait of the Duchess there were many immediate predecessors. Ibsen's Hedda Gabler, Wedekind's Lulu, Zola's Nana, are only some of the more familiar studies of an outstanding woman suffering as the victim of her time. While Mann continues this tradition in attempting a fresh, personal observation of feminine psychology, there is something new in this portrait which points to the particular inspiration of Nietzsche. Nietzsche's search to discover in a bourgeois age the qualities that make up a genuinely "noble" scale of values is a recurrent theme in much of his work. . . . The picture of the Duchess of Assy, for all her individual and personal qualities, reflects a similar search to reveal the characteristics that are the expression of a noble or aristocratic tradition. Mann is seeking in his own way to discover the values Nietzsche sought. . . . (pp. 165-66)

[The] Duchess remains in all her experiences of life untouched by the judgments of the outer world, indifferent to the opinion of the bourgeoisie among whom she lives. It is this unchallengeable self-respect that keeps her free from all the powerful dictates of what Nietzsche called "ressentiment." This is as essential for understanding Heinrich Mann here as it is for Nietzsche. Nietzsche later described his essay *Zur Genealogie der Moral* as the psychological exposition of the contrast between a noble morality and the morality of resentment, "the latter having sprung up as a denial of the former". . . .

The valuations of the bourgeois society with which the Duchess comes in contact are inextricably involved in a sense of reaction, envy, and revenge. Their judgments can never break free from these destructive forces. Their standards are necessarily those of the inferior, false, and biased because they are a form of protection, for the most part unconscious, against the outer world. Only she is able to live and make judgments freely, independently, disinterestedly. (p. 167)

[The] Duchess' life leaves us with a peculiar sense of dissatisfaction. There are too many uncertain elements. How are we to explain her recurring feeling that everything has been done before and seen before and painted before, every passion has been experienced, every valid action taken . . .? This is not only because the overcivilized outer world has become depressed and weary, but because she herself has so strong a sense of her own family's decline and is haunted by the fear her ancestors have used up its last energies. Hence the recurrent sense of "Is that all?" Is there no other joy to be looked for? Does life itself not offer more. . . . (pp. 168-69)

[The] fact emerges that the portrait of the Duchess is essentially a romantic one in disguise; it is emptiness and longing for life that impels her, not fullness or excess. She suffers from an impoverishment of everyday existence and seeks the "intoxication" and the "madness" of conviction and faith. She is, despite everything, the victim of her age. Her longing for a life worthy of her ancestors is in the end a form of romantic escape from her sense of decay.

In this respect we may point out how Mann's relationship to Nietzsche seems to have been influenced by the popular movement of "Renaissancism." Nietzsche's early fame coincided with a new outburst of enthusiasm for the amorality and overflowing passions of the Renaissance. Many of the more striking elements in Nietzsche—his cult of immoralism, his attacks on the slave-morality of modern times, the admiration he asserted for Cesare Borgia and the Renaissance "man of prey"—seemed to justify such an association. (p. 170)

Yet when we consider Mann's work from the point of view of the creative writer, it seems perhaps inevitable that his portrait should have these romantic qualities. Although Mann clearly intends the Duchess to stand apart from her bourgeois environment, she is not an abstract figure invented from theory alone. The Duchess is a part of life, created by the novelist as a human being in a human situation and envisioned very concretely by him. Thus she is necessarily a figure of the nineteenth century, a part of the world in which she lives. Mann's purpose itself is ambiguous, as we see in the fact that he chose a woman as the last of the Assy's. How are the positive, aggressive qualities that Nietzsche demands to be expressed here? We might expect a kind of "Überweib," but this would mean a complete sacrifice of Mann's critical sense. Instead, his actual

treatment of the woman is much closer to the genuine point of view of Nietzsche, who in an age of flourishing feminism emphasized the inescapably different roles of the sexes.

Heinrich Mann sees women as ultimately dependent on men; the very sense of emptiness the Duchess feels comes from the failure of the time and above all the failure of man. Since women are closer to nature than men, they retain more primitive strength, but they suffer all the more from the desperateness of the situation. They search for tasks which are essentially those of men. This is a frequently recurring theme in Mann's works. And the Duchess is not free from an experience that she shares with other women in the trilogy, the sculptress Properzia Ponti, for instance, or the world traveler Lady Olympia Ragg, and such other heroines as Ute Ende in *Die Jagd nach Liebe* and Lola Gabriel in *Zwischen den Rassen*. But to recognize this is to see the Duchess no longer as an external measure for the age, but as one who is herself involved in its complex problems. (p. 171)

[The] emphasis in Mann's work from *Im Schlaraffenland* through *Die Jagd nach Liebe* and *Professor Unrat* and on to the Wilhelminian trilogy *Der Untertan, Die Armen*, and *Der Kopf*, was a growing bitterness in his observation of the contemporary scene and a stern rejection of illusory reconciliations. In this development Mann's picture of Nietzsche did not change. In *Die Göttinnen* Nietzsche had been the principal source of criteria by which the age could be judged; Mann's work continues the exploration of modern decadence but never again in so explicitly Nietzschean terms. Mann's associations with Nietzsche were more and more with the unrestrained passions of the Renaissance cult. (p. 177)

*Roger A. Nicholls, "Heinrich Mann and Nietzsche,"* in Modern Language Quarterly (© 1960 University of Washington), Vol. XXI, No. 2, June, 1960, pp. 165-78.\**

## ULRICH WEISSTEIN (essay date 1960)

[*Weisstein is a prominent Mann scholar. In his essay on* Die kleine Stadt, *excerpted below, Weisstein discusses Mann's relationship to Italy and the modern Italian literary movement of Verism.*]

Whereas in his previous novels, where the aesthetic point of view prevails, his interest in politics is incidental, [Mann] has struck [in *Die Kleine Stadt*] a perfect balance between art, life and politics. . . .

In its sunny Mediterranean setting, *Die Kleine Stadt* bespeaks Heinrich Mann's artistic temperament just as *Buddenbrooks* and *Der Zauberberg* betoken that of his brother. The basic difference in their outlook is even more apparent in those of their works which lack the customary setting, Heinrich Mann's Germany turning into an object for satire, and Thomas Mann's Italy remaining a mythical country where metaphysical speculation still results in the Wagnerian death-wish. (p. 255)

The complex plot of *Die Kleine Stadt* begins to unfold when an operatic troupe arrives for a brief *stagione*. Liberating the emotions hitherto hidden under a cloak of tradition and respectability, this artistic event—serving as a catalyst by means of which the latent struggle between two opposing factions is brought into the open—has grave political and moral consequences. Rallying to the defence of art, the 'progressives', led by the lawyer Belotti, fight the 'conservatives' under the resolute leadership of Don Taddeo. Defeated in a pitched battle, Taddeo's forces are saved when a fire, which threatens to destroy the city, demands the attention of the entire populace. (p. 256)

I shall endeavour to describe the nature of the interrelation between art, life and politics within the framework of *Die Kleine Stadt*. Fortunately, such an undertaking is facilitated by the third chapter of the novel, where the operatic action on stage is skilfully integrated with the reaction of the audience and thus related to life in general. But it is pointless to discuss this topic in the absence of a definite historical perspective.

The Italy of our novel is a country in which the spirit of Garibaldi still lives and the art of Giuseppe Verdi is highly esteemed. But in addition to the historical names of Verdi and Garibaldi the reader will find those of fictitious personalities like Viviani (the composer of an opera entitled *Die Arme Tonietta*) and Enrico Dorlenghi, his follower. Viviani's opera is Heinrich Mann's contribution to Verism, a phase in the history of the lyric theatre which is represented in the works of Leoncavallo and Mascagni. While emulating the strictly naturalistic approach so dear to these masters, Mann also discovers its inherent limitations. In *Die Arme Tonietta* he transcends these limitations by introducing unrestrained lyricism of the kind which the mature Puccini permitted in his operas. (p. 257)

According to a well-known musicologist, it is the aim of Verism, 'simply to present a vivid, melodramatic plot, to arouse sensation by violent contrasts, to paint a cross-section of life without concerning itself with any general significance the action might have'. Veristic music 'aims simply and directly at the expression of intense passion through melodic or declamator phrases', everything being so arranged that 'the moments of excitement follow one another in swift climactic succession'. This intensity fully accounts for the brevity of many veristic operas, certain of which are derived from works like Giovanni Verga's concise *Novelle Rusticane*. In the process of transformation these works are sentimentalized, as can be shown in the case of Verga's *Cavalleria Rusticana*, a short story which the author himself adapted for the stage, and which was later transformed into the libretto of Mascagni's opera. Heinrich Mann showed his awareness of this stylistic trend by publishing in 1910, *Die arme Tonietta,* a *novella* based on the operatic plot described in the novel, but treating its ingredients in a manner compatible with literary Verism.

Instead of presenting the action of his opera-within-the-novel by way of a synopsis, Heinrich Mann makes it emerge from the scattered comments of his small-town audience. This goes to prove that in introducing the opera he was primarily concerned with the popular reaction to an artistic experience capable of being related to the personal experiences of each member of the audience. . . . Since it is a vital aspect of life in Italy, this interpenetration enables the author to establish a critical point of view outside either sphere of existence.

Like Flaubert in a famous scene of his *Madame Bovary*, Heinrich Mann skilfully interlaces several strands of action in order to produce the desired effect upon the reader. By showing life to be symbolized in the medium of art, he reminds us of the latter's life-enhancing values. By demonstrating how aesthetic categories can be erroneously applied to life, he warns us of the dangers inherent in the confusion of ethical with aesthetic standards.

Those readers of *Die Kleine Stadt* who are not familiar with the southern mentality will be struck by the lack of privacy which makes itself felt on every page of the novel. Without much exaggeration one could say that in Italy all manifestations

of life turn into public spectacles. Due to the quick temper of most individuals, the most trifling incidents are always on the verge of being comedy or tragedy. A noble action and a fine artistic performance are greeted with equal applause, just as an unpopular deed and an artistic failure meet with disapproval. As the reaction of the audience is spontaneous, however, approval and disapproval may follow closely upon each other. . . . Politically speaking, this fickleness is both fortunate and unfortunate: fortunate in that no systematic subversion of the existing order is possible (hence Savezzo's failure), unfortunate because the popular hero may become the victim of shifting opinion (hence Belotti's ordeal).

In the Italy of *Die Kleine Stadt,* 'il popolo è mobile,' the force which appeared to liberate the emotions soon undermines public morality. Instead of serving the cause of political freedom, the new libertinism (that which Belotti euphemistically terms 'die freie Menschlichkeit') furthers the breakthrough of anarchic sentiments. As rumour fans suspicion, all emotional controls are abandoned and the whole town is thrown into utter confusion. But the reign of terror is of brief duration. Deprived of its leader, Don Taddeo, the mass is split into its elements; and since, as individuals, the inhabitants are incapable of sustaining a heightened emotion, their rage subsides as quickly as it was aroused.

It was because of the volatility of the Italian character, so familiar to him, that Heinrich Mann ventured to present his theme in the gentle spirit of irony instead of handling it with the coarse tools of satire. In the little world of our novel, political consequences were to be feared only if anarchy were allowed to spread beyond the city limits. But since the scene of action is well contained, no such infection can be envisaged. Everything happens on an intimate scale, and no character forgets that the hostile faction, too, consists of neighbours and relatives. Political tragedy is possible only where the scale is large or where the horizon can be widened. Where the limitations are observed, human weakness appears in a mellow, conciliatory light. The tragic elements are moved to the periphery or altogether expelled. (pp. 258-59)

Although full of contradictions and inconsistencies, *Die Kleine Stadt* is a milestone on Heinrich Mann's way to artistic maturity and deserves comparison with *Der Untertan* and *Professor Unrat* as a minor classic of modern German literature. (p. 261)

*Ulrich Weisstein, " 'Die Kleine Stadt': Art, Life and Politics in Heinrich Mann's Novel," in* German Life & Letters, *n.s. Vol. XIII, No. 4, July, 1960, pp. 255-61.*

### W. E. YUILL (essay date 1963)

[It was Heinrich Mann's] aim to register the intellectual and emotional climate of an era, a social class or a nation. The climate rather than the geology, so to speak, for Mann is not a sociological novelist in the sense of one who painstakingly maps out the structure of society. His imagination is visual and poetic rather than primarily analytical: it is stimulated by patterns rather than diagrams and revels in gestures rather than graphs. . . .

Mann's mind not only absorbs and reproduces striking gestures—it magnifies them, too, for there is in it an element of the grotesque and the histrionic. But although his visions often have the quality of nightmare, they are rarely pure fantasy: they are simply the truth writ large. (p. 200)

Although he never achieved lasting success as a dramatist, Mann was fascinated throughout his life by the theatre, and there is hardly one of his novels, from *Im Schlaraffenland* to *Henri IV* in which a theatrical performance does not play a significant part. It is above all the glamorous figure of the actress that captivates his imagination: his work is full of characters like Ute Ende, Branzilla (in the *Novelle* of that name) and Flora Garlinda in *Die kleine Stadt,* bewitching monsters of artifice and pathological ambition. . . . But the actress is not only a siren, she is also an outcast; her art is a weakness as well as a weapon, requiring her to live on that razor-edge between truth and fiction, tragedy and comedy. Mann's understanding of this situation is shown in the short story *Schauspielerin* and the drama with the same title, which have plots differing only in the ending. The heroine in each case is loved by a wealthy man who, for family reasons, refuses to marry her. In the story (as in another *Novelle* entitled *Szene*) the actress survives the crisis precisely because of the release of tension offered by her art and the emotional resilience it has taught her. (pp. 202-03)

For the respectable citizen the stage can be a perilous lure: it represents a kind of pandemonium which threatens to overturn his well-ordered society. The moral balance of a community may in fact be judged by its reaction to the seductive world of the stage. This is essentially the theme of *Professor Unrat* and *Die kleine Stadt,* which depict the response of two very different communities to the irruption into their midst of a Bohemian element. *Professor Unrat* is more than a study of a personality grotesquely deformed by the exercise of authority and the burden of public scorn: Mann is concerned with the inner nature of a community as well as with the fate of an eccentric. When the grammar-school teacher is ostracized because he has succumbed to the grimy attractions of the "Blue Angel", he avenges himself on the community by turning on it the spell which caused his own downfall. Himself entangled in a web of hatred and jealousy, he uses the "artiste", Rosa Fröhlich, to ensnare and deprave his fellow-citizens. Unrat's revenge could not succeed, however, if he did not appeal to an element of anarchy and latent hysteria beneath the apparent respectability of this small town. (p. 203)

It is almost by chance that the hypnotic power of Unrat—or, rather, the power of the citizens' own vices—is broken: he is arrested for a minor offence and at once becomes a scapegoat instead of an ogre. (p. 204)

*Im Schlaraffenland, Die Göttinnen* and *Die Jagd nach Liebe* have an element of satire, but their social criticism is peripheral. *Professor Unrat, Die kleine Stadt* and the novel *Zwischen den Rassen,* which is concerned specifically with the schizophrenia of those who—like Mann—are situated between the Nordic and the Latin race: these are works which indicate growing concentration and a sharpening of focus. Mann begins to see his task as social critic more clearly; the pose of the outsider which may be detected in much of his early work, is dropped and the moralist and political thinker emerge more and more; Zola succeeds Nietzsche as Mann's model. Henceforth Heinrich Mann adheres to what he regards as a typically French tradition of liberal thought and writing. . . . In Heinrich Mann's view the modern German writer has betrayed his nation. . . . German poets have dwelt in an ivory tower, cut off from the concerns of the people. . . . There is, by and large, some truth in this view, although it does less than justice to the naturalistic writers and to an unruly genius like Frank Wedekind, for whom Mann elsewhere expresses great admiration. There is some

truth, too, in Mann's contention that German society does not know its own nature because the poets have thus failed it. As he was to write later, "It is split into strata which are ignorant of each other, and the ruling class looms vaguely behind the clouds." It was to remedy this situation that Heinrich Mann embarked on his second trilogy, *Das Kaiserreich,* in which he attempts to analyse the society of Imperial Germany as Zola had analysed that of the Second Empire.

Of the three novels, *Der Untertan, Die Armen* and *Der Kopf,* which deal respectively with the middle class, the workers and the political leadership, the first is undoubtedly the most accomplished. The very name of its hero, Diederich Heßling, with the mixture of hatred and weakness it suggests, is an imaginative triumph. Heßling is a complex figure, embodying the contradictions of his class and yet by no means forfeiting his plausibility. (pp. 205-06)

*Der Untertan* is a splendid satire, executed with the deftness and the controlled distortions of a *Simplicissimus* caricature; it is mordant but not pitiless, full of understanding as well as anger. It has humorous scenes of unforced symbolism: Heßling squatting in a puddle before his monarch, or pursuing him with frantic hurrahs across a Roman square; dedicating his wedding night to the Emperor, or crouching under the lectern to escape the thunderbolts which his oration has apparently called down. Mann's touch is less adroit in the sequel, *Die Armen,* perhaps because the tragedy of the German situation had become more obvious. This is a sombre work with lurid highlights. Heßling has developed fully the satanic features that the elder Buck had glimpsed in his dying moments; he rules, a neurotic tyrant and the father of degenerate sons, over a colony of workers who are degraded, like the workers in Brecht's *Heilige Johanna,* by their dependence and penury. . . . (p. 209)

The capitulation of the intellectual is the theme of *Der Kopf.* This final novel of the trilogy is not a sequel to the other two, and it differs from them in that it is a semi-fictional work, in which real events feature and leading German politicians appear under pseudonyms. The documentation of the story occupied Mann for years, and it was not published until 1925. The plot revolves round two men of Mann's own generation who embark on political careers. Wolf Mangolf chooses the path of the conformist; Claudius Terra is a much more problematic character, half-idealist, half-charlatan, a disreputable Marquis Posa, a mountebank who pursues humanitarian ideals. (pp. 209-10)

*Der Kopf* has not the clear contours of *Der Untertan* nor its uniformly satirical mood; it is a mixture of savage caricature and mystical symbolism. The language oscillates between brooding lyricism and the staccato style of "Neue Sachlichkeit". On the one hand there is the delicately equivocal relationship between Terra and his sister Lea—a recurrent theme in Mann's work, well illustrated in the story, *Der Bruder,* written about this time. On the other hand there is the nightmarish description of the hate-feast of militarists and industrialists. The novel is altogether a sad and tortured work. *Der Untertan* was a prophecy; *Der Kopf* is an epitaph on a lost generation of intellectuals who were forced by the social pressures of their age into disingenuousness and anarchy on the one hand, irresponsible ambition and compromise on the other. It is an epitaph, too, on a nation that rushed to its doom, hypnotized by the abyss. . . . (p. 210)

Like his short stories and plays, Mann's novels of this period mostly exude the typically hectic atmosphere of the 1920's. In common with Brecht, Feuchtwanger, Döblin and the artist George

Groß, Mann was fascinated by the jungle of the cities with their jazz, professional boxers, fast cars and ''big deals''. This was just the atmosphere to stimulate the romantic nerve in Mann's imagination, and often he seems less concerned with social criticism than with the fate of individuals in a milieu that is very much that of the detective story. In Mann, as in Brecht, mother-love is very nearly the only emotion that remains uncorrupted in this context, and in **Mutter Marie** and **Ein ernstes Leben** the theme is a mother's battle for her child against the criminal designs of the Berlin underworld. In both these stories Mann also explores the near-incestuous relationships that seemed to haunt him: the quasi-erotic feeling of Marie for Valentin, her son, is reminiscent of the relationship between Lili and her son in **Der Kopf,** while the intimacy of Terra and Lea is raised to daemonic pitch in Kurt and Vicki Meier in **Ein ernstes Leben.** (p. 213)

Cut off after 1933 from the nation whose social and political malaise he had so faithfully recorded, Mann at last departed from his resolve to write novels of contemporary society. The last phase of his work is dominated by the third great pillar that supports a span of nearly sixty years' creative writing—the two historical novels, **Die Jugend des Henri Quatre** and **Die Vollendung des Henri Quatre.** . . . Mann does not hesitate to idealize the character and aspirations of Henry, for the novel is designed to put into narrative patterns and symbolic scenes the liberal idealism of his political writing.

For Mann, Henry's excellence as a ruler stems from his qualities as a man: he has the emotional well-temperedness and the sound sensuality of the Mediterranean race, the critical reason of the Frenchman; he is both an intellectual and a man of action, a militant humanist. (pp. 214-15)

The two novels of Henry's life were not the last of Mann's works; they were followed by volumes of essays and reminiscences, as well as by a satirical novel of the Czech resistance, **Lidice,** and by a strange and involved account of the outbreak of the 1939 war in France (**Der Atem**), which falls far short of the standard of his other work. After his death the fragmentary dramatized novel on Frederick the Great was published. None of these later works, however, embodies the essence of Mann's thought or illustrates the maturity of his art as well as **Henry IV.** It is a work of epic stamina that moves at a steady, unhurried pace. Often the narrative gives way to pure dialogue, for which Mann showed an increasing fondness, and the author does not hesitate to employ elliptical epic phrases of his own devising. The style is terse and compact, not so much German in its syntax and rhythm as French—and, indeed, the periodic commentaries and the final vision of the transfigured hero are written in French. (p. 217)

In his determination to speak to the nation as a whole and to help shape its policies, Mann differs probably from the majority of German writers, who have tended to address themselves rather to the individual cultured mind. To some readers, Mann may seem naïve in his pursuit of political ideals, undiscriminating, for instance, in his unqualified enthusiasm for the Russian revolution as the worthy continuation of the revolution of 1789. It would be difficult, however, to doubt his integrity, his sincere devotion to principles which he is capable of formulating clearly and simply. (pp. 218-19)

> W. E. Yuill, ''Heinrich Mann,'' in German Men of Letters: Twelve Literary Essays, Vol. II, edited by Alex Natan (© 1963 Oswald Wolff (Publishers) Limited), Wolff, 1963, pp. 197-224.

## DAVID ROBERTS   (essay date 1971)

> [In the following excerpt from his study of Mann, Roberts divides Mann's works into three periods. The first period (1900-1914) includes works dealing with isolated individuals, usually artists, as in Im Schlaraffenland. The works of the second period (1914-1933), including the Kaiserreich trilogy, reveal Mann's reaction to political conditions in Germany. Mann's last period (1933-1939) examines the failure of nationalism and treats Europe as an interrelated cultural and political entity, most notably in the novel Henri Quatre.]

[An] identity of views over a period of fifteen years [1900-1914] reveals the depth and the extent of Heinrich Mann's problem: it is the key to the slow process of self-understanding of the anti-bourgeois who is a bourgeois, whose attacks on the Kaiserreich do not spare the dreams and illusions of the critic himself. The analysis of society is also self-analysis. It is from this point that we can understand the dual function of the central figure of **Im Schlaraffenland. Ein Roman unter feinen Leuten.** In taking Maupassant's *Bel Ami* as his model, Heinrich Mann renews a favorite theme of the 19 century novel: the provincial's attempts to gain a footing in high society—with the decisive variation, however, that the hero, who is worthy of the society he ''conquers'', serves now not only as the transparent medium of the social satire but also as the objectification, *via* the figure of the novelist Köpf, of Heinrich Mann's own relation to society. The author's lack of sympathy with his hero Andreas Zumsee—the type of the adventurer and confidence trickster, bourgeois and anti-bourgeois in one (cf. [Frank Wedekind's] *Der Marquis von Keith,* also published in 1900)—is the ironic corrective of the novelist to his own earlier ''Plan'' of 1894 (the year of the action of the novel) of a life of exclusive luxury in Paris—at least for a month! (p. 26)

The sum of the novel? Less its sum than the problem of its author: the problem of a writer in a society in which culture is governed by money. . . . Heinrich Mann's satire reveals in its absolute negativity the impossibility of engagement. The technique of the self-exposure by means of the self-presentation of society, in which dialogue plays a central role, is the form appropriate to this satirical position, and at the same time it points forward to the impersonal style of the dramatic novel. Imitation and parody, mimicry and caricature . . . are the weapons of Heinrich Mann's satire, against which the comic sense of the grotesque and self-irony—we must not overlook the achievement of **Im Schlaraffenland** as a comic novel—provide the defensive liberation from the urge to self-assertion. In attacking Berlin society Heinrich Mann must also attack his own illusions—the dream of ''Geist'' conquering ''Macht''. The study of power involves also the study of the writer's will to power.

Heinrich Mann's critical reception of Nietzsche, the psychologist of decadence and the philosopher of ''life'', of ''strength'', is one with his slow and painful search for a firm position in the years up to 1907. Nietzsche's influence is thus most clearly discernable in the ''artist'' figures in Heinrich Mann's work in this period, of which Mario Malvolto, if the best known, is only the most prominent of the long line of decadents and aesthetes who are ''malvolto''; others in this series are Jean Guignol, Mortoeil, Jakobus Halm (**Die Göttinnen**), Claude Marehn (**Die Jagd nach Liebe**), Arnold Acton (**Zwischen den Rassen**). The names Guignol, Halm, Mortoeil are revealing of the author's attitude. Mortoeil, for instance, destroys life, Midaslike, wherever he touches it. Guignol, Halm, Siebelind are the sick who preach health, who forget their cynicism and despair at the prospect of sexual satisfaction. In their heads and in their actions lives the antagonism of life and art. They long to experience all that is denied them. (pp. 29-31)

Heinrich Mann's artists and aesthetes are the bearers of the theme of impotence, of the defeat of spontaneous nature by intellect, which gives rise in their works to the fantasies of virility and beauty, even more, to the fatal desire to *live* what they *dream*. Basic to the analysis of the aesthete is the motif of the artist who plays with his own emotions and degrades life to the raw material of literature, where even the attempt to break out of this deadening self-consciousness turns out to be an irresponsible game. The sequence—the exploitation of life for the sake of art, the writer become the dramatist of his own emotions, who finally confuses the dream with reality— is given in paradigmatic form in the tragicomedy of Mario Malvolto. He can stand for all the efforts to escape to life, which have the purpose of denying the one real experience common to all these figures, the intolerable knowledge of their weakness and insufficiency. For these latecomers life is accordingly the unthinking strength of the condottiere, the passionate satisfaction of the instincts, that is to say, inhuman, superhuman. The antitheses are weak or strong, sick and healthy, ugly and beautiful, pedestrian and adventurous life. (pp. 33-4)

Only one element is missing—the human. It is inevitable that the works of this period end in catastrophe. Andreas Zumsee, the hero of *Im Schlaraffenland,* is plunged from the heights of social success back into well-deserved obscurity, Violante dies of hysteria, unable to have the child she wants, the last of her race; Unrat is locked up by his fellow-citizens, only too happy to find a scapegoat ("eine Fuhre Unrat") for their degeneration; Mario Malvolto is left the crushed survivor of a suicide pact; Claude Marehn (*Jagd nach Liebe*) . . . dies of his impotent longing.

When we turn to the bourgeois world—not the "Schlaraffenland" of Berlin or the international society of *Die Göttinnen* (the character Claire Pimbusch appears in both works)—we discover that the "Bürger" is only the unconscious counterpart of the outsider. The critique of the aesthete already contains the elements of analysis which bring to light the latent tendencies of provincial life in *Professor Unrat.* The hero of this novel—humanly speaking—is dead. Here the denial of the romantic impulse leads to the deformation of emotion in bitter satire. This is the precondition of the inhumanity of Unrat (which is not motivated but simply stated), whose late sensuality stands in grotesque contrast to his sentimental adulation of Rosa Fröhlich. Unrat's life is a struggle against a rebellious world—the classroom on which he seeks to impose the peace of the graveyard. Since his authority, however, stands in no relation to his tyrannic will his impotence in the face of the world produces in him a smouldering fury, the longing to destroy and the compensation of "Herrenmoral". . . . In Unrat we see once more, in modified form, the conflicts of the aesthete. . . . (p. 34)

The driving force of Heinrich Mann's development is the urge to overcome the split between art and life. We see first in *Flaubert* and then in *Zwischen den Rassen* und *Der Tyrann* how human and political emancipation converge (the inspiration is the French Revolution) to find at last their productive union in *Die Kleine Stadt.* Up to and including *Zwischen den Rassen* Heinrich Mann's path is contradictory for he cannot escape the false alternatives of art and life which govern the self-consciousness of the isolated rebel and determine the sharp antitheses of the Flaubert essay. Only when Heinrich Mann has

seized the real interconnexion of art and life, of the artist and bourgeois society, can the inner movement of his development become conscious—the striving to escape, through social engagement, the very role and function that bourgeois society has allotted the "artist". And yet as the radical democrat in the Kaiserreich it is this new, politically conscious, isolation which in the ground for his two pre-war masterpieces. Heinrich Mann's isolation has now become a source of strength. It is now the vantage point which makes him *the* political satirist of the Kaiserreich in *Der Untertan* and *the* democrat and humanist among the writers of pre-war Germany in *Die Kleine Stadt.* . . . (p. 50)

In [the essay] *Zola* we see the incipient crisis of Heinrich Mann's work and development. The impetus of his development reaches its highpoint in this theoretical statement of his beliefs, it carries him from liberalism to socialism, from the bourgeoisie to the workers as the new bearers of democracy. But where is the revolutionary class in Germany? All that follows reveals the essay as a last heroic but abstract statement of 19 century democratic, utopian faith. . . . This essay which grew out of *Der Untertan* is its ideal counterpart, and the ideal counterpart to the *Kaiserreich* trilogy. Here is the transcendence of the Kaiserreich and war which the novelist could not give and which the Weimar Republic did not give. Thus when Heinrich Mann writes the last part of his trilogy in the Weimar Republic, the Zola essay becomes part of the history of the Kaiserreich. (p. 135)

Heinrich Mann's second period of work is determined from without. It is encompassed by two violent breaks, 1914 and 1933, the end of the era of peace and the end of the Weimar Republic. We cannot look for an internal logic of development, an organic unity such as we saw in the growth to maturity and literary mastery in the years preceding the first world war. It is not a natural but a historically determined unit and thus we can only approach Heinrich Mann's work through the social and political upheavals of this period. Not surprisingly the fate of Germany dominates Heinrich Mann's thought almost to the exclusion of everything else and his work reflects this, most obviously in the six novels from *Die Armen* to *Ein ernstes Leben* . . . , which are all devoted to the German scene between 1871 and 1932, and of which half, and the more substantial half, return to "die bürgerliche Zeit" before 1914. Whereas in the first period of work the Italian novels and Novellen more than hold the balance with the novels about the Kaiserreich, now after 1914 Italy disappears altogether while France provides the subject only for the Novelle *Liliane und Paul* . . . and for the one play *Der Weg zur Macht,* in which Heinrich Mann is concerned above all—he is writing in 1917 and 1918—to examine through the French Revolution the parallels to the German situation. Although France plays a decisive role in Heinrich Mann's thought from the Flaubert essay onwards, as has often been pointed out, it does not provide— and this has not been stressed—the setting or subject for any of his novels before *Henri Quatre.* Only in exile does the novelist give direct expression to the civilisation which has moulded his development. The polemic opposition of France to the German reality is present already in 1910 in the essays *Geist und Tat* and *Voltaire—Goethe,* but with this opposition just as clearly the necessity of making the democratic alternative fruitful *for and in* Germany: the central and abortive concern of the years 1914-1932. Abortive politically because there was hardly a possibility of a Franco-German synthesis in these years, abortive artistically because Heinrich Mann could be true to himself only in opposition, given the actual course of events. 1933 thus signifies the "liberation" from the compulsion of a hopeless struggle. The advent of Hitler transfers the struggle from a vain defence of a Republic, dead in all but name, onto the level of a life and death resistance to the total challenge of Fascism, a challenge which restores the unity of heart and head, so hopelessly split between duty and insight in the Weimar Republic. The failure of the novelist must be the judgement on Heinrich Mann's second period of work. (pp. 136-37)

If the belief in democracy before 1914 means the conquest of the disruptive dichotomy of art and life (in art), the overcoming of the split plunges Heinrich Mann into the opposite extreme of the tension between life and art. The path to democracy inspires the artist before 1914, the struggle for democracy cripples the artist after 1914. The conscience of the "Bürger", his bitter indignation, was artistically productive in the political novel *Der Untertan*, but artistically destructive in *Die Armen*, the novel of a political writer, for whom the duty and the ambition to be the chronicler of the Kaiserreich (*Die Armen* and *Der Kopf*) dictated works which spring from no fruitful inner compulsion. The union of art and politics as the answer to isolation and as the road to a wide influence, as the expression of Heinrich Mann's belief in the word as a force, superceding the old sterile dualism of art and life, romanticism and realism, in fact results in the destruction of the precarious balance of tensions from which Heinrich Mann had won his pre-war masterpieces. The conflict of artist and citizen, individual and society (in itself the *subject-matter* of the writer) gives way, not to the sacrifice of intellect to "life", the earlier temptation of the aesthete, but to the sacrifice of art to the demands of the day, the temptation of the moralist. The logical consequence is to turn from art, and it would hardly be an exaggeration to see the half-hearted didacticism of the "Romane der Republik" (1926-1932) as a form of inner emigration from the realm of art.

Heinrich Mann is caught in the second period of work between his duty as a writer anxious not to escape his responsibilities (seeking to break down the barriers between the intellectual and the workers and to find new readers), and the bewildering reality of war, revolution and reaction, the failure to consolidate the Republic and the speedy confusion of democracy. It is here that we must situate Heinrich Mann's crisis of the novel. It is the crisis of the writer for whom the commission of the age—to be the novelist of a Republic which believed in itself—did not arrive. We cannot say that this explains the failure of Heinrich Mann at the height of his powers or justifies the weakness of the years which should have crowned his career, but it is the only approach which comes near to an adequate understanding: it is not the problematic nature of reality which shows us the way but the specific question of the impact of Germany's course on a writer, who, in proclaiming the identity of art and politics, reflects in the most direct manner the problem of the engaged writer. (pp. 137-38)

Heinrich Mann must go other ways if he is to escape the impasse of his art in a society he has inwardly given up and this way is into exile and to the France of Henri IV and the popular front. (p. 161)

The contradictions of Heinrich Mann's thinking in 1925 reveal the imperative need for a new synthesis—the United States of Europe as the only means to prevent the next European war. We can now attempt—from this point 1925—a unifying model of Heinrich Mann's development which embraces the dialectic of reality and its intellectual-artistic mastering.

*Stage one (Im Schlaraffenland* to *Zwischen den Rassen)* is determined the contradictions of the isolated individual, seen as the internal civil war of the heart and the head, which, extended to the problems of a repressive and authoritarian society, leads from psychology to politics. The dynamic ego structure of the individual is translated to the body politic. The contradictions of the *individual* demand a higher synthesis, the jump from the individual to the group. The love of power yields to the power of love.

This brings us to *stage two (Die Kleine Stadt):* Eros becomes the driving force of the polis democracy. We see the Social Contract in action, the civil war results in the strengthening of the general will. This in turn calls forth its contradiction—*Der Untertan,* in which individual psychology becomes group psychology, the "history of the public soul under Wilhelm II". Now the civil war against the "inner enemy" produces a dynamic of imbalance; the triumph of aggression is the triumph of the death wish. Private interest prevails over the public. Might becomes right, the Social Contract dissolves itself and as the German "civil war" (to which Heinrich Mann opposes the other civil war in *Zola,* the victory of right over might) crosses its national boundaries with the outbreak of war, Heinrich Mann is forced to the European synthesis to resolve the *national* contradictions.

Here we reach *stage three.* The interlinked fates of Germany and France meet in the prologue [to *Der Kopf*] "Neunzig Jahre vorher"—which calls forth its ideal counterpart "Die Memoiren Napoleons". The Napoleonic wars offers the chance of "une Europe des patries". . . . Heinrich Mann's horizons expand—of necessity: the progression from the individual to the nation to Europe is dictated by the course of events. Looking back from this point we can see how the dialectic of past and present, Europe (France) and Germany, which will find its most comprehensive expression in *Henri Quatre,* is the dialectic of the (revolutionary) idea and the (imperialist) reality. Thus *Der Untertan* is the correction to *Die Kleine Stadt, Zola* to *Der Untertan, Die Armen* and *Der Kopf* to *Zola.* The link between these two opposing groups of works is the French Revolution and Napoleon. (pp. 165-66)

It is the classical content of (continental) European political thought since Plato, whose most complete expression Heinrich Mann found in the French Revolution and Napoleon, the two basic models for the novelist—both for the thinker and the *artist,* the analyst and the *dramatist* of power—which are joined in *Henri Quatre.*

The two opposed possibilities are the revolution from below and the revolution from above. They are held in balance in *Zola* with the emphasis on the people. They are held in balance in *Henri Quatre* with the emphasis on the leader. These two *central* works of Heinrich Mann's political thinking are ideal constructions, the transfiguration of reality—the idea of the French Revolution and the idea of Napoleon. Two extreme possibilities which Heinrich Mann was forced to think to their conclusion against the course of German history, and it is precisely the German inheritance and the European situation which takes Heinrich Mann from the revolution from below—*Die Jugend*—to revolutionary authority—*Die Vollendung*. But the two possibilities remain to the last—the acceptance of Stalin the realist (the Hitler-Stalin Pact), the understanding of the Moscow trials as Jacobin terror . . . , the admiration of Napoleon but also of Robespierre, "der Unbestechliche", and St. Just, "ein gewappneter Erzengel". . . . The two possibilities in *Zola* and *Henri Quatre* but also the sceptical wisdom of the moralist, who sees only the provisional achievements of human reason. (pp. 188-89)

In all respects *Henri Quatre,* as the culmination of his historical perspective, imposes a regressive-progressive approach to tradition. To renew the novel Heinrich Mann seeks inspiration from the epic and he returns the "Entwicklungsroman" to its picaresque origins of a series of adventures, but at the same time Henri is not simply a hero in the old epic sense, he is seen from within not from outside. (p. 193)

In *Henri Quatre* Heinrich Mann seeks to renew the link with Germany's classical heritage just as his brother felt compelled to write *finis* in *Doktor Faustus;* and just as his brother saw his work at the last expression of the 19 century novel, Heinrich Mann seeks its renewal in *Henri Quatre. Faust* ends with salvation through grace, *Doktor Faustus* with a prayer for grace, *Henri Quatre* with the call to action to preserve the precarious reign of reason and civilisation against the devilish possibilities in man. (p. 223)

The first world war is the decisive break for Heinrich Mann. The fact that the main body of his work, from *Im Schlaraffenland* to *Die Vollendung des Königs Henri Quatre,* falls into the periods—1900-1914, 1914-1933, 1933-1939—indicates how closely Heinrich Mann's production is tied to the age, and it is from this standpoint that we have sought to analyse his work. These three periods of work, determined so directly by the political events of the time, crystallise in the discontinuity they reveal, in the three stages they represent, the problem of the novelist Heinrich Mann. That is to say, had Heinrich Mann written nothing after 1914 the question of his literary place and achievement would not pose the problems they do. (pp. 243-44)

[The] major problem of H. Mann's work after *Zola* is that of a *political* conscience sustained by no fruitful inner persuasion, a commitment lacking a *good* conscience: a split which allows only the moral exercises of the "novels of the Republic" after the tortured, self-critical study of political conscience in *Der Kopf.* The crisis of the engaged writer and the novelist of German society is all too apparent in this novel—*Der Kopf* indeed confirms that the natural epoch of Heinrich Mann the social novelist came to an end in 1914, for if Heinrich Mann's subject in *Die Armen* and *Der Kopf* is still the Kaiserreich, these two novels reveal that he is too much caught up in the new situation of war and post-war to find once more the unity of conception and purpose of *Der Untertan*—or indeed of its counterpart *Die kleine Stadt,* for which there is equally no continuation in the Weimar Republic. *Der Kopf* is the conclusion of the novelist's attempt at intellectual conquest of German society. . . . The novels of the Weimar Republic which follow register no more than the willingness to come to terms with a new, unstable and short-lived society. The deeper response to contemporary events passes after 1914 from the novel to the essay; the essay collections *Macht und Mensch, Diktatur der Vernunft, Sieben Jahre* and the essay *Bekenntnis zum Übernationalen,* published between 1919 and 1932, certainly deserve far closer attention than they have received so far. But in stressing the importance of the essays (for all their tendency to abstractness) we must see that this split between the essay and the novel, this inability—or reluctance—to integrate the essay into the novel, underlines once again the problem of the novelist. (p. 245)

If we can see the second period of work in the main as the negative pendant to the first period, and if the double uncertainty—both artistically and politically—of Heinrich Mann's work after 1914 goes far to explain his failure, at the same time it also points to Heinrich Mann's extreme unevenness as a writer. We need, as it were, the artistic achievement of *Henri Quatre* to confirm the quality of his pre-1914 masterpieces. This unevenness—in striking contrast to his brother's *oeuvre*—confronts us with a phenomenon, which, if it is by no means unique in German literature, assumes such dimensions in Heinrich Mann's case that it acquires central importance. Heinrich Mann fascinates not only as a political "case history" but equally as an artistic "case history", and in assessing his work we must see that these two aspects belong together, that they form one problem and that Heinrich Mann reflects in an unusually clear and direct fashion the interaction of literature and politics, of the writer and his age, as indeed the periods of his work document. That is to say, the achievement of the novelist Heinrich Mann derives from the political situation, the artistic *truth* of his work is tied to the *historical moment:* more concretely, the artistic and political synthesis of *Die Kleine Stadt, Der Untertan* and *Henri Quatre* draws (in the last resort) on the hidden roots of *potential* revolutionary change in Germany.

Seen in this light these three novels are not just fortunate accidents in puzzling contradiction to the rest of his work, but the exceptions which prove the rule. The inescapable power of the age over the writer—one of Heinrich Mann's earliest insights and convictions—is the *objective* source of both his strength and his weakness. (pp. 248-49)

> *David Roberts, in his* Artistic Consciousness and Political Conscience: The Novels of Heinrich Mann, 1900-1938 *(© Herbert Lang & Co. Ltd., 1971), Lang, 1971, 261 p.*

**EDMUND KOSTKA** (essay date 1975)

[*While many critics point to Mann's affinities with French authors, Kostka's well-known study points out his kinship to Russian author Fyodor Sologub, comparing his* Professor Unrat *to Sologub's* The Little Demon.]

[There] emerges at least one major work by Heinrich Mann, *Professor Unrat* . . . , which bears a perplexing resemblance to the great novel of a *Russian* poet and romancier, Fyodor Sologub's *The Little Demon.* . . . Its protagonist Peredonov (a proverbial figure in Russian literature), spreads fear and terror among his unfortunate students like his colleague Unrat. Furthermore, both novels envelop the reader in a very peculiar atmosphere of individualism, aestheticism, nihilism, and sexual perversion. Not only the established order of society but the reality and validity of life itself are challenged in the name of beauty, indicted before the tribunal of humanity, and inescapably condemned. The dreary melancholy of isolated existence assumes in both works a highly significative symbolic dimension which is suggestive of the hopeless melancholy of human existence. (p. 22)

The scene of Heinrich Mann's novel is a small German town, a provincial town inhabited by dull, malicious, gossiping, corrupted burghers. It is with exquisite skill that the author distributes the social motif among his numerous characters. The aristocracy is represented by von Ertzum, a young man of good manners and an amazing naïveté who stolidly believes in the innocence and virginity of a tavern singer. (p. 25)

Among the members of the middle class we meet drunkards like the port inspector Kieselack, religious fanatics like the shoemaker Rindfleisch, philistines in the disguise of free-thinkers like Professor Unrat. Both Unrat and Peredonov [in *The Little Demon*] embody the type of the hypocritical philistine who, although unbelieving, still insists on obedience, religion, and morality in his subordinates. Being despots by nature, they instinctively know how to maintain authority, keep slaves, rule the unenlightened rabble. (pp. 25-6)

The type of the demonized small bourgeois is by no means a sporadic phenomenon in the literary production of Heinrich Mann. Through many of his novels goes like a red thread his fervent "interest for the 'bad': demoniacal characters who are obsessed by themselves." The same is true of the works of Fyodor Sologub. Time and again the Russian writer depicts demoniacal figures in his stories, plays, and novels. The names of Peredonov, Login, Trirodov are links in a long chain of satanic characters.

The scene of the novel *The Little Demon* is likewise a small town. The hopeless triviality of life, however, knows no frontiers; and melancholy, corruption, anguish, and vice weigh heavily on the souls of the Russian burghers. The figure of Peredonov constitutes the physical focus of all the invisible and series of Russian provincial life. The demon embodied in Peredonov is, accordingly, a little demon that has nothing in common with the great spirit of negation and doubt by whom Faust and Ivan Karamazov had been tormented. (p. 27)

[There] are characters in both novels that seem to contradict the assumption that the "Peredonovshchina" represents a disease of universal dimensions. In Heinrich Mann's novel the student Lohmann is such an exceptional character. (p. 28)

A dreamer and creator of fairy tales (in the Sologubian sense) lives in the student Lohmann. He is the only representative of the spirit in Heinrich Mann's novel, the type of the eternally dissatisfied ponderer—a sort of decadent Faust. He loves the things "because of the reminiscences they produce, the love of women only on account of the bitter loneliness that follows, happiness at most for the sake of the choking longing it leaves in one's throat." But he is more than just a dreamer—he is also the author of exuberant love poems. One night, overwhelmed by the throbbing of his yearning heart, he ardently kissed the door of Dora Breetpoot's house. Later, in a fit of despair, he hid a rifle in his father's warehouse to shoot himself in case his agonizing secret was discovered. Yet no one ever discovered it and "Lohmann could keep playing to himself and experiencing the wild chastity, the voluptuous bitterness, the timid, conceited, comforting world-disdain of his seventeen years. . . ." As he grew older he arrived at a more objective perception of the world—and fear of life and its realities suddenly laid hold of him. The dreamer, "touched by the spirit" and imbued with the romanticism of Heinrich Heine, collided with the hard facts of every-day life and experienced the shock of awakening. His observing eyes soon saw through the comedy of human existence; disenchantment, weariness, and bitterness filled him "up to the neck." Empty and charred, without a spark in his heart, he finally went to the house of the actress Rosa Fröhlich. The specter of the "Peredonovshchina" had vanquished him.

There is poignant melancholy at the bottom of these seemingly comical novels, a profound sorrow at the utter helplessness of man in the face of an invincible enemy. Man, according to this gloomy philosophy, is but a pitiable prisoner—an hostage of implacable and monstrous life, and the only thing left to him is despair. Such is the reaction of vanquished Lohmann

when he finally realized "what life had made of him." God does not exist in this world of demoniacal paltriness, and even if he did exist he would not have any use for the wretched human worms. . . . However, from this self-deification does not necessarily follow the negation of God in an absolute sense. It may be a paradox, yet Sologub—like Ivan Karamazov—rejects not God but the world created by God. In this respect, the parallel to the religious and socio-political views of the German writer is far-reaching. Needless to say, neither Heinrich Mann nor Fyodor Sologub were philosophers in the strict sense of the word, nor did they dream of elaborating a philosophical system of their own. But a metaphysical aura pervades their works and an agonizing melancholy lurks at the bottom of their concepts and ideas—it is the same ominous melancholy by which their Unrats and Peredonovs are driven to despair and madness. (pp. 29-30)

At the first glance, both Peredonov and Unrat appear thoroughly guilty and worthy of punishment. The matter looks different, however, if considered *sub specie aeternitatis*. Then it becomes evident how cruelly they were treated by their fellow citizens, how circumstances and conditions implacably conspired to bring about their madness and destruction. There was no one in the whole town who understood Peredonov. No one understood his secret longing, his hidden dreams—no one understood his shuddering at the blear-eyed "Nedotykomka." Yet even Peredonov had his Dulcinea and yearned after a higher life with all the strength of his sluggish spirit. (p. 32)

It is not difficult to perceive that also Professor Unrat may be seen as a victim of human society and circumstances. There was little more in his pitiful life than loneliness, hate, and despair. Mocked and persecuted by the entire town, he became a social outcast. . . . No one understood his secret fears and ardent longings—no one except the whimsical dreamer Lohmann who occasionally took compassion on the wretched old man, "compassion and even a sort of reserved sympathy for this lonely enemy of all mankind. . . ." The solitary rainbow-chaser Lohmann intuitively understands that the solitary anarchist Unrat "is also only human" and that "one should not expect any meanness of him beyond his strength." But even Lohmann's penetrating eyes did not reach the last corners of the tyrant's soul. What could he know of its desperate flights over abysses, its agonizing incineration, its desolate loneliness? Neither he nor anyone else was able to divine the fearful scope of Unrat's destiny: to suffer infernal torments because of himself and because of society, to cremate ungratified longings in his own aching heart, to bury "screams of agony in the depths of his own bosom." Unrat's attempt to build a new life in the old environment propels him into conflict with established society. He fights back ferociously—but he is alone and the odds are against him. The isolated rebel is bound to succumb in the unequal struggle, "a moving, heroic figure surrounded by irony and melancholy, an erratic rock of a man, representative of all enslaved and proscribed creatures." Like Peredonov, he is a ruthless little tyrant—but also tyrants are haunted by hopes and fears and tormented by agonies. (pp. 33-4)

In the eyes of many *The Little Demon* ranks as a classic, and there are some who extol it as "the best and greatest Russian novel since *The Brothers Karamazov*." (p. 35)

It is in the same period of time, at the turn of the century, that we observe the unfolding of the talents of Heinrich Mann with little distance in the chronology. . . . [Heinrich Mann] laid the scene for the unfolding of a bizarre human destiny in the crooked lanes and gable houses of his home town. "After all his preceding experiences and trials, attainments and perceptions, it could not possibly become an idyl.'' And no mistake—far from being an idyl, *Professor Unrat* vies with *The Little Demon* in virulent satire on the German variety of ''Peredonovshchina.'' But as in *The Little Demon,* the macabre specter of disaster and insanity lurks behind the thin layer of comedy and grotesqueness. Unrat's crass individualism and eroticism afford another parallel and, of course, there is the same metaphysical symbolism which transposes the work to a sphere of timeless universality. As a result, even critics hostile to Heinrich Mann have grudgingly given their praise to the novel. His admirers, on the other hand, have not hesitated to elevate Professor Unrat to the rank of ''one of the greatest figures in German literature.'' (pp. 35-6)

> Edmund Kostka, ''A Literary Quandary: Fyodor Sologub and Heinrich Mann,'' in his Glimpses of Germanic-Slavic Relations from Pushkin to Heinrich·Mann (© 1975 by Associated University Presses, Inc.), Bucknell University Press, 1975, pp. 21-37.*

## J. E. ALLISON  (essay date 1979)

The articles which Heinrich Mann subsequently published in *Das Zwanzigste Jahrhundert* betray a deep admiration for Nietzsche's genius and herald him as a utopian philosopher. However, Heinrich Mann is not uncritical of much of Nietzsche's thought, particularly his invectives against German culture, and throughout his life Heinrich Mann's attitude to Nietzsche remains ambivalent, accepting Nietzsche's brutal yet realistic philosophy, whilst simultaneously endeavouring to temper it with humaneness.

The year 1905 marks a watershed in Heinrich Mann's thinking; his former support for an aristocratic individualism as advocated by Nietzsche is transformed into a demand for democracy. Many critics have termed this a rejection of Nietzschean ideology—this is not so. It is rather a development. Heinrich Mann does not totally renounce Nietzsche's doctrine but modifies it to suit his own 'Weltanschauung'. *Professor Unrat* highlights the evolution of Heinrich Mann's ideological beliefs, in particular his interpretation of the Nietzschean 'Wille zur Macht'. (p. 190)

Throughout Nietzsche's philosophical writings the concept of power is inextricably linked with the will. This 'Wille zur Macht' is a feature common to all men no matter how strong or weak they may be. It is a generic trait and more significantly it is not a drive alongside others, as for example the sexual drive, but all impulses and desires within man are modes and expressions of the 'Wille zur Macht'. (pp. 190-91)

Having ascertained that the 'Wille zur Macht' is the basic drive in man, Nietzsche proposes that it is the essence of all life. Whereas Darwin had only perceived a 'Kampf um's Leben' . . . ., a fight for existence, Nietzsche advanced the theory one step further. Man does not need to will his own existence. The supreme issue is not what we are but what we do. (p. 191)

The problem of the will and its freedom had occupied Heinrich Mann as early as the essay 'Neue Romantik' in 1892, when he postulated that Naturalism, with its emphasis on the effects of the environment on humanity, was seeking to destroy the concept of a 'freier Wille' . . . which he advocated. But what degree of freedom should the will be allowed, when it relentlessly and exclusively seeks the subjection and denigration of all others? And should not the will be controlled and guided by something other than a maniacal desire for 'Macht'? . . .

Heinrich Mann recognizes two fundamental kinds of power—the power of the individual and the power of the state. In his early creative period when the influence of Nietzsche upon him was at its zenith Heinrich Mann concentrates on the power of the individual.

At the time [*Professor Unrat*] was written satire on the German school system was quite prevalent. . . . It is Unrat's inability to come to terms with the discrepancy between his position in the school and his position in society which leads him down the stormy road to power. The irony with which Heinrich Mann regards his protagonist becomes evident as the power Unrat wields in the classroom has not had to be fought for or willed. It has rather been accorded to him by virtue of the position which he occupies in the school and thus he cannot be considered a 'Machthaber' in the true Nietzschean sense of the word. (pp. 192-93)

The most nefarious crime is to refer to this authoritarian schoolmaster by his nickname; his real name is Professor Raat (Unrat meaning 'rubbish' or 'filth'). Not only the pupils in the classroom employ this appellation but also the townsfolk and his fellow-teachers as soon as his back is turned. Unrat's priority in life is to catch these rogues whenever they refer to him by his nickname. Unrat has taught at the school for twenty-five years and has seen numerous pupils pass through his hands. He is thus acquainted with almost the entire population of the town. . . . In Unrat's mind the school is not restricted to the confines of the school-gates but extends over the walls and embraces the whole·town. The entire population deserves punishment in some form or other. (pp. 193-94)

Unrat recognizes a hierarchy in mankind and thus supports the status quo in order to preserve his own position. . . . [He] knows how best to keep those beneath him in check. Heinrich Mann has clearly depicted and adapted Nietzsche's doctrine of a universal will to power as all the teachers in the novel are opportunists seeking advancement either in their posts in the school or their positions in society. (p. 194)

Like so many of the tyrants in Heinrich Mann's works, as for example the dukes in 'Der Tyrann' and 'Auferstehung', Unrat lives in complete seclusion, at one remove from the rest of the community. He enjoys no relationships with others and in this respect can only be termed 'décadent'. Those without any sensuality cannot be regarded as alive, for in both Nietzsche's and Heinrich Mann's 'Weltanschauung' the life of the senses has a vital role to play. The human side of Unrat's character is only revealed when he falls in love with Rosa and this reawakening of the senses, this rebirth into the social world initiates his downfall as a 'Machthaber'. (p. 196)

The cardinal discrepancy between Nietzsche's concept of the 'Wille zur Macht' and Heinrich Mann's portrayal of it in this novel is Unrat's fear. His power is far from stable, primarily as a result of his own self-doubt. At the slightest hint of any defiance he is seized by terror and his calm exterior is instantaneously replaced by the loss of all self-control. Unrat is a 'Machthaber' who feels endangered at the first suggestion of dissent and we soon discover that his authoritarian attitude is in fact an attempt to conceal his inner debility. There are frequent references to 'die Panik des bedrohten Tyrannen' . . . , for Unrat experiences a deep inner insecurity if he is not treated like a 'Machthaber'. . . .

Fear is symptomatic of all tyrants in Heinrich Mann's works. Their unjust position is doomed from the start, (a fact of which they themselves are only too well aware) and the resultant fear is what spurs them on to their tyrannical acts. Unrat is the classic 'Allerweltsfeind' . . . who hates everyone and expects only their hatred in return. (p. 198)

Heinrich Mann is seeking to demonstrate the dangers which may befall mankind when power is placed in the hands of someone unfit to hold it. Nietzsche himself is most insistent that 'Macht' should only be entrusted to a man capable of wielding it correctly, what he terms the 'höhere Mensch'. . . . It would be catastrophic if power lay in the possession of a decadent type and this is precisely what Heinrich Mann depicts. (pp. 198-99)

A further development in Heinrich Mann's view of the Nietzschean 'Wille zur Macht' is the dichotomy between it and 'Geist'. In this novel the debate is between Lohmann (the representative of 'Geist') and Unrat (the representative of 'Macht'); they are the first characters to embody these notions in Heinrich Mann's works.

From the opening chapter of the novel Heinrich Mann points to Lohmann as the depiction of 'Geist'. He pays little attention in school as he is devoting his time to acquiring a literary education. . . .

'Geist' is inevitably the main antagonist of 'Macht' and thus it appears quite natural that Lohmann is the pupil whom Unrat detests the most. As Unrat's power is of a decadent nature it instinctively shies away from the influence of reason. (p. 199)

When Lohmann regards Unrat as a rather pathetic figure not worth troubling oneself about, Heinrich Mann is mocking the apathetic attitude of 'Geist'. What Lohmann considers unworthy of attention later reveals itself as highly dangerous. Although Heinrich Mann employs Lohmann as his mouthpiece, he does not totally identify with him but insists instead that 'Geist' must not remain content to sit back on its laurels. In the final analysis Lohmann's behaviour is ironicized. Instead of taking action himself when Unrat steals his wallet, Lohmann's only reaction is 'ganz bürgerlich'—he shouts for the police. . . . Heinrich Mann discerns little value in separating 'Geist' and 'Macht'; man must work towards a fusion of the two, as occurs in his next novel *Zwischen den Rassen* when Arnold Acton resorts to force to protect his beliefs. Lohmann is aware of what is right but does not possess the necessary 'Macht' to take steps himself. 'Geist' without 'Macht' ultimately remains ineffective. Progress then does not signify the control of one over the other but rather harmony between the two. (p. 201)

In Heinrich Mann's view, then, the Nietzschean 'Wille zur Macht' is recognized as a necessary component of life. There will always be a part of man which craves success and glory over other men. We must accept this but simultaneously seek to control this basic drive through the 'Geist' and thus benefit mankind in general. (p. 202)

*J. E. Allison, "An Analysis of the Nietzschean 'Wille Zur Macht' as Portrayed in Heinrich Mann's 'Professor Unrat'," in New German Studies, Vol. 7, No. 3, Autumn, 1979, pp. 189-204.*

## ADDITIONAL BIBLIOGRAPHY

Firda, Richard Arthur. "Literary Origins: Sternberg's Film *The Blue Angel*." Film/Literature Quarterly 7, No. 2 (1979): 126-36.
  Compares the novel *Professor Unrat* to Josef von Sternberg's film version. According to this essay, "Heinrich Mann's unholy alliance between sex and politics" in his novel is in the film "subordinate to Sternberg's filmic discovery of Lola as a Fatal Woman."

Hamilton, Nigel. *The Brothers Mann: The Lives of Heinrich and Thomas Mann, 1871-1950 and 1875-1955*. London: Secker & Warburg, 1978, 422 p.
  Noncritical biography chronicling the personal and literary relationship between Heinrich and Thomas Mann. There is not an extensive treatment of their lives individually.

Kayser, Rudolf. "Heinrich Mann." *Books Abroad* 15, No. 4 (Autumn 1941): 401-05.
  Biocritical sketch.

Linn, Rolf N. *Heinrich Mann*. New York: Twayne Publishers, 1967, 144 p.
  Critical introduction to Mann's major works.

Mackinnon, E. "Heinrich Mann's *Im Schlaraffenland*: The Aesthetic Reflection of the *Bürger*." *New German Studies* IV, No. 3 (Autumn 1976): 119-27.
  Political analysis of Mann's novel, treating its main characters as representatives of their respective social classes.

Shchurowsky, G. Roman, and Hart, Pierre R. "A Somber Madness: Dionysian Excess in *The Petty Demon* and *Professor Unrat*." *Germano-Slavica* III, No. 1 (Spring 1979): 33-44.
  Builds upon Edmund Kostka's thesis [see excerpt above] that Mann's *Professor Unrat* bears considerable resemblance to Sologub's *The Petty Demon*. While Kostka's focuses upon thematic similarities, this essay is concerned with the Nietzschean aspects of the protagonists of these novels.

Weisstein, Ulrich. "Humanism and the Novel: An Introduction to Heinrich Mann's *Henri Quatre*." *Monatshefte* LI, No. 1 (January 1959): 13-24.
  Evaluates Mann's techniques of characterization and his historical accuracy in *Henri Quatre*.

Weisstein, Ulrich. "*Die Arme Tonietta*: Heinrich Mann's Triple Version of an Operatic Plot." *Modern Language Quarterly* XX, No. 4 (December 1959): 371-77.
  Contrasts Mann's treatment of *Die Arme Tonietta* as a novella, and as an opera-within-a-novel in *Die Kleine Stadt*.

Weisstein, Ulrich. "Heinrich Mann's *Madame Legros*—Not a Revolutionary Drama." *The Germanic Review* XXXV, No. 1 (February 1960): 39-49.
  General discussion of themes, style, characterization, and historical background of Mann's drama.

# José Ortega y Gasset

## 1883-1955

Spanish philosopher and essayist.

Ortega is one of the most important and influential writers in twentieth-century philosophy. His works are noted for redefining individual existence in terms of a new freedom from the restrictions of pure reason and from the deterministic forces of society. He is also regarded as a highly original theorist and critic of art and literature. One of Ortega's most prominent achievements in his lifetime was the introduction of new ideas into Spanish philosophy, including the thought of such German philosophers as Wilhelm Dilthey and Edmund Husserl. His own writing and teaching effected a dramatic stimulation of intellectual activity and promoted an intellectual renaissance in his country. An elegant writer and thinker, Ortega was untiring in his efforts to "Europeanize Spain."

Ortega was born into an intellectual family; his father was a journalist and novelist, and his grandfather was founder of the newspaper *Imparcial*. Ortega frequently published in newspapers and himself founded the periodicals *Faro, Europa,* and the influential *Revista de Occidente.* He was educated at a Jesuit school in Miraflores del Palo, Málaga and then studied at the University of Madrid, where he earned a doctorate in philosophy in 1904. His studies in Germany during the next few years, a time when he discovered Neo-Kantian ideas, enriched his intellectual life and created a desire to establish in Spain an atmosphere of progressive thought. From 1910 until 1936 he was professor of metaphysics at the University of Madrid, and in 1948 he founded with Julián Marías the Instituto de Humanidades, a cultural center in Madrid. From this time until his death, Ortega lectured throughout Europe and wrote some of his most important works.

*Meditaciones del Quijote (Meditations on Quixote)* was Ortega's first major work. It was in the *Meditations* that his ideas about reality were introduced. These essays hold life to be the relationship between each man and his environment, reality breaking into "innumerable facets . . . each one of which faces a certain individual." This is summarized in Ortega's statement "I am my ego plus my circumstances." Ortega also maintained that circumstance is transcended by the individual effort to create life as one's own "project." *España invertebrada (Invertebrate Spain)* is an expansion of these ideas, and an examination of Spanish civil disorder. A popular and influential book, this work views society as "a fossilization of life, a mineralized excresence of human existence." It is important in Ortega's view that the individual retreat from stultification and respond authentically to his surroundings. Here Ortega also theorized that by finding developmental patterns in history, our immediate situations and needs could be best revealed. *El tema de nuestro tiempo (The Modern Theme)* again deals with contemporary problems and presents the philosopher's concept of perspectivism: the ideal of perceiving the various aspects of reality in their true proportions and relationships, rather than from a subjective, limited viewpoint. In *The Modern Theme* Ortega also discussed his concept of vital reason, writing that "the 'theme of our time' consists of subordinating reason to vitality, localizing it within the biological,

submitting it to the spontaneous. . . . Pure reason has to yield up its dominion to vital reason."

In his next important work, *La des humanización del arte. Ideas sobre la novela (The Dehumanization of Art. Notes on the Novel),* Ortega conceived art and reality as distinct phenomena which should not be interpreted in terms of each other, but which instead should be considered separate areas of experience. Among other subjects, the possibility of human freedom is examined in *¿Que es filosofía? (What Is Philosophy?)* and *Historia como sistema (Toward a Philosophy of History).* The drama of human life lies in the choices each person makes in a world whose meaning is defined by history. The inherent vacillation of individual life is itself freedom—the unfixed design of reality stimulating free choice. In *La rebelión de las masas (Revolt of the Masses),* Ortega created a distinction between the "common" man and the "superior" man, this being one of intellect, cultivation, and discipline. This work concerns itself with increasing the power of the masses and the resultant overthrow of an elite minority which has determined the course of civilization throughout history.

In addition to his intellectual importance, Ortega is noted for his prose style. George Pendle states that Ortega "has a complete and inborn mastery of language." Ortega did not communicate his philosophy systematically but rather used the essay form, with all the freedom it permits, to reflect his meditative style of thought. His elegant essays aspired to "the high Brahmanism of German academic thought, with all its great merits and its shortcomings," according to William Barrett.

Throughout his intellectual career, Ortega treated an impressive variety of subjects, including the novel, art, history, politics, language, love, and numerous philosophical topics. His ideas on modern art have sometimes been misinterpreted and disparaged as aesthetic elitism and his intuitive style of thought often sacrifices the rigor and consistency commonly valued in a philosopher. Nevertheless, Ortega's place in existential thought is significant and his contributions to the cultural development of Spain are among the most important of that country's history.

## PRINCIPAL WORKS

*Meditaciones del Quijote*   (essays)   1914
  [*Meditations on Quixote*, 1961]
*Personas, obras y cosas*   (essays)   1916
*España invertebrada*   (essays)   1921
  [*Invertebrate Spain*, 1937]
*El tema de nuestro tiempo*   (essays)   1923
  [*The Modern Theme*, 1931]
*Las Atlántidas*   (essay)   1924
*La deshumanización del arte. Ideas sobre la novela*
  (essays)   1925
  [*The Dehumanization of Art. Notes on the Novel*, 1948]
*La rebelión de las masas*   (essay)   1929
  [*The Revolt of the Masses*, 1932]
*Misión de la universidad*   (essay)   1930
  [*Mission of the University*, 1944]
*En torno a Galileo*   (lectures)   1933
  [*Man and Crisis*, 1958]
*Estudios sobre el amor*   (essays)   1939
  [*On Love*, 1957]
*\*Del imperio romano*   (essays)   1941
  [*Concord and Liberty*, 1946]
*\*Historia como sistema*   (essay)   1941
  [*Toward a Philosophy of History*, 1941]
*Obras completas. 6 vols.*   (essays and lectures)   1946-47
*El hombre y la gente*   (lectures)   1957
  [*Man and People*, 1957]
*\*\*¿Qué es filosofía?*   (lectures)   1957
  [*What Is Philosophy?*, 1960]
*La idea de principio en Leibniz y la evolución de la teoría
  deductiva*   (essay)   1958
  [*The Idea of Principle in Leibniz and the Evolution of
  Deductive Theory*, 1958]
*Idea del teatro*   (essays)   1958
  [*Idea of the Theater*, 1958]
*Una interpretación de la historia universal, en torno a
  Toynbee*   (lectures)   1959
  [*An Interpretation of Universal History*, 1960]
*Meditacion de Europa*   (essay)   1960
  [*Meditation on Europe*, 1960]
*Unas lecciones de metafisica*   (lectures)   1966
  [*Some Lessons in Metaphysics*, 1966]

*These works were published as *Historia como sistema y del imperio
  romano* in 1941.

**This work was originally written in 1929.

---

## JOSÉ ORTEGA y GASSET   (essay date 1914)

I consider philosophy to be the general science of love; it represents the greatest impulse toward an integrated whole within the intellectual sphere, with the result that a shade of difference between understanding and mere knowing becomes apparent in it. We know so many things that we do not understand! All knowledge of facts is really incomprehensive and can be justified only when used in the service of a theory.

Ideally speaking, philosophy is the opposite of information or erudition. Far be it from me to scorn the latter; factual knowledge has doubtless been a form of science. It had its hour. (p. 38)

[Erudition] occupies the outskirts of science because it is limited to accumulating facts, while philosophy represents its central aspiration, because it is pure synthesis. In the accumulating process the data are merely collected, and, forming a heap, each one asserts its independence, its separateness. In the synthesis of facts, on the contrary, the latter disappear like a well-assimilated food and only their essential vigor remains.

The ultimate ambition of philosophy would be to arrive at a single proposition which would express the whole truth. Thus the twelve hundred pages of Hegel's *Logik* are just the preparation which enables us to pronounce, in all the fullness of its meaning, this sentence: "The idea is the absolute." This sentence, so poor in appearance, has in reality a literally infinite meaning; and when one considers it as one should, the whole treasury of its significance bursts open suddenly and it illuminates for us at once the enormous perspective of the world. This supreme illumination I have called understanding. Particular formulas may prove to be erroneous, and even all those that have been tried may be wrong; but from their doctrinal ruins philosophy is reborn intact as an aspiration, as an urge.

Sexual pleasure seems to be a sudden discharge of nervous energy. Esthetic enjoyment is a sudden discharge of allusive emotions. By analogy, philosophy is like a sudden discharge of intellectual insight. (p. 39)

Man reaches his full capacity when he acquires complete consciousness of his circumstances. Through them he communicates with the universe.

Circumstance! *Circum stantia!* That is, the mute things which are all around us. Very close to us they raise their silent faces with an expression of humility and eagerness as if they needed our acceptance of their offering and at the same time were ashamed of the apparent simplicity of their gift. We walk blindly among them, our gaze fixed on remote enterprises, embarked upon the conquest of distant schematic cities. Few books have moved me as much as those stories in which the hero goes forward, impetuous and straight as an arrow, towards a glorious goal, without noticing the anonymous maiden who, secretly in love with him, walks beside him with a humble and suppliant look, carrying within her white body a heart which burns for him, like a red-hot coal on which incense is burned in his honor. We should like to signal to the hero for him to turn his eyes for a moment towards that passion-inflamed flower which is at his feet. All of us are heroes in varying degrees and we all arouse humble loves around us. "I have been a fighter / And this means I have been a man," exclaims Goethe. We are heroes, we are forever struggling for something far away, and trample upon fragrant violets as we go.

In my **"Essay on Limitation,"** I stop to meditate on this theme with leisurely delight. I believe very seriously that one of the most profound changes in the present as compared with the nineteenth century is going to consist in the changing of our sensitivity to environment. A sort of restlessness and impatience seemed to prevail in the past century—in its second half especially—which compelled people to disregard everything immediate and momentary in life. As distance lends a more synthesizing outline to the past century, its essentially political character becomes clearer to us. Western man underwent his apprenticeship in politics, a kind of life hitherto confined to ministers and palace councils. Political preoccupation, that is, consciousness of and activity in the social field, spreads among the masses, thanks to democracy. With a fierce exclusivism the problems of social life took over the first plane of attention, while the other element, individual life, was put aside as a matter of little consequence. It is especially significant that the only powerful affirmation of the individual in the nineteenth century—individualism—should be a political doctrine, that is to say, a social one, and that its whole tenet consisted in asking that the individual should not be annihilated. How can we doubt that some day soon this will appear incredible? (pp. 41-2)

Individual life, the immediate, the circumstance, are different names for the same thing: those parts of life from which their inner spirit, their *logos,* has not yet been extracted. Since spirit and *logos* are nothing but ''meaning,'' connectedness, and unity, all that is individual, immediate, and circumstantial appears to be accidental and meaningless.

We ought to consider that social life as well as the other forms of culture are given to us in the form of individual life, of the immediate. What we today receive already decorated with sublime aureoles once had to contract and shrink in order to pass through a man's heart. All that is recognized today as truth, as perfect beauty, as highly valuable, was once born in the inner spirit of an individual, mixed with his whims and humors. We should not let our acquired culture become hieratic, as it will if we are more concerned with repeating than increasing it.

The specifically cultural act is the creative, that in which we extract the *logos* from something which was still meaningless (*i-logico*). Acquired culture has value only as the instrument and weapon of new conquests. Therefore, in comparison with the immediate, with our spontaneous life, all that we have learned seems to be abstract, generic, schematic. It not only seems so, it is. The hammer is the abstraction of each one of its hammerings.

All that is general, all that has been learned, achieved in culture is only the tactical turn which we have to take in order to cope with the immediate. Those who live near a cataract do not notice its roar; it is necessary for us to put some distance between our immediate surroundings and ourselves so that they may acquire meaning in our eyes.

The Egyptians believed that the valley of the Nile was the whole world. Such a statement about a circumstance is monstrous and, contrary to what it might appear, impoverishes its significance. Certain minds show their basic weakness when they cannot become interested in a thing unless they delude themselves into thinking that it is the whole or the best in the world. This sticky and womanish idealism must be eradicated from our consciousness. Only parts do exist in fact; the whole is an abstraction of the parts and it depends on them. In the same way, there cannot be anything better except where there are other good things, and it is only by our being interested in the latter that the better or best acquires its rank. What is a captain without soldiers?

When shall we open our minds to the conviction that the ultimate reality of the world is neither matter nor spirit, is no definite thing, but a perspective? God is perspective and hierarchy; Satan's sin was an error of perspective. Now, a perspective is perfected by the multiplication of its viewpoints and the precision with which we react to each one of its planes. The intuition of higher values fertilizes our contact with the lesser ones, and love for what is near and small makes the sublime real and effective within our hearts. For the person for whom small things do not exist, the great is not great.

We must try to find for our circumstance, such as it is, and precisely in its very limitation and peculiarity, its appropriate place in the immense perspective of the world. We must not stop in perpetual ecstasy before hieratic values, but conquer the right place among them for our individual life. In short, the reabsorption of circumstance is the concrete destiny of man.

My natural exit toward the universe is through the mountain passes of the Guadarrama or the plain of Ontígola. This sector of circumstantial reality forms the other half of my person; only through it can I integrate myself and be fully myself. The most recent biological science studies the living organism as a unit composed of the body and its particular environment so that the life process consists not only of the adaptation of the body to its environment but also of the adaptation of the environment to its body. The hand tries to adjust itself to the material object in order to grasp it firmly; but, at the same time, each material object conceals a previous affinity with a particular hand.

I am myself plus my circumstance, and if I do not save it, I cannot save myself. *Benefac loco illi quo natus es,* as we read in the Bible. And in the Platonic school the task of all culture is given as ''to save the appearances,'' the phenomena; that is to say, to look for the meaning of what surrounds us. (pp. 43-6)

Nothing prevents heroism—which is the activity of the spirit—as much as considering it bound to certain specific contents of life. The possibility of heroism must subsist beneath the surface everywhere, and every man should be able to hope that a spring may come forth when he strikes vigorously the earth he treads. For Moses the Hero, every rock contains a spring. For Giordano Bruno, *est animal sanctum, sacrum et venerabile, mundus.* (p. 46)

*José Ortega y Gasset, ''To the Reader'' (1914), in his* Meditations on Quixote, *translated by Evelyn Rugg and Diego Marín (reprinted by permission of W. W. Norton & Company, Inc.; translation copyright © 1961 by W. W. Norton & Company, Inc.; originally published as* Obras completas: Meditaciones del Quijote, Vol. I, *Revista de Occidente, 1946), Norton, 1961, pp. 31-53.*

## PAUL ELMER MORE (essay date 1928)

Demon of the Absolute is nothing else but rationalism, what Francis Bacon called the *intellectus sibi permissus,* or, if you wish it in plainer English, reason run amuck. Now reason, so long as it is content to accept the actual data of experience, is manifestly one of our diviner faculties; at every step in life it is our guide and friend, and without it we can do nothing wisely or prosperously. And that is why it becomes so dangerous when, disregarding ''matters of fact, those unconcerning things,'' it sets up its own absolutes as the truth and asks us to act thereupon. For there are no absolutes in nature; they are phantoms created by reason itself in its own likeness, delusions which, when once evoked, usurp the field of reality and bring endless confusion in their train. Their close is chaos, in which Anarchy rules supreme. (p. 258)

I turn to the distinguished critic and philosopher of Spain, José Ortega y Gasset, and in particular to his essay published under the significant title of *The Dehumanization of Art.* Unless I mistake his language, Señor Ortega finds little satisfaction aesthetically in the extreme products of the movement he describes. But he believes that it is not the function of a critic to value works of art in accordance with his own taste or distaste. And especially today, when more than ever before it is a characteristic of art to divide mankind sharply into those who comprehend and those who do not, the business of criticism should be to enter into the intention of the artist, and not to judge his work from some alien point of view, least of all to condemn. Well, Señor Ortega in a sense comprehends; he states the various theories adopted by the *jóvenes* to justify their adventurous ways with admirable perspicuity and precision—and with that final confusion at the back of his mind which enables him to speak as one who belongs intellectually to the movement, however practically his taste may lag a little behind its utmost advance.

The central thesis of Señor Ortega's book, which at once justifies his title and summarizes the most advanced attitude towards art, is exactly this: ''To rejoice or suffer with the human lot which a work of art may incidentally suggest or present to us, is a very different thing from the true artistic pleasure. More than that: this occupation with the human element of the work is essentially incompatible with pure aesthetic fruition.''

That clearly is the voice of the Demon once more, appealing to the same lust for an irresponsible absolute as inspires the Crocean aesthetics. And now art is to be not only independent of morals but in its essence divided altogether from human nature; and if it still aims to please, its pleasure is of a kind peculiar to itself and unrelated to the coarse fodder of life. Suppose, to take the illustration given by Señor Ortega, a notable man is lying at the point of death. His wife will be standing by his bed, a physician will be counting his pulse, while elsewhere in the house a reporter awaits the news and a painter is engaged to depict the scene. All four persons—wife, physician, reporter, painter—are intent upon the same fact, but with varying degrees of intimacy and with different kinds of interest. To the wife the event is an occasion of grief and anxiety; she is, as it were, a part of it; whereas to the artist, at the other extreme, the situation is entirely divested of human sympathy or sentiment: ''his mind is set solely on the exterior, on certain lights and shadows, certain chromatic values.'' And so it happens that if the natural emotions felt on such an occasion by the wife, the physician, and even to a lesser degree by the news-reporter, are what the ordinary man (the ''philistine'' or ''bourgeois'' of the older romantic jargon) regards as the real stuff of life, then art to the ordinary man is removed to a sphere of incomprehensible unreality. ''An artistic object,'' says Señor Ortega, ''is artistic only in the measure in which it ceases to be real.'' Hence, in the scene just described, the actual death-bed and the artist's picture of it are two things ''absolutely different (*completamente distintos*).'' We may interest ourselves in one or the other; in one case we live with, or in, the event, in the other case we ''contemplate'' an object of art as such, with aesthetic pleasure perhaps, but with no human emotions. Just in so far as the picture shows any feeling for, or awakens in the beholder any response to, the signifi-

cance of death, it falls below the high function of art. The tragedy of loss, the frustration of ambition, the humility of surrender, the consolations of hope, the victory of love, the sanctities of religion,—any shadow of these resting upon the canvas will detract from the purity of aesthetic pleasure. The artist and the connoisseur in the presence of death find only an occasion for certain lines and colours. And further, as our power of contemplation becomes more refined, we cease to discern (or, if we are artists, to paint) even the unreal representation of a real event; a picture will cease to depend on, or suggest, any subject whatsoever. For art is like a window through which we look out upon a garden. The ordinary man sees only the flowers and leaves beyond, and is so absorbed in these as to be quite unaware of the pane of glass, the more so as the glass is purer and clearer. But with effort we can make ourselves conscious of the medium through which we are looking; and as our vision is thus concentrated on the glass, the garden fades into a confused blotch of colours or even passes out of conscious perception altogether.

That is Señor Ortega's vivid metaphor for the Crocean theory of art as pure intuition—which he professes to reach, however, by no theorizing of his own but from study of the actual practice of certain of the *jóvenes*. For those who believe in the divine mission of art the elevation of society might seem to lie in obeying the command of Mr. Skionar in Peacock's *Crotchet Castle:* ''Build *sacella* for transcendental oracles to teach the world how to see through a glass darkly.'' It all sounds rather funny to me. But I hope I am not laughing at an unfair caricature. What else in fact is the meaning of those sapient critics, who might join me in repudiating the language of metaphysics, yet insist that in judging a picture we shall pay no heed to the subject represented but consider it as pure representation, or who say that the value of a work of art depends not at all on the character of the human experience put into it but only on the sincerity of self-expression?—as if there were some mystical virtue in self-expression even when the self has no experience worthy to be expressed. It is, in fact, pedantic talk of this sort in the mouths of respected critics that indicates how far the depredations of the Demon have extended into the realm of common sense.

As for the creators, so called, there may be a young votary of art here and there who is trying honestly to put these abstractions into practice; and for him, I should suppose, the goal of dehumanization and derealization will have been attained when his pictures are simplified to a cunning design of line and colour with no suggestion of a definite subject, or still further to a spread of pure colour with no design at all; his music to a pure tone without melody or even variation; his poems to a succession of beautiful words unsullied by sense. That would seem to be the nearest practical equivalent to seeing a pure pane of glass. One wonders why the pilgrim of vacuity should be so slow and hesitant in his progress towards so easy a mark. Perhaps he foresees that absolute art, so reached, will cease to be art at all. Perhaps he has a foreboding that the prize if obtained would not be very valuable. It is hard to imagine the pleasure or profit to be derived from concentrating one's attention upon a pane of transparent glass until one sees nothing through it; most of us would prefer to retain our impure perception of the flowers in the garden beyond. Despite the majestic logic of youth we persist in thinking that such a picture as Leonardo da Vinci's *Last Supper* is a truer work of art than the deftest whirl of colours ever painted; that the *Æneid* is richer in poetical joy than *Kubla Khan* (not to mention the latest lyric from the American colony in Paris); that Bach's

*Mass in B Minor* is still a miracle and a rapture of sound. Yet all these—the painting and the epic and the mass—are brimming with human emotion and with a brooding sense of the eternal values of life. They are great for various reasons, no doubt; but certainly among those reasons is the fact that they are not art at all as the modernists would have us believe.

The simple truth is that the effort to create pure art is nothing more than idolatry to a fetish of abstract reason—unless you prefer to ticket it as empty conceit—and could never engage the practical interest of any but a few witless cranks. There is a profound confusion in Señor Ortega's interpretation of what is happening among the mass of the younger artists, as indeed there is often in their own statement of what they are endeavouring to do. They may be seeking an absolute, but it is not an absolute of purity in any sense of the word. (pp. 280-83)

> *Paul Elmer More, in an excerpt from his* The Demon of the Absolute *(copyright 1928 by Princeton University Press, copyright renewed © 1956 and assigned to Princeton University Press; reprinted by permission of Princeton University Press), Princeton University Press, 1928 (and reprinted as ''The Demon of the Absolute,'' in* American Literary Criticism 1900-1950, *edited by Charles I. Glicksberg, Hendricks House, Inc., 1952, pp. 258-87).\**

## HERMANN HESSE   (essay date 1931-1932)

Not all the works of this very estimable Spanish writer have appealed to me; occasionally from behind his bravado and cheerful aggressiveness there peeks out something like philistinism and professorial decorum. But [*The Revolt of the Masses*] I cannot commend too highly, because it is one of those books in which an age can be seen struggling toward consciousness and attempting to draw its own face. Ortega y Gasset chooses to present the spiritual structure of our time through popular, often almost banal examples, but he has pictured some of them, especially the run-of-the-mill scientist and the type he calls ''the self-satisfied young gentleman'' with such complete clarity and expressiveness that one cannot help but be stimulated. Ultimately the book is a warning cry of the intellectual addressed to the apathetic, of the aristocrat to the standard-bearers of collective ideals, a protest of personality against the mass, and on this most significant point I can only wholeheartedly agree with the author and rejoice that these thoughts, held by a few thousand people for a long time, have now found a gripping and, one hopes, popular presentation.

Though a trifle too popular in style—for this is basically a book for the few—and occasionally a trifle rhetorical, this remarkable volume is the work of one of the few men who have real knowledge of the nature of mankind, the nature of history, and therefore the state of mankind today. I am in unreserved agreement with the presentation and analysis of the mass man as Ortega gives it; it has never before been put forth so consistently and clearly. No less do I agree, and agree actively, with his conception of the state, and therefore with his conception of the only possibility for Europe's future—Europe must become a single nation. Among a series of clearly formulated and originally selected examples from history there are many individual passages of striking, witty comment, as, for example, this about historians: ''One sees of the past about as much as one guesses about the future.'' All in all, it is a rousing, demanding, thought-provoking work that is important to Europe. The majority of German youth, instead of wrangling over their teen-age problems that will have disappeared by tomorrow,

should read such books, not in order to be witty and clever about them in conversation, but to learn from them. (pp. 371-72)

> *Hermann Hesse, ''José Ortega y Gasset'' (1931-32; originally published as ''José Ortega y Gasset'' in* Schriften zur Literatur, *Suhrkamp Verlag, 1972), in his* My Belief: Essays on Life and Art, *edited by Theodore Ziolkowski, translated by Denver Lindley (reprinted by permission of Farrar, Straus and Giroux, Inc.; translation copyright © 1974 by Farrar, Straus and Giroux, Inc.), Farrar, Straus and Giroux, 1974, pp. 371-72.*

## H. L. MENCKEN   (essay date 1932)

The anonymous translator of [*The Revolt of the Masses*] says that ''in the Spanish histories of the future Don José Ortega y Gasset will probably be spoken of as one of the Fathers of the Republic.'' If so, then the definition of republic will have to be changed, at all events in Spain. For what Professor Ortega denounces most violently in his book is precisely the idea upon which the whole science and art of republicanism has always been based, to wit, the idea that there is some mystical virtue, and what is more, some mystical wisdom, in men in the mass—that what everyone believes is somehow likely to be true. Upon this doctrine he flings himself with great enthusiasm, and, save at moments when he loses the thread of his discourse and argues against himself, with considerable effect.

The liberation of the masses, he believes, has done Europe a lot of harm. It has upset the old scale of values, especially in the field of government, and substituted a kind of moony indifferentism, grounded upon simple and even childish desires. The mob is impatient of all ideas, and hence refuses to consider and discuss them. The one thing it esteems is a comfortable conformity, and that conformity is naturally pitched upon a low level. Moreover, it is quite irrational, for there is no coherent concept behind it, but only a yearning to be ''undifferentiated from other men,'' to pass unmarked and unmolested in a vague crowd. Thus mere quantity is substituted for quality, and all the high aspirations and emprises of superior men sink into desuetude.

Señor Ortega's thesis is here clear enough, but it cannot be said that he maintains it with unfailing consistency. It is hard to follow an argument which begins with an eloquent plea for aristocracy . . . , and ends with the conclusion that ''liberal democracy based on technical knowledge is the highest type of public life hitherto known.'' . . . Nor is it easy to agree, on the one hand, that the stupidities of the mob now engulf and smother *homo sapiens,* and on the other hand that his ''vital tone,'' which ''consists in his feeling himself possessed of greater potentiality than ever before,'' is now at its historic maximum.

But such confusions, of course, are apt to occur in a book which covers so wide a field, especially if it comes from the studio of a metaphysician. When Señor Ortega turns into by-paths he often writes with great clarity, and is pleasantly persuasive. In one of his later chapters, for example, he has an excellent short treatise on the nature of the state, along with a hearty denunciation of the current tendency to regard it as a stupendous Peruna bottle, with a cure in it for every ill. And he pleads with fine eloquence for some of the standards that democracy has tended to destroy. From his main contention few will dissent—that it is bad government which particularly afflicts the world, and especially Europe, today. But most readers will regret that he did not state it more simply, and argue for it with a more concentrated assiduity. (pp. 260-61)

*H. L. Mencken, "Spanish Katzenjammer," in* The Nation *(copyright 1932* The Nation *magazine, The Nation Associates, Inc.), Vol. 135, No. 3507, September 21, 1932, pp. 260-61.*

**JOSÉ SÁNCHEZ VILLASEÑOR, S.J.** (essay date 1943)

[*Evaluating Ortega's thought from a Christian perspective, Villaseñor's study—from which the excerpt below is taken—is among the most negative and severe appraisals of the Spanish philosopher.*]

In the Ortegan concept of life we can distinguish three periods. In the first, life is considered as the highest value. In the second, it is established as the fundamental reality, thanks to the existentialist influence. Finally, in *Ideas y creencias* all reality is declared unknowable and human life becomes an insoluble enigma.

One subject of Ortega's writings is the theme of life as the highest value, as reality which justifies itself. *The Modern Theme* shouts out like a battle cry the triumph of vital values. "Pure Reason must yield its supremacy to vital reason." Culture must be placed at the service of life. But what does it mean to speak of values immanent to life, superior to every other value? What does it mean to say that vitality contains the highest value? Pure vitality, no doubt, is worth while. Nevertheless, it is not true that it occupies the supreme distinction in the hierarchy of values. For the rest, the author does not take the trouble to prove his thesis. He is content with affirmations, and in passing offers us two examples which prove nothing. The first, concerning the pure-blooded horse, does not touch the point, for we are not treating of life in general but of human life. The second, in which he tells us of the magnificent, attractive human animal (referring to Napoleon), is disputable.

Aside from this, Ortega himself recognizes, at least implicitly, the falsity of this thesis when he affirms years later that man has no ambition to be in the world, "his desire is to be well; for him life means not merely to be but to be well."

Such a radical change is but in obedience to the influence of the new ideas. The concept of life as the highest value yields its position to the new current which establishes human existence as the fundamental reality. It should not be forgotten that for Ortega there is no other norm of truth than the docile submission to the message of the time.

The Ortegan theory of life as the fundamental reality is inspired in this second period by the ideas of Heidegger and Dilthey. The phrases in which he defines life as fundamental insecurity are in the Heideggerian style: "the feeling of a shipwrecked mariner in a mysterious element, strange and frequently hostile"; the falling prisoner to an inexorable environment in which we suddenly find ourselves without knowing how.

From Dilthey he adopts the term, "life as history," as vital, nontransferable history. From Fichte he receives the theory that life is mere activity, a task (*Tathandlung*), and the practical nature of all knowledge. This is a doctrine which Ortega shares with Heidegger and Dilthey.

Nevertheless, in Ortega the theory of human existence has an accentuated tinge of skepticism. Ortega clings to it as to a life

preserver, disillusioned with all other reality. With faith lost in God and in reason, "man retains only his disillusioned living." But Ortega even renounces that disillusioned living. Carrying the positivistic and agnostic principles to their extreme, he admits that the basic reality "is pure enigma." The intellectual interpretation which we form of it is fanciful and illusory. Every effort to explore the secret of man and of the universe is condemned to failure. In its very essence science is as imaginary as poetry. (pp. 172-74)

In Ortega's existentialist writings there is an expression which because of its mysteriousness and its repetition well merits a serious analysis. "For the sake of life," he says, "I have been flung out into environment, into the chaotic swarm of things." In another place we read: "Life is given to us, since we do not give it to ourselves, but we suddenly find ourselves in it and without knowing how." In the prologue to his complete works, Ortega asserts that "to live is to have fallen prisoner to an inexorable environment." But why multiply the references? Under a thin allusion a secret and weighty problem throbs throughout these phrases. Man has not given existence to himself. He finds himself thrown into it unexpectedly, without knowing how. (p. 176)

The Ortegan ethical panorama is desolate and bitter. As in the metaphysical sphere, so also in the moral field he aspires to grant indisputable hegemony to life. Influenced by Nietzsche, he endeavors to achieve a complete transformation of values.

For the morality which is based on reason and imposes inflexible norms he finds no other name than depravity. In his eyes, life is its own ethics. Illusion is more fruitful than duty. The new norm of morality eulogized by Ortega consists in "a religious docility to life," in preferring the corruptible to the immutable, the tremulous inconsistency of existence to a schematic and bloodless eternity. Such a theory is entirely immoral. (p. 224)

Ortega's pretensions to erect as the norm of morality a religious docility to life are . . . inacceptable, false, and immoral. Inacceptable, because they defend a subjective relativistic criterion, attentive only to the command of fashion and leading finally to moral skepticism. False, because the norm of morality is not a matter of emotional reactions, nor of vital impulses blind and confused. Immoral, because they open the door to wantonness and licentiousness. An example of this is Ortega's justification of the immoral acts of a great statesman; he gives free rein indiscriminately to noble and depraved tendencies of human nature under the futile pretext that life is ethical in itself. (pp. 226-27)

Ortega condemns culturalism, which after displacing God endeavored to justify life with the deification of reason and its cultural creations. In its place he enthrones life, existence worthy in itself and needing no extravital content to assert itself. This first faith is slowly extinguished in his spirit. Finally, he recognizes that life has value as the achievement of one's ego. "Be yourself," he repeats with Pindar and Fichte. He proclaims that life is drama, inexorable mission, destiny. . . . He aspires, consciously or unconsciously, to endow existence with a valuable content, without abandoning his naturalistic attitude, without going beyond the boundaries of the purely human. He nourishes his secret intention, as did Heidegger, of formulating a philosophical justification for atheism. But his plans failed. The last stage of Ortegan ideology is lost in the night of skeptical nihilism. (pp. 227-28)

Having without reasonable cause discarded the supernatural, Ortega wields his destructive mattock against the foundations of science and of culture. We are left only the "disillusioned living," an icy and skeptical pessimism. What does Ortega build on these ruins? His dithyrambs on the festive meaning of life, on vital energy and sumptuousness, on the values of youth are flowers which wither. In his heart he harbors the secret conviction that the enigma of life is insoluble. (p. 233)

> *José Sánchez Villaseñor, S.J., in his* Ortega y Gasset Existentialist: A Critical Study of His Thought and Its Source, *translated by Joseph Small, S.J. (originally a doctoral study submitted to the University of Mexico in 1943; translation copyright 1949 Henry Regnery Company; reprinted by permission of the Literary Estate of José Sánchez Villaseñor and the translator),* Henry Regnery, 1949, 264 p.

## HARRY LEVIN   (essay date 1948)

[In] the year 1925, when ["**The Dehumanization of Art**" and "**Notes on the Novel**"], two complementary essays, first appeared, Cubism was culminating with Picasso's "Three Dancers." Critical discussion was highlighted by the then current appearance of such novels as Dreiser's "American Tragedy," Fitzgerald's "Great Gatsby," Virginia Woolf's "Mrs. Dalloway," Gide's "Counterfeiters," Proust's "The Sweet Cheat Gone," and Kafka's "Trial."

Señor Ortega's observations are as keen as ever, while the polemics and manifestos of that decade make dull rereading, because he was "moved exclusively by the delight of trying to understand—and neither by ire nor by enthusiasm." The meditative habit, the spectatorial role of his earlier writing well befit the critic; though they have their political limitations, as he was subsequently to show. A generation whose rallying cry is engagement rather than detachment will not apply to him for its philosophy of history. Yet the intellectuality that chills, whenever he condescends to discuss the masses, illuminates his vivid interpretations of the cerebral life. His German training blends with his Latin temperament to produce a zest for ideas which is never dogmatic, a flair for epigrams which is seldom verbalistic....

The distinctive quality that Ortega perceives throughout the varied manifestations of modern art is its "will to style." Its consciousness of form is an iconoclastic recoil from its previous dependence on subject-matter, from the extrinsic appeal of both the romanticists and the realists to human interest and local color. Impure poetry, confessional fiction, melodramatic music, story-telling pictures—needless to say, such genres have been popular. Hence the process of purification, the tendency toward abstraction, is essentially an unpopular movement. Renewing the obligations of craftsmanship, as well as the accumulations of tradition, the artist becomes a technician par excellence. And Ortega is willing to face, with the mixed emotions of irony, the implications of art for art's sake: its narrowing horizons, its tongue-in-cheek attitudes. Poetry, for Eliot "a superior amusement," is for him "a higher algebra of metaphors." No one has more sharply or paradoxically formulated the alternative to the propagandistic and humanitarian position of Tolstoy's "What Is Art?"

Ortega's companion essay, which he calls "**Notes on the Novel,**" is an application of his esthetic theories to the most formless of literary forms. Though the present translation omits the relevant paragraphs, it was written to dissent from Pio Baroja, who—like so many novelists and novel-readers—regarded this medium as a kind of catch-all. Ortega demonstrates the im-

portance of structure, citing the *a fortiori* case of Dostoevsky. He also cites the contemporaneous examples of Proust and Joyce, who concentrated on detail to a highly imaginative degree, and thus turned fiction away from prose toward poetry. Responding to the challenge of psychology, he prefers description to narration, and points out that plot has gradually been superseded by character. He concedes the possibility, which more recent critics have vigorously pursued, that the novel itself may prove to be obsolete. If so, its decadence has been its age of final perfection: "Ulysses," "The Magic Mountain," "The Remembrance of Things Past."

> *Harry Levin, "'Modern' Art—and 'Modern' Novels," in* The New York Times Book Review *(© 1948 by The New York Times Company; reprinted by permission), January 6, 1948, p. 4.*

## ERNST ROBERT CURTIUS   (essay date 1950)

Real philosophy is rooted in a vital enthusiasm. It springs from a new contact with life, an intoxicating contact. I let Ortega speak: "I regard philosophy as the general science of love. Within the intellectual cosmos, it represents the strongest impulse toward a total union." Then he makes a bold comparison. "Sexual pleasure," he says, "appears to consist in a sudden discharge of nervous energy. . . . Similarly, philosophy is a sudden discharge of intellectual activity." . . .

That the enthusiasm of living philosophy should be restored to us by a Spaniard was one of the surprises in which the intellectual environment of the 1920's was so rich. (p. 260)

The cultural reawakening of Spain is one of the few heartwarming things that have taken place in the twentieth century. And it is no unimportant matter. . . .

An élite of Spanish society was exploring new modes of life and new ideas. The channel for modern ideas was the *Revista de Occidente,* which was edited by Ortega. It imported the best of the intellectual production of foreign countries. (p. 261)

[Ortega's] is a prose of intuition, its form is the newspaper article or the essay. This scandalizes the official philosophers. Ortega has answered them: "The newspaper or magazine article is today an indispensable form of thought, and anyone who pedantically scorns it has not the least conception of what is going on in history." Ortega's earlier books are observations upon persons, books, pictures, landscapes. But, however various the subjects, the impelling force is always the same: an intellectual love of the world, an *amor intellectualis.* And the aim is the same: to exhibit all these things in their full significance as directly as possible.

These early books radiate a bright, virile enthusiasm. The abundance of things and beings which they reveal, seems overwhelming. But the energy of the thought, the accuracy of the verbal formulations, keeps the richness of the matter under control. The observer's pleasure is the pleasure of the huntsman. He ambushes the game and brings it down. A holiday brightness pervades these books. The thirty-year-old thinker sees a new age beginning, an age which will be richer, more complex, healthier, nobler, and which will offer infinite possibilities of experience.

A wealth of possibilities for experience—but controlled by the primacy of thought. The point at which vitality and reason meet and intersect—that is the creative center of Ortega's philosophy. Here the electric contact is made. Here the sparks fly. Here is the focal point at which all rays meet. It is the place of tensions and decisions. (p. 263)

Vital force and inner discipline: here we have the synthesis of life and reason which Ortega demands. . . . (p. 264)

What made possible the development of the polarity "life—reason" which is one of the principal themes of Ortega's thought? Two things were necessary: belief in reason and belief in life. . . . He can remain satisfied neither with a human life without the organ of reason, nor yet with a truth which is outside the stream of life. There is no intellectuality without vitality. On the other hand, life, as Simmel correctly perceived, is always more than life. It comprises a transcendental function. Therefore the two powers, reason and life, are not to be opposed to each other. They must interpenetrate each other. A two-fold commandment applies: Life must be intellectual, but at the same time the intellect must be alive. In other words: Culture is only of value in so far as it is lived. Mere professions of culture, mere faith in it which surrounds it with religious veneration and which can degenerate into a false piety of culture, is of no value. The task of our time consists in finding the proper place for reason in biology. Pure reason must be replaced by vital reason.

Since Bergson's influence struck the first spark, there has been a long series of philosophies known as "vital philosophies." They have differed greatly in value. While they could not abolish abstract thinking, they nevertheless set intuition, inner vision, and the like, beside it, if not above it, as sources of knowledge.

With these "vital philosophies" Ortega's philosophy has no connection. He holds fast to the severe discipline of abstraction, he holds fast to reason. But he tries to find a place for reason in the vital. He demands a vital reason. And at the same time it is present in his thought like a new dimension of reason. He argues for his demand with the greatest intensity, and with the same intensity he turns against all the philosophical schools which had been successful in the last decades—for example, against the phenomenology of Husserl and Scheler, no less than against the "existence philosophy" of Heidegger. Whether he has succeeded, or will succeed, in founding, developing and effectively defending the system of vital reason, I do not know. (pp. 264-66)

History—not physics—is for Ortega the basic reality. Stars, plants, and animals have nature. Man, instead of nature, has history. Hence it is the task of thought to raise history to a system. The evolution of man is not merely change, it is growth. Each stage includes those which preceded it. Hence man understands himself only when he understands the entire past. History is, or ought to be, a systematic knowledge of the basic reality which is my life. But the intellectual activity which puts us in touch with truth is reason. Hence history must become a science of reason. When it accomplishes its task, it will be equivalent to a "new revelation." (pp. 267-68)

My life consists in the fact that I find myself under the necessity of existing in a particular environment or a particular situation—in a particular "circumstance" as Ortega puts it. There is no life *in abstracto*. I do not find myself to be merely a thinking consciousness, as idealism has taught since the time of Descartes. Rather, life means being the prisoner of surroundings that cannot be changed. We live here and now. In this sense, life is absolute actuality, bound to a particular point in space and time. Everything that I do is determined by that unique situation. And my life consists in what I do. One is what one does. . . .

For Ortega, the first moral postulate is sincerity. He advocates it with an absoluteness which leads to extreme consequences. What I cannot sincerely accept on the basis of my personal sense of life, I must reject. Hence there is no eternal pattern. There are no classics. (p. 268)

In his earliest writings Ortega criticized the "faith in culture," the bigoted Pharisaism of culture, which is rampant in the modern world. Nevertheless, at that period he was much interested in the modern literary movement. He wrote on Proust and on Cóngora, whose tercentenary in 1927 was of such great significance for modern Spanish criticism. But gradually symptoms of an estrangement from literature appeared. This found expression in 1932 in an essay on—and against—Goethe, which aroused much comment. His attitude toward French literature is critical too. It is, he writes, the "normal" literature—but, like everything normal, it has neither heights nor depths. He is suspicious of Pascal. "Long ago," he wrote in 1937, "I learned to beware when I hear anyone quoting Pascal. This is an elementary hygienic precaution." Rousseau, on the other hand, with his mad doctrine of the natural goodness of man, spoiled a century and a half of European history, until, after interminable catastrophes (the series of which is perhaps not yet closed) we have learned to re-discover the simple truth, known to almost all earlier centuries: that man is by birth an evil beast. Ortega has also made some caustic remarks on the subject of Paul Valéry. Such are a few of Ortega's opinions on the subject of French literature. For three hundred years, France has regarded herself—and perhaps rightly—as the country where the best writing is done. "But France has also hesitated the longest over convincing herself that in this day and age one can no longer live on literature."

Philosophers, when they have rightly understood themselves, have always been the enemies of poets. The Pre-Socratics rebuked Homer, and Plato wanted to banish poets from his republic. In his turn, Ortega has said: "We have grown accustomed to speaking of poetry without much emotion. If we say that it is not a *serious* matter, no one gets angry but the poets." In Germany too there have been cases of great poets being called to order by philosophers, as Goethe was by Jaspers. This is inevitable, because philosophy is by nature intensely intolerant. It is natural to philosophy to take nothing seriously but itself. But the philosopher finds poetry to be among the contents of the universe. He has to come to terms with it. I can imagine a brilliant essay by Ortega in which literature should be brought to trial. He opens his **"Considerations on Technique"** with the following sentences: "One of the themes which will be most eagerly discussed in the next few years is that of the meaning, advantages, disadvantages, and limits of technique. I have always been of the opinion that it is the writer's mission to anticipate the problems with which his reader will be confronted years later, and to offer him clear ideas on the questions at issue in good time—that is, before the controversy begins—so that he may go down into the dust of battle with the serene mind of a man who has already reached a decision in principle. *On ne doit écrire que pour faire connaître la vérité,*' said Malebranche, and turned his back on literature. For many years now, Western Man, whether he is aware of it or not, has ceased to hope anything from literature and once again hungers and thirsts for clear and intelligible ideas about the things that matter."

Every philosophy raises a total claim. But we can respect only those philosophies which know it and admit it. Ortega fulfils this expectation. Philosophy, he teaches, possesses a violence which is a part of its nature and which is in distinct opposition to the peaceful demeanor which the sect of philosophers assumed soon after it made its first appearance. Philosophers are generally too polite to discuss this point openly. But the very existence of philosophy implies a continuous and irreconcilable affront to the rest of humanity. It implies nothing less than that the man without philosophy is scarcely more than an animal. Where philosophy does not rule, sleep-walking rules. All of us who do not philosophize, spend our lives, so to say, in a state of somnolence.

A harsh judgment. But we shall find means to bear up under it. It is not proven, and it cannot be proven, that all men must philosophize. Once, in a criticism of modern physical science, Ortega referred to the "terrorism of the laboratories." We could object to him that he teaches a terrorism of clear ideas. Such a spectacle is not often offered us. There is something enthralling about it, as there is about every process in which thought establishes an extreme position.

Let us take a few final steps in philosophic perception under Ortega's guidance. His first problem was the antagonism between life and reason. The formula which should solve it was to be the concept of vital reason. Immediate life then revealed itself as an aspect of history. The task now became: a system of historical reason. But what place is science to have in human thought? What is the physical world? Does it affect the reality of our existence? Not at all. Physics is a conceptual system, which perhaps has a certain relation to reality, but which is first of all a construction of thought. These thoughts are not a matter of reality, and reality is not a matter of thought. Therefore the physicist lives in a world of ideas constructed by himself. His relation to it is like that of a reader to the imaginary world of the novel he is reading. We call such a world a "poetic world." It is a product of imagination, an "inner world." But is physics any different? Its concepts are intellectual constructions. Physics, philosophy, poetry, religion—they are all inner worlds, creations of the imagination which, according to Ortega, is the "principal organ" of our intellectual apparatus. The world of perception, then, is but one of the many inner worlds, and in what do these worlds consist? These are questions which will hardly be asked. Yet their solution would be of the greatest importance. Ortega clearly formulated the problem fifteen years ago. Anyone at all conversant with the history of philosophy will recognize that he is dealing with problems which had already arisen in the thought of Hegel and Schelling. Ortega earlier attacked philosophic idealism in all its forms, he scoffed at the "knights of the spirit." But this system of inner worlds which creative imagination produces out of itself is, in other terms, exactly what Hegel called "objective spirit." There are inescapable philosophical problems. They signify the meeting of mind with itself. (pp. 269-71)

> *Ernst Robert Curtius, "Ortega," translated by Willard R. Trask, in* Partisan Review *(copyright © 1950 by Partisan Review, Inc.), Vol. XVII, No. 3, March 1950, pp. 259-71.*

## ALFRED STERN   (essay date 1954)

In his *Revolt of the Masses* Ortega tried to show how, in our technological civilization, the mass man tends to supplant the élite. In this respect he is a spiritual brother of Nietzsche.

Ortega's philosophical education, however, was less Nietzschean than Kantian. His erudition is as universal and international as Unamuno's was; but while his broad outlook did

not prevent Unamuno from remaining deeply rooted in his Spanish mother earth, Ortega is much more European than Spaniard. And Europe means to him Germany, England, and France. Ortega studied philosophy in Berlin and Marburg, Germany. His teachers were the two leaders of the famous Neo-Kantian School of Marburg: Hermann Cohen and Paul Natorp. To these two prominent scholars Ortega owes, as he says himself, all his intellectual discipline but not his philosophical ideas. Among his closest spiritual relatives I should consider Wilhelm Dilthey, Max Scheler, and Henri Bergson. And in many respects Ortega anticipated the ideas of Heidegger and Sartre. (p. 318)

Unlike his teachers Cohen and Natorp, Ortega is not an idealist, because one never meets the ego without things. And he is not a realist, for one never meets things without the ego. As a matter of fact, man never meets "things" but only "difficulties" and "facilities" for his existence. Eight years after Ortega had expressed this idea in his *Historia como Sistema* . . . , Sartre expressed it in his *L'Etre et le Néant*. Also in denying human nature and in insisting that man is not a thing Sartre followed Ortega. To the Spanish thinker man is *drama* in the original sense of the Greek word δρᾶν to act. And the "radical reality" in which he believes is life, each man's life, prior to any theory.

*"Yo soy yo y mi circunstancia"*—"I am I and my circumstance"—Ortega wrote in 1914, in his *Meditaciones del Quijote*—thirteen years before Heidegger expressed a similar idea in his famous *Sein und Zeit,* where he defined existence as *"in-der-Welt-sein"* or "being-in-the-world." And as Heidegger characterized existence furthermore as "being-with-others," Ortega called it, seventeen years before him, *"convivir"* or *"coexistir."*

Ortega goes back to the etymological Latin roots of the word circumstance: *circum-stantia* are the things which stand around us, are referred to us, determine the outlook of each of us. It is what three decades later Sartre was to call *"situation"* or *"facticité."* This section of reality into which I am cast and which may be the Sierra of Guadarrama or the Broadway of New York is considered by Ortega as the natural exit which leads Gonzalez or Smith into the world. Thus, these *circum-stantia* form the other half of my person.

Life is that which I make with my circumstances, the things which encompass me. In order to maintain myself in my circumstance I have always to do something. But that which I have to do is not imposed upon me by the circumstances the same way an orbit is prescribed to each star. Man, every man, has to decide at every moment that which he is going to do and to be in the following moment.

If we had at every moment only one possibility in front of us, it would be a mere necessity. But man does not act out of pure necessity since he always finds himself confronted with diverse possibilities among which he has to decide. To live is thus to find oneself in a surrounding of some determined possibilities. The world is the repertoire of our vital possibilities; it is not something apart from us, but life's authentic periphery.

What is it that determines our decisions? It is a *project*, a vital project for each of us, by which each of us imagines what he will try to become under the specific conditions of his physical, cultural, and historical circumstances. To live is to *choose* among the possibilities which the circumstances offer. In so far I am free. "But I am *forcibly free*, whether I like it or not," says Ortega. Years later Sartre wrote, "I am *condemned* to be free,'' without referring to his Spanish predecessor. But Sartre developed and integrated these ideas into a kind of system, whose tonality is anxiety, as I show in my recent book *Sartre—His Philosophy and Psychoanalysis*. Ortega's system, however, is still to be published, as his disciple, Julián Marías, announces.

Long before Sartre, Ortega y Gasset insisted on the necessity of man's engagement in a definite project. Without a project life is demoralized, debased, he says rightfully. And as if he wanted to establish the antithesis to André Gide's doctrine of man's *''disponibilité,''* Ortega wrote: ''A disposable life is a greater negation of itself than death.'' The Spanish thinker showed convincingly that this was true, not only for individual lives but also for the lives of collectivities. To him a state is, above all, a project of action, a project of collaboration. ''A state is neither consanguinity nor linguistic unity, nor territorial unity. . . . It is pure dynamism—the will to do something together.'' With these words Ortega revealed the futility of Hitler's racial state fifteen years before it proved its futility by its collapse.

The United States and Latin America are probably the best examples to demonstrate the correctness of our philosopher's conceptions. At the end of the eighteenth century and the beginning of the nineteenth, neither the links of blood, nor those of language, culture, and a common historical past could prevent the separation of the United Colonies from England, and that of the Latin-American countries from Spain, for neither England nor Spain was any longer able to offer the Americas inspiring projects of a common collective future. It is the future which makes nations—counter-current-like—and Ortega is a futurist. He is convinced that the moral disintegration of Europe can be prevented only if the European nations can become engaged in a great common enterprise, in an inspiring project of a common collective future. This project which Ortega proposed to the Europeans in 1930 is that of the creation of a European supernation, the United States of Europe.

Ortega's suggestion is extremely timely, and it is not a utopia, for what the Europeans have in common weighs more heavily than their distinctive characters as Spaniards, Frenchmen, Germans, and Italians.

In his *Historia como Sistema* Ortega realized that the ''reason'' of physical science cannot tell us anything about man. ''The failure of physical reason opens the road for a vital and historical reason.'' Only a few words can be said about this important concept: Man has no nature but he has a history, i.e., his previous experiences, and this history, together with his circumstances, constitutes the basic limitation of his future possibilities. In order to be able to choose and to decide, man has to know his vital circumstances and his and his group's historical past, which, in fact, has become a part of his circumstances. Thereby man is guided by concrete reason, a *vital, historical reason*. While our philosopher denies that the physicomathematical reason—that of his teachers Cohen and Natorp—brings us into contact with a transcendent reality, he thinks that vital, historical reason does. For him life and its history is the basic reality. Vital reason understands life, because it is adapted to the fluidity of life. Bergson and Unamuno saw in reason the power which solidifies everything it touches. Their criticism holds for pure reason, but not for Ortega's vital, historical reason, which tries to ''liquefy'' (*fluidificar*) every fact, by revealing its becoming.

Thus Ortega's philosophy is—as indicated by the title of one of his essays—''neither vitalism nor rationalism.'' Although it places the problem of life in the center of its investigations, Ortega's thought cannot be termed as vitalism, because it does not admit any other kind of theoretical knowledge than that based on reason. It is, however, no rationalism either, because Ortega realizes that within reality reason is only a ''tiny island surrounded by irrationality.'' Thus ''to reason'' cannot mean to prescribe laws to reality, but only to combine elements which cannot be further penetrated by reason.

Reality can only be seen from the specific standpoint which each man occupies in the universe. Thus it is broken up into innumerable subjective ''facets'' or individual ''perspectives,'' which are determined by time, place, environment—in short, by the peculiar existential circumstances of each individual. ''Within mankind each race, and within each race every individual is an organ of perception distinct from all the others.'' Reality offers itself in individual perspectives. None of them exhausts reality, and in spite of their diversity these individual perspectives do not exclude each other; on the contrary, each requires the other as its complement, and all individual perspectives together build up the reality of life.

This is, in a nutshell, Ortega's doctrine of ''perspectivism.'' It is an inspiring doctrine, for it ascribes to each man and to each nation a specific mission of truth. (pp. 318-22)

> *Alfred Stern, ''Unamuno and Ortega: The Revival of Philosophy in Spain,'' in* The Pacific Spectator *(copyright © 1954 by The Pacific Coast Committee for the Humanities of the American Council of Learned Societies), Vol. VIII, No. 4, Autumn, 1954, pp. 310-24.\**

## DAVID WHITE (essay date 1956)

There is a definite Protestant quality to Ortega's concept of man's authentic being consisting in a mission, a vocation, a task. He had reacted against Roman Catholicism, not in the tradition of the rationalist free-thinker, the anticlerical so common in the Latin countries of both Europe and the Americas, but as one who intimately knew the structure of Roman Catholic thought and found it wanting. In later years he describes Thomism as an ''Aristotelian betrayal'' of the basic Christian genius, as the earlier Middle Ages had been a Platonist betrayal. He never seems as conversant with Protestant thought. He never came to profess any particular religious faith, although he never says he is not a Christian, only that he is not a Roman Catholic.

The Protestant flavor of his thought comes from his deep indebtedness to German thought and culture; and despite his opposition to the Kantian tradition as expressed in neo-Kantianism, the Kantian emphasis on duty—a Protestant heritage in Kant—shows through in Ortega's emphasis on responsibility in an individual, a nation, a generation. Those Protestant theologians who look sympathetically at existentialism as a possible philosophical medium will find much in Ortega's thought to recommend it, particularly in bringing Reformation thought on ''vocation'' into focus on the contemporary scene.

Along other lines one finds his philosophy extremely suggestive in its implications for the interplay between philosophical and theological thought, although as we pass from the philosophical to the theological we are in the realm of supposition and implication. Ortega himself says nothing in regard to it, and we may at times ask more of him than we have a right to ask. (pp. 255-56)

Both Thomistic and the various forms of Idealistic philosophy holding to the primacy of the intellect have created philosophic systems which rob the historical scene of most of its vitality and decisive importance. Reality is seen ultimately as static rather than dynamic. Even God becomes a part of the system and his action is restricted to what the system imposes upon him. Actually, he fulfills a function determined by the system. While some of these would attribute the reason to God's creative activity, the logical implications are that God is the creation of the intellect. The so-called theistic philosophies in effect so exalt man and limit God that man has little need of God.

The existential philosophy of Ortega y Gasset, which says little about God, actually leaves God free and man open to God's activity. Reality is not closed or static but open to the future and vital with possibility. Ortega's philosophy would rightfully condemn the gods of philosophical systems as creations of the intellect, as the creation of God in man's rational image. Here, however, God can never be known rationally except as a meditation after the fact of his activity. God must be met in a personal encounter within life, in such a philosophy, if he is to be other than a rational abstraction.

Ortega's philosophy of history gives the historical event vital importance. It is not a shadowy "moving image of eternity," but the very essence of life in the making. Both Idealism and Thomism tend to rob the historical event of any decisive significance. As a result they also rob the Incarnation of its decisive importance. They don't know exactly what to do with Christ. Ortega in his advocacy of the historical reason does one thing—he insures that all history must be taken seriously. While he does not give Christ decisive importance, he leaves the way open for such an acknowledgment to take place. To understand our own experience we must see our life in the light of history, and Christ is a part of history. Christ must be taken into account, he must be encountered whatever our reaction to the encounter might be, if we would know ourselves at all. What is lacking in Ortega's philosophy is that nothing leads us to give Christ that decisive significance he has in the life of the Christian over other historical figures and events.

But after all, Ortega is writing philosophy and not testimony. Each moment in time has its importance, but the question remains as to what gives what event the deciding importance. Personally, I feel it is just as well that the matter remains open in Ortega, for only in the encounter of each life with Christ does Christ become all-significant. He then illuminates history and "my life" as he becomes a reality of personal experience in a personal revealing encounter. It is that experience that then gives rise to creeds and doctrines and gives them whatever authenticity they may have. Without the encounter these creeds and doctrines are as tinkling cymbal and sounding brass.

The philosophy of Ortega y Gasset keeps man open toward the future, and incidentally open toward God. Life is not a closed affair already determined by the impervious demand of reason. Man is not some *thing,* but a conduct, a drama, a project. The man who seeks to realize a project seeks ends, ultimates, and eventually the ultimate. In his inability to realize them in himself, he is driven back upon his own insufficiency or shipwreck. This for the Christian is the first condition necessary in man's salvation in eventually turning him to God. It is not, as Ortega would have it, his salvation—to realize that one is shipwrecked is but the first step toward salvation. (pp. 256-57)

> David White, "'One of the Twelve': The Life and Thought of José Ortega y Gasset," in Religion in

*Life (copyright © 1956 by Abingdon Press), Vol. XXV, No. 2, Spring, 1956, pp. 247-58.*

## PAUL WEST (essay date 1959)

Ortega impresses and infuriates. He was determined to turn philosophy and history into belles lettres. Half of him was prophet and rather smug on that account. He sought in his prose for a Paterian radiance, and appeared to think metaphor and repetition essential to the expression of sincere thought. Most of his works—*The Revolt of the Masses* excluded—support a tribal dance of ideas, some of them huge and seminal. But his vatic repetition too often becomes erratic variation, and we have to read him with a potato-peeler. He puts nothing plainly until he's baffled us with adumbration. He is a self-celebrating writer and at his best only when he isn't trying too hard. This forefather of Malraux has much in common with Arnold Toynbee and the Algerian in Camus. Their ways of self-conception are his, and so are most of their ideas.

*Man and Crisis,* in the manner of a slow-motion whirlwind, suggests that we are now witnessing the end of the era that began with Galileo. We live in crisis—as did people in the change from paganism to Christianity and from the static world of the Middle Ages to the Renaissance. Before analysing these two earlier crises, Ortega clears the ground (but strains our patience) by establishing that in life's variety there is an unchanging basic structure; that 'man' is a drama of self-determining; that man has to have a cosmology; that the generation is the proper unit of historical change and that the 'tone of history' changes every fifteen years. Little of this substantially affects the beguiling argument and learned exemplification that follow.

Why, then, do crises come about? Why do we bring upon ourselves confusion, primitivism, *fay ce que vouldras,* cynicism, nihilism, bitterness (like Cicero's or Petrarch's), the cults of nature and of the man-of-action, and the *vita minima* of excessive socialization? For these, says Ortega, all come with crisis. The reason (the most sustainedly lucid exposition in the book) is this: each man inherits a cosmology and yet yearns to create it himself—he means each *intellectual* man; heirs develop inertia; and individual originality becomes subsumed under the collective inheritance. (pp. 241-42)

This is a high-falutin, intellectual's version of the seven-year itch; the scratching is gigantic. Ortega then gives a fascinating account of how man-worship developed: 'Ancient life was cosmocentric; medieval life was theocentric; modern life is anthropocentric.' (p. 242)

The first crisis began with repudiation of culture: 'God,' said St Paul, 'hath chosen the foolish things of the world.' And the second began similarly with Cusanus's praise of the idiot, *Moriae encomium* by Erasmus and Giordano Bruno's *Lode del asino.* This is absolutism—and Ortega has a sharp chapter on 'Extremism as a Way of Life'. But the Middle Ages worked towards their golden age, the thirteenth-century's well-caulked world: Augustine's *credo ut intelligam* yields to St Anselmo's eleventh-century motto, 'faith seeking intelligence'; but rational Thomism soon attracts the protests of Scotism, which wants inspiration back; and Occam completes the sabotage by toppling the universals. (pp. 242-43)

This is the sparkling panorama of *Man and Crisis*—a dithyrambic version of a Basil Willey Background. Ortega may at times founder in his own abundance, but his comprehension (in both senses) of our three main crises is patent. **Man and Crisis,** just as reiterative and seminal as **The Revolt of the Masses, The Mission of the University** and **The Dehumanization of Art,** has to be read along with Spengler, Toynbee and Ranke; with Cassirer's **Essay on Man,** Camus's **The Rebel,** and Hannah Arendt's **The Human Condition.** As synoptic books go, it is astonishingly free from the suppositious. Only one assertion seems questionable: 'To be centred within oneself is the opposite of living harried and confused.' 'Centred' seems to mean 'coherent'; but does it? This would make the assertion tautologous. The truth seems to be that Ortega, in his true colours as a humanist, has to identify introversion with the self-communing on which Christianity is based. His otherworldliness is a form of spiritual privacy, which puts him in a large and humane company.

This 'being centred within oneself' (*ensimismarse*) Ortega opposes to 'confused otherness' (*alteración*). And **Man and Crisis** is important because it explains why Ortega in **The Dehumanisation of Art** . . . could attack introverted art. He attacked not the introversion but the failure, after meditation or retreat or recharging of batteries, to reconfront the outside world of 'confused otherness'. In **The Theme of Our Time** . . . he had attacked both Christian and aesthetic otherworldliness; because modern art was a 'farce', because it was a mere fooling, Ortega was tempted to look for a new era impending as after the iconoclasm of St Paul and Erasmus's **Praise of Folly.** And yet such art was, in Ortega's own words, the result of the artist's seeking 'a new contact with his own self'—trying to 'create from nought'. This he identifies as the itch behind crisis, but he continues to berate secession even in **Man and Crisis.** . . . Ortega's position never changed; and it is an earnest of his integrity that up to his death in 1955 he understood and yet refused to cheer on those activities whose increasing vogue would vindicate his theories. Like Santayana and Camus, he was more of a humanist than a philosopher: for whatever reasons man withdrew into himself, his obligation (as Ortega saw it) was to emerge to confront the world again, however hopelessly, with renewed energy and craving for harmony. Ortega evokes Seneca's *sustine.* He thought that humanism, like art, should be organic, not abstract. He recognized and admitted that many men aspire to mysticism (whether through love or art); that crisis itself was attributable to a self-renewal that rejects inherited forms much as the fox submerges himself until all his fleas have collected on his snout and he can dispatch them with a sneeze. He knew that abstract art, like the revolt against images in Oriental Christendom, was an iconoclasm aiming at purity, at an absolute. As Ernst Cassirer rather heavily but rightly says: 'Mysticism attempts to arrive at the pure meaning of religion as such, free from all encumbrance with the "otherness" of empirical-sensuous existence and of sensuous images and representation.' The art, as Ortega said, was bound to revest itself in images, just as religion was bound to attend again to the mundane. What counts is not expectation of success but convinced resolution. Simplification, monism, purity, coherence and spiritual nudity cannot efface the 'confused otherness'; they merely precede and follow attempts to cope. The humanist trend is always back to the raw stuff of life, to the fertile muddle. Ortega approvingly quotes in **Man and Crisis** a Renaissance motto: *philosophia duce, regredimur.* That is obviously the motto which assembles such as Arnold, Pater, Santayana, Camus, Malraux, Hemingway, E. M. Forster, Gilbert Murray and Schweitzer.

But the humanist, more keenly than any other man, feels the urge to make his own system—something which relates him,

in all his personal peculiarity, to the cosmos. And he of course feels just as keenly the precarious arbitrariness of what he creates; like the romantic lover, he is never quite sure how much he has imagined and how much is real. From systems emerges culture, as Ortega says: one cannot contemplate a hostile or alien environment indefinitely. 'Vital reason' prevails. That is Ortega's point all along. Systems have to be exposed to the rough-and-tumble of everyday living; and the quality of the rough-and-tumble has somehow to be given to works of art. Coherence has to cope with muddle; muddle has to prevent coherence from becoming 'dehumanized'. For, at root, both pattern and chaos are human creations and the sources of crises other than that of our own time.

From all this we might turn to Ortega's **On Love** in anticipation of a relaxing master; and, true, the master does relax, but his light relief has a serious point that weighs down his lighter touches. He pontificates, pothers and bumbles. The prose is paunchy, and a good many of the ideas are subdued to the metaphors he works in. (pp. 243-45)

This is in fact no erotic guide-book, but further documentation of his historical-philosophical hypotheses: man is a drama; man always yearns to, sometimes convulsively has to, renew his sense of himself, even to the point of emulating the mystics.

**On Love** is dominated by familiar Ortega themes: in his choice of lover, man defines his individuality; he breaks out of one kind of mysticism, solitude, into another, love, which is really the equivalent of the artist's return from abstraction to reality. Yet man distorts that reality by concocting romantic love. It was not for nothing that Ortega called love 'a literary genre'. About all, it is an activity, a self-projection of a sort rare in Spain. (p. 246)

[Love] and meditation are the twin bases of humanism. And to encounter this lean, generous, paralyzingly aphoristic but literally coherent mind is to be reminded of humanism's positive side. The genteel heresy, the simplified inward pastoral, sheer fright and sheer retreat all haunted him. But he kept humanizing himself, kept squaring up to the world again. Such is the humanist's *vita maxima.* Bravely enough, the mind in solitude goes on erecting edifices of ideas and of sentiment. Systematic thought, like romantic love, is a precarious structure; both defy nature. But the most defiant form of such thought is its emotional version in such eclectic contrivances as Pater's House Beautiful, Malraux's Imaginary Museum, E. M. Forster's Love the Beloved Republic, Yeats's Vision—even Maritain's own cosmic whorls and cones in the diagrams for **On the Philosophy of History,** and Ortega's recipe for speeding up and thus dismissing the twentieth-century crisis. These are the fantasies that average man ignores. Yet they, like the romantic love Ortega recommends, seem to satisfy some spirits; they bring to their authors as much comfort and fulfilment as more orthodox systems bring to their own exponents. Even heresy, like idealization, is creative. And they are often the same thing. (p. 247)

*Paul West, "Ortega and the Humanist Illusion" (reprinted by permission of the author), in* The Twentieth Century, *Vol. 166, No. 992, October, 1959, pp. 241-47.*

### E. CORDEL McDONALD (essay date 1959)

In 1925 Ortega published some brief **Ideas sobre la novela,** at a time when a vast amount of interest was being directed toward this genre. An examination of his ideas, which have remained relatively unnoticed, proves fruitful for several reasons; they contain penetrating insights into various problems concerned with the novel; they provide a most revealing comparison with ideas of Pío Baroja, a practicing novelist; they show to what degree Ortega's thought has been attuned to one specific current critical preoccupation.

Ortega, aware of current discussions in literary circles in the rest of Europe, and sensitive to an "ausencia de más sólidas reflexiones" on the modern novel in current Spanish literary criticism . . . , drew his together around the development of two themes: a consideration of the nature of the then much talked about crisis of the novel, and an exposition of a few workable norms which he considered basic to a critical examination of the genre.

The crisis of the novel he summarized and explained. . . . The novelist must face the fact, according to Ortega, that there no longer exist any plots which have not been used as the basis of novels, and he must recognize a change in readers' tastes which have become more discriminating. . . . (p. 475)

Ortega turned attention to an examination and exposition of certain norms which he considered basic for an intelligent critical examination of the genre, norms which, if applied in an evaluation of fiction, can help determine its value and worth: a) the psychological foundations on which the novelist rests his novelistic structure; b) the peculiarly unique novelistic *cosmos* which he creates; c) the method and techniques by which he best achieves these ends. (p. 476)

If the explicit desire to publish these notes and to help fill an "ausencia de más sólidas reflexiones" on the subject in current Spanish literary criticism included the implicit urge to stimulate thought on the part of other critics and practicing novelists and thereby affect an exchange of opinion, Ortega did not have long to wait. Pío Baroja, in a reply which he facetiously called a "Prólogo casi doctrinal sobre la novela," directed an attack against almost every idea which Ortega had expressed.

To the remarks about the crisis of contemporary fiction and the difficulty of coming by new and better plots, Baroja teasingly objected. . . . (p. 477)

Baroja suggested that the real reason behind Ortega's having launched upon the theme of crisis was the simple fact that Ortega, "especialista en cuestiones pedagógicas," had quite willingly let himself be taken in by a current Parisian fad. . . .

Baroja was correct in suggesting that Ortega had been listening very intently to critical discussions then being carried on in Paris. Ortega always kept an ear attuned to all kinds of discussions, those literary being no exception. It is a fact that critics were about to turn the subject of the novel's crisis into almost a public issue in France. . . .

[But] Ortega was no mere mouthpiece for fads. His suggestions that the crisis stems from a change which involves author and reader is his unique contribution, one which he expanded in the exposition of very workable norms for the genre.

If Baroja's reaction to the first theme was a series of mild objections, his reaction to the second was a violent disagreement. He differs with all that Ortega suggested, for he holds that in art, and especially in literature, there are no ultimate norms to which author and critic can have recourse. Critics and "cultivadores del ensayo filosófico" should realize first, suggested Baroja, the relativity of their judgments. . . .

In his disagreements with Ortega's suggestions that certain norms might be helpful in approaching a consideration of fiction, Baroja proceeded on the hypothesis that there are many novelistic types, many methods and techniques, and that to suggest the superiority of any one is to suggest critical dogma. . . . The most extreme position taken by Baroja in disagreement with Ortega is that there can be no norms for fiction. . . . (p. 478)

Baroja's objections and disagreements pose one chief question: are there certain norms which can suggest a means of evaluating fiction in terms of character, setting, method and technique or, as Baroja suggested, is the novel a genre which is in such a plastic state of development, whose proteic form allows its adaption to any demands of the novelist, and are there so many novelistic types, methods and techniques, that to attempt to outline any system of standards of judgment is useless and better not begun? Baroja's objections do point out certain dangers in Ortega's tendency to synthesize and formulate rules. On the other hand, Baroja has shown the limitations of his own kind of approach. Granting that the novel is a loose form with many types and techniques does not deny that we can decide by means of some system of standards of judgment which types and techniques are better. Ortega's positive approach would seem superior to the negative attitude taken by Baroja; analyzing the nature of the "imaginative psychology," which permeates the novelist's concept and creation of character and human personality, examining the peculiar nature and values of the novel's *cosmos,* and understanding the method and technique by which he has achieved these goals provide a real means of arriving at both a better understanding and an evaluation of the genre.

It might be suggested that Ortega's *Ideas* are valuable not only within the framework of Spanish literary criticism, but also when viewed in a larger perspective and placed along side ideas of other European critics. Those studies on the novel written in the twenties which retain most relevance today are those in which critics were groping with the still very confused aesthetics of the novel. The chief critical preoccupation at the time was with method and technique conceived in terms of the problem of narration. As [René] Warren and [Austin] Wellek pointed out, at the central core of all novelistic method is the relation of the novelist to his material. Traditionally there had been one way of telling the story: the novelist narrated his story, using the third person, often as an omniscient narrator. He stood, as it were, at the side of his work, including his own comments, giving his own style to the narration. There are two ways of deviating from this mode of "natural narration." One is a kind of romantic-ironic method, which deliberately magnifies the role of the narrator, which delights in violating any possible illusion that is life and not art. The method closely resembles the natural method in that it emphasizes still further the literary character of the work. The second way of deviating from this method is the one that has come to be known as the objective. Ortega's ideas on what he called the *método autóptico* are related to this objective method.

Ideas discussed in the formulation of a theory of the objective method were not particularly new in the twenties. Their genesis springs from nineteenth century novelistic practice and critical thought. Most critics who developed the theory insisted on the idea of a voluntary absence of the author from his novel. They insisted that the author must not tell about but instead show his characters and their world functioning in their own right. Ortega, in the earlier essay *Meditaciones del Quijote* . . . , suggested an understanding of the nature of these developments in critical thought by his comments on the "presentative technique" of Cervantes. But the ideas of 1925 show that he was completely aware of the significance of all these developments in critical theory of the novel. . . . (p. 479)

Pursuing the matter further, may we suggest that what makes Ortega's ideas unique, valuable and worthy of a place within the current of critical writings being directed toward a theory of an objective-presentative method, are the aesthetic foundations on which he bases his ideas. Similar foundations do not seem to have been suggested until after the publication of Ortega's essay, when the French critic Ramon Fernandez repeated ideas concerning the aesthetic foundations of the method in his study of "La méthode de Balzac: le récit et l'esthétique du roman." The French critic separates all narrative fiction into two classes, recital and novel. The former is the narration of what has already taken place and is now being told, according to laws of exposition; the novel represents events as taking place in time and space, according to an order of living reproduction.

There is a strikingly similar parallel between the ideas of these two critics. Ortega's summary statement that "Peter was melancholy," exemplifies the technique of the recital, which uses a conceptual exposition of references, allusions, definitions and depends on what Fernandez calls rational proofs. On the other hand, the evocation and presentation of Peter's melancholy involves the creation of a novel, which uses a living production of Peter's speech, his actions, his thoughts, which actually take place, as it were, before the reader, and it depends on what Fernandez calls aesthetic proofs. (p. 480)

In summary, to suggest again what value Ortega's *Ideas* still possess, we would do well to return to the two basic themes around which he constructed his essay and which have served as our constant point of reference. The problem of the novel's crisis seems to be a perennial, favorite theme in critical discussions for it is surely still being considered today when the novel is said to be yet in a period of disorientation. This theme has lost none of its vitality although it might appear that one aspect of Ortega's treatment of it has. Surely, one may justly disagree with him in the matter of the non-existence of "new," never-before-used plots. Plots do exist, although they are built around a limited number of plot situations. And Ortega himself told the novelist to turn to the ever fecund examination of human personality. As to the novel's *how* having become as important as its *what*, we heartily agree. It must be hoped, at least, that readers' tastes have become more discriminatingly sensitive to such matters as setting, structure, style, method and technique. As for the second theme created by Ortega, it can be said that he laid out, in general terms, the fields in which novelistic theory and criticism must always continue to function. Herein is found much of the *Ideas* positive value. Ortega's *Ideas* brilliantly summarize the currents of critical thought being directed toward the novel at the time they were written. Although they place the subject within a broad aesthetic framework and thus leave problems of practical application to other critics, the *Ideas* treat in a stimulating and original fashion the chief problems with which novelistic creation, theory and criticism are still occupied. (pp. 480-81)

> *E. Cordel McDonald, "The Modern Novel As Viewed by Ortega," in* Hispania *(© 1959 The American Association of Teachers of Spanish and Portuguese, Inc.), Vol. XLII, No. 4, December, 1959, pp. 475-81.*

## JULIÁN MARÍAS    (essay date 1960)

> [*Marías's exhaustive study is considered the most important single work on Ortega's philosophy. The following excerpt from* José Ortega y Gassett: Circumstance and Vocation *concerns two of the philosopher's central concepts, those of "circumstance" and "perspectivism."*]

Among the truths which Ortega taught about human life, the following two are numbered: that everything man does, he does *in view of the circumstances,* and that to each of the actions of our lives, its justification intrinsically belongs. (p. 3)

Ortega occupies a unique place, by virtue of his quality and character, in the history of Spain and, in general, the history of the Hispanic peoples; in him the Spanish-speaking peoples have had for the first time the full and authentic experience of philosophy. By this I mean that before Ortega, philosophy had had among us a penultimate and deficient character, from the point of view of philosophy as well as the point of view of its condition in Spain. Either there have been immature philosophical attempts (gropings, rather), intuitions which have not attained the level of strict theory, or simple utilization of alien philosophical structures—not thought out from inside Spanish circumstances—set in motion by the need to interpret reality from this irreplaceable perspective. In Ortega—and not before him or after him—something decisive happened to the Spanish mind as such, something which makes it different from what it had been before, and which conditions its future: the incorporation of philosophy. And this, of course, becomes a new determination of Hispanic reality, to the extent that philosophy has begun to function within it, in a double sense: as an element with which it will have to reckon in the future, and as a possibility which will be at its disposal from now on. Before Ortega, an analysis of the essential content of the form of Spanish historical life did not reveal philosophy, except in the relatively abstract dimension where philosophy formed part of Europe and the West, realities in which Spain is implanted. Ortega's work signifies the inclusion of philosophy in the very texture of things Hispanic. (pp. 3-4)

It might be thought that, even though this were correct, interest in Ortega's works would be confined to Spanish-speaking countries. I do not believe that this is the case, for an extremely simple reason: if it is true that philosophy has happened to the Spanish mind, it is no less true that the *Spanish version* of philosophy has happened to Western philosophy through the work of Ortega. I mean that twentieth-century European thought has become part of a new, *irreducible* perspective, which works back on all the other perspectives and changes them. What Descartes, and possibly Giordano Bruno, and Bacon, and Leibniz and Kant—both of them, for Leibniz did not write in German—have meant for modern philosophy, Ortega has meant in our time, for he has contributed *a new way of looking at things,* without which Western philosophical thought would be mutilated, incomplete, anachronistic, and, in short, *less than itself.* Since, moreover, Ortega's philosophy includes decisive aspects which are not found, not even in other forms or versions, in the rest of the philosophical systems of our time, their incorporation into the common property of Western philosophy becomes as necessary as it is urgent: given the rhythm of historical transformation in our century, certain anomalies began to be observed some years ago in European and American thought which endanger a large part of their best possibilities, and which a sufficient presence of Orteguian philosophy would have prevented from the start.

This means that its *effective possession* is an inescapable condition for making a Spanish philosophy possible and for a Western philosophy to achieve its proper level. In other words, we need Ortega in order to be fully ourselves, in order to have available all the possibilities of our future. (p. 4)

In a thinker who possessed a maximum of profundity and authenticity, as Ortega did, the deepest and innermost part of his life is expressed and "realized" in his work; though, naturally, it is only accessible if his work is taken in its complex reality. We must take seriously the need, formulated by Ortega, to see the work as "interwoven with a whole vital trajectory"; but no less seriously the second part of that sentence in which he states that "each one of the pages collected here summed up my entire existence at the hour it was written, and, put together, they represent the melodic line of my personal destiny." Anything else would be like thinking that we knew who Beethoven was, however many things we might be told about him, if we were unaware of his symphonies. When it is said that, whatever the biographical events history may discover, Shakespeare is the author of Shakespeare's plays, Cervantes the man who wrote *Don Quixote*, and Homer the Homeric poems, this does not mean—it ought not to mean—the selfish triviality that it is the works themselves which interest us; rather that, at that level of creation, they are the most refined and personal expression of their authors, the thing in which those authors, when they existed, most properly *consisted;* and that, therefore, that is what we properly understand by the names of Beethoven, Shakespeare, Cervantes, and Homer, on condition that we see these works as human productions in which was made manifest and realized that ungraspable and ultimate project to which each of them alluded when he said, making a vague gesture toward his heart, "I."

That project, program, or aspiration, that arrow aimed at a target, that voice (or vocation) which calls us, that destiny which is "ours" and which we fundamentally are, is not separable from, nor does it have concrete reality apart from, a precise circumstance which we may call "our world." This has always been true, but Ortega is the first man who has understood it philosophically and has made it the very root of his doctrine. This is why that condition of human life has been still more true in him; I mean that in him this inexorable condition was *accepted;* and instead of fabricating another, as almost all Western thought has done, he made it the starting-point of his philosophy, at once resistance and point of support, servitude and spur. Everything human is circumstantial, but in Ortega it was so deliberately. To say the same thing in other words, we may add that Ortega's philosophy consisted, and very formally . . . in *freely deciding to be faithful to his destiny.* And this expression I have just written is perhaps the best possible definition of *authenticity.* (pp. 6-7)

If we consider Ortega's written work, we will see that there are several points of inflection in it. In the first place, whereas in its early stages the realization seems to coincide approximately with the projects, in the last stages a series of apparent chance occurrences constantly disturbs the plan and its configuration. In the second place, the continuity of aim, the sure fluency of the writer, is not always equally visible. Finally, on various occasions there are explicit references to the need for going to new forms of expression—and of intellectual creation—and it is never entirely clear whether this is what one is reading or whether what is before one's eyes is only a new postponement. At the end of his prologue to the first collected—though not complete—edition of his *Works,* he expressly stated this in a Platonic figure of speech: "A new task begins, then. Little boat, to sea once more! What Plato calls 'the second voyage' begins." (pp. 8-9)

The circumstantial character of Ortega's thought, of which he had such a clear consciousness from very early in his career, led him to the formation of the concept of *circumstance,* which became one of the pillars of his philosophy. (p. 353)

The theory of circumstance appears in Ortega in the *Meditations on Quixote.* The concrete form in which this notion is introduced, and therefore the foreshortening in which it is presented in this decisive context, must be kept in mind. Only thus can we attempt to understand what Ortega is thinking when he uses the term "circumstance"; other previous contexts will confirm for us the trajectory of this idea in his thought—that is, where it came from.

Ortega mentions the *themes* with which the *Meditations* he is about to present are to be concerned: besides the "glorious matters," "the most unimportant things," small manifestations in which the soul of a race is revealed. We must be careful not to confuse the large and the small; that is, we must affirm the *hierarchy* "without which the cosmos returns to chaos"; but, once this is assumed, we must also turn our attention to what is to be found *near* our person. And he at once introduces the concept of circumstance—*circum-stantia.* . . . Ortega thnks that one of the most profound changes in the twentieth century, compared to the preceding one, will be the mutation of "our sensitivity with regard to circumstances." This consideration leads him to sketch out a theory of *perspective* and of *culture.* . . . And then he adds: "We must search for our circumstance, precisely in what it possesses of limitation, of peculiarity, the one right place *in the immense perspective of the world.* We should not remain in perpetual ecstasy in the presence of hieratic values, but gain for our individual life the proper place among them. In short: *the reabsorption of the circumstance is the concrete destiny of man."* And he continues: "My natural outlet *toward the Universe* opens out over the Guadarrama passes or the countryside around Ontígola. This sector of circumstantial reality *forms the other half of my person;* only by means of it can I become integrated and be fully myself." (p. 360)

The concept of *circumstance* in Ortega is linked with that of *perspective.* This union is essential; I mean that to take them in an isolated manner has caused these concepts to be quite sterile in the philosophies—and these are very few—in which they have appeared. The idea of circumstance demands, in some measure, the presence of perspective, even though there is an attempt to avoid it. . . . When Ortega, however, says, "We must seek for our *circumstance* . . . the one right place in the immense *perspective* of the world," he introduces a new concept, different from the modest previous philosophical tradition. (p. 366)

The notion of perspective appears formally, using this precise term, in the *Meditations on Quixote.* The first text is as follows: "When will we become open to the conviction that the definitive being of the world is neither matter nor soul, that it is not any particular thing, but a perspective? God is the perspective and the hierarchy: Satan's sin was an error of perspective. Well then, the perspective becomes perfected through the multiplication of its terms and the exactness with which we react in the presence of each of its hierarchical ranks."

With this paragraph alone, Ortega turns his back on the idea of perspective introduced into contemporary philosophy by

Nietzsche, Vaihinger, and Teichmüller, and poses the question in a different, almost an opposite, form. For the first thing he says about perspective is that the definitive *being* of the world consists in it; that is, the first attribution of perspective is not to *knowledge* or any of its aspects, but to *the real*. Nor does he say that matter and soul are not real; rather, that the *definitive* being of the world does not consist in them, because this is not "any particular thing." This places us very far from any subjectivism, from any reduction of the real and the subject who observes it: from any "phenomenalism," from any projection of the subject and its point of view. In fact, the opposite is being dealt with: a reality with a rigorous structure of its own, to which one must hold in order to attain the truth. Perspective is made perfect by the multiplication of its terms and the exactness with which we react to each of its hierarchical ranks; that is, there is a structure of the real, which only presents itself perspectively, which needs to be integrated from multiple terms or points of view, and which demands *exactness* in our reaction. . . . Every time that a particular point of view is built into an absolute one, instead of placing it in its proper place within the total perspective, an error is committed which consists in usurping God's point of view—if the expression can be permitted—which is precisely the infinitude of all possible points of view, the hierarchical integration of all perspectives. This is why I often say that all claims to "absolutism of the intellect," to the affirmation of a particular system to the exclusion of all the rest, are forms of "Satanism," no matter how innocuous and even pious the intention may be.

Whereas in Nietzsche or Teichmüller perspective is contrasted to reality and means appearance, convention, illusion which vanishes when the perspectivist vision is suppressed, *in Ortega perspective is the condition of the real and the possibility of access to its truth*. Falsity consists in evading the perspective, in being unfaithful to it, or in making a *particular* point of view absolute; that is, *forgetting the perspective quality of every vision*. Or, expressed in other words, the need for each perspective to be integrated with others, for perspective means *one among various possible perspectives*, and a single perspective is a contradiction. (pp. 374-75)

*Vision, intelligence, valuation, imagination, desire, are ingredients of perspective*. But neither is perspective *static* nor *passive;* it is not limited to "reflecting" speculatively a reality which is simply there, but acts upon it; and further, reality is in part *not there*. Stated more strictly: *my reality* is also reality; it is a part, or, better still, *a constitutive ingredient of reality*. (pp. 378-79)

Without going beyond the level of the **Meditations on Quixote** and **"Truth and Perspective"**—that is, between the years 1914 and 1916, when for the first time Ortega takes philosophic possession of his original intuition—we find that the word "reality" lacks meaning for us outside of the perspective in which it is constituted and organized, in which *it is real*. We can say that for Ortega *reality only exists as such perspectively*, and that on this fact is based the possibility of its truth. (p. 379)

> *Julián Marías, in his* José Ortega y Gasset: Circumstance and Vocation, *translated by Frances M. López-Morillas (copyright 1970 by the University of Oklahoma Press; originally published as* Ortega, Revista de Occidente, *1960), University of Oklahoma Press, 1970, 479 p.*

**JOSEPH FRANK** (essay date 1963)

Despite its wide acceptance . . . Ortega's [*The Dehumanization of Art*] has been the subject of a good deal of misunderstanding.

For one thing, it is universally accepted as a *defense* of the movement it sets out to investigate, although Ortega emphatically declared that he was not attempting to assume the role of judge or advocate but solely that of philosophical observer. And when Ortega abandons this role for a moment, as he does from time to time, he makes it quite clear that his tastes by no means incline him toward modern art. "It may be said that the new art has so far produced nothing worth while," he observes at one point, "and I am inclined to think the same." Even more, Ortega's interest in modern art derives far more from his own philosophy than from any attraction to this art itself. And his reflections lead him into a *depreciation* of the function of art in modern culture which has gone largely unnoticed, and which, if understood, would hardly please the partisans of the moderns. Now that the passage of time has somewhat dimmed the immediate sense of illumination provided by Ortega's scintillating pages, it may thus prove useful to go back and reassess his book from a more balanced perspective.

Certainly the most valuable and perennial section of the work is Ortega's *description* of the main tendency of modern art. This remains as fresh today as when it was first written. Whether or not Ortega coined the word "dehumanization," it was first given currency by his book; and it has been used ever since to fix one of modern art's most dominating traits. What Ortega means is most obvious in the plastic arts, where the importance of recognizable human forms is no longer dependent on their specifically *human* expressiveness. . . . Ortega, it might be noted, does not apply this idea to so-called "pure" abstract art, which in any case he thinks impossible; and he remarks that the few attempts made by Picasso in this direction have been "failures."

A similar evolution has taken place in modern literature, and particularly modern poetry. In the past, simile and metaphor had been used to decorate and embellish the "real" subject or content of the poem, just as form and color had been used to express and convey the "real" subject of the plastic work of art. But now, exactly as in the plastic arts, the order of importance between these elements has been reversed, and what was merely instrumental has become essential. "Before, reality was overlaid with metaphors by way of ornament; now the tendency is to eliminate the extra-poetical, or real, prop and to 'realize' the metaphor, to make it the *res poetica*." . . . This objectification of metaphor, which Ortega finds beginning with Mallarmé, is the most radical method of dehumanization in literature. But he also discerns another method in such writers as Proust, Ramón Gomez de la Serna, and Joyce, who change the normal perspective on reality by shifting attention to, and placing in the foreground, aspects of life which are usually kept in the background or which escape attention altogether.

All these experiments of modern art move in the same direction—a direction that Ortega defines in terms of the epistemological relation between idea and thing. Ordinarily, ideas are used to orient action, to help us grasp reality; and so unconscious are we of this process that we constantly define reality in terms of our ideas, as if the two were naturally identical. "By means of ideas we see the world," Ortega notes, "but in a natural attitude of the mind we do not see the ideas—the same as the eye in seeing does not see itself." But modern art, by shifting attention away from the "reality" expressed in art, has inverted this natural relation between idea and thing. The artist no longer focuses on reality, surreptitiously using his ideas as a controlling framework, but rather turns back and displaces the artistic center of gravity to a *direct* expression of his ideas. The portrait painter is far more interested in *his* perception of the pattern created by a sitter than in the sitter himself; and Cubist paintings are what Ortega calls a ''symbolic cipher'' for certain ideas about the structure of reality. In his immensely suggestive essay **"On Point of View in the Arts,"** which serves as a valuable supplement to *The Dehumanization of Art,* Ortega sees modern art as the culmination of the entire history of Western painting. For the law which he persuasively deduces from its historical evolution is that ''first, things are painted; then sensations; finally, ideas.''

This displacement by modern art of the normal focus of interest—i.e., reality, the world, people and passions as they present themselves in ordinary human life and human affairs—has thus resulted in a purer distillation of the essence of art than ever before. And, while Ortega may have his doubts about the permanent value of the products of modern art, there can be no question that he is wholeheartedly in sympathy with this endeavor of the moderns to define boundaries rigorously and stringently. Ortega's thought, violently in reaction against the eclecticism of the second half of the nineteenth century, welcomes modern art's rejection of the confusion between art and life fostered by realism and naturalism—movements which he calls ''a maximum aberration in the history of taste.'' Also, he favors modern art, unexpectedly enough, for what he labels ''sociological'' reasons.

Modern art, he points out, separates its audience into those who are capable of a ''pure'' aesthetic experience and those who are not. It thereby distinguishes the select from the vulgar, and becomes an invaluable catalyst for the formation of that new aristocracy of the spirit which Ortega believed indispensable to the salvation of modern culture. Since this aspect of Ortega's aesthetics has usually been ignored, it is worth quoting a key passage. ''Through its mere presence,'' he argues, ''the art of the young compels the average citizen to realize that he is just this—the average citizen, a creature incapable of receiving the sacrament of art, blind and deaf to pure beauty. . . . On the other hand, the new art also helps the élite to recognize themselves and one another in the drab mass of society and to learn their mission which consists in being few and holding their own against the many.''

For all these reasons, Ortega spoke warmly and enthusiastically of the new trend as an inevitable and salutary historical phenomenon (which no doubt accounts for the mistaken belief that he was concerned to defend its particular manifestations and experiments). . . . Ortega's pages are filled with the same dash, defiance, and willful injustice toward the past that inspired modernism in its heyday; no other work communicates so vivid a sense of the youthful élan and bravado of this effervescent era. Nor has any writer since been able to compete with Ortega's trenchant book in synoptic grasp and power of conceptual penetration.

As we pursue the train of Ortega's ideas, however, we soon begin to find ourselves in strange and rather quagmirish territory. Dehumanized modern art, cutting itself off from the natural relation of mind to reality, has ceased, we are told, to have any ''connection with dramatic social or political movements, or with profound religious or philosophical currents.'' Art during the nineteenth century, particularly in the Romantic period, had been ready to take on itself nothing less than ''the salvation of mankind''; but modern art and the modern artist, Ortega asserts, will no longer have anything to do with such ponderous pretensions. Art has renounced its role, apparently

voluntarily, of being the spokesman and interpreter of the highest values of its culture and has retired to a realm where the pleasures and refinements of the aesthetic sensibility are cultivated exclusively for their own sake.

Most writers on modern art have seen this increasingly predominant aestheticism as stimulated by a sense of art's superiority to vulgar and ''impure'' reality. But here Ortega paradoxically takes the opposite view, that modern art is being modest rather than proud; and he points to the irony and self-mockery so characteristic of modern art (or at least of the modern art of the twenties) as proof of his contention. (pp. 164-69)

Modern art, then, is essentially negative, derisive, ironic. *It does not take itself seriously,* nor, in Ortega's opinion, does it expect anyone else to do so. (p. 169)

Ortega does not undertake the task of explaining in *The Dehumanization of Art* why art should have traveled this road in modern times; he refers for more details to an earlier work, *The Modern Theme.* And if we turn to this book we discover that Ortega's interpretation of modern art clearly derives from his general philosophical position at this period. *The Modern Theme* is the written version of a group of lectures, given in 1921-22, in which Ortega launches a Nietzschean attack on ''culture'' as a watered-down religion that places the ends of human existence in a sphere transcendent to life. ''Culturalism,'' he declares here, ''is a Christianity without God.'' According to Ortega, culturalism locates the values of life in the infinite future; it sets up a hierarchy of abstractions—science, art, ethics, justice—divorced from the possibility of their fulfillment under concrete biological and historical conditions. Ortega's thought is bitterly hostile to this deification of ''culture,'' and he searches for symptoms in modern life that a new era is impending. Such a symptom he finds in the disagreement over modern art which, in the early twenties, pitted the younger generation against the old. (pp. 169-70)

Ortega argues that the gap between the generations (a point he also stresses in *The Dehumanization of Art*) is one that cannot possibly be bridged. For the older generation, the lack of seriousness in art disqualifies it immediately; for the younger, this very lack of seriousness is the supreme value. And Ortega contends that the attitude of the younger generation reveals ''one of the most widespread features in the new reaction to existence; it was what I long ago called the sense of life as a sport and as a festivity.''

These last words take us back to Ortega's remark that the dehumanization of modern art is ''linked to the triumph of sport and games.'' For in the early twenties Ortega genuinely believed that the whole character of modern life was about to change. We must keep in mind that he was writing during the heyday of Dadaism in France, Ultraism in Spain, and the *Jugendbewegung* in Germany. Youth, vitality, athleticism, bullfighting, nude sunbathing, and the emancipation of the senses were being glorified almost everywhere. There was a gigantic explosion of frenzied *joie de vivre* (or what easily could be seen as such, despite its undertone of tragic despair) as a reaction against the intolerable psychic tensions of the war years.

At that moment it might well have seemed that biological values would replace those of the cultural ''beyond''; that the present would replace the future as the dominating temporal horizon; that youth would take precedence over age, and that the cult of the body would triumph over the moribund and senile cult of the mind. And a consequence of this triumph would be not only the dehumanization of art but its *devaluation*, its relegation to a secondary zone of cultural importance, the refusal any longer to invest it with the dignity and reverence it had formerly claimed—and received. ''What is behind this disgust at seeing art mixed up with life?'' Ortega asks suggestively. (pp. 171-72)

Ortega's thought, then, lands him in the awkward position of maintaining that a *victory* for the biological and organic values of life in our time has been responsible for the dehumanization of art. (p. 172)

Once we become aware of Ortega's underlying point of view, the dazzling sparkle of his perceptions cannot altogether blind us to the weak links in his chain of argument. To begin, we may note a purely internal contradiction. Ortega does not seem to be aware that, if art were really to shift to a secondary zone of interest in modern culture, then the beneficial sociological result he expected from such a shift would not occur. Such a result, we recall, was to be the polarization of society into the vulgar and the élite, the touchstone of selection being the capacity of each group to respond to the purely aesthetic appeal of a dehumanized art. The average citizen would become aware in this way that he was incapable of receiving ''the sacrament of art,'' and would thus, presumably, acknowledge his limitations. But this assumes that the average citizen will continue to think of the appreciation of art as conferring some sort of sacrament; in other words, it assumes that art will continue to retain its importance as one of the highest cultural values. If neither the average citizen *nor* the artist believes that art has any importance, it is difficult to understand why either should feel inferior or superior as a result of his response.

Another objection to Ortega is that the permanent unpopularity of modern art, which he unquestioningly accepted as an axiom, simply has been disproved by the passage of time. Movements such as Cubism and Expressionism, which seemed so scandalous and inacceptable when Ortega was writing, have now become thoroughly assimilated and domesticated. The new art created a new sensibility capable of absorbing its innovations, but not, as Ortega had hoped, a new culture based on a sharp distinction between the élite and the vulgar. (pp. 173-74)

Ortega's most glaring mistake, however, was to insist on viewing modern art only as its own self-negation—as a game which could be whimsical and witty, or strident and raucous, but which never took itself seriously. From our vantage point it is clear that modern culture did not take the road that Ortega predicted. The farcical phase of modern art had ended almost by the time Ortega's essay appeared; and no modern artist would accept Ortega's definition of his role. Indeed, we can easily argue that modern artists take themselves with a good deal more seriousness than did the artists of the past. Ortega is right in linking the dehumanization of art with a radical crisis in modern culture; but he misinterpreted the meaning of the symptoms of that crisis, and in doing so he misjudged the significance of the most revealing symptom of all—the dehumanization of art. (p. 174)

> *Joseph Frank, ''The Dehumanization of Art,'' in his* The Widening Gyre: Crisis and Mastery in Modern Literature *(copyright © 1963 by Rutgers, The State University; reprinted by permission of Rutgers University Press), Rutgers University Press, 1963 (and reprinted by Indiana University Press, 1968) pp. 163-77.*

**MARGUERITE HOWE**   (essay date 1973)

*An Interpretation of Universal History* is a compilation of [Ortega's lectures on Arnold Toynbee]. (p. 315)

*An Interpretation of Universal History* is very much about politics—particularly Spanish politics—and very much, as always with Ortega, a here-and-now didactic effort. His use of Roman history is parabolic—which gives the lectures a lively double focus. (pp. 315-16)

Dense but not difficult, the lectures display to advantage Ortega's positive genius for adapting (or perverting) other people's ideas. . . . Ortega rejects obstacle-and-reaction as the genesis of civilizations, merely. ''Man is essentially an unbalanced animal whose existence is always one of a greater and lesser degree of imbalance'' between himself and his ''medium,'' between his inner world of imaginary ideals, and his outer world of ''what is.'' Man ''needs to be what he is not,'' says Ortega, transforming challenge and response into a definition of perpetual existential disequilibrium.

*An Interpretation of Universal History* shows also Ortega's humanistic individualism, in which he differs radically from Toynbee and other speculative philosophers of history. Toynbee takes as his ''unit of study'' the civilization ''in its entirety''; Ortega strives to save the individual lost in the generalization (as he is, elsewhere, lost in the mass). Man does not yield his meaning to history studied as a natural science: ''should we not fear that [Toynbee] might minimize the intimate and secret elements in every human happening, and fail to take into account . . . that man in the abstract does not exist, and that a people . . . is made up of individuals?'' The aim of history is to project us into the individual distant in time, so that we can understand his existential involvement with his social medium, all with a view to applying it to our own lives—for what else is history but our ''pre-occupation'' with the future?

Ortega's prescriptive leap of faith is that somehow, magically, when the individual is perfected, the whole society will go right. Like *The Revolt of the Masses, An Interpretation of Universal History* counsels studious self-perfection, much as Matthew Arnold invokes an aristocracy of culture to cultivate disinterestedness, best ideas, sweetness and light, and the semimystical faculty of criticism—which resembles what Ortega elsewhere calls ''historical reason'': the speculative faculty with which we make the choices that constitute the act of living.

Historic reason requires the ability to see clearly and to ''reflect conceptually,'' two qualities Ortega perpetually blamed Spanish intellectuals for lacking. And Ortega's mission as an intellectual—apparent throughout this volume—is to provoke thought, rather than to provide a series of neatly boxed concepts, as Toynbee does. Contrasted with Toynbee's oversystematization, Ortega's approach to history has a quality of play. Sometimes as inaccurate as Toynbee, he is never as rigid. He stresses the relativity of the historian's perspective, the complexity and possibility of history—and of life itself.

The lecture is the form that suits Ortega best: moderately disorganized, improvisatory, eclectic, a dialogue with his audience that is elastic enough to allow him to prod and tease each individual into using his historic reason. (His philosophy, likewise, is a loose and open existential lesson; not intended to be a perfect abstraction, as a system of pure reason it is insignificant.) *An Interpretation of Universal History* lavishly condemns Toynbee, ''one who never yields to facts,'' as a ''representative sample of how an intellect can be out of shape.'' Ortega's attack is *ad hominem* abusive precisely because to him the individual, not the argument, is paramount. Toynbee's refusal to see clearly and "reflect conceptually" is a failure of historic reason, which makes him inauthentic. "In Toynbee's case [there is] hidden under what is called the 'empirical method' the totalitarian resolution that ideas which the English had previously in their minds shall echo the facts discovered." This is the pseudo-method and pseudo-experience of the mass man.

The central argument of *An Interpretation of Universal History* is the legitimacy of different kinds of government. Ortega (the method is late Heidegger) traces the use of *"Imperium,"* Right, through Roman history, to show how its meaning changed as power shifted. His conclusions represent a hash-up of Weber's three types of legitimacy (rational-legal, traditional and charismatic), and an inversion of Rousseau's definition of legitimacy as the rational agreement to effect the general will. The only originating, mystical and absolute legitimacy, says Ortega, belongs to a monarch, *rex sacrorum*, king "by the grace of God," whose *charisma* signifies that he is nearer the gods than all others. . . . Like Rome, our own civilization falls apart because it insists on the legitimacy of popular sovereignty, which is actually "unconsecrated public power, absolute and absolutely illegitimate."

In fact, Ortega's analysis of power is very much like Toynbee's. The "nemesis of creativity" resembles the failure of the elite to create and adapt, as detailed in *The Revolt of the Masses.* (pp. 316-17)

Ortega's consecration of power is actually a consecration of the past. He argues that to the Roman, law was sacred and inviolate. When law became a question of justice, it became manmade and transitory, no longer absolute, no longer the "connecting substance which unifies the life of a people." Rome lost faith in the *mos maiorum*, the usages of its ancestors, which had been "the firm, compact, and consecrated belief on which the pure legitimacy of the immemorial past was founded." So now with Europe.

*An Interpretation of Universal History* continues Ortega's unashamed battle with "modernity." He looks back to a legitimate past, claims that only the past can legitimatize the present, offers us mystical conservatism. (p. 317)

> Marguerite Howe, *"Two Prophets of the Absent God,"* in The Nation *(copyright 1973* The Nation *magazine, The Nation Associates, Inc.), Vol. 217, No. 10, October 1, 1973, pp. 315-17.\**

**PATRICK H. DUST**　(essay date 1979)

It is a well-known fact among Ortega scholars that at the heart of this philosopher's thinking there was a conflict between the persistent will to create a "system" and the quasi-literary devotion to his peculiarly Spanish "circumstance." Metaphysician in the classical sense on the one hand, literary artist and social reformer on the other, Ortega, it seems, never tired of striving to integrate the life of contemplation with the life of action. Thus one of his students, José Gaos, emphasizes the existential character of the master's writings, his distinctively spontaneous, even "voluptuous" encounter with ideas and reality, while a second disciple, Julián Marías, prefers to focus attention on the more rational and systematic dimension. And recently, a third writer, Ciriaco Morón Arroyo, has painstakingly documented the implicit presence of system throughout the long and arduous evolution of Ortega's philosophy. These

scholars are formidable thinkers in their own right and their contributions to our understanding of Ortega's complex thought are invaluable. My own effort . . . must of necessity be considerably more modest. I too am interested in the fundamental tension between systematic clarity and vital expression; but I shall limit the scope of inquiry here to a single essay that Ortega published in 1926 under the title of **"Amor en Stendhal."**

My central thesis may be summarized as follows: the basic philosophical premises that underlie much of the discussion in this particular essay are admirably unified and consistent. Whether these premises are made explicit for the reader or left relatively implicit, there is no confusion in the mind of the author about what they are nor about how they should be defined. In this sense, at the level of pre-expressed awareness, Ortega's style of thought is characterized by an undeniable clarity and system. At the same time, however, the Spaniard's "circumstantial" and literary bent, his desire to communicate in a nontechnical language that might make philosophy accessible to the masses, introduces into his essay a tendency toward fragmentation and digression which affects the order and clarity of the exposition. Rigorously clear in its presuppositions, fragmented and a little confused in its actual style of expression, **"Amor en Stendhal"** offers the reader the opportunity to take a journey at once gratifying and tortuous into the mind of a brilliant thinker.

Ortega holds at least three basic convictions which make his disagreement with Stendhal as uncompromising as it is inevitable: the first has to do with the very problem we have been discussing, the need for clarity and system; the second relates to the insufficiency of philosophical idealism; and the third involves the wider issue of an optimistic versus a pessimistic outlook.

According to Ortega, the seriousness of a writer's thought can be measured by the degree of systematicity that it does or does not possess. So crucial, in fact, is this issue for the author that it becomes the first theme to which he addresses himself in the opening paragraphs of the essay. Cautioning the reader not to be deceived by appearances, Ortega insists that writers like Stendhal and Baroja must not be confused with genuine philosophers. . . . [This idea] has a twofold source, stemming first from Ortega's acceptance of the intuition that reality is one, and second from his recognition that the human mind is essentially discontinuous and multiform. Given these two propositions, the thinker's responsibility may be defined as follows: he must patiently strive to eliminate contradiction from his ideas, and he must formulate a single, all-embracing theory that provides a systematic correspondence to the oneness of reality. Stendhal and Baroja ignore this grave responsibility and their thought, according to Ortega, is consequently more lyrical than metaphysical. They "sing" instead of "think," and their works ultimately speak to us not about reality but only about themselves. (pp. 266-67)

The second conviction that underlies Ortega's disagreement with Stendhal involves a rejection of philosophical idealism. This premise is even less explicit than the previous one, but it is not on that account any less influential. According to the Spaniard, idealism was a characteristic tendency of nineteenth-century thought, one which involved an arbitrary reduction of the objective world to a mere "idea" in man's mind. Kant's views on knowledge provide perhaps the best example of this attitude. But Stendhal's theory of crystallization fits the same basic mold. . . . Ortega's opposition to such a view is implied in the phrase "hacia el cual vivimos." . . . When he says that "we live toward" external objects, he suggests in passing one of the most seminal ideas of his philosophy, namely, that "reality" is neither mind nor world exclusively but the peculiar interaction of the two. "Reality" for Ortega is man's creative involvement with his circumstance. Now since this belief is incompatible with Stendhal's idealism, it becomes necessary for the Spaniard to repudiate the theory of crystallization.

The emphasis seen above on "system" and on man's basic "openness" to the world are both good examples of what Julián Marías would call the "iceberg" style of Ortega's thought. Neither idea receives any extended development; each makes a brief appearance on the shifting stage of the author's thought and quickly recedes into the background, to be replaced by another intuition, another idea. This peculiarly hidden or latent quality is less pronounced in the case of the third premise, that is, in the issue of optimism versus pessimism. In its fundamental outlines Ortega's overall attitude is clearly a hopeful one. Although he is not naive, the Spaniard does have a faith in human rationality and in man's capacity to relate himself meaningfully to the truth of reality. Stendhal, on the other hand, seems to have a somewhat negative outlook, one that implies that man's imagination continually condemns him to an inaccurate perception of reality. Seeking to be more reasonable in his approach to the problem, Ortega points out that all of our mental life involves, to some degree, a process of crystallization. . . . But immediately after admitting this fact, Ortega proceeds to affirm unambiguously an apprehension of reality which is nevertheless reliable. . . . (pp. 267-68)

It would be a mistake, however, to think that Ortega could rest content with such an unqualified expression of faith in man's capacity to perceive the real. While he is confident of his theory, he recognizes that in actual practice most men never succeed in deciphering the "great tectonic outlines" or latent structure of the world. . . . This is a typical expression of Ortega's notorious elitism, one which is rarely absent from his often paternalistic attempts to educate an unenlightened public. In this particular instance, it serves to qualify the optimism and to remind the reader that the author's faith in man is not indiscriminate.

A similar kind of conclusion is also reached in the more crucial question of love itself. Relying heavily on Abel Bonnard's biography of Stendhal, Ortega repeatedly stresses the for him indisputable fact that the Frenchman "ni verdaderamente amó ni, sobre todo, verdaderamente fue amada." . . . This alone would explain why Stendhal fabricated an erroneous theory of love: his personal failure with women led him to incorrectly assume that success was a fiction and that love was a self-imposed hallucination. Stendhal, we are given to understand, was deeply pessimistic because he could not believe in real love. Ortega, on the other hand, is of a quite different opinion. . . . Ortega does more than just proclaim the desirability of a normal, more healthy perspective on love; he seeks to provide that perspective in the most constructive parts of his essay. . . . Clearly, in comparison with Stendhal's more gloomy conclusions, Ortega's attitude toward love is refreshingly optimistic.

At this point an important qualification once again becomes necessary. On the one hand, Ortega may be certain that man can love and even love well, but, on the other, he feels obliged to point out that the majority of men do not achieve this noble experience. . . . As disconcerting as it may be, the belief that love is real for some but not for all is an integral part of his attitude toward the erotic phenomenon.

In the light of what has been discussed above, it can be affirmed that all three of the basic premises which have guided Ortega in his confrontation with Stendhal are unified and consistent among themselves. There is no conflict between the emphasis on system and the interest in man's openness to his circumstance. Nor is there any incompatibility between those ideas and the author's optimism concerning knowledge and love. Even the aggressive elitism turns out in the end to be more of a qualification than a real contradiction. What all of this amounts to saying is that at the implicit level of pre-expressed awareness, Ortega's thought is characterized by an undeniable clarity and system. Indeed, if we were to apply to **"Amor en Stendhal"** the same criterion for serious thinking that the author himself applied to Stendhal and Baroja at the beginning of the essay, Ortega would emerge as singularly faithful to his professed principles. His own style of thought, in other words, would be authentic because it is rigorously systematic.

The above impression of orderliness and system vanishes, however, when we turn our attention away from the status of ideas in the author's mind to the concrete development of these ideas in the actual mode of expression. Ortega knew that he was writing for an audience untrained in philosophy and, therefore, unreceptive to technical treatises which made relevant problems seem obscure. Furthermore, the Spaniard also nourished a literary ambition that went beyond the passing delight afforded by an occasional simile or metaphor. When he decided to combine these two concerns, the "circumstantial" and the artistic, with his philosophical aspiration, Ortega created the distinctively personal type of essay that was to become his trademark. **"Amor en Stendhal"** is only one example among hundreds in this sense, and as such it exhibits both the strengths and the weaknesses of an unusual style of expression.

One of the strengths derives from the use of metaphors which are calculated not only to entertain the reader but also to inform him. (pp. 268-70)

Another advantage of Ortega's essentially informal style is the way in which it allows him to provide dramatic recreations of scenes instead of conceptual abstractions. . . .

At the same time, however, it must be recognized that Ortega's style is not an unmixed blessing. Along with the advantages that make it genuinely rewarding in many moments, there are also disadvantages that make it confusing and a little frustrating for the reader in others. The reason for this ambiguity is not hard to find: Ortega was so fascinated by a multiplicity of perspectives and ideas that he often found it difficult to narrow his attention to only one or two themes. Reality to him seemed so rich, so pregnant with intellectual possibilities, that he continually indulged his enthusiasm and wrote about numerous subjects simultaneously.

The result, in terms of **"Amor en Stendhal,"** is a style that is characterized by a marked tendency toward fragmentation and digression. This is particularly evident in the exposition and development of the author's central theme. No sooner, for example, does he introduce his subject and begin to present his objections to the theory of crystallization, when he becomes sidetracked by an incursion into the Don Juan theme. . . . Now while it may be quite true that Ortega's views on the Don Juan phenomenon are both original and provocative, it must also be noted that they break up the logical development of the central theme and seriously affect the overall clarity of the exposition. Only if the reader is a relatively sophisticated one will he realize that he is being forced to make an adjustment, to be patient, and wait for the author to resume his confrontation with Stendhal.

There are numerous other digressions that are shorter and less notable than the one just described. Scattered at irregular intervals throughout the various sections, they give to the exposition a peculiar rhythm that is at once progressive and regressive. Starting and stopping, continually digressing and returning to the central theme, Ortega winds his way gradually toward his destination. (p. 270)

The foregoing observations seem to point to a single conclusion: the style of exposition in **"Amor en Stendhal"** is relatively disorganized and unclear. This arises from the frequent digressions with their progressive-regressive rhythm, the fragmentary nature of themes that are suggested but often undeveloped, and, a general incompleteness that characterizes the essay. Along with the positive techniques which promote a fuller understanding and enjoyment of the ideas—metaphors, dramatic recreations—there is also an undeniable degree of confusion in the overall development which can be seen as a stylistic weakness.

And yet, this is not the whole story, for the fact remains that **"Amor en Stendhal"** is a valuable essay, not in spite of its style, but in large measure *because* of it. The contradiction can be resolved if we examine the "disorder" in question from a wholly different point of view than the one that has been used so far. The fact that a high degree of clarity in exposition is normally a stylistic virtue does not mean that it cannot be subordinated to another, perhaps less familiar aspiration. We noted earlier that Ortega's style was ambiguous because it was animated by a fascination with a multiplicity of perspectives, one which made it difficult for the author to control his enthusiasm and to limit himself to a smaller number of themes. This rather free-ranging enthusiasm before the richness of reality should not be underestimated, for ultimately it provides the key for an understanding of Ortega's literary personality.

The reality which becomes especially relevant at this point is the Spaniard's persistent struggle against philosophical abstractions. . . . There are only numerous perspectives on the world, each tied to a particular time, place, and personality. (p. 271)

If Ortega's purpose in writing [**"Amor en Stendhal"**] had been to combat falsehoods with truths that were impersonal, if he had sought merely to present propositions contrived to inform, then the relative disorder in the exposition would be a serious weakness indeed. In fact, however, the Spaniard repudiated this more traditional approach to expression and did not try to be either impersonal or abstract. Writing in a modern, post-romantic age that convinced him that truth could not exist apart from its particular expressions, Ortega allowed his style to gravitate toward dialogue, he made the *logos* or meaning of his discourse "humanísima conversación." At the same time, therefore, that he advanced a healthy and objective psychology of love, he also cultivated a personal type of reflection that retained its existential bond with his concrete, lived experience.

The immediate result of this existential bias is that Ortega did not seek to eliminate his personality from the essay, allowing it to disappear into the pseudotruth of a systematic exposition. On the contrary, he deliberately accentuated the presence of that personality, not by talking about it directly (as Unamuno did), but *by reproducing the characteristic way in which his mind creatively encountered reality*. It is at this point that the author's fascination with multiple perspectives, his enthusiasm before the richness of reality, becomes so important. The uni-

verse the philosopher perceives is so filled with human significance, so alive with intellectual possibilities, that it produces an experience of wonder and excitement which demands some form of expression. In this sense, Ortega's reaction to his world might be compared to the reaction of a child to a journey through enchanted forest. There is so much to see and to do, there is such beauty in its variety and such delight in an active participation in its forms, that he can hardly be expected to stay on the path that reduces the trip to the shortest distance between two points. He cannot be blamed, in other words, if he digresses irresistibly to explore areas that others might consider "extraneous," or if he prefers to meander leisurely toward his destination rather than march toward it directly, half-blind and perhaps half-alive.

Seen in this light, the disorder that permeates the exposition in **"Amor en Stendhal"** ceases to be a weakness and becomes a genuine strength. Employed as the necessary means to an end, it reflects the author's uncompromising rejection of an abstract mode of thought and expresses the extraordinary vitality of his ideas. The tendency toward digression, the fragmentary nature of the themes, and the incompleteness that were examined above are simply the price Ortega willingly pays to capture the spontaneity and enthusiasm of his intensely personal encounter with reality. They are, in short, an essential part of a self-revelation that occurs in the midst of the very search for philosophical truth.

But the existential quality of the style should not be thought of as an end-in-itself. It derives its fullest value ultimately from a connection with the Spaniard's "circumstantial" aspiration, that is, with his desire to make philosophy accessible to the masses. It is not by chance, for example, that the reader of the essay is given such a vivid sense of Ortega's personal existence precisely in the moment when the latter acquires its greatest meaning in the discovery of truth. This is just as the author wanted it to be, for pedagogue and social reformer that he was, he nourished the hope that his own passion for thought, the excitement created by his own adventure in ideas, would be vicariously experienced in such a way as to awaken in his reader the "love of knowledge" that is the essence of philosophy. Compelling the reader not only to *think* like a philosopher but to *feel* like one as well, to live ideas, to let them enrich the whole fabric of his personal existence, Ortega sought to persuade the masses that philosophy was relevant to their lives.

It is evident that there is a notable contrast between the clear and systematic style of thought that Ortega took great pains to cultivate before actually writing, and the disordered, existential style of exposition that he subsequently employed with consummate literary skill. . . . By deliberately limiting our focus to an indepth examination of a single essay, we have been able to observe exactly how the conceptual rigor of three specific presuppositions influenced the Spaniard's discussion of Stendhal's theory of crystallization. We have been able to explore the relative disorder of the exposition in a perspective that reveals its underlying *raison d'être* and ultimate justification. And finally, we have been able to elucidate Ortega's unique articulation of "circumstantial" and artistic concerns with his philosophical aspiration, an articulation which allowed him to create the distinctively personal type of essay that became his trademark. **"Amor en Stendhal,"** we noted at the beginning of this inquiry, offers the reader an opportunity to take a journey, at once gratifying and tortuous, into the mind of a brilliant thinker. We can add at this point that, in the last analysis, that journey is immensely more gratifying than tortuous, because it succeeds in making us experience the delight and love that are philosophy. (pp. 272-73)

*Patrick H. Dust, "Style of Thought and Style of Expression in Ortega's 'Amor en Stendhal'," in Hispania (© 1979 The American Association of Teachers of Spanish and Portuguese, Inc.), Vol. LXII, No. 3, September, 1979, pp. 266-74.*

## VICTOR OUIMETTE   (essay date 1982)

[*Ouimette's recent study—from which this excerpt on Ortega's later and posthumous essay collections is taken—is a comprehensive survey of the philosopher's works.*]

[In *¿Qué es filosofía?* (What Is Philosophy?) Ortega's] purpose was not to provide an introduction to philosophy, but rather "to take the philosophical activity itself, philosophizing itself, and submit it to a radical analysis." . . . After more than three centuries in which philosophy had allowed itself to be reduced to mere theory of the knowledge that only the physical sciences had seemed capable of discovering, these latter had expanded to the stage where they had to philosophize about themselves in order to attempt to resolve a crisis brought on by the awareness that they represent a symbolic and, therefore, secondary and inferior form of knowledge. Having discovered that it could not do everything, however, had become a source of renewed vitality for physics. Now, philosophy, too, could reassume its proper role as the means of discovering and understanding the totality of the Universe, an act of "intellectual heroism" . . . in which the philosopher sets out in search of the absolutely unknown and the potentially unknowable, filled with an "appetite for the Universe." . . . Rather than aim to provide concrete solutions to concrete problems, as is the destiny of science, philosophy answers that uniquely human need to know that distinguishes *homo theoreticus* from both God and the beast.

Philosophy must consider part of its duty to be the demonstration of the insolubility of certain problems as it searches for the first principles that are constitutionally beyond the reach of physical science. It must always reexamine everything so as to discover "everything that there is," . . . regardless of whether it in fact exists. From the stump that we have, philosophy must try to discover the Whole, without even the certainty that the Whole is knowable, nor whether it is a Universe or a Multiverse. The world of which we are aware, like the forest in the *Meditations on Quixote,* is incomplete and has as its background all the things that we do not see, but whose absence we can sense and which philosophy attempts to make present. Only philosophy can have as its aim this absolute "other," for it is the only science that is truly autonomous in that it creates all its own suppositions. It is dedicated to that part of each thing that is universal, that makes it fit into the Whole, and so must achieve a communicable vision, a concept. It is the process of constant uncovering (*alétheia*) and saying: "if physics is everything that can be measured, philosophy is the whole of what can be said about the Universe." . . .

Ortega proposed an "absolute positivism" that would include intuitive evidence. In this way it would be possible to distinguish among three classes of things: "those that may be in the Universe, whether we know it or not; those that we erroneously believe there are; but which, in fact, there are not; and, finally, those that we can be sure that there are." . . . These last he called the "data of the Universe," for they can be neither doubted nor proven and are problematic only in that philosophy must begin by determining what they are.

Descartes began modern philosophy by systematically doubting the very existence of the outside world and recognizing that the unique characteristic of thought is that it is autogenous, independent of anything outside itself. Idealism took this to mean that external reality proceeds from thought, exists only as thought, and is thus contained within us. However, such a concept effectively seals us off from the outside world and leads to the discovery "that each self is, in its very essence, radical solitude." Man's intimacy thus includes the Universe and cannot be penetrated by external reality. Such an idea could not satisfy Ortega, for if the self is the center of our consciousness, then the external world, our "circumstance," forms the periphery; yet he agreed with Idealism that only the thinking of the thought, but not necessarily the object of the thought, is. Consequently, the external world is only when I think it; however, it is neither my thought nor an independent reality: "Without objects there is no subject." . . . This absolute coexistence of a self and its world is living, the radical reality and philosophy's fundamental problem. Being is "intimacy with oneself and with things." . . . (pp. 104-06)

The new definition of life, then, means to be aware of our living as an endless uncovering and a finding of ourselves in the world. Living is what we do and what happens to us, a taking account of and occupying ourselves with "the other," the world, the circumstance, but with no physical or temporal distance between our life and our world, no precedence of one over the other. This is our vital horizon, which we cannot choose, but within which we can make certain decisions: "Life is, at once, fatality and liberty, it is being free within a given fatality. . . . We accept the fatality and within it we decide on a destiny. Life is destiny." . . . Ortega thus began to touch upon the dramatic, problematic quality of life by stressing that it is a constant projection into the future, an endless series of decisions regarding what we are going to be next, and attempts to preform that future. Such decisions demand an awareness of what our life is and the extreme mode of this is philosophy, "the attempt life makes to transcend itself." . . . (p. 106)

Repeatedly, Ortega declared that any major alteration in the way of thinking appeared first in the arts. Spain had produced outstanding examples of two critical moments in European thought in two of her greatest painters: Velázquez, who was a member of the generation in which the Modern Age became consolidated; and Goya, who belonged to the generation that made the transition towards the decline of the Modern Age. (p. 129)

Ortega's interest in Velázquez was due to the fact that, alone among his Spanish contemporaries, he went against the current of his times, not in a spirit of rebellion, but merely of independence.

Painting begins where language and poetry leave off and, because of its muteness, always demands interpretation. Ortega called it "the most hermetic of the arts," . . . and found it ceaselessly dynamic because it is constitutionally inexhaustible. Interpretation, however, is necessarily historic, for the painter is always present and it is incumbent upon the viewer to attempt to understand what painting meant for him, what moved him to paint, what dictated his style, and what were the presuppositions from which he worked. (p. 130)

Ortega laid much importance by the necessary "derealization" carried out by all works of art. Velázquez effected a revolution by causing real, everyday objects to take on all the artistic prestige of the unreal and the imaginary that were still the nucleus of artistic attention. In his hands, the most banal subject matter became surprising as he stripped objects down and eliminated their tactile quality. He painted only the elements that presented themselves to the eye, "reality as appearance," . . . the object as it eternally comes into being in the eye of the viewer, as light and color, not as touch and form. There is added no apparent interpretation of the subject matter, but rather an interest limited to the mere presence of the objects, undeformed by any human idealization that gives them a convenient preciseness that they otherwise lack.

No less significant was his choice of themes. Because he believed that aesthetic emotion could be produced in ways other than the depiction of fantasies, his artistic world virtually never went beyond the limits of the known world. Alone among contemporary painters, "he senses a satiety of beauty and poetry, and a longing for prose." . . . The abstract ideal of Beauty, the essential deformation implied by "what things would be if they were as we want them," . . . characteristic of the Italian tradition, was banished as he returned to the "real object." Unlike his Baroque contemporaries, Velázquez painted not the synthesis of a series of movements, but a moment in the existence of his subjects, an instant rendered eternal. His independence and ultimate influence in painting were no less dramatic than those of Descartes in philosophy, for in both cases reality was allowed to appear as it is, unadorned, prosaic, and pure.

Ortega began his 1948 study of Goya with words similar to those that he applied to Goethe: "Goya is a fact of the first order, belonging to the destiny of the West." . . . Like his contemporaries Mirabeau and Goethe, he was the sharp edge between two ages and his work showed the continuation of the traditions of the past while representing a great and unexpected leap into the future. He offered a useful complement to Goethe in Ortega's analyses, for he knew instinctively, although not intellectually, from a very early age what he had to be and his life, seen from within, is a slow movement toward vital fulfillment. Rude and untutored, the rustic from Aragón moved gradually and inexorably to become the first painter of Spain and possibly of Europe. The pattern of his development reveals that, like Mirabeau, he carried this destiny within him in everything that he did. (pp. 131-32)

[Ortega] summed up his analysis with the observation that "Goya is an extreme example of the human situation that we may call 'the creative man'." . . . (p. 133)

Like pre-Christian religion, [the theater] provides another world to which man can escape; like sports and games, it provides a suspension of life.

In ["Idea del teatro" ("The Idea of the Theater")], Ortega considered the way this vital function is revealed in the modern theater's physical construction. First, it is a building that separates an inner space from the everyday world. Inside it consists of a series of three essential dualities. There is the architecture that divides the building into a section for the actors and another for the audience, separated by a proscenium arch that symbolizes both the division and the dynamic relationship that must exist between them. Thus arises the human duality, between activity and passivity. The furnishings demonstrate that the public is expected to remain still and attentive, while the actors, in their open space, are to be active but with the public in mind. The third duality is functional: one group is there to see

and the other to be seen. The literary element is secondary to the purely visual and Ortega's concern was directed towards the theater as a human activity.

Like the mask of the Bacchic orgy, the spectacle is pure metaphor in which the actor creates another being that subsumes his own: "So that what is *not* real, the unreal . . . has the strength, the magical power, to cause the real to disappear." . . . The materiality of the actors induces the viewer to forget who he "really" is. The essential character of the theater is phantasmagoric, and both the public and the actors must be sufficiently alert to retain their "sense of unreality," . . . so as to enter consciously the alternative world of fiction, farce, and fantasy.

The major result of Ortega's stay in Lisbon was [*La idea de principio en Leibniz y la evolución de la teoría deductiva* (**The Idea of Principle in Leibniz and the Evolution of Deductive Theory**)], his longest and most uncompromising work. The book was never finished, and ends on the very threshold of the problem announced in the first half of the working title: to reexamine according to his own philosophy the thought of one of the most important inspirations of the neo-Kantianism of Marburg. Moved once more by the crisis of principles in the physical sciences, Ortega took the principle as the basis for examining the philosophic pattern established by Aristotle and leading through the Stoics and Scholasticism up to Descartes and the beginning of modern thought. He set out from his conviction that philosophy is not, like other sciences, merely based on organizing principles that serve to explain, but has as its aim the very discovery of ultimate or radical principles. (pp. 134-35)

[*Del Imperio Romano* (**On the Roman Empire**)] was translated into English as *Concord and Liberty,* a felicitous title that shows that Ortega once more failed to fulfill the promise of his original title. He had intended to examine the history of Rome as the model that it was: an entire civilization whose creation, culmination, and decay were completely documented and well known to contemporary man, and that offered parallels with contemporary Europe. Cicero, like Ortega, had discerned in the crises of society "the very condition on which is founded and from which emerges the health of the State," . . . and his use of the terms *concordia* and *libertas* in *De re publica* appeared to offer the key to the lessons that might be derived from the history of the Empire. *Concordia* meant for Cicero the common agreement of a people on certain fundamental matters, the force that binds a state and underlies discord in less essential matters. When such basic agreement crumbles, however, the state and the community may be destroyed, confronting man with the sensation of a radically unstable universe in which beliefs and reality itself disintegrate. Both Cicero and Ortega confronted such a situation.

Nineteenth-century liberalism had fostered the notion that man is naturally social and that society is good, when Ortega in fact saw society as a utopian ideal, a seductress who conflicts with man's no less important antisocial impulses. Society, he claimed, is merely the endless attempt of one set of impulses to conquer another. It is not a spontaneous organism as liberalism claims, but a ceaseless pursuit that is essentially degrading because it demands authority and force, both of which must be exercised by those very levels that are better than the task required of them. Ortega now saw liberty as the historically normal form of European life and believed that, even in the face of the curtailment of certain specific freedoms, man could feel himself to be free. For Cicero, however, liberty was indivisible and meant freedom under a strict system of laws. He saw freedom broadly, socially, defined in the answer to the question of who shall rule, whereas modern Europe had seen it in terms of individual limits and man's degree of willingness to allow himself to be ruled. The Roman concept of liberty, then, believed that human nature had to be kept under control, whereas modern liberalism affirmed man's natural goodness and innate sociability. Freedom thus becomes the common agreement to live within a certain system of political inspiration, yet no state, however liberal, can fail to exert pressure.

Ortega postulated three conditions for freedom: a feeling of collective stability; a collective solution that occupies the collective mind and brings about desired change; and universal participation in the functioning of the state. The example of Rome shows to what extent a nation may create its own history, for as the social structure felt new needs, new institutions were developed to deal with them, so that "the State gradually molds itself to the social body as the skin forms itself over our own body." . . . The pressure and restraint exerted by the state in times of freedom are inseparable from the body itself and are not felt as a lack of liberty, for they best fit the circumstances and the collective preference. Such was the case of the development of Rome as long as the underlying concord existed. Her laws owed more to custom and usage than to abstract reason, and the political institutions that she created responded to a historic need. They were interrelated and sprang from the depths of the collectivity; the liberty that derived from them was part of a total, living system. (pp. 138-39)

[*El hombre y la gente* (**Man and People**)] represents more than twenty years of thought, having its development in many lectures and courses that Ortega gave over the last two decades of his life. Moved by what he considered to be the inadequacy of both sociology and linguistics, he employed an orientation that was clearly more sociological than historical as he attempted to determine whether society could be taken as an "irreducible reality" or whether the proper object of analysis was the individual.

The "social fact," he again observed, does not preexist in the individual, but is the result of the interrelationship between an individual, who acts through his relationship with his circumstance, and other individuals who do likewise. Ortega distinguished, however, between "interindividual" relationships and truly social ones which reveal themselves in many customs, traditions, and usages that are not the result of either reflection, emotion, or the will of the individual but are imposed on him from without: they are essentially as irrational as they are impersonal. Ortega rejected the idea of a "collective soul" and believed rather that such usages were the product of "the 'inhuman element' in which the person finds himself." . . . They make social coexistence feasible because they are as predictable in individuals whom one knows as in those whom one does not know. Moreover, they are dictated by the times in which one lives and to which one must therefore rise. Their mechanical nature serves to simplify relationships so that the individual may more easily devote himself to the creative potential of his personal life. (p. 143)

Society is public power to an extent that goes far beyond institutionalized structures, and some such tensions exist throughout even the most primitive of societies: "The collectivity—without proposing to do so—watches over every minute of individual life." . . . Such power is a force that counteracts other forces that go against the dominant opinions. Ortega concluded that society is "*constitutively* sick" . . . because it

represents the endless struggle between these two types of force, the institutional derivative of which is the state, charged with the task of enforcing public power.

Appropriately, Ortega's last major work looked to the future. [*Meditación de Europa* (**Meditation on Europe**)] is a revised but unfinished version of ideas presented in a lecture in Berlin in 1949, as well as in other talks and an article in the final years of Ortega's life. In those moments when the Continent was striving to recover from two decades of tension and war, the Free University in West Berlin seemed to be the appropriate locale for an intellectual to attempt to clarify the current European situation. The fundamental values upon which European civilization rests had been weakened, but Ortega was persuaded that the deepening crisis could be healthy: "I do not recall that any civilization has died from an attack of doubt." . . . Nowhere was such potential for creation more luminous than in defeated and divided Germany, whom he addressed from the viewpoint of a society accustomed to defeat, but always ready to face life on its own terms.

For nine centuries, European reality had been one of coexistence in a common atmosphere defined less by geography than by history. It constituted a society not because of laws or other abstractions, but because it had been "the living together of men within a determined system of usages," . . . and this reality predated any national units, all of which were the result of denser "socialization" that had arisen from these usages. Ortega believed, however, that the time for nations had passed and that the people of Europe must look not toward "international" units, as Toynbee suggested, but toward an "ultranational" one. . . . History moves inexorably toward larger social units. (pp. 147-48)

[Ortega's] standing among the great philosophers of the West remains to be determined by another age. His ideas are rarely difficult and the clarity of his style, when it does not merely dazzle, serves to facilitate the reader's task. Yet, in his concern to be original, he was often guilty of neglecting to be thorough. Few serious thinkers can have been so consistent in their refusal to see their intuitions and insights through to their logical conclusions. This fact in Ortega made it possible for so many conflicting critical approaches to exist side by side, with equal claims upon our allegiance. It is not enough even to rely on the primary texts, for the fact remains that Ortega did not say enough about almost any important subject. He allowed himself to be intellectually alluring, and all too often moved on, failing to complete even the project at hand, into which he had seduced the reader with unfulfilled promises. Yet his thought is evocative, and that is no small gift. Even in his most pessimistic works, he saw life as aesthetic and intellectual enjoyment; the scope of his enthusiasm was universal, but the ceaseless creation of introductory studies of themes left the door open for succeeding writers to presume conclusions that cannot be easily discarded, although common sense dictates that they are erroneous and ill-intentioned. And yet, he was never dull, never repetitive, never false, and never intellectually careless. He is one of the pillars of a new Spanish intellectual tradition. As Antonio Machado declared, he is "a new gesture." (pp. 152-53)

*Victor Ouimette, in his* José Ortega y Gasset *(copyright © 1982 by Twayne Publishers, Inc.; reprinted with the permission of Twayne Publishers, a Division of G. K. Hall & Co., Boston), Twayne, 1982, 176 p.*

## ADDITIONAL BIBLIOGRAPHY

Díaz, Janet Winecoff. *The Major Themes of Existentialism in the Work of José Ortega y Gasset*. Chapel Hill: The University of North Carolina Press, 1970, 233 p.
>   Integrates Ortega's major works into the existentialist philosophical tradition. This study also includes a useful survey of critical reaction to Ortega's writings.

Ferrater Mora, José. *Ortega y Gasset: An Outline of His Philosophy*. London: Bowes & Bowes, 1956, 69 p.
>   Employs a biographical method as the most effective approach to Ortega's "non-formalistic" philosophy.

Habershon, Nigel. "'España Invertebrada'." In *European Patterns: Contemporary Patterns in European Writing,* edited by T. B. Harward, pp. 76-81. Dublin: The Dolmen Press, 1964.
>   Examines Ortega's political assessment of Spain.

Holmes, Oliver W. *Human Reality and the Social World: Ortega's Philosophy of History*. Amherst: University of Massachusetts Press, 1975, 175 p.
>   Explains Ortega's view of humanity within a historical and sociological context.

Kilgore, William J. "Freedom in the Perspectivism of Ortega." *Philosophy and Phenomenological Research* XXXII, No. 4 (June 1972): 500-13.
>   Explains that in Ortega's view freedom within perspectivism is integral in determining individual character. Kilgore also considers how political factors affect personal freedom.

Livingstone, Leon. "Ortega y Gasset's Philosophy of Art." *PMLA* LXVII, No. 5 (September 1952): 609-54.
>   Integrates Ortega's aesthetic theories with his other principal concepts, such as perspectivism and vital reason.

Lopez-Morillas, Juan. "Ortega y Gasset: Historicism vs. Classicism." *Yale French Studies,* No. 6 (1950-51): 63-74.
>   Excellent explanation of several of Ortega's concepts, including ratio-vitalism, new classicism, and uchronia.

McClintock, Robert. *Man and His Circumstances: Ortega As Educator*. New York: Teachers College Press, 1971, 648 p.
>   Study of Ortega's role as an educator who defined a new vision of western society and its future.

Medina, Angel. "Action, Interaction and Reflection in the Ontology of Ortega y Gasset." In *Crosscurrents in Phenomenology,* edited by Ronald Bruzina and Bruce Wilshire, pp. 66-106. The Hague: Martinus Nijhoff, 1978.
>   Examines Ortega's ideas concerning "time, identity, and human interaction." Medina supports the claim that Ortega anticipated Heidegger in regard to several distinctive concepts.

Meregalli, Franco. "A Parallel Observer and Innovator: José Ortega y Gasset." In *Américo Castro and the Meaning of Spanish Civilization,* edited by José Rubia Barcia, pp. 267-91. Berkeley: University of California Press, 1976.
>   Reveals the analogous relationship of Ortega and Américo Castro "through the transformations of Castro's well-known and extensive works."

Niedermayer, Franz. *José Ortega y Gasset*. Translated by Peter Tirner. New York: Frederick Ungar Publishing Co., 1973, 138 p.
>   Introduction to Ortega and his works.

Orringer, Nelson R. "Ortega y Gasset's Sportive Theories of Communication." *Modern Language Notes* 85, No. 2 (March 1970): 207-34.
>   Shows that "the idea of 'sport' informs Ortega's view on words and gestures from about the mid-twenties onward."

Orringer, Nelson R. "Life As Shipwreck or As Sport in Ortega y Gasset?" *Romance Notes* XVII, No. 1 (Fall 1976): 70-5.
>   Contends that insecurity is overcome by one's sportive capacity.

Raley, Harold C. *José Ortega y Gasset: Philosopher of European Unity*. University: The University of Alabama Press, 1971, 247 p.
>   Emphasizes the importance of Ortega's ideas in European history.

Schwartz, Kessel. "Ortega y Gasset and Goethe." In his *The Meaning of Existence in Contemporary Hispanic Literature,* pp. 71-82. Hispanic-American Studies, no. 23. Coral Gables: University of Miami Press, 1969.*
>   Examines the importance of German thought and culture on Ortega's intellectual development and shows the similarity of his attitudes toward life to those of Goethe.

Sebastian, Elmer G. "José Ortega y Gasset: World Crises and the Unification of Europe." *Hispania* XLVI, No. 3 (September 1963): 490-95.
>   Ortega's ideas on the cause of and solution to historical crises.

Shaw, Donald L. *The Generation of 1898 in Spain*. London: Ernest Benn, 1975, 246 p.*
>   Overview of Ortega's philosophical concepts, concluding that "nothing is more opposed to the '98 view than Ortega's belief in the intelligibility of life as an ascending creative process."

Silver, Philip W. *Ortega As Phenomenologist: The Genesis of "Meditations on Quixote."* New York: Columbia University Press, 1978, 175 p.
>   Describes Ortega's early philosophical development as it relates to his first work, *Meditations on Quixote*.

# T(heodore) F(rancis) Powys

## 1875-1953

English novelist, short story writer, and essayist.

Powys is noted for a fictional technique which combines the methods of traditional allegorical narrative with those of modern literary realism. He repeatedly offers rural life and the rustic simplicity of its people as a universal representation of humanity, exploring the fundamental themes of love and death and good and evil. For the most part neglected by the public, Powys did receive recognition for *Mr. Weston's Good Wine*, his greatest literary achievement and the work most often referred to by critics as his masterpiece.

The son of an Evangelical clergyman, Powys was born in Shirley, Derbyshire, where his father served as vicar. While a strong religious sense remained with Powys all his life, his writing reflects an unorthodox view of Christianity, one that prefers a disillusioned acceptance of evil to a pretense of goodness. Rather than attend a university, as did his two writer brothers Llewelyn and John Cowper, Powys chose to become a farmer. Though farming was not a successful venture for him, the pastoral beauty and quietness of Dorsetshire, where he had settled with his own family, provided him with the privacy he desired.

Powys did not publish until he was over thirty years old. His first publications, the philosophical works *An Interpretation of Genesis* and *The Soliloquy of a Hermit*, drew little attention. His first work of fiction, the novella collection *The Left Leg*, displayed Powys's narrative power and his understanding of human feelings regardless of their grotesqueness or perversity. Stripped of conventional roles and illusions, his peasant characters reveal the bestial traits and expose the hypocrisies of humankind. This pessimism is prominently displayed in the novel *Mark Only*. The tragic title character, a simple man whose life is a total failure from beginning to end, is contrasted with a successful antagonist, who is the personification of evil. Such situations, in which evil prospers while goodness fails, are typical of Powys's work. *Mr. Tasker's Gods*, similar in its pessimism to *Mark Only*, is also a study of characters hopelessly victimized both by human weakness and by the inhuman evils of the world around them. These novels are stepping stones to what critics consider the culmination of Powys's craft, *Mr. Weston's Good Wine*.

Mr. Weston, a wine salesman, comes to a small village selling light and dark wines. In this allegory, Mr. Weston is God, and the light and dark wines symbolize Love and Death. Powys gives to *Mr. Weston's Good Wine* a degree of realism not achieved in his other work, and his portrait of a God with human feelings is masterfully drawn. Powys's preoccupation with love and death persists in his last novel, *Unclay*. As in *Mr. Weston's Good Wine*, the supernatural is immanent, this time in the character of John Death. In Powysian fashion Death is overcome by human frailty and falls in love with the young woman he was sent to "unclay." Death as a sensuous personality is striking and original, but critics maintain that the novel does not possess the flawless artistry or allegorical potency of *Mr. Weston's Good Wine*.

Powys was a prolific short story writer and many critics believe this was the genre best suited to his writing style. *Fables* is the most acclaimed of his short works, and these nineteen stories rival the moral lessons of Aesop for their philosophical breadth and originality. In his *Fables* Powys transforms inanimate objects into intelligent beings to convey his message to the reader. These objects range from the commonplace bucket and rope to the macabre skull and tombstone. His other short stories never reach the brilliance of *Fables*, but they do contain the odd, often brutal twists of plot and the mystical insights that are frequently described by critics as Powysian.

Powys's harsh form of mysticism is aptly conveyed by his writing style, which also provides a fit expression of his often primitive storylines and savage characters. His terse, monosyllabic language is often compared to John Bunyan's *The Pilgrim's Progress* and the Old Testament. This simple yet poetic style enlivens the author's equally simple themes, often achieving the complex artistry of modern literature.

Although critics find that Powys's style admirably suits his material, many find his rural settings and provincial characters monotonous. Except for *Mr. Weston's Good Wine*, Powys's books never gained a wide readership. But he never sought to be a popular writer, nor did he expect any great financial gain from his writings. On the matter of material success,

Powys stated: "The hack writer, the cheap, commercial artist—they are entirely excused if they write and paint for the sheer necessities of food and shelter. But as soon as a man has a bare sufficiency of these necessities, he should abandon the *getting* spirit before it is too late. Before it *gets* him." With the exception of a few minor short stories, Powys discontinued writing nearly fifteen years before his death, content with what he had achieved.

## PRINCIPAL WORKS

*An Interpretation of Genesis*  (dialogue)  1907
*The Soliloquy of a Hermit*  (essay)  1916; also published as *Soliloquies of a Hermit*, 1918
*Black Bryony*  (novel)  1923
*The Left Leg*  (novellas)  1923
*Mark Only*  (novel)  1924
*Mr. Tasker's Gods*  (novel)  1925
*Mockery Gap*  (novel)  1925
*Innocent Birds*  (novel)  1926
*Mr. Weston's Good Wine*  (novel)  1927
*The House with the Echo*  (short stories)  1928
*Fables*  (short stories)  1929; also published as *No Painted Plumage*, 1934
*Kindness in a Corner*  (novel)  1930
*The White Paternoster, and Other Stories*  (short stories)  1930
*The Only Penitent*  (novella)  1931
*Unclay*  (novel)  1931
*When Thou Wast Naked*  (novella)  1931
*The Two Thieves*  (novellas)  1932
*Captain Patch*  (short stories)  1935
*The Bottle's Path*  (short stories)  1946
*God's Eyes A-Twinkle*  (short stories)  1947
*Rosie Plum, and Other Stories*  (short stories)  1966
*Two Stories: "Come and Dine" and "Tadnol"*  (short stories)  1967

---

## THE DIAL (essay date 1916)

Baffling at first, and somewhat so to the end, is the whimsical monologue entitled **"The Soliloquy of a Hermit,"** by Mr. Theodore Francis Powys. Not exactly a hermit does he show himself to be, after all, for he walks and talks with his fellowmen and manifests a lively interest in the world about him. Better might he have called his book "The Soliloquy of a Satirist," since satire of a delightful sort crops out on almost every page. Of a certain Mr. Thomas (though that is not his real name) who inhabits a red house in the village of Blank, the author writes: "I cannot say that I think that God has expressed His divine purpose very well in this kind of a man,— a man that does not even know how to treat a tradesman, and who will thank a porter for doing what he is paid to do." And of himself, his chief theme, he says: "I take my life as I find it, and live it to myself as everyone does. As I am a priest, I never give anything away; it is a natural law of my nature not to give, but always to receive." Then he amusingly relates with ostensible frankness an incident illustrating his own alleged stinginess. Again, in characteristic vein, he writes: "It is much better, I have found, to love a chair than to love a person; there is often more of God in a chair." The fiction of

his priesthood is humorously maintained through the book. "Avoid the good ones," he counsels little children, near the close of his soliloquy, "and go and dance with those that take and eat honestly the lion's share. We know that Lion; there is something honest and open about him; the immortal laughters surround him as he gambols and frolics in new-mown hay." Truly, a satirist and humorist of a different kidney from the ordinary sort is this companionable hermit. There is many a chuckle in his little book.

> *"The Whimsical Monologue of a Man of Moods,"* in The Dial *(copyright, 1916, by The Dial Publishing Company, Inc.), Vol. LX, No. 713, March 2, 1916, p. 218.*

## LOUIS U. WILKINSON (essay date 1916)

[*A long-time friend of the Powys family, Wilkinson was determined to see T. F. Powys achieve recognition, and he wrote the following dialogue as a promotional device for* The Soliloquy of a Hermit. *Wilkinson contrasts* The Soliloquy of a Hermit *with John Cowper Powys's* Wood and Stone, *expressing his bias for the former work.*]

The Marquis:
Remy, I must talk to you quite seriously. Why do you go about praising unpardonable novels and sneering at works of art? You are my son. Your ineptitudes reflect upon me.

Remy:
Father! "Wood and Stone" an unpardonable novel! **"The Soliloquy of a Hermit"** a work of art,—*art!* What can you mean? Why is "Wood and Stone" unpardonable?

The Marquis:
Because it is frivolous.

Remy:
Good heavens, Father, but aren't you frivolous?

The Marquis:
Remy, why are you so ignorant? Don't you know yet that I am a religious man, that I believe and tremble . . .? The author of "Wood and Stone" blasphemes my faith. The author of **"The Soliloquy of a Hermit"** comforts it.

Remy:
But how?

The Marquis:
There are rituals of self-expression. . . . Not to observe them is the unpardonable offence. This John Cowper of yours has no sense of ritual, he has no religious care. Naturally: because there is no temple in his spirit. His soul is an echoing labyrinth without one holy place.

Remy:
But he has *ideas!* Think of the "Mythology of Power," the "Mythology of Sacrifice"!

The Marquis:
A couple of Rocking Horses. He went out and bought them.

Remy:
You are most unjust, sir. I am sure that he was genuinely moved to expression. He is a man of real feeling . . . his sympathy with the pariah! And surely you can't deny that he has real feeling for nature? That "Leonian stone"!

The Marquis:
Ah, yes! He is forever breaking into spiritual sweats. They

water his forehead: his soul keeps dry. Now his brother Theodore—

Remy:
A ponderous self-centred fool!

The Marquis:
Theodore remains calm. The disciples of John Cowper do not. Theodore is honest because honesty, for him, is worth its pains. He has something that is worth being honest for. John Cowper has nothing: nothing of his own. Nothing to evoke, nothing to realize, nothing to enhance, nothing to guard,—nothing that is sacred, nothing that demands its rite and will have it, in all devoted labour!

Remy:
And pray, sir, what is this precious possession of Theodore's own—evoked, guarded, enhanced and the rest, in **"The Soliloquy of a Hermit"**? What is it?

The Marquis:
Himself. Theodore possesses himself: and for that reason he can give himself—surely and completely. He has knowledge of what he is; and sincerity in the use of his knowledge. This is why **"The Soliloquy of a Hermit"** is a work of art.

Remy:
Well, he may be sincere, but his personality doesn't interest me. I'm not in sympathy with that type of mind.

The Marquis:
Becuase you are not grown up. **"The Soliloquy of a Hermit"** is not written for the half-educated. Theodore is not clever enough for them; he does not play their tricks. He cares only for saying what he feels. And his expression is complete; that vexes their comfort, their conventions . . . *Nom de Dieu!* He says everything that is necessary, nothing that is not. It is perfect. A perfect work of art.

Remy:
At least you'll admit, sir, that he has a very limited vocabulary.

The Marquis:
Ah! that is one of his greatest charms! No sought-out words, no laborious phrases, no smell of the literary laboratory. And yet none of that care-worn affectation of simplicity that your modern "spiritual" authors so tediously adopt! Theodore uses his natural speech; he does not refrain from lettered language; he has never learned it.

Remy:
Oh, that's all very well, but he writes like a rustic.

The Marquis:
Yes. He writes of *"summer blessedness,"* of *"cool places amidst great and fair trees,"* of *"rich banks of summer flowers."* . . . *"Under this blessed mood the winds of heaven are still."* . . . What you say is true. The grave and tender beauty of this man's style was not city-bred.

Remy:
Style, sir! Why, now and again his grammar is shaky.

The Marquis:
I wish the scholars would go to school to him. His little finger is thicker than their loins.—*"I have tried to hide amongst grassy hills; but the moods of God have hunted me out."*— That one sentence bears more weight than all the seven hundred pages of "Wood and Stone." Listen, Remy: the root of the matter is there. How did it happen to Theodore Powys to write

those words that I remember? He wrote them *under compulsion;* under stress of the feeling of his God's moods. He had indeed tried to hide; and indeed he had been hunted out. So, when he tells us, we respond, we are in union with the sense that held him. It is the thrilling communication of art. (pp. 5-8)

Remy:
About the **"Soliloquy,"** then. I confess you surprised me, sir. Theodore Powys is not at all like you.

The Marquis:
*Nom de Dieu!* I should think not. I dream of favourite slaves. I keep, urbanely, at a decorous distance from his God. If I knew this Hermit, there would be many days when I should send him off to dig for potatoes. My beard is pointed: Theodore's, I am sure, is not. But what of that? Do you think I care only for authors who are of my own mind? What they are is nothing: it is how they are what they are that matters. They must be themselves profoundly, they must confess themselves honestly: then they can be mystics or business men, buffoons or philosophers, lovers of lust or ascetics; they can be of the faith of power or the faith of humility—but they must go down to their own deeps, then speak what they know. And how many are thus profound and sincere? No more than there are men of genius.

Remy:
What! Theodore Powys a man of genius! With that one little book of harassed meditation!

The Marquis:
Even with one little sentence of that one little book. Yes. A man of genius. They'll be reading **"The Soliloquy of a Hermit"** in a hundred years. Remy,—my soul on that! The soul of a true Epicurean!

Remy:
Why, sir, you are actually excited.

The Marquis:
Genius is exciting, my dear. But you haven't discovered that yet. Go back to your "Wood and Stone" and get your little thrills. A very good makeshift for the "real right thing," at your age—good training, too; ah, things lead up; we pass on. In a few years, you will read the **"Soliloquy"** again. Theodore's novel will be out before then, but you had better wait. You had better wait. I'll keep a copy for your twenty-fifth birthday.

Remy:
Oh, come now, Father! I have my rights of preference. One shouldn't be too dogmatic. It's all a matter of taste.

The Marquis:
A matter of taste. *"I have tried to hide amongst grassy hills: but the moods of God have hunted me out."* (pp. 8-9)

> *Louis U. Wilkinson, in his* Blasphemy and Religion *(© Kenneth Hopkins and the Estate of Louis Wilkinson, 1969), G. A. Shaw, 1916 (and reprinted by Colgate University Press, 1969), 12 p.*

**CLIFTON P. FADIMAN**   (essay date 1924)

**"The Left Leg,"** **"Black Bryony,"** and now **"Mark Only,"** present pictures of life as it is lived in the south and west of modern England. Mr. Powys, ruthless, Dante-visioned, bitter with the agony of long and continuous contact with the environment he describes, strips this life of every possible idyllic association. We arise from these novels of the most exquisite realism with a vision of the mutilated corpse of the gentle Mrs. Gaskell, who saw life steadily but saw it over the rim of a teacup.

Those, however, who have read Mr. Powys's early book of confession, **"The Soliloquies of a Hermit,"** and who have patiently endeavored to define for themselves the rare, if bitter, savor of his novels, are convinced that he is more than a crusader against sentimentality. It is true that in **"Mark Only"** the hero Mark Andrews is technically a moron, the villain Tulk a despicable satyr of the most fiendish type, and the other characters either wandering in their wits or mudded with brutality. It is true that the story itself is a compound of every horror-inspiring melodramatic device known to the hack of fifty years ago. It is true that a bestial passion creeps through the pages of the story like a dirty white fog, compelling our nostrils to an involuntary quiver. Granted—Mr. Powys is not for the weak-stomached. He may very well be presenting a faithful, if revolting, portrait of country life; or he may not be. He overdraws at times, being given more particularly in **"Mark Only"** to piling horror upon horror with the persistence of a Sophocles. But all this does not so much matter—the importance of Mr. Powys is that his concern is with deeper things than mere truth to externals. What, for example, is the aesthetic problem that he has so successfully solved?

The people in Mr. Powys's world move so slowly that they seem to compose an almost static society. Their lives are so intensely primitive and simple that the intrusion of drama into them seems an impossibility. They are all governed by one or two elementary desires, or rather obsessions—the poor halfwit Mark by a half-realized desire to keep his life running or creeping in the old channels familiar to him, the lame Tulk by an uncomplicated lust for power over his immediate fellow-creatures, Emmie the little servant by a tragic and childlike sexual curiosity that masters her like a Greek Fate, Mr. Beggwell, prosperous farmer, by an overweening pride in the enormity of his prize mangelwurzels, and so on. The minds of these people stir like the thick mud at the bottom of a stagnant pond; it is as if they were being put through their paces by the operation of a slow-motion camera. Nothing surprises them. The flame of life has burned so low that they are the most passive of receptacles for the most limited of experiences. They do not seem organic; they are the agents through which operates a continual and relentless process of petrification. They live in a worn world; their environment is sessile. So quiescent are they, so slow in reaction, that it seems impossible to find any conflict among them—and narrative is born of conflict.

Mr. Powys in describing this negatively accelerated universe with sympathy and power has performed an amazing technical feat. He has synchronized the volatile motions of his brain with the unbelievably impeded tempo of the village of Dodderdown. His style is carefully graduated so as to approach monotony but never quite reach it. It is one of stark simplicity where the lacunae of human speech count for more than the words themselves, where omission lights up emotion. He wastes little time in reflection, none in characterization. He stamps his characters with the decision and accuracy of a minting machine: "Mr. Thomas had a wife who was in ill-health and made the most of it." Never is there the slightest concession to fine writing, although the flame of a twisted and tender beauty flickers through these pages. Mr. Powys, in short, has presented an organic picture of an almost static society. He is a splendid example of the adaptation of the artist to his material. And it

must not be thought that his people are dull. They are fascinating. We enter into their squalid but intensely poignant lives as if we were making an excursion into the mind of primitive man. Kinship we cannot feel, but the Balboan thrill of discovery is ours. Mr. Powys has described, it may be invented, a new world where Mr. Peach and Mr. Tolly discourse of the soul "which do be a hedgehog," where old Mrs. Andrews, patting her thin and greasy hair, gibbers the story of a tragic girlhood, where Mr. Hayball the parson escapes unwitting from the life around him by indulging a queer antiquarian taste for rainfall statistics. Mr. Powys has invented a new genre—the tragicomedy of rustic life seen by one as over-sensitive to ugliness as the flayed Marsyas was to pain. (pp. 524-25)

> *Clifton P. Fadiman, "A New Genre," in* The Nation *(copyright 1924 The Nation magazine, The Nation Associates, Inc.), Vol. 119, No. 3097, November 12, 1924, pp. 524-25.*

**JOHN COWPER POWYS**   (essay date 1925)

In the three long short-stories of **"The Left Leg,"** in **"Black Bryony,"** and in **"Mark Only,"** my brother Theodore has already established his position as one of the most arresting and formidable of modern writers of fiction.

Of the four of us [Powys brothers] he is undoubtedly the most original. He is indeed so original both in subject matter and in style that it is hard to find any literary analogies or comparisons wherewith to throw his extraordinary work into critical perspective.

Dealing with the same locale as has been so triumphantly exploited by Thomas Hardy, there is nothing even remotely Hardyesque about his manner of presentation. He seems to write of Dorset scenery and of Dorset peasants from a point of view that isolates that devoted section of the earth as completely from all others as the Limbo in Dante's "Divine Comedy" is isolated from earth and hell and purgatory and heaven. The stretch of country occupied by these luckless hamlets, overshadowed by the merciless "moods" of God, seems in fact to be lifted up or lowered down beyond the common earth-level; until it is so soaked by fairy rains and so blighted by magic moons as to become rather a projection of one man's creative mind than a reproduction of any actual human province. The country dialect, as T. F. Powys uses it, becomes itself a sort of modifying and transfiguring medium through which the events are seen remotely, at a distance, as if through a filmy mist. But within that mist, within this magic circle, how we become aware of every least gesture of these fantastic and unhappy persons, of every stick and stone in these haunted roads, of every crack and cranny in these persecuted houses!

My brother's humor, wrinkling his tragic mask, is utterly unlike any other humor that I have ever encountered. It has a directness that approaches its object with the tap of a raven's beak. It divides the just from the unjust with the physical assurance of a fork dividing a beard. It brings you into such palpable impact with the reality in question that you start back under the shock of it as if from the laugh of a hobgoblin when you are robbing a henroost, or from the "droppings" of an owl in a high tree when you're playing Peeping Tom. It is a humor that has a deep, sweet-bitter subterranean malice in it; a malice that moves close up to the thing it is handling and catches it off-guard and disarrayed; catches it, if it is alive, sneezing, gobbling, scratching, stretching, shivering with fear or with desire, prowling off on some affair "that has no relish of salvation in't."

And always, in these extraordinary books, one is uneasily aware, out there in the dim background, of the furtive hoofs of the great god Pan. The hills may lie lovely and quiet in the noon heat. The valleys may laugh and sing with daisies and children. Over the green bracken, amid the white clover, go those mysterious hoof-thuds, bringing a tremor of the dark underworld into every heart that hears them. For although religion enters profoundly into the texture of these stories, it cannot be said, except in the case of the allegorical and ambiguous Mr. Jar, that it enters with any reassurance or comfort. It "scatters hoarfrost like ashes"; and the good and the bad alike whinny and bleat as it skulks around their threshold.

There is something almost Manichean about T. F. Powys's attitude to life. "Pure Love," as in some Saturnian Pilgrim's Progress, finds herself so absolutely separated from her wicked brother "Profane Love" that a kind of dark Pauline curse falls upon all natural and normal sex impulses. And this vein is further accentuated by the presence of a deep-bitten, uncompromising, inveterate hostility to every form of careless strength or casual well-being.

Theodore Powys's world is indeed a world projected whole and entire out of the shadowy recesses of his own unusual subconsciousness. So original is his vision of things, so saturated with his extraordinary personality is every word he writes, that one feels certain that these strange tales are assured, if anything is assured, of a lasting hold upon certain troubled minds. The passages that are least affected by this unceasing and remorseless pursuit of the weak by the strong, this dark hunt that we follow with such mingled emotions—for the human heart is a colosseum of contradictions—are the passages in which the rambling choruses of old men and old women exchange their comments upon it all. In the **"Left Leg"** the women meet in the village shop. In **"Hester Dominy"** the men meet in the pound, in **"Mark Only,"** in Mark's stable. While in **"Black Bryony"** the meeting-place of men and women alike is the motor-van of the carrier. In all these scenes, where the gloom of the plot is relieved by a unique and elfish humor, one is aware of something mysteriously simple and yet mysteriously profound in the writer's philosophy—a philosophy to which door-handles and loaves of bread and wooden settles and church-porchbiers and spades and mugs and platters and pitchforks and horse-dung all contribute their quota of mystic intimation. It is a Hans Andersen world rather than a Grimm's fairy-tale world; for over it all hangs the shadow of the projection of man's heart, which remains desperately and stupidly wicked; but it is a world where there *are* Hester Dominys and where there *are* Mr. Thomases, and though their days on the earth are few and evil, and though none throw incense on their sacrifices, that they have existed at all redeems a little—more perhaps than we know—the pressure of the will to live. (pp. 558-59)

*John Cowper Powys, "Four Brothers: A Family Confession" (reprinted by permission of Lawrence Pollinger Ltd and the Estate of John Cowper Powys), in The Century, Vol. 110, No. 5, September, 1925, pp. 553-60.\**

### THOMAS BEER   (essay date 1928)

Mr. T. F. Powys, in **"Mr. Weston's Good Wine"** is not openly handling the pencil of a correspondent at Ragnarök. He brings about a little doomsday within terms of the Christian tradition. A god takes on the function of St. Nicholas or Madame the Virgin in the later Christian mythology, and graciously inter-feres with mankind in the village of Folly Down. This deity arrives in a Ford truck with his handsome assistant, Michael, a more tactful archangel than the fatigued lieutenant of "The High Place," but not as amusing. Mr. Weston is a placid, oldish person who once wrote a long prose poem in many books and was astonished when it came true. He is a weary, civilized I-Am-What-I-Am. He releases the Lion on sinners without any fuss about it, in rather the manner of the Home Secretary sending out a letter of admonition to a misbehaving coal baron. He keeps his performance inside the margins of his own celebrated publication, changing water into wine with an apologetic privacy and carefully uniting lovers on their hasty way to bed. . . .

It is a Northern fable. Mr. Weston's wine is what you like—love, faith, pitying death—and once, when Tamar Grobe comes into the archangel's human arms under the oak tree on the dark green, it is the love-death, the Northern passion that slays. When Mr. Weston confronts Ada Kibble's loutish seducer with her rotted body in the churchyard you are in the Scotch and Flemish folk lore. When the old sexton recognizes the deity you see a simple character from one of Breughels's pictures meeting another honest fellow; a finite body meets a finite god. Out beyond them is the Northern mist, and the nameless principles imposing dooms without an end. Even St. Francis of Assisi, intruding in Folly Down under the name of Luke Bird, is a homely, self-conscious little rhapsodist, somewhat more male than the Southern figure. Mrs. Vosper, the Celestina of the village, and the landlord of the Angel Inn, and the lewd Mumby brothers are all Northern carvings, and the mystery is that of a winter evening's tale beside the fire. . . . The mind arranging this is not the mind trained to discuss self-surrender. It can conceive an act of contrition, it comprehends pity, but it knows that justice is an irrational fiction and that the still, small voice is a voice contrived by man. The difference is that, please, of a "Crucifixion" by Grünewald and El Greco's "Nativity." The Alsatian stabs at your sympathy for the sons and hurt mothers of men, and places his emblems in front of a retiring shadow in which the mystery and the doom exist, away from you. The Greek, bred in the union of Syrian and European romance, demands that you follow the weaving gestures of an ecstatic acceptance. One of them sees a green and blue shadow, behind which—beyond Hela—is a Power. The other sees a light from heaven, glaring right on his face. . . . And there is no light from heaven in Mr. Weston's stay at Folly Down. At best the kindly wine merchant has just made the white stars into Gothic angels to comfort praying folk. His omnipotence is that of the All Father at the top of a German Judgment Day of the fifteenth century. He is good until Ragnarök and not a minute after.

Mr. Powys puts all this on paper in a languid simplicity of words and with notable smoothness. His error, on the whole, is that he falls back into an occasional, distressing mood of the Victorian romantics. You feel that he used to read Mr. Le Gallienne and Stevenson very seriously as you come on something like this: "When a young man is in love, that meek virgin, nature, weeps and hopes, sighs and longs with him. No movement of a tree stirred by the wind, no hurried scuttle and rush of a rabbit in a hedge, no cloud in the sky, but yearns with him and bids him hope." . . . There is a lot of dust on that, and it was always a frail chair, even when it was fresher and Mr. Le Gallienne handed it to you at his tea party for the Golden Girl. But Mr. Powys does not do it often. He is generally simple and effective. As his people and their emotions must never be allowed to become tense and real (three paragraphs of reality would smash the tale to bits) he winds them in and out of his misty fable in a series of easy artifices and comes through to a handsome success, in the school. It is a most agreeable book. The total gain is that of an advanced Robert Louis Stevenson who has risen above the wistfulness of "Will o' the Mill" and "The House of Eld" and is speculating tranquilly on the mental condition of a gentleman's god. . . .

As a comment on the idea of deity the book has no importance, but it has the merit of a parable against the surviving notions of good and evil, told gracefully and in terms of solid sense. . . . Presently a new god and the intermingling rhythms of what we call a culture will come from somewhere and the critics of the year 2628 will examine the transacted letters of the nineteenth and twentieth centuries as if they looked over a wall at children playing with ruined dolls below the sunlight. One begs to remind them that Ragnarök is not a comfortable occasion and, also, that it seems to be recurrent. All things tend to their end, Mr. Weston quotes to St. Michael as they drive away from Folly Down. All things do. And I mean, All. (p. 6)

> Thomas Beer, *"Little Doomsday,"* in New York Herald Tribune Books (© *I.H.T. Corporation; reprinted by permission*), March 4, 1928, pp. 1, 6.

## ERNEST DIMNET (essay date 1929)

["**An Interpretation of Genesis**"] is neither a commentary nor a dissertation; it is a dialogue. The Interlocutors are Moses, who, for majesty's sake, is called the Lawgiver of Israel, and an imaginary person who is called Zetetes, though, if what is left of one's Greek is not a delusion, he should have been called Eroton. This Zetetes, as is the rule in dialogues of this kind, is an intelligent fool who asks partly intelligent questions and sometimes gets informed for being intelligent, sometimes gets snubbed for being a fool. Once in a while the author forgets his cast and Zetetes goes quite out of his depth and of ours too.

As for the subject of this long conversation it is, or seems to be, "Genesis," which I had better remind you at the outset means Birth, for Birth or No-Birth means a great deal to Mr. Powys. . . . However the episodes of "Genesis" are commented upon, one after another, from the creation of the world to the death, if not of Joseph, as in the Bible, at least of Jacob "who gathered up his feet into the bed and gave up the ghost." Each story is briefly narrated, often in a quotation from the English Bible, whereupon Zetetes and the Lawgiver exchange wise sayings about it.

The language is, of course, poetic, prophetic and stately, with all the whereofs, thereofs, thereuntos, willests, wouldests, wist nots, perchances and what not which pertain to Biblical imitations. There is a continuous flow of images, quite a number of which are as satisfactory as images can be, and a great fund of allusion.

The vocabulary requires some study, at the beginning, and has to be watched all the time, because prophets are above philology, and the meaning of words in a rich kaleidoscopic work of this kind is likely to vary like the reflections in an *aurora borealis*. The Mother means Mother-Earth, no doubt, and Motherland is just earth, but in one place Rebekah is puzzlingly called the Mother too. The Father may mean God, but you have to be careful, for Mr. Powys has his own ideas about God which I shall recount in good time. It may also mean the

firmament, and above all it may mean Truth, about which (or whom) also more anon. The Fatherland sometimes means Eden, sometimes the other side of things generally. Darkness means stupidity, ignorance, vice, very bad vice, and seems to correspond to what used to be credited to sin and the devil. Nakedness varies in meaning, being sometimes sacred and beautiful, but later degenerating into something bestial and even sacerdotal. (p. 1)

[If in "**An Interpretation of Genesis**"] there is no theology of the theological school variety, there are traces all through the hundred beautifully printed pages of a philosophy of science, man and life, of morals, and even here and there some sociology and internationalism of the orthodox description. . . . Mr. Powys's theodicy is surprisingly clear. His idea of God is that He is only God—that is to say, not much, in comparison with Truth. In describing Jacob's wrestling with a supernatural champion he actually calls the latter "old darkness." He devotes thirty of the great full pages to Abraham or Abram, but the patriarch fares rather ill at his hands. . . . A great deal has been written, ably and eloquently, about him. But Mr. Powys does not follow suit. He rather thinks that the God made by Abraham, as well as by the fulsome being called priest, is a retrogression. He accuses the God of causing Abraham, at least for a time, to work against Truth. Finally Abraham discovers that the people are superior to God, and we suddenly find ourselves in full modernity. Mr. Powys is sure that Abraham's God is the God whose deeds fill the Bible, but fill it with murders of men and of truths. Mr. Powys, it can be said for him, reads serious books; I have no doubt but that he has read Marcion, who was a distinguished intellect and who is rather in fashion at the present moment.

I said above that Mr. Powys attaches an extraordinary importance to birth and to whatever is connected with birth. As early as Page 5 you find a little bit of Freudianism, which seems as unexpected here as a glacier boulder under a hot sun: "In the babe the first thought is food and the second is generation." (Freud, of course, would invert the order of these terms.) . . .

[Mr. Powys's] intention was to clothe the scientific history of the globe and of man in poetic Biblical language. The hardening of stars, the caveman, the humble beginnings of religion are here. Incongruous sentences almost on every page show the impossibility of such an attempt, although Mr. Powys is content with the most elementary statements of evolution and seems to know nothing of the spiritualization of matter by modern physics. Add that he is an optimist, sure that in the beginning all was well, yet compelled by evolution to say that primitive man was "but little removed from the nakedness of the beast." So his innocent boast: "I write the history of Truth in man," is only an innocent boast.

Shall we blame Mr. Powys for attempting the impossible? Undoubtedly. There is a shallowness over "**An Interpretation of Genesis**" and, to be frank, a charlatanry which must be severely censured. Writers *will* begin to write their books before they are finished, and that is the root of the evil. Probably Mr. Powys tried his hand at a few passages (do the same, it will amuse you and you will see how easy it is), and then he imagined he must write a hundred pages. If he had asked himself after those first essays what he really wished to do, he would have seen the impossibility of reconciling opposites. His book could only conceal the vagueness of its conception by the vagueness of its treatment, which is the fundamental criticism one must make of it. I should not mind a few incongruities of language: ("Abraham was Sarah's god," which would seem anachronistic even in "The Vicar of Wakefield"), and a number of platitudes which quotation would make worse than they are and which therefore I will not quote, but grandiloquent obscurity is unforgivable. "Darkness covers nothing." All the time you read hoping to be taught everything—for somehow Mr. Powys, or the Bible, or the beautiful print holds you and you cannot skip—but you learn nothing, and finally you say to the author in his own words: "Thy book is before thee, O man, and darkness is within it." I have no doubt that Mr. Powys answers, also in his own words: "Leave me upon my height amongst the desolate and great rocks, leave me, I say, and return to the Mother in the valley. Perchance thou canst not yet hear the thoughts of the Father." (p. 6)

Ernest Dimnet, "Truth in Man," in New York Herald Tribune Books (© I.H.T. Corporation; reprinted by permission), September 15, 1929, pp. 1, 6.

**WILLIAM HUNTER**   (essay date 1930)

[*Hunter's* The Novels and Stories of T. F. Powys *is one of the most thorough studies of the author's fiction, its symbols, themes, and techniques.*]

In this century, when a writer moves away from the conventional path, his achievement does not receive immediate recognition. T. F. Powys is one of the modern novelists to break new ground, and his recognition at present is so slight as to be almost negligible. One cannot, somehow, think of him as a revolutionary, in the sense that Joyce and Lawrence are revolutionaries, yet his contribution to literature is as original as theirs. He has given us a new formula. He is of the generation and yet not of it. His novels are only possible because he has cut himself off from twentieth-century civilisation, and yet could have been written in no other century but this. He owes little or nothing to contemporary literature; all his debts are to the past. He derives from no "school" and he will found none. But it is probable that future generations will regard him as standing in something of the same relation to this generation as Blake did to his. (p. 3)

There will be no complete acceptance of his work as long as it is regarded as realism. His novels are not pure fantasy; there is realism in them all, as there must be in novels which have their roots in actual life. Indeed, in the less mature novels, such as **Hester Dominy,** the realism outweighs the rest. . . . At his best, as in **Mark Only** or **Mr. Weston's Good Wine,** there is something more than realism, something which no one else has done in quite the same way before. His world is a unique world, and in dealing with a unique world it becomes difficult to find terms by which to describe it. It is a small world— Madder or Dodder or Folly Down are all the same. But it is sufficiently large, nevertheless—it is a world of poetic imagination. The books are a curious mixture of realism and mysticism, of symbolism and allegory, of "mud and Godhead." . . .

A frequent objection to his work is that the same characters constantly recur. But it must be remembered that all his work is a slow progression towards **Mr. Weston's Good Wine.** (p. 4)

If one must search for sources in a writer so original, one would have thought that his two great sources of inspiration were sufficiently obvious—The Authorised Version and John Bunyan. To probe beyond these is unprofitable. It is the something of his own which is important.

The novels may be roughly divided, for our purpose, into two groups, which we may call Experimental and Post-Experimental. In the first five novels he has not yet complete control of his medium, but they show an advancing maturity, which makes **The Left Leg** the most finished, and the one which may appropriately end the period of experiment. . . .

While in many ways the least mature of the nine [novels, **Mr. Tasker's Gods**] is not on that account the least interesting. A critical examination of **Mr. Tasker's Gods,** where the weaknesses of his method are most apparent, is the best clue to an understanding of the later novels, where the maturer craftsmanship is more cunningly concealed.

Mr. Tasker is a churchwarden and a dairyman who worships his pigs. (p. 5)

This is the character who gives the book its name. Powys' very methods of character-drawing are essentially non-realistic. His art is two- rather than three-dimensional, and only very occasionally is there so much even as an approach to a third dimension. In these novels a villain *is* a villain, and the lives of Mr. Tasker, Charlie Tulk, and Mrs. Vosper are perfectly harmonious works of art, from birth to death unmarred by a single good action; any good action or unselfish thought would destroy their purpose.

Mr. Tasker, then, is a simplified character. He is dominated by a particular characteristic, and at the same time he is a symbol. But to say that his character is the mere dominance of a humour or monomania is not to say everything. Although the characters are not realistic in the conventional sense, they are more than the fantastic creations of a disordered imagination. In the simplified, two-dimensional form in which they are presented to us, they exist only against their own background. But they are nevertheless fundamentally real. They are taken from life, and then stripped by the artist, who retains only the essential aspects of character, the aspects necessary for his purpose. His characters are not types, but simplified and somewhat distorted individuals with typical lusts or weaknesses or virtues. This simplification, and a kind of flat distortion in the drawing, is essential to his art, which is an art of caricature, of great and beautiful caricature.

With Powys we know at once what *kind* of a character it is, and almost at once all that we ever shall know of his *character*—not, of course, of his actions or behaviour. (pp. 6-7)

There is no gradual revealing of weaknesses. If there is weakness indicated in the beginning, there will be further weakness, but everything follows from what we know on [the character's] first entrance into the novel. (p. 7)

Much that is in the later novels subtly implied, is [in **Mr. Tasker's Gods**] explicitly stated. There is too sharp a division between good and evil, between black and white. There is none of the beautiful, subtle shadow of the later work. There are other faults too. There is a tendency to kill his characters off too indiscriminately, to use death as a convenient solution of all difficulties, and at times his bitterness overmasters his judgment and degenerates into violence. The book, in short, is immature. But in spite of serious faults it is an important book, containing the germ of his masterpiece. It is magnificently sincere, and the prose style is individual and distinguished; in places it reaches the level which it maintains consistently in the later [books]. . . . (p. 8)

The development is evident through the next four novels. After the violence of **Mr. Tasker's Gods, Black Bryony** seems a very quiet book. It contains nothing so good as the first novel at its best, but as a whole it is a better book, though on a lower and less ambitious plane. The symbolism, while still at times a little clumsy, is more definite, more under control. It is a slight book, "a summer's night fantasy," but as original as his first. The poisonous black bryony plant, the symbol of evil, is the real dominant of the book, and not Mary—a fine piece of drawing—or Matthew Hurd or Mr. Crossley. It is more subtle, and exhibits pervasively a restraint that is evident in *Mr. Tasker's Gods* only in patches.

*Hester Dominy* is the least successful of all the novels, because it is the nearest approach to the conventional representation of ordinary events. It is a good book, with writing of a quality that is rare nowadays. There are, for example, the conversations between Hester and Anthony Dine, and the two pathetic, unforgettable old maids, and if it does nothing else, it shows that the town is an uncongenial background for his characters.

As if Powys had realised this, Luke Bird, in *Abraham Men*, moves from the town into the country. The town never again becomes a background for his characters, except in the opening chapters of *Mr. Weston's Good Wine*. (pp. 8-9)

*The Left Leg* may end the experimental period. [Powys] is now on the verge of full maturity but not quite beyond it. And it is the first allegorical novel, with the "twisted" or "distorted" allegory. The allegory is of the Virgin Mary (Mary Gillet), and Joseph (Old Jar, the tinker), and the birth of Christ. The rape of Mary by rich Farmer Mew gives the ironic twist to the Biblical story, a twist which is repeated again, in *Mockery Gap*, for instance, in the allegory of the Resurrection. . . .

The character of Farmer Mew is significant. He is one of those characters who begin apparently as realistic portraits, and then, by passing beyond the bounds of possibility, become caricatures. (p. 10)

The mould in which [Powys'] style shall be cast is now decided. From the quotations the faults as well as the qualities of his style, which is an experiment as well as everything else, can be seen. It is a style modelled on Florio's Montaigne, The Authorised Version, and Bunyan, "a style that in no way dances in the air, but prefers clay as a medium." At a hasty reading it seems "quaint," to have an almost childish simplicity. It is a style that deceives many. At its best, it is extraordinarily complex, though apparently simple. By extreme concentration he gains the maximum effect; every word is used for a very definite purpose. (p. 11)

Sometimes there is an extraordinary sensuous rhythm in the prose—as, for example, in the superb passage in *Abraham Men* describing the country and the country people. . . . Very often he achieves his effect by the use of similes and metaphors. He takes grave risks, but the metaphors are never strained or inappropriate, the risks are always justified. (p. 12)

*The Left Leg* ends the experimental period. The expression is fuller in the later novels, the construction more skilfully engineered; but the form of his stories is now decided, and remains largely the same.

At this point the ordered progression ceases. *Innocent Birds* is not a definite advance on *Mark Only,* and *Mockery Gap* is certainly not an advance on either. *Innocent Birds* has not the tragic intensity of *Mark Only;* but it is an important book, with *Mark Only* the most significant of his work before *Mr. Weston's Good Wine.* There are the same single-trait characters, the same poetic imagery. An ironic humour is pervasive throughout the

book, but underneath there is a deeper note, and the three chapters dealing with the rape of Polly by Mr. Bugby, and the death of Fred and Polly—*Another Bird for Mr. Bugby, Scattered Bones,* and *The Foolish Guillemot*—are probably Powys' finest pieces of sustained writing, and one of the finest pieces of twentieth-century prose. After this novel and *Mark Only,* there can be no danger of Powys ever returning to "realism." . . . (p. 13)

It is with this novel that one must take account of Powys' preoccupation with Death. It is an important part of his work, that has been present in the earlier novels. But this is its most mature expression before *Mr. Weston's Good Wine.* It is the background of the book. God promises to Madder a perfect gift. The gift is Death, and the recipients the two innocent birds, Fred and Polly. In these novels it is the beautiful that passes away, Fred and Polly and Mark and the two Henries. It is "the everlasting mud," Mr. Tasker, James Andrews, and Mark's sisters, who triumph and remain.

To call *Mark Only* a great novel is not an exaggeration. It is, in its way, almost perfect. Nothing is irrelevant, and to take out any part would be to destroy the unity of the whole. Realism and mysticism are at last perfectly blended, and the lessons of the earlier work assimilated. . . .

The book offers very little opportunity for adverse criticism. Mr. Thomas, the sweep, is the only character about whose inclusion there can be any reasonable doubt. He seems to be brought in to save Emmie from tragedy, a kind of god out of the machine. But when one considers how slight her tragedy would be beside that of Mark and Nellie, and how unimportant she is beside these two and Charlie Tulk, Mr. Thomas' inclusion seems justified. (p. 14)

Mark is probably Powys' most complex character, his nearest successful approach to "roundness." He is a distortion, like all the others, but he is not so simplified, so consistent as the rest. Mr. Tasker, or Henry Turnbull, or Mrs. Vosper, or Old Jar, or the Nellie Bird are comparatively simple. Mark is more difficult. He is the first tragic figure—the tragic figure in *Mr. Tasker's Gods* are never big enough to be permanently tragic figures in themselves as Mark is. Mark Only is the common countryman, more imaginative, i.e. madder, than his fellows, raised from the ordinary realistic plane, and made by genius into a tragic figure. (p. 15)

The book owes more to *Mr. Tasker's Gods* than is immediately apparent. It is, so to speak, his first novel written in maturity. Mrs. Andrews has developed from an aspect of Mrs. Turnbull only sketched and never fully developed. (p. 16)

Mrs. Turnbull's "one beat out of place" has become Mrs. Andrews' "normal pulse," and Mark has become the idiot. Mark's brother James and his two sisters have taken the place of Henry's brothers; and Charlie Tulk has many important characteristics in common with Mr. Tasker, Mrs. Fancy, and Henry's brothers. There is a close resemblance, too, between the gradually accumulating tragedy of Henry and Neville and that of Mark. But *Mark Only* is on a grander scale altogether.

In the use of the minor characters, who have no effect on the main tragedy, but who are used to heighten and contrast it, Powys seems to me to be using a wholly unique type of comedy. (pp. 16-17)

These two novels show the limit to which Powys, in this phase of his development, has been able to go. *Mockery Gap* is a halt, a breathing-space in his progress. It is an ironic allegory, a dream fantasy. The quality of the prose is superb, and the dream atmosphere—in the death of Miss Pink, for instance—amazing. But in this dream world the advent of the Roddites is an alien and discordant intrusion. It may be coupled with **Kindness in a Corner,** a later and on the whole disappointing novel. In **Kindness in a Corner,** however, there is nothing but humour, with the exception of one magnificent chapter—*The Dirt of God.* In **Mockery Gap** the humour is ironical, and there is something more besides. In such a world one might suppose that the nearest approach to "seriousness" would be the quarrel of the Prings and the Pottles, and it is in itself a considerable achievement to have introduced a deeper note into the fantasy.

All these novels had definite limitations, and if one had only these by which to judge, Powys would have been a master, but only a minor master. **Mr. Weston's Good Wine,** however, leaves one in no doubt as to his place in English literature. He is now, without any doubt, a major writer. This book is a masterpiece which has transcended all the limitations of the earlier work. It is one of the greatest novels of this century, and one of the greatest allegories in the English language. His technique is perfected and at its most mature, his style at its most deceivingly simple. He triumphs over every difficulty. One has the impression of a man walking along the edge of a very steep precipice; one false step would mean disaster; but he never falters. There is a new tone about the book which had not been present in the others.

By means of the allegory, Christian myth is used to express a pagan philosophy. The book is indescribably subtle. It is a great tribute to his craftsmanship that even the attentive reader has read many pages before he arrives at the identity of Mr. Weston. (pp. 19-20)

The more one reads this book, the more one admires its astonishing beauty as a whole. Not even the severest critic could reasonably find any fault. In the first 68 pages, which are introductory, before Folly Down is reached, there are innumerable passages full of meaning, if the reader knows the book well, but which can be understood only in retrospect if the book has been read once only. For instance, Mr. Weston's behaviour on reading the name of Mr. Grobe in the book is very significant in view of later events. It is, too, an extremely subtle mind that makes Mr. Weston short-sighted. (pp. 21-2)

After the first ten explanatory chapters, the plot moves into its permanent background, Folly Down. Gradually, the characters are introduced—their names we have seen before in Mr. Weston's book—Tamar, the wonderful daughter of Mr. Grobe, Mr. Grunter, Mrs. Vosper, the Kiddles, Landlord Bunce and Jenny Bunce, Mr. Meek and the Mumbys—each one a different coloured thread in the stuff of which the novel is made, all mingling and cooperating to form a complete and beautiful design.

The stopping of all the clocks at seven places the action in a plane where time does not exist. Time has stopped, and Eternity has come. It is incredible that Landlord Bunce's clock should stop. As a result, the villagers are sure that strange happenings are to take place, and so is the reader. On this plane, everything is possible. (p. 23)

What *is* Mr. Weston's Good Wine? Mr. Weston himself says that it is "as sweet as love and as strong as death." And stated crudely, the two are Love and Death, always for Powys the two great realities. The deadlier draught is reserved only for those whom he loves especially. (p. 26)

Powys has a pagan philosophy of life. But it is a paganism that is neither lighthearted nor stoic, a wide paganism of which Christian ethic is a part. His attitude to physical love, pervasive throughout the book is essentially tolerant, approving, non-Christian—"country manners," laughed Mr. Weston. "A rare vintage" sometimes "do mean a pretty an' plump maiden wi' buttons to unfasten,"—an attitude which it would be difficult to find in Christian teaching. And it is significant that when the oak tree, the symbol of lust, has been struck down, the mossy bed remains. His attitude, in effect, is: "Drink of the light wine by all means. But the dark wine is preferable. You will want to drink that when you have tired of the other." Mr. Weston himself wishes to drink his own dark wine, and on that day the firm will end, and all his customers will drink of it too.

"All things tend to their end." And when the strange tangle of Folly Down life has been unravelled, Mr. Weston leaves, and the book closes as magnificently as it had begun. (p. 30)

Powys is as much a master of the short story as of the novel, and his later work, such stories as *The Key of the Field* and *Darkness and Nathaniel,* make it possible to claim for him the position of the greatest English short story writer. Indeed, there is no writer in English in this form who has written so many stories at such a consistently high level.

His stories, like his novels, conveniently group themselves into two periods; the earlier period is represented by the stories contained in *The House with the Echo,* the later period by *Fables* and *The Key of the Field.*

The stories in his first volume range from immature and on the whole unsuccessful work, such as the title story, to more finished work, such as **Nor Iron Bars.** There is here, as in the novels, the same extreme concentration and compressed imagery, the elimination of all but the essential, the same stylisation, ironic humour and tragic intensity. The best of this early work is perfect, but perfect only in a limited range. They have not the depth and variety of attitudes of his later work. Nevertheless, even if he had achieved nothing better than the best of these tales, if we had to judge him as a short story writer by **Nor Iron Bars, In Dull Devonshire, The Dewpond,** and **What Lack I Yet?,** he would remain one of the finest and most individual of English short story writers. **What Lack I Yet?,** in fact, transcends his limitations and can stand beside the best.

With the publication of **Fables** and **The Key of the Field** there is no longer any question. None excels, and few equal him. **The Key of the Field** can be compared in English only with such work as *The Woman who Rode Away.* In this work there is no question of a limited range. He is doing with prose, as in the novels, the work of poetry. (pp. 31-2)

**Fables** represents, too, the logical step forward which the attitude to life exhibited in **Mr. Weston's Good Wine** had promised. There was there the light as well as the dark wine. But the dark wine was the ultimate solace, which we will drink when we have tired of the lighter brand. Here there is little or no trace of the light wine. . . .

In all the best of these stories, as well as in **The Key of the Field**—an achievement more apparently impossible even than **Mr. Weston's Good Wine**—death is the dominant note. **Darkness and Nathaniel,** perhaps the most magnificent story in the book, shows in a very short space Powys' attitude in the later work, and in addition sums up the attitude of his earlier work. (p. 33)

William Hunter, in his The Novels and Stories of T. F. Powys, Gordon Fraser, Minority Press, 1930, 34 p.

## DONALD MacCAMPBELL (essay date 1934)

"All our little moral sensations are upon the surface of our lives; it is the great immoralist that lies beneath. And you have not got to go very far into the lives of the people before you come upon him." In these words, taken from the pages of *Soliloquies of a Hermit,* one finds an adequate expression of a thesis which Theodore Francis Powys attempts in all of his works to develop. Man, stripped of his virtuous mask, is little better—morally speaking—than the lower animals: greedy, cruel, and lustful. Yet by living, unmasked, on a naturalistic plane, and by yielding himself shamelessly to the various "moods of God" which normally would pass through his being, Man might more fully realize his mission on earth, which is simply to seize and enjoy the life around him, to pass his hours lazily in the sunlight, and to wax old by the measure of common, sensuous experience, assured that nothing in the end can really matter. (p. 461)

There is much in the *Soliloquies of a Hermit* that suggests both Llewelyn and John Cowper Powys—two more popular, though decidedly less talented, younger brothers. . . . In all three alike there is the same rugged individualism, the same contempt for hypocrisy, the same naïve respect for simple sensuous experience as an end in itself. And yet it were impossible, considering their efforts as a whole, to regard them as other than three distinct personalities, with the strange, ugly, almost terrifying, genius of Theodore standing well above the very capable talents of the other two. (p. 462)

Can it be that the world of T. F. Powys is too perverse, too unremittingly satanic, to gain any real hold upon the average discriminating reader? Of the many explanations which critics have given for his neglect, certainly this is not the least plausible. Indeed, there are those who believe that, were it not for the indescribable charm of his style, Powys would lose even the respect of the press. As it is, he may safely be called an author's author, for there is no man writing in England or America today who asserts a greater command over the various technicalities of prose fiction; and few excel him in sheer narrative power. Within a narrow, but carefully chosen, field he has found a new form for the novel—of which *Mr. Weston's Good Wine* should live as a classic example. But there are times when one feels certain that Powys has plotted his course through dangerous territory.

In using his peasants for the purpose of symbolizing the less attractive vices of civilized men and women—thus exposing the latter to mockery—the author has not only maligned the innocent folk whom he obviously loves but has needlessly exaggerated the vices themselves. Moreover, while he describes with humane tolerance and tireless humor the antics of his village immoralists—ever reminding us that beneath the surface we are all equally as vicious, and that honest vices are more lovable than dishonest virtues—one is still nothing loth to cleave to the traditional belief that, as Goethe once put it, Man must retain the essential illusions of life. And although in reality humanity be every bit as lustful, greedy and cruel as Powys would have us to believe, it is still consoling to defend ourselves at risk of self-deception with the thought that natural

human goodness can sometimes exist apart from imbecility. Nowhere in the world of this author's fantastic imagination can encouragement for such an idea be found. With his ugly, cynical understanding of depravity, he has peopled his little villages—Mockery Gap, Norbury, Folly Down, Tadnol, and the others—with a grotesque assortment of lunatics, harlots, libertines, procuresses, unbelieving clergymen, and insatiable monsters of brutality. If presented seriously, in the manner of the modern realistic novel, these characters would disgust even the most misanthropic of readers. But fortunately Powys is anything but a realist, and much of the ugliness which he describes is redeemed by his method of approach which is always to a considerable degree poetical, and frequently intensely humorous as well. His peasants speak in the quaint Dorsetshire dialect, and they live in the picturesque Wessex countryside—both of which facts account for much of the poetic side of his work. And while they are mere symbols—each standing for a particular human failing which is allowed to color his every action—their behaviour is so exaggerated, so distorted, that much of their wickedness can pass for pure nonsense. Critics have frequently described Powys' peasants as being both fantastic and true: fantastic inasmuch as their deportment is unreal; true inasmuch as the passions which direct their behaviour are invariably and unmistakably natural. (pp. 463-65)

[While Powys] is laying bare in his narrative the hidden animal in Man, he is implying at the same time—by means of an ingenious stylistic trick—that this animal can be not only charming but occasionally even amiable to behold. The trick itself is not easy to explain: it involves, for one thing, an ability to speak through form as well as through expression—through style as well as through narrative. By using an artificially simple vocabulary, which alone imparts a sort of innocency to the story, and by using beautiful, even poetic, phraseology in describing such things as rapes and murders, the author seems to feel that he can not only expose the natural propensities of civilized human-beings, but can lead the reader to believe that crimes such as these, when committed honestly, are not entirely unattractive—not without their peculiar charm. One must not forget for a moment that this peculiar charm lies not in the crimes narrated but rather in the narrator of the crimes. . . .

Powys, like most naturalists, is primarily interested in problems of Love and Death. Because he has assumed a Freudian attitude toward sex he is able to arrive at the conclusion that man is essentially an immoralist; and because he sees in death the annihilation of life—with all of its values—he has come to believe that it is best to ruminate like a cow. In short, God has but two gifts to offer the children of the world: the privilege of loving, and the privilege of dying. Such is the underlying philosophy of the author's masterpiece, *Mr. Weston's Good Wine.* (pp. 466-67)

In most of his books, Powys has employed some one of his characters as a mouth-piece. For example, in *Innocent Birds* he is Reverend Thomas Tucker, who believes that "whoever adds one tittle to the work of the world, or prevents one child from playing, commits the sin that can never be pardoned". In *Kindness in a Corner* he is Reverend Silas Dottery, who asks: "How can it be possible when all things die with us when we die—every candle going out like our candle—to hurt and torment one another as we do, when we are, as we all must be, in present view of utter destruction?" (p. 468)

In *Mr. Weston's Good Wine* one finds convincing proof of [Powys'] astounding powers of craftsmanship. Indeed, as William Hunter has pointed out in an admirable monograph [see excerpt above], the sly facility with which the author succeeds in introducing his symbolism into this work is truly remarkable. Actually it is not until the reader has advanced well into the body of the novel that he becomes conscious of the fact that Mr. Weston is the Almighty, that his Ford car is a symbol of the world, that the good wine which he offers is the wine of Love and Death, and that the lion is none other than Satan himself—this despite the carefully placed hints which are scattered throughout the pages from the very beginning. The same subtle method, incidentally, is used by Powys in presenting the symbol of the old oak tree in the same novel: not until many strangely amorous happenings have occurred thereunder does the reader suspect the tree to be the seat of ancient phallic love. Indeed, one must be ever on the lookout for such symbols, for Powys is as well grounded in Hellenism as in our own Hebraic mythology—although the Bible is unquestionably nearer to him, and represents perhaps his most constant source of inspiration.

The Bible—and, next to the Bible, John Bunyan—has exerted the strongest influence over him. But one must not assume from this that Powys' love for the Scriptures has been extended to the Church itself. On the contrary, never does his power of irony appear to better advantage than in those passages where he has set out to mock Christianity. (pp. 469-70)

Closely related to Powys' masterly power of ironic expression—which has been shown to be both bitter and playful—is another important aspect of his genius which, for want of a better word, may be called simply subtlety. By using the simplest language, and the most concentrated phraseology, he produces an atmosphere of innocence and naïveté which contrasts strangely with the wise and sophisticated outlook upon human perversities as revealed in the narratives themselves. It is just this facility for clothing a twentieth century sophistication in language as simple as the Authorized Version of the Holy Bible that makes T. F. Powys so extremely subtle. Indeed, judging from style alone, one might readily mistake him for a seventeenth century divine—contemporary with Jeremy Taylor and John Bunyan; but after examining the content of his stories—with their numerous examples of exhibitionism, nympholepsy, sadism, and masochism—one realizes at once that he belongs to the age of Sigmund Freud. (p. 471)

Perhaps this basic contradiction in Powys has had much to do with his being so frequently misunderstood. Despite the fact that he has written about what appear on the surface to be very simple people, and despite his numerous references to such quaint and child-like souls as Jeremy Taylor, Thomas Fuller, or John Bunyan, it is yet difficult to believe that the creator of such fantastic monsters as Charlie Tulk and Farmer Mew can honestly and boldly declare, as he does in his *Soliloquies of a Hermit,* that two of his greatest pleasures in life are digging in his little garden, and mending his broken fence-posts with pieces of string.

No novelist even in this Freudian era has made freer use of sex in his stories than has he. And yet one may rest assured that—to borrow the famous words of Bunyan—If all the fornicators and adulterers in England were hanged by the neck till they be dead, Theodore Francis Powys would still be alive and well! (p. 473)

*Donald MacCampbell, "The Art of T. F. Powys,"
in* The Sewanee Review *(reprinted by permission of
the editor; published in 1934 by The University of the South), Vol. XLII, No. 4, October-December,
1934, pp. 461-73.

### A. G. VAN KRANENDONK   (essay date 1944)

[T. F. Powys's novel *Unclay* is] in my opinion a veritable masterpiece of originality, written in the same simple, ironically prattling style as most of [his] others. In it he begins as usual by drawing an attractive, almost idyllic picture of the hunt and more especially of its leader, the abominable, blundering tyrant, hardly conscious of his own aims: Lord Bullman. A simple parson, Mr. Hayhoe, who happens to draw near, startled by the humming sound of bad curses, is able to render his noble lordship a slight service, whereupon the latter throws down from his saddle like a piece of liver to a poor dog the promise of the living of Dodder, the village recurring in almost every one of Powys' books. (p. 104)

In brief, the reader soon finds that the story is symbolic, that he has to do here with a modern "dance of death", and that one of the best and most moving ever written. We meet with a great variety of figures in the course of the tale, with many experiences and happenings and quaintly formulated meditations, some terrible or disgusting, others tender, others again lovely or funny or most often slily ironical, all very impressive and rendering the whole sphere of village life in a truly marvellous way. The principal love-story of the book, the deep young love between the simple Joseph Bridle, a type of the poor, honest, hard-working peasant and the beautiful but weakly Susie Dawe, the daughter of a grotesquely coarse, selfish, sadistically cruel farmer. One of the most moving scenes is the one where Joe to his intense sorrow sees Susie making advances to John Death, walking about with him on a chilly evening in the lanes, after which she makes it up again to Joe by her loveliness and passionate fervour, trying in vain, however, to keep away from John, who continues to attract her mysteriously. He has meanwhile found the awful paper again, on which is written "Unclay Susie Dawe and Joseph Bridle", "unclay", of course, meaning "put to death", and though he has not yet found his scythe, which has been stolen by the sadist farmer, he manages to obey the command of his High Master, the two lovers committing suicide in a dirty pond.

From time to time the allegorical figure of this master, of God himself, appears in the story, in the shape this time of a poor, melancholy tinker, who walks about near a hill in the neighbourhood, sometimes issuing from his hiding-place to chase away his servant John when the latter, teased by a village-maid, a real little hussy, tries to do her harm. But mostly even He seems unable to stop the fatal course of events, and one of the most touching passages in the whole book is that in which we see the melancholy Tinker, after some village outrage which He has not been able to prevent, creeping away in the dusk to his hill, shedding bitter tears.

John Death, innocently believing in his master's omnipotence, stays on in Dodder still, on the whole a pleasant companion, especially to the young, subtly influencing the lives of all the villagers, occasionally secretly "unclaying" some one, the dreaded enemy of the bad, the benefactor of the suffering good. His presence, and the antics of a few queer, of many stupid and some wise men, their curious relations and interactions, constitute a strange, varied story, with many unforgettable and some moving scenes, the like of which has but seldom been seen. Majestically it steers its high and difficult course to the very end, the current of its simple, babbling, but highly effective and pellucid style continuing unweakened, unfailing. It is a book containing vivid pictures of quaint and quiet village life, much wisdom and some bitterly sarcastic comments on life in general, yet mostly resigned, trusting in an ultimate that will prove good; the irony always disguised in seemingly inconsequential, or merely pleasant, chatting. (pp. 105-06)

*A. G. Van Kranendonk, "T. F. Powys," in* English Studies *(© 1944 by Swets & Zeitlinger B.V.), Vol. XXVI, No. 4, August, 1944, pp. 97-107.*

## MARTIN STEINMANN, Jr.  (essay date 1957)

Of the Georgians, T. F. Powys is surely the furthest removed from realism and naturalism and the farthest gone in symbolism (though the former are so influential that his novels and stories have been read—and both admired and loathed—as both true and false *reportage,* and though his sort of symbolism is hardly fashionable.) He is, indeed, so given to symbolism as to be almost literally incapable of writing in any other mode. His fiction is impersonal and universal, and at the same time individual: impersonal because it is autobiographical only in embodying his values and beliefs; universal because it is not "timely" and has no program; and individual because it is impersonal and universal and, hence, not naturalistic, and because its symbolism is in a different tradition from that of the other Georgians. (p. 49)

Most of Powys' characters are quite beyond the pale of realism and naturalism. . . . The good characters are innocents dominated by two principles, love and passivity. Though full of kindness and incapable of evil, they are infamously used by the villains and rewarded only by death, "God's best gift"; and they neither know how nor wish to resist evil. The villains are personifications of what are, for Powys, the four cardinal sins—greed, which entails the other three; anger; pride, which has first place because last to leave the sinful; and cruelty, the most potent of all. Inherent in these is lust, and hypocrisy sometimes masks (but intensifies) them.

Many of both the good and the evil characters, particularly in the early works, express or symbolize their virtues or vices in one or a pair of humors, interests which give not only pleasure but meaning and direction to existence and which sum up all there is to say about their characters. Mr. Tasker, for instance, has his pigs, Mrs. Crossley (**Black Bryony**), computations. Mrs. Dominy (**"Hester Dominy"**), rats and false teeth; the Reverend Robert Herrick (**"In Dull Devonshire"**), cider; Mr. Thursby (**"The White Weathercock"**), manners, stocks, and shares; Mr. Beggwell (**Mark Only**), mangel-wurzels; Mr. Hayhoe (**Unclay**), Jane Austen's novels; and John Chew (**"God"**), a hat.

Powys emphasizes the symbolic function of many of these "humorous" interests by identifying or associating them with religion. For the character, they objectify and symbolize his temperament or his plight; for the reader, abstract qualities. (pp. 51-2)

Some characters, moreover, systematically or momentarily, instead of or in addition to symbolizing virtues or vices, symbolize Biblical figures or saints. (p. 52)

Unlike the characters of the other Georgians, these characters have little complexity; they are usually characterized, for once and for all, and by their moral rather than their physical qualities, upon their first appearance; and they rarely develop. (p. 53)

There are, however, two important exceptions to [this generalization]. . . . In two of the early novels, **Black Bryony** and **Mark Only,** Powys essays with some success the creation of complex characters, many-sided characters who, moreover, are delineated—not in a block, by a portrait or a gesture—but gradually and through their actions. Second, the symbolical identity of those characters who stand for Biblical figures or saints—Mr. Weston is the most distinguished example—is seldom revealed at a stroke, though their moral natures—another dimension of their total significance—usually is; it is rather—and this is the source of the greatest esthetic pleasure—revealed gradually and with the subtlest kind of art. (pp. 54-5)

[Powys'] characters are not his spokesmen; and for this reason, and because of their simplification, distortion, and consequent lack of verisimilitude, the reader does not, and cannot, project himself into them. Unlike real people and the creations of the naturalist, they are interesting not as individuals but as symbols. Judged by realistic and naturalistic standards, they are failures. The innocents are improbable idiots, and the villains unbelievable monsters—but only if we lift them out of their stories and novels and set them down in Dorset or Bloomsbury; in the imaginative world of Powys' fiction, which has its own standards of normality, each has his place, ordained by the exigencies of theme. They take on interest and meaning only when viewed as part of the total pattern that is the story or the novel. Though they are related to life, they are not slices of life; the relation is indirect, through theme. Their coherence is internal, not external; they are consistent, not with life, but with one another and with the total pattern. These characters—as Eliot says of Jonson's (and the comparison is instructive)—"conform to the logic of the emotion of their world. They are not fancy, because they have a logic of their own; and this logic illuminates the actual world, because it gives us a new point of view from which to inspect it" ("Ben Jonson," *Selected Essays* 1917-1932).

Collectively, Powys' characters and his settings, like Faulkner's, constitute a mythical world. At least fifty of his characters, major and minor, appear, or are alluded to, in two or more stories or novels. Fewer than fifty mythical villages or towns suffice for the settings of the one-hundred and forty-two published works of fiction, and fewer than a dozen do service for perhaps three quarters of these works. (pp. 55-6)

[This] mythical world has a symbolic (and a linguistic) rather than a strictly literal unity—a moral rather than, for example, a geographical consistency—; and this unity, far from detracting from the artistic unity of individual works, makes that unity more evident. . . . Powys' fiction is in no sense a continuous, consistent, literal collective history or survey of his world. Though each work illuminates every other work in the way that *King Lear* illuminated *Antony and Cleopatra,* each work is an artistic unity in itself; or—if, as is sometimes the case (in **Mr. Tasker's Gods,** for example), it is not—the fault is internal and not the world's. The reader's previous acquaintance with a given character or setting can heighten his pleasure in, or provide him a clue to the interpretation of, a work that renews that acquaintance; but such previous acquaintance is neither a necessary nor a sufficient condition of his interpretation of that work, and sometimes, indeed . . . , it can be downright misleading. Such literal unity as Powys' world has—and, as we have seen, it has considerable—results from its technical and thematic unity, and not vice versa. The real unity is a unity of attitudes and ideas, and of tone, symbolic devices, and language. (pp. 56-8)

Powys' plots, like his characters and his settings, exist in a world far removed from that of strict cause and effect operating in accordance with psychological and sociological laws. It is an allegorical world in which the interactions of symbolic characters in symbolic settings figure a meaning: theme, rather than scientific law, is its master. The allegory—while in, and drawing much of its force from, the native English tradition—is yet different from the typical product of that tradition; and the difference is not simply of the sort that might result from (say) providing Christian with a Ford or Everyman with a television receiver. It is a modification in method as well as a substitution of matter, and it is in the creation of this "twisted" allegory—in William Hunter's fine phrase [see excerpt above] . . .—that Powys' great originality lies. In the uses to which he puts this allegory is a subtle art that an account of his simplified, typical characters would not lead us to look for. (pp. 58-9)

Powys' allegory is of two kinds. In both, there is a symbolic surface populated with concretes—people, animals, vegetables, minerals, artifacts—; and in both, the interactions of these concretes are a key to a meaning—a theme, a "significacio"—; and, in both, there is a subsurface populated with things that bear a one-to-one correspondence to the concretes on the symbolic surface and whose interactions correspond to the interactions of the concretes. In one, however, the concretes on the surface correspond to abstractions—virtues and vices, and such things as love and death—on the subsurface; while in the other, they correspond to other concretes.

And these two kinds of allegory may be, and usually are, mixed in various ways. On the symbolic surface of *Mr. Weston's Good Wine,* for instance, some of the concretes—notably the light and the dark wines—correspond to abstractions on the subsurface—love and death—; while others—Mr. Weston himself, for example—correspond to other concretes—God, in his case.

There is, moreover, a difference in the ways in which these two kinds of allegory figure themes. In the first kind, the abstractions on the subsurface are the real subjects of fictional discourse: *Mr. Weston's Good Wine* is a novel about love and death. In the second, however, the concretes on the subsurface are not the real subject: *Mr. Weston's Good Wine* is not a novel about God. Mr. Weston is the hero of his novel. He is in every way indispensable, and the two kinds of allegory are mixed there; but the subject of this novel is not God or any other concretes on the subsurface. . . . In the first kind of allegory, the concretes on the subsurface are (to use I. A. Richards' terminology) the vehicle, and the abstractions on the subsurface the tenor (Mr. Weston's wines, for example, are metaphors for love and death). In the second kind, the relationships between the concretes on the surface and those on the subsurface are various and complex. Typically, the concretes on the surface are the tenor, and the concretes on the subsurface the vehicle; there is, moreover, a kind of ironical tension between tenor and vehicle; and, finally, the allegory is so mixed with the first kind as to make the mixture three-dimensional. In *Innocent Birds,* for example, Deborah and Solly, *in respect of Moses and Joshua,* are the tenor, and Moses and Joshua the vehicles; and the comparison draws its force as much from differences as similarities. But, *in another dimension,* Deborah and Solly are not the tenor but the vehicle; in that dimension, Deborah is a personification of goodness, and Solly of modesty. Similarly, God's gift, a concrète on the surface, turns out to be death; and death as the greatest salvation, rather than the deliverance of the Israelites, is one of the themes of *Innocent Birds.* God (or nature) promises a great gift on both the surface

and the subsurface, and Deborah and Solly are His agents or interpreters on the surface as Moses and Joshua are on the subsurface. But how different the two surfaces are in other respects. Deborah is no stern lawgiver; Solly, no relentless warrior. On the contrary, both are unassuming, impractical, and endearingly unsententious; and both, though in one sense unworldly, are more concerned with the things of this world than with God (or—better, perhaps—more with Powys' god, who is nature, than with Moses'). This tension between the surface and the subsurface has the effect both of universalizing the specific events in the novel (that is, of giving a third dimension to the allegory, of establishing a synecdochic relationship between these events as vehicle and other events outside the novel as tenor, of making death the greatest gift, not only for Fred Pim and Polly Wimple, but for all mankind) and of understating the themes.

Powys' second kind of allegory, in its richness and complexity, does indeed deserve the epithet "twisted." But this account of it may suggest that the first kind, where concretes on the surface correspond to abstractions on the subsurface, the kind that sometimes gives a third dimension to the second kind, is (in the words of Coleridge's definition) . "but a translation of abstract notions into a picture language . . ." (*The Statesman's Manual,* where he contrasts "allegory" and "symbol"), an arbitrary and confusing (though elaborate and perhaps ornamental) way of saying something that could just as well—in fact better—be said in literal language, a cipher without the justification of secrecy. Such, however, is not the case. . . . Farmer Mew, in **"The Left Leg,"** for instance, is a concrete corresponding to an abstraction, avarice; but, far from being an arbitrarily chosen symbol of avarice, he "partakes of the reality which" he "renders intelligible"; he represents avarice in the only way that we do (or can) experience that quality: he embodies it, he enacts it. To say that a man is avaricious is to say that he behaves in certain specified ways; and Farmer Mew is a perfect symbol of this quality because he behaves in these ways, and in these ways only. The relation between the symbol and the thing symbolized is surely the fittest one possible: synecdochic—that between the class member and the class, between the individual and the special; such a symbol is surely an instance of the "translucence of the special in the individual." (pp. 59-61)

The relation between symbol and thing symbolized in this first kind of allegory is not, of course, always synecdochic. That between Mr. Weston's light and dark wines, on the one hand, and, on the other, love and death, for example, is metaphorical. But these symbols, like Farmer Mew, though (to be sure) for another reason, are not arbitrary. They are validated by the overall allegorical plan of the novel; and, granted Powys' attitudes towards, and beliefs about, love and death, they are naturally fitting metaphors.

Allegory of this first kind is the staple of Powys' fiction (as it is, indeed, of fiction generally); the second kind, where concrete corresponds to concrete, occurs only in fits and flashes in the early fiction and is used systematically—and then, of course, usually in a three-dimensional mixture with the first kind—only in *Innocent Birds, Mr. Weston's Good Wine,* and *Unclay.* (p. 62)

*Fables,* a collection of nineteen apologues or beast fables and Powys' favorite among his books, deserves special mention as something of a special case. In these stories, as I remarked earlier, animals, vegetables, minerals, artifacts, and even sensations—all equipped with such distinctively human attributes as speech—as well as people are characters; and the doings of these motley characters figure themes by means of both kinds of allegory. In **"Darkness and Nathaniel,"** for instance, one of the finest of these fables, the three main characters—Light, Darkness, and Nathaniel—figure the theme that man's true happiness lies, not in life and love, but in death. Light symbolizes the abstractions life and love, and Darkness the abstraction death; and Nathaniel symbolizes the concrete man or mankind. (p. 63)

Martin Steinmann, Jr., "The Symbolism of T. F. Powys," in Critique: Studies in Modern Fiction (copyright © by Critique, 1957), Vol. 1, No. 2, 1957, pp. 49-63.

## H. COOMBES  (essay date 1960)

[*Mr. Weston's Good Wine*] is Powys's masterpiece because it is his fullest and most perfect artistic utterance. It is without the faults that mar many of the longer works: exaggerated intensities and violences, Dickensian repetitiousness in the matter of idiosyncrasies and fancies, lack of satisfying positive values as embodied in people (as distinct from enriching pleasure in nature and contemplation), the flatness of an unforceful realism, whims of structure both in chapter- and paragraph-sequence. One or more of these is likely to be found, in these works, jostling the corresponding things of force, delicacy, and beauty. This is not so in *Mr. Weston,* where the communication of a mastery over a wide range of experience is achieved with scarcely a jarring note.

It has been my experience to hear more than one reader speak warmly and admiringly of *Mr. Weston's Good Wine,* while at the same time being uneasy about its 'meaning'. Everything that happens is clearly enough understood, but the character and function of Mr. Weston, and with him Michael, do not for many readers fit into either allegory or realism. It is somehow felt to be disconcerting to receive the impact of so much actual village life at the same time as having to keep in mind throughout that Mr. Weston is 'God'. And yet, do we have to keep it in mind? Once realised, is not the allegorical significance taken up, with an easy perfection, into the whole work? There ought to be no more difficulty in accepting the *Good Wine* than there is in accepting *The Tempest.* The power and nature of its language should be its warranty.

Acceptance of the mode doesn't of course guarantee immediate understanding of the whole novel. There are cruxes in the *Good Wine* which require a good deal of pondering. But despite their presence, and however puzzling they may be, the novel as a whole is no more 'strange' than (say) *The Scarlet Letter* or *What Maisie Knew.* (pp. 47-8)

One of the effects of the inclusiveness of Powys's imaginative sympathies is to give to his writing the kind of force and interest which is found often in, say, Langland and Bunyan, and sometimes in Swift. The harmonising of heterogeneous elements in story and in style springs out of a spirit that is fine because it is truly democratic. (p. 63)

The juxtapositions, the kind of wit involved, are not autonomous clevernesses but are inseparable from the progress and totality of the story. Moreover there are many passages of an easy-flowing eloquence, which, while it is controlled towards the significant issues and ends in view, is eager and warm. Quotation would have to be inconveniently lengthy to support these points, but I do not think they are likely to be disputed

by anyone who recalls or turns up the pages where (say) Michael explains the difference wrought on the earth and on people by the coming of darkness, or where he describes the sorrowing state of Mr. Grobe, or where Mr. Weston stands on the hill and surveys Folly Down, or where the spirit of the Angel Inn (at the end of chapter XVII) is conveyed.

There is no need here to demonstrate in any fullness the effectiveness of the specifically dramatic moments in the novel, of the evocations of atmosphere, of the humour of the rustic dialogue as distinct from the profounder colloquies. These things are there for all to see. The numerous realistic descriptions and the gestures and speech of every day mingle with scenes like that in which chilly horror descends on Mrs. Vosper's 'love'-parlour, when the 'clammy damp wound in coils about the girls', with the momentous silence and the stopping of time in the Angel Inn parlour, with the exultant encounter in love of Tamar and Michael, with strange steps heard, with the moments when the words 'Mr. Weston's Good Wine' are spoken, and so on: they add up to a total 'atmosphere' where actuality and the temporal are firmly grasped and at the same time given a visionary quality embracing both physical and moral significances.

Nor is it necessary at this juncture to do more than touch upon the presence of topics and themes which enrich and diversify the whole. For instance, there is the question of responsibility, of man's free will: is it God or Mr. Grunter who is responsible for the troubles of Folly Down? Then there is the life of nature, self-contained, apart from man. . . . Luke Bird, the simple idealist, finds that the geese which he would like to baptise have a 'hatred of religion', a 'contempt for Christianity'. The relationship of Nature and art, primal matter and civilisation, is referred to more than once. . . . (pp. 64-5)

The variety of life, of Nature, seen and enjoyed and suffered and pondered, is shaped into the work of art which is *Mr. Weston's Good Wine.* The omnipresent wine unifies all. The language, easily collocating familiar and solemn, comic and transcendental, is beautifully controlled to dramatic, ironic, 'atmospheric' ends. The wonderful conclusion of the book again reminds one of *The Tempest* or *A Winter's Tale* in the way it gathers strands together and culminates in a certain rich relief and establishes a kind of peace. (pp. 65-6)

Without insisting on further possibilities of comparison, it can justly be said that *Mr. Weston's Good Wine* is among the finest of those 'novels as dramatic poems' which hold more of the English body and spirit, more essential Englishness than any other *genre* since Jacobean times. And for those who may not care to consider Powys a novelist at all, as not providing a sufficient wealth of 'realistic' character and fact, there is the choice between allegorist and fabulist. But considering what a variety of writers come under the term 'novelist' it would seem that Powys is most satisfactorily included among them. (p. 68)

To say that T. F. Powys is among our great short story writers is to say that his finest achievements in this *genre* engaged his full creative energies. They are an expression, subtly and movingly presented, of certain profound interests and preoccupations, and a reader who doesn't approach them with a set expectation of the conventional short story ingredients and methods can hardly fail to be struck by their power and originality. Of the hundred or so short stories that Powys wrote, the fables and a few others, perhaps some thirty works in all, have the quality we hint at when we speak of fineness and permanence. Many of the rest are in one way or another attractive and interesting, and quite a number are very small affairs. (p. 69)

The fables conform to what we understand as such, in that feelings and speech and actions are given to animals and inanimate things, and the narratives and interactions and dialogues become ways of presenting human situations. But no simple moral of the Æsop kind is to be drawn from them. It is not the conclusions that count but the full liberating and widening effect (as in, say, *Volpone,* or *Middlemarch* or *St. Mawr*) of the interplay of various feelings and attitudes, the pattern of humour, irony, anger, warm affirmation, wit gentle or sardonic. We are made to feel the wisdom of avoiding simple comprehensive judgments. Issues which may at first appear simple are shown to be delicate and ambiguous. In listening to discussion between a tombstone and a skull, between a withered leaf and a green one, between a hassock and a psalter, our sympathies and assent are likely to veer from one to the other and are often not settled even by the final, seemingly clinching episode, the smashing of the skull, the (green) leaf blown off in the storm, the burning of the hassock. The moral effect of the fables lies in their art: by their incident and dialogue, by the finely sustained tone, they move, invigorate, and enlighten. They add up to a humane vision of life, rendered with beauty and power. (p. 70)

In *The Stone and Mr. Thomas* the intense appreciation of lived actualities is balanced with a no less complete knowledge of annihilation and oblivion. The skull of Mr. Thomas, lying upon a rubbish-heap, in an argument with his gravestone will not believe that he, who enjoyed so much, is forgotten. . . . The stone is unmoved by all the 'fine talk'; it alone will last. In the end the poor skull is reduced to admitting the futility of his former life. But the homely confident tone of the stone, while utterly and unfeelingly nullifying the pretensions of the skull, and virtually negating his being, nevertheless contains the suggestion, unexpected but spontaneous, of new life and usefulness in 'excellent cool dung for spring onions'. (p. 80)

When Powys reduces pretensions, when he puts egocentricity and the over-grand and the inflated into perspective, it is rarely that mockery is the sole or chief impulsion. His dealings with solemnities real or factitious are more often than not touched or suffused with a compassionate humour; there is a quiet regardfulness for all forms of life, a concrn for the moderate pleasures of everyday. (p. 81)

The fables, simple in a superficial sense—never an unusual and rarely a long word, never an involved sentence—and developing with plenty of external action and incident and lively dialogue—. . . the fables, simple-seeming, often work with a subtle interplay of viewpoints in a presentment of complexities. (p. 87)

The remaining eighty-odd of Powys's short stories are not fables; almost all of these are very short. With a few exceptions, they could fairly readily be grouped into categories: humorous, serious-moral, whimsical, pathetic, sentimental-melodramatic, allegorical-supernatural, horror.

On the whole, although Powys's humour finds felicitous expression over and over again, the lighter stories are the weaker. Too often the story is a mere elaboration of a fancy. . . .

In some of the stories the moral is less illustrated than integral, and this is so because genuine feeling, even though without any very great strength or depth, accompanies the small, neatly executed structure of character, event, and sometimes symbol. In *Jane Mollet's Box,* for instance, there is something more than fanciful embroidering of a common Christian-virtue theme. (p. 89)

These particular stories seem to me to be just on the credit side of sentimentality. Without great force, they nevertheless impress with a certain warmth and a certain sharpness of statement. This sharpness, effectively employed for narrative and simple dramatic purposes in a number of Powys's short stories (in some, the material and intention being so slight, it is little more than a mannerism) is not of course the same thing as the compactness and pregnant economy of the fables proper. It is nonetheless original and remarkable. *Lie Thee Down, Oddity!* with its significance of contrast between lawn and heath, its Mr. Cronch who obeys his profound impulse to do good though he knows the dangers of so doing in a world organised as ours is, its suggestive touches of description, its skilful juxtaposing of social wrongs with Mr. Cronch's actions—he is unsanctimonious like Christ—is one of several realistic-allegorical stories whose excellence depends largely upon that concise manner. In this connection *Uriah on the Hill, What Lack I Yet?* and *The Dewpond* come to mind.

Extreme instances of greed and cruelty—cruelty in particular—and of terror and anxiety, make up the material for Powys's purely 'horror' stories. They are without any Poe-like luridness, but whether they are direct-overt accounts or skilful structures of ironies and innuendoes, they can be classed 'horror' because of their intensity. They all have, it seems to me, a basis of psychological truth even though the facts of the story are on occasions like those of the most highly-coloured and bizarre occurrences reported in the most sensational newspapers. They are real enough to be shocking, especially to those who believe that there are certain things about human nature that are best left unrecognised. The proportion of ostriches among those who read Powys is likely to be very small, though it can be admitted that if a man spent his writing-life predominantly on works of this kind he would be stamped as narrow, unfree, sombre, obsessed. Powys never forgot the force and incidence of human depravity of the darkest kind, but the short stories dealing exclusively with that are very few, perhaps half a dozen. (pp. 90-1)

Selfishness, grossness, callousness, perverse sexuality, are portrayed in an astonishing short story called *The Barometer.* It is astonishing because of the force generated by the perfectly deliberate laconic unfolding of a vicious situation and action; nothing is commented on, the writer seems to be merely narrating and describing; but echoes and cross-references, odd facts and occurrences are seen finally to link up in the whole pattern. The pattern is not a big and rich one, and the range of feeling is narrow. But even when the manner of functioning of the barometer is known, and the identity of the pig, and the significance of certain things which at a first reading are likely to seem merely irrelevant, the duplicity and the completeness of the callousness continue to make themselves felt both in the structure and in the deadly detachment of the telling. The closeness of the organisation is such that quotation would not be helpful without a more complete exposition of the story. . . . If *The Barometer* fails to be a great short story it is because its concern is with a corner and not with a central node of human affairs. Perhaps its quality is best suggested by calling it a striking *tour de force,* where preoccupation with the human problem counts for less, if only a little less, than technique. There is not quite the fusion that is so perfect in the fables.

Several of the longer short stories, on the other hand, with deeply felt themes and containing magnificent passages, seem to me faulty technically, inclined to looseness and rambling. The allegorical **When Thou Wast Naked,** for instance, despite the interest and the convincingness of the presentment of good-natured Mr. Priddle, and the odd charm of much of the incident, involving (say) snobbery, or social ambition, or modern rush, has too many Biblical analogies and too much barely-relevant material. There is some excellent writing, as when the source of the quite innocent Mr. Priddle's money is indicated—the Great War. . . . And the conclusion, too lengthy to quote here, admirably suggests the trivial-minded worldliness of the gossipers as well as the pathos of the defeated and ruined Priddles. That the impression we have, notwithstanding our discovery of the (neat but not very significant) references to many details in Ezekiel XXIII and in spite of our seeing Mr. Priddle as another version, well presented, of that prophet—the Word of the Lord, but kindly and charitable—is one of pathos and not tragedy, perhaps indicates the general feeling-tone of this interesting tale. (pp. 92-3)

In making the generalisation that the writings of T. F. Powys (with the possible exception of his first book, the **Interpretation of Genesis**) are marked by an original style, the sort of originality that is meant is not one that is striking merely by virtue of novelty. Although it is possible to isolate certain qualities of that originality, T. F. Powys's writing is one of those cases where style and substance are in the last analysis inseparable.

If diction were the main criterion, there would not be a simpler writer in the language than T. F. Powys. He is content with the words of everyday use, and he never gives them arbitrary meanings. Likewise there are no inversions or convolutions of language. Yet his use of the ordinary yields a style which gives us as a main impression the sense of successful endeavour to write as if from scratch, starting again with a new and fresh and simple language to convey a new and fresh vision of things and happenings and people. (pp. 111-12)

[Powys] found man's moral life a theme for amusement as well as compassion, but his mockery was not frivolity; and the fascination that he found in the forms of everyday life did not turn him into a superior spectator. A church in Powys is always a country church with its quiet architectural beauty and the feeling it gives of what the centuries have left there; and at the unfrequented back of the church are a heap of sweet grass-cuttings, a rusty wheelbarrow, and a lean-to shed with a few tools and an ash-bin. It is because human living, around us now and always, is never forgotten by Powys, that his style is unique in its combination of homeliness and strength. (pp. 121-22)

> *H. Coombes, in his* T. F. Powys *(© 1960 by H. Coombes; reprinted by permission of Joy Coombes), Barrie and Rockliff, 1960, 173 p.*

## W. I. CARR (essay date 1964)

It may be said at once that T. F. Powys was not a great creative writer. The reader who has been disturbed and moved by what is truly significant, truly living, in Powys's art will say this with reluctance. Not many English writers of the present century can offer so humane and so unrelenting a scrutiny of fundamental preoccupations, and there is more than enough reason for supposing that the critical function has not served him well. (p. 8)

Some of the reasons for Powys's neglect, however, may be ascribed to the kind and degree of his originality. His was an intensely English genius, and yet one which has nothing to do with the development of the English novel. His achievement was carried out in absolute isolation from everything except his Dorset experience and the singular list of writers who positively fed his imagination: Shakespeare, certain seventeenth-century divines, Bunyan, Jane Austen, and, of course, the Bible. (Also, one feels, though without the relevant evidence, the George Eliot of *Silas Marner*.) Powys obviously had the kind of vision which unerringly selects what is vital to its own nourishment.

Yet one has to admit a certain monotony of creation and a constricted sensibility. There are villains who reappear in Powys's fictions, archetypes of greed, cruelty, and selfishness, whom the reader soon comes to know and begins to lose interest in. We have Mrs. Vosper, triumphantly, in **Mr. Weston's Good Wine,** and the bland, ironic comedy of Miss Pettifer in **Innocent Birds;** but we have also Charlie Tulk, Mr. Bugby, Jimmy Peddle, and Mr. Tasker's father, who could be interchanged without important alteration to their different tales. They are really all the same person, and one is driven to reservations about an art which seemed to need that degree of provocation to warm it into life. These reservations become sharper in proportion as the central characters appear inertly acted upon, rendered through simple, reiterated gestures, or are just not present with any conviction at all. Human vindictiveness is permitted to act as too large a stimulus in the creation of the particular fable; or rather—and this is the more generous way of putting it—Powys's apprehension of it is so stringent that it becomes the dominant element in his experience; having the compelling force of an obsession, the artistic account of it tends towards the mechanical. That Powys's 'good' characters are nearly always on the edge of events suggests an impairing of real vitality. Powys had not consistently the creative resources for embodying the horrifying intensities of his inner experience, and one finds him frozen into a posture of resignation or savage contempt. It is a little as though (by analogy) Shakespeare had not progressed beyond *Troilus and Cressida*.

The impression left by a novel like **Mr. Tasker's Gods**, for example, is finally one of disordered repulsion. The Reverend Hector Turnbull, one of the principal characters in the book, is initially a masterly study in cruel hypocrisy, present through that disturbingly idiosyncratic style of Powys's, a mixture of surface simplicity and profound metaphorical economy. . . . But it is not with the inevitability of art that the Reverend Hector Turnbull is made to die a contemptible death in pursuit of a young girl in a dingy back bedroom. And the different weaknesses of his sons, genteel and venal, appear as things tacked on, as trailing behind the character. . . . The prim stiffness of the prose and the tone of uplift remind one of a Victorian children's book. There is the risk of real unfairness, of course, in suggesting without qualification that the malevolence is mechanically induced. There is nothing prefabricated about Powys's moral horror, no intent to trap the reader by automatic violence. **Mr. Tasker's Gods** has moments of genuinely shocking power in its diagnosis of what men can do to each other—all accepted by Powys with a kind of terrifying calm (an advantage he has over Faulkner with his rather down-at-heel apologetic liberalism).

But the scales are unfairly weighted: there seems to have been some profound disorganization in Powys's being, evident in the strains and false resolutions of the work. His moments of refuge from the claims of a tormenting imagination are to be found in a work like *The White Paternoster*, a collection of tales, mostly frail pieces recording some fitful perception of good or evil. (pp. 9-10)

The best things, however, those to which a reader might be unreservedly directed, are *Innocent Birds, In Good Earth, No Painted Plumage*, and *Mr. Weston's Good Wine*—a work which ought to find a natural place in any responsible discussion of the achievement of the English novel, a work of profoundly original imagination. It is Powys's major work, a rich, moving, comic meditation upon the gift of life and the death which gives it significance, a generous quest for the sources of value and the evil which seeks to thwart them. . . . The art is that of allegory, but without the simplifications and evasions that allegory (including that of Powys himself) is skilful at concealing. The presentation is without portentousness, without that deft juggling that can be found at times in, say, Hawthorne (another great allegorist), where the detail, the local perception, seems to offer a vitality that does not inform the whole. How much better Powys could have handled things like *Ethan Brand* and *Wakefield*!

The instinct behind *Mr. Weston's Good Wine* is one of profound affirmation, immediately present in the varieties of tone and inflexion, the shades of emphasis that indicate a close and delicate relation with all the complexities of the theme. One has, for example, in the marriage of Jenny Bunce and Luke Bird (who is much more than the sometimes rather unimpressive Holy Fool) the whole creative significance of sexual desire, its mingled joy and pain, and the sanctities which should attend its consummation. It is handled with charitable and sensitive comedy, and a humane awareness of implication and attitude that speaks for itself against the infelicity of Richard Hoggart's reference to the 'apples be ripe bucolics of T. F. Powys'. Here is an imaginative and moving presentiment of what can be between a man and a woman, of a quality that sends the reader to Lawrence for a fuller understanding. Powys is the lesser writer, of course, but he has his own way of developing his awareness of the relationship: the suffering involved, the splendid comedy of Luke's growing realization of what is happening to him, from his absurd but touching speech on temperance to the owner of a brewery, his sermons to the bulls, and his marriage to Jenny, his whole life, indeed, assuming shape and proportion, stature and significance. The art that can give us this, the sense of Luke's innocence as something unreal and uncreated without Jenny, is a conduit of life, and the novel as a whole is the work of a writer at the full maturity of very individual powers. The one weakness is in the treatment of Tamar Grobe and her dealings with Michael. Tamar's father is so poignantly present in his isolation from life, with his one brief glimpse of happiness so terribly denied him, that Tamar herself suggests a certain insistent 'business', a groping for a significance which is not actual to Powys himself. The scenes between Tamar and Michael have enough lingering beauty of effect to qualify, a little, the central purposes of the book. A nimbus of ambiguity surrounds them. If the love/death urge which they seem to embody is so important to Powys the moral balance of the novel is out of true. Most readers are bound to feel that, among the human characters, it is Mr. Grunter who really counts in his contemplation of death and his realization of the destiny of Ada Kiddle.

The implications of the Tamar/Michael relationship are insistently present (in differing ways) in *In Good Earth* and *Unclay*. The feeling that death gives significance to life, is almost the source of life's strenuous attraction, has become disconcertingly relaxed. Death has assumed such proportions of sweetness that life hardly seems worth living. In *In Good Earth* John Gidden's anguished pursuit of what is really important to him, his progress through the pride of possession, the pride of lust, and the pride of reputation, against the background (or rather as an aspect) of the seasons and the barren hopeless farm he has to till, is done with the fertile economy of a master of the Morality. But his final awareness of death (the Good Earth) as providing the great moment of release and fulfilment is merely disconcerting. What we are invited to endorse is suicide. In *Unclay* the attraction of death is so insistent a presence, and yet essentially so vague in what it might mean for human beings, that the actual living of the hero and the heroine are drained of vital content. The reader comes away exasperated from his grappling with an elusive and unrealized significance.

*Innocent Birds* is weakened by the thinness, the externally established pathos, that invests its two central figures. The strengths of the book lie in the ironic dealings with Miss Pettifer, and the rich assertion of the power of kindness and the reality of human dignity; of the maturity of those who have a courageous and unsentimental feeling for human life as they are obliged to live it, whose endurance of what is daily their ranks among the great human qualities. Mr. Solly with his garden and *History of the Americans*, Mr. Hayhoe's behaviour in the situation which lack of imagination has forced upon him, Mr. Chick's timid dodging of the gravedigger, and Mr. Pym's puzzled awe before the mysteries of conception, birth, and death—these challenge the reader's own narrowly drawn assurances. And mention must be made of *Fables* (reprinted as *No Painted Plumage*). . . . The fables themselves are not all of the same power, though even the slighter require careful attention. *The Seaweed and the Cuckoo-clock* may be briefly noted as a fine comic treatment of the wilful curtailment of experience, the rigorous imposition of our preconceptions upon the variety which surrounds us. But almost none of the fables are capable of simple reduction; their ambiguity derives from the nature of their subjects, from the tensions within and the possibilities which confront any deeply felt human situation.

At the centre of Powys's art there is the profoundest respect for human beings and the life they are given. His hold upon the experience which he turns into art is sometimes perilous enough, in ways already suggested; but he has with his impressive seriousness of purpose and his moral cast of mind (which is nearly always so much more than harsh, simple-minded conclusiveness) qualities which relate him to the great masters. His individuality is evident both in the form he chose for expression and in the themes he commands. His treatment of sexual relations, for instance, exemplifies a humanitarian common sense that has nothing at all to do with the buttock-slapping and prurient sniggers of which his work has been frequently accused. Indeed, he should be felt as a cleansing agent in any discussion of sexual morality (a role which would seem to have been committed to the charge of Mr. Nabokov). He really sees what one usually thinks one sees, with unflinching attention to what he feels to be the conditions of experience. There are times when the reader will not be with him, but there will be no relaxing of sympathy for an effort at understanding so tenacious and so delicate: understanding of the dense texture of appetite, moral decision, and human feeling, the finally tragic attempt to present an allegory of how we live. T. F. Powys has no relation to the dominant literary interests and movements of the last thirty years or so, but it is a signal lack in one's experience as a reader not to know him. (pp. 10-12)

W. I. Carr, "T. F. Powys: A Comment," in English, Vol. XV, No. 85, Spring, 1964, pp. 8-12.

## M. BUNING (essay date 1969)

[Powys's short story] *Come and Dine* can be seen as a modern adaptation of the biblical parable as related in S. Matthew 22: 1-10, where the Realm of Heaven is compared to a king, giving a marriage banquet in honour of his Son. The official guests refusing to come, the servants are ordered to go out in the streets inviting good and bad alike. . . . The title of the story itself refers to the words spoken by Jesus to his disciples at the Last Supper. It is an invitation to share ritually in the mysteries of Life and Death. There are many other New Testament references, notably to the Beatitudes (S. Matthew, chapter V), where the humble and the pure in heart are promised inheritance of the earth and the sight of God, and to the various warnings against the rich, personified in this story by Miss Pettifer and the squire's family.

In this story the central symbol of food and drink suggests spontaneous living and communication with the others. The religious overtones are unobtrusively woven into the story without any moralizing or dogmatizing. In fact the implied author celebrates a modern, 'horizontal' view of religion: to believe is to be in solidarity with one's fellow beings. From this solidarity Miss Pettifer and the Cosser family are excluded; for them religion is an outward coat. They are the archetypes of hypocrisy, selfishness and pride. Their negative nature is rendered symbolically in images associated with Hell, and through bland irony. (pp. 595-96)

This short-story contains some characteristically Powysian characters and situations, such as the character of Mr. Dirdoe, who sides with his parishioners against officialdom, and who shows a sympathetic understanding of human weakness and imperfection, symbolized in the village whore Ann Loop. A similar situation is described in the novel *Unclay* in the relationship between Mr. Hayhoe and Daisy. It is interesting to note that John Death, the main character in that novel, is referred to in passing. The similarities with Powys's major work *Mr Weston's Good Wine,* however, are of greater importance, since they relate to theme as well as technique. Both deal with the metaphysical question about God's presence in daily circumstances and human contacts. Is it a hallucination, a hoax or a reality?

In both works this question is put by the innkeeper, and the answer is given in symbolic terms in the presence of Mr Weston. In the novel the scene of revelation is the local pub, where the epiphany is enacted; in the short-story the scene is transferred to the church. In either case Mr Weston is the mediator and agent of ultimate discovery. Both works are allegories, being based upon earlier story frames, which are themselves double-levelled. The central, archetypal symbol in each work is the wine which becomes real and makes reality appear an illusion. Both stories are presented with much authorial control (see, for example, the introduction of Jessie Barret in chapter V), explicit side comments and scenic presentation. There is a perfect fusion of idiosyncratic, colloquial diction—much of it in stylized Dorset dialect—and biblical speech.

Interestingly enough the lion which plays such an important and haunting part in the novel, as the instrument of wrath and punishment, appears again in the later story, though only in a minor way, when this Apocalyptic Beast is chased by one of Mr Weston's servants with a 'flaming sword'.

In relation to the novel *Come and Dine* is, of course, a limited achievement. It does not possess the same degree of rich texture, allegorical complexity and symbolic significance as *Mr Weston's Good Wine.* Yet it will surely come to occupy a unique position in Powys's oeuvre. There is nothing of the macabre or the obsessional qualities which at times disturb the total impact of his other works. The sexual undertones are there, such as in Mr Board's strange dealings with women (including his own wife), or in the hint of Miss Pettifer's fear of masculinity, and in the presentation of God as the fulfillment of female desire, but they are integrated within the total framework. Likewise, though Death is present, it is organically controlled by the theme.

*Come and Dine* is positive and affirmative in tone, showing a profound respect for human beings and the lives they lead. Powys has succeeded in fusing the realistic and the symbolic modes and levels of style and theme, endowing them with the simplicity of a Christmas story, as well as with the integrity and profundity of a moral fable. (pp. 596-97)

M. Buning, "Folly Down Revisited: Some New Light on T. F. Powys," in English Studies (© 1969 by Swets & Zeitlinger B.V.) Vol. 50, No. 6, December, 1969, pp. 588-97.

## GLEN CAVALIERO (essay date 1977)

[In T. F. Powys's] early books rustic society has no romantic qualities. **'Hester Dominy',** the second story in *The Left Leg* volume, is especially concerned with the sheer boredom of much village life (a boredom reflected too in the flatness of the writing and the listless nature of the tale). It is a classic statement of futility. Religion has become a matter of listening to the church-bells: with a quiet effectiveness peculiarly his own, Powys anatomises the stultifying effects of conventional Christianity. . . . There is no denunciation of man or fate, only weary resignation. What lightens the tale is compassion, nowhere in Powys's work so touchingly evidenced as in his treatment of the old village women. The chapter called 'Old Feet', besides anticipating his later use of mythological elements, is notable for the tenderness with which he treats the willing victims of that living death symbolised by the message of the bells. (pp. 176-77)

*Black Bryony* is similarly pessimistic, and its title contains an unpleasant pun, since the bryony refers not only to the weed of that name—a symbol here of sexuality—but also to the baby who is burnt to death in the fire at Norbury Rectory. This is the poorest of the novels, disjointed in construction and implausibly motivated; but it has its moments of intensity, as in the strange opening when the Salvation Army girl binds the black bryony wreaths about her head, or when the kind old rector, Mr Crossley, watching the flames devour his house, learns to love his flock—fire, in this novel, being a symbol of purging, though it is also one of destruction. In Powys's world the two concepts are usually the same.

*Mark Only* is the last and most accomplished of this early group of 'dark' novels. It is the life story of a ploughman, a quiet, simple man born to be cheated and oppressed. The tone of the book is almost entirely negative, its action determined by the author's pessimistic vision. Mark, misnamed at the very font, is exploited by his family and the evil Charlie Tulk; even the love of his young wife Nellie cannot stand up to the brutality in man. Death, once more, is the rescuer, personified in Mark's vision of the dogs who are pursuing him. At the end 'the dogs had him, the good dogs'.

The wickedness of man is here seen as endemic in nature itself. In no other of Powys's novels is the country painted in such austere, drab colours, the action taking place against a predominantly winter landscape, with a great emphasis on dirt and smells. In places the book attains a Hardy-like grandeur, as in those moments when the figure of the ploughman is seen upon the skyline; but the narrative is overloaded with authorial comment and an almost mechanical insistence upon gloom. What gives it solidity and persuasiveness is the sensibility with which the character of Mark himself is presented, and the robustness and roundedness of the 'good' characters, who are treated here far more convincingly than are the innocents of Powys's later work: the friendly farmer Peter Andrews is alive in a way that few of Powys's puppet-like characters are alive. Moreover there begins to appear in this book that black humour which is one of Powys's most distinctive characteristics. . . . (pp. 177-78)

There is still more humour in the novels of the middle period. . . . [*Mockery Gap, Innocent Birds,* and *Mr Weston's Good Wine*] are mellower in tone than the earlier ones, partly because the author postulates some kind of alleviating activity within the general horror of existence. The figures of Tinker Jar, the Fisherman, and Mr Weston are attempts to define and illustrate what might be called this internal providence. (p. 178)

[A] sense of irrational disturbance is frequent in Powys's work; and it develops from novel to novel. In **'The Left Leg'**, the earliest of the tales to treat of providence, the disturbance takes the form of Tinker Jar's vengeance upon the cruel and greedy Farmer Mew; but Jar is little more than a figure of retribution. He is not integrated into the nature of the surrounding world like the Fisherman in *Mockery Gap* or the incomparable Mr Weston. Indeed Powys seems unsure as to whom Mr Jar represents. His name suggests identification with the God of the Old Testament, his come-and-go existence with the Son of Man wandering upon the face of the earth. But God is Himself invoked by name in a passage recalling Powys's earlier speculations in *Soliloquies of a Hermit*. . . .

This book, a collection of meditations in rural solitude, belongs to a genre frequently to be published at this time. . . . [In *Soliloquies of a Hermit*] Powys transcends the sensibility and attendant diction of his age. He creates the rural experience anew, and in doing so he sees the Deity revealed in the life of nature. (p. 179)

In *Mockery Gap* the interest is transferred from God to man. The book is a study of a village community, and of the nature of human desire and its fulfilment. In its quiet way it is a critique of romanticism. The villagers are stirred up to expect something exciting to happen, something symbolised by the elusive Nellie-bird, which is interpreted in various manners and according to their own natures by those who believe in its coming. But their real desires are met by the Fisherman, who for a while takes up his residence by the sea, which they are too unadventurous to visit.

The Fisherman is an interesting variant on Powys's figures of remedial providence. He is the youngest and sexually the most attractive of them, and while he influences the action he takes no part in it. (p. 181)

But *Mockery Gap* is remarkable less for its picture of the providence of God than for its portrayal of village life. The little community near the sea is more realistically treated than in the rest of Powys's work, the children especially, viewed as they are from the standpoint of an alarmed adult. The feud between the Prings and the Pottles has all the rancour and venom of something observed and experienced; and the particular quality of Powys's awareness is caught in his remark that 'In every village almost that we can think of . . . there is a blind lane that leads nowhere, or at least, if it does lead somewhere, 'tis but to a cottage and a pond, and there the lane ends.' Close familiarity with his village world informs all Powys's writing; he conveys, for all the mannered quality of his prose, a keen sense of the slowness and monotony of rural life, and the feel, as much as the look, of stiles and paths and hedgerows. (pp. 181-82)

*Innocent Birds, Mockery Gap*'s companion, is an altogether grimmer affair, and is among the more reflective novels. Here too we are presented with a village community, but the inhabitants of Madder (*Innocent Birds* is a kind of sequel to **'The Left Leg'**) are more crudely contrasted in their good and evil. (p. 182)

The central weakness of *Innocent Birds,* as of *Mockery Gap,* is the feebleness of the forces for good; to be good in Powys's world seems to necessitate being a little stupid also. A naïvety of moral presentation is coupled with a theological uncertainty: this robs the books of an energy sufficient to keep them credible. Both *Mark Only* and *Mr Tasker's Gods* have more conviction. But these intermediate novels, the preludes to Powys's supreme achievements, are stronger than their predecessors in more important qualities than narrative power or certainty of aim—they are richer in compassion and more secure in their hold on the actualities of human life. There is a beautifully controlled pathos in the story, in *Mockery Gap,* of the lovelorn Miss Pink, while *Innocent Birds* is rich in moments of humorous melancholy. . . . (p. 184)

[Humanity] is abundantly present in *Mr Weston's Good Wine,* which is Powys's undisputed masterpiece. (p. 185)

*Mr Weston's Good Wine* would not be the masterpiece it is if it did not incorporate the darker side of Powys's imagination; but there is no morbidity. The crude brutalities of the early novels are exchanged for a more genuine realism. The scene in which the Mumby brothers are taken to the graveyard to see the decomposing body of the girl whom they have raped and driven to suicide has a Webster-like gruesomeness; but it is also sombrely moral. (p. 186)

It is [the] timeless element in the book which gives it its artistic unity. The ingredients of the novel are those familiar to us from Powys's other work; but here they all subserve a central purpose, and centre upon a particular theme. It is the most optimistic of the books, suffused with a genial peacefulness that comprehends its darker insights. We are a long way from the bitterness of *Mr Tasker's Gods.* (It is also free from the archness and whimsicality that mar all the other novels, *Mark Only* excepted: the youthful and lamented Mrs Grobe is a great improvement upon all the tiresome merry maidens who frisk and skip their way through too many of Powys's pages.) The novel is the affirmation of an eternal world of values which underlies and supports the limited world of Folly Down, so that the oak-tree bed where the Mumby twins seduce the village girls can also be seen as the meeting place of earth and heaven. But there is nothing portentous about the treatment: all is seen as being natural, part of a single reality.

But perhaps because of this timeless element, *Mr Weston's Good Wine* is less vivid as a picture of country life than are the other novels. The bucolic element subserves the symbolic end; and, real as Landlord Bunce, Mr Grunter and the rest are, we see them always in the light of Mr Weston's visit. It is this which most clearly demonstrates Powys's particular significance as a novelist of rural life. He used his knowledge of the country to create a representative world within which he could work out his speculations on the nature of God and man. Far from being a narrowly 'rustic' writer or the mere exploiter of a particular region, Powys is more in the nature of a seer—as his first champion, Louis Wilkinson, suggested [see excerpt above]. (pp. 187-88)

[Powys's work] stands outside time or fashion. And although its bucolic world can feel monotonous and small, it *is* a world, a distillation of the rustic experience through which Powys's supremely original mind and sensibility could express their responses to the fundamental experiences of human life. He has nothing ostensibly to say to the twentieth century—in this respect he is the rural novelist *par excellence*—and he often utters the great platitudes in a voice that does little to disguise them; but for the most part it is the manner in which he works, his gifts as a literary artist, that put a new perspective on familiar matter, his style at its best being so clean-cut that simply to read it is to be mentally quickened and invigorated. Above all he celebrates the rural world, not by exploiting its historical aspect, not by any working up of regional scenery, but by relating it to the permanent realities of human existence. His originality provides a methodology; the quietness of his tone has a steady insistence comparable to the working of a mole. His own sophistication of mind prevents him from being an 'earthy' writer in the crude sense—though it is surprising how much one is aware, despite the absence of descriptive set-pieces, of the actual landscape and of primitive natural forces as one reads his work.

Powys succeeded in making out of the rural experience something entirely new in fiction. His success is a paradoxical one not least because it has in no way commended itself to a large audience. His account of village life does in some ways epitomise all that is wrong in the approach of the alienated townsman, and in this respect it deserves Stella Gibbons's burlesque. This is ironic in view of Powys's deliberate rusticity of life; but the oddity of his work, its mannered dialect and self-mockery, is a deliberate distortion of carefully observed realities. Powys plays on and exaggerates the remoteness of his pastoral world in order to make of it a symbol of human life in general. Even at his most prosaic he is a fabulist; meaning is organic in his work, not arbitrarily imposed or merely collocated. Compared with that of Lawrence, his achievement seems extremely limited, but this is less a matter of his skill as an artist than of the scale on which he chose to write. The geographical restrictions of the rural novel made it insufficient to meet the imaginative needs of an age of ever greater dispersion and mobility; instead it catered all too easily, as has been seen, to its emotions. T. F. Powys outraged those emotions, which accounts for his particular distinction; but, as was the case with Hardy and *Jude The Obscure*, it also accounts for his unpopularity with many admirers of the rural fictional tradition. Nonetheless his work, by its very power to disturb, represents that tradition at its most forceful and effective. (pp. 194-95)

> *Glen Cavaliero, "Rural Symbolism: T. F. Powys,"*
> *in his* The Rural Tradition in the English Novel: 1900-
> 1939 *(© Glen Cavaliero 1977), Rowman and Little-*
> *field, 1977, pp. 173-95.*

**JOANNA CIECIERSKA**　(essay date 1978)

T. F. Powys's strength as a writer is revealed in his ability to limit the props or remarks which may be helpful towards a proper interpretation of the work to the text itself. Unlike, for example, another contemporary English allegorical novelist, William Golding, he manages to convey the intended meaning without resorting to additional lectures, essays, interviews, etc. on the subject. The organization of the work itself directs the reader from the vehicle, a semi-mimetic account of a pathological rural community in the South of England, to the tenor, a picture of human life dominated by the clash between elements of good and evil inherent in human beings.

The world vision presented by T. F. Powys's writing is effected by two contrasting modes of imagination, anthropomorphizing and reifying.

The first finds its most complete expression in *Fables*. . . . Unlike the remaining more than eighty short prose works by T. F. Powys, none of the fables had been published before the book edition appeared, according to A. P. Riley, the writer's bibliographer. The fact seems to confirm the hypothesis that T. F. Powys considered *Fables* a consciously arranged entity with the main idea and organization identical in all its component parts, rather than a largely accidental collection of stories of similar form. The *dramatis personae* of *Fables* are objects, plants, animals and natural phenomena which the writer anthropomorphizes by attributing to them the ability to perceive, reason and communicate both among themselves and with the human world. All the stories of the volume follow the convention of the pathetic fallacy, which is employed in three different variants.

In fables such as "**The Clout and the Pan**" and "*The Bucket and the Rope*", objects are impassionate witnesses of dramatic events (a widow's ambiguous attitude after the death of her miser husband and a man's suicide after his wife's treachery) taking place in the world of men, undoubtedly interesting but foreign to them. The questions of love and death, which fascinated T. F. Powys throughout all of his writing, are observed from a certain distance, by a different consciousness which is able to place particular events in chronological order but does not attempt to find any relevant relationship of cause and effect between them. Observed without the filter of emotion, people appear as a-logical creatures behaving in an inexplicable manner, rather than beings which are fascinating because of the complexity of their feelings and perceptions.

The stories "**The Blind Hen and the Earthworm**" and "**The Withered Leaf and the Green**" are obviously modelled on the classical fable where the events in the anthropomorphous world of animals and inanimate nature, or the opinions expressed by their representatives, serve to illustrate the author's theses concerning typical human traits, often with a strong critical and moralizing colouring. The first story is a parable of morbid egotism which leads to the arbitrary choice of a hierarchy of values and demanding a sacrifice of one for the benefit of others without any justification whatsoever—a blind hen orders a worm to submit to her eating him ' for the worms are given by the grand creator to the birds to be their meat". The second story presents a contrast between the optimism of youth and the pessimism of old age resulting from the experience of a lifetime. The oak tree thus derides the chesnut-tree: "When I heard you to praise the world so finely I could not but laugh a little, for I knew you to be a new and ignorant being, whereas I lived long enough to have learned better"

Two stories about the unusual encounter of people with animals and objects able to reason and communicate their observations constitute the third division. For Mr. Bonnet (**"The Hat and the Post"**) and Mr. Pim (**"Mr. Pim and the Holy Crumb"**) these encounters are not only exercises in moral instruction, suddenly making them aware of some obvious although hitherto unrealized truth. The fables also introduce the protagonists as well as the readers to that peculiar allegorizing vision of the world characteristic of Powys. The most despised thing may provide "clothing" for some concept of infinite greatness, as a crumb of bread lying on the church floor may prove to be another impersonation of God converting Mr. Pim, who had previously never had the least idea what the ceremony of the holy communion actually meant. This tendency to show complex notions and relationships through trivialities occurs throughout T. F. Powys's writing. A travelling wine salesman distributing his merchandise and an itinerant tinker are actually God, a stranger appearing in a rural community and bearing a common Suffolk surname turns out to be Death.

If animals, plants and inanimate objects are provided with certain features of human personality, man is subjected to a reverse process. This is accomplished by means of depriving him of his individual nature, through certain peculiar dean-imization and objectivization. Characters do not interest the writer as individuals but as definite types characteristic of any human community or as archetypes of virtues and, more frequently, vices, and thus are important merely because of the function they have there. Hence there is a certain monotony in T. F. Powys's fiction, since fascination with the same subject matter entails the constant re-introduction of virtually identical characters.

Psychization of the world of nature and inanimate objects combined with the reification of human beings has manifold purposes. The reversal of roles typical of the fairy-tale world introduces an element of fantasy which disturbs the "real" character of the presented world, thus contributing to its fabulation and depriving it of the status of a set of verifiable information. At the same time it provides the key to its interpretation. That process consists in making the reader aware of the necessity of adopting the convention of surprise whereby the unexpected looms behind the familiar. Shifts in the "natural" hierarchy of things on the one hand help to create a suggestive picture of a homogenous universe where the human being loses his arbitrarily usurped superior position, and on the other hand affect the linguistic make-up of the work, since such shifts justify a metaphorical account of man's emotional conditioning and the dominant traits of his personality. Putting man on the same footing as other creatures leads to the feeling of empathy between the two levels which are usually not able to intercommunicate, and thus enables the author to create brief allegories reminiscent of the medieval exempla. For instance, the death of a hare torn into pieces by hounds, brings to Luke the threatening cruelty inseparable from the desire he feels for Jenny (**Mr. Weston's Good Wine**).

The ancillary function of the literal stratum referring not to the verifiable extra-fictitious reality, but to the superior meaning hidden behind it, is emphasized by conscious moulding of the vehicle as a created literary utterance, rather than as a *quasi* live-account. A discernible manipulation of plots, manifested in advanced selectiveness, and the frequently employed device of retrospection constitute the dominant feature of a Powysian narrative. The characteristic function of the time element plays an important part in this respect. T. F. Powys hardly ever introduces an undisturbed linear order. Most often he goes back into the past, referring to the relevant previous experiences which precede the present action, as if he tried to project the condensed selective character of a parable.

Since T. F. Powys does not concern himself with actual communities placed in a particular period but with mankind in general, a deep conviction about the eternal character of the problems presented seems to be another reason for rejecting the linear shape of plot in favour of the balanced circular pattern founded upon a recurring order whose particular stages are determined by birth, life and death, and their equivalents, the seasons. The everlasting repetition of things as time passes is a preoccupation of T. F. Powys's thought. The chronology of physical time measured with clocks is usually abandoned in the metaphorical time-space of Powysland. . . . The most extreme instance of this occurs in **Mr Weston's Good Wine,** when all the clocks stop during Mr. Weston's visit at Folly Down.

A similar purpose is served by a common use of self-quotation and self-reference. The same characters and places often appear in several works, or one novel contains numerous references to the events depicted in another (cf. **Mr. Weston's Good Wine** and **Unclay**). This brings about the illusion of peculiar autonomy and homogeneity of the country of T. F. Powys, although it must have prompted Dylan Thomas to dismiss the body of T. F.Powys's fiction as "Biblical stories about old sextons called Parsnip and Dottle"

Identification of characters inhabiting the self-contained territory is achieved mostly by references to the cultural tradition shared by the author and his readers. The Bible, folklore, certain literary works deeply rooted in the audience's consciousness, all serve the purpose of guideposts scattered throughout the texts. Paraphrases of the Scriptures, for instance Mr. Weston mentioning his predilection for inns with their stables which obviously leads to Luke, 2:7; Death presented as a male figure (so unlike for instance that of Slavonic tradition) and speaking of his "vasty hall" which is an obvious quotation from the popular "Requiescat" by Matthew Arnold, are but a few instances of relying on the reader's power to infer the half-hidden meaning.

T. F. Powys's vision of the world, marked by an extreme level of reification and concentration, attempts to draw the reader's attention to the dangerous forces beneath the appearances of everyday life. His deceptively simple stories of the crude reality of a rural community are in fact manifestations of a search for the truth about man and his place in the universe. (pp. 183-86)

*Joanna Ciecierska, "The World of T. F. Powys's Fiction" (reprinted by permission of the author), in* Kwartalnik Neofilologiczny, *Vol. XXV, No. 2, 1978, pp. 179-86.*

---

## ADDITIONAL BIBLIOGRAPHY

Govan, Gilbert E. "The Powys Family." *The Sewanee Review* XLVI, No. 1 (January 1938): 74-90.*
  Comparative study of the writings of the Powys brothers. The section on T. F. Powys focuses on *Mr. Weston's Good Wine.*

Holbrook, David. "Metaphor and Maturity: T. F. Powys and Dylan Thomas." In *The Modern Age*, pp. 415-28. *Penguin Guide to English*

*Literature,* edited by Boris Ford, vol. 7. Baltimore: Penguin Books, 1963.*

> Views *Mr. Weston's Good Wine* as a "spiritual autobiography of a man seeking to comprehend some possible meaning in life."

Hopkins, Kenneth. *The Powys Brothers: A Biographical Appreciation.* London: Phoenix House, 1967, 275 p.*

> Chronicles the lives of the Powys brothers and renders critical comments and comparison of their literary works.

Humfrey, Belinda, ed. *Recollections of the Powys Brothers: Llewelyn, Theodore, and John Cowper.* London: Peter Owen, 1980, 288 p.*

> Offers ten essays and character sketches on T. F. Powys by his friends, family, and critics. In her introduction, Humfrey gives an overview of the personalities and writing style of the three brothers.

Marlow, Louis [pseudonym of Louis Umfreville Wilkinson]. *Welsh Ambassadors: Powys Lives and Letters.* London: Bertram Rota, 1971, 274 p.*

> Intimate biographical look at the Powyses through their personal letters, with an introduction by another Powys biographer, Kenneth Hopkins. Hopkins calls *Welsh Ambassadors* "an essential text for any reader wishing to study the Powys brothers."

Prentice, Charles. Preface to *God's Eyes A-Twinkle,* by T. F. Powys, pp. ix-xv. London: Chatto & Windus, 1947.

> Study of Powys as a short story writer.

Riley, Peter. *A Bibliography of T. F. Powys.* Hastings, England: R. A. Brimmell, 1967, 72 p.

> Most extensive Powys bibliography, with a list of selected criticism. Stories never before collected as well as Powys's non-fiction contributions to periodicals and anthologies are noted in this bibliography.

Sewall, Father Brocard, ed. *Theodore: Essays on T. F. Powys.* Aylesford, England: Saint Albert Press, 1964, 74 p.

> Reminiscences and criticism by such intimates as Powys's son Francis, his brother John Cowper Powys, and close friend, author Louis Wilkinson. The previously unpublished short story "The Useless Woman" by Powys, and several of his personal letters are also gathered in this book.

Steinmann, Martin, Jr. "Water and Animal Symbolism in T. F. Powys." *English Studies* XLI (December 1960): 359-65.

> Studies water and animal symbolism as two facets of the overall nature symbolism of Powys's work.

# John (Silas) Reed

## 1887-1920

American journalist, historian, poet, short story writer, and dramatist.

Reed is best known for his account of the Russian Revolution, *Ten Days That Shook the World*. Praised for its emotional impact as well as its factual detail, this work is representative of Reed's passionate, often subjective approach to journalism. While this approach may have lessened Reed's stature as a journalist in the eyes of some critics, it has also caused his works to be appreciated for their purely literary qualities.

Reed was raised in Portland, Oregon, the son of prosperous parents. He began writing at an early age and hist first short stories and poems were published in high school literary magazines. At Harvard, Reed expanded his literary interests as a member of the editorial boards of the *Harvard Lampoon* and *Harvard Monthly*. Following his graduation, he moved to Greenwich Village where, with the help of renowned journalist, social critic, and family friend Lincoln Steffens, he became a contributor and editor for *American Magazine*.

Even though he pursued a career in journalism, Reed still considered himself a poet and fiction writer. *The Smart Set* and the *Metropolitan Magazine* bought some of his short fiction, and a slim volume of his poetry was published by a friend under the title *Tamburlaine and Other Verses*. But his success in these genres was limited, and it was in journalism that his reputation was made. Reed earned his living by writing for traditional publications like *American Magazine* and the *Metropolitan* but, according to John Stuart, his best work was done for *The Masses*, a radical publication edited by Max Eastman, which featured a roster of young American writers that included Amy Lowell and Sherwood Anderson. In *The Masses*, Reed published a famous account of the silk workers' strike in Paterson, New Jersey, which won him notoriety as a capable reporter who had a feeling for working-class politics. Several magazine articles and the book *Insurgent Mexico*—which came out of an assignment from the *Metropolitan* to cover the Mexican Revolution—attracted even more attention from editors and critics, who called Reed "the American Kipling." Reed's popularity soon withered, however, when his opposition to U.S. involvement in World War I and his participation in the Socialist Party became widely publicized. Afterward, the pages of most mainstream publications were closed to him.

Unable to sell his articles, Reed became involved with the Provincetown Players, producing short plays which he co-wrote with his future wife Louise Bryant, and with Eugene O'Neill. Shortly thereafter, he set out with Bryant to cover the impending revolution in Russia. Already a supporter of the communist cause, Reed immediately sided with V. I. Lenin and his followers upon arriving in Russia in August, 1917. *Ten Days That Shook the World*, written during the next few months, is a sympathetic, insider's view of the Bolshevik bureaucracy, of life among Lenin's soldiers, and of the events surrounding the overthrow of Aleksandr Kerensky's provisional government. Returning to the United States, Reed founded the Communist Labor Party and edited its journal, *The Voice of Labor*.

*The Granger Collection, New York*

The radical nature of his activities and the partisan stance revealed in *Ten Days That Shook of World* led to Reed's indictment as a communist leader during the post-World War I "Red Scare." He fled to Russia, where he died of typhus in Moscow. Regarded as a Soviet hero, Reed was buried with honors at the Kremlin wall.

Reed's journalistic style is highly impressionistic—he often rearranged the chronology of events he covered to heighten the emotional impact of his description. For this reason, his reliability as a reporter has often been questioned. While many critics applaud Reed's vivid presentation of the strikes and revolutions he covered, few would consider him an objective observer. But Reed's work is often a secondary consideration in discussions of his career. For many, he is the epitome of the socially committed writer, a literary man-of-action who was fortunate enough both to make history and to write about it. Some critics deplore this romanticization of Reed, but few would deny the power he wielded as a writer who could move his readers with scenes of working-class struggles, and who captured the sense and sound of history as he saw it.

## PRINCIPAL WORKS

*The Day in Bohemia; or, Life among the Artists*  (poetry)
  1913

---

## WALTER LIPPMANN  (essay date 1914)

[After the *Metropolitan Magazine* sent him to Mexico, the public discovered] that whatever John Reed could touch or see or smell he could convey. The variety of his impressions, the resources and color of his language seemed inexhaustible. The articles which he sent back from the border were as hot as the Mexican desert, and Villa's revolution, till then reported only as a nuisance, began to unfold itself into throngs of moving people in a gorgeous panorama of earth and sky. . . .

[Reed] did not judge, he identified himself with the struggle, and gradually what he saw mingled with what he hoped. Wherever his sympathies marched with the facts, Reed was superb. His interview with Carranza almost a year ago was so sensationally accurate in its estimate of the feeling between Carranza and Villa that he suppressed it at the time out of loyalty to the success of the revolution. But where his feeling conflicted with the facts, his vision flickered. He seems totally to have misjudged the power of Villa.

Reed has no detachment, and is proud of it, I think. By temperament he is not a professional writer or reporter. He is a person who enjoys himself. Revolution, literature, poetry, they are only things which hold him at times, incidents merely of his living. Now and then he finds adventure by imagining it, oftener he transforms his own experience. He is one of those people who treat as serious possibilities such stock fantasies as shipping before the mast, rescuing women, hunting lions, or trying to fly around the world in an aeroplane. He is the only fellow I know who gets himself pursued by men with revolvers, who is always once more just about to ruin himself. (p. 15)

Walter Lippmann, *"Legendary John Reed,"* in The New Republic *(©1914 The New Republic, Inc.), Vol. I, No. 8, December 26, 1914, pp. 15-16.*

## THE NATION  (essay date 1915)

[Although the author of **"Insurgent Mexico"**] has been proclaimed "the Kipling of Mexico," he has no right to that title except in an extreme sense, for Mr. Reed at his best resembles Mr. Kipling at his worst. As a presentation of conditions and problems now existing in Mexico, the book is a lurid exaggeration of some few aspects, and the frenzied manner of the whole composition aims not so much at depicting sober truths as at shocking the reader by disgusting naturalism in describing an irregular assortment of horrors such as were to be found nowhere else in the world at the time Mr. Reed wrote.

**"Insurgent Mexico"** consists of six parts, of varying length, apparently selected at random, and composed of the superfluous local color deleted by a wise news-editor from the dis-

patches of an active war correspondent. Vivid impressions of Desert War, Francisco Villa, and Jiminez and Points West comprise the first three. Villa he describes sympathetically, making him out a very agreeable robber-captain. To the fourth, narrating the attack on Torreon, is given the title, now so portentous, of A People in Arms! Carranza—an Impression, reproduces an unfavorable interview by Mr. Reed with the First Chief. The last part, Mexican Nights, indicates a lack of feeling for unity, since it concludes the whole book with the account of a crude miracle play.

The quantity of blood spilled throughout **"Insurgent Mexico"** is revolting. The book is soaked and clotted with it; every page drips gore. Detailed accounts are furnished of amateur, impromptu surgery. . . . Later on, among other bloody pages, we have a most precise and circumstantial recital of the killing of some *rurales*, and the condition of their corpses when found by Reed and his companions of the revolutionary forces. Again there occur pictures of wounded such as none of the dispatches from abroad have dared to give.

Mannerisms in the use of words, and disregard of such trifles as ordinary punctuation and paragraphing, are commonplaces of **"Insurgent Mexico."** Mr. Reed says of "Captain Fernando, a grizzled giant of a man in tight trousers, who had fought twenty-one battles," that "he took the keenest delight in my fragmentary Spanish, and every word I spoke sent him into bellows of laughter that shook down the adobe from the ceiling." Yet rare is the page which has not its sprinkling of italicized Spanish words, often misspelled; and further to display his rapid progress after Captain Fernando's amusement, he unblushingly quotes numerous specimens of the unintelligent, obscene expressions which in Mexico fill the office of Anglo-Saxon profanity.

After the rout at La Cadena, Mr. Reed tells us of his terror-stricken flight: "I ran. . . . I kept thinking to myself: 'Well, this is certainly an experience. I'm going to have something to write about.'" This fully states the function of **"Insurgent Mexico"**—something for Mr. Reed to write about. (pp. 82-3)

*"A Gory Volume," in* The Nation *(copyright 1915 The Nation magazine, The Nation Associates, Inc.), Vol. 100, No. 2586, January 21, 1915, pp. 82-3.*

## JOHN REED  (essay date 1917)

The *Metropolitan Magazine* asked me to go to Mexico as war correspondent, and I knew that I must do it. (p. 335)

Altogether I was four months with the Constitutionalist armies in Mexico. When I first crossed the border deadliest fear gripped me. I was afraid of death, of mutilation, of a strange land and strange people whose speech and thought I did not know. But a terrible curiosity urged me on; I felt I *had to know* how I would act under fire, how I would get along with these primitive folks at war. And I discovered that bullets are not very terrifying, that the fear of death is not such a great thing, and that the Mexicans are wonderfully congenial. That four months of riding hundreds of miles across the blazing plains, sleeping on the ground with the *hombres*, dancing and carousing in looted haciendas all night after an all-day ride, being with them intimately in play, in battle, was perhaps the most satisfactory period of my life. I made good with these wild fighting men, and with myself. I loved them and I loved the life. I found myself again. I wrote better than I have ever written. (pp. 335-36)

John Reed, "Almost Thirty" (1917, reprinted by permission of the Literary Estate of John Reed), in The New Republic, Vol. LXXXVI, No. 1117, April 29, 1936, pp. 332-36.

## HAROLD STEARNS   (essay date 1919)

Shall we have to say that the most impartial histories are those written by prejudiced persons? . . .

[In *Ten Days That Shook the World*], the reader knows what the author wanted; the cards are on the table. It is not the things which are said in a historical volume that do harm; it is the things which are left unsaid—and it is a curious fact that Mr. Reed quotes more anti-Bolshevik statements and gives more generously the anti-Bolshevik point of view than do most of those industrious apologists so anxious to prove Bolshevism a menace to all civilization and decent living. Furthermore, Mr. Reed had the advantage of being on the side that won: he began with the conviction that eventually it was going to win, and if to be a good prophet is to be a bad historian, Mr. Reed will have to put up with his critics. For when your interpretation of anything is justified later by the course of events, you can afford to be generous with your opponents. (p. 301)

Mr. Reed, then, has the initial advantages of straight-forwardness and of guessing right. But he discloses other virtues in the book itself. Those who remember Mr. Reed for his fine impressionistic descriptions of the revolution in Mexico will perhaps be taken aback at the almost severe quality of this present narrative. With opportunity after opportunity for "purple patches" Mr. Reed shows a restraint which practically vacuum-cleans the book of any mere rhetorical passages. He is content to let the narrative flow on naturally and quietly, welded together by the hammer of relevant fact after relevant fact, in short paragraphs which frequently end in a tiny row of dots, a happy incorporation of the technique of Wellsian suggestiveness. Often he includes proclamations of the various parties and statements and speeches of the party leaders in the text itself, although the more important of the documentary material is included in an appendix which historians of the future will find as invaluable as the living observers of today. The story does not lack emotional thrill because of this deliberately chosen method of unemphatic presentation. If anything, it gains. Mr. Reed has taken only ten days of the Bolshevik Revolution—the vital ten days—with short glimpses before them and few after. Consequently there is some inevitable repetition. But the effect is cumulative. A picture of the state of mind which made the Bolsheviki uprising inevitable emerges gradually, with the outlines of the picture becoming sharper and sharper, until finally it stands forth etched with unforgetable definiteness. The author, for instance, seldom tells you what he thinks the proletariat, the toiling masses, the soldiers, the workers and peasants, are saying. He lets them speak for themselves at just the correct dramatic moment. He selects their spokesmen not only with the unerring precision of the partisan but also with the wisdom of the journalist in choosing those who are truly representative. (pp. 301-02)

Mr. Reed has pictured the conflict of classes with such precision and finality that his account of Petrograd during those ten days furnishes a sort of microcosm of what happened all over Russia shortly afterwards, and what we have already seen happen in parts of Germany. It takes no great gift of prophecy to see that it is also a microcosm of what, in varying forms, is certain to take place in many other countries, perhaps even here in safe America where nobody yet believes in a Soviet revolution except the Overman Committee, army officers, and government officials, who are being driven by their fear to just those actions most nicely calculated to encourage such a revolution. (p. 302)

Harold Stearns, "The Unending Revolution," in The Dial (copyright, 1919, by The Dial Publishing Company, Inc.), Vol. LXVI, No. 786, March 22, 1919, pp. 301-03.

## V. I. LENIN   (essay date 1919)

With the greatest interest and with never slackening attention I read John Reed's book, *Ten Days That Shook the World*. Unreservedly do I recommend it to the workers of the world. Here is a book which I should like to see published in millions of copies and translated into all languages. It gives a truthful and most vivid exposition of the events so significant to the comprehension of what really is the Proletarian Revolution and the Dictatorship of the Proletariat. These problems are widely discussed, but before one can accept or reject these ideas, he must understand the full significance of his decision. John Reed's book will undoubtedly help to clear this question, which is the fundamental problem of the international labor movement.

V. I. Lenin, "Foreword" (1919), in Ten Days That Shook the World by John Reed (copyright, 1919, by Boni & Liveright, Inc.; copyright, 1935, by The Modern Library), Modern Library, 1935 (and reprinted by Vintage Books, 1960, p. xivi).

## HARRIET MONROE   (essay date 1921)

The recent death of two poets enforces a sharp contrast between their characters and careers. John Reed and Louise Imogen Guiney were alike only in their courage and spiritual integrity, and in their love of the art, which they practised too fitfully; in all other details no two human beings could be more different than the shy recluse who died in Oxford, and the rash adventurer of countless wars who died in Moscow.

John Reed was so active in radical politics as to have too little time left for poetry; but in this place it is proper to record that his neglect of the art was accident and not intention. Like Jack London, he was always dreaming of tomorrow's masterpiece. Knowing himself for a poet, he hoped to prove his vocation by many poems worthy to endure; but life was so exciting, and the social struggle in these States and Mexico, in Finland, Russia—everywhere—so tempting to a fighting radical, that poetry had to wait for the leisure which—alas!—never came.

My too slight acquaintance with John Reed dates from a letter of September 11, 1912, written at Porland, Oregon. . . . (pp. 208-09)

Enclosed in this letter came the beautiful ballad *Sangar*, dedicated to Lincoln Steffens and symbolizing what Reed called his "magnificent try for peace during the trial of the Mc-Namaras." Today we might almost apply the poem to Reed himself; for although he loved a fight as well as any soldier, his dream was of a peaceful, co-operative world which, I fear, he would have found very dull—that wonderful "new world" in which, as Gorky says of Lenin's dream, "all men are reasonable," and "the earth is a gigantic jewel, facetted with beautiful evidences of the labor of a free humanity." (p. 210)

They were true to the vision, both these dead poets, even though their achievement was, as with all the high-desiring, imperfect and incomplete. (p. 212)

Harriet Monroe, "Two Poets Have Died," in Poetry (©1921 by The Modern Poetry Association), Vol. XVII, No. 4, January, 1921, pp. 208-12.*

## THOMAS BOYD (essay date 1927)

If the ability to make memorable pictures by words used with the keenest economy, to handle material with sympathy and understanding, to transcribe bizarre scenes and unusual motives in a way that makes them familiar to the reader—if these things count for anything then ["**Daughter of the Revolution**"] should have a notable place among contemporary books. . . .

What Reed heard and saw and felt he wrote about with a realistic vitality. Not that he recorded adventure in terms of himself; he wasn't one of those great-souled people who could stand at the edge of a fire and be so engaged in feeling their own tremors that they would fail to see fifty who were perishing. On the contrary, though most of the tales in "**Daughter of the Revolution**" are written in the first person, they celebrate humanity as a whole and their comment is bound up with its destiny. He was what H. L. Mencken recently called a mushhead; that is to say he had a belief that as men had come out of savagery into barbarism and from barbarism into civilization, so might they some day live a more agreeable, socialized life than they are living at present.

It was because of this belief that Reed took notice of conditions that lay below the surface, which enabled him to catch the spirit of Paris during the war and to fuse it into the title story which, if seen from a distance, possibly, would possess a strange, inexplicable grandeur akin to that in Hans Andersen's "Great Claus and Little Claus." That is the tale of three generations of Frenchmen taking up civil bushwhacking one after the other, fighting, starving and being beaten for a word called freedom, and of a woman who achieved it by an easier, shoddier means; there is also the story of "**Mac-American**" who had betrayed his brother and helped to lynch a negro but who hated living in Mexico because the people there were unfriendly and hadn't any heart; the story of a captain of a Serbian artillery company who once had dreamed of the rebirth of the world but whose thoughts dwelt so continuously on the care and firing of his guns—trained on the Austrians—that even his feeling for his family became unimportant to him and nothing mattered but the perfection of the guns—a dozen or more stories in all.

Coming today, when every college freshman reads his Antole France, Cabell and Mencken and when a writer can't be contemporary unless he is heavily ironical, the wide satire and youthful irony of "**Daughter of the Revolution and Other Stories**" are not unusual qualities. But the work in this volume was written from ten to fifteen years ago—John Reed has been dead almost exactly seven years—and in that period reality was confused with the stories of Kipling, Davis and O. Henry; and Dreiser still had many a storm to weather. Moreover, the pitch struck in these swift and vivid stories comes naturally to them, for they are above all ingenuous. And though many of them are broader than they are long there is enough youth and color and fineness in them to warrant their salvaging.

Thomas Boyd, "John Reed As an Ironic Realist before His Time," in the New York Evening Post (reprinted by permission of The New York Post), Vol. 126, No. 305, November 12, 1927, p. 12.

## GRANVILLE HICKS (essay date 1936)

[During his nights in Mexico, Reed] as he scribbled in his notebook, the scenes of the day stood sharply before him, and he described them in phrases that scarcely needed to be modified when his articles were composed. He did not hesitate to re-arrange incidents to suit whatever pattern he desired, but he was rigorously faithful to the visual impression of each event. He was indifferent to the accuracy of the historian, but he had the integrity of a poet.

***Insurgent Mexico,*** made out of his articles for the *Metropolitan* and the *Masses,* is a book for the eye. But John Reed was not merely recording surfaces. The book has its own kind of insight. He made little effort to understand the history of the country and its revolutions, and his researches into economics were impressionistic. Steffens could have told him more about Federal and Constitutionalist policies than he could have learned if his four months' stay had been prolonged for four years. But he knew something that Steffens did not, and something that, in his mind, was more important than all Steffens' knowledge, he knew the people of Mexico. "He did not judge," Lippmann wrote . . . ; "he identified himself with the struggle, and gradually what he saw mingled with what he hoped. Whenever his sympathies marched with the facts, Reed was superb" [see excerpt above]. (pp. 134-35)

[Reed was also interested in plays. His ***Enter Dibble***] derived straight from Bernard Shaw. Reed had tried to write an intellectual farce, the story of an upper-class revolutionary and superman who disrupts a bourgeois family. (p. 175)

[The play was] alive, in spite of its debt to Shaw and its immaturity and weak construction. The revolutionary comedy of ideas, as Steffens could have told him, was not the best possible form for John Reed to attempt, but the artificiality of the medium and its uncongeniality could not completely conceal the vitality of the man. Reed's whole indictment of the bourgeoisie centered in their stifling of life. He wanted freedom and beauty—but not merely for himself. His own generous passions escaped into the play. The dialogue was mostly feeble in its groping after Shavian wit, but it had moments of fire. (p. 176)

[When he went to Russia], Reed had become a different kind of reporter. In Mexico he had looked for color; in Russia he sought substance. He had filled his Mexican notebooks with poetic phrases, so that he might render with precision the look of the sky or the cast of a man's face. His Russian notebooks were devoted to figures and exact quotations. . . . He had not lost his sharp awareness of appearances, and he created phrases as vivid as any he had written in Mexico, but he was not content with catching the surface of events.

The articles that he somehow found time to hammer out on his typewriter between visits to Smolny and explorations of the Petrograd streets, were shaped by his eagerness to understand and to interpret. . . . He shared in the Bolsheviks' understanding of what they were doing. This was not, so far as the leaders were concerned, a blind revolt, such as he had watched and welcomed in Mexico; the leaders knew precisely where they were going. For this event twenty years of Marxian study had prepared Lenin, and Reed could look through Lenin's eyes. (p. 283)

Granville Hicks, in his John Reed: The Making of a Revolutionary (reprinted by permission of Russell & Volkening, Inc., as agents for the author; © 1936 *by Macmillan Publishing Co., Inc.), Macmillan, 1936, 445 p.*

## MAX EASTMAN (essay date 1942)

[Poetry] to Reed was not only a matter of writing words but of living life. We were carrying realism so far in those days that it walked us right out of our books. We had a certain scorn of books. We wanted to live our poetry. Jack Reed did especially. His comradeship with Louise Bryant was based on a joint determination to smash through the hulls of custom and tradition and all polite and proper forms of behavior, and touch at all times and all over the earth the raw current of life. . . . It was as though they had agreed to inscribe at least two audacious, deep, and real lives in the book of time and let the gods call it poetry. (p. 213)

Hicks has been perspicuous in describing the change in John Reed's style when he came back from Russia after the revolution [see excerpt above]. He was subdued. He was never again so brilliant. Color and metaphor gave place to naked information—and even, let me add, statistics—in his writing. From having been a flashing and imaginatively adventuring reporter-poet, he became an earnest propagandist and prose teacher—almost the embodiment of Lenin's austere term, "professional revolutionist." (p. 221)

> *Max Eastman, "Contribution to an Apotheosis: John Reed and the Russian Revolution," in his* Heroes I Have Known: Twelve Who Lived Great Lives *(copyright, 1942 by Max Eastman; copyright renewed © 1970 by Yvette Eastman; reprinted by permission of Yvette Sakay Eastman), Simon and Schuster, 1942, pp. 201-37.*

## JOHN STUART (essay date 1955)

In the 1913 strike of silk workers in Paterson, New Jersey, [Reed] had his first taste of labor in active warfare. (p. 17)

He saw the oppressors and how they squeezed and crushed the life of the workers; and brought home to him in more concrete terms was "the hard knowledge that the manufacturers get all they can out of labor, pay as little as they must, and permit the existence of great masses of the miserable unemployed in order to keep wages down; that the forces of the state are on the side of property against the propertyless." . . .

After he returned to New York, Reed was asked to cover the revolt of the peons in Mexico against a new set of dictators, the offer coming from the *Metropolitan*. . . . (p. 18)

What he wrote from Mexico had a loving ring. Under his amazing descriptive power landscape and men were transformed into a lyrical, vibrant picture. He captured the spirit of the guerrillas, their fighting lives, their miseries. He sang with them, wrote down their ballads and put them into English. (p. 19)

[After] he came up from Mexico, he saw more of Wall Street's tyranny. At Ludlow, Col., mine guards aided by the state militia had burned a tent colony of striking miners and their families who had been evicted from their homes. . . . He wrote about the strike with scrupulous attention to details. It was a study as much as it was a colorful report. He hunted for evidence not apparent to the eye, and the whole effort marked his growth as a class-conscious writer not easily satisfied with

recording his impressions but who must dig deeper into the play of forces behind them. (pp. 20-1)

When Reed left for Europe in the summer of 1914 to cover the western front for the *Metropolitan,* he . . . saw nothing with which to identify himself on either side of the belligerents. He was depressed and disgusted by the whole damned business, and because he hated it he found it impossible to write what the *Metropolitan* wanted—color, glory, thunder. He gave them what he had actually seen, and it was not pretty. He would not do a thing to influence his readers away from neutrality. (pp. 22-3)

[The Russian] revolution was the kind of school in which John Reed could learn quickly. It taught him convincingly "that in the last analysis the property-owning class is loyal only to its own property. That the property-owning class will never readily compromise with the working class. That the masses of workers are not only capable of great dreams but have in them the power to make dreams come true." And this had been the core of his inner conflict and now it no longer stabbed at him. Paterson, Mexico, Ludlow, the war itself, prepared him for the revolution, and in Petrograd and Moscow he knew what to look for and how to look at it, and thus knitted together were the loose threads of the years past. It was a hard but steady growth.

He could no longer content himself with the mere recording of impressions, however lyrically he expressed them. More than ever before he sought the inter-connection between things, the continuous process of shift and change. The difference between most of his earlier writing and that on the revolution was the difference between the close sympathizer and the participant. In Mexico he had shared the life of the guerrillas to satisfy his quest for experience and to lend dramatic color to his reports. His identification was limited to the work in hand and by the very character of the uprising itself. But in Russia his identification with the revolution was complete and lasting, for not only had he finally come to know that the militant labor movement was the anchor of his life, but he knew that here was the revolution that had opened a new future to all oppressed. His writing thus gained an emotional charge and an intellectual dimension beyond a skilled use of words in a rhythmically constructed sentence. There was now an acute sense of history, a deeper appreciation of theory. What he wrote about the Russian Revolution in *Ten Days That Shook The World,* with its extraordinary weaving of significant detail into a triumphal theme, was a measure of the great leap forward he had made.

*Ten Days* was the first major account in America of the revolution's universal impact. Reed had mastered its broad fundamentals, although he was not familiar with the complex politics which characterized the revolution from the beginning of 1917. (pp. 29-30)

[Yet], *Ten Days* was a unique document. It became in its time a force for socialism by rousing others in the same way Reed had been roused. It helped to break the cordon of censorship thrown around Russia by a bitterly hostile imperialist world, and it compelled its many readers to think hard on the great historic event of their time. (p. 30)

If in all this turmoil there was an occasional moment of grief for Reed, it was that he had no time for poetry. He had always thought of himself as a poet and the rich cadences of his prose, the power of his images, derived from his poetic skill. And now there was hardly a moment to spare for it. He yielded to his political commitments but not without the hope that some day in the future he would be able to return to poetry. Most of his poetry was written when he was younger and under the influence of conventional forms into which he fitted conventional themes. Without doubt, had he been able to give it time, it would have reflected his newer consciousness. As it stood, it had genuine poetic feeling, a music and technical facility that were undeniable. Yet on the whole it hinged on sensation and merely glimpsed life, for in the past he had thought of poetry as a world apart from everything else. It thus happened that his verse often lapsed into the mystical and the platitudinous. But in "**America, 1918**," a long poem he began in revolutionary Petrograd and finished in New York, he displayed a fresher approach. The poem was autobiographical with the seeming purpose of rearranging his feelings, his impressions, to a new pattern. (pp. 32-3)

Judged by Reed's convictions it was not a successful piece of work. The poem as a whole lacked the quality of struggle. It was unconsciously chauvinistic in a few of its lines and it was quite removed, for all his intentions, from the actual America of 1918. But for what he had to say, the old masters he followed in the past were not entirely useful. He needed to borrow the method, the strength and spirit of the Whitman tradition. And because he was unpracticed in it, the poem suffered from overcataloguing as though he were trying to pile under an enlarging glass the thirty-odd tumbling years of his life. What did come through was Reed's deep love of country, his faith in the untold possibilities before it. He was beginning to rethink in newer poetic terms much of his experience and if he had had the leisure, he might have been able in time to fuse his beliefs into a poetry as vital as his prose. (pp. 34-5)

The articles and such other theoretical writing as he did showed crudities which were as much the evidence of his own inexperience with theory as they were of a movement that had not yet found itself and in which non-Marxist influences were strong. But the special stamp of this writing was his effort to find those features of American history and the labor movement that had handicapped the unfolding of a truly Marxist party of the American working class. Up until the time he had begun this examination—although he came prepared with a unique range of experience—his political knowledge was empirical and chaotic. It made for an impetuousness not lessened by the anarchic society in which he moved and by the conflict between what he willed and what he saw actually happening. By digging into the past without losing the focal point of the present, he separated from the confusion of experience those elements in American life that would give sustenance to a new militant party. (p. 36)

*John Stuart, in his introduction to* The Education of John Reed: Selected Writings *by John Reed (© by International Publishers Co. Inc., 1955), International, 1955, pp. 7-38.*

## BERTRAM D. WOLFE (essay date 1965)

To Reed the Mexican Revolution was a pageant, a succession of adventures, a delight to the eye, a chance to discover that he was not afraid of bullets. His reports overflow with life and movement: simple, savage men, capricious cruelty, warm comradeship, splashes of color, bits of song, fragments of social and political dreams, personal peril, gay humor, reckless daring. Neither Steffens, who joined and counted on Venustiano Carranza, nor Reed, who celebrated the pastoral dreams and

bold deeds of Pancho Villa, had any real notion of the Mexican maze. But Reed's mingling of personal adventure with camera-eye close-ups lighted by a poet's vision made superb reporting. The book he made of them, *Insurgent Mexico*, despite its careless ignorance of men, events, and forces, and even of Spanish, which he mangled in the ballads he quoted, was closer to the feeling of Mexico in revolution than most things that Americans have written on it. (p. 39)

Of Lenin's authoritarian party structure and organization creed [Reed] knew nothing: so much the freer was his fancy to endow the conflict and chaos [of the Russian Revolution] he was to witness with the form and substance of his own dream. (p. 41)

With his poet's blood and rebel's heart he decided what to believe. Then, with the artist's gift for selection, heightening and unifying, he assimilated all the chaotic impressions into a picture more impressive and more beautiful than life itself.

When Boardman Robinson reproached him once with "But it didn't happen that way!" his answer was an *ad hominem* of artist to artist. "What the hell difference does it make?" And, seizing one of Robinson's sketches: "She didn't have a bundle as big as that . . . he didn't have so full a beard." Drawing, Robinson explained, was not a matter of photographic accuracy but of over-all impression. "Exactly," Reed cried in triumph, "that is just what I am trying to do!"

Yet there is nothing of the mean, deliberate lie about John Reed's *Ten Days That Shook the World*. A good reporter, always in the thick of things, he possessed an honest sense of vivid detail that makes one page refute another.

He idealized the masses. He believed the ridiculous legend, born perhaps of his own dream, that the Bolshevik Central Committee, after having rejected the idea of an insurrection, was made to reverse itself by a single speech of a rank and file workingman (There was such a reversal, but the "rank and file workingman" was Lenin!) (pp. 42-3)

Though his "vision" raced ahead of his eyes, creating its own illusion, yet his eyes were everywhere. And his person, too. He tried to see it all and put it all on paper. The dream of the Bolsheviks, the realities of their deeds, and the tension between the dream and the reality are in his pages. If he did not comprehend the meaning of the large events, what observer or participant did? He understood less and misunderstood more than many, so that one of the personages of whom he wrote would say to me of his book: "The work of an innocent who did not know whether he was attending a wedding or a funeral!" It was a funeral—of Russia's newly won liberties, achieved after a century of struggle. If Jack thought that he was witnessing the wedding of liberty and justice destined to live together happily ever after, so well does he report that we can see the acts of burial even as he sings of nuptials.

As a repository of facts for the historian, his book is bursting with precious material: interviews, speeches, resolutions, press clippings. One of his habits was to tear down a specimen of every poster or proclamation for future translation. The book is full of quotations from these documents, and illustrated by photos of many of them—a priceless opportunity for the historian to enter into a time that has passed.

Whether because of or despite the dream that possessed him, as literature Reed's book is the finest piece of eye-witness reporting the Revolution produced. It is his true monument, more enduring than the name carved on the Kremlin wall. (p. 45)

Bertram D. Wolfe, "The Harvard Man in the Kremlin Wall," in his Strange Communists I Have Known (copyright © 1965 by Bertram D. Wolfe; reprinted with permission of Stein and Day Publishers), Stein and Day, 1965, pp. 23-51.

**RENATO LEDUC** (essay date 1968)

In the stories of *Insurgent Mexico,* whether about fiestas or fiascos, a penetrating literary sensibility bursts at every paragraph, a rare poetic flair, an indefinable grace, a mischievous joy which no longer is present in the monolithic monument to *Ten Days That Shook the World.* French journalist Paul Nizan once defined the diplomatic correspondent as "the historian of the present." The definition applies also to the political journalist, to the war correspondent. *Ten Days That Shook the World* and *Insurgent Mexico* are history, but if I may be allowed a comparison, the first is Tacitus at work, and the second is Suetonius, biographer of Hadrian.

*Ten Days* is an objective document, exact, minute, incontrovertibly authentic. The penetrating political sensibility of the author did not lose sight of the immense importance of the events he witnessed in those days in the streets of the tsarist capital. But by then Reed had ceased to be "the troubadour" in quest of "the lady of his sonnets," as Waldo Frank put it, to become the exemplary, exacting chronicler. Reed stifled his emotions to the point that he himself, as a kind of exonerating plea, wrote in the preface to his magnificent reportage: "In the struggle my sympathies were not neutral. But in telling the story of those great days I have tried to see events with the eye of a conscientious reporter, interested in setting down the truth." (pp. xiii-xiv)

*Insurgent Mexico* is something else. Alfredo Varela defines Reed quite well when he says in his preface [to an Argentine edition]: "In the end he is a mural painter. The great fresco is his specialty, the panoramic picture which reveals history in a thousand details." Even as late as 1914, war, and particularly a revolutionary war of guerrillas as was being fought in Mexico, still had a marked romantic quality which appealed greatly to the temperament of a troubadour which Waldo Frank attributed to Reed. In his journalistic war adventure in Mexico Reed came in contact with truly destitute miserable masses, with authentically popular leaders, with disorganized armies, ill-armed, dressed in rags, but determined to die for an ideal—allow me a paradox—which was totally materialistic: for a piece of land on which to raise a bare sustenance.

During the months he lived with the Mexican guerrillas, Reed was not only a witness and chronicler, but also a participant in many of the incidents he recorded. So much so, that on the pages of *Insurgent Mexico* he lavished such literary qualities as grace, emotion, humor—but, on the other hand, forgot totally to follow a chronology, indispensable requirement of the journalist. (pp. xiv-xv)

Renato Leduc, "Preface," translated by Tana de Gámez (1968), to Insurgent Mexico by John Reed (copyright © 1969 by International Publishers Co., Inc.), International, 1969, pp. vii-xxiv.

**HARRY HENDERSON III** (essay date 1973)

There is, I recognize, something of a feeling of shock in applying the terms of formal literary criticism to Reed's book. *Ten Days* is most often regarded as a journalistic fluke, as the great case in the history of eye-witness accounts of the right reporter being in the right place at the right time. Almost all published discussion of the book has been devoted to explaining how Reed became that "right" man: the leftward progress of a gifted Harvard dilettante from the Paterson strike and the I.W.W. to Mexico, to the Colorado Coal Fields, to both fronts in the Great War and at last to Revolutionary Petrograd. Reed's classic has been accepted as a happy (or unhappy, depending on one's political sympathies) juncture of man and moment, of the enthusiasm of a red romantic with an event large enough to give him scope.

The application of the generic terms of major literary art to Reed's work may seem especially inappropriate in view of his career as a journalist and propagandist and the sharp distinction usually made in critical theory between these two modes and that of art. Art is typically distinguished from journalism by its appeal to a unity based on probability rather than randomness of phenomenal detail. Art is distinguished in turn from propaganda by the integrity of aesthetic order and its freedom from ulterior ends. Yet one's acceptance of the validity of these distinctions should not prevent a recognition of the way the great generic forms dominate one's thinking about extraliterary matters nor how they help to organize emotional responses to contemporary history. . . . Nor should one ignore the gropings towards major form which created in Reed's masterpiece a new genre—the urban comedy of revolution.

That Reed had to grope is not surprising considering that his models had little to teach him about structural form. His writing mentor at Harvard, Charles Townsend Copeland, the beloved "Copey" to whom he dedicated his first book, was an aficionado of the sharply rendered detail, and was uninterested in the grand pattern. As another student of his, Van Wyck Brooks, wrote later, he stressed "emphasis, or the striking phrase, or Kipling's kind of vividness" as opposed to "Anatole France's *pas d'emphase,* vividness without effect and the phrase that is not striking but that haunts the mind." Copey taught the virtues of the anecdote and vignette rather than the orientation of overall structure and form. Reed wrote him in later years, "I would never have seen what I did had it not been for your teaching me." Copeland's training explains Reed's vividness as a reporter but also helps to account for his difficulties in puzzling through the structural problems of his narratives.

One of Reed's first and most famous pieces of committed journalism was on the Paterson silk strike of 1913, in which Reed was first arrested, and then went on to produce a pageant of the strike, performed by the striking workers themselves, in Madison Square Garden. . . . [The article's] rhetorical strategy, insisting on an equality of the battleground between two adversaries and denying to the state's power in the service of management any sanction of impartiality, was crucial to Reed's rhetoric as it has always been as essential part of Marxian ideology. As the I.W.W. put it, the state was only "the slugging committee of the ruling class." And Reed carried this strategy on, into his articles on the Colorado mine strikes (**"The Colorado War"**) and the Chicago trial of the I.W.W. The war metaphor dominates his treatment of these events because war is seen by him as legitimizing the economic struggle. It legitimizes, paradoxically enough, by negating the civil law, and transcending the legalistic bonds which define social action in times of social stability. The war metaphor is extralegal in two senses: it is not within the purview of the law of capitalist society; and it is free of the taint of revolutionary tribunals.

Thus through the metaphor of armed, open conflict, Reed could open up comic potentialities within the traditionally dark and tragic subject of violence and class struggle. (pp. 424-25)

In a war with but two sides, the writer must *choose,* and Reed's point of view in his pieces on labor-conflict reflects the unity that Reed always sought with the working class "veterans." Yet this self-conscious unity of the middle-class radical intellectual with the struggling masses, achieved in the fellowship of a metaphorical foxhole, would not sustain a longer narrative, as Reed showed in his first book, *Insurgent Mexico.* . . .

[*Insurgent Mexico*] can best be characterized as a form of revolutionary picaresque, a picaresque with pastoral overtones. The pastorality is appropriate not only because it is an agrarian revolution which Reed is dramatizing (although this circumstance is critical) but because the adventuresome narrator sees the action with the sophisticated eyes of an urban intellectual. The cultural distance between the intellectual advocate and his working class comrades, which had been for Reed a problem to circumvent rhetorically in his earliest reporting, now becomes dramatically problematic as well, a source of tension with artistic potentialities. (p. 426)

Grotesque humor is the dominant note of the first part of *Mexico*: a man who has lost his wife weeping for his missing spurs, a woman who has lost her lover spending a chaste night with Reed before mindlessly taking a new protector, Reed repeatedly leaving violent brawls he has helped precipitate. The incidents serve Reed's new persona as the tough, committed, worldly writer who turns off pathos and resists a sentimental attitude towards either himself or the masses.

The new persona has an important implication, for its adoption means Reed cannot enforce an identity between himself and the forces of the Revolution as he had with striking workers at home. Only the ambiguous dispensation of the war metaphor—here no metaphor but a fact—saves him from retreating to an aloof stance before the violent action he describes. Reed drains the pathos and menace from revolutionary violence by constantly drawing attention to the comic potential of a picaresque, urbane intellectual encamped among pastoral revolutionaries.

Reed insists on the pastoral nature of his subject because it helps him reflect on the nature of his problematic art. The concluding chapter of this book, *"Los Pastores,"* describes a medieval mystery play performed by Mexican villagers which is fully and spontaneously entered into by the audience. The performance creates itself as an art form which has an authentic and direct function in the lives of the common people. In so doing, it suggests the possibility of a literature which is not moralized like protest fiction and muckraking journalism, nor sensationalized like the reportorial derring-do of Richard Harding Davis, which Reed ironically mocks in *Mexico.* *"Los Pastores"* implicitly raises the idea of Reed's journalism—perhaps—as the new form for his own urbane culture. It is as colorful and as expressive of its subject, the common people as historical actors, as Reed can make it. It embodies, however covertly, an informed awareness of modern politics, technology and ideology. It creates two new literary figures: the revolutionary peasant and the unalienated revolutionary intellectual. In other words, it tries to give the cultures of Villa and Reed each their full artistic rights. (pp. 427-28)

Measured against these standards, Reed's next book, *The War in Eastern Europe,* was a dismal failure. Superficially it is identical in form to *Mexico,* detailing the picaresque adventures of the socialist reporter in the midst of vast events, filled with local color and amusing escapades. The problem is that history has played an ironic joke on Reed by realizing his favorite metaphor in its ugliest form. Reed's purpose is sabotaged by his method. Without the framework of the war metaphor to legitimize his struggle and his unity with the revolutionary masses, Reed becomes entirely disoriented as a narrator.

The want of structure destroys even his political perspective, and his stance degenerates to a mixture of disgust and facetiousness. His local color, when bereft of pastoral logic, becomes chauvinism: "And always Jews, Jews, Jews: bowed, their men in rusty derbies and greasy long coats, with stringy beards and crafty, desperate eyes . . . a race inbred and poisoned with its narrow learning. . . ." [When] Reed wrote *Ten Days That Shook the World,* its very title suggestively parodying the "shot heard round the world" of Emerson's "Concord Hymn," he was no longer a picaresque reporter, but an impassioned documentary artificer, creating through an elaborate comedy of manners the emergence of Red Petrograd itself as a comic hero.

The importance of this comic perspective may not be immediately clear, and yet the creation of major comedy from revolutionary materials had been almost unthinkable since the last days of the French Revolution. (pp. 428-29)

For Reed the holiday—the Revolution—is proposed as a kind of consciousness which can extend itself beyond ten days. This is the comic faith of Reed's account: that the revolution (in which crucial nights in Petrograd significantly pass without a robbery or crime of any kind), that the enchanted period of return of men to their full potentiality, will not be a transitory part of a cycle, but a restoration and new establishment of natural desires and natural order.

One serious objection to this discussion of *Ten Days* as a comic answer to a century of revolutionary tragedies intrudes itself. This is the argument that Reed could write in a comic vein only because he wrote of a comic *stage* of the Revolution. It is as if one restricted one's apprehension of the French Revolution to the fall of the Bastille, to that time when "Bliss was it in that hour to be alive / But to be young was very heaven." The argument would emphasize the nature of the subject rather than Reed's striving for a formal structuring of reality. Even Trotsky, who was certainly anything but an uncritical apologist for the later stages of the Russian Revolution, followed Reed in treating both February and October in comic and often in farcical tones. (pp. 431-32)

Thus it may have been only Reed's reportorial alacrity and early death which saved him from having to deal with the later stages, when the Bolsheviks must confront workers, peasants and revolutionary intellectuals rather than monarchists, liberals, and a new, vulgar bourgeoisie. . . .

One may pose the problem in terms of apparently contradictory theses. The first would say that Reed was a mere journalist and an enthusiastic supporter of the Russian Revolution, and so wrote early and in the light of comedy. The second would declare Reed's book a conscious rebuke to a century of "tragedies." Yet because Reed neglects to plant the seeds of future conflict in terms of bloody violence, dictatorial attitudes of party members, and a clearly drawn division between temporary goals and tactics and long-term strategy, Reed must be pronounced a conscious, but a profoundly undialectical writer. (p. 432)

Reed was able to realize his comic intention in *Ten Days* because the idea of the city, of Red Petrograd, could contain his brilliantly dramatic and impressionistic grasp of detail without the constrictions and distortion of an outgrown picaresque narrative mask. In *Mexico* Reed had exploited the distance between him and the peons making the *Revolucion* by playing on pastoral conventions. In *Ten Days* the setting of an imperial capital allows Reed to bring his urban vision to bear without self-conscious posing. It is not for exotic detail alone that Petrograd is valuable to Reed's purpose. Whether revolutionary comedy is seen as the happy completion of a significant historical action or as the execution of a periodic collective ritual, its highly formalized treatment is possible only in the capital, the symbolic center of a civilization.

The comic pattern can best be seen in terms of the emergence of a new collective hero as the proletariat of Red Petrograd take their place on the stage of history and literature at the same moment. The urban environment is crucial to Reed's comic strategy because it mediates the comic reactions to the appearance of this hero. The developing stages of reaction represent a change in consciousness which is far more important to Reed's drama than the capture of the Winter Palace.

The emergence of the hero occurs on three levels. The first level of reaction to the revolutionary proletariat is that of the bourgeoisie, liberals, and non-Bolshevik socialists, many of them veteran "revolutionaries." Much of the first part of the book is devoted to unmasking the pretensions of the non-Bolshevik intelligentsia, as in scenes like the . . . encounter of student and soldier. . . .

Unmasking must be the main focus for Reed rather than the overthrow of the old regime, for *Ten Days* discovers the comedy of revolution not so much in the displacement of the propertied as in the discomfiture of the intellectuals. The edge of the wit is delicious when the intellectuals are exposed as fatuously self-decieved rather than as hypocrites consciously disguising their motives. (p. 433)

The next level of emergence, that of the "adventures of the hero," is enacted largely in the period of dangers the proletariat must weather after the capture of the Winter Palace. Reed builds up the suspense of the days when the return of Kerensky is feared, raising expectation of a climactic, bloody struggle of resolute foes. Instead, the conflict materializes primarily as a bloodless psychological struggle for the loyalty of the troops. Reed blows a bubble menacing tragic violence, and then pricks it. (p. 434)

The ultimate level of Reed's myth is the self-recognition of the hero as an actor on the stage of history. The collective hero at first cannot be distinguished; the babel of "revolutionary" voices resembles a classic fairy tale in which many suitors contend for the hand of a princess, with one alone her true love. It is worth noting that it is not the Party itself which is hailed as authentic by Reed, but rather the figures of Lenin and Trotsky, the new historical character made *articulate*.

The finale of the book is a sequence of rituals: a real funeral in Moscow and a symbolic wedding in Petrograd. In Moscow, the martyrs of the battles in that city are interred by a triumphant working class in mourning. The ceremony is devout but secular and imbued with revolutionary consciousness. Reed says: "I suddenly realized that the devout Russian people no longer needed priests to pray them into heaven. On earth they were building a kingdom more bright than any heaven had to offer, and for which it was a glory to die. . . ."

The symbolic wedding resolves a very significant political problem, for the proletariat of the cities were only a small minority when compared to the masses of Russian peasantry. The symbolic wedding rites of city and country, workers and peasants (with the return of the defecting prodigal sons) conclude the book. . . .

The collective urban hero has emerged from the shifting appearances of the metropolis. First the pretenders to his name were unmasked. Then Reed's collective protagonist braved the ordeal of violence in facing the threat of counterrevolution without flinching or arbitrary force. At last a voice is added to his will and Red Petrograd is finally prepared to recognize and be recognized by his rural mate, the revolutionary peasantry. And so Reed closes his comedy. (p. 435)

> *Harry Henderson III, "John Reed's Urban Comedy of Revolution," in* The Massachusetts Review (*reprinted from* The Massachusetts Review; © 1973 The Massachusetts Review, Inc.), *Vol. XIV, No. 2, Spring, 1973, pp. 421-35.*

### LAWRENCE FERLINGHETTI  (essay date 1975)

There is indeed, in some of [Reed's] descriptions of the "poor and downtrodden," a sense of the upperclass adventurer doing a little slumming. One can almost see the five-pound wingtip shoes and the Ivy League suit, one of the world's most boring costumes. And Reed did have a fatal innocence about him, a political naiveté which led directly to his death in Moscow. "On earth they were building a kingdom," he wrote from there in 1917, "more bright than any heaven had to offer, and for which it was a glory to die." He did. But when he did, he muttered over and over, "Caught in a trap, caught in a trap." He had painted himself into that corner which a whole generation of American radicals was to paint itself into—that of the totalitarian State which refused to "wither away" as it was supposed to.

Yet Reed's time has come again because his writing also embodies that still insurgent spirit in American life which is much closer to Whitman than to Lenin. (Reed in fact knew Whitman's writing better.) This insurgent spirit is more anarchist and libertarian than authoritarian. It is the spirit of his fiction, not his political reportage, and yet this fiction has generally been considered beneath notice, and no American publisher saw fit to print [the stories of *Adventures of a Young Man*] in the decade since they were published abroad. What also comes through to us in them is a gusto and a love-of-life, an acute and often euphoric observation of the world, coupled with the defiance of youth. And we can use this kind of native solar energy today, in this too-cool post-SLA "time of the ostrich." (pp. 7-8)

> *Lawrence Ferlinghetti, in his preface to* Adventures of a Young Man: Short Stories from Life *by John Reed (© 1975 by City Lights Books; reprinted by permission of City Lights Books), City Lights Books, 1975, pp. 7-8.*

### ROBERT A. ROSENSTONE  (essay date 1975)

More fantastic [than his poetry] was Reed's fiction. Even works set in the present were touched with mystery: the **"Red Hand"** tale with its magic potions and bizarre conspirators; the story of an invasion of modern England turned back by the arrival of King Arthur bearing Excalibur; . . . the **"Story About Kubac,"** a decaying kingdom lost in the backwash of time.

Such strange tales suited Jack's talents. Description was his real strength, tone his métier. Mood was the best element in his stories: the solemn Greek valley haunted by memories of hoplites marching to war; the clangor of Thebes as a torch-bearing army storms a temple; the ghostly lighthouse shrouded by fog on a pine-clad headland; the excitement of shadowy Round Table knights sweeping across a plain into battle. (p. 58)

*Insurgent Mexico* is a book for the eye, a vast panorama like one of the great murals of the Mexican painters, full of color, motion and the life-and-death struggle of a people. Its power comes from the close identification of the author with his subject. Friends of Reed realized this, Lippmann by noting that the writing was "alive with Mexico and you," Dave Carb in saying, "It's so much Reed that I suspect it is very little Mexico." Obviously conscious of this approach, Jack told a story not only of Mexico in arms, but also of an American radical's reaction to revolution. Less clearly did he realize that he was writing an important slice of autobiography, a kind of modern picaresque tale of one man's education in an arena of danger, an adventure yarn about how an American poet becomes a man.

In composing the book, the poet was stronger than the journalist, making *Insurgent Mexico* more encompassing than any straight factual account. Its artistically arranged scenes have a balance, coherence and integrity that daily experience lacks. Skies often turn blood-red after battles, simple peons speak with uncanny folk wisdom, the narrator has sudden flashing insights into the symbolic meanings of complex events—such things occur too often to be taken as a literal transcription of what Reed saw, heard and did. Yet the rearrangement, careful selection and poetic rendering allowed him to create a deep feeling for the texture and quality of a land in the throes of a vast, historic change. (pp. 167-68)

Unlike the predecessor on Mexico, with its rearrangement of material for both personal and dramatic effect, [*The War in Eastern Europe*] was a generally straight-forward, chronological account. The amount of artistry used was no different from that in all Reed's reporting. (p. 232)

Despite fine individual sections, the lack of overall dramatic shape makes *The War in Eastern Europe* less interesting than *Insurgent Mexico*. For all the evocative descriptions of lands and people, and the harrowing and humorous adventures of the narrator, it is a work that conforms to the contours of experience rather than art. The explanation for this is simple enough. Reed's time in Mexico had been a period when a sense of manhood emerged, when individual concern fused with a larger, meaningful cause, and when self and cause could be united through the medium of words. In the Balkans there was no such unity, no John Reed aching to test himself against death, no figure like Villa to personify a movement, no people whose viewpoint could be wholly embraced. There was only a good reporter doing a job under difficult conditions, sometimes allowing an active imagination to roam, but usually remaining planted on the stubborn ground of fact.

If it lacks dramatic impact, *The War in Eastern Europe* fairly crackles with the author's world-view. Peasants and workers are lionized, the overly sophisticated viewed with suspicion, politicians and the wealthy treated with contempt. Sometimes Reed's accuracy of observation conflicted with his preconceptions. Horrified at the "boundless territorial ambitions"—a

recurrent phrase—of all the Balkan states, he would have liked to blame them solely on corrupt leaders. Yet honesty compelled him to report similar views often expressed by unlettered peasants. Much as Jack would have liked to wriggle out of this, it was impossible, and the work's pages have the feeling that imperial ambitions have sunk deep into the hearts of the populace. Certainly this is a main reason that, for all the attraction of Serbs and Bulgars, Reed could never feel at one with them or wholly consider their cause his own. (pp. 232-33)

Compared to his past work, the book on Russia is a major stride forward. For all the brilliant descriptions and set pieces, *Insurgent Mexico* is disjointed, a series of episodes held together by the theme of a young man finding himself amid the violence of agrarian revolution, while *The War in Eastern Europe* has little focus or tension, sustaining interest only through the sharp eyes of the narrator. *Ten Days That Shook the World* is far different. If there is still an "I" relating the action, this narrator is in the background, no more than a camera recording history that dwarfs the story of any individual or group of men.

The structure of the book is that of drama. Three historical-background chapters stand as a prologue; two are a first act in which the people rise; three describe the counterrevolutionary offensive; two more form a final act in which the people emerge triumphant, while a two-chapter epilogue forms a slow denouement, summarizing subsequent events. Underlying the story is an epic theme, the avenging of historic injustice by a trial of arms, the rising of the oppressed and underprivileged to regain power and freedom. The hero is mass man rather than the individual, the epic seen from below rather than above. Standing tradition on its head in this way, Reed was only following a writer's instinct toward a new kind of truth. Living at that point when the mass was entering history with a vengeance, he fixed an image of the crowd as hero for a new age.

Structure and theme keep *Ten Days That Shook the World* focused and tight, providing a driving power. With descriptions toned down, with far fewer consciously poetic flights than in earlier books, Reed keeps the eye centered on concrete places and events—Petrograd with its meeting halls and shabby factories, Smolny and the languid flow of crowds in the streets, idle conversation in cafés and grandiloquent speeches of ministers, proclamations tacked on walls and newspapers fresh with rumors. The work is heavily documented, but the lengthy texts of decrees and speeches become more than idle words to skim. Realizing the feeling inherent in the events, the eloquence of men speaking their hearts in moments of passion and crisis, the author lets their own words create drama and excitement. In this way the vacillating moods, the doubts, hesitation, debates, confusion, anger, betrayal, surprise, purpose and hostility of a revolutionary city are conveyed. Broadening the scope, brief references to decrees, articles, resolutions and actions from the rest of Russia give a sense of the tides of history beating against Smolny, the Marinsky, the Winter Palace, and place Petrograd in a context of anguish and triumph of workers, soldiers and Soviets. The capital city is a test case, a model of struggle that drastically changed the course of a nation. By implication it is also a model for other countries and for all mankind.

*Ten Days That Shook the World* is a distillation, a summation of Reed's feeling about the revolution and its importance. Being that, it is streaked with bias. (pp. 335-37)

In writing *Ten Days That Shook the World,* John Reed was working at the limit of his artistic capacities. For years he had believed himself a poet, but only recently, in a few brief works, had he been free and brave enough to bare those inner regions of pain that forge a bond of images between people. The Russian revolution allowed him to do the same on a broad canvas. A movement rooted in objective conditions that simultaneously oppressed people's bodies and stunted their imaginations, it was much more than a series of external events. The fullness of the revolution could be encompassed only by a writer sensitive to its emotional basis and overtones, and Reed was such a man. Because he shared the commitment and vision of the participants, he was able to capture the emotions that people pour into waking dreams. Inaccurate in details, biased in point of view, *Ten Days That Shook the World* conveys the kind of truth that is beyond fact, that creates fact. More than history, it is poetry, the poetry of revolution. (p. 337)

> *Robert A. Rosenstone, in his* Romantic Revolutionary: A Biography of John Reed *(copyright © 1975 by Robert A. Rosenstone; reprinted by permission of Alfred A. Knopf, Inc.), Knopf, 1975, 430 p.*

## A.J.P. TAYLOR   (essay date 1977)

George Kennan, the American diplomat and historian, has written: 'Reed's account of the events of that time rises above every other contemporary record for its literary power, its penetration, its command of detail. It will be remembered when all the others are forgotten'. Reed's [*Ten Days That Shook the World*] is not only the best account of the Bolshevik revolution, it comes near to being the best account of any revolution. (p. vii)

[Reed] was too good a journalist to write propaganda, but he made no secret of where his sympathies lay. He had one further quality which completed the others. He was a great writer. To quote Kennan again, 'Reed was a poet of the first order'. This book is evidence that he was a prose artist of the first order also.

Dazzled by Reed's achievement, we may fail to appreciate exactly what it was. This is not history written in detachment, with a large bibliography and a fuller understanding than men had at the time. The book is a contribution to history, not an analysis composed afterwards. It is first-hand evidence when Reed described what he saw and experienced. But much of it is not first-hand. Often Reed sat in the quiet of his hotel room, cigarette in mouth, tapping out on his typewriter copy for *The Masses*. He would piece together fragments of conversations, add imaginative detail of what was likely to have happened and crown all with a brilliant phrase.

For instance Reed often says that Smolny, which housed the Petrograd Soviet, was 'humming with activity', lights blazing all night, messengers and Red Guards crowding its corridors. Smolny appears as a sort of beehive and with little detail of what the bees were up to. Reed did not in fact know. He was a foreign journalist, though a sympathetic one, and the Bolsheviks revealed to him few of their secrets. Again Reed, like any good reporter, gives the impression of an unflagging excitement. In reality nothing was happening for much of the time, and Reed himself was occupied only in talking with other American journalists. (pp. xiii-ix)

Reed's book is not reliable in every detail. Its achievement is to recapture the spirit of those stirring days. As with most writers, Reed heightened the drama, and this drama sometimes took over from reality. Bolshevik participants, when they looked back, often based their recollections more on Reed's book than on their own memories. This often happens. Veterans of the First World War saw the trenches through the eyes of Robert Graves, Edmund Blunden and Siegfried Sassoon, and their own memories became blurred. In this sense, Reed's book founded a legend, one which has largely triumphed over the facts. (p. ix)

> *A.J.P. Taylor, "Introduction" (copyright © 1977 by A.J.P. Taylor; reprinted by permission of Penguin Books Ltd), to* Ten Days That Shook the World *by John Reed, Penguin Books, 1977, pp. vii-xix.*

## PAUL BERMAN   (essay date 1982)

In *Insurgent Mexico* [Reed] followed the Jack London example of rebel writer on the road, and pursued adventure to an extreme. The book was about a trip with notebook and camera to the front lines of the Mexican Revolution. . . .

[In] Mexico Reed found a revolutionary leader who made Big Bill [Haywood] look like white bread: Pancho Villa, the ferocious bandit, whom Reed once saw wandering along the front of a major battle encouraging his men, cigar in one hand, bomb in the other, ready to light the fuse and let go. . . .

Reed pictured Villa as a kind of perfect primitive king: abysmally, even comically, ignorant, dependent on the suggestions of his educated followers, but able to weigh and choose among these suggestions with the trueness of his emotions and the simplicity of his moral sense. . . .

The portrait laid it on so thick that Reed's coolness and judgment were called into question. He did seem to have been flamboozled by the brutal bandit leader. Yet the portrait suggested a powerful idea. At the center of revolutionary events, Reed seemed to be saying, stands a heroic figure—in this case a primitive himself and spokesman for a primitive class, a man of will, no bohemian dilettante or trade union piecard corrupted by ties to the middle class, but a violent doer, a bandit, by God, a man so strong he could put his shoulder to history and butt it forward a few feet. . . . (p. 6)

[In] *Ten Days That Shook the World,* Reed produced a book that does indeed occupy a place in the hsitory of politics, America's one great contribution to the classics of international Communism. How was he able to do this? The question was first asked by N. K. Krupskaya, the Bolshevik leader who also happened to be Lenin's wife, in her preface to the first Russian edition in 1923. The Russians themselves don't write this way about the October Revolution, she observed. Reed was a foreigner who hardly knew the customs of Russia, could barely speak the language. And yet he had grasped the meaning of the revolution and had written an "epochal" book. He did this, she explained, by being a revolutionary in spirit, a true Communist.

The structure of *Ten Days* suggests that Reed had changed considerably since *Insurgent Mexico*. He had grown up some (he was 32 when he wrote *Ten Days*) and no longer doted quite so boyishly on swashbuckles. He had always had a sense of economy in drawing scenes, but now speeded up to the pace of a teletype machine. By no means did he give up on self-conscious literary techniques; he still threw in Whitmanesque flourishes about the "terrible dawn gray-rising over Russia" or the "world red-tide," some of which were, in combination with the teletype pace, very effective. But *Insurgent Mexico* was organized around these techniques, and the new book wasn't. Stephen Crane lay behind him. Instead he filled *Ten Days* with facts, dozens of documents, speeches, placards, debates, sometimes reproduced in full. He included copies of leaflets, Cyrillic letters staring up from the page. The mass of material is confusing, fatiguing, almost too breathless to get through. Reading it is like deciphering one of those walls covered with a thousand posters. Then again, it has extraordinary energy, and a sense of extraordinary fidelity. *Insurgent Mexico* read like a novel. *Ten Days That Shook the World* was a report from the front. (p. 6-7)

Only in the portraits of Lenin and Trotsky did *Ten Days* depart from Reed's earlier ideas, and even here the departure was not obvious. Lenin and Trotsky stand at the center of *Ten Days* just as Villa stood at the center of *Insurgent Mexico*. Like Villa, they radiate fierceness and strength. . . .

But the difference between Villa and the Bolsheviks is that the Bolsheviks don't lug bombs to the front, they lug a theory of history, and at each little step in the Petrograd struggle detonate a new assertion about how history is moving along. . . .

These Bolsheviks were intellectuals, more intellectual even than Reed and the bohemian writers. There was nothing romantic about them in Reed's old sense. He described Lenin as physically "unimpressive," "colorless," "without picturesque idiosyncrasies." But this Lenin had fashioned an altogether new notion of what intellectuals could do. He and the Bolsheviks had shouldered aside the natural leaders of the working class and put themselves at the head of the proletariat, and in doing so they had made the revolution. This was not the same as having wild adventures, Reed-style, or being a writer for *The Masses* and hoping vaguely that one's literary labors would help the proletariat. The Bolshevik example was far more serious, far grander, and there was no room in it for the old bohemian gaiety. (p. 7)

> *Paul Berman, "To Russia with Love" (reprinted by permission of* The Village Voice *and the author; copyright © News Group Publications, Inc., 1982), in* The Village Voice, *Vol. XXVII, No. 6, February 3-9, 1982, pp. 6-9.\**

## ADDITIONAL BIBLIOGRAPHY

Aaron, Daniel. "Four Radicals." In his *Writers on the Left*, pp. 30-67. New York: Harcourt, Brace & World, 1961.*
   Explores Reed's relationship to such radical writers and activists as Max Eastman and Floyd Dell.

Dell, Floyd. Introduction to *Daughter of the Revolution and Other Stories*, by John Reed, pp. v-ix. New York: Vanguard Press, 1927.
   Guarded praise for the short stories collected in *Daughter of the Revolution and Other Stories*.

Dos Passos, John. "Jack Reed." *New Masses* 6, No. 5 (October 1930): 6-7.
   An impressionistic biocritical sketch.

Gelb, Barbara. *So Short a Time: A Biography of John Reed and Louise Bryant*. New York: W. W. Norton and Co., 1973, 304 p.
   Traces the professional and personal relationship between Reed and Bryant and includes substantial quotations from their books and letters.

Lerner, Max. "John Reed: No Legend." In his *Ideas Are Weapons: The History and Uses of Ideas*, pp. 174-77. New York: The Viking Press, 1940.
   Characterizes Reed as a writer villified by historians who are more interested in the man's exploits than in the man himself. Lerner applauds Reed's thirst for "freedom and action and joyousness . . . that gives his life importance for us and makes the incidents of it credible."

Madison, Charles A. "John Reed: Rebel into Revolutionary." In his *Critics and Crusaders: A Century of American Protest*, pp. 507-27. New York: Henry Holt and Co., 1947.
   Highlights elements from the author's background that informed his major works.

Startsey, Able. "Writer and Revolutionary." *Soviet Literature*, No. 10 (1977): 165-68.
   An excerpt from Startsey's Russian-language introduction to *The Russian Note-Books of John Reed*. The author focuses upon Reed's political development, naming the individuals and movements that most influenced him.

# Olive (Emilie Albertina) Schreiner (Cronwright)

## 1855-1920

(Also wrote under pseudonym of Ralph Iron) South African novelist, essayist, short story writer, and critic.

Schreiner was an important feminist and social critic. Her polemic *Woman and Labour* was once regarded as "the Bible of the international feminist movement," and her novel *The Story of an African Farm* introduced Victorian England to modern ideas on sexuality and the nature of truth. Her fiction, set in her native South Africa, brought that country's natural beauty, people, and racial problems to the world's attention.

Schreiner was born in Basutoland, South Africa of missionary parents. She was self-educated but well-read, and supported herself working as a governess to Boer children. While still in her teens, Schreiner began writing her semiautobiographical novel, *The Story of an African Farm*. In 1883, she took the manuscript to London, where it came to the attention of George Meredith, a reader for the publisher Chapman and Hall. Meredith urged publication of the book, which appeared under the author's pseudonym, Ralph Iron. *African Farm* was an immediate critical and popular success, appealing to Victorian readers because of its original subject matter, exotic setting, and unconventional views of religion and marriage. But when the public discovered that the author of *African Farm* was a woman, fame turned to notoriety and the book was reassessed as un-Christian and antifeminine. No longer able to publish her work in England, Schreiner returned to South Africa. There, she married Samuel Cronwright, a lawyer and politician who occasionally collaborated with her in writing broadsides on social issues. Schreiner published numerous essays on women's issues and on South Africa's racial concerns, attacking the policies of Prime Minister Cecil Rhodes in *Trooper Peter Halket of Mashonaland*. But *Woman and Labour* is considered her most important social statement. The book attacks the economic and personal oppression of working women, and was hailed throughout the Western world as a persuasive, timely document. During her career, Schreiner also produced three volumes of allegorical, mystical short stories and worked on two novels left unfinished at her death, *Undine* and *From Man to Man*.

All of Schreiner's novels are concerned with women's search for equality, love, and fulfillment. They share characteristics common to Victorian fiction: the tendency to ramble and to appeal to the emotions rather than to the intellect. Schreiner drew credible characterizations of children, but her depictions of adults, and especially her male characters, are often considered unrealistic. However, many critics contend that Schreiner is best appraised as something other than a fiction writer. In her novels, the artist often gives way to the social reformer, and some critics view *Trooper Peter Halket of Mashonaland* as a political and economic tract rather than a novel. In her short stories, Schreiner's bold, lively, and realistic style takes on a quasi-biblical aura. These stories offer vibrant, optimistic visions of life, contrasting sharply with her novels in style and tone. Based upon readings of Schreiner's stories, some critics have described her as essentially a poet and a prophet, and not a fiction writer.

BBC Hulton Picture Library

Modern feminists consider Schreiner one of the most important voices of the movement's early days. Her role as an influence upon other writers is also widely acknowledged. According to some critics, D. H. Lawrence's early novels owe much to Schreiner's daring treatment of human sexuality. Her pioneering essays on the repressed plight of women and South African blacks, as well as her imaginative depiction of her homeland, have influenced many writers around the world.

## PRINCIPAL WORKS

*The Story of an African Farm* [as Ralph Iron]   (novel) 1883
*Dreams*  (short stories)  1890
*Trooper Peter Halket of Mashonaland*  (novel)  1897
*Woman and Labour*  (essay)  1911
*Stories, Dreams, and Allegories*  (short stories)  1923
*The Letters of Olive Schreiner: 1876-1920*  (letters)  1924
*From Man to Man*  (unfinished novel)  1926
*Undine*  (unfinished novel)  1928

## HENRY NORMAN   (essay date 1883)

In spite of the very masculine name on the title-page [*The Story of an African Farm*] is clearly the work of a woman, and almost equally clearly of a very young one, which makes it all the more remarkable. The hand of the beginner, too, is betrayed by a number of faults of proportion and perspective. The modest title gives no clue to the contents. It is the story of the growth of a human mind cut off from all but the most commonplace influences, facing its own doubts, crushing its own and others' deceits, and at last beating out a music which is not very melodious, but which is thoroughly honest. On the solitary ''Kopje,'' in the growth of the mind of the little Dutch Waldo, there comes up for solution one after another the simple questions of human nature and human action that the world has labelled with many big names; and this young lady historian of Boer life—if the above surmise is correct—faces them as they rise with refreshing temerity, and what is still more surpising and refreshing, she has the right word to say about almost all. Orthodox Christianity, Unitarian Christianity, woman suffrage, marriage, Malthusianism, immortality—they all arise, though not with these names, over the horizon of this African farm. The book might well be called the *Romance of the New Ethics,* and to those to whom the New Ethics embodies the hopes and the promises of the future, this novel offers a rare treat, for its author has a just appreciation of the terms and the solution of most of the problems to which this ethics applies. It is, too, an unspeakable relief to escape from the domains of the ordinary novelist—from Homburg and the Highlands, from yachts, clubs, hansoms, and Piccadilly. This book teaches the lesson that wherever there are human hearts beating with natural impulses there is scene enough for all the tragedy and all the comedy of life—that for the delineation of the highest interests of men and women *una domus sufficit.* The characters are all original—we have met none of them before; the style is fresh and full of humour; and, in spite of its occasional youthful lapses, the whole story is of fascinating interest, and, what is more, of great moral power. (p. 882)

> *Henry Norman, ''Theories and Practice of Modern Fiction,'' in* The Fortnightly Review *(reprinted by permission of Contemporary Review Company Limited), n.s. Vol. XXXIV, December 1, 1883, pp. 870-86.**

## RALPH IRON [Olive Schreiner]   (essay date 1883)

I have to thank cordially the public and my critics for the reception they have given [*The Story of an African Farm*].

Dealing with a subject that is far removed from the round of English daily life, it of necessity lacks the charm that hangs about the ideal representation of familiar things, and its reception has therefore been the more kindly.

A word of explanation is necessary. Two strangers appear on the scene, and some have fancied that in the second they have again the first, who returns in a new guise. Why this should be we cannot tell; unless there is a feeling that a man should not appear upon the scene, and then disappear, leaving behind him no more substantial trace than a mere book; that he should return later on as husband or lover, to fill some more important part than that of the mere stimulator of thought.

Human life may be painted according to two methods. There is the stage method. According to that each character is duly marshalled at first, and ticketed; we know with an immutable certainty that at the right crises each one will reappear and act his part, and, when the curtain falls, all will stand before it bowing. There is a sense of satisfaction in this, and of completeness. But there is another method—the method of the life we all lead. Here nothing can be prophesied. There is a strange coming and going of feet. Men appear, act and react upon each other, and pass away. When the crisis comes, the man who would fit it does not return. When the curtain falls, no one is ready. When the footlights are brightest, they are blown out; and what the name of the play is no one knows. (pp. 7-8)

It has been suggested by a kind critic that he would better have liked the little book if it had been a history of wild adventure; of cattle driven into inaccessible ''kranzes'' by Bushmen; ''of encounters with ravening lions, and hair-breadth escapes.'' This could not be. Such works are best written in Piccadilly or in the Strand; there the gifts of the creative imagination, untrammelled by contact with any fact, may spread their wings.

But should one sit down to paint the scenes among which he has grown, he will find that the facts creep in upon him. Those brilliant phases and shapes which the imagination sees in far-off lands are not for him to portray. Sadly he must squeeze the color from his brush, and dip it into the gray pigments around him. He must paint what lies before him. (pp. 8-9)

> *Ralph Iron [pseudonym of Olive Schreiner], ''Preface'' (1883), in her* The Story of an African Farm, *second edition, Roberts Brothers, 1894, pp. 7-9.*

## [ARTHUR SYMONS]   (essay date 1891)

It is nearly ten years since the publication of that wonderful book '**The Story of an African Farm**.'. . . It is by this time recognized, as a matter on which there can be no further question, that, as we ventured to say when reviewing it, the '**African Farm**' is a work of genius—immature in parts, and unequal as a whole, certainly, but a novel which has brought something new into literature. Here was a new voice, and the voice came from the heart to the heart. The style of the book is so simple as to seem childlike, and sometimes almost childish; there are occasional idioms which betray a foreign origin; whether by natural instinct or supreme art, there is something enchantingly artless about the manner of saying things. The book itself is a confession; it is so profoundly and intensely personal that it has seemed to many to express the deepest of their own feelings, the most intimate and secret of their thoughts. With much speculation, with much that might be called controversial in it, '**The Story of an African Farm**' is really great by reason of its simple human element. It would be hard to find in literature anything more poignant than certain pages—pages in which the agony of suffering, of loss, of death, seems to throb in the words like an actual wound in the body, an actual distress in the soul. The narrative of the death of Lyndall makes the reader think: ''The woman who wrote this must have herself died!'' The pathos is so keen as to become at times oppressive, like some unbearable suffering in which one has to share. For all its humour there never was a book less cheerful; its most supporting quality is a sort of gallant despair.

Miss Schreiner's new book will be a surprise, and probably a disappointment, to many of her admirers. ['**Dreams**'] is a book of allegories. One of them, it is true, had already appeared in the '**African Farm**,' where it seems to gather up into itself all the tangled threads of the narrative, expressing its deeper meaning. Some of the others have been printed in magazines. Brought together now, they make but a small volume, and a volume of so new a kind in so old a form that they are in danger of being either overlooked or misunderstood. Most people have a prejudice against allegories, and very justly. The form is dangerous for the artist, and rarely acceptable to the public. . . . But the allegories of Miss Schreiner are something entirely new; they can be compared only with the painted allegories of Mr. [George Frederic] Watts. Written in exquisite prose—somewhat less spontaneously simple than the prose of the **'African Farm,'** but with more colour and harmony—they have the essential qualities of poetry, and are, indeed, poems in prose. The book is like nothing else in English. Probably it will have no successors, as it has had no forerunners. Into these allegories Miss Schreiner seems to have put the soul of her soul; they express, in the only form possible, that passion for abstract ideas which in her lies deeper than any other. They are profoundly human, yet in no limited sense. Apprehended thus, the allegory may be considered the essence of art, all art being symbol, and allegories themselves pure symbols. Having felt that the whole book of the **'African Farm'** was condensed into that allegory about the hunter, Miss Schreiner has realized more and more the capacity of the form, its power in her hands, and she has given us, in this volume of allegories, her most deeply-felt "message."

**'The Sunlight lay across my Bed,'** the longest and most elaborate of these **'Dreams,'** is a vision of heaven and hell. It is at once music and a picture. Beautiful and terrible shapes move, as in a remote distance, before us; the words seem to chant themselves to a music which we do not hear. To appreciate all that is meant by this new kind of prose the writer demands some assistance from the reader, for printed words in prose cannot become audible, as words in verse may more easily do, in the precise tone and rhythm intended without some sympathetic aid from without. (pp. 46-7)

None of the other allegories is written in quite so lyrical a prose as this; they are not less poetical. And they are so many aspirations after the good, the true, the beautiful—so many expressions of sympathy with man who cannot find truth, who will not seek beauty, who has wandered away from good. Some of them are consecrated, in a yet more special sense, to the cause of woman: the **'Three Dreams in a Desert,'** for instance, and **'I thought I stood.'** The message of the book is a word of hope—ascetic, unrestful hope, born painfully of the brave, acquiescent despair of the earlier book; but still, hope. That signifies an advance in intellectual grasp, in intellectual control, and consequently in artistic mastery. (p. 47)

> [*Arthur Symons,*] "'*Dreams*'," in *The Athenaeum*, *No. 3298, January 10, 1891, pp. 46-7.*

### J. A. HOBSON  (essay date 1911)

The most essential character of the modern Woman's Movement, as Mrs. Schreiner sees it, is that of a half-instinctive, half-conscious struggle against certain social-economic forces driving women in the civilised world into a state of sex-parasitism. . . .

This "sex-parasitism" which Mrs. Schreiner sees growing in all civilised nations will, unless it is counteracted, drag down into physical, mental, and moral feebleness large numbers of women, widening the gulf of sympathy and co-operation between the sexes, and degrading by tradition and inheritance the character and ideals of the race. (p. 33)

Though the argument is by no means new, the force of Mrs. Schreiner's reasoned eloquence raises it to a higher power which sweeps aside the flimsy barriers that usage, prejudice, or sex interest have set up against it. For it is not merely the interests and aspirations of the sex, or of a little ambitious or excitable section of it, as is often held, that are at stake. Setting her issue in the full stream of a sociological interpretation, Mrs. Schreiner shows that what is at stake is the progress of humanity. For so inextricably knit by nature are the fates and characters of the sexes, that every denial of full liberty to woman must react on man and upon history, which is their joint life. Mrs. Schreiner does not, for instance, hesitate to insist that the survival of the horrors and iniquities of war is a result of male monopoly in politics. The equal weighting of women with men in critical determinations of policy will turn the scale against war. . . .

Though in [*Woman and Labour*] many highly disputable points are raised, and some of them settled in too arbitrary a manner, there is nowhere discernable that strain of sex antagonism which has of late, especially in this country, been far too prominent. Mrs. Schreiner does not see woman striving as a sex against a conspiracy of male monopolists and oppressors, the "new woman" against an inevitable "old man." On the contrary, she recognises everywhere a change in the sex attitude and disposition of man as large and as significant in its way as that of woman. She sees a "new man" preparing to grasp hands with the "new woman" in a spirit of equal comradeship, reforming on a sounder basis the structure not only of industry, but of marital and family relations, a gain and not a loss of sympathy between the sexes, a finer, because a freer, co-operation for all the purposes sexual, intellectual, and spiritual which contribute to the fuller life of humanity. (p. 34)

> *J. A. Hobson, "The Economic Freedom of Woman,"* in The Bookman, *London, Vol. XL, No. 235, April, 1911, pp. 33-4.**

### REBECCA WEST  (essay date 1912)

Olive Schreiner is less a woman than a geographical fact. Just as one thinks of Egypt as a foreground for the Pyramids, so South Africa seems the setting of that warm, attractive, aggressive personality. Her work is far inferior to her. **"Woman and Labour"** was slow and vague, though its heart was in the right place. **"The Story of a South African Farm"** was a good novel spoilt by an illicit attempt to improve the reader's morals. In **"Dreams"** she wrote of an abstract spiritual woman, just as Adam Smith wrote about an abstract economic man. To avoid the incomplete conclusions which are consequent on writing about abstractions she attempted to write in a poetic style, although at all times she has lacked the "fundamental brainwork" needed for poetry. Her real line was probably realism, for that, in its surrender of the selective power, needs little brainwork; Zola wrote charming novels on no basis whatsoever. Moreover, her style is too humourless for poetry. When Woman and Wine come leaping towards the Hunter they announce themselves as "the twins, Sensuality," as if sensuality would ever be anything so morally unassailable as twins, which are most commonly found among the more respectable poor in rural districts. The occasional note of private and confidential enlightenment over commonplace facts is subtly absurd. "Then the sun passed down behind the hills: but I knew that the next day he would rise again."

Her philosophy tends towards the most undiscriminating asceticism. (p. 391)

Rebecca West, *"So Simple" (reprinted by permission of A D Peters & Co Ltd), in* The Freewoman, *Vol. II, No. 46, October 3, 1912, pp. 390-91.\**

### FLOYD DELL  (essay date 1913)

Mrs. Olive Schreiner stands, by virtue of her latest book, **"Women and Labor,"** as an exponent of the doctrine that would send women into every field of economic activity; or, rather, the doctrine that finds in the forces which are driving them there a savior of her sex from the degradation of parasitism. In behalf of this doctrine she has expended all that eloquence and passion which have made her one of the figures in modern literature and a spokesman for all women who have not learned to speak that hieratic language which is heard, as the inexpressive speech of daily life is not heard, across space and time. (pp. 42-3)

*Floyd Dell, "Olive Schreiner and Isadora Duncan," in his* Women As World Builders: Studies in Modern Feminism *(copyright, 1913, by Forbes and Company), Forbes, 1913, pp. 41-51.\**

### HAVELOCK ELLIS  (essay date 1921)

Now that I have re-read Emily Brontë's [*Wuthering Heights*] I see that there is no later book in its class that can profitably be compared to it except **The Story of an African Farm**. There are more inequalities and extravagances and crudities of art in **The African Farm** than in the sober unbroken harmony of *Wuthering Heights,* and this is more than the difference between the hard grey gloom of Yorkshire—though the light and waters of Yorkshire can sparkle—and the fierce brilliance of the Karoo, for "Ellis Bell" was two or three years older than "Ralph Iron," at an age when two or three years make a great difference. On the other hand, there is in **The African Farm** an incomparable splendour of style, a poet's imagination, an audacity of thought, a flaming aspiration of social vision which were beyond the orbit of Emily Brontë's narrow and dark genius. They were alike in that each of them possessed masculine intellect in a feminine temperament, and that each embodied in her book the concentrated youthful passion of a solitary soul of the rarest intensity. (pp. 82-3)

*Havelock Ellis, in his journal entry of July 8, 1921, in his* Impressions and Comments: 1920-1923, third series *(copyright, 1924, by Havelock Ellis; copyright renewed © 1952 by Françoise Lafitte Cyon; reprinted by permission of Françoise Lafitte for the Literary Estate of Havelock Ellis), Houghton Mifflin, 1924, pp. 81-5.\**

### PHYLLIS BOTTOME  (essay date 1924)

[Olive Schreiner's] few writings show the maturity and weight of style, the simple and exquisite precision of a finished workman. But no great artist, not cut short by death, has ever expressed so little out of such vast stores. In reading the sincere and faithful account of her life written by her devoted husband, this great secret presses on the reader at the turn of every page: "How could she be so great, and consent to produce so little?" (pp. 624-25)

[Her] great first novel [**The Story of an African Farm**] is difficult to place in literature. In some ways it takes the place for South Africa that Harriet Beecher Stowe's *Uncle Tom's Cabin* took for the Southern States; but it is artistically a much greater book than *Uncle Tom's Cabin* and a far greater departure from all conventional law. It was the work of a first-rate, if ignorant mind, at work upon a second-rate and mature world. (p. 627)

[She produced] one brave, crude authentic piece of South African history, at the age of twenty-one, in **The Story of an African Farm;** a scarcely veiled attack on Rhodes in **Trooper Peter Halkett;** a clear and excellent study on **Woman and Labour,** and two wonderful short volumes of **Dreams** which should take a permanent place in English literature; and the memory of a great soul who lived upon its own inner wisdom with absolute integrity. (p. 630)

*Phyllis Bottome, "The Life of Olive Schreiner," in* Contemporary Review, *Vol. CXXV, May, 1924, pp. 624-30.*

### VIRGINIA WOOLF  (essay date 1925)

Olive Schreiner was neither a born letterwriter nor did she choose to make herself become one. She wrote carelessly, egotistically, of her health, of her sufferings, of her beliefs and desires, as if she were talking in the privacy of her room to a friend whom she trusted. This carelessness, while it has its charm, imposes some strain on the reader [of **The Letters of Olive Schreiner**]. If he is not to drop the book, dispirited by the jumble and muddle of odds and ends, plans and arrangements, bulletins of health and complaints of landladies—all of which are related as if Olive Schreiner were a figure of the highest importance—he must seek some point of view which imposes unity, some revelation in the light of which this rather distant and unfamiliar figure becomes of interest. He will find it perhaps in two sentences written in the same letter the year before she died. "Nothing matters in life but love and a great pity for all our fellows," she writes. That, indeed, was her teaching. A few lines lower down she adds, "It's ten days ago since I've spoken to anyone except the girl who brings up my coals and water." That was her fate. The discrepancy between what she desired and what she achieved can be felt, jarring and confusing, throughout the book. Always she is striving for something which escapes her grasp. Always some fault or misfortune interferes with her success. She loves the world at large, but cannot endure any individual in particular. Such would seem to be an outline snapshot of her position. But it is difficult to say further where the fault or misfortune lay. . . . She herself had a profound belief in her genius, and an overwhelming enthusiasm for her convictions. Nevertheless, all the strife and agony which ring through her letters—"The hidden agony of my life no human being understands"; "I am a fine genius, a celebrity, and tomorrow all these people would tread me under their feet"—resulted in one remarkable novel and a few other fragmentary works which no admirer of **The Story of an African Farm** would care to place beside it. But that famous book itself provides some explanation of her failure to become, as she bade fair to become, the equal of our greatest novelists. In its brilliance and power it reminds us inevitably of the Brontë novels. In it, as in them, we feel ourselves in the presence of a powerful nature which can make us see what it saw, and feel what it felt with astounding vividness. But it has the limitations of those egotistical masterpieces without a full measure of their strength. The writer's interests are local, her passions personal, and we cannot help suspecting that she has neither the width nor the strength to enter with sympathy into the experiences of minds differing from her own, or to debate questions calmly and reasonably.

Unfortunately for her fame as a writer, it was into debate and politics, and not into thought and literature, that she was impelled, chiefly by her passionate interest in sex questions. She was driven to teach, to dream and prophesy. Questions affecting women, in particular the relations between the sexes, obsessed her. There is scarcely a letter in the present volume in which she does not discuss them with passion, insight, and force, but interminably, in season and out, while her gifts as a writer were bestowed upon a stupendous work upon woman, which, though it took up her time and thought for years, remained, unfortunately, an unfinished masterpiece.

Her private life, disclosed very openly in the present book, seems equally thwarted and disappointed. . . . Her obsessions and her egotism are perfectly obvious in her letters; but so, too, are her convictions, her ruthless sincerity, and the masterly sanity which so often contrasts on the same page with childish outbursts of unreason. Olive Schreiner was one half of a great writer; a diamond marred by a flaw.

> *Virginia Woolf, "Olive Schreiner" (reprinted by permission of the Literary Estate of Virginia Woolf and The Hogarth Press Ltd.), in* The New Republic, *Vol. XLII, No. 537, March 18, 1925, p. 103.*

### ARNOLD BENNETT (essay date 1928)

In addition to being a long book, [*From Man to Man*] is certainly a full book, and the work of a very full mind. And to a marked degree it is propagandist literature. In these days, when the social conscience is so lively, sensitive, and inconvenient, every serious novelist must be a propagandist of something; otherwise his novels will not "rank." Olive Schreiner always ranged herself with the Left wing of critical and constructive thought. She was a vehement and even furious reformer. (p. 307)

I think that *From Man to Man* carries propaganda to excess. True, it is far less propagandist than [H. G. Wells's *The World of William Clissold*] but then *Clissold* is clearly, by the very spirit of its conception, a propagandist work. It is a political-social testament. The same cannot be said of *From Man to Man,* which is primarily a South African domestic story of two sisters, of whom the elder, Rebekah (the heroine), suffers desolation at the hands of a too temperamental husband and defeats the dog, and the younger, Baby-Bertie, drops somewhat casually into prostitution. The propaganda, though excellent of its kind, is not in the least essential to the story. A hundred pages might be cut out of the book, still leaving the story intact. When the two chief propagandists open their mouths they talk just like Olive Schreiner writes: which fact does not make for convincingness. And neither of them has humour or gaiety. Only the wicked ones are allowed by their creator to be gay. All the same, Rebekah is a big character; she is drawn, and successfully drawn, on the Valkyrie scale. Pity she is a shade too good, tremendous, and sublime for any husband's daily food!

Impossible to conceal that I have been a little, indeed more than a little, disappointed with *From Man to Man.* I had both heard and read rapturous praise of it. Such unmeasured laudation might well have prejudiced me against the book had I not had an intense, almost life-long, admiration for Olive Schreiner. I read *The Story of an African Farm* in 1889. It is one of the three novels that have kept me up all night. . . . Some passages in it are inferior to the rest, but taken as a whole it is a mighty affair.

Disagreeing with the majority, I thought *Trooper Peter Halket* extremely fine. As for the *Dreams* ("**The sunlight lay across my bed**"), I shall never forget the impression they made on me when they appeared in the *New Review*. Nothing like them before in English literature! Nor have they been even tolerably imitated. Yes, I was handsomely prepared and apparelled to be ecstatic about *From Man to Man.* 100 pages, and the thrill didn't come. 200, 300, 400 pages. No thrill! I felt cheated,—but solemnly cheated. I respected, I admired, but I wanted to admire much more.

To pass an adverse verdict on the book is not to pass an adverse verdict on the author. Because the book was never finished, and probably the completed parts were not finally revised. The most difficult chapters were not even sketched out. Yet *From Man to Man* was begun in 1873, and the author was still working at it in 1907. Now no novelist can write a satisfactory, coherent novel in 34 years. . . . The critical faculty is blurred. The work is bound to go wrong somewhere. This particular work seems in the latter half of it to be vitiated by a curious sentimentality.

But the gravest fault of the book, in my opinion, lies in the conception of the heroine. No woman so big, and politically so constructive, could possibly have continued throughout life to give her main attention to children and domesticity and the sacrificial diplomacy demanded by endless conjugal misfortune. Her genius, in fulfilling itself, would have forced her to put these matters in their proper secondary place. Neither the Karoo nor Cape Town could have confined her scope. She would have compelled the attention of the whole Anglo-Saxon literary world—as Olive Schreiner did. Rebekah is consistently too prodigious for her environment.

Her grand protest to the light husband takes the form of a letter which she sits up all night to compose. This letter is the equivalent of a book, and a remarkable book. It is, I calculated, 20,000 words long. Rebekah, though the author says she wore no stays, couldn't have written that book in a night. One feels, while reading on and on and on—and every intelligent reader must feel—that one is being asked to believe the impossible. (pp. 307-11)

Withal, *From Man to Man* demands, extorts, laudation. It is a very considerable book, by a genius who unfortunately was not content to be a genius. The unhappy woman was beset by her visions of the imperfectness of this world. In the end these visions overcame the artist in her. (p. 311)

> *Arnold Bennett, "Books of the Year," in his* The Savour of Life: Essays in Gusto *(copyright © 1928 by Doubleday, Doran & Company, Inc.; copyright renewed © 1952 by Marie Marguerite Bennett; reprinted by permission of the publisher), Doubleday, 1928, pp. 293-313.\**

### J. C. SMUTS (essay date 1948)

What struck me most in my personal contacts with Olive Schreiner was the intensity of her genius. She was a flame which burnt too fiercely, and, I fear, in the end frustrated and consumed herself. In this respect she resembled Emily Brontë, whose genius had the same, and an even higher, intensity, and whose characters all express this extreme quality.

In both cases their creations were simply the expression of the intense personality of the writers. Both reveal the mystery of the human personality in their art. Both had a great capacity for love, and love at a pitch of intensity which was almost demonic in its quality. In fact, *Wuthering Heights* is the finest example of demonic love, of fierce love which is almost one with hatred, in literature. With Olive Schreiner this intensity of love was given to all the good causes which she so vehemently championed, and the result was often detrimental to her artistic work. Art has its balance, as all great performance has. She had a passion for the cause of women which has seldom been equalled, and which gives immortal value to her *Story of an African Farm*. (pp. 13-14)

I love her as I love Emily Brontë. . . . Such women cast a radiance on this sombre scene in which we carry on the human struggle. (p. 14)

> *J. C. Smuts, in his introduction to* Not without Honour: The Life and Writings of Olive Schreiner *by Vera Buchanan-Gould, Hutchinson & Co. (Publishers) Limited, 1948, pp. 13-14.*

### D. L. HOBMAN   (essay date 1955)

Although [Olive Schreiner] wrote three novels, several volumes of allegories, and two full-length studies, one on South Africa and one dealing with the question of Women's Rights, her reputation now rests on *The Story of an African Farm*, and perhaps also on one collection of allegorical sketches called *Dreams*. Her contemporaries would have been surprised indeed to know how modest a place she was to occupy in the world of literature, and modern readers might be equally astonished to learn how profound and how extensive was the influence which she exerted not so very long ago. There was a time when this woman was acclaimed as poet, prophet, and pioneer. (pp. 1-2)

All her life she fought against injustice. She combined within herself the poet's special sensitivity to the hidden currents of existence and the reformer's zeal to have them canalized: an Emily Brontë with less of genius, an unmethodical Beatrice Webb. (pp. 2-3)

Some novels resemble paintings, word pictures of scenes and events, or portraits of persons; others, like music, are poured out in a flow of melody, harmonious only if the listener's ear is attuned to the same wave-length. *The Story of an African Farm* belongs to the second category; its plot is confused; its characters are vague, and the heroine herself, like any Shavian puppet, is nothing more than a speaking-tube for the author's most cherished opinions. Yet the book radiates some mysterious quality, not unlike that of *Wuthering Heights,* although less powerful, which made itself felt immediately and has not wholly faded from the pages more than half a century after its first appearance. (p. 50)

In *Wuthering Heights* and *The Story of an African Farm*, the plot in each case is confused and not important. . . .

Both novels are set against a wild and lonely background remote from the usual restraints of civilization, and both reveal a certain voluptuous preoccupation with physical violence and cruelty. Emily Brontë deals with this much more fully than Olive Schreiner; the latter is less elemental, more reflective; more concerned with large issues of belief and conduct than her predecessor. (p. 56)

The secret of the success of Olive Schreiner's first novel lay in the minds of her readers, which were in tune with her own attitude towards the world—doubting, questioning, yet always

passionately desiring to face the positive aspect of life: not superstition but truth, not cruelty but justice, not hatred but love. (p. 57)

Olive Schreiner wrote two other novels, both published after her death. The first one, *Undine*, was actually written before *The Story of an African Farm*. It is, as might have been expected, an immature and very ill-constructed book with a distinctly novelettish flavour. (p. 58)

The novel *From Man to Man,* richer and fuller than *Undine,* had been written in early girlhood but was re-written later, some of it while she was travelling about Europe, and it seems to have been more real and dear to her than any of her other books. (p. 60)

The plot is interrupted by endlessly long dissertations on philosophy, art, evolution, and any other subject with which the author was concerned. The novel is unfinished, but the ending which she had planned was known and is added to the book in an appendix. (p. 61)

*Woman and Labour* is one of the noblest books which have ever appeared in defence of feminism. *Trooper Peter Halket of Mashonaland* is a pacifist allegory, which was characteristic of her method. Through them she exercised a profound influence on many of her contemporaries. (pp. 62-3)

If *The Story of an African Farm* was not the only contribution which Olive Schreiner made to literature, it was undoubtedly the most important. Her name was made by it and is still linked to that one book. (p. 63)

> *D. L. Hobman, in her* Olive Schreiner: Her Friends and Times *(reprinted by permission of the Literary Estate of Mrs. D. L. Hobman), Watts & Co, 1955, 182 p.*

### UYS KRIGE   (essay date 1968)

A careful study of Olive Schreiner's novels today does not reveal her, to the dispassionate critic, as the great novelist so many of her contemporaries claimed her to be. The faults of *The Story of an African Farm,* generally considered by her admirers as her masterpiece, have become obvious. Yet what is as clear from her writings as the Karoo sunlight she loved so passionately all her life long is that she is both poet and prophet, and a truly great South African.

Perhaps the main fault of *The Story of an African Farm* flows from the fact that Olive Schreiner is not basically a novelist but a poet, highly individual and subjective with all the passionately intense inner life characteristic of the poet's unique personality. In all her novels she is more lyrical than epic, she lacks balance and poise, objectivity, detachment not only from her own feelings but also from the characters she wishes to portray—that strange detachment which is present in the novelist even when he is *corps à corps* with his characters and has the most piercing insight into them and their deepest motives; that 'majestic indifference' which marks the authentic novelist.

The novelist is, in a sense, a great immanent presence like the light or the air around us. He is everywhere and yet nowhere in his work. One senses his presence but one cannot define it. The novelist, Flaubert once said, should see his characters as God would see them. Olive Schreiner hardly ever sees her characters as God would see them; because of her emotional involvement with them she often sees them with too personal a vision, too narrow a focus.

At times in *The Story of an African Farm* Olive Schreiner almost burns herself up with her fierce lyricism—the lyricism of her proud, rebellious spirit, of her fiery revolt against woman's lot in the man-made world of the nineteenth century, and of the sorrows and despairs of her lonely adolescence on the desolate Karoo farm where as a girl still in her teens she started writing her first novel. Then she is at loggerheads with the novelist, of whom it is demanded that he should see life straight and see it whole, with the result that the harmony and unity of her novel are seriously impaired.

This youthful lyricism has an even more harmful effect on her other three novels. (Not only was her first novel completed on that Karoo farm but also most if not all of *Undine* and large portions of *From Man to Man*.) Olive Schreiner had completed *The Story of an African Farm* before she was 23. Up to her death, more than forty years later, she had added only three novels, *Trooper Peter Halket of Mashonaland*—her impassioned defence of the black man against British Imperialism—*Undine* and *From Man to Man*, not one of them in any way superior to her first flawed but strangely moving book. With maturity, her many years spent in England and on the continent of Europe, the inspiration of her lifelong friendship with some of the best minds and most gifted writers of her time, all the wealth of experience and knowledge of life and men the years had brought, and her complete dedication to the writer's craft, Olive Schreiner gained nothing as a novelist: her first novel remained easily her best. Does this lack of any development in her art, her *métier*, not seem to corroborate my contention that she was not, intrinsically, a novelist? (pp. 1-2)

There is a flaw that runs right through *The Story of an African Farm:* the split in her vision or presentation of her characters. About half of her characters are seen from the outside and the other half from the inside.

Of the 'outer' characters Napoleon Blenkins reminds one of a Dickens caricature. If ever there was a 'devil out of the machine', Napoleon is such a one. Not the slightest effort is made to explain him, to motivate his cruelty and sadism to the boy Waldo by reference, for instance, to his life as a slum child in London and the blighting influence of that life on the ambitious guttersnipe.

Perhaps Olive Schreiner conceived Napoleon contrapuntally—as a contrast to the gentle, good, lovable Otto, Waldo's father. But Napoleon is so bad and Otto so good, we often do not believe in Napoleon and are at times even inclined to disbelieve in the existence as a living character of Otto himself. Also, Napoleon practically dominates the first half of the book, then disappears completely from the second half, only to pop up again at the end as the successful suitor of a completely extraneous character, Tant Trana. But this is a minor defect in the book's pattern or construction; and Napoleon has at times a vitality comic in its preposterousness.

Tant Sannie, too, strikes one now and again as being a caricature; only here, more often than in the case of Napoleon, the hard, over-emphasized lines are softened, and so redeemed, by humour.

Waldo's Stranger drops in among us straight out of the blue. We have never heard of him before and we never hear of him again. Lyndall's Stranger is an even more unsatisfactory shadow or figment. As Lyndall's lover and father of her child whose birth is the cause of her death, he is one of the most important characters in the book. Yet we are told nothing about him except for a brief description of his external appearance on the

one occasion that he secretly visits the farm. This, it seems, is construction, even when judged by not very exacting standards, at its most rudimentary. And if both these Strangers are to be seen as symbols and not as human characters, then their disembodiedness, their vagueness, clashes surely with the concrete realism of characters such as Napoleon, Tant Sannie and others?

Of the 'inner' characters Waldo is perhaps the most convincing; although why as a strong, healthy young man he should, in the last page of the book, lie down in the sun and just die, is difficult to understand.

Even about that extraordinary character Lyndall—whose passionate, rigidly uncompromising nature gives the book its impetus and, in her death at the end, its deep cathartic emotion—we have at times our doubts. She will not marry her Stranger, the father of her child, since she realizes she loves him only physically. But despite her high ideals and integrity, for a long time she seriously contemplates marrying the feeble, pathetic Gregory, whom she loves not at all, neither physically nor spiritually. Must we conclude that the lofty-minded Lyndall is here about to stoop to a piece of trickery as mean to herself as to Gregory?

Perhaps, also, there is too marked a resemblance in character between Lyndall and Waldo. Are they not two, in many respects identical, idealized projections of the novelist herself? And is this not yet another sign of Olive Schreiner's over-subjectivity as a novelist?

The novel has other constructional defects such as Waldo's going away and coming back to the farm and telling in detail the story of everything that has happened to him; Gregory's leaving the farm soon after and, on his return, telling his story. . . . And the whole episode of Gregory, disguised as a woman, serving as Lyndall's 'female nurse' is clumsy and hardly credible.

Yet, notwithstanding all its faults, *The Story of an African Farm* is still after more than eighty years the most significant novel to have come out of South Africa, of so direct an appeal and so haunting a quality that the reader never forgets it. Its conclusion, particularly, is fine, sweeping aside all one's objections and reservations and purging one's feeling with an effect that approaches tragedy.

To explain partly this apparent contradiction, I think I should return here to my original suggestion: the book should be seen rather as a poem than as a novel; a poem written by a young woman hardly out of her teens in which—often deeply disturbed by the sudden violences, griefs and exaltations of her emotional, still-adolescent nature, tortured by her agonizing insight into the modern woman's needs in a hostile male world, racked by her 'thirst for the absolute', her profound doubts in the God of her fathers, and yearning for the full life waiting for her beyond the wide circle of those far, blue koppies—she speaks of her sorrows and ecstasies in so pure and passionate a voice that criticism is silenced.

And nowhere is her poet's gift more apparent than in her evocative power. How this African farm lives! How clearly one sees it, even when it is not directly described but its presence or atmosphere only suggested: shimmering, almost afloat in the haze of early summer; distorted into a phantasmagoria of shape and contour, sky, land and water in the drought's mocking mirage; etched in the sharp white light of winter; fresh and with a fragrance of its own in the desert dawn; parched and bleak in the hot glare of noon; glowing in the immense golden and crimson sunset; or touched at night to a still, mysterious beauty by the moon.

Indeed, so vividly does it come to life that at times one is tempted to say that the hero or main character of *The Story of an African Farm* is neither Lyndall nor Waldo, but the farm itself.

The faults of *The Story of an African Farm* are also the faults of Olive Schreiner's three other novels. In all there is the same intrusion upon her main characters of the writer's personality, of her views and opinions on the great problems of her day—such as the Women's Movement, the place of the 'fallen woman' in the hypocritical Puritan society of Victorian times, the question of subject races or minorities in an era of expanding Imperialism, war and the necessity of preventing it. . . . And in all, especially in *Undine* and *Trooper Peter Halket*, there is a lack of character delineation or, when Olive Schreiner does attempt a full portrayal of character, a contradiction in her presentation, and an identical failure of her constructional powers.

*Trooper Peter Halket* is hardly a novel. Despite a few moving passages and the excellence of its free-flowing, rhythmic style, it falls fairly and squarely between two stools. Olive Schreiner is here so obsessed by her moral indignation at the havoc wrought by Rhodes's Chartered Company upon the people of Mashonaland that she does not see Trooper Halket as a real human being. Only if we could believe in his reality, would the situation in which he is involved become true and valid for us. Lacking as it does this truth of human character, the book therefore makes little impact. At the end Trooper Halket dies under what Olive Schreiner would have liked us to believe are tragic circumstances. But they are not tragic.

Since Halket has not come alive, his death does not move us. It has been said before in one form or another but it is worth repeating: nobility of intention is certainly not enough for the novelist.

Perhaps Olive Schreiner should have tried in *Trooper Peter Halket* to write not a novel but a modern morality or allegory obeying its own laws and having little or no relation to the novel form. If it is objected here that that was precisely her intention, then it would seem to me that she was not sufficiently conscious of writing with this aim. *Trooper Peter Halket,* being neither a novel nor an allegory, therefore lacks balance, tonal unity.

*From Man to Man* is a curiously baffling book. In spite of its obvious defects it continued through its 480-odd pages to fascinate me. And this fascination persisted at a second and even a third reading. It is the 'poetic' quality of its writing, I think, that is the book's main attraction: the description of the Karoo farm, the mountain and kloof, the farm's many moods by day and night; the vignettes of Cape Town, Wynberg, of the little Karoo dorp of Cradock; and the sad brooding evocation at the end of the book of a London—with its everlasting grey mists or thick, damp fog, its ragged cold and the incessant drip-drip of its rain—with which South Africans who have experienced an English winter are only too familiar.

The portrayal of the human relationships in *From Man to Man* is much less satisfactory. The love of the two young women, the sisters Rebekah and Bertie, for each other is beautifully depicted while they are still on their Karoo farm at the beginning of the book. But where *From Man to Man* goes wrong is

in the presentation of its male characters. The three main male characters, Percy Lawrie, John-Ferdinand and Frank—the first Bertie's lover, the second the man who later wants to marry her, and the third Rebekah's husband—are just no men at all. They are *strooipoppe,* men of straw in more sense than one. Here we have a repetition of Lyndall's Stranger, for they all three remain figments. When placed in a major concrete situation with the women they love or are supposed to love, they are such poor surface creatures or their actions appear so completely unmotivated that we never for a moment suspend our complete disbelief in them.

(In *Undine,* incidentally, Olive Schreiner's incapacity to see a male character in the round—especially when that character is portrayed in a love relationship with a woman—comes close to absurdity: George Blair is a monstrosity in several ways; his one son, Harry, is an abject weakling whose weakness has no human validity for us; and the other, the flashy, arrogant Albert, seems to have stepped straight out of a Victorian barnstormer.)

The failure of Olive Schreiner's imagination with her male characters becomes such a constant that one asks oneself whether at some stage of her impressionable adolescence or youth she did not suffer a profound psychological shock in her relationship with a young man she loved dearly; and a shock of so basic a nature that it jarred her intuitive powers, subconsciously distorting for her as a creative artist her outlook on the male sex and so making her as a novelist incapable of creating a nuanced and completely credible male character, especially one involved in a deeply personal relationship with a woman. (pp. 3-7)

Even the relationship between the two sisters, once they are both settled in Cape Town, is open to criticism. (p. 7)

*From Man to Man* has other faults. There are the long 'liberal' talks Rebekah has with her children in their bedroom at night. These conversations or interpolations are well written and contain a great deal of clean, honest thinking, but they are more appropriate to a book like *Woman and Labour* or a sociological treatise than a novel with its own clearly defined needs. Coming as they do in great, solid chunks soon after the shattering revelation to Rebekah of her husband's highly dramatic betrayal of her love, these passages stick out from the rest of the book like the exposed scaffolding of an uncompleted building.

One has only to compare *From Man to Man* with Flaubert's *Madame Bovary* to become acutely aware of the lack of depth or nuance in the delineation of Bertie's character as against the full portrait Flaubert has painted for us of his equally ill-fated heroine, Emma. In Emma's gradual disintegration everything is motivated, logical, inevitable. In Bertie's almost everything is circumstantial, coincidental, fortuitous. Flaubert analyses Emma's character and downfall relentlessly—but with a deep underlying compassion that has a certain concealed quality about it the more poignant for its concealment, and that in its cumulative effect gives this masterpiece an ending terrifying in its force and finality. Olive Schreiner has much compassion for Bertie but little if any understanding of her.

Also there is an ineluctability about the whole slow, fatal progression of events leading to Emma's pitiful suicide that despite the lack of any heroic stature in Emma, is reminiscent of Greek tragedy. In *Madame Bovary* everything flows naturally from character and situation and from the reciprocal action of character and situation upon each other, whereas in *From Man to*

*Man* there is no such subtle interplay of character and situation. (pp. 7-8)

*The Story of an African Farm* was Olive Schreiner's first great blow for the emancipation of women although many of today's readers would hardly see it in this light. *Woman and Labour* . . . was the second. It is the most profound study of the women's question and the most eloquent plea for feminism I have read. Though the cause which it so powerfully advocates has long since triumphed and some of its pages contain for us only faint echoes of 'old, unhappy far-off things, and battles long ago', Olive Schreiner's supple, swift prose has here such a sustained power, such a Karoo-like cleanness and clarity that much of it is as readable today as it must have been on its first appearance.

Quotation by no means does justice to its peculiar quality. Coming with acute observation upon actue observation, piling telling argument upon telling argument, giving time and again striking proof of the wide range of her mind—her grasp of anthropology, zoology, economy, sociology, history and other branches of knowledge is extensive—Olive Schreiner does not here shock one into awareness with a single brilliant snatch of prose, but slowly, methodically, cumulatively she convinces one of the rightness of the great cause she is pleading.

Her allegories when published in the collection entitled *Dreams* in 1890 achieved an immediate popular success. . . . Yet these literary efforts to which she devoted so much time and care—as well as her later allegories and 'dreams' published posthumously in *Stories, Dreams and Allegories* in 1923—make in the main unsatisfactory reading today.

Perhaps this form of symbolism is somewhat 'dated', is too *fin de siècle*, appears a little facile and even sentimental at times. And her prose, usually so impressive, has now and again a faintly hollow sound. One has only to place these allegories beside the *poèmes en prose* of a dozen French poets of the nineteenth century to note the difference in tonal values and subtlety. I have made only two choices from Olive Schreiner's many allegories; the first, **'A Dream of Prayer'**, to my mind has all the concision, interior movement and rhythm, intensity and controlled emotional power characteristic of a fine poem.

The stark, deeply compassionate **'Two Women'** is far and away her best short story. Here, the writer's symbolism has nothing forced or strained, nothing 'Victorian' about it; but the figure of the old Boer woman who in the South African War suffers once again a deep personal loss in the death in battle of a beloved son and a grandchild, becomes symbolic by suggestion and implication—the implication slowly but surely impinging upon our consciousness out of the tragic situation itself and all its attendant circumstances of war and violent death, as well as out of the truth of the characters involved in that situation. And she is symbolic not only of her people's sorrow but of the suffering of all humanity.

At the end, in her unutterable pain and her courageous and stoic acceptance of that pain, she becomes archetypal, rises to a Hecuba-like stature of grief and resignation: we see her as 'a tower beyond tragedy'. And the closing scene of the old woman and her daughter as they stand out clear-cut against the setting sun, sowing as their menfolk, now both dead, would have sown in times of peace the fallow fields, moves us in its desolation and dignity to pity and awe.

I have suggested that Olive Schreiner had a poet's nature rather than a novelist's. In yet another aspect of her life and work

she was the true poet. The word is used here in its original sense: that of the *vates*, the seer or prophet. In *Thoughts on South Africa*, in my opinion her richest work, her prophetic gifts find their most explicit utterance.

Reading it today, one is time and again astonished by its profound intuitions, its acute perceptions of the essential nature of the different South African peoples, their joint problems and their common destiny. But what particularly strikes one in this embarrassment of riches is the author's visionary power. Much of what one reads here on page after page could have appeared in an intelligent leading article this very day in any of the more enlightened of our newspapers—with the difference that Olive Schreiner's prose is of a superior order. (pp. 8-10)

[In] *Thoughts on South Africa* Olive Schreiner's gift of prophecy was not confined only to things South African. As a universal human being her searching gaze scanned many horizons. When materialist Europe seemed to be drunk with power, when the scramble for Africa was in full swing, and leaders of world finance appeared to have a limitless faith in 'progress' and yet more profits, she saw through this combination of greed and facile optimism, pointed out its hallowness and inhumanity, and predicted its decline and ultimate collapse. (p. 17)

In *Thoughts on South Africa* we find . . . many signposts to South Africa's future. But it is in her discussion of a united South Africa in **'Closer Union'** . . . that Olive Schreiner's farsightedness is most apparent, that her prophetic voice comes to us from beyond the grave with a clarity and conviction startling in their urgency; and that in the agonized searchings of our conscience we should profit from the immediacy of her warning, the boldness of her vision and the generosity of her dream of a happy united South Africa. (pp. 21-2)

*Uys Krige, "Olive Schreiner: Poet and Prophet," in* Olive Schreiner: A Selection, *by Olive Schreiner, edited by Uys Krige (reprinted by permission of Oxford University Press, South Africa), Oxford University Press, Cape Town, 1968, pp. 1-30.*

### DORIS LESSING (essay date 1968)

I read [*The Story of an African Farm*] when I was fourteen or so; understanding very well the isolation described in it; responding to her sense of Africa the magnificent—mine, and everyone's who knows Africa; realising that this was one of the few rare books. For it is on that small number of novels, with *Moby Dick, Jude the Obscure, Wuthering Heights*, perhaps one or two others, which is on a frontier of the human mind. Also, this was the first "real" book I'd met with that had Africa for a setting. Here was the substance of truth, and not from England or Russia or France or America, necessitating all kinds of mental translations, switches, correspondences, but reflecting what I knew and could see. And the book became part of me, as the few rare books do. A decade or so later, meeting people who talked of books, they talked of this one, mentioning this or that character, or scene; and I discovered that while I held the strongest sense of the novel, I couldn't remember anything about it. Yet I had only to hear the title, or "Olive Schreiner," and my deepest self was touched.

I read it again, for the first time as an experienced reader, able to judge and compare—and criticise. The first shock was that Olive Schreiner, who had always felt so close, like a sister, could have been my grandmother. The second was that, if I used the rules that turn out a thousand good forgettable novels a year, let the book spread out from the capsuled essence of it I had held, so that it became a matter of characters and a plot, it was not a good novel. But, then, of course, neither is *Wuthering Heights*. Well, then, what are these rules? Faced with one of the rare books, one has to ask such questions, to discover, again, that there aren't any. Nor can there be; the novel being that hybrid, the mixture of journalism and the *Zeitgeist* and autobiography that comes out a part of the human consciousness which is always trying to understand itself, to come into the light. Not on the level where poetry works, or music, or mathematics, the high arts; no, but on the rawest and most workaday level, like earthworms making new soil where things can grow. True lovers of the novel must love it as the wise man in the fable did the crippled beauty whose complaint against fate was that she was beautiful—for what use was her beauty? She was always trying for humanity and failing. And he replied that it was because of the trying that he loved her.

The true novel wrestles on the edge of understanding, lying about on all sides desperately, for every sort of experience, pressing into use every flash of intuition or correspondence, trying to fuse together the crudest of materials, and the humblest, which the higher arts can't include. But it is precisely here, where the writer fights with the raw, the intractable, that poetry is born. Poetry, that is, of the novel: appropriate to it. *The Story of an African Farm* is a poetic novel; and when one has done with the "plot" and the characters, that is what remains: an endeavour, a kind of hunger, that passionate desire for growth and understanding, which is the deepest pulse of human beings. (pp. 2-3)

[Parts of the story] are well done by the conventional yardstick: the scenes of rural Boer life; the dance, the scene where the young man comes in "his hopeless resignation" to court Tant' Sannie; . . . Tant' Sannie on progress: "Not that I believe in this new plan of putting soda into the pot. If the dear Father had meant soda to be put into soap, what would He have made milkbushes for, and stuck them all over the veld, as thick as lambs in lambing season." This woman, as near animal as they come, is written with love and with humour—a triumph. Em, too, the maiden dreaming of motherhood: "I always come to watch the milking. That red cow with the short horns is bringing up the calf of the white cow that died. She loves it so—just as if it were her own. It is so nice to see her lick its little ears. Just look!" Now, these are characters that could have appeared in any good novel called *Scenes from the Karroo, 18—*. It did not take Olive Schreiner to create them. The novel's greatness lies precisely in where it breaks from "lifelike" characters, and an easily recognisable probability.

There is the question of Bonaparte Blenkins, the charlatan. Later Olive said she was sorry that she had given him no real humanity, made him two-dimensional. But her first instinct was right. Evil is not personified in this book—neither is goodness. Human beings are small things in the grip of gigantic forces. They cry out and fight and struggle to understand the incomprehensible, which is beyond good and evil. Had Bonaparte been given depth and weight, we would have had to ask questions about the saintliness of the old German, Bonaparte's counterweight, and whom he has to destroy. He is saintly: but very silly. And Bonaparte is wicked—and silly. Not damaging? Indeed, yes: his persecution of the old German, his treatment of Waldo, the brutal beating he gave him, scarred Waldo, and taught him his helplessness; taught Lyndall her helplessness, and enforced her determination to free herself. But he was stupid, undid himself—and ran away. Wickedness

is arbitrary, almost grotesque. And innocent childlike goodness is impotent. But—does it matter all that much? The sun burns down over the Karroo; the pitilessly indifferent stars wheel and deploy; and two young creatures look up at the skies where they see their unimportance written, and ask questions, can find no answers—and suffer most frightfully.

Lyndall and Waldo: Olive said that in these two she had put herself. They share a soul; and when Lyndall dies, Waldo has to die. But it is Waldo who is the heart of the book, a ragged, sullen, clumsy farm boy, all inarticulate hunger—not for education, like Lyndall, but for the unknown. And it is to Waldo that Olive gave the chapter that is the core, not only of this novel, but of all her work. It is called "Waldo's stranger," and in it a man travelling through the Cape stops to rest on the farm for an hour. Waldo has carved a piece of wood. "It was by no means lovely. The men and birds were almost grotesque in their laboured resemblance to nature, and bore signs of patient thought. The stranger turns the thing over on his knee . . ." and offers to buy it for £5. Waldo, whom he sees as "a hind" says no: it is for his father's grave. The visitor is touched, presses the boy to talk, and finally, understanding his need, puts what Waldo has carved on the stick into a story. This is the legend of The Hunter. . . . The Hunter of the Stranger's tale has tried all his life to climb the mountains whose summits hold the Truth, cutting steps in the rock so that he, and others after him, can climb. He lies dying, alone. Long ago he has shed the childish arrogance that let him believe he could find Truth: what matters is that he has spent his life trying. Then: "Slowly from the white sky above, through the still air, came something falling, falling, falling. Softly it fluttered down and dropped on the breast of the dying man. He felt it with his hands. It was a feather. He died holding it." What Olive makes of this tale is both all her own, and from that region of the human mind called Anon. (pp. 5-7)

Lyndall has given her name to dozens of little South African girls: the beautiful young woman who chooses to die alone rather than marry a man she cannot respect. Lyndall is that projection of a novelist created as a means of psychic self-preservation. Olive, at that time, was very much alone. If not estranged from her family, she could not get from it the moral support she so badly needed. She was very young. She was ill: was to be ill all her life. She had been through violent religious conflicts that had left her drained, exhausted. She had been in love with, possibly jilted by, a man who found her socially inadequate, and morally and mentally his superior—or so the evidence suggests. That Olive should have needed Lyndall is not surprising: she had to love Lyndall, and stand by her, and protect her—and explain her; for Lyndall was the first of her kind in fiction. Of her we can say: that kind of embattled woman was the product of that kind of society, where women had a hard time of it. But Waldo is the truth of Lyndall, and he is timeless. (pp. 8-9)

Waldo is the first appearance in women's writing of the true hero, in a form appropriate to the novel; here a kind of Caliban who mysteriously embodies Prospero's spirit, or Faust's. (p. 9)

*Doris Lessing, "Afterword" (copyright © 1968 by Doris Lessing; reprinted by permission of Curtis Brown Ltd., London, on behalf of Doris Lessing), in* The Story of an African Farm *by Olive Schreiner, Fawcett, 1968 (and reprinted as the introduction to* The Story of an African Farm *by Olive Schreiner, Schocken Books, 1976, pp. 1-18).*

**DAN JACOBSON** (essay date 1971)

It is impossible to read *From Man to Man* without feeling an almost overwhelming sense of talents wasted and frustrated in what appears to be a perversely deliberate way. From such a spectacle, from the wreckage of this potentially major work, one cannot turn with any sense of real satisfaction to [Schreiner's] political writings on South Africa, admirable though some of her insights are. Much the same is true of *Woman and Labour*, her one extended attempt at dealing with 'The Woman Question', which caused some stir in Europe and the United States on its publication in 1911. My own dissatisfaction with *Woman and Labour*, at any rate, does not spring from an inclination automatically to put a higher value on 'art' than on a preoccupation with social or political issues; or from a lack of sympathy with her plea for greater equality between men and women; or even from the feeling that conditions have so changed that everything she had to say has simply gone out of date. In fact, as with her writings on South Africa, *Woman and Labour* is not only of value as a document from the past, but contains insights which still have a certain relevance today: even if it is difficult to see it as 'the bible of the women's movement', as some of its more enthusiastic admirers declared it to be at the time. (pp. 15-16)

[Theoretical] or polemical writings of any kind presented peculiar temptations to Olive Schreiner; and in a book like *Woman and Labour* she fell into them with the greatest readiness and regularity. Paradoxical though it may seem, for her to write on such topical issues of the day as the condition of women, or the relationship which should exist between white and black, was all too often not an act of engagement with the world immediately around her, but a sanctioned escape from it. She invariably took upon herself the pain of speaking up for the humiliated and oppressed—Boers, blacks, women, Jews; and what could be more selfless than that? She always pleaded for tenderness and candour in human relationships; and what could be more generous? She always tried to envisage a future in which man's finest aspirations would be realized; and what could be more hopeful and undaunted? But again and again the effect would be to transcend the torments of the present by a feat of moral and rhetorical levitation which ultimately strikes the reader as having an inner meaning or impulsion quite opposite to that intended. It begins to strike him as strangely selfish, uncaring, preoccupied far more with reassuring the speaker than with ministering to the needs of those to whom, or of whom, she is speaking. She is not the only writer espousing a love of humanity in whose work such a process can be observed.

The relevance of this mode of lacerated self-exaltation to several passages of *The Story of an African Farm* should be plain enough to any reader of the novel. Take, for example, the fable of The Hunter, which the stranger tells to Waldo in a central scene of the novel. (It was subsequently reprinted separately in a volume entitled *Dreams*, of which Olive Schreiner was particularly proud.) The fable describes how a Hunter leaves the comfortable valleys where the mass of mankind lives, and begins to scale an impassable mountain in search of the great white bird of truth he believes he will find on its summit. His utter loneliness and suffering are described at some length, and so too is the recompense he at last receives, when a single feather from the wing of the bird flutters down to him as he is on the point of dying. But within this allegory, one can't help noticing, is buried another allegory of whose meaning the author was quite unconscious. The truth whose value and beauty we are so pressingly asked to believe in has, by definition, no

connection whatsoever with any life we could actually live; and the same goes for the Hunter's manner of pursuing it. His truth hasn't even the merit of being death itself. No wonder he never asks himself what he could possibly do with the bird if he were ever to get his hands on it.

No, a much more modest truth we can catch on the wing is that it is only as a novelist, and only so far as she was one, that Olive Schreiner ever managed to engage herself wholly with the realities of the world as she had experienced it. It is a wonderful illustration of the unpredictability of the creative impulse that this desperately unhappy woman, so given to a solemn, high-flown rhetoric of human brotherhood, should have demonstrated her real gifts of sympathy and understanding, her real seriousness if you like, in those passages of broad, shameless farce which help so much to make *The Story of an African Farm* still a living book today.

Olive Schreiner's first, adolescent attempt at a novel, *Undine*, was for the most part set in England: a never-never England taken entirely from books, where, when the characters are not drinking tea on the lawn or walking through vaguely described woods, the snow is incessantly falling. From the hundreds of pages of *Undine* devoted to that fantasy-land we can judge just how difficult it was for her to make *plausible* to herself the material around her as a source of fiction: her snow-less, wood-less, lawn-less Karroo, about which not a word had ever appeared in any novel. To anyone who reflects seriously on what it must be like to grow up within a society that has never been given any kind of a voice of its own, there must appear something almost heroic about the opening of *The Story of an African Farm*, with its first fine sentence: 'The full African moon poured down its light from the blue sky into the wide, lonely plain . . .' and its description of the kopje near the homestead, the sheep *kraals*, the Kaffir huts, and 'Tant' Sannie, the Boer housewife, in bed, in her clothes, dreaming of the sheep's trotters she had eaten for supper that night. 'She dreamed that one stuck fast in her throat, and she rolled her huge form from side to side, and snorted horribly.'

The African moon, by the way, *is* bright enough to fill the sky with a hard blue radiance; the sentence I have quoted is not an inaccurate one. Which suggests another way of conveying the initial difficulty Olive Schreiner had to overcome as a novelist: when I read her novel for the first time, some sixty years after it was first published, I had to struggle with my own incredulity that the kopjes, *kraals* and cactus plants she mentions were of the same kind as those I was familiar with; so little experience had I had of encountering them within the pages of a book. For it isn't only the hitherto undescribed, uncelebrated, wordless quality of the life around him that makes it seem implausible to the colonial as a fit subject for fiction; it is also (no matter how bright the moonlight may be) its appearance of drabness, its thinness, its lack of richness and variety in comparison with what he has read about in the books that come to him from abroad. So much so, that when a writer from such a society presents it as simply bursting with 'life' and 'colour' one must suspect him of having chosen to see it from without, as his metropolitan readers would want to see it, and not as he himself has experienced it. It is not accidental that in her introduction to the second edition of the book, Olive Schreiner used the metaphor of squeezing the colours from her brush and dipping it into the grey pigments around her.

This is not to deny that *The Story of an African Farm* is in many respects, some of them damaging to it, a very 'literary' piece of work; the fruit in places more of reading than of life.

It could hardly be otherwise. Even Bonaparte Blenkins—tramp, rogue, sadist, and comic, one of the liveliest of the novel's inventions—owes much to other books. Sometimes he talks like Mr. Jingle of *The Pickwick Papers;* sometimes he preaches like Mr. Chadband of *Bleak House.* As for Lyndall, the doomed, imperious heroine, who goes through the novel complaining that her heart is dead, that she is incapable of feeling, but who is shown to us as never finding anyone worthy of her high emotions—she, too, is not an unfamiliar figure to any reader of Victorian fiction. (The portentous loquacity of Lyndall's feminist convictions is more of a novelty; but one can't say that it is entirely a welcome one.) And there is no need to dwell on the second-hand lyricism of such chapters as the interlude, 'Times and Seasons', describing the growth of a child's consciousness, or Waldo's meeting with the stranger.

Altogether, the faults of the book are glaring, and it would be pointless to try to gloss over them. But it would be even more of a mistake to allow the faults to obscure the novel's considerable merits. (pp. 16-19)

Two grounds for my admiration of the novel I have already given: its passages of comedy, which are often outrightly farcical, and none the worse in my opinion for being so; and the power and originality of its evocation of the Karroo landscapes the author knew so well. But there is another, which—given what we know of Olive Schreiner's life and temperament, and the urgency of the passions she poured into the book—is almost as surprising as the comic spirit it displays. That quality I would describe as the book's calmness. She manages to display repeatedly a degree of disinterestedness towards her own characters which is the mark of the true novelist: a readiness not to bear grudges against them; to allow them to develop or change (and change back again to what they were before); to let the events of the novel make their own impersonal comment, as it were, upon what the people do or say. I am not speaking here merely of charity on the part of the writer towards her own characters; but of something harder to achieve, beyond either charity or animus. (p. 20)

Thus there is nothing clownish about Bonaparte when he flogs Waldo in one of the most disturbing scenes in the book. But his cruelty does not transform him into a wholly villainous figure; just as in the later slapstick of his humiliation, when a barrel of pickled meat is poured over him, there is still a touch of pathos. . . .

Tant' Sannie is credulous, sensual, lazy, and ready to acquiesce in every one of Bonaparte's cruelties; but she is also—what she is; and at the end of the book we see her telling Emily how to boil soap, and fondly wishing her as many children in five years as a cow has calves.

There is one further small example of the author's creative detachment I would like to mention. *The Story of an African Farm* is about the white people on the farm, not the black; it is far from being the novel of 'race relations' which many people have come to expect every South African novel to be. The black people in it are merely extras, supernumeraries, part of the background. But in one brief scene we are made aware of the possibilities that such a background can contain. When Tant' Sannie drives Waldo's father off the farm because of the lies Bonaparte has told about him, the old German turns in bewilderment to her coloured maid. . . . (p. 21)

The servant isn't deflected from her pleasure by the fact that of all the people on the farm, the old man had always been the most tender-hearted to black and white alike. Nor is Olive

Schreiner deflected by the pleasure or pain of either from her pursuit of the truth.

Creative detachment? Creative immersion might be a better phrase to describe so complex a mode of artistic apprehension. Only in *The Story of an African Farm* was she capable of it for long enough to bring the work, however flawed it might be, to a conclusion. Neither her own unhappiness, nor her quasi-religious insistence that such unhappiness somehow be exorcized from the experience of all mankind, ever permitted it to happen again. (pp. 21-2)

> *Dan Jacobson, "Introduction" (copyright © by Dan Jacobson 1971; reprinted by permission of Penguin Books Ltd), in* The Story of an African Farm *by Olive Schreiner, Penguin Books, 1971, pp. 7-26.*

### ELAINE SHOWALTER (essay date 1977)

In Schreiner's novels, the quintessential female role is frequently associated with a grotesque obesity, like pregnancy or dropsy. In *Story of an African Farm,* Em, the passive domestic farm girl is "grown into a premature little old woman of sixteen, ridiculously fat." Tante Sannie, the Boer woman, weighs 250 pounds and is too fat to kneel; she dreams of sheeps-trotters and snorts in her sleep. A gross parody of womanhood, a sort of Hottentot Venus, she devours three husbands, the last being her nineteen-year-old albino nephew. . . . Reduced to their sexual functions, women in Schreiner's novels seem monstrous, swollen, and destructive. They are the parasites described in *Woman and Labour,* whose better nature has atrophied through disuse. In *From Man to Man* . . . , the innocent Baby Bertie, seduced and betrayed, ends up as the prisoner of a rich Jew who keeps her in overheated rooms where she grows fatter and fatter, although she scarcely eats. At last, her body too heavy for her tiny feet, she is practically immobile. In an effort to alleviate her despair, the Jew buys her three kittens, and she acts out a fantastic motherhood, embroidering tiny garments for them and putting them to bed in little cradles. Schreiner's fictional world is obsessed with a femaleness grown monstrous in confinement—a world full of Bertha Masons. (pp. 196-97)

Yet Schreiner made an important contribution to the female tradition. Her use of female symbolism, her commitment to feminist theory, and her harshly physical allegories, which the suffragettes read to each other in Holloway Prison, were part of her effort to articulate the tense, indirect perceptions of a new womanhood. Even her insistent and sometimes nagging narrative voice takes us to the reality of female experience. That voice, soft, heavy, continuous, is a genuine accent of womanhood, one of the chorus of secret voices speaking out of our bones, dreadful and irritating but instantly recognizable. Other women whom she influenced—Virginia Woolf, Dorothy Richardson, and Doris Lessing—were to make much better use of it, but Schreiner hit upon it first. It is the fitful, fretful rhythm of women's daily lives, a Beckett monolog without a beginning or an end.

Schreiner's male contemporaries failed to understand this quality in her books, although George Meredith was the reader who recommended that Chapman and Hall publish *Story of an African Farm.* Other male novelists very naturally tended to see Schreiner's work as deficient in the qualities they themselves possessed. (pp. 198-99)

In adopting the pseudonym ''Ralph Iron'' and in calling two main characters Waldo and Em, Schreiner was paying homage to her favorite philosopher, Ralph Waldo Emerson, and indicating that her tone would be ironic. She intended *African Farm* to represent her vision of life; at one point she had considered titling it *Mirage: A Series of Abortions*. The book is about man's moral redemption in a meaningless universe, through identification with female suffering. Its plot is diffuse, but the central situation of the persecuted orphan, Waldo, who falls in love with his childhood ally, Lyndall, has reminded many readers of *Wuthering Heights*.

Schreiner's Lyndall is the first wholly serious feminist heroine in the English novel, and she remains one of the few who is not patronized by her author. Through Lyndall's monologs, Schreiner analyzes the connections' between sex-role conditioning, narcissism, parasitism, and frustration. The tragedies of Victorian heroines like Maggie Tulliver and Dorothea Casaubon become the sources of Schreiner's powerful analysis. . . . (p. 199)

For someone so keenly aware of female oppression, Schreiner is sadly underambitious. When all is said and done, the novels are depressing and claustrophobic. The heroines are granted only the narrowest of possibilities; the treatment of them is disconcertingly unadventurous, even timid. Lyndall dies after childbirth; Bertie meets a fate worse than death; Rebekah retreats, daydreams, and desultorily cultivates a fragmented and undisciplined art. Like Schreiner, they give up too easily and too soon. In his introduction to *African Farm,* the South African novelist Dan Jacobson writes regretfully about the ''almost overwhelming sense of talents wasted and frustrated in what appears to be a perversely deliberate way.'' [See excerpt above.] (pp. 203-04)

And yet, as Jacobson fully recognizes, there is ''something almost heroic'' in Schreiner's effort to make art out of ''a society that has never been given any kind of a voice of its own.'' Schreiner's first book, *Undine,* was set in a fantasized England, copied from the novels of Jane Austen. *African Farm* confronted the drab reality of kopjes and cactus. The real problem of the colonial writer, Jacobson suggests, is not just the ''hitherto undescribed, uncelebrated wordless quality'' of the life around him, but its inferiority in contrast to the apparent richness and color of the parent literature. As a South African and as a woman, Schreiner was writing out of a double colonialism. The uncelebrated landscapes she was trying to record were both the barren Karoo and the claustrophobic, inner landscape of the new woman. The authenticity of her struggle— its rawness, its personality—touched readers, especially women readers, and awakened their deepest selves; these qualities made Schreiner important for other women writers. Doris Lessing remembered *African Farm* as the first book she had read that reflected what she herself ''knew and could see,'' and also, ultimately, ''an endeavor, a kind of hunger, that passionate desire for growth and understanding, which is the deepest pulse of human beings'' [see excerpt above]. (p. 204)

> *Elaine Showalter, ''The Feminist Novelists,'' in her* A Literature of Their Own: British Women Novelists from Brontë to Lessing *(copyright © 1977 by Princeton University Press; reprinted by permission of Princeton University Press), Princeton University Press, 1977, pp. 182-215.** 

## JANE MARCUS  (essay date 1979)

Olive Schreiner's *Woman and Labour* . . . was called the Bible of the international woman's movement. It still retains its el-

emental prophetic power. And its outmoded anthropological and social darwinist trappings, its dream of matriarchal origins based in Bebel and Spencer, only add to its Old Testament hunger and thirst for justice and freedom. It expresses the need of the oppressed to see themselves as a chosen people. Women are for Olive Schreiner a lost tribe, keeping the memory of original sexual freedom alive in the slavery of centuries of diaspora. Like the Old Testament, *Woman and Labour* combines history and poetry. It curses the enemy, bewails woman's fate, urges her on with tales of the trials and tribulations of her forebears, sings her to sleep with a lullaby of revenge on her enemies and hope of peace after struggle, for her daughters. It is a text for ''keeping the faith,'' that is, woman's faith in herself, and was meant to be chanted aloud in small groups of struggling, persecuted women, as the books of the Bible were read by persecuted Jews and Christians. (p. 58)

If *Woman and Labour* is her Old Testament, *Trooper Peter Halket of Mashonaland* is her New Testament. Christ himself is one of Olive Schreiner's characters in his most endearing role as friend of the common man. But in the allegories of *Dreams* . . . she wrote her prophetic books for womankind. *Dreams* is a feminist *Pilgrim's Progress*. In her hands, as in Bunyan's, the spiritual journey, the moral tale, is political as well as religious. The teller, the reader and the listener (for surely these allegories were meant to be spoken, sister to sisters) form a conspiracy. The wretchedness of their lives is to be redeemed by hope. . . .

It is a mistake to read Olive Schreiner as sophisticated intellectuals do, dismissing her power because her prose lacks logic or her biology a scientific basis. Some books can best be judged by their readers, and *Dreams* is one of them. One can have visions of freedom over a washtub or on one's knees with a scrubbing brush, and the cooperative working women who contributed to *Life As We Have Known It* give ample testimony to the influence of *Dreams*. (p. 59)

The critics who are discomforted by Olive Schreiner's prose style have been taught that irony, not allegory, is the sharpest tool for shaping the literature of dissent. But irony is only the last resort of the defenseless intellectual, not the hapless black, woman or working class prophet. Irony is an upper-class weapon. It can utterly defeat its enemies by the assumption of mental superiority. (pp. 59-60)

But Olive Schreiner's allegories never mock the common reader. Here it is the skilled reader who is confused and disturbed by the primitive outcry, the naked dream and wish, the language of scripture and the archetypal image. The dreams are the ''scraps, orts and fragments'' of a lost culture, like Miss La Trobe's pageant in wartime Britain in [Virginia Woolf's] *Between the Acts*. There too, as in the Bible, there is an ache after evolutionary knowledge. Fear for the end of the world prompts a desire to know its beginnings. The songs and stories in the novel, the allegories and the scriptures are fragmentary records of a lost world. While for Virginia Woolf it was a swamp which spawned us (and she is always hankering after Mother Water) Olive Schreiner's territory is the biblical desert. Her native South African *karoo* was a natural landscape for the exercise of the biblical imagination. The land leant itself to the mysterious mixture of mythical and scientific speculation about human origins which distinguishes her writing.

All exiles are experts at their native geography. When Olive Schreiner mapped out Adam and Eve's garden in ''darkest Africa'' where the desert meets the sea and the mountains rise into the clouds from a flat plain, the result was a geography of both literary and historical interest. Moral and political geography is a commonplace literary result of the disasters of the twentieth century. But in Olive Schreiner's case there is a particular prophetic poignancy about the method, for she foresaw all that torments us about South Africa today. She dreamed of an African desert where the human race began and her life was spent in a political struggle for an end there, in that very soil, of nationalism and racism, sexism and antisemitism. (p. 60)

Her hopes for political unity were . . . severely dashed by the Boer War. *Trooper Peter Halket* . . . is one of the finest pieces of antiwar propaganda ever written. . . . A young English conscript loses his way in the desert, is found by Christ and told that he is fighting in a race war for gold, not for his queen and country, that he is a mercenary in Rhodes' private army. He returns to his company, frees a black prisoner who is being tortured like Christ and is shot by his officer whose fellows rally round to declare that Peter was a deserter. It is a crude and simple allegory, as crude and simple as the war itself. Primitive Christianity becomes a weapon for political rebellion. Its allegory is aimed not at intellectuals but at the souls of English working class men who had been seduced by hopes of buying houses for their mothers with the spoils of a capitalist war. (p. 61)

Olive Schreiner is the great cartographer of the spirit who maps the world of our dreams. Doris Lessing, fellow female South African exile, radical champion of the same causes, carries on this vision, this capacity to see and say, as our exiled young women dream dreams and our old ones see visions. The visionary gleam in Schreiner and Lessing is not like Woolf's with its Quaker and Clapham Sect restraint, rationality and asceticism, mental mirrorings of inner light. Schreiner is broader, baptist, Bunyanesque. There is a primitive pastoralism which derives from experience and a political lesson in the vision which derives from the literature of dissent and resembles Mother Ann Lee and the sectarian women preachers. Schreiner's is an outer, physical radiance.

Yet they do share one subversive element, the attempt to restore the myth of female power. . . . In **"The Sunlight Lay Across My Bed,"** [Schreiner] shows the seeker after light that the sun and its "shine" are in human effort, in a collective and historical struggle toward the truth. . . . Her most famous allegory "The Hunter," from *Story of an African Farm*, envisions the white bird of truth and pursuit of it up the most difficult mountain as the highest human goal. For the asthmatic exile, these breathless exploits over African mountains under the relentless sun, transform her own physical struggles into moral allegories which reach the hearts of many other weary toilers. (pp. 63-4)

For Virginia Woolf, Olive Schreiner was "one half of a great writer, a diamond marred by a flaw" [see excerpt above]. She had the diamond's sheen, its brilliance without its hardness. In her youth South African mines yielded untold riches in diamonds and gold at an untold expense of human life and labor. She chose iron as her own symbol, opaque, dark and useful in contrast to bright gold and diamonds which imprisoned their owners in greed. Her pseudonym was "Ralph Iron," she chose "Ralph" in an age of all those female "Georges," both famous and forgotten. The "Ralph," like Waldo in *African Farm* was a tribute to Ralph Waldo Emerson, whose transcendental idealism and ideas of duty and self-reliance were her mainstay. "Iron," reproaches the despoilers of her native

land and it was also an evolutionary feminist dream back to the Iron Age of women's power. (p. 64)

*Dreams* is a feminist archetype and many will struggle along the path Olive Schreiner cleared, hoping for a glimpse of one feather of the White Bird of Truth. . . . [She] is not only a geographical fact [as Rebecca West has claimed] but a political and spiritual fact as well in the great literature of feminist dissent. On our inner maps she has enlarged the territorial imperative for women, Jews, blacks and the working class. The barbed wire of South African camps cannot imprison dreams. (p. 66)

> *Jane Marcus, "Olive Schreiner: Cartographer of the Spirit—A Review Article" (reprinted by permission of the author), in* The Minnesota Review, *n.s. No. 12, Spring, 1979, pp. 58-66.*

## RUTH FIRST and ANN SCOTT (essay date 1980)

The tension between writing as an omnipotent activity and her sense of her characters being utterly real and beyond her control led Olive Schreiner to experiment with three novels [*Undine, The Story of an African Farm,* and *From Man to Man*]—gather material that was later used in her allegories, and work on a number of short stories over the eight years to 1881. She herself felt she was most successful when her characters led her and not the other way round; thus *Undine,* the most closely autobiographical of the three, pleased her least. . . . (p. 83)

'I was tired of being called queer and strange and odd.' The novel *Undine,* which opens in this way, is both Undine's and Olive's story. As narrator Olive makes an explicit critique of sexual oppression; as Undine she provides her reader with the development of her subjective world; as narrator, again, she exposes Undine's mistakes. Using themes of love, identity and death the work attempted, not unsuccessfully, to situate different kinds of female experience within a series of confrontations, longings, and power relationships. (pp. 84-5)

In one way the novel is a simple exposé of the impossibility of Undine's fantasy of what 'womanhood' brings—knowledge and love—for the proper female sphere is defined once and for all by her grandmother's generation. Women should be attractive and receptive to men, but without views, especially 'idiotic' religious views like Undine's. In terms of religion and sexuality women therefore have no real access to culture, no active space of their own; indeed, a dialogue about literature within the novel mirrors that division in culture. Her cousin Jonathan asks her if she's reading Elizabeth Barrett Browning, referring to it as 'poetry and effete nonsense'. Undine retorts that she's reading Mill: 'Nothing very sentimental in that.' So non-sense and non-sentiment are polarzied, as though symbolizing the meaning of female and male.

Throughout the novel, Undine's perception of herself, however confused, is at odds with others' perceptions of her. Her governess in Africa sees her as stupid and wicked because she would rather go to hell than be good and go to heaven merely because she was afraid of hell; cousin Jonathan in England sees her as having a cold, feelingless shell. She agrees to marry a wealthy middle-aged man on condition that he make over a large amount of money before their marriage—which she intends to give to his son Albert, whom she loves and he has disinherited—and the loathing that Albert Blair, ignorant of her plan, then feels for her makes him take up his father's position that 'all women have their value in coins, though some mount high'. Undine is thus taken as representative of the schemer by the world she has characterized as scheming. At every step she is disconfirmed by an outside world which reads her generosity as manipulation and her relationships as immorality.

One very early moment, however, marks a decisive transition for her sense of herself. It comes when [her brother] Frank drowns—in circumstances remarkably similar to Shelley's death in Italy in 1822—and Aunt Margaret has 'gone mad', accusing Undine of being the devil, and hence responsible for his death. Undine's formulation of the event is that her childhood is over and a strange 'deadness' seems to have settled; now she becomes a very self-punishing young woman. When asked what she thinks of Albert Blair—to whom she is tremendously attracted—she refers to Eve and the story of the fall, inferring her own fall from her concern with her gloves and her hair. So when she sees Albert she can't integrate the attraction she feels, and loses her identity as an intellectual: she literally drops the book she's been reading, prepared to do anything to gain his approval.

It was through overhearing her grandmother's friends' gossip about the local loose woman that Undine lost what she terms her 'ignorance of evil':

> Much . . . was made clear to me that night, and I was wretched; for alas! is it not the old, old story—that the tree of knowledge is the tree of pain, and that 'In the day wherein thou eatest thou shalt surely die', stands written on every fruit of the wonderful tree?

But Undine also knows that women are abused by men when she compares the 'unenviable fate of both women and pictures'—to be possessed by a man. She splits body and soul, however, when she refers to gold as God of the body and love as God of the soul. At the same time she identifies with the 'very wicked woman' who has an illegitimate child because her child is a child 'of love', unlike her own, the child 'of loathing'. And she will defend love when it is misrepresented, particularly when it is associated with an affront to conventional morality. To the shabby woman on board ship to South Africa who had been told Shelley was wicked, Undine says it's always right to love. . . . (pp. 86-8)

Undine's advocacy of love, however, bears little relation to the actual condition of her life, which is one of repeated loss. When one of the men for whom she irons falls ill and she nurses him, the practice of love becomes one of renunciation: Undine uses the money she has saved to pay for his return to England. On the day of his departure he tells her he's sure they'll meet again. The narrator mocks him:

> Meet again! Who ever met again? The child we love goes from us and comes back to us a man, and all others praise the change; but we, even while we run our fingers through his curls, we hunger for the little child that sat upon our knee.

> Only when we come so close that nothing separates us can we meet again, only when what binds us is not my need of you or your need of me nor any chance circumstance, but a deep ingrained likeness of nature that cannot pass away.

This concept of love is abstract—'not my need of you nor your need of me'; belittles the significance of daily reality in forming bonds between people—'nor any chance circumstance'; and narcissistic—'a deep ingrained likeness of nature'. The clear understanding of men's degradation of women which informs the novel is then confused by the proposal of a love whose meaning can be found only in loss and, ultimately, in death.

The sharpness of the novel's critique of religion derived from the support Olive Schreiner's reading provided—an awareness, however theoretical or self-contained, that such issues mattered to others. Her account of women's attraction to men, on the other hand, has a derivative quality, as though she is working from a male model of the female. This sentimentality may have been a product of a patriarchal culture in which female sexuality was diffused into notions of service, and women had no access to their specifically sexual feelings. So Undine's rejection of her social situation as a married woman represents a kind of sexual rebellion, but one that can be concluded only by a de-sexing: her return to Africa and her childhood. The shabby woman on board ship who befriends her had experienced something of the same kind of regression, but hers was into silence. In the context of a basically passive orientation on life, she had loved her man friend because he wanted to have someone care for him; but there was also the paradox that this fantasy lover—for the man was married, and the relationship covert—made all the other people in her life seem like dreams: a double irreality. Love had to be invisible, and sexuality restricted to touch: the woman liked simply to touch his coat and his brushes in the hall. She came to feel she could tolerate her own wickedness in 'seducing' him, but not his in deceiving his wife. As she sewed stockings one day, she realized she must leave him, but she could make it right for him 'if I worked for other people all my life'. She became a nurse, basing her loveless penance on the archaic moral assumption that suffering annuls the bad consequences of an act.

All these confusions about loving are organized around the Biblical image of Eve. The Bible appears in **Undine** both in dialogue within religious meetings, and as part of a literary form; as when Undine has 'taken the first bite at the forbidden tree'. For Undine believes that women corrupt men, and Eve is an explicit personification of evil. Yet both Undine and Olive are also working through a belief in female self-expression, in the validity of women's emotional and—however inexplicitly expressed—sexual feeling. There are bound to be conflicting models of behaviour: on the one hand the bad Eve, who corrupts because she feels desire; on the other the defence of Shelley and the advocacy of love. The contradictions which emerge can only be resolved through death: in Undine's words, 'only that which has no existence lasts for ever.'

The dénouement, in Undine's death, tells of peace, escape, and rescue from struggle. Olive sought to transcend the constraining world she was placed in by an ahistorical displacement of the self: backwards and forwards in death, and backwards and forwards in a Spencerian concept of change. The constant presence of illness and death in her environment—one of high infant and maternal mortality, with little or no diagnostic or 'scientific' medicine—took on a mystical quality of release in her fiction. The distinction between *living* and *dying* is made to seem unimportant and death is always an option. In **Undine** the issue is brought out in an allegory Undine tells Diogenes, her friend at the Diamond Fields, in which a dying woman asks Life to take her child.

Death and Life take it in turns to tell her what they can give: Death, very tall and calm, is presented as a strange and mysterious individual, in no way frightening—'his eyelids were half closed and in the eyes beneath them lay the shadows of wonderful dreams'—and as an alternative world in which to live. Life is beautiful, 'but when the mother looked at her forehead, knit with thought and pain . . . she feared her also'. Death offers rest and sleep, but the mother eventually offers the child to Life, since 'your best is bitter sweet, but it is sweet'. Even so, death always has the ultimate moral force: when Undine almost dies in childbirth and is then nursed back to health, her riches are made tawdry by their juxtaposition and death: the dressing gown and shawl symbolize recovery, but falsehood as well.

'Medical' reasons for death or recovery are never given, only their moral associations indicated. Concepts of illness are always vague, as when Undine asks the African who comes to order Mrs. Blair's mourning what her husband died of: 'he took ill, something wrong inside'; and whereas Albert Blair's wife is unable to deal with his death and has his body put outside the house, Undine has no fear. Their different responses become a statement about their worth as individuals. Albert's death enables Undine to reveal the truth about her feeling for him. She goes to the shed where he has been laid out and takes the sheet from his face:

> In his ear she whispered the wild words of love that to the living she would never utter—wild passionate words, the outpourings of a life's crushed-out love, the breaking forth of a fiercely suppressed passion. And the dead man lies so still; he does not send her from him; he does not silence her; he understands her now; he loves her now.

Here death creates both equality and exclusive possession.

Undine's own fatal illness is equally unexplained, though Albert's death seems to deprive her of life, a sensation that she displaces onto an empty barrel the next morning in a search for water: 'There must be some living thing withholding life from her.' But death is an old attraction, though not that of the Christian deathbed. When Undine leaves her tent that night and looks up in the sky, she remembers the stars who shed their light on the Karoo and looked at the child who read the Testament so long ago. One star in particular describes himself as her brother, a few million years older than she, who has 'seen that the thing which you call death is the father of all life and beauty . . . to make a man a million million forms have been and are not. Without death there is no change, without change no life.' . . . It is a comfort as ideological as was Undine's attempt to live by rationality in her first days at New Rush.

Olive never wanted *Undine* to be published. She told Ellis in 1884 that she had not looked at it since she wrote it, and 'ought to have burnt it long ago', but the autobiographical element in it made her 'soft' to it. . . . In some ways, in fact, it is harder to interpret than *The Story of an African Farm,* precisely because it *is* so raw, so unclearly differentiated from its author's experience, so overtly split between a critique of culture and a sentimental endorsement of it. (pp. 88-92)

> *Ruth First and Ann Scott, in their* Olive Schreiner *(reprinted by permission of Schocken Books Inc.; in Canada by Andre Deutsch; copyright © 1980 by Ruth First and Ann Scott), Schocken Books, 1980, Andre Deutsch, 1980, 383 p.*

## ADDITIONAL BIBLIOGRAPHY

Beeton, Ridley. "In Search of Olive Schreiner in Texas." *The Texas Quarterly* XVII, No. 3 (Autumn 1974): 105-54.
  Researches the University of Texas's holdings of Schreiner's correspondence, revealing her psychological complexity.

Berkman, Joyce Avrech. *Olive Schreiner: Feminism on the Frontier.* Monographs in Women's Studies, edited by Sherri Clarkson. St. Albens, Vt.: Eden Press, 1979, 88 p.
  Defines Schreiner's feminist vision and explores its expression in her work.

Cronwright-Schreiner, S.C. *The Life of Olive Schreiner.* Boston: Little, Brown, and Co., 1924, 414 p.
  Detailed biography by Schreiner's husband.

Davis, Roslyn. *Olive Schreiner: 1920-1971.* Johannesburg: University of the Witwatersrand Department of Bibliography, Librarianship, and Typography, 1972, 24 p.
  Supplements E. Verster's bibliography, emphasizing biographical and critical materials published between 1920 and 1971.

Fairley, Margaret A. "The Novels of Olive Schreiner." *The Dalhousie Review* IX, No. 2 (July 1929): pp. 168-80.
  Considers characters in *The Story of an African Farm* and *From Man to Man,* finding Waldo and Rebecca to be reflections of Olive Shreiner's personality.

Friedlander, Zelda. *Until the Heart Changes: A Garland for Olive Schreiner.* Capetown: Tafelberg-Uitgewers, 1967, 158 p.
  Brief critical estimates of Schreiner arranged under headings to reflect her many literary and personal aspects.

Friedmann, Marion V. *Olive Schreiner: A Study in Latent Meanings.* Johannesburg: Witwatersrand University Press, 1955, 69 p.
  Explores the penetration of Schreiner's personal psychology into her work.

Gregg, Lyndall (Schreiner). *Memories of Olive Schreiner.* London: W. & R. Chambers, 1957, 77 p.
  Fictionalized biography by one of Schreiner's nieces.

Laredo, Ursula. "Olive Schreiner." *Journal of Commonwealth Literature,* No. 8 (December 1969): 107-24.
  A critical discussion of Schreiner's novels, paying close attention to the rhetorical and allegorical elements of *The Story of an African Farm,* concluding that the author's interests "lay in sociological analysis, and in political prediction, not in plot-making or creation of character."

Lawrence, Margaret. *The School of Femininity.* New York: Frederick A. Stokes Co., 1936, 382 p.
  Sociological essay, comparing Schreiner's works and thoughts with those of other feminist writers.

Meintjes, Johannes. *Olive Schreiner: Portrait of a South African Woman.* Johannesburg: Hugh Keartland (Publishers), 1965, 196 p.
  A perceptive critical biography.

Plomer, William. "Olive Schreiner." In his *Electric Delights,* pp. 113-17. London: Jonathan Cape, 1978.
  Biographical sketch. Plomer concludes that the reformer and propagandist in Schreiner overshadowed the thinker and the artist.

Tessitore, John. "Olive Schreiner's *The Story of an African Farm:* Prototype of Lawrence's Early Novels." *English Language Notes* XIV, No. 1 (September 1976): 44-50.
  Identifies Schreiner's themes and her method of character development, noting their influence on Lawrence's *The Rainbow* and *Women in Love.*

Toth, Emily. "The Independent Woman and 'Free' Love." *The Massachusetts Review* XVI, No. 4 (Autumn 1975): 647-64.*
  Compares Schreiner's heroine Lyndall with feminist characters created by George Sands, Kate Chopin, and Alexandra Kollantai.

Verster, E. *Olive Emilie Albertina Schreiner*. Capetown: University of Capetown, School of Librarianship, 1946, 21 p.
> Lists English and foreign language publication information and includes directions to early critical reviews.

Walsh, William. "Olive Schreiner." In his *A Manifold Voice: Studies in Commonwealth Literature*, pp. 36-47. London: Chatto & Windus, 1970.
> Indepth examination of *The Story of an African Farm* as "the only thing of note Olive Schreiner produced."

Wilson, Elaine. "Pervasive Symbolism in *The Story of an African Farm*." *English Studies in Africa* XIV, No. 2 (September 1971): pp. 179-86.
> Traces the symbolism of sleep throughout *The Story of an African Farm*.

# (George) Bernard Shaw

## 1856-1950

(Also wrote under pseudonym of Corno di Bassetto) Irish dramatist, essayist, critic, novelist, short story writer, and poet.

Shaw is generally considered the greatest and best-known dramatist to write in the English language since Shakespeare. Following the example of Henrik Ibsen, he succeeded in revolutionizing the English stage, disposing of the romantic conventions and devices of the "well-made" play, and instituting the theater of ideas, grounded in realism. During his lifetime, he was equally famous as an iconoclastic and outspoken public figure. Essentially a shy man, Shaw created the public persona of G.B.S.: showman, satirist, pundit, and intellectual jester, who challenged established political and social beliefs.

Shaw was born into genteel poverty in Dublin. His father was an alcoholic. His mother, a woman of some refinement and culture, introduced her son to music and art at an early age. In 1876 Shaw moved to London and was supported by his mother for nine years while he tended to his self-education. During this period, he wrote five unsuccessful novels and, through intensive reading, acquired a strong background in economics and politics. Shaw established himself as a persuasive orator during the 1880s, rising to prominence in the socialist Fabian Society. He also became prominent as a literary critic, an art critic, a music critic, and, in 1895, the drama critic for *The Saturday Review*. G.B.S., as he now signed his work, began to be widely recognized for reviews that were witty, biting, and often brilliant.

Shaw had the unusual distinction of being a playwright whose work was successful in book form before its success on the stage. His early plays aroused the interest of a small, enthusiastic audience, although several were rejected for performance because they were believed to be unactable or risqué. Nevertheless, six of his early dramas were collected in *Plays: Pleasant and Unpleasant,* and were accompanied by lengthy explanatory prefaces that many critics consider as significant as the plays themselves. The critical and popular success of this endeavor, along with his marriage in 1898 to Charlotte Payne-Townshend, a rich Fabian, proved a turning point in Shaw's fortunes. From that time on, Shaw was closely associated with the intellectual revival of the English theater, two of his greatest critical successes being *Man and Superman* and *St. Joan.* The comedy *Pygmalion*, highlighting the absurdities of class distinction, was his most outstanding commercial success. Constantly revived, *Pygmalion* was adapted into the popular, long-running musical, *My Fair Lady.* During his sixty years of literary activity, Shaw produced a tremendous body of work, and never hesitated to publicly express his views on such subjects as feminism, war, religion, imperialism, individualism, and socialism with frankness and wit. He declined the Order of Merit, but was persuaded to accept the 1925 Nobel Prize in literature.

Central to Shaw's philosophy was a belief in the Life Force: an impersonal god of sorts, which accomplishes its purpose through creative evolution. This doctrine is described in *Man and Superman.* Human beings are themselves agents of the Life Force; males, however, are also motivated by the creative

Pictorial Parade

intellect, which inspires them to develop a race and world superior to their own. Shaw's idea of the dramatic hero was one "whose passions are those which have produced the philosophy, the poetry, the art, and the stagecraft of the world, and not merely [the type] who have produced its weddings, coroners' inquests, and executions." Shaw's dramas present characters who undergo a synthesis of outlook following a clash between other characters or with the moral and religious conventions of their time. The heroes are often reflections of Shaw himself: vivacious, sophisticated, and lucid.

Not surprisingly, the central criticism directed at Shaw as a dramatist is that his characters are intellectual rather than human creations. From the time of Shaw's first dramas, critics have claimed that he peoples his stage with cleverly disguised strawmen, only to have his favored protagonists knock them down with Shavian declamations by the final curtain. But many critics find this to be his greatest strength. They regard Shaw's art as one in which intellectual conflicts are animated and enlivened. For this reason, Shaw is often considered a great dramatic teacher, with the theater as his classroom.

As Samuel Hynes has noted, Shaw was driven by *weltverbesserungswahn*—a rage to better the world. His vivid characters and clever dialogue only disguise his moral purpose, called Puritan by some: to expose the dilemmas, absurdities, and injustices of society. Shaw turned away from the nineteenth-century concept of the English theater as a source of light entertainment, and made acceptable the drama of ideas. In this he altered the course of twentieth-century drama.

(See also *TCLC*, Vol. 3, and *Dictionary of Literary Biography*, Vol. 10: *Modern British Dramatists, 1910-1945*.)

## PRINCIPAL WORKS

*Cashel Byron's Profession* (novel) 1886
*An Unsocial Socialist* (novel) 1887
*The Quintessence of Ibsenism* (criticism) 1891
*Widowers' Houses* (drama) 1892
*Arms and the Man* (drama) 1894
*Candida* (drama) 1897
*The Devil's Disciple* (drama) 1897
*The Perfect Wagnerite* (essay) 1898
*Plays: Pleasant and Unpleasant* [first publication] (dramas) 1898
*You Never Can Tell* (drama) 1899
*Captain Brassbound's Conversion* (drama) 1900
*Love among the Artists* (novel) 1900
*Socialism for Millionaires* (essay) 1901
*Three Plays for Puritans* [first publication] (dramas) 1901
*Mrs. Warren's Profession* (drama) 1902
*\*The Admirable Bashville; or, Constancy Unrewarded* (drama) 1903
*How He Lied to Her Husband* (drama) 1904
*John Bull's Other Island* (drama) 1904
*The Irrational Knot* (novel) 1905
*Major Barbara* (drama) 1905
*Man and Superman: A Comedy and a Philosophy* (drama) 1905
*On Going to Church* (essay) 1905
*The Philanderer* (drama) 1905
*Caesar and Cleopatra* (drama) 1906
*The Doctor's Dilemma* (drama) 1906
*Dramatic Opinions and Essays* (essays) 1906
*Getting Married* (drama) 1908
*The Shewing-Up of Blanco Posnet* (drama) 1909
*Misalliance* (drama) 1910
*Fanny's First Play* (drama) 1911
*Androcles and the Lion* (drama) 1912
*Pygmalion* (drama) 1913
*Heartbreak House* (drama) 1920
*Back to Methuselah* (drama) 1922
*Saint Joan* (drama) 1923
*The Intelligent Woman's Guide to Socialism* (essay) 1928
*The Apple Cart* (drama) 1929
*Immaturity* (novel) 1930
*The Adventures of the Black Girl in Her Search for God* (short story) 1932
*Music in London, 1890-94* (criticism) 1932
*Too True to Be Good* (drama) 1932
*The Simpleton of the Unexpected Isles* (drama) 1935
*London Music in 1888-89* (criticism) 1937
*Geneva* (drama) 1938
*Bernard Shaw's Rhyming Picture Guide to Ayot St. Lawrence* (poetry) 1950

*This drama is an adaptation of the novel *Cashel Byron's Profession*.

---

### THE ATHENAEUM (essay date 1887)

[In *An Unsocial Socialist*], Mr. Shaw seems to have sat down with the purpose of writing a perfectly unconventional story, and to have devised for that end a thoroughly unnatural situation. . . . If the morals which he suggests or enforces are mostly extravagant and frequently perverted, he is certainly shrewd enough at times to start in the mind of his reader a train of thought which is worth following out. The hero's Socialism appears to rest on a basis of uncompromising cynicism; his guiding principle, if he has one, is to relieve all the undeserved misery which comes in his way and to destroy all the undeserved happiness—his own included. There might be method in this madness if he did not go a step or two further, and create fresh happiness in order to destroy it. Mr. Shaw's story must be taken as a burlesque, and in that sense it will afford perhaps more than the average amusement of highly imaginative romance.

> *"Novels of the Week: 'An Unsocial Socialist',"* in
> *The Athenaeum, No. 3097, March 5, 1887, p. 318.*

### BERNARD SHAW (essay date 1898)

[*In this preface, Shaw provides an overview of his work to-date and discusses some of his theories of drama.*]

There is an old saying that if a man has not fallen in love before forty, he had better not fall in love after. I long ago perceived that this rule applied to many other matters as well: for example, to the writing of plays; and I made a rough memorandum for my own guidance that unless I could produce at least half a dozen plays before I was forty, I had better let playwriting alone. It was not so easy to comply with this provision as might be supposed. Not that I lacked the dramatist's gift. As far as that is concerned, I have encountered no limit but my own laziness to my power of conjuring up imaginary people in imaginary places, and finding pretexts for theatrical scenes between them. But to obtain a livelihood by this insane gift, I must have conjured so as to interest not only my own imagination, but that of at least some seventy or a hundred thousand contemporary London playgoers. To fulfil this condition was hopelessly out of my power. I had no taste for what is called popular art, no respect for popular morality, no belief in popular religion, no admiration for popular heroics. As an Irishman I could pretend to patriotism neither for the country I had abandoned nor the country that had ruined it. As a humane person I detested violence and slaughter, whether in war, sport, or the butcher's yard. I was a Socialist, detesting our anarchical scramble for money, and believing in equality as the only possible permanent basis of social organization, discipline, subordination, good manners, and selection of fit persons for high functions. Fashionable life, open on indulgent terms to unencumbered 'brilliant' persons, I could not endure, even if I had not feared its demoralizing effect on a character which required looking after as much as my own. I was neither a sceptic nor a cynic in these matters: I simply understood life differently from the average respectable man; and as I certainly enjoyed myself more—mostly in ways which would have made him unbearably miserable—I was not splenetic over our variance.

Judge then, how impossible it was for me to write fiction that should delight the public. (pp. 7-8)

The matter, once I gave up writing novels, was not so very difficult. Every despot must have one disloyal subject to keep him sane. Even Louis the Eleventh had to tolerate his confessor, standing for the eternal against the temporal throne. Democracy has now handed the sceptre of the despot to the sovereign people; but they, too, must have their confessor, whom they call Critic. Criticism is not only medicinally salutary: it has positive popular attractions in its cruelty, its gladiatorship, and the gratification given to envy by its attacks on the great, and to enthusiasm by its praises. It may say things which many would like to say, but dare not, and indeed for want of skill could not even if they durst. Its iconoclasms, seditions, and blasphemies, if well turned, tickle those whom they shock; so that the critic adds the privileges of the court jester to those of the confessor. . . .

It was as Punch, then, that I emerged from obscurity. All I had to do was to open my normal eyes, and with my utmost literary skill put the case exactly as it struck me, or describe the thing exactly as I saw it, to be applauded as the most humorously extravagant paradoxer in London. The only reproach with which I became familiar was the everlasting 'Why can you not be serious?' Soon my privileges were enormous and my wealth immense. (p. 9)

But alas! the world grew younger as I grew older: its vision cleared as mine dimmed: it began to read with the naked eye the writing on the wall which now began to remind me that the age of spectacles was at hand. . . . In my weekly columns, which I once filled full from a magic well that never ran dry or lost its sparkle provided I pumped hard enough, I began to repeat myself; to fall into a style which, to my great peril, was recognized as at least partly serious; to find the pump tiring me and the water lower in the well; and, worst symptom of all, to reflect with little tremors on the fact that my mystic wealth could not, like the money for which other men threw it away, be stored up against my second childhood. (p. 10)

I then raked out, from my dustiest pile of discarded and rejected manuscripts, two acts of a play I had begun in 1885, shortly after the close of my novel writing period, in collaboration with my friend William Archer.

Archer has himself described how I proved the most impossible of collaborators. Laying violent hands on his thoroughly planned scheme for a sympathetically romantic 'well made play' of the Parisian type then in vogue, I perversely distorted it into a grotesquely realistic exposure of slum landlordism, municipal jobbery, and the pecuniary and matrimonial ties between them and the pleasant people with 'independent' incomes who imagine that such sordid matters do not touch their own lives. The result was revoltingly incongruous; for though I took my theme seriously enough, I did not then take the theatre quite seriously, even in taking it more seriously than it took itself. The farcical trivialities in which I followed the fashion of the times became silly and irritating beyond all endurance when intruded upon a subject of such depth, reality, and force as that into which I had plunged my drama. . . . Exhuming this as aforesaid seven years later, I saw that the very qualities which had made it impossible for ordinary commercial purposes in 1885 might be exactly those needed by the Independent Theatre in 1892. So I completed it by a third act; gave it the farfetched Scriptural title of *Widowers' Houses;* and . . . launched it at the public in the Royalty Theatre with all its original tomfooleries on its head. It made a sensation out of all proportion to its merits or even its demerits; and I at once became infamous as a playwright. (pp. 12-13)

Had the two performances of *Widowers' Houses* . . . been multiplied by fifty, it would still have remained unknown to those who either dwell out of reach of a theatre, or, as a matter of habit, prejudice, comfort, health or age, abstain altogether from playgoing. Many people who read with delight all the classic dramatists, from Eschylus to Ibsen, only go to the theatre on the rare occasions when they are offered a play by an author whose work they have already learnt to value as literature, or a performance by an actor of the first rank. (pp. 17-18)

[The] presentation of plays through the literary medium has not yet become an art; and the result is that it is very difficult to induce the English public to buy and read plays. Indeed, why should they, when they find nothing in them except the bare words, with a few carpenter's and costumier's directions as to the heroine's father having a grey beard, and the drawing room having three doors on the right, two doors and an entrance through the conservatory on the left, and a French window in the middle? . . . Who will deny that the resultant occasional mysteriousness of effect, enchanting though it may be, is produced at the cost of intellectual obscurity? (p. 23)

Finally, may I put in a plea for the actors themselves? Born actors have a susceptibility to dramatic emotion which enables them to seize the moods of their parts intuitively. But to expect them to be intuitive as to intellectual meaning and circumstantial conditions as well, is to demand powers of divination from them: one might as well expect the Astronomer Royal to tell the time in a catacomb. And yet the actor generally finds his part full of emotional directions which he could supply as well or better than the author, whilst he is left quite in the dark as to the political or religious conditions under which the character he impersonates is supposed to be acting. Definite conceptions of these are always implicit in the best plays, and are often the key to their appropriate rendering; but most actors are so accustomed to do without them that they would object to being troubled with them, although it is only by such educative trouble that an actor's profession can place him on the level of the lawyer, the physician, the churchman, and the statesman. Even as it is, Shylock as a Jew and usurer, Othello as a Moor and a soldier, Caesar, Cleopatra and Antony as figures in defined political circumstances, are enormously more real to the actor than the countless heroes as to whom nothing is ever known except that they wear nice clothes, love the heroine, baffle the villain, and live happily ever after.

The case, then, is overwhelming not only for printing and publishing the dialogue of plays, but for a serious effort to convey their full content to the reader. This means the institution of a new art; and I daresay that before these two volumes are ten years old, the bald attempt they make at it will be left far behind, and that the customary brief and unreadable scene specification at the head of an act will have expanded into a chapter, or even a series of chapters. No doubt one result of this will be the production, under cover of the above arguments, of works of a mixture of kinds, part narrative, part homily, part description, part dialogue, and (possibly) part drama: works that could be read, but not acted. I have no objection to such works; but my own aim has been that of the practical dramatist: if anything my eye has been too much on the stage. At all events, I have tried to put down nothing that is irrelevant to the actor's performance, and, through it, to the audience's comprehension of the play. I have of course been compelled to omit many things that a stage representation could convey, simply because the art of letters, though highly developed grammatically, is still in its infancy as a technical speech notation: for example, there are fifty ways of saying Yes, and five hundred of saying No, but only one way of writing them down. Even the use of spaced letters instead of italics for underlining though familiar to foreign readers, will have to be learned by the English public before it becomes effective. But if my readers do their fair share of the work, I daresay they will understand nearly as much of the plays as I do myself.

Finally, a word as to why I have labelled the three plays in this first volume [*Widowers' Houses, The Philanderer*, and *Mrs. Warren's Profession*] Unpleasant. The reason is pretty obvious: their dramatic power is used to force the spectator to face unpleasant facts. No doubt all plays which deal sincerely with humanity must wound the monstrous conceit which it is the business of romance to flatter. But here we are confronted, not only with the comedy and tragedy of individual character and destiny, but with those social horrors which arise from the fact that the average homebred Englishman, however honorable and goodnatured he may be in his private capacity, is, as a citizen, a wretched creature who, whilst clamoring for a gratuitous millennium, will shut his eyes to the most villainous abuses if the remedy threatens to add another penny in the pound to the rates and taxes which he has to be half cheated, half coerced into paying. In *Widowers' Houses* I have shewn middle-class respectability and younger son gentility fattening on the poverty of the slum as flies fatten on filth. That is not a pleasant theme.

In *The Philanderer* I have shewn the grotesque sexual compacts made between men and women under marriage laws which represent to some of us a political necessity (especially for other people), to some a divine ordinance, to some a romantic ideal, to some a domestic profession for women, and to some that worst of blundering abominations, an institution which society has outgrown but not modified, and which 'advanced' individuals are therefore forced to evade. The scene with which *The Philanderer* opens, the atmosphere in which it proceeds, and the marriage with which it ends, are, for the intellectually and artistically conscious classes in modern society, typical; and it will hardly be denied, I think, that they are unpleasant.

In *Mrs. Warren's Profession* I have gone straight at the fact that, as Mrs. Warren puts it, 'the only way for a woman to provide for herself decently is for her to be good to some man that can afford to be good to her.' There are certain questions on which I am, like most Socialists, an extreme Individualist. I believe that any society which desires to found itself on a high standard of integrity of character in its units should organize itself in such a fashion as to make it possible for all men and all women to maintain themselves in reasonable comfort by their industry without selling their affections and their convictions. At present we not only condemn women as a sex to attach themselves to breadwinners, licitly or illicitly, on pain of heavy privation and disadvantage; but we have great prostitute classes of men: for instance, the playwrights and journalists, to whom I myself belong, not to mention the legions of lawyers, doctors, clergymen, and platform politicians who are daily using their highest faculties to belie their real sentiments: a sin compared to which that of a woman who sells the use of her person for a few hours is too venial to be worth mentioning; for rich men without conviction are more dangerous in modern society than poor women without chastity. Hardly a pleasant subject, this!

I must, however, warn my readers that my attacks are directed against themselves, not against my stage figures. They cannot too throughly understand that the guilt of defective social organization does not lie alone on the people who actually work the commercial makeshifts which the defects make inevitable, and who often, like Sartorius and Mrs. Warren, display valu-

able executive capacities and even high moral virtues in their administration, but with the whole body of citizens whose public opinion, public action, and public contribution as ratepayers, alone can replace Sartorius's slums with decent dwellings, Charteris's intrigues with reasonable marriage contracts, and Mrs. Warren's profession with honorable industries guarded by a humane industrial code and a 'moral minimum' wage. (pp. 24-7)

> *Bernard Shaw, "Mainly About Myself," in his* Plays: Pleasant and Unpleasant, Vol. I *(reprinted by permission of The Society of Authors on behalf of the Bernard Shaw Estate), Gilbert S. Stone and Company, 1898 (and reprinted in his* Plays Unpleasant: Widower's Houses, The Philanderer, Mrs. Warren's Profession, *Penguin Books, 1961, pp. 7-27).*

## W. B. YEATS  (letter date 1904)

[*John Bull's Other Island, a drama concerning the effects of imperialism on the conqueror as well as the vanquished, draws high praise from Yeats in the following letter, written during a time of growing Irish nationalism.*]

My Dear Shaw: I have been very long about thanking you for the play [*John Bull's Other Island*]. (p. 122)

I was disappointed by the first act and a half. The stage Irishman who wasn't an Irishman was very amusing, but then I said to myself 'What the devil did Shaw mean by all this Union of Hearts-like Conversation? What do we care here in this country, which despite the Act of Union is still an island, about the English liberal party and the Tariff, and the difference between English and Irish character, or whatever else it was all about. Being raw people,' I said, 'we do care about human nature in action, and that he's not giving us.' Then my interest began to awake. That young woman who persuaded that Englishman, full of impulsiveness that comes from a good banking account, that he was drunk on nothing more serious than poteen, was altogether a delight. The motor car too, the choosing the member of Parliament, and so on right to the end, often exciting and mostly to the point. I thought in reading the first act that you had forgotten Ireland, but I found in the other acts that [it] is the only subject on which you are entirely serious. In fact you are so serious that sometimes your seriousness leaps upon the stage, knocks the characters over, and insists on having all the conversation to himself. However the inevitable cutting (the play is as you say immensely too long) is certain to send your seriousness back to the front row of the stalls. You have said things in this play which are entirely true about Ireland, things which nobody has ever said before, and these are the very things that are most part of the action. It astonishes me that you should have been so long in London and yet have remembered so much. To some extent this play is unlike anything you have done before. Hitherto you have taken your situations from melodrama, and called up logic to make them ridiculous. Your process here seems to be quite different, you are taking your situations more from life, you are for the first time trying to get the atmosphere of a place, you have for the first time a geographical conscience. (For instance you have not made the landlords the winning side, as you did the Servians in the first version of *Arms and the Man*.)

Synge who is as good an opinion as I know, thinks that 'it will hold a Dublin audience, and at times move them if even tolerably played.' . . . To my surprise I must say, I do not consider the play dangerous. There may be a phrase, but I cannot think of one at this moment. Here again, you show your wonderful knowledge of the country. You have laughed at all the things that are ripe for laughter, and not where the ear is still green. I don't mean to say that there won't be indignation about one thing or another, and a great deal of talk about it all, but I mean that we can play it, and survive to play something else. (pp. 123-24)

*W. B. Yeats, in his letter to Bernard Shaw on October 5, 1904 (reprinted by permission of Michael and Anne Yeats), in* Shaw: The Critical Heritage, *edited by T. F. Evans, Routledge & Kegan Paul, 1976, pp. 122-24.*

## GILBERT K. CHESTERTON (essay date 1909)

[*Chesterton and Shaw were personal friends but professional enemies. At the time he wrote* George Bernard Shaw, *Chesterton was embracing orthodox Christianity, while Shaw was well established as an iconoclast and promoter of creative evolution. Chesterton's study is, hence, alternately admiring and vengeful in tone.*]

No one who was alive at the time and interested in such matters will ever forget the first acting of *Arms and the Man.* It was applauded by that indescribable element in all of us which rejoices to see the genuine thing prevail against the plausible; that element which rejoices that even its enemies are alive. Apart from the problems raised in the play, the very form of it was an attractive and forcible innovation. Classic plays which were wholly heroic, comic plays which were wholly and even heartlessly ironical, were common enough. Commonest of all in this particular time was the play that began playfully, with plenty of comic business, and was gradually sobered by sentiment until it ended on a note of romance or even of pathos. . . . The first thing that Bernard Shaw did when he stepped before the footlights was to reverse this process. He resolved to build a play not on pathos, but on bathos. . . . This merely technical originality is indicated in the very title of the play. The *Arma Virumque* of Virgil is a mounting and ascending phrase, the man is more than his weapons. The Latin line suggests a superb procession which should bring on to the stage the brazen and resounding armour, the shield and shattering axe, but end with the hero himself, taller and more terrible because unarmed. The technical effect of Shaw's scheme is like the same scene, in which a crowd should carry even more gigantic shapes of shield and helmet, but when the horns and howls were at their highest, should end with the figure of Little Tich. The name itself is meant to be a bathos; arms—and the man.

It is well to begin with the superficial; and this is the superficial effectiveness of Shaw; the brilliancy of bathos. But of course the vitality and value of his plays does not lie merely in this; any more than the value of Swinburne lies in alliteration or the value of Hood in puns. This is not his message; but it is his method; it is his style. The first taste we had of it was in this play of *Arms and the Man;* but even at the very first it was evident that there was much more in the play than that. Among other things there was one thing not unimportant; there was savage sincerity. . . . It is all very well to accuse Mr. Shaw of standing on his head; but if you stand on your head you must have a hard and solid head to stand on. In *Arms and the Man* the bathos of form was strictly the incarnation of a strong satire in the idea. (pp. 118-20)

The dramatic volume with which Shaw [first] dazzled the public was called, *Plays, Pleasant and Unpleasant.* I think the most striking and typical thing about it was that he did not know very clearly which plays were unpleasant and which were pleasant. . . . First in fame and contemporary importance came the reprint of *Arms and the Man,* of which I have already spoken. Over all the rest towered unquestionably the two figures of Mrs. Warren and of Candida. (pp. 123-24)

I fancy that the author rather dislikes *Candida* because it is so generally liked. I give my own feeling for what it is worth (a foolish phrase), but I think that there were only two moments when this powerful writer was truly, in the ancient and popular sense, inspired; that is, breathing from a bigger self and telling more truth than he knew. One is that scene in a later play where after the secrets and revenges of Egypt have rioted and rotted all round him, the colossal sanity of Caesar is suddenly acclaimed with swords. The other is that great last scene in *Candida* where the wife, stung into final speech, declared her purpose of remaining with the strong man because he is the weak man. . . . Even among the plain and ringing paradoxes of the Shaw play this is one of the best reversals or turnovers ever effected. A paradoxical writer like Bernard Shaw is perpetually and tiresomely told that he stands on his head. But all romance and all religion consist in making the whole universe stand on its head. That reversal is the whole idea of virtue; that the last shall be first and the first last. Considered as a pure piece of Shaw therefore, the thing is of the best. (pp. 124-25)

There are one or two errors in the play; and they are all due to the primary error of despising the mental attitude of romance, which is the only key to real human conduct. . . . For dramatic purposes, G.B.S., even if he despises romance, ought to comprehend it. But then, if once he comprehended romance, he would not despise it.

The series contained, besides its more substantial work, tragic and comic, a comparative frivolity called *The Man of Destiny.* It is a little comedy about Napoleon, and is chiefly interesting as a foreshadowing of his after sketches of heroes and strong men; it is a kind of parody of *Caesar and Cleopatra* before it was written. In this connection the mere title of this Napoleonic play is of interest. All Shaw's generation and school of thought remembered Napoleon only by his late and corrupt title of ''The Man of Destiny,'' a title only given to him when he was already fat and tired and destined to exile. They forgot that through all the really thrilling and creative part of his career he was not the man of destiny, but the man who defied destiny. Shaw's sketch is extraordinarily clever; but it is tinged with this unmilitary notion of an inevitable conquest; and this we must remember when we come to those larger canvases on which he painted his more serious heroes. As for the play, it is packed with good things, of which the last is perhaps the best. The long duologue between Bonaparte and the Irish lady ends with the General declaring that he will only be beaten when he meets an English army under an Irish general. It has always been one of Shaw's paradoxes that the English mind has the force to fulfil orders, while the Irish mind has the intelligence to give them, and it is among those of his paradoxes which contain a certain truth.

A far more important play is *The Philanderer,* an ironic comedy which is full of fine strokes and real satire; it is more especially the vehicle of some of Shaw's best satire upon physical science. Nothing could be cleverer than the picture of the young strenuous doctor, in the utter innocence of his professional ambition, who has discovered a new disease, and is delighted when he finds people suffering from it and cast down to despair when he finds that it does not exist. The point is worth a pause, because it is a good, short way of stating Shaw's attitude, right or wrong, upon the whole of formal morality. What he dislikes in young Dr. Paramore is that he has interposed a secondary and false conscience between himself and the facts. When his disease is disproved, instead of seeing the escape of a human being who thought he was going to die of it, Paramore sees the downfall of a kind of flag or cause. This is the whole contention of *The Quintessence of Ibsenism,* put better than the book puts it; it is a really sharp exposition of the dangers of "idealism," the sacrifice of people to principles, and Shaw is even wiser in his suggestion that this excessive idealism exists nowhere so strongly as in the world of physical science. He shows that the scientist tends to be more concerned about the sickness than about the sick man; but it was certainly in his mind to suggest here also that the idealist is more concerned about the sin than about the sinner.

This business of Dr. Paramore's disease while it is the most farcical thing in the play is also the most philosophic and important. The rest of the figures, including the Philanderer himself, are in the full sense of those blasting and obliterating words "funny without being vulgar," that is, funny without being of any importance to the masses of men. (pp. 128-33)

In *The Philanderer* there are five hundred excellent and about five magnificent things. The rattle of repartees between the doctor and the soldier about the humanity of their two trades is admirable. Or again, when the colonel tells Chartaris that "in his young days" he would have no more behaved like Chartaris than he would have cheated at cards. After a pause Chartaris says, "You're getting old, Craven, and you make a virtue of it as usual." (p. 134)

There is an acrid taste in *The Philanderer;* and certainly he might be considered a supersensitive person who should find anything acrid in *You Never Can Tell.* This play is the nearest approach to frank and objectless exuberance in the whole of Shaw's work. (pp. 134-35)

The only one out of this brilliant batch of plays in which I think that the [farcical method] really fails, is the one called *Widowers' Houses.* The best touch of Shaw is simply in the title. The simple substitution of widowers for widows contains almost the whole bitter and yet boisterous protest of Shaw; all his preference for undignified fact over dignified phrase; all his dislike of those subtle trends of sex or mystery which swing the logician off the straight line. We can imagine him crying "Why in the name of death and conscience should it be tragic to be a widow but comic to be a widower?" (pp. 135-36)

The play of *Mrs. Warren's Profession* is concerned with a coarse mother and a cold daughter; the mother drives the ordinary and dirty trade of harlotry; the daughter does not know until the end the atrocious origin of all her own comfort and refinement. . . . Undoubtedly the upshot is that a brothel is a miserable business, and a brothel-keeper a miserable woman. The whole dramatic art of Shaw is in the literal sense of the word, tragi-comic; I mean that the comic part comes after the tragedy. But just as *You Never Can Tell* represents the nearest approach of Shaw to the purely comic, so *Mrs. Warren's Profession* represents his only complete, or nearly complete, tragedy. There is no twopenny modernism in it, as in *The Philanderer.* Mrs. Warren is as old as the Old Testament; "for she hath cast down many wounded, yea, many strong men have been slain by her; her house is in the gates of hell, going down into the chamber of death." Here is no subtle ethics, as in *Widowers'*

*Houses;* for even those moderns who think it noble that a woman should throw away her honour, surely cannot think it especially noble that she should sell it. Here is no lighting up by laughter, astonishment, and happy coincidence, as in *You Never Can Tell.* The play is a pure tragedy about a permanent and quite plain human problem; the problem is as plain and permanent, the tragedy is as proud and pure, as in *Oedipus* or *Macbeth.* (pp. 137-39)

Bernard Shaw is a Puritan and his work is Puritan work. He has all the essentials of the old, virile and extinct Protestant type. In his work he is as ugly as a Puritan. He is as indecent as a Puritan. He is as full of gross words and sensual facts as a sermon of the seventeenth century. Up to this point of his life indeed hardly anyone would have dreamed of calling him a Puritan; he was called sometimes an anarchist, sometimes a buffoon, sometimes (by the more discerning stupid people) a prig. His attitude towards current problems was felt to be arresting and even indecent; I do not think that anyone thought of connecting it with the old Calvinistic morality. But Shaw, who knew better than the Shavians, was at this moment on the very eve of confessing his moral origin. The next book of plays he produced (including *The Devil's Disciple, Captain Brassbound's Conversion,* and *Caesar and Cleopatra*), actually bore the title of *Plays for Puritans.*

The play called *The Devil's Disciple* has great merits, but the merits are incidental. Some of its jokes are serious and important, but its general plan can only be called a joke. Almost alone among Bernard Shaw's plays (except of course such things as *How he lied to her Husband* and *The Admirable Bashville*) this drama does not turn on any very plain pivot of ethical or philosophical conviction. The artistic idea seems to be the notion of a melodrama in which all the conventional melodramatic situations shall suddenly take unconventional turns. Just where the melodramatic clergyman would show courage he appears to show cowardice; just where the melodramatic sinner would confess his love he confesses his indifference. This is a little too like the Shaw of the newspaper critics rather than the Shaw of reality. There are indeed present in the play two of the writer's principal moral conceptions. The first is the idea of a great heroic action coming in a sense from nowhere; that is, not coming from any commonplace motive; being born in the soul in naked beauty, coming with its own authority and testifying only to itself. Shaw's agent does not act towards something, but from something. The hero dies, not because he desires heroism, but because he has it. So in this particular play the Devil's Disciple finds that his own nature will not permit him to put the rope round another man's neck; he has no reasons of desire, affection, or even equity; his death is a sort of divine whim. And in connection with this the dramatist introduces another favourite moral; the objection to perpetual playing upon the motive of sex. He deliberately lures the onlooker into the net of Cupid in order to tell him with salutary decision that Cupid is not there at all. Millions of melodramatic dramatists have made a man face death for the woman he loves; Shaw makes him face death for the woman he does not love—merely in order to put woman in her palace. He objects to that idolatry of sexualism which makes it the fountain of all forcible enthusiasms; he dislikes the amorous drama which makes the female the only key to the male. He is Feminist in politics, but Anti-feminist in emotion. His key to most problems is "Ne cherchez pas la femme." (pp. 147-49)

The third play in order in the series called *Plays for Puritans* is a very charming one; *Captain Brassbound's Conversion.* This also turns, as does so much of the Caesar drama, on the idea of vanity of revenge—the idea that it is too slight and silly a thing for a man to allow to occupy and corrupt his consciousness. It is not, of course, the morality that is new here, but the touch of cold laughter in the core of the morality. Many saints and sages have denounced vengeance. But they treated vengeance as something too great for man. ''Vengeance is Mine, saith the Lord; I will repay.'' Shaw treats vengeance as something too small for man—a monkey trick he ought to have outlived, a childish storm of tears which he ought to be able to control. (pp. 151-52)

We may now pass to the more important of the plays. For some time Bernard Shaw would seem to have been brooding upon the soul of Julius Caesar. . . . The conjunction of Shaw and Caesar has about it something smooth and inevitable; for this decisive reason, that Caesar is really the only great man of history to whom the Shaw theories apply. Caesar *was* a Shaw hero. (p. 154)

[Whether] the Shavian Caesar is a sound ideal or no, there can be little doubt that he is a very fine reality. Shaw has done nothing greater as a piece of artistic creation. (p. 157)

His primary and defiant proposition is the Calvinistic proposition: that the elect do not earn virtue, but possess it. The goodness of a man does not consist in trying to be good, but in being good. Julius Caesar prevails over other people by possessing more *virtus* than they; not by having striven or suffered or bought his virtue; not because he has struggled heroically, but because he is a hero. (pp. 160-61)

Some of the incidental wit in the Caesarian drama is excellent, although it is upon the whole less spontaneous and perfect than in the previous plays. One of its jests may be mentioned in passing, not merely to draw attention to its failure (though Shaw is brilliant enough to afford many failures), but because it is the best opportunity for mentioning one of the writer's minor notions to which he obstinately adheres. He describes the Ancient Briton in Caesar's train as being exactly like a modern respectable Englishman. As a joke for a Christmas pantomime this would be all very well; but one expects the jokes of Bernard Shaw to have some intellectual root, however fantastic the flower. And obviously all historic common sense is against the idea that that dim Druid people, whoever they were, who dwelt in our land before it was lit up by Rome or loaded with varied invasions, were a precise facsimile of the commercial society of Birmingham or Brighton. (pp. 164-65)

[This] is as good an instance as any we are likely to come across of a certain almost extraneous fault which does deface the work of Bernard Shaw. It is a fault only to be mentioned when we have made the solidity of the merits quite clear. . . . [If] any real student of Shaw says that Shaw is only making a fool of him, we can only say that of that student it is very superfluous for anyone to make a fool. But though the dramatist's jests are always serious and generally obvious, he is really affected from time to time by a certain spirit of which that climate theory is a case—a spirit that can only be called one of senseless ingenuity. I suppose it is a sort of nemesis of wit; the skidding of a wheel in the height of its speed. Perhaps it is connected with the nomadic nature of his mind. That lack of roots, this remoteness from ancient instincts and traditions is responsible for a certain bleak and heartless extravagance of statement on certain subjects which makes the author really unconvincing as well as exaggerative; satires that are *saugrenu*, jokes that are rather silly than wild, statements which even

considered as lies have no symbolic relation to truth. They are exaggerations of something that does not exist. For instance, if a man called Christmas Day a mere hypocritical excuse for drunkenness and gluttony that would be false, but it would have a fact hidden in it somewhere. But when Bernard Shaw says that Christmas Day is only a conspiracy kept up by poulterers and wine merchants from strictly business motives, then he says something which is not so much false as startlingly and arrestingly foolish. He might as well say that the two sexes were invented by jewellers who wanted to sell wedding rings. (pp. 167-69)

[There] must be some truth in every popular impression. And the impression that Shaw, the most savagely serious man of his time, is a mere music-hall artist must have reference to such rare outbreaks as these. As a rule his speeches are full, not only of substance, but of substances, materials like pork, mahogany, lead, and leather. There is no man whose arguments cover a more Napoleonic map of detail. It is true that he jokes; but wherever he is he has topical jokes, one might almost say family jokes. If he talks to tailors he can allude to the last absurdity about buttons. If he talks to soldiers he can see the exquisite and exact humour of the last gun-carriage. But when all his powerful practicality is allowed, there does run through him this erratic levity, an explosion of ineptitude. It is a queer quality in literature. It is a sort of cold extravagance; and it has made him all his enemies. (pp. 169-70)

> *Gilbert K. Chesterton, in his* George Bernard Shaw, *John Lane Company, 1909, 258 p.*

## H. L. MENCKEN (essay date 1916)

[*Mencken's first book, disregarding an immature poetry collection, was a laudatory survey of Shaw's work,* George Bernard Shaw: His Plays *(see excerpt in* TCLC, *Vol. 3). Written early in Mencken's career, the work stands in sharp contrast, in style and tone, to the following attack on Shaw, written during the critic's years as editor and book reviewer of* The Smart Set.]

Practically all of the sagacity of George Bernard Shaw consists of bellowing vociferously what every one knows. I think I am as well acquainted with his works, both hortatory and dramatic, as the next man. I wrote the first book ever devoted to a discussion of them, and I read them pretty steadily, even today, and with endless enjoyment. Yet, so far as I know, I have never found an original idea in them—never a single statement of fact or opinion that was not anteriorly familiar, and almost commonplace. Put the thesis of any of his plays into a plain proposition, and I doubt that you could find a literate man in Christendom who had not heard it before, or who would seriously dispute it. The roots of each one of them are in platitude; the roots of *every* effective stage-play are in platitude; that a dramatist is inevitably a platitudinarian is itself a platitude double damned. But Shaw clings to the obvious even when he is not hampered by the suffocating conventions of the stage. His Fabian tracts and his pamphlets on the war are veritable compendiums of the undeniable; what is seriously stated in them is quite beyond logical dispute. They have excited a great deal of ire, they have brought down upon him a great deal of amusing abuse, but I have yet to hear of any one actually controverting them. As well try to controvert the Copernican astronomy. They are as bullet-proof in essence as the multiplication table, and vastly more bullet-proof than the Ten Commandments or the Constitution of the United States.

Well, then, why does the Ulsterman kick up such a pother? Why is he regarded as an arch-heretic, almost comparable to Galileo, Nietzsche or Simon Magnus? For the simplest of reasons. Because he practices with great zest and skill the fine art of exhibiting the obvious in unexpected and terrifying lights—because he is a master of the logical trick of so matching two apparently safe premises that they yield an incongruous and inconvenient conclusion—above all, because he is a fellow of the utmost charm and address, quick-witted, bold, limbertongued, persuasive, humorous, iconoclastic, ingratiating—in brief, a true Kelt, and so the exact antithesis of the solemn Sassenachs who ordinarily instruct and exhort us. Turn to his **"Man and Superman,"** and you will see the whole Shaw machine at work. What he starts out with is the self-evident fact, disputed by no one not idiotic, that a woman has vastly more to gain by marriage, under Christian monogamy, than a man. That fact is as old as monogamy itself; it was, I daresay, the admitted basis of the palace revolution which brought monogamy into the world. But now comes Shaw with an implication that the sentimentality of the world chooses to conceal—with a deduction plainly resident in the original proposition, but kept in safe silence there by a preposterous and hypocritical taboo—to wit, the deduction that women are well aware of the profit that marriage yields for them, and that they are thus much more eager to marry than men are, and ever alert to take the lead in the business. This second fact, to any man who has passed through the terrible years between twenty-five and forty, is as plain as the first, but by a sort of general consent it is not openly stated. Violate that general consent and you are guilty of *scandalum magnatum.* Shaw is simply one who is guilty of *scandalum magnatum* habitually, a professional criminal in that department. It is his life work to announce the obvious in terms of the scandalous. (pp. 181-83)

Read his critical writings from end to end, and you will not find the slightest hint that objects of art were passing before him as he wrote. . . . Always the ethical obsession, the hallmark of the Scotch Puritan, is visible in him. His politics is mere moral indignation. His aesthetic theory is cannibalism upon aesthetics. And in his general writing he is forever discovering an atrocity in what was hitherto passed as no more than a human weakness; he is forever inventing new sins, and demanding their punishment; he always sees his opponent, not only as wrong, but also as a scoundrel. I have called him a Presbyterian. Need I add that he flirts with predestination under the quasi-scientific *nom de guerre* of determinism—that he seems to be convinced that, while men may not be responsible for their virtues, they are undoubtedly responsible for their offendings, and deserve to be clubbed therefor? . . .

And this is Shaw the revolutionist, the heretic! Next, perhaps, we shall be hearing of Benedict XV, the atheist. . . . (pp. 189-90)

> *H. L. Mencken, "The Ulster Polonius" (originally published in* The Smart Set, *Vol. XLIX, No. 4, August, 1916), in his* Prejudices, *first series (copyright © 1919 by Alfred A. Knopf, Inc.), Knopf, 1919, pp. 181-90.*

## LUIGI PIRANDELLO   (essay date 1924)

[*Pirandello expresses high praise for Shaw as an artist, finding* St. Joan *to be a powerful work of poetry and not, as some critics have concluded, a sermon disguised as a drama.*]

I have a strong impression that for some time past George Bernard Shaw has been growing more and more serious. He has always believed in himself, and with good reason. But in a number of plays, after his first successes, he did not seem to believe very much in what he was doing. This, at least may properly be suspected, since it cannot be denied that in his eagerness to defend his own intellectual position against the so-called 'bourgeois morality', he not infrequently abandoned all pretensions to seriousness as an artist. Now, however, he seems to be believing less in himself, and more in what he is doing. From the epilogue of this drama on Joan of Arc we may gather almost explicitly the reason for which Shaw wrote it. This world, he seems to say, is not made for saints to live in. We must take the people who live in it for what they are, since it is not vouchsafed them to be anything else.

In fact, as we look carefully and deeply at this work of Shaw, taken as a whole, we cannot help detecting in it that curious half-humorous melancholy which is peculiar to the disillusioned idealist. Shaw has always had too keen a sense of reality not to be aware of the conflict between it and his social and moral ideals. The various phases of reality, as they were yesterday, as they are today, as they will be tomorrow, come forward in the persons who represent them before the ideal phantom of Joan (now a Saint without her knowing it). Each of these type persons justifies his own manner of being, and confesses the sin of which he was guilty, but in such a way as to show that he is unable really to mend his ways—so true is it that each is today as he was yesterday, and will be tomorrow as he is today. Joan listens to them all, but she is not angry. She has for them just a tolerant pity. She can only pray that the world may some time be made beautiful enough to be a worthy abode for the saints!

This new tolerance and pity rise from the most secret depths of poetry that exist in Shaw. Whenever, instead of tolerating, instead of pitying, he loses his temper at the shock of reality against his ideals, and then, for fear of betraying his anger—which would be bad mannered—begins to harass himself and his hearers with the dazzling brilliance of his paradoxes, Shaw, the artist properly speaking, suffers more or less seriously—he falls to the level of the jeu d'esprit which is amusing in itself, though it irremediably spoils the work of art. I may cite in point a passage in the second act of *Saint Joan* where the Archbishop expatiates on the differences between fraud and miracles. 'Frauds deceive,' says he. 'An event which creates faith does not deceive, therefore it is not a fraud but a miracle.' Such word play is for amusement only. A work that would do something more than amuse must always respect the deeper demands of art, and so respecting these, the witticism is no longer a witticism but true art.

In none of Shaw's work that I can think of have considerations of art been so thoroughly respected as in *Saint Joan.* The four acts of this drama begin, as they must begin, with Joan's request for soldiers of Robert de Baudricourt to use in driving the English from 'the sweet land of France'. And they end, as they must end, with the trial and execution of Joan. Shaw calls this play a chronicle. In fact, the drama is built up episode by episode, moment by moment, some of them rigorously particular and free from generality—truly in the style of the chroniclers—though usually they tend to be what I call deliberate 'constructiveness'. The hens have not been laying, when suddenly, they begin to lay. The wind has long been blowing from the east, and suddenly it begins blowing from the west. Two miracles! Then there are other simple, naïve things, such as the recognition of the 'blood royal' in the third act, which likewise seems to be a miracle.

But these moments are interspersed with other moments of irony and satire, of which either the Church or the English are the victims. However, this attempt to present the chronicle inside what is really history does not seem to me quite as happy as it was in *Caesar and Cleopatra*. In *Saint Joan*, history, or rather character historically conceived, weighs a bit too heavily on the living fluid objectivity of the chronicle, and the events in the play somehow lose that sense of the unexpected which is the breath of true life. We know in advance where we are going to come out. The characters, whether historical or typical, do not quite free themselves from the fixity that history has forced upon them and from the significant role they are to play in history.

Joan herself, who is presented to us as a fresh creature of the open fields, full of burning faith and self-confidence, remains that way from the beginning to the end of the play; and she makes a little too obvious her intention not to be reciting a historical role and to remain that dear, frank, innocent, inspired child that she is. Yes, Joan, as she really was in her own little individual history, must have been much as Shaw imagined her. But he seems to look on her once and for all, so to speak, quite without regard for the various situations in which she will meet life in the course of the story.

And she is kept thus simple and unilinear by the author just to bring her airy, refreshing ingenuousness into contrast with the artificial, sophisticated—or, as I say, 'deliberate' or 'constructed'—complexity of her accusers. There is, in other words, something mechanical, foreordained, fixed, about her character. Much more free and unobstructed in his natural impulses, much more independent of any deliberate restraints, and accordingly much more 'living' (from my point of view) is the Chaplain, de Stogumber, the truly admirable creation in this drama, and a persongage on which Shaw has surely expended a great deal of affectionate effort.

At a certain moment Joan's faith in her 'voices' is shaken. And this charming little creature, hitherto steadfastly confident in the divine inspiration which has many times saved her from death in battle, is suddenly filled with terror at the torment awaiting her. (pp. 280-82)

At this moment Shaw carries his protagonists to a summit of noble poetry with which any other author would be content; and we may be sure that any other author would have lowered the curtain on this scene. But Shaw cannot resist the pressure and the inspiration of the life he well knows must be surging in such circumstances in his other character—the Chaplain. He rushes on toward a second climax of not less noble poetry, depicting with magnificent elan the mad remorse, the hopeless penitence of Stogumber, thus adding to our first crisis of exquisite anguish another not less potent and overwhelming.

Rarely has George Bernard Shaw attained higher altitudes of poetic emotion than here. There is a truly great poet in Shaw; but this combative Anglo-Irishman is often willing to forget that he is a poet, so immersed is he in being a citizen of his country, or a man of the twentieth century society, with a number of respectable ideas to defend, a number of sermons to preach, a number of antagonists to rout from the intellectual battlefield. But here, in *Saint Joan,* the poet comes into his own again, with only a subordinate role left, as a demanded compensation, to irony and satire. To be sure *Saint Joan* has all the savor and all the attractiveness of Shaw's witty polemical

dialogue. But for all of these keen and cutting thrusts to left and right in Shaw's usual style of propaganda, *Saint Joan* is a work of poetry from beginning to end.

This play represents in marvellous fashion what, among so many elements of negation, is the positive element, indeed the fundamental underpinning, in the character, thought and art of this great writer—an outspoken Puritanism, which brooks no go-betweens and no mediations between man and God; a vigorous and independent vital energy, that frees itself restlessly and with joyous scorn from all the stupid and burdensome shackles of habit, routine and tradition, to conquer for itself a natural law more consonant with the poet's own being, and therefore more rational and more sound. (p. 283)

Joan, at bottom, quite without knowing it, and still declaring herself a faithful daughter of the Church, is a Puritan, like Shaw himself—affirming her own life impulse, her unshakable, her even tyrannical will to live, by accepting death itself. Joan, like Shaw, cannot exist without a life that is free and fruitful. When she tears up her recantation in the face of her deaf and blind accusers, she exemplifies the basic germ of Shaw's art, which is the germ also of his spiritual life. (p. 284)

> Luigi Pirandello, "Pirandello Distills Shaw: The Italian Playwright Discovers the Puritan Poet Idealist Sublimated in 'Saint Joan'," in The New York Times, Section 7 (© 1924 by The New York Times Company; reprinted by permission), January 13, 1924 (and reprinted in Shaw: The Critical Heritage, edited by T. F. Evans, Routledge & Kegan Paul, 1976, pp. 279-84).

## CRITES [pseudonym of T. S. ELIOT]  (essay date 1924)

[*In contrast to Pirandello (see excerpt above), Eliot finds* St. Joan *to be a travesty of the Joan of Arc story.*]

The true "dominant" of our time (with "the inevitable price of diminished progress") is Mr. Bernard Shaw. Mr. Shaw stands in fact for "the great middle-class liberalism" (I am not now quoting from Professor [F. W.] Gamble) "as Dr. Newman saw it, and as it really broke the Oxford movement." *St. Joan* has been called his masterpiece. I should be inclined to contest this judgment in favour of *Man and Superman,* but certainly (unless we owe our clairvoyance solely to the lapse of time) *St. Joan* seems to illustrate Mr. Shaw's mind more clearly than anything he has written before. No one can grasp more firmly an idea which he does not maintain, or expound it with more cogency, than Mr. Shaw. He manipulates every idea so brilliantly that he blinds us when we attempt to look for the ideas *with which he works.* And the ideas with which he works, are they more than the residue of the great Victorian labours of Darwin, and Huxley, and Cobden? We must not be deceived by the fact that he scandalised many people of the type to which we say he belongs: he scandalised them, not because his first principles were fundamentally different, but because he was much cleverer, because his thought was more rapid, because he looked farther in the same direction. The animosity which he aroused was the animosity of the dull toward the intelligent. And we cannot forget on the other hand that Mr. Shaw was the intellectual stimulant and the dramatic delight of twenty years which had little enough of either: London owes him a twenty years' debt. Yet his Joan of Arc is perhaps the greatest sacrilege of all Joans: for instead of the saint or the strumpet of the legends to which he objects, he has turned her into a great middle-class reformer, and her place is a little higher than Mrs. Pankhurst. If Mr. Shaw is an artist, he may contemplate his work with ecstasy. (pp. 4-5)

> Crites [*pseudonym of T. S. Eliot*], "A Commentary"
> (*reprinted by permission of Mrs. Valerie Eliot and
> Faber and Faber Ltd*), in The Criterion, *Vol. III,
> No. IX, October, 1924, pp. 1-5.**

## BERTOLT BRECHT   (essay date 1926)

[*In the following essay, Brecht discusses Shaw's aim and technique.*]

It should be clear by now that Shaw is a terrorist. The Shavian terror is an unusual one, and he employs an unusual weapon—that of humor. This unusual man seems to be of the opinion that there is nothing fearful in the world except the calm and incorruptible eye of the common man. But this eye must be feared, always and unconditionally. This theory endows him with a remarkable natural superiority; and by his unfaltering practice in accordance with it, he has made it impossible for anyone who ever comes into contact with him—be it in person, through his books, or through his theater—to assume that he ever committed a deed or uttered a sentence without fearful respect for this incorruptible eye. In fact, young people, whose main qualification is often their love of mettle, are often held to a minimum of aggressiveness by their premonition that any attack on Shaw's habits, even if it were his insistence on wear-ing peculiar underwear, would inevitably result in a terrible defeat of their own thoughtlessly selected apparel. If one adds to this his exploding of the thoughtless, habitual assumption that anything that might possibly be considered venerable should be treated in a subdued manner instead of energetically and joyously; if one adds to this his successful proof that in the face of truly significant ideas a relaxed (even snotty) attitude is the only proper one, since it alone facilitates true concen-tration, it becomes evident what measure of personal freedom he has achieved.

The Shavian terror consists of Shaw's insistence on the pre-rogative of every man to act decently, logically, and with a sense of humor, and on the obligation to act in this manner even in the face of opposition. He knows very well how much courage it takes to laugh about the ridiculous and how much seriounsess it takes to discover the amusing. And, like all purposeful people, he knows, on the other hand, that the most time-consuming and distracting pursuit is a certain kind of seriousness which pervades literature but does not exist any-where else. (Like us, the young generation, he considers it naive to write for the theater, and he does not show the slightest inclination to pretend that he is not aware of this: he makes far-reaching use of his naivete. He furnishes the theater with as much fun as it can take. And it can take a lot. What draws people to the theater is, strictly speaking, so much nonsense, which constitutes a tremendous buoyancy for those problems which really interest the progressive dramatic writer and which are the real value of his pieces. It follows that his problems must be so pertinent that he can be as buoyant about them as he wishes to be, for the buoyancy is what people want.)

I seem to remember that Shaw recently expressed his opinion about the future of the drama. He says that in the future people will no longer go to the theater in order to understand. He probably means that mere reproduction of reality curiously fails to give the impression of verisimilitude. The younger gener-ation will not contradict Shaw on this point. But I feel that Shaw's own dramatic works were able to overshadow those of his contemporaries exactly because they unflinchingly appealed to the intellect. His world is composed of opinions. The fate of his characters is identical with their opinions. Shaw, in order to have a play, invents some complications which provide his characters with opportunities to vent their opinions extensively and to have them clash with ours. (These complications can never be old and familiar enough to suit Shaw; here he really has no ambition whatever: a thoroughly ordinary usurer is worth his weight in gold; he stumbles on a patriotic girl in history, and the only important thing is that his audience be equally familiar with the story of this girl, that the sad end of the usurer be well known and gleefully anticipated, so that he can upset all the more completely our old-fashioned concepts of these types and—above all—our notions of the way these types think.)

Probably all of his characters, in all their traits, are the result of Shaw's delight in upsetting our habitual prejudices. He knows that we have the terrible habit of forcing all the attributes of a certain kind of people into one preconceived, stereotyped concept. In our imagination the usurer is cowardly, sneaky, and brutal. We would not think of permitting him to be even a little courageous, sentimental, or soft hearted. Shaw does.

Concerning heroes, Shaw's degenerate successors have awk-wardly amplified his refreshing conviction—that heroes are not exemplary scholars and that heroism is a very inscrutable, but very real conglomeration of contradictory traits—to mean that neither heroism nor heroes exist. But even this does not bother Shaw. It seems he considers it healthier to live among common people than among heroes.

In the composition of his works Shaw proceeds with utmost frankness. He does not mind writing under the continuous scrutiny of the public. In order to make his judgments more emphatic, he facilitates this scrutiny: he unremittingly stresses his own peculiarities, his very individualistic taste, even his own (little) weaknesses. Thus he cannot fail to reap gratitude. Even where his opinions clash with those of the younger gen-eration, he is listened to with glee: he is—and what more can be said about a man—a good fellow. Besides, his time pre-serves opinions better than emotions and moods. It seems that of all the things produced in this epoch opinions are the most durable.

It is characteristically difficult to find out the opinions of other European authors. But I assume that concerning literature they hold approximately the same view, to wit, that writing is a melancholy business. Shaw, whose opinions about everything are widely known throughout the world, clearly sets himself deliberately apart from this view of his colleagues. . . . Shaw likes to write. On his head there is no room for the crown of a martyr. His literary preoccupation does not separate him from life. On the contrary. I do not know whether it is an indication of talent, but the effect of his unmistakeable serenity and his contagious good humor is extraordinary. Shaw actually suc-ceeds in giving the impression that his mental and bodily health increases with every sentence he writes. Reading him is perhaps not exhilarating in a dionysean manner, but it is undeniable that it is amazingly conducive to good health. And his only enemies—if we must mention them at all—are obviously ex-clusively people to whom health is much less of a concern.

I cannot remember a single one of Shaw's "characteristic" ideas, although I know, of course, that he has many; but I remember many things which he discovers to be characteristic of other people. In his own estimate, at any rate, his temper is more important than his individual opinions. And that speaks well for a man like him.

I feel that a theory of evolution is central for him, one which, in his opinion, differs considerably and significantly from another theory of evolution of definitely lower calibre. At any rate, his faith that man is capable of infinite improvement plays an important rôle in his works. It will be clearly recognized as a sincere ovation for Shaw when I admit without blushing that I unconditionally subscribe to Shaw's view although I am not thoroughly acquainted with either of the two theories mentioned above. The reason? A man with such keen intellect and courageous eloquence simply deserves my complete confidence. This is all the more true as I have considered—always and in any situation—the forcefulness of an expression more important than its immediate applicability and a man of stature more important than the sphere of his activity. (pp. 184-87)

> *Bertolt Brecht, "Ovation for Shaw," translated by Gerhard H. W. Zuther (originally published under a different title in* Berliner Borsen-Courier, *July 25, 1926; copyright © 1959; reprinted by permission of* Modern Drama, University of Toronto,*) in* Modern Drama, *Vol. 2, No. 2, September, 1959, pp. 184-87.*

## H. G. WELLS (essay date 1934)

[*Wells was one of the few persons of whom Shaw could write: "I never met such a chap. I could not survive such another." In this section from his autobiography, Wells compares his own style and thought with that of Shaw.*]

We were both atheists and socialists; we were both attacking an apparently fixed and invincible social system from the outside; but this much resemblance did not prevent our carrying ourselves with a certain sustained defensiveness towards each other that remains to this day. . . . To him, I guess, I have always appeared heavily and sometimes formidably facty and close-set; to me his judgments, arrived at by feeling and expression, have always had a flimsiness. I want to get hold of Fact, strip off her inessentials and, if she behaves badly put her in stays and irons; but Shaw dances round her and weaves a wilful veil of confident assurances about her as her true presentment. He thinks one can "put things over" on Fact and I do not. He philanders with her. I have no delusions about the natural goodness and wisdom of human beings and at bottom I am grimly and desperately educational. But Shaw's conception of education is to let dear old Nature rip. He has got no further in that respect than Rousseau. Then I know, fundamentally, the heartless impartiality of natural causation, but Shaw makes Evolution something brighter and softer, by endowing it with an ultimately benevolent Life Force, acquired, quite uncritically I feel, from his friend and adviser Samuel Butler. We have been fighting this battle with each other all our lives. (pp. 455-56)

> *H. G. Wells, "Fairly Launched at Last," in his* Experiment in Autobiography: Discoveries and Conclusions of a Very Ordinary Brain (Since 1866) *(reprinted with the permission of the estate of H. G. Wells;* ©*1934 by H. G. Wells; copyright renewed* © *1962 by George Philip Wells and Francis Richard Wells),* The Macmillan Company, *1934, pp. 425-548.**

## JOHN MASON BROWN (essay date 1950)

[*Brown, long the drama critic for* The Saturday Review of Literature, *discusses* Caesar and Cleopatra.]

When in 1898 Shaw decided to invade Egypt, to come to grips with the mighty Julius, and as a vegetable-fed Puritan to run the risks of Cleopatra, he had something very much his own to say, which, as usual, he managed to get said in his own way. (p. 247)

Shaw, being Shaw, did not hesitate to offer ***Caesar and Cleopatra*** to the public as an improvement on Shakespeare. "Better than Shakespeare" was the title he chose for his preface. By this, he pointed out with surprising modesty, he did not mean that he professed to write better plays than Shakespeare. He did, however, claim the right to criticize Shakespeare, to discard and discredit his romantic notions of passion and history, and to substitute new ideas and a new approach born of a new age.

The first change, an inevitable one in Shaw's case, was that where Shakespeare had written a tragedy Shaw wrote a comedy. The side of Shaw which is John Bunyan pretended to be shocked by Shakespeare's Cleopatra. He dismissed her as a Circe who, instead of turning heroes into hogs, turned hogs into heroes. He would have nothing to do with the mature woman, a tawdry wanton as he saw her, whose lustfulness had transformed a world leader into a strumpet's fool. For that matter, he would have nothing to do with the youthful Cleopatra who, according to history, had a child by Caesar. In her place he preferred to draw, and drew delectably, the portrait of a kittenish girl who under Caesar's tutelage flowered into a queen. His Cleopatra's youth was more than a puritanic evasion. It was a Shavian device by means of which superstitions could be mocked and Caesar, the conqueror, humanized by being seen through the irreverent eyes of a child. In other words, it was Shaw's characteristic way of taking the starch out of the stuffed-shirt approach to history.

As for Shakespeare's Caesar, Shaw had only contempt for him. His contention was that Shakespeare, who knew human weakness so well, never knew human strength of the Caesarian type. Just why Shaw, also a man of words, felt that he had a greater claim to understanding the inner workings of a man of action, is something he did not bother to explain. But that he succeeded with his Caesar where Shakespeare failed with his, few would deny.

In his preface to ***Caesar and Cleopatra*** G.B.S. described himself as a crow who has followed many plows. Surely none of these had led him down stranger furrows than his flirtations with the dictator principle. The champion of the superman, who was fascinated by Napoleon and who has had kind words to say about Stalin and even Mussolini, was bound sooner or later to be drawn to Caesar.

The major source of his Julius was not Plutarch. As he confessed, it was Mommsen, the nineteenth-century German historian. He liked Mommsen's account of the Egyptian visit and agreed with his estimate of Caesar. Shaw also admitted his debt to Carlyle for his concept of the historical hero capable of bearing "the weight of life" realistically rather than suffering from a passion to die gallantly.

The Caesar Shaw drew would not have been recognized by Suetonius or Plutarch, neither of whom liked him. But the man who wrote *The Gallic War* would have recognized this Shavian Julius—with gratitude and relief. The clemency and statesmanship, the largeness of mind and spirit, which for the sake of the record he had been careful to establish as his, are qualities that shine in Shaw's Caesar. Caesar's self-love could not have been greater than Shaw's almost romantic infatuation with the benevolent despot he depicted.

But there was a difference—an immeasurable difference. Where Plutarch was dignified, Suetonius scurrilous, Caesar determinedly official, and Shakespeare rhetorically athletic, Shaw was Shavian. This in itself represented a complete abandonment of the orthodox ways of writing not only history but historical plays. It meant that, more than upsetting an applecart, Shaw had brought about a one-man revolution in the theatre and in literature.

He approached the past unawed, anxious to see it in contemporary terms, eager for a laugh, and with a wit which, though impudent, was wonderfully humanizing. The effects of his innovations are still with us, though in lesser hands they have never achieved the same dimensions and have sometimes been downright sophomoric. Quite rightly, it has been pointed out that what is widely thought of as Lytton Strachey's method was something for which Shaw prepared the way. But what is often overlooked is that G.B.S., regardless of his impertinences, was never a debunker. His spirit was always too positive for that, his intellect too superior.

*Caesar and Cleopatra* is a proof of this. However flippant or hilarious its means may be, its concerns are serious and sizable. For Shaw's real interest, so gaily presented in a very funny play, is nothing less than a study of the anatomy of earthly power and greatness. Although his Caesar may laugh and be laughed at, he is palpably a great man misunderstood by those around him and even by the Cleopatra he has instructed in queenship. If in delineating this greatness Shaw deliberately substitutes colloquial prose for what he had once condemned as the melodious fustian and mechanical lilt of Shakespeare's blank verse, he is nonetheless able in speech after speech to rise to a glorious eloquence of his own.

Caesar's apostrophe to the Sphinx is a sample. Other samples are the wisdom of Caesar's "He who has never hoped can never despair" and his "One year of Rome is like another, except that I grow older whilst the crowd in the Appian Way is always the same age." Or the beauty of his leave-taking of Cleopatra, when he describes Mark Antony to her. . . . In almost every instance the organ plays full and strong, only to be interrupted by a jest. Even so, the sense of greatness is not lost. *Caesar and Cleopatra* makes the past provocative, history human, and greatness gay. (pp. 247-49)

> *John Mason Brown, " 'Caesar and Cleopatra'," in his* Still Seeing Things *(copyright 1950 by John Mason Brown; copyright renewed © 1981 by Meredith M. Brown; reprinted by permission of the Literary Estate of John Mason Brown), McGraw-Hill, 1950 (and reprinted in* George Bernard Shaw: A Critical Survey, *edited by Louis Kronenberger, The World Publishing Company, 1953, pp. 247-49).*

## JORGE LUIS BORGES   (essay date 1951)

[*Borges praises Shaw as a liberator of the human spirit and as a pre-eminent creator of characters.*]

Can an author create characters that are superior to himself? I would reply that he cannot, and my negation would apply to the intellectual as well as the moral levels. I believe that creatures who are more lucid or more noble than our best moments will not issue from us. On that opinion I base my conviction of the pre-eminence of Shaw. The problems about labor unions

and municipalities of his early works will cease to be interesting, or else have already done so; the jokes of the Pleasant Plays bid fair to being, some day, no less awkward than Shakespeare's (humor, I suspect, is an oral genre, a sudden spark in conversation, not a written thing); the ideas expressed in the prologues and the eloquent tirades will be sought in Schopenhauer and in Samuel Butler; but Lavinia, Blanco Posnet, Keegan, Shotover, Richard Dudgeon, and, above all, Julius Caesar, surpass any character imagined by the art of our time. To think of Monsieur Teste or the histrionic Zarathustra of Nietzsche alongside them is to apprehend, with surprise or even astonishment, the primacy of Shaw. In 1911 Albert Soergel was able to write, repeating a commonplace of the time, "Bernard Shaw is an annihilator of the heroic concept, a killer of heroes" . . . ; he did not understand that the heroic was completely independent from the romantic and was embodied in Captain Bluntschli of *Arms and the Man,* not in Sergius Saranoff.

The biography of Bernard Shaw by Frank Harris contains an admirable letter written by Shaw, in which he says: "I understand everything and everyone, and am nobody and nothing." . . . From that nothingness (so comparable to the nothingness of God before He created the world, so comparable to the primordial divinity that another Irishman, Johannes Scotus Erigena, called *Nihil*), Bernard Shaw educed almost innumerable persons, or dramatis personae: the most ephemeral, I suspect, is G.B.S., who represented him to the public and who supplied such a wealth of easy witticisms for newspaper columns.

Shaw's basic subjects are philosophy and ethics: it is natural and inevitable that he is not esteemed in Argentina, or that he is remembered in that country only for a few epigrams. The Argentine feels that the universe is nothing but a manifestation of chance, the fortuitous combination of atoms conceived by Democritus; philosophy does not interest him. Nor does ethics: for him, social problems are nothing but a conflict of individuals or classes or nations, in which everything is licit—except ridicule or defeat.

Man's character and its variations constitute the essential theme of the novel of our time; the lyric is the complacent magnification of amorous fortunes or misfortunes; the philosophies of Heidegger or Jaspers transform each one of us into the interesting interlocutor of a secret and continuous dialogue with nothingness or with divinity; these disciplines, which may be formally admirable, foster the illusion of the self that Vedanta condemns as a capital error. They may play at desperation and anguish, but at bottom they flatter the vanity; in that sense, they are immoral. Shaw's work, on the other hand, leaves an aftertaste of liberation. The taste of the doctrines of Zeno's Porch and the taste of the sagas. (pp. 165-66)

> *Jorge Luis Borges, "For Bernard Shaw" (1951), in his* Other Inquisitions: 1937-1952, *translated by Ruth L. C. Simms (copyright © 1964 by the University of Texas Press), University of Texas Press, 1964, pp. 163-66.*

## GORE VIDAL   (essay date 1959)

[*Vidal critically attacks* Heartbreak House, *though he acknowledges Shaw as "the best and most useful dramatist in English" since Shakespeare.*]

''Heartbreak House . . . rhapsodized about love; but it believed in cruelty. It was afraid of the cruel people; and it saw that cruelty was at least effective. Cruelty did things that made money, whereas Love did nothing but prove the soundness of La Rochefoucauld's saying that very few people would fall in love if they had never read about it. Heartbreak House in short did not know how to live, at which point at that was left to it was the boast that at least it knew how to die: a melancholy accomplishment which the outbreak of war presently gave it practically unlimited opportunities of displaying. Thus were the first-born of Heartbreak House smitten; and the young, the innocent, the hopeful expiated the folly and worthlessness of their elders.''

That is from Bernard Shaw's odd preface to his even odder play, [*Heartbreak House*]. . . . The preface is odd, among other things, because it is written with the wrong sort of hindsight. Shaw did not know when he began the play in 1913 that the first-born were going to be struck down. Nor is there any reference to war, actual or impending, in the first two acts. The third act, however, was completed after the first aerial bombardments in history, and Shaw, rather casually, uses this to drop a bomb and end the play. Yet it is not the residents of Heartbreak House or their first-born who get blown up; only a businessman and a burglar expiate the folly and worthlessness of what? Not Heartbreak House certainly; capitalism, perhaps.

Everything about the play is queer. . . . I should put quite plainly here at the beginning that I regard Bernard Shaw as the best and most useful dramatist in English since the author of *Much Ado About Nothing* turned gentleman and let fall the feather.

What is Heartbreak House? In the context of the play it stands for the ruling class of England pre-1914: the ''nice people,'' somewhat educated, somewhat sensitive, somewhat independent financially (their cousins the hearties lived over at Horseback Hall). They were devotees of laissez-faire; they rhapsodized about love—but I have already quoted Shaw's indictment. Heartbreak House, of course, is only another name for our new friend the Establishment, a protective association made up of public-school boys who come down from Oxbridge to take over Whitehall, the Church of England, the BBC, Fleet Sheet, the better-looking girls, and everything else that's fun, while (so young writers tell us) sneering at the newly articulate *Lumpenproletariat* who have gone to red-brick colleges where, if one reads the new novels accurately, the main course given is Opportunism: Don't reform, adapt. . . . To put it plain, Shaw's target was important; and he knew what he wanted, which was not to adapt, or to make his own way, but to reform.

I think we know pretty much what Shaw intended to do in *Heartbreak House,* yet what actually did he do in the play itself? For one thing, it is improvised work. Shaw admitted he made it up as he went along, not knowing from day to day what his characters would do or say or become. He always tended to work this way, regarding a play essentially as an organism with a life of its own; one need only nurture it and let it assume its own shape. He even used to keep a checkerboard at hand to remind him who was onstage and who was off at any given moment in the writing. There is no doubt that this method served him as well as any other; his night mind was not, to say the least, fantastic. I am sure deep in his unconscious there lurked not the usual nightmare monsters of the rest of us but yards of thesis, antithesis, and synthesis, all neatly labeled and filed. Yet in *Heartbreak House* Shaw's im-

provisatory genius breaks down; he keeps marching into conversational culs-de-sac.

For example, in the second act the play comes to a grinding halt after Boss Mangan, recovered from hypnotic trance, denounces and is denounced by those who happen to be onstage at the moment, and exits. Then Captain Shotover tosses a Delphic phrase or two upon the night and paddles off. (Later the Captain, while again trying for an exit, says, almost apologetically: ''I must go in and out,'' a compulsion he shares with everyone else in this play; they all go in and out at whim.) This ill-madeness is often beguiling except on those occasions when it defeats the author, who finds himself with nobody left onstage except a couple who don't have much of anything to say to one another at the moment. It is then that Shaw invariably, shamelessly, brings on the New Character, who is very often a member of the lower classes with a colorful speech pattern usually written out phonetically in the text. This time he is the Burglar, a comic character right out of Dickens, where Shaw claimed, not entirely facetiously, to have got most of his characters, at least those who are not himself. The Burglar is one of Shaw's standbys, used in play after play; he is awful, but at least he starts the second act moving again and gives it a certain vivacity. As usual, Shaw, delighted with his own cunning, starts tying up ends; the Burglar is really the Captain's old bos'n, the nurse's husband, etc., etc. And now let's have a long chat about the poor and the exploited, the exploiters and the *rentiers,* and then end the act.

As a rule, Shaw's arbitrariness does not disturb. After all, he is conducting a seminar with enormous wit and style and we don't much mind his more casual contrivances. But in this play they don't come off. I think it has to do with a fundamental conflict between characters and settings. The characters, of course, are our old friends the Bernard Shaw Team of Fabian Debaters; we know each one of them already. But what are they doing in this peculiar Midsummer's Eve *ambiance?* They seem a bit puzzled, too. As they debate with their usual ease they tend nervously to eye the shrubbery: are there elves at the bottom of that garden? Have we been booked into an allegory? Are we going to find out we're all dead or something? Steady, chaps, the old boy's got us into one of *those* plays. They rattle on bravely but they are clearly ill at ease, and so is the audience. I think it was one of the New York daily reviewers who observed that the mood is not Chekhov but J. M. Barrie. Which is exactly right. We are led to expect magic, fey girls upon the heath, and revelation through fantasy. But we get none of it. Instead we are offered the old Debating Team in top form but in the wrong place and mood (oh, for that dentist's office!). As a result the debaters recede as characters; we grow indifferent to them; they are too humorous in the original sense of the word. Especially Ellie, Shaw's super-girl. In this version she is more than ever iron, ready to mother not heroes but heroines. Shaw dotes on Ellie; I found her purest drip-torture. . . . Of all the debaters assembled, I liked only Captain Shotover, because his dottiness contrasted agreeably with the uneasy predictability of his teammates.

Finally, at the play's end, I found myself entirely confused as to what Shaw intended. Shaw is not, even when he would like to be, an impressionist, a Chekhov turning life before our eyes to no end but that life observed is sufficient. Look, we live, we are, says Chekhov. While Shaw declares briskly: Pull up your socks! Fall in line there. Come along now. Double-quick march and we'll overtake the future by morning! One loves Shaw for his optimism, but moonlight is not a time for marching, and *Heartbreak House* is a moonlight play, suitable for recapturing the past. Elegy and debate cancel one another out. Nor is the work really satiric, an attack on "folly and worthlessness." These people are splendid and unique, and Shaw knows it. He cannot blow them up at the end.

Shaw's prefaces—no matter how proudly irrelevant their content may, at first, seem to the play that follows (sometimes a bit forlornly)—usually turn out to be apposite or at least complementary. But not this preface. In fact, it is misleading. Shaw talks about Chekhov. He finds the country-house mentality Chekhov *seems* to be writing about endemic to Europe, part of the sweet sickness of the bourgeoisie. Therefore Shaw will examine the same house in the same way, only in English terms. Ever since that preface, we have all dutifully considered this play in terms of Chekhov. Does it compare? Is it as good? Why is it *un*like? It is true that both are dealing with the same dying society of "nice people," but where Chekhov's interest was the "nice people," Shaw's interest was the dying society and the birth pains of the new.

Shaw once told Sir Cedric Hardwicke that he had no idea how to end the play until the first bombs fell. I suspect he had originally planned to allow Captain Shotover to attain "the Seventh Degree of concentration," thereby detonating the dynamite he had stored in the gravel pit and blowing up the enemy Mangan. As it was, at the last minute, the bomb from the Zeppelin did the trick even better, providing Shaw quite literally with a god from the machine. Then, almost as an afterthought, Shaw comes to the point. . . . (pp. 58-63)

Captain Shotover, supposed to have sold his soul to the devil, to have meddled with mysticism, to have mastered the *non sequitur,* turns out to be a good Fabian socialist after all. Obviously, Shotover was a humbug mystic, excusably deranged by the setting Shaw put him in; not until faced with his world's extinction does he throw off the mask of dottiness to reveal the bright, hard, intelligent face of Bernard Shaw, who to this day has a good deal to tell us about the danger of a society drifting as opposed to one which has learned the virtue of setting a deliberate course by fixed stars. To navigate is to plan. Laissez-faire, though always delightful for a few, in crisis is disastrous for all. There is no alternative to a planned society; that is the burden of the Shaw debate. Almost as an afterthought he makes this familiar point as the bomb drops near Heartbreak House. (pp. 63-4)

> *Gore Vidal, "Bernard Shaw's 'Heartbreak House'" (originally published in* The Reporter *November 26, 1959), in his* Homage to Daniel Shays: Collected Essays 1952-1972 *(copyright © 1959 by Gore Vidal; reprinted by permission of Random House, Inc.),* Vintage Books, 1972, pp. 58-66.

## ROBERT HOGAN (essay date 1965)

In his five novels, Shaw has created a world that is inimitible, full and convincing. It is one unified world, impelled by the same single view, discussed in the same single language. Its characters are constant, and when Harriet Russell or Isabella Woodward or Ned Conolly stand on the sidelines of a story not their own, they lend a kind of depth of reality to it. I refer, of course, to the reality of art; that kind of reality Shaw's people have. One will surely remember Owen Jack much, much longer than all of the faceless, forgotten characters in *Germinal* or *U.S.A.* If those characters are supposed to be

"real" characters in a "real" world, then this critic has very little understanding of what reality is.

Archibald Henderson remarked that each of Shaw's novels was better then the preceding one. I would disagree. It may seem a perverse opinion, but the most artistically finished of the novels, the novel most complete and satisfactory as a work of art, seems to me the second one, *The Irrational Knot.* In this novel, the plot is well handled, fully developed, and satisfyingly rounded off. The theme arises naturally and convincingly from the plot. The characters are well realized types, and Conolly himself is quite original. The dialogue is generally easy and fluent, and for the most part strikes a happy compromise between a formal use of rhetorical devices and an idiomatic softening of them. The novel is studded with witty turns of speech, with epigrams and with pungent observations, as well as with several extended comic scenes that are quite happily executed and that may be compared without folly to the better comic scenes in the mature plays.

*Immaturity* is extraordinarily interesting, as, indeed, are all of the novels, but this first attempt has too many faults for a memorable work of art. The first fourth is dull, the plot is uncoordinated, and the characters shift disconcertingly in and out of focus.

*Love among the Artists* is, by a narrow margin, my own favorite, but it is not the most successful. Its major theme of courtship and marriage is not fully worked out, and the book gives the impression of being awkwardly abridged, as if the author's invention had flagged or his spirit had wearied. The characters are once again well drawn types, and Owen Jack is a vital and delightful one. Indeed, he probably generates more vitality and delight than many of Shaw's more famous characters—more, I should say, than Bluntschli, more even than Jack Tanner and Henry Higgins. The comic scenes are more effective than those in *The Irrational Knot,* and the language is the brightest, deftest, and most polished in all of the five novels. Nevertheless, because of its plot, the novel is not fully satisfying as a novel; it remains an immense and masterly fragment.

*Cashel Byron's Profession* is a successful but minor work. It is the shortest, slightest, most popular, most conventional, and least ambitious. Lydia and Cashel are nicely drawn; the other characters are easily forgettable. The novel has none of the superb scenes of comedy of the previous books, and the language, although more idiomatic than the other novels, more often tiredly lapses into the conventionally formal.

*An Unsocial Socialist* probably ranks next to *Immaturity* as the least successful of the novels. Its first half is Shaw at his brilliant best, but its last half is curiously slow and dull. The characters in the last half are merely types or stereotypes that are not particularly interesting. The excellent Agatha of the first half shows only a glimpse or two of her former quality, while her foils, Jane and Gertrude, have similarly shrunk. The two new characters of the baronet and the poet are respectively stereotypical and undeveloped. Perhaps these qualities are especially noticeable because of the superior vitality and inventiveness of the book's first half. A greater flaw is that the plot has nothing to do with the theme. The plot concerns courtship and marriage; the theme concerns socialism and capitalism and can only be introduced arbitrarily by long harangues from Trefusis. Trefusis is the ultimate rock upon which the novel flounders. He is that rare and inartistic creation, a character as full and contradictory as a person from real life, and such a character is much too complex for a work of art. Nevertheless, because of Trefusis and because of its first half and because of its criticisms of fiction in its last half, this volume is fully as valuable as *Love among the Artists*—which is merely to say that it is invaluable.

To sum up, these five novels chart the rise and fall of Shaw's involvement with fiction. His later fiction was, despite its frequent excellence, the casual after-thought of the artist, that brimming overflow of exuberance that was not entirely used up by the plays. It is true that Shaw's dismissal of fiction arose partly because of the failure of his novels and partly because of his new interest in socialism, but it is also true that his criticism of fiction still stands as a cogent indictment of most novels. The traditional form of most novels he found inadequate either to portray life fully or to contain an intelligent discussion of the issues most crucial to man.

By his own standards, these novels were jejune work, and the term "jejune" has been applied to them by most of their critics. It might be argued that by Shaw's own standards the novels of Lever and Dickens and Thackeray and Trollope were also jejune work, and that compared to those novels Shaw's have a curious air of maturity. His novels have significant faults of form not usually found in the best work of the traditional English novelists, but they have also significant qualities of excellence not to be found elsewhere in English fiction. (pp. 108-09)

> Robert Hogan, "The Novels of Bernard Shaw," in English Literature in Transition (*copyright © 1965 Helga S. Gerber*), *Vol. 8, No. 2, 1965, pp. 63-114.*

## TREVOR WHITTOCK   (essay date 1978)

[*Whittock's is the standard reading of* Major Barbara.]

Shakespeare and Shaw are still the great figures in English comic drama. With Shakespeare comedy was only one facet of the universal genius. With Shaw it was the quintessential achievement of a lively and provocative man: music critic, drama critic, Fabian socialist, debater and propagandist, philosopher, wit, self-proclaimed professor of natural scientific history, and dramatist. In his best comedies all his talents meet and compound, and for us still explode in scintillating entertainment. The best of Shaw's best includes *Major Barbara*. Not only is it a delightful play, it is a great one. (p. 1)

The arguments of the play are presented by means of two interrelated plots which form the basis of the play's action. The first plot, derived from conventional melodrama, is the search for an heir to Undershaft's armament industry. (With typical effrontery Shaw inverts the convention: the heir will turn out to be not a foundling who must prove the legitimacy of his birth but a legitimate child who must prove he was really a foundling.) The second plot turns on Barbara's challenge that she may convert Undershaft to the Salvation Army, and his counter-challenge to her. . . . What connects the two plots is that Cusins too must be 'converted' before he will accept his true inheritance, and Barbara does not declare herself until he has chosen.

Shaw portrays Barbara as a truly religious person. Rejecting the meaninglessness of her secure and pampered existence at Wilton Crescent, Barbara seeks to serve a cause greater than herself, and thinks she has found it in the Salvation Army where she can bring spiritual enlightenment and practical help to the needy poor. Cusins, on the other hand, is a humanist—

intellectual and sceptical—though as a scholar he is extremely well-read in the history of religions. His profession, Professor of Greek, allies him to the great, rational civilisations of Greece and Rome. He combines the best learning of the past with contemporary aspirations for justice and equality. (The character is acknowledgedly based on that of Gilbert Murray.) Behind Cusins' mild demeanour lies a strong and determined man; his pursuit of Barbara is one indication of this. To ensure that Barbara and Cusins are fitting opponents for the struggle with Undershaft, Shaw is careful in the first and second acts to show their strength: Barbara's vitality and fervour, Cusins' determination and intelligence. (pp. 6-7)

Undershaft breaks Barbara's faith when he demonstrates that the Salvation Army can, like any other organisation of that nature, be bought. By his cheque to the Army he proves that the pipers who call the tune are Undershaft and Bodger. The full implications of this emerge gradually. One implication is that Barbara's faith rested on shaky foundations because it assumed that spiritual welfare could be separated from the material circumstances of life. Man does not live by bread alone: but without bread he may not live at all. No faith can be sustained which ignores the basic conditions of existence. Furthermore, however the Salvation Army may wish to alleviate the misery of the poor, it is incapable of abolishing the circumstances that create poverty and hardship. Should it attempt to change these circumstances it would be squashed by people whose wealth depends on their existence, and indeed it is only tolerated by the power-holders because it conditions the poor to accept their lot and thus prevents them rising in revolt for a better deal. Nor can people who are starving and scraping be brought to spiritual enlightenment: they can only be bribed by charity to pay lip-service to religious doctrines. . . . True religion is only possible when people have the energy and the freedom from want to pursue it. Undershaft argues that material prosperity must be given priority, and only when people are paid and productive, and can afford homes and food and clothing, only then can the works of the spirit really begin. The lives his employees lead at his factory prove his point: they have security and dignity, and they worship at a multitude of churches. (pp. 7-9)

Undershaft's strength of feeling about the evils of poverty springs from his own sufferings and hardships as a youth. It was in that period he became resolved to be a full-fed free man at all costs, even if he had to kill to do it. Here Shaw provides another contrast: that between Peter Shirley and Andrew Undershaft. Peter is a humble and honest man; though he is not a professing Christian he does live the life of a Christian. And where does it get him? He is sacked and forgotten. In the harsh capitalist world of competition and exploitation the Christian virtues are not only irrelevant: they are actually a handicap. The price of survival is to scrap them. Undershaft chooses to be the exploiter rather than the exploited, and flourishes.

Undershaft's creed is a capitalist one, but Undershaft speaks as a capitalist who knows what his wealth has delivered him from (and delivered his family from); he knows the benefits he can obtain for himself and his employees, the benefits of material security. This knowledge gives authority to his arguments. Now the question arises, how far is Shaw the socialist endorsing the argument of Undershaft the capitalist? To answer this we must consider another question and a much more important one. Why does Shaw make Undershaft a manufacturer of cannons, a merchant of death and destruction? The answers to this question will take us to the very heart of the play.

If Shaw had wished he could have given Undershaft some more socially approved occupation: he could have made him a capitalist of a more benevolent kind—a ship builder, a clothing magnate, or even an oil baron. But by making him an armaments manufacturer, Shaw is able to emphasize an aspect of capitalism that might otherwise be played down, namely, its ruthlessness. Undershaft, Lazarus and their employees are secure and comfortable because the goods they make murder and maim countless other people. This serves as a metaphor to describe all capitalism. Though capitalism may abolish pockets of poverty and exploitation, it will not abolish poverty and exploitation themselves: indeed its own success depends on their existence. Thus Shaw the socialist is only endorsing the gospel of Undershaft to a qualified extent. Something more adequate must be sought. This brings us to the choices that face Barbara and Cusins.

Their dilemma is greater than the one Undershaft faced as a young man; for him it was starvation or a full belly; for them the course they adopt must satisfy the demands of their consciences which tell them they must serve the spiritual and material welfare, not only of themselves or a select group, but of all men. Without this hope they cannot be reconciled to accepting the inheritance awaiting them. Earlier I said Undershaft had to convert them, but what he does is not strictly speaking a 'conversion' at all. They don't accept the capitalist aspect of his creed; rather they take from him the challenge and the pointer to how mankind may move beyond capitalism. Undershaft rallies Barbara with the challenge: 'Try your hand on my men: their souls are hungry because their bellies are full'; and Cusins he recruits with, 'Dare you make war on war?' They accept their inheritance: Barbara so that she may do God's work for its own sake when material prosperity has rendered bribes unnecessary; Cusins so that he can use the armaments works to give weapons to the poor that they may through force and revolution create a society where the necessities of life will be guaranteed to all. Undershaft's ruthless capitalism, which has demonstrated the importance of material security, points the way to socialist revolution and spiritual evolution.

At several points in the play itself Undershaft is associated with the ancient Greek god, Dionysus. Cusins calls him Dionysus several times, and also quotes lines from the Greek dramatist Euripides whose play, *The Bacchae*, was about the Dionysian religion. (pp. 9-10)

Shaw not only makes reference to Euripides' great tragedy: his own play actually echoes it. Undershaft/Dionysus comes to the Salvation Army, possesses the women (Mrs. Baines, Jenny Hill and their like) by means of his 'charity' and leads them triumphantly in religious procession (Undershaft blowing a trombone), having torn Barbara/Pentheus to pieces—figuratively only, of course—by rending apart her religious assumptions. Through this analogy between Undershaft and Dionysus, and the parallels in the action of the two plays, Shaw emphasises how, when a form of belief arises, its assault on the old assumptions will seem savage and cruel. In the arrival of the new will be apprehended fear, cruelty, madness, destruction, as well as exhilaration, joy and release. But the spirit of life is remorseless, and bears down any opposition. 'Blood and fire' is as appropriate a motto for the Dionysian force as it is for the maker of cannons.

Cusins, the Euripidean scholar, naturally spots the analogy and, expressing it, he gives vent to his own alarm before the challenging figure of Undershaft. Cusins again, and Shaw through him, makes further use of literary mythology when he associates Undershaft with another legendary figure, that of the Prince of Darkness. Certainly the reference to Mephistophilis conjures up the story of the scholar Faust who was tempted to sell his soul to the devil, and reveals how the scholar Cusins initially responds to Undershaft's challenge to forget the pursuit of a dead language and seize the power of life and death. But the Mephistophelean portrait Shaw sketches of Undershaft owes less to the dramatists Marlowe and Goethe than it does to the poet William Blake. For Blake, particularly in *The Marriage of Heaven and Hell*, presented a new way of conceiving the devil which enormously fascinated and influenced Shaw. Briefly and oversimply, Blake envisaged life as a progression created through the clash of contraries, in particular the contraries of Reason and Energy. His Satanic figure is not a force of evil, but rather of rebellious energy denounced by the sour Jehovah of intellect and repression whom Blake sometimes called Urizen (Your reason). Blake's devil then is a force of life, of instinct, trying to break the bonds established by arid intellect and established morality. Like Blake's devil, Undershaft comes with the gifts of energy and liberation. His so-called immoral doctrines assault conventional pieties; his vitality breeds enthusiasm and commitment; even his trade testifies to his destroying in order to liberate. As Blake puts it in one of his proverbs of Hell, 'The tygers of wrath are wiser than the horses of instruction.' (Some of Undershaft's aphorisms are almost straight from Blake: for example. 'There is only one true morality for every man; but every man has not the same true morality,' is implied in Blake's, 'One Law for the Lion and Ox is Oppression.')

By bringing in these associations of godhead, Shaw gives a greater substance to the effect of Undershaft. But how does he present Undershaft's own picture of himself? In Act I he makes Undershaft describe himself as a 'mystic': this remark is not explained until the following exchange in Act III:

> UNDERSHAFT: From the moment when you became Andrew Undershaft, you will never do as you please again. Don't come here lusting for power, young man.
>
> CUSINS: If power were my aim I should not come here for it. You have no power.
>
> UNDERSHAFT: None of my own, certainly.
>
> CUSINS: I have more power than you, more will. You do not drive this place: it drives you. And what drives the place?
>
> UNDERSHAFT: *(enigmatically)* A will of which I am a part.

The will of which Undershaft is merely a part is the will of Creative Evolution—life striving ever upward in its drive to greater comprehension. The vital spirits in each generation pass the task on to those who succeed them: so Undershaft's handing on of the inheritance is really a handing on of the creative destiny. The 'blood and fire' Barbara and Cusins choose to serve is the life and energy of godhead using its human creatures in the evolutionary surge. Hence the speeches of Barbara and Cusins, very near the end, are life-celebratory. In particular, Major Barbara who thought her soul had died in West Ham finds it resurrected in Perivale St. Andrews. She recovers her pride, and recovers her joy—the joy of submission to a Purpose, to a Life Force. (pp. 11-13)

Here is the real affirmation of the play. Now too is it possible to see how the comedy is at one with the meaning, the structure of the play with the argument. Shaw once defined comedy as 'nothing less than the destruction of old-fashioned morals.' The play begins with people set in their complacent beliefs and established illusions, as Lady Britomart is described in the first stage direction ('limited in the oddest way with domestic and class limitations, conceiving the universe exactly as if it were a large house in Wilton Crescent . . .'). Till life comes along in the shape of Dionysus Mephistophilis Undershaft to kick that little world to pieces about them. But despite the pain of loss they must welcome the actions of life because it pushes mankind forward. Life shatters and destroys, only to rebuild and re-create; at first the destructive element terrifies, later with liberation the energy and power are celebrated. Hence the answer to the question posed earlier, why did Shaw make Undershaft a manufacturer of explosives? As the agent of the Life Force he comes to demolish so that reconstruction can begin. . . . The newer and better religion, morality, political constitution, whatever, must fit the facts: that is, accept the conditions life lays down. The political level of the play—the arguments that Christian morality and liberal humanism are no longer adequate to cope with the world of the twentieth century, that the achievements of technology and capitalism must give way to social equality—these arguments are only an illustration of the more fundamental issue: that men must move forward with the movement of life itself, serving with their creative energy that ultimate Creative Energy which makes what will be. Shaw's play does more than preach this doctrine: it enacts it. In the very structure and unfolding of the play the audience is made to *experience* that movement of life within and through the mode of comedy: the dismay, the disillusion, the challenge, the doubt, the celebration. Just as Shakespeare's comedies move to a glimpse and promise of the divine harmony, so ***Major Barbara*** may be described as a divine comedy of creative evolution. (pp. 13-14)

> *Trevor Whittock, "'Major Barbara': Comic Masterpiece," in* Theoria, *No. LI, October, 1978, pp. 1-14.*

### COLIN WILSON    (essay date 1979)

[*A major Shaw scholar, Wilson offers the following discussion of Shaw as a life-affirming promoter of "sanity and optimism."*]

[Although] I had read every Shaw play by the time I was seventeen and most of the novels and prefaces, I never became a 'complete Shavian'. I felt that after ***Man and Superman***, Shaw had made no real effort to analyse the central problem of *what human beings are supposed to do with their lives*. Don Juan could speak about the need to 'help life in its struggle upward', about 'Life's incessant aspiration to higher organisation, wider, deeper intenser self-consciousness and clearer self-understanding' but how does the individual actually go about it? Shaw's political solutions always aroused my deepest scepticism. Shaw once remarked that Jesus's miracles were irrelevant because it would be absurd to say: 'You should love your enemies; and to convince you of this, I will now proceed to cure this gentleman of a cataract.' It seemed to me equally irrelevant when Shaw said: 'Life aims at deeper self awareness, therefore we must abolish capitalism.' Then, as now, Shaw's socialist dogmas struck me as largely fallacious. Similarly, the intellectual content of most of the major plays seemed to me oddly disappointing. I wanted him to talk about ultimate problems of philosophy, and he insisted on talking about politics and ed-

ucation and marriage and the iniquities of the medical profession (another matter on which I felt he was mildly cranky). The result was that in my first book on Shaw (*The Quintessence of Shavianism,* written at sixteen) I remained more than a little critical, and ended by implying that I would one day do better.

But then, the moment I actually opened a volume of Shaw, this hypercritical attitude vanished; I found it impossible not to keep on reading with a kind of excited approval, like a spectator at a boxing match who has to shout his enthusiasm. . . . Within a few lines, I was chuckling, then shouting with laughter—not so much because I found it funny as because it was so exhilirating. It made no difference whether I opened the ***Collected Plays*** at ***Widowers' Houses*** or ***Farfetched Fables;*** the effect was always the same: a sense of revitalization, of excitement, like setting out on a holiday.

Oddly enough, it never struck me to try and analyse the source of this effect until I was asked to write the present essay. And then I found it fairly easy to track down. It is the fact that, embedded in its very syntax, Shaw's prose has an irresistibly *optimistic* forward movement.

> Then there was my Uncle William, a most amiable man, with great natural dignity. In early manhood he was not only an inveterate smoker, but so insistent a toper that a man who made a bet that he would produce Barney Shaw sober, and knocked him up at six in the morning with that object, lost his bet. But this might have happened to any common drunkard. What gave the peculiar Shaw finish and humour to the case was that my uncle suddenly and instantly gave up smoking and drinking at one blow, and devoted himself to the accomplishment of playing the ophicleide. . . .

As I now read these words, I find myself beginning to smile halfway through the first sentence: 'a most amiable man, with great natural dignity'—for I know this is going to be the prelude to some anticlimactic absurdity. And then there is an element in the prose which in a comedian like Groucho Marx would be called perfect timing. If Shaw had written: 'my uncle suddenly gave up smoking and drinking, and devoted himself . . . ' etc., it would not be funny; to say: ''suddenly and instantly gave up smoking and drinking at one blow' produces a kind of shock effect, like a clown walking into a custard pie.

All Shaw's prose produces an effect of determined clarity, and it is this clarity that causes our ears to prick up: he is obviously saying something important or he wouldn't be making such an effort. And the air of optimism is a consequence of the directness. Inability to express ourselves makes us feel depressed and defeated—a gloomy conviction that the world is too complicated for our limited powers of assimilation. Kafka's effects of nightmare are produced by piling up dreamlike ambiguities and complications until the mind is hypnotized into a sense of helplessness. Shaw's clarity produces exactly the opposite effect, for it is obviously inspired by a conviction that any problem will yield to a combination of reason, courage and determination. 'The brain will not fail when the will is in earnest.' No matter what Shaw happens to be saying—whether he is talking about human evolution or municipal trading—it is this underlying tone of sanity and optimism that produces the exhilarating effect. (pp. 226-27)

And what about Shaw as a thinker? Shaw liked to regard himself as an artist-philosopher. Most of us will concede that he was an artist, but we have our doubts about the philosopher. Again that could be due to our lack of perspective. We think of a list of typical philosophers—Plato, Spinoza, Locke, Hegel, Whitehead—ask if Shaw belongs on it, and decide he doesn't fit. But philosophers cannot be judged simply as abstract thinkers; what is equally important is their place in the history of ideas. And here Shaw undoubtedly qualifies. He was born in the middle of the Romantic era, the century of pessimism. . . . When Shaw came on the literary scene, in the early 1880s, the romantics had decided that mankind can be split into two groups: the stupid go-getters and the sensitive world-rejectors. You were either a shallow-minded optimist or an intelligent pessimist. (Thomas Mann made this antimony the basis of all his work.)

Shaw's revolt was instinctive. If he was a romantic, it was not of the self-pitying variety that regards the universe as cruel and meaningless because it refuses to treat them as exceptions. And it was Shaw's intuitive intelligence that made him aware that no healthy civilization can embrace a philosophy of pessimism. In *Man and Superman* he points out that man is the only animal who can be nerved to bravery by putting an *idea* into his head: that is to say, that man's inner strength depends on his beliefs; in *Back to Methuselah* he shows the other side of the coin when Pygmalion's two human creations lie down and die when they feel discouraged. It follows that a civilization that believes that Darwin and Freud are right about human nature is going to deflate like a tyre with a slow puncture. Shaw was not capable of analysing the history of philosophy since Descartes, the history of science since Newton, the history of religion since Luther, the history of romanticism since Rousseau and writing his own *Decline of the West*, yet he recognized that all have converged into the conviction that made Sartre write: 'Man is a useless passion.' He knew only one thing: *that somehow, sooner or later, the trend will have to be reversed.* His own age was not ready for that insight, and a younger generation of writers—Proust, Eliot, Joyce *et al*—continued the tradition of romantic pessimism as if Shaw had never existed. Most of them took the opportunity to denounce Shaw for failing to recognize the seriousness of the situation. Yet as this century of confusion and anxiety enters its last decades, it becomes clear that Shaw's instinct was correct. Somehow, whether we like it or not, we have to start believing in the future, and in man's power to transform it. At the end of *Too True to be Good,* the rascally clergyman declares: 'We have outgrown our religion, outgrown our political system, outgrown our own strength of mind and character. . . . But what next? Is NO enough? For a boy, yes: for a man, never. Are we any the less obsessed with a belief when we are denying it than when we are affirming it? No, I must have affirmations to preach. . . .'

The affirmations are still in the painful process of being born. When it finally happens, we shall recognize that Shaw did more than any other man to bring them into being. (pp. 228-29)

> Colin Wilson, "A Personal View" (copyright © 1979 by Colin Wilson; copyright © 1979 by George Rainbird Limited; reprinted by permission of Holt, Rinehart and Winston, Publishers), in The Genius of Shaw: A Symposium, edited by Michael Holroyd, Holt, Rinehart and Winston, 1979, pp. 223-29.

## ARNOLD SILVER (essay date 1982)

[*Silver's* Bernard Shaw: The Darker Side, *from which the following excerpt is taken, is a psychological examination of Shaw, and* a radical departure in Shaw scholarship. Rejecting the common perception of Shaw as a genial, intellectual wit, Silver attempts to demonstrate the existence of an undercurrent of sadistic, masochistic, and homocidal tendencies in Shaw's life, stemming from his difficult childhood, celibate marriage, and troubled extramarital affairs with Alice Lockett and Mrs. Patrick Campbell. Silver finds expression of this "darker side" of Shaw's life evident in his defense of fascist and communist dictatorships, and in elements of certain of his works, among them, Man and Superman, discussed below.]

In its formal structure and as an experiment in playwriting, *Man and Superman* is clearly one of Shaw's most unusual works. The experiment was, in its conception, audacious and yet simple: to include in a romantic comedy a philosophic interlude of dramatic interest which would also elucidate events in the play. Perhaps challenged by the complaint that his comedies were slowed down by too much discussion, Shaw may have determined to extend the discussion beyond all earlier limits, make it as lively as the physical action, and yet blend it within a traditional play—even at the risk of excessive length. He further intended the dream interlude to provide not only philosophic implications but also musical and literary references, for the strains of Mozart's *Don Giovanni* heralding the interlude, and the legendary names of the participants, set the dialogue against a background of other versions of Don Juan's story. (p. 120)

The unusual length, it should immediately be settled, is not at all a fault. Long plays can be staged quite successfully—witness Ibsen's *Peer Gynt*, for example, or O'Neill's *A Long Day's Journey Into Night*. Yet the length of Shaw's dream interlude, by itself, does do damage because it suspends interest in the surrounding play for too great a time. . . . The ninety-minute dream sequence, both by its length and its intellectual intensity, distracts attention from the play, and even Shaw's best efforts in writing the final act, inventive and fast-paced as that act is, can never quite recapture our full interest or the necessary theatrical illusion.

Yet this defect might have been more apparent than real if the dream actually did illuminate the surrounding comedy. In fact it does not, because the ideas relating to the play have already been explicitly presented and are now mostly redundant. For instance Tanner, the revolutionary propagandist, talks at great length of the general conflict of the sexes, of the particular conflict between the artist-man and the mother-woman, of the irresistible Life Force; Don Juan then simply restates these notions, often in the same terms. As for the other ideas in the interlude, most are either irrelevant to the play or actually contradict it. In sum, Shaw has really written two plays, very different in mode and only superficially integrated. (pp. 120-21)

[Theatrically] the Hell sequence is static and its conflicts, even when intense, are mostly cerebral; it curbs the emotional range of drama and converts the stage into a platform of costumed debaters. Shaw declared that he was writing for "a pit of philosophers," but such an intention deliberately thwarts the expectations of the intelligent layman as much as it misconceives the reasons why the philosopher himself might go to the theater. And if the latter does go only in his professional capacity rather than as a man, then he may find himself smiling for reasons Shaw never intended, smiling at the meretriciousness of many of the ideas for all their verbal dazzle, at the confusion, the inconsistencies, and the evasions. (pp. 121-22)

[But why], we may first wonder, did Shaw allow the play to fall into two detachable segments? Was he truly unequal to the technical challenge of his experiment? I think not. Rather, I believe that the form was created as a way of dealing with some extremely intimate experiences and that the conflicting nature of these experiences, the raw content of the work, required two separate plays. The disunity of the play's structure reflects a disunity in Shaw himself and not merely an unsolved technical difficulty. Hence in pursuing our new approach to the play we must concentrate, not on the ideas he picked up here and there from earlier writers, but on the root experiences that made him responsive to those ideas. And we must address ourselves to such questions as the following: What was the experiential material that made it difficult for Shaw to write a unified work? What are the virtues and the faults of the romantic comedy and how might we account for them? Why did Shaw allow the dream sequence to run on at such length? What is the nature and source of its confusions? What is the dream's true relationship to the surrounding play? Fortunately the answers to these questions are tightly linked, and all signify that **Man and Superman,** whatever its artistic inadequacies, marks a critical change in Shaw's outlook even as it deals with the most significant experience of his adult life.

The nub of this experience, to anticipate, may be suggested by a remark of the play's heroine to the poet Octavius: "You are like the bird that presses its breast against the sharp thorn to make itself sing." Similarly, I believe, the energies Shaw poured into his play were aroused by pressing himself against the sharp thorn of his recent marriage to Charlotte Payne-Townshend. The song was a prolonged one, with intricate variations on a plaintive yet hidden theme; but I think that if we listen closely we can come to hear the muffled cry from the heart sounding in the very depths of the work. (pp. 122-23)

[In **Man and Superman**] the woman is entirely the aggressor, controlling the man against his will. He bears no responsibility for his relations with women up to marriage and, by implication, after marriage as well. If the woman decides on motherhood, as presumably the domineering Violet decided, the man must accommodate her. If she chooses not to be a mother, that choice also is hers, imposed on her by the Life Force. Ann Whitefield, we may imagine, will take the initiative on the honeymoon as she has throughout the courtship, for the Life Force, acting through the woman, will determine what sort of erotic activity will occur.

Shaw's notion of the aggressiveness of the woman and the passivity of the man is of course a comic reversal of the usual formula of the duel of the sexes. As a theatrical conceit it had most recently been exploited by W. S. Gilbert, whose contraltos throb with menacing lust. Shaw domesticates the lust, makes its possessor more youthful, and turns her into a central figure. To some extent he follows Gilbert in using the reversal solely for comic purposes, but he also seeks to establish it as the real truth about the relationship between the sexes. And his failure to take his idea comically enough, his insistent attempt to convert its partial truth into the total truth, contributes to the implausibility of the main romance and to the play's frequent sense of strain.

Why was he so insistent? Why, furthermore, was he so hostile to Ann as to reduce her appeal as the embodiment of the Life Force? I believe that the answer in the most general terms is that Shaw's hidden feelings toward his wife entered into the portrait of Ann Whitefield. To substantiate this, we must first remind ourselves of Shaw's close personal identification with Tanner and his counterpart Don Juan of the dream sequence.

That identification was made visible in the first London staging when the actor who played Tanner adopted Shaw's own style of dressing, on Shaw's orders, and thereby began a practice which is still current. Long before his marriage Shaw had fancied himself as "an Irish Don Juan" (as he confided in a letter in 1890), and he was called Don Giovanni by his Fabian friends in recognition of his love of Mozart's opera as well as his supposedly incorrigible philandering. In 1887 he had written a little story **"Don Giovanni Explains,"** which draws on his own amatory adventures and pretends to lament the problems the Don faced from pursuing women. The portrait of Tanner, it is true, is based in some minor respects on the radical politician H. M. Hyndman, but in a fashion typical of many Shaw plays and novels, the central figure soon became a satirized self-portrait; and he finally made the matter explicit in 1919 when in one of his autobiographical sketches he admitted his personal degree of identification with Tanner and acknowledged that the last scene, "in which the hero revolts from marriage and struggles against it without any hope of escape, is a poignantly sincere utterance" which came "from personal experience."

In the same letter in which he mentioned being an Irish Don Juan, Shaw also admits that he has "an Irishman's habit of treating women with a certain gallantry." Perhaps it was this gallantry as well as his playwright's obligation to transmute any living models that prompted him to keep Ann from resembling his wife, Charlotte, too noticeably, and he introduces several calculated dissimilarities. Ann is considerably younger than Charlotte was when she met Shaw, and Ann unlike Charlotte knew her future husband from childhood. Ann, again unlike Charlotte, takes no interest in political matters. Yet on the other hand both women are heiresses. Both have a younger sister. Both revere the memory of their dead father. Both are women of strong will yet models of respectability. Both are attracted to intellectual men and are looking for husbands. Just as Shaw in his correspondence singled out Charlotte's handsome eyes for especial comment, so too he singled out Ann's "ensnaring eyes" in the stage description of his heroine. In sum the playwright, self-admittedly identifying to a large extent with Tanner, creates in Ann a woman who has several key points of resemblance to Charlotte, and Shaw may have felt that his portrait of the relationship between the man and the woman was a fundamentally accurate version of his own courtship.

That he did believe this is evident from his latter-day comments on Charlotte's initiative in capturing him, which parallels the way Ann pursued Tanner into marriage. Whether Shaw was correct in his belief is not in itself important. Nor was he obliged in writing the work to duplicate in any respect his private life. But an acquaintance with the biographic matrix is nonetheless helpful in clarifying both the play and the dream sequence. (pp. 129-31)

[St. John Ervine] asserts that Shaw "in his old age expressed regret that his marriage had been fruitless, and thought that he ought to have been firmer with Charlotte about sexual relations. But Charlotte's will was as firm as his." In this matter, surely, it was firmer than his, for according to the same biographer, Shaw "was a man who delighted in women and enjoyed carnal concurrence with them"—a formulation that for the moment may be accepted. There is no reason to believe that his desires or potency suddenly atrophied on the day he married at the age of forty-one. Nor is there any evidence, direct or indirect, that the conflict of wills occurred before marriage. Indeed, Shaw's own statement—"As man and wife we found a new relation in which sex had no part"—obviously suggests a postmarital decision. My belief is that Charlotte announced her decision very soon after the wedding, that Shaw was profoundly shocked by it, and that he lost the battle of wills which then ensued. The Irish Don Juan had been more than caught: he had been emasculated.

But it seems likely that Shaw lost the battle of wills because his own will was more divided than he may have realized. An ambivalence toward sexuality is clearly evident in his early writings. And equally evident in his private life is a sexual passivity, a need for a woman to take the lead, as did Jenny Patterson when she seduced him on his twenty-ninth birthday. (p. 135)

Shaw's postmarital writings, [notably his prefaces to **Misalliance** and **Getting Married**], indicate his troubled and vacillating attitude toward sexuality and also his lifelong effort to reconcile himself to his strange marriage. His most considerable single effort was in the play he began to work on soon after the marriage, and we may now return to that play more adequately prepared to see how it reflects his private difficulties, especially the difficulty in facing the truth. . . . Shaw had sought to fascinate Charlotte and to fulfill his role as an Irish Don Juan. Tanner, by contrast, even though absurdly claiming to be a modern Don Juan, is completely passive with Ann. At the cost of credibility, Shaw has now to insist—in plot, characterization, and preachment—on the woman as ruthless aggressor and the man as helpless victim. Male passivity has to be made a general truth so as to minimize the particular truth of his own postmarital passivity. A cosmic Life Force has to be invoked to explain marriage and to obscure thereby the individual's own responsibility for his marital fate. Shaw has to annul retroactively his personal initiative *before* marriage in order to reduce anxiety over his insufficient sexual initiative *after* marriage. Perhaps his outrage at what he may have regarded as Charlotte's trickery is being vented in Tanner's contempt for Ann's trickery, but this makes it hard to understand why Tanner would succumb to her. In sum, it was Shaw's exigent postmarital adjustments as a man that curbed his ability as a playwright to capture the truth of his early relationship to Charlotte, to make the heroine unequivocally appealing and the romance wholly convincing.

His need to fantasize the past in ways that would diminish his accountability for the present also prompted him to omit from the play certain embarrassing motives which seem to have entered into his courtship of Charlotte, namely, an eye for her money and apprehension over a rival male. (p. 142)

If the complicating elements of financial self-interest and jealousy were too threatening for Shaw to include, their omission nevertheless allowed him to keep intact the principle of the woman as the aggressor and necessary victor in the duel of sex. The superior man, however, could still rescue his masculinity by claiming an inviolate realm of his own—his work. This idea is developed in the course of the longest private conversation in the play, as Tanner and Ann recount their childhood friendship. (p. 144)

The dialogue between Tanner and Ann . . . is one of several passages in which the "discussion" bears very little relationship to the play, and it is this lack of pertinence rather than the mere length of Tanner's speeches that contributes to the sense of strain in the play. All of the irrelevant passages can be understood as Shaw's further efforts to rationalize his pre-

sent, postmarital situation. The need to do this was far more pressing than the need to reshape the past, though such reshaping was itself part of the total rationalization. However Shaw might overlay the courtship between Tanner and Ann with his present feelings, and thereby distort the reality he had lived, the story of a woman capturing a man could not resolve in imagination his immediate situation. The mortifying personal events following upon that supposed capture required another play, and really another form than any play he could then allow himself to imagine. For the unconsummated marriage was too painful and without action to be suitable for a comic drama, and the traditional form of a play, even as he had modified it in his own earlier work to accommodate discussion, was too restrictive in that he would have to attend to plot and characters and action. The essence of his postmarital adjustment was to talk himself into accepting the situation, and talk was all there was. Hence to give adequate space to the inner debate, he boldly adopted the ancient form of the philosophic dialogue, in which ideas had more reality than characters and in which issues could be fully explored. He wrote, that is to say, the famous Don Juan in Hell sequence, whose intensity is so much greater than the romantic play surrounding it precisely because it grapples with his imperative present problem. Moreover its dialogue form, inviting comparisons to Plato and Diderot and Hume, was part of his attempt to cancel his body's defeat by a triumph of mind. We have seen Tanner dismiss the importance of all passions other than that moral seriousness through which he defines his manhood; similarly, Shaw now has to define his own manhood by emphasizing his moral seriousness, by regarding himself as more than an entertainer, a writer of romantic comedies, a "pander, buffoon, beauty monger, sentimentalizer," which "rich people" would force the artist to be. He must regard himself as a serious thinker, "no mere artist, but an artist philosopher," and to make his claim unmistakable he subtitles the play "a Comedy *and a Philosophy*." The comedy is almost a concession to public taste and theatrical requirements, merely "a trumpery story of modern London life," as he calls it in the same preface from which the above quotations are drawn. Thus the philosophic dialogue, though he recognizes it as "totally extraneous" to the play, reflects his now urgent need to establish his credentials as a thinker.

Indeed he began writing the philosophic section before writing the play; and keeping this fact in mind enables us to avoid much of the usual critical confusion about the work as a whole. Because Tanner is referred to in the play as a descendant of Don Juan, and because the Hell sequence in Act III is ostensibly Tanner's dream of his ancestor, commentators have assumed that Shaw was giving his own version of the legendary Don Juan, and Shaw himself tried to make it appear so in the interests of connecting the two parts of the work. Yet the integration of the parts is superficial because on a psychic level Shaw was recreating Don Juan as Tanner's successor, not his ancestor. Tanner is the earlier Shaw, the one who supposedly capitulated to marriage; Don Juan, turning contemptuously away from women, is the present Shaw, the Irish Don Juan with a virginal wife, struggling to renounce a desire for women. In short, the best way to comprehend the inner drama of **Man and Superman** is to view the romantic play section as Shaw's attempt to incorporate into his art the events leading up to his marriage to Charlotte—though those events are infiltrated by his later feelings and distorted to suit his present needs—and to view the dream sequence as his attempt to incorporate and expand the rationalizations that he developed after his marriage. (pp. 147-48)

The Don Juan in Hell scene purports to be Tanner's "dream" as he dozes in the Sierra Nevada, and certainly never in dramatic literature have we had a dream like this one, in substance so talkative and argumentative, and with such an appearance of rational control. Yet . . . however undreamlike it may seem to be, and however out of character for Tanner ever to have had such a dream, in relation to Shaw himself the sequence is pervaded by the same fundamental urges as lie within actual dreams, and that these urges—sexual and aggressive—emerge just as they do in actual dreams, with disguises imposed by a censor, meanings turned inside out, logic suspended, and time distinctions nullified. Indeed the very talkativeness of the dream, as well as its apparent rationality and impersonality, are the chief disguises beneath which Shaw permits himself to express his sexual and aggressive urges. The Hell scene, in a word, is Shaw's own therapeutic daydream as "an Irish Don Juan," newly emasculated. Its resolutely cerebral form seeks to place the dreamer as far as possible from his wounded psyche and to establish himself as a philosopher, superior to mere bodily appetites. Fearing in the depths of his being that he might be less than a man, he fantasizes himself as a Superman, enlisting his humor in a task somewhat beyond its resources and selecting whatever he finds suitable from Nietzsche's doctrines even while avoiding Nietzsche's disconcerting theory of *ressentiment*. As a Superman, he assures himself, his brain is the culminating achievement of the evolutionary process and the very tool for Nature to bring its further purposes to consciousness. But since such grave responsibilities would render mere human pleasure frivolous, Shaw summons up an alternate fantasy in which Nature's most immediately discernible purpose is for him to transmit his mental superiority to a succeeding generation. Admittedly, to advocate eugenics as a means of creating the Superman lessens his claim to Superman status in the present, but it does rescue the possibility of having sexual relations with women: far better to be a near-Superman if women will still be available than to be a full-fledged abstinent one, though of course such relations will be undertaken only as a solemn social obligation and not for brute pleasure.

Yet alongside these improbable fantasies Shaw cannot refrain from venting his resentment toward all males who happen to have less forbidding wives. Hence the proposal to eliminate sex from marriage (establishing his own marriage as the model for all others) and to confine sex to an elite (conspicuously including himself) who could improve the race through selective breeding, both proposals reflecting the same malice that had prompted him to emasculate all the men in the play. Shaw's resentment further led him to call for civil carnage, when men would "rise up, father against son, and brother against brother, and kill one another." In fact he yearned for the extinction of the whole human race, though he hid this yearning within the folds of a handsome idealism, a putative Life Force driving toward a race of Supermen to replace the present race of men. The Superman's transcendence of ordinary moral codes enhanced his appeal for Shaw, nagged as he was by a social conscience which cautioned him that the Superman would regard men and women as indifferently as he would a collection of cats. The Superman's omnipotence also exerted a particularly strong appeal to a man in Shaw's state of enforced continence, and it embodied the classic compensatory longing of the impotent. The deliberate omission of benevolence from among the Superman's attributes further points to the more sinister attraction Shaw found in the Superman's limitless power—the power to kill with impunity and a clear conscience.

Since the yearning to kill more fortunate men and to possess omnipotence drew its strength from envy, it was accompanied by a self-hatred which even a determined narcissism could not truly hide, and this made Shaw perfectly ready to destroy himself along with the rest of mankind. His surrogate Tanner reveals this impulse to Ann at the climactic moment in the final act: "If we two stood now on the edge of a precipice, I would hold you tight and jump." This desire to coalesce murder and suicide, though it carries the dual components of sadomasochism to their ultimate ecstasy, simultaneously destroys the peculiar pleasures they afford, and Shaw therefore usually contents himself with expressing his sadomasochistic impulses well on the near side of fantasized death. Both impulses are present throughout *Man and Superman*, the sadism more prominently in the dream sequence as Don Juan lashes men and women for every fault he can name, and the masochism in the romantic comedy as Shaw endlessly embarrasses Tanner, that protagonist who was even clothed to look like himself. From this psychological angle we can also see why making Tanner credible as a superior man received so little of Shaw's attention, busy as he was enjoying Tanner's humiliations.

In several ways, then, *Man and Superman: A Comedy and a Philosophy* validates the warning that Shaw had once uttered to Alice Lockett: "Beware. When all the love has gone out of me, I am remorseless: I hurl the truth about like destroying lightning." Certainly the remorselessness and the destructiveness underlie the entire work, and the truth that Shaw unintentionally offers is that the frustrations of his unconsummated marriage aroused his malevolent impulses and corrupted his idealism. (pp. 171-73)

> *Arnold Silver, in his* Bernard Shaw: The Darker Side *(with the permission of the publishers, Stanford University Press; copyright 1982 by the Board of Trustees of the Leland Stanford Junior University), Stanford University Press, 1982, 353 p.*

---

## ADDITIONAL BIBLIOGRAPHY

Allen, Walter. "Bernard Shaw: The Intoxication of Ideas." *The Times Literary Supplement*, No. 2839 (27 July 1956): 441-42.
   Examination of Shaw's beliefs and his works.

Anderson, Maxwell. "St. Bernard." In his *Off Broadway: Essays about the Theater*, pp. 12-17. New York: William Sloane Associates, 1947.
   A laudatory appraisal of Shaw and his work, originally delivered as a lecture at Rutgers University. Anderson concludes of Shaw: "The worth of his work lies in this—that in expounding, defending, attacking, and laying bare all the conceivable aspects of belief and all the possible motives for action he has irradiated almost the whole of a century with the unquenchable wildfire of an extraordinary brain."

Bentley, Eric. "Bernard Shaw." In his *The Playwright As Thinker: A Study of Drama in Modern Times*, pp. 137-57. New York: Reynal & Hitchcock, 1946.
   Attempts "to set forth the theory and practice of Shavian drama as forthrightly as possible."

Bentley, Eric. *Bernard Shaw*. New York: New Directions Publishing Corp., 1947, 242 p.
   A seminal analysis of Shaw's dramas which was highly regarded by Shaw himself.

Bentley, Eric. "The Making of a Dramatist (Shaw: 1892-1903)." In *Theater in the Twentieth Century,* edited by Robert W. Corrigan, pp. 282-303. Freeport, N.Y.: Books for Libraries Press, 1970.
    Examination of the deceptive qualities that sometimes mask Shaw's dramatic brilliance.

Bridie, James. "Shaw As Playwright." *The New Statesman and Nation* XL, No. 1027 (11 November 1950): 422.
    Praise of Shaw, written shortly after his death.

Chesterton, G. K. "The Last of the Rationalists (A Reply to Mr. Bernard Shaw)." *The New Age* n.s. II, No. 18 (29 February 1908): 348-49.
    A rebuttal to Shaw's famous essay "Chesterton and Belloc," an article in which the derisive term "Chesterbelloc" was first used. In reply, Chesterton compares the Chesterbelloc's beliefs to those of Shaw and H. G. Wells, on the subjects of socialism, the supernatural, evolution, and beer-drinking.

Clarke, Arthur C. "Shaw and the Sound Barrier." *The Virginia Quarterly Review* 36, No. 1 (Winter 1960): 72-7.
    An interesting sidelight on Shaw's interest in supersonic flight and space travel, including the contents of short letters sent by Shaw to Clarke.

Ervine, St. John. *Bernard Shaw.* New York: William Morrow and Co., 1956, 628 p.
    Biography of Shaw written by his intimate friend. Ervine's work contains many excerpts from Shaw's early diaries.

Ganz, Arthur. "Chekhov, Shaw, Giraudoux." In his *Realms of the Self: Variations on a Theme in Modern Drama,* pp. 37-104. New York: New York University Press, 1980.*
    Studies several of Shaw's plays, revealing their embodiment of the playwright's ambivalent attraction to revolutionary action and transcendent withdrawal.

Hale, Edward Everett, Jr. "Bernard Shaw." In his *Dramatists of Today: Rostand, Hauptmann, Sudermann, Pinero, Shaw, Phillips, Maeterlinck,* pp. 112-47. New York: Henry Holt and Co., 1911.
    A study of Shaw which claims that "Mr. Shaw is nowadays no mere dramatist: he is an Artist-Philosopher: he has a mission, a gospel, a message . . . : he is an Interpreter of Life."

Henderson, Archibald. *George Bernard Shaw: Man of the Century.* New York: Appleton-Century-Crofts, 1956, 969 p.
    Authorized biography of Shaw, prepared over a period of fifty years with the playwright's full cooperation. Henderson's work contains memoirs written by Shaw expressly for the biography, and reprints many letters.

Hind, C. Lewis. "George Bernard Shaw." In his *Authors and I,* pp. 256-61. New York: John Lane, 1921.
    Tribute to Shaw's lively writing and lively character.

Lewis, C. S. "What Lies behind the Law." In his *Mere Christianity,* pp. 31-5. New York: Macmillan Publishing Co., 1960.*
    Examines crucial problems in the Life-Force philosophy. "The wittiest expositions of it come in the works of Bernard Shaw," writes Lewis, "but the most profound ones in those of Bergson."

Lewis denounces the Life Force as an insupportable hobby horse— "a sort of tame God. You can switch it on when you want, but it will not bother you. All the thrills of religion and none of the cost."

MacCarthy, Desmond. *Shaw.* London: MacGibbon & Dee, 1951, 217 p.
    Criticism of Shaw's plays, written over a forty-year period. MacCarthy includes reviews of performances of the plays, as well as criticism of the texts.

Masur, Gerhard. "The Confident Years." In his *Prophets of Yesterday: Studies in European Culture 1890-1914,* pp. 252-97. New York: The Macmillan Co., 1961.*
    Examination of Shaw's many beliefs.

Murry, J. Middleton. "On Dependable Writers." In his *Pencillings,* pp. 90-8. New York: Thomas Seltzer, 1925.
    Laudatory appraisal of Shaw's literary criticism.

Pritchard, William H. "England Through." In his *Seeing through Everything: English Writers 1918-1940,* pp. 23-50. New York: Oxford University Press, 1977.*
    Examination of *Heartbreak House* and brief critique of *Saint Joan.*

Purdom, C. B. *A Guide to the Plays of Bernard Shaw.* London: Methuen and Co., 1963, 233 p.
    Plot outlines, summaries and some discussion of Shaw's life, themes, and the Shaw-vs.-Shakespeare controversy.

Stewart, J.I.M. "Shaw." In *Eight Modern Writers,* edited by F. P. Wilson and Bonamy Dobree, pp. 122-83. Clarendon: Oxford University Press, 1963.
    Critical overview of Shaw's work.

Trilling, Lionel. *"The Doctor's Dilemma."* In his *Prefaces to the Experience of Literature,* pp. 37-44. New York: Harcourt Brace Jovanovich, 1979.
    Discussion of *The Doctor's Dilemma,* examining the play's strengths and weaknesses.

Vogt, Sally Peters. "*Heartbreak House:* Shaw's Ship of Fools." *Modern Drama* XXI, No. 3 (September 1978): 267-86.
    Explores the dual theme of the ship of state and the ship of fools as the key to interpreting *Heartbreak House.*

Ward, A. C. *Bernard Shaw.* Harlow, England: British Council, 1970, 60 p.
    Biography of Shaw tracing his career and illuminating his philosophies.

Weintraub, Rodelle, ed. *Fabian Feminist: Bernard Shaw and Woman.* University Park: The Pennsylvania State University Press, 1977, 271 p.
    A collection of essays on Shaw's thoughts on women as revealed in his essays and dramas. Essayists include Germaine Greer, Sally Peters Vogt, Barbara Bellow Watson, and Stanley Weintraub, among others. Several essays by Shaw are also reprinted.

Yeats, W. B. "Unity of Being: Unity of Culture." In *Major British Writers, Vol. II,* edited by G. G. Harrison, pp. 652-53. New York: Harcourt Brace and Co., 1954.*
    Impressions of the first performances of *Arms and the Man,* noting the play's rousing reception by its audiences.

# Fyodor Sologub

## 1863-1927

(Pseudonym of Fyodor Kuzmich Teternikov; also transliterated as Fëdor, Fiodor, Fedor, Thedor) Russian poet, novelist, short story writer, dramatist, essayist, and critic.

Sologub is best-known for the novel *Melkii bes (The Petty Demon)*, in which he introduced to Russian literature a new character type: the evil, tormented cynic, personified in Peredonov, whose sole diversion in life lies in blighting the joy of others. But Sologub was also the first Russian Symbolist poet to receive wide recognition, and many critics consider him to be among the finest Russian poets in the mastery of form.

Born in St. Petersburg, Sologub came from a lower-class family. He received a modest education at the St. Petersburg Teachers Institute and, upon finishing his studies, began a career as a schoolmaster in a number of small provincial towns, many of which are recreated in his short stories and his novels *Tyazhelye sny (Bad Dreams)* and *The Petty Demon*. Though he began writing early in the eighties, it wasn't until 1896 that his first works appeared—two volumes of verse, a collection of short stories, and the novel *Bad Dreams*. Sologub was eventually made a district inspector of elementary schools, and he continued in this position until 1907 when the success of *The Petty Demon* allowed him to devote himself to literature. But his later work did not meet with the same success, and after 1910 critics began to note signs of diminishing power. Like many Symbolists, Sologub was fundamentally apolitical, and after the 1917 revolution he withdrew from both social and political activities. In 1921 his wife committed suicide after the couple were refused permission to emigrate from Russia. Her death left Sologub bitter, and he did not continue his literary career. Though he was eventually granted a visa to leave Russia, he spent his final years in Leningrad.

The vulgarity of the external world and the beauty of the human imagination are two elements apparent in all of Sologub's work. Sologub rejected the visible world as ugly and vulgar—an evil from which the individual must seek escape in beautiful dreams, in death, or both. *The Petty Demon* most clearly demonstrates this Manichaean view of life. The joyless character of Peredonov is contrasted with the idyllic loves of Sasha and Ludmila, two people who dared to create their own artificial world in a cruel environment. Peredonov is the most compelling figure in the book; he is an object of pity as well as an oppressor. Slowly consumed in madness, the victim of a meaningless, inarticulate world, Peredonov has been described by Roman S. Struc as "the negative counterpart of Myshkin in *The Idiot*." *The Petty Demon* is praised for its insightful examination of the human mind and spirit, and for its portrayal of the human propensity for evil.

Although Sologub was a Symbolist his entire career, he exhibited a peculiar poetic style. Unlike most other Symbolists of his time, he scorned complex metaphors, unusual structure, and an exotic vocabulary. His rhymes are simple and exact, his meters monotonous but exquisite, and his vocabulary quite small. But the simplicity and exactness of imagery in Sologub's verse have earned him praise as a poet who refined his art to the utmost degree of perfection. His short stories and plays

are more fantastic than his poetry and novels. In these works he gave free reign to his morbid sensual demands and his belief in death as a great comforter and source of emancipation. Elements of sensuous despair, tortuous sexuality, the glorification of pain and death, and the juxtaposition of the real and the fantastic consistently appear throughout Sologub's canon.

Like many Russian writers at the turn of the century, Sologub suffered an almost total eclipse after the 1917 revolution. Recently critics have begun to reappraise his work. Although his poetry has been highly praised, Sologub's novels and plays have received less critical acclaim. With the exception of *The Petty Demon*, many critics argue that the eroticism in his novels and stories is often repulsive and at times an insurmountable obstacle to the enjoyment of his work. Others claim that his later efforts are marred by irritating mannerisms and do not have the clearness and balance of his early works. His plays are generally regarded as less important than his poetry and of little dramatic merit. But despite the critical debate over his work, Sologub's single masterpiece, *The Petty Demon*, is regarded by many, in D. S. Mirsky's words, as "the most perfect Russian novel since the death of Dostoevsky."

## PRINCIPAL WORKS

*Stikhi. Kniga I-II*   (poetry)   1896

*Tyazhelye sny* (novel) 1896
[*Bad Dreams*, 1978]
*Sobranie stikhov. Kniga III-IV* (poetry) 1904
*Kniga skazok* (fairy tales) 1905
*Političeskie skazčki* (fairy tales) 1906
*Rodine* (poetry) 1906
*Dar mudrykh pchol* (drama) 1907
*Melkii bes* (novel) 1907
[*The Little Demon*, 1916; also published as *The Petty Demon*, 1962]
*Pobeda smerti* (drama) 1907
[*The Triumph of Death*, 1916]
*Zmii* (poetry) 1907
*Plamennyi krug* (poetry) 1908
*\*Tvorimaja legenda*. 3 vols. (novels) 1908-12
[*The Created Legend* (partial translation), 1916; also published as *The Created Legend* (complete translation), 1979]
*Nochnyi plyaski* (drama) 1909
*Vanka klyuchnik i pazh Zhean* (drama) 1909
*Zalozhniki zhizni* (drama) 1912
*Sobranie sochinenii*. 20 vols. (poetry, dramas, novels, short stories, and fairy tales) 1913-14
*The Old House, and Other Tales* (fables and short stories) 1915
*The Sweet-Scented Name, and Other Fairy Tales, Fables, and Stories* (fables, fairy tales, and short stories) 1915
*Voina* (poetry) 1915
*Alyi mak* (poetry) 1917
*Fimiamy* (poetry) 1921
*Nebo goluboe* (poetry) 1921
*Odna lyubov'* (poetry) 1921
*Charodjnaja chasha* (poetry) 1922
*Koster dorozhnyj* (poetry) 1922
*Svirel'* (poetry) 1922
*Velikii blagovest* (poetry) 1923
*The Kiss of the Unborn and Other Stories* (short stories) 1977

*\*This work includes the novels Dym i pepel (Smoke and Ash), Kapli krovi (Drops of Blood) and Koroleva Ortruda (Queen Ortruda).*

---

## FYODOR SOLOGUB (essay date 1908)

Of all that ever has been created by the genius of man, the theatre is perhaps the lightest creation on its visible surface and the most frightful in its perceived depths. The fatal steps:—playing—spectacle—sacrament. . . . High tragedy to the same degree as light comedy and popular farce. . . .

The fatal steps. We played when we were children—and then we died in our hearts for simple play, and we came out of curiosity to watch a spectacle—and the hour will come when we, in a transformation of body and soul, will reach true unity in the liturgical act, in the mysterious rite. . . . (p. 87)

A theatrical spectacle, which people come to watch for amusement and for entertainment, will not long remain for us simply a spectacle. And very quickly the spectator, tired by the change of spectacles alien to him, will wish to become a participant in the mystery, as he was once a participant in the playing. Expelled from Eden, he will soon knock with a bold hand on the door behind which the bridegroom feasts with the wise virgins. He was a participant in innocent play when he was still alive, when he still dwelt in paradise, in My beautiful garden between two great rivers. And now the sole way to resurrection for him lies in becoming a participant in the mystery, in joining hands with his brother and with his sister in the liturgical rite, and in pressing his lips, eternally parched from thirst, against the mysteriously filled cup where I "shall mix blood with water." To do in a brightly lighted temple open to all the people what can only be done now in the catacombs. (p. 88)

The contemporary theatre presents a sad spectacle of a fragmented will and thus of a disunified action. "People are different," thinks the simple-minded playwright, "every fellow according to this own pattern." He goes various places, notices the setting, the way of life and the customs, observes various people, and depicts it all very faithfully. . . . The audience is in ecstasy—it recognizes its own acquaintances and non-acquaintances and feels itself at an undoubted advantage: no matter what widespread faults have been displayed upon the stage, for all that each spectator, except for a small number of those portrayed, sees clearly that it is not he who is depicted, but someone else.

And none of this is at all needed. There is no everyday life, and there are no customs and manners—there is only the playing out of the eternal mystery. There are no stories and intrigues, and all the plots have long ago been plotted, and all the denouements long ago foretold—and only the eternal liturgy takes place. And what about all the words and dialog? One eternal dialog is being conducted, and the questioner himself responds and thirsts for the answer. And what are the themes? Only Love, only Death.

There are no different people—there is only one single man, only one single I in the entire universe, willing, acting, suffering, burning in the inextinguishable fire, and from the fury of a horrible and hideous life finding salvation in the cool and comforting embraces of the eternal consoler—Death.

I put on my guises according to My will, but always and everything I remain myself—as a certain Shalyapin is the same in all his roles. Both beneath the frightful mask of the tragic hero, and beneath the ludicrous countenance of the fool who is the laughing stock of comedy, and in the motley overalls made of many-colored rags enveloping the fair-booth clown's body as it goes into contortions to amuse the gallery—beneath all these coverings the spectator must discover Me. The theatrical spectacle is presented before him as a problem with one unknown quantity.

If the spectator has come to the theatre as the simpleminded idler goes out into the world "in order to see the sun," then it is I, the poet, who create the drama in order to recreate the world according to My new conception. As in the great world, My single will alone rules, so in the small circle of the theatrical spectacle only a single will should rule—the will of the poet. (pp. 90-1)

[My] word must sound openly and loudly. The visitor to the theatrical spectacle must hear the poet before the actor. (p. 91)

Tragedy tears off from the face of the world its entrancing guise, and there, where harmony had seemed to exist for us, either pre-established or in the process of being created, the tragic muse discloses before us the eternal contradictoriness of the world, the eternal identity of good and evil and other polarities. Tragedy affirms every kind of contradiction; to every claim of life, be it true or false, tragedy responds with an equally ironic *Yes!* Neither to good nor to evil will it give a lyrical *No!* Tragedy is always irony, and it never takes the form of the lyric. And this is the way that tragedy must be put on. (p. 94)

Chief spokesman of My will, the hero of the tragedy stands at the furthest remove from the spectator, and the path to an understanding of him is the longest of all; the spectator is required to climb up a steep flight of stairs toward him, and to overcome and triumph over much that lies within and without. But the further the distance from the hero, the closer to the spectator, and the more comprehensible for him, until finally the characters in the drama become so close to the spectator that they more or less completely coincide with him. They are similar to the chorus of ancient tragedy, giving voice to what any of those sitting on the steps of the amphitheatre might say. (p. 95)

The whole world is only the scenery behind which is hidden the creative soul—My soul. Every earthly face and every earthly body is only a guise, only a marionette destined for one playing each, for an earthly tragicomedy—a marionette set in motion for word, gesture, laughter, and tears. But tragedy arrives upon the scene, attenuates the settings and appearances and through the scenery there appears translucent a world transfigured by Me, the world of My soul, the realization of My sole will—and through the guises and appearances there shines My sole image and My sole transfigured flesh. Flesh beautiful and liberated.

The rhythm of liberation is the rhythm of the dance. The grandeur of liberation is the joy of the beautiful, bare body.

The dancing spectator, both male and female, will come to the theatre, and at the threshold they will leave behind their crude, their petty-bourgeois clothes. And they race along in the light dance.

So the crowd, which has come to look on, will be transformed in the round dance, which has come to participate in the tragic action. (p. 99)

> *Fyodor Sologub, "The Theatre of One Will," translated by Daniel Gerould (1908; translation © copyright 1977 Daniel Gerould; reprinted by permission; all rights reserved), in* The Drama Review, *No. 4, 1977, pp. 84-99.*

## ZINAIDA GIPPIUS   (essay date 1911)

[*Gippius, a contemporary of Sologub, offers a novel reaction to* The Petty Demon, *suggesting that we view Peredonov not only as the incarnation of evil but that we ask, in the name of love, how such a person comes to exist. For the standard interpretation of* The Petty Demon, *see the essays of D. S. Mirsky and Roman S. Struc excerpted below.*]

Perhaps—and this may even be a good thing—Sologub himself fails to understand his own hero Peredonov (*The Petty Demon*) and to relate to him as he should. Here I am not concerned with whether this is good or bad. I am only establishing the fact that both the author and the public, which was enthusiastic about *The Petty Demon*, understood and interpreted Peredonov in exactly the same way—and further, that such an interpretation was simple, understandable and natural. (p. 145)

No matter how we settle the argument of who is depicted in the figure of Peredonov, the central issue remains unchanged. For this argument is peripheral. *The Petty Demon* remains a "satire," a venomous tangle of snakes; it is a magic mirror *which exposes* defects . . . whether of all people or almost all matters little. What is important is that it *exposes*. . . .

It should be said that in no way do I deny this primary accusatory and repelling aspect of the novel or the mirroring quality of Peredonov. The novel supports this interpretation and may be understood in this sense. It is difficult, very difficult to pass beyond the thrice-locked doors, deep into that region where even the father of Peredonov and the *nedotikomka* has not penetrated. But in the final analysis it is impossible not to go there.

I remember my first meeting with Peredonov many years ago. I remember the stack of blue student notebooks from Polyakov's store, covered with Sologub's high, clear script. . . . At that time the novel still contained a number of coarse spots, later omitted by the author; but Peredonov stood as he stands today: in his full stature. And—one must be truthful—my first impression was identical with that received by almost everyone who reads the novel today. I was enchanted by Ludmila and the symphony of spirits; I was horrified by the revolting truth, the living filth of Peredonov. What could be more hateful than a vulgar fool going out of his mind? Yes, yes, here is an object truly worthy of our hatred, and if, in each of us, there sits this indecent fool who will certainly go mad, then we have all the more reason to hate him. I was delighted by the author's disinterested art, excited by a sordid hatred towards the living Peredonov. And I experienced then the strong conviction that Peredonov exists, not only somewhere in ourselves, partially, but that he is alive and actual—complete, real. If he does not exist today—he will exist tomorrow, he existed yesterday. In a word, he *can* exist. (p. 146)

[Since] the time of the blue notebooks I felt no need to re-read the novel. I thought I knew Peredonov as many know him today; oh, of course, he is the most absolute, most revolting "image of evil." How could one not hate him?

Finally, I open the book. The author's brilliant foreword prepares me for the familiar feelings. I wait for them—and I read.

Here he is, the dirty and dull Ardalion in all his obscenity, rotting and stinking, not even going upright out of his mind, but creeping off its edge. . . . Nothing goes right for Peredonov, the *nedotikomka* slowly sucks him in; he feels that he is drowning, that everyone is against him . . . and is it madness that makes him feel this? Such feelings can drive one mad, of course, but Peredonov is not yet mad, for in actual fact everyone and everything *is* against him.

A strange, new, as yet inarticulate feeling for Peredonov stirred within me. And the last thing it resembled was hatred. Not the printed pages of the story about Peredonov, but Peredonov himself, with his gray, embittered face, passed before me. And I fervently wished *that things had happened differently*, that Varvara had not deceived him, that the Director had not thrown him out, that the *nedotikomka* had been caught and killed. It is impossible not to wish this. You can wish not to wish—but you will wish it anyway. Why the devil do we say "satire," "embodiment of evil," when a living man, yesterday's, tomorrow's Ardalion Peredonov finds himself in such desperate, unparalleled misery! Before misery like this all the horrors so laboriously heaped up by Leonid Andreev are mere trifles. . . . In all suffering there is hope; but in Peredonov's there is none.

No one will intercede for him. He is ugly, evil, dirty and full; he has nothing, nothing at all. And nevertheless he is created, he *is;* he is an "I" like any other "I," he matters first to himself and is everything to himself. The gray, slowly contracting ring has seized him, is suffocating him, and he cannot do anything; he possesses nothing beyond the agony of suffocation. (pp. 146-48)

Peredonov's misery is not just, but somehow *extremely unjust.* It is incumbent upon us to justify the "little tear of the tormented child" because we must know: for what crime? why? for what purpose? But similarly, it is incumbent, strongly incumbent upon me to justify each of Peredonov's elephant tears, each of his shudders at the sight of the *nedotikomka,* each heel blow against his physiognomy, which he "justly" receives from a good man, each of his shrieks and wails in the madhouse where he will inevitably be sent. If we continue to live in and even to love this world full of tormented children and rocks which may fall on our heads tomorrow—it is only because we say our "I do not wish it" and with stubborn, instinctive hope wait for an answer to "for what crime?" "for what purpose?"...

Beyond the limit of pure justice, the simple definiton of guilt, of human culpability or innocence, disappears, The question "for what crime?" disappears too. We cease to judge Peredonov; we protect him. And, protecting him, we ask: *How did He dare* to create his creature? And how will He *answer for him?*

Of course, it is another matter entirely if no such person as Peredonov exists, if all this is the fabrication of a talented novelist, if, speaking plainly, Peredonov was created by Sologub. There is no point in turning to such a creator of Peredonov with the question "how did you dare" and "will you answer for him." Clearly, Sologub depicted him against his own desires, does not know him and will in no way answer for him. The feeling of lack of responsibility for his hero is very clear in Sologub's novel. *He does not love* Peredonov and this underscores the fact that he did not give birth to him, but merely found him and exposed him....

Thank you, nonetheless, for exposing, for remembering him who must be remembered. (p. 148)

[For there] are many tormented children, many innocently and guiltily suffering people..., but the tribe of Peredonovs, suffering hopelessly, poor in everything and cursed by all, is even *more numerous.* (p. 149)

> Zinaida Gippius, "Peredonov's Little Tear (What Sologub Doesn't Know)," translated by Sharon Leiter, (originally published as "Slezinka Peredonova," in O Fedore Sologube, edited by A.N. Cebotarevskaja, Sipovnik, 1911), in Russian Literature Triquarterly (copyright © 1972 by Ardis Publishers), No. 4, Fall, 1972, pp. 145-49.

## JOHN COURNOS (essay date 1916)

[Fedor Sologub is] the author of twenty bulky volumes.... Best known as a novelist—whose *Little Demon*,... is already considered a classic—he has actually mastered every medium he has tried. He is hardly less famous for his short stories, which are a curious blend of Chekhov and Poe; his poems are as exquisite as any in Russian and are distinguished for their seductive word music.... (p. 329)

[It] is a curious thing, and the thing which proves Sologub's genius, that the contents of all his twenty volumes radiate, as it were, and converge towards a single point. As he himself says in his foreword to his play, *The Triumph of Death,* "By means of all the words he can find he calls unwearyingly to one and the same thing." Again, he makes the poet Trirodov, of *The Created Legend,* say: "A man's whole life is barely enough to think out a single idea properly. . . . If people should but grasp this fact human knowledge would take an unprecedented step forward." (p. 330)

With the eye of a great artist, Sologub reduces life to an esthetic phenomenon, a legend, a decoration, One Face, a mask, apparently tranquil on the surface, but suggesting infinite depths of experience and pain. He would have the drama a thing without excess of grimace and gesture—for art is not violence. (p. 340)

*The Triumph of Death* is perhaps the best of Sologub's plays. . . . It is not a realistic play, and the characters in it are more or less abstractioned—let us say, Love, Beauty and Death. Sologub reiterates here the idea he has expressed more than once elsewhere, an idea which he conceived by his early and unceasing admiration of Cervantes' *Don Quixote.* He takes the story of Aldonza, transformed by the gallant Don Quixote into Dulcinea, as a symbol of the poet's mission in the world: the discernment of beauty, wherever and under whatsoever guise it may be found. And there he develops a philosophic theory, that beauty does not achieve perfection but is always in the making, and a given element of it is therefore always a creative force, forever seeking realization, forever discontented, forever trying to find a lover, a poet, or a king to crown her.

In this play we find Malgista (Dulcinea) sending out her wise and beautiful young daughter Algista (Aldonza) to a great deed, that of deposing ugliness, symbolized in the person of Queen Bertha, and usurping the throne for herself, Algista, that is Beauty, until now the Queen's maid-servant. The argument of the play is clearly and beautifully worked out in the Prologue. The peasant girl Aldonza enters upon the scene, bearing across her young shoulders a yoke with two pails, of living and of dead water, which, if sprinkled on the world, might create a new and beautiful life. But people don't understand this: they regard the sweet water of beauty as bitter and harsh, fit only for washing floors with—just as they do not acknowledge beauty herself as the supreme thing in life and subject her to a secondary role, that of a servant. The king refuses to crown her, the poet to sing her praises—the latter indeed pays more attention to the lady who is a mere chance acquaintance, a fellow traveller; they call her Aldonza, and refuse to recognize her as Dulcinea. . . . [All] her magic and charms fail to win over the king and the poet and the young lover, Page Dagobert. (pp. 341-42)

One cannot avoid the reflection that these spectators are as blind as those critics of *The Little Demon* who could see only slime and filth in it and were too obtuse to see that it was a criticism of life. There can be no better retort than this play.

As a pendant to *The Triumph of Death,* you have Sologub's tragedy, *The Gift of the Wise Bees* based on a story from Greek mythology. (pp. 342-43)

And the interesting thing about this play is that in spite of its Greek theme, and to a large extent its observances of the form of ancient tragedy, it remains essentially modern, and essentially Sologubian, in that it reveals the author's own soul, in the hope, as he says somewhere, "that the intimate part of me shall become the universal."

But Sologub has also written realistic plays. Putting aside his dramatization of **The Little Demon,** his most successful play is **Hostages of Life.** Even here the realism is only external; actually it is a thoroughly symbolist play. It presents the same fundamental idea, the eternal antagonism of Dream and Reality, of Art and Life, of Dulcinea and Aldonza. (pp. 343-44)

[In] spite of the absolutely realistic appearance of the play, the theme remains the same; it is again the story of Dulcinea—unrecognized and uncrowned Beauty—and people, like Katya and Mikhail, are shown to be only poor prisoners, Mere "hostages of life." The hour of their triumph will come, but it will be only a partial triumph, earthly and merely over themselves, over their own individual lives, and that is why weariness and sadness sound in their triumph. For at best one must deny in order to affirm, even as in the case of Ivan Karamazov.

And so from the first page of his works to the last we truly find Sologub "calling unwearyingly " towards one and the same thing by means "of the charms of words obedient to him." And indeed no writer in Russia knows the magic of words more then he. (pp. 344-45)

> *John Cournos, "Feodor Sologub As a Dramatist,"*
> *in* The Drama *(copyright, 1916, by Drama League*
> *of America), No. 23, August, 1916, pp. 329-45.*

## WILLIAM LYON PHELPS  (essay date 1916)

Sologub is a brilliant and original man, and I hope that all his work may eventually appear in an accessible form. His short stories are full of imagination, beauty, and charm—which will surprise those who are acquainted only with **"The Little Demon."** If there were an international prize for the shortest of all short stories, Sologub would assuredly win it, for many of his stories occupy only half a page of print. Yet his genius appears, though in a disagreeable form, in [**"The Little Demon"**]. This is a strange story of original sin, in which the leading character is not meant to be a type but rather an illustration of the undoubted truth that every man and woman—no matter how noble—have within them natural tendencies to evil. Usually these are held in check, and occasionally conquered; in this novel the sombre results are shown where sin remains in control. As a teacher, I found another source of interest in this book; the devilish hero is a school-teacher, and the pictures of Russian schools with the relations existing between master and pupils are exotically attractive. (p. 210)

> *William Lyon Phelps, "Russian Novels in New*
> *Translations," in* The Yale Review *(© 1916 by Yale*
> *University), Vol. VI, No. 1, October, 1916, pp. 207-*
> *12.**

## D. S. MIRSKY  (essay date 1926)

[*Mirsky is considered one of the foremost critics on Russian literature. In the essay below he offers the standard assessment of Sologub's work.*]

Sologub's poetry developed along different lines from that of the other Symbolists. His vocabulary, his diction, and his images are closely akin to those of the eclectic poetry of the "Victorians." His metres are simple and ordinary, but refined to the utmost degree of perfection. His vocabulary is almost as small as Racine's, but he uses it with almost equal precision

and felicity. He is a Symbolist in that his words are *symbols,* with a double meaning, and are used in their secondary, not in their ordinary sense. But the completeness of his philosophy allows him to use them with an exactness that is almost classical. This, however, refers only to that part of his poetry which reflects his ideal heaven, or his yearning for it. There is another series of poems which are, as his *Inferno,* dark and cruel evocations of the evil diversity of the world, and in them his language becomes cruder and richer and more racy. . . . As for his idealistic lyrics, which are, after all, his greatest achievement, it is useless, except one be a master of English verse, to attempt any translation of them. Their beauty is classical; it depends on the imponderables of rhythm and meaning. As in all classic poetry, the poet's silences are as important as his words, that which is left unsaid as that which he says. It is the most refined and most delicate of all modern Russian poetry.

Although his verse is the most perfect and rarest flower of Sologub's genius, his fame at home, and especially abroad, is based on his novels rather than on his poetry. The first of these, **Bad Dreams,** is autobiographical and lyrical. The hero, Login, a schoolmaster in an out-of-the-way provincial town, has the same perverse obsessions and the same ideal visions as haunt Sologub's own poetry. The novel is the history of the man capable of reaching the ideal, in the thick of a world of vulgarity, cruelty, selfishness, stupidity, and lewdness. Russian provincial society is portrayed with incisive cruelty, a cruelty reminiscent of Gogol. But it is not realism in the good old Russian sense of the word, for it is all meant as a symbol of more than Russian vastness. Sologub's second novel, **Melki Bes** . . . , is the most famous of all his writings, and it may be recognized as the most perfect Russian novel since the death of Dostoevsky. Like **Bad Dreams,** it is apparently realistic, but internally symbolical. It transcends realism not because Sologub introduces the mysterious demon *Nedotykomka,* which, after all, may be explained away as a hallucination of Peredonov's, but because his aim is not to paint the life of a Russian provincial town, but life, the evil creation of God, as a whole. The satirical drawing is admirable, a touch more grotesque, and consequently more poetical, than in the earlier novel, but the town is only a microcosm of all life. The novel has two planes: the life of Peredonov, the incarnation of the joyless evils of life, and the idyllic loves of the boy Sasha Pylnikov and Ludmila Rutilova. These two are the emanation of Beauty, but their beauty is not pure, it has been polluted by the evil touch of life. The Sasha and Ludmila episode has a subtle sensual flavour, and is introduced not only for its symbolical and constructive value, but also to answer the demands of the poet's *libido.* Peredonov has become a famous figure, in fact the most famous and memorable character of Russian fiction since *The Brothers Karamazov,* and his name is now a word of the literary language. It stands for the incarnation of sullen evil, which knows no joy and resents others' knowing it; one of the most terrible figures ever created by a poet. He lives in constant hatred of him. He loves to inflict cruelty, and to dash to the ground the joys of others. He finally succumbs to a mania of persecution and commits murder in a state of insanity.

Sologub's third novel, **The Created Legend** . . . , is his longest. It consists of three parts, each of which is a self-contained novel. In the first part the scene is laid in Russia in 1905. The hero is Trirodov, a Satanist after the heart of Sologub. He is also a revolutionary, though only a contemplative one. Sologub's political attitude was then strongly revolutionary: it is natural that with his philosophy the existing order of things, the forces of reaction and conservatism, should appear as the fullest expression of evil life. The volume is full of scenes of horror and cruelty in the suppression of the revolutionary movement: hence its title, **Drops of Blood.** Trirodov is the ideal man who has nearest approached the serenity of death, and sheds around himself a cool and calm atmosphere, symbolized in his colony of "quiet boys"—a weird vision of Sologub's perverse imagination. In the second and third parts (**Queen Ortruda** and **Smoke and Ashes**) the scene is shifted to the Kingdom of the United Islands, an imaginary volcanic group in the Mediterranean. These volumes have a powerful and subtle, if suspicious, charm. Unlike most Russian novels, they may be read for the interest of the story. It is a very complicated story of love and political intrigue. It is all dominated by the ever present danger, the volcano, and in the third part the eruption occurs. The story is symbolical, but, as I have said, contains quite sufficient charm apart from its symbolism. (pp. 198-201)

Sologub's short stories are a link between his poetry and his novels. Some of them are shorter sketches in the style of **Bad Dreams** and **Melki Bes.** Others, especially after 1905, are frankly fantastic and symbolical. In these more than anywhere else Sologub gave free reign to his morbid sensual demands. **The Dear Page** and . . . **The Lady in Fetters** are typical examples of this kind. **The Miracle of the Boy Linus,** a revolutionary story in a conventional poetical setting, is one of the most beautiful pieces of modern Russian prose. In general, Sologub's prose is beautiful: limpid, clear, balanced, poetical, but with a keen sense of measure. In his later writings it is marred by certain irritating mannerisms. Apart from his other prose writings stand his **Political Fables** . . . , admirable both for the scathing point of their satire, and for their remarkably elaborate popular language, rich in verbal effects (as all popular speech is) and reminiscent of the grotesque manner of [Nikolay Semyonovich] Leskov.

His plays are not on a level with his other writings. Of peculiar dramatic merit they have but little. Such as **The Sting of Death** and **The Gift of the Wise Bees** are academic pageants symbolizing the concepts of his philosophy. They are less genuine than his poetry and constantly fall into the false beautiful. More interesting is **Vanka the Butler and the Page Jehan** an amusing piece of irony: the familiar history of the young servant who seduces the lady of the house is developed in two parallel variations: in mediæval France and in Muscovite Russia. It is a satire on Russian civilization, with its crudeness and poverty of forms, and is at the same time a symbol of the essential sameness of the evil diversity of life all over the world and throughout the ages. (p. 201)

> *D. S. Mirsky, "Sologub," in his* Contemporary Russian Literature: 1881-1925 *(copyright 1926 by Alfred A. Knopf, Inc.; reprinted by permission of the publisher), Knopf, 1926, G. Routledge & Sons, 1926, pp. 196-201.*

## JANKO LAVRIN (essay date 1942)

The interest in religion, before the [Bolshevik] revolution, became quite a vogue. So did the interest in occultism, or rather in inverted religion, indulged in by the most talented of all the Russian decadents, Fyodor K. Sologub. . . . [Sologub] wrote much poetry and prose of a morbid type. As though under the weight of an irreparable injury, he adopted a Manichean attitude towards life, in the name of which he rejected the entire visible world as something unworthy of acceptance. In this manner he carried Gogol's aversion to reality to those limits

where negation passes into rancorous anti-religion of a Satanic kind. To this he adapted his own theory of aestheticism, conjuring up in its hothouse atmosphere a compensatory world— dreamy and ghostlike, over which he ruled like a necromancer. . . . This was the only world in which he felt perfectly at home. The world of our everyday actualities aroused in him nothing but disgust and negation. The symbol of his romantic negation was Satan—the Satan of Baudelaire rather than of Carducci.

Sologub's writings thus became largely an apology of a decadent who looks upon art as a shelter from the ugliness and vulgarity of life. Not only his poems, but also his novels and stories are, in a sense, autobiographic. His method is distilled realism of indictment, mixed with symbolic and allegorical fancies. . . . Like Gogol, he regarded vulgarity as something which has a metaphysical existence of its own, and is beyond man's control. But if life be devoid of beauty, man is still free to create a beautiful legend of his own—both as a refuge from and a reproach against life as it is. Such deliberate quixotism became a cult with Sologub, threatening now and then to pass into aesthetic sentimentality, at least after his remarkable novel, **The Petty Demon**. . . . (pp. 150-51)

This work is one of the masterpieces of Russian modernism, most of whose ingredients it contains. Indictment, strengthened by several Dostoevskian elements (the very title of the novel was taken from Ivan Karamazov's nightmare), is deepened into a frightening symbol of human vulgarity and squalor. (p. 151)

In his intense aversion to actual life, Sologub turned aestheticism into a cult and built out of his dreams a 'legend', an imaginary counter-reality of his own. The series of novels in which he embodied this attitude bears the general title, [**The Created Legend**]. . . . Trirodov, the chief character of the series, is a Russian des Esseintes and a modern Prospero in one— with a magic power over nature and human beings. Interesting as a transposed confession, this series is a pastiche of allegorism, reality, and sentimental-romantic fancies of a decadent escapist. Sologub sums up life as a disgusting fat slut, whose touch makes everything appear gross and ugly. This is the leit motiv of most of his stories and novels. . . . The same attitude pervades Sologub's plays—most of them rather forced and therefore inferior to his novels, as well as to his poetry in which he achieved real greatness. (p. 152)

> *Janko Lavrin, "The Modernist Movement," in his* An Introduction to the Russian Novel *(reprinted by permission of the author), Methuen & Co. Ltd., 1942, pp. 145-59.**

## RENATO POGGIOLI (essay date 1960)

Sologub's fame will rest primarily on **A Petty Devil;** yet, had he written only that, he would be remembered merely as a Russian Barbey d'Aurevilly, or at most, as a Russian Villiers de l'Isle-Adam. His name will, however, be recommended to posterity by his lyrics, which have earned their author a place of his own within the poetry of his time. Sologub's verse, no less than his prose, is ruled by a negative vision of life, expressed in terse images and sober speech. Here the "bad dreams" of his fiction become clear and lucid as objective visions; and one could fairly say that Sologub was better able than any of his Decadent brethren to fix languid and morbid moods into classic molds. His temperament was neurotic, but there was no hysteria in his art. The material of his inspiration is unhealthy; yet, unlike his peers, all too naturally led to express the sickly and the perverse in allusive and elusive terms, he always controls his frenzy and submits his own pathos to the severe ethos of form.

The Satanism of many other Decadent poets . . . is often hardly more than a pose; and, as such, it is merely the reverse of Romantic sentimentalism. Sologub's Satanism is, however, a genuine reflection of his view of human life. Existence, especially that of modern man, seems to him a kind of nonexistence. Man goes through the limbo of being like a living corpse. Life is demonic not merely because it denies God, but also because God denies life, or, as the poet says, "God does not want life, and life does not want God." By identifying the human and the earthly with the demonic, Sologub lowers the human to the level of the subhuman and sinks the earthly underground. The demonic obsesses Sologub's imagination as much as that of Gogol' and Dostoevskij, yet the evil spirits he conjures resemble more the impish sprites of Gogol' than the black angels of Dostoevskij. . . . It was perhaps from Dostoevskij that Sologub took the idea, and even the title, of his main novel; yet there are no "petty devils" in the work of that master, while the fiction of Gogol' and the poetry of Sologub are full of them. The regions or elements producing those perverse creatures are fancy and superstition; and this origin, while depriving them of symbolic power, strengthens their psychological significance, and endows them with a sense of reality which is at once eerie and grotesque. Sologub's mean demons may not be the evil geniuses of the soul, but they certainly are the malicious trolls of the psyche. Perhaps this is the reason why the poet treats them with the familiarity which one reserves for one's intimates or friends. (pp. 109-10)

[One] could say that all of Sologub's best poems are as light and shapely as an ancient vase, pure in form, even when impure in content. That Sologub must have been aware of this quality of his creation is shown by the poem **"Amphora,"** in which he chose to describe his art as a beautiful vessel which a slave carries on his shoulder in perfect equilibrium, to prevent the liquid it holds from being spilled, since that liquid is not a drink but a poison. This ethical awareness redeems Sologub's poetry from the cheap and vulgar immoralism which stains such a large body of Decadent writing, and, along with his formal mastery, saves his work from neglect. It was not the vanity of an aesthete, but a lucid self-criticism, which led him to claim in one of his lyrics that all his sins as a man and as a poet would be remitted and forgiven because of a single merit, which was the purity of his craft. Sologub was right in this expectation: his name will be spared by the judgment of posterity; his poetry will escape that oblivion which is the nemesis of all artists who sin against their calling by bad faith, even more than by bad works. (p. 111)

> *Renato Poggioli, "The Decadents," in his* The Poets of Russia 1890-1930 *(copyright ©1960 by the President and Fellows of Harvard College; excerpted by permission), Cambridge, Mass.: Harvard University Press, 1960, pp. 89-115.\**

## ANDREW FIELD (essay date 1961)

[*Field is considered one of the leading critics on Sologub and his study of the political undertones in* The Created Legend *is a notable example of a symbolist interpretation.*]

Perhaps the most difficult of all Sologub's works is his trilogy, *Tvorimaja legenda.* . . . Yet, in spite of its complexity, the trilogy is a good point from which to examine Sologub's art

as a whole precisely because it is, as it were, a meeting place for all the ideas in his poetry, stories, dramas, and other novels. (p. 341)

[The plot of *The Created Legend*] at first appears incredible and incomprehensible. A closer examination reveals, however, that *The Created Legend* is an intricate field of symbols which are often all the more confusing for their very clarity and boldness. The trilogy is, above all, an ambitious experimental novel, and it attempts to encompass symbolism and realism, history and utopia. The failure of the trilogy lies in its most interesting feature, namely, its lack of a unified structure. For one cannot deal with *The Created Legend* on the basis of only the narrative and the characters. . . . *The Created Legend* has many separate levels of meaning, but, because of its unorthodox structure, it cannot, like *The Petty Demon,* be understood apart from its symbolism.

The most obvious level of a significance in the novel is its political meaning. *Drops of Blood* and *Smoke and Ash* portray the effect of social turmoil upon individual lives, while *Queen Ortruda* reflects the broader, national significance of the years leading up to the 1905 revolution. In this way, *The Created Legend* furnishes one of the most comprehensive artistic records of the period.

In *Queen Ortruda* the actual characters and events have been altered and "re-created" by Sologub. The position of the Russian monarchy is shown through Ortruda and Tankred in such a way that each has certain qualities of both Nicholas II and Tsaritsa Aleksandra Fedorovna. The circumstances of the accession of the young Nicholas, his initial popularity, and his romantic marriage are reflected in the early events of Ortruda's reign. On the other hand, in reality it was Aleksandra Fedorovna who was a German and was greatly mistrusted, while in the novel it is Prince Tankred who is in this position. In Tankred's plans for a fleet and an empire are depicted the desires of Nicholas to develop a powerful navy and to extend the territory of Russia to include Korea and Manchuria. Tankred's fleet (which has more admirals than ships and which is caught totally unprepared when actually called upon) recalls the situation of the Russian navy limping to certain defeat at the hands of the Japanese in 1905. Ortruda reflects the fatalistic attitude of Nicholas and his desire to deny the urgent facts of political reality. The revolutionary, Phillipo Mecchio, is Lenin—as shown by the name of Mecchio's revolutionary newspaper, *Vpered.* Lenin founded a paper with that name in December 1904. (pp. 342-43)

In *Drops of Blood* and *Smoke and Ash,* Sologub depicts the spread of terrorism in Russia: the Cossack militia, the murder of an innocent Jewess by hooligans, the attempted assassination of Vice-Governor Peredonov. The humiliating position of the intelligentsia is vividly shown in the stupid and coarse search of Dr. Svetilovič's house and guests during an evening party. (p. 343)

But Sologub assigns politics . . . to the background of the novel. In the oft-quoted opening to the trilogy, he makes a statement which at once challenges the conventions and traditions of life and the art of fiction itself. . . . No longer is Sologub's art even pretending to be, in the terms he himself once used, a "mirror of life."

If *The Created Legend* has a prototype, it is Shakespeare's own symbolic fantasy, *The Tempest.* The importance of *The Tempest* lies beyond its action and characters. . . . It is no coincidence that *Queen Ortruda* is given the same setting as *The Tempest*—an imaginary Mediterranean island.

Trirodov, Sologub's Prospero, is an arch-magician who skillfully strives towards good through the manipulation of magic forces around him. He exists "on the border between dream and waking." Trirodov is a complex symbol, and an understanding of the roots of his character furnishes a key to the novel itself. Like Prospero, Trirodov stands in close proximity to his author. Sologub not only makes no effort to conceal this similarity, he frequently plays upon it. . . . The most striking indication of their similarity is the way in which Trirodov often restates, almost verbatim, lines from Sologub's poetry. (pp. 344-45)

But Trirodov is not only a reflection of Sologub. Trirodov—as his name, "Mr. Trinity," indicates—is really three characters: himself, Sologub, and Prince Tankred. The basis of Sologub's conception of man as a multiple being lies in his Hindu-like conception of fundamental personality, the mystical "I" which includes all creatures. . . . The characters in Sologub's prose form a continuous chain of being, stretching from Peredonov to Trirodov. Any given character is but a single component and manifestation of a larger, more universal Self. Each character, therefore, has hidden in his past, his subconscious, and his future—as well as in *other* characters, the elements and potentialities of different existences. Each Aldonsa is capable of becoming a Dulcinea and each Dulcinea is perhaps really only an Aldonsa. Sologub's characters are aspects of each other, or they "co-habit" the same form.

The notions of the fragmentary man and the *homo multiplex* are by no means new and play an important role in nineteenth century Russian literature. . . . Sologub's chain of characters . . . is nothing unusual in itself. What is new is the degree to which he develops the device, the openness with which he presents it, and the symbolic importance which he attaches to it. (pp. 345-46)

The character of Elisaveta is fully as complex as that of Trirodov. . . . In the novel Elisaveta dresses only in shades of yellow and green, and we are told that this preference arises from "a very distant, subconscious remembrance, as though from another, previous life." . . . Thus, the character of Elisaveta too has varying representations: herself, Ortruda, and the Queen she will finally become. At two points in *Drops of Blood* the presence of Ortruda within Elisaveta is revealed. The first moment occurs when Elisaveta confesses to herself at night that she longs for Petr Matov, a rejected suitor, to come to her. . . . The second is when two tramps attack her in the woods and attempt to rape her. In the depths of her subconscious suddenly arises the strong desire "to submit, to submit sweetly." . . . (pp. 346-47)

Both Ortruda and Ljudmila commit themselves to pleasure and beauty as the solution to the unsatisfactory world that surrounds them. They each have young boys for lovers. The scenes in which young Astolf declares that Ortruda is a pagan . . . and in which she slaps him . . . are inversions of corresponding scenes from *The Petty Demon*. Ortruda's world of fantasy, however, is not a tiny bedroom but a huge and mysterious cavern. This cavern is not just her escape, it is literally herself, and when in it she feels "as if she were cut off from all the world." . . . It is another world, a world where, in the same words Ivan Karamazov used, "all is permitted." . . . But the underground world is also a terrible place which seems to Ortruda like "a journey through hell," . . . and the more

frequently she visits the cavern the more strongly the desire to torment and to see blood is awakened within her.

Ortruda is at last totally estranged from "real" life, and it soon becomes clear that death is the only solution for her. Perhaps by Ortruda's death Sologub also signifies the defeat of the erotic and the sensual as an alternative to the repulsiveness of ordinary life. The secret of access to the underground cavern is lost, and it is Elisaveta who survives and eventually will occupy her alter ego's throne not to escape from, but to transform life.

What distinguishes *The Created Legend* from Sologub's previous work is precisely this unusual—for him—atmosphere of optimism which is evident from the very beginning of the novel. . . . Sologub envisions the coming years as a cleansing flame through which people will pass and emerge purified. This aspect of the novel—the visionary—contains the author's plans and hopes for a life based upon a transcendental freedom. There will be, in addition to the class struggle, a much broader dialectic movement between two philosophies, one affirmative and the other negative, a synthesis between Christianity and Buddhism. From Christianity Sologub would take the lyrical elements: paradise, freedom, innocence. From Eastern religious thought he would take the concepts of non-being, reincarnation, and Self.

Children play a central role in Sologub's plan for the future. They are the most innocent and the least deformed by society. Children for Sologub symbolize freedom, beauty, and life itself—in short, all that he sees as lacking in society. In Sologub's future society the system of education will be drastically reformed, presumably after the model of Trirodov's colony. Children will no longer be made "to see the world through others' eyes, the eyes of the dead." . . . (pp. 347-48)

Sologub uses the image of barefoot children running and playing as a symbol of freedom from the prohibitions and unhealthy restraints of society. For this he has been criticized as having had a "foot fixation." In fact, however, this image, like many other of Sologub's symbolic themes, is drawn from Puškin. . . . The image of bare feet in both Puškin and Sologub is not a sexual fetish, but a conscious symbol of freedom, beauty, and simplicity. The prophetic vision of *The Created Legend*, quite simply put, is a return to innocence.

In the last book Trirodov arrives from Russia to become king of the United Islands, and, although we were not granted a glimpse of the "brave new world" he has come to create, that world already exists in our imaginations. A new fantasy, the future, takes the place of the old fantasy that was reality, and the novel ends, like *The Tempest*, at the beginning. (p. 348)

*Andrew Field, "'The Created Legend': Sologub's Symbolic Universe," in* Slavic and East European Journal *(© 1961 by AATSEEL of the U.S., Inc.), Vol. V, No. 4, Winter, 1961, pp. 341-49.*

**ANDREW FIELD**   (essay date 1962)

The two most important directors of the Russian symbolist theatre were Vsevolod Meyerhol'd and Nikolay Yevreinov, each of whom treated the problem of symbolist drama in a different manner. Both directors produced plays written by Sologub.

Meyerhol'd's productions were characterised by great emphasis upon form. He was concerned mainly with problems of dimension and movement, and extended the stage platform down-stage, thus bringing the action closer to the audience and rendering illusory stage techniques less feasible. Two other effects which he employed to do away with theatrical pretense were the absence of any curtain and the use of house lights during the performance. . . .

Nikolay Yevreinov, on the other hand, was concerned with achieving precisely that mood of *teatral'nost'* (theatricality) that Meyerhol'd eschewed. He argued that the unsophisticated and intentionally theatrical *balagan* or farce was the sole natural form for the theatre. He sought to convey meaning through exaggeration, humorous scenery, and unexpected representations of objects and characters. The theatre, in other words, was to be a parody of itself. Such a theatre turned naturally to fantasy and myth for its material. (p. 80)

[In his article **'Teatr odnoy volya'** (**The Theatre of One Will**)], Sologub said that the theatre should strive towards free play of mind and body through mystery, dance, music, and rapture [see excerpt above]. He declared that all we really want from the theatre is what we once wished from our childhood play: youthful, flaming ecstasy. Sologub perceived that symbols have a natural place in the mimicry and make-believe of children, and he wanted the drama and the stage to pattern themselves on the freedom of this playfulness. He gave his plays mythological, exotic, and, occasionally, frankly ironic settings, and these settings themselves—like children's make-believe—create a natural climate for symbolism and fantasy. Sologub felt that the traditional theatre served only to anger or to flatter the spectator and did not allow him to identify himself with the action and progression of the play at a level which transcends moral judgment and easy sympathy. The theatre, he felt, should not imitate life but create a life of its own that will draw the spectator away from the illusion of reality.

All these principles are associated with the work of Yevreinov. . . . (pp. 81-2)

A certain number of the ideas expressed in Sologub's article are compatible with the views of both Meyerhol'd and Yevreinov, and it is difficult in the mass of theoretical articles that were written during this period to determine exact priority of authorship. Perhaps the most important of these 'common ideas' was the notion of the actor as a puppet. Sologub claimed that a play exists only by its relation to and expression of its author. From this point of view, the more talented the actor is, the more he 'acts', the more harmful is his influence on the play. (p. 82)

There is, finally, a third group of ideas in Sologub's essay which differ from those associated with Yevreinov and those which were held in common, namely, those which correspond closely to the principles of dramatic production followed by Meyerhol'd. Like Meyerhol'd, Sologub said that it was necessary to destroy the illusion of the theatre. He felt that, in a very real sense, there are no parts, no actors. Action, said Sologub, must unfold slowly, picture after picture. The actors should recite their lines calmly and coldly, and their movements should be slow and beautiful. All minor characters are only steps leading up to the main character. Desdemona, for example, is important to Sologub only as a cause of Othello's tragic illumination. The main point of disagreement between Meyerhol'd and Sologub (the reason for which is not difficult to understand) was that Meyerhol'd wanted all meaning to come through the director, while Sologub insisted that the 'one will' in the theatre must be the author's.

It should by now be readily apparent that, in agreeing with both Meyerhol'd and Yevreinov in his essay, Sologub often contradicted himself. How is it possible for a play to be free and full of child-like make-believe and, at the same time, to proceed at a restrained and solemn pace towards a tragic conclusion? How is it possible for an actor to combine 'flaming ecstasy' with 'calm and cold enunciation'? In effect then Sologub had not one, but two loosely related dramatic theories, and these theories reflect the two main tendencies in Russian symbolist drama as a whole. It will be useful, therefore, in approaching Sologub's plays to regard them as being either 'Meyerhol'd-plays' or 'Yevreinov-plays', even though Sologub's essay precedes the theoretical works of both directors and not all of Sologub's plays, of course, were staged by them.

Sologub wrote two full length dramas in 1907, and they are the best of his 'Meyerhol'd-plays'. The first, *Dar mudrykh pchol* (The Gift of the Wise Bees) is a lyric drama based upon a Greek myth. Both Sologub and Meyerhol'd were very interested in Greek drama, and Meyerhol'd referred to **'The Gift of the Wise Bees'** as one of the most beautiful of modern plays.

The drama involves dance, gods and goddesses, and even a chorus. The story concerns Laodamia, whose husband, King Protesilaus, left for the Trojan war immediately after his wedding night. He was the first of the Greeks to set foot on shore and the first to be killed. The goddess Aphrodite, angry with him for having left his new wife so soon, appears on earth in the form of a servant girl and gives Laodamia an enchanted wax statue of her husband. Laodamia becomes so attached to the image that, when her husband has won permission to return to earth for a day, she tells him, 'Go away, deceitful ghost. Don't frighten me. My Protesilaus is with me'. Here the wax image and Protesilaus symbolise the conflict that exists between art and life, dream and reality. Sologub uses wax—the gift of the wise bees—as a symbol in many ways. As the material from which masks are made, wax symbolises the false outward shell of appearance. Also, molten wax is a symbol of death, and the grieving Laodamia wishes that she were like wax. The bees themselves, buzzing against her window, symbolise life. (pp. 82-3)

The other full length play that Sologub wrote in the same year was *Pobeda smerti* (The Victory of Death). It too was adapted from a legend, the old French myth, 'Berthe au grand pied', in which a beautiful servant takes the place of her mistress, an ugly princess who has just been married to a king. . . .

There is a short one act prologue to **'The Victory of Death'**. In it Sologub sets forth the symbolic significance which he attaches to the myth. As in the play, the servant Aldonsa (who is really Dulcinea) is rejected and mocked by all. . . . The Aldonsa-Dulcinea motif was, of course, one of Sologub's favourite symbolic themes. (p. 84)

**'The Victory of Death'** was Sologub's best 'Meyerhol'd-play', and it is one of the plays on which his claim to an important place among symbolist dramatists depends. (p. 85)

It was in his 'Yevreinov-plays' that Sologub achieved his best artistic results. He is even said to have written several of his shorter plays especially for production at Yevreinov's theatre. . . . Sologub's most successful 'Yevreinov-plays' are the two longer plays he wrote in 1909, *Nochnyye plyaski* (**Night Dances**) and *Van'ka-Klyuchnik i pazh Zhean* (**Van'ka the Lackey and Jean the Page**).

**'Night Dances'** uses many of the same structural techniques—dance, mythology, a chorus—as **'The Gift of the Wise Bees'**, but its mood is entirely different. It is a light and buoyant play; Sologub correctly subtitled it: 'a dramatic *shazka*'. The story, again, is a variation of a folktale. (pp. 85-6)

Sologub's other 1909 play, **'Van'ka the Lackey and Jean the Page'**, is far the best he wrote, and it is also the play that was most often staged. . . . The most startling thing about **'Van'ka'** is that it is really two plays which proceed side by side. First a scene is enacted in 16th-century Russia, and then, immediately following that, the same scene is presented in 16th-century France. This theme of parallel existences also figures in his trilogy and many of his short stories and was a particular favourite of the symbolists as a whole. The basic plot was adapted from a well-known Russian folk song. Indeed Sologub's greatest talent lay in taking an old legend, myth, or song and, by changing it slightly, endowing it with rich symbolic and dramatic properties which it did not have before. In **'Van'ka'** he has taken a simple story that is not in itself suitable for a play and has placed it in juxtaposition to itself in different settings. The result is a single play that is interesting, clever, and abounding in satirical overtones. (pp. 86-7)

Sologub's plays, like the rest of his prose, present a sharply contrasting picture and defy any simple label. They are representative of the best and the worst in symbolist drama. If many of the plays seem artificial and awkward, it must be remembered that this is because the symbolist dramatist has a more difficult task than the 'realistic' dramatist. Certainly, there are among them plays of unquestionable value. **'Van'ka'** stands out above all, followed closely by **'The Victory of Death'**, **'Night Dances'**, and, to a less extent, **'The Gift of the Wise Bees'**. Because they are not conventional plays they require their own special kind of theatre—an intimate, symbolist theatre. Until such a theatre again exists there can be little hope that Sologub's plays will appear on the stage, but this in itself does not constitute a judgment of their dramatic value. (p. 88)

*Andrew Field, ''The Theatre of Two Wills: Sologub's Plays,'' in* The Slavonic and East European Review *(© University of London (School of Slavonic and East European Studies) 1962; reprinted by permission), Vol. XLI, No. 96, December, 1962, pp. 80-8.*

### ALEXANDR BLOK   (essay date 1962)

The works of Fyodor Sologub stand apart in contemporary literature. He has his own devices, his own language, and his own literary forms. His versatility is also notable, for his prose is as strong as his poetry. His works may be approached from many points of view and cannot be measured by any one literary theory. The reader will find in them both moral instruction and amusement, both light and solemn reading, and, finally and simply, a beautiful style and poetic mood.

Sologub's novels and stories are mottled with the colors of life. A realistic storyteller, he relates everyday scenes and makes intelligent observations on life. The strength of his expression is close to Gogol's. There is not a trace of bookishness or artificiality, and little-known local words fit so comfortably into the framework of his story and so quickly acquire the status of ordinary words that one is amazed how seldom such words were used before.

The peculiarity of Sologub's works does not lie only in their language. Most likely their peculiarity is rooted in the reader's feeling, in the simple realistic scenes, that the writer is getting ready for something. It is as if everything we have been reading has been observed through a translucent curtain which has softened the harsh features, but now the author will lift the curtain, revealing, if only for a moment, *the monstrousness of life*.

This chaos requires immediate casting, like liquid metal which threatens to spill over the brim. The master directs all his energy toward ordering this chaos. He wants to show the reader something monstrously stupid in such a way that the reader may calmly observe it as though it were a caged beast. This beast is human vulgarity . . . , and Sologub's cage is his technique of stylization, of symmetry. In his symmetry, however, there is something shapeless and formless, a waft of something from the beyond, the unreal, the realm of nonexistence, a diabolical visage, the chaos of the nether regions. This is really a higher, bared reality, an instant which flares and impresses itself deeply in our memory, just as in life we remember those furious and fiery moments, whether good or evil, which have made our heads spin and ache.

In Sologub's first novel, **Bad Dreams,** after many pages of vividly depicting the stilted life of a small provincial town, the author tells how his hero falls into the living room of the Representative of the Nobility, a retired general. The General's appearance, conversation, surroundings are all uniformly vulgar. This atmosphere of vulgarity reaches its boiling point when the absurdity becomes sharp and terrifying: the General forces his children, ''with dull and restless eyes, with reddened and trembling lips,'' to fall down, knocking the backs of their heads against the floor, and to sneeze, weep, and dance on command. (pp. 181-82)

The tempest of vulgarity subsides and life returns into its ordinary cycle. Sologub's bright instant of chaos sweeps down from the nether world and is given flesh in some demicreature. The hero of Sologub's greatest novel, the schoolteacher Peredonov, a dirty and stupid animal, a ''petty demon,'' is threatened by a corporeal terror, both a creature and not a creature, whirling in the dust by the side of the road when he goes to be married. Perhaps it is the terror of life's vulgarity and ordinariness, or, if you prefer, it is a threatening image of fear, despondency, despair, helplessness. Sologub christened this terror, ''Nedotykomka.'' . . . (p. 182)

If Sologub's prose most frequently embodies the horror of life, he speaks more often in his poetry about the beauties of life and about quiet. His muse is either mad or sad. The object of his poetry is more the soul interpreting the world itself than the world interpreted within the soul.

All of Sologub's work is characterized by tragic humor. The most lively, the most sensitive artists of our century have been stricken with an illness unknown to physicians and psychologists. This illness is like a spiritual disorder and may be called ''irony.'' . . .

Dostoevsky, Leonid Andreev, and Sologub are, of course, Russian satirists, revealers of social vices and sores, but God save us from their destructive laughter, from their irony. (p. 183)

[Sologub] does not say no to his Nedotykomka; he is tied to it with a secret vow of faithfulness. Sologub would not change the gloom of the existence he knows for any other existence. Only a foolish reader would take Sologub's songs to be complaints. The enchanter Sologub, the ironical Russian Verlaine, will not complain to anyone. . . .

A sacred formula which continually reoccurs in Sologub is repeated in one way or another by all writers: ''For one's own sake, and not for Russia, renounce oneself'' (Gogol). ''In order to be oneself, one must renounce oneself'' (Ibsen). Literally everyone repeats this formula, unavoidably stumbles onto it, if he lives a spiritual life that is deep. This formula would be banal if it were not sacred. It is the most difficult thing to understand. (p. 184)

> Alexandr Blok, ''Alexandr Blok on Fyodor Sologub'' (originally published in two parts in his Sobranie sochinenee, Vol. 5, State Publisher of Arts and Letters, 1962), in The Complection of Russian Literature: A Cento, edited by Andrew Field (copyright © 1971 by Andrew Field; reprinted with the permission of Atheneum Publishers, New York), Atheneum, 1971, pp. 181-84.

## F. D. REEVE (essay date 1966)

[Reeve goes beyond the standard interpretation of The Petty Demon, as demonstrated by D. S. Mirsky (see excerpt above) and Roman S. Struc (see excerpt below), suggesting that the novel presents a total view of society and, in particular, demonstrates the power of language to shape one's perception of reality.]

[The Petty Demon] has been read either as a libidinal nightmare or, in terms of another prejudice, as an instance of the absurd polarities of Sologub's symbolism. A step toward understanding it is to consider it in relation to the Russian symbolist movement (from about 1895 to 1910), whose adherents, much like the French symbolists earlier, considered art to be a total view of society, a dramatization of social and political ''problems'' and their solution by the ''logic of imagination,'' the revitalization of language and artistic form. (p. 303)

In *The Petty Demon* we are given a society out-of-joint that has lost all value and all chance of communion, a society with an inadequate language. Prevailing social abuse of language occasions Sologub's exploitation of words to restore reality, an exploitation that, in a sense, leads Sologub away from the very society he is trying to circumscribe. The reader is taken as the norm of that society, an individual consumed by the confusion of his own subjectivity and the loss of significant communication with anyone on any level. Because the language lacks suppleness, refinement, and the precision of gesture—because there is no such thing as what Edmund Wilson has called ''the ordinary language of literature''—and because the relations perceived are dynamic, Sologub is prevented from narrating or from allegorizing. He has to move from the world as he perceives it into his book. He must create in his book special situations which in themselves symbolize the intended meaning. He must invent his form as he goes along in order to bring back to his reader the compelling ''logic'' of a real perception. His book is a sign of how far away he has been taken, and he must fight through it back to the world he first perceived. When he says, in the preface to the second edition, that his novel is a scientifically accurate mirror and that ''both the deformed and the beautiful are reflected in it equally exactly,'' he means not only that men are good and bad for the same reasons and in much the same ways, but also that the ''duality'' of man is finally judged or made real by the power and excellence of uncaused talent. The precision is within the book, not in the applicability of the book to life. (pp. 308-09)

But it is not consequently accountable to life. It is neither an awkward poem nor a moral documentary. It makes its own life—it is symbolic action made—consciously out of inadequate words. When it is made, the words are, as in a library book, expired. . . . (p. 309)

The depravity—the fascination with self-abuse and the meaningless defacing of what is an extension of someone else in a frenzy of self-affirmation—the seduction into self-righteous barbarity, as presented in the book, is the mark of the success of evil. Corruption that is respectable, like the Devil in *The Karamazov Brothers*, is real corruption. It is undefinable and incorrigible. What is Anthony's advantage in his picture is that the horrors come as symbols. Or, that is our advantage as we look at the picture. They are frightening but not invincible. Peredonov, however, has no anagogical or moral ladder up which to escape from his vision of horror.

The first moment in the process of self-destruction is the self-enforced delusion of superiority. One is not merely different in one's corruption; one is better. Peredonov is satisfied by what he feeds on—himself—since he has excluded all other possible relations. He is charmed by his turpitude and afraid of usual people. In contradistinction to Don Quixote, that moral visionary whose books were burned for him, Peredonov—the ''Don done over''—burns his books himself. . . . He is afraid that he will be read out of his corrupt mediocrity. . . .

The world given the reader is peopled with devils and fools. The devils impose on the fools because the fools yield to any attraction. (Evil in any form is at least initially attractive.) The devils enjoy success up to that point at which their activity becomes wholly introverted and they absurdly and pathetically avenge themselves on themselves. At that point, all common value is lost—this is the given condition—and whatever has worked has generated its own validity. The signs, like empty words, reveal internal pauperism and barbarity. (pp. 311-13)

The curse of insensibility—the noise of dumbness—threatens life. Words fascinate people, playing on the surface of consciousness as light and shadow play on water. But because the words are perverted or broken, they are tools of torture. (p. 313)

Words evaluate behavior, arrange celebrations, provoke fights, cast spells. The tacit power that works among men is imported into understanding by the ambivalent but precise turns of words. When Peredonov grasps his nose, he shows he is under the spell of the language. When, later, he talks of having been seduced by black magic and says, ''Until I recited the countercharm, I was completely drugged,'' he understands that he got over the spell of words with words. The language, itself a possible response to fear, has made him afraid. And his demonic activity consists of practicing a kind of verbal duplicity or legerdemain: he wants the princess to write the words he needs—announcement of promotion—and he goes around talking deceptively to others to secure his own best advantage.

Each man's total, or mythic, view of reality impinges on the others' to force, somewhere, the inevitable disillusion of discovered self-deception. The reality which the symbols are intended to apprehend is, for each man, only the ''reality'' of one consciousness. The continual and necessary effort at judgment is ironic. The quest for power is both ridiculous and true. In this book, among these fragmentary characters, it is ultimately self-destruction. It is partly comic, since there is the common, systematic denominator of desire or power, and partly horrible, since it is, like the activity of Kafka's beetle, plausible.

The book as a whole stands against the characters: that is, the book comes to judgment. The ''petty demon'' is a symbol of a total understanding, a motionless figure of despair, in a mind outside the book.

Literally, the *nedotykomka* represents a deliberate symbolization by the author—retained from an earlier poem which begins with it as a dramatic persona—characterizing not so much Peredonov's state of mind (he clearly is a paranoiac) as his contact with another reality. (pp. 314-15)

Sologub assumes, like Aristotle, that essential conflict is individual and ethical, but, unlike Aristotle, that rational solutions or demonstrations of solutions are implausible because the intellect is neither virtuous nor vicious. Who asks for solution only discusses himself. The "problem" is the system of problems which people live by. The "solution" is the game of animating the problems—that is, of playing them off against each other so that one problem is both the impulse to and the resolution of the next. The whole is a huge ethical gesture which, because it is ineffable gesture, yields only to a series of particular dramatizations. In this sense, reality is a group of essentially moral scenes each moving away from and back into the others and pointing toward an ultimate vision, presented as reality contemporaneous with us, to which we must assent.

The vision as symbol has perhaps two directly analogous moments elsewhere in the book: the dreams and the murder of the bug. Lyudmila's first dream, for example, makes both her and us conscious of her reality. It functions in the book as an expression of the naturally secret, the private, in the only way we do express it. It is a particular, sexual dream, a sudden revelation to and of Lyudmila. . . . It also serves, literally and allegorically, as an obvious symbol of physical and spiritual Eden in the book's general moral structure.

Peredonov's murder of the bug is an image given as dramatic action. It symbolizes the reality of individual consciousness moved against the pattern of consciousness. . . . At the end of the book, when he kills a man, not a bug, he effectually kills himself—he loses consciousness. He, like his words, is used up. But when he kills the bug, he celebrates the act. He takes his new sense of size from the fact of having killed, of having accumulated enough power in evil to transcend more defamation. This also leads to the irony of his delusion. . . . Self-gratification works against the self: because there is no system in corruption, either, the delusion is like the obverse of a two-sided mirror. As one tries to get to that invisible reality in the middle, which does not move but is, one seems only to get smaller and smaller, that is, farther and farther away. Against the series of conflicts taken in Freudian terms, the book, as form, is the imposition of laws of meaning on the chimerical and passionate violence of all the devils. (pp. 316-18)

The dichtomy between what seems to be and what seems to be able to be is terrifying and humiliating, like any perception of implausible contrast. The original esthetic impulse that identified the moment or the thing as real has discovered that that moment belongs in a system made intelligible by the life of the symbol. . . . But everything except the symbols, being transient and outside a communicable system, lacks reality. Everything else turns against the person who mistakes it as real. (pp. 318-19)

Since Peredonov lives off his delusion and depends, for his life, on others taking his delusion at face value, he is surrendered in all his subjectivity to the overwhelming and chaotic subjectivities of everybody else. He cannot see what they want or think, and they cannot see him except as a madman. Everyone is afraid of losing himself—his position. Nobody can do

anything to help anybody. . . . Serious efforts at self-explanation are, consequently, bad jokes, that sort of twisted irony which is barely instructive and very painful. At one point, for example, Peredonov and Volodin wear neckties as emblems expressing hidden feelings. The preposterous fantasy of the situation quickly shatters illusions, but, in this world of damned isolation, no one's attitude toward himself is ever altered. (p. 319)

Self-revelation to another person is also keeping oneself socially concealed. The alternative, rather mystical, even Christian, is equally real. Whichever way one moves one also simultaneously moves in the opposite way. One is always doubly exposed.

Peredonov deliberately, madly exposes himself. He attaches his delusions to (most charming symbol of all) the society of cards and blinds all the men and women there. Cards are not only a symbol of social games in the present but also, like the tarot pack, a means for revealing the mysteries of the future. They are mysterious in their self-sufficient competency, which all the more poignantly measures Peredonov's impotency. . . . He cannot tolerate their self-confidence. He cannot endure their authority. So he kills them. He arranges an *auto da fé* which turns on its inquisitor. His martyrs and victims mock and frighten him. The murder is a bitter joke. (p. 321)

The symbols themselves become further, purer symbols through the alchemy of gesture, and we as readers are prepared to accept the mockery because of the sympathy which Sologub provokes. As we read, we soon become aware that even Peredonov's ambitions are only half credible. If they were wholly credible, the book would be a sort of humorous, medieval allegory of Hell. The structure of the book, however, makes all the personae plausible. They believe one another, and they love themselves.

As Peredonov moves through his comedy into his agony, as he tries to grasp his illusions, like Quixote at the beginning of his quest, we condone his acquisitiveness and destructiveness. But, because he, unlike Quixote, wholly fails, we are removed from him to an understanding of the book itself as symbol of an actual relation and an artistic perception. The closer we, like Peredonov, try to get to invisible reality in the center of the circle, the smaller we seem to become, the farther away we seem from ourselves. Outside the symbols there is no truth, for outside them there is nothing real. Finally, even Peredonov himself becomes a symbol. We understand the book as a symbol, and we reject the life within it. Our symbolic response is the real solution. (pp. 322-23)

Although perhaps no more sensitive to primordial Dionysian ecstasies or to an Eden of love than Peredonov, we know that he, like the book that encompasses the "problem" of his society, is not decadent. The author's disillusionment is not romantic. For him, society is a system of uncaused problems operating fortuitously without value or meaning. It cannot cause its own solution. Love, like hatred, is only a necessary invention for personal security. Usually, it amounts to less. What life adds up to—short of the mystery which Sologub assumes lies beyond, at the center—is known only as a sum of obvious absurdities. What it means is the burden of his book's words. (pp. 323-24)

*F. D. Reeve, "Art As Solution: Sologub's Devil,"* in Modern Fiction Studies (© 1957 by Purdue Research Foundation, West Lafayette, Indiana 47907, U.S.A.), Vol. III, No. 2, Summer, 1957 (and reprinted in a different form as "'The Petty Demon',"* *in his* The Russian Novel, *McGraw-Hill Book Company, 1966, pp. 302-24).*

## EVELYN BRISTOL (essay date 1971)

Most of Sologub's collections of verse can be understood as the work of a skeptical idealist. The transcendental world that once seemed near to Blok was the aim too of Sologub. He was among the first of the Symbolist poets in Russia, and his work reflected the evolutions of that movement; like most Symbolists he retained to the end a spiritual nostalgia which was lost in the next generation.

His first two volumes of verse appeared in 1896. In *Book I* [*Stikhi. Kniga I*] he is barely distinguishable from the vapid ''art-for-art'' poets of the eighties; his subjects are theirs—melancholia and the beauties of nature. But even this book has some notes straight from French decadence, a perverseness that indicates that some underlying frustration is at work. In the second book [*Stikhi. Kniga II*] he is definitely a man of the new school. He now shows an irresistible attraction to reveries and dreams, the significant theme that came from Poe through Baudelaire. His melancholia is deepened by metaphysical causes: He hates time and space and longs for the absolute. He continues to admire nature, the poet's ally and refuge and a reminder of an otherworldly beauty. Konstantia Balmont was his only rival as a serious new poet at this time. Both were labeled decadent and were derivative of the French movement, both dealt, so far, in pessimism and isolation in nature.

In 1904, when Sologub brought out his next two volumes of verse, [*Sobranie stikhov. Kniga III-IV*], the Symbolists formed a coterie of poets who restively accepted the aegis of Valery Briusov. . . . Sologub remained pessimistic, gloomy, and resentful. In *Book III* fruitless dreaming alternates with frustrated idealism. He invented a fantasy world to depict the utopia that was the object of his longing. (p. 268)

The discrepancy between his vision and reality made Sologub the most forceful poet of metaphysical despair within the Russian Symbolist movement. . . .

Sologub's *Book IV* is still more explicitly philosophical. In it two arch Symbolist positions contend with each other. Here the extreme individualistic current of the school finds expression in Sologub's notorious solipsism; the world is his own creation. On the other hand, the desire of Symbolists to perceive a spiritual unity pervading the universe is also present. But, given Sologub's pessimism, he imagines the universe as an evil process emanating from a malevolent, tyrannical spirit-of-becoming. Only nature can instill the idea of a beneficent source. Now the pale melancholia of *Book I* has become a mordantly pessimistic philosophy that is a perversion of German romantic idealism. (p. 269)

[When the Russo-Japanese War and Revolution of 1905 took place, Sologub published] a small book called *For the Homeland* [*Rodine*]. It is offered as a patriotic book expressing devotion to the country and the opening poems are ''Hymns to the Homeland.'' The war is injected into the volume with laments for the dead. But allusions to civic strife and abuse make up the better part of the book, and it ends pessimistically with a depiction of the dead victims of a violent repression. This book marks the first eruption of actuality into Sologub's poetic world.

His next slim volume, *The Serpent* [*Zmii*], appears to be a return to metaphysics. It consists of an outburst of vitriolic resentment against the sun, the creator and sustainer of life, which is equated with the ancient symbol of evil, the serpent. Emotionally, the sun has the same role as the hostile spirit-of-becoming of *Book IV*. However, *The Serpent* coincided with deep public disillusionment, and some of its heat may be due to an underlying political frustration.

Having published a volume of translations from Verlaine, Sologub again appeared with a full-length book in 1908. *The Flaming Circle* [*Plamennyi krug*] reads like an anthology of Sologub's concerns and resources as a poet. . . . The main problem of *The Flaming Circle* is again the plight of the individual longing for a non-existent ideal. Sologub's imagery is generally imaginative. He opens the book with a section of poems purporting to deal with his own past lives, beginning with Adam, who pines for his first wife Lilith. Elsewhere he is a dog at a royal court. A second theme is hatred for the material world, which is depicted as crass and base. (p. 270)

[In] the vein of a moody diary, the poet escapes into a life of inertia, dreams, and magic. In passing, he creates a new idyll, this time on earth, of consoling nature and innocent love. But he closes with his dilemmas unresolved and with a consideration of the philosophical meaning of death—the last consolation.

In the prewar period the Symbolists had become distinguished writers, and their collected works began to appear, Sologub's among them. It was an era of immense literary ferment and the younger poets now reacted against the metaphysical premises of Symbolism. Some returned to realism; others went on to experiments that foreshadowed surrealism in Europe. For his *Collected Works* [*Sobranie sochenenii*], Sologub rearranged the poems from his first seven volumes into four new ones, adding later as well as previously unpublished poems. Each of these volumes is like a lyrical diary, with its own predominant mood. But all share a conclusion that was new for Sologub: spiritual optimism and an acceptance of the real world.

*Azure Mountains* [*Lazurnye gory*] opens with Sologub's underlying theme: nostalgia for an ideal. From here, he proceeds to the metaphysical despair of *Book III*, on through a long escape into a ''night life'' of dreams and sorrow, and arrives at a contemplation of divinity in nature. He closes with the earthly paradise that seemed a simplified idyll in *The Flaming Circle*, but which here turns out to be real. Sologub couches his modern, metaphysical musings with their startling imagery in clear and polished language. He never cultivated the elusiveness and nuances that are associated with the Symbolists. His verse forms too are conventional and even old-fashioned.

For *Ascents* [*Voskhozhdeniia*], Sologub reserved his sharper statements of metaphysical resentment. The book opens in a mood of emotional loss and peevishness. Its cause is the impasse of *Book IV*: either the universe is an endless, meaningless, suffering process or only the creation of a poet-solipsist. Poems on nature and love relieve the gloom. Suddenly the actual world of *For the Homeland* interrupts these pessimistic thoughts. Having broken out of their circle, he ends again with the quiet world of nature and love which closed the first volume.

In *Serpent Eyes* [*Zmeinye ochi*] the poems are arranged, for the first time, in chronological order, and yet basically the same ''story'' arises. For the most part, the book is another protest against reality, but without the philosophical underpinning of *Ascents*. The poet's emphasis here is on the attendant moods, particularly a spiritual emptiness that is distracted by passing fancies. A number of poems dated 1905 and later are new. Among them are hints that romantic rebelliousness might be forgotten through a turn to humanism. Beyond this, there is no resolution in attitudes. However, there is a genuine change in Sologub's language. He achieves an increased flexibility in style and vividness of detail, so that subjects appear in sharper focus, as though the atmosphere had cleared.

In *Orbs of Pearl* [*Zhemchuzhnye svetila*], which is also chronologically arranged, Sologub's poetic evolution is plainly seen. An introductory poem shows his love for nature as the basis for his acceptance of the world. (pp. 271-72)

The text opens in the 1880s with wistful and rural poems. The nineties show that social utopianism and Christian aspirations originally preceded his nostalgia for an otherworldly ideal. Metaphysical disillusionment reigns from 1900 to 1904; this was also a time of fantastic imagery and figurative style. The period 1905 to 1912 is life-affirming, though the universe is still conceived in tragic terms. The poet resigns himself to the unattainability of the ideal, remains reverent before the good (Christ in Gethsemane), renounces his dream life, and turns to love the world, imperfect as it is. His imagery returns to the everyday and his language assumes the intonations of a bookish mind in conversation. This closing reconciliation is the most convincing yet.

*Charms of the Earth* [*Ocharovaniia zemli*] bears out, as its title suggests, the life-loving direction of the earlier volumes. It consists entirely of new poems written in 1913. Quite startlingly, 178 of them are triolets, a short verse form with rigorous repetitions; this was a playful act on Sologub's part. There are also thirteen regular poems. Many of the triolets are travel impressions written on lecture tours. In them Sologub greets not only nature, but also a whole new world of commonplace settings, whether provincial locales or the petit-bourgeois crowds of the city. The amount of sympathetic observation and lightheartedness is entirely new for Sologub. Yet art, especially in its ability to transform and elevate reality, is also an essential part of this book.

In 1915, Sologub responded to the war with a small, patriotic book, *War* [*Voina*], in which he lauds Russia's purposes, depreciates an expansionist Germany, and depicts the horrors of fighting. In the following year he returned to his metaphysical concerns in *The Red Poppy* [*Alyi mak*], which follows a cycle resembling that of the first four volumes of the *Collected Works*. The opening sections concern the pleasures of life, but soon our attention is turned to the negative through a short section in which the world is seen through the eyes of dogs. Then the world seems empty and society mean. In this situation Sologub calls for staunchness and resoluteness. The final section includes the poems from *War*, but other poems have been added which broaden the book's scope: The war must awaken the people to efforts which will transform the world toward the ideal. Thus Sologub's anxiety about World War I coincided with a humanizing of his Symbolist aspirations.

After the Revolution, Sologub remained in Russia, a prestigious if half-forgotten figure, active in some literary organizations. He published eight small books of verse, two on civic and revolutionary themes. *The Toll of the Great Church Bell* [*Velikii blagovest*] is an enlargement of *The Toll of the Cathedral Bell*. Both are mainly collections of poems written before 1917. They record Sologub's early utopianism, the rising tide of the revolution, and a very few post-revolutionary speculations. Six of the last books deal with familiar themes such as nature, love, and death. (pp. 273-74)

Each of the six books has its own thematic slant. In *Incense* [*Fimiamy*], Sologub takes up man's place in the universe; there are echoes of his romantic rebellion in a certain atmosphere of violent contradiction and passionate involvement. In *One Love* [*Odna lyubov*] he extols erotic love as the one vital source of life and the origin of transforming inspiration as well. *Blue Sky* [*Nebo goluboe*] has no philosophical point; it expresses an unthinking love for life, usually in connection with nature or love. Its last section was published separately with the title *Panpipes* [*Svirel'*]. This is a remarkable cycle of imitations of French classical pastoral poems on shepherds and shepherdesses, all written in a twelve-day period in the spring of the famine year 1921 in Petrograd. In *The Enchanted Cup* [*Charodeinaia chasha*] the poet turns to nature in its intoxicating aspects and to the mysterious in life. *The Wayside Fire* [*Koster dorozhnyi*] again has notes of philosophical restiveness, and the presence of death is felt. Among the poems written after 1917 are some of Sologub's best; he continued to grow in stature as long as he wrote. The later poems are devoid, whatever their convictions, of any Symbolist prettiness. They have a stark clarity that brings to mind a honed and elegant classicism. In the end, Sologub saw poetry itself as the creative effort whereby man transforms the world and reaches toward the perfect and mysterious. (pp. 275-76)

> *Evelyn Bristol, "Fedor Sologub As Lyric Poet," in* The Russian Review *(copyright 1971 by The Russian Review, Inc.), Vol. 30, No. 3, July, 1971, pp. 268-76.*

### ROMAN S. STRUC (essay date 1972)

[*Struc's focus on Sologub's Manichaean view of life as demonstrated in* The Petty Demon *is considered the standard interpretation of that novel.*]

If the *nedotykomka* [in Sologub's *The Petty Demon* (*Melkii bes*)] is one of the most repulsive products of the artistic imagination, its nominal progenitor, Peredonov, outdoes this creature in ugliness, imaginative cruelty, malice, dishonesty, and sly stupidity. But Peredonov is no exception. All the characters of the novel, the whole town, in fact, live either in a slumber of vulgar complacency or, upon awakening, in a frenzy of destructiveness. (p. 77)

The saner townspeople are no less frightening than the guests of Peredonov. Just as Chichikov of *Dead Souls* visits the local worthies to buy up "dead souls," another Don Quixote, Peredonov, makes a series of calls on the local officials in order to ingratiate himself with them with a view to a possible promotion. He proceeds by slandering his colleagues and students, dropping hints reflecting on their political and moral unreliability, and tries to exonerate himself of imaginary charges brought against him; in short, he plays the game according to the prevailing rules. Although the man is clearly insane—the novel is also an account of a rapidly developing psychosis—none of his hosts seems to notice it; indeed, some of them are as insane as he is. During one such visit, this time with the local district attorney, Peredonov is assumed to be a criminal who has come to confess his crime, although one must also assume that the two know each other personally. Thus Peredonov's paranoia is only an enlargement upon the pathological suspiciousness and basic corruption of the town and its inhabitants. I do not mean to claim that the novel . . . contains an intentionally realistic account of affairs in a small Russian town. Indeed, the novel creates a rather hermetic universe which, neither

Russian nor foreign, should be seen in the spirit of an inverted utopia rather than as a commentary on social reality. It is primarily an artistic vision, and a grim one at that. Sologub's "Platonic" eye strips reality of its nonessentials and exposes it as an inferno in which man is a beast guided by the lowest instincts. The social reality of Sologub's utopia is the result of savage internecine war, with Peredonov as its chief protagonist, a man whose pockets are stuffed with caramels which he bestows on his favorites as a sign of his grace. Nothing in his personality can even remotely redeem him. Everything about him is "unbeautiful." . . . Nothing Peredonov touches remains unsoiled, often in a physical sense, just as often by his obscene imagination. If Dostoevsky's protagonists are projected as complex men whose basic dualism (insect-angel) drives them to debauchery and crime, Sologub's hero appears as a uniquely monolithic character. Peredonov is the negative counterpart of Myshkin in *The Idiot;* the latter's unqualified innocence has its reverse analogy in the former's total corruption. Yet it would be wrong to assume that Peredonov is a happy "petty demon." Obliquely, Sologub shows in the mad restlessness, the gloom, the pensiveness of his protagonist, his essential dissatisfaction with himself. To be sure, his horizon is strictly circumscribed. The target of his pathological activity is a school inspectorship and the respect of his peers. But his distorted vision does not allow him to transcend the self-created magic circle of intrigue, gossip, and calumny. Corruption within and without places Peredonov in the darkest corner of the Platonic cave, with no ray penetrating its recesses. (pp. 77-8)

It has often been said that Peredonov and his kind are a caricature, an exaggerated picture of provincial Russia, with all its boredom, vulgarity, hopeless pettiness. In a novel of even implicit social criticism, one expects and finds a much more explicit identification of the causes of unsatisfactory conditions; one also expects, if only implicitly, some suggestion of a solution to the problems described. Sologub's novel, however, contains neither overt nor implied criticism, except in the very general sense that a novel, as a verbal construct, unintentionally partakes of phenomenal reality and, by implication, social reality. (p. 79)

Yet there is a realm in *The Petty Demon* which escapes the ugly tentacles of Peredonov. The connection between the Peredonov-plot and the Sasha-Ludmila episode is rather flimsy. Sasha is a pupil of Peredonov's whom he singles out for persecution and slander because of a fantastic suspicion that his pupil is a girl masquerading as a boy, but primarily because of his extraordinary physical beauty and his disgust for ugliness. The somewhat older Ludmila, however, plays the aggressive part in the affair. The feats of sensuality Ludmila and Sasha celebrate stand in direct opposition to the vulgar sensuality of Peredonov. The eroticism does not seek sexual consummation; indeed that seems to be one of the taboos imposed upon the relationship by Lumila, and therefore it is a relationship which is at once daringly wanton and esthetically restrictive. Beauty, in Ludmila's view, does not involve ethical considerations. She manifestly worships the beauty of the human body, yet without the ethical implications present in Gogol and Dostoevsky. (p. 80)

The title of a less successful though no less curious trilogy is *The Created Legend (Tvorimaya legenda).* This title, which in Russian more than in English suggests both a "created" legend and a legend in the process of being created, perhaps best explains the significance of the Ludmila-Sasha episode. Created or perhaps even contrived beauty seems to be the answer to a world ugly and evil. Sologub's literary hero is Don Quixote, who has the ability to do precisely what Ludmila and Sasha are doing. In the midst of ugliness, vulgarity, and repulsive sexuality, they are creating a world totally apart. It is created by Ludmila, who painstakingly scents herself and her lover with the most exquisite perfumes from Paris and develops the legend of beauty by continuously trying on new dresses and dressing her lover in girls' clothes. She and Sasha taste the thrill of being new people—gypsies, nymphs, and pages—and thus they remove themselves from the laws of the ugly world in which they are obliged to live. . . . It is obvious, then, that it is the poet, the creator of magic, illusions, and beautiful falsehoods, who is projected as the antipode to the world created ugly and evil. Sologub more than anyone realized the precariousness of "the created legend," for he knew what a vulnerable dwelling it had to be. Such a realization frequently becomes the source of his irony. Can Dulcinea survive the confrontation with Aldonsa? At the local masquerade ball Sasha appears as a beautifully attired geisha; it is only by mere chance that he is not discovered and beaten up by the vulgar company of guests. Shivering and in tears, he makes his escape. The legend ends with a rather sordid scandal. No one, including perhaps the creators of the legend, is safe from the all-pervasive vulgarity of the age. (pp. 80-1)

> *Roman S. Struc, "'Petty Demons' and Beauty: Gogol, Dostoevsky, Sologub,"* in Essays on European Literature, *Peter Uwe Hohendahl, Herbert Lindenberger, Egon Schwarz, eds. (copyright 1972 by Washington University Press), Washington University Press, 1972, pp. 61-82.*

## MURL G. BARKER   (essay date 1977)

The controlling force in [Sologub's] legend-making, that which praises madness and courts death, is the author's "I." It is an oversimplification to label Sologub a solipsist, for it was not merely a preoccupation with the self that he was condoning. Sologub sees his inner world, the "I," or ego, as a dynamic force, an entity of reserve energy, capable of creating new worlds to escape the evils inherent in the existing order of things. And Sologub even defended the solipsist by asserting that seeing the world through one's own experiences puts the responsibility for what happens in the world on the individual. And in this way, man strives for that merging of the self with the One Will.

This world of Sologub's unfolds through his short stories and indeed, he was a prolific writer in the genre: there are nine volumes in his published works. The strictures of the short story curtail the author's tendency to become diffuse as he often does in his less successful novels. The combination of realistic detail with symbolism is both startling and haunting. [The stories presented in *The Kiss of the Unborn and Other Stories*] bring the reader into this decadent, solipsistic, erotic, Manichean, escapist world of Sologub's.

The first story of the collection, **"The Wall and the Shadows"** is a masterpiece of the genre. Published in 1894, it is a chilling combination of realism (the study of madness) and symbolism (a testament to the author's view of reality and his inherent escapism). Volodya is a typical portrait in the Sologubian gallery: being twelve years old, he stands at the abyss of maturity, where he can comprehend the evil raging around him. This is particularly true of the school, a setting Sologub will return to over and over again to dramatize the suffering of innocent children. It is a microcosm of the real world, where Gogol's hierarchy of Very Important Personages sets up a chain reaction of brutality ending with the children who become the real victims. Ivan Karamazov's question about the injustice of innocent childrens' suffering is immediately brought to mind.

Volodya's physical appearance is lightly sketched by the author and suggests his vulnerability. The boy's paleness is also symbolic: he has not been touched by the "Dragon" or "Serpent," Sologub's symbolic reference to the sun which incites destructive passions. And those large eyes are significant, for they are the receptors through which the boy is burdened by the truths of reality.

The emotional relationship between Volodya and his mother borders on the perverse. Their vexations and fears and the intense affection they share, plus the fact that Volodya speaks like an adult, force the boy into the role of a surrogate husband.

The shadows evolve into a symbolic world starting with the funny girl in a peaked hat and developing into the image of a helpless and homeless old man being felled by hostile elements. At first the shadows seem to offer Volodya an escape from a reality which is defined as repulsive through the scenes at school and the descriptions of nature. But the shadows gradually gain control over Volodya and become his master. And since Sologub has stated, through Volodya, that man is trapped by walls, then the only escape is madness or death. In this early story, death is not courted by Sologub. Here, the legend-making does not result in beauty, but rather Volodya, and later, his mother, create legends on those symbolic walls, legends which control their creators and drive them mad.

Religion, another possibility for escape, is rejected in **"The Wall and the Shadows."** Sologub's attitude toward organized religion will change with time, but here, the mother's prayers are ineffectual and the icons and church appear alien and offer no consolation. One shadow is likened to an angel that is flying off to heaven from a "depraved and grieving world." There is a heaven then, and there are angels, but Volodya and his mother are isolated and trapped within the walls of reality. Sologub asks, "Isn't there something significant, yet scorned, being carried away from the world in the gentle hands of the angel?" Perhaps it is Volodya's (and his mother's) innocence, or their creative will. But while the angel is able to soar above those symbolic walls, Volodya and his mother turn to them for their escape which is shadow-making. But their ultimate escape from reality is madness. (pp. xxiii-xxv)

The gloomy drama of a youth destroyed in a historical setting is found in . . . **"The Youth Linus."** . . . [The] story is a realistic account of a miraculous event: the resurrection of the slain Linus, an innocent victim of ruthless brute force and savage slaughter, who comes back again and again to haunt the troops with his blood-stained body as a symbol of their wanton destructiveness. Linus belongs to the same genus as the suffering child who figures so prominently in the works of Dostoevsky. Linus is a child in age only; he possesses a wisdom far beyond his years. The boy is catapulted into the adult world by his recognition of the evil which the Roman soldiers represent. The adult perception of the child is reflected in his speech: he addresses the old centurion in a linguistically mature style; and the content of his address strains for credulity when the reader remembers that a youth is speaking. His speech symbolically addresses a far wider audience than the group of soldiers: Linus is speaking for all of the insulted and injured who have been victims of destructive forces.

**"The Youth Linus"** is an example of Sologub at his most pessimistic. There is no light-hearted or even sardonic character

. . . to relieve the all-pervading gloom. The syntax is complicated, the prose heavy, the repetitions monotonous. The heavy tread of the horses' hoofs pounding down on a despairing earth, and the evil Dragon-Serpent inflaming the man-beast with the desire for blood allow for no escape: the natural world, the animal world, and the human world unite into one repulsive and horrifying image. The reappearances of Linus do not offer the antithetical escape which is usually found in Sologub. The story presents no alternative to the brutality. The miracle of Linus's appearance is no escape, and death is no escape. No one is triumphant; the reader is left only with a sense of all-pervading horror. (pp. xxix-xxx)

[**"Death by Advertisement"**] contains a bit of Sologubian self-debunking. In this story, the author mixes the highest form of abstract symbolism with Gogolian humor. Some of Sologub's critics were appalled at his "decadent" preoccupation with death, and this story might be interpreted as the author's parodying his purported attitude towards the theme when the hero, Rezanov, advertises for someone to play the role of his Death.

Here are the blurred edges so favored by the symbolists: there is a "someone" who talks to Rezanov; and the whole mood of a dreamlike reality and the hallucinations (when he does not know whether or not he is speaking or thinking). The dialogue between Rezanov and Death is loaded with symbolic overtones and undercurrents: the repetition of such words as "melancholy," "pining," "sadness," "yearning," "torment," and the abundance of exclamation points parody the symbolists' significant preoccupations. And Death herself ("death" has a feminine gender in Russian) mocks the symbolists' myths with her vision of their ruler sprinkling the stars with a mixture made from Rezanov's soul juices and her quiet tears.

What is particularly bizarre in this story is Death's death. In his rather sly twist of events at the end, was Sologub symbolically killing off his preoccupation with death? Perhaps the author meant to imply that he was releasing himself from symbolism's obtuse legends and the decadents' handmaiden of finality.

The characters Rezanov observes in the post office are true Gogolian types. Their behavior depresses the hero and intensifies his desire for death. In this scene, Sologub piles up insignificant detail about inconsequential persons and the result is a study of the grotesque. A perfect example is the woman with the wart who is not only characterized by that wart, but also is fated to carry a ridiculous and hilarious name. (Ruslan is the hero of Pushkin's poetic fairy tale "Ruslan and Ludmila." "Zvonareva" might be translated as "trumpeter." She stands isolated from equally bizarre caricatures by a wart and an absurd name.

The longest story in the collection, **"In The Crowd,"** . . . is an entirely different matter. The story is based on fact: on May 18, 1896, some three thousand people perished and many more were injured in a crush on the Khodynka field near Moscow. (pp. xxx-xxxi)

**"In The Crowd"** is an excellent example of Sologub's complete control over the genre of the short story: it is a forceful blending of realism and symbolism, and its cohesiveness in content and form is impressive. The narrator plays an active role in the story from the very beginning where, as he is matter-of-factly describing the events in Mstislavl, he adds a judiciously wry comment or outright condemnation of human folly. There is that Gogolian stratification of society when we are presented with a picture of very important people who are as petty and vulgar as the lowliest peasant. The Udoev children are somewhere in the middle: not only do they represent the innocence of youth, but they also stand in the middle as a kind of collective Everyman. Their individual personalities are rather sketchily presented; it is their innocence, naïveté, and good will that are important.

The nightmare is built up gradually. The metaphysical horror keeps pace with the physical. Sologub utilizes opposites again to develop the tension: the expanse of the heavens in contrast to the crowd, darkness versus daylight, children against adults, coolness and heat.

It is through the children that the reader views the metamorphosis of man-beast into man-devil. The cohesion which existed at the beginning is fragmented into a bedlam, which is reflected in the author's style: from conventional descriptive prose and the narrator's tone of indulgent irony, the style changes to elusive, elliptical sentences and the expressions "it seemed" and "for some reason" describe the chaos. As the story develops, realistic detail gives way to symbolic constructions by the narrator. And at the end, the title takes on a more symbolic than realistic denotation: Sologub has dramatized here the fact that by the individual being in a crowd, he is, as Volodya said in **"The Wall and the Shadows,"** surrounded by walls from which one cannot escape. Here they are human walls—oppressive, repulsive, and deadly. (pp. xxxi-xxxii)

Sologub's attitudes toward death and religion vacillated between attraction and revulsion. Certainly death offers the ultimate escape from a dark and evil world. Religion—or at least Christianity, with its ritual, fine trappings, and mystery—holds some allure (and Christ on the cross delights Ludmila, who sees the suffering through eyes that seek out the sadistic). But in story after story, religion appears as a mechanical response and prayers go unanswered. There is no spiritual solace in blind faith. However, in the story **"The Red-Lipped Guest"** written in 1909, we see a curious reversal in Sologub's treatment of the theme.

The myth of Lilith is much favored by Sologub and he uses her extensively in his works. Lilith, according to Semitic belief, was Adam's first wife before Eve. Rather than submit to him, she became a female demon, belonging to the night. Traditionally, this evil spirit is especially dangerous to children. In Sologub's symbolic world, however, Lilith is generally regarded as a positive symbol: she belongs to the moon and the night; she is in that lyrical company where Dulcinea also reposes. Lydia Rothstein, who is the Lilith in **"The Red-Lipped Guest,"** reverses Sologub's usual treatment of the myths; here she takes on her traditionally evil personality. A certain tension in her person is evident from the outset when her physical appearance is described by Vargolsky's servant, Victor, in his clumsy attempts at eloquence: she is compared to both a Greek statue (Tanagra) and a French courtesan of the turn of the century (Cleo de Mérode). Thus she is primarily a woman of the flesh, and while she promises a legend for escape, it must be paid for by physical sacrifice.

Many of Sologub's later stories show that the author ultimately did profess a belief in God. And **"The Red-Lipped Guest"** dramatizes the possible appeal of religion for him. The antithetical myth presented here by the Youth of the spirit and protector of life underscores the Bible's "wise and simple stories" as opposed to the destructive complexities of the Lilith symbol. (Equally appealing to Sologub's aesthetics is the victory of a beautiful, innocent boy over the destructiveness of a demanding woman.)

Another miracle occurs in **"The Kiss of the Unborn."** . . . The story of Seryozha's suicide brings another portrait of youth catapulted into adulthood by the realization that life is a nightmare. Seryozha is obviously referring to Tolstoy when he talks to his Aunt Nadya about "the best of all people," who, as an old man, ran away from his home and died because he "glimpsed the terror in which we all live and could not bear it." This is an oversimplification of the spiritual crisis, involving moral, aesthetic, philosophic, and religious questions that compelled Tolstoy to leave his home, Yasnaya Polyana. Tolstoy was not seeking out death as the ultimate escape, but this is what Seryozha does by his act of suicide. One reason that Seryozha is so drawn to the mid-nineteenth-century poet Nekrasov is because the writer had great compassion for suffering. (pp. xxxiv-xxxv)

The miracle in **"The Kiss of the Unborn"** occurs at the end of the story when Nadya sits on the stairs before going in to comfort her sister (Seryozha's mother). Nadya had had an abortion some years before, but she has been visited by the image of her son over the years. While he would sometimes press his lips to her cheeks, he had never kissed her on the lips. At the end of the story, her child appears to her again and this time he does kiss her and forgives her for depriving him of life. ("I don't want to live" he assures her.) Seryozha's death brings about this resurrection of love, a symbolic "birth" of Nadya's son. Seryozha's death is a rejection of reality; her unborn son is an affirmation of the dream, and a reaffirmation of the rejection of life and reality. (p. xxxvi)

> *Murl G. Barker, in his introduction to* The Kiss of the Unborn and Other Stories *by Fedor Sologub, translated by Murl G. Barker (copyright © 1977 by The University of Tennessee Press; reprinted by permission of The University of Tennessee Press), University of Tennessee Press, 1977, pp. xii-xxxvi.*

**STANLEY J. RABINOWITZ**   (essay date 1980)

The theme of the creative and redemptive power of language becomes ever important in Sologub's *oeuvre* and the child's particular relationship to it is most evident in the writer's *Fairy Tales (Skazki)*. . . . The year 1905 saw the publication of his **Book of Fairy Tales (Kniga skazok),** which was followed a year later by the **Political Fairy Tales (Političeskie skazočki),** a slim volume of fifty pages, roughly two thirds the length of its predecessor. Most of Volume Ten of the **Collected Works**—nearly one hundred and twenty pages—is devoted to over seventy of these tales. . . . (p. 132)

[For] all the crucial points of intersection between Sologub's fairy tales and the typical representatives of this genre, his tales contain a special quality, they exude a certain magic, a particular kind of poetry which set them apart as works of a highly original order. Sologub's writing attempts, and often successfully, to follow Trirodov's injunction in Part One of *A Legend in Creation,* that art, first and foremost, say or achieve something new. . . . The *Fairy Tales* work within an old and established tradition but move beyond it to achieve a singular effect. Indeed, to examine the idiosyncratic nature of these pieces is to discover the writer's peculiar understanding of this mode and his attempt to employ its aesthetic and philosophical potential in new ways.

Curiously downplayed in Sologub's fairy tale world are some of the principal sources of its customary wonder: magic potions and objects, dwarfs, dragons, witches, kings, queens, princes and princesses, and the like. In this collection of over seventy *skazki*, only a handful contains characters who are stock figures in the fairy or magical tale proper. . . . (pp. 136-37)

This phenomenon immediately signals the specialness of Sologub's fairy tales. . . . He can, and seeks to, derive the miraculous from the here and now; he is able to find it in the special status of childhood. . . . As Trirodov creates a fantastic order of "quiet children" from perfectly natural and everyday creatures such as Egorka, so Sologub constructs an enchanted universe solely by reproducing the unique perspective of the child. Enchantment here depends less on the presence of fantastic places, objects, or creatures than it does on the freshness, purity, and lovely wonderment of the child's outlook. At its most essential, fairy tale in Sologub is synonymous with seeing the world through the child's eye. (p. 137)

Sologub does more than *imply* the uniqueness of the child's frame of thinking in his fairy tales. He actually populates them largely with these characters (roughly half of them contain children), and shows how the child's mere everyday experience is the most wondrous, the most fairy-tale like form of existence. (p. 139)

We are, in Sologub's *Fairy Tales,* midway between poetry and prose. The colloquialisms, the use of conversation, of paired words and alliteration, yield a texture which is less "refined" and literary in nature and one which more faithfully approximates the oral, folk-poetic style. But the collection attains to poetry in other ways. The compactness, intensity, and imaginativeness of the language, the lovely, lilting quality of the "young" diction, the wonderful way Sologub gives life to words as he conveys them through the prism of the child's psychic apparatus, and the brevity of the tales, which almost *look* like verse on the printed page—all of this contributes to what is surely an ingenious linguistic performance. [Roman] Jakobson has insisted that "the originality of the Russian fairy tale lies not in plot but . . . in its stylistic adornments," and Sologub's fairy tales admirably adhere to this tradition. (pp. 142-43)

[The *Political Fairy Tales*] are especially noteworthy for the way in which their pleasant form contains, and almost conceals, their bitter, even scathing content. At least initially these works are deceptively innocent because their harsh sociopolitical criticism lies embedded beneath the simplicity and charm of their language. (p. 143)

And indeed one can appreciate even Sologub's political fairy tales solely as brilliant verbal performances, for one tends to assess their subject matter only after marveling at their linguistic effects, which no translation can convey. . . . What ultimately unites all the fairy tales, what constitutes their lowest common denominator, is their sheer poetic beauty. This is all the more reason why it is so difficult to agree with Dolinin's generalization that Sologub's style is marked by "its monotony, by its unusually severe finish, and by what I would say is its rather deliberate coldness." A proper reading of the *Fairy Tales* should permanently set to rest the long-held fallacy that Sologub's artistic universe possesses a singularly sluggish, static, and lifeless quality.

As the *Political Fairy Tales* demonstrate, words such as "simple" and "miniature" may describe the form of Sologub's works in this genre, but they do not apply to their content, which is often grave and complex in nature. Even less so do such words apply to the ideological position which these works hold in the overall scheme of the writer's creative universe.

Written at a critical and transitional period in Sologub's development, the fairy tale express a central aspect of his artistic and philosophical credo. Instead of expressing a bleaker, more pessimistic and apocalyptic tone after the dismal failure of the Revolution of 1905, Sologub gradually turned away from his previously gloomy outlook to a more positive and upbeat one. (pp. 144-45)

[The] fairy tales represent the most sustained and self-contained examples of the writer's desired world of dream. Sologub's vision attains cosmic dimensions here, for the entire earthly community is elevated to the more imaginative level of poetry and fantasy. The simplest details, the most inconsequential objects and routine situations are transfigured, such that they occupy a more exalted status.

Take, for example, **"A Drop of Rain and a Speck of Dust"** (**"Kaplja i pylinka"**). In five lines Sologub narrates how a falling drop decides to merge with something solid rather than merely swimming in a puddle. So it joins together with a speck of dust and lies on the ground as a ball of dirt. What we have is a trifling phenomenon: a bit of mud on the street, explained in a fresh and delightful manner. So it is in **"The Yellowed Birch Leaf, the Drop of Rain and the Lower Sky"** (**"Poželtevšij berezovyj list, kaplja i nižnee nebo"**). The existence of a yellow leaf is provided a history, a reason and, by extension, a dignity of its own. A raindrop falls on it and enjoys its stay, but convinced that there is a lower sky beneath the leaf, it gladly falls to the ground, certain that it hears the swaying branches whispering: "lower sky." Abandoned and grief-stricken, the birch leaf turns yellow. Once again, an ordinary phenomenon is endowed with meaning and magic: in content, as in form, this brief incident conveys a sense of loveliness, it achieves a uniqueness otherwise absent. (p. 146)

We have, then, yet another definition, a different use, of fairy tale in Sologub. It is a means of explaining the existence of mundane events and, even more so, of imparting to them a new and more beautiful meaning and, therefore, a higher significance. Sologub does not reject or ignore the everyday world, rather he poeticizes it and creates from its common matter different orders of reality. These tales are cosmogenies—each one creating its own universe by providing original explanations of the particular phenomenon described within it. These phenomena and the stories about their existence are infinite, and in writing the *Fairy Tales* Sologub paves the way for Trirodov's later statement about the need to create many everchanging realities. (pp. 146-47)

The apparent merging of dream and reality in the *Fairy Tales* does not mean that the world which is presented in them is a homogenized one, purged of human foibles. As we evidence particularly in the *Political Fairy Tales,* man's negative impulses are every bit as present here as they are in Sologub's prose fiction. The content of many fairy tales speaks to the futility of human existence in a world ruled by arbitrary fate and inhabited by people who are limited by their selfish interests and narrow outlooks. Yet in the fairy tales the predominant vision of life is markedly less tortured and contradictory than in Sologub's other writing. Evil and virtue are equally present but, unlike reality, the fairy tale world is purged of ambiguous grey areas. Moreover, no infraction ever attains metaphysical proportions and the mood is thus free from what Bryusov labels as heaviness. The adult perspective, Bryusov's "all too earthly body," disappears and with it vanishes the emotional anguish, which many critics had accused Sologub of often transferring unconvincingly onto his child-heroes. A psyche which is ordinarily torn, and fully colored, by a dualistic world view yields to a different domain. Evil is acknowledged but only as a natural part of a much larger universe in which optimism and enchantment still predominate. As Bryusov understood, the fairy tales reflect to a far less significant degree than Sologub's other writing the alternation between moments of doubt and belief, between reality and dream. Rather, the antipodes coalesce because the presentation of even negative, potentially agony-producing elements is filtered through the child's wondrous, pure, and simple imagination.

Not that Sologub has any illusions about the child's world: it is filled with acts of dishonesty, greed, selfishness, and even violence. In **"White, Gray, Black, Red"** (**"Belye, serye, černye, krasnye"**) a spoiled child's incendiary impulses result in a destroyed house and his death. . . . There are no happy endings in the sense of justness or fairness prevailing; there is often no resolution of unpleasantness, but merely the affirmation of its existence.

The lack of justice notwithstanding, the situations in these tales never approach tragic or gloomy proportions, for the tone remains light and the language familiar and entertaining. (pp. 148-49)

With metaphysical doubt absent and psychological conflict eliminated, genuine humor, devoid of the black or sinister overtones which one finds in *The Petty Demon,* is allowed to prevail. We could say of these tales what Ivanov-Razumnik remarked about Remizov's equally charming collection of juvenilia, *Posolon,* that "there is nothing terrible, nothing incomprehensible; there are no tears or drama, and if there are, they are only simple and innocent tragic-comedies." Sologub's fairy tales contain a comic, often frivolous and whimsical tone, which make them unique in his entire *oeuvre.* (p. 149)

The humorousness of the *skazki* results ultimately from the writer's ability to stand outside himself and to abandon his traditionally contemplative attitude toward life. Of all Sologub's writing, the *Fairy Tales* are where the authorial persona is most conspicuously absent. As such these works may be viewed as Sologub's fullest attempt at escape. Ordinarily concerned with his own adult ego, obsessed with his lyrical "I," Sologub abandons his self-centered world. In this fairy-tale existence, the painful consciousness of evil is noticeably absent because Sologub flees his metaphorical cell of claustrophobic guilt and sin. We are at the furthest reaches of Login's oppressive burden in *Bad Dreams* which, as he says, increases with the passage of time. The fairy tales present a world unencumbered by physical and temporal concerns, a realm, like the child's, where all is a state of continuous becoming and endless potential. (pp. 149-50)

The theme of transformation, of man's need and ability to change himself and his surroundings in ways that are infinitely diverse and exciting, runs constantly through Sologub's writing. . . . But it is the *Fairy Tales* where transformation reaches its apogee. Throughout the work, in the form of the narrator, the adult becomes fully and permanently what is most precious of all to Sologub—the child himself, and all of life undergoes a marvelous transfiguration. (p. 150)

Sologub's life-long goal of conflict-free innocence and purity is achieved, if anywhere, in his most fantastic works. In them the writer perceives life through the transluscent shroud of reverie and they might just as easily have been called "sny"—dreams. He is concerned far less with possibility than with desirability, and this is as it should be in fairy tales. . . . And

Sologub's *Fairy Tales* do indeed represent the highest fulfillment, the clearest exemplification of Trirodov's credo that "all that is beautiful in life has become real through dream."

Sologub, then, accomplishes on the literary level what his artist-hero will call for spiritually—the complete return to the special status of childhood. With this comes the greater feeling of oneness with the beautiful world which the writer believes accompanies, and truly defines, this state. Only in the works where the child's presence predominates completely is the Sologubian ideal of enchanting transcendental otherness reached. Of his numerous works which deal with children, it is his *Fairy Tales* which, perhaps, most fully capture the landscape and tone of childhood. And that the transformation, indeed the creation, of this ideal state comes about essentially through the medium of the child's special vision and language corroborates Trirodov's seminal idea that higher worlds can be produced through creative fantasy and artistic imagination, that is, through *words.* The fairy tales stand as a confirmation of Trirodov's— and Sologub's—cherished belief that art is the most beautiful means of escape and the securist refuge from the tedium of life. (pp. 150-51)

*Stanley J. Rabinowitz, in his* Sologub's Literary Children: Keys to a Symbolist's Prose *(copyright © 1980 by Stanley J. Rabinowitz; reprinted by permission of the author), Slavica Publishers, Inc., 1980, 176 p.*

---

## ADDITIONAL BIBLIOGRAPHY

Barker, Murl G. "Erotic Themes in Sologub's Prose." *Modern Fiction Studies* 26, No. 2 (Summer 1980): 241-48.
  Analysis of the erotic themes in some of Sologub's short stories and *The Petty Demon.* Barker concludes that Sologub's eroticism is an escape from the vulgarity of reality, but that "the ideal is seldom triumphant—it is always temporal and often despoiled by the very forces it seeks to escape."

Bristol, Evelyn. "Fedor Sologub's Postrevolutionary Poetry." *The American Slavic and East European Review* XIX, No. 3 (October 1960): 414-22.
  Studies the eight volumes of poetry published between 1921 and 1924, finding in their themes and techniques a return to the Symbolistic method Sologub had abandoned for modernism during the prerevolutionary years.

Chandler, Frank W. "The Little Eccentrics: Artzybashev, Sologub, Evreinov." In his *Modern Continental Playwrights,* pp. 94-110. New York: Harper & Brothers, 1931.*
  Discussion of Sologub's unconventional conception of the theater.

Connolly, Julian W. "The Role of Duality in Sologub's *Tvorimaja legenda.*" *Die Welt der Slaven* XIX-XX, No. 1 (1974-75): 25-36.
  Finds that the symbolist theme of duality plays "a central role on all levels in Tvorimaja legenda, from the expression of Sologub's philosophic vision to the organizing principles of the work itself." Connolly traces and interprets the many doubles occurring throughout the novel.

Dienes, L. "Creative Imagination in Fedor Sologub's *Tvorimaja legenda.*" *Die Welt der Slaven* XXIII, No. 1 (1978): 176-86.
  Posits that the apparent formlessness of certain sections of *Tvorimaja legenda* was done intentionally to illustrate the working of the author's creative mind rather than to tell a story. Dienes's organizing hypothesis is that "*Tvorimaja legenda* is a work *on* literary creation."

Hansson, Carola. *Fedor Sologub As a Short Story Writer.* Stockholm: Almquist e Wiksell International, 1975, 194 p.

Close study of the style of "Svet i teni," "Belaja sobaka," and "Mudrye devy": stories chosen as typical among Sologub's short fiction.

Kostka, Edmund. "A Literary Quandary: Fyodor Sologub and Heinrich Mann." In his *Glimpses of Germanic-Slavic Relations from Pushkin to Heinrich Mann*, pp. 21-37. London: Associated University Presses, 1975.*

Comparative study of Heinrich Mann's *Professor Unrat* and Sologub's *The Petty Demon*. Kostka argues that Mann's novel bears numerous similarities to Sologub's with respect to the main character of each and the depiction of the "hopeless melancholy of human existence."

Rabinowitz, Stanley J. "Fedor Sologub and His Nineteenth-Century Russian Antecedents." *Slavic and East European Journal* 22, No. 3 (Fall 1978): 324-25.

Traces Sologub's debt to Dostoevsky, Gogol, Nekrasov, and others, using as evidence common themes culled from Sologub's work.

Rabinowitz, Stanley J. "Bely and Sologub: Toward the History of a Friendship." In *Andrey Bely: A Critical Review*, edited by Gerald Janecek, pp. 157-68. Lexington: The University Press of Kentucky, 1978.*

Biocritical discussion of Andrey Bely's relationship with Sologub. By using available published and unpublished material, Rabinowitz reconstructs the personal and professional aspects of Bely's relationship with Sologub, stressing the similarities and differences in their views on Symbolism and Russian literature.

Smith, Vassar. "On *Bad Dreams*." *Russian Literature Triquarterly*, No. 16 (1979): 86-91.

A short examination of Sologub's first novel.

Zamyatin, Yevgeny. "Fyodor Sologub." In his *A Soviet Heretic: Essays by Yevgeny Zamyatin*, edited and translated by Mirra Ginsburg, pp. 217-23. Chicago: University of Chicago Press, 1970.

Review of Sologub's art by a fellow-Russian author. Zamyatin considers Sologub one of Russia's leading writers because of his satire and his experimentation with form.

# (Newton) Booth Tarkington

## 1869-1946

(Also wrote under pseudonyms of John Corburton, Cecil Woodford, and Milton Kilgalen) American novelist, dramatist, short story writer, essayist, poet, and autobiographer.

Tarkington was a popular Midwestern writer who worked in the realistic tradition of William Dean Howells and Mark Twain. He is best remembered today for his adventure-filled, wholesome young-adult fiction, most notably the *Penrod* series and *Seventeen*. The small-town Midwestern settings of his novels and his informal, homey style attracted a wide readership. Tarkington also contributed significantly to American literature in his portrayal of early twentieth-century Midwestern mores and in his fictional accounts of the personal and social consequences of industrialization. Prominent among these works are his Pulitzer Prize-winning novels *Alice Adams* and *The Magnificent Ambersons*.

Tarkington was born in Indianapolis to a financially comfortable, middle-class family. He spent one year at Purdue University, but the most important part of his education was spent at Princeton, where he became the editor of three major campus publications. After leaving Princeton, Tarkington returned to Indiana with hopes of earning a living by writing. For six years he endured publisher rejection slips until the acceptance, in 1899, of *The Gentleman from Indiana*, which was an immediate success. Readers felt the novel captured the essence of the American heartland and readily identified with the hero and heroine of the story. Tarkington's next work, the romance *Monsieur Beaucaire*, was also immensely popular, and a dramatic adaptation of the novel has had a long life on the stage and in films. Tarkington's success made his name so familiar in his home state that in 1902 he was elected to the Indiana House of Representatives without actively campaigning. His legislative career was cut short by illness, though his brief experience with politics was later worked into a collection of short stories, *In the Arena*. In 1905, Tarkington turned his attention to the theater, and for six years he worked in collaboration with dramatist Harry Leon Wilson. Together they wrote only one financially successful and enduring play, *The Man from Home*. These years, which were marred by alcoholism and marital problems that resulted in divorce, marked a low point in Tarkington's life. However, the emotional support of his family and a new love interest helped revitalize his creative efforts, and with the publication of *The Flirt* in 1913 there came a turning point in Tarkington's career. *The Flirt* is not one of his better known novels, but it foreshadows his successful young-adult tales in its attempt at realistic characterization and narration.

With *Penrod* and *Seventeen*, Tarkington created classic portraits of the all-American boy at the turn of the century. Tarkington used his own childhood experiences to recount the realities and dreams that complicate a boy's life, and the realism with which they are evoked is attributed by some critics to his careful use of novel situations and the avoidance of gimmicky "kid talk." In all his young adult tales Tarkington emphasized sharp delineation of character rather than development of a complicated plot. Tarkington's characterizations and humorous, occasionally painful depictions of the adven-

tures of Penrod Schofield and Willy Baxter have been critically acclaimed, and Penrod has often been favorably compared to Twain's Tom Sawyer.

Tarkington broke new artistic ground with his trilogy of urban life, *Growth*. *The Turmoil*, *The Magnificent Ambersons* and *The Midlander* were inspired by the transformation Tarkington observed as the Midwest responded to America's growing industrialization. In these novels the author explored the grotesque consequences of sudden wealth. Chronicling three generations of a family's rags-to-riches-to-rags fortunes, *The Magnificent Ambersons* is viewed as the best novel of the trilogy, although many critics believe it is flawed by an illogical, sentimental conclusion.

*Alice Adams*, often regarded as an extension of the *Growth* trilogy, is considered Tarkington's greatest novel. Alice is poignantly rendered as she seeks upward social mobility as an escape from her unhappy life. Critics agree that *Alice Adams* is Tarkington's most mature and important work, citing the artistic representation of the Adamses as a realistic portrayal of a family caught in the social and economic binds of industrial changeover. Moreover, some critics view the opportunistic schemes leading to Alice's downfall as symbolic of the opportunism and eventual collapse of the American economy in the twenties. Tarkington's work retained a high standard of quality throughout the rest of his career, although he never regained the power displayed during the years between *The Flirt* and *The Midlander*.

According to James Woodress, Tarkington's attention to social themes, as in *Alice Adams* and his later works, "put him in the mainstream of literary protest," dealing with such subjects as materialism and progress. As much as Tarkington contributed in this vein, many critics contend that he ignored other important issues of the day, such as sexuality and war, and that his idealistic approach to life blinded him to life's darker elements. Tarkington's optimistic world view colors much of his work, echoing Howells's belief that "the smiling aspects of life" are the "most American." Even in the darker socio-economic novels of the *Growth* trilogy, Tarkington is able to view the ever-present sooty smokestacks as a phase of progress which will eventually produce a better life for his Midwestern neighbors. He believed that readers wanted to be entertained, not reminded of sorrow. Not surprisingly, his books were widely read during the Great Depression.

That Tarkington's realism often lapsed to romanticism did not diminish his popularity with readers as much as with critics, who considered his novels naive and old-fashioned. But his works are still admired today for their well-crafted plots, interesting portraits of America in transition, and for their sheer entertainment value.

(See also *Dictionary of Literary Biography*, Vol. 9: *American Novelists, 1910-1945.*)

## PRINCIPAL WORKS

*The Gentleman from Indiana* (novel) 1899
*Monsieur Beaucaire* (novel) 1900
*Monsieur Beaucaire* [with Evelyn Greenleaf Sutherland] (drama) 1901
*Cherry* (novel) 1903
*In the Arena* (short stories) 1905
*The Man from Home* [with Harry Leon Wilson] (drama) 1907
*The Flirt* (novel) 1913
*Penrod* (novel) 1914
*\*The Turmoil* (novel) 1915
*Penrod and Sam* (novel) 1916
*Seventeen* (novel) 1916
*\*The Magnificent Ambersons* (novel) 1918
*Clarence* (drama) 1919
*Alice Adams* (novel) 1921
*Gentle Julia* (novel) 1922
*\*The Midlander* (novel) 1924; also published as *National Avenue*, 1927
*Women* (novel) 1925
*The Plutocrat* (novel) 1927
*The World Does Move* (autobiography) 1928
*Penrod Jashber* (novel) 1929
*The Heritage of Hatcher Ide* (novel) 1941
*Kate Fennigate* (novel) 1943
*The Show Piece* (unfinished novel) 1943

\*These works were published as *Growth* in 1927.

---

## THE INDEPENDENT (essay date 1900)

As a young man's first book [*The Gentleman from Indiana*] has many pleasing points of promise, if the alliteration is not offensive, and notwithstanding frequent crudities, the dramatic composition of the story shows considerable cleverness. The style is redundant to a degree, and the author seems to affect uncommon words and phraseology. He gets his botany mixed by growing green wheat, low corn, blooming dog-fennel and purple iron weeds all at once. He tells of a distance that "sped malignantly," and of the heroine humming a song of "an ineffably gentle, slow movement;" he describes, when he comes to ornithology, flocks of blackbirds in June, and we could easily fill a column with similar slips and inaccuracies evidently due to carelessness or lack of knowledge. The hero is a newspaper editor in a small Indiana town; but Mr. Tarkington's description of him does not disclose any good reason for believing that he knows anything whatever about country newspaper work. Indeed the chief weakness of the story lies in the author's inability to impress his people and facts with the authentic influence. His characters, scenes, incidents, landscapes are interesting, but they do not seem quite imbued with real life. There is almost nothing of the genuine Indiana in the book. It is all romance out of the whole cloth. Having said this much regarding the crudities of *The Gentleman from Indiana*, we hasten to add that it is brim full of a certain boyish enthusiasm which is delightful. The pages have a fine flavor of youth. We can feel that Mr. Tarkington came to his task with all the novelty of literary fascination upon him. He plunged into the writing of his story as a boy into a summer stream. What if he couldn't swim; he could welter and splash; he could shout and paddle and feel all the joy of the water. The result is a charming story, bristling with faults and saturated with absurdity, yet charming all the same—a story of Indiana life with scarcely a trace of Indiana life in it. Mr. Tarkington's lovers are silly and sweet, as lovers mostly are; they do most unconventional things; the hero reforms politics in his district as if by magic; the heroine, in the hero's absence, by the same magic, runs his newspaper and nominates him for Congress. A settlement of "White-caps"—an actual colony of them—openly figures in the story, and we have some wonderful performances on their part, to the tune of "Old John Brown." It is difficult not to give a wrong impression, however, in a short notice of this story. We think that every reader qualified to judge will decide that it is a remarkable romance—remarkable for its crudity, its touch of genius, its curious lack of taste here and there, and its charming taste in other places, its platitudes, its brilliant passages, its hysterical love scenes, its beautiful sketches of landscape, its atmosphere of high youthful enthusiasm, its eloquent exaggerations and its unbridled romantic movement. We have read it with just such pleasure as comes of hearing the noise of a distant base ball game of a dreamy June afternoon, when the roads are dusty and the wind is from the West. (pp. 67-8)

*"Book Reviews: 'The Gentleman from Indiana',"* in The Independent, *Vol. LII, No. 2666, January 4, 1900, pp. 67-8.*

## W. D. HOWELLS (essay date 1915)

[*Howells was considered "The father of American realism"; his praise of* The Turmoil *was therefore significant as an indication of Tarkington's acceptance as a serious artist. According to his biographers, Tarkington was flattered by the following essay and in a letter to Howells, whom he held in high esteem, he wrote: "Any writer in America would rather have a word from you than*] *any other man. . . . It has helped my self-esteem as nothing else could. . . . You are responsible for whatever good we produce."*]

[We] New Yorkers, and especially we adoptive New Yorkers, must not ask an exclusive attention from literature. If Mr. Booth Tarkington chooses that the scene of his great drama *The Turmoil* shall rather pass in whatever Mid-Western metropolis of the remorseless industries, we must patiently await the arrival of his art in this supreme theater. In certain dimensions, in fact, that metropolis is not less adequate than our stage to the demands of his tragedy. . . . The action of *The Turmoil* is possible everywhere that the human passions and volitions have play, but they seem more characterized as American by the greater geographical remoteness from Europe. This apparently makes them more intensely ours because there is less in that new *entourage* to cast even a reflected light from finer ideals upon their crude ugliness. There is something peculiarly touching in the defeat of the dreams by the events . . .—those very intense passages in which the father and son oppose their diverse motives, and the gentler prevails against the stronger, only to be precipitated in ultimate defeat. It is of course an accident which effects the tragical result, and the tragedy is softened as much as may be by the happy close of the love-affair involved. But though Mary Vertrees is a woman soul beautifully painted, and offered us for all consolation in the fatality through which her lover wins her, we are not sure but the author means us to feel that the frustration of Bibbs Sheridan's ideal by his father's ambition is not something too dire for consolation, except through the sense that there is something to come which shall "trammel up the consequence" now left so heavy with the witness. The story so powerful in expression abounds in subtle intimations, and this may be one of them. As it stands, the tragedy appeals to us like one of those conceptions which Rodin has learned from Michelangelo to leave half emerging from the stone. But could the author himself bid it wholly appear?

Perhaps he means the reader's imagination, which has been his silent partner in the work, to complete the work. In that case we should like to let our fancy play, not about the happiness of Bibbs and Mary (for they must be happy), but about the misery which the sisters-in-law, Edith and Sibyl, are fated to. These two personages are rendered to the last effect of their atrocious vulgarity. Yet vulgarity is not quite the word for egotism so simple and sincere, so unspared and unsparing in their hate of each other and of any whose will crosses theirs. Of the two, Sibyl seems to us the more triumphant characterization, with that touch of pity in her for her drink-sodden husband whom her abominable folly has ruined. The scene where she raves to the doctor from her sick-bed and pours out the gall of her bitterness on Mary, who has snubbed her, and on Edith, who has won her lover from her, is possibly equaled in another sort by the fatuous message which Edith sends home to her family telling them she has married the scoundrel she was sent away to save her from. (p. 961)

> W. D. Howells, "Editor's Easy Chair" (reprinted by permission of the Literary Estate of W. D. Howells), in Harper's, Vol. CXXX, No. DCCLXXX, May, 1915, pp. 958-61.*

## WILLIAM LYON PHELPS (essay date 1916)

Booth Tarkington has exactly what Winston Churchill has not—humour, charm, lightness of touch, a certain winsomeness of style as pervasive as sunshine. The difference between the two men is immediately apparent when we compare *Mr. Crewe's Career* with *The Gentleman from Indiana*. . . . *Richard Carvel* and *The Gentleman from Indiana* were published the same year, 1899, one a historical romance, in the correct fashion of the moment, the other a realistic portrayal of journalistic and political life in a small town. Since that date these two popular favourites have written side by side, unconsciously inviting comparative criticism. In choosing between them the public has taken both.

It is rather interesting that in the year 1915 our two novelists should each have produced a book that is intended to be, and is, an indictment of modern American conditions in the commercial life of big cities. Now there is surely more humanity in *The Turmoil* than in *A Far Country*. The hero of the latter novel is a mechanism merely, a representative of the evil tendencies condemned by the author; whereas in *The Turmoil,* both father and son are real persons, full of individuality. This story is a skilful accusation of the American love of bigness, with its concomitant evils of smoke, dirt, noise, especially noise. The son is as unlike his father as the sons of rich Americans are likely to be: in the end the enormous distance between them is spanned by the longest bridge in the universe—love. The son is so much like the author of the novel that we hope his apparent surrender to big business at the end does not mean the surrender of Mr. Tarkington to the demands of the reading public. Four or five years ago I feared that the brilliant gifts of this Hoosier were going to be degraded to the production of the girl-model of the year—he is much too able a writer to become a caterer and to fall under the temptation of immediate success. (pp. 277-79)

*The Turmoil* is the most ambitious and on the whole the best of Mr. Tarkington's novels; without too much didacticism, it is an unsparing and honest diagnosis of the great American disease. Its author has proved that he can write a novel full of cerebration without losing any of his charm. In spite of that delightful miniature historical romance, *Monsieur Beaucaire,* Mr. Tarkington is a realist; he hates pretence, sham, cant in just the way a typical undergraduate hates them; perhaps if he did not hate them so much, perhaps if his sense of humour were not such a conservative force in his nature, he might attain to even higher ground. In his study of the American boy, *Penrod,* we see his shrewd knowledge of life and his original mirth-sense. The first half of the book is second-rate; it seems like a copy of some original; but the second half is wonderful, with its feeling for reality as against cant; and those two nigger-boys are worthy of Mark Twain at his best. The sense of fact is the dominant quality in Booth Tarkington, as it was in Mark Twain. It accounts for his artistic virtues, and for his lack of range. But *The Turmoil* proves that he is growing in spiritual grace.

Every man and woman over fifty ought to read *Seventeen*. It is not only a skilful analysis of adolescent love, it is, with all its side-splitting mirth, a tragedy. No mature person who reads this novel will ever seriously regret his "lost youth" or wish he were young again. (pp. 279-81)

> William Lyon Phelps, "Twentieth Century American Novelists" (originally published as "The Advance of the English Novel," in The Bookman, New York, Vol. XLIII, No. 5, July, 1916), in his The Advance of the English Novel (copyright, 1915 by Dodd, Mead and Company; copyright, 1916 by Dodd, Mead and Company, Inc.), Dodd, Mead, 1916, pp. 267-301.

**JAMES BRANCH CABELL** (essay date 1919)

[*Tarkington's sentimentality is the subject of this derisive essay.*]

[Mr. Booth Tarkington] is a very popular novelist. . . . But that I take to be one of the most tragic items in all the long list of misfortunes which have befallen American literature. It is a fact that merits its threnody, since the loss of an artist demands lamentation, even when he commits suicide.

For if, as Stevenson declared, the fairies were tipsy at Mr. Kipling's christening, at Mr. Tarkington's they must have been in the last stage of maudlin generosity. Poetic insight they gave him; and the knack of story building; and all their own authentic elfin liveliness of fancy; and actually perceptive eyes, by virtue of which his more truly Tarkingtonian pages are enriched with countless happy little miracles of observation; and the dramatic gift, of contriving and causing to move convincingly a wide variety of puppets in nothing resembling the puppet-master; and the not uncommon desire to "write," with just enough deficiency in common-sense to make him willing to put up with the laboriousness of writing fairly well. In fine, there is hardly one natural endowment requisite to grace in a creative author that was omitted by these inebriated fairies. And to all this Mr. Tarkington has since added, through lonesome and grinding toil, an astounding proficiency at the indoor sport of adroit verbal expression. No living manipulator of English employs the contents of his dictionary more artfully or, in the general hackneyed and misleading phrase, has a better "style." (pp. 300-02)

Mr. Tarkington has published nothing that does not make very "pleasant" reading. He has in fact re-written the quaint legend, that virtue and honest worth must rise inevitably to be the target both of rice-throwing and of respectful consideration by the bank cashier, as indefatigably as human optimism and the endurance of the human wrist would reasonably permit. For the rest, his plots are the sort of thing that makes criticism seem cruel. His ventriloquism is startling in its excellence; but his marionettes, under the most life-like of exteriors, have either hearts of gold or entrails of sawdust; there is no medium: and as touches their behavior, all the Tarkingtonian puppets "form themselves" after the example of the not unfamous young person who had a curl in the middle of her forehead. And Mr. Tarkington's auctorial philosophy was summed up long ago, in *The Gentleman from Indiana*. "Look," said Helen. "Aren't they good dear people?"—"The beautiful people!" he answered.

Now this, precisely this, Mr. Tarkington has been answering ever since to every riddle in life. To-day he is still murmuring, for publication, "The good dear people, the beautiful people!"—who, according to his very latest bulletin at the moment I speak, are presently to be awarded suitable residences in "a noble and joyous city, unbelievably white." Questionless, the apostrophe, no less than the prediction, is "pleasant" to the apostrophized, his chosen and enormous audience; and as such is well received by the majority, who according to our theories of government are always right. Yet to some carping few of us (who read the daily papers, say) this sentiment now seems peculiarly anachronistic and irrational. (pp. 302-04)

Mr. Tarkington has not mere talent but an uncontrollable wizardry that defies concealment, even by the livery of a popular novelist. The winding-up of the William Sylvanus Baxter stories [in *Seventeen*], for example, is just the species of necromancy attainable by no other living author; so that a theatre wherein but now the humor of sitting upon wet paint and the

mirthful aspect of a person vomiting have made their bids for popular applause, is shaken to its low foundation by the departing rumble of a "pompous train," and unsuspected casements open upon Fairy Land. Nor is the ending of *The Turmoil,* technically, a whit inferior. Here, though, with due respect to the recorded verdict of Mr. W. D. Howells, one does not "stand on tiptoe" to reach an effect so beautiful and unpredictable and so eminently "as it ought to be." Instead, one is rather inclined to kneel.

For here—and in how many other places!—Mr. Tarkington displays a form of wealth which should not be exempt from fair taxation. . . . And in fine, it all comes back to this: to write "best sellers" is by ordinary a harmless and very often a philanthropic performance; but in Mr. Tarkington's case it is a misappropriation of funds. (pp. 304-05)

Mr. Tarkington is a gentleman whose ability none of us has any choice save cordially to love, and to revere. It is for that reason I resent its waste, and voice my resentment unwillingly. In short, I throw my brick with one hand, and with the other remove my hat. And to many this well may seem the inkiest ingratitude, for one half-moment to begrudge prosperity and wide applause to a person who has purveyed so many enjoyable half-hours. But in cold earnest one of the most dire calamities that ever befell American literature was the commercial success of *The Gentleman from Indiana,* so closely followed by the popular triumph of *Monsieur Beaucaire.* For this double misfortune has since bred such concessions by Mr. Tarkington, to the necessity of being "pleasant," as would seem amply to justify a remission of that necessity, at all events among the admirers of his ability as distinguished from its employment. And the pathos of it all is but augmented by the circumstance that both of these novels were quite fine enough to have "fallen flat," and so have left Mr. Tarkington to write in rational obscurity a book commensurate with his intelligence.

"Is that time dead?—lo, with a little Penrod he has but touched the honey of romance" since then, and thus has very, very slightly dissipated its saccharinity. Still, we who have read all his stories with resentful admiration cannot but hopefully consider the date of Mr. Tarkington's birth, and reflect that the really incurable optimism of senility remains a comfortably remote affair. Religion too assures us that there is always hope for a change of heart, if not for any actual regaining of the Biblical view—which, to be sure, is peculiarly ophthalmic as to the far-and-wide existence of "good and dear and beautiful people" and is unlikely ever to be taken seriously by Americans. No less, the fact remains that out of forty-nine years of living Mr. Tarkington has thus far given us only *Seventeen.* Nor would this matter were Mr. Tarkington a Barclay or a Harrison, or even the mental and artistic equal of the trio's far more popular rival, Mr. Harold Bell Wright. But Mr. Tarkington had genius. That is even more tragic than the "pleasant" ending of *The Magnificent Ambersons*. . . . (pp. 305-07)

*James Branch Cabell, "Which Defers to the Arbiters," in his* Beyond Life: Dizain des démiurges *(copyright © 1919, copyright renewed © 1945, by James Branch Cabell; reprinted by permission of Margaret Freeman Cabell), R. M. McBride and Company, 1919 (and reprinted by The Modern Library, 1923), pp. 277-322.*

**HEYWOOD BROUN** (essay date 1921)

Booth Tarkington seems to us to lead almost every other American in technical finish. His facility is so great that he has been known to trade upon it. There was a time when he was in danger of establishing himself as just a funny man. That passed beyond recall with **"Alice Adams."** . . . No more poignant tragedy has been written in the year. . . . The tragic method of **"Alice Adams"** sways us utterly because it is a tragedy in which nobody dies, nobody goes mad, nobody commits suicide. Indeed the people who go down are still fighting at the end and that is characteristic of man in the face of adversity. They dream even after disaster. The study of Alice herself is masterly in its insight and the picture of her father is just as good. Ironically enough, it has been said that Booth Tarkington did not like **"Main Street"** and planned **"Alice Adams"** as an answer. To be sure he has bettered the contentions of Sinclair Lewis but nothing has been offered in rebuttal. The dinner on the hot night completes one of the most devastating pictures of American life which has ever been drawn. And incidentally no living writer can do more with temperature than Tarkington. F. Scott Fitzgerald in a short story called **"The Ice Palace"** made us feel almost as cold as we ever feared to be, but Tarkington cannot be matched for bringing home humidity. **"Alice Adams"** is a book to move the heart and wilt the collar. (pp. 394-95)

> *Heywood Broun, "A Group of Books Worth Reading: 'Alice Adams',"* in The Bookman, *New York (copyright, 1921, by George H. Doran Company), Vol. LIV, No. 4, December, 1921, pp. 394-95.*

## CARL VAN DOREN (essay date 1922)

Booth Tarkington is the glass of adolescence and the mold of Indiana. The hero of his earliest novel, Harkless in **The Gentleman from Indiana,** drifts through that narrative with a melancholy stride because he has been seven long years out of college and has not yet set the prairie on fire. But Mr. Tarkington, at the time of writing distant from Princeton by about the same number of years and also not yet famous, could not put up with failure in a hero. So Harkless appears as a mine of latent splendors. Carlow County idolizes him, evil-doers hate him, grateful old men worship him, devoted young men shadow his unsuspecting steps at night in order to protect him from the villains of Six-Cross-Roads, sweet girls adore him, fortune saves him from dire adventures, and in the end his fellow-voters choose him to represent their innumerable virtues in the Congress of their country without his even dreaming what affectionate game they are at. This from the creator of Penrod, who at the comical age of twelve so often lays large plans for proving to the heedless world that he, too, has been a hero all along! In somewhat happier hours Mr. Tarkington wrote **Monsieur Beaucaire,** that dainty romantic episode in the life of Prince Louis-Philippe de Valois, who masquerades as a barber and then as a gambler at Bath, is misjudged on the evidence of his own disguises, just escapes catastrophe, and in the end gracefully forgives the gentlemen and ladies who have been wrong, parting with an exquisite gesture from Lady Mary Carlisle, the beauty of Bath, who loves him but who for a few fatal days had doubted. This from the creator of William Sylvanus Baxter, who at the preposterous age of seventeen imagines himself another Sydney Carton and after a silent, agonizing, condescending farewell goes out to the imaginary tumbril!

Just such postures and phantasms of adolescence lie behind all Mr. Tarkington's more serious plots—and not merely those earlier ones which he constructed a score of years ago when the mode in fiction was historical and rococo. Van Revel in

**The Two Van Revels,** convinced and passionate abolitionist, nevertheless becomes as hungry as any fire-eater of them all the moment Polk moves for war on Mexico, though to Van Revel the war is an evil madness. In **The Conquest of Canaan** Louden plays Prince Hal among the lowest his town affords, only to mount with a rush to the mayoralty when he is ready. **The Guest of Quesnay** takes a hero who is soiled with every vileness, smashes his head in an automobile accident, and thus transforms him into that glorious kind of creature known as a "Greek god"—beautiful and innocent beyond belief or endurance. **The Turmoil** is really not much more veracious, with its ugly duckling, Bibbs Sheridan, who has ideas, loves beauty, and writes verse, but who after years of futile dreaming becomes a master of capital almost overnight. Even **The Magnificent Ambersons,** with its wealth of admirable satire, does not satirize its own conclusion but rounds out its narrative with a hasty regeneration. And what can a critic say of such blatant nonsense as arises from the frenzy of propaganda in **Ramsey Milholland**?

Perhaps it is truer to call Mr. Tarkington's plots sophomoric than to call them adolescent. Indeed, the mark of the undergraduate almost covers them, especially of the undergraduate as he fondly imagines himself in his callow days and as he is foolishly instructed to regard himself by the more vinous and more hilarious of the old graduates who annually come back to a college to offer themselves—though this is not their conscious purpose—as an object lesson in the loud triviality peculiar and traditional to such hours of reunion. Adolescence, however, when left to itself, has other and very different hours which Mr. Tarkington shows almost no signs of comprehending.

The author of **Penrod,** of **Penrod and Sam,** and of **Seventeen** passes for an expert in youth; rarely has so persistent a reputation been so insecurely founded. What all these books primarily recall is the winks that adults exchange over the heads of children who are minding their own business, as the adults are not; the winks, moreover, of adults who have forgotten the inner concerns of adolescence and now observe only its surface awkwardnesses. Real adolescence, like any other age of man, has its own passions, its own poetry, its own tragedies and felicities; the adolescence of Mr. Tarkington's tales is almost nothing but farce—staged for outsiders. Not one of the characters is an individual; they are all little monsters—amusing monsters, it is true—dressed up to display the stock ambitions and the stock resentments and the stock affectations and the stock perturbations of the heart which attend the middle teens. The pranks of Penrod Schofield are merely those of Tom Sawyer repeated in another town, without the touches of poetry or of the informing imagination lent by Mark Twain. The sighs of "Silly Bill" Baxter—at first diverting, it is also true—are exorbitantly multiplied till reality drops out of the semblance. Calf-love does not always remain a joke merely because there are mature spectators to stand by nudging one another and roaring at the discomfort which love causes its least experienced victims. Those knowing asides which accompany these juvenile records have been mistaken too often for shrewd, even for profound, analyses of human nature. Actually they are only knowing, as sophomores are knowing with respect to their juniors by a few years. In contemporary American fiction Mr. Tarkington is the perennial sophomore.

If he may be said never to have outgrown Purdue and Princeton, so also may he be said never to have outgrown Indiana. In any larger sense, of course, he has not needed to. A novelist does not require a universe in which to find the universe, which lies folded, for the sufficiently perceptive eye, in any village. Thoreau and Emerson found it in Concord; Thomas Hardy in Wessex has watched the world move by without himself moving. But Mr. Tarkington has toward his native state the conscious attitude of the booster. Smile as he may at the too emphatic patriotism of this or that of her sons, he himself nevertheless expands under a similar stimulus. The impulse of Harkless to clasp all Carlow County to his broad breast obviously sprang from a mood which Mr. Tarkington himself had felt. And that impulse of that first novel has been repeated again and again in the later characters. *In the Arena,* fruit of Mr. Tarkington's term in the Indiana legislature, is a study in complacency. Setting out to take the world of politics as he finds it, he comes perilously near to ending on the note of approval for it as it stands—as good, on the whole, as any possible world. His satire, at least, is on the side of the established order. A certain soundness and rightness of feeling, a natural hearty democratic instinct, which appears in the novels, must not be allowed to mislead the analyst of his art. More than once, to his credit, he satirically recurs to the spectacle of those young Indianians who come back from their travels with a secret condescension, as did George Amberson Minafer: "His politeness was of a kind which democratic people found hard to bear. In a word, M. le Duc had returned from the gay life of the capital to show himself for a week among the loyal peasants belonging to the old chateau, and their quaint habits and costumes afforded him a mild amusement." Such passages, however, may be matched with irritating dozens in which Mr. Tarkington swallows Indiana whole. (pp. 84-9)

To practise an art which is genuinely characteristic of some section of the folk anywhere is to do what may be important and is sure to be interesting. But Mr. Tarkington no more displays the naïveté of a true folk-novelist than he displays the serene vision that can lift a novelist above the accidents of his particular time and place. This Indianian constantly appears, by his allusions, to be a citizen of the world. He knows Europe; he knows New York. Again and again, particularly in the superb opening chapters of *The Magnificent Ambersons,* he rises above the local prejudices of his special parish and observes with a finely critical eye. But whenever he comes to a crisis in the building of a plot or in the truthful representation of a character he sags down to the level of Indiana sentimentality. George Minafer departs from the Hoosier average by being a snob; time—and Mr. Tarkington's plot—drags the cub back to normality. Bibbs Sheridan departs from the Hoosier average by being a poet; time—and Mr. Tarkington's plot—drags the cub back to normality. Both processes are the same. Perhaps Mr. Tarkington would not deliberately say that snobbery and poetry are equivalent offenses, but he does not particularly distinguish. Sympathize as he may with these two aberrant youths, he knows no other solution than in the end to reduce them to the ranks. He accepts, that is, the casual Hoosier valuation, not with pity because so many of the creative hopes of youth come to naught or with regret that the flock in the end so frequently prevails over individual talent, but with a sort of exultant hurrah at seeing all the wandering sheep brought back in the last chapter and tucked safely away in the good old Hoosier fold.

Viewed critically this attitude of Mr. Tarkington's is of course not even a compliment to Indiana, any more than it is a compliment to women to take always the high chivalrous tone toward them, as if they were flawless creatures; any more than it is a compliment to the poor to assume that they are all virtuous

or to the rich to assume that they are all malefactors of a tyrannical disposition. If Indiana plays microcosm to Mr. Tarkington's art, he owes it to his state to find more there than he has found—or has cared to set down; he owes it to his state now and then to quarrel with the dominant majority, for majorities occasionally go wrong, as well as men; he owes it to his state to give up his method of starting his narrative himself and then calling in popular sentimentalism to advise him how to bring it to an end.

According to all the codes of the more serious kinds of fiction, the unwillingness—or the inability—to conduct a plot to its legitimate ending implies some weakness in the artistic character; and this weakness has been Mr. Tarkington's principal defect. Nor does it in any way appear that he excuses himself by citing the immemorial license of the romancer. Mr. Tarkington apparently believes in his own conclusions. Now this causes the more regret for the reason that he has what is next best to character in a novelist—that is, knack. He has the knack of romance when he wants to employ it: a light, allusive manner; a sufficient acquaintance with certain charming historical epochs and the "properties" thereto pertaining—frills, ruffs, rapiers, insinuation; a considerable expertness in the ways of the "world"; gay colors, swift moods, the note of tender elegy. He has also the knack of satire, which he employs more frequently than romance. With what a rapid, joyous, accurate eye he has surveyed the processes of culture in "the Midland town"! How quickly he catches the first gesture of affectation and how deftly he sets it forth, entertained and entertaining! From the chuckling exordium of *The Magnificent Ambersons* it is but a step to *The Age of Innocence* and *Main Street.* Little reflective as he has allowed himself to be, he has by shrewd observation alone succeeded in writing not a few chapters which have texture, substance, "thickness." He has movement, he has energy, he has invention, he has good temper, he has the leisure to write as well as he can if he wishes to. And, unlike those dozens of living American writers who once each wrote one good book and then lapsed into dull oblivion or duller repetition, he has traveled a long way from the methods of his greener days.

Why then does he continue to trifle with his threadbare adolescents, as if he were afraid to write candidly about his coevals? Why does he drift with the sentimental tide and make propaganda for provincial complacency? He must know better. He can do better. (pp. 90-3)

POSTSCRIPT.—He has done better. Almost as if to prove a somewhat somber critic in the wrong and to show that newer novelists have no monopoly of the new style of seriousness, Mr. Tarkington has in *Alice Adams* held himself veracious to the end and has produced a genuinely significant book. Alice is, indeed, less strictly a tragic figure than she appears to be. Desire, in any of the deeper senses, she shows no signs of feeling; what she loves in Russell is but incidentally himself and actually his assured position and his assured prosperity. So considered, her machinations to enchant and hold him have a comic aspect; one touch more of exaggeration and she would pass over to join those sorry ladies of the world of farce who take a larger visible hand in wooing than human customs happen to approve. But Mr. Tarkington withholds that one touch more of exaggeration. He understands that Alice's instinct to win a husband is an instinct as powerful as any that she has and is all that she has been taught by her society to have. In his handling she becomes important; her struggle, without the aid of guardian dowager or beguiling dot, becomes increasingly pathetic as the narrative advances; and her eventual failure, though signalized merely by her resolution to desert the inhospitable circles of privilege for the wider universe of work, carries with it the sting of tragedy.

Mr. Tarkington might have gone further than he has behind the bourgeois assumptions which his story takes for granted, but he has probably been wiser not to. Sticking to familiar territory, he writes with the confident touch of a man unconfused by speculation. His style is still swift, still easy, still flexible, still accurate in its conformity to the vernacular. He attempts no sentimental detours and permits himself no popular superfluities. He has retained all his tried qualities of observation and dexterity while admitting to his work the element of a sterner conscience than it has heretofore betrayed. With the honesty of his conclusion goes the mingling of mirth and sadness in *Alice Adams* as another trait of its superiority. The manners of the young which have always seemed so amusing to Mr. Tarkington and which he has kept on watching and laughing at as his principal material, now practically for the first time have evoked from him a considerate sense of the pathos of youth. It strengthens the pathos of Alice's fate that the comedy holds out so well; it enlarges the comedy of it that its pathos is so essential to the action. Even the most comic things have their tears. (pp. 93-4)

> Carl Van Doren, "Contemporary American Novelists: Booth Tarkington," in The Nation (copyright 1921 The Nation magazine, The Nation Associates, Inc.), Vol. CXII, No. 2901, February 9, 1921 (and reprinted in a slightly different form in his Contemporary American Novelists 1900-1920, The Macmillan Company, 1922, pp. 84-94).

## PERCY H. BOYNTON (essay date 1923)

To anyone who is interested in stories not as narrative formulas—hero, heroine, obstacle, happy dénouement—but as the chronicles of natural people, the popular endings of the Tarkington novels are usually anything but pleasant. For Mr. Tarkington is a composite of sensitive tenderness and brutal disregard. He naturally inclines toward the finer sorts of people for whom the man on the street has little use. He develops them with sympathy and a great deal of insight, and he does it well enough to endear them to the reader who can understand them. The impractical idealist of his pages is a grown-up Willy Baxter; Tarkington makes a real man of him—like Bibbs Sheridan, for example. He develops more than one young woman of beauty and strength. He gives them a genuinely maternal wisdom and patience. But having brought them into being in the midst of the turmoil, he faces an awkward dilemma. He must let the story dispose of them as it will, or he must dispose of them himself as the man on the street and his sentimental daughter would prefer. This is according to the commercial formula, "to be prosperous is to be happy," or the romance formula, "to be married is to be happy." But, as a matter of fact, such a disposition is often an affront to the reader and a cruel injustice to the character. . . . Yet it is quite apparent that Mr. Tarkington directed their fortunes out of a mistaken tenderness of heart, hoping for the best, and that the man on the street and his matinée daughter will be quite satisfied. As long as everything is pleasant when the curtain goes down. . . .

Another reason for the popular acclaim of Mr. Tarkington is his ability to deal as amiably with period background as with character. And the two are very closely related. Penrod and Clarence rejoice their irresponsible uncles, not only because

their endearing young charms are amusing in themselves, but because they are so amusingly like the boyhoods that their uncles look smilingly back to. Those boyhoods were spent somewhere from 1875 on, in social circumstances which have lapsed into a colorless half-oblivion except as someone with a vivid memory recalls them. Then the kindly smile of reminiscence rises. The illustrated section of the Sunday magazine capitalizes this feeling with its pictorial Do-You-Remember-Way-Back-When section. Mr. Tarkington makes a second appeal to his own generation in recalling the backgrounds as well as the years of their youth.

However, Mr. Tarkington has other qualities than those inherent in the salesmanship that makes "best sellers." If he did not mark the obvious distinction between mere popularity and solid excellence, Harold Bell Wright, Edgar Guest, George M. Cohan, and Dr. Frank Crane would be walking off with the Pulitzer prizes.

He has a clear eye for character, and he has created some that have won the widest of reputations. Since the Dickens triumphs of two generations ago Tom Sawyer has been the only boy to gain a celebrity as general as that of Mr. Tarkington's two protégés of eleven and seventeen. . . . [You] are safe in alluding to Penrod or to the boy who was Seventeen in any company.

It is in a measure true that these boys, and particularly the older one, have been presented for the benefit of older readers; but this comment has too often been made by critics as though it were an accusation instead of an appraisement; and, oddly enough, the same critics who have deplored Tarkington's softness of heart and sentimentalism in the matter of his plot-building, have deprecated his ironical and altogether unsentimental attitude toward childhood. They have apparently wanted to "get him going and coming," as if unwilling to be caught in the admission that he had done anything commendable of any kind. In forcing home this latter charge they have disparaged *Penrod* by citing *Tom Sawyer*. (pp. 114-18)

If the novelist is subject to indictment unless he writes to champion a social thesis, then unintelligence should be presented as a tragic fact. But if the novelist has a right and a duty to present life as he sees it, then he is bound—if he sees them—to hold the mirror up to some of the vast majority of unthinking people who perhaps ought to be bored to the verge of suicide by the utter tameness of their lots, but who in truth are having a very good time with life because unfortunately they do not know enough to be unhappy. Mr. Tarkington has a special gift for the delineation of this stratum because the individuals in it are children in all but years, and because he has a native aptitude for drawing children; and he is able, as Mr. Howells was before him, to demonstrate that, after all, the degree of interest in human subject-matter is determined chiefly by the magnifying power of the lens through which it is seen. At the same time the author is indubitably bigger than his characters. His sympathy with them is usually tinged with irony. He understands their mental and emotional processes but never identifies himself with them. He is affectionate but detached.

So, too, he is with the region and the period of his boyhood that he thoroughly enjoys. Always there is in his feeling the combination of affection and conscious appraisal that we recall in Daniel Webster's attitude toward Dartmouth College or in Touchstone's toward Audrey. So in his treatment of the nineties, Mr. Tarkington sees them not merely in themselves but with the historian's realization of what they were moving away from and what they were drifting toward. In this spirit he presents the social side of the end of the century with the fashions in dress, the domestic architecture and ménage, the favorite dances, songs, and plays, the prevailing leisure, . . . and the prevailing thrift. . . . (pp. 120-22)

Mr. Tarkington is neither an original nor an independent thinker. He is a not too searching realist, tinged with sentimentalism, and his mind is not unlike that of William Sylvanus Baxter's uncle. It is observant but untroubled by intense convictions. . . . On the whole, dear old Indiana is good enough for Mr. Baxter, and what is good enough for him ought to be good enough for the next generation. From which sentiments Mr. Tarkington shows no inclination to demur. Crowns and thrones may perish, Kingdoms rise and wane, But old Indiana, Constant shall remain.

He has been said never to have outgrown Princeton and Purdue. He has been a long time coming to it; but in his latest work Mr. Tarkington has finally come to the point where he could leave his friends in the hands of fate, where he could doom them to the consequences of their own personalities. In *Alice Adams* there are no eleventh-hour reprieves. Perhaps he has turned a corner. If this proves to be the case the many will applaud him less, but the wise will approve him more. (pp. 122-24)

> *Percy H. Boynton, "Booth Tarkington" (originally published in* English Journal, *Vol. XII, No. 2, February, 1923), in his* Some Contemporary Americans: The Personal Equation in Literature, *University of Chicago Press, 1924, pp. 108-25.*

### CHARLES C. BALDWIN    (essay date 1924)

Mr. Tarkington is that most incorrigible person, the parson's next of kin; and it follows that his sins are many. He is, for one thing, our most consummate liar; and—but that should suffice as a first count.

Take the end tacked onto *The Magnificent Ambersons.*

*The Magnificent Ambersons* retells the story of *The Egoist* in terms of a fast-growing city in our own Middle-West; and up to a certain point the retelling is admirable. Mr. Tarkington's hero is despicable: and Mr. Tarkington knows it. No pains are spared to deal out to him a fair and even justice. He is the gilded calf; but his feet are clay and Mr. Tarkington wastes no time in idle worship. Mr. Tarkington is fair—up to a certain point. . . .

The magnificence of the Ambersons began in 1873 when Major Amberson made a fortune; and the book tells of the blaze of glory in which his daughter marries, of the devotion with which she spoils her son and the arrogance in which that son grows up. He rides roughshod over friend and foe; and we wait, with his distracted neighbors, while fate (in the person of Mr. Tarkington) plays out to him the rope with which, soon or late, he must hang himself. We can bide our wrath, for time is with us. The world moves and he will be left standing, alone and forlorn, in his distorted attitude of graceless nobility. (pp. 474-75)

It is the old story of King Robert of Sicily—the mighty shall be cast down from their seats. We need no monks chanting the *Magnificat* to point the moral. We know. As I have said, we have Mr. Tarkington's word for it.

But have we? And even though that word be given can we rely upon it? Apparently not. George marries an heiress. (p. 476)

*Alice Adams* purports to be the true story of a true girl growing up in a pinched and stupid family, pretending to be at least as good as she is, making a friend and becoming engaged to him only to have the engagement broken when he meets the family.

As you can see, an ambitious plan carried (this time) to a fitting climax. It is perhaps a little too sentimental in its avowed sympathy for Alice; it may be less lively than is usual with Mr. Tarkington. . . . But it is good. The only fault that I can find is that again Mr. Tarkington has allowed his readers to do the writing for him. *Alice Adams* is every girl's idea of her own superiority to her miserable family. Mr. Tarkington shows us what she could have been, what she hoped to be, and then excuses her for not being all that one might expect because—well, look at the family!

Nor is Alice a tragic figure. All this pother is about nothing very much—except, of course, that she would rather marry than go to work. But desire, in any real sense, she never feels. It is not Russell that she loves but his assured prosperity and the assured position a marriage with him would give her. Indeed, her queer efforts to enchant her lover are of the stuff from which countless farces have been made. But that stuff is never farcical in the hands of Mr. Tarkington. And that is the true significance of *Alice Adams*. After so many years spent in laughing at and with adolescence, Mr. Tarkington has at last come to an understanding of the essential pathos of youth in a world dedicated to the pursuit of power and wealth.

It is a step forward. But Mr. Tarkington steps right back again in the latest of his offerings, *The Midlander. The Midlander*—if we are to believe Robert Morse Lovett; and I do believe him—is a feeble presentation of the Indiana superman, by conventional methods from material which has become trite.

Mr. Tarkington does not change. Indiana supermen, conventional methods, material that has become trite—these are his humanity, his wit and wisdom. For twenty-five years he has been writing about the Midlands and for twenty-five years, with one benign smile or another, he has murmured, with Harkless in *The Gentleman from Indiana*, "the dear, good people." The dear people, the good people—that, and that alone, is his comment on the emptiness and loneliness of life in the Middle-West, the futility of it, the shallow pretence, crowding together in hail-fellow clubs, bargaining with bootleggers, smirking when graver passions are mentioned, corrupting the language in feeble imitations of vaudeville actors doing the more expensive movie theaters. It may sicken his heroes; they may rebel; but it does not sicken Mr. Tarkington. You can always climb out of it, he says—always, mind you, and especially when Tarkington is your creator—and seen from above it's not so bad. . . .

That is the moral of *The Turmoil*. And the windup of *The Turmoil* is Bibbs Sheridan, an ugly duckling, with wasted years of dreaming behind him, suddenly, over night, to leave a good taste in the reader's mouth, become a master of capital and the lord of beauty. (pp. 477-79)

Mr. Tarkington has only one or two plots—in that being about three ahead of Mark Twain. "Don't worry about plot," Tarkington says. "The characters make their own plot—all the plot they should have. Think of them in their relation to one another and they will make your story. Your struggle should be against everything extraneous. It is unusual poignancy that makes a book unusual, not unusual plot. Treatment is the big thing.''

And it has been the big thing with Mr. Tarkington. (pp. 484-85)

*Seventeen* is ·Mr. Tarkington's high water mark. It is farce, without passion, without poetry, palpably insincere and shallow—but it is hilarious. The fool in every boy is made a hero and offers himself up as another Sidney Carton to the implacable stupidity of the world. Baxter never comes alive, but he is nonetheless a creation with his calf-love, his sighs, his fastidious scorn for the mere business of living; and I should no more think of criticizing him than I shall think of criticizing *Bunker Bean.*

Indeed it is folly to criticize Mr. Tarkington or to expect great things of him. Books are written to be read; and that would be his answer, as it was Dr. Johnson's long ago—the answer to a thousand cavils. There remains only a doubt as to whether it be answer enough. Dr. Johnson, at any rate, did not always truckle to the prejudices of his readers. (pp. 485-86)

> *Charles C. Baldwin, "Booth Tarkington," in his The Men Who Make Our Novels (reprinted by permission of Dodd, Mead & Company, Inc.; copyright 1919, 1924 by Dodd, Mead and Company, Inc.), revised edition, Dodd, Mead, 1924, pp. 474-86.*

**JOSEPH COLLINS**  (essay date 1927)

Booth Tarkington is one of our literary assets whose value has not been subject to profound fluctuation, and that is the more remarkable since he has made a complete *volte-face* from pure romance to sheer realism. Apparently, ideas and beliefs which crowded his mind and obstructed his vision in early maturity have been modified or dislodged by life and experience. This metamorphosis may account for his steady ascent from the exclusively idealized picture of Helen Fisbee in **"The Gentleman from Indiana"** to the realistic revelation of the Beautiful Widow, or of Mrs. Dodge in **"Women"**. In his later novels, there is abundant evidence that he is determined to cast off every vestige of romanticism. Yet he never quite succeeds. He still allows his dreams to come true, though never with such violence or success as in his early books. . . .

There is a striking similarity between Howells's novels and Mr. Tarkington's; but the style of the former is smooth, agreeable to the eye and harmonious to the ear, whereas Mr. Tarkington often does profound injury to the English language. . . .

It is possible that this was done with a purpose; the influence of some ultra-modern writer may have been weighing upon his mind. Yet when plain grammar is tampered with, the question of style for style's sake is no longer a matter of taste, but of rules. (p. 12)

Howells was a beacon light to Mr. Tarkington in his early years. From him, he derived the sense of reality, the artistic touch to everyday details, and the composition of a central figure, consistent with itself, true to its makeup and environment.

Mr. Tarkington does not let us watch life, with him, in his mirror. His method is not a direct one: he surveys his men and women and constantly interferes between them and us, telling us what to believe and what to see, what they do and what they like, but not what they think or what they feel. His views

are purely objective, and because he does not mingle with the intimate life of his characters he deprives us of a fine feeling of complete harmony with them.

It is difficult to say whether the Tarkington heroes are idealized pictures of what he himself would like to be, or the expression of a valiant struggle to bring romance and ideals to an alien land. There can be little doubt that John Harkless, his first fullfledged westerner, is a self portrait. In that novel, reality was distorted in an effort to create a "type". (pp. 12, 14)

The refusal to admit that materialism has superseded ideals may be traced in all his novels. It may be camouflaged a bit, as in Bibbs Sheridan's efforts to get away from "big business" or in Harlan Oliphant's determination to turn a deaf ear to progress and development; in George Minafer's ambition to redeem himself from his moral crime against his mother, or in Alice Adams's purposeful blindness to the obvious, in search of false values she cannot reconcile to reality. But it is there none the less.

Mr. Tarkington has an eye for the particular, a talent for details which, in its great lines, rivets his attention to local interest, to the detriment of the universal scheme. With the exception of a few exotic tales which reveal him as a gifted cosmopolitan, Indiana is the beginning and the end of his world. In his most widely read novels, he is Indianian through and through. When his eye seeks repose and new interests, it lands on the virtues of his own people, on their gifts and the blessings that have been lavishly dispensed to them.

Mr. Tarkington is not often concerned with plot. In **"Monsieur Beaucaire"** and **"The Magnificent Ambersons"** he displays ability to handle it, but in **"The Turmoil"** and **"The Two Vanrevels"** it deserts him. His preoccupation is to show characters rather than to tell a story, and it is a wise determination, because he is never more successful than when he focuses his power on character depicting. No one can say that **"Penrod"**, **"Women"**, **"Penrod and Sam"**, or even **"Alice Adams"** has a definite action, yet they are Tarkington's most popular books and, from the literary standpoint, the most worthwhile of his stories.

The same men live through every one of his novels, under different masks, in diverse walks of life, and with personal characteristics which change their patterns enough to make them outstanding as individuals, not members of one family. (p. 14)

**"The Two Vanrevels"** is the halfway house on Mr. Tarkington's literary road: change of scenery, new passengers, added impedimenta. Young girls and their psychology, their dreams and their fancies, urges, pretenses, and motives now absorb the driver's mind. It cannot be said that the Tarkington youths, so long admired, are typical of what young girls and boys are known to be; they are true only in certain respects. But Betty Carewe satisfies us that Tarkington found his new interest engrossing and meant to concentrate upon it in the future. Not that he relinquishes his hold on the romantico-real man, or on the traditional villain, for he gives us of both, and plenty, in each novel; he merely adds to his palette the softer hues of girlish youth, and sharp tones of humor. . . . Generally the humorous touches and the "strike home" truths are left to the younger members of the family—the naughty, incorrigible boy makes fun of his sister, while the young sister is a pest in the eyes and estimation of her older brother. **"The Gentleman from Indiana"** had as little humor as a baby has, but as Tarkington's literary family grew, they developed it until **"Women"** fairly reeks of it.

After **"The Two Vanrevels"** the author gives himself two short rides, one abroad and one into politics. No long description of places, no intimate revelations of the size and furnishing of houses, no small town talk and local preoccupations are to be found in the short stories of abroad. Brevity is the soul of his wit in those, in which he reveals a facility for handling the surprise element, especially in **"His Own People"**, which smacks of the O. Henry quality.

**"In the Arena"** depicts the men who go into politics for a living. Through the mire and the groveling souls of his characters, there still shines the ideal of the author: the honest man, not strikingly intelligent, but incapable of bargaining with his conscience or shirking his duty: the Dago, Pietro Tobigli; the Democrat, Uncle Billy Rollinson; Joe Lane and Melville Bickner—all a composite picture of idealism, western sentimentality, painful virtue.

Advancing steadily down the line of Mr. Tarkington's characters, we come to **"The Guest of Quesnay"**, in which plot is the essential element. Character depicting gives way to the telling of a story full of romantic possibilities. The great woman has now replaced the great man; men fall in love with her at first sight; her eyes are magnetic and her soul is as fair as her body; her heart vibrates in unison with the just, and injustice makes it arhythmic; her happiness is complete only in love and sacrifice. In each novel, Mr. Tarkington endows at least one woman with perfection; he loves the swooning type so fashionable in the last century.

I have met many admirers of Edith Wharton who have not read "Sanctuary", one of the gems of her collection, and many readers of Tarkington who are not familiar with **"Cherry"**, one of his most artistic tales. The first thing that strikes one in **"Cherry"** is the repressed humor which he has so well under control. There is no hint that he does not take Mr. Sudgeberry seriously. William Fentriss is an eighteenth century John Harkless, an amusing Tom Vanrevel, a grown up Penrod. The tale is told with gusto and charm, refrained and tempered by dry wit. (pp. 15-16)

The romantic candle of Booth Tarkington held a dying sputter when he wrote **"Beauty and the Jacobin"**. It has the intangible loveliness of old music, the softness of faded daguerreotypes, but none of the qualities that make rarefied air breathable to the few. It was indeed his last effort at pure romance.

In **"The Flirt"** he leaves behind him the foreign, the exotic, the intangible; the middle west, his own state, its people and their problems, seem suddenly to engross him. He knows them, loves them, understands the pathetic and the comic side of their makeup, and he is confident that he has discernment in his affections and critical power in his attachments.

For the first time, we have the Tarkington "boy" in a novel. He is a foil for Booth Tarkington's views and thoughts. Henrick Madison is as typical of what we think boys are as Penrod is, and more, because he is the mouthpiece of the world at large in his relations with his sister, his family, his life, and life in general.

The new departure of Tarkington did not much affect his views of idealism and romance, although he blended them with pictures of appalling reality. The world around his characters is as concrete and real as beef and cabbage. The small Indiana town is there, fully painted, drearily accurate. So are the Tar-

kington heroes. Somehow, the good men of the Tarkington world are unattractive because they are so absolutely uninteresting. **"The Flirt"** is undoubtedly the dividing line between the two Tarkington manners: pure romance and a semblance of realism. It divides the story teller and the painter of characters; it removes its author from the chronicler of men's doings and puts him in the limited class of propagandist for the west, its defender and champion.

**"The Turmoil"** is the great, everlasting story of love accomplishing what neither doctors nor sanatoriums, parental threats nor thought taking could achieve: the evolution from impotency to power, from a dreamer of useless dreams to a quick witted, active, useful individual; from a discouraged, dull, dismal person to an articulate, ambitious, accomplished husband. Bibbs Sheridan is typical of Tarkingtonian heroes in his search for something beyond everyday interests; in his attempts at poetry and essay writing we have a glimpse of the never dying romancer, as convincingly portrayed as in **"Monsieur Beaucaire"** but chastened, hardened, "made" by life—not broken. (p. 16)

Big business, giving wealth of the mushroom sort to men of otherwise uncouth and uncultured extraction, must of necessity do so at the expense of the older family of a medium size Indiana town; this is the foundation of **"The Magnificent Ambersons"**, one of Tarkington's most significant novels. It remains powerful until the closing episode wrecks it irretrievably. . . .

**"The Midlander"** is the last of Tarkington's novels depicting his typical hero in familiar guise. It is another stone to his edifice which rests on the belief that progress means ugliness, and that the western world is a constantly moving and shifting process of adjustment. (p. 17)

Mr. Tarkington's women, like his men, are all of one psychological pattern. The relationship which exists between the men of Booth Tarkington's creation may be traced between his women. From the first, Helen Fisbee of **"The Gentleman from Indiana"**, we have a picture of the author's ideal woman, and he remains as true to that picture as he does to his conception of male ideals.

His women, however, may be divided into several groups. First, the Helen Fisbee type, a miniature of the perfection of the cosmos, endowed with every quality of nobility. To her group belong the strong, faithful, loyal, somewhat masochist girls of later novels. . . . (pp. 17-18)

Besides that group, there is the "eternal woman", vivacious and beautiful. She begins with Betty Carewe of **"The Two Vanrevels"** and goes on down the line with Sylvia of **"Cherry"**, Cora Madison of **"The Flirt"**, who is in some ways the twin sister of Alice Adams, and a first but unsophisticated cousin of Lucy Oliphant.

The Tarkington women are either too reckless or not enough. They are either kind, self sacrificing, or impetuous, wilful, stubborn, like Edith Sheridan of **"The Turmoil"** or Cora Madison. . . . Or else they are too good to be true, too idealized to be real, too saintly to be human.

Alice Adams is the exception; she is as real as Emma Bovary. She is as true of today as of any time since there have been women—and men. None of Mr. Tarkington's pictures of small town life in Indiana are more real than those of **"Alice Adams"**. He saw it with a woman's eye, and women make the social life of the community. Its gossipy interest, its spirit of rivalry, the humiliations and little victories one suffers and enjoys are all there, ''as big as life and twice as natural''.

Alice is true to life and true to herself. Her weakness is perhaps the protraction of her pretense. (p. 18)

''**Gentle Julia**'' is not Alice's sister: she belongs to the Tarkington women who wrought havoc with the men they inspired to heroic deeds: the Cora Madison and Edith Sheridan types. She gets away with everything, a conspicuous attribute of pretty, angelic looking, devilish acting women the world over.

The last of Booth Tarkington's women came in all at once in ''**Women**''. There is no denying that he learned women's minds and hearts from keen observation, and he knows how to make them stand out in a background of familiar environment. ''**Cornelia's Happiest Hour**'' is a gem of understanding, and the fact that Mr. Tarkington forgets that he is a champion when he writes of women makes him hold up the mirror to reality in the proper light. His women act, talk, think, and suffer much as women do in real life; they have hysterics and sharp tongues like many women, and they are done with the fine end of a pen dipped in subtle ink. By going from one house to another, raising roofs and looking in, Mr. Tarkington has done a gallery of feminine pictures which reveal him as a serious student and painter of character. (pp. 18-19)

The youngest child is often the star in the family firmament, but the reverse is frequently true of literary children. The first is often brilliant, the last a dunce. ''**The Plutocrat**'' is the most unpromising child of Mr. Tarkington's mind. (p. 19)

It is somewhat pathetic to witness the struggle of a stubborn individual, bent on putting over an idea in a world that no longer wants to accept it. And yet ''**The Plutocrat**'' is just that; it leaves a sense of the uselessness and waste of time in writing such a story. (p. 20)

Much can be said, and has been said, in praise of Mr. Tarkington's novels. The reading world is indebted to him for much pleasure and some enlightenment. It regrets that he did not give equally of both: save in few instances we know very little about his men and women. All we know is what he tells us, for his is not the subtle gift which implies an idea with such power that it soon becomes our own. His bulk stands conspicuously between us and the inner light that would illumine the characters. We remain strangers to the fate of the men and women of his creation because we are not allowed a peep into their fundamental makeup. We are attentive listeners to their tales, never participants of their dreams.

His stories create pictures and situations, all in the impersonal, Tarkington manner; there is no effort at analysis, at critical understanding, at profound search into individual reactions, at semblance of logic in actions. We accept them as he gives them to us, and we are constantly confronted with Alice Adamses, Penrods, Mrs. Dodges and Sheridans. But none of the Tarkington heroes remain in our hearts and help us over the rough passages, as those of Howells or Maupassant do. It is all superficial and external, and it lacks, more than anything, the sacred fire of inspiration. Perfect background and an eye for incidental details make for greatness, but do not constitute it.

It is Tarkington's belief that primitive passions have no play in human characters. Lust and lustful desires, yielding to temptations that have been part and parcel of man's makeup since time immemorial, seem abhorrent to him. He will not admit that men and women have passions that may carry them away

from the accepted code of morality. His heroes fall in love, but they seldom feel the call of the flesh; they dream about women, but they do not seem to mind much if their dreams never come true. They are as sexless as angels are reputed to be. There is never a time, in the lives of these men and women who breathe and suffer, when passions become so overwhelming in intensity as to make them lose sight of the way approved by convention.

The characters of Tarkington who are affected by love are generally sentimental and romantic, yet temptation never gets beyond their control. To deny passion its potency is to deny man and woman the greatest source of happiness and of inspiration that has been vouchsafed them. In none of Tarkington's novels is there one gallant surrender, one all powerful surge of emotion that sweeps convention to the winds and scatters its ashes on the way to a higher aim. We deal with the commonplace, the drab, the narrow side of realism, and we do not even have, as compensation, the beauty and the power of realism. The ideals with which Tarkington endows his men and women are of the sort that are not encountered in life, save in rare instances; whereas the struggle for beauty, the effort to rise from the daily drivel and drudge of life, are absent in his novels—such effort would require a code of morals not always in keeping with that of the ''nice'' people of the nineties who aimed at snuffing out self expression and self indulgence.

The Tarkington men work for an ideal, generally a woman, but they seldom have the courage to go after it as they do after success. They are in love with love, on an impractical and intangible basis; they love a picture of something their minds tell them is ''ideal''; and they conform their conduct to the dictates of their heads, regardless of the claims of their hearts.

Heart, meaning emotion, is an unknown quantity in his world. For it he substitutes accuracy in details, a firm determination to remain within the narrow confines of western ideals. His books may be read without expense of innocence. (pp. 20-1)

> *Joseph Collins, ''The New Mr. Tarkington'' (reprinted by permission of the Literary Estate of Joseph Collins), in* The Bookman, *New York, Vol. LXV, No. 1, March, 1927, pp. 12-21.*

**BARRETT H. CLARK** (essay date 1938)

[Tarkington's] novels of midwestern life are notable contributions to our own peculiar brand of naturalism: his best novels, that is, like ''**The Magnificent Ambersons.**'' In ''**Seventeen**'' and the lighter works he has achieved success in the depiction of young people, their sorrows and joys, above all their pathetic attempts to grow up.

But the theater has always attracted this enormously successful novelist, and for nearly twenty years he has sought—either alone or in collaboration—to win success in the theater. The truth of the matter seems to be that he never took playwriting seriously: he appears, in all his early plays, to have learned the tricks, but none of the art of playwriting. . . . But with ''**Clarence**,'' in 1920, it was evident that Tarkington could write as distinguished a work for the stage as he ever wrote in narrative form, and the plays he has since written are, if not as well-sustained as ''**Clarence**,'' at least skillful examples of playwriting. (pp. 399-400)

''**Clarence**'' is (with one exception) the first play written by the author without the aid of a collaborator, and it is by all odds his best. In playwriting—as in many other things—it is by no means true that two minds are better than one. Tarkington and Wilson are both first-rate novelists, but the plays they have written together are, with perhaps one exception, in no way comparable to their novels. . . .

**"Clarence"** is a true comedy of character. Tarkington has discarded most of the stage tricks he evidently thought indispensable in his early work, and produced a play that is well-written, amusing, and a real revelation of character. (p. 401)

**"Clarence"** is, *of its kind,* a brilliant comedy of pure character; but there is little use in comparing it with the mature work of Hauptmann. The most we can say is that it is not so full of overtones, it is not so deeply impregnated with the sense of life, as certain other plays are.

"Of its kind." What is its "kind"? A comedy of character. Are not all comedies comedies of character? The more character the less plot is not an immutable rule, but it is generally a fact. (p. 402)

Tarkington does not, it would seem, care much for Gorky or Shaw or Wedekind. He expresses the "happy" viewpoint that is characteristic of most healthy Americans. Grant Overton relates that in his novels, Tarkington sees no use in delving down into the sex-life of his characters.

We go, and ought to go, to the theater for pleasure, and if "sex" and "gloomy thoughts" do not give you pleasure, then you have only to keep away from theaters where the plays of Chekhov and O'Neill and Hauptmann are performed. Still, sex and gloomy thoughts are part of life, and any artist who makes up his mind to have absolutely nothing to do with them will (to say the least) find himself very limited in his subject-matter. (pp. 403-04)

Consider **"Clarence"**; does the author's optimistic view of life prevent his telling anything essential about his characters? Certainly, he *could* have revealed many "unpleasant" aspects of temperament and character in all the personages. Was it necessary, however?

Can you imagine **"Clarence"** written by Wedekind, or Chekhov, or Andreyev? (p. 404)

> *Barrett H. Clark, "The American Drama," in his* A Study of the Modern Drama: A Handbook for the Study and Appreciation of Typical Plays, European, English, and American, of the Last Three-Quarters of a Century *(copyright, 1925, 1928 by D. Appleton and Company; copyright, 1938, by D. Appleton-Century Company, Inc.; reprinted by permission of the Estate of Barrett H. Clark), revised edition, Appleton, 1938, pp. 359-410.*

**BOOTH TARKINGTON**   (essay date 1941)

[*In the following excerpt Tarkington describes how he wrote his first published novel,* The Gentleman from Indiana.]

One day as I sat facing the fact that I'd been working for four years with blank results, I remembered the novel I'd begun when I came home after Princeton [*The Gentleman from Indiana*], and abruptly I saw why it had jammed itself into a blind alley. I got the manuscript out, began it again, found that I had some control over the story, and, though I was without any hope that it would ever see print—I couldn't imagine anything of mine doing that—I worked month after month after month upon it.

I tried to keep out of it any imitation of my literary gods, Alphonse Daudet, Victor Cherbuliez, Dickens, Irving, Henry James, Howells, Mark Twain, Stevenson, Thomas Hardy, Thackeray and George Meredith—I'd at last grown up enough to come round to Meredith—but of course bits and echoes of all of them got into it. Mark Twain was the hardest to keep out, because I tried to pitch the style principally in the key of Middle West ordinary speech. My father's talk, recorded literally, was like Mark Twain's writing; so were the spoken words of most of the intelligent midland men I knew of that generation, and daily I heard that way of speech all about me. It was the native way, just as it was natural to Mark Twain, himself a midland man of the same period; and as he talked, so he customarily wrote.

The texture of my novel thus couldn't wholly avoid being pseudo-Mark Twainish in spots if kept faithful, and, though of course romance and even melodrama got into the made-up events, I kept the telling as homely as I youthfully could.

There was something behind the story—a young hurt and a young championage. I'd first begun to feel the hurt, rather puzzledly, when from Princeton I visited Eastern classmates and their families, and observed that my Hoosier origin was ignored with conscious tact by these kindhearted people. It was as if I had a physical defect, they so thoughtfully avoided seeming to be aware of it. . . . Eastern newspapers then cherished the legend that Indiana was a backwoods state; our rusticity was an established mark for mechanized journalistic humor.

Sensitive and even resentful, I tried to make my novel answer all this nonsense. That heaven of my boyhood, Marshall, was just over the Indiana border and in Illinois; but out of fond memories I built it into an Indiana county seat and set the scene of my story there. A thing the novel tried to say was that in the matter of human character the people of such an out-of-the-way midland village were as estimable as any others anywhere, maybe rather more so—indeed, that even in its most bucolic aspect Indiana belonged to the beautiful and the good. This, in my sensitive young fervor, was my emotional tribute to the land of my birth. (p. 85)

> *Booth Tarkington, "As I Seem to Me" (© 1941 The Curtis Publishing Company; copyright renewed © 1968 by Merchants National Bank & Trust Company of Indianapolis, executor of the Literary Estate of the author Booth Tarkington; reprinted by permission of the Literary Estate of Booth Tarkington), in* The Saturday Evening Post, *Vol. 214, No. 8, August 23, 1941, pp. 27, 80-8.*

**VAN WYCK BROOKS**   (essay date 1952)

[*This excerpt, from the fifth volume of Brooks's history of American literature to 1915, gives a balanced retrospective evaluation of Tarkington's work.*]

Booth Tarkington and William Allen White, native realists, as they were called, prolonged in their novels and stories the genial note of the horse-and-buggy age. Many of their characters suggested the Kentons, the normal kindly folksy souls of whom William Dean Howells had written with such affection, the "really happy people" whom Theodore Dreiser had also found in Indiana towns that he described as vigorous and hopeful. . . . Both retained in their native scene the faith that Dreiser had only lost because, as he explained it, he had "seen

Pittsburgh,'' and democracy for them was a reality rather than a dream. This was partly because their small-town world was ''one big jolly family'' still, like the Plattsville of Tarkington's *The Gentleman from Indiana*. In a sense their America was the ''nation of villagers'' that Bernard Shaw called the country, still racially simple, still largely agricultural and rural, a world to which the young editor Harkless had wished to come back for his career because people were ''kinder'' there than they were in New York. (pp. 328-29)

It was true that both Tarkington and William Allen White found much to condemn in this genial scene, which they were disposed to chasten because they loved it,—the ''certain rich man,'' for example, who presently appeared in the novel of White and who rose to great wealth by chicanery, though he fell in the end. For Tarkington's subtler and abler mind much was amiss with the world of his youth, especially its tendency to become like other regions, lover that he was of the old village life, the whittler on the fence-rail, the rusty silk hat, the buggy, the alpaca coat and the tilted chair. . . . All his more sensitive characters disliked the growth of their Midland city, the noise, the dirt and the rush of machinery and bigness, the ''mere shapelessness on the run'' that befouled itself and darkened the sky as lines of houses shot out all over the country. They remembered what one of them called in *The Turmoil* the ''pleasant big town of neighbourly people,'' leisurely, kindly, homelike, of much the same type, who jogged about in their phaetons and surreys for a family drive on Sunday through the placid fields and woodlands that surrounded the town. It had all been happier and wiser when it was smaller and cleaner, when, with plenty of time to live, there had been few of the snobberies of wealth that caused so much of the heartache of Alice Adams.

But, as Tarkington himself observed, his people had always longed for ''size,'' though they sometimes disliked the consequences when they achieved it, and, while Tarkington recoiled from the ''bigger and better,'' he shared many of the tastes that led to it,—he was quite at home with the folksy Hoosier boosters. He was to draw in *The Plutocrat* one of the few sympathetic pictures of the big booming Western business man, and his young poet Bibbs in *The Turmoil*, who detested business at the start, gladly joined in the end in the money-shuffle. Was not business leading to ''some good future''? So Bibbs,—and his creator,—thought; but was not this just the future of more good plumbing and more paved streets that also gladdened the heart of William Allen White? (pp. 329-30)

Booth Tarkington, who was more complex, could never have shared White's satisfaction with the somewhat militant mediocrity of this typical town. All the ''park systems'' in the world would not have been enough for him, or even his old Sheridan's ''carloads'' of ''culture and refinement.'' But he was still further removed from the writers whose heroes disgustedly left the town or saw only its drabness and dullness, its errors and frustrations. He was aware of the delusions and foibles of its cult of prosperity and progress. . . . In *Young Mrs. Greeley* he described the banalities of a corporation banquet as inimitably as Sinclair Lewis could ever have done it. But how fiercely in *The Plutocrat* he turned on the three young highbrow snobs who sneered at his ''middle-class Middle Western'' hero and the smoky twilight in which he and his friends ''groped ignobly for money'' and babbled in their Western dialect about their grubbing. How astonished they were that Madame Momoro, the beautiful sphinx on the voyage to Algiers, was drawn to this shocking type of the prosperous vulgar who was so afraid

of ''Honey'' and ''Baby,'' as he called his wife and daughter, and behaved like an infantile barbarian on ship and on shore. In Algiers he saw nothing but dirt and backward people who needed a ''good live snappy Board of Health,'' while, scattering his money on every side, with his friendly concern and hearty voice, he was ''like a sack of sugar spilled in the sun for the bees and ants.'' The Easterners could not understand how really good he was because, as his daughter told them, they lived ''in New York.''

Now this portrait of Tinker, the ''plutocrat,'' was one of Booth Tarkington's triumphs, which was only equalled by Sinclair Lewis's Dodsworth, though the story was not quite subtle enough and the humour was laid on too thick for the book to be an authentic masterpiece. This big broad-faced midlander was a type of the American business man whom no other novelist had ever portrayed so well. . . . Tarkington loved his Tinker as Balzac was said to have loved his Valérie, as Lewis loved Dodsworth and Howells loved Silas Lapham. So Mark Twain had loved his Philistine Connecticut Yankee.

This element of love in a novelist's work was misprized in days to come when even the creation of character was not greatly valued, when the sympathetic picture of American life was distrusted by the advance-guard, who could only credit a picture that was unsympathetic. But the older novelists who created characters when so to create was the novelist's aim frequently loved the figures they called out of the void, and there was no reason to suppose that the future would demand a *mise en scène* that was always and exclusively frustrating, drab and evil. That Tarkington loved Tinker and Indiana was not the weakness one quarrelled with when one quarrelled, as one did inevitably, with Tarkington's work, and it might even have been supposed that his affection for his people and scenes enabled him all the better to understand them. . . . This feeling of Tarkington's helped him to write *The Magnificent Ambersons*, perhaps his best novel, a typical story of an American family and town,—the great family that locally ruled the roost and vanished virtually in a day as the town spread and darkened into a city. This novel no doubt was a permanent page in the social history of the United States, so admirably conceived and written was the tale of the Ambersons, their house, their fate and the growth of the community in which they were submerged in the end. (pp. 331-34)

[Only] Booth Tarkington's feeling for the people and the town made this book, like *The Plutocrat*, a memorable novel, more memorable even than *Alice Adams*, a tragedy of caste in the Middle West that was much more nearly perfect as a work of art. For the central character in *Alice Adams* was permitted to create its own story, and this was all but unique in Tarkington's work, his weakness being that his novels did not follow their logical course but were modified to conform to Hoosier folkways. *The Magnificent Ambersons* might have been a great symbolical American story if the family had been irrevocably engulfed and lost in the town, but the arrogant George Amberson, suddenly poor, becomes a considerate, hard-working young man, already on the way to retrieve the family fortunes. Just so old Sheridan, the tyrant in *The Turmoil*, bull-headed, stubborn and hard, becomes in the end imaginative, kind and gentle, while Bibbs, the ineffectual dreamer and poet, when he gets down to brass tacks, becomes the master-capitalist overnight. These swift regenerations and lightning-like changes of character destroyed the coherence and integrity of Tarkington's novels, and it was notable that in his failure to conduct his stories to their logical end he always wound up in a fashion that pleased his neighbours. That is to say, he adjusted his characters, whatever they were, to the point of view that the best thing is to get on and make money, for, although the tables might quite as well have been turned the other way, the business men always have the laugh of the poets and the highbrows. Tarkington's implication is that poetry is "woman's work," as old Sheridan says before Bibbs awakens from his trance, and the trouble with Tarkington was not that he loved the well-to-do Hoosiers he wrote about but that he accepted so readily their Philistine standards. He was not sufficiently detached from his world to criticize its values,—which is merely a way of saying that he never grew up, that he remained the college boy who failed to establish his independence in his prosperous Hoosier lawyer father's house.

So Tarkington, the prince of popular novelists, was never taken seriously,—in critical circles he sat below the salt,—in spite of a brilliant satirical gift that rivalled Sinclair Lewis's and a feeling like Scott Fitzgerald's for the glamour of youth. For who could evoke better than he the magic of the "last waltz together"? (pp. 334-35)

> Van Wyck Brooks, "Looking Westward," in his The Confident Years: 1885-1915 (copyright, 1952, by Van Wyck Brooks; copyright renewed © 1980 by Mrs. Van Wyck Brooks; reprinted by permission of the publishers, E. P. Dutton, Inc.), Dutton, 1952, pp. 321-36.*

**ALBERT VAN NOSTRAND** (essay date 1955)

With one or two exceptions, Tarkington's plays dramatize the subjects of his novels: the American abroad, the ideology of capitalism, and the domestic comedy. Moreover, the plays tend to caricature these subjects. The American tourist, for instance, so thoroughly treated in the novels, becomes in the plays the prototype of the provincial who is thrust into one exotic and urban society after another, whether abroad or at home; and the humor arises inevitably from this incongruity. To this group belong [*The Man from Home, Foreign Exchange, Getting a Polish, Mister Antonio, The Country Cousin,* and *Up from Nowhere*]. . . . (p. 16)

These are all variations on *The Man from Home,* the saga of Daniel Voorhees Pike, the Indiana lawyer who travels to Italy to rescue his ward from her misalliance with a degenerate aristocrat. This play was so enthusiastically received that the intended satire of Pike's chauvinism never materialized, as Tarkington later reminded [producer George C.] Tyler:

> When we made our hero say absurd things which we not infrequently heard first-trip Americans saying, in Europe, we were not very well understood, I fear. We had been in the habit of collecting naive patriotics, and found the collection handy—but the effect of them, as given forth by Daniel Voorhees Pike, was unforeseen and astonishing. When he declared "I wouldn't trade our State Insane Asylum for the worst ruined ruin in Europe" we were laughing at him; thought the audience would laugh at him, as we did, forgivingly. The New York critics thought we meant that we wouldn't trade the asylum for Pompeii, and reproved us for bunkum and for attacking the culture of Europe. Of course, I don't mean that this play could be thought a proper piece of work today; thank

heaven it couldn't! The "types" and the co-incidental impossibilities of plot have long since become stock stuff in the general discard, but the thing wasn't contemporaneously attacked for the coincidental impossibilities—it was attacked, as I say, principally for its "Middle Westness."

The "stock stuff" which Tarkington mentions in his letter, the melodrama, and the polarity of the characterization as regards moral behavior, was at the time part of its tremendous appeal. Nearly twenty years after the play's opening, when Tarkington had agreed to Tyler's request that he revise it for a new production, he wrote to the producer analyzing what had made this appeal, and acknowledging the need to conform to new fashions. Structurally, he wrote, the play was good and not to be interfered with; it merely needed "resurfacing." But to the purpose of conforming to present fashion, he declared, the "exaggerated coloring" must go. With the encouragement of his audiences, Will Hodge made the character of Pike into a braggart. Pike must be made genuinely modest, yet conscious of no social inferiority. His adversaries—the aristocratic pretenders—must also be made more credible.

For all his humorous idiosyncrasies, nevertheless, Pike's convictions were meant to be taken seriously, and the temptation to draw a moral from the discrepancy between provincial virtues and cosmopolitan vices was even more evident in the next play of Tarkington and Wilson, *Foreign Exchange.* . . . Located in France and concerned with an American couple on the grand tour, visiting their daughter whom they have married into a titled French family, this play is a caricature of most of Henry James's early novels. It dramatizes the rescue of an American girl and her child from her husband, the Count of Savergne. Like James's Madame de Mauves, this heroine has married an idea, a distorted notion of aristocracy, only to find herself surrounded by a strange and frightening code of morals. But, unlike the formidable heroine of James, this girl contrives to run away. The plot of her escape involves a series of episodes which cure the girl's mother of social climbing. The play closed a week after it opened, in Chicago's Grand Opera House, and it was immediately followed by another one like it. *If I Had Money* . . . again demonstrates the disparity between provincial and suburban societies. The adversaries belong respectively to Yellow Dog, Montana, and New York's Fifth Avenue. (pp. 16-18)

*If I Had Money* marked one more development in the treatment of the provincial. The authors discovered that this character did not have to be sent abroad in order to manifest his kind of Americanism. There might, in fact, be some advantage in juxtaposing his virtues with the dubious type of person who apparently denied these same virtues right here at home. George Tyler suggested this some years later to Tarkington, pointing out that the plot of *The Man from Home* could be readily adapted with a young lady fulfilling the function of Daniel Voorhees Pike. The playwright was amenable. In the summer of 1915 Tarkington set to work with a collaborator, Julian Street, and their first draft was completed in two months. Revised considerably, it was produced as *The Ohio Lady* . . . , and completely rewritten it appeared the following season as *The Country Cousin.* . . . (p. 18)

It is a permutation of *The Man from Home.* The expatriate in the new play is a young lady from Ohio, the legatee of a wealthy uncle, who yearns to escape from the Midwest and to live like the people in the rotogravures. She goes to Long Island to live with her father and her stepmother, who allow her to rent for them an expensive suburban estate. When it becomes evident that the girl is being victimized by her parents, her elder cousin, Nancy Price, is sent to her rescue. Miss Price is the counterpart of Daniel Voorhees Pike in *The Man from Home*, and her adversaries, the socialites, are equally familiar. They are represented primarily by the character of George Tewksbery Reynolds, III, ''a superior and triumphant youth of twenty-eight; very smart, half-Bostonese English, yet altogether a New Yorker,'' whose action signifies the capitulation of this whole group to the superiority of Middle Western virtues. . . . [The intention] was to make the hero and heroine represent opposing kinds of Americanism, and to convey an attitude toward this disparity by means of the plot. The Ohio spinster tames the cosmopolite by ignoring his pretensions and judging him on her own terms. Moreover, 1917 offered a ready market for the play's chauvinism. Miss Price's continual iteration that these bounders are wasting their time when they might more profitably employ themselves in the service of their country finally rouses the hero, who enlists in the army and goes off in the last act to begin his training at Plattsburg. (pp. 18-19)

One other play in this group, *Mister Antonio* . . . , develops the antipathy between urban and provincial. The play is an account of small town hypocrisy, and it anticipates Tarkington's later novels, in which he assumes ''provincial'' to be a relative term, and champions that character who most represents the homely virtues. His method is to contrast the uncomplicated faith of the hero in himself to the pretension of his antagonists. Mr. Antonio is an Italian hand-organ man who rescues a tourist about to be thrown out of a New York bar. The disgraced tourist is next discovered in his professional capacity as the mayor of a small Pennsylvania town, about to ostracize one of his servants for her harmless indiscretion in patronizing a local roadhouse. Tony's arrival on the scene, and his threat—in the girl's behalf—to expose the mayor's own indiscretion, prompts the mayor to try to have him shot. There is an unconvincing reconciliation, but the play's worst offense is mistaking comedy for melodrama. (p. 19)

Tarkington also wrote several thesis plays about the ideology of capitalism. These are associated with his economic novels, although developing more bluntly than the novels the conservative attitude toward free enterprise. The most important of these plays was *Poldekin*. . . . It was the single occasion on which the author frankly used the stage for editorial comment; and its failure caused him sharp disappointment. The play concerns the fortunes of a missionary band sent by Soviet Russia to hasten, by whatever means at its disposal, a proletarian regime in the United States. One of the revolutionaries is Poldekin, despised by his colleagues for his inclination to doubt the wisdom of his party's policies. From the back yard of a New York tenement, where the group has established its headquarters, Poldekin sets out to find his own America. . . . (p. 20)

The play is an informal debate, and its characters are embodied points of view. At the time the author was criticized for setting up and knocking down a ''Bolshevist strawman,'' and for portraying as well an Americanism equally unformidable, even smug. But by his caricature of the revolutionaries Tarkington did achieve their absolute humorlessness and, hence, a suggestion of the sinister. . . .

Tarkington was after a tone of whimsy and pathos, as he made clear in an issue which arose over the ending of the play. As originally written, Poldekin was slain by his comrades after revealing what he had printed. But in the out-of-town tryouts

George Arliss made the character so winning that the audiences were dissatisfied with his death. Arliss and Tyler both demanded a new ending, one in which Poldekin would somehow escape harm, winning at the same time the sympathies of the daughter of one of the revolutionaries. This the playwright stubbornly opposed. He conceded the validity of the box office, but pointed out that a happy ending would be insipid; that it would belie the characters of the antagonists. . . . The happy ending, he wrote, was a palpable between-the-eyes lie, and there was no way to tell it without getting caught. The alternative of having someone shoot at Poldekin but miss he impatiently rejected, and his argument was a comment on the kind of play he was attempting. (p. 21)

In contrast to the thesis plays are others singularly unburdened by editorial comment. These are the domestic comedies dramatizing the family scene, and corresponding to the domestic novels. . . . [*Clarence, The Wren, The Intimate Strangers, Rose Briar*, and *Tweedles*] belong to this group. . . . Similar in theme, his domestic novels and domestic plays move, however, in different directions. The novels are preoccupied with the mutual involvement of the characters in a given domestic situation. (p. 22)

*Colonel Satan* belongs to a group of Tarkington's period plays, which share exotic settings, sentimentalism, the perilous joining of comedy and melodrama, and the fact that they were all vehicles for particular actors. Like Tarkington's occasional historical novels, these plays represent a recurrent interest of the author and what he thought to be a recurrent interest of his audiences. The first of these was *Monsieur Beaucaire* . . . , a dramatization of his own novel to suit the talents of Richard Mansfield. The action of the original story was extended; the conflict between Beaucaire and his adversaries was underscored; a duel not called for in the original was written into the script and fought onstage; there was a new and more passionate scene between the hero and heroine; and the ending was changed to make certain their reconciliation. The effect of these changes was to elaborate the character of Beaucaire, and, in fact, under Mansfield's direction the other characters were allowed even less individuality than in the original story. (p. 26)

From Tarkington's first stage production, in which he modified the role of Beaucaire to suit Mansfield, to his last, which he wrote for [George] Arliss, the genesis of nearly every one of his plays lay in the personality of some particular individual. Nearly a third of them were written at the request either of actors themselves or of producers with certain players in mind. (pp. 26-7)

The New York critics came to expect skillful casting of each new Tarkington play. They took for granted the author's insistent attention to what he called ''balance.'' It was his search for ''balance,'' for the right combination of players, which delayed so long the production of *The Country Cousin*. . . . Whether to modify a character or to make the player adapt himself to it was ultimately determined by this concept of balance, as Tarkington understood it. (p. 28)

In view of the lack of formal criticism of Tarkington's plays, the reviews must be considered contemporary official opinion. In these reviews there is a great deal of speculation over why Tarkington's plays are not more impressive ''art,'' why they do not present more authoritative comment on contemporary problems, why, in short, they are not more conspicuously successful. Most reviewers speculated that since he was a novelist he took his plays less seriously. But this does not hold up. The similarity between plays and novels in theme and in language is extraordinary. The novels, in fact, often approximating a stage dialogue, and with their technique of advancing the narrative by scenes, frequently suggest the presence of a stage production. Moreover, the only distinction Tarkington made between his plays and his novels was that his plays were intended to be, if anything, the more popular. . . . Quite to the contrary of the reviewers' opinions, the fate of his plays was precisely because they were so like his novels. The discrepancy which the reviewers sought between Tarkington's plays and his novels was a property not of his writing but of the audiences for which he wrote. (p. 32)

[He] refused to make concessions to the prevailing opinion of his critics; and notwithstanding his statement that he tried to satisfy the inclinations of his audiences, he evidently disbelieved that they might want any startling departure from what was in his fiction. The marked tone of provincialism and the deliberate lack of sophistication remained stable elements in his plays, yet, as he continued to write through the nineteen twenties, the New York engagements of his plays became less impressive. Conversely, a number of his plays which barely survived a respectable Broadway engagement nevertheless succeeded eminently on the road.

Whether consciously or not, Tarkington actually represented the interests of a larger audience than that which he discovered on Broadway. He believed that it demanded entertainment; a well-defined narrative, with characters into which a reader or viewer could easily project himself, although with heroes and heroines perceptibly above normal; the assurance of a moral world, in which these characters could determine their own actions, and in which a just retribution afforded a final security. Upon these conditions, he believed, this audience would tolerate benevolent satire on its own shortcomings. (p. 33)

> Albert Van Nostrand, "The Plays of Booth Tarkington," in The Princeton University Library Chronicle (copyright © 1955 by Princeton University Library), Vol. XVII, No. 1, Autumn, 1955, pp. 13-39.

## JAMES WOODRESS   (essay date 1955)

[*Woodress's* Booth Tarkington *is the most complete study of Tarkington's life and works.*]

Even though Tarkington in his maturity disparaged his early fiction, [*Monsieur Beaucaire*] was a deservedly popular and well-constructed example of its literary genre, the costume romance; and its charm lies not only in the evocation of eighteenth-century England but also in the employment in its plot of the always appealing underdog who comes out on top. The story has won many admirers, one of whom—the hard-bitten Damon Runyon—wrote in 1937: "'**Monsieur Beaucaire**' is ever green. It is a little literary cameo, and we read it over at least once a year." (p. 72)

[Tarkington's first published novel, *The Gentleman from Indiana,*] was inspired by a genuine desire to extol the virtues of his native state. . . . With youthful tenderness and championship he set about to tell the story of John Harkless, stalwart young newspaperman who comes out of the East to settle in Plattville, Indiana. . . .

Although it is sentimentally romantic, the novel is overlaid with a realistic patina deriving from the author's memories of Marshall, Illinois. The setting evokes an historical epoch, much

as Mark Twain's Mississippi River locales hark back to his youth in Missouri, but the action is nominally contemporary, Harkless being a recent college graduate of the author's own generation. Part of the interest in the novel also lies in its use of the Whitecaps as the evil force against which the heroic Harkless is opposed. . . .

The real popularity of *The Gentleman from Indiana,* however, rested on the manly virtues of the hero and feminine charm of the heroine. By snaring his readers through the attractiveness of his idealized characters, Tarkington produced a novel that he later held in low critical esteem. (p. 82)

While Tarkington's [critical] theories looked forward towards realism, his practice also was moving slowly in that direction. One of his most curious works is *Cherry,* a burlesqued historical romance, which he laid in eighteenth-century Princeton and environs. When *Richard Carvel* appeared in 1899, it was "so rotten clumsy in the hero's telling what people said to him about himself" that it made Tarkington laugh and determine to satirize the awkward first-person narrative device. (p. 86)

"'**Cherry**' will get by," Tarkington wrote later, "if taken on the ground of its intention—but if you read it as a *story* it's all off!" Since most readers were expecting entertainment, the serial attracted little attention, and the book version, even with extensive revisions, made no great splash. . . . Tarkington's mistake in *Cherry* perhaps lay in his effort to combine two disparate kinds of satire—satire of historical fiction and of priggish human nature. Had he placed his story in Princeton in 1893, he might have managed to create an amusing comedy of manners; but unfortunately, as he later realized, "No one ever saw what I was up to!" (p. 87)

*The Two Vanrevels,* his last obeisance for thirty years to the "incredibly prevalent . . . entertainment for the 'tired businessman'"—the historical romance. Like Maurice Thompson's *Alice of Old Vincennes* (1900), it made use of Indiana history and was a popular success and best seller.

Laid in Terre Haute (Rouen in the novel) at the time of the Mexican War, Tarkington's new story drew its inspiration partly from his mother's memories of her schooldays at St. Mary-of-the-Woods. The heroine of this romantic tale, who is named Elizabeth for his mother, returns home from St. Mary's as the story opens, and her experience with the world outside the convent walls provides the plot of the novel. (p. 92)

[The] novel is a sentimental melodrama in which Betty's tyrannical father carries on a bitter but unsuccessful feud with his daughter's lover. The story, moreover, uses an elaborate case of mistaken identity and a cold-blooded murder to sustain the reader's interest. Yet Tarkington's selection of material capable of supporting a novel of manners indicates perhaps the transitional nature of the story. He gradually was working himself out of the stereotypes of the historical romance and laying the groundwork for his later studies of contemporary Indiana life. (pp. 92-3)

Although he modestly doubted his ability to write a political novel based on his recent term of office, he set to work . . . [on] the short stories that eventually grew into the collection *In the Arena*. . . . One was "**Boss Gorgett,**" a tale of machine politics in a mayoralty campaign. . . . This is a neatly plotted and well-spun little comedy using politics effectively as background coloring. Quite different, however, is "**The Aliens,**" . . . for it is a small, unrelieved tragedy, "a story of politics in a tough precinct," in which Tarkington's observation of ward politics at their slimiest produced a work of naturalistic fiction. (p. 112)

Tarkington's life breaks sharply at the critical date of January 16, 1912. After the emotional knots of the divorce had been unraveled and the physical specter of alcoholism conquered, he went back to his desk, and gradually the old delight in work returned; and with it came the old capacity to see and to do. . . . [The] amount of writing that he accomplished during the next ten years is prodigious, and its quality is uniformly high. (p. 166)

[He] told an interviewer that he planned to get back to prose fiction by warming up with short stories. Playwriting and fiction are two very different types of work, he said, "and I feel that I am very far away from fiction now." Accordingly, he began with one of his best stories, "**Mary Smith,**" a tale of a college sophomore on vacation. . . . (p. 167)

A first-rate story of adolescence, this tale foreshadows the better known *Seventeen*. . . . At last Tarkington was working with material close at hand and shaping it with a wonderfully acute comic sense. "**Mary Smith**" was the type of thing his talents best qualified him to write, for he was always the interested and sympathetic uncle who enjoyed observing and recording the activities of his nephews. His humorously exaggerated accounts of the problems of children and adolescents mirrored faithfully the comedy in American middle-class life.

Tarkington knew that he was following the right path in the work he had begun, and his next project was *The Flirt*, the first novel in his later manner. In it he abandoned elaborate plot, which had been his "stumbling block and curse for years," and let the characters make their own story. (pp. 167-68)

In several respects *The Flirt* was a proving ground for fictional materials that were subsequently to occupy a great deal of Tarkington's attention. Not only is it his first domestic novel, but it also is his first long fiction making significant use of a Midwestern city that is Indianapolis thinly disguised. The Madison family, moreover, belongs to the same submerging middle-class group that is treated later in *Alice Adams,* and the history of the Corlisses, who have been one of the city's great families, suggests the family dynasty chronicled in *The Magnificent Ambersons*. Cora, the flirt, is also the first of a good many selfish, egoistic women who make life a hell for their lovers and husbands in Tarkington's novels, and finally, it should be noted, Hedrick Madison, Cora's younger brother, is the earliest of Tarkington's juveniles, the prototype of Penrod Schofield. (pp. 168-69)

Tarkington was in full mastery of his literary medium when he wrote *Penrod*. His style, which is supple, articulate, witty, is equal to all the demands he makes of it and succeeds simultaneously in entertaining children and delighting adults. His management of detail is so deft and subtle that the juvenile reader enjoys vicariously the activities of Penrod and his gang and the adult takes pleasure in Penrod's "*suffering* and his mental processes, not what *happens* to him." Tarkington's episodes have traces of the tall tale, but in essence they are everyday incidents in which style and arrangement of detail are everything. The successive chapters detailing Penrod's secret authorship of "Harold Ramorez the Roadagent or Wild Life among the Rocky Mts." and the humiliating actualities of the Round Table are a brilliant juxtaposition of humorous irony; and the linking of Penrod's schoolroom dreams with the realities of arithmetic is a similarly effective stroke. The language of the boys, too, is fresh and the situations avoid triteness. (p. 179)

When he wrote *The Flirt*, [Tarkington] was chiefly interested in character development and noted only briefly the physical disparities between his home town before and after his years away. In the Penrod stories that followed he placed his action nostalgically "in the days when the stable was empty but not yet rebuilt into a garage" and did not have to grapple with either the tangible or intangible problems of the change.

Then early in 1914 he wrote *The Turmoil,* in which he indicted angrily the great despoiler, business. Once he had begun scrutinizing the social and economic life of his native community, the impulse continued for ten years and three more novels: [*The Magnificent Ambersons, Alice Adams,* and *The Midlander*]. . . . Intrinsically, these are well-made novels written in the tradition of commonplace realism as pioneered by Howells, and taken as a whole, they represent Tarkington in his major phase. All four are Indiana family chronicles against a business background, and together they paint a valuable picture of the urban Midwest during the early decades of this century. When the time comes that American life of this period must be reconstructed from documents, Tarkington's tetralogy will be immensely useful to the social historian. It is also worth noting that Tarkington was attacking American materialism a decade before Mencken and Sinclair Lewis discovered the "booboisie." (p. 182)

*The Turmoil* is the story of an ascending family, first-generation makers of the wealth. James Sheridan at the outset of the novel is the owner of the biggest skyscraper, the biggest trust company, and the biggest manufacturing works in the city. . . . His success in business has not prepared him for success in human relations, and while he possesses a Midas touch, his acquisitive genius is no more able than the fabled king's to buy happiness. . . . Sheridan wins his main contest, however, which involves his youngest son Bibbs, a fragile, poetic young man who wants no part in the family enterprises. Bibbs ultimately suppresses his own desire to write and by an act of will makes himself into the image of his father. In doing this he succumbs to the historic force that always bends the creators in society to the will of the acquisitors, and thus Tarkington anticipated the problem posed by Van Wyck Brooks in *The Ordeal of Mark Twain* (1920) and O'Neill in *The Great God Brown* (1926). (pp. 185-86)

Having preached against materialism in *The Turmoil,* Tarkington next demonstrated his versatility by returning to comedy. The lode that he had struck in "**Mary Smith**" remained rich and unworked, and he soon created in Willie Baxter in *Seventeen* a character almost as well known as Penrod. (p. 188)

*Seventeen* is a nostalgic tale that was compounded from the author's memories of adolescence. . . . It is one of the superb comedies of adolescence and one of the happiest moments in Tarkington's literary career. (p. 189)

The huge success of Tarkington's stories of children and adolescents, plus a return to the theater, kept him for three years from continuing his social and economic studies of Midwestern growth. Then early in 1917 he began his first Pulitzer Prize novel, *The Magnificent Ambersons*. Where he had built *The Turmoil* around the rising Sheridans, he picked a completely opposite group, a descending family, for his next novel. (p. 194)

*The Magnificent Ambersons* is a book to conjure with, for Tarkington not only told a good story against the social and economic background of Indianapolis, but he also worked out appropriate themes to give the novel significance. George is the victim of the dead hand of tradition, which is represented by the inherited self-esteem of the Amberson clan and rests on no firmer a foundation than the physical accumulation of wealth. . . . When the family fortune finally is dissipated and George has to go to work, the moral rebirth of the Ambersons takes place and the family begins to grow again. In Tarkington's moral order, work was the cornerstone.

Allied with the theme of work and regeneration is another interesting motif represented by the mother-son relationship. Isabel is a possessive mother whose smothering love leaves her son incomplete. In fact, it reduces him to moral idiocy and results in the destruction of her romance, her subsequent death, and the near ruin of George's own life. (pp. 196-97)

The unifying factor in Tarkington's writing of the Twenties is his strong sense of historical movement. Implicit or explicit, it appears in most of his fiction and nonfiction and even slips sometimes into his titles. When he collected his trilogy of family chronicles, all set against the socio-economic background of Indianapolis, he called the single volume **Growth,** and when he published a volume of autobiographical and reflective essays, he named it **The World Does Move.** The changes during his lifetime indeed had been startling: immigration, industrialization, mechanization, urbanization had transformed the world of his youth. (p. 244)

Tarkington began the new decade with **Alice Adams,** his tenth full-length novel. Written in the summer of 1920 at Kennebunkport and published the following year, it is very likely the best work of his entire career. (p. 245)

*Alice Adams* is a further probing of the materialism amid change that Tarkington saw about him. . . . The desire for money, which seemed the universal motivation in 1920, pursues the characters in the story like an avenging fury. It makes a monster out of Alice's mother, wrecks her father's life, physically and spiritually, corrupts her brother, and blights her own youth. With the corroding mania for riches goes the foolish longing for social position, which money can buy; but the Adamses are not an emerging midland family like the Sheridans or the Morgans and are destined not to rise above the surface. Because they are unimaginative, unsuccessful, and average, damaged by the false idol of materialism, they are left at the end with nothing to compensate for their loss of self-respect. The story is both depressing and comic when stripped to its thematic content, but Tarkington is an adroit storyteller who keeps his ethic well concealed. Alice alone emerges from the ordeal with the mental and physical resiliency to adjust herself to the realities of life. For all but her the story is low-keyed tragedy. (pp. 245-46)

*The Midlander* is both a somber story reflecting the bleak events of its composition and the summation and conclusion which gives direction and significance to the phenomenon of twentieth-century change. . . . Although the story is tragic, Tarkington wrote Barton Currie that he did not feel it so: "Certainly it's no more tragic than almost the happiest *actual* life." He was chiefly interested in finding design in "what *seems* haphazard and almost ironically tragic," though he admitted that "we don't know, of course," what life really is.

*The Midlander* is the story of Dan Oliphant, an attractive young man with a vision of his city's future glory. (pp. 256-57)

Dan is a symbolic figure in Tarkington's study—both the creator and the victim of industrial America. Like the inventor and builder in Melville's "The Bell Tower," Dan is destroyed by the mechanism that he has fashioned. . . . Dan is a casualty

in the growth of the city, and he finds no more happiness in his life than the millionaire automobile maker Dodsworth whom Sinclair Lewis created five years later. Whether Dan's sacrifice is worth while, Tarkington does not say. If the growth is to take place, his immolation is necessary; and if one regards the change as a good, Dan's death is not in vain. Elsewhere Tarkington argues that change is progress and hence beneficent, but here he does not feel obliged to pass explicit judgment on the inevitable historic process. (pp. 257-58)

Tarkington began using his new stock of memories [of a 1925 visit to Europe] in **The Plutocrat,** which he wrote the next year in a renewed burst of creative energy. The inspiration for the novel came from both North Africa and his traveling companion Howard Fisher of Pittsburgh. (p. 265)

Although Fisher served as model for the fictional plutocrat, he was not easily recognizable in the character of Earl Tinker. In the novel Fisher appears as a fairly uncomplicated piece of human machinery with a quite different background. "My fellow," explained Tarkington, pointing out that Fisher had been only a point of departure, "is a big, bragging, noisy Illinois manufacturer—he gets drunk, lies to his wife, chases women, makes himself a spectacle, and is a real show, I think." In addition he supports hospitals, employs five thousand persons in a business that he built all by himself, and is so completely good-natured, generous, and unpretentious that even his severest critic in the novel ends up liking him. Tinker is a superb creation, almost a legendary figure; but it is not the actual detail of Tinker's magnificent sweep across Algeria, showering silver as he goes, that is important. The significance of the book lies in Tarkington's concept of Tinker as a modern Roman. Tarkington saw America's impact on Western Europe in the twentieth century as similar to Rome's collision with Greek civilization at the beginning of the Christian era. Just as Rome had borrowed, diluted, and overwhelmed Greek culture, so was America repeating the process. (p. 266)

Paradoxically, Tarkington found himself at the peak of his grass-roots popularity during the depression but scorned by many critics. Certainly his most enduring books had been written at least ten years before, but he was still a conscientious craftsman and superb stylist, and the reason for the critical abuse he received lay outside his art. He was a conservative in an age of social revolution, felt uncomfortable in the new climate of opinion, and admitted publicly that the days of McKinley and Theodore Roosevelt had seemed pretty good; yet he did not engage in polemics, and his late novels are nearly all contemporary in action, albeit implicitly old-fashioned in their point of view. (p. 286)

In 1935 after several years of large-scale collecting, Tarkington had accumulated a great deal of information about the mechanics of selling expensive pictures. More than once he had been talked into buying old paintings for more than he wanted to spend, or he had been persuaded to snap up bargains before other collectors saw them. He bought some of his pictures from the Robert C. Vose Galleries of Boston, . . . but most of his transactions were made with Abris and David Silberman, New York dealers. . . . From the Silbermans he gathered anecdotes of the trade as well as first-hand experiences. Both brothers sat for the portrait of Mr. Rumbin, but David, who was fat and spoke a gorgeous broken-English, supplied the major part of the character. The Rumbin stories began in the *Post* in January, 1936, and continued sporadically for ten years, though half of them appeared within twelve months. Collected into a novel, *Rumbin Galleries* . . . , the first six stories made a highly entertaining book.

Although the Rumbin tales paid for a good many of his paintings, Tarkington lavished even more literary skill and knowledge of art on his essays. There was no magazine market for art essays, but Tarkington wrote them because he wanted to, and Doubleday brought them out in a handsome volume, excellently illustrated, under the title *Some Old Portraits*. . . . Tarkington described twenty-two of his own paintings in this volume, writing with affection amounting to inspiration, and the result is an exquisite book that tells the interested nonspecialist more about its subject than an entire course in "art appreciation." Furthermore, the essays also contain insights for the specialist, for Tarkington had made himself an expert on his own collection, and concentrating on the English portrait painters of the eighteenth century, he mastered not only the art history of the period but also the political and social background. His knowledge of art was accurate, extensive, and perceptive.

What makes these essays valuable for layman and expert alike is their unusual approach to the subject. Tarkington writes about art like a novelist who "did gather humours of men dayly," as John Aubrey once said of Shakespeare and Jonson. Not only was he interested in the artist and the picture, but he was attracted equally to the subject. He considered the usual matters of form, space, mass, line, movement, color, and light, then added another dimension to his criticism—a complete knowledge of the sitter; and with this special competence he produced illuminating commentaries. (pp. 298-99)

During the last years of his life Tarkington returned from the literary byways to the main thoroughfare of his ripest creative period—the Indiana scene. (p. 307)

*The Heritage of Hatcher Ide* is perhaps Tarkington's best late novel, a well-constructed piece of fiction with depth and breadth. Hatcher is a vivid life-sized figure, and Sarah Florian, in the words of Kenneth Roberts, is "a terrible lady, beautifully done. I wish to God I could do it a quarter as well." The plot also is managed with real skill, especially in the interweaving of the business and social narratives. When Frederic Ide's business partner, Harry Aldrich, commits suicide and Sarah Florian's malice is fully revealed, Tarkington brings the novel to a powerful conclusion. The story is not tragedy, however, for the new generation is left afloat after their elders founder in the economic storm. Tarkington's prognosis that life would go on richly and more vigorously under young leadership was optimistic and, as subsequent events have shown, sound. (p. 308)

His next novel, *The Fighting Littles*, which is loosely episodic and grew by accretion in the manner of *Women* or *Mary's Neck*, concerns the lively activities of the Little family, mostly in their comfortable midland city home. The inmates of this establishment include Filmer, fifteen, a youth to whom something always is happening; Goody, his eighteen-year-old sister, who is besieged by hare-brained males her own age; Ripley Little, the most irascible man in town; the fluttering and ineffectual Mrs. Little; and Cousin Olita Filmer, a middle-aged poor relation, who acts as housekeeper. This is not Tarkington at his best, though there are in the collection a good many amusing scenes. Filmer's first attempts at smoking, for example, are hilarious, and some of the adolescent capers of Goody and her boy friends are excellent Tarkington; but at its worst the novel descends to slapstick farce. (p. 309)

*Kate Fennigate* appeals more to women than to men, especially to the type of reader that Tarkington deprecated, the vicarious

adventurer. Kate is a shrewd, brilliant woman who manages people without their being conscious of her doing it. Her assets are not all plus, for Tarkington made her "a dry little gal . . . generally lacking in what we used to call 'charm.'" But she married Ames Lanning at the nadir of his career and is in great measure responsible for the subsequent realization of his early promise. She is the fictional embodiment of what all women believe (and what often is the truth): that behind every successful man there is always a woman. Ames is, moreover, a somewhat contemptible figure, as he was intended to be; but he also is, indefensibly, slightly incredible. Although Tarkington recognized this weakness, his attention was fully engrossed by his heroine, whose portrait is undeniably interesting. (p. 311)

Tarkington went on with his use of the Indianapolis milieu in his last completed long fiction, *Image of Josephine,* written two years later. Economic and social history, however, were employed only tangentially, for in this novel he combined his interest in art collecting and his experience as a museum trustee. The germ of the story had been in his mind a dozen years, during which time he had become more and more interested in art galleries. He thought that a "house attached to a museum might engender a situation in human lives that could be studied as the basis for a novel." To implement this notion Tarkington created Josephine Oaklin, proud, spoiled granddaughter of a Midwestern millionaire, Thomas Oaklin, who gives his city an art museum. (p. 312)

The soldier, Bailey Fount, inevitably clashes with and is attracted to Josephine, but the outcome is not conventional. Bailey plays Petruchio, but Josephine is no ordinary Katharina, as he realizes, and the novel ends with the couple engaged but not destined for an easy life together, if indeed they ever are to get married. Josephine does not change.

Since the novel ends with an engagement, most readers probably discounted the author's explicit denial of Josephine's reformation. They bought well over half a million copies, making the novel one of Tarkington's most widely distributed works; but the fact remains that the heroine is purposely an elusive figure. "No man knows himself and even the shrewdest women have but a sketchy notion of themselves," wrote Tarkington at the time of the book's publication. "No two people have the same concept of a third person, and the person concerned has a third opinion of himself." (pp. 312-13)

Tarkington's uncompleted last novel, *The Show Piece,* continued the fictional preoccupation of his final years. Like *Kate Fennigate* and *Image of Josephine,* it too is what he called an "investigatory novel," which is simply another name for realism that refuses to be bound by any set of rules. . . . Irvie Pease, the protagonist in *The Show Piece,* is developed by this investigatory method and also like Kate and Josephine is a character not destined to be loved by the reader. (pp. 313-14)

The really interesting thing about *The Show Piece* is its final demonstration of a subject that held lifelong fascination for Tarkington. Studies of egoism, male and female, as we have seen, abound in his large output of novels, stories, and plays. . . .

"Egoism," he wrote, "is the main and controlling force operative among human beings." Yet Tarkington himself focused outwardly on the world about him, a trait which is perhaps the essential requirement for a novelist who combines realism and social history. (pp. 314-15)

*James Woodress, in his* Booth Tarkington: Gentleman from Indiana *(copyright, 1954, 1955 by James*

Woodress; reprinted by permission of the author),
*J. B. Lippincott Company, 1955, 350 p.*

**JOHN D. SEELYE** (essay date 1961)

Booth Tarkington's **"Penrod,"** has withstood the test of time, but not the demands of maturity. It remains a book for boys, and if the adult reader retreats into its pages in the afternoon hope of a delightful moral discovery, he is foredoomed to failure. Not that such an excursion is a waste of time—far from it. Discoveries are to be made in **"Penrod,"** as in "Huckleberry Finn," and if they are not wonderful, at least they are fascinating.

The **"Penrod"** books were once particular favorites of mine, for different, although equally valid, reasons from those which drew me to "Huckleberry Finn." For although Huck undergoes a magnificent adventure, to a child of the middle classes he represents foreign ways of thought and life. Huck is an admirable exotic, but Penrod is definitely a child of the twentieth century, a boy whose adventures are limited to the backyards of suburbia. If he is never forced into a major moral decision, he nonetheless stretches the limits of his ingenuity in search of diversion, he is still the progenitor of a consumer economy. Thus, Penrod is a lesser Tom Sawyer, a creation whose integrity, whose desire for adventure, has been sacrificed to his and the reader's desire for entertainment. There is no heroism in Penrod, therefore no boyish derring-do, no fiendish mischief: nothing but a desire to fill his days with senseless activity, as if waiting for that ultimate reward of childhood, growing up. Of this urge, Tarkington wrote: "Being human, though boys, they considered their present estate too commonplace to be dwelt upon." Though Huck's bravery and Tom's love of romantic adventure are very fine things, and admirable, yet they are as far from the adult-oriented sphere of the modern boy as Jim Hawkins and his apple-barrel. On the other hand, for the child of the middle classes, at least, Penrod is the very thing itself.

Since at one time I held Penrod to be my *alter ego,* I recently reread his book out of feelings of nostalgia and idle curiosity. Although I knew it to be a book of far less stature than "Huckleberry Finn" (or "Tom Sawyer"), I nevertheless opened it with certain expectations, perhaps warmed by the glowing eulogies that marked Tarkington's death not so many years ago. . . . I soon found myself, however, in the uncomfortable position of looking down upon the old, fondly-remembered Penrod and Sam as children, a strangely unique experience. It was as if I had gone home again to find a childhood friend in a state of arrested development, even down to the ubiquitous cap and knickers. I felt, in short, a certain sense of betrayal, of having been involved years ago and all unknowing in some kind of trick upon myself. For although it can never be said that one laughs *with* Penrod—he is too much the scapegoat of youth's follies—still, the average boy doubtlessly feels a certain sympathetic identification with the hapless victim, and when he laughs at him (as when an adult laughs at Chaplin), he laughs at himself. There is for the older reader, on the other hand, no such bond of sympathy: laughing at Penrod, he laughs at boyhood. There seems to be a seed of treachery hiding in this synecdoche, a bitter kernel only slightly sweetened by the thought that Tarkington's amusement was made possible by his unawareness of the fear and prejudice unconsciously reflected in his hilarious microcosm. The myth underlying **"Penrod"** is not that of innocence and delight, as in "Huckleberry Finn," but of the peculiar fairyland lurking in the dark side of the

"urban, middle-class, Midwestern America" that Tarkington is credited with having "portrayed . . . better than anyone else."

To begin with, no one familiar with the book can ever forget the uproarious antics of Herman and Verman, the two stage Negroes with which Tarkington stocks his back-yard "Big Show"; like the darkies of Twain, Joel Chandler Harris, and William Faulkner, they are with us always as part of our minstrel heritage. But how many readers, as children, noted the specific identity of little Maurice Levy? Or now—as adults—can even remember him as anything other than a duplicate of Georgie Bassett, contemptible as Sid Sawyer is contemptible, because of his damned "little gentlemanness"? Yet Maurice is one of Penrod's chief antagonists, and occupies at least as much space as the two Negro boys, who are not.

Admittedly, there is not much that is Semitic about Maurice Levy save his tribal name, his curly black hair, and his dark complexion (faithfully reproduced in the Gordon Grant illustrations). That he is a Jew, however, cannot be denied. . . . Tarkington was an authentic Hoosier, a middle-class, Midwestern American, and a lot can be learned about this kind of authentic American by keeping a careful eye on Maurice, as well as on Herman and Verman, as he moves through the book.

Although none of the major characters in the Penrod series are what one would call psychologically motivated (we would probably be shocked to find that they were) nonetheless the book contains types suspiciously reflective of a uniform psyche, namely, that of Tarkington and the society to which he belonged. First, there is Penrod, and as befits the central character of a book dedicated to the ideals of entertainment, our hero never becomes more than an uneasy generality. Unlike Huck and Tom, or even the little men of Louisa May Alcott, Penrod never seems motivated by anything more than the impulse of the moment, an impulse that appears at times almost masochistically oriented, as the boy throws himself into one misadventure after another.

The superficiality of Penrod's characterization is indicated by a lack of detailed personal description. . . . Penrod's girl friend, Marjorie Jones (could any name suggest less character?) is similarly an anonym. She has auburn hair, is heavily freckled; yet the rest is not mystery, but vacuum. Unlike Huck, Tom, and Becky Thatcher, who stand in a greater or less degree for themselves, as individuals, Penrod, Sam, and Marjorie stand for those great homogenies, American boy- and girlhood. Maurice, as well as Herman and Verman, stands for something else again.

Despite his lineage, Maurice figures predominantly as the boy most often graced with little Marjorie's favors: even in America, the course of generalized, homogenized love never does run smooth. This, of course, is a device bracing the necessities of plot—*somebody* has to keep Marjorie out of Penrod's way until the dénouement. But there is more to Maurice than mere stuffing designed to fill out structural exigencies, for it is quickly made apparent that his popularity with Marjorie is not based on any particular virtue of his own, but is achieved through luck precipitated by his papa's fortune. Not only is Maurice a Jew, he is placed still further outside the pale of authentic American boyhood by the fact that he is also *rich*. Thus, slowly, do the fairyland aspects of this tale emerge.

Although little Levy is Penrod's chief antagonist, he is abetted by other forces, omnipotent influences that threaten to degrade Penrod at every turn of his tortuous, aimless pilgrimage. Most of these forces, ironically, haunt hearth and home—Penrod knows no asylum save his bower in the barn. (Significantly, this turn-of-the-century anachronism is no longer a stable and not yet a garage. Abandoned by adults, it is Penrod's version of Huck's raft: instead of being brought to events, Penrod often arranges them.) (pp. 591-95)

Still, life goes on, as does the book, and Maurice tends to withdraw to the forests of circumstance as other monsters of antagonism make themselves known. The lower class, in the form of a tough named Rupe Collins, has its effect on our hero, besmutting his armor while adding more style to his violence: "Within five days from his first encounter with Rupe Collins, Penrod had become unbearable. He even almost alienated Sam Williams, who for a time submitted to finger twisting and neck squeezing and the new style of conversation, but finally declared that Penrod made him 'sick.'" Herman and Verman are also the victims of Rupe's talented pupil, and although delighted by Penrod's rough ministrations, they are roused to combat when Rupe unfortunately usurps the prerogatives of a friend.

The immediate influence put to bloody rout by the ferocious brothers, Penrod nevertheless remains at general odds with the world, odds that are suddenly and terrifically evened by means of the baptismal "Great Tar Fight," an almost indescribable incident in which the disparate elements of Penrod's world, including Maurice, are leveled by total immersion in the black element. Significantly, Herman and Verman are absent from this fracas, for they are already black by nature, as black as the ink-drawn caricatures accompanying the story. Black seems to have had as many values for Tarkington as white held for Melville (the evil of the Licorice Water, the ambiguity of the Tar), and a certain complexity is hinted at in the conception of the Negro brothers. For one thing, unlike Maurice, who remains obnoxious to the end ("I got a stronger voice than anybody here") they are sympathetically treated.

Even before Penrod encounters the hilarious brothers, Tarkington's attitude towards the domesticated African is clearly revealed. . . . Leslie Fiedler has already outlined certain black and white aspects of American male relationships, and regard his proposition as we may, there can be little doubt that the Negro has become (*vide* Norman Mailer's recent pronouncement on the "White Negro") an archetypal antithesis to the work-and-duty-bound American businessman. And though Penrod, by his own assertion, is no "little gentleman," he is certainly a little businessman: In the sequel, **"Penrod and Sam,"** Tarkington speaks of his hero's adventures as "the crises which prepare a boy for the business difficulties of his later life," and of "the executive Penrod." (Considering the violence with which the boy meets his crises, this does not speak well of the authentic American businessman.)

Consequently, as the authentic American compensates for his envy of the Negro's freedom and lyricism by putting him in Uncle Tom rags and pitying him or, better yet, in minstrel-show finery and laughing at him, so Penrod elaborates on the colored brothers' already abundant grotesqueness by painting them elaborately (as tattooed savages) for his "Big Show," one of the key incidents in the book. Like Jim at the end of Huck's "Adventures," Herman and Verman are free, but as Tom Sawyer makes the Negro pay a humiliating price for the news of his freedom, so Penrod continues to levy a tax of ridicule upon his dark companions.

Furthermore, Tarkington never ceases to remind the reader of the Negroes' jungle ancestry, and in the sanguinary encounter

with Rupe Collins, he allows the two brothers a primitive display of temperament: "When Herman and Verman set to't the record must be no more than few fragments left by the expurgator. . . . Verman struck from behind. He struck as hard as he could. And he struck with the [rake] tines down. For, in his simple, direct African way he wished to kill his enemy, and he wished to kill him as soon as possible. That was his single, earnest purpose." Herman and Verman, according to biographer-critic James Woodress, are "young savages whose battle is primitive in its ferocity and refreshingly amoral." Penrod and Sam, however, seem unrefreshed: "appalled," they "retreated to the doorway nearest the yard, where they stood dumbly watching the cataclysm." Only the two dogs, "Dan and Duke, mistaking all for mirth, barked gayly," as in a violent presage of the Tar Fight, black and white mingle in a terrifying tangle of mayhem: "The struggle increased in primitive simplicity: time and again the howling Rupe got to his knees only to go down again as the earnest brothers, in their own way, assisted him to a more reclining position. Primal forces operated here, and the two blanched, slightly higher products of evolution, Sam and Penrod, no more thought of interfering than they would have thought of interfering with an earthquake." As Ahab discovers too late, it is foolhardy to meddle with raw nature, to collide "with beings in one of those lower stages of evolution wherein theories about 'hitting below the belt' have not yet made their appearance." Beneath the Negro's thick, chocolate layer of jolly good-humor is the vanilla-white heat of jungle ferocity.

But the chocolate is the predominate flavor; despite their primitive indiscretions, Herman and Verman are good fellows, full of fun and laughter. For the authentic American has little to fear, economically speaking, from his black brethren. He may be jealous of their freedom of action (translated by Fiedler into terms of sexual prowess), but that is all, and he compensates for this by ridiculing the Negro (an act of emasculation) into a safe position within the American hierarchy of values. (Little Verman, it might be added, is tongue-tied: "'Talk some, Verman. . . .'") Then too, the black man's savagery can often be turned to good purposes, for not only is his chuckle-headed irresponsibility a welcome, dog-like companion, his ferocity is a useful ally in an alley fight, or in any other kind of battle.

In the latter half of the book, as has been noted, Maurice sinks into the background, as the antagonism between him and Penrod is ignored rather than resolved. Again, this is due to the demands of the narrative, for Tarkington is preparing his scenery for the grand finale, Penrod's twelfth birthday, in which the boy comes into his own. It is best that the Jew's power and wealth be dimmed by distance, for through no other apparent virtue than being Penrod (he is his own talisman), the protagonist is enabled to bypass Maurice, leaving his rival to disappear uncomprehendingly into the darker shadows of the stage. To be authentically American is to have destiny on your side, and all the money and all the guile in the world cannot block Penrod's fated passage through life.

It is not without some struggle on the part of the fairy princess, however, that this revolution is brought about. Although Marjorie is at first acquiescent to Maurice's attentions and somewhat hostile to Penrod's ("*Penrod Schofield, don't you dare ever to speak to me again as long as you live!*"), she appears at the last to possess authentic, true-blue American blood: not only has she had Penrod in her sights all along, she also quickly disposes of her one possible rival, the dark lady of the piece, little, phony, cosmopolitan Fanchon Gelbraith. (All in all, Marjorie is quite a contrast to the frail, pusillanimous Becky Thatcher.) The main point is, of course, that little Master and Miss America are meant irrevocably for each other ("'Oh, *Penrod!*'"), and that, in the end, this mystic confluence of the sexes will be brought about, despite all the money and magic of little Maurices and Fanchons. Ever since Royall Tyler's "The Contrast," authentic American plain virtue (the common-sense *mystique*) has triumphed, while spurious talent, wealth, and foreign manners and costume have gone under the righteous heel.

It is in this tradition that Tarkington is writing, for **"Penrod"** is a romance, a myth of a certain kind of boyhood. . . . [If] Penrod emerges as something other than Huckleberry Finn, he is nonetheless a formidable figure of entertainment; since his appearance almost fifty years ago, no other has arrived on the scene to rival his particular claim to the backyards of American suburbia.

In a final judgment, moreover, Tarkington's prejudices are never so bitter or so overwhelming as to obscure the fine humor of the book, and however deep-seated his fears may have been, they are put forth in a predominantly genial myth. Like Lamb's "imperfect sympathies," however, they do exist, and cannot be extricated from his book without destroying its fabric, indicating that the creative psyche of the author—of any author— is shaped inexorably by the society to which he belongs. As Winfield Townley Scott has pointed out, Tarkington "meant to tell the truth about such facets of American middle-class society as he knew most intimately, and he meant to tell it well." All one might add to this is that he told it a little better than he himself imagined. (pp. 599-604)

> John D. Seelye, "That Marvelous Boy—Penrod Once Again," in The Virginia Quarterly Review *(copyright, 1961, by* The Virginia Quarterly Review, *The University of Virginia), Vol. 37, No. 4 (Autumn, 1961), pp. 591-604.*

**WINFIELD TOWNLEY SCOTT**   (essay date 1961)

In his success and fame Tarkington seemed to a vast number of readers the literary ornament of the times. F. Scott Fitzgerald's friend Edmund Wilson, for one, knew better; nevertheless Fitzgerald, right out of Princeton, became an immediate celebrity with *This Side of Paradise*, much of which is nothing but bad emulation of Booth Tarkington. Now all the literary historians of the 1920's know better. They know so much better that they ignore Tarkington lock, stock, and barrel. They are unaware that in his novel *Alice Adams*, Tarkington made a far more significant contribution to American fiction in the 1920's than many an admired rover of the Riviera, Paris, Provincetown, and Greenwich Village could possibly have made.

*Alice Adams*, much lauded in its day, is sometimes referred to, if at all, as "probably his best novel." In the past it has ever been in part misread by critics, and I cannot find it has ever been read with any perception of its adumbration of American society in the decade that lay ahead. *Alice Adams* was written in 1920 and published in 1921. Commentators at the time could not have foreseen its prophetic accuracy; later they did not bother. In the general collapse of Tarkington's reputation following his death, *Alice* is among a few survivors in print. But think of the novelists more or less Tarkington's contemporaries whose names are a part of the brightness of his era: Edith Wharton, Ellen Glasgow, Joseph Hergesheimer, Carl Van Vechten, the somewhat younger Sinclair Lewis. Fade is on

some of these, yet nobody judges it gauche to account for them; and yet, again, none of them wrote a better novel than *Alice Adams*. (p. 95)

[In America during the 1920's, there was still] a sense of small world, of neighborhood, one of the indigenous qualities Tarkington's better novels are saturated with; and there was the felt rhythmic round of the year. Falling leaves in the swifter dark, then the deep snows, then spring again. And from summer I remember the lights on the screened-in porches, sometimes as late as nine o'clock at night; after that there might be low voices, talking and laughing, where a daughter of seventeen or so had a caller; and the regular chain creak of a hammock hidden beyond the rusty hydrangea bushes dim in the arclight on the silent street. . . . *Alice Adams* best of all our novels records that experience and in symbol foreshadows the crash which demolished its brief world.

The time in *Alice Adams* is contemporary with the novel's composition, 1920. We know this because Arthur Russell, the well-connected young man so attracted to Alice, is a fairly recent veteran of the World War; he has come to the Midwestern city to settle down and begin a business career. As in *The Turmoil* and *The Magnificent Ambersons,* this is a virile, expanding community, and Alice's convalescent father, Virgil Adams, is aware of its vigor as he intermittently drowses and wakes through the night of April 30. (pp. 104-05)

Although we do not cross the hall until the second chapter and meet the pretty daughter around whom all the action is to revolve, the first chapter sounds the theme of the book; we know within these ten pages that Mrs. Adams habitually nags her husband to leave his lifelong, modest job with the J. A. Lamb Company and somehow to launch at fifty-five into something that will make much more money, and we know her reiterant reason for nagging him is "you owe it to your children." In a word, the theme *is* money. (p. 105)

Much later in the story we discover that Mrs. Adams' specific plan is for her husband to set himself up as a glue manufacturer, and that in his mind were he to do so his position, to say the least, would be ambiguous. Years before, Adams (and another young man long since dead) had worked out for J. A. Lamb a glue formula. Mr. Lamb had lost interest and done nothing with it in his business. So there is a very real moral conflict involved. Mrs. Adams insists the formula belongs to her husband. He is not convinced of any such right, and furthermore, "an oldfashioned man," Virgil Adams has a loyalty amounting to love for his rich and powerful employer. The crisis of Tarkington's book is the breakdown of Adams' standards. Mrs. Adams precipitates it but her instrument is Alice. The novel is not mistitled.

No one who has read *Alice Adams* ever forgets two huge scenes: the dance at the Palmers' and the dinner for Arthur Russell at the Adamses'. Tarkington's own phrase for that ghastly dinner in the steaming little house is "tragic-comic," and it applies as well to Alice's tortures as a wallflower at the Palmers'. In each, every grim or ludicrous detail builds mercilessly the atmosphere of hectic pretension with, at the same time, its overtones of moving pathos. The scenes ache with taut emotions. From the moment Alice gathers violets in the rain for her corsage until, home after the dance, she collapses in sobs in her mother's arms, an empathy of foolish suffering is forced upon the reader. Alice in her out-of-date organdy and her wilting violets, arriving with her vulgar brother Walter (her unwilling escort) in a rickety flivver Walter has borrowed, then painfully passing the hours with one desperate device after another in the attempt to conceal that she is mostly ignored—it is made at once fascinating and all but unbearable by the brilliance of the writing. And the humid dinner amidst the dying roses is no less a triumph of execution as step by step poor Alice's airily erected implications of grandeur go down before Russell's eyes to the mean reality. (p. 106)

Tarkington's hand is utterly certain in creating Alice. She has elements he could do with a turn of the wrist as in the novel called *The Flirt* or exaggerate to caricature as with Lola Pratt in *Seventeen*. But Alice Adams, for all her posturing and flirtations, is seen with such understanding she is an infinitely more mature creation than any of her sisters in his fiction. (p. 108)

Underlying *Alice Adams* is a philosophy so mundane that Tarkington feels no need to call attention to it: that is, that some people have the ability to make money and a great many people have not. He does not ask if the larger class should have *more* money for services rendered. No more in *Alice Adams* than elsewhere in his work does it occur to him to question the *status quo* of free capitalism. There is a bland innocence here which is a part of his automatic limitation of view. Nevertheless I think we cannot question the truth of his portraiture or of the situation *as it is*. And before leaping fiercely on the limitation we might, for instance, imagine what a proletarian novelist of the following decade would have done with the same theme. (pp. 108-09)

Tarkington is going well everywhere in *Alice Adams*. There are no youngsters to captivate him. Another weakness of his, to bring on Negroes as comedy relief, appears very little in *Alice* and only once offensively. His realism probes no more here into sexual matters, or anything else impolite, than in his other novels; but here it is consistent on its own terms without contrivance of plot or falsifyings of situation. It has so much revelation that we need nothing further. We are convinced that we ''know all about'' these people.

There are those in the past who have praised *Alice Adams* and deplored its ''sentimental'' ending. This is a misreading based, I think, upon other Tarkington novels. In no conventional sense does *Alice* have a happy ending. Walter has fled in disgrace. Mrs. Adams, querulous as ever, is rearranging the house to take in boarders and roomers. Adams himself is helpless and to Alice he defies his state in one of the brilliant passages of the book. . . . (p. 110)

But Alice feels pretty sure that her father will [finish his life as ''a landlady's husband''] and she goes downtown to begin a working girl's life by entering Frincke's Business College. (pp. 110-11)

From far back in the narrative, and on more than one occasion, we have known Alice's special feeling about the Business College. ''She hated the place. . . .'' [Now] she enters and goes up the stairs. ''Halfway up the shadows were heaviest, but after that the place began to seem brighter. There was an open window overhead somewhere, she found, and the steps at the top were gay with sunshine.'' All of Alice's pretentious dreams have perished and her possible marriage to the well-connected, well-to-do Russell has perished with them, and her family is worse off than ever before. That mitigating sunlight on the stairs is only the warrant of the rightness of her common sense, integrity, bravery; she has come down in the world and has discovered her real world. In her active acceptance is her ma-

turity. In Tarkington's way it is gently put, but no other reading is plausible in that best ending of his best novel. (p. 111)

In the Midwest-city trilogy of novels, his focus was upon the Sheridans, the Ambersons, and the Oliphants, and these families are of a social cast similar to that of the Lambs and the Palmers in *Alice Adams*. But in *Alice* it is the Adamses who are at front stage, Virgil Adams and his modest job and his unforgettably thin-walled house with its front porch and bad pictures and worn furniture. Tarkington could not exclude gallantry in portraying Alice nor some sort of understanding pity toward her and her family; indeed, he thought it unlikely anybody would want to read about these people whom, nonetheless, he went passionately ahead writing about. But who can doubt that Tarkington hated the threadbare, pinch-penny, insecure life represented by the Adamses? Or that from his superiority to it—in part a self-achieved superiority—he was able to write *Alice Adams*? (pp. 112-13)

With its class of everyday, semi-anonymous folk he was uninvolved. For himself, he knew what their place was, wrote a drama of their struggle to better it, and concluded by putting them firmly in their place. He was guaranteed for once in his career a clinical detachment. Here, he felt no need for apologetics. His focus, so generally softened by fondness for the ''better people,'' in *Alice Adams* flicked on sharply to dissect the ''little people.'' Fortunately, Tarkington also had the gifts of humor and compassion. The Adamses are seen in the round as only an artist could have seen them and made them live with significance. By an accident of economics in real life, the Adamses represent a special American era of ambition and disaster. They are the creation of a novelist whose general success and failure arise from his conformity to the very world against which the young expatriates of Paris and Greenwich Village were rebelling. The ironic triumph in the writing of *Alice Adams* is that of conformity with a difference. The Adamses' meaning and their pathos are not limited to a calendar date; but no other novelist made quite the same contribution to the record of the 1920's. (p. 113)

*Winfield Townley Scott, ''Tarkington and the 1920's'' (copyright © 1957 by Winfield Townley Scott; reprinted by permission of the Literary Estate of Winfield Townley Scott), in* The American Scholar, *Vol. 26, No. 2, Spring, 1957 (and reprinted in a slightly altered version in his* Exiles and Fabrications, *Doubleday & Company, Inc., 1961, pp. 92-113).*

## KEITH J. FENNIMORE  (essay date 1974)

[*Fennimore's* Booth Tarkington *is the most recent book-length biographical and critical appraisal of Tarkington.*]

Through the *Growth* trilogy, *The Plutocrat, The Heritage of Hatcher Ide,* as well as a sprinkling of related titles, Tarkington expressed steady faith in the American dream of social betterment, the American scheme of free enterprise, and the American theme of optimistic progressivism. Although he found it increasingly difficult to preserve the delicate balance between practicality and idealism, Tarkington clung to his basic convictions during two world wars and a major depression. (p. 77)

[These] novels of social concern also reflect the serious craftsman in such fundamental areas as characterization and literary style. Together with *Alice Adams,* they exemplify the type of ''selective Realism'' which Howells admired so warmly in the mature Tarkington and which gained him critical esteem as a ''serious novelist.'' Although not unmarred by occasional lapses into melodrama and sentimentality, these works maintain a high level of objectivity in their turn of events and in the shaping of characters. Here, more than anywhere else in his writings, Tarkington devoted his considerable talent to subject matter worthy of his sharpest insight. In these products of his major phase, Tarkington merits appreciably more recognition as a perceptive witness of his time and place, as well as a talented craftsman in casting the social novel, than present-day judgment accords him. (pp. 77-8)

[Tarkington's] deft touch in the sketching of word-portraits and his keen ear in the cross-play of dialogue created descriptive drama in the depiction of the commonplace. So familiar a phenomenon as a thunderstorm assumes an almost poetic quality in the lyric sweep of his figurative language; so homely a bit of Americana as the front parlor takes on an aura of nostalgia in his evocative details. His authentic descriptions duplicate the reader's own experiences; his accurate settings partake of social history. (p. 138)

Tarkington was a strong advocate of clarity in prose style. Although he often resorted to verbose circumlocutions for humorous effects in his lighter works (especially in the juveniles), he ordinarily employed a transparent, open style. Wherever the obscurantist appears in a Tarkington novel, his outré efforts were intended to lead only to ridicule. Tarkington held that communication is the first responsibility of the artist in any medium; hence, he insisted upon lucidity. In literature, the only bridge between author and reader is the written word, and Tarkington found scant justification for a writer's setting up barriers to obstruct his own purposes. Consequently, we search the Tarkington canon in vain for the contorted prose of a William Faulkner or for the involutions of a James Joyce.

For much the same reason, Tarkington resorted sparingly to the obliquities of symbolism in his writing. In *The Show Piece*, a sudden squall puts a trio of youngsters at the mercy of the sea; the incident, however, remains solely a device to reveal the egoism of Irvie Pease. "Dat ol' debbil sea" has no symbolic significance in the Eugene O'Neill sense, nor is it any cosmic force as with Herman Melville. Scattered details do have extended implications at rare intervals, but these are not abtruse by contemporary standards. In *The Midlander*, the falling of the cloud-shadow over Ornaby Addition certainly is imbued with prophetic import. In *Alice Adams*, the knot of violets, gathered at such cost by the girl, wilt and die at the dancing party quite as her summer hopes do. The building and demolition of the Amberson mansion in *The Magnificent Ambersons* surely symbolize the rise and fall of the family as well; and the union of George and Lucy is clearly a figurative merging of tradition and change. Throughout the other two novels in the *Growth* trilogy rises the most pervasive symbol in Tarkington fiction—the sooty plumes of industrial smoke. Even there, however, we sense more the limitations of the device in Tarkington's hands rather than its range. Although used more frequently than his detractors concede, the symbolism of Tarkington lacks the dimension and the intricacy which modern criticism prefers. Whether Tarkington himself would consider this a deficiency in his literary competence is open to question. Perhaps he realized that relatively few of his readers would recognize the subtleties of symbolism; in any case, he sacrificed cleverness for clarity.

In a similar vein, Tarkington took little issue with a problem that has vexed many a critic: the distinctions between a literature to "entertain" and a literature to "instruct." From the first, he placed a high premium upon the entertainment quality of his fiction. It was his conviction that even a reflective novel of social substance might well include the texture of plot and the color of romance if these factors will aid the author in "saying something" to his readers. In fact, he contended, any novel which fails to capture its reader by its narrative can never hold him by its abstract implications. (pp. 139-40)

Closely akin to entertainment as a prime factor in fiction is humor. In the words of Tarkington, "comedy is, so far, the only alleviation of life, except work and what is called faith. I should call it the third best thing in life." As a matter of fact, he went, upon occasion, so far as to rank comedy above tragedy, both in its composition and its function. Quite aware of the lowly position of the comic element within critical circles, Tarkington himself accorded humor a high respect and devoted to it the same artistry with which he treated serious subjects. (p. 140)

Let it be said also, however, that this same sense of humor has been a persistent stumbling block in academic appraisals of him. . . . With Tarkington, there is some justification for critical complaint, for he did resort to humor upon occasion as an easy way out of painful situations. As "the third best thing in life," it may indeed function as a vital stabilizing factor amid the adversities of life; it also may emerge as grotesquery when used under false pretenses.

Perhaps the best explanation for these occasional lapses in comic judgment is Tarkington's indomitable optimism. The reader should recall that the national crises of the last decade and a half of his career might well have overwhelmed a less resilient spirit. (p. 141)

Indeed, amid the vagaries of a world tensed for "future shock," he felt that there now rests upon authors in general a grave obligation to assist in restoring the dignity of the human spirit. . . . Amid the perplexities of the everyday, he was aware that "there are fewer tears of joy than sorrow"; hence his justification in the domain of fiction for a dash of romance, touches of humor, moments of nostalgia. Whatever his method, Tarkington felt the sincere writer can perform no higher service than "to lift the human spirit." (pp. 141-42)

> *Keith J. Fennimore, in his* Booth Tarkington *(copyright © 1974 by Twayne Publishers, Inc.; reprinted with permission of Twayne Publishers, a Division of G. K. Hall & Co., Boston), Twayne, 1974, 167 p.*

## PARK DIXON GOIST   (essay date 1977)

Booth Tarkington is best remembered for his stories of midwest boyhood. Penrod Schofield and his friends in the *Penrod* tales—the first of which was published in 1913—have joined Tom Sawyer and Huck Finn as the most enduring of American literary adolescents. Tarkington also chronicled a number of the social changes taking place in the urban Midwest during the early years of the twentieth century in a series of novels which appeared in the ten years between 1914 and 1924. These works were, in part, the writer's response to and reflection on those processes—mechanization, industrialization, bureaucratization, immigration, and urbanization—which were transforming his world. His boy stories, on the other hand, owe their popularity to the creation of a nostalgic atmosphere in which youngsters roam about in an environment largely untouched by these forces. But the book that most clearly expresses Tarkington's image of the town as ideal community was the first one he wrote, *The Gentleman from Indiana*, published in 1899. (pp. 14-15)

*The Gentleman from Indiana* is the story of John Harkless, a newspaper editor, and his involvement with the small Hoosier town of Plattville. Young Harkless is in search of something to which he can belong, a community which he defines as "home." Born in Indiana, he moves to the East at an early age, remaining there until shortly after his graduation from college. Later he has nostalgic memories of his college days when he was "the Great Harkless." "Yet he could remember no home that had ever been his since he was a little child, neither father nor mother, no one who belonged to him or to whom he belonged. . . ." . . . In this sense, John is a prototype of the American Adam: a man without a background. (p. 15)

He hears of a newspaper for sale in his native state and, sight unseen, buys the rundown Carlow County *Herald,* located in Plattville. While it is quite by chance that he comes to this particular town, he has consciously chosen to return to Indiana. "I always had a dim sort of feeling that the people out in these parts knew more—had more *sense* and were less artificial, I mean—and were kinder, and tried less to be somebody else, than almost any other people anywhere." . . . (pp. 15-16)

In the next five years Harkless turns the *Herald* into a reform newspaper, checks rowdyism and political corruption in the district, and emerges as a power in local politics. (p. 16)

[By the end of the book] John has realized himself amid the "good dear" and "beautiful people" of Plattville, and once again he feels himself to be the Great Harkless. He has come home, the favorite son of an "awakened" town marked by a daily newspaper, a developing oil industry, and a soon-to-be-asphalted Main Street. He has routed vice and political corruption and won the love of a beautiful and talented young woman. He has found love, home, and community in Plattville. He is a model for ambitious youth, but also a reminder that one's ambitions are best realized within the context of the homey, middle class qualities of small town life.

For John Harkless community functions in a specific place. It means living, working, interacting with good and honest townfolk. It means sharing a deep respect for such virtues as fearlessness, honor, and kindness. It means enjoying a sense of solidarity among one's own kind. It means realizing one's potential among these people, having a social role to play which is recognized as valuable by them. For Harkless's creator community meant the same things. Booth Tarkington lived the majority of the remainder of his life in Indianapolis—though he was forced to move away from his family's cherished homestead as it became encircled by the expanding city . . .—but his image of community was forever what it had been when he created Plattville. (p. 17)

[For Zona Gale], Tarkington, and many of their contemporaries community was made up of the same characteristics which recent sociologists have located as essential. But contrary to some contemporary thought, they insisted on the importance of place as a basic element of community. For them community existed in small town America; for them the small town meant community. (p. 20)

> *Park Dixon Goist, "The Town As Ideal Community: Booth Tarkington and Zona Gale," in his* From Main Street to State Street: Town, City, and Community

in America *(reprinted by permission of Kennikat Press Corp.; copyright 1977 by Kennikat Press Corp.),* Kennikat, 1977, pp. 13-20.*

---

## ADDITIONAL BIBLIOGRAPHY

Basso, Hamilton. "The World of Booth Tarkington." *The New Yorker* XXII, No. 50 (25 January 1947): 83-4.
  Critique of Tarkington's unfinished novel, *The Show Piece.* Basso contends the ending of *The Show Piece* (left in sketch form), is true to Tarkington's Midwestern middle-class values.

Cooper, Frederic Taber. "Newton Booth Tarkington." In his *Some American Story Tellers,* pp. 196-224. New York: Henry Holt and Co., 1911.
  Early survey of Tarkington's work.

Crowley, Richard. "Booth Tarkington: Time for Revival." *America* XC, No. 20 (13 February 1954): 508-10.
  Calls for a reevaluation of Tarkington's work. Crowley argues that Tarkington deserves a rightful place in American letters and should no longer be ignored by today's public.

Hamblen, Abigail Ann. "Booth Tarkington's Classic of Adolescence." *The Southern Humanities Review* III, No. 3 (Summer 1969): 225-31.
  Interesting comparison between the classic turn-of-the-century adolescents in *Seventeen* and the youth of the sixties.

Karsner, David. "Booth Tarkington." In his *Sixteen Authors to One: Intimate Sketches of Leading American Story Tellers,* pp. 83-100. New York: Lewis Copeland Co., 1928.
  Ambient interview with Tarkington. Karsner gives the reader an informal look at Tarkington, the man.

Quinn, Arthur Hobson. "Booth Tarkington and the Later Romance." In his *American Fiction: An Historical and Critical Survey,* pp. 596-622. New York: Appleton-Century-Crofts, 1936.
  Critical survey of Tarkington's literary works. Quinn illuminates Tarkington as a romanticist not a realist.

Russo, Dorothy Ritter; and Sullivan, Thelma L. *A Bibliography of Booth Tarkington: 1869-1946.* Indianapolis: Indiana Historical Society, 1949, 303 p.
  Invaluable Tarkington bibliography with a thorough section on "periodicals containing first appearances" of his much serialized work.

Schwartz, Nancy L. "Alice Adams: From American Tragedy to Small-Town-Dream-Come-True." In *The Classic American Novel and the Movies,* edited by Gerald Peary and Roger Shatzkin, pp. 218-25. New York: Frederick Ungar Publishing Co., 1977.
  Insightful comparative study of *Alice Adams* the novel and *Alice Adams* the movie.

Sorkin, Adam J. " 'She Doesn't Last, Apparently': A Reconsideration of Booth Tarkington's *Alice Adams.*" *American Literature* XLVI, No. 2 (May 1974): 182-99.
  Discusses realism in *Alice Adams* and the novel's accurate depiction of American life in the 1920s.

Wagenknecht, Edward. "Booth Tarkington, Success." In his *Cavalcade of the American Novel: From the Birth of the Nation to the Middle of the Twentieth Century,* pp. 224-51. New York: Henry Holt and Co., 1952.
  Views Tarkington as satirist, romanticist, and a chronicler of the times.

Woollcott, Alexander. "The Gentle Julians." In his *The Portable Woollcott,* edited by Joseph Hennessey, pp. 343-46. Westport, Conn.: Greenwood Press, 1972.
  Affectionate appraisal of a lesser known Tarkington work, *Gentle Julia.*

# (Marie Joseph) Pierre Teilhard de Chardin

## 1881-1955

French philosopher and essayist.

The writings of Teilhard represent one of the most extensive efforts on the part of a Catholic thinker to harmonize the fundamental doctrines of Catholicism with the principles and discoveries of modern science. A background in both the natural sciences and religious thought enabled Teilhard to perceive new relationships between the material and spiritual worlds—primarily their mutual function in the progressive evolution of the physical universe toward ultimate union with God. From his observations as a student of mammalian paleontology, Teilhard reasoned that the world was developing through a series of phases which began with nonliving forms and later yielded living forms with the potential for higher states of existence. The introduction of human consciousness into the universe signaled a major event in this process, allowing consciously willed action to further the evolutionary sequence that Teilhard believed would result in both the personal immortality of individuals and all creation's ascendance into the divine. This forms the central argument of almost all his work.

Born in Sarcenat, France, Teilhard was raised in an aristocratic, devoutly Catholic household. From an early age he was drawn toward a spiritual vocation, and he entered the Jesuit order when he was eighteen years old, his ordination as a priest taking place in 1911. During his novitiate period he sought a thorough education in the sciences, later focusing on paleontology. He participated in paleontological expeditions all over the world, including the excavation in China that led to the discovery of Peking man. Teilhard's acceptance of Charles Darwin's theories of biological evolution and Henri Bergson's philosophy based on the evolution of human consciousness presented a challenge to the static conception of human nature inherent to his Catholic faith. In an attempt to resolve this apparently insoluble conflict of ideologies, Teilhard revised both his religious beliefs and his scientific knowledge, viewing them as unified aspects of a single philosophical system—a synthesis of science and Christianity. Teilhard's unorthodox works were not acceptable to the hierarchy of the Catholic Church, who disapproved of their "heretical implications" and denied him the right to publish them. Despite his unhappiness, Teilhard remained loyal to the Church, but he gave his unpublished writings to a friend in Paris. After Teilhard's death, his manuscripts were released for publication, resulting in immediate and widespread interest in his work.

In such volumes as *Le phénomène humain* (*The Phenomenon of Man*) and *Le milieu divin* (*The Divine Milieu*), Teilhard attempted a comprehensive history of the universe. His philosophy extends the concept of biological evolution indefinitely into the past and indefinitely into the future, thus plotting a series of well-defined steps through which progressively more complex forms of existence evolve. This process of evolution is assumed to be "convergent," that is, one destined for final unity. The process begins in the "lithosphere" of inorganic matter, next proceeding into the "biosphere" of primary living forms, and then, with the advent of humans, emerges into the "noosphere" of human consciousness. The noosphere, ac-

cording to Teilhard, marks the present phase of the evolutionary process; it is characterized by growing interdependence of cultures and improved means of communication among them. In *L'avenir de l'homme* (*The Future of Man*) Teilhard explains how evolution is now at work in the noosphere and contends that in this stage it is the role of humans to extend their awareness of themselves as part of the collective whole of humanity.

The final stage in Teilhard's universal evolution is the "theosphere," also referred to as the "omega point," in which the paramount importance of Catholic theology becomes most evident. The omega point is a "radiation of divine altruistic love *incarnated* in Christ," all physical matter having undergone the spiritual metamorphosis which Teilhard calls "Christification." This represents Teilhard's most mystical concept and the aspect of his philosophy most open to criticism. Though he is praised, even by such non-Christian scientists as Julian Huxley, for not resorting to supernatural explanations in order to comprehend material phenomena not understood by science, he is criticized for regarding unsubstantiated theories as truth. Commentators point out that a particular weakness of spiritual evolution lies in the fact that scientists are not yet agreed that biological evolution indeed works in the way the Jesuit thinker assumes it does.

For many, however, the value of Teilhard's work is founded in its remarkable, though not flawless, coordination of scientific erudition and religious feeling, along with a lyric expressiveness that in such works as *Hymne de l'univers (Hymn of the Universe)* is sometimes considered the most compelling aspect of his thought. Whatever their personal convictions, most commentators agree that in Teilhard's philosophy the integrated doctrines of science and Catholicism serve to generate one of the most original mystical prophecies of the twentieth century.

## PRINCIPAL WORKS

*Le phénomène humain* (essays) 1955
 [*The Phenomenon of Man*, 1959]
*L'apparition de l'homme* (essays) 1956
 [*The Appearance of Man*, 1965]
*Lettres de voyage (1923-1939)* (letters) 1956
 [*Letters from a Traveler* (partial translation), 1962]
*Le milieu divin* (essay) 1957
 [*The Divine Milieu*, 1960]
*Nouvelles lettres de voyage (1939-1955)* (letters) 1957
 [*Letters from a Traveler* (partial translation), 1962]
*La vision du passé* (essays) 1957
 [*The Vision of the Past*, 1966]
*L'avenir de l'homme* (essays) 1959
 [*The Future of Man*, 1965]
*Genèse d'une pensée: Lettres 1914-1919* (letters) 1961
 [*The Making of a Mind: Letters from a Soldier-Priest, 1914-1919*, 1965]
*Hymne de l'univers* (essays) 1961
 [*Hymn of the Universe*, 1965]
*L'énergie humaine* (essays) 1962
 [*Human Energy*, 1969]
*L'activation de l'énergie* (essays) 1963
 [*Activation of Energy*, 1970]
*Lettres d'Égypte, 1905-1908* (letters) 1963
 [*Letters from Egypt, 1905-1908*, 1965]
*La place de l'homme dans la nature* (essays) 1963
 [*Man's Place in Nature*, 1966]
*Écrits du temps de la guerre (1916-1919)* (essays) 1965
 [*Writings in Time of War*, 1968]
*Lettres d'Hastings et de Paris, 1908-1914* (letters) 1965
 [Published in two volumes: *Letters from Paris, 1912-1914*, 1967; *Letters from Hastings, 1908-1912*, 1968]
*Science et Christ* (essays) 1965
 [*Science and Christ*, 1968]
*Comment je crois* (essays) 1969
 [*Christianity and Evolution*, 1971]

---

**PIERRE TEILHARD DE CHARDIN** (essay date 1947)

If [*The Phenomenon of Man*] is to be properly understood, it must be read not as a work on metaphysics, still less as a sort of theological essay, but purely and simply as a scientific treatise. The title itself indicates that. This book deals with man *solely* as a phenomenon; but it also deals with the *whole* phenomenon of man.

In the first place, it deals with man *solely* as a phenomenon. [Its pages] do not attempt to give an explanation of the world, but only an introduction to such an explanation. Put quite simply, what I have tried to do is this; I have chosen man as the centre, and around him I have tried to establish a coherent order between antecedents and consequences. I have not tried to discover a system of ontological and causal relations between the elements of the universe, but only an experimental law of recurrence which would express their successive appearance in time. Beyond these first purely *scientific* reflections, there is obviously ample room for the most far-reaching speculations of the philosopher and the theologian. Of set purpose, I have at all times carefully avoided venturing into that field of the essence of being. At most I am confident that, on the plane of experience, I have identified with some accuracy the combined movement towards unity, and have marked the places where philosophical and religious thinkers, in pursuing the matter further, would be entitled, for reasons of a higher order, to look for breaches of continuity.

But this book also deals with the *whole* phenomenon of man. Without contradicting what I have just said (however much it may appear to do so) it is this aspect which might possibly make my suggestions *look* like a philosophy. During the last fifty years or so, the investigations of science have proved beyond all doubt that there is no fact which exists in pure isolation, but that every experience, however objective it may seem, inevitably becomes enveloped in a complex of assumptions as soon as the scientist attempts to explain it. But while this aura of subjective interpretation may remain imperceptible where the field of observation is limited, it is bound to become practically dominant as soon as the field of vision extends to the whole. Like the meridians as they approach the poles, science, philosophy and religion are bound to converge as they draw nearer to the whole. I say 'converge' advisedly, but without merging, and without ceasing, to the very end, to assail the real from different angles and on different planes. Take any book about the universe written by one of the great modern scientists, such as Poincaré, Einstein or Jeans, and you will see that it is impossible to attempt a general scientific interpretation of the universe without *giving the impression* of trying to explain it through and through. But look a little more closely and you will see that this 'hyperphysics' is still not a metaphysic.

In the course of every effort of this kind to give a scientific description of the whole, it is natural that certain basic assumptions, on which the whole superstructure rests, should make their influence felt to the fullest possible extent. In the specific instance of [*The Phenomenon of Man*], I think it important to point out that two basic assumptions go hand in hand to support and govern every development of the theme. The first is the primacy accorded to the psychic and to thought in the stuff of the universe, and the second is the 'biological' value attributed to the social fact around us.

The pre-eminent significance of man in nature, and the organic nature of mankind; these are two assumptions that one may start by trying to reject, but without accepting them, I do not see how it is possible to give a full and coherent account of the phenomenon of man. (pp. 29-30)

*Pierre Teilhard de Chardin, "Preface" (1947), in his* The Phenomenon of Man, *translated by Bernard Wall (translation © 1959 by William Collins Sons & Co., Ltd., and Harper & Row, Publishers, Inc.; reprinted by permission of Harper & Row, Publishers, Inc.; in Canada by William Collins Sons & Co., Ltd.; originally published as* Le phénomène humain *(copyright 1955 by Editions du Seuil), Editions du Seuil, 1955), Harper & Row, 1959, pp. 29-30.*

**ARTHUR KNODEL**  (essay date 1957)

[It] is clear that Teilhard, whose deeply felt mission was "to hear and to make others hear, even to intoxication, the immense music of things," . . . bases his whole approach to theological questions on his interpretation of the sensible universe, of the Phenomenon—as he himself calls it. Hence, it is fitting that a brief introduction confine itself to a summary of Teilhard's conception of the Phenomenon. To facilitate this task, I shall list, in as logical a sequence as the material will permit, six main points around which the main lines of Teilhard's thought may be oriented. These points may be arbitrarily designated as:

1. Integral evolutionism.
2. Evolutionary plateaus and thresholds.
3. The law of complexification.
4. Tangential and radial energy.
5. Phyletic convergence of *Homo sapiens*.
6. The Point Omega.

1. *Integral evolutionism.*—Evolution for Teilhard is not hypothetical; neither does it apply merely to the biological realm. . . . [Biological] evolution is only one part of a much greater continuum, a continuum that is quite simply the whole cosmos, in time as well as space. Evolution begins with the undifferentiated primordial energy that modern physics lets us glimpse at the outset of things, and it proceeds uninterruptedly through the subatomic, the atomic, the molecular, the protoplasmic and beyond. (pp. 348-49)

This "integral evolutionism" necessitates a kind of hylozoism, and Teilhard tells us that "inert matter" is an inaccurate term. We should say, instead, "pre-vital matter." And thus, biology becomes simply a special kind of physics, and psychology an extension of biology.

2. *Evolutionary plateaus and thresholds.*—Following this view, it is clear that any exclusive antinomy between matter and life is untenable. (Here, it may be noted, is one of several important points of contrast between Teilhard and Bergson, with whom he is often rather uncritically compared.) For Teilhard, Evolution does not represent a steady ascent with a constant rate of change. Evolution, he tells us, always goes forward, but at certain critical junctures, transformations are so great and so rapid that, lacking the necessary patience and scientific apparatus, men are understandably prone to resort to miraculous or "extra-phenomenal" explanations. The comparison used by Teilhard to clarify his view is the familiar one of water that is put to boil. The basic stuff is water, first in a liquid state; then, suddenly and without warning, at 100° C. the liquid changes to something with very different properties, namely a gaseous vapor—but it is still water, and there is no extra-phenomenal intrusion that takes place every time 100° C. is reached. Water at that critical temperature is analogous to Evolution at one of the "thresholds" (*seuil*) occurring at the end of each longer, steadier stretch or "plateau" (*palier* = stair-landing). When subatomic elements polarize into atoms, a threshold is crossed. Similarly for the formation of the first molecules, and then again at the moment of emergence of the first cells capable of reproducing themselves. But, as we shall see, the threshold leading into the Biosphere is not the last one for Teilhard. Moreover, this evolutive drive from threshold to threshold operates irreversibly. Teilhard, along with many other biologists, feels that the weight of empirical evidence establishes this overall irreversibility beyond reasonable doubt.

3. *The law of complexification.*—Perhaps the most characteristic aspect of this irreversibility is revealed in what Teilhard calls the Law of Complexity-Consciousness, or more simply, of Complexification. As scientists continue to scrutinize the Phenomenon, it becomes increasingly evident that more complex units keep appearing—not uniformly and everywhere, but at different levels, yet emerging always from less complex units. The idea of complexity, however, requires definition. An increase in complexity is achieved only when each of a limited number of elements (a closed field) establishes more and more of all the possible relationships with the other elements—a process that is, it would seem, concomitant with another phenomenon, not so readily definable in purely quantitative terms, namely, the phenomenon of "centration." As a unit becomes more complex, its "center" becomes more massive and more far-reaching in its effects. Thus, an atom must have a nucleus; molecules polarize in certain ways. A protozoan cell has a nucleus; and metazoan aggregates always polarize in some way, usually, in the higher forms, around a nerve-center and finally, in the mammals, around the brain (a trend called "cephalization" by Teilhard). It is clear, then, that in view of the integral character of Teilhard's evolutionism, consciousness is the expression of the highest degrees of complexification yet observed. But consciousness as a property of matter is present everywhere, even though most often in imperceptible amounts. And the most complex and highly centered form of consciousness is, of course, the conceptual self-consciousness of *Homo sapiens*.

4. *Tangential and radial energy.*—Since biology is simply "the physics of higher complexes," consciousness is a manifestation of energy. Or rather, consciousness is a highly concentrated form of one aspect of energy—of the aspect Teilhard calls *radial*. The other aspect of energy, the one to which the laws of thermodynamics are applicable, Teilhard calls *tangential*. He is fully aware that radial energy cannot be treated in terms of the laws of conservation and degradation that are universally applicable to tangential energy. Yet a profound relationship between the two, as yet very dimly understood, *does* exist. For, in the crudest terms, one must eat, *i.e.*, provide tangential energy, to live and, all the more, to think. But in purely statistical terms the relationship is utterly baffling, since very small amounts of tangential energy suffice to support overwhelming manifestations of radial energy. (pp. 349-51)

In all this speculation, however, of one thing Teilhard is convinced, and that is, that to regard the isolated and so pathetically limited phenomenon of life and consciousness as a transitory epiphenomenon of no importance in the total Phenomenon is to be unintelligent and blind as the physicists would have been if, some sixty years ago, they had persisted in regarding radioactivity—that isolated curiosity discovered by the Curies—as a mere epiphenomenon instead of as the key to a whole new physics. . . .

5. *Phyletic Convergence of Homo sapiens.*—Now the most intense expression of life that we yet know is to be found among mammals, and especially among the primates. Here Teilhard is on much surer ground than in his speculations about Energy, for he was one of the world's great authorities on the hominians and pre-hominians. Going about the work of systematizing the primate family, Teilhard was struck, as indeed many other biologists have been, by certain irreducible peculiarities which the species *Homo sapiens* does not share with any other primate or, in fact, with any other known form of life. (p. 352)

[Arriving] at true man—that is, a primate capable of making fire and producing utensils—a great novelty occurs. Instead of the various "sub-species" (Teilhard at one place ingeniously refers to them as "isotopes") of *Homo sapiens* fanning out and becoming full-blown, mutually exclusive species, they *converge,* coalescing successfully. . . .

In view of these two "peculiarities" it is clear, says Teilhard, that biologists must admit that the appearance of man at the end of Pliocene times marks the crossing of a new evolutive threshold upon our planet; we pass from the Biosphere or envelope of life, into the Noösphere or envelope of thought.

In the Noösphere certain properties that are all but imperceptible on previous plateaus begin to show up massively. The property which in primordial matter appears only as a physical principle of indeterminacy manifests itself in *Homo sapiens* as acute consciousness of choice, as free will. And the force of evil, which on the lower plateaus is chiefly a matter of prodigal waste and painful trial-and-error, becomes in the Noösphere an aggressive force that man can and must struggle against. Indeed, human history—which is simply Evolution working itself out in the Noösphere—is the tragic record of this struggle.

But the direction of human history is clear: It has proceeded and is now more acutely than ever proceeding towards a consolidation of the species in the Noösphere, thanks to the combined advantages of conceptual consciousness and phyletic convergence. It is obvious that, in a way no other species of life has ever done, man is, in narrowly biological terms, successfully dominating every nook and recess of the earth's surface and subjugating all the other forms of life to his will. (p. 353)

6. *The Point Omega.*—Finally, it is evident that the phyletic convergence which is translating itself into increasing social convergence will in its turn reach a saturation point. This critical maximum Teilhard calls the Point Omega. . . .

From the point of view of the evolutionist, the Point Omega is simply another threshold. As such, it results from the interplay of the same forces and trends apparent on lower plateaus. It will represent, for example, a new height of complexification. Now complexification may be viewed as "interiorization," as increasing consciousness; and in the Biosphere this increasing consciousness takes the form of increasing personalization. The Point Omega, then, is a threshold where new heights of personalization may be achieved. Here, says Teilhard, Evolution confirms common sense:

> . . .Common sense is right. It is impossible to give one's self, body and soul, to the Anonymous Many. But let the Universe that lies ahead take on a face and a heart; let it personify itself, so to speak. And immediately in the atmosphere emanating therefrom elemental forces of attraction will be able to come into full play. And then, most surely, under the unavoidable pressure of an Earth closing in on itself, there will burst forth the tremendous energies of attraction that still lie dormant in the human molecules. . . .
>
> (p. 354)

Here, of course, we have left the realm of the Phenomenon, or at least of the Phenomenon as we know it at the present point in space and time. And here our schematic presentation comes to an end. But in fairness to Teilhard's profoundly Christian orientation, an expression of the fundamental zoölogical convergence of the species. And the phenomenon of more and

more intense socialization one must add that it is here, at the personalized Point Omega, that Christianity is introduced into the picture. Christ is, for Teilhard, the finest manifestation of God personalized, of God who once took on the guise of man. (pp. 354-55)

There is, I think, little doubt that Teilhard's multifarious views will prove of widely varying validity. But one thing is certain: Even in his most daring and—some would say—fanciful speculative flights one is conscious of Teilhard's solid scientific grounding and of his agonized good faith. (p. 355)

*Arthur Knodel, "An Introduction to the Integral Evolutionism of Teilhard de Chardin," in* The Personalist, *Vol. XXXVIII, No. 4, October, 1957, pp. 347-55.*

## JULIAN HUXLEY  (essay date 1958)

*The Phenomenon of Man* is a very remarkable work by a very remarkable human being. Père Teilhard de Chardin was at the same time a Jesuit Father and a distinguished palaeontologist. In *The Phenomenon of Man* he has effected a threefold synthesis—of the material and physical world with the world of mind and spirit; of the past with the future; and of variety with unity, the many with the one. He achieves this by examining every fact and every subject of his investigation *sub specie evolutionis,* with reference to its development in time and to its evolutionary position. Conversely, he is able to envisage the whole of knowable reality not as a static mechanism but as a process. In consequence, he is driven to search for human significance in relation to the trends of that enduring and comprehensive process; the measure of his stature is that he so largely succeeded in the search. (p. 11)

*The Phenomenon of Man* is certainly the most important of Père Teilhard's published works. Of the rest, some, including the essays in *La Vision du Passè,* reveal earlier developments or later elaborations of his general thought; while others, like *L'Apparition de l'Homme,* are rather more technical.

Père Teilhard starts from the position that mankind in its totality is a phenomenon to be described and analysed like any other phenomenon: it and all its manifestations, including human history and human values, are proper objects for scientific study.

His second and perhaps most fundamental point is the absolute necessity of adopting an evolutionary point of view. Though for certain limited purposes it may be useful to think of phenomena as isolated statically in time, they are in point of fact never static: they are always processes or parts of processes. The different branches of science combine to demonstrate that the universe in its entirety must be regarded as one gigantic process, a process of becoming, of attaining new levels of existence and organization, which can properly be called a genesis or an evolution. For this reason, he uses words like *noogenesis,* to mean the gradual evolution of mind or mental properties, and repeatedly stresses that we should no longer speak of a cosmology but of a *cosmogenesis.* Similarly, he likes to use a pregnant term like *hominisation* to denote the process by which the original proto-human stock became (and is still becoming) more truly human, the process by which potential man realized more and more of his possibilities. Indeed, he extends this evolutionary terminology by employing terms like *ultra-hominisation* to denote the deducible future stage of the process in which man will have so far transcended himself as to demand some new appellation.

With this approach he is rightly and indeed inevitably driven to the conclusion that, since evolutionary phenomena (of course including the phenomenon known as man) are processes, they can never be evaluated or even adequately described solely or mainly in terms of their origins: they must be defined by their direction, their inherent possibilities (including of course also their limitations), and their deducible future trends. He quotes with approval Nietzsche's view that man is unfinished and must be surpassed or completed; and proceeds to deduce the steps needed for his completion.

Père Teilhard was keenly aware of the importance of vivid and arresting terminology. Thus in 1925 he coined the term *noosphere* to denote the sphere of mind, as opposed to, or rather superposed on, the biosphere or sphere of life, and acting as a transforming agency promoting hominisation (or as I would put it, progressive psychosocial evolution). He may perhaps be criticized for not defining the term more explicitly. By *noosphere* did he intend simply the total pattern of thinking organisms (i.e. human beings) and their activity, including the patterns of their interrelations: or did he intend the special environment of man, the systems of organized thought and its products in which men move and have their being, as fish swim and reproduce in rivers and the sea? Perhaps it might have been better to restrict *noosphere* to the first-named sense, and to use something like *noosystem* for the second. But certainly *noosphere* is a valuable and thought-provoking word.

He usually uses *convergence* to denote the tendency of mankind, during its evolution, to superpose centripetal on centrifugal trends, so as to prevent centrifugal differentiation from leading to fragmentation, and eventually to incorporate the results of differentiation in an organized and unified pattern. Human convergence was first manifested on the genetic or biological level: after *Homo sapiens* began to differentiate into distinct races (or *subspecies,* in more scientific terminology) migration and intermarriage prevented the pioneers from going further, and led to increasing interbreeding between all human variants. As a result, man is the only successful type which has remained as a single interbreeding group or species, and has not radiated out into a number of biologically separated assemblages (like the birds, with about 8,500 species, or the insects with over half a million).

Cultural differentiation set in later, producing a number of psychosocial units with different cultures. However, these 'interthinking groups,' as one writer has called them, are never so sharply separated as are biological species; and with time, the process known to anthropologists as cultural diffusion, facilitated by migration and improved communications, led to an accelerating counter-process of cultural convergence, and so towards the union of the whole human species into a single interthinking group based on a single self-developing framework of thought (or noosystem).

In parenthesis, Père Teilhard showed himself aware of the danger that his tendency might destroy the valuable results of cultural diversification, and lead to drab uniformity instead of to a rich and potent pattern of variety-in-unity. However, perhaps because he was (rightly) so deeply concerned with establishing a global unification of human awareness as a necessary prerequisite for any real future progress of mankind, and perhaps also because he was by nature and inclination more interested in rational and scientific thought than in the arts, he

did not discuss the evolutionary value of cultural variety in any detail, but contented himself by maintaining that East and West are culturally complementary, and that both are needed for the further synthesis and unification of world thought. (pp. 12-15)

In Père Teilhard's view, the increase of human numbers combined with the improvement of human communications has fused all the parts of the noosphere together, has increased the tension within it, and has caused it to become 'infolded' upon itself, and therefore more highly organised. In the process of convergence and coalescence, what we may metaphorically describe as the psychosocial temperature rises. Mankind as a whole will accordingly achieve more intense, more complex, and more integrated mental activity, which can guide the human species up the path of progress to higher levels of hominisation. (p. 17)

Père Teilhard, extrapolating from the past into the future, envisaged the process of human convergence as tending to a final state, which he called 'point *Omega*,' as opposed to the *Alpha* of elementary material particles and their energies. If I understand him aright, he considers that two factors are co-operating to promote this further complexification of the noosphere. One is the increase of knowledge about the universe at large, from the galaxies and stars to human societies and individuals. The other is the increase of psychosocial pressure on the surface of our planet. The result of the one is that the noosphere incorporates ever more facts of the cosmos, including the facts of its general direction and its trends in time, so as to become more truly a microcosm, which (like all incorporated knowledge) is both a mirror and a directive agency. The result of the other is the increased unification and the increased intensity of the system of human thought. The combined result, according to Père Teilhard, will be the attainment of point Omega, where the noosphere will be intensely unified and will have achieved a 'hyperpersonal' organisation.

Here his thought is not fully clear to me. Sometimes he seems to equate this future hyperpersonal psychosocial organisation with an emergent Divinity: at one place, for instance, he speaks of the trend as a *Christogenesis;* and elsewhere he appears not to be guarding himself sufficiently against the dangers of personifying the nonpersonal elements of reality. Sometimes, too, he seems to envisage as desirable the merging of individual human variety in this new unity. Though many scientists may, as I do, find it impossible to follow him all the way in his gallant attempt to reconcile the supernatural elements in Christianity with the facts and implications of evolution, this in no way detracts from the positive value of his naturalistic general approach. (pp. 18-19)

The biologist may perhaps consider that in *The Phenomenon of Man* [Teilhard] paid insufficient attention to genetics and the possibilities and limitations of natural selection, the theologian that his treatment of the problems of sin and suffering was inadequate or at least unorthodox, the social scientist that he failed to take sufficient account of the facts of political and social history. But he saw that what was needed at the moment was a broad sweep and a comprehensive treatment. This was what he essayed in *The Phenomenon of Man.* In my view he achieved a remarkable success, and opened up vast territories of thought to further exploration and detailed mapping. (p. 21)

*Julian Huxley, "Introduction" (1958) in* The Phenomenon of Man *by Pierre Teilhard de Chardin, translated by Bernard Wall (translation copyright © 1959 by Wm. Collins Sons & Co., Ltd., and Harper & Brothers; reprinted by permission of Harper &*

Row, Publishers, Inc.; in Canada by William Collins Sons & Co., Ltd.), Harper & Row, 1959, pp. 11-28.

## CLAUDE CUÉNOT (essay date 1958)

What influenced [Teilhard's] conversion to evolutionism? His reading of Bergson's *L'Évolution créatrice* was but one occasion that made him realize where he stood, the coincidence of his own inner conviction with the need to understand the data of science, which only evolution could make intelligible. This twofold awareness blended into a single certitude. Evolution, a simple hypothesis of nineteenth-century biology, revealed itself to Teilhard as a necessary condition of all scientific thought, since henceforth evolution (whatever might be the disputes among biologists about its mechanism and its modalities) was to invade and include every field, including physics, and was to dominate all cosmology. In his view, the unity of the world was of a dynamic or evolutive character, no longer an immobile cosmos, but a cosmogenesis, with everything unfolding in a biological space-time. In this Teilhard's view of evolution differed radically from Bergson's. Teilhard rejected the Bergsonian cosmos, which took the form of a *divergent* irradiation, originating at a central source, whereas his own was essentially *convergent,* and he rejected the Bergsonian idea of a vital impulse having no finality. Teilhard, although a vitalist—or, more exactly, a supporter of orthogenesis—did allow mechanisms their part (their very great part, particularly in elementary forms of life), but he credited them with only a minor role in complex forms of life—man above all—and maintained that life is, at bottom, of a psychic character.

If Teilhard's cosmology is indissolubly wedded to evolutionism, he deduced from the latter doctrine some original conclusions. By a purely apparent paradox—and in contrast with the philosophy of Herbert Spencer—his view of reality invalidated, in his mind, the hypothesis according to which the truly substantial is what is elementary and undifferentiated. The radical dualism of matter and spirit, of body and soul, dissolved before his eyes "like fog before rising sun". Matter and spirit seemed no longer two things, the latter reducible to the former, but two states, two aspects of one and the same cosmic "stuff". Spirit, which slowly emerges from matter, takes precedence of the physical and chemical, and it is in spirit, in the highly complex, that all substantiality, all "consistence" resides, so that to find it we must not "look backwards, to matter" but "forwards, to spirit".

This step towards "spiritualized evolution" was taken about 1914, and so coincided with Teilhard's introduction to war. From the first, life in the trenches seemed to act as a catalyst upon his mind; the first essay produced under its influence was *La vie cosmique* (24 March 1916). . . . Teilhard's intention here was to voice his love of matter and of life, but in harmony with his adoration of the one, absolute, undevelopable divinity. His point of departure was the initial, basic fact that each one of us is connected by all the fibres of his being, material, organic, and psychic, with everything else around him; for the human monad, like every other monad, is essentially cosmic. He saw the problem, then, for a Christian, in these terms: Must one, in order to be united to Christ, detach one's self from the cosmic tide?

Teilhard had become convinced that the basis of our supernatural growth is not detachment from all the things that give charm and interest to our natural life. Thus we need not reject the impulses growing out of our awareness of the cosmos, provided we do not divorce from "sacred evolution" its orientation towards eternal hope and beatitude. In the section entitled "sacred Evolution" Teilhard speaks with happiness of his feeling of God's presence everywhere, of the mystic's total abandonment to God's will, and of the effort to communicate with the invisible through the visible world and to reconcile the claims of the Kingdom of God with love of the cosmos. . . . (p. 36)

In *La vie cosmique* we find two basic ideas, one cosmological (governed by the evolutionist viewpoint), the other Christological, together with an early effort to combine the two. In fact in this early work Christ, as God-man who synthesizes all things, is already assigned a cosmic function, as is suggested in the conclusion:

> There is a communion with God, and a communion with the earth, and a communion with God through the earth.

The very title of a later essay is something of a shock: *La nostalgie du front* (September, 1917). That Teilhard could feel homesick for the ugliness and evil of the front line is explained by the fact that it was there that he was able to discover the third basic factor in his spiritual life. Until that time he had lived a sheltered, circumscribe life, at home, and as a young Jesuit, with few outside contacts. He now came up against man in the mass and realized that he was spiritually one with a wider humanity, a collective entity with riches past and future. This partial loss of individuality gave him an entrancing sense of a new freedom.

Moreover, the experience brought to him, as a priest, the revelation that, higher than the care of single souls, there is a universal function to be fulfilled, the offering to God of the entire world. (p. 38)

Some of Teilhard's writings at this time were brief essays in ontology; they were rough hewn, and the thought was sometimes incomplete, abstract, and uneven. Nevertheless, underneath this thin veneer of scholasticism an extremely original mind was at work, and we find the germ of a number of his more important themes. For instance, just as in the view of twentieth-century physicists matter is no longer an absolute, but merely a function of its own rate of motion, so, in Teilhard's view, *being* is no longer the fundamental concept, yielding its place to *uniting.* Creation, then, he considered above all an act of union; and it is this union that produces being. This idea was to underlie his whole metaphysics, as was still evident in 1948 in *Comment je vois.* To this same period belong some valuable meditations on the role of the priest and on "the mystic milieu", important as closely presaging [*La messe sur le monde* and *Le milieu divin*]. . . . (p. 39)

Sometimes Teilhard set down half-poetic, half-religious fancies, containing, however, clearly authentic philosophical intuitions, and thus useful as source-material to professional philosophers. Teilhard, however, was not a mystic who, out of modesty, presented his visions under the disguise of literature. His *Trois histoires comme Benson* are an exact depiction of things he himself experienced and understood. (p. 40)

The form of the *Trois histoires comme Benson* is of an unusual beauty, for in them he is the poet at once of earth, fire, and light. He takes anything as a starting point—a lamp of his cousin's, or one of those Saint-Sulpice pictures of the Sacred Heart—and proceeds to transfigure it. The lamp becomes the terrestrial globe, lighted by the translucent Christ; the Heart of Jesus (a childhood devotion that grew with him) flames out, shines forth, projects its rays into the darkest corners of matter, which is transformed thus into an immense Mount Thabor.

His quality as a poet is shown in the astonishing rhythms of [*Le puissance spirituelle de la matière, La messe sur le monde,* certain passages in *Le coeur de la matière,* and *En regardant un cyclotron*]. . . . His lyric works rank with the finest of the world's religious poetry.

The inspiration of Teilhard's poetry was threefold: mystical, derived from the cosmic Christ revealed by St. Paul; epic, derived from a palaeontologist's familiarity with the vast story of man, his origins, and the origin of the universe in which he lives; and finally eschatological, derived from his semi-prophetic view of man's future. We may think of him as continuing the great line of Hebrew prophets, as a Pascal freed from Jansenism and with no fear of the silence of infinite space, or as a Lucretius without the crude materialism of the *De Rerum Natura.*

His poetic talent was accompanied by the power to handle abstract ideas and construct a solidly framed argument. His thought, particularly in his early and late periods, was necessarily abstract, close-packed, difficult, at times almost cryptic, and expressed in a highly personal vocabulary. Under this complex exterior burned a volcano, which gave vigour and richness to his work, as the hot streams of lava enrich the grapes and olives that grow on the slopes of Vesuvius. (pp. 41-2)

[In *From Cosmos to Cosmogenesis*] Teilhard emphasizes that, in spite of setbacks, man has just crossed a new threshold, an intellectual step forward from seeing things in the context of a cosmos (an immobile world, with a cyclic time) to seeing things as a cosmogenesis. . . . The concept of cosmogenesis is well defined in Teilhard's own words: "An organic universe in which no element and no event can appear except by birth, i.e. in association with the development of the whole. . . . Since the days of St Thomas the Universe has taken on a new dimension: *organicity.*" (pp. 291-92)

From this dynamic unity of the universe there follow religious consequences. The God of the Bible is also the God of the still-to-come, the God of evolution (as the "days" of Genesis seem to suggest), but men could not see him as such until the universe was seen as a cosmogenesis. In such a concept, while God still remains essentially transcendent, the relation between creator and created world cannot still be simply divergence and change, but primarily a movement of convergence, synthesis, and union. And how could God unite without immersing himself in the world, and so participating in the world's suffering, which is the fruit of unrealized union? Thus Creation and Incarnation are not simply isolated, revolutionary, events in the history of the world. Creation is still going on all around us; as a phenomenon, it is a daily experience. On the other hand, while the Incarnation is still, in the human-divine "cell" of Jesus, an isolated event, it is clear that when God immerses himself in the world he cannot but Christify himself. The foreshadowing of Christ runs through the Old Testament; and, through the Church, Christ's activity still continues in the Eucharist, which extends the effects of the Incarnation. (pp. 292-93)

The synthesis between the Above and the still-to-come operates, *essentially,* at the moment of the Incarnation. It continues through the Eucharist. It will be consummated in the Parousia.

But this Parousia, like Creation, must have an experimental aspect. There must be a maturation of cosmic noogenesis through a social effect of totalization, through a super-evolution, that is, by a sort of super-creation constituting a decisive progress in union.

And at the Parousia the Omega point, the centre of human convergence, and Christ the Omega (that is, the eternal Word) will coincide and be seen to be one and the same. The perfect synthesis of the two faiths will be realized. . . .

If noogenesis is to reach that term it is vitally urgent to foster and nourish man's "appetite for life", the evolutive pressure that is without any doubt the most fundamental of cosmic energies. Mankind is, at the moment, passing through a formidable crisis. Evolution has become conscious in man. Instinct and the hidden life-forces are no longer sufficient to keep it moving. Man asks himself the meaning of his existence in the world, and is plagued by *taedium vitae,* with its external "what's the good?". Conscious evolution can escape this only if it is irreversible, that is, immortal: and that is not a matter of emotion, or logic, but simply of energetics. (p. 294)

Thus we see how Père Teilhard's thought progresses. Faced by the urgent problems of the time, he chose two crucial points, and pursued them with vigour. If there is a rupture between Christianity and science, we must reconcile, or rather synthesize them. If a part of the *élite* has lost the appetite for life, and is afraid of our growing socialization, we must restore its courage and make it understand the meaning of this evolution. (p. 295)

Teilhard's great discovery, in the thirties, was the recognition of a cosmic focus in evolution, with all the consequences implied in the notion of cosmic convergence: the law of complexity-consciousness; the confluence of human branches, the existence at the summit of noogenesis of an Omega point, the rebound of evolution through the energy released by the conjunction of cosmic and Christic. One fruit of his genius, then, was to indicate an apologetic for biologists and anthropologists.

Even if, as with Teilhard, an apologetic proposes a series of progressively ascending acts of faith, which is necessary to a conscious evolution's continual forward progress, it must still employ the method of immanence; it must, that is, endeavour to show God as already present in the universe, positive reality, suitably interpreted, being already pre-Christian or peri-Christian. In other words, the sculptor has left the mark of his thumb on the clay of reality, so that the modelling of the universe bears the imprint of its God. *Caeli enarrant gloriam Dei.* Teilhard's task, then, was not to construct a metaphysic but a sort of ultra-physics that would bring together in harmony all the fruit of scientific experience. In crossing this bridge he could not lean too heavily on any philosophical system; he had to confine himself to scientific facts and so discover the significance and direction, if such existed, of evolution. He developed, therefore, a phenomenology—which has practically nothing in common with that of Husserl and still less with that of Hegel. Unlike the former, so far from turning his back on science in order to discover a pre-reflective *cogito,* it is on science that he relies. Again, in his view, an essential feature of the phenomenon is not that it is perceived by an individual consciousness, but that it forms part of a noogenesis. According to Teilhard, phenomenologists of Husserl's school forget that science is a common act of perception, the manifestation of a collective consciousness, and that one of the essential marks of the phenomenon is to be convergent. With a keen awareness of universal interdependence, he sees the world as one whole, and, rising above the close-knit totality of beings and phenomena, he perceives a global reality that must be much more essentially necessary than any of the individual things it embraces, just as the organ is less real than the organism which is the only justification of its existence.

Within this phenomenology we still find the three main components of Teilhard's thought, the cosmic, the Human, and the Christic, the three completed by his energetics. Now, however, they live in symbiosis, reducible one to another, or deducible one from another; we may, too, pass freely from one to another. The notion of the Universal Christ—the Christ of the Universe, Christ the King, Pantocrator—achieves the synthesis between the cosmic and the Christic, and so, by a stroke of genius, what might have been pantheistic becomes a pan-Christicism—God in all of us—that preserves human personality while drawing all to converge upon a "Universal-Person", Christ-Omega. This synthesis between the "God above" (the classical transcendent God) and the "God of the future" (the immanent God whose face has been revealed in evolution) is not simply a synthesis on paper. Even though Teilhard first disclosed the cosmic function of Christ, this explanation, grand though it might be as a concept of the concrete reality of the Incarnation, would have seemed barren to an unbeliever had he not, by studying evolution as a phenomenologist, gone on to disclose, too, the Christic function of the universe—the ascent of the world towards Christ the King with the irresistible surge of the ocean tides under the pull of moon and sun. The Human, the third component, falls similarly into place as the first reflective mirror in which God can be reflected over the universe. Thus the Human is the necessary unit between the cosmic and the Christic, for the noosphere is an essential stage between the biosphere and ultra-human. And so cosmogenesis, proceeding through anthropogenesis, culminates in a Christogenesis. (pp. 375-77)

Teilhard's greatness lay in this, that in a world ravaged by neurosis he provided an answer to our modern anguish and reconciled man with the cosmos and with himself by offering him an "ideal of humanity that, through a higher and consciously willed synthesis, would restore the instinctive equilibrium enjoyed in ages of primitive simplicity". To put it more exactly, what he did was to replace man at the head, not of a cosmos but of a cosmogenesis, and thus to present in its true dimensions a Christogenesis, identified, in the light of the risen Christ, with cosmic evolution. No longer do we have geocentrism, or monogeism (Teilhard's speculation . . . on the other inhabited planets may be remembered), or an immobile hierarchically arranged cosmos, or anthropocentrism. All these have gone, but man is still left as the spearhead of evolution and has recovered his true place in the universe. Man ceases to be an enigma, between the two infinities of the great and the small, for he constitutes a third infinity, that of complexity. No doubt the cosmos, being unconscious, or rather pre-conscious, does not know him, but Christ the Evolver, who lies at the heart of cosmogenesis, knows him, as the still incomplete species progressing, through countless trials and troubles, towards a transcendent future. By a master stroke Teilhard, by reconciling twentieth-century man with himself, reconciles Christianity with evolutionist science, substitutes progressive optimism for static pessimism, and finds again a treasure buried since the days of St Paul and St Irenaeus, "the meaning of the cosmic component of salvation", of Christ, in whom all things are taken up. (p. 399)

*Claude Cuénot, in his* Teilhard de Chardin: A Biographical Study, *edited by René Hague, translated by Vincent Colimore (translation © 1965 by Helicon Press, Inc.; reprinted by permission of Helicon Press, Inc., 200 E. Biadle Street, Baltimore, MD 21202; originally published as* Pierre Teilhard de Chardin: Les grandes étapes de son évolution, Librairie Plon, *1958), Helicon Press, 1965, 492 p.*

## GEORGE VASS, S.J. (essay date 1961)

*Le Milieu Divin* would seem to call for some reflections not entirely confined to that comparatively short essay on the interior life. For this book 'is not specifically addressed to Christians who are firmly established in their faith' but is rather 'written for the waverers'. Such a disclaimer, however, should not deceive. The book is one of intense vision: it is the expression of a spiritual seer whose inward experience it does not fail to reflect, in such a way that the reader of necessity seeks to place the original in the wider setting of the whole man, the savant as well as the spiritual visionary.

For this Jesuit anthropologist it is the universal evolution of our cosmos which leads inevitably to Christ. In Christian revelation he seems to have found for himself and for his disciples the ultimate answer to the destiny of mankind. It is sufficient to page through *The Phenomenon of Man,* and in the French *L'Apparition de l'Homme* as well as *La Vision du Passé* to be aware that this is no spiritual or scientific banality. A greater glimpse is to be had into the intense spiritual and intellectual life of Teilhard by means of the published correspondence; and this is true also of *Le Milieu Divin*. . . . The extent to which Teilhard has enlisted evolution in the service of Christian thought can now be gauged in its interior and personal depth. While the currents of cosmic progress flow to the universal Christ, it is maintained that even on the scale of individual human effort, the faithful efforts of the individual life in Christ are also a real factor in evolution as such. (p. 237)

There is on the one hand for Teilhard the all-embracing fact of evolution, and on the other the future destiny of mankind as revealed by God. Can the first help the understanding and the realization of the second? It is Teilhard's 'history of a soul', which little by little weaves the detailed problems of life into a pattern containing two motifs. The scientist and the religious priest had to find his home in two different worlds. (p. 239)

The harmonization called for by Teilhard's dilemma already had its classic formula which ran: 'perform your worldly actions with a good intention and they will help your soul to reach perfection'. For the soul is on its way to God, and the whole man had according to this maxim to be forced into the pattern dictated by the good intention. Thus would arise a certain divine all-embracingness since the things of the world are to be *used as instruments* for the greater good of the soul.

However clear cut and reasonable all this might seem, it could not satisfy a man of Teilhard's spiritual ambitions. For him in fact it is not only the soul which is in evolution towards God, but the whole world as well. And in this ever-developing world, the intellectual and reflective soul is an essential force. This evolution of the universe towards God is carried on by the spirit of man. Consequently every human action must be an infinitesimal step furthering universal progress. For Teilhard to see sanctity only in the goodness of intention is to divide the world into one of static 'matter' over against another one of ever-increasing spirit. Thus in his view the things of this earth, if merely used or rejected for a higher purpose, remain in themselves indifferent. They should do so, but they do not become more human, or more spiritualized, in their ontological being so long as man in performing his actions is merely utilizing them with a good conscience. The effect according to Teilhard is that the good intention can indeed sanctify the human action, but it still fails to make the Christian life more human; '— either to make man's endeavour holy, or to give the Christian life the full flavour of humanity'. . . . Pure intention is able to create a certain divine *milieu* for the soul, but it fails—according to Teilhard—to give to our bodies the hope of resurrection in the new Jerusalem: 'The divinization of our endeavour by the value of the intention put into it, pours a priceless *soul* [sic] into all our actions; but *it does not confer the hope of resurrection upon their bodies*'. . . .

In the alternative solution suggested by Teilhard, the soul will proceed towards its perfection *through* worldly activities—and the world will be reshaped by human perfection in God. Man will love God *in the world,* and the world in God. This very book of Teilhard's spirituality [*Le Mileu Divin*] is written also 'For those who love the world' (Pour ceux qui aiment le monde). (pp. 241-42)

[This] is where the view of Teilhard makes its distinctive contribution: the existence of the whole sensible world *is for* the soul; and on this point he speaks more emphatically than ever. Human spirit, by being and acting in the world, draws the elements of its environment into its own action. Hence the whole world is spiritualized *through* the soul, and *with* the soul it will be divinized in the fullness of Jesus Christ. Thus, in the Christian sense, human action not only makes the world more human, but it is the source of further evolution. It is welded into the vast 'ontogenesis', until the whole earth is re-shaped in Christ. 'With each one of our *works,* we labour—in individual separation, but no less really to build the Pleroma; that is to say we bring Christ to fulfilment'. . . . Perfection of the soul, everday work with its manifold human activities, and the development of the world itself, have become one and the same objective in the vision of Teilhard de Chardin. (pp. 242-43)

Our activities and our sufferings share the progress of an expanding world, and by that fact they bring about a divine openness in it. But the idea of the divine *milieu* is not yet clearly put. For Teilhard it is already discernible in the natural taste for life which is the first appearance of the divine Reality incarnate on this earth. He can write: 'With that reservation [the false trails of pantheism], it remains true that, physiologically, the so-called 'natural' taste for being is, in each life, the first dawn of the divine illumination—the first tremor perceived of the world animated by the Incarnation'. . . . Teilhard is rightly careful in his own footnote to this passage to emphasize that he is dealing with a 'psychological' description, not a theological explanation. For ourselves we can discover this taste and its correlative as a fine modification in the very being of things that are ordained to expand to new perfections. It is already in the structure of creation converging upon Christ. And in this way, there is no doubt, Christ is everywhere in this Universe: 'the *divine omnipresence* translates itself within our universe by the network of organizing forces of the total Christ'. . . . The divine *milieu* is the universal Christ as manifested by his action in the progressing world, and as shared by our human efforts and sufferings. Christ attracts the whole universe into his fullness and man takes part with his whole life in creating step by step this new universe where God will be all in everything. (p. 244)

*George Vass, S.J., "Teilhard de Chardin and Inward Vision," in* The Heythrop Journal, *(Robert Murray © 1961), Vol. II, No. 3, July, 1961, pp. 237-49.*

**MICHAEL STOCK, O.P.** (essay date 1962)

[There] are those who find the greatest attractiveness in Teilhard's view as it seems to be an authentic interpretation of the Sacred Scriptures—more profound, more stirring, more open to grace, more apostolically effective than any other. But here there might be appended some reservations about the metaphysical or scientific aspects of the theory. . . . (p. 369)

In short, even where Teilhard's point of view has excited the greatest enthusiasm, it has not evoked the kind of total commitment it seems to call for. What I should like to do here is examine the basic idea in itself, to see if possible why it does not seem to hold together in its entirety. Teilhard said: "This work may be summed up as an attempt to see." "I intend to develop a simplified but structural representation of life evolving on earth; a vision so homogeneous and coherent that its truth is irresistible. I provide no minor details, but only a perspective that the reader may see and accept—or not see." I want to defend the reader who perhaps does not see. (pp. 369-70)

[For Teilhard] the universe is essentially homogeneous. To understand it, you have to discover those laws which are basically identical at every level of organization, no matter how these levels may be apparently or superficially diversified.

But is the homogeneity of the universe a fact so well established scientifically? It does not seem to be regarded this way. In his paper on "The Origin of Life," Hans Gaffron at the Darwin Centennial expressed the widely held view of the opposition:

> It is a prime experience of modern man that only life produces life. Together with the mind-body problem (how consciousness arises in living matter) and the problem of reason (how the incomprehensible can be comprehended), the question "What is life," is considered one of the primary problems of existence.

With regard to biogenesis in nature, he adds:

> There is a nice theory, but no shred of evidence, no single fact whatever, forces us to believe in it. What exists is only the scientists' wish not to admit a discontinuity in nature and not to assume a creative act forever beyond comprehension.

> An extremely plausible proposition is no guarantee against committing a fundamental error. It is quite possible that life and its origin are truly insolvable problems.

He sums up, saying:

> The more clearly we perceive the "grand design" of science, the sharper the lines which mark the limits of scientific endeavors. For centuries philosophers have meditated upon these limits, with the result that the three gaps in the continuity of verifiable knowledge are now generally accepted as absolute.

These citations do not, of course, prove that nature is not homogeneous. But they do underline the fact that at present the only way to bridge the interstices in nature is with a wish and a hope. And, needless to say, Teilhard, in confessing the supernatural order of Christian revelation, acknowledges a fourth interstice in reality, which science, if not all properly human thought, must fail to include in its legitimate scope and method.

In effect, these four gaps in the smooth character of reality as we know it are four breakdowns in Teilhard's vision, when it is viewed as a whole, as all-embracing. But even within the stretches of reality, as defined by these gaps, where homogeneity of some sort may be acknowledged, how effective is the evolutionary concept as an explicative principle? Is Teilhard justified at least here? (pp. 370-72)

[The theory of evolution] offers us an intelligible process and a unifying principle with which to view and explain an enormous number of facts. It has, moreover, been a fruitful source of new lines of scientific investigation.

But is its applicability so all-pervasive, is its explanatory power so illuminating, that we can accept a theory of evolution as the—if not unique, at least decisive—principle in life sciences? Do we here, in Teilhard's terms, *see* something that imposes itself so irresistibly on our intelligence that we are compelled to acknowledge it as our essential insight?

Perhaps not, for even here, where Chardin's view might be expected to find its most thorough verification, it fails to attract absolutely, not because evolutionary theory is not attractive, but because it remains, for most scientists, still only hypothetical. As a hypothesis, some obscurities, some difficulties are tolerable—a hypothesis is formulated to be productive, to be suggestive, to coordinate efforts and direct them. As long as it is hypothetical, it can afford some little incoherence. But in Teilhard's system, evolution is not a hypothesis, it is a dogma. It purports to supply the ultimate foundation on which all else stands firm, to give the ultimate certitude from which all other conclusions derive their force. Elevated to a dogma, all the inadequacies which bedevil evolutionary theorizing assume critical importance, and a dogma, to be a good dogma, cannot afford critical inadequacies, at least not in this day and age. (pp. 373-74)

[There] are serious criticisms from men who are working in the field of evolution. Their effect was cited by Everett C. Olson at the Darwin Centennial, when he said:

> . . . much that is to be known about evolution is, at least in broad outline, now known. There are, of course, degrees of difference in evaluation of successes, from healthy scepticism to confidence that the final word has been said, and there are still some among the biologists who feel that much of the fabric of theory accepted by the majority today is actually false. . . . There exists, as well, a generally silent group of students engaged in biological pursuits who tend to disagree with much of the current thought but say and write little . . . many who are not satisfied with current theory are to be found in the ranks of the paleontologists and morphologists.

In fine, the theory of evolution is still in a state of suspension. Teilhard did not fully appreciate this, and that is why he brought down on himself the censures of scientists. (p. 376)

A fortiori, to make of evolution the fundamental principle in whose light all the progress of the universe is explained from its primordial beginnings to its final consummation in the vision of God, seems rash and unjustifiable. Even in the biological order strictly taken, the theory of evolution is not that effective.

There is only one point to make concerning the noosphere and its evolution, as described in *The Phenomenon of Man*. Teilhard accepts the advent of man—the conscious, thinking organism—as a crisis in evolutionary development, after which evolution took a new turn with new laws superseding the old and rendering them obsolete. This cannot be denied, i.e., that the movement of culture or civilization, as products of the mind, presents itself as a movement of progressive growth. But what a difference it displays. It is no longer evolution in the biological sense, it has nothing to do now with genetic mutation and propagation, natural selection and adaptation; it has in fact become Lamarckian evolution. It is evolution in which mutation is supplied by intelligence and deliberation, by inventiveness, insight and discovery in every field of thought, technology, art, political organization and in all branches of human endeavor, and inventiveness which more often than not has been mothered by necessity, just as Lamarck would have had it. Moreover the "mutations" supplied by invention are easily propagated and passed on without need for recourse to genetic mechanisms—all the arts of communication combine to spread and establish far and wide and for successive generations the innovations of one time and place. There are no significant gaps in the evidence for the evolution of cultures, or where there are gaps, they are easily explained by the known capacities of intelligent originality. There are no real problems of heritibility because inheritance is accomplished by the facile modes of human communication.

The only problem is: what is the significance of calling the flourishing of human culture and the proliferation of living forms by the one name, "evolution." Is it instructive and does it signify anything more than a metaphor? Does it suggest any new ideas or deepen our understanding of the nature of things? At least the question should be raised, for if there are two processes operating in different orders of beings, by laws fundamentally different, it is not always meaningful to name them by the same name. W. W. Howells of Harvard University, in his review of the second volume of the Darwin Centennial proceedings, makes an explicit point of this anomaly.

> The happiest of these writers [on cultural evolution] seem to be those least bothered by biological parallels or the traditional baggage of evolutionary ideas. Bordes, in a fine paper on paleolithic cultures, does not even pause to genuflect to Darwin. . . .

(pp. 378-79)

[Therefore, summing up] it would seem to be safe to say that the scientific fraternity does not give unqualified support to the kind of evolutionary picture proposed by Teilhard de Chardin. They do not agree that the whole range of natural phenomena can be united under one evolutionary principle, nor even that any but the most limited successions of specific types are clearly and certainly explained by it. Evolution is certainly a process which has occurred in the course of this world's development, but the extent to which it has occurred is still open to argument. The proposition that there is a meaningful sense of the theory of evolution which consistently explains the history of the universe is, at present, only a guess and a wish.

A final point should perhaps be made. The charge is sometimes made against those who criticize *The Phenomenon of Man* unfavorably, that the ideas expressed in the book are not being judged in the sense in which they are proposed. The approach of Teilhard is, as he says, scientific and phenomenological. He is concerned with the arrangement of appearances, with their connections and the successions they manifest, and with the law of recurrence by which the universe is structured. He is not concerned with ontology; the phenomena make up his field of study. His work is akin, says one of his commentators, to Aristotelian physics. With this in mind, we have also tried to avoid comments in terms of metaphysics, limiting the discussion to the appearances, mostly by restricting it to the observations and judgments of other men who are also interested primarily in the appearances, and precisely in their scientific import. The conclusion which emerges is that these men do not see what Teilhard claims is there to be seen. His vision does not seem to be objectively substantiated. On the objective evidence, to which all truths must ultimately submit, it fails. (pp. 379-80)

> *Michael Stock, O.P., "Scientific vs. Phenomenological Evolution: A Critique of Teilhard de Chardin," in* New Scholasticism *(© copyright 1962 by American Catholic Philosophical Association), Vol. XXXVI, No. 3, July, 1962, pp. 368-80.*

## CHARLES E. RAVEN (essay date 1962)

Teilhard's full-scale interpretation of cosmic evolution in terms of the universal Christ disposes at once of the versions of creation and fall which depose God from his world and assign to man the power to frustrate God's purpose, and to Satan the role of Lord of the Earth. With his vision of a universe measured in light-years and even so unbounded, of an earth in which succeeding realms bathysphere, lithosphere, hydrosphere, atmosphere and stratosphere . . . give rise to its biosphere and noosphere, and of the immense onward and upward movement manifested throughout its history, the old dualisms of matter and mind, body and spirit, God and devil are plainly transcended. In such a setting the denial of progress becomes an impossible arrogance: "Has it even occurred", asks Teilhard, "to those who say that the new generation, less ingenuous than their elders, no longer believes in a perfecting of the world, that if they are right all spiritual effort on earth would be virtually brought to a stop?" . . . Surely no Christian can deny his conclusion that "If progress is a myth, our efforts will flag. With that the whole of evolution will come to a halt—because we are evolution," and "All conscious energy is, like love (and because it is love), founded upon hope." We are "saved by hope", and the sort of despair so prevalent among us is in fact a repudiation of salvation. It is an apostasy.

Nor is it in any way a valid protest to urge that Teilhard "has no sense of sin". That is a charge easily brought against anyone who defends the unique supremacy of God; like pantheism it is easily applied to all who take seriously the "divinisation" attainable in Christ and described by his Apostle. Teilhard was, of course, fully aware of his liability to both criticisms. Early in his work he took occasion to protest that pantheism in the sense in which alone it is heretical was very different from his own insistence upon the universal presence and sustaining energy of God. "The sojourner in the divine *milieu* is not a pantheist." . . . Diversity is integrated and consummated in unity: it is not absorbed or nullified in it. "Christianity saves the essential aspiration of all mysticism: *to be united* (that is

to become the other) while *remaining oneself.*" . . . Though he admits, as any honest student must, that on occasion St. Paul's emphasis upon the wholeness of God, the totality of Christ, and our identification with him is so full as to suggest that for us Christification implies individual perfection, yet rightly appreciated it is fulfilled only by membership in and total involvement with the divine community, the "body" of Christ. For him as for St. Paul the master-text is Ephesians iv. 13, "Until we all come home into the oneness of our faith and our full awareness of the Son of God, into mature humanity, into the measure of the stature of the fullness of Christ"; and this does not assert the equal perfection of each individual, but the total integration of each in the full development of the whole. Pantheism, as Dean Inge used to say, is not equivalent to Panentheism; the latter does not involve the former; the "cell" does not become the body though its whole life is fulfilled within the body. Teilhard emphasised this distinction in one of his last essays on the Spirit of identification and the Spirit of unification.

So with the fact of sin, he declares that as "his aim is solely to show how all things can help the believer to unite himslf to God there is no need to concern ourselves directly with bad actions, that is with positive gestures of disunion." . . . And realising as he always does the need to take all the field of experience into account he deals at the end of the book with this factor in its extreme form—with the traditional view of hell and of eternal damnation. No one reading those pages could fail to admit that for Teilhard as for any sensitive soul the problem of evil constitutes, with that of suffering and even more profoundly, the paradox and testing-point of belief.

Here, as in other matters, for example his admission that all religious truth was revealed only through the Church (a confession very hard for some of us to reconcile with his general outlook), he accepted explicitly the traditional belief in hell—though claiming that he was "forbidden to hold with absolute certainty that any single man has been damned." . . . Moreover, although he admits to praying that the flames may never touch anyone, he reaches for his own mind a recognition that somehow "the damned are not excluded from the Pleroma . . . they lose it but are not lost to it" . . . , and does not find this an insurmountable obstacle. And as such though we may be unable to follow him, we have no ground for denying his sense of sin—still less for insinuating that his faith is shallow or incomplete. Those who feel that the primary quality of Christ is "to seek and to save that which is lost" (Lk. xix. II) will share the conviction that since divinisation is ultimately universal, eternal damnation as commonly understood must remain for us a contradiction in terms. Gehenna is surely the destruction of that which has forfeited all value, the rubbish dump of Jerusalem, not the everlasting torture-chamber. Immortality is not a physical condition of individual existence but a relationship with God and the community. (pp. 177-80)

Teilhard claims in *Le Milieu* that his concern does not admit of detailed discussion of evil: his life, according to the universal testimony of his friends and of his works, was similarly preoccupied with God. "No man can serve two masters" (Matt. vi. 24 and Lk. xvi. 13): by the law of reversed effort too much anxiety about avoiding sin, as most of us know by experience, easily produces the very disease which it dreads. (pp. 180-81)

Teilhard's confession of faith dating from July 1933 and printed by Cuénot [in his biography of Teilhard] summarises his convictions. "We can be fundamentally happy only in a personal union with something personal (with the personality of everything) in everything. This is the ultimate appeal of what we call 'love'. In consequence the essential quality of the joy of life discloses itself in the knowledge or feeling that in everything that we taste, create, undertake, discover or suffer in ourselves or in others, in every possible line of life or death, organic, social, artistic or scientific, we are increasing gradually and are ourselves gradually incorporated in the growth of the universal soul or spirit.'' For this conviction all that is needed is an impassioned human heart and the acceptance of three points:

(1) That Evolution or the birth of the universe is by nature convergent not divergent, making for a final unity; (2) that this unity, built up gradually by the world's labour, is by nature spiritual—spirit being understood *not* as a withdrawal from but as a transformation or sublimation or culmination of matter; (3) that the centre of this spiritualised matter, of this totality of what is by nature spiritual, must in consequence be supremely conscious and personal: the Ocean which gathers all the spiritual tides of the universe is not only something but someone: he is in himself face and heart. If one accepts these three points the whole of life, including death, becomes for each one of us a discovery and continual conquest of a divine and irresistible Presence. This Presence illuminates the secrecies and inmost depths of everything and every man around us. We can attain a full realisation not a simple enjoyment of everything and every man. And we cannot be deprived of it by anything or anyone. That is Teilhard's creed.

And if we are to express it theologically we find him convinced that evil is no accident or regrettable mistake. We have no right to suppose that God would have created a world without evil and suffering: they are, however we explain it, an integral part of the process. All we can say is that the world is so constructed that evil and death occur in it. ''Suffering'' said Teilhard in his *La Vie cosmique* . . . ''is the consequence and the price of the labour of development.'' ''Creation groans and travails until now,'' as St. Paul put it, ''Creation, Incarnation, Redemption, each marking a stage in the divine operation, are they not three phases indissolubly joined in the manifestation of the divine?'' (pp. 183-84)

> *Charles E. Raven, in his* Teilhard de Chardin: Scientist and Seer *(© Charles E. Raven 1962; reprinted by permission of William Collins Sons & Co Ltd), Collins, 1962, 221 p.*

## JOSEPH F. DONCEEL, S.J.  (essay date 1965)

There seems to have occurred a definite change from the younger to the older Teilhard. In 1930 he agreed with the majority of his fellow scientists, who prefer to keep philosophical explanations out of their scientific system. In 1955 he had given up the distinction which he used to emphasize. Or more correctly, he wanted both explanations included in science. That shift had already occurred in 1947, the year in which he wrote in the *Avertissement* (Warning) for *Le phénomène humain:* ''If this book is to be properly understood, it must be read not as a work on metaphysics, still less as a sort of theological essay, but purely and simply as a scientific memoir.''

Obviously Teilhard had widened his conception of pure science. He has not erased the boundaries between science and philosophy, since, in the same *Warning* he wrote, ''Beyond these first purely scientific reflections, there is obviously ample room for the most far-reaching speculations of the philosopher and the theologian.'' But he has definitely moved up the bound-

ary line. He has pulled up the stakes where he found them in 1930, and transplanted them inside what he formerly considered as philosophical territory.

Quite a number of scientists and of philosophers, even among those who admire Teilhard, prefer his position of 1930 to that of 1947. I agree with them. *The Phenomenon of Man* is not a ''purely scientific memoir.'' Teilhard himself seems to doubt it since, in that very book, he speaks of ''the conviction, *strictly undemonstrable to science,* that the universe has a direction,'' and of the access of thought as a ''threshold which had to be crossed at a single stride: a 'transexperimental' interval about which scientifically we can say nothing.''

Summarizing I would say that the scientist, as scientist, in his strictly scientific work, should only consider the empirical sequences of antecedents and consequents. He will steadily make more progress in that kind of explanation, but he will never reach the end of it, he will never explain the totality of the phenomena. But there is quite a difference between ignoring another explanation and denying its existence. A scientist who ignores the other explanation is confining himself to his task; a scientist who denies its existence is no longer speaking as a scientist, he is indulging in philosophy. (pp. 254-55)

Although I believe that the later Teilhard was mistaken when he tried to include both levels of explanation within the compass of science, it seems to me that he was right when he insisted upon the need of both of them for a complete theory of life and evolution. (p. 255)

Whenever man knows something, he knows it with his whole mind. But there are different levels in the human mind. . . .

In the objects which we know the several levels of our mind attain being or reality, but they attain it under different aspects. That which is reached by the senses is sensible being, reality as known by the senses, empirical reality, which is the object of everyday and of scientific knowledge. That which is reached by the intellect is intelligible being, being as being, noumenal reality. These two aspects of reality never exist separately. They always go together. (p. 257)

Teilhard felt that a complete explanation of reality was impossible unless one takes into account both the ''without'' and the ''within'' of things, their empirical and their intelligible aspect. It seems to me that he was right. Moreover, during the second half of his career he insisted that it was the scientist's task to provide this double explanation. This might be misunderstood; here I have my doubts. If he meant that it was up to the scientist as a man, as a philosopher, to build up a complete interpretation of reality, I would go along with him. But it seems evident that he meant that the scientist as such should combine the study of the without with that of the within, should explain things in terms both of tangential and of radial energy. It is a fact that the majority of the scientists do not follow him in this direction. I believe that they are right. Teilhard invites them to modify the traditional conception of experimental science, to widen it considerably, to include within its scope what has, until now, been considered as belonging to the domain of philosophy. I am afraid that most scientists will not accept this expansion of the domain of natural science, and rightly so, because the traditional boundaries between science and philosophy, even though they may be vague in certain instances, are not the result of mere conventions or of practical compromises, but . . . they are deeply rooted in the nature of reality and of human knowledge. (pp. 264-65)

Because he was at once a scientist and a philosopher, Teilhard de Chardin could afford to build a comprehensive explanation of the world all by himself. His pioneering efforts might best be carried on in occasional meetings and discussions of scientists and philosophers, who would bring to bear upon reality their *complementary* ways of approaching and interpreting the wide panorama of the universe. (p. 266)

> *Joseph F. Donceel, S.J., "Teilhard de Chardin: Scientist or Philosopher?" in* International Philosophical Quarterly, *Vol. V, No. 2, May, 1965, pp. 248-66.*

## JACOB BRONOWSKI  (essay date 1965)

[Teilhard de Chardin and Margaret Mead] mark the two ends of the spectrum of speculation: Mead is searching for the smallest step of social change, and Teilhard de Chardin by contrast looked only for its cosmic direction. They are equally at extremes in the relative importance that they give to the individual man and to his society; it is ironic that Mead, the social anthropologist, stresses the part played by the individual, and that Teilhard de Chardin, the shepherd of souls, pictured a society without men. . . . [Both] writers understand what makes a theory scientific, the demands for order and coherence that it must meet, and they hold to this scrupulous standard. (p. 155)

The speculations of Teilhard de Chardin are, I have said, at the opposite extreme to Mead's. His vision was of macroevolution, on a cosmic scale. Moreover, to still his own religious scruples and those of his superiors in the Jesuit order, he colored his vision with a rich mystic lacquer. But the essence of what he had to say is plain, and it is particularly plain in this book of essays, which collects what Teilhard thought as he thought it, over thirty years. *The Future of Man* says nothing unexpected, yet it is to me much the most interesting of Teilhard de Chardin's books.

Teilhard held that what his fellow biologists call the higher animals are higher, not only on the scale of biological complexity, but on any scale of values which makes sense to us. And on that scale we are, of course, highest among the animals. This is (in Teilhard's view) an absolute scale: evolution has labored most elaborately on God's behalf to produce man. The complexity which places man absolutely above the other animals is expressed in his possession of mind. So far (apart from the religious intrusions) few biologists would find fault with Teilhard.

Man's mind enables him to form concepts, use language, build societies and cultures; above all, it enables him to work in intellectual community with others. Human groups are not mere packs of wolves or monkeys (in whose communal habits Teilhard was not interested), but are societies in which knowledge is fixed and handed on, and in which the intellectual and emotional life of each man is sustained by his unity with others— for the glory of God. So far (apart from the religious intrusions) few anthropologists would find fault with Teilhard.

What Teilhard did now was to project the direction of evolution forward, beyond man as he is to that which his endowments seem to design him for. He concluded that the social use of the intellect is the peak of man's talents, and would become their ultimate realization. . . . (pp. 159-60)

Teilhard foresaw a universal community of men who no longer have individual minds, but flow into one all-embracing mind, "an envelope of thinking substance" around the world. It was as if all mankind would become a single clone of cells—or a single insect colony, informed by a common unity of mind instead of common instincts.

This is of course a cultural, not a biological dream: what Teilhard called "an irresistible physical process: the collectivization of mankind." (p. 160)

It has been thought that Teilhard was silenced by his superiors, and died in 1955 with his work unpublished, because they would not acknowledge that man has evolved as the other animals have, without a special act of creation. But it seems to me that they must also have shuddered at his picture of the future, in which man will lose his identity in a God who has become a sort of queen bee of mind. Indeed, they cannot have approved his wish to see man saved by collective rather than personal grace.

Teilhard de Chardin was, beneath the faith and the hallelujahs, a pessimist about the fate of man; Margaret Mead, pouring her torrential prose over the coffee tables, is an optimist. I am on her side. But I am conscious that when any one of us thinks about the future, what we see is still hopelessly vague and idealized. (pp. 160-61)

> *Jacob Bronowski, "Where Do We Go from Here," in* The New York Review of Books *(reprinted with permission from* The New York Review of Books; *copyright © 1965 Nyrev, Inc.), Vol. IV, No. 2, February 25, 1965 (and reprinted in his* A Sense of the Future: Essays in Natural Philosophy, *edited by Piero E. Ariotti with Rita Bronowski, The MIT Press, 1977, pp. 155-62).* *

## IAN G. BARBOUR  (essay date 1967)

Teilhard was not trained in philosophy as he was in science and to some extent in theology. Nevertheless his *process metaphysics,* though not formally developed, seems to have been the "middle term" through which his evolutionary outlook influenced his theology and vice versa. Where *being* and *substance* were scholastic philosophy's basic categories, *becoming* and *process* are Teilhard's. Time, change and interaction are constitutive of reality. Ours is a world in flux, a network of interacting influences spread through time and space. Teilhard's metaphysics strikingly resembles that of the philosopher Alfred North Whitehead—in part, no doubt, because of their common indebtedness to evolutionary thought in general and to Henri Bergson in particular. Both men stress the continuity of evolutionary history and of the levels of life today. The capacities of higher organisms were present in rudimentary form in the lower. . . .

Teilhard, like Whitehead, pictures every entity as a center of spontaneity and responsiveness. Of course neither thinker imputes to simpler organisms any self-consciousness or reflection, but only an incipient "*within,*" an elementary beginning of perception and anticipation "in extremely attenuated versions." (p. 1099)

Teilhard's process metaphysics . . . influenced his theology, especially his rendering of the doctrines of *creation, redemption* and *eschatology*. These themes are implicit in the *Phenomenon* and explicit in *The Divine Milieu* and in some of his shorter essays. . . . Teilhard urges us to think of creation "not as an instantaneous act, but in the manner of a process or synthesizing action. . . . Its act is a great continuous movement spread out over the totality of time. It is still going on." That is to say, we are part of an embryonic cosmos still in birth. Our understanding of God's relation to the world must take into account our knowledge of the temporal character of that world. Divine creativity is not arbitrary but has a definite structure, "the unification of the multiple" and "the creative transformation of earlier forms."

His evolutionary outlook leads Teilhard to declare *the unity of creation and redemption*. In his view the purpose of the incarnation is less the "remedial" work of making satisfaction for man's sin than the "constructive" work of uniting all reality and bringing it to fulfillment in God. Grace is not primarily an antidote for moral evil but a creative force at work throughout the world and human life. Where Western tradition has stressed the juridical and moral functions of Christ, Teilhard stresses his cosmic and ontological significance. Christ is not a foreign intruder sent arbitrarily to an alien realm to rescue individuals from it. He is the world's true fulfillment, integrally related to whatever is creative in the world. Redemption is the continuation of creation and vice versa. Here are ideas reminiscent of the Greek Fathers' "Universal Lord," John's "Logos" and Paul's "Christ in whom all things cohere." Teilhard sets forth a strong *theology of the secular*, affirming the positive potentialities of the world and rejecting any dualism which considers matter inherently evil. If God is involved in the world—in continuous creation and in the person of Christ—the Christian life must likewise entail involvement in the world. In this appreciation of the values in secularity Teilhard is not unlike Bonhoeffer, Cox and other exponents of "worldly Christianity." . . .

Teilhard portrays a *reciprocal interaction* between God and the world. The universe is not "useless" and "superfluous" to God, nor is he "indifferent" to it. "Truly it is not the notion of the contingency of the created but the sense of the mutual completion of God and the world which makes Christianity live." Teilhard argues that when men believed the world was created instantaneously it was difficult to reconcile the *presence of evil* with the goodness and power of God; but in an evolutionary creation God is exonerated because evil is an inevitable by-product. "There can be no order in process of formation that does not at all stages involve disorder." The pain of failure and death are structural concomitants of evolutionary growth. Suffering is "the consequence and price of a labor of development."

The orthodoxy of some of Teilhard's teachings has been questioned by his more conservative theological critics. The accusation of pantheism seems unfounded, since he explicitly defends God's transcendence even if he puts the emphasis on immanence. Like the Christian mystics, he speaks of personal union with God rather than of absorption of the individual in an impersonal All. A more serious deficiency may be present in his treatment of sin as simply one form of inescapable evil in the world; he tends to neglect the moral dimensions of individual freedom and divine forgiveness. But there can be no question about his personal devotion to Christ and the Roman Catholic Church. . . . (p. 1100)

In the later chapters of the *Phenomenon,* in *The Future of Man* and in *Man's Place in Nature,* he extrapolates the apparent direction of past evolution to a future global convergence of mankind into an interthinking fabric of humanity, a collectivity of consciousness ("the Noosphere"). Believing that the universe is "personalizing" and "individuating," he is confident that this new "social organism" will be informed by freedom and diversity rather than totalitarian uniformity. The bond un-

iting the new humanity will be love. Perhaps Teilhard gives too little attention to the differences between biological and cultural evolution, and extrapolates too readily from one to the other. He seems to underestimate the tragic and ambiguous character of human history. True, he acknowledges that, with the advent of reflective thought, man—who is "evolution conscious of itself"—chooses his own destiny and now has the power to destroy himself. Nevertheless he is convinced that the cosmic process, having gone so far as it has, will inevitably progress further. One wonders whether this assurance about the future did not derive as much from his Christian faith as from his empirical study of man.

The Teilhardian view of *the final fulfillment* combines an evolutionary optimism with a Christian eschatology in which the activity of man and the world contribute to the actualization of the Kingdom. The maturation of man is "a condition (not indeed sufficient and determinative but necessary) for the Parousia of Christ." Man and nature collaborate with God in bringing the cosmos to completion; evolutionary development and human endeavor cooperate with the unifying and creative divine action. Salvation is not an escape from the world but its completion and sanctification. Yet the ending is not merely the intrinsic climax of a process ascending "on its own" without God. For God is at work throughout history, and the consummation of history is a gift of his grace. This is neither a purely "natural ascent" nor an arbitrary "supernatural finale" unrelated to what went before; the action is both "natural" and "supernatural" throughout, until the ultimate consummation which is the culmination of Teilhard's cosmic vision. (pp. 1100-01)

Teilhard's writings can profitably be read in a variety of ways: as science, as poetry, as natural theology, as process philosophy, and as Christian theology. Many interpreters have sharply contrasted his various works, classifying the *Phenomenon,* for instance, as natural theology and *The Divine Milieu* as Christian theology. I have suggested, however, that there is unity in his thought and that both evolutionary and biblical assumptions influenced all his writing, though obviously in varying degrees. The role of Teilhard's process metaphysics as a "middle term" here has often been overlooked. Whether he intended to or not, he deals with questions that have traditionally been the province of metaphysics: mind and matter, purpose and mechanism, the relationship between nature, man and God. It is precisely his temporalistic metaphysics that enables him to develop a process theology emphasizing such genuinely biblical themes as the importance of time and history, affirmation of "secular" life, the unity of man as a total being, belief in a living God involved in the world, and the cosmic significance of Christ. As I see it, Teilhard's most original work is his exploration of the nature of man and the meaning of creation, redemption and eschatology in an evolving world. (p. 1101)

> *Ian G. Barbour, "The Significance of Teilhard," in* The Christian Century *(copyright 1967 Christian Century Foundation; reprinted by permission from the August, 1967 issue of* The Christian Century*), Vol. LXXXIV, No. 35, August 30, 1967, pp. 1098-1102.*

### THEODOSIUS DOBZHANSKY　(essay date 1967)

"Men's minds are reluctant to recognize that evolution has a precise *orientation* and a privileged *axis*." This is the cardinal postulate of the Teilhardian synthesis. Evolution, human and biological and cosmic, is not simply a lot of whirl and flutter going nowhere in particular. It is, at least in its general trend, progressive. (p. 116)

Teilhard's assertion that the evolutionary process has a definite orientation must be very carefully examined. Evolutionary changes taking place at any given time are conditioned by the changes which preceded them, and they will condition the changes that take place in the future. This is especially obvious in biological evolution—the evolutionary past of a living species is, as it were, inscribed in its genes. (p. 117)

Now, it is the totality of evolution that occupies Teilhard's attention almost exclusively. The only particular evolutionary line which interests him is that of man, and this because he believes that in man evolution as a whole is, as it were, brought into focus. (p. 119)

Concerning the causes of evolution he had actually little to say. Although the latter part of his life coincided with the development of the modern biological (synthetic) theory of evolution, he had only a hazy idea about it. And yet his general conception of the nature of evolution harmonizes with the fundamentals of biological theory far better than with that of orthogenesis. And let this be made clear: what is here involved is not a technical biological problem; the issue is critical for the whole Teilhardian synthesis.

If evolution follows a path which is predestined (orthogenesis), or if it is propelled and guided toward some goal by divine interventions (finalism), then its meaning becomes a tantalizing, and even distressing, puzzle. If the universe was designed to advance toward some state of absolute beauty and goodness, the design was incredibly faulty. (p. 120)

The evolution of the universe must be conceived as having been in some sense a struggle for a gradual emergence of freedom. The outcome of evolution is not predestined because, in Teilhard's words, "There is a danger that the elements of the world should refuse to serve the world—because they think; or more precisely that the world should refuse itself from perceiving itself through reflection." (pp. 120-21)

Teilhard describes the method of evolution as "groping." He also claims that "Groping is directed chance." This requires careful examination. Among Teilhard's many metaphors, "groping" is perhaps the most ingenious one. Natural selection operates with mutations and gene combinations in the origin of which "chance" plays an important role. Natural selection "directs" this "chance" into adaptive channels. One must, however, beware of personalizing natural selection. It is not some kind of spirit or demon who directs evolution to accomplish some set purpose. "Groping" in the dark is, indeed, the only way natural selection can proceed. Now, groping may lead to discovery of openings toward new opportunities for living. It may also end in a fall from a precipice. It may preserve and enhance life, or it may lead to extinction. Teilhard was a paleontologist, and he was quite familiar with extinction of evolutionary lines. Yet he devoted strangely little attention to this phenomenon in his writings. It would have caused him no difficulty had he realized that natural selection is necessarily opportunistic and shortsighted in its gropings. (p. 128)

"No evolutionary future awaits man except in association with all other men." Reluctant to admit it, Teilhard enters here the realm of prophecy. Yet he does not allow his prophetic vision to soar out of sight of the solid ground of cumulative knowledge. His prophecy is not scientifically provable; if it were so it would be prediction rather than prophecy. However, a prophecy may be compatible with, or contradictory to, scientific knowledge. This gives us a warrant to examine Teilhard's prophecy from the point of view of evolutionary biology, which is, after all, the same point from which Teilhard himself takes his departure.

The trend prevailing in the evolution of the noosphere, the noogenesis, is toward "planetization" and the "megasynthesis." This implies a radical convergence and integration of the physical, cultural, and ideological branches of mankind. . . . Like the diversity on the biological level, human diversity served to "try everything so as to find everything." The other side of the coin is not pretty; differences among men have often inflamed hatreds, cruelty, strife, war (hot and cold), genocide, concentration camps. Social Darwinists, as un-Darwinian as they are antisocial, contend that strife and all its grim consequences are merely the wages which mankind has to pay for progress. (pp. 132-33)

Teilhard rejects social Darwinism. In noogenesis, the most powerful impetus toward progress comes not from strife or waste but from love. Replacement of strife by love already began in biological evolution, biogenesis. The classics of evolutionism described natural selection as a consequence of the struggle for existence. The "struggle" does not, however, always mean strife. Our modern view of natural selection sees it promoted by cooperation as well as by competition. Moreover, the importance of cooperation relative to competition has been growing as biological evolution has advanced. By and large, it is greater among higher than among lower animals. (p. 133)

The "planetization" of mankind is, in Teilhard's view, made inevitable by the swiftly increasing facility of communication and by increasing knowledge. Mankind inhabits the surface of only one rather small planet. Unless means are found to emigrate and to colonize other planets, people will finally have to learn to live harmoniously or at least peacefully with more and more numerous neighbors. (p. 134)

Is there anything more than Teilhard's burning faith to bear out the bright hope of the megasynthesis? Can one rule out the polar opposite: disunion, dispersion, and arrogant self-assertion of the individual against mankind? The antithesis to megasynthesis is the ideal of the Dostoevskian Grand Inquisitor and the Nietzschean Superman. Without specifically mentioning Dostoevsky or Nietzsche, Teilhard recognizes the danger. Human freedom enables man to choose also a direction away from megasynthesis. Mankind may become a dust of independent and dissociated sparks of consciousness. Some of those sparks, being stronger, brighter, or perhaps simply luckier, than the rest, will "eventually find the road always sought by the Consciousness towards its consummation." Teilhard rejects this possibility as leading into an evolutionary blind alley. Spiritually matured mankind should be able to extricate itself from such a blind alley, because man is the only form of life which need not accept the direction of the evolutionary forces acting upon him, but can direct his evolution. (pp. 135-36)

The eventual consummation of all evolution is envisaged by Teilhard as a convergence in the Omega. (p. 136)

It is evidently the inspiration of a mystic, not a process of inference from scientific data, that lifts Teilhard to the heights of his eschatological vision. Yet he remains a consistent evolutionist throughout. The point which he stresses again and again is that man is not to be a passive witness but a participant in the evolutionary process. (p. 137)

*Theodosius Dobzhansky, "The Teilhardian Synthesis," in his* The Biology of Ultimate Concern *(copyright © 1967 by Theodosius Dobzhansky; reprinted by permission of the Literary Estate of Theodosius Dobzhansky),* The New American Library, 1967, pp. 108-37.

## ROBERT SPEAIGHT (essay date 1967)

Between the outbreak of war and the end of 1918 [Teilhard] composed thirteen essays which contain, in germ, the future development of his thought. He described them as his 'intellectual honeymoon'. (p. 75)

[*La Vie Cosmique* was written, as Teilhard] admitted, out of sheer exuberance and the necessity of living, to express his passionate vision of the universe. The essay was a prayer rather than an argument; Teilhard described it as his *'testament d'intellectuel'*. In Christ was resumed the 'implacable grandeur of the world'; He was union and multitude, spirit and matter, the personal and the infinity, the part and the whole. He was sweetness and intimacy and power. Life on earth only continued because the cosmic Christ was still in the act of formation; he was the natural as well as the supernatural consummation of all created activity; and for that reason evolution was 'holy'. The sole business of the world was the physical incorporation of the faithful in Christ, and this work proceeded with 'the rigour and harmony of a natural evolution'. But it was the transcendent *fiat* of the Incarnation which made it possible. (pp. 76-7)

In a note adjoined to his MS Teilhard made an important distinction between two conceptions of Christian asceticism. According to the one, suffering was above all 'a punishment and an expiation'. The fruit of original sin, its efficacy was sacrificial; it was a way of reparation. According to the other, suffering was the consequence and the price of a work still in process of development. It was the sign of a continual effort, and its efficacy lay in this. Physical and moral evil were the result of what was coming to be; everything in evolution had to endure its travail and commit its faults. The Cross—Teilhard went on boldly to assert—was an evolutionary no less than an expiatory symbol. The two points of view coincided if one admitted that the natural consequence of original sin was to make mankind work 'with the sweat of his brow', but Teilhard recognized the sharp difference of emphasis, and thought it only loyal that he should point it out. Nevertheless in doing so he exposed his failure to see that 'the only guarantee of evolution's success was Christ's conquest of man's capacity for disunion and hatred on the personal level', and at the same time he exposed a flank of which his adversaries were quick to take advantage.

In September of the same year (1916) Teilhard turned from his personal testament to the task which he saw confronting him. The Church was still under the spell of a pessimism which the Syllabus of Pius IX had disastrously confirmed, whatever historical reasons might be pleaded in its excuse. The protest of the Reformation, the paganism of the Renaissance, the scepticism of the Enlightenment, and the raucous clamour of political and industrial democracy had reduced the magisterium to panic. It confused the world which Christ had redeemed with the world he had condemned. To save his soul the Christian would do better to avoid the contamination of secular concerns. Against this emasculated pietism Teilhard set his face. He saw the 'intensive socialization' of a world in the throes of transforming itself as a movement of the Absolute

rejoining the forces of renewal and inviting their response. The very idea of evolution was meaningless unless it posited a term—and for Teilhard, secure in the option of faith, this could only be the transfiguring image of Christ. To synthesize the truths of revelation with the just, and inevitable, advance of knowledge—this was the task he assigned himself; and he described his acceptance of it as a 'conversion'.

He began to elaborate his ideas in *La Maîtrise du Monde et le Règne de Dieu.* Christ was 'the principle of unity who saves a culpable creation in process of returning to dust'; critics of Teilhard should here note the admission of culpability. The evolution of matter was a scientific truth so clear as to need no further demonstration, but now mind itself was evolving. Less evident was his contention that history, in spite of its accidental convulsions which were all around him as he wrote, was infallible in its phases and fortunate in its results. 'After each new crisis Humanity must yield to the evidence that it has progressed, that it has changed to its own advantage. For Life, and Life alone, knows what is good for its children.' Here was the Teilhardian optimism which would survive all the shocks that the twentieth century had in store for it. . . . In Teilhard's view the conquests the humanity were irreversible; it would make its mistakes, but it was incapable of permanent regression; and it was here that revelation proposed an apex to the ascending pyramid of man's endeavour. (pp. 77-8)

[There followed, later in the same year] *Le Christ dans la Matière: Trois Histoires comme Benson.* These stories, although their narrative content is very slight, were inspired by a reading of Robert Hugh Benson, and they expressed ideas which Benson might have developed. Teilhard gives himself the alibi of a friend with whom he imagines himself in conversation. The friend has died at Verdun and Teilhard recalls an evening when he had spoken of his vision of Christ, of how the universe had come to assume for him the lineaments of the divine figure. (p. 79)

In the second story Teilhard, or his *alter ego* interlocutor, watches the expansion of the Host in the monstrance till it becomes incandescent, consuming and transforming all the energies of love in the universe. The white patch of consecrated bread then contracts slowly, leaving behind it 'certain refractory elements' in outer darkness. The third story, *La Custode,* is even more directly autobiographical. Teilhard takes the reader back to the time when his regiment was in the line near Verdun, and he was carrying the Blessed Sacrament on his own person. How was it possible, he asks, that the springs of life and the richness of the world should be so close to him and yet defy his penetration? Even at the moment of communion he feels that they are still not truly a part of him. All his powers of recollection are in vain; the centre of what he holds attracts him but eludes his grasp. But at last, and in proportion as his efforts are redoubled, the Host takes on the form of a brother who needs his love or consolation, the memory of some joy or suffering, the thought of some work to be accomplished. The entire universe is reconstituted in the particle of bread and borrows its appearances. Teilhard then understands the nature of the obstacle which bars him from a perfect union with the object of his love and his pursuit—namely 'the whole substance and surface of the years which remain for him to live and to divinize'. . . . And so he looked forward to a day when the 'vast décor' of the universe might wither or collapse—looked forward to the imminent possibility of his own death—without any diminution of joy because 'the substantial Reality would remain intact'. The rays of energy would retire upon their source and he would still embrace them. (pp. 79-80)

[In *La Lutte contre la Multitude*] Teilhard broached the problem of the one and the many—a question that was to haunt him for many years to come as the socialization of human life made such rapid, and often such disconcerting, progress. The philosophical importance of the essay seemed to him 'obviously very limited', but it brought him to a precious definition of the 'pure in heart'. For Teilhard, purity of heart simply consisted in loving God above everything else and in seeing his presence everywhere in a world that was waiting to be conquered and perfected by him. Thus individual objects lost their superficial multiplicity. The natural privilege of the pure soul was to move at the heart of an immense and superior unity. Where the carnal sinner was dispersed in his passions, the saint escaped from their complexity and made himself to that extent immaterial. For him, everything was God and God was everything, and Jesus was 'God and everything combined'. The specification of purity was to unify the interior powers of the soul in the activity of a single passion. Overcoming the multiple and distracting appeal of objects, the pure soul steeped its unity in 'the ardours of the divine simplicity'. For Teilhard de Chardin purity of soul was only another name for singleness of mind. And where purity operated in solitude, charity operated in society. This was the chief work of human life; and it was by this that we should be justified or condemned. (pp. 81-2)

[*Le Milieu Mystique* is the] most important perhaps of Teilhard's earlier essays because it prefigured *Le Milieu Divin*. . . . In summing up, Teilhard disclaimed any intention of describing the mystical life in itself; he wished only to disentangle its 'natural and cosmic roots'. Just as there was a single matter created to support the additions of consciousness, so there was a single, fundamental idea and aspiration at the base of every variety of mysticism—the innate love of the human person extended to the whole universe. This was liable to many deviations. It might evaporate into an empty poetizing or degenerate into a pagan pantheism. Nevertheless it was here, and here alone, that mysticism had its primitive beginnings. Once again Teilhard's passionate quest for unity is troubled by the multitude of created beings; he shares the mystic's obstinate passion for 'the stable, the unchanging and the absolute'; but then he perceives that 'the Real is not only transparent but solid'. The world is 'full' and its fullness is the fullness of the Absolute. In loving an object he discovers that the opacity of that object, and the barrier of separation between itself and him, are dissolved into a unifying transparency by the intensity of his own attachment. In and through his perception of another, he has come to possess everything in himself.

The creative activity of God does not knead us, as the potter kneads his clay; it is more like a vivifying fire, and it is through living that we surrender ourselves to its possession. This surrender is in fact an incessant task of self-correction and self-development, in which the soul can have no rest until every least discordance has ceased between its own vibration and the *milieu divin*. . . . As the thought takes him, Teilhard passes from analysis to reflection and from reflection to prayer. For a moment a cloud of pessimism overshadows him; nature is a bungler and progress a fraud; all that we see and hear is inert and gross; and only in the wheatfields of the catalyzing Spirit is there a harvest of energy and good will. And so he dreams of a common centre where the liveliest energies and sharpest sensibilities of the cosmos will put down their roots. This is the *milieu mystique;* this is the *milieu divin*. But the source is

personal; and it is to a person that Teilhard directs his prayer. . . . (pp. 82-3)

*La Nostalgie du Front* resumed Teilhard's feelings about the war very much as he had expressed them in letters to Marguerite Teillard-Chambon. . . .

So far from dreading his first advance to the trenches, he was not only curious as to what the experience would bring him but envious of those already inured to it. Whenever his regiment was withdrawn from the front line he could not understand why those who worked in the rear—the ambulance drivers, chauffeurs, and radio technicians—were not as curious and envious as he. He proposed the paradox—and proposed it without fear of contradiction—that to go up into the line was to go forward into peace. This sensation of peace was in fact a sensation of liberty. One night in particular he called to mind. Among the poplar trees, not far ahead, there still lingered the deadly aroma of poison gas; a bomb exploded in the wood; but the crickets continued to chirp, and Teilhard could wander at will, picking up a stray apple, and sleeping in the first shell hole that took his fancy. He had not forgotten the interests and anxieties which normally beset him, but he saw them in a new light and a more distant perspective. He was their master; and he described the sensation as one of 'inexplicable lightheartedness'.

But these were only the negative aspects of a more positive and creative liberty. The material and spiritual forces that the war had unleashed were an appeal to life, even though they were often a vocation to death—they engaged the last ounce of human energies. This freedom was a liberation of powers usually dormant for want of space for their expansion. As he wrote his essay in the rear, Teilhard felt that he had travelled an immense distance: 'I feel as if I had lost a Soul, a Soul greater than my own that inhabits the front line, and I feel that I have left it there.' (p. 88)

In January 1918 Teilhard composed *L'Âme du Monde.* Here the title begged the rather big question as to how far one could speak, with any precision, about 'the soul of the world'. In Teilhard's later writings the phrase disappears, but in 1918 he was struck by the religious character of so many secular aspirations; the best minds of his time seemed to find Christianity too selfish for their altruism. Charity was not dead in them, but it looked elsewhere for its source and its sanction. . . . Teilhard appealed to the basic principles of revelation to show that 'Christ and the Soul of the World are not two opposed and independent realities, nor are they adequately to be distinguished *in natura rerum*, but that the one is the milieu in which we are transformed into the Other'. Teilhard was again looking forward to the elaboration of his theory in *Le Milieu Divin,* and to his conception of the *noosphère*—a conception less open to theological objection than 'the soul of the world'. (pp. 89-90)

Only a month later he completed *La Grande Monade*—described as a *'fantaisie sérieuse—au clair de lune'*. Watching the moon rise above trenches and its light filter across the coils of barbed wire, he saluted it as a 'symbolic star' prefiguring a new earth more conscious of itself and more unified—which was even now coming to birth in the trenches in front of him. For it was in the struggle against itself that humanity was achieving its solidarity; this was the law of secular strife and progress. But the moon was also the symbol of loneliness and death; it came to resemble the whitened skull which was the object of the ascetic's contemplation. Humanity would grow and multiply, but as its powers expanded it would find itself 'bound to a corpse'. The stiff crust of the moon's unchanging outline was a mocking reminder of the prison-house in which all human effort was confined. 'The only true death, the only good death', Teilhard wrote, was 'a paroxysm of life'; and it could only be achieved 'by a desperate effort of the living towards a greater purity, a greater dispossession of self, and a greater reaching out beyond the zone of its confinement. Happy is the world which comes to an end in ecstasy!' (pp. 90-1)

Teilhard's next essay has a particular biographical interest. He entitled it *L'Éternel Féminin,* and it is the only one of these early writings to carry a dedication as distinct from an epigraph. The connection is plain between the *Béatrix* of the dedication and the Beatrice of the Divine Comedy—a figure in whom Teilhard's vision of *le féminin* is made luminously clear; and the emotional resonance of the essay—or poem, for that is what it really is—will hardly escape the sensitive ear. It is woman who speaks in the person of eternal Wisdom, taking her text from the Book of Proverbs: *'ab initio creata sum'* ['I was created from the beginning']. She is also the *Ewig-Weibliche* of Goethe's *Faust;* the 'charm' introduced into the world to assist its grouping, and the 'ideal suspended above it' to encourage its ascent. She is always a few steps ahead of it, and 'the appropriate form of its beatitude'. She is the cause of violence in man who thinks he has found in her a companion, only to discover that in touching her he has touched the secret forces of life. (p. 91)

[Teilhard] saw in the Christian ideal of virginity a principle of fecundity, not impoverishment. Here was the supreme crystallization of feminine power, the most radiant manifestation of its charm—'Christ has left men all his jewels'. The Blessed Virgin was both woman and mother; the Eternal Feminine remade; she was 'the incorruptible beauty of the times to come', the Bride of Christ, the Church which he had founded. Both the thought and style of *L'Éternel Féminin* are very reminiscent of Claudel, who more than once celebrated the mystical unity of the Church and the Blessed Virgin. As in Claudel, the eloquence breaks in irregular waves of rhapsody under the stress of emotion mastered by mind.

Even the friends to whom Teilhard had sent his writings were disconcerted, in varying degrees, by his ideas; and it was to explain these ideas more precisely to himself and to facilitate their correction by others that he set about the composition of *Mon Univers.* He looked back to his childhood and the 'stones' he had collected at Sarcenat. He was still only happy in the possession, or the contemplation, of consistent and unchanging things. His passion for natural phenomena was less scientific than religious, and in comparison with the universe and its limitless potentialities, the agitations of humanity seemed of very small account. Human activity was completely satisfying only when it went hand in hand with the movement of the cosmos towards its own perfection. . . . (p. 92)

*Le Prêtre,* written shortly before [Teilhard] took his solemn vows, summed up the whole sense of his priesthood, and his vocation to a world which believed it could dispense with Christ. He would be the first to take cognizance of the world's travail and aspirations; the first to suffer, to sympathize and to search; the first to sacrifice himself, in becoming 'more broadly human and more nobly of this earth than any servant of the world'. Meditating once more upon his vows, he resolved to recover in the very act of renunciation 'whatever of heavenly flame might be contained in the triple concupiscence; to sanc-

tify in chastity, poverty, and obedience the power residing in love and gold and independence'. Here the last word is significant. Teilhard did not understand by obedience the abandonment of liberty, but rather its exercise in a special relationship with others. (pp. 94-5)

[In *Forma Christi* Teilhard was concerned] to counteract the tendencies of a Christianity 'too extrinsic and particularist', a dogmatic structure which seemed to have no attachment to the universe. It was not surprising that men in close touch with concrete reality found the Christian revelation 'cold and infantile' if they were only shown its 'scholastic and disciplinary aspects'. This led Teilhard to consider the 'dual respiration' of Christian asceticism, its active and passive functioning. . . . One 'had to have loved the world a great deal to feel the need of getting beyond it', and it was for want of this love that religion had become anaemic. In preaching renunciation for the wrong reasons, it had lost the power to practise it for the right ones.

These two components of the interior life—spiritual growth and natural diminution in Christ—were not mutually exclusive. They might be alternating or simultaneous, directed towards a 'mobile and supple equilibrium'. The action of Christ in his 'information' of the universe was at once a cosmic and a personal possession, restricted only by the recalcitrance of human liberties. Finally Teilhard broached the article of Christian faith most difficult to imagine, if not to believe—the resurrection of the body. He saw this as a 'cosmic rather than individual phenomenon', and for this reason its apparition was plausibly postponed until the end of time. But here and now, 'thanks to an immense sum of infinitesimal efforts, and the accumulated effect of good desires and good communions, an indestructible world is in course of construction by our souls and bodies, under the shelter of Christ incarnate'. In so far as the universe of monads was moulded in the *'forma Christi'*, it would assume, in its eventual perfection, the shape and substance of his body as well as his soul.

No doubt these early essays of Teilhard are repetitive and to some degree imprecise. Each is carefully organized, but in their sum they are redundant, and their effect is occasionally rhapsodic. To read them is to be reminded of music where now one theme, and now another, is taken up and developed, and where the same theme constantly recurs. They belong to the order of poetry and meditation, less exactly to the order of analysis. (pp. 97-8)

> *Robert Speaight, in his* Teilhard de Chardin: A Biography (© *1967 Robert Speaight; reprinted by permission of William Collins Sons & Co Ltd), Collins, 1967, 360 p.*

### N. M. WILDIERS  (essay date 1968)

We must dare to face the truth: from the Renaissance on, a deep split gradually arose between the Church and modern culture, and often we are not even aware of the width and depth of this gap.

How clearly Teilhard de Chardin realized this problem appears even in his first writings. It is not exaggerated to claim that this contradiction between modern culture and Christianity occupied his mind from his youth and formed the major theme of his meditations. The spiritual climate in which he grew up at the beginning of this century must have filled him with discontent and dissatisfaction; it could not be otherwise. The separation between earth and heaven, between science and faith, between the modern world and Christianity, put him in an untenable situation.

His whole life as a matter of fact derives its deepest meaning from the striving toward unity between these two worlds. He cannot be at peace with a human culture which lacks every religious consecration, and cannot acquiesce in a Christianity which underestimates the greatness of human labor and effort. How can we justify the world in the eye of faith and faith in the eye of science? How can we be fully Christian, without falling short to both? These questions do not leave him for an instant.

Even during the years of his novitiate he is tormented by the question whether he would not do better to forego the religious life in order to follow more closely his scientific vocation. Was there no conflict in wanting to consecrate himself at one and the same time to God and to the study of this world? . . . [From his first writings, *Ecrits du temps de la guerre*] it clearly appears how his thinking in those years was entirely focused on the building-up of a Christ-centered philosophy of life, which would fully do justice to the terrestrial vocation of man. Even with the beginning of his first essay **"La vie cosmique,"** written in Nieuwpoort in 1916, we can read these remarkable lines: "I write these lines . . . in order to express an ardent view of the Earth, and in order to seek a solution to the doubts of my actions; because I love the Universe, its energies, its secrets, its hopes, and because, at the same time, I am dedicated to God, the single Beginning, the single Solution, the single End." The same problem is found again in most of the essays dating from the period. (pp. 528-29)

From all this it is evident how a work such as *The Divine Milieu* is to be viewed against the background of a historical and psychological context. Teilhard de Chardin fully sensed the inner discord which characterized the Christian consciousness at the beginning of our century. From this personal experience this book derives its meaning and authenticity.

Let us now turn our attention to the results Teilhard arrived at after many years of search and reflection. In what does the terrestrial vocation of man consist? In what does his heavenly vocation consist? How can this double vocation be lived as a single task, so that both missions reciprocally complement and complete each other? By means of these three questions the teaching of Teilhard will become clear for us.

[1. In what does the terrestrial vocation of man consist?]

Summarized in a concise way we could answer this question as follows: Man is called to carry on evolution and, through his work and effort, to bring the world to completion. In order to understand this answer well, we must recall the whole Teilhardian anthropology. Man, we learn there, is no heterogenous being who, so to say, has been brought from outside into the world. We are not, as Plato thought, descended from another and totally different world, only accidentally connected with this material world. No; man is linked with this earth with his whole being, he is an incarnated-consciousness-in-the-world, and this bond with the world is not merely external and accidental. He has risen from the earth, "the flower on the stem of the world" as Julian Huxley put it, and he is in the continuation of matter, of plant and animal. Even more: in man the deepest reality of the cosmos reveals itself as bifacial reality. This vision of man flows from the evolutionary world-image. The cosmos appears to us as a great historical process, as an evolving happening, as a world-in-the-making, and this evolv-

ing process in its great lines is characterized by a growth in the direction of an ever-increasing complexity and an ever-increasing consciousness. Along intricate and inscrutable ways matter gradually built itself up; atoms, molecules, stars, planets arose. On the outskirts of one of these planets the first forms of living matter arose, and these first forms of life gradually developed further in great variety and increasing wealth of life. As life arose in the bosom of matter, so finally man arose in the bosom of life. He is not loose from the world: he has risen from it and is in his existence continually dependent on the material and living beings which surround him.

But if man is in the continuation of all that has preceded him in time, he also radically differs from all this. Man is a discontinuity in the continuity. He is according to Herder "the first freedman of nature." In him the whole world receives a new dimension, the dimension of self-consciousness and freedom. Seen in the whole of the cosmic history, it is the mission of man to contribute in a conscious and deliberate way to the progress and the completion of the cosmos. In him the cosmos awoke, in him the cosmos came to consciousness, in him the cosmos conquered its freedom, in him it will continue its way—consciously and deliberately—unto its final destination. (pp. 529-31)

[2. In what does man's heavenly vocation consist?]

This question, too, needs reflection. The true vocation of the Christian is not merely to attain his personal salvation in the other life. The true vocation of the Christian is to cooperate in the building-up of the total Christ; he is called to cooperate in the building-up of the Church—*aedificatio ecclesiae*—of the *Corpus Mysticum*, and to attain in this way his ultimate salvation as a natural consequence of his striving toward the completion of Christ.

Whoever sees Christianity only as a way toward a more or less egoistically conceived happiness in the hereafter has but a very poor and shortsighted view of Christianity. The integral goal toward which Christianity orientates us lies endlessly farther. "The essence of Christianity," Teilhard de Chardin writes, "is nothing else than the unification of the world in God through the Incarnation." It is the new heaven and the new earth about which Scripture speaks to us. It is the Kingdom of God, whose advent we daily implore in the Our Father. It is necessary to revive in us this great vision of Christianity. All too often we have been satisfied with a narrow, restricted and provincial conception of Christianity. Christianity has been misused to keep people good, submissive. It has been reduced to a set of puerile and pious practices, to a form of external good manners and social conformism, not to mention the many forms of sentimentality, of bigotry, of bad taste, and even of superstition with which it has been draped. In its external appearance Christianity has been counterfeited unto the unrecognizable.

We are to free our faith from these wrong and narrow presentations. Christianity is endlessly much more than just leading a good and virtuous life in this world and then attaining eternal happiness in the hereafter. Christianity has a world-encompassing significance. It is focused on the completion of the cosmos in Christ. Christ is the meaning, the end of the whole creation: in Him everything exists. Through Him and in Him everything has to receive its completion.

The vocation of the Christian is, then, also endlessly greater and farther reaching than the personal happiness of the individual in the hereafter. All of us are called to cooperate in the building-up of the world in Christ and to complement what according to St. Paul's word is lacking to Christ's work. We are called to cooperate in the building-up of the total Christ, who according to St. Augustine consists of head and members. We are to be aware again of the greatness and the true content of Christianity.

3. Our integral vocation as man is thus the building-up and completion of creation. Our integral vocation as Christians is the building-up and completion of the *Corpus Mysticum*. The question which arises now for us is: Is there any connection between the building-up of the world and the building-up of the *Corpus Mysticum?* Are both realms and missions entirely apart from each other, without having the least in common, or are they related in one way or another, so that they can be lived, to a certain extent, as a unity? This is the central question with which Teilhard is concerned.

The answer he proposes can be summarized as follows: There is to be a certain relation between the completion of the world and the building-up of the *Corpus Mysticum,* as creation and incarnation are also related, as nature and grace, too, are in harmony with each other. It is after all unthinkable that there would not be any relation between God's self-revelation in creation and God's self-revelation in incarnation. Is it not rather that the second is to be seen as the continuation of the first? The world is created in Christ and has in Him its existence: both the natural and supernatural order have their existence in Christ. If man's vocation is to bring to completion both the creation and the redemption of the world, through his cooperation, then there must exist a deep inner connection between this double mission.

To bring to light this inner connection constitutes the great theme of Teilhard's theological reflection and especially of his work **The Divine Milieu.** In a highly nuanced way he shows us how through our work and our suffering, through our total living out of our being man, we really can approach God and contribute to the redemption of the world in Christ. Since it is the same God who reveals Himself in the creation and in the incarnation, so man must realize himself in his double mission: to complete the world and to build up the *Corpus Mysticum.*

How this is possible will become clear when we ask ourselves of what the completion of the world and the building-up of the *Corpus Mysticum* concretely consist. By means of a scientific phenomenology Teilhard de Chardin demonstrates (in his **The Human Phenomenon**) that the completion of the world ultimately consists of a process of unification and spiritualization which reaches its climax in the point omega. The building-up of the *Corpus Mysticum,* however, consists of the unification of the world in Christ: the *recapitulare omnia in Christo,* of which St. Paul tells us. If we now accept the idea that there exists a harmonious relation between the order of nature and the order of supernature, and that nature is destined to be sanctified and completed by grace, is it then not obvious to conclude that everything which contributes to the unification of the world possesses an intrinsic orientation to Christ and that the sanctification of our profane activities must thus consist in becoming conscious of this deeper dimension of all human labor?

"In the eyes of such a believer," Teilhard de Chardin writes, "the history of the world takes shape of a vast cosmogenesis, during which all the lines of the Real converge, without confusion, in a Christ, who is, at the same time, personal and universal. Strictly speaking and without metaphor, the Christian who understands, at the same time, the essence of his Credo and the space-time connections of nature, finds himself in the happy situation of being able to express himself by the whole variety of his activities in union with the whole of humanity in one great gesture of communion." . . . (pp. 531-34)

That is the reason why Teilhard thinks he may conclude: "With each one of our *works,* we labor—in individual separation, but no less really—to build the Pleroma; that is to say, we bring to Christ a little fulfillment. Each one of our works, by its more or less remote or direct effect upon the spiritual world, helps to make perfect Christ in his mystical totality." (p. 534)

[This Teilhardian synthesis is] in part indebted to anthropology and cosmology as conceived by the author. Here we are no longer in the terrain of theology, but of natural sciences and of natural philosophy. Insofar as the real theological aspect of the synthesis is concerned, his doctrine is fully defensible and cannot give rise to any serious difficulty.

Where to find, then, the originality and the importance of his work? It seems to me that if we are to understand the significance of this work, we must not only situate it on the theological level, but even more so on the historical and the sociological plane. What Teilhard de Chardin was pursuing most of all was to bring about a change, a conversion in the concrete attitude of the Catholic milieus vs. modern culture. (p. 535)

*N. M. Wildiers, "The New Christian of Teilhard de Chardin," in* THOUGHT *(reprinted by permission of Fordham University Press, New York; copyright © 1968 by Fordham University Press), Vol. XLIII, No. 171, December, 1968, pp. 523-38.*

## DONALD P. GRAY   (essay date 1969)

[According] to Teilhard, "science, philosophy, and religion alike have all been basically concerned with the resolution of but one single problem: that of the relationship between multiplicity and unity." (p. 156)

[For] Teilhard the problem of the one and the many is fundamentally a threefold problem. When man reflects upon the relationship between spirit and matter, or between the person and the community, or between God and his creatures, in each instance, according to Teilhard, he is brought face to face with the problem of the one and the many. And in each case Teilhard tries to understand these relationships in such a way that the multiple can be unified without being destroyed. His thought is not monistic but, rather, dipolar or dialectical in character, seeking always to safeguard diversity within unity. The essence of Teilhard's approach is capsulized in his own formula "union differentiates." This is Teilhard's law, if one may so state the matter, and at no point in his system does he violate it in the interests of a simplistic solution which would sacrifice authentic union in favor of an undifferentiated identity.

Given Teilhard's overarching concern with the problem of the one and the many and his determination to avoid the simple elimination of the many, we have taken the notion of union to be the basic category of Teilhard's system. The whole purpose and meaning of the evolutionary process is to achieve increasingly higher forms of union. And the ultimate goal of this process is the union of all things in God, the pleroma or Omega Point of evolutionary history. Thus for Teilhard the evolutionary process begins from a state of extreme multiplicity, the multiplicity of a primitive *Weltstoff,* proceeds through various stages of union (pre-life, life, man), and culminates in the union of all things in God.

When we consider the beginning of the evolutionary process in relation to its end, it is only too obvious that through the intervening stages something new has come into being through union; novelty has appeared. The end is not the beginning. The evolutionary process does not consist in a return to its beginning. Something new has been created between the beginning and the end. Union is thus seen to be properly creative in the sense that novelty emerges. The dynamism of the evolutionary process may therefore be characterized as a creative union. Evolution or creation, depending on one's point of view, proceeds through union. Creation cannot be reduced to a single or even a series of divine acts in the remote past but must, rather, be considered as a continuous process of unification and synthesis. "Creation takes place through a process of unification; and true union comes about only through creation. These two propositions are correlative." Union appears to be the modality of God's creative activity. The theory of creative union may be said to constitute an attempt to grasp the dynamics of creation understood as a continuous evolutionary process rather than as an act in the past.

If the theory of creative union is meant to be employed as a hermeneutical tool for the interpretation of the dynamics of an evolutionary creation, can it effectively deal with the problem of the one and the many as a threefold problem of the relationship of matter and spirit, person and community, creatures and God? In other words, how does the theory of creative union delineate the structure of the creative movement in terms of these three relationships?

Picturing the initial state of creation under the form of an extreme multiplicity, a multiplicity of *Weltstoff* which is neither matter nor spirit alone but rather matter-spirit, Teilhard argues that the complexification of the material pole of this primitive *Weltstoff* is accompanied by a growth of the pole of spirit. The difficult question of causality is deliberately left aside here because Teilhard maintains that he is proceeding descriptively or phenomenologically and is not concerned with philosophical issues. In point of fact, the causal question is not particularly relevant to Teilhard's deepest intention, inasmuch as he is trying to discern a pattern of development, to discover purpose and meaning in the phenomenological evidence. The process of complexification seems indeed to Teilhard to be a directed one, and its directionality can be expressed in the term "spiritualization." The process of unification is directed towards higher forms of spirit and consciousness.

This movement which characterizes the stages of pre-life and life attains to a critical threshold which is successfully crossed with the step of reflection, the appearance of man. Something truly new has now appeared which is continuous with the past stages of evolution, but which at the same time is discontinuous with them in that it marks a transformation, a hominization, of matter-spirit. If the problematic of the stages of pre-life and life can accurately be characterized in terms of the relationship between spirit (the one) and matter (the many), the problematic of the stage of hominized life must be characterized rather in terms of the person (the many) and the community (the one), although the matter-spirit relationship will still continue to play a subsidiary role within this problematic and also serve to provide helpful analogues for the understanding of the person-community relationship.

The law of complexity-consciousness which provides what Teilhard terms an "Ariadne's thread" through the maze of pre-

life and life continues to be relevant at the stage of hominization, since the complexification of the material matrix of man's communal relationships plays an important part in the growth of human consciousness. However, here again it can be allowed to play but a subsidiary role in the resolution of the problem of the one and the many in its hominized form. For the problem at this stage of evolution is how to unify persons together in community, how to achieve an authentic union of persons which will be properly creative of genuine personhood. The complexification of the material matrix of man's life is insufficient, if nonetheless indispensable, for this.

A new unifying factor enters into the picture at this point, although it has not been absent at the pre-hominized stages of evolution. That factor is love. Only love can achieve the unification of human persons in community at the same time that it safeguards and indeed leads to authentic personhood. However, when Teilhard comes to inspect the forms of love-energy immediately available to man in the noosphere for the accomplishing of this task, he finds them all to be both limited and ambiguous. While they do indeed unite, they only unite limited segments of the noosphere at the same time that they tend to create new antagonisms and divisions. What is clearly needed is a form of love capable of embracing the whole noosphere. It is the quest for this universal form of love which leads Teilhard to the Church as a phenomenologically observable constituent of the noosphere which claims, however, to be grounded in a reality and power which transcends the purely immanent factors in the evolutionary movement.

The Church serves to prove for Teilhard that the universl form of love necessary for the completion of evolution is both psychologically possible and historically realizable for man. Man is thus given a meaningful future by the Church, for he is allowed through the example of the Church to see that the unity which he desires and knows to be necessary is not merely an ideal but a realizable possibility. The Church also serves to point beyond itself to Christ as the transcendent personal Center capable of activating within the whole of humanity the kind of love neded for final unity. It also can be shown, Teilhard believes, that the Christ experienced in faith by the Christian community correlates in a striking way with the Omega Point whose existence has to be postulated by reason on the basis of the exigencies of the evolutionary movement.

This whole line of argument, beginning with the hominized form of the problem of the one and the many and culminating in the correlation of the cosmic Christ with Omega Point, may properly be characterized as the apologetical side of Teilhard's system, but it is intimately connected with the theme of union which in the context of hominization increasingly depends upon the activation of a universal form of love. What we are here calling the "apologetical side" of Teilhard's system also corresponds for the most part with the structure of *The Phenomenon of Man,* but seen in the light of the notion of creative union. Although Teilhard does not employ this expression in that work, he does invite us to read it from such a point of view when he says that "fuller being consists in closer union: such is the kernel and conclusion of this book." (pp. 156-60)

It has often enough been contended that Teilhard's view of evolutionary process is unduly and unwarrantedly optimistic. . . . Do we in fact find in Teilhard simply an evolutionary process of unification moving blissfully towards its completion in God? Is it not rather the case that it is the problem of evil as Teilhard understands it which really makes the problem of the one and the many a genuinely acute one for him? Matter is not simply a fertile matrix for the growth of spirit; in fact, it can be characterized as a directional vector towards multiplicity which spells death for spirit. The person does not enter easily and readily into the interests and purposes of the communal growth of mankind; in fact, the creature represents still another directional vector towards the non-being which is multiplicity. In short, the many resist unity, and hence union can be achieved only by overcoming this resistance through struggle.

The problem of evil is neither sleighted nor under-estimated by Teilhard, but he is compelled to reinterpret it in the light of his understanding of creation as a continuous process. If we may describe Teilhard's understanding of evil fundamentally as a flight from union, then evil is concomitant with creation itself. Matter flees from spirit, the person flees from community, the creature flees from God. What is the origin of this inclination towards flight into multiplicity and non-being? It can hardly originate with man in an evolutionary world view. However, it is hardly more satisfactory to say, as Teilhard does, that evil is simply a by-product of the evolutionary process, a statistical necessity. At any rate, Teilhard's real contribution to an understanding of the problem of evil is not in terms of origins but, rather, in terms of the phenomenological description of evil as the flight into multiplicity, as the attempt to make the world of creation irreducibly pluralistic.

The tendency of matter towards disintegration finds expression in Teilhard's thought in the concept of entropy, whereas the tendency of the person towards the disintegration of community through pride and sensuality finds expression in the concept of original sin. However, for Teilhard the term "original sin," like the term "creation," can only be understood in a rather limited sense as an act in the remote past. Which is only to say that his principal concern is not with the traditional notion of origianl sin as an act of mankind's first parents at all but, rather, with the problem of evil in general which he illegitimately tries to treat under the single rubric of original sin. Teilhard can only logically say that evil is modalized in different ways at different stages of the evolutionary movement, that physical and moral evil are different modalities of evil in general, and that they are causally unconnected even if physical evil is considerably aggravated by the appearance of a properly hominized form of evil.

Because for Teilhard the evolutionary process involves a growth in consciousness, it also necessarily involves a growth in the possibilities for evil, and these possibilities are frequently enough actualized through sin. However, the disintegrative force of sin is not allowed to develop unchecked inasmuch as Teilhard thinks of the redemptive activity of God as also being coextensive with his total creative activity. In fact, it may be said that the divine redemptive activity is to be considered a modality of the divine creative activity, and that it expresses the necessity of God's entering into struggle with the forces of disintegration in order to create by unifying. Both God's creative and redemptive activity are thus understood in terms of the notion of unification, just as evil is understood in terms of fragmentation and disintegration. The theory of creative union is also a theory of redemptive union. The problem of evil and the doctrine of redemption are understood strictly in relation to the problem of the one and the many as a problem of how to unify the many in the face of the disruptive force of evil.

The Christian's participation in this struggle for unity involves a spirituality of creative and redemptive union which seeks "in all things, to promote and undergo the organic unity of the world." It is thus essentially a spirituality of both activity and passivity lived within the unifying ambiance of the divine milieu or Body of Christ. It is a spirituality centered on the Eucharist, the sacrament of both union and creative transformation. It is a spirituality focused on the cultivation of the virtues of purity and love, virtues whose function it is to unify the person and the community respectively. And even in his treatment of the virtues, we see that Teilhard is seeking once again to resolve the problem of the one and the many as it is caught up in the problem of evil, for purity and love are seen to be engaged in a struggle with sensuality and pride, vices which fragment and scatter the person and the community into multiplicity.

If Teilhardian spirituality is ecclesiological, sacramental, and ethical in its orientation, it is also mystical in its aspirations. It seeks not only to discover the divine presence immanent in the world, but also to be open to the unifying influence of that presence in oneself and in the larger community of creation. Teilhardian spirituality is a mysticism of union, creative and personalizing union, whose goal is nothing less than the union of all things in God. (pp. 161-64)

*Donald P. Gray, in his* The One and the Many: Teilhard de Chardin's Vision of Unity *(copyright © 1969 Herder and Herder, Inc.; used by permission of the publisher), Herder & Herder, 1969, 183 p.*

### F. A. TURK   (essay date 1970)

[How] shall we ourselves—given some vague feeling of consent to the proposition that Teilhard's intuitions may be of value to us—deal with this extraordinary system which is demonstrably not scientific, is philosophically *'jejune'* and logically faulty? That some scientific 'fact' enters into it is undeniable. That it is in some sense a philosophy has been admitted by most of his readers, and yet the more sophisticated or less committed will surely be uncomfortably aware that it is perilously near those metaphysical systems which, I believe, the great Kant said were to be likened to a man holding a sieve and another attempting to milk a billy goat into it!

But if it is not a philosophy; if neither the method nor the conclusions may, in any strict sense, be accounted scientific, what, in fact, is it? Has it value? If so, how best may we use it? . . . If we discard Teilhard's system because it is not 'scientific' or even because it is often grossly illogical in its exposition, we shall, in my view, be guilty of maximum error. It differs from Newton's apocalyptic writings and Blake's visionary ones precisely because it is more relevant to our own climate of knowledge than the first and is potentially more generative of further 'gestalts' than the second. (pp. 4-6)

[If] we read Teilhard's account of evolution in isolation, then his facts are 'coloured' by his theory, both as to selection, interpretation and presentation. If, however, we look at Teilhard's evolutionary theory in relation to, and in the context of, other theories, we should, it seems, eventually be able to make adjustments and modifications which will provide us with an 'objective', if only very partial, 'apparatus criticus' of Teilhard's whole system. (pp. 6-7)

In reading his biographers, and more so in reading Teilhard's letters, I have come to the inescapable conclusion that he had a deep emotional need to be assured of the reality of progress. (p. 8)

Progress—the belief in progress—was an essential part of Teilhard's troubled spirit: it was this that did most to reconcile in later life his scientific knowledge which his spiritual yearnings, his guilt feelings about his urge to speculation and his irrepressible need to feel that he comprehended what the otherwise to him incomprehensible Christian God was about.

As one of several pieces of supporting evidence we need only cite a passage in a letter on the 9th May, 1940 to his cousin in which he says 'Are not such moments (i.e. of suffering) necessary to accustom us to that gesture, essential not only in death but in life, which consists in allowing ourselves to rest upon Him who sustains and upholds us right outside all the tangible things to which we feel so strong an instinct to cling? It is undoubtedly by being accustomed in this way that we shall finally be released from speculation.' But this Islamic surrender to the will of God was not for him—or not for long; his could never be the mysticism of the *via negativa*. Less than a year later (12 January, 1941) he is writing 'Everything can be forced and led out by a group of men united by a common faith in the spiritual future of the earth. We must take up again on a sounder scientific basis and as a more exact philosophical concept the idea (or if you prefer it the 'myth') of progress. This is essentially the setting in which I see the simultaneous rebirth of humanism and Christianity.' Yet, by the time **The Phenomenon of Man** appears that prudent phrase about the 'myth' of progress has disappeared. On page 230 of the English edition we find him saying 'If progress is a myth, that is to say, if faced by the work involved we can say: "what's the good of it all", our efforts will flag. With that the whole of evolution will come to a halt—because we are evolution.' He himself had to hope before he could summon energy for any activity—a sure indication of the incipient neurosis with which he made such valiant and successful attempts to come to terms, for, as he says in a footnote to page 233 of **The Phenomenon:** 'All conscious energy is, like love, founded on hope.' That others should labour for the solace of the work, from pleasurable interest of activity, even simply for the fulfilment of their own nature, was apparently an experience he neither shared nor understood.

To me, it seems clear enough that Teilhard had a great and ever erupting need to convince himself that progress was real and that it could, in a sense, be controlled by Man. This was essential to his system and his system was essential to reconcile this spiritual need with what he conceived to be the truths of science and it had to act as a catalyst upon all the conflicting elements that tormented him for sixty years albeit apparently hidden from his friends and close associates. . . . Progress then is an essential element, perhaps *the* essential element, in his philosophy and yet, by a strange and possibly revealing quirk of circumstance, I do not think that you will find this word as an item in the index of any one of his major works. (pp. 10-11)

If progress means directional movement as, for example, from lower to higher or simpler to complex, then indeed this is progress and Teilhard was on firm enough ground in invoking it as a pattern inherent in the evolution of life. But if by progress we mean movement towards a goal and, by implication, the fulfilment of either purpose or promise, we shall have to look both harder and further, for this second kind of progress (one which is, of course, the whole *raison d'être* of Teilhard's system) is not easily to be derived, in any illative sense, from the first. (p. 14)

[Our] difficulties are not at an end in the consideration which must be given to the views that have been held of the nature of biological progress. To make a fair exposition of this we must notice the conclusions of another group of biologists of whom [E.] Hennig may well stand as a somewhat typical exponent. He says 'All progressive development from the simplest cell to the vertebrate animal and the highest type of plant can only be regarded as a pure progress *in a certain field*, and it is definitely *not* a progress towards biological perfection. The trend of evolution results in enormous complication; no biological sense can be traced in it with certainty.' This indeed is a lion in the path of our speculation! Teilhard, I suppose, would have ignored this view as untenable and unworthy and passed along believing that he would never be bitten in the rear! Others of us are more timorous. (p. 21)

Undoubtedly there is a sense, it seems to me, in which Hennig is right: there is *no* progress to perfection. Yet there *is* another sense in which it seems to have some meaning for us—and that one that is constantly overlooked by Teilhard. I refer to the performance of function by increased economy of means. Thus the six paired aortic arches of the primitive vertebrate are quickly reduced to four pairs in the dipnoid fish and these themselves undergo still further but *differing* reduction in reptiles, birds and mammals. The reduction therefore takes several forms and has appeared along different developmental lines in the course of evolution. Teilhard stressed 'The Law of Complexification' (**Phenomenon** . . .) and the law of the 'fixity' of basic type. Of course, he was right in doing so, but everywhere there is a law of increasing economy of means of which he made little or nothing. (pp. 21-2)

Finally, in considering Teilhard's views of progress and how it is brought about in evolution, there is one other matter that must concern us, the more so because it has a bearing on the theme of social progress. This is the concept of macromutation; the belief that evolution sometimes, if rarely, takes place, not only by the infinite 'addition' of small variants moulded by natural selection, but by large-scale 'quanta' occurring as it were instantaneously. In a former paper I have argued this technically by considering the evolutionary patterns of the Arachnida. Teilhard is not, with one exception, much concerned with this and one cannot assess his views on it with certainty. His one unequivocal statement on this matter appears to be that on page 171 of **The Phenomenon;** discussing the birth of intelligence he says 'What at first sight disconcerts us, on the other hand, is the need to accept that this step could only be achieved *at one single stroke*'. This appears to invoke something very like macromutation, a concept of considerable importance to evolution as it must, naturally, be to social progress.

There are possibly no clearer or more lucid passages in **The Phenomenon** than those . . . in which the author argues the unique nature of Man as a consciously reflective being. Much depends upon this: the proof that life, 'like all growing magnitudes in the world' needs 'to become different so as to remain itself', and the growing awareness of mankind as a real entity and not just a vague concept, are perhaps the most important. Yet it is obvious in reading these that Teilhard has convinced himself entirely that Man is indeed separated from the animals by an apparently unbridgeable chasm: 'Admittedly the animal knows. *But it cannot know that it knows.*'

This, I think, is an argument difficult to support from what is known of animal behaviour. Professor N. J. Berrill, in whose fine book [*Man's Emerging Mind*] most readers of Teilhard de Chardin would find much to their taste and not a little for their correction, makes the point that for every planned action 'a certain form of imagination' is necessary. The animal must, in some sense, picture itself going through this or that performance *in the future*. . . . So complete is this evidence that morphologically there is every reason to suppose that Man's ability to reflect was of gradual emergence. (pp. 22-4)

[Now to Teilhard's proposition of the growing awareness of mankind] it appears to me we are on much firmer ground and it is much to the point that he admits this to be 'a *growing* awareness'. As the American anthropologist Prof. Kluckhorn says, '. . . as men of all nations struggle to adjust themselves to the new demands of the international situation, they steadily modify their conceptions of themselves and others. Slowly but surely, a new social order and new personality trends will emerge in the process.' Many of us have seen this happen, not just in our own life-times but in the last two decades! Undeniably, there is much here that supports Teilhard's views of the nature of Man and perhaps even of the emergence of a super-consciousness. This is one face of the theme of social progress.

But there is another and antithetical one, it seems to me, that is almost completely neglected by Teilhard because inconsistent with his vision of the distant horizons upon which he best loves (and needs) to dwell. This is the tendency of the human society to fractionate into ever smaller groups; nor is this solely a thing of the past or of the primitive. As an example one has only to think of the numerous sub-groups in our own technological society, each often with its own argot like that of criminals, or the members of Winchester College with its language synthesised from mediaeval latin and generations of schoolboy slang. There was a just point to Bernard Shaw's witticism, 'The Golden Rule is really: don't do unto others as you would have them do unto you—their tastes may be different'. Indeed, are there not likely to be more closely defined limits to the convergence on which Teilhard placed so much emphasis and hope, and may we not just as easily see in evolution a pattern for Teilhard's super-consciousness, such that the component parts—each widely diversified—co-operate together like the different tissues of an organic body or the many castes of a termitary? One cannot help thinking in this connection that Prof. Bosanquet's view of the individual in relation to the Absolute, whilst having much in it that is very similar to Teilhard's, is yet more pregnant with significance for us and more justly renders the patterns we can extract from nature, in so far as he holds purpose secondary to individuality and tells us that we must understand the world, not in terms of purpose, but of the principle of individuality.

If one thing is definite in Teilhard's theories it is that civilisation is itself a great step forward to the realization of the omega point; that social progress is real, is possible, is directional and almost that (if we believe in his philosophy) it is certain. Moreover he believes he can demonstrate all of this from the observable facts of nature. But were those facts *all* that were to be observed? For all his concern to expound his philosophy from the standpoint of evolution, one senses that he would not altogether easily have accepted a thesis such as that put forward by Desmond Morris [in *The Naked Ape*]. Teilhard's fastidiousness would surely have felt this too much of the ancient ape in the old Adam.

Perhaps it is a useful corrective, providing an illuminated perspective, if we recall that not all writers have seen social progress as real, inevitable or even desirable. If such writers are seldom to the purposes of the modern state, or to the modern taste, that is possibly all the greater reason for mentioning them here. The Cambridge philosopher F.C.S. Schiller early in this

century had this to say [in his *Tantalus*]: 'It appears that we can extract no guarantee of progress from the nature of man or from the nature of human institutions. . . .' (pp. 24-6)

Whatever social progress may be, it seems to me that it is nothing if not relative—a view from which a careful reading of Teilhard's works has failed to dissuade me. (p. 27)

[Yet] I am quite fully persuaded that Teilhard is correct in seeing that the whole course of evolution is towards 'more consciousness, more personality'. Moreover, in connection with social progress it seems to me he makes a valuable contribution in calling attention to the following properties of consciousness: (1) that it centres everything partially upon itself and (2) that it centres itself upon itself constantly and increasingly. That it seems impossible to reconcile these two kinds of 'pattern extraction' suggests that all the theories we have are inadequate (including Teilhard's) and that we must wait for further rethinking of the many issues involved. (pp. 27-8)

Nowhere, that I can find, in all the vast mirage of the future to which Teilhard would lead us, nor in that long pathway to the beginnings of life along which he hurries us, is there a hint of the wonder and meaning of memory. Whatever else has evolved with Man surely this is demonstrably at the heart of his progress. And yet how near this power of memory lies to Teilhard's purposes had he not wished to convince us of his 'Omega-point'! Since Proust's great novel [*A la recherche du temps perdu*], we have all been able to be aware of the possibility which memory opens to life,—the possibility of a certain 'deliverance from time'—that time which has shackled all other species to the inevitabilities of its own passage. How closely this conforms with some of Teilhard's views about us may be glimpsed in the following passage from the philosopher Santayana. Only transpose such terms in it as 'reflective', 'intelligent' and 'apprehension' with those of Teilhard's system and you will see the point: 'Ever since substance became at some sensitive point intelligent and reflective, ever since time made room and pause for memory, for history, for the consciousness of time, a god, as it were, became incarnate in mortality and some vision of truth, some self-forgetful satisfaction, became a heritage that moment could transmit to moment and man to man. . . . To participate in this vision is to participate at once in humanity and divinity, since all other bonds are material and perishable, but the bond between two thoughts that have grasped the same truth, of two instants that have caught the same beauty, is a spiritual and imperishable bond.'

To many of us this will seem a more demonstrable pattern than that which Teilhard eventually produces and moreover one derived from much the same range of facts. To most who feel this, it will seem a persistent sadness that finally he fails so far and by so much. As for the cause of his failure, it is perhaps inherent in the nature of his task. The whole history of the type of Christian apologetics based on science is an unfortunate and embarrassing one. Very few among its practitioners have been able to deal anything but tendentiously with either the one or the other—or both! (pp. 30-1)

All writers who base a system of Christian apologetics on the mutabilities of science seem to hold particularly *jejune* views of this history of science—not excepting Teilhard himself. (pp. 31-2)

But there exists a greater and wholly ineradicable reason for the failure of Teilhard's system as it presents itself in the theme of progress. It is this: anyone who would erect an all inclusive metaphysic solely on the real or imagined groundwork of evolution and the assumption of the 'primacy of matter' must have an intellect, however exalted, flawed in some measure with 'hubris'. Teilhard's failure is basically and fatally a lack of the essential intellectual humility that there must be to accept the relativism with which all ideas of such an order are forever and essentially tinged. And to this there must be added his extremely naïve ideas about the nature of science and its relation to actuality; just how naïve these ideas must be will be demonstrated to any one reading Cassirer's work. Yet, because he gives us, as it were, one more in a plurality of definitions of nature—all of which add a little to the scope of our insights into natural phenomena—we shall forgive him these failings if only because it is to our own advantage to do so—or even, perhaps, because they are, in a measure, equally our own. (p. 32)

> *F. A. Turk, "The Idea of Biological and Social Progress in the System of Teilhard de Chardin," in* Teilhard Reassessed: A Symposium of Critical Studies in the Thought of Père Teilhard de Chardin Attempting an Evaluation of His Place in Contemporary Christian Thinking, *edited by Anthony Hanson (© 1970 by Anthony Hanson), Darton, Longman & Todd, 1970, pp. 1-32.*

### R. B. SMITH  (essay date 1970)

Teilhard de Chardin claimed that the discovery of evolution, in particular, provides fresh evidence to explain the place of evil in the world and also indicates an approach whereby evil may be overcome. (p. 59)

[We] face the difficulty that there is no systematic treatment of the problem of evil anywhere in Teilhard's writings, published or unpublished. . . . However, although he never explored evil systematically as a whole, Teilhard says enough about it in some of his writings and implies enough in others—e.g. in *The Phenomenon of Man,* where, as he says, it 'seeps out through every nook and cranny, every joint and sinew'—that it is possible to construct a fairly detailed and systematic account of the place of evil, seen in the light of his thought.

There is a second difficulty. Some critics object that Teilhard has no doctrine of evil, and a few go so far as to deny that he was willing to recognise evil and imply that his vision of the world is an over-optimistic caricature of reality. Others, more sympathetic, nevertheless suggest that Teilhard did not give sufficient consideration to the place of evil and to Christ's victory over evil on the cross. On the other hand, Henri de Lubac insists that Teilhard's insights into the nature of evil are of very great value. We must admit that Teilhard provides evidence to support either position. He spoke of blindness to evil as a 'mortal flaw', and mentioned the fact that evil increases with the advance of evolution, so that 'the more man becomes man, the more the question of evil adheres and aggravates, in his flesh, in his nerves, in his spirit. But then in other passages he gives the impression of being a naïve optimist:

> As a result of deeply rooted habits, the problem of evil continues automatically to be called insoluble. We must really ask why. . . . In our modern perspectives of a universe in the state of cosmogenesis, how is it that so many intelligent people obstinately refuse to see that, in-

tellectually speaking, the famous problem *no longer exists*?

In addition to examining these two approaches to the problem of evil, the one stressing its great importance and the other claiming that it is a non-existent problem, there are two other attitudes towards evil which we must investigate. The first is concerned with the difficulty of maintaining our belief in God's goodness in the face of the undoubted fact of evil. Teilhard maintains that evil is an inevitable accompaniment to creation, and adds that 'God seems to have been unable to create without entering into a struggle against evil'. Evil is not the will of God, but something he will ultimately overcome. Yet in spite of his love, God cannot simply do away with evil at this stage of evolution: 'God *cannot,* now and at a single stroke, heal us and show himself'. This is not because of any defect in God's power or goodness or in his love for us and concern for our well-being, but because of the nature of the creation itself.

The last attitude towards evil which we have to examine is exemplified by a passage in **'The Mystical Milieu',** in which Teilhard seems to welcome evil, at least in some of its forms, and hail it as a friend. While it remains evil and must be resisted, evil can nevertheless be used by God to bring us into closer union with him:

> Blessed then be the disappointments which snatch the cup from our lips; blessed be the chains which force us to go where we would not. Blessed be relentless time and the unending thraldom in which it holds us. . . . Blessed, above all, be death and the horror of falling back into the cosmic forces.

These four very different attitudes to evil all form part of the system of Teilhard de Chardin, and we cannot safely ignore any of them without running the risk of destroying something valuable in his thought. They appear contradictory, but in fact they must all be understood in their relation to the central and unifying concept of evolution. (pp. 59-62)

[Because] evil does appear in an especially acute form at the highest point of evolution, it is here that it must be defined. Seeing man in the context of evolution, Teilhard defines the 'good' as that which tends towards the increase of complexity and consciousness, or, in different terms, that which tends towards further development of the personal, in both its individual and its collective forms. Similarly, we may . . . define evil as movement which opposes or limits the growth of complexity and consciousness or the personal. But just as consciousness itself appears clearly for the first time in man, and as it is only in the light of human consciousness that an 'inward' aspect is attributed to the rest of creation, so also evil appears clearly for the first time in man, and the disorders and pain on the lower levels of evolution are said to be evil only because they are part of the process that leads to human evil.

Treating evil as a part of the total phenomenon of man in the universe, we may distinguish three basic types of evil, each characteristic of one of the major 'zones' of evolution:

*(a)* There is a form of evil which is a tendency towards disorder and disunion, found throughout the universe along with a tendency towards order and union. In the zone of the pre-living this is the only kind of evil discernible. At that stage also, the question of its 'evilness' may be disputed; it appears as a necessary condition for advance, and a small enough price for the success of so valuable a project as evolution. On the human

level, however, it appears clearly as an evil. It is not only a small portion of humanity that must advance, as happened with material particles, but humanity as a whole. Evolution can no longer afford wastage or drop-outs. Mankind is converging on itself, being welded into one personal unit, and therefore any advance must be the advance of the whole, for we can no longer tolerate the idea of a portion of humanity failing to evolve any farther or another part falling back to a lower level. We are part of each other, and what affects one affects all.

*(b)* There is the evil of suffering and pain, in which man is one with all living creatures. Like disintegration, this kind of evil is in its origin related to progress, and therefore its appearance in the world seems quite natural. Reproduction and *death* are a means of advance primarily, and suffering is associated largely with the death. In man, however, pain has become not so much a spur to advance as a dissuasive against it, because we are able to foresee further suffering as a result of our efforts to advance. Teilhard's main concern was to show how suffering may be transformed and used constructively, by offering it to God for the advance of the world, to bring out to a greater extent the 'within', the spiritual.

*(c)* Moral evil is the specifically human form of evil. Its effects are seen in nature but it originates in man. The possibility of moral evil follows from the fact of human freedom or self-evolution. It appears as a turning aside from the true line of advance. This is not necessarily a guilty opposition to evolution, because it is very often the result of a necessary experiment which goes in the wrong direction, a consequence of ignorance or of groping for the right way and failing to find it. Other times, it can only be attributed to sheer perversity. There is no question about the evil nature of this. It is obviously evil, and it must be overcome.

Looking at evil in the perspective of evolution we may now be able to see the pattern of its development. It originates from the disunity at the base of evolution, and in its most elementary form is simply the tendency of the products of evolution to decompose or to develop in directions that preclude further advance. There is no particular problem left here. Disorder and the tendency to disunity are clearly part of the material basis on which evolution is built, and evil extends from there throughout creation. Pain and suffering are a transformation of this elementary form of evil at a higher stage of being. In itself, suffering is often an incentive to progress, even though it results in a part from progress. Even moral evil, understood as primarily a groping towards further evolutionary advance, either of the individual or of mankind as a whole, has quite a reasonable place in a world which is in evolution.

However, we must never forget that Teilhard's analysis of evolution shows that something beyond evolution is necessary for its continuation and stability. While it is not legitimate to conclude that science, or a philosophy based on science, requires belief in God, Teilhard maintains that a synthesis of scientific belief in evolution and the Christian doctrine of God leads to new strength and new insights for both, and therefore he accepts and integrates into his system not only a phenomenology but also a full Christian belief. Now the question of evil reappears, but it is a slightly different question this time. Christian faith is not content to accept the fact that evil may have an easily explained place in evolution. It demands why this is so—how is it that there can be evil in God's creation if God is both loving and all-powerful? This is an old question for Christians, both as a practical problem in our own lives

and as a theoretical one when non-Christians point to the undoubted fact of evil as an argument against God. (pp. 64-6)

[Surely] it will be objected, God might have made a creation which did not include evil as a side-effect? Possibly indeed, for who can say what is possible with God? However, Teilhard rightly refused to consider the question. There is no point at all in speculating about hypothetical possible worlds; *this* world is the one we are concerned with. God could only create a world which is evolving towards a free union of persons with him in the way he did create it. Therefore we must maintain that evil is to some extent unavoidable as a side-effect of a process leading to the personal. (p. 69)

One of the major aims of Teilhard's writings is to assure men that evil cannot finally triumph. If the universe were such that man was headed towards total death, then the universe would be revealed as senseless and as incapable of producing the sort of creatures it has produced. We must maintain that in order for man to function in a self-evolutionary manner, which he is doing at the present time, there must be ahead of men an Omega, the 'Prime Mover ahead', whose function it is to bring evolution to its completion, which lies in the direction of more personality, not less, of good, not evil. Finally, Teilhard writes, we come to escape from evil of all kinds through joining in a centre-to-centre union with Omega, which may come as a detachment from the womb of matter and may have the appearance of death, but is actually death and resurrection, 'the *hominisation* of death itself'.

Christianity provides a final assurance for human action. The death and resurrection of Christ are evidence that God can overcome evil and that he has acted to overcome it. In the work of Christ on the Cross, suffering and evil must be continued unceasingly in the direction of increasing complexity/consciousness; human personality must press on towards its completion and totalisation in Christ. In God's acceptance and transformation of our efforts and ourselves, we shall find the final solution to the problem of evil. (pp. 76-7)

*R. B. Smith, "The Place of Evil in a World of Evolution," in* Teilhard Reassessed: A Symposium of Critical Studies in the Thought of Père Teilhard de Chardin Attempting an Evaluation of His Place in Contemporary Christian Thinking, *edited by Anthony Hanson (© 1970 by Anthony Hanson), Darton, Longman & Todd, 1970, pp. 59-77.*

### G. F. PENN ANTHONY (essay date 1975)

The immense significance of Teilhard lies in this, that he has brought to bear upon his thesis a powerful and trained scientific mind together with a deep religious insight—a unique blend that enabled this highly qualified scientist-priest to present to the world a stupendous vision. Teilhard boldly proclaims, "From the depths of Matter to the highest peak of Spirit there is only *one evolution.*" . . .

[It] is to a large extent the inwardness of Teilhard's own thesis that compels the asking of certain questions which it does not itself answer. They are: *What* "evolves"? Does it *have* to "evolve"? and, Does it in fact "evolve" at all? (p. 71)

Teilhard presents a consistent picture of complexifying aggregation in the stuff of the universe, which raises it from the rudiments of physical matter to the enormously intricate qualitative complexities of the human physical unit. As to the effect of the process, it may be summed up in one word: *emergence.*

Teilhard shows clearly that every "whole," from the simplest unit at the atomic level, to the most complex, has an "emergent" that characterizes and unifies the complex. The emergent of every complex is that which identifies it as "*a whole.*" But in doing so, it is not merely a sum of the functions of its components: it transcends them all by constituting *the function of their sum.*

Inevitably, "emergence" implies a "within" *which* emerges. And, just as inevitably, the fact of multiplicity in the created order underlines a "without." But the enormous *diversity* of the created order results, in Teilhard's view, from the evolutionary activity that plays through and through it. "True union," says Teilhard, "does not confound: it differentiates. Teilhard seeks to trace the operation of this principle from rudimentary atomic structure upwards through the entire variegated efflorescence of the created order as we find it today. It is diversified *because* combinative additivity functions that way.

But when one comes down to it, what does emergence "differentiate"? The interpretation of the created order in terms of an evolutionary pattern is, after all, a rational application of hindsight. The pattern emerges in a context of unimaginable vistas of time. Evolution is thinkable only within duration; and, conversely, duration seems to tell only one story, evolution.

Teilhard ascribes specific types of energy to the "within" and the "without": they are a "radial energy," and a "tangential energy," respectively. Talking about these two energies, Teilhard says, "The two energies—of mind and matter—spread respectively through the two layers of the world (the *within* and the *without*), have, taken as a whole, much the same demeanour." But he seems to feel uncomfortable at the thought of a fundamental duality at the heart of things. This he tries hard to minimize:

> To avoid a fundamental duality, at once impossible and unscientific, and at the same time to safeguard the natural complexity of the stuff of the universe, . . . we shall assume that, essentially, all energy is psychical in nature; but add that in each particular element this fundamental energy is divided into two distinct components. . . .

Notwithstanding his obvious distaste for a fundamental duality at the heart of things, Teilhard seems reluctant to probe to its logical conclusion his own insight that the prime mover of both the "within" and the "without" is psychic in nature and content. He does not suggest by what means a unitary psychic energy manifests itself in such apparently irreconcilable modes as "mind" and "matter."

In fact, reading between the lines, each term of the dualism seems to be evolving in its own right, albeit that they do so only in close collaboration with each other. The "diversification" Teilhard draws attention to seems to relate only to the "matter" side of the equation, the "without": the complexification-aggregation process constantly produces units of greater and greater bodily complexity. But the "within" is pictured as *a homogeneous quality* that emerges in ever greater freedom. This homogeneous emergent is consciousness. Although the *nature* of this emergent becomes recognizable *as* consciousness only after life takes the stage, Teilhard, by implication, extends the concept backwards and construes that the varying properties of matter in its pre-life evolutionary phase are also emergent manifestations of virtual consciousness at those lowlier levels

of complexity. In this regard, Teilhard calls attention to ". . . the preference of Nature for Being over non-Being, for life over non-life—Being and Life manifesting and evaluating themselves through the growth of consciousness." And again, "What is really going on . . . is the super-organisation of Matter upon itself, which as it continues to advance produces the habitual, specific effect, the further liberation of consciousness." That is to say, the "within" and the "without" *both evolve* through a process of forming successive "wholes."

An alternative reading, perhaps more valid, is possible. This results from the supposition that while evolution *actively brings into being successive complexities,* it does not bring consciousness *into being.* Consciousness *always inherently is;* it merely *"emerges"* in *freer expression* of itself. This would mean, further, that "the stuff of the universe," whose "natural complexity" Teilhard is concerned to safeguard, is identifiable *only* with the *matter*-content of wholes, that is to say, the "without." It is true that in one of his essays, Teilhard says, "There is neither spirit nor matter in the world; the 'stuff of the universe' is *spirit-matter.*" Nevertheless, the *process,* so far as it "creates" complexes, creates complexities of form. The emergent is not created—it *emerges* as a function that inherently invests the units of the complex before they aggregate, but which emerges by virtue of the combination.

*What,* then, is the essential nature of the "within"—consciousness? Teilhard offers no answer. If, however, we *must* "avoid a fundamental dualism" *because* it is "at once impossible and unscientific," we are left with no option but to acknowledge that a homogeneous, unitary "something" *operates* in ever greater freedom *by manifesting* itself *as* "the stuff of the universe" in ever greater qualitative complexities.

Teilhard seems to see it in much the same way. He says, ". . . every spirit derives its reality and nature from a particular type of universal synthesis. Whatever its 'purity,' however great its purity, it is the crown and expression of a genesis. The 'higher' a being is in duration, the greater and more finely unified the complexity that contains its solid parts." (Mark the "duration," and the "solid parts." They seem fundamental to Teilhard's thesis.)

It would simplify the situation if consciousness were taken to be not merely a term describing the emergent "within" in the psychosomatic octaves of the created order, but as being that very homogeneous, unitary "something" that once and for all abolishes duality at the heart of being. If, therefore, anything evolves, it is consciousness—or, more correctly, the *modalities of its manifestation.* (pp. 72-4)

Teilhard contends that evolution is now at work in the "noosphere"—the supra-physical dimension of thought. The process of complexity-aggregation is progressively shifting its focus from the physical to the supra-physical. Teilhard says, "It is most striking that morphological change of living creatures seems to have slowed down at the precise moment when Thought appeared on Earth." "By virtue of the emergence of Thought," he says, "a special and novel environment has been evolved among human individuals within which they acquire a faculty of associating together, and reacting upon one another, no longer primarily for the preservation and continuance of the species but for the creation of a common consciousness." Teilhard feels that "life shows signs . . . of requiring us, by virtue of its movement towards a state of higher Being, to sacrifice our individuality." (pp. 76-7)

We may say that phenomena behave in the way they do because it is in their nature to do so. No more, and no less. But whether this spells "evolution" is something else again. (p. 77)

By "evolution" we mean the attempted interpretation of the totality of interactions throughout the created order, not merely in its "being," but in a presumed process of its "becoming." Teilhard introduces his thesis with these words: "My only aim in these pages—and to this aim all my powers are bent—is to *see;* that is to say, to develop a *homogeneous* and *coherent* perspective of our general extended experience of man. A *whole* which unfolds." Again, he says, ". . . everything in the world appears and exists as a function of the whole. This is the broadest, deepest and most unassailable meaning of the idea of Evolution."

The backdrop of this process is Duration: ". . . the stuff of the universe," says Teilhard, "spreads and radiates outwardly from ourselves, without limit, spatially from the Immense to the Infinitesimal and temporally from the abyss of the past to the abyss of the future." Also, ". . . the Space-Time Continuum is . . . the only framework within which our thoughts can continue to progress." It must be conceded that if orderliness is the single greatest and most ubiquitous fact in our experience, it implies sequentiality, which is the mode in which we (the general run of humanity), apprehend change. (pp. 77-8)

[Inasmuch as] the *combining* of units to form new wholes . . . takes time there would appear to be something about a unit that resists combining. . . . [What] makes a unit distinguishable is its delimiting form. This form, at all levels of phenomenality up to and including organisms of every complexity, is composed of physical matter. In combining with other units to form more complex wholes, it is this individualistic form that the unit must surrender. Its erstwhile individuality is lost in the new whole. The new whole in turn must be broken down, its wholeness must be destroyed by dismemberment, if the identity of any component unit is again to be perceived in its individuality. So while the "without" of a unit stands to lose its distinguishability in combinative additivity, its "within" loses nothing; rather, indeed, if Teilhard is right in saying that the "within" is homogeneous consciousness, the "within" *gains* by bringing more of its inhering potential into active play. Resistance to combination must then be a feature of that which stands to lose its identity by combining, namely, the form-component of a unit. That is to say, that which makes for duration is a feature of the "without"—a feature of the activity of physical matter. (p. 79)

Teilhard does not deal at all with *psi* phenomena [telephathy, clairvoyance, clairaudience, telekinesis, retrocognition, and precognition] and has therefore nothing to say regarding their significance and implications. But inasmuch as *psi* phenomena and mystical experience are both valid and genuine areas within which human consciousness is known to operate, the experience so gained must be given *as much* consideration and weight as those other experiences (of what Teilhard calls "the whole") in the light of which a process of evolution is construed by human understanding. Indeed, to the mystic, the mystical experience is overwhelmingly more "real," more compelling, more coherent and cohesive, and more integrating, than any experience obtained within day-to-day levels of waking awareness. (pp. 79-80)

What are we to make of the fact that the essentially supraphysical activity of the "within" is *always* in temporal and spatial perspectives when it is filtered through the physically material component of a complex, and *only* when it is so filtered? Surely the only admissible conclusion must be that physical matter is a mode of limitation of consciousness at which the "within" apprehends spatio-temporally; or, putting it another way, that spatio-temporality is the mode of activity of consciousness at the degree of limitation where consciousness constitutes physical matter. And when consciousness demonstrates activity which is non-spatial and non-temporal, notwithstanding that the whole demonstrating it exhibits a material element in its complexity, it only means that physical matter is not a necessary and inevitable condition for the activity of consciousness. It means that the nature of activity and experience *at varying levels are specific to those levels, and,* more importantly, *cannot be validly extrapolated.*

For example, a cell is a unit-mass of living matter by itself, or associated with others in a higher unity. The whole consciousness of a cell, its whole activity, its whole experience, is concerned with metabolic functioning alone. But although the human body is a complex of some thousands of millions of cells, metabolic functioning alone is very far from being the sole activity of consciousness *as* the human unit. Even at the level of Teilhard's "Noosphere" it is notoriously true that mass psychology can never be predicated upon individual psychology.

That emergents and their activity are specific to specific limitations of phenomena amply accounts for the immense diversity of the manifested Whole. From being specific properties at the levels of simple structure, consciousness manifests itself in ever greater freedom, its range and character always being specific to the precise complex of the whole concerned. Indeed, so individualistic, so personalized, is consciousness at the human spectrum that "What is evil, material, for me, is good, spiritual, for another advancing by my side. And the climber ahead of me on the mountain would be corrupted if he used what gives me unity."

Teilhard confesses that, "I know as a scientist how dangerous it is to extend a curve beyond the facts, that is to say, to extrapolate." Neverhteless, he extrapolates space-time perspectives far beyond their valid application. This is all the more surprising because he holds that "True wisdom consists in retaining the obscurities of the world at the points at which they do in reality appear, and not in shifting them artificially on the pretext of respecting principles that are only apparently evident."

It is indeed unfortunate that Teilhard did not "see" the implications of ESP and mystical experience. Had he done so, his sterling integrity would not have permitted him to submit so extensively to the momentum of his own argument. But having failed to see them, what he seeks to establish as "a *homogeneous* and *coherent* perspective of our general extended experience of man" in fact omits a crucially significant area of that experience that has immense importance in actually establishing homogeneity and coherence. "Everything" does indeed appear and exist "as a function of the whole," but the whole of Teilhard's *evolutionary* vision, which is entirely spatio-temporal, falls short of The Whole as it demonstrably functions here and now. Spatio-temporality cannot be extrapolated beyond the limits of its function. it is simply not sustainable that "From the depths of Matter to the highest peak of Spirit there is only *one evolution.*" At best, evolution may be *one* interpretation of Reality. . . . (pp. 80-2)

*G. F. Penn Anthony, "Whither Evolution? Some Questions to Teilhard de Chardin," in* International

Philosophical Quarterly, *Vol. XV, No. 1, March, 1975, pp. 71-82.*

**JOHN H. MORGAN**  (essay date 1978)

[A] small collection of rather brief but lucid and eloquent essays by Teilhard, entitled, *Building the Earth,* constitutes the best and most jargon-free exposition of his ideas. (pp. 86-7)

There is no recurrent theme so common nor topic so frequently discussed as that of the future of man. And the drive of Teilhard to demonstrate the inevitable convergence of every possible truth often led him to attempted syntheses of what on the surface appeared to be mutually alien if not outright hostile subjects.

One of the best illustrations of this point is his somewhat controversial perspective on democracy, communism, and fascism, i.e., an attempt to ferret out the deep complementary truths of what are normally considered mutually exclusive ideologies. Though his success or failure in such an endeavor is much debated, nevertheless, the attempted synthesis bespeaks his sincere belief that truth rises, and that all "that rises must converge." The "besetting temptation of our time," observes Teilhard, is a too quick willingness to adopt a defeatist attitude toward the world. It is too easy to "find an excuse for inaction," says Teilhard, "by pleading the decadence of civilization, or even the imminent end of the world. . . ." Man must not dwell upon his all too obvious depravity, his animality, but must press on towards the future, a future wherein man arises as he grows in love and truth. (p. 87)

[The] disorder and chaos which so often characterize the profound depths of human society today decry an absence of progress, of order and direction. "There are three major influences," Teilhard argues, "confronting each other and struggling for possession of the earth. . . ." They are Democracy, Communism, Fascism (all forms of authoritarian nationalism). How can anyone propose that these three world-forces are or can be positively related in the face of the global struggles that characterize their relationship?

The answer must come by way of an examination of the source of their strength. In spite of their supposed and real conflicting differences, they each in a unique and positively important way exemplify "three aspirations which are characteristic of a faith in the future," says Teilhard, and they are: "A passion for the future, a passion for the universal, and a passion for the individual." Though positive in their own right, when misunderstood or imperfectly comprehended, they rain tension and conflict upon the global community. Each ideology attempts to enact these three aspirations of man's faith in the future, only to fail here or there in such a way as to perpetuate human unification. (p. 88)

There is now such a dissatisfaction among the peoples of the world with these systems—their internal logic and their external hostilities—and a growing expectation that something new is about to emerge as to elicit from those who seek and see the coming higher synthesis a desire to rise and speak. "It is not the fear of perishing," says Teilhard, "which has thrown man into the exploration of nature, the conquest of the atmosphere and the heavens . . . but the ambition to live. . . ." And though this ambition has rightly expressed itself in a science passionately seeking "to unveil the mysteries concealed in matter infinitely great and infinitesimally small," the time is coming (and indeed has now arrived) when scientists will seek ever grander things, viz., "the study of psychic currents and attractions" in what Teilhard calls a "science of spiritual energy." (p. 90)

As man looks to his future, he musters within himself a common hope, a shared aspiration, a feeling of corporate confidence and expectation about the destiny of man. And this destiny is wrapped up in the future of earth itself. These feelings of hope and expectation, though they "awaken so belatedly," rise out of and give expression to what Teilhard has called, "the Spirit of Earth." This phrase Teilhard understands to mean "the passionate concern of our common destiny which draws the thinking part of life ever further onward. . . ." This Spirit is intrinsic to nature itself, and though it is slow to awaken, it is the firm foundation upon which cosmic evolution is centered. The discovery that "the only truly natural and real human Unity is the Spirit of Earth" is gradually made as human consciousness, still somewhat restricted by circles of "family, country, and race," expands its perimeters.

This growing consciousness of the Spirit of Earth, which is resulting from the increasingly sophisticated discoveries of social and scientific import, is "a conquering passion," says Teilhard, which is sweeping away and transforming earlier premature models of earth. The three-fold nature of this passion is awakening and ordering human consciousness towards the future of earth. The three expressions of this passion are: "The emancipated forces of love, the dormant forces of human unity, and the hesitant forces of research." To understand these three passions is to grasp a "Sense of Earth," and to use these three passions wisely and creatively is to facilitate the cosmic evolution towards God. (pp. 90-1)

The danger inherent in this scenario of optimism is that immature men will think themselves no longer in need of religion. For such men—pretenders to the title of mature, liberated, scientific moderns—God is a psychological need whose projection declines with the rise of science and culture. Yet, says Teilhard, the very process of scientific research, emancipated love, and human unity all are in support of a world in need of faith, for the Spirit of Earth increases man's need to "adore." Therefore, "out of universal evolution God emerges in our consciousness as greater and more necessary than ever." (p. 92)

The Earth has become conscious through the agency of the human mind, the very mind which the earth through its supportive evolutionary processes has produced. And now, since evolution has become conscious of itself, it will not progress without the concerted effort of man. Evolution "will not happen by itself," warns Teilhard, for now with its increasingly sophisticated mechanism of syntheses, evolution "is constantly acquiring greater freedom," and with increased freedom, an equal capacity for evil and destruction as for good and creativity. In answer to his own question as to "what steps must we take in relation to this forward march?," he answers in five words: *"a great hope, in common. . . ."* (p. 93)

The Spirit of Earth with its imperative "to build the Earth" brings with it the problem and challenge of *human unification*. Of all the demands and pressures of our current times—individual cares, political, economic, and psychic turmoils—none are so formidable as is this one. In the not too distant past, it was a common belief that the increasing aggregation of mankind on the earth was little more than a simple demonstration of man's search for a more comfortable life. Today, such a view is pristinely naive, for now we are in a position to better understand through a closer scrutiny of Time and Space those forces which operate under the "veil of human socialization." (p. 95)

In view of this evolutionary scheme, Teilhard makes three important observations about the historical and biological position of modern man. First, granted the truth of this scheme of the movement of social totalization as a "drift of cosmic magnitude," then, says Teilhard, "we may be confident that it points the safest (and probably the only) way in which we can engage ourselves if we wish not only to survive, but to live abundantly (supervive)." Second, and because of the "growing compression of expanding Mankind over the closed surface of the Earth," Teilhard contends that "the unifying process in which we are caught is to some extent, not only healing, but *irresistible*." Third, and in spite of the evolutionary movement and its irresistibility, it is theoretically possible that if we misuse the liberty which our consciousness has given us relative to our responsibility towards evolution, we could escape the transformation." (pp. 95-6)

Teilhard derides those well-meaning but inordinately narrow people who bewail the misuse of the world's resources of thermal energy and food. Even if man could perpetually replenish the heaps of wheat, the mountains of uranium and coal, and oceans of oil, mankind "will starve and decay," warns Teilhard, "unless it guards and feeds the source of its vital passion for more power and more vision." No external pressure will facilitate the preservation of the human species unless Man first and foremost, from deep within, "believes passionately in the future of his evolution. . . ."

In the closing pages of **Building the Earth,** Teilhard explores both the objective and the subjective conditions "necessary for the preservation and the growth in humanity of the psychical ardor which is physically indispensable for the completion of its biological development," i.e., the psychological conditions of human unification. In his considerations of the objective conditions for unification, Teilhard suggests that the world must possess both the character of *openness* and a center of *convergency* at the final end of its development. Man is unable to creatively and responsibly carry on his life's work in a world devoid of hope towards the future. (p. 96)

This focus of unification and completion Teilhard understands to have two dimensions—that of a "clarified sense of the irreversible," and also of a "corrected and generalized sense of the Cosmic or of the Universal . . .". We are now entering a new age, a new spirit, a new world, wherein these two-fold senses of the Irreversible and the Cosmic are converging in human consciousness such that our primary attention in psychological research will increasingly be focused upon the human experience of the Spirit of Earth. "Ultimately," says Teilhard, "there is no other fuel, no other blood, able to feed (and to humanize at the same time) the giant organism built up by human socialization, but a *new type of faith* in the future of the Species and in a spiritual climaxing of the World. . . ." (p. 97)

*John H. Morgan, "Faith in the Future," in his* In Search of Meaning: From Freud to Teilhard de Chardin *(copyright © 1978 by University Press of America), University Press of America, 1978, pp. 85-98.*

**ROBERT E. DOUD**   (essay date 1980)

In a way that can only be naive because no method exists for its execution, Teilhard synthesizes fields that are highly differentiated, technically structured, and methodologically distinct.

With a respect for and even an internal expertise in the various disciplines, Teilhard launches into the program of fusing knowledge and vision, faith and fact, the empirical and the metaphysical in a synthetic activity that refuses to believe that truth is as compartmentalized as we have allowed it to become. . . . This anthropological approach, transcending all disciplinary lines, is necessary insofar as man is a unity transcending his own rich diversity and that of the universe. He is both product and process, result and director of the evolutionary process. He must find in and give wholeness to the process, if he is to orchestrate it intelligently. . . .

Man himself is the phenomenon that Teilhard is examining. (p. 91)

For Teilhard, phenomenology represented a physics in which man could be included. Up to now man had systematically excluded himself from his science. Now he might find his own inner dynamisms the very clue he needs to unlock further secrets of science. (p. 93)

The word "seeing" in Teilhard de Chardin refers to much more than visual perception. It refers to certain facts that are empirically verifiable, and also to a rich context in which those facts are meaningful. This meaning does exist on a pre-reflective level, but it exists more importantly on a level requiring rational insight and inquiry. (p. 95)

For Teilhard, to see more really is to become more. Deeper vision is really fuller being, and we should look closely at things and ourselves in order to increase our capacity to live. To try to see more and better is not a matter of whim or curiosity or self-indulgence. We are to develop ever more perfect eyes within a cosmos in which there always is something more to be seen. By an increase in vision or in seeing, Teilhard refers to an increase in consciousness. (p. 96)

The biological and spiritual ultimate future is called Omega by Teilhard. It is the goal of the universe in evolution. It is the present center of the convergence for the entire evolutionary process. It is the body of Jesus as the historical midpoint of the process. Originally, it is God as Spirit breathing existence and evolutionary direction into the Alpha Particles, or first stuff out of which all things eventually will evolve in increasing degrees of complexity.

The Omega is spiritually and physically the center of a super-consciousness that is divine, but which radiates transparently through all creation in an intimacy best described now as organic. Teilhard does not go into detail on how this universe as one body will develop. He does point to the New Testament in which Christ becomes all in all, and in which the resurrection of the body is the highest cipher for bodily beatitude and interpersonal communication. The only new thing Teilhard adds is something he insists was there all along; that the consummation of the universe will be physical and material, bodily and hyperpersonal.

Human solidarity in the Omega will be beyond our powers to imagine now. It is true in evolution that the powers to appreciate a new development only come with the arrival of the development itself. The faculty follows the fact. . . . Teilhard looks forward to new emotions, new feelings, both aesthetic and ethical, which are to be future products of divinely guided emergent evolution. We will have to develop new capacities for loving each other if we are to enjoy the compression of living in one body together. Of course, Teilhard insists that he is extending the idea of body greatly to include whatever the future brings. He is definitely not using the word "body" in a metaphorical sense.

Human solidarity and personal autonomy increase, for Teilhard, in direct and not in inverse proportion with one another. Only in intimacy with God and with others, enveloped in the super-consciousness of the Omega, does our individual identity, consciousness, and self-determination in freedom reach fever pitch. Here we see the full sense of freedom; not just the power to choose, but the power to choose the best consistently. The best in Omega will at last admit of no contrariety between the personal and the social welfare.

There is no indication that Teilhard intended the bliss of Omega to be a return of the world process to absolute rest and everlasting stasis. The Omega will mean the undisturbed equilibrium of all forces forever, but it would not mean the cessation of all change. Like a kaleidoscope, a variety of patterns is possible without any lack of balance. It might mean the acceleration of change, where change would no longer suffer a margin of disorientation, pain, and dizziness. So, Teilhard's eschatology, while more explicit than that of other process philosophers, might not oppose the unceasing ongoingness of Alfred North Whitehead and others.

Teilhard's Omega is both bodily and organic, but is it not also material? (p. 99)

[In] the vision of Teilhard [matter] will be elevated, consecrated, absorbed into spirit. Not achieving this of its own inner energies and properties, it will be uplifted and glorified in a new gratuitous activity on the part of spirit. Such will be the bodiliness and organicity of Omega, physical and material, though transformed, everlasting, though not of itself eternal. (p. 100)

If it is important to phenomenology to deal with a phenomenon that is bodily, organic, and material. It is also important to deal with a phenomenon that is temporal and that is realized primarily in the present. Can we affirm the primacy of the present in Teilhard de Chardin? We can insofar as we affirm in him the primacy of Christ as a sustaining presence to the evolutionary advance, and insofar as we affirm in Teilhard the attention to have all he says about the Omega serve as motivation for personal contribution to the process in the here and now. (p. 101)

It is in man's present effort primarily that he encounters God and pushes forward the world process toward Omega. Teilhard intends his Omega to be a perceived phenomenon and not a Utopian dream. It is available in some sense to the non-Christian as well as to the Christian. It is a perception of the progress of the world process and the hope that the progress will continue. It is energy for active participation in the forwarding of the world process. Omega is not fully actualized already and, although it is concomitantly a divine gratuity, it is the supreme achievement of human effort. . . .

Teilhard de Chardin projects his vision of Omega from his measurement of progress in the past. Tracing ages of sidereal, geological, and paleontological sediment, he conjectures as to how the process will go on. No age or moment is determined ahead of time, but is a novel configuration of forces. He is fond of saying that the process is determined if viewed from without, but free if viewed from within. His phenomenological vision is ambiguous, requiring us to do both at the same time. (p. 102)

Robert E. Doud, "Wholeness As Phenomenon in Teilhard de Chardin and Merleau-Ponty," in Philosophy Today (copyright 1980 by the Messenger Press; reprinted by permission of the Messenger Press, Carthagena Station, Celino, Ohio 45822), Vol. XXIV, No. 2, Summer, 1980, pp. 90-103.*

---

## ADDITIONAL BIBLIOGRAPHY

Corte, Nicolas. *Pierre Teilhard de Chardin: His Life and Spirit*. Translated by Martin Jarrett-Kerr. New York: The Macmillan Co., 1960, 120 p.
>    Early full-length study introducing Teilhard's theological writings.

De Lubac, Henri. *Teilhard de Chardin: The Man and His Meaning*. Translated by René Hague. New York: Hawthorn Books, 1965, 204 p.
>    Traces Teilhard's spiritual development and examines the dual bases of the rational and the spiritual in his writings.

De Terra, Helmut. *Memories of Teilhard de Chardin*. Translated by J. Maxwell Brownjohn. New York: Harper & Row, 1962, 142 p.
>    Reminiscences by a geologist whom Teilhard accompanied on scientific expeditions in the East Indies, Burma, Java, and China.

Grenet, Abbé Paul. *Teilhard de Chardin: The Man and His Theories*. Translated by R. A. Rudorff. London: Souvenir Press, 1965, 196 p.
>    Introductory biocritical study, including a selection of Teilhard's writings.

Hanson, Anthony, ed. *Teilhard Reassessed: A Symposium of Critical Studies in the Thought of Père Teilhard de Chardin Attempting an Evaluation of His Place in Contemporary Christian Thinking*. London: Darton, Longman & Todd, 1970, 184 p.
>    Essays exploring theological, sociological, philosophical, scientific, and religious themes in Teilhards works.

Hefner, Philip. *The Promise of Teilhard: The Meaning of the Twentieth Century in Christian Perspective*. Philadelphia, New York: J. B. Lippincott Co., 1970, 127 p.
>    Interprets Teilhard as a Christian humanist rather than as a professional theologian.

Isaye, Gaston. "The Method of Teilhard de Chardin: A Critical Study." *New Scholasticism* XLI (Winter 1967): 31-57.
>    Defends the basic validity of Teilhard's method of "seeing" by mixing science and metaphysics. The critic finds that while this method lacks "sufficient rigor and precision" as applied by Teilhard, its value lies in bringing about a "fertile collaboration" between science and metaphysics.

Lukas, Mary and Lukas, Ellen. *Teilhard*. Garden City, N.Y.: Doubleday and Co., 1977, 360 p.
>    Designed to narrate Teilhard's "extraordinary story as accurately and graphically as possible, drawing on primary sources, putting his philosophic work in its psychological, historical, and political environment, translating into common speech as clearly as we can his groping neologisms."

Rabut, Olivier. *Teilhard de Chardin: A Critical Study*. New York: Sheed and Ward, 1961, 247 p.
>    Examines the "chief problems" raised by the religious and scientific claims of Teilhard's writings, finding fragments of valuable insights among the "hit-or-miss" conclusions regarding progressive evolution.

Stiernotte, Alfred P. "An Interpretation of Teilhard As Reflected in Recent Literature." *Zygon* 3, No. 4 (December 1968): 377-425.
>    Introduction to the main points of Teilhard's works, with a survey of reaction and interpretation.

# Miguel de Unamuno (y Jugo)

## 1864-1936

Spanish poet, essayist, novelist, novella writer, poet, dramatist, and journalist.

A mystic, a pioneer of existentialism, and a leader of the Generation of 1898, Unamuno was one of the most influential Spanish writers and thinkers of his era. His essay collection *En torno al casticismo* was the earliest significant examination of Spain's decline as a cultural and military world power, a concern characteristic of the Generation of 1898. Unamuno saw parallels between the search by Spain for self-renewal and world recognition and the struggle of an individual for purpose and immortality, and this analogy is a motif explored throughout his work. His first fiction, *Paz en la guerra*, examines this theme, and is sometimes regarded as the first existentialist novel. Unamuno's work is preoccupied with such eternal dilemmas as immortality versus death, faith versus doubt, and illusion versus reality.

A native of the Basque provinces, Unamuno was profoundly affected during his childhood by Spain's political tension and unrest, particularly the Carlist siege of his home city, Bilbao. In 1891, he was appointed professor of Greek at the University of Salamanca, where he spent most of his life. His first published work, *En torno al casticisimo*, appeared in the journal *La españa moderna* in 1895. In these essays, Unamuno called for Spain to cease its cultural isolation from the rest of Europe, and receive new ideas from the rest of the world. Two years later, *Paz en la guerra* appeared, an event which coincided with an intense religious crisis, from which Unamuno emerged devoid of orthodox faith in God. He struggled with the philosophical conflict between faith and reason in *Amor y pedagogía*, *Vida de Don Quijote y Sancho (The Life of Don Quixote and Sancho)*, and his most famous work, *Del sentimiento trágico de la vida en los hombres y en los pueblos (The Tragic Sense of Life in Men and Peoples)*. In his essays, Unamuno attacked the policies of Alfonso XIII and the dictatorship of Primo de Riviera. Considered both a religious and political heretic, he was dismissed from the University of Salamanca in 1914 and exiled to the Canary Islands ten years later. With the fall of the dictatorship, Unamuno returned to Spain and his university position, finishing his best-crafted work of fiction, *San Manuel Bueno, mártir (Saint Emmanuel the Good, Martyr)* in 1932. An outspoken opponent of both factions during the Spanish civil war, Unamuno was confined by military order to his house, where he died in 1936.

Unamuno was extremely well-read in Western literature and philosophy. His first two works exhibit the influence of Georg Hegel's theory of dialectic synthesis. After the religious crisis of 1897, the Hegelian theories were supplanted by those of Sören Kierkegaard, Henri Bergson, and William James. The resulting philosophy of anguish was shaped over several years, resolving at last in Unamuno's definitive philosophical statement, *The Tragic Sense of Life in Men and Peoples*. In this essay, he demonstrated the incompatability of faith and reason, as represented by philosophy or religion and science. Acknowledging the inability of science to give meaning to life, Unamuno rejected nihilism, calling for humanity to live according to religiously-based ethical values in spite of their

ultimate invalidity. For this idealistic alternative to spiritual inertia, Unamuno's name is often linked to that of his literary hero, Don Quixote de la Mancha. In conjunction with his philosophy, Unamuno stresses the importance of the individual and human perceptions of reality and fate: milieu becomes unimportant, while the struggle against annihilation and toward self-awareness is paramount. In *Amor y pedagogía*, characters exist independent of their setting, and in later works, they become independent of Unamuno himself. In *Niebla (Mist)* the protagonist challenges his creator, confronting Unamuno with the knowledge of his own transience. Unamuno's technique in these nivolas, as he called them, was designed to present common ideas in an original, unexpected manner, provoking the reader to think and act with a fresh outlook.

Unamuno considered himself primarily a poet, and a poetic sensitivity pervades all his work. Milton, Dante, Gustavo Bécquer, and the English Romantics were the foremost influences on his poetry, which is notable for its unique, rich blend of philosophical directness and romanticism. In their depictions of the Spanish countryside, the poems demonstrate a sense of tranquility, evoking the meditative twilight hour, Unamuno's favorite time of day.

Because of the complexity, idealism, rationality, and depth of his work, Unamuno has inspired much scholarly study during the twentieth century. He does not fit easily into any literary category, but is acknowledged as an individualist: a philosopher who scorned philosophy, an innovator of both form and idea, and a strong influence on the course of European literature. His writings were instrumental in overthrowing the Spanish monarchy and guiding Spain toward a twentieth-century cultural renaissance. John A. MacKay has written: "The truth is that no one can understand the Spanish soul who does not study the personality and writings of Unamuno."

(See also *TCLC*, Vol. 2.)

## PRINCIPAL WORKS

*Paz en la guerra*  (novel)  1897
*Amor y pedagogía*  (novel)  1902
*En torno al casticismo*  (essays)  1902
*Paisajes*  (essays)  1902
*Vida de Don Quijote y Sancho*  (essay)  1905
 [*The Life of Don Quixote and Sancho*, 1927]
*Poesías*  (poetry)  1907
*La esfinge*  (drama)  1909
*La difunta*  (drama)  1910
*Rosario de sonetos líricos*  (poetry)  1911
*Del sentimiento trágico de la vida en los hombres y en los
 pueblos*  (essay)  1913
 [*The Tragic Sense of Life in Men and in Peoples*, 1921]
*Niebla (Nivola)*  (novel)  1914
 [*Mist (Niebla)*, 1928]
*Abel Sánchez*  (novel)  1917
 [*Abel Sánchez*, 1947]
*Fedra*  (drama)  1918
*El Cristo de Velázquez*  (poetry)  1920
 [*The Christ of Velázques*, 1951]
*Tres novelas ejemplares y un prólogo*  (novellas)  1920
 [*Three Exemplary Novels and a Prologue*, 1930]
*La tía Tula*  (novella)  1921
 [*Tía Tula* published in *Ficciones*, 1976]
*La venda*  (drama)  1921
*El pasado que vuelve*  (drama)  1923
*Rimas de dentro*  (poetry)  1923
*Teresa*  (poetry)  1924
*L'agonie du christianisme*  (essay)  1925; also published as
 *La agonía del Christianismo*, 1931
 [*The Agony of Christianity*, 1928]
*Raguel encadenada*  (drama)  1926
*Cómo se hace una novela*  (essay)  1927
*Sombras de sueño*  (drama)  1930
*El otro*  (drama)  1932
 [*The Other* published in *Ficciones*, 1976]
*San Manuel Bueno, mártir, y tres historias más*  (novellas)
 1933
 [*Saint Emmanuel the Good, Martyr* published in *Abel
 Sánchez and Other Stories*, 1956]
*El hermano Juan; o, El mundo es teatro* [first publication]
 (drama)  1934
*Obras completas*. 15 vols.  (novels, essays, poetry, dramas,
 and novellas)  1950-63
*Ensayos*. 7 vols.  (essays)  1951
*Poems*  (poetry)  1952
*Cancionero, Diario poético*  (poetry)  1953
*Soledad*  (drama)  1953
*Abel Sanchez and Other Stories*  (novella and short stories)
 1956
*The Last Poems of Miguel de Unamuno*  (poetry)  1974

## HAVELOCK ELLIS  (essay date 1908)

[Miguel de Unamuno] is one of the most brilliant of Spanish writers and a penetrative critic, especially the critic, caustic more often than sympathetic, of his countrymen's characteristics and shortcomings. His recent *Vida de Don Quijote y Sancho* is a curious attempt to present an essay of Spanish philosophy expressed in terms of the two figures who together sum up the whole attitude of the Spanish mind towards life. Of more significance, however, from our present point of view, is the volume entitled *En Torno al Casticismo,* published in 1902, although it was really written in substance during 1895, and thus belongs to the same period as [Ángel] Ganivet's *Idearium Español,* to which it forms an interesting counterpart. Ganivet, living a cosmopolitan life outside his country, concentrated his devout reflections on the permanently vital and precious elements in the Spanish spirit, the sole source, it seemed to him, of any national regeneration. Unamuno, a less deliberate writer perhaps, a less fascinatingly individual thinker, possesses a larger outlook, the charm of a spontaneous and ardent style, a wide acquaintance as well with books as with the younger generation of Spaniards, and an eager impatience with the obstacles in the road of progress which leads him to throw an air of satire even over his serious attempts to define precisely the essence of the Castilian spirit. The word *casticismo* by which he designates this spirit—a word which occurs so often in the writings of Spanish critics—may be said to correspond to our "breed" or "race" in the more popular use of the words as an indication of approval. It is in the golden age of Castilian literature, especially in the drama, and above all in Calderon,—the "poeta españolissimo," as Menendez y Pelayo terms him,—that Unamuno finds the purest manifestations of *casticismo*. In that word are concentrated the special valour and virtue of Castile, just as some have attempted to concentrate the special valour and virtue of Japan in the word *bushido*. But Unamuno, while by no means wishing to cast contempt on what is *castizo*, reveals that he is not himself a true child of Castile, by pointing out how largely it is characterised by sterility and impracticability. . . . Unamuno contrasts the narrow sterility of this *casticismo* with the universally human spirit of Cervantes, and urges his countrymen to recognise that it is only in the larger and more vital ideas of old Spain that they can find help to grapple with the problems of the modern world. (pp. 401-03)

[Unamuno] deprecates the Spanish emphasis on individuality and distinguishes between individuality and personality. . . . The Castilian soul was great only when it opened itself to the four winds and scattered itself across the world. It is only by opening our windows to the winds of Europe, Unamuno finally repeats, in the faith that we shall not thereby lose our own personality, that we can hope to regenerate the exhausted moral soil of Spain. (pp. 407-08)

Havelock Ellis, "Spanish Ideals of To-Day," in his The Soul of Spain *(reprinted by permission of Houghton Mifflin Company), Houghton Mifflin, 1908 (and reprinted by Houghton Mifflin, 1924), pp. 386-414.\**

## SALVADOR DE MADARIAGA  (essay date 1921)

[Unamuno] is what he wants to be, a man—in the striking expression which he chose as a title for one of his short stories, *nothing less than a whole man*. Not a mere thinking machine, set to prove a theory, nor an actor on the world stage, singing a well-built poem, well built at the price of many a compromise; but a whole man, with all his affirmations and all his negations, all the pitiless thoughts of a penetrating mind that denies, and all the desperate self-assertions of a soul that yearns for eternal life.

This strife between enemy truths, the truth thought and the truth felt, or, as he himself puts it, between veracity and sincerity, is Unamuno's *raison d'être*. And it is because the *Tragic Sense of Life* is the most direct expression of it that this book is his masterpiece. The conflict is here seen as reflected in the person of the author. The book opens by a definition of the Spanish man, the 'man of flesh and bones', illustrated by the consideration of the real living men who stood behind the bookish figures of great philosophers and consciously or unconsciously shaped and misshaped their doctrines in order to satisfy their own vital yearnings. This is followed by the statement of the will to live or hunger for immortality, in the course of which the usual subterfuges with which this all-important issue is evaded in philosophy, theology, or mystic literature, are exposed, and the real, concrete, 'flesh and bones' character of the immortality which men desire is reaffirmed. The Catholic position is then explained as the *vital* attitude in the matter, summed up in Tertullian's *Credo quia absurdum,* and this is opposed to the critical attitude which denies the possibility of individual survival in the sense previously defined. Thus Unamuno leads us to his inner deadlock: his reason can rise no higher than scepticism, and, unable to become vital, dies sterile; his faith, exacting anti-rational affirmations and unable therefore to be apprehended by the logical mind, remains incommunicable. From the bottom of this abyss Unamuno builds up his theory of life. But is it a theory? Unamuno does not claim for it such an intellectual dignity. He knows too well that in the constructive part of his book his vital self takes the leading part and repeatedly warns his reader of the fact, lest critical objections might be raised against this or that assumption or self-contradiction. It is on the survival of his will to live, after all the onslaughts of his critical intellect, that he finds the basis for his belief—or rather for his effort to believe. Self-compassion leads to self-love, and this self-love, founded as it is on a universal conflict, widens into love of all that lives and therefore wants to survive. So, by an act of love, springing from our own hunger for immortality, we are led to give a conscience to the Universe—that is, to create God.

Such is the process by which Unamuno, from the transcendental pessimism of his inner contradiction, extracts an everyday optimism founded on love. His symbol of this attitude is the figure of Don Quixote, of whom he truly says that his creed 'can hardly be called idealism, since he did not fight for ideas: it was spiritualism, for he fought for the spirit'. Thus he opposes a synthetical to an analytical attitude; a religious to an ethico-scientific ideal; Spain, his Spain, i.e. the spiritual manifestation of the Spanish race, to Europe, his Europe, i.e. the intellectual manifestation of the white race, which he sees in Franco-Germany; and heroic love, even when comically unpractical, to culture, which, in this book, written in 1912, is already prophetically spelt Kultura.

This courageous work is written in a style which is the man—for [Georges] Buffon's saying, seldom true, applies here to the letter. It is written as Carlyle wrote, not merely with the brain, but with the whole soul and the whole body of the man, and in such a vivid manner that one can without much effort imagine the eager gesticulation which now and then underlines, inter-

prets, despises, argues, denies, and above all asserts. In his absolute subservience to the matter in hand this manner of writing has its great precedent in Santa Teresa. The differences, and they are considerable, are not of art, absent in either case, but of nature. They are such deep and obvious differences as obtain between the devout, ignorant, graceful nun of sixteenth-century Avila and the free-thinking, learned, wilful professor of twentieth-century Salamanca. In the one case, as in the other, the language is the most direct and simple required. It is also the least literary and the most popular. Unamuno, who lives in close touch with the people, has enriched the Spanish literary language by returning to it many a popular term. His vocabulary abounds in words racy of the soil, and his writings gain from them an almost peasant-like pith and directness which suits his own Basque primitive nature. His expression occurs simultaneously with the thoughts and feelings to be expressed, the flow of which, but loosely controlled by the critical mind, often breaks through the meshes of established diction and gives birth to new forms created under the pressure of the moment. This feature Unamuno has also in common with Santa Teresa, but what in the Saint was a self-ignorant charm becomes in Unamuno à deliberate manner inspired, partly by an acute sense of the symbolical and psychological value of word-connexions, partly by that genuine need for expansion of the language which all true original thinkers or 'feelers' must experience, but partly also by an acquired habit of juggling with words which is but natural in a philologist endowed with a vigorous imagination. Unamuno revels in words. He positively enjoys stretching them beyond their usual meaning, twisting them, composing, opposing, and transposing them in all sorts of possible ways. This game—not wholly unrewarded now and then by striking intellectual finds—seems to be the only relaxation which he allows his usually austere mind. It certainly is the only light feature of a style the merit of which lies in its being the close-fitting expression of a great mind earnestly concentrated on a great idea.

The earnestness, the intensity, and the oneness of his predominant passion are the main cause of the strength of Unamuno's philosophic work. They remain his main asset, yet become also the principal cause of his weakness, as a creative artist. Great art can only flourish in the temperate zone of the passions, on the return journey from the torrid. Unamuno, as a creator, has none of the failings of those artists who have never felt deeply. But he does show the limitations of those artists who cannot cool down. And the most striking of them is that at bottom he is seldom able to put himself in a purely aesthetical mood. In this, as in many other features, Unamuno curiously resembles Wordsworth. . . . Like him, Unamuno is an essentially purposeful and utilitarian mind. Of the two qualities which the work of art requires for its inception—earnestness and detachment—both Unamuno and Wordsworth possess the first; both are deficient in the second. Their interest in their respective leading thought—survival in the first, virtue in the second—is too direct, too pressing, to allow them the 'distance' necessary for artistic work. Both are urged to work by a lofty utilitarianism—the search for God through the individual soul in Unamuno, the search for God through the social soul in Wordsworth—so that their thoughts and sensations are polarized and their spirit loses that impartial transparence for nature's lights without which no great art is possible. . . . There are no doubt important differences. The Englishman's sense of nature is both keener and more concrete; while the Spaniard's knowledge of human nature is not barred by the subtle inhibitions and innate limitations which tend to blind its more unpleasant aspects to the eye of the Englishman. There is more courage and passion in the Spaniard; more harmony and good-will in the Englishman; the one is more like fire, the other like light. For Wordsworth, a poem is above all an essay, a means for conveying a lesson in forcible and easily remembered terms to those who are in need of improvement. For Unamuno, a poem or a novel (and he holds that a novel is but a poem) is the outpouring of a man's passion, the overflow of the heart which cannot help itself and lets go. And it may be that the essential difference between the two is to be found in this difference between their respective purposes: Unamuno's purpose is more intimately personal and individual; Wordsworth's is more social and objective. Thus both miss the temperate zone, where emotion takes shape into the moulds of art; but while Wordsworth is driven by his ideal of social service this side of it, into the cold light of both moral and intellectual self-control, Unamuno remains beyond, where the molten metal is too near the fire of passion, and cannot cool down into shape.

Unamuno is therefore not unlike Wordsworth in the insufficiency of his sense of form. We have just seen the essential cause of this insufficiency to lie in the non-aesthetical attitude of his mind, and we have tried to show one of the roots of such an attitude in the very loftiness and earnestness of his purpose. Yet, there are others, for living nature is many-rooted as it is many-branched. It cannot be doubted that a certain refractoriness to form is a typical feature of the Basque character. The sense of form is closely in sympathy with the feminine element in human nature, and the Basque race is strongly masculine. The predominance of the masculine element—strength without grace—is as typical of Unamuno as it is of Wordsworth. The literary gifts which might for the sake of synthesis be symbolized in a smile are absent in both. There is as little humour in the one as in the other. Humour, however, sometimes occurs in Unamuno, but only in his ill-humoured moments, and then with a curious bite of its own which adds an unconscious element to its comic effect. Grace only visits them in moments of inspiration, and then it is of a noble character, enhanced as it is by the ever-present gift of strength. And as for the sense for rhythm and music, both Unamuno and Wordsworth seem to be limited to the most vigorous and masculine gaits. This feature is particularly pronounced in Unamuno, for while Wordsworth is painstaking, all-observant, and too good a 'teacher' to underestimate the importance of pleasure in man's progress, Unamuno knows no compromise. His aim is not to please but to strike, and he deliberately seeks the naked, the forceful, even the brutal word for truth. There is in him, however, a cause of formlessness of which Wordsworth is free—namely, an eagerness for sincerity and veracity which brushes aside all preparation, ordering or planning of ideas as suspect of 'dishing up', intellectual trickery, and juggling with spontaneous truths.

Such qualities—both the positive and the negative—are apparent in his poetry. In it, the appeal of force and sincerity is usually stronger than that of art. This is particularly the case in his first volume (*Poesías*, . . .), in which a lofty inspiration, a noble attitude of mind, a rich and racy vocabulary, a keen insight into the spirit of places, and above all the overflowing vitality of a strong man in the force of ripeness, contend against the still awkward gait of the Basque and a certain rebelliousness of rhyme. The dough of the poetic language is here seen heavily pounded by a powerful hand, bent on reducing its angularities and on improving its plasticity. Nor do we need to wait for further works in order to enjoy the reward of such efforts, for it is attained in this very volume more than once, as for instance in *Muere en el mar el ave que voló del buque*, a beautiful poem

in which emotion and thought are happily blended into exquisite form.

In his last poem, *El Cristo de Velázquez* . . . , Unamuno undertakes the task of giving a poetical rendering of his tragic sense of life, in the form of a meditation on the Christ of [Rodríguez de Silva y Velázquez] the beautiful and pathetic picture in the Prado. Why Velázquez's and not Christ himself? The fact is that, though in his references to actual forms, Unamuno closely follows Velázquez's picture, the spiritual interpretation of it which he develops as the poem unfolds itself is wholly personal. It would be difficult to find two great Spaniards wider apart than Unamuno and Velázquez, for if Unamuno is the very incarnation of the masculine spirit of the North—all strength and substance—Velázquez is the image of the feminine spirit of the South—all grace and form. Velázquez is a limpid mirror, with a human depth, yet a mirror. That Unamuno has departed from the image of Christ which the great Sevillian reflected on his immortal canvas therefore was to be expected. But then Unamuno has, while speaking of Don Quixote, whom he has also freely and personally interpreted, taken great care to point out that a work of art is, for each of us, all that we see in it. And, moreover, Unamuno has not so much departed from Velázquez's image of Christ as delved into its depths, expanded, enlarged it, or, if you prefer, seen in its limpid surface the immense figure of his own inner Christ. However free and unorthodox in its wide scope of images and ideas, the poem is in its form a regular meditation in the manner approved by the Catholic Church, and it is therefore meet that it should rise from a concrete, tangible object as it is recommended to the faithful. To this concrete character of its origin, the poem owes much of its suggestiveness. . . (pp. 94-102)

The poem, despite its length, easily maintains [a] lofty level throughout, and if he had written nothing else Unamuno would still remain as having given to Spanish letters the noblest and most sustained lyrical flight in the language. It abounds in passages of ample beauty, and often strikes a note of primitive strength in the true Old Testament style. It is most distinctively a poem in a major key, in a group with *Paradise Lost* and *The Excursion*, but in a tone half-way between the two; and, as coming from the most Northern-minded and substantial poet that Spain ever had, wholly free from that tendency towards grandiloquence and Ciceronian drapery which blighted previous similar efforts in Spain. Its weakness lies in a certain monotony due to the interplay of Unamuno's two main limitations as an artist: the absolute surrender to one dominant thought and a certain deficiency of form bordering here on contempt. The plan is but a loose sequence of meditations on successive aspects of Christ as suggested by images or ascriptions of His Divine person, or even of parts of His human body: Lion, Bull, Lily, Sword, Crown, Head, Knees. Each meditation is treated in a period of blank verse, usually of a beautiful texture, the splendour of which is due less to actual images than to the inner vigour of ideas and the eagerness with which even the simplest facts are interpreted into significant symbols. Yet, sometimes, this blank verse becomes hard and stony under the stubborn hammering of a too insistent mind, and the device of ending each meditation with a line accented on its last syllable tends but to increase the monotony of the whole. (p. 103)

Unamuno's best poetry, as Wordsworth's, is in his sonnets. His *Rosario de Sonetos líricos* . . . contains some of the finest sonnets in the Spanish language. There is variety in this volume—more at least than is usual in Unamuno: from comments on events of local politics (sonnet lii) which savour of the more prosaic side of Wordsworth, to meditations on space and time such as that sonnet xxxvii, so reminiscent of Shelley's *Ozymandias of Egypt;* from a suggestive homily to a 'Don Juan of Ideas' whose thirst for knowledge is 'not love of truth, but intellectual lust', and whose 'thought is therefore sterile' (sonnet cvii), to an exquisitely rendered moonlight love scene (sonnet civ). The author's main theme itself, which of course occupies a prominent part in the series, appears treated under many different lights and in genuinely poetical moods which truly do justice to the inherent wealth of poetical inspiration which it contains. Many a sonnet might be quoted here, and in particular that sombre and fateful poem *Nihil Novum sub sole* (cxxiii), which defeats its own theme by the striking originality of its inspiration.

So active, so positive is the inspiration of this poetry that the question of outside influences does not even arise. Unamuno is probably the Spanish contemporary poet whose manner owes least, if anything at all, to modern developments of poetry such as those which take their source in Baudelaire and Verlaine. . . . Unamuno is too genuine a representative of the spiritual and masculine variety of Spanish genius, ever impervious to French, and generally, to intellectual, influences, to be affected by the aesthetic excellence of this art. Yet, for all his disregard of the modern resources which it adds to the poetic craft, Unamuno loses none of his modernity. He is indeed more than modern. When, as he often does, he strikes the true poetic note, he is outside time. His appeal is not in complexity but in strength. He is not refined: he is final.

In the preface to his *Tres Novelas Ejemplares y un Prólogo* . . . Unamuno says: '. . . novelist—that is, poet . . . a novel—that is, a poem.' Thus, with characteristic decision, he sides with the lyrical conception of the novel. . . . It is the recognition of his own lyrical inward-looking nature which makes Unamuno pronounce the identity of the novel and the poem.

Whatever we may think of it as a general theory, there is little doubt that this opinion is in the main sound in so far as it refers to Unamuno's own work. His novels are created within. They are—and their author is the first to declare it so—novels which happen in the kingdom of the spirit. Outward points of reference in time and space are sparingly given—in fact, reduced to a bare minimum. In some of them, as for instance *Niebla* . . . the name of the town in which the action takes place is not given, and such scanty references to the topography and general features as are supplied would equally apply to any other provincial town of Spain. Action, in the current sense of the word, is correspondingly simplified, since the material and local elements on which it usually exerts itself are schematized, and in their turn made, as it were, spiritual. Thus a street, a river of colour for some, for others a series of accurately described shops and dwellings, becomes in Unamuno (see *Niebla*) a loom where the passions and desires of men and women cross and recross each other and weave the cloth of daily life. Even the physical description of characters is reduced to a standard of the utmost simplicity. So that, in fine, Unamuno's novels, by eliminating all other material, appear, if the boldness of the metaphor be permitted, as the spiritual skeletons of novels, conflicts between souls.

Nor is this the last stage in his deepening and narrowing of the creative furrow. For these souls are in their turn concentrated so that the whole of their vitality burns into one passion. If a somewhat fanciful comparison from another art may throw any light on this feature of his work, we might say that his characters are to those of Galdós, for instance, as counterpoint

music to the complex modern symphony. Joaquín Monegro, the true hero of his *Abel Sánchez* . . . is the personification of hatred. Raquel in *Dos Madres* and Catalina in *El Marqués de Lumbría* are two widely different but vigorous, almost barbarous, 'maternities'. Alejandro, the hero of his powerful *Nada menos que todo un Hombre,* is masculine will, pure and unconquerable, save by death. Further still, in most if not all of his main characters, we can trace the dominant passion which is their whole being to a mere variety of the one and only passion which obsesses Unamuno himself, the hunger for life, a full life, here and after. (pp. 104-07)

There are critics who conclude from this observation that these characters do not exist, that they are mere arguments on legs, personified ideas. Here and there, in Unamuno's novels, there are passages which lend some colour of plausibility to this view. Yet, it is in my opinion mistaken. Unamuno's characters may be schematized, stripped of their complexities, reduced to the mainspring of their nature; they may, moreover, reveal mainsprings made of the same steel. But that they are alive no one could deny who has a sense for life. The very restraint in the use of physical details which Unamuno has made a feature of his creative work may have led his critics to forget the intensity of those—admirably chosen—which are given. It is significant that the eyes play an important part in his description of characters and in his narrative too. His sense of the interpenetration of body and soul is so deep that he does not for one moment let us forget how bodily his 'souls' are, and how pregnant with spiritual significance is every one of their words and gestures. No. These characters are not arguments on legs. They truly are men and women of 'flesh and bones', human, terribly human.

In thus emphasizing a particular feature in their nature, Unamuno imparts to his creations a certain deformity which savours of romantic days. Yet Unamuno is not a romanticist, mainly because Romanticism was an aesthetic attitude, and his attitude is seldom purely aesthetic. For all their show of passion true Romanticists seldom gave their real selves to their art. They created a stage double of their own selves for public exhibitions. They sought the picturesque. Their form was lyrical, but their substance was dramatic. Unamuno, on the contrary, even though he often seeks expression in dramatic form, is essentially lyrical. And if he is always intense, he never is exuberant. He follows the Spanish tradition for restraint—for there is one, along with its opposite tradition for grandiloquence—and, true to the spirit of it, he seeks the maximum of effect through the minimum of means. Then he never shouts. (pp. 108-09)

Miguel de Unamuno is to-day the greatest literary figure of Spain. Baroja may surpass him in variety of external experience, Azorín in delicate art, Ortega y Gasset in philosophical subtlety, Ayala in intellectual elegance, Valle Inclán in rhythmical grace. Even in vitality he may have to yield the first place to that overwhelming athlete of literature, Blasco Ibáñez. But Unamuno is head and shoulders above them all in the highness of his purpose and in the earnestness and loyalty with which, Quixote-like, he has served all through his life his unattainable Dulcinea. Then there is another and most important reason which explains his position as first, *princeps,* of Spanish letters, and it is that Unamuno, by the cross which he has chosen to bear, incarnates the spirit of modern Spain. His eternal conflict between faith and reason, between life and thought, between spirit and intellect, between heaven and civilization, is the conflict of Spain herself. A border country, like Russia, in which East and West mix their spiritual waters, Spain wavers between two life-philosophies and cannot rest. In Russia, this conflict emerges in literature during the nineteenth century, when Dostoievsky and Tolstoy stand for the East while Turgeniev becomes the West's advocate. . . . Unamuno is our Dostoievsky, but painfully aware of the strength of the other side within him, and full of misgivings. . . . Unamuno, whose literary qualities and defects make him a genuine representative of the more masculine variety of the Spanish genius, becomes in his spiritual life the true living symbol of his country and his time. And that he is great enough to bear this incarnation is a sufficient measure of his greatness. (pp. 109-10)

> *Salvador de Madariaga, in his introduction to* The Tragic Sense of Life in Men and Peoples *by Miguel de Unamuno, translated by J. E. Crawford Flitch (reprinted by permission of Macmillan, London and Basingstoke), Macmillan, 1921 (and reprinted as "Miguel de Unamuno" in his* The Genius of Spain, and Other Essays on Spanish Contemporary Literature, *Oxford University Press, Oxford, 1923, pp. 87-110).*

### MARK VAN DOREN   (essay date 1922)

Don Quixote lives in Spain again in the person, or rather in the mind, of a professor of Greek at the University of Salamanca. Miguel de Unamuno, poet, novelist, metaphysician, whom Salvador de Madariaga, assuming the worshipful role of Sancho Panza, calls "the greatest literary figure in Spain" [see excerpt above], and who if he is not that is one of the five or six leaders of the intellectual renaissance in that fascinating country today, fights the windmills of despair. His masterpiece, **"Del Sentimiento Trágico de la Vida,"** . . . is modern Catholicism's richest, most passionate, most brilliant statement of the grounds that exist for faith in immortality, now that reason and science have done their worst.

One need not be interested in immortality to appreciate this book, but one should be interested in windmills; one should be able to like a losing fight. Unamuno fights because he knows there is not a chance in the world to win. He has tasted the glory of absurdity. He has decided to hope what he cannot believe. He has discovered grounds for faith in the very fact that there are no grounds.

He accepts reason and science to their last syllable, and curiously enough he begins where Bertrand Russell, in "A Free Man's Worship," begins—with despair. . . . The two philosophers proceed thenceforth in opposite directions—Russell to the consideration of what man as man can know, Unamuno to the consideration of what man as man can feel—both, however, convinced that the profoundest of man's creations is Tragedy. . . .

The tragic sense of life is nothing more or less than a sense of the disparity between what we know we can be and what we can think of being, between the limitations Nature has imposed upon us and the limits of our imagination; or, as Unamuno puts it, between the necessities of reason and the necessities of life. . . .

We begin to live, says Unamuno, as soon as we have become aware of our limitations. Men live in different ways; Unamuno lives in faith. Let it be said again that one need not be interested in faith to follow him in his flight, which is not, of course, orthodox. Sancho Panza was never deceived about Don Quixote, but Don Quixote was never dull. He was exhilarating in his madness, and so is Unamuno. He leaps from metaphor to metaphor; he writes like fire. Above all, there is none of the nonsense in him of "reconciliation" between knowledge and belief. Supremely intelligent, he never believes; religiously alive, he hopes. His book is very absurd, but it is tremendous work and fun for the mind.

> *Mark Van Doren, "Don Quixote of Salamanca," in* The Nation *(copyright 1922 The Nation magazine, The Nation Associates, Inc.), Vol. 114, No. 2967, May 17, 1922, p. 600.*

### JOHN DOS PASSOS   (essay date 1922)

Unamuno is the champion of death. (p. 220)

Unamuno's idols are the mystics and saints and sensualists of Castile, hard stalwart men who walked with God, Loyola, Torquemada, Pizarro, Narváez, who governed with whips and thumbscrews and drank death down greedily like heady wine. He is excited by the amorous madness of the mysticism of Santa Teresa and San Juan de la Cruz. His religion is paradoxical, unreasonable, of faith alone, full of furious yearning other-worldliness. His style, it follows perforce, is headlong, gruff, redundant, full of tremendous pounding phrases. There is a vigorous angry insistence about his dogmas that makes his essays unforgettable, even if one objects as violently as I do to his asceticism and death-worship. There is an anarchic fury about his crying in the wilderness that will win many a man from the fleshpots and chain gangs.

In the apse of the old cathedral of Salamanca is a fresco of the Last Judgment, perhaps by the Castilian painter Gallegos. Over the retablo on a black ground a tremendous figure of the avenging angel brandishes a sword while behind him unrolls the scroll of the *Dies Irae* and huddled clusters of plump little naked people fall away into space from under his feet. There are moments in **"Del Sentimiento Trágico de la Vida"** and in the **"Vida de Don Quijote y Sancho"** when in the rolling earthy Castilian phrases one can feel the brandishing of the sword of that very angel. . . . Unamuno is constantly attacking sturdily those who clamor for the modernization, Europeanization of Spanish life and Spanish thought: he is the counterpoise to the northward-yearning apostles of Giner de los Ríos. (pp. 224-26)

> *John Dos Passos, "A Funeral in Madrid," in his* Rosinante to the Road Again *(copyright, 1922, by George H. Doran Company; copyright renewed © 1949 by John Dos Passos; reprinted by the Literary Estate of John Dos Passos), Doran, 1922, pp. 202-29.\**

### ERNEST BOYD   (essay date 1925)

Miguel de Unamuno is a humanist and a Hellenist, and the influence of his classical studies is deeply imprinted upon his style with its Latin lucidity and Socratic subtleties. As befits a true Hellenist, Unamuno is both an artist and a philosopher, and if *The Tragic Sense of Life* is the only formal exposition of his philosophy, his teachings are scattered through the seven volumes of *Ensayos* and that charming book *La Vida de Don Quijote y Sancho,* which many hold to be his masterpiece. Don Miguel is a philologist by profession and a philosopher by vocation, but he is also a poet and a novelist; he is of the true lineage of Cervantes.

His most recent book, *Andanzas y Visiones Españolas,* is a volume of travel sketches, making a companion book to the earlier collection *Por Tierras de España y Portugal.* In the preface he explains the genesis of the work rather curiously when he says that these *Walks and Visions* are to make up for the lack of descriptive passages in his novels. "Those who follow my work and who have read my novels will have noticed that, except in the first, *Paz en la Guerra,* I have avoided descriptions of landscapes and even definite settings of time and place and local color. . . . I obeyed my desire to give the stories the greatest possible intensity and dramatic character by reducing them, where possible, to dialogue and the narrative of action and feeling—the latter in dialogue form—and by avoiding what the dramatists call asides. I might easily have put into my novels the descriptions of lands and houses, of mountains, valleys, and villages which I have collected here, but I did not do so in order to lighten them. Whoever reads a novel, like a playgoer in a theatre, is held by the development of the argument, by the interplay of the actions and passions of the characters, and is strongly inclined to skip the descriptions of landscapes, however beautiful they may be." (pp. 63-4)

In the light of his theories of novel-writing Unamuno's novels are of peculiar interest. They are five in number, *Paz en la Guerra, Amor y Pedagogía, El Espejo de la Muerte, Niebla, Abel Sánchez, La Tía Tula,* and *Tres Novelas Ejemplares.* The first of these to meet with any success was *Niebla,* which has the distinction of anticipating the method of Pirandello in his *Six Characters in Search of an Author.* The fable is exceedingly simple: the contrast between the intelligence of a dog and the stupidity of men. The dog, guided by his instincts, unfailingly finds his way through life, but man, confused by his illusions, his desires, and his dreams, cannot thread his way through the labyrinth of existence. (p. 65)

The book is a curious and original piece of work. There is no narrative, for the story unfolds in dialogues and soliloquies, not because Unamuno believes that character is revealed by speech, but for the contrary reason. Speech, he holds, is a social convention and therefore artificial and insincere. "Man lies in so far as he speaks, and he lies to himself when he talks to himself, that is, when he thinks deliberately and consciously." Unamuno's theory is that we speak first, then think what we say, then do what we think.

The same paradoxical, sceptical note is discernible in *Abel Sánchez,* ironically described as a "story of passion." As in *Niebla,* the form is as rigid as a geometrical figure, and the incidents develop as though moved by a mechanism. Here . . . two couples are confronted: Abel Sánchez, the painter; Joaquín Monegro, the doctor; their wives and children. The artist, whose eyes are fixed on the surface of things, because his art is concerned with the appearance and color of life, is an easygoing person, easy to get on with, sympathetic, successful. The doctor, on the other hand, whose studies have forced him to look for the secret ills, the internal weaknesses, of humanity, is as complicated, as sad, as profound as the painter is simple, good-humored, and superficial. He is suspected of envying and hating his popular friend. What is called hate is merely the antithesis between happiness and grief, wealth and poverty, and has no psychological basis. It is there just as shade is inseparable from light. . . . In this novel Unamuno shows us the paradoxical play of human destiny, which delights in representing the human soul in absurd and contradictory postures. The narrative is rigorously suppressed, and the story is told in short dialogues, ironical, logical, full of incisive observation. Unamuno has turned the art of fiction back to the technic of the Platonic dialogue.

*The Tragic Sentiment of Life* is a work which comes in direct line from the literature of the Spanish mystics. It is the reply of a Spaniard of to-day to self-sufficient radicalism, and in it is heard the note of Pascal, torn between the logic of reason and the irrepressible demands of faith. The visionary passion of a mind which refuses to accept the denial of spiritual hopes and is yet conscious of the sovereignty of the reasoning faculties finds dramatic expression in his book. Unamuno confesses an impotence of feeling when confronted by the unanswerable arguments of reason. The desire for immortality can find no rational confirmation, but reason leaves us no object in life and gives it no finality. Thought and feeling thus meet in a common despair. (pp. 66-8)

In its own defense life finds the weak point in reason, which is scepticism, and from the despair engendered by scepticism is born "the holy, sweet, redeeming uncertainty, our supreme consolation." There are, then, three solutions to the problem of existence—either there is no after-life, which means despair in resignation and the eternal struggle, which is the theme of Unamuno. . . . His book will be read by us rather for its poignant drama of the human soul than for its doctrine, which rests too easily upon assumptions which have long since ceased to be taken for granted outside Spain. Don Miguel de Unamuno is a rebel in his own country, but we are more likely to be surprised by his orthodoxy. (pp. 68-9)

The doctrines of Unamuno will never stir the typical Western mind, but, as Salvador de Madariaga points out in *The Genius of Spain,* Unamuno's country, like Russia, is "a border country," in which "East and West mix their spiritual waters," and he incarnates the spirit of modern Spain "astride two enemy ideals" [see excerpt above]. Hence his importance, and the tributes which have been paid to his genius by men as dissimilar as Havelock Ellis [see excerpt above] and [Giovanni] Papini. (p. 70)

> *Ernest Boyd, "Don Miguel de Unamuno," in his* Studies from Ten Literatures *(copyright © 1925 by Charles Scribner's Sons; reprinted with permission of Charles Scribner's Sons), Charles Scribner's Sons, 1925, pp. 61-71.*

## ÁNGEL DEL RÍO and AMELIA A. DE DEL RÍO (essay date 1947)

Unamuno cultivated all the literary forms—the novel, the short story, the drama, the essay, poetry—but the last two dominate and set the tone of his work since they are the forms most suited to personal expression. In Unamuno's case, specifically, they serve to express his anxieties, emotions, and preoccupations, and permit him to discourse poetically and to reason about the problems which absorb him: God, immortality, Don Quixote, Spain, and the conflict between science and life, and between reason and feeling.

In the last analysis, it is useless to attempt to define the subject matter, the ideas, and the substance of Unamuno's writing because his combined work, his life, and his personality, have for root and impulse a dynamic or dialectical contradiction whose import Unamuno formulated again and again, especially in the essay entitled *Mi religión.* (p. 10)

The principles of his spiritual life were, then, struggle, negation, and doubt. And from them, like his masters, Pascal and Kierkegaard, he drew his metaphysical concepts of desperation, anguish, and agony, which he expounds with aggressive insistence in his essays, which he incarnates starkly in the characters of his novels and dramas, and which are at the core of the religious inspiration of his poetry. They are, for him, the essence of the Spanish spirit, composed of dissonances, with its perpetual conflict between the ideal and reality, between heaven and earth, between its Sancho Panza-like sense of the immediate and its quixotic yearning for immortality.

The incidental themes of Unamuno's essays vary, but, in reality, the only theme of all his works is Unamuno himself and, as he frequently said, his philosophy, his poetry, like his novels and his plays, are always a self-critical and spiritual autobiography. The ideas appear in his work charged with personal emotion, and, vice versa, the emotion, the profound lyricism of his poetry is the result of his intellectual and religious anguish. Hence his style, rather than the clear, orderly style of a philosopher, is always that of a poet, impassioned, full of images, sometimes difficult because of the abundance of allusions, paradoxes, digressions, parentheses, exclamations, and ingenious plays upon words and ideas (called in Spanish *"conceptos,"* and, technically, in English, "conceits"), which pile themselves up in a kind of prophetic and poetic vertigo, contrasting at times with a starkness of expression that is direct and cutting.

Unamuno collected a part of his work as an essayist in some twenty volumes; another very considerable part, the thousands of articles which he wrote for the daily press and the reviews, is still to be compiled. Perhaps the part of Unamuno which is most alive consists of these brief, unconnected essays inspired by momentary passions, such as the ones contained in the seven volumes of *Ensayos,* or those of *Mi religión y otros ensayos, Contra esto y aquello, Soliloquios y conversaciones,* or the impressions of landscapes, countryside and cities, in *Andanzas y visiones españolas* and *Por tierras de Portugal y de España.* Aside from these books, the three principal works of Unamuno as an essayist, particularly important because of their broader, somewhat systematic development of his thought, are [*En torno al casticismo; Vida de don Quijote y Sancho según Miguel de Cervantes Saavedra, explicada y comentada;* and *Del sentimiento trágico de la vida en los hombres y en los pueblos*]. . . . (pp. 10-12)

The first, conceived in the atmosphere of criticism and reappraisal of Spain's past which prevailed prior to the disaster of '98, is an interpretation in five essays of Spanish history and literature, in which Unamuno seeks, not the accidental and local phases of that history and literature, but what is eternal and universal at their core. His tone is pessimistic, and his censure of the official academic Spain, harsh. Unamuno proposes two courses for the regeneration of Spain: one, to return to the deeply rooted, eternal traditions, to become more Spanish, "chapuzándose en el pueblo," (immersing oneself in the people), those who keep those traditions alive; the other, apparently contradictory, to become Europeanized, opening the windows of Spanish life to all the winds of Western, European culture. Owing to the combative, dialectical tone of all his thought, Unamuno changed a great deal, and came to contradict almost all the ideas which he was defending in this book, but in it may be found the basis for all his later ideas concerning Spain. Together with the *Idearium español* of Ángel Ganivet, written a short time afterward, it constitutes the first step toward a new view of Spanish values. (p. 12)

[*La vida de don Quijote y Sancho*] is a personal commentary upon Cervantes' novel, or rather a eulogistic interpretation of its two immortal characters as symbols of the Spanish soul. It is a profession of quixotic faith, and an appeal for the revival of the ideals of the *hidalgo* from La Mancha as a road to spiritual redemption. Unamuno ignores the literary significance of the *Quijote* in order the better to understand its human significance. This book marks the change of direction in Unamuno's ideas, his turning away from European culture. He no longer advocates the Europeanizing of Spain but urges a re-affirmation of the values of the *Quijote:* faith, glory, goodness, the longing for immortality, heroism, action, as an antidote for modern rationalistic and utilitarian society.

This attitude on Unamuno's part in opposition to modern European culture is fully defined in *Del sentimiento trágico de la vida,* his masterpiece, and the most profound and difficult of his works. It is an attempt on the part of a writer so unsystematic as Unamuno to explain more systematically his thought in regard to the problem of human destiny in modern culture, and the impossibility of solving it rationally because of the incompatibility of reason and faith.

Starting with the concept of individuality, of the "hombre de carne y hueso" ["man of flesh and bone"], Unamuno analyzes what he calls the tragic essence of modern civilization, resulting from the longing for knowledge which, guided by reason, has destroyed man's faith in God and in immortality, a faith necessary for his emotional life. Hence, modern humanity, incapable of solving the problem, is forced to struggle in uncertainty, and at the same time to strive after truth, a struggle and agony inherently tragic.

In connection with this central thought, which is more poetical than logical, and is fundamentally existentialist, a reflection of Kierkegaard's ideas about anguish, Unamuno gives us a fruitful series of comments upon and evaluations of culture in many fields, especially Spanish culture. He believes that Spain retains at the root of her medieval, Catholic culture that living faith in immortality, incarnated by her greatest hero, Don Quixote, and that she should rally to him, as a living symbol, to cry in the wilderness of the intellectualized world. She should remain faithful to her mission of maintaining moral and human values, and of creating, not ideas and techniques, as the modern materialistic, industrial, and scientific world has done, but human souls. (pp. 12-13)

Unamuno develops this philosophy of anguish in a still more extreme form in *La agonía del cristianismo,* in essays and brief articles, and later in his poetry, his novels, and his plays, the creative forms toward which his literary activity was increasingly directed.

Not far behind Unamuno the essayist and thinker should stand Unamuno the poet of *Rosario de sonetos líricos, El Cristo de Velázquez, Teresa,* etc. We refer here specifically to his work in verse, for Unamuno is always and above all a poet, not only in the quality and tone of his prose, but in the always lyrical and personal character of his philosophy. (p. 14)

[In] his poetry, which is entirely independent of formulas and schools, perhaps more than in the rest of his work, we find the essence of his religious and very personal attitude toward life, his philosophy of anguish, his very human and very Spanish, but universal emotion, mingled with a concrete feeling for everyday reality; the transitory and individual side by side with the universal and eternal, the constant poles of Unamuno's combative soul.

But his lyre has many strings. Together with the pure emotion of his philosophical poetry or his impressions of the Spanish landscape and of Spanish life—constant themes in Unamuno—

of which poems like *Castilla* and *Salamanca* may serve as examples, we find the polemical tone of his ballads and sonnets written in exile; together with the metaphorical exuberance of *El Cristo de Velázquez,* the sober language of some of his lyrical sonnets; and in contrast to the fanciful ingeniousness of many of his plays on words and rhythms, inspired by a dry humor, we find the bareness of many of his verses, in which artifice is reduced to a minimum. It is no less characteristic of the immense variety of his poetical inspiration, always bearing, however, an unmistakable, personal accent, that this poet, apparently so abstract and intellectual, has written some of the most beautiful verses in contemporary Spanish poetry when inspired by very human themes of personal feeling.

Power, lyricism, ideas and feeling, a very rich vocabulary, varied forms and rhythms, ingenious plays upon words and ideas (*conceptos*), the aggressive words of a polemicist, the apocalyptical vision of a poet, and tender humanity—all that is Unamuno, rich, changing, indefinable. He is not an easy poet, but he will always be—in spite of a certain hard quality, and an occasional lapse into harshness and prosiness—one of the great poets of the Spanish language wherever that language is spoken.

Unamuno's narrative and dramatic work is not so well known as his essays and poetry. It is not, however, less original. Unamuno's strong personality is present in every page which he wrote, and his novels, stories, and plays have an intensity which is heightened by their bareness of form, their lack of realistic detail and of anything which might distract attention from the story—which is almost always a study of human passions—or from the dramatic theme.

Unamuno divided his novels into two groups. In the first, he placed his first novel, which is also one of his earliest works: *Paz en la guerra.* . . . In the other, he placed the rest of his novels, which are very different from the first in technique and choice of theme: [*Amor y pedagogía, Niebla, Abel Sánchez, Tres novelas ejemplares, La tía Tula,* and *San Manuel Bueno, mártir*]. . . . (pp. 14-16)

The theme of *Paz en la guerra* is the siege of Bilbao in 1874 by the Carlist troops. . . . It relates the events of the siege, merging them with an evocation of the sufferings of the two factions and with the recollections of his own childhood. Moreover, Unamuno, through the anxieties of Pachico Zabalbide, reveals the perplexities of his own youth, which continued to harass him throughout his life. In its lyrical tone, its delineation of character from within rather than from without, and in the ideas which it conveys, this novel differs radically from the realistic novels of the nineteenth century, although superficially its technique retains a certain resemblance to them. In every field, Unamuno was an initiator, and *Paz en la guerra* is one of the first, if not the first, Spanish novel with a truly contemporary spirit.

In his later novels, Unamuno abandoned entirely all semblance of realistic technique. . . . (p. 16)

[*Amor y pedagogía*] is the result of Unamuno's rebellion against the scientific spirit. The hero, Avito Carrascal, wishes to marry a strong, healthy woman who will give him a son who will be a genius, but love plays a trick on him and he falls in love with the friend of the woman he had chosen. He marries, a son is born (Apolodoro), and Avito subjects him to so scientific a plan of education that his life is ruined. Apolodoro ends by hanging himself. Unamuno presents the characters and incidents with a dry humor, without ever falling directly into satire,

although his intention undoubtedly approaches the satirical. The disquieting questions which nourish Unamuno's thought remain unsettled. Does Avito learn from his failure? Is this the logical end of the scientist? Can science be the mistress of life?

A minor character, don Fulgencio Entrambosmares, Apolodoro's teacher, expresses the doubts which are always present in the author's essays and poetry. At times he speaks with the anguished cry which years later will serve as a stylistic device in the philosophical digressions in *Del sentimiento trágico de la vida.* (pp. 16-17)

Unamuno's next novel or ''nivola,'' *Niebla,* is one of his most original, and the one that has been most translated. . . . A German critic has called it ''a fantastic novel,'' and Werner Fite, ''a tragi-comedy.'' It has also been said that it is a precursor of Pirandello's *Six Characters in Search of an Author* in representing the independence of fictional characters with respect to their creators. All this is true. It is the most philosophical and intellectual of Unamuno's novels, and at the same time one of the most human. Its humor is more subtle than that of *Amor y pedagogía.* (p. 17)

In *Niebla,* love appears arm in arm with chance and the mystery of physical attraction, represented in this case by Eugenia's eyes, which seem to stir and attract the apathetic Augusto. . . . The unexpected encounter with those eyes decides his fate and his tragedy. As always in Unamuno, it is life which triumphs.

*Niebla* abounds in ingenious conceptions and paradoxes. The whole novel rests on an idea that is eminently paradoxical, as Unamuno's ideas regularly are. (p. 18)

[With *Abel Sánchez*] Unamuno introduces a different type of novel. The two which precede it take their conception, one might say, from ideas, and are of an intellectual and humorous character. All of those which follow turn upon intense and forthright passions. They have a tragic, human character. They are personal dramas, analyses of the ego in characters which, because of their very humanness, and their being dominated by a passion, almost turn into condensed, abstract beings. These characters are all impelled by the urge, so characteristic of Unamuno's philosophy, to assert their personalities even at the cost of destroying those who surround them, and at times of destroying themselves.

That is what happens, in one form or another, in the novelettes collected in *Tres novelas ejemplares.* The three are variations of the same theme, an assertion of will-power. In [*Dos madres* and *El marqués de Lumbría*], that will, or wilfullness, is incarnated in the woman and centers upon the maternal instinct which impels the principal feminine characters to incredible acts. (pp. 18-19)

The last of these three novels, *Nada menos que todo un hombre* (dramatized by Julio de Hoyos with the title of *Todo un hombre*), is the most intense. Here, as the title indicates, it is the man, Alejandro Gómez, who personifies the dominating will. Out of love, but with complete disregard for sentimentality, he seeks to impose his ego on the weak and sentimental Julia, his wife, and brings her finally to adultery, almost to insanity, and at last to death. (p. 19)

After *Tres novelas ejemplares* came *La tía Tula,* inspired, like two of the novelettes, by the maternal instinct, which now appears glorified in the figure of a strong and firm woman, one who is all love, incapable of meanness. Unamuno's novels are mellowing, becoming more human. . . .

This process, which we may call a humanizing and at the same time a poetizing of Unamuno's novels, tempering the passionate and tragic tone which culminates in *Abel Sánchez,* is fully perceptible in *San Manuel Bueno, mártir,* the last and perhaps the finest of all his great novels. (p. 20)

In *San Manuel Bueno, mártir,* Unamuno returns to the use of natural scenery, and to a lyrical, descriptive tone. The background of landscape throughout the book, and the intimate feelings of the principal character raise the novel, without loss of reality, to a poetic plane. (p. 21)

[Unamuno's] dramatic works are related to his novels, although they are much fewer and on the whole less important. The reader will have noticed that all the novels which we have examined have an eminently dramatic character and are, strictly speaking, dramas, presenting with tragic intensity the conflict of souls and the clash of passions. They are, moreover, predominantly in the form of dialogues or monologues—what Unamuno used to call *"autodiálogos"*—in order to emphasize their dramatic significance.

What he does in his theatrical works—*Fedra, El otro, El hermano Juan o el mundo es teatro*—is to adapt the novel technique to the requirements of stage production. His dialogue is the same sharp-edged dialogue of his novels; his tone, that of overpowering passions; and his themes, eminently tragic: the classic theme of Euripides, Seneca, and Racine in *Fedra;* the theme of the seducer in *El hermano Juan o el mundo es teatro;* and of a personality asserting itself through a Cain-like hatred and envy in *El otro.* This last theme is directly related to that of *Abel Sánchez,* except that here the hatred arises between twin brothers. Because of this resemblance, *El otro* is of particular interest to the reader of this novel, of which the play is, in a way, a sequel and a further development. (p. 22)

In regard to style, Unamuno's narrative work shares the general characteristics of his language, one of the richest, most complex, and difficult to study in all Spanish literature. The style of his novels, like that of his essays or poems, is always dynamic, fraught with suggestion, and almost electrifying in its tense, abrupt dialogues; with short, aggressive sentences, numerous exclamations, and perturbing interrogations—a poetic and philosophical style. (pp. 24-5)

> Amelia A. de del Río and Ángel del Río "Introduction" (copyright 1947 by Holt, Rinehart and Winston, Inc.; reprinted by permission of Holt, Rinehart and Winston, Publishers, CBS College Publishing), Abel Sanchez *by Miguel de Unamuno, edited by Angel del Río and Amelia de del Río, Holt, Rinehart and Winston, 1947 (and reprinted by Holt, Rinehart and Winston, 1968), pp. 5-29.*

**RICARDO GULLÓN** (essay date 1967)

Paradoxically, the principle that acting leads to feeling could be stated this way: the more a character acts out a role, the better he affirms his reality. In the extensive introduction to his play *El hermano Juan ("Brother Juan"),* Unamuno specifies: "All the ideal greatness of Don Juan Tenorio, his whole universal and external—that is, historical—reality, consists of his being the most eminently theatrical, representational, historical character there is; of the fact that he is always acting, always playing himself."

The Don-less Juan in Unamuno's play lives, or allows his life to be lived, in the theater, which is his world. He is both at the heart of the action and apart from it, like an airplane pilot flying perilously in the hurricane's eye to gauge its strength. He is the center because he is surrounded, hedged in, squeezed by the others, and pressed on. He feels himself to be the axis on which events turn, yet at the same time he feels impelled by them. While the others come and go, he stays where he is, awaiting them perhaps, knowing beforehand when they will come and what for.

These "others"—Inés, Elvira, Antonio, Benito, and so on— give rise to disconnected scenes in which Juan participates without committing himself. A spectator as much as an actor, he seems to watch with relative curiosity the events woven around him, but always keeps his distance. Sometimes he is not sure of anything, not even of his feelings. Seeing him move about in the vagueness of a legend that has shrunken into a trivial Don Juanism, one could well ask him, just as a patient in the Sarriá sanatorium once asked Unamuno himself, if he was really the authentic one, "the real one, and not the one they're always writing about." And the character in the play would be quick to ask himself, as his author did, "whether the poor lunatic was not right," because he realizes that his awareness of himself is a reflection of what is written about him, or of the role he plays.

Is there any other "authentic" self? Unamuno himself replied by asserting that among the possible men one may be, only God knows which is the authentic one. We must resign ourselves to what is within our reach, to discover, or at least try to discover, reality in our playing of roles. (pp. 139-40)

[Juan] is not unprecedented. Unamuno had already created a character concerned only with his own inner life, in his first novel: *Paz en la guerra ("Peace in war")*. . . . Don Joaquín, a pious old man, considered his soul a field where battles were being fought against the devil, and the civil war that was then bleeding his country dry seemed to him to be of little moment when compared with such transcendent warfare. As grave and sensational as events in the exterior world were, they seemed monotonous against "the inexhaustible variety" of a conscience in motion.

In the final analysis Juan, like Unamuno, depends on no audience other than himself: Juan the spectator watching Juan the person exhibiting himself in the performance. Brother Juan is not trying to convince an audience: he is trying to convince himself. He plays his role to fill the emptiness of his soul; and if he turns to the others, it is to look for a reflection of the legend he would like to incarnate. If they believe in him, they will literally bring him to life, just as the characters do out of whose acting he is constituted. The first thing he says when the play opens is that he simply cannot understand himself. Naturally! That is a never-ending process. What was his life like before the play began? Does he have a secret? The others believe he does, and they act on this assumption, even though all along they suspect the truth, which he neither hides nor denies. He says: "In this theater, which is the world itself, everyone is born condemned to a role, and everyone must play it for life."

In *Niebla ("Mist"),* the protagonist, Augusto Pérez, had posed the same problem in one of his monologues addressed to his dog, Orfeo: "All we do is play each one our role. All of us, characters, masks, actors! No one suffers or enjoys what he says and expresses and maybe believes he is enjoying and suffering; otherwise life would be impossible. Basically, we are quite unmoved." This tranquillity is disconcerting in Brother

Juan, whose will to be is not strong enough to induce him to act. Like Augusto, he is conscious that his anxieties and concerns are essentially figments of his imagination. (pp. 140-41)

*Brother Juan* is one of those rare works in which soul and idea coincide. Long before writing the play, Unamuno had said: "For each soul there is an idea that belongs to it and is something like its formula; and souls and ideas move in search of each other." In this instance they have met and fused to the point of inseparability: what impels him to be incessantly playing a role is his soul's desire to be in accordance with what the idea is. The will to identification is nothing more or less than the ardent wish to create the man according to the idea that turns into the animating project of our lives. Therefore, whoever plays a role lives, because his acting proceeds from his desire to be and to seem in accordance with project and idea. Indifference to the role playing of others has a positive and almost dynamic aspect: Juan will accept from the others what is useful for his own needs, and will ignore or look askance at the rest. In dealing with them and with the world, he will apply one inflexible criterion, that of their utility for the constitution of his *I*. This throws a new light on Juan's willingness to let women do as they wish with his image: his willingness is a subtle control mechanism, and his indifference is a weapon to help him get what he wants—himself.

Juan applies his criterion spontaneously; and as he does, he reveals the Unamunian texture, the projection of Unamuno's spirit in that of the character. Unamuno knew what he was acting out and why, as he dreamt his dream of himself. The indifferentiation of living, dreaming, and acting is straight Unamuno, as is his feeling of being on stage, his longing to be dreamt in their dreams by others and to leave behind a name— a name in which scattered longings adhere and take form; a name to make comprehensible and definable the substance, the idea that will give his soul authenticity or an eagerness for authenticity, and at the same time, fill it with anguish. He cannot have one without the other: he cannot achieve authentic being without struggle, and that struggle will cause doubting and suffering—suffering because the play or dream of life leads to an end that supposes the extinction of the dreaming actor. Death definitively ends the drama—and the man. But isn't it then childish to sustain the prolonged effort to live by playing oneself, inventing a being destined to disappear when the curtain falls on the last act? Isn't creating oneself for nothing and nothingness a mad enterprise? In the uncertainty caused by these questions, anguish burgeons; and to overcome it, there is the precarious consolation of survival in the myth.

The existential question remains unanswered or, to be more precise, open. Death, the final and irrevocable scene, is not an answer, although it does help us form an opinion, which is the most we should risk in replying to the "Who am I?" of Brother Juan, Unamuno, or our own selves. The mystery will continue to exist, because proper to it is its insolubility; if it had a "solution," it would be not a mystery but a problem and within the reach of intelligences capable of solving it.

At the end, Elvira asks Juan who he is "really"—in reality, not in fiction. There was only one possible response: "Do you think I know?" And he bursts out at her in the unmistakable style of his author: "We are nothing less than every inch a theater!" Not "every inch a man," like Alejandro Gómez, the character in one of Unamuno's most famous stories, but a theater, a theater in the mind, the stage of our drama where our shadow and the shadows of others pass and act in the exchange of auto-dialogues which constitutes life. Since he is

a reincarnation of a theatrical figure, Juan's consistency can be only theatrical: he is really only a fiction, and in fiction he seeks truth. He discovers the devil, Satan, and discovers him to be a character playing a role. And God, can he also be a character in the play? Is that His substance? If so, the only truth is performed truth, and it lasts only as long as the performance. Appearance, as Unamuno said over and over, is the foundation, the inner core, all there is.

"A stage of ghosts" is the term Unamuno used to define both life and the theater. In a play he planned to write but never did (*Maese Pedro* was to be its title), the protagonist was to engage in a dialogue with the marionettes of his show just as Juan, or Unamuno, does with the linear figures in the present play. At the end of *La tía Tula,* the protagonist Tula murmured the confession implicit in *Brother Juan:* "Marionettes all!" And in her desolate conclusion, in the depths of despair—for that "all" includes Tula as well as you, my reader, and me— I believe I detect the expression of a secret, abysmal, irrational belief; for if we are puppets or marionettes, it means that there is someone moving the strings, and that the someone, the creator of the farce and the puppets, could convoke them— and convoke us—later on for a new and lasting performance. (pp. 152-55)

*Ricardo Gullón, "The Soul on Stage," in* Unamuno: Creator and Creation, *edited by José Rubia Barcia and M. A. Zeitlin (© 1967 by The Regents of the University of California; reprinted by permission of the University of California Press), University of California Press, 1967, pp. 139-55.*

**J. F. TULL, JR.** (essay date 1970)

Spanish authors of the last two centuries, like many of their counterparts in other Western countries, have been dealing with the themes of both psychological and metaphysical alienation while, generally, not attempting to label them as such. . . .

But it was in the social, political and spiritual crisis of Spain at the turn of the century that writers came to the fore who spoke, in the clearest terms, of the intimately related concepts of psychological and metaphysical estrangement. (p. 27)

[It was] for Unamuno, a figure who transcends the notion of generations and who speaks, at one and the same time, as both modern and universal man, to synthesize and spell out in his poetry, essays and, especially, in his "nivolas" the dilemma of the individual "of flesh and bones," as he was fond of saying, alienated both psychologically and metaphysically in the twentieth century. In this study, I should like to single out, as examples of this synthesis, three characters in the three "nivolas," *Niebla,* ("Film" [that dims the sight]), *Nada menos que todo un hombre,* ("Every Inch a Man"), and *San Manuel Bueno, mártir,* ("Saint Immanuel the Good, Martyr"). (p. 28)

The first case in point is that of Augusto Pérez, protagonist of *Niebla,* who suffers both pathological and spiritual alienation. Upon his death, the doctor in attendance remarks under his breath: "Who knows whether Augusto existed or not, especially he himself . . .? The individual is one who knows least of his existence . . . He exists only for others."

The truth is that Augusto did not even appear to exist even for others. As he says in a monologue to his dog, Orfeo: "Many times it has occurred to me to think, Orfeo, that there is no me, and I went through the streets with the impression that other people couldn't see me . . . ." Augusto did exist for some:

for his friend, Victor Goti; for his fiancée, Eugenia, "the woman of the future," as her uncle called her; for Rosario, the young laundress who befriended him; for the servants of his household. Yet it was his good friend, Victor, who advised him to "devour himself," and his fiancée, Eugenia, believed that he existed only as means to secure the money to flee with her lover, Mauricio. Rosario thought that he "must be mad," and the servants could make no sense of his actions.

If we overlook for a moment the ubiquitous presence of Unamuno as creator of the novel, and if we accept Augusto as a fictional being as real as Unamuno himself—(Augusto, in a dramatic scene toward the end of the work asks his creator: "Was it not you who, not once but many times, said that Don Quijote and Sancho are not only as real, but even more real than Cervantes?")—if we accept these two conditions, we can examine Augusto as a prototype not only of the young Spaniard alienated from his society, but also as a typical instance of the psychological alienation of many modern men.

If we were Freudian in approach, we might say that this estrangement began with the early death of Augusto's father and the resultant relationship of emotional dependence on his mother which deprived him of a sense of self and inhibited his relations with others. But here Unamuno, as in most of his works, does not concern himself with describing the details and traumas of the childhood of his characters. Rather, he presents them as adults already moulded in their ways, beings immersed in their particular view of things. In point of fact, the greatest cause of the adult Augusto's existential problems, as is seen throughout *Niebla,* is his concept of the relationship of love. It is very possible that a mature, reciprocated love—not Augusto's concept of love as a mixture of romantic fantasy and physical attraction—might have redeemed him from his alienation, as it did in the case of Alejandro Gómez, in *Nada menos.* For as he himself exclaims to Rosario: "To dream together! Not to be together, each one dreaming his own dream, but dreaming together a single dream!" (pp. 28-9)

The irony is that the alienated man does not fall in love in a fashion that might redeem him. Augusto's "love" for Eugenia begins when "not a dog, but a graceful young woman passed along the street, and like one drawn by a magnet without realizing it, Augusto followed, in pursuit of her eyes." Augusto, "adrift" on the street, fell in love with a woman who proved to be totally incompatible and, in the end, appallingly cruel.

There are other characteristics of the alienated man that appear in Augusto's psychology. As Victor says, he is a "loner," a "little Hamlet." He has few friends, most of them male, and seems able to relate completely only with non-human creatures, in this instance, the stray dog, Orfeo, that he takes off the streets. After a scene in which he learns that Eugenia's lover, Mauricio, knows all about his confession to Rosario and after a succinct letter from Eugenia, informing him that she is leaving with Mauricio, aided by Augusto's generous financial help, the latter's mental state worsens, and the process of further retreat into psychological alienation begins to unfold. The aberrations of Augusto's conduct cause extreme uneasiness in his servants and even in Rosario, who for a moment fears for her life. Totally defeated in his attempts to pierce through the film which has progressively blinded his eyes, Augusto commits suicide.

I say "suicide" because I share the belief of Victor Goti, in his prologue to the novel, that he did so and not that he died

as a whim of his creator. As Augusto's faithful servant, Liduvina, observes after his death: "Well, I think my master got it into his head to die and obviously if one insists on dying, he ends up by doing so." Augusto's suicide is psychic, as in many cases in the "nivolas" of Unamuno. He died as a result of his steadily increasing alienation, and if Unamuno was a God who dictated his death, he did so as an impersonal God who destroyed a man according to the necessities of the latter's own "inner logic," to use Augusto's own words.

"One exists only for others" was the comment of the doctor. I find this observation fallacious. It is true that there is among men a constant interaction which gives them a superficial conception of their social being, but the belief of Augusto on seeing himself in the mirror: "I end up by doubting my own existence . . ." is, on a deeper, metaphysical level, the reaction of an individual who has never experienced the profound, integrated core of his inner self that is the essential inheritance of all men, alienated or fully incorporated in their world.

Julia Yáñez, in *Nada menos,* combines the same aspects of psychological and metaphysical alienation found in *Niebla,* in a slightly different form. For her father, Don Victorino, "a person of very dubious moral background" she and her beauty were the key to his hopes of economic redemption. (pp. 29-30)

Then came her suitors: first, Enrique, "an incipient Don Juan," who sought a way to end his relationship with Julia "once he succeeded in making it known in all of Renada that its sacred regional beauty had admitted him to her window." Next it was Pedro "more stout-hearted" than Enrique, who exclaimed that Julia was mad when she suggested the idea of a mutual suicide pact, an act that would put an end to the maneuverings of her father toward her. . . . Julia believed that her father was capable of selling her favors to [the wealthy landowner] Don Alberto, that, for him, it would not seem a bad idea.

At this point, the *indiano,* Alejandro Gómez, arrived on the scene. He is described by Unamuno as "very willful and very stubborn and very self-centered." He courted Julia and won her hand in marriage. . . . Nevertheless, like her father, he made no display of affection toward her, regarded her as a possession and caused her to ask herself repeatedly "Does he love *me,* or is it only that he wants to show off my beauty?"

Unquestionably, the exclamation "your beauty will cause your ruin!," a thought which obsessed Julia at the beginning of the story, seems to be the key to the understanding of her state of constant emotional and spiritual crisis throughout the work. Like Pedro, Alejandro views Julia as "neurasthenic," and Unamuno confirms the idea of acute psychological stress when he comments, shortly before her death, "All these tortures of her spirit destroyed Julia's life, and she became gravely ill, mentally ill." This mental illness caused her death, a psychic suicide comparable to that of Augusto in *Niebla.* The enigma of Julia's pathological state and consequent death is not clarified by Unamuno and must rest upon interpretation.

At first glance it would seem that Julia's beauty "caused her ruin" and death because of the cruelty and avarice of her father, a sense of betrayal by her suitors, Alejandro's hermetic nature, in other words, because of her relationship with the men she regarded as most important in her life.

There is, however, another interpretation which explains more profoundly Julia's spiritual crisis, her psychic suicide. "This interpretation has to do not only with her beauty, but with her concept of beauty, with her concept of her own being. As has been pointed out, Julia constantly asked herself whether Alejandro loves her or her beauty. And, in similar fashion, when Enrique abandons her, she exclaims, "And he said he loved me! No, he didn't love me, he loved my beauty." After Pedro leaves her, she thinks to herself: "He didn't love me either, he didn't either. They fall in love with my beauty, not with me."

This thorough identification with an internal "ego" separated from her body seems to indicate that Julia suffered from a dualistic alienation between her psyche and her external appearance. She despised her body. . . . In fact, we might conclude that there is not one Julia, complete and integrated, but a woman split in two by an illusory dualism between inward personality and outward physical appearance. Julia is both psychologically and metaphysically alienated because she has not understood and accepted the fusion of corporeal elements and psychic aspects which constitute the totality of every individual and, consequently, she dies.

Spanish criticism of the "Christian atheist," Don Manuel, in *San Manuel Bueno, mártir* has seen in him "the most complete personification of the tormented incredulity of [the work's] author," Unamuno. It has also recognized that Don Manuel's consolation was "to console myself by consoling others, even though the consolation I give them may not be mine." This body of criticism recognizes, moreover, the existential base of Don Manuel's metaphysical anxiety and alienation and his search "to do! to do!," to flee from "idle thoughts, alone," and that, for him, "the truth . . . is perhaps something terrible, something intolerable, something mortal; simple folk could not live with it." The most recent criticism that suggests that Unamuno, with this statement, had repented rather belatedly "for having agitated others with his own religious doubts and anxieties" has been that of Marín, in his introduction to *San Manuel* in *Literatura española, selección.* (pp. 30-1)

I should like to expound, at this point, the hypothesis that both creator and fictional character sensed in this late fruit of Unamuno's literary output intuitive glimpses of the possibility of a resolution of the "tortured incredulity" of both. I make reference, specifically, to the curious juxtaposition of three incidents in the very heart of the story, quoted by Lázaro, brother of the narrator and confidante of Don Manuel.

The first episode that Lázaro relates is a scene at the edge of the omnipresent lake when Don Manuel comments: "This is my greatest temptation." He continues by describing his perpetual combat against a suicidal impulse. The second incident, immediately following, is the scene of the shepherdess, in which Don Manuel says: "Look, it seems as if time had come to an end, as if this shepherdess had been there always, and just as she is, and singing as she is, and as if she were going to continue being there always, as she was before my consciousness began, as she will be when it ends. That shepherdess forms a part, with the rocks, the clouds, the trees, the water, of nature and not history". The juxtaposition of episodes ends with Lázaro's commentary on the day of the snow storm when Don Manuel said: "Have you ever seen, Lázaro, a mystery greater than that of the snow falling in the lake and dying in it . . ."

To me, these three incidents represent three phases in the process of spiritual maturation, intuitive at first, which occur to many individuals, in different cultures and different times, tormented like Don Manuel by incredulity before the meaning of their own existence. In the first episode, I do not believe, with Marín, that the lake represents "the death and oblivion in which men are interred," but rather Don Manuel's intuitive aspiration toward a sublimation—a "suicide," if you will—of his conscious ego, imprisoned until now by his alienation, his doubts and anxieties, into a wider vision of human existence, manifested, as will be seen, in the scene of the shepherdess. The rest which Don Manuel aspires to achieve in his last hours (once again, as *Niebla* and *Nada menos,* a psychically motivated death) is not the rest of oblivion with physical death, but rather the spiritual rest after the individual's conscious ego sees itself not as an isolated object, alienated from a foreign and impersonal universe, but as an integral part of a process which both incorporates and transcends its individual existence.

Unamuno—Don Manuel intuits this interpretation of existence in the moments of the shepherdess and the snow storm. The shepherdess—the man freed from his metaphysical alienation—is outside of history, or of the conventional, linear concept we hold of history and life in general. The shepherdess lives in an eternal present, "as if time had come to an end," in intimate contact with her environment. This is precisely the sensation of existence that Don Manuel has intuited, but has not experienced. It might be added that his constant "via negativa," his "neti neti," the negation which he embraces in his interpretation of life, has led many individuals, paradoxically, to an affirmation of life not as an occasion to "console others", but as an experience which we shall now examine in the incident of the snow storm.

In the storm, the last phase of spiritual development, the snowflake, the individual, senses that he is fused as an integral part of the cosmos. His alienation and incredulity end, not with respect to the convention of a life after death, but rather with respect to the intimate and sometimes ecstatic relationship that exists between the individual and his universe.

We may thus conclude that Unamuno intuited in these three key incidents the possibility of a concept, a feeling of existence, that is immensely wider for the individual alienated from the rest of nature by his incredulity. Yet Unamuno, like Don Manuel, never achieved the full sensation of this vision of the world simply because he could never completely "let go," in the words of the French psychiatrist, Hubert Benoit; he could not go beyond his concept of human personality as an ego imprisoned and alienated. He did not recognize totally the abandonment of this ego in a "suicide" which, again paradoxically, results in a sense of the eternal present and an awareness of man's fusion with the "lake" which is the cosmos.

Unamuno, in these three "nivolas," wrote of modern man's psychological alienation and universal man's metaphysical alienation because he had experienced both to the depths of his being. In fact, as may be seen from this study, it is very difficult to draw the line between the two aspects of alienation, the best solution possibly being to recognise that they are conventional distinctions made by an intellect that is habituated to categorizing and defining. In any event, . . . while alienation as a term is in danger of abuse, as a literary theme in the hands of an author with the creative powers of an Unamuno, it can strike us with particular force that this is the way that many men "of flesh and bones" live and have lived. (pp. 31-2)

*J. F. Tull, Jr., "Alienation, Psychological and Metaphysical, in Three 'Nivolas' of Unamuno," in* The Humanities Association Bulletin, *Vol. XXI, No. 1, Winter, 1970, pp. 27-33.*

**FRANCES WYERS**  (essay date 1976)

[Miguel de Unamuno] is an exemplary figure in our age. The violent contradictions of his thought reflect and predict the violent contradictions of our culture. The frenzied shifts and turns of his conceptual formulations are a model of contemporary intellectual disjunction and splintered feelings. His doubts about his own existence, his frantic pursuit of the self, and the loneliness of that solipsistic quest, have come to be the common experience of many. Unamuno's works give a vivid picture of the sense of separation and frightening isolation that are central and pervasive themes in modern literature. Although Unamuno denied (sometimes by a paradoxical affirmation) and obfuscated his internal conflicts, he was often enough aware of his evasive strategies; his writings constitute an extensive and almost lucid record of internal cleavage. (p. ix)

One of the most striking features of Unamuno's thought is his apparent inability or unwillingness to come to grips with the feelings that most troubled him. He made much of his religious doubts, his yearning for faith, and his desire for immortality. . . . Although religion and the problem of personality are certainly the ostensible topics of much of what he wrote, we sense underneath them a personal struggle that does not rise to the level of conscious expression. Unamuno talks a great deal about faith, doubt, the mystery of the self, the problematic relation between the real and the fictitious, but one looks in vain for the intellectual ordering that would tie together these themes in any comprehensible way. Of course, everyone knows and repeats that Unamuno was not and did not want to be a systematic philosopher. His often proclaimed aversion to system and dogma (for him almost synonyms) and his manifest pride in disorder would seem to tell us that we can hardly fault him for what he quite defiantly chose not to do.

The opposition to systematization or to strict intellectual patterning could have taken other forms; Unamuno might have cultivated the kind of playful subversiveness found in the prose of Antonio Machado or Jorge Luis Borges, or he might have abandoned the essay entirely and devoted himself to fiction, theater, and poetry. But he produced a prodigious number of articles and longer prose works of a loosely philosophical nature in which, while denying the value of coherent argument, he tries to convince the reader of the truth of what he says. Although we should not ignore the purely economic side of this productivity (that most Spanish writers relied heavily on the fees paid by journals and newspapers must be considered in any evaluation of the prose of the period), Unamuno apparently also felt a great personal need to communicate with his readers through this medium. He clearly conceived of his essays (and of all his literature) as a way of baring his soul and exposing to others his inmost desires and torments. Because he saw the essay as an emotional outpouring he naturally took very few pains in its construction; they all more or less follow the principle of the one titled "A lo que salga"—the rule of chance. He composed with a determined disregard for structure and coherence; frequently enough, one can scarcely find any single unifying topic so that the title seems an arbitrary afterthought. The reader of Unamuno's essays is plunged into a chaos of paradoxical affirmations and negations; he feels he cannot touch ground or find any path to a clearing in the tangle of prose. Eventually it becomes evident that all the conceptual shifts and turns obey principles that are never enunciated. Nothing can be taken at face value and we must search for an undisclosed fabric of meaning that the author seems to be almost purposely obfuscating. So the soul-baring and the exhibitionist stance is also a cover-up; the actor, as Unamuno says in one of his essays, acts in order to conceal his true self.

This simultaneous showing and hiding explains the oddly disjunctive quality of his writing. True concerns are replaced by an enormous verbal mass that obscures or, at best, hints at what lies beneath. There is, in other words, a marked separation between what he talks about and what he says.

This duplicity of style and thought also explains the lack of any genuine intellectual evolution; what we perceive in its stead is an increasingly complicated psychological division. Although at least one critic goes so far as to argue that all of Unamuno's contradictions would disappear if we read his works in strictly chronological order, I see at most a very general shift in emphasis. And contradictions abound even in a single essay. Throughout all his works we find a persistent contrariness, an almost desperate need to set up oppositions and then collapse them into a single entity, to take sides and then switch, to deny and then deny the denial or to assert that what was denied was really affirmed. The reader is confounded and ensnared in a rhetoric of perpetual self-reversal.

As for the consistency of his themes, from the 1897 Diary to his death we find him worrying the same ones (he often said that great writers play out only one or two basic themes). Over and over he returns to the same subject. But the consistency is a mere surface phenomenon because his concepts and verbal images continually alter; a careful reading of the texts shows that a single word or topic may represent a series of significations that are often mutually exclusive. These continual transmutations give his language a curiously autonomous quality, as if certain key phrases at one moment set in motion one train of thought, at another, one that is quite distinct. The intellectual coherence that many of his admirers like to find in his works rests on this verbal illusion. The same words are set to quite different tunes which sometimes are played simultaneously in an essay so that one must imagine two or more intersecting scores.

The critics who have discussed the contradictory nature of his writings have either explained it in terms of a rationalist/mystical dichotomy in his personality, attributable to a biographical event (the loss of faith during his university years) or have spoken of hypocrisy and inauthenticity. . . . In a way both are correct. But I think a more accurate description would be of a self-deceiving consciousness that does not recognize the true roots of its despair. Thus the critics who turn Unamuno's existential conflict into an existentialist philosophy confuse the symptom with its philosophical formulation. Most of Unamuno's prose makes clear what Sartre meant by "bad faith".

Yet Unamuno himself appears to recognize his elaborate and devious facade for what it is. "I never reveal my thinking more clearly to myself than when I am trying to conceal it." Self-deception would here seem to become a means of self-disclosure. And it is, in a sense. But what he conceals . . . is not really the same thing as what he reveals; there is always a gap between the confession and the hidden thought. The same might be said of Unamuno's well-known fondness for paradox. Unamuno's paradoxes are the result of an unexamined, almost frantic, effort to tie together opposing aspirations. They are expressions of an emotional ambivalence that he would pass off in the guise of an intellectual riddle. This becomes evident when, as so often happens, the paradox suddenly dissolves and one term is absorbed into its opposite. Coalescence replaces contradiction. (pp. xv-xvii)

In *Del sentimiento trágico de la vida,* and in several other places as well, Unamuno wrote that the inner biography of a man is what explains most about his philosophy. . . . We do not have to look far in Unamuno's life for the emotional correlates of these conceptual gyrations. Unamuno was very much aware of the discontinuities in his own life and they evidently caused him considerable uneasiness. He had been a Christian and then an agnostic. The socialist concerned with the problems of this world suddenly found himself looking for consolation in the other. The failure to achieve it sent him once more in search of renown. At any moment in this series of transformations he could not help but remember that he had felt otherwise, that he was, as he so often said, "el otro", the other, another— the rationalist or the Catholic. And, he always added, if one is another, he is not himself. Being another means "ceasing to be". Change, for Unamuno, is a kind of death.

One might take the biographical considerations a little further back. We move beyond available information and into the zone of speculation. Unamuno must have experienced very early in life an intense insecurity about his very being. His works show us a man who seems to doubt that he is there at all. In an effort to counter that frightful possibility he seeks to affirm the solidity of his self, his personality. Throughout his writings he speaks of an inner substance, an inner core, and his language is colored with nostalgia and longing. When he claims that the soul is the most substantial part of a man and that the body is a mere husk or shell, he expresses a disdain for the visible and the concrete in favor of an invisible "concreteness" that can exist nowhere. But that impossible substance is exactly what he aims at—his own substance, his own inner core. Unamuno tried constantly to grasp his own self. He imagines it as something stable and solid. Characteristically he thinks of it in physical terms, firm as bedrock, yet sensually inviting and throbbing with life. He speaks of searching out one's soul and embracing it, rubbing up against it and feeling its substance and warmth. Although this never quite becomes an explicit topic, it is clear that he seeks union with himself, a kind of magical self-copulation in a hidden and invisible place. Behind Unamuno's preferences for certain gut words—blood, bones, marrow, palpitating entrails—stands a private mythology about a secret world to which he longs to gain access and a secret substance which is his very own.

Inner reality also represents a refuge from the external world. He escapes inwards. But Unamuno is even less explicit about this aspect of his goal. Indeed, nowhere does he fully describe for his readers the notion of the inner self; one must piece it together on the basis of passages scattered throughout his work. It is not part of an intellectual scheme but a kind of wishful fantasy that appears in moments of need. Unamuno developed no psychological theory but he did dramatize—sometimes as if unaware—the essential features of his own psychic life.

The need to take possession of his self also found a contrary form—the outward self that Unamuno longed to get hold of and to see ("If one could only see oneself from without!" he wrote in his Diary). He lusted for fame not so much in order to perpetuate himself as to acquire a visible and tangible self. He would become his own legend. He would make himself an image in the eyes of others and then get back this reflection— a pseudo-substance—in their admiring looks. He thought he could achieve an identity in and through his readers. But the legendary self is visible; it exists in the world subject to the judgements of others, and we have seen that one of the functions of the notion of inwardness is protection from the external world and, ultimately, from the gaze of others. What is visible and external can be appropriated by others; the legend can turn out to be a way of losing the self. Usually Unamuno's search for fame calls up the counter-movement of retreat inwards. But he cannot long be satisfied with what is, after all, only an imaginary internal substance. So he veers from one to the other.

Longing for something solid and unchangeable, Unamuno searches for a self, sometimes within, sometimes without. To the flux and uncertainty of experience he opposes the notion of stability and permanence. Yet the fulfillment of either wish would also mean its destruction. A totally private self has no contact with the world and, as a pure subjectivity, loses the very "substance" that is craved; a self created through fame becomes detached from the life that feeds it. In both cases the image he pursues alienates him from lived experience—from himself and from others. Unamuno's wishes only heighten the fear of the void. In the Diary he several times described his terror of non-being as a consequence of the aim of self-possession. "Would not an eternity of solitude, alone with one's void, be more horrible than nothingness? Since you have thought only of yourself and searched only for yourself . . . you will be with yourself and only yourself for all eternity, with your inner world, your senses closed to the external one, and thus you will sink into your own nothingness and have it for eternal company." Realizing full well that the fixity he dreamed of could exist only outside of life, he feared it at the same time that he wished for it. The fear sometimes pushed him to a complete self-renunciation; then he longed to lose himself in his people or his readers, in nature, in eternity, in God, in unconsciousness. Death would be his mother and his bride (the protagonist's vision at the end of the play *El hermano Juan*).

Two patterns of oscillation can be traced in his works, the one including the other: the first alternates between, on the one hand, the search for a solid inner core and, on the other, the wish to grasp the self as an image in the eyes of others; the second moves between the dream of self-possession and the dream of self-dissolution. He sometimes desires the very thing he most fears. The feeling of alientation makes him long for union, yet the dread of being submerged by the world (or God) sends him back in pursuit of a lonely and constricted identity. This double set of reversing mechanisms is in perpetual motion because each wish inevitably calls up its contrary.

Unamuno was aware of his inner division but he was not aware of its true polarities nor of the way they functioned in his thoughts and feelings. Instead of confronting the specific nature of his contradictions, he described them in terms that were much in fashion among the '98 writers in their discussions of the crisis of Spanish culture and the problem of national personality; he spoke of the dichotomy between action and contemplation. "These are my two great longings, action and repose. I have within me, and doubtless all men do, two men, one active, and one contemplative, one warlike and one pacific, one enamored of agitation, the other of calm." . . . What Unamuno does here is make use of a ready-made formula that has very little to do with the complicated shifts between the fear of insubstantiality, the craving for personal substance or external image and the opposite self-negating desire for dissolution and absorption. Nor does he come any closer to an accurate picture of his dramatic imbalance in his many references to the war between reason and sentiment, heart and head: "I do not want to find inner peace in harmonies, concordances, and compromises that lead to inert stability; I do not want my heart to make peace with my head, but both to do battle with each other . . . I am, and want to continue to be, an antinomic, dualistic spirit . . . my whole life moves by a principle of inner contradiction.'' This description too simplifies and displaces the real contradiction and turns it into a romantic duel between equally respected antagonists. The claim that he shuns peace and harmony is typical of Unamuno's continual effort to make his suffering a proof of his solidity, strength, and superiority, an effort which underlies the whole conception of *Del sentimiento trágico de la vida.* The apparent and prideful acceptance of the inner war is, however, belied by every page in which Unamuno attempts to fuse contraries and to turn reality into a dream-like fiction.

The action/contemplation duality has provided several critics with a model of psychological division; they speak of an ''agonic'' and a contemplative Unamuno or of a man who retained in some way his childhood religious faith while professing publicly his doubts; they refer to a clash between an original disposition (what Unamuno always referred to as his childhood self) and a subsequent intellectual and/or histrionic development. These critics see a basic stratum of personality overlaid with contrary attitudes and they do not move beyond the fact of alternating positions. But the supposedly underlying childhood self, the contemplative one, is clearly as much a creation of Unamuno's fears and internal opposition as the self that seeks its confirmation in fame. Indeed, Unamuno's whole concern with religion must have sprung out of the need to support an originally precarious sense of being. Everything that he wrote about God, from the Diary to *La agonía del cristianismo,* indicates that his principal concern was finding some guarantee for personal immortality. God's primary if not only function for Unamuno is the maintenance and perpetuation of individual existence. The faith he lost must have itself evolved out of an early and great fear of non-being. Its loss aggravated an already desperate need.

Unamuno's works do not show us an ''agonic'' writer who sometimes slips into a prior mode but a person who veers ceaselessly between mutually exclusive and ultimately self-defeating aims. Yet the contrary aims have a common root—the fear of insubstantiality, a primary doubt about the very existence of the self. It is this common root which makes inevitable the frenzied and dizzying fluctuations. Dreading annihilation he devises protective images that turn out to menace him with the very destruction he flees from. So he darts back and forth among them, sometimes shifting course in the middle of an argument or jumping from one level of opposition (inner self/outer self) to the other (possession of self/loss of self).

Of course Unamuno knew very well his terror of nothingness; he referred to it over and over. He made it the core of his book *Del sentimiento trágico de la vida* in which his personal dilemma is elevated to an ontological conflict. Yet though he says there that every philosophy has its roots in the author's emotional life, he does not really describe the concrete connections between his own feelings and their conceptualizations. Instead, he remains on the level of general emotional antitheses—reason and sentiment, heart and head, and, more ominously, ''all or nothing''. Unamuno is unable to make explicit the links between his fears and the ideological and verbal maneuvers employed to overcome them.

The strategies are apparent but they do not seem to be controlled by the author. Unamuno talks about his pain, but the causes of that pain surface on their own; they become evident in spite of him, in spite of the intended or apparent thrust of his declarations. (pp. xviii-xxi)

In his fictional works Unamuno seems in general clearer about his own meanings. Yet many of them too reveal strange cross purposes and apparent reversals; his own comments about them in prefaces or subsequent references are sometimes totally disconcerting because they express attitudes which run counter to those that emerge from the fictions themselves.

That Unamuno became such an important figure in the Hispanic world is due in part to the relative isolation of Spanish from European culture since the seventeenth century. He brought before Spain's small reading public certain central intellectual and existential concerns of the late nineteenth and early twentieth centuries. It is true that he wrote about them in the somewhat anachronistic language of religious faith and doubt and that when he approached ''the problem of personality'' his own egocentricity (which he always defended) sometimes obscured the real philosophical issues. The most serious failing of his work is its complicated deviousness; yet that is also one source of its interest. Unamuno the thinker and essayist gives way to Unamuno as a personality that embodies and dramatizes certain contemporary modes of intellectual and emotional disjunction. He is neither the first nor the last writer to formulate a mystique of inwardness and to deal with the contrary pulls between an inaccessible inner truth and the deceits of actions aimed only at impressing others. His work is best viewed as what Unamuno himself called an ''exemplary novel''. (pp. xxi-xxii)

> *Frances Wyers, ''Introduction: The Divided Self,''*
> *in her* Miguel de Unamuno: The Contrary Self *(©*
> *by Tamesis Books Limited, 1976), Tamesis Books,*
> *1976, pp. ix-xxii.*

### DEBRA HARPER LOVE    (essay date 1979)

[Walt Whitman and Miguel de Unamuno] held parallel beliefs concerning the utility of language in achieving a higher sense of spiritual identity while living in the three-dimensional world, in assuring the perpetuation of the thoughts of the souls of all men in the collective memory of future mankind, and in establishing the individual historical and spiritual identity of the poet himself so that his thoughts might live on in the minds of those who read his works after his death.

In the philosophy of Whitman and Unamuno, the soul of man is given its identity through birth, at which time the soul begins one step in its long journey toward immortality in the Absolute. Man may accelerate the process of achieving perfection for his soul, thus moving one step closer to immortality, by exercising the intuitive faculty through the use of words. Language and literature stimulate the imagination, making objects real. By naming objects, the poet can establish a 'oneness' with them, creating reality, and thus wholeness for himself by bringing the spirit of the objects into direct relationship with his own spirit. Language makes possible the absorption of all things, which contributes toward the further development of the spiritual identity. (pp. 66-7)

Unamuno asserts his belief in the power of words to evoke the imagination to create reality in *Tragic Sense of Life:* 'Is it not written in the Scriptures that God creates with His word—that is to say, with his thought—and that by this word, by His word, He made everything that exists?' In 'Democratic Vistas,' Whitman expresses this same belief—that all things are created by words in the imagination, that objects are not real until they are given existence in the human mind. For Whitman, words create a reality that is otherwise impossible. . . . For Unamuno, also, the reality created by words of thought is the actual reality. In *Tragic Sense of Life,* he states that 'Language is that which gives us reality, and not as a mere vehicle of reality, but as its true flesh, of which all the rest, dumb or inarticulate representation, is merely the skeleton.'

Language is essential as a stimulus for the imagination. Without words which invoke images in the mind, nothing exists; and if an object does not exist for a person, he cannot absorb it into himself, and he cannot achieve that sense of wholeness which contributes toward the perfection of his soul. (p. 67)

Ultimately, Whitman and Unamuno use the wonder of words to attribute consciousness to things so that they may absorb them and feel them within. In *Tragic Sense of Life,* Unamuno says that, 'Proceeding from ourselves, from our own human consciousness, the only consciousness which we feel from within, and in which feeling is identical with being, we attribute some sort of consciousness, . . . to all living things. . . .' In much of Whitman's poetry, and specifically in his search for identity in 'Song of Myself,' he uses catalogues in which he names people and objects, in total disregard for time and space; by naming these things, he is making them come alive in his imagination, feeling them within. This feeling which Unamuno and Whitman have is that of absorption, which contributes to the wholeness of their spiritual identities, enabling them to move up the spiritual ladder toward 'oneness' with the Absolute and immortality of the human soul.

In addition to facilitating the movement toward perfection of the individual soul, language assures a form of 'general immortality' for the souls of men in the collective memory of mankind; the thought of men of the past is to be found in the language of today, and the thought of the present will live on in the minds and language of future men. The basis for this belief in 'general immortality' for human souls may be found in the works of Whitman and Unamuno, in which each man asserts that the thought of today is a culmination of all past thoughts, expressed in the language of the world. . . . In *Tragic Sense of Life,* Unamuno asserts that 'When we think, we are obliged to set out, whether we know it not and whether we will or not, from what has been thought by others who came before us and who environ us.' He states in *The Agony of Christianity* that language is essential because, 'In order to express a feeling or thought that sprouts from the roots of our soul, we must express it in the language of the world . . .'

Language, which Unamuno describes as the spoken thought, is a product of the past. We should 'Examine language, for language carries along with it, under pressure of the centuries, the secular sediment which is the richest alluvium of the collective spirit.' Whitman alludes to this same belief when he says in 'A Backward Glance O'er Travel'd Roads,' 'As America fully and fairly construed is the legitimate result and evolutionary outcome of the past, so I would dare to claim for my verse.' . . . The thoughts of mankind live on in later generations in the language of the world, and the man of today will achieve a form of immortality through stimulating the thought of later generations. (pp. 68-9)

Stemming from the belief that the souls of the persons who utter thought will be preserved by language in the minds of future generations, Whitman and Unamuno view their written thoughts as a means of perserving their individual historical and spiritual identities after their deaths.

Both men admit that the desire for the preservation of the historical image was one factor which motivated them to write. Unamuno, who was more preoccupied than Whitman by the fear of death, used his writing as insurance for a lesser form of immortality in the event that no better form exists. He

comments, '. . . if I do not create my legend, I will die altogether. . . .' 'This Unamuno of my legend, of my novel . . . this Unamuno gives me life and death. . . .' Whitman expresses the fact that *Leaves of Grass* was written out of a desire to preserve his historical identity. . . . (p. 70)

The two men demonstrate that, in addition to preserving the images of themselves in their particular eras of existence as three-dimensional figures, they believe that their spirits will be given a vicarious form of continuing existence through their work and their readers. Unamuno writes, 'The immortality of the soul is a spiritual matter, a social matter. Whosoever creates a work, lives in it and through it lives in other men. . . .' In **'Farewell, Go with God,'** Unamuno addresses his poems, the 'children of his soul,' expressing his wish that they should pave a pathway to eternity for his soul, and that they should find a home in the minds of his readers. . . . (p. 71)

That Whitman and Unamuno shared a common belief in the importance of language in achieving immortality becomes quite evident in much of their work. The two men use words to stimulate the imagination to make objects exist for themselves so that they may absorb the spirit of the objects, thus achieving a sense of wholeness and moving up the ladder toward perfection of the human soul and immortality in the Absolute. They use thought expressed in language to plant ideas in the minds of future generations to ensure for themselves a place in the collective memory of future generations by promoting the continuing growth of knowledge and ideas in human minds. Finally, they view their writing as a means of preserving their individual historical and spiritual identities here on Earth, so that as long as people read their works, they may have a vicarious form of continuing existence. (p. 72)

*Debra Harper Love, ''Whitman and Unamuno: Language for Immortality,''* in Walt Whitman Review *(reprinted by permission of the Wayne State University Press; copyright © 1979 by Wayne State University Press), Vol. 25, No. 2, June, 1979, pp. 66-72.*

### C. A. LONGHURST (essay date 1981)

Unamuno's *San Manuel Bueno, mártir* has often been called the most perfect, most satisfying of Unamuno's novels, and more than one critic has described it as a prose poem. Yet almost the entire critical debate on this novel has revolved around the mainly theological or philosophical question of whether the protagonist exemplifies religious scepticism or uncertainty or an unusual kind of faith. There are indeed a whole host of questions about the nature of Don Manuel's beliefs which the work poses, questions which have understandably, if inconclusively, aroused a good deal of critical interest. But in pursuing these questions which have to do with finding the meaning *of* the work, other questions more specifically directed to finding meaning *in* the work have largely been ignored. Why did Unamuno employ a personalized narrator? Why did he choose a female narrator? Why should Angela want to write down Don Manuel's story anyway? (p. 582)

The following proposition will serve as my basic premise: there is no way we can get to know the truth about Don Manuel because we do not see Don Manuel directly; all we see is Angela's reconstruction of him. We get absolutely no other view of Don Manuel, not even Lázaro's, because Lázaro's account of him is given through Angela. The only objective knowledge we possess of Don Manuel (objective within the fiction, of course) is that he had a reputation for sanctity and that because of this reputation the bishop of the diocese is promoting the process of beatification. Indeed the reader learns this fact (i.e. the promotion of the beatification process) in the very first sentence of Angela's narrative: it stands out as a significant fact. Obviously for beatification to take place the Church will require not only sanctity but also orthodoxy: it is not going to beatify someone who does not believe in the resurrection of Christ. The bishop and the villagers appear to have no doubts about Don Manuel's orthodoxy. Now suppose that Angela's memoir fell into the hands of the bishop and the ecclesiastical court considering Don Manuel's beatification: how would they react to it? This, after all, is exactly the position the reader of Angela's account is in at the start of the novel. Like the bishop and the ecclesiastical court of inquiry the reader will want to establish the truth about Don Manuel. The bishop and other members of the court of inquiry, then (and by analogy the reader), if they were honest and conscientious, would want to consider two questions in connexion with Angela's account: (1) Is there any external evidence to support Angela's view of Don Manuel? (2) What sort of a person is the writer of this document: is she a completely reliable witness, reliable enough for what she says to be taken literally? The answer to the first question must be no; Angela has not a single supporting witness upon whom to call. Lázaro, who might have shed further light, is by now dead (and the notes which he left behind appear to contain Don Manuel's teachings, not evidence of his disbelief—Angela never actually quotes from these notes). The answer to the second question is of course crucial to the interpretation of the novel. (pp. 582-83)

Angela's personal re-creation of Don Manuel is an equivocal and contradictory one, governed by her own ambiguous relationship with him. It is a portrayal of Don Manuel in which the overt aim of presenting him in a saintly light is undermined by a covert reprobation which has no very clear cause but which reflects her lonely and unhappy situation at the time of writing. If speculation about a fictitious character's real motives were not such a debatable exercise one might conjecture that she is suffering from a suppressed resentment caused by rebuff or frustration. But in any case what emerges perfectly clearly without any need to speculate is her mental confusion and disorientation, her bewilderment and even perturbation. This is not merely implicit in her ambivalent portrayal of Don Manuel but is explicitly recognized by her at the end of her story: she confesses that she can no longer tell truth from falsehood, reality from imagination; she wonders whether what she relates actually happened the way she relates it. Curiously she brings in the idea of conscience . . . , suggesting that writing down her memoir has some therapeutic or cathartic value. Angela had forged a relationship with Don Manuel which, on her side, clearly went further than the normal one between confessor and penitent or between priest and acolyte. For Angela, Don Manuel became a father-figure with a latent sexual role. Just as a nun entering a convent and taking her vows becomes 'the bride of Christ', so Angela on entering her own convent of Valverde de Lucerna (as she herself calls it) becomes in her own imagination the bride of Don Manuel. Psychologically this ties in perfectly with what we learn of Angela's childhood. The loss of her own father when very young provokes a search for a surrogate father, and given her mother's devotion to Don Manuel, the child's attention is drawn towards the priest. This initial conditioning is reinforced by Angela coming under the tutelage of the priest at a particularly impressionable age: sixteen. On returning to the village from school she immediately becomes emotionally involved (as is evident from her first

encounter with Don Manuel) with the figure of the priest whom her mother has for so long held up to her as a father-figure; the surrogate father becomes a surrogate husband. What is recognized by developmental psychology as being only a passing phase in female adolescence becomes, in Angela's case, a permanent state of affairs; indeed this possibility has already been adumbrated by the early reference in the text to the lure of the convent and the visions of romantic and matrimonial adventures all in the same breath. Angela *qua* narrator and Angela *qua* character are thus beautifully consistent.

This view of Angela not only appears to fit the facts of her life-story, but also goes some way towards explaining why she writes. For her, Don Manuel has been at the centre of her life. When he dies, she still has Lázaro to help maintain alive the image of the priest and to act as a link with her past. . . . Lázaro's death signifies a break in Angela's life, and this break, exacerbated by the bishop's insistent questioning and by his decision to write a book about Don Manuel thus threatening to take over from Angela the creative function of keeping alive the image of the priest, precipitates a crisis that leads directly to her memoir. (Angela's references to the present, that is the time of narration, indicate that she writes not long after Lázaro's death and at the time of the ecclesiastical inquiry into Don Manuel's life.) For Angela, now old and lonely ('desolada', 'envejecida'), the memoir is a life-support: it enables her to relive in fantasy her association with Don Manuel, to try and find meaning and consolation in the past as she searches for some sense of purpose in the present. As she consciously consigns her memories to paper she also subconsciously betrays feelings of perplexity and regret at having given her life to Don Manuel's spiritual cause only to find herself in the end sad, lonely, and confused. It is evident that Angela's reconstruction of Don Manuel's life, her revelation of his 'secreto trágico' or of his 'piadoso fraude', represents a reply and a challenge to the orthodox biography that the bishop is preparing. Angela, who has been a doubting Thomas all her life, from the time she started reading her father's books to the moment of writing her memoir, makes an even greater one of Don Manuel. This 'togetherness in doubt' compensates for the simple fact that she never succeeded in being as close to Don Manuel as Lázaro and Blasillo: she did not enjoy the affection of Don Manuel as the village idiot did, nor did she enjoy the confidence of Don Manuel as her brother did. The unconscious recognition that Don Manuel did not fully reciprocate her infatuation leads her to write a double-edged account of the priest's life, encomiastic yet subtly critical. But the memoir allows us to infer much more about Angela herself than about the priest: *she* is the real doubter. The only real truth in the novel is the truth of the narrator herself; the real Don Manuel, hidden behind the impenetrable barrier of Angela's personality, uncertainties, and emotions, is inaccessible. One could in theory go further and put forward the view that the entire memoir was conceived by the novelist as a mere piece of fantasy on the part of the fictional narrator, with no basis in reality (fictional reality, that is). But such an explanation, though perfectly admissible in the case of certain stories by Poe, Borges, and others, seems to me unhelpful in this particular case. The theme and tone of the story suggest that what Unamuno had in mind was not a stark true/false alternative but an exploration of the nature of perception and belief, that is, of an individual's own intimate reasons, motivations, or pressures for accepting or not accepting something as true and real. At any rate we can be fairly certain that one of the reasons why Unamuno chose a personalized narrator, and a very particular one at that, was in order to eschew the 'truth' or the 'reality' within the fiction, in other words to provide us, the readers, with sufficient grounds on which to question the exactitude of Angela's account. One of the aims of Unamuno in *San Manuel Bueno, mártir*—at any rate one of the results of the technique he employs—is to raise the question of narrative authority, in which he was deeply interested, with special reference to the Gospels. Narratives, whether historical or fictitious, speak in hidden and personal ways and cannot simply be taken as mere records of facts. Just as the Gospels of Christ written by Matthew, Mark, Luke, and John were described by Unamuno (both in this work and elsewhere) as novels and not history, so the gospel of San Manuel written by Angela is her novel: not a record of a life but a personal interpretation of it, the work of Angela's imagination and fantasy having only partial links with an external reality, as she herself comes close to recognizing at the end. If we were to examine Angela's memoir from the point of view of its documentary value, several levels of factualness would be clearly distinguished, ranging from the totally factual to the non-factual. These levels could be schematized briefly as follows:

*Totally factual*

The basic elements of Angela's story: her family circumstances and certain events in her life; the existence of Don Manuel, his reputation for sanctity, the process of beatification; Lázaro's public conversion.

*Semi-factual*

A good deal of information about Don Manuel: Angela's anecdotes about him (she was not present), her impressions, recollections, reminiscences and reconstruction of distant events and conversations, all of which merge in her memory to give the account its oft-noticed dreamlike and poetic qualities.

*Uncertain*

The motives behind Lázaro's conversion and his relationship with Don Manuel: did Don Manuel tell Lázaro the complete truth about himself?; did Lázaro tell Angela the complete truth about Don Manuel?; did he tell her the truth about his own motives? A certain amount of critical information about Don Manuel is allegedly obtained through Lázaro; but Lázaro is not a neutral witness: according to Angela he is an atheist who thinks Don Manuel 'demasiado inteligente para creer todo lo que tiene que enseñar' ['too intelligent to believe everything he teaches'.] . . . Has Angela been unduly influenced by her brother? Or is Lázaro the excuse for her subtle denunciation of the priest?

*Non-factual*

Angela's personal interpretation of Don Manuel's religious ideology; her constant insinuations in the direction of unbelief.

*Unconscious*

Angela's self-portrayal: certain anecdotes about herself and her use of particular words and phrases in the account of Don Manuel which betray the submerged and unconfessed nature of her attachment to the priest and her ambivalent attitude towards him.

In giving his novel a structure based on levels of factualness or truth, Unamuno is moving away from an extra-literary reality and towards the fictive form itself. Indeed it is not even enough to talk conventionally of structure in this particular instance; it is the novel's *infrastructure* that gives it its special quality and ambiguity. But this ambiguity is not that of a capricious writer who merely seeks to mystify his readers or deviously to defend his own personal ideology; it is not the obfuscation and the 'aesthetic ambiguity' denounced by Frances Wyers [see excerpt above] . . . ; for while the work is certainly ambiguous, this ambiguity has its own internal justification: it is more than just a cheap attempt at fashionable obscurity; it is an integral part of the story, an essential dimension without which this particular novel would collapse. Another kind of narrator would write quite another kind of work. Angela's history, her personality, her circumstances, create the fiction. On this level the work is perfectly meaningful and intelligible and there is no need to resort to Unamuno's own biography in search of the rosetta stone with which to decipher his novelistic hieroglyphics. (pp. 592-96)

I should like to conclude this article by briefly considering the relevance of part of Unamuno's authorial interpolation to Angela's account.

Having first acknowledged the creative role of the narrator, that is, the crucial nature of her intervention, Unamuno goes on to insert a short paragraph which is both obscure and at the same time potentially decisive in any attempt to infer the author's attitude towards his fictional narrator. The paragraph ends with . . . a phrase of biblical origin which functions as an invitation to look beyond the surface for the deeper implication of the speaker's words. In this cryptic paragraph, on the face of it rather superfluous, Unamuno, quoting the epistle of St Jude, verse 9, reminds us of St Michael the Archangel's reproof to the Devil, who was claiming Moses's body: 'El Señor te reprenda' ['The Lord rebuke you']. There are three entities involved in this biblical anecdote: Moses, St Michael and the Devil. Since (1) Don Manuel has earlier been explicitly associated with Moses, since (2) Unamuno is explicitly identifying with St Michael (he reminds us that St Michael is his patron saint), and since (3) the only other person responsible for transmitting the story is Angela (as Unamuno has just reminded us in the immediately preceding paragraph), the clear possibility arises that Angela is being associated with the Devil (the association of angels with devils occurs in St Jude's epistle too), and that the dispute between St Michael and the Devil over who was to have jurisdiction over the body of Moses is meant to represent a divergence of views between Unamuno and his narrator. But why, one might well ask, should Unamuno choose this strange way of giving an authorial nod to the reader? Why should he cast Angela in the role of the Devil? The answer to this is beautifully simple and says a great deal for Unamuno's artistry, for the explanation is contained in the circumstances of composition of the life-story of Don Manuel. What prompts Angela to write her memoir is the beatification process initiated by the bishop of the diocese (this is mentioned twice by Angela, at the beginning and at the end of her memoir). Don Manuel is now the subject of an inquiry by an ecclesiastical court that will have to sit in judgement and decide whether he is a worthy candidate for beatification. In such a court of inquiry the Church always appoints a prosecutor (technically *promotor fidei* but more widely referred to as *advocatus diavoli*) whose function it is to oppose the promoters of the beatification process by questioning the evidence put forward for beatification and by looking for contrary evidence. In the case of Don Manuel it is the bishop (in accordance with canonical procedure) who is promoting the process of beatification and who is writing his life as an example of perfect priestliness. Contrariwise Angela, in her testimony, is presenting Don Manuel as a man lacking in faith, and is consequently hitting at the very heart of the case for beatification. In the context of a canonical beatification process (the starting-point for Angela's story), Angela and the bishop are antagonists. It follows that Angela is cast in the role of *advocatus diavoli*. There is further evidence that this is indeed what Unamuno was getting at, for in the very same paragraph he includes, at first sight gratuitously, a definition of the Devil which fits in exactly with the role of Angela as *advocatus diavoli:* ['the devil means accuser, prosecutor']. (pp. 596-97)

Having given us what amounts to a cryptic but intelligible warning not to take Angela's account of Don Manuel at face value, Unamuno ends his interpolation by claiming the superiority of imaginative literature over historiography, of *novela* over *cronicón*, and he goes on to say that his *relato* is not history because in it nothing happens: ['but I hope that in it everything remains, as lakes and mountains do remain'.] . . . If these symbols of permanence are going to attain their full value, it will be only by virtue of the opportunity that imaginative literature gives to the reader to respond to and keep alive the creative consciousness not of the individual, for that is lost forever, but of the artist. An approach to Unamuno's fiction based on a theological, philosophical, or biographical search for the meaning or the message is unlikely to get to the hub of Unamuno's art. Most novelists after all do not write novels to voice meanings; they turn to novels in order to construct artefacts out of language. In Western fiction of the post-realist mode, of which Unamuno is a prime example, the clear tendency was to allow the narrative to speak with its own voice. The meaning or the message was banished as something extra-literary; but what remained had its own kind of truth, its poem-like structure, its internal justification for existing. In **San Manuel Bueno, mártir** Unamuno has given us an artistic 'document', as he calls it, which invites the reader to search for the truth within the story. But the skilful arrangement of the narrative—with its subtle use of personalized narration and of Janus-like symbols and suggestive language—keeps the truth tantalizingly beyond our reach. The fact that ultimately there can be no truth, no reality, except that of the story itself, the fact that we the readers can never hope to be in possession of the truth about Don Manuel, is but a reflection on one level of man's limited access to knowledge of others and on another of the potential that literature has for creating self-contained worlds that are ever-beckoning but ever-mysterious. Angela will have one view of reality, we may have another one; but the truth itself must always elude us. (p. 597)

> C. A. Longhurst, "The Problem of Truth in 'San Manuel Bueno, Mártir'," in The Modern Language Review (© Modern Humanities Research Association 1981), Vol. 76, No. 3, July, 1981, pp. 581-97.

---

# ADDITIONAL BIBLIOGRAPHY

Balseiro, José A. "The Quixote of Contemporary Spain: Miguel de Unamuno." *PMLA* 49, No. 2 (June 1934): 645-56.
> A biocritical survey of Unamuno's life and work, stressing his role as a Quixotic awakener of the Spanish spirit.

Barcía, José Rubia, and Zeitlin, M. A., eds. *Unamuno: Creator and Creation*. Berkeley, Los Angeles: University of California Press, 1967, 253 p.
> Reprints fourteen scholarly essays presented to the symposium "Unamuno: The Man and His Work," from 22 October through 6 November 1964. The essays, written in observance of the Unamuno centenary, were contributed by Américo Castro, Leon Livingstone, José Rubia Barcía, and others.

Basdekis, Demetrios. *Unamuno and Spanish Literature*. University of California Publications in Modern Philology, vol. 85. Berkeley, Los Angeles: University of California Press, 1967, 101 p.
> Examines Unamuno's ideas on literature in general, in an attempt to understand his approach to specific works of Spanish literature. Basdekis also traces the effect of these earlier Spanish works on Unamuno's writings.

Eoff, Sherman H. "Creative Doubt: Miguel de Unamuno." In his *The Modern Spanish Novel: Comparative Essays Examining the Philosophical Impact of Science on Fiction*, pp. 186-212. New York: New York University Press, 1961.
> Discussion of Unamuno's philosophy, and examination of its application in *Niebla*, *Abel Sánchez*, and *San Manuel bueno, mártir*.

Foster, David William. "The Novel As Metaphor in *Niebla*." *Renascence* XVIII, No. 4 (Summer 1966): 201-08.
> Examines *Niebla* as an expression of Unamuno's preoccupation with existential self-awareness.

Huertas-Jourda, José. *The Existentialism of Miguel de Unamuno*. University of Florida Monographs: Humanities, no. 13. Gainesville: University of Florida Press, 1963, 70 p.
> Explores Unamuno's Quixotic vision and its expression in his work.

Jimenez-Fajardo, Salvador. "Unamuno's *Abel Sánchez*: Envy As a Work of Art." *Journal of Spanish Studies: Twentieth Century* 4, No. 2 (Fall 1976): 89-103.
> A close study of the role of envy as a life-giving force in *Abel Sánchez*.

Lacy, Allen. *Miguel de Unamuno: The Rhetoric of Existence*. Studies in Philosophy, vol. XII. The Hague: Mouton & Co., 1967, 289 p.
> A helpful study of Unamuno and his work, written as an aid to readers who know little about him.

MacKay, John A. Foreword to *Poems*, by Miguel de Unamuno, translated by Eleanor L. Turnbull, pp. vii-ix. Baltimore: The Johns Hopkins Press, 1952.
> An astute appraisal of Unamuno's life, work, and influence.

Olson, Paul R. "Unamuno's Lacquered Boxes: *Cómo se hace una novela* and the Ontology of Writing." *Revista Hispanica Moderna* XXXVI, No. 4 (1970-1971): 186-99.
> A close examination of *Cómo se hace una novela*, particularly of the Kantian elements contained therein.

Rudd, Margaret Thomas. *The Lone Heretic: A Biography of Miguel de Unamuno y Jugo*. Austin: University of Texas Press, 1963, 349 p.
> An excellent biography.

Stevens, James R. "Unamuno's *Don Sandalio*: Two Opposed Concepts of Fiction." *Romance Notes* XI, No. 2 (Winter 1969): 266-71.
> Examines the symbolism of the oak and the chess game in *Don Sandalio*, finding them to be symbols of escape from life's seeming meaninglessness.

Turner, David G. *Unamuno's Webs of Fatality*. London: Tamesis Books, 1974, 170 p.
> Detailed textual analysis of Unamuno's novels, tracing the author's use of imagery in expressing his constant theme of fate and its workings.

Valdes, Mario J. *Death in the Literature of Unamuno*. Urbana: University of Illinois Press, 1966, 173 p.
> A philosophical and literary discussion of Unamuno's vision of life and the reflection of that philosophy in his work.

Walker, Leslie J. "A Spanish Humanist." *The Dublin Review* 171, No. 342 (July/August/September 1922): 32-43.
> Unamuno's philosophy as revealed in *The Tragic Sense of Life*. Walker finds Unamuno to be a Christian humanist, whose book serves to reconcile faith and reason.

# Boris Vian

## 1920-1959

(Also wrote under pseudonyms of Vernon Sullivan, Baron Visi, Adolph Schmürz, and Bison Ravi) French novelist, dramatist, short story writer, poet, critic, translator, essayist, journalist, librettist, and song writer.

Vian belongs to the absurdist tradition in French literature which began with Alfred Jarry and was perpetuated, in varying forms, by Dadaism, Surrealism, and the Theater of the Absurd. His fiction and dramas are consistently fantastic in both plot and structure, conveying their author's bleak vision of human existence with black humor and an imagination unrestricted by codes of logic or morality. To some extent, Vian's pessimism is counteracted in his works by his energetic and inventive use of language, just as it was alleviated in his life by his abandonment to intense emotional experience.

Vian was born in a suburb of Paris to middle-class parents. When he was twelve years old, a bout with rheumatic fever left him with a lifelong cardiac condition. This infirmity is often cited as one source for the general preoccupation with death and disaster found throughout Vian's works, as well as being the origin of particular symbols and episodes involving physical violations of the heart. Vian received his education in Paris schools and later studied for a career in engineering, which he abandoned for a career as a writer. To support himself he produced thousands of magazine articles on various subjects. His first novel to receive wide attention was *J'irai cracher sur vos tombes,* a work which in 1948 became the subject of an obscenity trial due to its imitation, and deliberate exaggeration, of the sex and brutality of American hard-boiled detective fiction. In his defense, Vian claimed that he had merely translated an American author named Vernon Sullivan, who in reality was only Vian's invention. In its spirit of both seriousness and defiant frivolity, such a hoax is indicative of much of the author's works and his absurdist approach to life. Throughout the 1950s Vian turned out a prolific amount of writing. He died in 1959, following a heart attack he suffered while previewing a film adapted from *J'irai cracher sur vos tombes.*

The type of works Vian produced is perhaps best indicated by their link with the writings of Alfred Jarry, whose *Exploits and Opinions of Doctor Faustroll, Pataphysician* later became the basis for the worldwide College of Pataphysicians, which Vian officially joined in 1952. Pataphysics is a casual ideological doctrine that rejects all doctrines. For the most part it designates an attitude of mind that abjures any scientific, religious, or philosophical explanation of life, as well as recognizing no moral or aesthetic values. It is "the science of imaginary solutions," and as life-member Pataphysician and author Roger Shattuck explains: "The idea of 'truth' is the most imaginary of solutions." Characteristic of the influence of Pataphysics in Vian's work is an interweaving of the trivial with the extremely grave which is the hallmark of this philosophy. The novel *L'écume des jours (Froth on the Daydream)*—in which Jean-Sol Partre is murdered by having his heart ripped out— is compared by Donald Heiney to a Marx Brother's farce. While the violence in Vian's works is often comic, the humor is a means of underlining absurdist despair. The absurd, which

existentialism considers the basic condition of human existence and the paradoxical source of all human values, appears in Vian's works as a naked fact generating only random behavior. This is most strikingly disclosed in *L'arrache-coeur (The Heartsnatcher)*, whose main character, a psychiatrist visiting a small village, finds a confusion of forces and motives beneath the surface of this life and nothingness beyond it.

The aim of Pataphysics, according to Shattuck, is "imperturbability" in the face of the absurd. While Vian characters usually realize no such achievement, their lives are often lived to their emotional and sensual height. If the characters in such novels as *Vercoquin et le plancton* and *L'automne à Pékin* are inhabitants of an absurd world, they have freely derived from it what pleasures they could as a consolation. The greater victims are represented in Vian's works by those who, like the generals in the drama *Le goûter des généraux (The Generals' Tea-Party)*, are destroyed by their own self-important illusions of purpose and order in the universe. Vian's pessimistic world view is particularly apparent in his dramas, which critics group with the absurdist plays of Samuel Beckett, Fernando Arrabal, and Eugene Ionesco. *Les bâtisseurs d'empire; ou, Le schmürz (The Empire Builders)*, a bitter farce denigrating middle-class life, is considered his most important work in this genre.

Among Vian's numerous other works are short stories, opera libretti and ballet scenarios, translations of August Strindberg and other foreign authors, and popular songs, all produced in a relatively brief literary career. Although some have found Vian's pessimism objectionable, and his literary antics artistically trivial, a number of critics, most notably Alfred Cismaru, have placed his works among those which most successfully express the negative and disordered vision of modernist literature.

## PRINCIPAL WORKS

*Vercoquin et le plancton*   (novel)   1946
*L'automne à Pékin*   (drama)   1947
*L'écume des jours*   (novel)   1947
  [*Froth on the Daydream*, 1967; also published as *Mood Indigo*, 1969]
*J'irai cracher sur vos tombes* [as Vernon Sullivan]   1947
*Les morts ont tous la même peau* [as Vernon Sullivan]
  (novel)   1947
*Barnum's Digest*   (poetry)   1948
*Et on tuera tous les affreux* [as Vernon Sullivan]   (novel)
  1948
*\*J'irai cracher sur vos tombes*   (drama)   1948
*Les fourmis*   (short stories)   1949
*Cantilènes en gelée*   (poetry)   1950
*Le dernier des métiers*   (drama)   1950
*Elles se rendent pas compte* [as Vernon Sullivan]   (novel)
  1950
*L'équarrissage pour tous*   (drama)   1950
  [*The Knacker's ABC*, 1968]
*L'herbe rouge*   (novel)   1950
*L'arrache-cœur*   (novel)   1953
  [*The Heartsnatcher*, 1968]
*En avant la zizique*   (essay)   1958
*Fiesta*   (libretto)   1958
*Les bâtisseurs d'empire; ou, Le schmürz*   (drama)   1959
  [*The Empire Builders*, 1962]
*Je voudrais pas crever*   (poetry)   1962
*Les lurettes fourrés*   (short stories)   1962
*Le goûter des généraux*   (drama)   1965
  [*The General's Tea-Party*, 1967]
*Textes et chansons*   (songs)   1966
*Trouble dans les Andains*   (novel)   1966

*This drama is an adaptation of the novel *J'irai cracher sur vos tombes*.

---

### *THE TIMES LITERARY SUPPLEMENT* (essay date 1966)

[The] most pleasingly pataphysical piece of evidence that one can now admire the late Transcendant Satrap Boris Vian and still be intellectually respectable is his presence in the *Classiques du Vingtième Siècle* series, where his neighbours are Freud and Alain. . . .

What is happening now, according to Raymond Queneau, is that "Boris Vian va devenir Boris Vian" ["Boris Vian is going to become Boris Vian"]. There is a lot of point to this prediction. At the time of his death Vian was known to plenty of people as a typically insolent *chansonnier*, composing and performing, in front of frequently unamused audiences, songs like "Le Déserteur", which he himself looked on as being less anti-military than pro-civilian, a distinction that does him credit, and also as the "translator" of the novels of Vernon Sullivan, enthusiastic if often fanciful imitations of the "tough" Amer-

ican school of detective fiction. He died, as it happens, in a Paris cinema, at the preview of a film version of *J'irai cracher sur vos tombes,* the first of the four novels he published under this pseudonym and the one which caused the greatest scandal. The book was a simple piece of James M. Chicainery, written in ten days as the result of a characteristically generous promise made to a publisher in search of a modish best-seller. It sold by the thousand and fought several sparkling rounds with the censorship. Leader of those who claimed that the novel was an incitement to acts of adolescent debauchery was Daniel Parker, an architect, whose reward was the role of hero in the next Vernon Sullivan novel, where Dan Parker is the randy bouncer in a New York night-club, as well as a murderer. Everyone with whom Boris Vian came into contact at this time of his life was equally liable to be rushed into print, and it is this unpremeditated commitment to the people and values he lived among that gives his earlier books much of their attraction. . . .

Boris Vian [was] a man who wrote books in the first place to entertain a limited number of flesh and blood people, rather than any faceless public or non-existent posterity.

His first novel, *Vercoquin et le Plancton,* shows this very clearly. It is written in celebration of the "surprise-parties" which he loved to arrange, and the dancing, the jokes and the love-making that went with them. At the time Boris Vian was working, of all places, at the Association Française de Normalisation, and this institution naturally turns up in the novel with a predictable and rather sinister function—that of attempting to control the festival behaviour of the young people in the dusty interests of standardization. Spontaneity is seen to have enemies, and this is the battle which is fought over and over again in Boris Vian's books. But as he comes to realize how hopelessly powerful the forces are which exist to stifle life the bright lights are dimmed, and what begins as a stomp ends as a blues. In *Vercoquin* all is still well, and the violence is sublimated with true adolescent elegance. This is a good book for potential addicts to try out Vian's "loufoquerie", the sense of humour which he was happy to admit is that of children, for whom language is literal or nothing. Many of his comic effects both here and later are achieved simply by dropping little dabs of salt on the tails of metaphors, and by refusing to recognize any natural laws less flexible than those of language. . . .

Many grown-up people will be much too proud to take to this sort of thing, of course, and it is not surprising to learn from a recent article in *Le Figaro Littéraire* that it is the young who have rediscovered Boris Vian. . . . Boris Vian's is a desperately anthropomorphic world, in which the climate is as capricious as any young lover and in which buildings can shrink or even disappear in sympathy with their occupants. But this is a fantasy that cuts both ways; when things are going happily we may let out angry shouts of "whimsy", but once they turn sour the same sort of inventiveness can become a source of real pathos.

But where Vian shows himself most of all to be a young man writing for those simple souls who prefer making love to making war is in his vigorous sensuality. The nearest thing he recognizes to a sacred act is the act of love; intercourse with an inventive Negress indeed makes a highly popular "acte saint" for Claude Léon, a hermit in the Exopotamian desert in *L'Automne à Pékin*. . . .

But the minds in Boris Vian's books grow less and less easy; sex is not the last resting-place. His own heart, enlarged by a childhood illness, could sometimes be heard beating by the people he stood talking to, and it was never likely that a simple hedonism would be his last word on human relationships. The first tax on our pleasures we pay in the deterioration of our bodies, the second, particularly in the last novels, by the obsessions that can separate a man from a woman. In *L'Herbe Rouge* there is a case of impotence through guilt, in *L'Arrache-Coeur* there is the awful Clémentine, a wife turned Mother, whose husband takes to the sea as she encloses her beloved triplets inside a "wall of nothing", before finally having cages made for them. . . .

Innocence can be recognized in Boris Vian by the lack of a surname, but this innocence cannot survive the double threat from inside and out. Candid young lovers must submit to wasting and death, or in the later novels to deviations of the mind and senses. But Vian is surely at his most beneficial to us when he plots their lasting quarrels with our institutions, chief among them death's younger sister, work. Going into Vian's house, so someone said, was like going on holiday, and going into *L'Écume des Jours* is much the same. But once the trouble starts there come desolate scenes of manual labour, and an attack on the people who preach that work is sacred. The degraded copper miners leer at the young honeymooners as they drive by, because they are the stupid victims of a generalization which, like all generalizations, is evil, in this case the idea that work is good for people. Work is only to be tolerated when it leads to an escape from work. Instead of working to live—and so making sure we have no time to live— we should be working to install the substitute techniques which would enable us to live without working, that is to say that we produce eggs instead of hens. The simplicity of the argument is a sign of despair, but we ought to find it disturbing as well as sympathetic. As far as Boris Vian is concerned so long as there is work the young will go on being exploited like the pitiful apprentices in *L'Arrache-Coeur*, who live and die as easily replaceable implements.

It is this threat from the faceless powers which annihilate us under some embracing label that causes the deepest horror in Vian. When the policemen turn out under their seneschal in *L'Écume des Jours* they all answer to the same name. . . . But of all those whose particular costume is seen as the biggest hindrance to an open mind it is the priests who crop up most often. [Vian] presents them as entertainers, as men who are not serious. The Abbé in *Le Dernier des Métiers,* for example, has a dressing room where he is interviewed by reporters after a star sermon, while in *L'Arrache-Coeur* the incumbent of the egg-shaped church preaches with enormous conviction that God is luxury, is by definition useless, and is therefore more interested in according grace to the faithful than rainfall. . . .

In the face of doom Boris Vian can only offer a refusal to grow old. The blossom which ripens into fruit is denatured. We must go on wanting things and rage against the dying of our light, unlike the awful father in his best play, *Les Bâtisseurs d'Empire,* who is always ready to adjust himself to his ever-shrinking environment. Boris Vian was a man for whom whatever was predictable was bad. . . . Exopotamia, the desert country he invented for his autumn in Peking, defeats all attempts to impose a railway line on it, and at the end of the book we are told that the future of this country is perfectly unpredictable, that anything might happen there. It may seem odd that a man with this passion for leaving things open should ever have wanted to let his life congeal into print, but Boris Vian lived and wrote by the senses and knew all about the "illusion sémantique" which mistakes the word for the thing, the "map"

for the "territory" as he liked to put it himself. So his books build no walls to keep out death, but they do leave us with rare evidence of a generous man, uncritically in favour of every living thing. . . .

*"Man from Exopotamia," in* The Times Literary Supplement *(© Times Newspapers Ltd. (London) 1966; reproduced from* The Times Literary Supplement *by permission), No. 3349, May 5, 1966, p. 386.*

## ROBERT GARIS (essay date 1969)

The dustjacket on *Mood Indigo* reports that Boris Vian "died in 1959 at the age of thirty-eight. . . . His literary reputation has grown so greatly since his death that he is currently one of the 'cult' figures in French letters." *Mood Indigo,* which the dust-jacket also tells me is Vian's masterpiece, was in fact finished in New Orleans in 1946 but apparently not published until 1963, under the title *L'Ecume des Jours.* I think I can see how it all happened. Vian's little nonsense-pastoral is as mildly funny, as inoffensively silly—in short as inconsequential—now as it must have seemed in 1946. But a change in literary fashion, together with a certain coincidence of subject and a calculated misreading of Vian's tone and manner have sufficed to turn this little cream-puff of a novel into a Precursor of Pop-art, after which the formation of a Vian-cult was a foregone conclusion. The subject-matter Vian might be thought to share with Pop-art is his acceptance of consumer-culture, but the effect doesn't really feel like Pop at all. Vian falls short of the sternness of the radical Pop-esthetic, on the one hand; on the other hand, he hasn't a glimmer of the Beatles' energetic enjoyment or exhaustive knowledge of pop-culture, much less of their extraordinary ability to imitate it. Their kind of affectionate parody is really new, not just the old kind of ambiguity. But Vian doesn't even have the old ambiguity; his nonsense-wit is just a veneer over his sentimentality. When he goes behind the pages of glossy magazines to enter the world of their luxury ads, he is in Arcadia and he thinks the shepherds there are really sweet: Colin and Chick and Chloe and Alise, pretty androids with empty heads and smooth bodies covered with the nylon and cellophane which, alas, was as far as Vian's knowledge of high synthetic living could take him in 1946. Colin and Chloe's love affair is a shameless tear-jerker, though its terms are carefully bizarre. They are threatened by ugliness, you see. Chloe exquisitely wastes away because there's a water-lily growing inside her, draining her life away (this fatuity is below the level of the book as a whole, but it takes up a lot of its pages); expensive doctors simultaneously drain away Colin's entire trunkful of "double-zoons" (this *must* be more successful in French) and he has to go to work, which isn't at all agreeable. In the end the vision of his unappeasable grief drives his faithful and sensitive pet mouse to suicide. . . . I could tell you about the "pianocktail," a computer sort of thing that mixes very special cocktails when you program it with a Duke Ellington tune; I could tell you about Chick's fatal obsession of collecting all the editions and effects of a detestable writer named Jean-Sol Partre; and if it were worth the trouble I could report that Vian is much less amusing than a very long list of writers including Raymond Queneau, whom he occasionally imitates and who has called *Mood Indigo* "the greatest love novel of our time." (pp. 160-61)

*Robert Garis, "Fiction Chronicle," in* The Hudson Review *(copyright © 1969 by The Hudson Review, Inc.; reprinted by permission), Vol. XXII, No. 1, Spring, 1969, pp. 148-64.**

**JACQUES GUICHARNAUD** (essay date 1969)

It took some time for the dramatic works of Boris Vian, who died in 1959, to finally be performed. A poet, novelist, trumpet player, and dramatist, Vian was a kind of new Jarry—but a melancholy and tender Jarry. His works convey a taste for life in all its forms and also—like those of Ionesco or Raymond Queneau—an obsession with death. Death is not the sumptuous horror of decaying flesh or the supernatural phenomenon that it was for Ghelderode, but extinction in itself, a nothingness in the face of which man's agitation has little value.

This attitude led Vian, in two of his plays (*L'Equarrissage pour tous* and *Le Goûter des généraux*), to poke fun at the ambitions and incoherencies displayed by mankind in performing the act it would seem to take most seriously: war. Greedy, opportunistic, or simply childish. Vian's characters—generals, politicians, soldiers, and civilians of all nationalities and all leanings—take part, with an almost Ubuesque lack of awareness, in what seem like cabaret acts. According to a tradition dear to French children, the generals, properly dressed in the uniforms of today's army, have a tea party, during which they take a few alcoholic drinks on the sly (out of fear of an overpowering mother) and organize a war in all its detail—until they realize that they have forgotten to choose an enemy (*Le Goûter des généraux*). Similarly, amid the ravages of a war involving the French, the Americans, and the Germans, a wedding is being prepared—that of a French girl to a German soldier, who is fighting a hundred yards away and is called to the wedding by telephone (*L'Equarrissage pour tous*). War being absurd, Vian improves on its absurdity; but his method consists essentially in treating it with nonchalance.

The spectator at such plays is, in a sense, struck by the horrors of massacre and the general incoherence, but far more by the absolute irreverence with which things are minimized—even those that in reality are the most shattering. In *L'Equarrissage,* for example, everything is set up for a torture scene, but the torture consists in tickling the victim. Vian's intention is to shock, but the shock comes less from aggressive provocation than from total disrespect in both form and substance. The tension in *Le Goûter* and *L'Equarrissage* is created by the enormous incongruity between bad jokes, intentionally superficial in nature, and the seriousness of the values involved. An antimilitarist and author of the well-known French song "Chanson du déserteur," Vian is subversive by way of frivolity. In the face of the universal phenomenon of death, the social and political problems melt away and are not even worthy of being attacked seriously.

As a final disrespectful and facile gesture, Vian does away with all his characters at the end of both plays. The generals and politicians of *Le Goûter* kill themselves one after another during a collective game of Russian roulette which they find highly amusing; the setting of *L'Equarrissage* having disappeared in an explosion, the few survivors kill each other to the sound of the "Marseillaise." Vian may well be saying that mankind, both military and civilian, entertains a death-wish for collective annihilation, falsely glorified by big words and noble pretexts. But his burlesque and spectacular finales are also a sign that he is the last to take his own creations really seriously: his game is altogether subversive in that it itself is an object of subversion.

In a third play, *Les Bâtisseurs d'empire,* Vian presents the reality in relation to which all human values and ambitions become equalized in their indignity and comic absurdity: death. *Les Bâtisseurs* approaches allegory but, as in Beckett and most of Ionesco, stops short of it to the extent that the equation between what is seen or heard and the concepts suggested remains ambiguous, polyvalent, and thus not intellectually translatable. The play as a whole follows a rigorous movement from progressive suffocation and isolation to final and complete obscurity. Taken literally, it is a nightmare of invasion from the outside: as a family flees from apartment to apartment, its members disappear one after another, until only the Father is left, and his last refuge is then invaded, in the dark, by the deadly enemies. Confronted by this mysterious destruction of the world, the characters try—very comically—to justify their existence or their achievements, using a language made up of clichés and paralogisms, and doing their best to ignore the invasion, the shrinking space of their successive lodgings, and the gradual disappearance of the members of the family.

With more obviously social and political implications, Georges Michel has recently picked up this theme in his *Promenade du Dimanche,* but Vian's play goes beyond that level of a "plague" à la Camus. It is also concerned with a metaphor of individual death and in this respect may be compared to one of Ionesco's later plays, *Le Roi se meurt.* While the family disappears and the living space gets progressively smaller and shabbier, one realizes that the Father's flight from room to room is illusory, for he is always accompanied by his Schmürz, an ignoble, bloody, and permanent witness-scapegoat. The Schmürz is sometimes ignored and sometimes—in fact, quite regularly—beaten up, but he is always there, silent. If he is meant to represent anything, it would be, in a very general way, an aggregate of outer and inner realities (evil, bad faith, sadistic impulses, and the desire to subject others, hence the shame and joy of being a master) which men sometimes recognize in distrust or hate and try to destroy or frequently prefer to ignore so that they may contrive to live with it in some measure of satisfaction. Scenically, the Schmürz is an embodiment of malaise—the malaise of reality, which is actually the unacknowledged awareness of future annihilation, of a death which keeps men from *really* living: a few seconds before the final obscurity, the Schmürz dies, but he does so just before the door is smashed in and the invaders at last make their entrance. The invaders are never seen, but they are "perhaps," says Boris Vian, "Schmürzes."

In fact, the Schmürz is the image that gives Vian's dramatic works their meaning. For the nightmare horror of *Les Bâtisseurs d'empire,* along with its implacable rigor, is what justifies the nonchalance and burlesque elements of his other two plays. None of this, however, excludes a touch of infinite tenderness, which is far more obvious in certain of Vian's poems or in a novel such as *L'Ecume des jours,* in which the heroine dies from a flower that grows in her chest, and the hero, in charge of "growing" guns, manages to produce them, but each with, at the end of its barrel, a rose. (pp. 181-84)

> *Jacques Guicharnaud, "The Absurd Has Many Faces: Vian, Arrabal, Duras, Dubillard," in his* Modern French Theatre: From Giraudoux to Genet *(copyright © 1967 by Yale University), Yale University Press, 1969, pp. 178-95.\**

**MARTIN ESSLIN** (essay date 1969)

Boris Vian's first play, *L'Equarrissage pour Tous* (which might be rendered in English as *Knackery Made Easy . . .* ), already shows him as a master of a bitter, black humour, although the play, a tragicomic farce, still fits into a traditional pattern, in spite of the fact that Jean Cocteau greeted it as an event comparable to Apollinaire's *Les Mamelles de Tirésias* and his own *Mariés de la Tour Eiffel.* Described as 'a paramilitary vaudeville in one long act', *L'Equarrissage pour Tous* takes place in a knacker's yard at Arromanches on the day of the Allied landings there, 6 June 1944. While the knacker's eccentric family go about their peaceful business of horse-slaughtering and arranging the marriage of one of their daughters to a German soldier, the place is continually invaded by military personnel of various nations, ranging from a Japanese parachutist to a Soviet Russian woman soldier, who inexplicably is one of the daughters of the house. There are also numerous Americans and members of the Free French forces. The hilarious and bawdy proceedings end when the knacker's house is blown up to make room for the glorious rebuilding schemes of the future. By this time the whole family has been killed, and the curtain falls to the strains of the 'Marseillaise'.

So soon after the war, this sardonic play provoked veritable howls of indignation from all sides, particularly for its irreverent portrayal of members of the Free French forces, although they are expressly shown as opportunists who have joined the Resistance only that very day, and spend their time looking for cards they can requisition. In fact, the play is as harmless a piece of satire as it is a brilliant example of *l'humour noir* at its blackest.

*Les Bâtisseurs d'Empire* also has its touches of humour, but is a play of an altogether different kind—a poetic image of mortality and the fear of death. (pp. 207-08)

[There] is a mysterious, silent character, a half-human being, called a *schmürz*, 'covered in bandages, dressed in rags, one arm in a sling, he holds a walking-stick in the other. He limps, bleeds, and is ugly to look at.' This silent figure seems not to be noticed by the characters. Nevertheless they constantly rain brutal blows on him.

Simple in structure and relentless in its progression, *Les Bâtisseurs d'Empire* is a powerful and very personal statement. Proud as we are, confident that we are building our own world, our personal empire on earth, we are in fact constantly on the run; far from growing wider, our world contracts. As we approach death, we get more and more lonely, our range of vision and action becomes more and more narrow. It is increasingly difficult to communicate with the younger generation, and the subterranean noise of death grows louder and louder.

All this is clear enough. But what does the *schmürz* stand for? It is perhaps significant that Boris Vian wrote some of his contributions to the more popular magazines under the pseudonym Adolphe Schmürz. There can be little doubt that *Les Bâtisseurs d'Empire* dramatizes Vian's own feelings. He knew he was suffering from a serious heart condition, the after-effect of a fever attack. He had to give up playing his beloved jazz trumpet: 'Each note played on the trumpet shortens my life by a day,' he said. It was his own life he saw narrowing. Does the *schmürz* therefore stand for the mortal part of ourselves that we brutally flog and maltreat without noticing what we are doing? The fact that the *schmürz* collapses and dies just before the hero of the play does points in this direction. On the other hand, after the hero's death other *schmürzes* are seen invading the stage. Are they the messengers of death and is the hero's own *schmürz* his own death, silently waiting for him, thoughtlessly flogged by the hero when he is *not* aware of his own mortality? Or is *schmürz*, derived from the German word for pain—*Schmerz*—simply the silent, ever-present pain of heart disease? (pp. 208-09)

*Martin Esslin, "Parallels and Proselytes," in his* The Theatre of the Absurd *(copyright © 1961, 1968, 1969 by Martin Esslin; reprinted by permission of Doubleday & Company, Inc.), revised edition, Anchor Books, 1969, pp. 198-280.** *

### THE TIMES LITERARY SUPPLEMENT (essay date 1971)

None of the three plays in *Théâtre inédit* would stand up to the pressure of an actual production, but they all make dynamic reading. *Tête de méduse* is balanced shakily on the satirical proposition that you have got to suffer emotionally if you want to write a masterpiece: Vian's hero is an aspirant writer whose wife sleeps around at his direction so that he can be fruitfully tortured by jealousy. If this basic device is rather wooden, *Tête de méduse* does have plenty of sharp, period exchanges between young men about Paris which prove, once again, what an admirably direct spokesman Vian was for those of his postwar generation who refused to be neutered by the higher solemnities of Existentialism.

*Série blême,* the second play (cf. "série noire"), is a bit of comic guignol written largely in slang and wholly in verse. The plot out-Ubus Ubu as the hero, another writer, eliminates one by one a party of toothpaste salesmen who have crash-landed and broken the peace of his snowbound mountain retreat. Much of the play is comprehensible only in its general drift, so dense is the argot which Vian has managed to work into it. *Série blême,* in fact, is a full and most ingenious guide to the slang of its day. . . .

*Le Chasseur français* also relies on an extensive use of argot, this time put incongruously into the mouth of a marquise. The play is prodigally constructed in terms of scene and character and is intended as a musical, with some fetching lyrics mixed in with cod detectives, disguises, joke homosexuals and other *Vianesquerie.* The mixture suggests a genre in which Vian might have prospered, given time: the *opérette policière,* or Gilbert and Vernon Sullivan.

*"Deft and Dense," in* The Times Literary Supplement *(© Times Newspapers Ltd. (London) 1971; reproduced from* The Times Literary Supplement *by permission), No. 3593, January 8, 1971, p. 30.*

### JENNIFER WALTERS (essay date 1972)

[The] central theme of Vian's prose work is the way man moves incessantly and irrevocably toward death. His books are liberally bestrewn with corpses of all kinds, and rare is the story which does not end with the death of one or more of the protagonists. Three aspects of dying are depicted overtly: the usual attitude to the death of strangers, reaction to personal tragedy, and the intimate emotion involved in facing one's own imminent extinction.

Writing during and immediately after the Second World War, Vian presents death as violent, sudden, unexpected, and unimportant. It happens at any time to anybody. The ice skaters in *L'Ecume des Jours* are swept off the ice and forgotten, bodies are pushed into the knacker's pit in *L'Equarissage pour tous* and other people arrive to take the place of the dead, fragments of people are collected in helmets in *Les Fourmis,* and the violently and picturesquely slain are mere theatrical properties in *Et on tuera tous les affreux* and the other Vernon Sullivan thrillers.

The behavior of the living is unaltered by the alarming number of fatalities around them. The reader is surprised at the heartlessness, perhaps, but he too remains essentially untouched by the carnage. Presumably such a response is due to an awareness that Vian's world is psychologically true to the world in which the reader lives. The novelist creates his absurd universe by transposing into visual terms the emotional attitudes of postwar society. The people of Arromanches in *L'Equarissage pour tous* kill and exploit all soldiers irrespective of nationality because they are interested only in personal gain. Amadis Dudu's experience with the bus at the beginning of *L'Automne à Pékin* and the attitudes of Lune and Paton in **"Les bons élèves"** (one of the stories in *Les Fourmis*) are symptomatic of the general treatment meted out to the anonymous public by the equally undifferentiated authorities. Bits of the human body float in open drains in the medical quarter in *L'Ecume des Jours* as an indication of the doctors' reaction to their work. Vian's world thus is an undisguised manifestation of the true mass response to sickness and death. It is dangerous, unfeeling, and quite beyond the control of the individual.

Set off in contrast against this picture of society, the author's treatment of personal relationships is poignant in the extreme. Again the same technique is used. And again the same movement toward destruction occurs. When Colin falls in love with Chloé his home is full of sunshine, but as she becomes increasingly ill and his life accordingly is more constrained, the walls tarnish and the rooms get smaller. His depression is translated into physical terms, as is his joy: the bedroom becomes spherical. As Chloé approaches death, the bed and the ceiling get nearer and nearer to the ground. Similarly in *L'Arrache-Coeur,* as Joël, Noël, and Citroën grow and hence have more responsibilities imposed upon them by their mother and by society, first they are shod by the village blacksmith and finally are kept in cages. Had the tale continued, it may be assumed that the cages would decrease in size as the occupants approached death, following the pattern established in *Les bâtisseurs d'empire,* in which the apartments had one room less each time the father ran away from the noise.

In these novels the outside world is controlled by the character's mood. His modified perception is actualized. Similarly the actions of many of the protagonists are exteriorizations of emotional responses. In *L'Automne à Pékin* Angel pushes Ann down the mine because he would like to be rid of his rival. He then kills Rochelle because he is unable to express his love for her. (His attitude would have stifled her inner life.) The father in *Les bâtisseurs d'empire* sends Zénobie out of the apartment to her death at the moment when he is rejecting her habit of questioning his precepts. (pp. 97-9)

Perhaps the most telling illustrations of Vian's attitude to death occur in one story of *Les Fourmis* and in the last chapter of *L'Ecume des Jours,* in which the mouse lies with its head in the mouth of a cat and waits for twelve little blind orphans to pass by, singing. The title story of *Les Fourmis* depicts the solitude and the ultimate absurdity of death. . . .

Thus far I have noted nothing unusual in Vian's attitude to death except that he explores the subject with unusual thoroughness. A closer look at the details of his work shows a more personal story, however. Vian had a heart condition and expected to die at any moment. . . . Hence the unfeeling world in which his characters move suddenly becomes the world he perceived around himself. His is a world from which people disappear, unmourned, unmissed. Was Vian attempting to accustom himself to this idea, or did he perhaps resent the thought

that he too would be peeled off the ice-rink barrier and thrown away? Is the world he created an expression of his personal bitterness? His preoccupation with physical health and perfection and with success in a life of sex and violence was perhaps wish fulfillment. (p. 99)

Chloé dies of a flower which grows inside her and which must at all costs be prevented from blooming. Le Père runs away from a noise. What could be more evocative of consciousness of a heart than these two images which dominate the stories in which they are found? Each time the father hears the noise, he moves into more restricted quarters. The treatment of Chloé's water lily reduces Colin's income, and also his freedom and, as in *Les bâtisseurs d'empire*, restricts the physical conditions under which they live. Colin's love for Chloé imprisons him as surely as Clementine imprisons Joël, Noël, and Citroën. He is left standing on the edge of the water, waiting to die. These conditions are representative of Vian's own life and of his struggle against the restrictions imposed by his illness.

Most of his images and situations are threatening in some way, and those that are not are obviously self-protective. Guns are grown from body heat, the flowers around a sickbed have a menacing air, a wedding procession from the door of the church to the altar becomes a ghost-train ride. In *L'Herbe Rouge* Lazuli dies when all the different aspects of himself have been murdered one by one by his interest in Folavril. When Chloé and Colin drive past unpleasant sights, they tint the windows of the car with the colors of the rainbow. The doctor Mangemanche builds model aircraft to avoid thinking of the patients he has killed and those he might yet kill. Joël, Noël, and Citroën eat blue beetles and fly. Only by escaping from the surface of the earth are they free. It is therefore significant that many scenes are set in enclosed places, frequently underground. Doctor Schutz's laboratories where he creates uniformly perfect human beings are underground in *Et on tuera tous les affreux;* so are the excavations that cause the collapse of the railway and death of most of the people involved in the project in *L'Automne à Pékin.* Both are telling images of the absurdity of human endeavour.

The structure of the books enforces the tone of their themes. They are either episodic, giving the impression that there is no knowing what will happen next nor who will survive to see it, or claustrophobic, leading in plot and atmosphere toward constraint and death. A story like **"L'Oie bleue"** in *Les Fourmis,* where this theme is weakened to a simple missed opportunity and the disappointment which ensues, is very unusual.

In contrast to the reduction apparent in the structure is the freedom of Vian's language. He plays with words and grammatical constructions as notes and themes are used in jazz. By breaking down accepted linguistic forms, he is able to intertwine and juxtapose symbol and idea. Words create their own logic, which reflects a different world from the one in which the logic of concept is current. A new awareness is produced, and the world of objects, dependent for its effect on the way in which it is perceived, is modified in its turn. By means of the words the author chooses to express his personal view of the world, his interpretation achieves a place within reality.

Vian's use of language translates his attitude to the world in which he lives. Its inventiveness, freshness, and freedom of movement show his love of life and active awareness of it. But the way in which he destroys expected forms transmits his uncertainty, and the mental shock thus produced creates an impression of an absurd world over which man has no control.

He stimulates excitement together with uneasiness, combined in the bittersweet idiom of jazz.

The author discusses death openly because he has come to terms with it on the surface, but all the linguistic, thematic, and structural details in his writing transmit his emotional horror at his fate. His works fall into two categories: those in which he plays with death to savor it and keep it at bay; and the much smaller group formed by his most powerful works— *L'Ecume des Jours, Les bâtisseurs d'empire,* and *L'Arrache-Coeur*—in which he cries out in anguish: "Je voudrais pas crever." (pp. 99-101)

Jennifer Walters, *"Death and Boris Vian," in* Papers on Language and Literature *(copyright © 1972 by the Board of Trustees, Southern Illinois University at Edwardsville), Vol. VIII, No. 1, Winter, 1972, pp. 97-101.*

## ALFRED CISMARU  (essay date 1972)

Readers and theater-goers of the 1960's, having been exposed to the anti-novel and the anti-theater, to what is called the Literature of the Absurd or Aliterature, have discovered Boris Vian to be a writer in whose prolific work they could recognize a heretofore unknown pertinence: for his preoccupations and obsessions are indeed those of today. The intriguing, engaging, and cathartic qualities of Vian's writing may easily be seen in two representative works: "**Le Rappel**," a short story written in 1947 but published in 1962, and . . . *Les Batisseurs d'empire*.

"**Le Rappel**" relates how an anonymous protagonist climbs to the top of the Empire State Building, checks the direction of the wind by throwing a piece of paper into the abyss below, then jumps. In the course of the fall he looks through the open windows of the offices and apartments that fly by, and fragments of memories are awakened in his mind through associations of words and images. Thus, the reasons which have prompted the suicide are evoked, venial and vague, through bits of recalled conversations and broken interior monologues. As the rapidity of the fall is increased by the gravitational pull, the onrush of souvenirs is accelerated, the real and the fantastic become intermingled, and we are suddenly aware that the irony and the pathos of death are, in fact, the only means we can use in order to escape from the painful banality of terrestrial existence: for the actual plunge into the unknown below is complemented, for the hero, by a concomitant spiritual descent into the past, and the two tumbles result into a heretofore unexperienced awareness of his former existence, of his present aspirations, of what death is really like.

Of course, Boris Vian, suffering, as he did all his life, of a cardiac insufficiency, went through a not-too-unsimilar slow plunge into death. "I should not want to die," he said, "no Sir, no Ma'am, before having tasted the aroma of death which torments me . . . before having tasted the aroma of death." The hero of "**Le Rappel**" does taste, savor, masticate, swallow, and become impregnated with the feeling of physical annihilation in the course of his fall. In fact, the fall transforms him and awakens in him a variety of contradictory and complex reactions, colored and reinforced by the bits of memories invading his brain. . . . The smell of freshly brewed coffee emerging from an open window on the seventeenth floor tickles his taste buds and results in a renewed interest in life, pushing aside, temporarily, the attraction of death, and making him enter, miraculously, the room, where a mystifying conversation

ensues between him and a young girl residing or visiting there.

In the episode just mentioned, among the several points debated is that of the similarity of things and situations. The protagonist maintains that what he saw on the way down differed from the agreeable to the abominable; the girl suggests that everything he saw was alike, that in fact, had he decided to enter through another window, on another floor, he would have found the same decor, the same tenants, and she too would have been there, for everything and everyone are nowhere and everywhere. He opposes a mild resistance to such a pessimistic view but is perhaps convinced in the end because when he asks, "What if I remained?" her curt reply is "You cannot remain . . . it is too late." And so he has nothing left to do but to take the elevator up again and to throw himself once more into the emptiness below—this time, one suspects, without curiosity, eyes shut until his head "makes a medusa on the Fifth Avenue asphalt."

In spite of the seriousness of the situation, the story is not devoid of humorous passages. In addition to obvious ones describing the appearance and disappearance of objects and persons in the speed of the plunge, and the fantastic episode relating the stop on the seventeenth floor, there are numerous laugh-provoking allusions, innuendos, and just plain funny, often invented words. (pp. 18-20)

These comic interplays lard through the gravity of the main character's suicidal act. Not only do they provide a necessary humorous relief, but they point to a singular ability on the part of the author to combine the lightest fantasies with the most profound pathos emerging from the threat of death. This ability prevents him from falling into the trap of trite sentimentality. On the contrary, like the procedures used by Louis-Ferdinand Celine and Raymond Queneau, his verbal fireworks deepen the underlying tragic fabric of the story, while at the same time imparting an attitude of consolation and catharsis.

As in most contemporary Aliterature, this narration written almost a quarter of a century ago has little thematic link between the episodes recollected and alternating with the sights perceived in the course of the fall. Memories tumble through the mind of the protagonist just as his body does along the facade of the skyscraper. Besides, logical perusal of thoughts and associations would not have been appropriate to the hero's physical position in space. Moreover, the lack of link plays an even more important role than that of complementing the precarious condition of the protagonist: it creates, supports, and heightens the mood of catastrophe which is going to end in violent death. The fleeting moments preceding the leap into nothingness, the last spasms of life, become as confused, as alogical as all the years of struggles and defeats which have led to the decision to commit suicide, with the difference, however, that now, the hero no longer has any secrets: while the reader may indeed find the intermittent recollections mysterious, and the unfinished allusions puzzling, the *post-sight* of Vian's character permits him to view the past more clearly than before, to understand perfectly the present, and therefore to nourish only sporadic and vague regrets. That is why he does not oppose the dismissal flung at him by the young woman on the seventeenth floor; that is why he does not hesitate to climb once more to the top of the building and, having seen, having understood in the course of the previous plunge, to dive again without paying any attention to the sights available to him.

The cathartic quality of the narrative emerges from the very ability of the character to repeat his desperate gesture, to accept death as a solution once more, no longer in the heat of passion but after having been able to view the past again and to contemplate other possibilities (such as remaining on the seventeenth floor, establishing a rapport with his interlocutor, resuming life). The reader, who is not altogether up to date with the events leading to the initial gesture, can accept the second with a feeling of detachment, if not one of superiority: for he knows the past, or thinks he does, and he is not contemplating a step similar to the one undertaken by the hero. (pp. 20-1)

*Les Batisseurs d'empire* is considered to be the author's only play which is likely to survive. This drama of the absurd, written in only a few days, has been hailed as a masterpiece of humor and tragedy, moving and surpassing the personal obsessions of the dramatist who, in such plays as *Le Dernier des metiers* . . . and *Gouter des generaux* . . . , had limited himself merely to haranguing on his two pet peeves: clericalism and militarism. On the contrary, in *Les Batisseurs d'empire* he breaks away from strictly personal preoccupations and espouses those marring the existence of all men living under the threat of pain and death.

The threat has a twofold manifestation in the play: one is The Sound, which is heard at various degrees of intensity throughout the three acts, and which represents the menace of existence of physical annihilation; the other is the presence of The Schmurz . . . , suggestive of the German *Schmerz*, or pain. The dual threat is recognized by Zenobie, the young girl; it is ignored, to a large extent, by the parents and the servant who refuse to acknowledge openly the presence of any imminent danger. In fact, Father, Mother, and Cruche intermittently strike The Schmurz much as sick persons stab blindly at physical ills paining them with pills and palliatives of questionable value, but refuse to speak of or admit to the presence of chronic and incurable disease. Father and Mother, obstinately declining to acquiesce the catastrophe around them, become nevertheless incensed at trivial problems, such as which way a screwdriver (that they do not have) must be turned in order to put a screw into a piece of wood. Their responses to the daughter's insistence that steps be taken to deal with the dangers she sees, proceed, not according to logic, but by word and thought association. To the humor resulting is added the servant's comic accumulation of synonyms and antonyms in numerous senseless speeches, a dizzying and laugh-provoking device reminiscent of the *fabliaux* of the Middle Ages and Rabelais.

As in **"Le Rappel,"** The exploitation of comic techniques, far from rendering the human condition palatable, enhances and maximizes the tragedy of characters caught between an invisible Sound and a visible Schmurz. Against the first menace, one can do absolutely nothing short of pretending not to hear it; against the second, all attitudes remain futile: neither the parents' or Cruche's ignorance of it (a modified ignorance, of course, for it is accompanied by repeated and robot-like blows administered at times with passion), nor Zenobie's direct admittance that he exists and that more effective measures must be taken against it, have a satisfactory result. The Schmurz is a being that exists in and for itself, an unavoidable manifestation of reality which could only disappear when and if reality does. At the end of the play, after servant, daughter, and wife have vanished and left Father alone on the stage, The Schmurz remains, invulnerable even when shot at, and dies only when Father himself does. The final stage instructions specify that after the hero's death, a "door opens and enter, vague silhouettes in the dark, a number of Schmurz." Such multiple entries at the end suggest that while the specific Schmurz of Father disappears with his death, pain as such remains.

The success of *Les Batisseurs d'empire* with the European intelligentsia was due, in part, to its many affinities with other anti-plays, and with a number of literary currents preceding and following its composition. For example, Mother's and Father's lack of memory (they forget the shape and size of their previous apartment, their past in general, and just about everything they say once they have said it) can be linked to similar defects of characters in plays of Beckett and Arrabal, as well as novels and plays of Marguerite Duras. In contemporary literature defective memory is indeed a frequent trait of personages, pointing at once to their innocence and to their physical and spiritual decomposition. Many associations can also be found with Existentialism: Mother's and Father's refusal to *see* reality, their *bad faith*, their living for *autrui*, for example. Vian, of course, was a devotee of Existentialist circles and a friend of Sartre, who had published his very first works in *Les Temps modernes* and was satirized as Jean-Sol-Partre in Vian's novel *L'Ecume des jours*. Cruche's semi-symphonic variations on words and, in general, the characters' persistence in alogical conversational pursuits, are reminiscent of a host of contemporary writers and works, those of Beckett and Ionesco in particular. The same can be said of the frequent literal interpretations of idiomatic expressions, a device used by such famous writers of farce as Georges Feydeau, and brilliantly exploited by many later playwrights. The distortion, misuse, or overuse of cliches likewise adds to the humor of the play and points to familiar dramatic procedures. Finally, the scene in Act II in which Father mimics his *aventure* (the story of his life) can be compared to the dream sequence in the second act of Ionesco's *Amedee ou comment s'en debarrasser*, to the first tableau of Jacques Audiberti's *Quoat-Quoat*, and to many similar scenes in the plays of Beckett.

These affinities with Aliterature which apparently "sold" the play to the European public were the very ones which have made acceptance difficult in the United States. Edith Oliver, for example, defines Mother's and Father's speeches as "chatterings in a silly, mock-bright fashion to divert her [the *daughter*] as if Ionesco were trying to cheer up Anne Frank." What the reviewer failed to see was that, often, neither Ionesco nor Vian is interested in diverting anyone; that the role of humor in their plays is to evoke and deepen the tragedy while providing, at the same time, sufficient comic relief to make the spectator bear and withstand the onrush of pathos flung at him. Were this comic relief absent, the tragic human situation suggested would elicit either total despair, becoming a philosophical treatise (as Sartre's plays are frequently considered today), or sentimental tears, becoming a soap opera. The anonymous reviewer of *Time*, less belligerent, underlined what the American audiences find constantly objectionable in plays of this type: "What is The Schmurz—the awful awareness of one's death? Is despair the Sound that drives this man into an ever-narrowing corner? There are no answers, and the final moments of the play suffer somewhat from a lack of resolution." The two comments mentioned, representative of the American reception of *Les Batisseurs d'empire*, point to an inability or an unwillingness to look or dig beyond the "chatterings," and to accept a "lack of resolution" as a resolution of some sort, no matter how unsettling. Neither Beckett, Ionesco, nor Vian have ever viewed the act of writing as a means of providing answers to the questions inherent in man's terrestrial existence. Their intent is divorced from definitions, categorizations, and solutions. More aware of limitations and impossibilities, they strive to point out problems, to suggest areas of confusion and conflict, leaving to philosophers, priests, social and political leaders, to the reading public, that is, the consuming task of searching for remedies.

**"Le Rappel"** and *Les Batisseurs d'empire*, then, central in the literary work of Boris Vian, reveal an author able to anticipate a number of currents in today's letters, to use other contemporary ones, and to combine astutely his tragic vision of life with the comically derisory aspects of daily existence. (pp. 22-5)

> Alfred Cismaru, *"An Introduction to Boris Vian,"* in Critique: Studies in Modern Fiction *(copyright © by* Critique, *1972), Vol. XIV, No. 1, 1972, pp. 17-26.*

## MICHAEL G. LERNER  (essay date 1974)

[It] is through his style that Vian reveals both his highly critical "drop-out" attitude to life and society and also his talents as an imaginative, almost allegorical writer of the tragically humorous and strangely human in these as he experienced them from his own somewhat schizophrenic yet poetic point of view.

*L'Arrache-Coeur* shows Vian applying a literal Freudian interpretation to everyday affairs epitomised in the life of the village and one of its married couples, Angel and Clémentine, which his main character, a psychiatrist named Jacquemort discovers on a casual visit to the region. Born with a sort of existential emptiness within himself, Jacquemort wants to assume the desires and emotions of those he meets and wishes to psycho-analyse; and the village provides him with plenty to study from the very beginning when he is suddenly called upon to help in the delivery of Clémentine's triplets and becomes involved in the effects of her dominant matriarchy and subsequent rejection of her husband in favour of her children. Apart from her role as *l'arrache-coeur*, other psychological and social attitudes laid bare in their most literal form by Vian's critical, sick-humorous, grotesque imagination are represented by the *foire aux vieux* where old people are got rid of by auction in the most brutal way, the carpenter who uses orphaned weaklings as cheap, easily replacable labour instead of machines, the Acheron-like boatman La Gloïre who is the scapegoat for the sins of the community (elsewhere in Vian called the *Schmürz*, as in *Les Bâtisseurs d'Empire*), and the priest in the cuckoo-clock-like pulpit who stages fights with the Devil. The landscape—such as the blood-red stream La Gloïre sails on, the paths Jacquemort walks along to the white house with their symbolic rock formations and queer-goat excrement, and the cliff-face Clémentine climbs—is like the crucified stallion and the trees felled in the garden an integral part of Vian's imaginatively literal transposition of the instincts and neuroses—particularly sexual ones—that psycho-analysis reveals beneath the conventional and respectable veneer of normal society; this critical attitude is supported by the number of speaking animals in Vian's work which reflect on human attitudes latent in his characters. It is the empty Jacquemort's confrontation with these powerful forces not normally visible but grotesquely displayed here that forms the plot of the novel and his inability to integrate himself into the villagers' personalities as he desires that provides the main interest. Vian's style reflects the impact of these experiences with the villagers on Jacquemort's being. . . . (pp. 195-96)

The brevity of [Chapter XXI, the concluding chapter of Part One] is fairly typical of the structure of *L'Arrache-Coeur*; the chapters are short so that Jacquemort's experiences of events in the village as a whole are constantly juxtaposed with the relations of Angel and Clémentine and the latter's maternal complex as if to underline the *dédoublement* of Jacquemort and Angel as complementary aspects of the human personality, in fact Vian's own, and the selfishness, hatred, and other emotions in society that Clémentine's case exemplifies. Also, the quick succession of chapters each with its strange content or happening both creates a dynamic cohesiveness in the narrative—to which short, simple sentences also contribute—and at the same time maintains thereby its startling quality essential to the evocation of a strange, microcosmic atmosphere. Chapter XXI follows the scene in Chapter XIX of Jacquemort's inability to psycho-analyse Clémentine's nurse Culblanc—so named because of her rustic sexuality—because he cannot resist her invitation to have sex with her instead and the scene of Chapter XX where Clémentine finally ejects Angel from her bed forever; it thus follows a demonstration in the two previous scenes of the dilemma of man's sexual desire and the puppet-like role it reduces him to on an animal level at the hands of women; Jacquemort's experiment is halted and Angel's role is simply abandoned. This is a favourite theme in Vian's work and is very much to the fore in *L'Arrache-Coeur* because of events in Vian's conjugal life at the time of his writing the novel. Furthermore, the juxtaposition of the two scenes points out more clearly the complementary *dédoublement* of Jacquemort and Angel and the contrast between them: the former empty, free, and aspiring to the active feelings of others in his largely voyeuristic passivity and submission to circumstances; the latter actively struggling for survival in the world of Clémentine and the villagers as an individual with personal feelings and desires. [Chapter XXI] sums up both in its content and in its style Jacquemort's attitude to life in the village. (p. 196)

Although [Chapter XXI] is not wholly representative of Vian's style, it does show some of its characteristics which contribute to the psychological notion of *dédoublement* in his characters and the strangeness of his novel's *milieu:* his use of the short sentence; of the juxtaposition of concrete and abstract; of abstract nouns; of English or American words (here, *la nurse*); of technical or precious vocabulary for parts of the body, architecture, machinery, carpentry, etc.; of slightly unusual adjectives (here, *insolites, lointains*); and his enjoyment in playing with words as in the assonance of the last line here and in using those words with allusive or punning possibilities by their several levels of meaning or in juggling with words sounding or looking the same or taking proverbs or jargon at a literal level. All these devices reflect Vian's neo-Surrealistic desire to rebel and startle his reader and make him see life from a new "outsider's" angle—essentially a darker one born of his own neuroses—while being entertained at the same time by the author's stylistic box of tricks of neologisms, words taken literarily, technical vocabulary, and the juxtaposing of abstract and concrete. As in the novel, where the mixture of concrete and abstract provides a sort of hallucinatory impression of being and non-being in the characters such as has been seen with regard to Jacquemort in the passage above, so in the style there is a similar feeling of an active, meaningful rhetoric for humourous-critical effect and a great deal of gratuitous sensationalism. Both are sincere in their intended uses, but while the one is of literary and linguistic value, the other is merely obvious and naïve. (pp. 197-98)

> Michael G. Lerner, *"Boris Vian's 'L'arrache-coeur': Some Comments on His Style,"* in Neophilologus *(© 1974 H. D. Tjeenk Willink), Vol. LVIII, No. 2, April, 1974, pp. 195-98.*

**DONALD HEINEY** (essay date 1975)

Unfortunately not possessing genius, [Vian] was unable to follow Wilde's advice that one should put his genius into his life and only his talent into his work. His solution, at best a compromise, was to divide a considerable talent among so many realms that to judge him in any one of them would be most unfair. In a short lifetime—he was born in 1920 and died in 1959 of heart disease—he produced about twenty volumes of novels, stories, plays, poems and sketches, not counting the four pastiche novels which he offered as translations of the non-existent American novelist Vernon Sullivan. But even in this work there is a failure of total commitment—a kind of left-handed and negligent agility—that on the one hand makes it difficult to assess Vian seriously as a writer, and on the other hand constitutes one of his main charms. His dramas are absurd in several different senses; his fiction is fractured, paratactic, resembling a carelessly constructed kaleidoscope. In his first novel, *Vercoquin et le plancton,* there is a character named Emmanuel Pigeon who kills a giraffe by combing it excessively. This is exactly the Vian touch: the gentleness, the quality of the grotesque, the ultimate pessimism residing in the knowledge that gentleness is not enough. To this is added an element of outrage which derives from, or at least resembles, Jarry and the dadaists. The mixture is indigestible, like those cocktails made of horse-bones or gasoline which characters in Vian are always giving to their guests.

During his lifetime Vian's only successful book among the general public was *J'irai cracher sur vos tombes,* the best known of the Vernon Sullivan novels, and this was in large part a notoriety set off by its scabrous content and the lawsuit it entailed. By 1970, however—only eleven years after his death—Vian and his work, his legend, were in full revival. . . . Maurice Nadeau remarks of this phenomenon, "This youthful group is obviously less sensible to the value of the work itself than it is to the spirit in which the work was written, to the attitude toward life of an individual who shattered artistic categories, to the perpetual adolescent (with all the virtues and the insolence of adolescence) that was and remains Boris Vian." But the response to Vian is bifurcated; on the other hand there is "the value of the work," which is regarded quite seriously, even perhaps a little too solemnly in some academic circles. (pp. 66-7)

Like all pataphysicians (he is not only an admirer of Jarry but a contributor to the Cahiers du Collège de Pataphysique), Vian is the enemy of the serious, or at least must pretend to be. The element of parody in his fiction is chiefly parody of naturalism and of the well-made novel. In *L'automne à Pékin* we start off, in the Sartrian-Zolaesque mode, with the impression we are going to learn something about how the Paris bus system operates, along with some comments on the alienation of modern man in an urban environment. But when Amadis Dudu finally catches Bus 975 it takes him, after a twenty-four hour trip, to the imaginary country of Exopotamia, where some engineers are building a railroad on a completely featureless desert precisely because a railroad is not needed there. The setting of *La nausée* has turned into a landscape by Dali. The quality of discontinuity, of incohesion (although perhaps not of incoherence) is the most characteristic feature of the novels. In *L'arrache-coeur* there are two stories running side by side: the effort of the psychiatrist Jacquemort to obtain a soul for himself by "psychoanalyzing" one out of somebody, and the attack on motherhood in the portrayal of Clémentine and her grossly obsessive relations with her children. These two plots are not really integrated, or rather the technical efforts that

Vian makes to do so are themselves parodistic. Often the Jarryesque bawdiness, the outrage, is replaced by a fragile and poetic eroticism that, like the combing of the giraffe, ends in pathos. The love of Colin and Chloé in *L'écume des jours* is blighted by a nenuphar that grows slowly in her chest, dooming her to a death that is as artificial and operatic as it is touching. The invention of the water-lily as an agent of death suggests Blake ("Rose, thou art sick") more than it does the ordinary tragic romanticism of Dumas *fils* or—to take a rather flimsy modern example—Erich Segal's *Love Story.* This latter comparison is not entirely far-fetched, because Vian, especially in *L'écume des jours,* is always in danger of falling into a conventional sentimentalism; the risk is there as well in the relations of Angel and Rochelle in *L'automne à Pékin.* If he manages to elude this trap it is because, perhaps, he lacks the perseverance to sustain any one theme or mood for long, and soon deflates the sentiment with a sample of his black humor: a model airplane constructed by Professor Mangemanche plunges through the wall of the hotel in the desert, leaving an exactly airplane-shaped hole (as in cartoons) and shattering the cranium of the proprietor Pipo.

Not only is the narrative of *L'automne à Pékin* full of *actes gratuits,* like the building of the railroad in Exopotamia in the first place, and like the decision to run the tracks directly through the hotel which is the only substantial building in the country; but the novel (any novel by Vian) is itself a gratuitous artifact with no particular reason for its existence other than its own oneiric solidity and brilliance, its internal pyrotechnics. (*Feux d'artifices* would be an excellent title for a Vian novel, or for his work in general.) Henri Baudin in *Boris Vian humoriste* has elaborately classified these various forms of outrage to common sense, ranging from simple plays on words, to bad jokes, to false causality: "The tides of September . . . have the curious effect on the trees of reddening the leaves." Some of his leaps of logic are worthy of Groucho Marx: "Gentlemen of the jury, let's put aside the motive for the murder, the circumstances under which it was accomplished, and even the murder itself. In this case, what have you got to hold against my client?" . . . Certain passages in Vian, like the Old Folks' Fair in *L'arrache-coeur,* have exactly the same tone—outrage to human dignity combined with the utmost matter-of-factness—as the scene in *A Night at the Opera* in which the Marx Brothers try to crowd into a tiny ship's cabin along with fifteen or twenty other people. This lack of surprise in Vian's characters, their equanimity or resignation in the face of the general absurdity, is a consistent quality in both his fiction and his drama.

Oddly enough, this element of absurdity in Vian's work proves to be the link between the ridiculous and the sublime, between low comedy and any philosophy we are likely to find in it. Nadeau classifies the unclassifiable Vian under "L'existentialisme et ses à-côtés," and this label is probably less unsatisfactory than any other. In addition to the Colin-Chloé love plot in *L'écume des jours* there is a rather transparent roman à clef referring to Vian's own circle of acquaintances. Chick, a friend of Colin, is a fanatic disciple of a philosopher called Jean-Sol Partre; he spends all his money for Partre's books and borrows to buy more, and the obsession finally blights his romance with Alise, the fourth main character of the novel. Partre, disclaiming responsibility, merely remarks in existentialist jargon that Chick has "made his choice." Alise goes to see Partre and begs him to stop writing so many books. He refuses, and she slays him with an *arrache-coeur,* a tool she has brought along for the purpose. Partre dies quickly, only a little astonished at the discovery that his heart when extracted is tetrahedral in shape. His funeral resembles a scene from *Ubu Roi*. Vian was a personal friend of Sartre and Simone de Beauvoir (who appears in the novel as the Duchess of Bovouart), and, according to accounts, they were not offended by the novel and even found it amusing and witty. But there is still a fissure, an unbridgeable gulf, between the thought-systems of Vian and Sartre. Vian's whole life and work reflect an effort, and a successful one, to remain *dégagé* in a number of senses, politically and personally, ideologically and in literary technique. The notion of *littérature dégagé* was the guiding principle of the *Cahiers de la Pléiade,* founded by Jean Paulhan, with which Vian was closely associated and which printed an early version of *L'équarrissage pour tous* in 1948 in full tide of the rage for Sartrism. He rejected the premise that existence precedes essence, not because the order of the terms was wrong but because he didn't believe in essences. "What Vian failed to accept," [Alfred] Cismaru summarizes, "and wanted everyone else to refuse as well, is the process of the diminution of man, of his physical and spiritual assets, of the dignity which is at the core of his definition. Chloé dies, Wolf dies, Jacquemort deteriorates into La Gloïre. Time, age, and other people corrupt the zest and zeal of youth, cause it to decay, ultimately to disintegrate and vanish. This is beyond comprehension, Vian suggests, and also beyond our will or capacity to acquiesce." In short Vian rejects commitment but retains angst and rebellion. His stance is analogous to that of the fallen Christian, who, no longer believing in any means to salvation, continues to fear God and to accept the ultimate premises of the divine structure of power. Vian's answer is a laugh, a rather sickly one but one which he enjoys.

If Vian's work is existentialist or "on the fringes of existentialism" in its conceptual implications, it is surrealistic or neo-surrealistic in technique or, more precisely, in tone and image. It would be rather fruitless to attempt to make him out an important writer on the level of ideology or concept; at best he is a parodist of Sartre. But this other aspect of his work, the Jarryesque or surrealist, is probably a more significant contribution. For sheer verve and energy there is scarcely anyone to match him in postwar French fiction; Queneau is more precise, more intelligent, but less inventive. Vian's effects are not often sustained, but when he does manage to maintain the same tone for a half-dozen pages the results are often pointed or even eerie in their effect. When Jacquemort in *L'arrache-coeur* gives up his attempt to find a human patient and turns to psychoanalyze a cat, it has some peculiar effects on him: he develops a taste for catnip and is able to catch fish with his bare hands. But it affects the cat even more markedly. Soulless and dessicated, an "empty envelope," magically light, it is blown away by a chance puff of air in a scene which nobody witnesses, neither Jacquemort nor the cat itself. (pp. 67-9)

Vian [is] worthy of being saved from the overly enthusiastic Zazous of St.-Germain-des-Prés on the one hand, and from the solemn writers of dissertations on the other. And there is another kind of genuine quality, of integrity, in plays like *Les bâtisseurs d'empire* and *Le goûter des généraux,* a quality that stands up capably to comparison with the Ionesco of *La leçon* and *La cantatrice chauve.* The work of Vian portrays the same "cadaverous universe" as that of Ionesco and Beckett. Vian more closely resembles Ionesco, in that his universe is not delineated in any kind of coherent or even incoherent intellectual scheme, like the dialogues in *Endgame,* but sheerly in image and incident. Like the American jazz he so much admired, his work is improvised from phrase to phrase yet con-

trolled by the maker's inner sense of the fitness of each part to the whole. It is impossible to say why the wind should "stretch sharp threads of noise across the grass," except that this image is fitting to the whole vision of the blown-away cat. This is a Vian who, with a bad heart, was not well enough to be a jazz trumpeter and instead became a poet. (p. 69)

*Donald Heiney, "Boris Vian, the Marx Brothers, and Jean-Sol Partre," in* Books Abroad *(copyright 1975 by the University of Oklahoma Press), Vol. 49, No. 1, Winter, 1975, pp. 66-9.*

### D. McDOWELL (essay date 1978)

"With three boards, four rags and six guys, to show the spectator ten times more than he will ever see in all the *Obérons* on Opera Square." With this bold statement, Boris Vian, one of the most compelling members of the College of Pataphysics, expressed his desire to renew the Parisian stage of the forties. Heir of Jarry and Artaud, with *Le goûter des Généraux, L'e-quarissage pour tous* and *Les bâtisseurs d'empire,* he did just that—posthumously however. . . . [*Petits spectacles*] consists of ten skits written between 1947 and 1949 for the nightclubs and experimental theatres of the Left Bank.

Composed of dialogues enlivened by a confusion of all genres, songs, music, mime and dance, they tend to reflect a cruel, disconcerting and absurd reality but do not embody, however, Artaud's "theatre of cruelty." Vian's familiar themes—obsession with death, antimilitarism, anticlericalism, antipatriotism, antiheroism et cetera—as well as his liking for science fiction are all present but greatly weakened by traditional and unimaginative situations. He pokes fun, for instance, at the typical national idiosyncrasies or parodies the popular movies of the forties. The humor, so poetical and innovative in his major works, is facile, heavy and disappointing here. The comic element, a combination of funny gestures and situations, remains throughout the book totally superficial. Neither the burlesque nor the cruelty succeeds in creating a dramatic tension.

Watching the homosexual serpent—completely innocent, by the way, of Adam and Eve's Fall (*A chacun son serpent*)—or seeing tuxedoed Livingstone and Stanley eat rat with mint sauce while toasting their Queen and plotting to replace all lands by sea to reconquer England's supremacy (*Fluctuat nec mergitur*), the spectator will probably smile, but he will not be shattered nor concerned and certainly not enchanted. Vian's ten skits provide for an evening of light entertainment, but they are indeed "petits spectacles" which do not do justice to the author of *L'herbe rouge* or *L'écume des jours.* (pp. 436-37)

*D. McDowell, "French: 'Petits spectacles'," in* World Literature Today *(copyright 1978 by the University of Oklahoma Press), Vol. 52, No. 3, Summer, 1978, pp. 436-37.*

### ANNE L. GIBSON (essay date 1979)

*Le Goûter des généraux* is a delightful comedy wherein politicians, diplomats, and generals fall victim to Vian's skill at caricature and parody. Has it, however, any deeper significance than has been attributed to it? While it is apparently just a light-hearted spoof of Machiavellian politics and politicians, there is a singularly consistent and realistic manipulation of characters and plot through words alone. Can such consistency be attributed solely to the farcical situations or the childish personalities created by the author? Even though it does not deal with ultimate questions, is none of it to be taken seriously, or can we perceive something other than a purely comic intent on the part of the writer? (pp. 203-04)

The action of the play concerns the evolution of a war, from the initial stages of diplomatic manoeuvring to an ironic dénouement. Léon Plantin, Président du Conseil de France, has decided that France needs a war to solve her economic difficulties.

Léon goes to the home of his Chief of Staff, General James Audubon Wilson, to discuss the necessity for war and to convince Audubon that he must prepare the army. After much hesitation, Audubon agrees and calls in the General Staff to begin arrangements for the conflict. Later, he confers with Léon and the diplomatic representatives of the USA, China, and Russia, who are consulted about a suitable opponent for France. After much discussion, Morocco and Algeria are chosen for the honour and the war begins. The preliminaries make up the first two acts. The last act takes place in the generals' underground bunker above which the war is being fought.

From this description of the action, it will be apparent that the business of making war is treated like a game. There are, in fact, games within games, as further analysis of the play will show. It must be remembered that the basic feature of games is manipulation of counters, pieces, or 'men', according to fixed rules. In *Le Goûter des généraux,* the manipulation of counters will be readily apparent, but the rules that govern the game may not be so easily distinguishable.

The game of logic as played in *Le Goûter des généraux* parodies (although perhaps only slightly) the way in which wars are arranged by the very real people who share our own world. Vian manages to expose the logic of practical politics as a kind of primitive word magic.

The game resembles the diplomatic deals which the twentieth century knows too well, yet the scene with the diplomats is a funny scene. This is made possible through the comic relief provided by Audubon, and because the deals are not couched in diplomatic language. The diplomats are singularly blunt and honest. For this reason, perhaps, they no longer resemble their real-life counterparts, but become caricatures. The aims of the game, at least of the stage diplomats, are frankly stated. Each nation will benefit; the only losers will be people—who are just pawns anyway.

With this decision, the game is ready to begin. The opponents have been chosen, the rules agreed upon, and in Act III the game is in full swing, but already the generals have become bored with it. They are seeking another game which they can play in their bunker.

A game of cards would be amusing, but no one can remember the rules for cards, although Laveste claims to know one called 'tirelarigot'. . . .

When the diplomats visit the bunker to see how things are going, Korkiloff suggests that they 'play' the game of Russian roulette, which, he explains, is quite easy. Delighted at the simplicity of the rules, all agree to play. . . . Each takes a turn with the pistol while one of the others sing. . . .

Every time the song ends, the gun goes off, killing another player. The innocuous word 'game' obscures the mortal danger, and everyone 'plays' in turn until all are dead. It is a proper end for all who 'play' the 'game' known as war. (p. 208)

The politicians and diplomats whom Vian portrays as cynical manoeuvrers are devoid of human feeling. Consequently they are rarely funny except when they, too, fall victim to word games. In the game of Russian roulette, the diplomats behave as childishly as the generals.

All the characters react to words *as if* they were things, *as if* a word had the precise and equal force of its referent. Now it is the essence of magic to regard the object and its symbol as one and the same thing so that either may be invoked in order to bring about effects on the other. This is why, in Act III, the generals forbid anyone to use such words as 'tuant', 'bataille', 'mourir', or any other words which suggest death. To articulate them might invoke that condition.

The diplomats, no less than the infantile generals, are mesmerized by language. Their word games are the result of Vian's continuous exposure of 'batailles de mots qui tuent les hommes de chair'. Vian examines the words of demagoguery and exposes their essential hollowness. If words are not more powerful than reality, people act *as if* they were.

In *Le Goûter des généraux* the tragic consequences are shrouded in comedy, but the lesson is clear. The jargon of chauvinism can be a powerful goal for the ingenuous who mistake highsounding phrases for fact and thus endow words with semimagic properties. (p. 209)

> *Anne L. Gibson, ''Boris Vian's 'Le gouter des generaux' or Word Battles in Wonderland,'' in* Modern Languages, *Vol. LX, No. 4, December, 1979, pp. 203-10.*

---

## ADDITIONAL BIBLIOGRAPHY

Cismaru, Alfred. *Boris Vian.* New York: Twayne Publishers, 1974, 143 p.
> Critical survey of Vian's major and minor works.

Cismaru, Alfred. ''Antimilitarism in Boris Vian's First Play.'' *South Atlantic Bulletin* XL, No. 2 (May 1975): 24-32.
> Examines Vian's pacifist sentiments in *L'equarrissage pour tous,* an antiwar farce.

Gerrard, Charlotte F. ''Vian's Priest as Showman in *Le dernier des métiers.*'' *The French Review* XLVII, No. 6 (May 1974): 1123-24.
> Examines Vian's anticlericalism in *Le dernier des métiers.*

Mankin, Paul A. ''The Fight Against Institutions in the Parodic Discourse of Nathanael West and Boris Vian.'' In *Proceedings of the 7th Congress of the International Comparative Literature Association, Vol. 1,* edited by Milan V. Dimic and Juan Ferraté, pp. 507-10. Stuttgart: Kunst and Wissen, Erich Bieber, 1979.
> Compares satirical techniques of West's *A Cool Million* and Vian's *Froth on the Daydream.*

Roza, Robert. ''A Freedom beyond Dignity: Two Pataphysical Novels.'' *The American Society Legion of Honor Magazine* XLIV, No. 3: 139-49.*
> Compares Raymond Queneau's *Zazie dans le Métro* and Vian's *L'écume des jours.*

Walters, Jennifer R. ''The Disquieting Worlds of Lewis Carroll and Boris Vian.'' *Revue de Litterature Comparee* XLVI, No. 2 (April-June 1972): 284-94.*
> Detailed comparison of Lewis Carroll and Vian.

# Edith (Newbold Jones) Wharton

## 1862-1937

American novelist, short story writer, critic, autobiographer, and poet.

Wharton is best known as a novelist of manners whose fiction exposed the cruel excesses of aristocratic society at the turn of the century. Her subject matter, tone, and style have often been compared with those of Henry James, her friend and mentor. Many critics also point to Wharton's affinities with Jane Austen and George Eliot, who shared her concern for the constricted status of women in a modern society.

Born into a wealthy New York family, Wharton was privately educated by governesses and tutors both at home and in Europe. From this upper-class perspective, she observed power and wealth shift from the hands of New York's established gentry to the nouveau riche of the Industrial Revolution. Wharton considered many of the nouveau riche, whose obsession for economic status overshadowed personal and moral concerns, to be cultural philistines, and she drew some of her richest fictional characters and situations from this group. Dissatisfied with society life and ill-matched in marriage, Wharton turned to writing for a measure of fulfillment. Against her husband's wishes, she wrote several nonfictional books on architecture and interior decoration, as well as a number of novels and short story collections. *The Greater Inclination* and *The House of Mirth* were especially well received by critics and readers during the earliest years of Wharton's career. With the breakup of her marriage in 1912, Wharton took up permanent residence in France, where she wrote one of her most famous and long-lived books, *Ethan Frome*. In this novella, the author used the background of rural New England to explore her characteristic concern over the difficulties involved in male-female relationships, revealing her loathing of society's rigid, unpitying standards of decency, propriety, and loyalty. During World War I, Wharton organized relief efforts in France and cared for Belgian orphans, work that earned her the French Legion of Honor. However, her war novels *The Marne* and *A Son at the Front* are undistinguished. In 1921, she became the first female recipient of the Pulitzer Prize, awarded to her for *The Age of Innocence*. Like her other long masterpieces, *The House of Mirth, The Custom of the Country,* and *The Reef,* this novel focuses primarily on the tradition of marriage which, in Wharton's estimation, had been grossly misused by New York society to maintain its own male-dominated order. Wharton's later novels reflect the author's growing disillusionment with postwar America and the Jazz Age. With few exceptions, Wharton never again achieved the brilliant characterizations and settings which so enlivened her prewar works. When she died in St. Brice-sous-Forêt, her final novel, *The Buccaneers,* lay unfinished.

From the start of her professional career and for many years afterward, Wharton was advised and encouraged by her cousin and friend, Walter Berry. Romantic allusions about them have been made by various biographers, and Wharton's few sympathetic male characters are said to be modelled after either Berry or, as scholars have recently claimed, her lover, Morton Fullerton. The understanding, intellectual stimulation, and sexual fulfillment that Wharton belatedly found are tran-

*Pictorial Parade*

scribed in her fiction as a welcome refuge from the life-smothering deadness of the social values of America's upper class. The "smothered life," whether revealed in the treatment of women as mindless ornaments or in the denial by marriage of love for others, is one of Wharton's common themes. The man-chasing Lily Bart of *The House of Mirth* and Undine Spragg of *The Custom of the Country* may be foolish and grotesque, but society has conditioned them to be parasitic, a position Wharton despised.

Readers and critics have often failed to recognize Wharton's concerns and have mistakenly viewed her as an outdated novelist of manners, whose settings, style, and slow-moving pace belong to the nineteenth century. Comparisons of Wharton's work to that of Henry James are frequent; critics find the early short stories and *The Reef* the most Jamesian of her works. Some, however, notably Irving Howe, believe claims of James's influence to be exaggerated, the result of superficial readings of Wharton's work. With the rise of the women's movement during the 1970s, criticism has tended to focus on Wharton's expression of feminist issues, occasionally to the exclusion of the author's other concerns.

However, the feminist movement has spurred renewed interest in Wharton's moving and insightful portrayals of the position of women at the turn of the century. As Elizabeth Ammons has commented, Wharton's fiction "is both a record of one brilliant and intellectually independent woman's thinking about women and a map of feminism's ferment and failure in America in the decades surrounding the Great War." Furthermore, according to Margaret McDowell, she provided an important "link between the morally and psychologically oriented works of Hawthorne and James, who preceded her, and the later realists like Sinclair Lewis or F. Scott Fitzgerald with their tendency toward the sardonic and iconoclastic."

(See also *TCLC*, Vol. 3, and *Dictionary of Literary Biography*, Vol. 4: *American Writers in Paris, 1920-1939;* Vol. 9: *American Novelists, 1910-1945;* Vol. 12: *American Realists and Naturalists.*)

## PRINCIPAL WORKS

*The Decoration of Houses* [with Ogden Codman, Jr.]
    (nonfiction)   1897
*The Greater Inclination*   (short stories)   1899
*The Touchstone*   (novella)   1900; also published as *A Gift from the Grave*, 1900
*Crucial Instances*   (short stories)   1901
*The Valley of Decision*   (novel)   1902
*Sanctuary*   (novella)   1903
*The Descent of Man*   (short stories)   1904
*Italian Villas and Their Gardens*   (essays)   1904
*The House of Mirth*   (novel)   1905
*Italian Backgrounds*   (memoirs)   1905
*The Fruit of the Tree*   (novel)   1907
*Madame de Treymes*   (novella)   1907
*The Hermit and the Wild Woman, and Other Stories*   (short stories)   1908
*Tales of Ghosts and Men*   (short stories)   1910
*Ethan Frome*   (novella)   1911
*The Reef*   (novel)   1912
*The Custom of the Country*   (novel)   1913
*Xingu, and Other Stories*   (short stories and novella)   1916
*Summer*   (novel)   1917
*The Marne*   (novella)   1918
*French Ways and Their Meanings*   (essays)   1919
*The Age of Innocence*   (novel)   1920
*The Glimpses of the Moon*   (novel)   1922
*A Son at the Front*   (novel)   1923
*Old New York*   (novellas)   1924
*The Mother's Recompense*   (novel)   1925
*The Writing of Fiction*   (criticism)   1925
*Here and Beyond*   (short stories)   1926
*Twilight Sleep*   (novel)   1927
*The Children*   (novel)   1928
*Hudson River Bracketed*   (novel)   1929
*Certain People*   (short stories)   1930
*The Gods Arrive*   (novel)   1932
*A Backward Glance*   (autobiography)   1934
*The World Over*   (short stories)   1936
*Ghosts*   (short stories)   1937
*The Buccaneers*   (unfinished novel)   1938
*The Collected Short Stories*. 2 vols.   (short stories)   1968
*The Edith Wharton Omnibus*   (novels)   1978

*This work includes the novellas *False Dawn: The 'Forties, The Old Maid: The 'Fifties, The Spark: The 'Sixties,* and *New Year's Day: The 'Seventies.*

---

*THE CRITIC*   (essay date 1899)

[*Affinities with Henry James were noted by Wharton's critics from the time her first short story collection appeared. The Critic's anonymous reviewer was one of the first to write of the similarities.*]

Two hundred years ago things happened. Defoe, stringing together the fascinating series of events known as "Captain Singleton," was the artist of an age that found its play in events rather than in experience. . . . It is a far cry from the time when things happened to this new day, wherein, Mr. James tells us, "It is an incident for a woman to stand up with her hand resting on a table and look out at you in a certain way,"—or, as he goes on to suggest, "if it be not an incident, I think it will be hard to say what it is." The distance from Defoe to Henry James must somehow be spanned if one is to appreciate the artistic quality of such work as **"The Greater Inclination."**

It is not enough to say that these stories are realistic and that Henry James is their artistic sponsor. The reader is startled into a new appreciation of Mr. James and of the realistic method in general. So much keenness of insight, so much cleverness of phrase were not born, one is inclined to believe, of a day. It is realism carried to the $n$th power. Every character feels and thinks and reflects and feels again. But nothing happens—unless it can be called happening for a young woman, alone in a room in a New York hotel, to be pointing a revolver at her head; or for a man with staring eyes and small pinched face to lie dead in his berth in the flying express. The revolver never goes off. The dead man tells no tales. But the interest holds. Each minutest detail is selected and related with the exactness that befits a tragedy. The outcome may be death, or the birth of a new soul. The method in either case is the same, in the daily newspaper as in the realistic novel, that of circumstantial and exact detail. That one sometimes fails to see the wood for the trees, or the story for the telling, is only a phase of realism. That the stories have sometimes the effect of having been related so minutely that there is neither room nor time for the end is perhaps only another phase of realism. But that the interest never flags is pure art. (pp. 746-47)

The stories in **"The Greater Inclination"** inevitably recall the work of Henry James. Nor is the suggestion merely one of method. In very substance, even in titular phrase, the author pays Mr. James the sincere flattery of imitation. What is **"The Muse's Tragedy,"** but "The Tragic Muse" turned other end to; or **"The Pelican,"** who lectures "for the sake of the baby," but a more clever and youthful "Greville Fane" and her ungrateful offspring? Doubtless when Miss Wharton sketched **"The Portrait"** she was unconscious of other model than Vard, the political rascal, or of other artist than Lillo, the psychic interpreter of character. But the reader is liable to be reminded—in more than shadowy fashion—of that remarkable story "The Liar," in which the sitter is likewise a scoundrel and the artist a man of psychic trend. The pointing out of plagiarism, or unconscious adaptation or imitation, is a task neither pleasant nor difficult nor lofty. It falls now and then, however, to the lot of the reviewer and becomes more imperative in proportion as the work considered is more clever.

It is Miss Wharton's cleverness that betrays her and assigns her to her place. It is her cleverness, indeed, that differentiates her from her master and from artists of like calibre. One questions whether the whole range of Mr. James's work would yield as many epigrams, as much striking phrase, as **"The Pelican"** alone could furnish. It is in the power to weld clever phrase into fibre, to subordinate epigram to end, that the author of "The Pelican" is lacking—the power of self-restraint. The soft harmonious haze of an autumn day is not hers, nor the quick stinging touch of twilight in winter, nor the waking of a morning in spring. Spring, summer, and winter shall sooner lie down together some peaceful autumn day than the clever bits of writing in Miss Wharton's work efface themselves for the sake of anything so mild as style. In the meantime one may well be grateful for the cleverness and sparkle and interest. Whatever rank Miss Wharton shall ultimately choose to take, she has at least not fallen into the vulgar error of mistaking inanity for realism or the common fault of being able to see only with her eyes open. (pp. 747-48)

> *"Book Reviews: 'The Greater Inclination',"* in The Critic (© The Critic 1899), Vol. 35, No. 866, August, 1899, pp. 746-48.

### W. D. HOWELLS (essay date 1901)

[*The most influential American literary critic of the nineteenth century, and a close friend of Henry James, Howells was quick to spot Jamesian elements in Wharton's style and subject matter. From "The Editor's Easy Chair" at* Harper's Monthly, *he gave ringing approval of* Crucial Instances.]

[If] Mrs. Edith Wharton writes so well as she does almost too much in the manner of Mr. Henry James, those who know her writing need not be assured that its likeness to that master's work is not a condition of its excellence. At her best, in those moments when the poetic impulse which is the heart of her endeavor fulfils itself in some lyrical picture singing to the eye, she writes as wholly upon her own authority as any one can after so many thousand years of writing. The reader can make our dim meaning clearer to himself by turning to the opening passage of that study of mediaeval Italy called *The Duchess at Prayer,* which opens Mrs. Wharton's latest book, **"Crucial Instances."** "From the loggia, with its vanishing frescoes, I looked down an avenue *barred by a ladder of cypress shadows* to the ducal escutcheon and mutilated vases of the gate. *Flat noon* lay on the gardens, on fountains, porticoes, and grottoes. Below the terrace, *where a chrome-colored lichen had sheeted the balustrade as with fine laminae of gold,* vineyards stooped to the rich valley clasped in hills. The lower slopes were strewn with white villages like stars spangling a summer dusk; and beyond these, fold on fold of blue mountain, clear as gauze against the sky." This is such very Italy that one who has truly known Italy could name the very moment and place of it all; and the phrases which we have italicized lest the reader should miss any implication of them are those effects of emotion by which the poet shares with the reader what she felt as well as what she thought in beholding the things.

A poet Mrs. Wharton is always, and not least a poet in her defeats. She fails as the poet often fails with such material as that of *The Duchess at Prayer,* with the brute facts of the sin and the crime. The time and the place are wonderfully painted, but the action is so weak that one finds one's self not much caring whether the statue of the praying duchess is placed over her hidden lover in the crypt or not. The action is compensatingly strong in the other Italian piece, *The Confessional,* which closes the volume. This again is very Italy, not mediaeval Italy, but revolutionary Italy, the Italy of day before yesterday, whose generous hopes have been blighted in the Italy of to-day. The translation of the drama to our own land and hour, and to such a sordid scene and instant as an actual

manufacturing town on Long Island, gives proof of the author's power upon reality which makes one doubt whether she was not baffled by the essential unreality of *The Duchess at Prayer.* But, after all, she seems at her best in *The Recovery.* The study of the painter overrated by home criticism and liberated to self-knowledge by a visit to Paris, where his intrinsic honesty gets the better of all the mistaken admiration of his worshippers and he begins anew, is of many precious psychological imports suggested with a constant and delicately sarcastic humor. Something of the same humor qualifies that charming sketch *The Rembrandt,* but there it is a little sharper; in *The Angel at the Grave* it is felt rather as a pensive light on the pathetic event. It is this humor, in whatever force or phase it shows itself, which should enable the author to be solely herself. A poet may be unconsciously like some one else, even such a genuine poet as Mrs. Wharton, but a humorist cannot well reflect another method and another manner without knowing it. (pp. 823-24)

> W. D. Howells, "Editor's Easy Chair," in Harper's Monthly Magazine (copyright © 1901 by Harper's Magazine), Vol. CIII, No. DCXVII, October, 1901, pp. 822-27.*

### H. L. MENCKEN (essay date 1913)

["The Reef"] is so far below **"Ethan Frome"** that it seems to be by a different novelist. . . . A tawdry story, almost bad enough for a best seller, but relieved and embellished, of course, by Mrs. Wharton's keen wit, her skillful management of situation, her dramatic sense, her finished and admirable craftsmanship. However, I cannot recommend it as a fair specimen of her work, nor even as a passable specimen. That would be unjust to you, and more unjust to Mrs. Wharton. (p. 157)

> H. L. Mencken, "The Burden of Humor" (used by permission of The Enoch Pratt Free Library of Baltimore in accordance with the terms of the will of H. L. Mencken), in The Smart Set, Vol. XXXIX, No. 2, February, 1913, pp. 151-58.*

### JAMES HUNEKER (essay date 1914)

[*In his article "Three Disagreeable Girls," Huneker examined Henrik Ibsen's Hedda Gabler, George Moore's Mildred Lawson, and Wharton's Undine Spragg, relating them to the New Women of his era. Of the three, Huneker views Undine with unreserved disgust.*]

Perhaps there is more than a nuance of caricature in the choice of such a name as "Undine Spragg" for the heroine of Edith Wharton's *The Custom of the Country.* Throughout that book, with its brilliant enamel-like surfaces, there is a tendency to make sport of our national weakness for resounding names. Undine Spragg—hideous collocation—is not the only offence. There is Indiana Frusk of Apex City, and Millard Binch, a combination in which the Dickens of *American Notes* would have found amusement. Hotels with titles like The Stentorian are not exaggerated. Miss Spragg's ancestor had invented "a hair waver"; hence the name Undine: "from undoolay, you know, the French for crimping," as the simple-hearted mother of the girl explained to a suitor. Mrs. Wharton has been cruel, with a glacial cruelty, to her countrywomen of the Spragg type. But they abound. They come from the North, East, South, West to conquer New York, and thanks to untiring energy, a handsome exterior, and much money, they "arrive" sooner or later. With all her overaccentuated traits and the metallic quality of technique in the handling of her portrait, Undine Spragg is both a type and an individual—she is the newest variation of Daisy Miller—and compared with her brazen charmlessness the figures of Hedda Gabler and Mildred Lawson seem melting with tenderness, aglow with subtle charm and muffled exaltation. Undine—shades of La Motte Fouqué—is quite the most disagreeable girl in our fiction. She has been put under a glass and subjected to the air-pump pressure of Mrs. Wharton's art. She is a much more viable creature than the author's earlier Lily Bart, the heroine of *The House of Mirth*. At least Undine is not sloppy or sentimental, and that is a distinct claim on the suffrages of the intelligent reader. Furthermore, the clear hard atmosphere of the book is tempered by a tragic and humorous irony, a welcome astringent for the mental palate.

In Apex City Undine made up her mind to have her own way. She elopes and marries a vulgar "hustler," but is speedily divorced. She is very beautiful when she reaches New York. No emotional experience would leave a blur on her radiant youth, because love for her is a sensation, not a sentiment. By indirect and cumulative touches the novelist evokes for us her image. Truly a lovely apparition, almost mindless, with great sympathetic eyes and a sweet mouth. She exists, does Undine. She is not the barren fruit of a satirical pen. Foreigners, both men and women, puzzle over her freedom, chilliness, and commercial horse-sense. She doesn't long intrigue their curiosity, her brain is poorly furnished and conversation with her is not a fine art. She is temperamental in the sense that she lives on her nerves; without the hum and glitter of the opera, fashionable restaurants, or dances she relapses into a sullen stupor, or rages wildly at the fate that made her poor. She, too, like Hedda and Emma [Bovary], lives in the moment, a silly moth enamoured of a millionaire. Mildred Lawson is positively intellectual in comparison, for she has a "go" at picture-making, while the only pictures Undine cares for are those produced by her own exquisitely plastic figure. No wonder Ralph Marvell fell in love with her, or, rather, in love with his poetic vision of her. He was, poor man, an idealist, and his fine porcelain was soon cracked in contact with her brassy egotism.

He is of the old Washington Square stock, as antique—and as honourable—as Methuselah. Undine soon tires of him; above all, tires of his family and their old-fashioned social code. For her the rowdy joys of Peter Van Degen and his set. The Odyssey of Undine is set forth for us by an accomplished artist in prose. . . . We leave her in a blaze of rubies and glory at her French château, and she isn't happy, for she has just learned that, being divorced, she can never be an ambassadress, and that her major detestation, the "Jim Driscolls," had been appointed to the English court as ambassador from America. The novel ends with this coda: "She could never be an ambassador's wife; and as she advanced to welcome her first guests, she said to herself, that it was the one part she was really made for." The truth is she was bored as a wife, and like Emma Bovary, found in adultery all the platitudes of marriage. (pp. 323-27)

To my way of thinking, it is principally the craving for novelty in characterisation that has wrought the change in our heroines of fiction, although new freedom and responsibilities have evolved new types. . . . But it would be a mistake to call Hedda, or Mildred, or Undine, new women. Mildred is the most "advanced," Hedda the most dangerous—she pulled the trigger far too early—and Undine the most selfish of the three. The three are disagreeable, but the trio is transitional in type.

Each girl is a compromiser, Undine being the boldest; she did a lot of shifting and indulged in much cowardly evasion. Vulgarians all, they are yet too complex to be pinned down by a formula. Old wine in these three new bottles makes for disaster. Undine Spragg is the worst failure of the three. She got what she wanted for she wanted only dross. . . . And Undine Spragg hadn't the courage to become downright wicked; the game she played was so pitiful that it wasn't worth the poor little tallow-dip. What is her own is the will-to-silliness. As Princess Estradina exclaimed in her brutally frank fashion: "My dear, it's what I always say when people talk to me about fast Americans: you're the only innocent women left in the world. . . ." This is far from being a compliment. No, Undine is voluble, vulgar, and "catty," but she isn't wicked. It takes brains to be wicked in the grand manner. She is only disagreeable and fashionable; and she is as impersonal and monotonous as a self-playing pianoforte. (pp. 327-28)

> James Huneker, *"Three Disagreeable Girls"* (originally published in Forum, Vol. LII, No. 5, November, 1914), in his Ivory, Apes and Peacocks: Joseph Conrad, Walt Whitman, Jules Laforgue, Dostoïevsky and Tolstoy, Schoenberg, Wedenkind, Moussorgsky, Cézanne, Vermeer, Matisse, Van Gogh, Gauguin, Italian Futurists, Various Latter-Day Poets, Painters, Composers and Dramatists (copyright © 1915 Charles Scribner's Sons), Charles Scribner's Sons, 1915, pp. 311-28.*

## REBECCA WEST   (essay date 1922)

Every now and then some writer—either critic or novelist—announces that the novel is an art-form that is played out. The statement is, of course, not true. . . . But one can understand the mood of despair that makes people declare that all is up with the novel when one reads Mrs. Wharton's *The Glimpses of the Moon.*

Nothing more competent than this book could possibly be imagined. Mrs. Wharton has left undone nothing which she ought to have done; and on the other count, of doing nothing that she ought not to have done, her score is even higher. It has flashes of insight, as in that scene at the end of the book where the husband and wife, after a separation that has nearly terminated in their divorce, are sitting quietly together, and the husband's mind ranges back to the partners whom they had tentatively selected for consolation and remarriage. He thinks of the girl who had been willing to marry him, who will be cruelly disappointed by his return to his wife, with compunction and tenderness; and he is shocked by his certainty that his wife has utterly banished from her mind all thoughts of her dismissed suitor, whose goodness and affection deserved respect. But he remembers the next moment that whereas he had treated the girl very nearly like a cad, his wife treated her suitor with sincerity and courage. It is the neatest possible exhibition of the essential differences between Nick and Susy Branch. Yet, for all these occasional reminders that the hand that wrote this wrote **Ethan Frome,** and for all its perpetual, vigilant competence, the book is a dead thing. It is as well done as it possibly could be; but it is not worth doing. There is a very great temptation to say that since here is a novel which is written with supreme accomplishment and which is as dust in the mouth, there must be something wrong with the novel as an art-form. But if one examines the case more closely the failure of *The Glimpses of the Moon* may be seen to proceed, not from any inadequacy of the novel, but from two circumstances attending on the development of Mrs. Wharton's talent, which act on it as adversely as if they were innate defects.

The first of these is that Mrs. Wharton was born in America at exactly the wrong time. One does not mean that it was unfortunate that Mrs. Wharton was able to win (as she did with *The Age of Innocence*) the thousand-dollar Pulitzer prize. . . . Though indeed this is unfortunate, for that there is something within Mrs. Wharton which responds to this note is demonstrated by her choice of a title, for with a certain lack of sympathy with Dr. Donne she uses the line as a metaphor for the fleeting vision of the moral good which two persons pursue through the obscurities of a murky environment. But the real misfortune of Mrs. Wharton's uprising is that it happened at a time when fastidious spirits of the kind to which she markedly belonged were obsessed by a particular literary method, and in a place where every day revealed situations which were bound to attract an eager intelligence of the kind she undoubtedly possessed but which could not be appropriately treated by that favoured method. The method was that of William Dean Howells and Henry James. The situations were those arising out of the establishment of the American plutocracy; and they were large, bold situations, blatancies in a marble setting, that could not be dealt with by the method that in Mr. Howells' hands was adjusted to the nice balancing of integrities in a little town, and in Mr. James' to the aesthetic consideration of conduct in a society where the gross is simply put out of mind. The moral problem in *The Glimpses of the Moon* is as coarse as one can imagine anything self-consciously concerned with morality possibly being. Nick and Susy are two penniless persons of charm who find it easy to pick up a good living by sponging on their millionaire friends. They fall in love and marry, and then their way of living suddenly fails them, for it involves them in actions which people in love cannot bear to see each other performing. They sulk over it. They separate. Each meditates divorce and a mercenary marriage. They are drawn together and toward independence by a certain fundamental worthiness in both of them. About this situation of crude primary colours Mrs. Wharton writes with an air of discussing fine shades in neutral tints. It is as disconcerting as if, say, Mrs. Gaskell had written *Mary Barton* in exactly the same style as *Cranford*.

The second circumstance of Mrs. Wharton's uprising which has been adverse to her development was the unfashionability at that moment of the truth that novelty is a test of the authenticity of art. Tradition is a necessity to the artist; he must realise that he is only a bud on the tree. The America into which Mrs. Wharton was born was almost extravagantly conscious of that necessity, destitute as it was of traditions, terrified lest ill-advised patriotism should hinder it from affiliation to European tradition. But he must also realise that no bud is exactly like another bud. Imitation has its place in life; it is of considerable service in enabling people who have beautiful things in their minds, but who are not possessed of the necessary initiative to find the shape for them.

*Rebecca West, "Notes on Novels: 'The Glimpses of the Moon'," in* New Statesman *(© 1922 The Statesman Publishing Co. Ltd.), Vol. XIX, No. 490, September 2, 1922, p. 588.*

## EDITH WHARTON　(essay date 1922)

[*Wharton discusses her technique in the construction of* Ethan Frome.]

The problem before me [in writing *Ethan Frome*], as I saw in the first flash, was this: I had to deal with a subject of which the dramatic climax, or rather the anti-climax, occurs a generation later than the first acts of the tragedy. This enforced lapse of time would seem to anyone persuaded—as I have always been—that every subject (in the novelist's sense of the term) implicitly *contains its own form and dimensions*, to mark Ethan Frome as the subject for a novel. But I never thought this for a moment, for I had felt, at the same time, that the theme of my tale was not one on which many variations could be played. It must be treated as starkly and summarily as life had always presented itself to my protagonists; any attempt to elaborate and complicate their sentiments would necessarily have falsified the whole. (p. vi)

It appears to me, indeed, that, while an air of artificiality is lent to a tale of complex and sophisticated people which the novelist causes to be guessed at and interpreted by any mere looker-on, there need be no such drawback if the looker-on is sophisticated, and the people he interprets are simple. If he is capable of seeing all around them, no violence is done to probability in allowing him to exercise this faculty; it is natural enough that he should act as the sympathizing intermediary between his rudimentary characters and the more complicated minds to whom he is trying to present them. (p. viii)

The real merit of my construction seems to me to lie in a minor detail. I had to find means to bring my tragedy, in a way at once natural and picture-making, to the knowledge of its narrator. I might have sat him down before a village gossip who would have poured out the whole affair to him in a breath, but in doing this I should have been false to two essential elements of my picture: first, the deep-rooted reticence and inarticulateness of the people I was trying to draw, and secondly the effect of "roundness" (in the plastic sense) produced by letting their case be seen through eyes as different as those of Harmon Gow and Mrs. Ned Hale. Each of my chroniclers contributes to the narrative *just so much as he or she is capable of understanding* of what, to them, is a complicated and mysterious case; and only the narrator of the tale has scope enough to see it all, to resolve it back into simplicity, and to put it in its rightful place among his larger categories. (pp. viii-ix)

I can imagine nothing of any value to his readers except a statement as to why he decided to attempt the work in question, and why he selected one form rather than another for its embodiment. These primary aims, the only ones that can be explicitly stated, must, by the artist, be almost instinctively felt and acted upon before there can pass into his creation that imponderable something more which causes life to circulate in it, and preserves it for a little from decay. (p. x)

*Edith Wharton, "Introduction" (copyright, 1922 by Charles Scribner's Sons), in her* Ethan Frome, *Charles Scribner's Sons, 1922, pp. v-x.*

## E. M. FORSTER　(essay date 1934)

[*Forster finds* A Backward Glance *to be a fitting reflection of Wharton's dying aristocracy: interesting in spots, but mostly monotonous.*]

Goethe made a rather bitter epigram on Good Society: it is "good," he said, if it offers no opportunity whatever to poetry. Mrs. Wharton applies this epigram without bitterness; she would certainly prefer poetry to society, and a performance of *Bérénice* to a polo match, but she is not emphatic, and more inclined to chaff her worldlings than to excommunicate them. For this reason her career (or such of it as she has chosen to describe [in *A Backward Glance*]) has few moments of high tension; the dominant impression is comfort—comfort honestly enjoyed and generously shared, but extending uninterruptedly from a New York childhood through Continental trips down to a residence in France. . . . Because of her intelligence and self-control, this constant prosperity does not spoil her work, but it does make for autobiographical monotony. (p. 950)

Mrs. Wharton belongs to a tradition which is ending. She realises this, and surveys without asperity the succeeding chaos. It is essentially an American tradition, though not one which has been able to flourish in America. Rooted in Puritanism and financial stability, it has put forth in Europe the flowers of a conscientious and distinguished art—an art which could not bloom until it had been transplanted. (pp. 950, 952)

The atmosphere, though artificial, is not exotic. And the art, though cosmopolitan, is never international. It is connected with great cities and with the country houses dependent on them, and takes no stock of a new social order.

Though Mrs. Wharton is an excellent gossip and well-informed *diseuse* she is at her best when she talks about this beloved art. The chapters on her own work and on Henry James', and the references to that neglected novelist Howard Sturgis, are all illuminating. She tells us, for instance, that her characters come into her mind with their names attached, that she is still seeking a fictional home for a lady called Laura Testvalley. If Mrs. Testvalley gets as well suited as was another homeless character, the Princess Estradina, who finally arrived into the *Custom of the Country,* she will not have waited in vain. But, as her creator realises, she may take some suiting. All this discussion about books and the ways they are created and worked up is stimulating for readers as well as writers. And Henry James! She knew James well and was devoted to him, and her patience with his fussifications and affectations will strike the outsider as miraculous. But she is detached enough when she comes to his work, for the reason that she is serious about literature. She passes some very shrewd remarks about his later novels and she sees that his very conscientiousness as an artist led him to be a narrow critic, because he required all writers to be conscientious in exactly the same way.

She was also a friend of Howard Sturgis, her account of whom made me take down *Belchamber* again. . . . [If his work is revived], Mrs. Wharton will have promoted it by her amusing and sympathetic tribute. . . .

How much did the war destroy? It destroyed ''good society'' though the butler still brings the tea out under the cedar on occasion. Did it damage poetry too? And will writers ever recover that peculiar blend of security and alertness which characterises Mrs. Wharton and her tradition, and which has served her art so well? (p. 952)

*E. M. Forster, ''Good Society,'' in* The New States-man & Nation *(© 1934 The Statesman & Nation Publishing Co. Ltd.), n.s. Vol. VII, No. 174, June 23, 1934, pp. 950, 952.*

**EDMUND WILSON**   (essay date 1938)

[*Wilson notes Wharton's change of heart toward American society in* The Buccaneers *and her skill at limning characters, while acknowledging her last novel as ''banal and perhaps a shade trashy.''*]

Edith Wharton had been working on [''The Buccaneers''] dur-ing the last four or five years of her life, but died before she was able to finish it. The first section has a certain brilliance. It is concerned with the children of the *nouveaux riches* at Saratoga during the seventies, when the post-Civil War fortunes were rolling up, and it makes a counterpart to the picture in ''**The Age of Innocence**'' of the older well-to-do New Yorkers of this period. It all comes back rather diminished in memory but in lively and charming colors, like a slide in one of those magic lanterns which are mentioned as a contemporary form of entertainment: the pretty girls who are not in society but who get so much attention from the young men, while their parents try to prevent them from running wild, in the atmo-sphere of the Saratoga race track and the old Grand Union Hotel.

Later, she takes her Americans to London and has the girls make what are regarded by their parents as highly successful marriages with men of the aristocracy and of the rich industrial middle class. But Edith Wharton was never anything like so good when she was dealing with French or English society as she was with the United States; and this part of ''**The Buc-caneers**,'' even allowing for the fact that a good deal of it was left in the form of an unworked-over first draft, seems banal and perhaps a shade trashy. Also, the mellowness of Mrs. Wharton's later years here as elsewhere dulled the sharpness of her fiction. There are passages in ''**The Buccaneers**'' which read like an old-fashioned story for girls.

Something more interesting appears in her scenario for the unfinished part of the tale. In this last novel, Edith Wharton has more or less reversed the values of her embittered ''**Custom of the Country**'': instead of playing off the culture and tradition of Europe against the vulgar rich Americans, who are insensible to them, she dramatizes the climbing young ladies as a revi-vifying and air-cleaning force. But in the last pages she wrote, she made it plain that the hard-boiled commercial elements which were on the rise in both civilizations, representing fun-damentally the same thing, were to understand each other per-fectly. In what was to follow, the English governerness who has helped to engineer the success of the Americans and who is the child of Italian revolutionaries and a cousin of Dante Gabriel Rossetti, was to have sacrificed her own hopes of capturing an amateur esthete of the older generation of the nobility by aiding his son to elope with the most interesting of the American girls. (p. 342)

Miss Testvalley is much the best thing in the book; and there is a peculiar appropriateness and felicity in the fact that Edith Wharton should have left as the last human symbol of her fiction this figure who embodies the revolutionary principle implicit in all her work. As the light of her art grows dim and goes out before she has finished this last novel, the image still lingers on our retina of the large dark eyes of the clever spinster, who, like her creator, in trading in worldly values, has given a rebuff to the values of the world; in following a destiny solitary and disciplined, has fought a campaign for what, in that generation would have been called the rights of the heart. (p. 343)

*Edmund Wilson, ''The Revolutionary Governess'' (reprinted by permission of Farrar, Straus and Gi-roux, Inc.; copyright 1938), in* The New Republic, *Vol. LXXXXVI, No. 1246, October 26, 1938, pp. 342-43.*

**V. S. PRITCHETT** (essay date 1964)

*[Pritchett discusses Wharton's curious love-hate relationship with the social standards of old New York.]*

A novel by Mrs. Wharton in her best period is a correcting experience, a pain when the correction seems to be directed at ourselves, a pleasure when it is being handed out to other people. She is—so many of the important women novelists have been this—a mother-figure, determined, pragmatic, critical and alarming. How inevitable not to come up to her moral, intellectual, above all her social standards. Once we get out of the room where we have been sitting alone with the formidable lady, we foresee that we shall break out or go downhill once more. We know she is no fool; she can startle us by her range of observation; but we shall suspect that what she calls discipline is really first cousin to puritanism and fear, and that what she calls the Eumenides are really projections of the aunts who run the conventions and man the barricades of the taboos. The acerbity of a novelist, like Mrs. Wharton is *mondain* before it is intellectual; it denotes a positive pleasure in the fact that worldly error has to be heavily paid for spiritually. Her sense of tragedy is linked to a terrifying sense of propriety. It is steely and has the hard efficiency of the property market into which she was born. When, in *The House of Mirth*, Lily Bart is told that she will have to choose between the values of the smart set in New York and the "republic of the spirit," we are not absolutely convinced that this republic is not a new kind of puritan snobbery. The men who belong to this republic signally fail to rush the women off their feet into this excellent world, and Mrs. Wharton is drily aware of their failure. In its first decades the rise of American Big Business created an upper class whose sensitive men cut themselves off from a crude society that shocked them and which was dominated by women. She noted this in her autobiography and it is plain in all her books. Her own interesting situation is that there is an emotional force held back in her, which resents the things her mind approves of and it is this dilemma that gives her mind its cutting edge—at any rate in the books she wrote before she found personal happiness. That happiness, it now seems, dulled her talent.

There is, of course, more than all this to Mrs. Wharton, both as person and novelist. She elaborated the balance sheet of renunciation and became the accountant-historian of a rich society, and nothing passed her merciless eye. She wrote best when the pressure had been hardest to bear, even though that pressure may have frozen the imaginative and enhanced the critical character of her talent. Her prose has a presentable cold pomp: "The cushioned chairs, disposed expectantly under the wide awning, showed no signs of recent occupancy." Under great bitterness and frustration we have learned to expect outbursts of sentimentality—as a far greater writer, like Mauriac, has shown us—and when she drags the Eumenides into three or four melodramatic pages of her best novel, *The House of Mirth,* we are embarrassed. But it is exceptional for her control to go. Her study of rich New York in the early 1900's in that book will pass for smart sets anywhere and at any time, for even in our day, when most conventions have gone, when people no longer behave like "deaf mutes in an asylum," the cheerless figure of the socialite remains. The smart set is the quintessential dust bowl. In a later comment on this novel Mrs. Wharton wrote "that a frivolous society can acquire dramatic significance only through what its frivolity destroys. Its tragic implication lies in its power of debasing people and ideals." The idea is Jamesian and if the execution of it lacks the poetry, the heightened recitative of Henry James, we do get from Mrs. Wharton the hard, unpitying moralist who will forgive but not forget, and the derisive critic of social architecture.

Indignation about the sins of another social class is, of course, easy money, and does not, of itself, get a novelist very far. One strongly suspects that Mrs. Wharton did not like new people getting rich. But she did examine her subject with scientific efficiency, and in Lily Bart she created the most rewarding kind of socialite: one who was morally a cut above the rest of her circle, but who had been fatally conditioned from the first. Lily Bart is a beautiful and very intelligent girl, delightful company and really too clever for any of the men her society was likely to offer. On the lowest level, she is hopeless about money, about pushing her way in first, about intrigue, about using people, about the main chance. Her own view is that she behaves as she does because she has no money. It is Becky Sharp's cry: virtue on five thousand a year. But this is only half her case. She is a superb artist in the business of being in the swim, a brilliant contriver of success; she has a wonderful sense of timing—when to be in the spotlight and when not. Her startling weakness is that she sows but she does not reap. At the last moment she is wrecked by the sudden boredom and carelessness of the very clever. On the day of victory she oversleeps. Her self-confidence is such that she does not bother to play her ace; and she imagines her gift for dispensing with success at the last minute will make her impervious to her enemies. It does not. Selden, who wants to marry her, imagines that her last-minute failures are signs of grace, impulses from the unconscious. They make her very likable, but they must be considered as opportunities for further displays of courage and sangfroid rather than happy, nonsocial backslidings into "the republic of the spirit." Her courage is half vanity. So low are the standards of her set that she is encouraged thereby to mistake thrilled nerve for an access of intelligence:

> She . . . listened to Ned Silverton reading Theocritus by moonlight, as the yacht rounded the Sicilian promontories, with a thrill of the nerves that confirmed her belief in her intellectual superiority.

Theocritus is, in fact, the right poet, at the right moment, among the right people, at the height of the season. A venial folly; after all, are we quite sure that the enlightened Selden is any better for cutting himself off from the life of his country and reading La Bruyère?

Lily Bart has the beauty and vanity which George Eliot thought so wicked in women, but Lily's attractions are energy, an occasional capacity for honesty and innocence. She is not ashamed of her cunning in getting money out of a married man like Gus Trenor for she has used her brains; what really shocks her is the price demanded. Her match is Rosedale, the rich rising Jew who reads her character perfectly, who puts his price up as hers goes down and, in the end, out of sheer admiration for her abilities, is willing to behave disinterestedly. But he is defeated by her gift for last-minute failure: she refuses to silence the women who have ruined her. Pride or a sense of virtue? Neither, I think—and here Mrs. Wharton is very penetrating: those who believe in their star believe also in despair. Lily Bart is a gambler. One enjoys her as one enjoys the electric shocks of roulette, as one enjoys the incorrigible and the plunger. And one enjoys her also because Mrs. Wharton turns her inside out. . . . (pp. 269-73)

The only element missing from Lily Bart's character is her obvious sexual coldness to which, when the novel was written, Mrs. Wharton could hardly have referred even if—to suppose the impossible—she had desired to do so.

New York's social scene is expertly set down in *The House of Mirth* with an anthropologist's thoroughness and the novel is remarkable for its skillful visits from one smart set to the smart set on the stair below. These tours are conducted with all Mrs. Wharton's superlative snobbery. (pp. 273-74)

Mrs. Wharton hated the smart set she had been brought up in and she is good in this novel no doubt because she is anatomizing the monster whose stupidities and provincialities might have crushed her. But the making of her as a novelist is her power to create incident and to conduct great scenes. Strangely enough her ironical power and gift of surprise often recall those of an utterly different novelist—Thomas Hardy. She has—usually under iron control—a persistent sense of fate, a skill in entangling her characters before striking them down. The scene at Gus Trenor's when this magnate turns nasty and looks like going to the point of sexual assault is wonderfully handled and Lily is marvelous in it; every cliché in this well-known situation is avoided, every truth in it discerned and the end is perfect. And Bertha Dorset's revenge on Lily: that is as brilliant a *volte-face* and surprise as one can remember in any plot in social comedy. Mrs. Wharton did not touch these heights afterwards, though even in her weaker novels, there is the same astringency, the same readiness of invention.

Again and again we find that novelists who have attacked the conventions because they stultify the spirit, who attack the group for its cruelty to individuals, will end by pointing out the virtues of submission. Mrs. Wharton may have hated old New York, but she hated the new New York even more. She disliked the prison of silent hypocrisy, but she drew in her skirts when candor came in. Especially after her long life, *en grande luxe* in Europe. What indignation denounces creeps back in the name of sentiment. *The Age of Innocence* shows a man giving in, loyally marrying the conventional girl he does not love, throwing over the Europeanized woman who is his natural equal. It is the surrender to the established bourgeois standard. No great harms come of it; only dullness and disappointment. The sweet young girl he was engaged to was slyer than he thought. She became like her mother-in-law to whose face "a lifelong mastery over trifles had given factitious authority." Perhaps, after all, her husband reflects, that old New York which would not "know" a divorced woman, was rather charming and quite right. Better renunciation than a hole-in-corner affair. Mrs. Wharton always believed in the sterner condition; but her brain resented it. (pp. 274-75)

*V. S. Pritchett, "New York, 1900," in his* The Living Novel and Later Appreciations *(copyright 1947, © 1964 and renewed 1975 by V. S. Pritchett; reprinted by permission of Literistic, Ltd.), revised edition, Random House, 1964, pp. 269-75.*

### R.W.B. LEWIS (essay date 1968)

[*Lewis examines a representative selection of Wharton's short stories, finding them reflective of the author's multi-faceted personality.*]

[What distinguishes the best of Edith Wharton's short stories] must be specified with some care. It cannot be said, for example, that Mrs. Wharton significantly modified the genre itself—as during her lifetime, James Joyce and D. H. Lawrence and Ernest Hemingway were so differently doing. On the formal side, she was, to borrow a phrase from Louis Auchincloss, "a caretaker." She was the dedicated preserver of classical form in narrative, of the orderly progression in time and the carefully managed emphasis which, she reminds us in "**Telling a Short Story**," the French writers of *contes* had derived from the Latin tradition and the English in turn had taken over from the French. In "**Telling a Short Story**" (the second chapter of her book, *The Writing of Fiction* . . . ), Mrs. Wharton says much that is engrossing and valid, but virtually nothing that is new, at least to a reader of late Victorian literature. Perhaps the one surprising element—I shall come back to this—is her special admiration for the ghost story, "the peculiar category of the eerie" to which she turns her attention at once, even before getting down to questions about subject matter, characterization and the proper degree of economy in the short story proper. Elsewhere, she talks sensibly about "unity of vision," the strategically chosen "register" or point of view by which the experience is to be seen and by which it is to be shaped, with due acknowledgment to Henry James for first establishing the primacy of this fictional resource. She observes that the development and exploration of character is not the business of the short story, but rather that of the novel. And she lays it down that "situation is the main concern of the short story," so that "the effect produced by the short story depends entirely on its form, or presentation." (pp. vii-viii)

Early stories like "**That Good May Come**" and "**A Cup of Cold Water**" do in fact consist in the *working out* of a given situation, the active resolution, happily or unhappily, of some moral dilemma. But in the best of her stories—in "**Souls Belated**," "**The Other Two**," "**The Eyes**," "**Autres Temps . . . ,**" "**A Bottle of Perrier**" and others—it is rather that the situation itself is gradually revealed in all its complexity and finality. What we know at the end, in these "crucial instances," is not so much how some problem got resolved, but the full nature, usually the insurmountable nature, of the problem itself. (p. viii)

The situations she chose so to treat and to enlarge upon are not, at first glance, very original or unusual ones. . . . There was, however, one area of experience which she was perhaps the first *American* writer to make almost exclusively her own: even more, I dare say, than Henry James, who would in any event be her only rival in this respect. This is what . . . I call the marriage question. (p. ix)

[The] whole domain of the marriage question was the domain in which Edith Wharton sought the truth of human experience; it was where she tested the limits of human freedom and found the terms to define the human mystery.

"**Souls Belated**" is an excellent case in point. The situation there is that of Mrs. Lydia Tillotson, who has abandoned her husband and come to Europe with her lover Ralph Gannett to spend a year wandering through Italy and then to settle for a time, registered as man and wife, at a resort hotel on one of the Italian lakes. Her divorce decree is at this moment granted, and the lovers are free to marry; but Lydia, to Gannett's astonishment, is passionately opposed to remarrying. She is appalled at the thought of yielding to that conventional necessity, of returning to the social fold and eventually of being received by the very people she had hoped to escape. . . . [It] is evident that on this occasion Gannett speaks for Edith Wharton. The impossibility of founding a new ethic—of a man and woman arranging their life together on a new and socially unconventional basis—was one of Mrs. Wharton's most somber convictions, and a conviction all the stronger because (partly out of her own anguish) she tested it again and again in her stories. (pp. x-xi)

For Edith Wharton, . . . society, crushing as it might be, was all there was. . . . So it is in **"Souls Belated"**: Lydia tries to leave Gannett, but she knows she has literally no place to go; she comes wearily back to him, and at the story's end they are heading for Paris and the ceremony which will marry them back into respectable society. (p. xi)

Edith Wharton seriously treated the question of divorce in some of her most successful stories—among them, **"The Reckoning," "The Last Asset," "Autres Temps . . ."** and **"The Other Two."** She caught at the subject during the period when divorce was changing from the scandalous to the acceptable and even the commonplace; and it is just the shifting, uncertain *status* or the act on which Mrs. Wharton so knowingly concentrated. In her treatment, it was not so much the grounds for divorce that interested her (though she could be both amusing and bitter on this score), and much less the technicalities involved. It was the process by which an individual might be forced to confront the fact itself—especially in its psychological and social consequences—as something irreversible and yet sometimes wickedly paradoxical. . . . Divorce, thus considered, was also the source of a revelation: about manners and the stubborn attitudes they may equally express or conceal; about the essential nature of the sexual relation; about the lingering injuries to the psyche that divorce, given certain social pressures and prejudices, may inflict on all concerned.

It is all those things that Julia Westall is driven to understand in **"The Reckoning."** Julia had been a young woman with "her own views on the immorality of marriage"; she had been a leading practitioner, in New York Bohemia, of "the new dispensation . . . *Thou shalt not be unfaithful—to thyself.*" She had only acted on her own foolishly selfish ideas when she brusquely demanded release from her first husband; now she is reduced to hysteria and almost to madness when her second husband, who had been her disciple in these matters, makes the same demand of her. **"The Reckoning"** is somewhat overwritten, and it is uneven in tone; it is an anecdote, really, about the biter bit, though by no means unmoving. (pp. xiii-xiv)

**"The Other Two"** is a yet more brilliant dissection of the mannered life, and it is very likely the best story Mrs. Wharton ever wrote. It can stand as the measure of her achievement in the short story form; for it has scarcely any plot—it has no real arrangement of incidents, there being too few incidents to arrange—but consists almost entirely in the leisurely, coolly comic process by which a situation is revealed to those involved in it. It is revealed in particular to Waythorn, his wife's third husband, who discovers himself in mysterious but indissoluble league with "the other two," as exceedingly different in background or in style as all three are from one another. Waythorn comes by degrees to perceive that the wife he adores, and who had seemed to him so vivid and above all so unique a personality, is in fact (and in a disconcertingly appropriate figure) "'as easy as an old shoe'—a shoe that too many feet had worn. . . . Alice Haskett—Alice Varick—Alice Waythorn— she had been each in turn, and had left hanging to each name a little of her privacy, a little of her personality, a little of the inmost self where the unknown god abides." (pp. xiv-xv)

[Mrs. Wharton's] ghost stories are a provocatively mixed lot, [and] she displayed her skill in this category often enough to

be ranked among its modern masters. For an addict like the present commentator, **"Kerfol," "Mr. Jones," "Pomegranate Seed,"** and **"All Souls'"** are thoroughly beguiling and rereadable; while **"The Eyes"** verges on the extraordinary and contains something of "the appalling moral significance" Mrs. Wharton discerned in "The Turn of the Screw," that novella of Henry James for which she had a sort of absolute admiration.

Most of these stories deal, as I have said, with the marriage question, but they deal with it in an atmosphere which is a curious and artful blend of the passionate and violent with the muted and remote. (p. xv)

With the ghostly tales of Mrs. Wharton, in any event, one is inevitably interested not only in what happens in the plot, but in what happens in the telling of it. **"Pomegranate Seed"** offers one kind of clue. In the preface to *Ghosts,* while lamenting a decline in the practice and enjoyment of ghost stories, Mrs. Wharton speaks of the many inquiries she had received about the title of **"Pomegranate Seed,"** and refers a bit cryptically to the deplorable contemporary ignorance of "classical fairy lore." The reference is no doubt to the legend of Persephone (in the Latin-version), who was abducted by Pluto, god of the underworld, and who would have been entirely liberated by Jupiter if she had not broken her vow to Pluto—of total abstinence from food—by eating some pomegranate seeds; whereafter she was required to spend the dark winter months of each year in the underworld, returning to earth only with the arrival of spring.

The connection with Mrs. Wharton's tale is superficially slender, especially since the Persephone story is usually interpreted as a seasonal myth—the annual return of winter darkness and sterility, the annual rebirth of nature in the spring. But theorists of a Freudian or, alternately, a Jungian persuasion, have made out a strong sexual motif in most ancient mythology, and find the sources of myth as much in sexual struggles and yearnings as in the cycle of nature. The story of Persephone yields quickly to such an interpretation, and so obviously does **"Pomegranate Seed."** (p. xvi)

In this and other tales, in short, Mrs. Wharton's imagination was moving in the direction of the mythic, but arriving only at the way station of the ghostly and fantastic. This, for Mrs. Wharton, was far enough; for she was doing no more than adopting the Victorian habit (itself a gesture toward the mythic) of "distancing" the most intense and private sexual feelings by projecting them in the various forms of fantasy. It is notable, for example, that the ghostly context permits a more direct acknowledgment of sexual experience than we normally find in the dramas of manners and the social life. (p. xvii)

[To the degree that Mrs. Wharton] was great at all, she was great *as* a woman, with a distinctively feminine sensibility. We recognize it in the sometimes excessive concern with the details of female dress, and in her minute observation of interior *décor* (rooms and the furnishings of rooms are also her chief source of metaphor in the short stories). We see it even more in her subtle apprehension of the many "live filaments" that, Merrick remarks in **"The Long Run,"** individuals throw out to one another when a relationship is forming; of "the thousand imperceptible signs," according to Mrs. Anerton in **"The Muse's Tragedy,"** "by which one gropes one's way through the labyrinth of human nature"; of character and motive and the human relation as comprising delicate clusters of vibrations (to use one of her favorite words). At the same time, everyone who knew her has commented on a certain masculinity in her make-up; in her devotion to the orderly, in the vigorous play of her mind—and in her energetic sense of the satirical. (p. xxi)

*R.W.B. Lewis, "Introduction" (copyright © 1968 Charles Scribner's Sons; reprinted with permission of Charles Scribner's Sons), in* The Collected Short Stories of Edith Wharton, Vol. I, *edited by R.W.B. Lewis, Charles Scribner's Sons, 1968, pp. vii-xxv.*

## GEOFFREY WALTON    (essay date 1971)

[*Walton provides a survey of Wharton's career as an introduction to his study,* Edith Wharton: A Critical Interpretation.]

Edith Wharton's first written effort, at the age of eleven, which began: "'Oh, how do you do, Mrs. Brown?' said Mrs. Tompkins. 'If only I had known you were coming to call I should have tidied up the drawing-room'" shows that she was indeed almost predestined to become an interpreter of upper-class life, while her mother's crushing comment: "'Drawing-rooms are always tidy'" forms an excellent indication of her need for observation and experience. She seems equally to have been predestined to become a follower of Henry James and one early novel is plainly derivative from his early work. When, after achieving celebrity with her collaborative book on *The Decoration of Houses* (with several drawing-rooms) and establishing herself as a novelist, she eventually became a close friend of the Master, she was, Percy Lubbock tells us, the only woman whom he regarded as an equal and they were "more and more never apart." He was critical of her and she of him, he wishing to "tether" her "to native pastures," she deploring the lack of local habitation for the characters in his later work. Both, however, laid great stress on organic unity and close writing in the novel. (p. 21)

The all-embracing theme of Edith Wharton's earlier work is the relationship, usually a hostile relationship, between the individual and society. . . . [She] came of a small and in many respects obsolescent community, but its basic ideals were taken over by the more grandiose and expansive commercial dynasties that succeeded it. Social ambitions soared and moral codes loosened, but merely doing as one liked was still inconceivable. . . . [Edith Wharton presents] a conflict between two distinct upper middle classes running through parts of *The House of Mirth* and, more obviously, with foreign noble allies on the wing, in *The Custom of the Country. Madame de Treymes* has a foreign setting and *The Reef* is mainly concerned with individual conflict against a Franco-American upper-class background. In *The Fruit of the Tree,* where part of the conflict is shifted down the social scale and becomes a phase in the class war, the main interest is again focused on individuals. In all these books the individual involves himself—or herself, for Edith Wharton was a great creator of heroines—in a prolonged and complicated struggle with the conventions of manners and morality, both public and private, which had been so long established among the upper classes of Western Europe and the eastern states of America before the First World War that they could be taken for granted as an unquestioned and unquestionable code of civilization. . . . In her very early historical novel, *The Valley of Decision,* Edith Wharton had carried the theme of individual rebellion back into Italy in the age of enlightened despotism. In the New England novels she shows us the plight of the individual, rather than his rebellion, within the equally distinct and stable lower social strata. Everywhere she shows a deep sense of the value of mutual understanding and toleration and also of the meaning and value of forms and

decencies; her friend, the historian Gaillard Lapsley, once remarked that "she was possessed of a sense of compassion deeper and more authentic than [he had] ever seen in any human being."

In these earlier novels and stories she presents her chief characters against the background of a complex and changing, if still restricted, society, the whole studied with a depth of understanding that gives it the quality of a microcosm. This work has a richness and solidity that make it at least comparable to the early work of James. Physical detail and details of social custom are much more precisely and thoroughly presented than in his work, without losing their lasting and, as one says, universal appeal. The tremendous sense of the social hierarchy and of the meaning of class relationships, which one sees both in her novels and in her autobiography, reminds one not only of James but also of her other close friend and compatriot, Howard Sturgis. (pp. 22-4)

It seems to be a generally accepted opinion that Edith Wharton's powers declined beyond recovery during the 1920s and that her later novels were fit for no better public than that of the women's magazines where they were serialized before publication in book form. There is some speculation as to whether the decline was not rather an enforced and deliberate effort to meet the taste of a public whose purveyors presumably paid handsomely for the prestige that her name must have given to their journals. . . . Her powers as a novelist did not collapse, though all her later work may not be of equal merit. She gives us in *A Backward Glance* an account of her artistic circumstances that seems in the main immediately acceptable, whatever objections may be raised against certain details in the book. *The Age of Innocence* was an escape into "childish memories of a long-vanished America." It is a *tour de force,* but should not be overrated to the detriment of all her later work. She finally attempted to put her war experience into serious artistic form in *A Son at the Front,* which she had brooded over for more than four years, but the result, despite certain powerful lines of irony, is heavily sentimental in outlook and crude in detailed treatment. After it she thought of ceasing to write; she felt, very much as E. M. Forster has told us he also felt, "incapable of transmuting the raw material of the after-war world into a work of art." Her attempt to do so in *The Mother's Recompense* justifies her fears. But in *Twilight Sleep* and *The Children* we find a revival of her old creative energy and narrative skill along with the play of irony, albeit of a rather less subtle kind, which is the distinguishing feature of her best work. As a writer Edith Wharton deals as surely and decisively with the world of Scott Fitzgerald as she did with him in person at the famous tea-party (or was it luncheon?) at the Pavillon Colombe. The fact that she based her accounts of New York on hearsay, which, as Percy Lubbock tells us, she received with fascinated disgust, makes them the more remarkable in their vitality.

Edith Wharton's main interest as a novelist remained social. The early work, as has been indicated, records the conflicts of the individual with the conventions and customs of a still strong and organized community; *The Custom of the Country* is the comedy of a pyrrhic victory by an individual. The novels from *Twilight Sleep* onwards deal with the helplessness of individuals—the plural is appropriate here—in a Society scattered without much differentiation on both sides of the Atlantic, where conflict that can lead to tragedy is no longer possible. Edith Wharton is very critical indeed of the world in which Gatsby flourished and Dick Diver disintegrated, quite as critical as she was of the pre-1914 millionaire world, but the problem is different. Now there are neither established forms of humbug nor established forms of goodness to which the humbug can cling. In *The Writing of Fiction* Edith Wharton says that a novelist's work should bear "a recognizable relation to a familiar social and moral standard." The standard, as she presents it in these books, has lost its group sanctions and become a matter of individual sincerity and generosity.

Mrs. Wharton reviewed her relationship to the prose fiction of her native land and replied to her critics, contemporary and future, in a fine article, **"The Great American Novel."** From this she went on, in *Hudson River Bracketed* and *The Gods Arrive,* to deal with the problem of the individual and society in an extreme form, namely that of the modern artist. Her last and unfinished novel, *The Buccaneers,* represents a significant new development. One senses that a vision of social reintegration would have emerged from the completed work. In fact Edith Wharton's work as a whole gives one a sense of continuous growth and inner development. A fine sensibility is responding imaginatively to changing circumstances. It is not however of the widest imaginative grasp and adaptability. It is decidedly a critical and a judging sensibility. Mrs. Wharton was also a pioneer realist who remembered that she had once been asked, "'Have you ever known a respectable woman? If you have, in the name of decency write about her!'" and, though she satirized them severely, she did not flinch from the 1920s. She never saw much interest in "the man with the dinner-pail," as she described him. Her main achievement belongs to her "few yards of town-pavement"; but, as with James, how much takes place there! (pp. 25-7)

> *Geoffrey Walton, in his* Edith Wharton: A Critical Interpretation *(© 1970 by Geoffrey Walton), Fairleigh Dickinson University Press, 1971, 216 p.*

## GORDON MILNE (essay date 1977)

[*Milne discusses Wharton's novels as portraits of old New York's retreat before the advancing philistines.*]

A dominant theme in many of [Mrs. Wharton's] novels and stories is . . . the retreat of little old New York of the 1870s, the Knickerbocker aristocracy, marching backward when faced with the invasion of the plutocracy, the Astors and Vanderbilts, "the men who have risen," in the 1880s and 1890s. Mrs. Wharton knew well that the latter dynasty was to succeed, indeed, had succeeded, as symbolized in many cases by marriages uniting aristocrat and merchant. Her interest lay in contrasting the two social groups. Though her dislike of the arriviste—the Looty Arlingtons, the Indiana Frusks, the Undine Spraggs, even the Julius Beauforts, all those people from Pruneville, Nebraska—is more than apparent, and though her sympathy is drawn to the aristocrats proudly affirming their caste, she views the struggle between the two societies with detachment, not allowing her sympathies to warp her judgment. So, in *The Age of Innocence* . . . , the "first families" are shown wavering before the onslaught (the weeds pushing up between the ordered rows of social vegetables) of tasteless materialism, but deserving to be upset because their ostrichlike attitudes and dread of scandal indicate a declining culture. Similarly, in *The Buccaneers* . . . , Mrs. Wharton's last—and uncompleted—novel, the merchant class is conquering even the last stronghold of the aristocracy, England, a process that the author by no means wholly regrets, since the fresh charm

of "the buccaneers," the invading American girls, counteracts the stodgy narrowness of the old society.

To explore this "old order changeth" theme, Mrs. Wharton makes full use of the novel of manners format. Her best-known novel, *The Age of Innocence,* may serve, initially, as our prototype, since it distinctly illustrates many characteristics of the genre. In the first place, the novel, from beginning to end, gives us a strong sense of contrasting social groups, the aristocrats and the plutocrats. (p. 118)

Endless examples, some positive, some negative, are proffered of the manners of the ruling—if threatened—class. Its members are wholeheartedly governed by "the thing," for example, the convention of arriving late at the opera. Such conventions, the reader is told, play as important a part in social circles as did the inscrutable totem terrors that had ruled the destinies of the forefathers of this society thousands of years ago. Life is molded by the conventions and the forms, with considerable deference paid to the arbiters of these. (pp. 118-19)

*The Age of Innocence* is given enormous sparkle by the tone of light irony maintained throughout the work. The narrator tempers her sympathy for her subject, the established rich, with a tart quality. Recoiling as she does from "society's" matriarchal aspect, its shrinking from responsibility, its dread of innovation, and its confining innocence and distrust of the creative intelligence, while at the same time approving of its *douceur de vivre,* she presents a frank, often satiric, occasionally nostalgic picture.

The setting of *The Age of Innocence* is vividly and quite extensively treated, as is apt to be the case in a novel of manners, in which the reader must see the people against the background that conditions them. Mrs. Wharton, herself very sensitive about both exterior and interior decoration, lovingly describes the houses in which her principals dwell. (pp. 120-21)

Mrs. Wharton's theme in *The Age of Innocence* is derived from an examination of the interrelationship among Countess Olenska, May Welland, and Newland Archer. In the novel she expounds, as she had before and would several times again, upon the cruelty of social convention and the tyranny of the "in" group. The social arbiters militate against the individual, forcing him to give up his happiness for the duty that they dictate, causing him to yield his ideals, which they regard as impractical in the social order. Here, Ellen Olenska and Newland Archer must sacrifice their ideal of love, since she is married (and subsequently, he) and the scandal of divorce is unthinkable. (p. 124)

*The Age of Innocence,* like the majority of Mrs. Wharton's novels, and, indeed, like the majority of novels of manners, is a well-constructed work of fiction, subscribing, one might readily say, to the author's dictum that "every great novel must first of all be based on a profound sense of moral values, and then constructed with a classical unity and economy of means." Mrs. Wharton places her "situation" before us, a conflict between group and individual standards, then develops it crisply. Beginning in a lively manner, offering "signposts" in the form of revelatory little scenes along the way, then mounting to a striking and ironic climax, she creates a focused yet naturally unfolded story. The narrative in *The Age of Innocence* falls into two segments: the events leading up to the setting of the marriage date, and those following, with the climax occurring when the marriage is saved at a threatening point later on. A quiet denouement ensues, the account of Archer's visit to Paris with his son thirty years after the novel's principal incidents, and his refusal at this time to see Madame Olenska. The "overness" of the affair is thus lightly accentuated. Throughout the novel, the affair, or "situation," remains central, and lying behind it the dissection of a certain social sphere.

Contributing to the sense of unity is the author's reliance on the restricted point of view as the means by which the story is told. Most of the action is channeled through Newland Archer, who appears in almost every scene and whose viewpoint on these scenes very much coincides with that of the reader. What the reader knows and thinks of Ellen Olenska, for example, is pretty much what Archer knows and thinks. The novel is given reality, intensity, *and* suspense by this device, with the question of the actual character and status of Ellen—and thus the larger question of whether society or the individual is "right"—remaining in doubt for a long time.

Mrs. Wharton tells her story in a style that is pungent, facile, and witty—again, one ventures to say, all but a requirement of this particular genre, which demands a sophisticated manner of writing in order to preserve its urbane air. The novel abounds, for one thing, in similes and metaphors, arresting in the satiric picture they conjure up. Thus, Mrs. Manson Mingott's appearance: "a flight of smooth double chins led down to the dizzy depths of a still-snowy bosom . . . with two tiny hands poised like gulls on the surface of the billows." (pp. 125-26)

The balanced sentences that predominate in the novel often contain flashing ironies (Mrs. Welland "signed a haggard welcome"; Mrs. van der Luyden shines on Ellen "with the dim benevolence which was her nearest approach to cordiality") and/or an epigrammatic cast ("our legislation favors divorce; our social customs do not"; "the worst of doing one's duty was that it apparently unfitted one for anything else"). The diction supports the syntax in conveying the book's ironic flavor, especially when Mrs. Wharton overstates (Mrs. Mingott's bedroom is on the ground floor "in *flagrant* violation of all the New York proprieties") in order to mock the social legalism of the Knickerbocker group, using the serious word for trivialities, or the one with moral overtones for conventions. Some of the proper names may symbolize ironically, too: Archer as the ineffectual bowman, Ellen a misplaced Helen, May as innocence, overlapped, here, with conformity. (pp. 127-28)

With its consistently ironic style, precisely delineated characters and settings, and carefully worked-out theme, *The Age of Innocence* qualifies as an excellent novel. More particularly, it qualifies as an excellent novel of manners, being devoted to so thorough a discussion of the mores of old New York. (p. 128)

*The House of Mirth* . . . offers an early example, the novel unfolding the tragedy of Lily Bart, a young lady brought up in "society," but lacking the necessary money to retain her place and therefore forced into the unenviable role of a social parasite. (pp. 132-33)

While unfolding Lily's conflict between the claims of "sense" and "spirit," the author lays out the social topography against which the conflict is posed, the settled aristocracy over here, the moving plutocracy over there. As a student of manners, Mrs. Wharton is able to "fix" both groups, the former, tepidly devoted to family, form, and culture, the latter, more concerned about the distribution of wealth and the social privileges resulting from it. Mrs. Wharton very effectively dramatizes the plutocracy's social-climbing adventure, outlining a "hundred shades of aspect and manner" as she describes how its representatives are engaged in determining their status in society. The climbing action of the plutocracy suggests society's py-

ramidal structure, and indeed *The House of Mirth* indicates several gradations. (p. 133)

The book's well-bred surface does not conceal its dark texture. The plight of its half-belonging, half-rebelling protagonist produces a somber reaction and reminds the reader that the novel of manners "can register both the surface of social life and the inner vibrations of spirit that surface reveals, suppresses and distorts." The subject of "civilization and its discontents"—to use Freud's phrase—does not promote levity.

Successor to *The House of Mirth, The Custom of the Country* . . . follows the former's lead in toning down the comic note as it deals with the standard Wharton topic of societal realignments. Shifting, in her choice of protagonists, from defender (Lily Bart) to invader (Undine Spragg), Mrs. Wharton grimly—almost too grimly—delineates the "climb" of Miss Spragg, all the way from Apex City to Paris. (p. 134)

The rampant state of the new materialism is mirrored in the meteoric rise of Undine Spragg. Very harshly Mrs. Wharton depicts her as amoral, unsentimental, conscienceless, and cheap, yet with society now constituted as it is, she can forge ahead unimpeded. Mrs. Wharton has concluded that the "custom of the country" decrees money to be the open sesame, with social convention now transmogrified into a superficial veneer of good manners, which hardly mask an essential vulgarity. The main characteristic of the social structure of the day, Mrs. Wharton implies, is instability, its hierarchy being rearranged on a simple pecuniary basis, thus leaving the field open to the social adventurer.

Inevitably disturbed by this phenomenon, Mrs. Wharton, in her subsequent fiction, looks to the ordered past and nostalgically—though the satiric edge is always there—summons up the pre-assault era. . . . [*Old New York*], a collection of novelettes (*False Dawn, The Old Maid, The Spark,* and *New Year's Day*), is devoted to picturing the 1840-1870 world of formidable brownstone mansions, academies of music, and "downtown"—the vaguely described place of business, where people, it would seem, seldom had to be. It is a world of sober precedence—the grandmother's carriage preceding the aunt's—of order and form, of leisure, and of a fair amount of taste. Houses are carefully appointed, clothes are carefully chosen, dinners are carefully given.

From the novelettes the reader learns of the self-assured nature of the New Yorkers, their clannishness, their adherence to custom (betrothals, weddings, and funerals all have their pattern—the mourning crape at a precise length—in this "most totem-ridden of communities"), their narrow point of view, and their esthetic limitations. However charming the surface, those polished manners, and tasteful ceremonies, the environment exudes an airless atmosphere. Delia Ralston in *The Old Maid* sees the walls of her own grave in her surroundings. Attitudes are reactionary, family pressure is too intense, the values are often distorted (if society would not condone drink and dishonesty, it did condone almost everything else, including the double standard of morality, hypocrisy, and snobbery), and the culture is decidedly barren. (pp. 135-36)

If perhaps more masked in *Old New York*, still the money motif is discernible, and the class barriers are demonstrably breaking down. Everyone; even the Wesson clan, now goes to the parties of the shoe-polish heiress Mrs. Struthers.

Mrs. Wharton continues her discussion of the amalgamation of the aristocracy with the plutocracy in *The Mother's Rec-*

*ompense,* where one sees the union accomplished under the heading of the "new tolerance." When Kate Clephane returns to America, after many years abroad, she is impressed by the sense of change in this essentially "manner-less-age." . . . It would appear that the merger of the old and new societies has cost each its true character and has introduced an inane composite face.

This somewhat petulant disdain for the "modern age" marred Mrs. Wharton's later novels (e.g., *Hudson River Bracketed* and *The Gods Arrive*), most critics agreeing that her treatment of the aristocracy's yielding to the predatory arrivistes grew into a sour caricature. But her last novel, the unfinished *The Buccaneers* . . . , proves a late-in-the-day exception. In this interesting and amusing tale, the Wharton touch returns, and a new-found sympathy with the parvenus considerably mitigates the caricature. Looking backward from the mid-thirties, the author regards the invasion of the "buccaneers" forty years earlier as perhaps a healthy movement, for, awkward, uncultured, and superficial though they were, still, they introduced new blood and vitality into both the effete New York society and into the English aristocracy as well. The charming invaders are now sanctioned by Mrs. Wharton, especially Nan St. George, a happy blend of the new world conjoined to a sensitive appreciation of the tradition and continuity of the old. (pp. 136-38)

Mrs. Wharton is most concerned with the marriage of Nan St. George to the Duke of Tintagel, a marriage that appears the best of all but which proves the least workable. Nan, far more sensitive than her fellow Americans and more in key with the British love of tradition—"At least life in England had a background"—is the most receptive to the English atmosphere, but her husband, if superficially typifying glorious old Albion, turns out to be an incredibly stuffy and empty individual, and their marriage is loveless and hollow. Nan *should* have married Guy Thwaite, one who is slightly less blue-blooded but infinitely more intelligent and worthy. Mrs. Wharton's working plan for the uncompleted portion of *The Buccaneers* reveals that Nan will run off with Thwaite to South Africa, thus utterly defying convention but very possibly achieving happiness. The novel would have become morally as well as socially radical! (p. 140)

The exploration in *The Buccaneers*—as in its predecessors—of the "art" of manners involved all the resources of Mrs. Wharton's formidable technique. *The Buccaneers* is as craftsmanlike a performance as *The Age of Innocence,* and the same might be said of *The House of Mirth,* of *Old New York,* and of most of her other work. (p. 142)

> Gordon Milne, "Edith Wharton," in his *The Sense of Society: A History of the American Novel of Manners* (©1977, by Associated University Presses, Inc.), Fairleigh Dickinson University Press, 1977, pp. 116-49.

## GORE VIDAL (essay date 1978)

[*Vidal takes issue with the common conception of Wharton as a stuffy* grande dame. *He offers a short overview of her work and judges her, as an artist, to be the equal of Henry James.*]

[To] my mind, Henry James and Edith Wharton are the two great American masters of the novel. Most of our celebrated writers have not been, properly speaking, novelists at all. . . . Mark Twain was a memoirist. William Dean Howells was

indeed a true novelist but as Edith Wharton remarked (they were friendly acquaintances), Howells's "incurable moral timidity . . . again and again checked him on the verge of a masterpiece." She herself was never timid. Somehow in recent years a notion has got about that she was a stuffy grand old lady who wrote primly decorous novels about upper-class people of a sort that are no longer supposed to exist. She was indeed a grand lady, but she was not at all stuffy. Quite the contrary. She was witty. She was tough as nails. (p. viii)

Despite her reputation as being a stuffy *grande dame,* she had always been the most direct and masculine (old sense of the word, naturally) of writers; far more so than her somewhat fussy and hesitant friend Henry James. Spades got called spades in Edith Wharton's novels. As a result, she was always at war with "editorial timidity." Early on, she was told by one of the few good editors of the day that no American magazine would publish anything that might offend "a non-existent clergyman in the Mississippi valley; . . . [I] made up my mind from the first that I would never sacrifice my literary conscience to this ghostly censor." (p. xi)

The four stories that made up the volume *Old New York* together with *The Age of Innocence* can be read as a history of New York Society from the 1840s to the 1870s, all told from the vantage point of a brilliant middle-aged woman, looking back on a world that had already become as strange to her as that of the Pharaohs. . . .

[*Ethan Frome*] stands somewhat outside the canon of her work. For one thing, she herself is plainly outside the world that she is describing. Yet she is able to describe in a most convincing way a New England village filled with people of a sort that she could never have known well. The story is both readable and oddly remote. It could have been written by Daudet but not by her master Flaubert. Although she was very much under the influence of the French realists at the time, she does pay sly homage to Nathaniel Hawthorne, who had worked the same New England territory: a principal character in *Ethan Frome* is called Zenobia after the heroine of Hawthorne's *The Blithedale Romance.*

With the four New York stories and *The Age of Innocence* we are back in a world that she knew as intimately as Proust knew the Paris of much the same era. The stories begin. . . . But I am not going to say anything about them other than to note that they are precise and lucid, witty and passionate (there is no woman in American literature as fascinating as the doomed Madame Olenska). Not only does one live again in that lost world through Edith Wharton's art (and rather better to live in a far-off time through the medium of a great artist than to experience the real and probably awful age itself), but one is struck by the marvelous golden light that illuminates the world she reveals to us. How is this done? Through a total mastery of English. (p. xii)

In *The Age of Innocence* the language is unusually beautiful. That is to say, the prose is simple, straightforward, loved. When it comes to rounding off her great scene where Madame Olenska is decorously destroyed by the Old New Yorkers at a dinner, Edith Wharton writes with the graceful directness of the Recording Angel: "It was the old New York way of taking life 'without effusion of blood': the way of people who dreaded scandal more than disease, who placed decency above courage, and who considered that nothing was more ill-bred than 'scenes,' except the behavior of those who gave rise to them." . . .

Traditionally, Henry James has always been placed slightly higher up the slope of Parnassus than Edith Wharton. But now that the prejudice against the female writer is on the wane, they look to be exactly what they are: giants, equals, the tutelary and benign gods of our American literature. (p. xiii)

*Gore Vidal, "Introduction" (copyright © 1978 Gore Vidal; reprinted with permission of Charles Scribner's Sons), in* The Edith Wharton Omnibus *by Edith Wharton, Charles Scribner's Sons, 1978, pp. vii-xiii.*

## ELIZABETH AMMONS (essay date 1980)

[*Ammons studies* The Reef *as Wharton's feminist indictment of idealized, fairy-tale conceptions of erotic love.*]

Between the publication of *The Fruit of the Tree* in 1907 and *Ethan Frome* in 1911, Edith Wharton fell into, and what is more important, out of love. (p. 56)

What is most striking is how little, finally, the affair [with Morton Fullerton] changed Edith Wharton's argument. It did give her new respect for erotic motivation, which makes characters like Anna Leath and Sophy Viner, Charity Royall and Ellen Olenska more complicated and therefore more real, psychologically, than Lily Bart or Justine Brent. Analytically, however, it only deepened her developing argument with America. Despite the four-year break (a significant gap for a novelist as prolific as Wharton), Edith Wharton picked up almost where she left off in terms of her realistic social criticism: *The House of Mirth* and *The Fruit of The Tree* stand in a direct line with *Ethan Frome* and *The Reef* and *The Custom of the Country*. All five study work and marriage as the key problems affecting women.

Where *Ethan Frome* and *The Reef* deepen the argument, and the depth gained is considerable, is in taking fully into account the idea of love. In *The House of Mirth* love is barely an issue. In *The Fruit of the Tree* it is secondary. But in *Ethan Frome* and *The Reef,* love as we have been taught to expect it, as it is dreamed of for us in our fairy tales with their eternally happy endings, is Wharton's subject; and her verdict in both books is simple and harsh. She argues that until fairy-tale notions about romance and marriage are relinquished—which, given their psychological tenacity and political utility, seems unlikely in her view to happen—equality between the sexes, and thus the full emancipation of women, rich or poor, "new" or old-fashioned, will not come to pass. (p. 57)

*Ethan Frome* is complex but not subtle. Like the world it images, the mood of the piece is dark and obviously pessimistic. . . . *The Reef,* in contrast, is done in pastels. It too dramatizes sexual repression and bitter disillusion with love; but, perhaps because Wharton had already worked the themes through in one context and perspective in *Ethan Frome,* the use of fairy-tale imagery and symbolism in *The Reef* does not result in a new fairy tale but in a normal, full-length novel highly shaded by fairy-tale motifs and themes. *The Reef,*, in other words, is not an original fairy tale; it is a conventional novel whose meaning in large measure derives from allusions to two well-known, indeed probably the best-known, fairy tales: *Cinderella* and *Sleeping Beauty.*

The novel is a long, realistic narrative about genteel, sophisticated people whom Wharton brings together at a French château of picture-book charm and beauty. In this setting she interlocks the fates of two couples: the publicly affianced Anna Leath and George Darrow, mature people who have known each other for many years, and the secretly pledged Sophy Viner and Owen Leath, young lovers who have just recently

met. Both prospective brides—one a "lady" and the other a New Woman—harbor romantic dreams of female salvation through love and marriage. . . . No marriage takes place in *The Reef,* and each woman's dream of deliverance by a man ends in disillusionment to expose the fraudulent romantic visions fostered by the limitations imposed on women—in Sophy's case, economic dependence; in Anna's, sexual repression.

Wharton's older heroine, Anna, grew up (like Wharton herself) in old New York, where she was praised as "a model of ladylike repression." . . . Yet long before the novel opens the child began to tire of her sheltered and restricted life. "Love, she told herself, would one day release her from this spell of unreality." . . . She concludes that marriage, which she envisions as "passion in action, romance converted to reality," will be for her "the magic bridge between West Fifty-fifth Street and life." . . . Rhetoric signals theme. Anna dreamed of becoming a "heroine" who would be "transfigured" by the love of "a man" who would "release her" from a "spell" and with whom marriage would provide the "magic bridge" to "life," the "eternal theme" of which would be their love. . . . This language comes from fairy tales because the fantasy itself, not of escaping but of passively being freed, being saved, being awakened and reborn into life by the love of a man—the fantasy, in short, of Sleeping Beauty's being awakened by Prince Charming—comes from fairy tales. (pp. 79-80)

Before the novel opens, Anna thought she found her Prince Charming, her liberator and hero. But marriage soon showed her that the change in her last name from Summers to Leath had contrary significance. The summers of her life were chillingly replaced by a lethean existence at his château de Givré: palace of rime, hoarfrost. The French château which "had called up to her youthful fancy a throng of romantic associations, poetic, pictorial, and emotional," the château which was for Anna "a castle of dreams, evoker of fair images and romantic legend," . . . turned into a chamber of horrors where "life, to Mr. Leath, was like a walk through a carefully classified museum . . . [while] to his wife it was like groping about in a huge dark lumber-room where the exploring ray of curiosity lit up now some shape of breathing beauty and now a mummy's grin." . . . This was definitely the wrong fairy tale. Anna wanted to be awakened into "contact with the actual business of living;" . . . she wanted to be freed, not imprisoned. (p. 82)

Into this midnight tale of frustrated desires comes a rescuer in *The Reef.* Fraser Leath failed, but his widow blames the man, not the dream, and therefore looks forward to marriage with her old friend George Darrow. . . . Anna is ready for Darrow. Gradually awakening out of a lifetime of abnegation—first as a model daughter, then an obedient wife, finally a decorous widow—the woman's sense of impending freedom erupts. She runs across the grounds like a schoolgirl with "the feeling, which sometimes came to her in dreams, of skimming miraculously over short bright waves." (pp. 82-3)

Anna's running feels dreamlike because, exuberantly uninhibited at last, the "old vicious distinction between romance and reality" . . . for the moment disappears: the prospect of Darrow's arrival arouses the sensuous, carefree spirit so long dormant within Wharton's Sleeping Beauty.

Darrow shares Anna's romantic view of himself. Diplomacy, a princely vocation, will soon send him on a mission to South America, a distant and unfamiliar land, and he means to take his bride with him. Even his kiss is perfect. As in a fairy tale, he is masterful, she responsive. . . . Like the Prince in *Sleeping Beauty*, handsome George Darrow awakens Anna with a kiss, and her dream finally becomes real.

Out of all keeping with fairy-tale expectations, Anna's Prince Charming turns out to be a liar, a hypocrite, a coward, and a libertine. The discovery shocks her into admitting that. . . .

> She had believed it would be possible to sep-
> arate the image of the man she had thought him
> from that of the man he was. . . . but now she
> had begun to understand that the two men were
> really one. The Darrow she worshipped was
> inseparable from the Darrow she abhorred. . . .

As the image of Darrow as two men emphasizes, the double standard forms "the reef" on which Anna's dream shatters. (pp. 83-4)

The structure of the novel charts the crash of [Anna's] fantasy. In contrast to the gloomy weather and dingy urban settings of book 1, Anna's idyllic world of latent animation at the château in book 2 does seem a fairy-tale world coming to life. However, the harder she clings to her dream in the face of realities it cannot accommodate, the more inhospitable and enclosed the atmosphere becomes. In book 3 she has "the eerie feeling of having been overswept by a shadow which there had been no cloud to cast." . . . The day turns rainy and its two main events are Anna's visit to an injured child and Darrow's secret meeting with Sophy in a decaying summerhouse. In book 4 Anna does not leave Givré where her dream of perfect love is attenuated as she learns the truth about Darrow's character. The dream dissolves altogether in book 5, which like book 1 takes place mainly in Paris. The atmosphere grows stormy and dark, the action consists of frantic journeys and conferences in hotel rooms, and Anna last appears not at the château but in the bedroom of a strange woman in a shabby Parisian hotel.

This last scene is upsetting, even cruel, as critics often remark. But Wharton makes it so for a reason. Although Anna can no longer delude herself about marrying Darrow, she still clings to her hope of being saved by someone other than herself. She decides "it was Sophy Viner only who could save her—Sophy Viner only who could give her back her lost serenity. She would seek the girl out and tell her that she had given Darrow up; and that step once taken there would be no retracing it, and she would perforce have to go forward alone." . . . If successful, the plan will reanimate her dream: Darrow and Sophy's careless affair will be transformed into a beautiful love-match, and Anna will be transfigured into a self-sacrific-ing heroine. But Wharton does not let Anna find Sophy and therefore be saved by her. Instead she has her find herself among strangers in a tawdry hotel love-nest, and there all illusion about fairy-tale love explodes. In the person of the slovenly Mrs. McTarvie-Birch at the Hôtel Chicago we finally see the embodiment of Anna's earlier image of the woman in love as "a slave, and a goddess, and a girl in her teens": a prostitute who is bought and owned like a slave, enthroned on her bed like a goddess, and distracted by her pet poodle like a girl in her teens. That Anna mistakes this woman and her pimp for husband and wife simply emphasizes how pathetically naive she still is about the whole subject of love, sex, and marriage.

Wharton does not mock Anna in *The Reef*. (The irony of the final scene is sobering, not amusing or contemptuous.) . . . The target of criticism in *The Reef* is not Anna and not really

even women as a class, although the book does attack ideas held by women—held because they are carefully taught to hold them. (No one is born knowing, or believing in, the myth of Sleeping Beauty.) Wharton's object of attack is the culture that represses women and encourages them to believe that love and marriage will someday release them into "reality." Love and marriage as the culture defines them are not a release. Anna's dream cannot even withstand an engagement, let alone mar-riage, which, as her first union demonstrated and her relation-ship with Darrow suggests, simply delivers a woman from one subservient life into another. (pp. 86-8)

[Anna Leath's foil, Sophy Viner,] is a twentieth-century woman, a New Woman: she is modern, self-confident, practical. She is also completely unable to free herself from certain traditional notions and impediments. Her lack of marketable skills, her vulnerability to the double standard, and her own romantic infatuation with George Darrow keep her from gaining au-thority over her own life. She ends where she began, the un-happy appendage to a loud American dowager on the loose in Europe. (p. 89)

The notion sometimes advanced by critics that Wharton is cruel to Sophy because she makes her sister, Mrs. McTarvie-Birch, a prostitute and has Anna (and bear in mind it is not Wharton, but Anna) see a resemblance between the two sisters at the end of *The Reef* is as misguided as accusing Wharton of cruelty toward Mattie Silver or Lily Bart. The fact is, the novel's last scene implicitly admires rather than punishes Sophy Viner: against all odds, she has managed so far to avoid her sister's fate.

In addition to its realistic social criticism, Sophy's plot com-pletes Wharton's commentary on fairy tales in *The Reef*. Lit-erally Sophy serves as a foil for Anna; she is the New Woman whose experience with life highlights the older woman's na-iveté. But as with Zeena and Mattie, symbolically more im-portant than the contrasts between the two women are the similarities and connections. Both love the same man, Darrow. Both are closely attached to another man, Owen—Sophy as his fiancée, Anna as his stepmother (making her, in an echo of the sexual rivalry in *Ethan Frome,* a potential stepmother figure for Sophy). But, because Anna and Owen "have always been on odd kind of brother-and-sister terms," . . . Anna usu-ally thinks of herself as Owen's sister, which makes Sophy more like Anna's future sister than daughter-in-law. Indeed, if Sophy were to marry Owen, Anna and Sophy, like sisters, would share the same mother-figure (Madame de Chantelle) just as they now share the care of the same child (Effie). The intertwining of the two women's identities to imply figurative sisterhood suggests that symbolically Anna Leath and Sophy Viner represent a split heroine, a dichotomous embodiment of one basic identity. That basic identity in *The Reef* is the would-be fairy-tale heroine who is rescued from a miserable life by some sort of Prince Charming hero. For if Anna Leath resem-bles Sleeping Beauty, waiting for a man's passion to animate her, Sophy Viner in her way recalls the tale of Cinderella—a poor, neglected, down-to-earth girl who is transported to riches by her Prince Charming.

Especially reminiscent of Cinderella in book 1, Sophy Viner appears remarkably cheerful in the face of hardship; and for a woman in her middle twenties, she has an uncommonly fresh, juvenile quality. Her physical appearance and movements often look "boyish" to Darrow, so spontaneous and guileless she seems, while her earthy "naturalness" is so pronounced that she, like Mattie Silver before her, reminds the man who desires her of "a dryad in a dew-drenched forest" (. . . note also her surname). Like Cinderella setting out for the ball, Sophy emerges dressed for the theater "looking as if she had been plunged into some sparkling element which had curled up all her drooping tendrils and wrapped her in a shimmer of fresh leaves." . . . (pp. 91-2)

In the character of George Darrow, Wharton reveals the real values implicit in the Prince Charming fantasy. The self-acknowledged savior of women, Darrow believes they exist solely for his pleasure, and he has no difficulty fitting Sophy Viner and Anna Leath into his two categories of women: sexual objects or decorative objects but in neither case autonomous people. Women, in effect, represent human property at his disposal. (p. 95)

It is against this concept of female destiny that Edith Wharton argues in *The Reef*. The fairy-tale fantasy of deliverance by a man appears to be but is not a dream of freedom for women. It is a glorification of the status quo: a culturally perpetuated myth of female liberation which in reality celebrates masculine dominance, proprietorship, and privilege. That reality, for both of Edith Wharton's heroines, in the end marks "the reef." . . .

Prince Charming, properly understood, "liberates" his heroine into a life of permanent dependence. Exactly that happens in morbid *Ethan Frome*, just as it threatens to happen in *The Reef*; and love based on a model of slavery, even if that model comes from splendid fairy tales, can in Wharton's opinion free no one, man or woman. (p. 96)

> Elizabeth Ammons, "Fairy-Tale Love and 'The Reef'," in American Literature (reprinted by permission of the Publisher; copyright © 1976 by Duke University Press, Durham, North Carolina), Vol. XLVII, No. 4, January, 1976 (and reprinted in a different form in her Edith Wharton's Argument with America, University of Georgia Press, 1980, pp. 56-96).

---

## ADDITIONAL BIBLIOGRAPHY

Anderson, Hilton. "Edith Wharton as Fictional Heroine." *South Atlantic Quarterly* 69, No. 1 (Winter 1970): 118-23.
Interesting look at the parallels between Wharton's heroines and her own life.

Andrews, Wayne. "The World of Edith Wharton: Fragment of a Biography in Progress." In *The Best Short Stories of Edith Wharton*, by Edith Wharton, edited by Wayne Andrews, pp. vii-xxvii. New York: Charles Scribner's Sons, 1958.
Short biography of Wharton, including excerpts from her journal concerning her love for Walter Berry.

Auchincloss, Louis. "Edith Wharton and Her New Yorks." *Partisan Review* XVIII, No. 4 (July-August 1951): 411-19.
Overview of Wharton's novels illustrating Wharton's love-hate relationship with American values.

Bell, Millicent. "The Eagle and the Worm." *London Magazine* 6, No. 4 (July 1966): 5-46.
An account of Henry James's friendships with Edward and Edith Wharton, and Walter Berry, told largely through excerpts from James's letters.

Brooks, Van Wyck. "Edith Wharton." In his *The Confident Years: 1885-1915*, pp. 283-300. New York: E. P. Dutton & Co., 1952.
A thoughtful, general essay on Wharton's life and work, finding her to be more European than American in outlook, and more a writer of the nineteenth than the twentieth century.

Clough, David. "Edith Wharton's War Novels: A Reappraisal." *Twentieth Century Literature* 19, No. 1 (January 1973): 1-14.
Examines *The Marne* and *A Son at the Front*, illuminating American attitudes of World War I and the significance the war held for Wharton.

Coolidge, Olivia. *Edith Wharton, 1862-1937*. New York: Charles Scribner's Sons, 1964, 221 p.
Biography of Wharton.

Coxe, Louis O. "What Edith Wharton Saw in Innocence." *The New Republic* 132, No. 26 (27 June 1955): 16-18.
Examination of *The Age of Innocence*, in which the critic attempts to reintroduce "one of the fine novels of our century" to the contemporary reader.

French, Marilyn. Introduction to *The House of Mirth*, by Edith Wharton, pp. v-xxxviii. New York: Berkley Books, 1981.
Illuminates feminist concerns in Wharton's canon.

Hopkins, Viola. "The Ordering Style of *The Age of Innocence*." *American Literature* XXX, No. 3 (November 1958): 345-57.
Examination of the stylistic elements within *The Age of Innocence*.

Jessup, Josephine Lurie. "Edith Wharton: Drawing-Room Devotee." In her *The Faith of Our Feminists*, pp. 14-33. New York: Richard R. Smith, 1950.
Study of the male-female conflicts in Wharton's fiction. The critic sees women portrayed as preeminent beings, with their men "trailing at heel."

Kronenberger, Louis. "Mrs. Wharton's Literary Museum." *The Atlantic Monthly* 222, No. 3 (September 1968): 98-100, 102.
Critical overview of many of Wharton's short stories and novels.

Kronenberger, Louis. "Edith Wharton: *The Age of Innocence* and *The House of Mirth*." In his *The Polished Surface: Essays in the Literature of Worldliness*, pp. 246-70. New York: Alfred A. Knopf, 1969.
Explores two of Wharton's best-known novels, emphasizing their reflection of upper-class priggishness, rigidity, and corruption.

Lewis, R.W.B. *Edith Wharton: A Biography*. New York: Harper & Row, Publishers, 1975, 592 p.
The definitive biography.

Lidoff, Joan. "Another Sleeping Beauty: Narcissism in *The House of Mirth*." *American Quarterly* 32, No. 5 (Winter 1980): 519-39.
Examines *The House of Mirth* as "a romance of identity," in which Lily Bart is portrayed as a self-obsessed child-woman, whose maturation destroys her.

Lindberg, Gary H. *Edith Wharton and the Novel of Manners*. Charlottesville: University Press of Virginia, 1975, 186 p.
Close examination of *The House of Mirth*, *The Custom of the Country*, and *The Age of Innocence*.

Lubbock, Percy. *Portrait of Edith Wharton*. London: Jonathan Cape, 1947, 222 p.
Genteel biography of Wharton, consisting of reminiscences of her friends and excerpts from letters.

McDowell, Margaret B. "Viewing the Custom of Her Country: Edith Wharton's Feminism." *Contemporary Literature* XV, No. 4 (Autumn 1974): 521-38.
Thoughtful study of Wharton's implicit feminist concerns and her changing attitudes toward women throughout her life.

McDowell, Margaret B. *Edith Wharton*. Boston: Twayne Publishers, 1976, 158 p.
Insightful biography and analysis of Wharton's canon.

McManis, Jo Agnew. "Edith Wharton's Hymns to Respectability." *The Southern Review* 7, No. 4 (October 1971): 986-93.
Study of the theme of self-sacrifice in Wharton's characters and the motives behind their sacrifice.

Plante, Patricia R. "Edith Wharton As Short Story Writer." *The Mid-west Quarterly* IV, No. 4 (July 1963): 363-79.
> Careful study of the various collections of Wharton's short stories and critical reactions to them.

Thorp, Willard. *"The Age of Innocence."* In his *American Writing in the Twentieth Century,* pp. 1-24. Cambridge: Harvard University Press, 1960.
> Critical look at Wharton's works and assessment of her strengths as a writer.

Trilling, Diana. *"The House of Mirth* Revisited." *Harper's Bazaar* LXXXI, No. 12 (December 1947): 126-27, 181-86.
> Examination of *The House of Mirth* and biographical sketch of Wharton the aristocrat.

Trilling, Lionel. "The Morality of Inertia (Edith Wharton: *Ethan Frome*)." In *Great Moral Dilemmas in Literature, Past and Present,* edited by R. M. MacIver, pp. 37-46. New York: Cooper Square Publishers, 1964.
> Discussion of *Ethan Frome* and the "morality of inertia" presented within: morality imposed by social demand, circumstances, habit, and biology.

Wegelin, Christof. "Edith Wharton and the Twilight of the International Novel." *The Southern Review* 5, No. 2 (Spring 1969): 398-418.
> Examines Wharton's international novels and the European-American cultural clashes presented within them.

Wolff, Cynthia Griffin. *A Feast of Words: The Triumph of Edith Wharton.* New York: Oxford University Press, 1977, 453 p.
> Biography of Wharton, and examination of the author's major works as reflections of her psychological development.

# Appendix

**THE EXCERPTS IN TCLC, VOLUME 9, WERE REPRINTED FROM THE FOLLOWING PERIODICALS:**

The American Fabian
American Literary Realism 1870-1910
American Literature
American Quarterly
American Scholar
The Arena
The Athenaeum
The Atlantic Monthly
Book Week—The Washington Post
The Bookman (London)
The Bookman (New York)
Books Abroad
Bulletin of the John Rylands University
  Library of Manchester
Canadian Literature
Canadian Review of Comparative Literature
The Century
The Christian Century
Contemporary Review
The Cosmopolitan
The Criterion
The Critic
Critique: Studies in Modern Fiction
The Dial
Dissent
The Drama
Drama Review
Egoist
English Journal
English Literature in Transition
English Studies
The Fortnightly Review
Forum
The Freewoman
The French-American Review
German Life & Letters
The Germanic Review
Harper's
Harper's Monthly Magazine
Harper's New Monthly Magazine
The Heythrop Journal
The Hindu Review
Hispania
The Hound and Horn
The Humanities Association Bulletin

The Independent
International Philosophical Quarterly
Jack London Newsletter
Journal of Arabic Literature
Journal of English and German Philology
Kentucky Foreign Language Quarterly
Kwartalnik Neofilologiczny
Literature East and West
Living Age
The Masses
MELUS
The Methodist Review
The Minnesota Review
MLN
Modern Drama
Modern Fiction Studies
The Modern Language Journal
Modern Language Quarterly
The Modern Language Review
Modern Languages
Monatshefte
The Nation
The Nation and The Athenaeum
The New Age
The New England Quarterly
New German Studies
New International
New Masses
The New Republic
New Statesman
The New Statesman & Nation
New York Evening Post
New York Herald Tribune Books
The New York Review of Books
New York Times
The New York Times Book Review
The Nineteenth Century
Novel: A Forum on Fiction
Outlook
The Overland Monthly
Oxford German Studies
The Pacific Spectator
Papers on Language and Literature
Partisan Review
The Personalist

Philosophy Today
Poet Lore
Poetry
Poetry Wales
The Polish Review
The Princeton University Library Chronicle
Religion in Life
The Reporter
A Review of English Literature
Review of National Literatures
Russian Language Journal
Russian Literature Triquarterly
Russian Review
The Saturday Evening Post
The Saturday Review of Literature
The Sewanee Review
The Shaw Review
Shenandoah
Slavic and East European Journal
The Slavonic and East European Review
The Smart Set
The Southern Review
The Spectator
Studies in American Fiction
Studies in Short Fiction
The Symposium: A Critical Review
Theoria
Thought
The Times Literary Supplement
The Times, London
Tomorrow
The Tulane Drama Review
The Twentieth Century
The Village Voice
Virginia Quarterly Review
Walt Whitman Review
Die Welt der Slaven
Western Comrade
Wisconsin Studies in Contemporary
  Literature
World Literature Today
Yale French Studies
The Yale Review
Yellow Book

**THE EXCERPTS IN TCLC, VOLUME 9, WERE REPRINTED FROM THE FOLLOWING BOOKS:**

*Aiken, Conrad.* Collected Criticism. *Oxford University Press, 1968.*

*Ammons, Elizabeth.* Edith Wharton's Argument with America. *University of Georgia Press, 1980.*

*Auden, W. H.* Introduction to The Visionary Novels of George MacDonald: Lilith, Phantastes, *by George MacDonald. Edited by Anne Fremantle. Noonday Press, 1954.*

*Baldwin, Charles C.* The Men Who Make Our Novels. *Rev. ed. Dodd Mead, 1924.*

*Barcia, José Rubia, and Zeitlin, M.A., eds.* Unamuno: Creator and Creation. *University of California Press, 1967.*

*Barker, Murl G.* Introduction to The Kiss of the Unborn and Other Stories. *Translated by Murl G. Barker. University of Tennessee Press, 1977.*

*Bennett, Arnold.* Books and Persons: Being Comments on a Past Epoch, 1908-1911. *George H. Doran Company, 1917.*

*Bennett, Arnold.* The Savour of Life: Essays in Gusto. *Doubleday, 1928.*

*Bertaux, Félix.* A Panorama of German Literature from 1871 to 1931. *Translated by John J. Troustine. Whittlesey House, 1935, Cooper Square Publishers, Inc., 1970.*

*Besterman, Theodore.* Mrs. Annie Besant: A Modern Prophet. *Kegan Paul, Trench, Trubner, 1934.*

*Booth, Wayne C.* Introduction to Thais, *by Anatole France. Translated by Basia Gulatio. University of Chicago Press, 1976.*

*Bosmajian, Hamida.* Metaphors of Evil: Contemporary German Literature and the Shadow of Nazism. *University of Iowa Press, 1979.*

*Boyd, Ernest.* Studies from Ten Literatures. *Charles Scribner's Sons, 1925.*

*Boynton, Percy H.* Some Contemporary Americans: The Personal Equation in Literature. *University of Chicago Press, 1924.*

*Boynton, Percy H.* More Contemporary Americans. *University of Chicago Press, 1927.*

*Bresky, Dushan.* The Art of Anatole France. *Mouton Publishers, 1969.*

*Bronowski, Jacob.* A Sense of the Future: Essays in Natural Philosophy. *Edited by Piero E. Ariotti with Rita Bronowski. The MIT Press, 1977.*

*Brooks, Van Wyck.* The Confident Years: 1885-1915. *Dutton, 1952.*

*Brown, John.* Valery Larbaud. *Twayne, 1981.*

*Brown, John Mason.* Still Seeing Things. *McGraw-Hill, 1950.*

*Buchanon-Gould, Vera.* The Life and Writings of Olive Schreiner. *Hutchinson & Co. (Publishers) Limited, 1948.*

*Cabell, James Branch.* Beyond Life: Dizain des demiureges. *Modern Library, 1923.*

*Carroll, Lewis.* The Diaries of Lewis Carroll, Vol. 1. *Edited by Roger Lancelyn Green. Oxford University Press, 1954.*

*Cavaliero, Glen.* The Rural Tradition in the English Novel: 1900-1939. *Rowman and Littlefield, 1977.*

*Chamberlain, Basil Hall.* Things Japanese: Being Notes on Various Subjects Connected with Japan for the Use of Travellers and Others. *Rev. Ed. John Murray, 1905.*

*Chapman, Robert T.* Wyndham Lewis: Fictions and Satires. *Barnes & Noble, 1973.*

*Chesterton, G. K.* All Things Considered. *John Lane Company, 1908.*

*Chesterton, G. K.* George Bernard Shaw. *John Lane Company, 1909.*

*Clark, Barrett H.* A Study of the Modern Drama: A Handbook for the Study and Appreciation of Typical Plays, European, English and American, of the Last Three-Quarters of a Century. *Rev. ed. Appleton, 1938.*

*Conrad, Joseph.* Notes on Life and Letters. *J. M. Dent and Sons Ltd., 1921.*

*Coombes, H.* Edward Thomas. *Chatto & Windus, 1956.*

*Coombes, H.* T. F. Powys. *Barrie and Rockliff, 1960.*

*Cowley, Malcolm.* A Many-Windowed House: Collected Essays on American Writers and American Writing. *Edited by Henry Dan Piper. Southern Illinois University Press, 1970.*

*Cowley, Malcolm. Introduction to* The Selected Writings of Lafcadio Hearn. *Edited by Henry Goodman. Citadel Press, 1949.*

*Cuénot, Claude.* Teilhard de Chardin: A Biographical Study. *Edited by Rene Hague. Translated by Vincent Colimore. Helicon Press, 1965.*

*Davies, Barrie. Introduction to* At the Mermaid Inn: Wilfred Campbell, Archibald Lampman, Duncan Campbell Scott in ''The Globe'' 1892-93. *Edited by Douglas Lochhead. University of Toronto Press, 1979.*

*Degler, Carl N. Introduction to* Women and Economics, *by Charlotte Perkins Gilman. Edited by Carl N. Degler. Harper & Row, 1966.*

*De la Mare, Walter. Foreword to* Collected Poems, *by Edward Thomas. Selwyn & Blount, 1920.*

*Dell, Floyd.* Women As World Builders: Studies in Modern Feminism. *Forbes and Company, 1913.*

*Dell, Floyd. Introduction to* Daughter of the Revolution, *by John Reed. Edited by Floyd Dell. Vanguard Press, 1927.*

*Del Río, Ángel, and del Río, Amelia A. de. Introduction to* Abel Sánchez, *by Miguel de Unamuno. Edited by Ángel del Río and Amelia A. de del Río. Holt, Rinehart and Winston, 1968.*

*Dobzhansky, Theodius.* The Biology of Ultimate Concern. *The New American Library, 1967.*

*Dos Passos, John.* Rosinante to the Road Again. *Doran, 1922.*

*Drake, William A.* Contemporary European Writers. *The John Day Company, 1928.*

*Draper, Ronald P.* D. H. Lawrence. *Twayne, 1964.*

*Dukes, Ashley.* The Youngest Drama: Studies of Fifty Dramatists. *Ernest Benn, Limited, 1923.*

*Eastman, Max.* Heroes I Have Known: Twelve Who Lived Great Lives. *Simon and Schuster, 1942.*

*Ellis, Havelock.* Impressions and Comments: 1920-1923. *3d series. Houghton Mifflin, 1924.*

*Ellis, Havelock.* The Soul of Spain. *Houghton Mifflin, 1924.*

*Erskine, John. Introduction to* Interpretations of Literature, *by Lafcadio Hearn. Edited by John Erskine. Dodd Mead 1915, Kennikat Press, 1965.*

*Esslin, Martin.* The Theatre of the Absurd. *Anchor, 1969.*

*Etulain, Richard W. Introduction to* Jack London on the Road: The Tramp Diary and Other Hobo Writings. *Edited by Richard W. Etulain. Utah State University Press, 1979.*

*Evans, Ifor.* English Poetry in the Later Nineteenth Century. *Rev. ed. Barnes & Noble, 1966.*

*Evans, T. F., ed.* Shaw: The Critical Heritage. *Routledge and Kegan Paul, 1976.*

*Fennimore, Keith J.* Booth Tarkington. *Twayne, 1974.*

*Ferlinghetti, Lawrence. Preface to* Adventures of a Young Man: Short Stories from Life, *by John Reed. City Lights Books, 1975.*

*Field, Andrew, ed.* The Complection of Russian Literature: A. Cento, *Atheneum, 1971.*

*First, Ruth and Scott, Ann.* Olive Schreiner. A. *Andre Deutsch, 1980.*

*Forster, E. M.* Aspects of the Novel. *Harcourt, 1927.*

*Foster, Edward.* Mary E. Wilkins Freeman. *Hendricks House, 1956.*

*Frank, Joseph.* The Widening Gyre: Crisis and Mastery in Modern Literature. *Rutgers University Press, 1963, Indiana University Press, 1968.*

*Frank, Waldo.* Our America. *Boni and Liveright, 1919.*

*Fruchter, Moses Joseph.* The Social Dialectic in Georg Kaiser's Dramatic Works. *Philadelphia, 1933.*

*Frye, Northrop.* Northrop Frye on Culture and Literature: A Collection of Reviews and Essays. *The University of Chicago Press, 1978.*

*Gale, Zona.* Foreword to The Living of Charlotte Perkins Gilman: An Autobiography, *by Charlotte Perkins Gilman. D. Appleton-Century Company, 1935.*

*Galsworthy, John.* Candelabra: Selected Essays and Addresses. *Charles Scribner's Sons, 1933.*

*Geismar, Maxwell.* Rebels and Ancestors: The American Novel, 1890-1915. *Houghton Mifflin, 1953.*

*Gilbert, Sandra M.* Acts of Attention: The Poems of D. H. Lawrence. *Cornell University Press, 1972.*

*Glicksberg, Charles I., ed.* American Literary Criticism 1900-1950. *Hendricks House, Inc., 1952.*

*Gohdes, Clarence, ed.* Essays on American Literature in Honor of Jay B. Hubbell. *Duke University Press, 1967.*

*Goist, Park Dixon.* From Main Street to State Street: Town, City, and Community in America. *Kennikat, 1977.*

*Gosse, Edmund.* French Profiles. *Rev. ed. William Heinemann, 1913.*

*Gray, Donald P.* The One and the Many: Teilhard de Chardin's Vision of Unity. *Herder & Herder, 1969.*

*Greenslet, Ferris.* Introduction to Leaves from the Diary of an Impressionist: Early Writings by Lafcadio Hearn. *Houghton Mifflin, 1911.*

*Guicharnaud, Jacques.* Modern French Theatre: From Giraudoux to Genet. *Yale University Press, 1969.*

*Hamblen, Abigail Ann.* The New England Art of Mary E. Wilkins Freeman. *The Green Knight Press, 1966.*

*Hanson, Anthony, ed.* Teilhard Reassessed: A Symposium of Critical Studies in the Thought of Père Teilhard de Chardin Attempting an Evaluation of His Place in Contemporary Christian Thinking. *Darton, Longman & Todd, 1970.*

*Harrison, John R.* The Reactionaries: A Study of the Anti-Democratic Intelligentsia. *Gollancz, 1966.*

*Hart, Francis Russell.* The Scottish Novel: From Smollett to Spark. *Harvard University Press, 1978.*

*Hawi, Khalil S.* Kahlil Gibran: His Background, Character and Works. *The Arab Institute for Research and Publishing, 1972.*

*Hearn, Lafcadio.* Introduction to The Crime of Sylvestre Bonnard, *by Anatole France. Harper & Brothers, 1890.*

*Hedges, Elaine R.* Afterword to The Yellow Wallpaper, *by Charlotte Perkins Gilman. The Feminist Press, 1973.*

*Hendricks, King, ed.* Creator and Critic: A Controversy Between Jack London and Philo M. Buck, Jr. *Utah State University Press, 1961.*

*Hesse, Hermann.* My Belief: Essays on Life and Art. *Edited by Theodore Ziolkowski. Translated by Denver Lindley. Farrar, Straus and Giroux, 1974.*

*Hicks, Granville.* The Great Tradition: An Interpretation of American Literature since the Civil War. *Rev. ed. Macmillan, 1935, Quadrangle Books, 1969.*

*Hicks, Granville.* John Reed: The Making of a Revolutionary. *Macmillan, 1936.*

*Hillyer, Robert. Introduction to* A Tear and a Smile, *by Kahlil Gibran. Knopf, 1950.*

*Hobman, D. L.* Olive Schreiner: Her Friends and Times. *Watts & Co., 1955.*

*Hoffman, Frederick H., and Moore, Harry T., eds.* The Achievement of D. H. Lawrence. *University of Oklahoma, 1953.*

*Hohendahl, Peter Uwe, & others, eds.* Essays on European Literature. *Washington University Press, 1972.*

*Holroyd, Michael, ed.* The Genius of Shaw: A Symposium. *Holt, Rinehart and Winston, 1979.*

*Howells, William Dean. Introduction to* The Great Modern American Stories. *Boni and Liveright, 1920.*

*Huneker, James.* Ivory, Apes and Peacocks: Joseph Conrad, Jules Laforgue, Dostoievsky and Tolstoy, Schoenberg, Wedekind, Moussorgsky, Cézanne, Vermeer, Matisse, Van Gogh, Gauguin, Italian Futurists, Various Latter-day Poets, Painters, Composers and Dramatists. *Charles Scribner's Sons, 1922.*

*Hunter, William.* The Novels and Stories of T. F. Powys. *Minority Press, 1930.*

*Huttar, Charles A., ed.* Imagination and the Spirit: Essays in Literature and the Christian Faith Presented to Clyde S. Kilby. *Eerdmans, 1971.*

*Huxley, Aldous.* On the Margin: Notes and Essays. *George H. Doran, 1923.*

*Jackson, Rosemary.* Fantasy: The Literature of Subversion. *Methuen, 1981.*

*Jacobson, Dan. Introduction to* The Story of an African Farm, *by Olive Schreiner. Penguin Books, Inc., 1971.*

*Jameson, Fredric.* Fables of Aggression: Wyndham Lewis, the Modernist as Fascist. *University of California Press, 1979.*

*Josephson, Matthew.* Portrait of the Artist As American. *Harcourt Brace Jovanovich, 1930.*

*Karlinsky, Simon. Introduction to* A Difficult Soul: Zinaida Gippius, *by Vladimir Zlobin. University of California Press, 1980.*

*Kazin, Alfred.* On Native Grounds: An Interpretation of Modern American Prose Literature. *Reynal & Hitchcock, 1942.*

*Keith, W. J.* The Poetry of Nature: Rural Perspectives in Poetry from Wordsworth to the Present. *University of Toronto Press, 1980.*

*Kenworthy, B. J.* Georg Kaiser. *Basil Blackwell, 1957.*

*Kilmer, Joyce.* The Circus and Other Essays and Fugitive Pieces. *Edited by Robert Cortes Holliday. Doran, 1921.*

*Klinck, Carl F.* Wilfred Campbell: A Study in Provincial Victorianism. *Ryerson Press, 1942.*

*Kostka, Edmund.* Glimpses of Germanic-Slavic Relations from Pushkin to Heinrich Mann. *Bucknell University Press, 1975.*

*Kott, Jan. Introduction to* This Way to the Gas Ladies and Gentlemen, and Other Short Stories, *by Tadeusz Borowski. Translated by Barbara Vedder. Penguin, 1976.*

*Krige, Uys. Introduction to* Olive Schreiner: A Selection, *by Olive Schreiner. Edited by Uys Krige. Oxford University Press, 1968.*

*Krispyn, Egbert.* Georg Heym: A Reluctant Rebel. *University of Florida Press, 1968.*

*Kronenberger, Louis, ed.* George Bernard Shaw: A Critical Survey. *The World Publishing Company, 1953.*

*Kunst, Arthur E.* Lafcadio Hearn. *Twayne, 1969.*

*Labor, Earle.* Jack London. *Twayne, 1974.*

*Lalou, René.* Contemporary French Literature. *Translated by William Aspenwall Bradley. Knopf, 1924.*

*Lane, Ann J. Introduction to* Herland, *by Charlotte Perkins Gilman. Pantheon, 1979.*

Lane, Ann J. *Introduction to* The Charlotte Perkins Gilman Reader, *by Charlotte Perkins Gilman. Edited by Ann J. Lane. Pantheon, 1980.*

Lange, Victor. *Introduction to* The Coral: A Play in Five Acts, *by Georg Kaiser. Translated by Winifred Katzin. Frederick Unger Publishing Co., Inc., 1963.*

Langer, Lawrence L. Versions of Survival: The Holocaust and the Human Spirit. *State University of New York Press, 1982.*

Larbaud, Valery. Poems of a Multimillionaire. *Translated by William Jay Smith. Bonacio & Saul, 1955.*

Last, R. W. Periods in German Literature: Text and Contexts, Vol. II. *Edited by J. M. Ritchie. Wolff, 1969.*

Lavrin, Janko. An Introduction to the Russian Novel. *Methuen & Co. Ltd., 1942.*

Leary, Lewis. Southern Excursions: Essays on Mark Twain and Others. *Louisiana State University Press, 1971.*

Leavis, F. R. New Bearings in English Poetry: A Study of the Contemporary Situation. *Chatto & Windus, 1932.*

Leduc, Renato. *Preface to* Insurgent Mexico, *by John Reed. International, 1969.*

Lehmann, John. The Open Night. *Longmans, Green and Co., 1952.*

Lemaître, Jules. Literary Impressions. *Translated by A. W. Evans. Daniel O'Connor, 1921.*

Lenin, V. I. *Foreword to* Ten Days That Shook the World, *by John Reed. Vintage Books, 1960.*

Lessing, Doris. *Afterword to* The Story of an African Farm, *by Olive Schreiner. Fawcett, 1968.*

Lessing, Doris. *Introduction to* The Story of an African Farm, *by Olive Schreiner. Schocken Books, 1976.*

Lessing, Otto Eduard. Masters in His Modern German Literature. *Verlag Von Carl Reissner, 1912, Books for Libraries Press, 1967.*

Levy, Diane Wolfe. Techniques of Irony in Anatole France: Essay on "Les sept femmes de la Barbe-Blene." *U.N.C. Department of Romance Languages, 1978.*

Lewis, C. S. *Preface to* George MacDonald: An Anthology, *by George MacDonald. Edited by C. S. Lewis. Macmillan, 1947.*

Lewis, C. S. They Stand Together: The Letters of C. S. Lewis to Arthur Greeves (1914-1963). *Edited by Walter Hooper. Collins, 1979.*

Lewis, R.W.B. *Introduction to* The Collected Short Stories of Edith Wharton, Vol. I., *by Edith Wharton. Charles Scribner's Sons, 1968.*

Lukács, George. The Historical Novel. *Translated by Hannah Mitchell and Stanley Mitchell. Merlin Press, 1962.*

MacDonald, Greville. George MacDonald and His Wife. *Dial Press, 1924.*

Machen, Arthur. Hieroglyphics: A Note upon Ecstasy in Literature. *Knopf, 1923.*

MacNeice, Louis. Varieties of Parable. *Cambridge University Press, 1965.*

Macy, John, ed. American Writers on American Literature. *Liveright, 1931.*

Madariaga, Salvador de. The Genius of Spain, and Other Essays on Spanish Contemporary Literature. *Oxford University Press, 1923.*

Madariaga, Salvador de. *Introduction to* The Tragic Sense of Life in Men and Peoples, *by Miguel de Unamuno. Translated by J. E. Crawford Flitch. Macmillan, 1921.*

Mann, Thomas. Letters of Thomas Mann. *Edited and translated by Richard Winston and Clara Winston. Knopf, 1971.*

Mansfield, Katherine. Novels and Novelists. *Edited by J. Middleton Murry. Knopf, 1930.*

Marías, Julián. José Ortega y Gasset: Circumstance and Vocation. *Translated by Frances M. López-Morillas. University of Oklahoma Press, 1970.*

Materer, Timothy. Wyndham Lewis the Novelist. *Wayne State University Press, 1976.*

*Matich, Olga.* Paradox in the Religious Poetry of Zinaida Gippius. *Wilhelm Fink, 1972.*

*Maurois, André.* Prophets and Poets. *Harper & Row, 1935.*

*Maurois, André. Introduction to* The Gods Are A-Thirst, *by Anatole France. Translated by Alfred Allinson. Nonesuch Press, 1942.*

*McClintock, James I.* White Logic: Jack London's Short Stories. *Wolf House Books, 1975.*

*Mencken, H. L.* H. L. Mencken's "Smart Set" Criticism. *Edited by William H. Nolte. Cornell University Press, 1968.*

*Mencken, H. L.* Prejudices: First Series. *Knopf, 1919.*

*Milne, Gordon.* The Sense of Society: A History of the American Novel of Manners. *Fairleigh Dickinson University Press, 1977.*

*Milosz, Czeslaw.* The History of Polish Literature. *Macmillan, 1969.*

*Miner, Earl.* The Japanese Tradition in British and American Literature. *Princeton University Press, 1958.*

*Mirsky, D. S.* Contemporary Russian Literature: 1881-1925. *Knopf, 1926, G. Routledge & Sons, 1926.*

*Mirsky, D. S.* A History of Russian Literature Comprising: "A History of Russian Literature" and "Contemporary Russian Literature." *Edited by Francis J. Whitfield. Knopf, 1973.*

*More, Paul Elmer.* The Demon of the Absolute. *Princeton University Press, 1928.*

*Motion, Andrew. Introduction to* The Poetry of Edward Thomas, *by Edward Thomas. Routledge & Kegan Paul, 1980.*

*Mumford, Lewis.* Values for Survival: Essays, Addresses, and Letters on Politics and Education. *Harcourt Brace Jovanovich, 1946.*

*Murry, J. Middleton.* Aspects of Literature. *W. Collins Sons & Co. Ltd., 1920.*

*Murry, J. Middleton.* Reminiscences of D. H. Lawrence. *J. Cape, 1933.*

*Murry, J. Middleton.* Selected Criticism 1916-1957. *Edited by Richard Rees. Oxford University Press, 1960.*

*Naimy, Mikhail.* Kahlil Gibran: A Biography. *Philosophical Library, 1950.*

*O'Brien, Justin.* The French Literary Horizon. *Rutgers University Press, 1967.*

*O'Brien, Justin, ed.* From the N.R.F.: An Image of the Twentieth Century from the Pages of the "Nouvelle revue francaise." *Farrar, Straus and Cudahy, 1958.*

*Ortega y Gasset, José.* Meditations on Quixote. *Translated by Evelyn Rugg and Diego Marín. Norton, 1961.*

*Ouimette, Victor.* José Ortega y Gasset. *Twayne, 1982.*

*Pachmuss, Temira.* Zinaida Hippius: An Intellectual Profile. *Southern Illinois University Press, 1971.*

*Pal, Bepin Chandra.* Mrs. Annie Besant: A Psychological Study. *Ganesh, 1917.*

*Pattee, Fred Lewis.* The New American Literature 1890-1930. *Century, 1930, Cooper Square Publishers, Inc., 1968.*

*Pattee, Fred Lewis. Introduction to* A New England Nun, and Other Stories, *by Mary E. Wilkins Freeman. Harper & Brothers, 1920.*

*Peabody, A. P. Introduction to* The Imagination and Other Essays, *by George MacDonald. Lothrup, 1883.*

*Phelps, William Lyon.* The Advance of the English Novel. *Dodd, Mead, 1916.*

*Pickar, Gertrud Bauer, and Webb, Karl Eugene, eds.* Expressionism Reconsidered: Relationships and Affinities, Vol. 1. *Fink, 1979.*

*Poggioli, Renato.* The Poets of Russia: 1890-1930. *Harvard University Press, 1960.*

*Priestley, J. B.* Literature and Western Man. *Harper & Brothers, 1960.*

*Pritchett, V. S.* The Living Novel and Later Appreciations. *Rev. ed. Random House, 1964.*

*Raabe, Paul, ed.* The Era of German Expressionism. *Translated by J. M. Ritchie. The Overlook Press, 1974, Calder & Boyars, 1974.*

*Rabinowitz, Stanley J.* Sologub's Literary Children: Keys to a Symbolist's Prose. *Slavica Publishers, Inc., 1980.*

*Rabkin, Eric S.* The Fantastic in Literature. *Princeton University Press, 1976.*

*Raven, Charles E.* Teilhard de Chardin: Scientist and Seer. *Collins, 1962.*

*Reeve, F. D.* The Russian Novel. *McGraw-Hill Book Company, 1966.*

*Reis, Richard H.* George MacDonald. *Twayne, 1972.*

*Rexroth, Kenneth.* The Buddhist Writings of Lafcadio Hearn, *by Lafcadio Hearn. Ross-Erikson, Inc., Publishers, 1977.*

*Ritchie, J. M. Introduction to* Five Plays, *by Georg Kaiser. Translated by B. J. Kenworthy, Rex Last, and J. M. Ritchie. Calder and Boyars, 1971.*

*Roberts, David.* Artistic Consciousness and Political Conscience: The Novels of Heinrich Mann, 1900-1938. *Lang, 1971.*

*Rosenstone, Robert A.* Romantic Revolutionary: A Biography of John Reed. *Knopf, 1975.*

*Rowe, Anne.* The Enchanted Country: Northern Writers in the South 1865-1910. *Louisiana State University Press, 1978.*

*Sachs, Murray.* Anatole France: The Short Stories. *Edward Arnold, 1974.*

*Sanders, Scott.* D. H. Lawrence: The World of the Major Novels. *Vision, 1973, Viking Press, 1974.*

*Scannell, Vernon.* Edward Thomas. *British Council, 1963.*

*Schürer, Ernst.* Georg Kaiser. *Twayne, 1971.*

*Scott, Winfield Townley.* Exiles and Fabrications. *Doubleday, 1961.*

*Segel, Harold B.* Twentieth-Century Russian Drama: From Gorky to the Present. *Columbia University Press, 1979.*

*Shaw, Bernard.* Plays Unpleasant: Widowers' Houses, The Philanderer, Mrs. Warren's Profession. *Penguin Books Inc., 1946.*

*Shaw, Leroy R.* The Playwright & Historical Change: Dramatic Strategies in Brecht, Hauptmann, Kaiser & Wedekind. *University of Wisconsin Press, 1970.*

*Showalter, Elaine.* A Literature of Their Own: British Women Novelists from Brontë to Lessing. *Princeton University Press, 1977.*

*Silver, Arnold.* Bernard Shaw: The Darker Side. *Stanford University Press, 1982.*

*Slochower, Harry.* No Voice Is Wholly Lost ... Writers and Thinkers in War and Peace. *Creative Age Press, Inc., 1945.*

*Smith, William Jay.* The Streaks of the Tulip: Selected Criticism. *Delacorte Press, 1972.*

*Sokel, Walter H.* The Writer in Extremis: Expressionism in Twentieth-Century German Literature. *Stanford University Press, 1959.*

*Speaight, Robert.* Teilhard de Chardin: A Biography. *Collins, 1967.*

*Stuart, John. Introduction to* The Education of John Reed: Selected Writings, *by John Reed. International, 1955.*

*Styan, J. L.* Modern Drama in Theory and Practice: Expressionism and Epic Theatre, Vol. 3. *Cambridge University Press, 1981.*

*Swinnerton, Frank.* The Georgian Scene: A Literary Panorama. *Farrar & Rinehart, 1934.*

*Taylor, A.J.P. Introduction to* Ten Days That Shook the World, *by John Reed. Penguin Books, 1977.*

*Tiverton, W.* D. H. Lawrence and Human Existence. *Philosophical Library, 1951.*

*Trotsky, Leon.* Leon Trotsky on Literature and Art. *Edited by Paul N. Siegel. Pathfinder Press, 1970.*

*Trotsky, Leon.* Literature and Revolution. *Translated by Rose Strunsky. Allen & Unwin, 1925, Russell & Russell, 1957.*

*Van Doren, Carl.* Contemporary American Novelists 1900-1920. *Macmillan, 1922.*

*Vidal, Gore.* Homage to Daniel Shays: Collected Essays 1952-1972. *Vintage Books, 1972.*

*Vidal, Gore.* Introduction to *The Edith Wharton Omnibus, by Edith Wharton. Charles Scribner's Sons, 1978.*

*Villaseñor, S.J., José Sánchez.* Ortega y Gasset Existentialist: A Critical Study of His Thought and Its Source. *Translated by Joseph Small, S.J. Henry Regnery, 1949.*

*Walton, Geoffrey.* Edith Wharton: A Critical Interpretation. *Fairleigh Dickinson University Press, 1971.*

*Wells, H. G.* Experiment in Autobiography: Discoveries and Conclusions of a Very Ordinary Brain (since 1866). *The Macmillan Company, 1934.*

*West, Geoffrey.* Annie Besant. *Viking, 1928.*

*Westbrook, Perry D.* Mary Wilkins Freeman. *Twayne, 1967.*

*Weygandt, Cornelius.* The Time of Yeats: English Poetry of To-Day against an American Background. *D. Appleton-Century Company, Inc., 1937.*

*Wilkinson, Louis U.* Blasphemy and Religion. *G. A. Shaw, 1916.*

*Wilson, Edmund.* To the Finland Station. *Harcourt, Brace and Company, 1940, Farrar, Straus and Giroux, 1953.*

*Wolfe, Bertram D.* Strange Communists I Have Known. *Stein and Day, 1965.*

*Wolff, Robert Lee.* The Golden Key: A Study of George MacDonald. *Yale University Press, 1961.*

*Woodress, James.* Booth Tarkington: Gentleman from Indiana. *Lippincott, 1955.*

*Wyers, Frances.* Miguel de Unamuno: The Contrary Self. *Tamesis Books, 1976.*

*Yu, Beongcheon.* An Ape of Gods: The Art and Thought of Lafcadio Hearn. *Wayne State University Press, 1964.*

*Yuill, W. E.* German Men of Letters: Twelve Literary Essays, Vol. II. *Edited by Alex Natan. Wolff, 1963.*

*Zamyatin, Yevgeny.* A Soviet Heretic: Essays by Yevgeny Zamyatin. *Edited and translated by Mirra Ginsburg. University of Chicago Press, 1970.*

*Zlobin, Vladimir.* A Difficult Soul: Zinaida Gippius. *Edited and translated by Simon Karlinsky. University of California Press, 1980.*

# Cumulative Index to Authors

Author Index

Author Index

# Cumulative Index to Nationalities

# Cumulative Index to Critics

**Aaron, Daniel**
Nathanael West **1**:485

**Abcarian, Richard**
Sherwood Anderson **1**:59

**Abel, Lionel**
Bertolt Brecht **1**:109
Henrik Ibsen **2**:232

**Abercrombie, Lascelles**
Thomas Hardy **4**:153

**Abrams, Ivan B.**
Sholom Aleichem **1**:24

**Abramson, Doris E.**
Wallace Thurman **6**:449

**Abril, Xavier**
César Vallejo **3**:526

**Adams, Henry**
William Dean Howells **7**:363

**Adams, J. Donald**
F. Scott Fitzgerald **1**:239

**Adams, Marion**
Gottfried Benn **3**:111

**Adams, Phoebe-Lou**
Malcolm Lowry **6**:237

**Adams, Robert M.**
Gabriele D'Annunzio **6**:140

**Adams, Robert Martin**
James Joyce **3**:273

**Adams, Samuel Hopkins**
Alexander Woollcott **5**:524

**Adams, Walter S.**
Thomas Wolfe **4**:506

**Adcock, A. St. John**
Wilfred Campbell **9**:31
O. Henry **1**:347
Bernard Shaw **3**:386

**Adell, Alberto**
Ramón del Valle-Inclán **5**:484

**Adrian, John**
Paul Heyse **8**:123

**Aguirre, Ángel Manuel**
Juan Ramón Jiménez **4**:223

**Aguinaga, Carlos Blanco**
Miguel de Unamuno **2**:561

**Aiken, Conrad**
Sherwood Anderson **1**:37
Robert Bridges **1**:127
James Branch Cabell **6**:62
Walter de la Mare **4**:71
F. Scott Fitzgerald **1**:237
John Galsworthy **1**:296
Federico García Lorca **1**:308
Thomas Hardy **4**:155
D. H. Lawrence **2**:344
Wyndham Lewis **9**:236
Edgar Lee Masters **2**:460
Eugene O'Neill **1**:383
Dorothy Richardson **3**:349
Rainer Maria Rilke **1**:414
Edwin Arlington Robinson
**5**:403
Gertrude Stein **6**:406
Dylan Thomas **1**:466
Virginia Woolf **1**:529

**Akhsharumov, N. D.**
Leo Tolstoy **4**:446

**Alcott, Louisa May**
Rebecca Harding Davis **6**:148

**Aldington, Richard**
Oscar Wilde **1**:499

**Aldiss, Brian W.**
Jules Verne **6**:497

**Aldridge, John**
F. Scott Fitzgerald **1**:246

**Alexandrova, Vera**
Sergei Esenin **4**:113

**Allen, Paul M.**
Jakob Wassermann **6**:520

**Allen, Walter**
Arnold Bennett **5**:40
Wyndham Lewis **2**:394
Dorothy Richardson **3**:358

**Allison, J. E.**
Heinrich Mann **9**:331

**Alpers, Antony**
Katherine Mansfield **8**:291

**Alpert, Hollis**
O. Henry **1**:350

**Alsen, Eberhard**
Hamlin Garland **3**:200

**Altrocchi, Rudolph**
Gabriele D'Annunzio **6**:135

**Alvarez, A.**
Hart Crane **2**:118
D. H. Lawrence **2**:364
Wallace Stevens **3**:454
William Butler Yeats **1**:564

**Alworth, E. Paul**
Will Rogers **8**:336

**Amann, Clarence A.**
James Weldon Johnson **3**:247

**Amis, Kingsley**
G. K. Chesterton **1**:185
C. M. Kornbluth **8**:213
Jules Verne **6**:493

**Ammons, Elizabeth**
Edith Wharton **9**:552

**Amoia, Alba della Fazia**
Edmond Rostand **6**:381

**Amon, Frank**
D. H. Lawrence **9**:220

**Anders, Gunther**
Franz Kafka **2**:302

**Anderson, David D.**
Sherwood Anderson **1**:52

**Anderson, Isaac**
Raymond Chandler **7**:167

**Anderson, Maxwell**
Edna St. Vincent Millay **4**:306

**Anderson, Quentin**
Willa Cather **1**:163

**Anderson, Sherwood**
Gertrude Stein **6**:407
Mark Twain **6**:459

**Andrews, William L.**
Charles Waddel Chesnutt **5**:136

**Angenot, Marc**
Jules Verne **6**:501

**Annenkov, P. V.**
Leo Tolstoy **4**:444

**Anouilh, Jean**
Jean Giraudoux **7**:320

**Anthony, Edward**
Don Marquis **7**:443

**Anthony, G. F. Penn**
Pierre Teilhard de Chardin
**9**:501

**Antoninus, Brother**
Hart Crane **2**:119

**Aquilar, Helene J.F. de**
Federico García Lorca **7**:302

Critic Index

**Critic Index**

**Critic Index**

**Critic Index**

Critic Index

Władysław Stanisław Reymont
5:390
Bernard Shaw 3:397
Robert E. Sherwood 3:412
May Sinclair 3:438
August Strindberg 1:450
Oscar Wilde 1:502
Jakob Wassermann 6:508
Alexander Woollcott 5:521

**Krzyzanowski, Jerzy R.**
Władysław Stanisław Reymont
5:395
Stanisław Ignacy Witkiewicz
8:509

**Kunst, Arthur E.**
Lafcadio Hearn 9:135

**Kurrick, Maire Jaanus**
Georg Trakl 5:466

**Kustow, Michael**
Bertolt Brecht 1:122

**Labor, Earle**
Jack London 9:272

**Lafourcade, Georges**
Arnold Bennett 5:38

**Lagerkvist, Pär**
August Strindberg 1:456

**Lagerroth, Erland**
Selma Lagerlöf 4:241

**Lago, Mary M.**
Rabindranath Tagore 3:498,
499

**Lakshin, Vladimir**
Mikhail Bulgakov 2:73

**Lalou, René**
Valéry Larbaud 9:196

**Lambasa, Frank**
Franz Werfel 8:474

**Lambert, J. W.**
John Galsworthy 1:304
Saki 3:369

**Lamm, Martin**
Federico García Lorca 1:314
August Strindberg 1:444

**Lampan, Archibald**
Charles G. D. Roberts 8:313

**Landis, Joseph C.**
Sholem Asch 3:70

**Lane, Ann J.**
Charlotte Gilman 9:108, 112

**Lang, Andrew**
Anatole France 9:44
Rudyard Kipling 8:176
George MacDonald 9:288
Émile Zola 6:559

**Lang, Cecil Y.**
Charles Swinburne 8:439

**Lange, Victor**
Georg Kaiser 9:184

**Langer, Lawrence L.**
Tadeusz Borowski 9:25

**Lapp, John C.**
Émile Zola 6:568

**Larsen, Erling**
James Agee 1:16

**Larsen, Hanna Astrup**
Knut Hamsun 2:202
Selma Lagerlöf 4:234
Sigrid Undset 3:511

**Larson, Harold**
Bjørnstjerne Bjørnson 7:109

**Last, R. W.**
Georg Kaiser 9:185

**Lauterbach, Charles E.**
W. S. Gilbert 3:212

**Lavrin, Janko**
Leonid Andreyev 3:26
Andrey Bely 7:49
Aleksandr Blok 5:98
Sergei Esenin 4:110
Maxim Gorky 8:76
Knut Hamsun 2:203
Fyodor Sologub 9:436

**Lawler, James R.**
Paul Claudel 2:109

**Lawrence, D. H.**
Thomas Hardy 4:162
D. H. Lawrence 9:217
Giovanni Verga 3:539, 543
H. G. Wells 6:529

**Lawrence, Margaret**
Rose Macaulay 7:423

**Lawrence, Thomas Edward**
Charlotte Mew 8:296

**Lawson, Henry**
Miles Franklin 7:264

**Lawson, John Howard**
Robert E. Sherwood 3:410

**Lawson, Richard H.**
Edith Wharton 3:579

**Lawson, Robb**
Algernon Blackwood 5:70

**Layton, Susan**
Yevgeny Ivanovich Zamyatin
8:555

**Lea, Henry A.**
Franz Werfel 8:481

**Leach, Henry Goddard**
Selma Lagerlöf 4:230

**Leacock, Stephen**
O. Henry 1:346

**Leal, Luis**
Mariano Azuela 3:80

**Leary, Lewis**
Kate Chopin 5:150
Lafcadio Hearn 9:134
Mark Twain 6:475

**Leaska, Mitchell A.**
Virginia Woolf 5:512

**Leavis, F. R.**
Joseph Conrad 1:204
Thomas Hardy 4:164
Henry James 2:262
D. H. Lawrence 2:360

**Leavis, Q. D.**
Dorothy L. Sayers 2:528
Edith Wharton 3:564

**Leblanc-Maeterlinck, Georgette**
Maurice Maeterlinck 3:320

**Lebowitz, Naomi**
Italo Svevo 2:554

**Lederman, Marie Jean**
Katherine Mansfield 2:456

**Lednicki, Waclaw**
Henryk Sienkiewicz 3:427

**Leduc, Renato**
John Reed 9:386

**Lee, Alice**
Isaak Babel 2:23

**Lee, Lynn**
Don Marquis 7:450

**Le Gallienne, Richard**
Rudyard Kipling 8:179
Don Marquis 7:435
Alfred Noyes 7:504

**Legh-Jones, J.**
Guillaume Apollinaire 3:40

**Lehan, Richard**
F. Scott Fitzgerald 1:267
Ford Madox Ford 1:287

**Lehmann, John**
Rupert Brooke 7:129
Lewis Grassic Gibbon 4:121
Alun Lewis 3:287
Virginia Woolf 1:538

**Lehnert, Herbert**
Georg Heym 9:151

**Leiber, Fritz, Jr.**
Robert E. Howard 8:130
H. P. Lovecraft 4:267

**Leibowitz, Herbert A.**
Hart Crane 2:122

**Lemaitre, Georges**
André Gide 5:216
Jean Giraudoux 2:169

**Lemaître, Jules**
Anatole France 9:46

**Lenin, Nikolai**
Vladimir Mayakovsky 4:289

**Lenin, V. I.**
John Reed 9:382
Leo Tolstoy 4:452

**Leon, Derrick**
Marcel Proust 7:527

**Lerner, Michael G.**
Boris Vian 9:535

**LeSage, Laurent**
Jean Giraudoux 2:163

**Lessing, Doris**
A. E. Coppard 5:181
Olive Schreiner 9:400

**Lessing, Otto**
Heinrich Mann 9:314

**Levey, Michael**
Francis Thompson 4:441

**Levin, Harry**
James Joyce 3:272
José Ortega y Gasset 9:339
Marcel Proust 7:540
Émile Zola 6:566

**Levine, Robert T.**
Franz Kafka 6:229

**Levitt, Morton P.**
Nikos Kazantzakis 2:318

**Levy, Babette May**
Mary Wilkins Freeman 9:67

**Levy, Diane Wolfe**
Anatole France 9:57

**Levy, Karen D.**
Alain-Fournier 6:28

**Levy, Kurt L.**
Mariano Azuela 3:82

**Lewis, Allan**
Maxim Gorky 8:88
Federico García Lorca 7:296

**Lewis, C. Day**
Wilfred Owen 5:368
Dylan Thomas 8:450

**Lewis, C. S.**
G. K. Chesterton 6:99
Rudyard Kipling 8:192
George MacDonald 9:293
George Orwell 2:501
Charles Williams 1:511

**Lewis, Charlton M.**
Francis Thompson 4:437

**Lewis, Peter**
Charlotte Gilman 9:115

**Lewis, R. W. B.**
Joseph Conrad 1:210
Hart Crane 5:191
F. Scott Fitzgerald 1:245
Henry James 2:267
Edith Wharton 3:575; 9:546

**Lewis, Sinclair**
Willa Cather 1:151
Hamlin Garland 3:194
William Dean Howells 7:374

**Lewis, Theophilus**
Wallace Thurman 6:445

**Lewis, Wyndham**
James Joyce 3:253

**Lewisohn, Ludwig**
A. E. Coppard 5:176
Zona Gale 7:278
John Galsworthy 1:295
Gerhart Hauptmann 4:197
William Dean Howells 7:374
Georg Kaiser 9:171
Luigi Pirandello 4:327
Rainer Maria Rilke 1:408

**Lid, R. W.**
Raymond Chandler 7:168

**Liddell, Robert**
C. P. Cavafy 7:152

**Light, James F.**
Nathanael West 1:486

**Lima, Robert**
Federico García Lorca 1:321
Ramón del Valle-Inclán 5:485

**Lindenberger, Herbert**
Georg Trakl 5:462

**Lindbergh, Anne Morrow**
Antoine de Saint-Exupéry 2:516

**Linklater, Eric**
James Bridie 3:131

**Linn, Rolf N.**
Heinrich Mann 9:320

**Lippmann, Walter**
Amy Lowell 8:223
John Reed 9:381

Critic Index

Critic Index

Critic Index

**Critic Index**

**Critic Index**

Critic Index